BRITTEN'S
OLD CLOCKS
AND
WATCHES
AND THEIR MAKERS

FRONTISPIECE

Table clock by John Ellicott the younger, circa 1750–60. The case is veneered in amboyna wood and the exceptionally fine silver-gilt mounts are probably by Georg Michael Moser. The spandrel mounts of the dial also are silver-gilt and the chapter ring is of solid silver. This must be reckoned as one of the finest eighteenth-century bracket or table clocks.
(Victoria and Albert Museum)

BRITTEN'S

OLD CLOCKS

AND

WATCHES

AND THEIR MAKERS

A HISTORICAL AND DESCRIPTIVE ACCOUNT
OF THE DIFFERENT STYLES OF CLOCKS AND WATCHES
OF THE PAST IN ENGLAND AND ABROAD
CONTAINING A LIST OF NEARLY
FOURTEEN THOUSAND
MAKERS

Eighth edition by CECIL CLUTTON, CBE, FSA,
and the late G. H. BAILLIE, FBHI, and C. A. ILBERT, FBHI,
revised and enlarged by Cecil Clutton

with diagrams by F. JANČA
and endpapers by L. H. CRESSWELL

EYRE METHUEN · LONDON
in association with
E. & F. N. SPON LTD · LONDON

'Former Clock and Watchmakers
and Their Work', 1894
'Old Clocks and Watches' :

1st Edition 1899
2nd Edition 1904
3rd Edition 1911
4th Edition 1920
5th Edition 1922
6th Edition 1933
7th Edition 1956
New impression with corrections 1969
8th Edition 1973
Reprinted 1975

Printed in Great Britain for Eyre Methuen Ltd
in association with
E. & F. N. Spon Ltd, 11 New Fetter Lane, London EC4P 4EE
by Fletcher & Son Ltd, Norwich

ISBN 0 413 28700 9

Editors' Preface to the Seventh Edition

IN 1894 the late Mr. F. J. Britten published a book entitled *Former Clock and Watchmakers and their Work* and in 1899 this was remodelled and expanded into what was to prove itself the standard work on horological history: *Old Clocks and Watches and their Makers*. After running through six editions the book has been out of print for nearly twenty years, yet despite the spate of horological works which has been published during those years its position has remained unassailed and its second-hand value has risen steadily.

With the sixth edition of 1932 it was apparent that the original frame-work had been developed to its utmost, while many of the photographic blocks had reached the end of their useful life. It was therefore clear that any subsequent edition, to be successful, must involve a major re-arrangement of the book; and as the guiding hand of Mr. Britten is, unfortunately, no longer available (he died in 1913) it is with the greatest trepidation that the formidable task has been approached by the present editors. Moreover, the work had not progressed very far before that great horological historian and writer, Mr. G. H. Baillie, who was to have been the leader of the team, himself died. Fortunately, he had already written portions of the work which could hardly have been completed otherwise. Much of what is good in this edition must be attributed to Mr. Baillie; his survivors gladly accept any blame for the rest.

In its sixth edition form *Old Clocks and Watches and their Makers* had to some extent lost its pattern; some parts were unduly long; others insufficiently detailed. The illustrations appeared to follow no very definite plan. In compiling the present edition the Editors have had two cardinal factors in mind:

Firstly, that 'Britten' has become the 'bible' of the amateur collector and professional dealer. They are most interested in instruments of a kind likely to pass through their hands. Except insofar as they may provide some essential link in the historical sequence of events, unique examples are not of such great interest to the average collector and dealer, and this premise has largely guided the choice of illustrations. Similarly, the more unusual and complicated forms of mechanism have not been described in detail and the diagrams have been confined to typical examples. In these, and their explanatory captions, the aim has been to produce something which would be understood readily by the average collector, rather than precise accuracy of terminology and draughtsmanship.

Secondly, that since 'Britten' first appeared in print, innumerable books have been written on horology, many of great importance and highly specialised. With these, a general work like 'Britten' cannot hope to compete on their own ground, but what it can do is to present the picture as a whole, with all its parts in perspective. The thrilling story of Longitude has been told incomparably by the late Lt. Commdr. R. T. Gould, R.N., in *The Marine Chronometer*, of which a new edition is now being prepared, while Tompion and Breguet, the two giants of horology, have their biographers in R. W. Symonds and the late Sir David Salomons Bt., respectively. For detailed information on these and other specialised aspects of horology the curious reader can now be referred by our bibliography to the appropriate work.

Even in the list of makers, that was for so long the stand-by of collectors and dealers, 'Britten' has been far outstripped by *Watchmakers and Clockmakers of the World* by our own late co-editor, G. H. Baillie, with his list of 35,000 makers. Yet, by its very comprehensiveness, Baillie's great list perforce lacks a good deal of valuable detail to be found in Britten. Many men in Britten's list never made a watch in their lives, but put their names on movements supplied to them by the trade; yet so great is the tradition which has grown up around Britten's list that the Editors and Publishers have been reluctant to delete names from it, and then have only done so for some very good reason or in the case of makers only active after 1830, which has been adopted as the terminating date of the new edition. On the other hand, many important English, Continental and American makers have been added to make the list more complete.

As will be seen, much alteration and re-arrangement has gone into the present edition, but the Editors and Publishers have the temerity to believe that, however inadequate their achievement, the method is that which Mr. Britten would have adopted had he been alive. It was he who laid the foundation for the whole modern study of horological history and it has been the guiding hope of all concerned that this edition should perpetuate his pioneer work in the most generally useful modern shape.

As to whether they have succeeded in this, the reader must now judge for himself.

C. A. I.
C. C.

London, 1955.

Editor's Preface to the Eighth Edition

SINCE the publication of the seventh edition in 1956 the sixth edition has been republished in facsimile and this is a valuable work for collectors. With the culmination of the previous five editions, it had become, in effect, a great scrap-book and a mine of information and illustration.

However, it had become extremely difficult to use as a consecutive history of styles and it was for that reason that the seventh edition was written, being an almost entirely new book. That, and its reprint in 1969 are now out of print. In the intervening years no other overall history of the subject has been written, and since, as has been said, the sixth edition is an almost entirely different book, it has been felt that an eighth edition is merited. The opportunity has been taken to add a chapter bringing the history up to date from the year 1830 at which the seventh edition terminated.

Throughout the book, minor corrections have been made in the light of modern knowledge, especially in the section on Breguet in Chapter IX. Much has been discovered about his numbering system since the publication of the seventh edition.

Of the three co-authors of the seventh edition, G. H. Baillie died before it had hardly got under way and Courtenay Ilbert lived only just long enough to hold an advance copy of the book in his hands. He stood head and shoulders above all his contemporaries in historical horological knowledge and as the survivor of the team I can now say that while the actual writing of the seventh edition fell almost entirely upon my pen, the information in it was entirely his. His great knowledge was matched by his incomparable collection, from which most of the illustrations were taken. At his death, thanks to a massive donation by Gilbert Edgar, C.B.E. the whole collection has been secured by the nation and may now be seen in the British Museum, which may thus claim to have the world's premier collection of clocks and watches.

Many of the clocks and watches (mostly clocks) illustrated in the seventh edition which did not belong to Mr Ilbert have subsequently changed hands or their owners have died, and the present owners are not known. Acknowledgements of ownership have, therefore, been omitted from the present edition, except as to those in public ownership or appearing for the first time. It is hoped that their present owners will accept the necessity for these omissions.

Of all the people thanked in 'acknowledgements' many, alas, are now dead, but it is appropriate to renew the thanks then expressed for the exceptional help given by Mr F. J. B. Watson, C.V.O., F.S.A., Director of the Wallace Collection and Surveyor of the Queen's Works of Art, in writing the chapter on French Clocks; to Mr A. W. Van Lennep in connection with Dutch Clocks; and Dr H. Von Bertele in connection with Austrian Clocks.

My thanks are due to the Victoria and Albert Museum for permission to reproduce, in colour, pictures of several of their fine decorative watches, and the superb Ellicott clock which forms the frontispiece; and also to the staff of the museum for their help and patience during the taking of the photographs.

LONDON, 1972   C.C.

Contents

Contents

Contents

Contents

List of Plates

xv

CHAPTER IV

List of Diagrams

Endpapers: Cut-away drawing of a typical Tompion bracket clock

BRITTEN'S
OLD CLOCKS
AND
WATCHES
AND THEIR MAKERS

CHAPTER I

Counting the hours: from the beginning to 1550

INTRODUCTORY – TIME AND ITS MEASUREMENT

IT is unnecessary for the antiquarian horologist to have any wide knowledge of the theory of time and of the different systems of measuring it, but he should possess a rudimentary understanding of the problems involved. Throughout the history of civilisation the measurement of time has exercised man's utmost ingenuity and until within the last two hundred years the mechanism of clocks far exceeded all other sorts of contemporary machinery in complexity.

Time may be measured by the sun, or the stars, or by a man-made device of one kind or another.

SOLAR TIME

A solar day is the period which elapses between two successive returns of the sun to the meridian. Owing to the rotation of the earth about the sun, and the varying inclination of its own axis the length of the solar day varies throughout the year, and the moment at which the sun crosses the meridian will therefore coincide but rarely with midday as recorded by a perfectly accurate timekeeper. The dates of greatest variation are February 11th, when the sun lags 14 minutes 28 seconds behind mean time, and November 3rd, when it is 16 minutes 18 seconds in advance. Solar and mean time only coincide on April 15th, June 14th, September 1st and December 25th.

A cycle of the sun is a period of 28 years after which the days of the week again fall on the same days of the month as during the first year of the former cycle.

SIDEREAL TIME

Sidereal time, the standard used by astronomers, is measured by the diurnal rotation of the earth which turns on its axis in 23 hours 56 minutes and 4.1 seconds. Owing to its annual rotation round the sun the earth revolves once more in a year than is apparently the case. The sidereal day is therefore 3 minutes 56 seconds less than the mean solar day, and a clock showing sidereal time must have its pendulum a trifle shorter than a mean time clock with the same train. Mean time clocks can be regulated by the stars with greater facility than by the sun, for the motion of the earth in relationship to the fixed stars is uniform and a star will always cross the meridian 3 minutes 56 seconds sooner than it did on the preceding day.

DURATION OF A YEAR

The sidereal year starts with the spring equinox, when the sun crosses the equator from south to north. The earth in its revolution round the sun makes rather over 366 rotations, or 366 sidereal days, which are equal to 365 solar days. The sidereal year is equal to 365 days, 6 hours, 9 minutes, 11 seconds (nearly) of mean solar time. The earth, on completion of its revolution, returns to the same place among the stars, but not exactly at the spring equinox, owing to the precession of the equinoxes; so in order that the year may accord with the seasons the sidereal year is disregarded in favour of the equinoctial, or solar year, taken as 365 days, 5 hours, 48 minutes, 48 seconds. Among the Romans no regular account was taken of the difference between the true year and 365 days until 45 B.C., when the surplus was reckoned at 6 hours, and every fourth year was a leap-year. This produced an error of about seven days in 900 years. In 1582 Pope Gregory XII struck out ten days, which represented the accumulated error, from the calendar, and ordained that three leap-years should be omitted every 400 years. Thus, as 1600 was a leap-year, 1700, 1800 and 1900 were not, but 2000 will be a leap-year. This rectification was not adopted in England until 1752, and then only in face of bitter opposition. Eleven days were omitted from the calendar and the amended calendar was known as 'New Time'. As our year still exceeds the true year, although by a very small fraction, another leap-year in addition will have to be omitted once in 4000 years.

Timekeepers are primarily concerned with the subdivisions of a day and many forms of division have been used at different times and places, of which one or two examples may be cited as relevant to our subject.

Our present system of time-measurement is closely related to that adopted by the Sumerians at the very dawn of our civilization. They appear to have had two systems. In one, the day commenced at midnight and had six main divisions, each subdivided into sixty parts. In the other system, the day began at sunset and had twelve divisions, each subdivided into thirty parts. While the day commencing at a fixed moment, such as midnight, is more logical where mechanical time-keepers are concerned; when none is available, the moment of sunset is more readily observed, and it is therefore not surprising that the latter system prevailed to become the bane of the early clockmakers. We accordingly find it adopted in ancient Greece, but with a further subdivision of sixty parts (i.e. 4 seconds each).

Rome, in turn, and Italy, throughout the middle ages, used a 24-hour day starting at sunset, yet despite the extreme inconvenience of this arrangement in conjunction with mechanical time-keepers, it prevailed in Italy, even into the nineteenth century. Other localities had their own arrangements— the Persians, for example, used 24 hours starting at sunrise, while in Nuremberg the day consisted of 24 hours, but it was divided into two unequal parts, conforming to day and night. The number of hours in each part was announced monthly by proclamation and clocks frequently had dials painted in dark and light blue with movable shutters, indicating the proportion of official light and darkness. This system was not abandoned until the seventeenth century. In south Germany the day comprised two cycles of 12 hours each, starting at midnight, and as soon as clocks became fairly common (about 1400) this system was generally adopted for the ordering of civil affairs.

As will shortly be seen, mechanical clocks almost certainly originated in monasteries where the inmates were primarily interested in irregularly spaced canonical hours dependent upon sunset and sunrise. With them, day was started by Matins at the third quarter of the night followed by Prima at sunrise; Tertia fell half-way between sunrise and mid-day, Sexta was at mid-day, Nona mid-afternoon, Vespers one hour before sunset and Compline at the close of day. Later, Tertia and Sexta were combined and Nona moved back to mid-day, whence the term 'Noon'.

PRIMITIVE TIMEKEEPERS

The passage of the sun across the sky provided primitive man with a rough and ready means of judging the time of day but he soon felt the need of some more exact means of telling one hour from another. Sundials provided an easy solution and examples exist from prehistoric times. The sun, however, did not always shine and various devices were invented to do duty in its absence. These were all flow-meters of one sort or another, sand and water being the most popular, in a variety of forms. A burning lamp was another expedient, the lamp oil being kept in a vessel with graduated markings whereby the time could be told from the level of the fuel. All these systems were more or less unreliable, although the water-clock, or Clepsydra, showed the most promise and was even revived in the seventeenth century to the accompaniment of considerable ingenuity. But its performance varied with the temperature and no method of compensation could be devised. Very few early water clocks have survived and even seventeenth century examples are virtually non-existent, although there are many modern copies.

One example may be quoted to show the amount of ingenuity devoted to the clepsydra, even in the early centuries of the Christian era. In A.D. 807 a water clock of bronze inlaid with gold was presented by the King of Persia to Charlemagne. It is reported that the dial was composed of twelve small doors which represented the hours; each door opened at the hour it was intended to represent and out of it came the same number of little balls, which fell, one by one, at equal intervals of time, on a brass drum. When it was twelve o'clock twelve horsemen in miniature issued forth and shut all the doors.

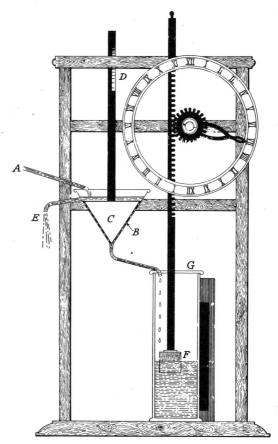

FIGURE 1. *Clepsydra or water clock. Water is fed into the clock from pipe A into funnel B. Inverted cone C is the 'regulator'. The regulator scale D is unequally calibrated since, the more closely the cone approaches the funnel, the more difference in rate a small movement of it will make. Surplus water escapes via overflow pipe E. The indicator hand on the dial is driven by a rack carried on a float F which rises as the metered flow of water from B gradually fills the canister G.*

Sand glasses have remained popular and useful until the present day when they are still used for recording short passages of time, such as that necessary for the boiling of an egg.

MECHANICAL TIMEKEEPERS

It is not known who made the first clock, nor when. Probably it was evolved by different experimenters working independently of each other, towards the end of the thirteenth century. Some Italian historians, however, claim that mechanical clocks existed in the twelfth century. In the middle ages, scientific knowledge was almost the prerogative of the church and it is generally assumed that the first clocks were made in and for the monasteries. While the middle ages afford numerous references to a 'horologium', unfortunately this may refer to a sundial, clepsydra, bell, or mechanical clock, and only in the fourteenth century do references become sufficiently precise for us to be sure that a mechanical clock is intended.

The notebook of the mid-thirteenth century French architect, Wilard de Honnecourt, shows a device which has been put forward as a first step towards a genuine escapement. It was designed to turn an angel (probably on a church roof) to indicate the time of day and consisted of a weighted rope passed round the vertical shaft on which the angel was fixed, and then through the spokes of a flywheel. The falling weight, drawing the rope through the spokes, would tend to turn the flywheel with it until the spokes gripped the rope, bringing the weight up with a jerk. A recoil would follow, after which a short length of rope would succeed in slipping through the spokes before the process started again. The arrangement does therefore contain the germ of an escapement and swinging balance, but it is mainly of interest as showing that a serious mechanical clock was unknown to this much-travelled architect in about 1250.

When an escapement was finally evolved it took the form of the 'verge and foliot' and for nearly four centuries this remained the only form of escapement in regular use. It remained in regular manufacture for a further two hundred years (300,000 verge watches were made in Switzerland in 1887) giving a total span of six centuries.

In its primitive form it consisted of an escape wheel (also called a 'crown wheel', because of its shape) of

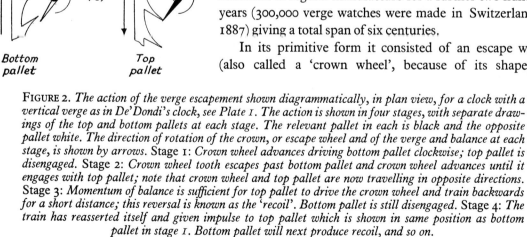

Bottom   Top
pallet   pallet

FIGURE 2. *The action of the verge escapement shown diagrammatically, in plan view, for a clock with a vertical verge as in De'Dondi's clock, see Plate 1. The action is shown in four stages, with separate drawings of the top and bottom pallets at each stage. The relevant pallet in each is black and the opposite pallet white. The direction of rotation of the crown, or escape wheel and of the verge and balance at each stage, is shown by arrows. Stage 1: Crown wheel advances driving bottom pallet clockwise; top pallet is disengaged. Stage 2: Crown wheel tooth escapes past bottom pallet and crown wheel advances until it engages with top pallet; note that crown wheel and top pallet are now travelling in opposite directions. Stage 3: Momentum of balance is sufficient for top pallet to drive the crown wheel and train backwards for a short distance; this reversal is known as the 'recoil'. Bottom pallet is still disengaged. Stage 4: The train has reasserted itself and given impulse to top pallet which is shown in same position as bottom pallet in stage 1. Bottom pallet will next produce recoil, and so on.*

contrate formation, with an odd number of triangular-shaped teeth pointing in the direction of rotation. The arbor of the crown wheel lay horizontal. Across the plane of this wheel was placed the arbor of the balance, known as the verge, and on its upper end was the balance itself, consisting either of a cross-bar, known as a 'foliot' or of a wheel. Projecting from the verge were two flag-shaped excrescences known as the 'pallets'. These were spaced at roughly a right angle to each other and at a distance apart on the balance staff corresponding to the diameter of the crown wheel, in the path of whose teeth they lay. The crown wheel being driven round by the motive power of the clock, one of its teeth came into contact with one of the pallets, thus imparting circular motion to the balance until the tooth escaped past the pallet, leaving the crown wheel free to advance. Immediately, however, a tooth on the opposite side of the wheel found itself obstructed by the other pallet and the process was repeated in the opposite direction. And so it continued, the balance swinging to and fro, while the teeth of the crown wheel escaped past the pallets one at a time. Thus the passage of time was measured by the even beats of the balance.

Since the design and construction of such an escape wheel from first principles would present considerable problems, it seems not unlikely that the first attempts took the shape of a pin-wheel, the pins projecting at right angles to the surface of the wheel. This arrangement is found in primitive Black Forest Clocks quite late into the seventeenth century.

Towards the end of the thirteenth century literary references to horologia are found which make it reasonable to assume that mechanical time-keepers are intended, but it is not until 1335 that conclusive evidence is forthcoming. On the other hand, writers between 1335–50 describe in detail clocks of such advanced design and complexity that at least half a century of previous development must be assumed. It may therefore be accepted that weight-driven clocks with a verge escapement existed in the last quarter of the thirteenth century.

It has been suggested that Italy is the birth-place of the mechanical clock and that the invention spread gradually northwards, reaching England only in the third quarter of the fourteenth century.

Nevertheless, there are early references to English Clocks which may well have had escapements and the possibility of their having been invented simultaneously in other countries besides Italy cannot be discounted.

St. Paul's Cathedral in London had a clock of some kind in 1286 when Bartholomew the Orologius received a loaf of bread a day and an allowance of beer for attending to it. This might equally well refer to a water or an escapement clock, but in 1344 it was replaced by a machine of which the description can hardly refer to anything less than an escapement. In this year the Dean & Chapter entered into an agreement with Walter 'Lorgoner' of Southwark for making . . . 'une dyal en lorloge demesme leglise od roofs et totes maneres de ustimentz appartenantz al dit Dyal et an tourner del Angel per amunt lorloge . . .'. The complete passage is translated as follows:

"The said Walter shall make a dial for the clock of the same church with roofs and all manner of apparatus appertaining to the said dial and for turning the Angel in front of the clock so that the said clock may be good and suitable and profitable to show the hours of the day and night. The said clock is to remain without defects and in case defects shall be found afterwards in the same clock the said Walter binds himself by this indenture to make the repairs whenever he shall be summoned by the ministers of the Church. And for this work well and duly done and completed the aforesaid Dean and Chapter shall pay him six pounds sterling—and the said Walter shall find at his own cost the iron, brass and all manner of other things for carrying out the said work: and shall have for himself the old apparatus which will no longer serve.''

In 1292 Canterbury followed with a 'great new clock' and four years earlier is a much disputed reference to the setting up of a clock tower and horologium in Westminster. This was built with the proceeds of a fine imposed upon Judge Ralph de Hengham for altering the record of a judgement; but the story rests on a 14th century tradition, so it is not completely reliable.

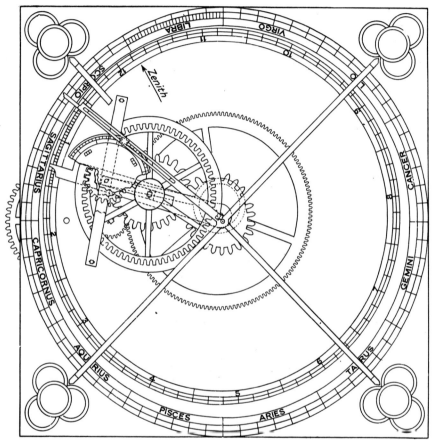

FIGURE 3. *The gearing for the planet Mercury in De'Dondi's fourteenth century planetarium clock, drawn by the late G. H. Baillie from the original manuscript prepared by De'Dondi. Note the elliptical-shaped gear wheels and sun and planet gears.*

Records from before 1300 at Exeter and Ely Cathedrals and Dunstable Priory point fairly strongly to mechanical escapement clocks and by 1325 Norwich Cathedral had a complicated automata and astronomical clock.

The monk, Peter Lightfoot, has been credited at one time or another with practically every mediaeval English clock but in fact his fame rests solely on a remark by Leland, referring to Glastonbury Abbey, to the effect that 'Horologium Petrus Lightfoote Monachus fecit hoc opus'—but there is no evidence that this horologium was an escapement clock.

Returning to Italy, references which appear to relate to mechanical clocks are found from 1300. In the Chronicle of Galvano Fiamma, for the year 1306, writing of the church of Sant Eustorgio at Milan, he says '—horologium fereum fabricatur', but in 1335 he was evidently far more greatly impressed by the clock of the Beata Vergine, later San Gottardo, also at Milan, of which he wrote 'There is there a wonderful clock, because there is a very large clapper which strikes a bell 24 times according to the 24 hours of the day and night, and thus at the first hour of the night gives one sound, at the second two strokes—and so distinguishes one hour from another, which is of the greatest use to men of every degree'. These two entries are of considerable interest, because Fiamma very briefly dismisses a clock in 1306 as quite a matter of course, but nearly 30 years later he is profoundly moved by a striking clock, indicating that it was then a novelty. We come next to two entirely remarkable achievements. The first was a clock made by Richard of Wallingford, the Abbot of St Albans, between 1327 and his death in 1336. It struck the hours and had dials for the astrolabe, motion of the sun, phases of the moon and (perhaps) the motions of the planets. Even more remarkable was the achievement by Giovanni De'Dondi, who was born in 1318. He was professor of astronomy at the University of Padua up to 1356 and died in 1389. In 1348 he started to make a planetarium clock which he completed in 1364. The clock appears to have been destroyed by fire in the sixteenth century but fortunately De'Dondi left a detailed and lucid description of it, extending to 85 closely written pages.

For complexity, it has seldom if ever been surpassed and the mechanical problems solved by Richard of Wallingford and by De'Dondi, apparently with hardly any precedent to work from, must be regarded as nearly miraculous, when compared with the very scant mechanical achievements of their century.

To reproduce the movements of the five known planets, sun and moon, according to the geocentric system, demanded some extremely complicated gearing; especially in the case of the planet Mercury, with its retrogradations and pronouncedly elliptical orbit. Under the Ptolemaic system Mercury moves round a circle whose centre in turn revolves around a point which in turn revolves around a centre slightly removed from the earth, which is the fixed centre of the whole universe. To illustrate this mechanical nightmare, De'Dondi resorted to a pair of elliptical shaped gear-wheels and also a sun-and-planet gear. He illustrates the layout

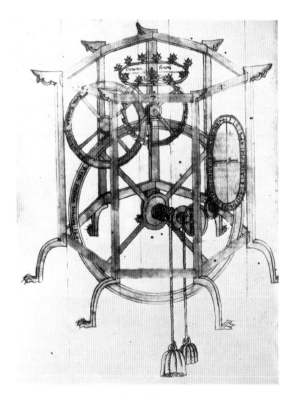

PLATE 1

The mid-fourteenth century Clock of De'Dondi as illustrated in his own descriptive manuscript. Note wheel-type balance (called by De'Dondi the 'Corona freni'); early use of leaf pinions; revolving chapter ring; counterweight for winding. The planetarium mechanism was in a separate frame on top of the clock proper, see also Fig. 3.

for each body in his MS. but the full complexity of the situation is best shown by a cutaway plan drawn by G. H. Baillie, in connection with a lecture to the British Horological Institute on March 14th, 1934, of the movement for Mercury. De'Dondi apologises for having got his gearing wrong by one part in 1600, and explains how to correct when the error becomes apparent. Similar, but less complicated gearings, exist for the six other planets (the sun and moon then being accounted as such). Now that such things have so long been commonplace it is difficult to appreciate the piercing mental clarity necessary to invent the sun-and-planet gear and calculate its movements, at a time when nothing but the simplest gearing previously existed.

The entire machine consisted of a heptagonal clock on top of which was placed the planetarium, driven from the clock, with one planet on each of the seven sides. The planetarium was slightly larger than the clock. De'Dondi does not give a complete picture but he does draw the clock (in very erratic perspective). The making of the clock is briefly dismissed as follows: 'the framework of the model having been constructed, it remains to arrange a common clock within the sides of the lower framework. But the method of making this clock will not be discussed in such detail as the rest because its construction is well known, and there are many varieties of them, and however it is made the diversity of methods does not come within the scope of this work since we desire nothing more from it than the uniform and equal motion of a wheel which shall complete its course in the space of a natural day, and such a wheel in common clocks, is called the horary sphere.'

A great wheel, on the barrel, has 120 teeth driving a pinion of 12 on a wheel of 80 teeth. This drives a pinion of 10 on the escape wheel which has 27 teeth. The balance takes the form of a crown and beats 1800 per hour which is said to be the usual rate. It is interesting that the earliest known clocks have a foliot balance (two arms with serrated extremities upon which weights can be hung at varying distances from the centre, to adjust for rate). De'Dondi's clock with its wheel-type balance had therefore no means of adjusting for rate except by varying the size of the driving weight, or the depth of engagement of the balance with the escape wheel.

The barrel, by description, has a ratchet not shown in the illustration and winding is effected by pulling down the counterweight which is wound on to the barrel so as to rise as the main weight descends. As was universal before about 1400, the dial revolves, the time being indicated by a fixed pointer. It is driven from a wheel on the barrel, via a small pinion which is a sliding fit on its arbor so that the dial may be set to time by disengaging it. The escapement is the ordinary verge, differing only from later examples in that instead of the escape wheel arbor being carried in a potence, it continues past the verge staff which therefore has to be cranked to avoid it.

A contemporary report relates that such was the genius and skill of De'Dondi that 'with his own hands and without assistance, he fabricated the clock all of brass and copper; and he did nothing else for sixteen years'. If correct, this mention of brass and copper is interesting since brass wheelwork does not begin to appear until the sixteenth century.

De'Dondi's masterpiece was of such a size that it could be accommodated within a large room, but one other complicated fourteenth century clock which must be mentioned was of a monumental nature more than 20 feet high. This was the first of the celebrated Strasburg clocks, constructed in two years and completed and set up in the Cathedral in 1354. It consisted of a calendar, representing in a painting some indications relative to the principal movable feasts. In the middle part there was an astrolabe, whose pointers showed the movement of the sun and moon, the hours and their subdivisions. There was placed at the same elevation the prime mover, and the other wheelwork which caused the clock to go. The upper compartment was adorned with a statuette of the Virgin before whom, at noon, the three Magi bowed themselves. A cock placed upon the crown of the case, crowed at the same moment, moving its beak and flapping its wings. A small set of chimes, composed of several cymbals, was also incorporated in the work. This famous clock has twice been replaced by others no less complex, but of the original clock only the cock survives.

As has been show, the first striking clocks seem to have been evolved in Italy soon after 1330, but Salisbury Cathedral may perhaps have had one by 1306. In 1365–6 Edward III caused a stone clock-tower to be erected at Westminster, opposite the hall and it 'contained a clock which struck every hour on a great bell, to be heard into the hall in sitting time of the Courts and the same clock on a clear night might be heard in the City of London'. In 1368 three Dutch clockmakers received a passport to carry on their craft in England, so it is reasonable to assume that they were imported to construct this first English striking clock. Probably also referring to it is a note in the Chronicle of the Monk of Malmesbury, for the year 1373: 'hoc anno horologia distinguentia 24 horas primo inventa sunt.' This has been interpreted as meaning that there were no clocks in England before 1373; but it seems more logical to suppose that 'distinguentia' means 'striking' and it was only that aspect of the clock which was then new to this country.

Whatever England's claims to priority of invention may be, she is certainly richest in surviving mechanisms of very early date. Two quite complete examples may be attributed with reasonable certainty to the fourteenth century and while France can claim two clocks of comparable date at Dijon and Rouen, only that at Rouen is reasonably complete; at Dijon nothing but the framework survives. Apart from these two, no known continental clock possesses any considerable amount of its mechanism dating back to the fourteenth century.

Apart from Rouen, probably the earliest complete continental clock is in the museum at Nuremburg, and while a date of circa 1400 is attributed to it, it may well be a later clock of archaic type. In any case, however, great interest attaches to its striking mechanism which is unique, employing the principle of the early alarum clock in conjunction with an hourly operation.

The Great wheel revolves hourly and has a pin projecting from it which lets off the striking

PLATE 2

The earliest known, and possibly only surviving example of a type of alarum clock made in Italy from the fifteenth (or even fourteenth) century. The wheels are of brass and the actual date of the clock cannot be closely determined. Overall height 9¾ inches. Note crenellated, wheel-type balance; revolving 24-hour chapter ring (seldom found after 1500) with holes for alarum pins (see page 10); detent at bottom of dial for setting off alarum.

train by a simple detent. The bell-hammer is worked by a crown wheel and verge identical with that of the clock escapement, and when its crown wheel has completed half a turn, a projection from the crown wheel returns the detent to its normal position, so that on completion of a full turn the detent again stops the crown wheel. It is thus able to repeat its action hourly until the weight is fully unwound.

As has already been mentioned, the monastic institutions mainly required to be warned of the hours for their duties, especially during the night, and it is therefore probable that an alarum mechanism was developed before the more complicated train necessary to strike the correct number of strokes at each hour. It may well be that the Nuremburg clock marks the transition from the alarum to the striking clock.

Apart from the Nuremburg clock, no very early alarum clocks have survived but there are several very early Italian illustrations with a bell.

It was long supposed that the ringing gear was solely hand-operated by the clock-keeper. However, recent researches, and the discovery in Italy of an actual example of fifteenth century type, show that the alarum was fully automatic.

A rope with a weight attached, was wound round the arbor of the crown wheel of the striking mechanism, and this was wound up by the cranked handle, the verge staff being lifted so that the verges were clear of the teeth of the crown wheel during winding.

What appears to be merely a fixed pointer against which the hours could be read off the revolving dial, was in fact also a pivoted detent which held the handle after the rope had been wound up. The dial had holes in it and a peg was inserted into the hole according to the hour at which the alarum was next needed. This peg in due course came in contact with the detent and, pushing it to one side, released the alarum handle and the falling weight caused the crown wheel to revolve and the bell to sound, the alarum continuing until the rope was fully unwound.

Preceding both these primitive types in actual age are the two English striking clocks from Salisbury and Wells cathedrals. These were almost certainly made within ten years of each other and their remarkable similarity of detail and design suggest that they were made by one man. That at Salisbury, illustrated in plate 3, is the older, and the Cathedral accounts show that it was bought in 1386. As no other clock is known to have been bought for the cathedral for the next five centuries, it is reasonable to suppose that the clock still at Salisbury is the original one of 1386. It was at first installed in a thirteenth century bell-tower in the close, but when this was demolished in the eighteenth century the clock was removed to the cathedral spire, and at or about this time it was fitted with a pendulum and anchor escapement. Here it remained in use until 1884 when it was superseded and lay unnoticed until 1928 when it was rediscovered and set up in the nave where it may now be seen. The clock possesses going and striking trains but there is no trace of a dial and it may be that none ever existed.

Apart from the actual escapement the mechanism appears to be substantially original and it may therefore claim to be the oldest reasonably complete clock in England and perhaps in the world. Even the very incomplete clock at Dijon only antedates it by three years. That at Rouen was completed in 1389.

At Wells the Cathedral expenses accounts exist for the years 1343–4, 1392–5, 1400–1 and 1407–9. There is no mention of a clock keeper in the first group but his wages are recorded in 1392 and subsequently. On this, and the evidence of the clock itself, it seems reasonable to date it a little earlier than 1392.

As at Salisbury, a pendulum and anchor escapement were fitted at some stage in the clock's

PLATE 3

The clock in Salisbury Cathedral, made in 1386 and almost certainly the oldest surviving complete clock. Iron movement; going and striking trains; there never was a dial. Note lantern pinions; internally-toothed count wheel; hand wheel for winding; gothic finials and detail. The crown-wheel, verge and foliot are restorations.

11

history, and it remained in use at Wells until 1831. After 40 years of neglect it was put into repair, some modern brass motion-work added, and set up in the old Patent Office Museum, whence it was removed to its present home in the Science Museum, South Kensington, London.

In addition to the going and striking trains the Wells clock has a quarter-striking train which might argue against a very early date if the other evidence was not so strong. In other respects it is remarkably similar to Salisbury. The whole machine is constructed of iron, and no screws are used, all joints being riveted or wedged. The rims of the wheels are forged and although they can hardly have been made in one piece, no weld joints are visible. The four spokes are split at their ends, the rim fitting into the slot and the whole being clamped together and welded under heat. The spokes of the great wheel have elegant trefoil-shaped ends where they overlap the rim. This arrangement appears to have been usual in early clocks, but an alternative was to attach the spokes to one side only of the rim, the two being riveted together.

The almost square-shaped teeth engage with lantern pinions having octagonal end-plates. The arbors are also mostly of octagonal section. It has been said that lantern pinions were of fairly late invention, but most mediaeval gearing was carried out in wood in which, owing to the grain, a leaf pinion would be impracticable. Pin-toothed contrate wheels had been known from the first century A.D. and from this it was but a short and obvious step to make a complete lantern pinion by the addition of a second plate. On the evidence of surviving examples it seems clear that lantern pinions are a good indication of early date.

The Wells clock originally operated an astronomical dial while at the hour, knights jousted with each other and, a puppet known as 'Jack Blandifer' moved his head and struck the hour on a bell. All this mechanism still exists and is in use, although actuated by a modern clock. The striking puppets are known as 'Jacks', of which Jack Blandifer is the oldest surviving example in England, but many others of varying antiquity are to be seen up and down England and the Continent.

The mechanisms of early clocks tend to be so much alike that they afford little help as evidence of precise age; the framework is usually a better guide. All clocks of established antiquity (fourteenth or fifteenth century) have posts with short vertical finials, and those at Salisbury and Wells have a small castellated ornamentation. The moulding of the bases is also consistent with the fourteenth century style of gothic architecture. Seventeenth century turret clocks very generally have finials bent outwards with a variety of bun-shaped terminals and this bent feature is never found in earlier clocks

Of this pattern is the ancient clock discovered at Dover Castle in the middle of the nineteenth century, which was long supposed to be by far the oldest clock existing, and an entirely fallacious date of 1348 was confidently attributed to it. Nevertheless, its general design and striking gear clearly belong to a much later period, and the bent-out, bud-shaped finials put it fairly conclusively not earlier than 1600. The very corroded surface of all the metal parts gives it an air of great antiquity, but this is a natural consequence of the sea air at Dover. The pinions throughout are of leaf formation and there is no provision for a dial. What does make the clock of great interest is the survival of the original foliot balance, which is most unusual in an early turret clock. There are, therefore, several mechanisms as old as the Dover Clock, especially in the South West of England, which seems to have been an active centre of clockmaking in the fifteenth and sixteenth centuries. The oldest English clock still working in its original position is at Rye Church, completed in 1515, and later converted

PLATE 4

*Turret clock from Cassiobury Park, Hertfordshire, circa 1600. One of the very few early turret clocks
to have retained the foliot type of balance. Note the general similarity to the Salisbury Cathedral clock,
Plate 3 but the outward bent, bud-shaped finials indicate its comparatively late date.*
(British Museum)

to pendulum escapement. Of other examples of early turret clocks and automata of various kinds
there is now no space to write here, but they may be found in a number of writings referred to in the
Bibliography.

DOMESTIC CLOCKS

As long as weights were the only motive power, house clocks were not easily movable and they either stood on brackets or were spiked to the wall. Early examples are exceedingly rare but a very few can with some confidence be attributed to the late fifteenth century. Nevertheless, such clocks had become quite common by the end of the sixteenth century, and there are references going back much earlier. An inventory of the belongings of Philippe-le-Bel of France, who reigned from 1285 to 1314, refers to 'un reloge d'argent tout entièrement sans fer—avec deux contrepoids d'argent emplis de plon'. If this is correct it is undoubtedly the earliest domestic clock known, but it is possible that some changes had taken place between the king's death in 1314 and the preparation of the inventory in 1380. However, the accounts of the Vatican refer to a clock in the Pope's garderobe in 1343, and in 1363 26 florins were paid for a clock in his 'arrière Chambre'. In 1359 King John of France, while a prisoner in England, paid 7 nobles for a clock and in 1365 at the Louvre we read of 'un estuy de bois d'illande pour herbergier l'orloge de M. le Dauphin qui sonne les heures audit Louvre'. The earliest English reference to a domestic clock is found in one of the Paston letters, written in the spring of 1469. 'I praye you speke wt Harcourt off the Abbeye ffor a lytell clokke whyche I sent him by James Gressham to ament and yt ye woll get it off him an it be redy, and send it me, as ffor mony for his labour, he hath another clok of myn which St. Thoms Lyndes, God have hys soule, gave me. He maye kepe that tyll I paye him. This klok is my Lordys Archebysshopis but late him not wote off it.'

Prior to 1550 surviving domestic clocks are of the utmost rarity but for the most part the weight-driven variety seem to have followed the gothic pattern which was really a scaled down turret clock. The movement was entirely unenclosed, being contained in an open framework. The trains varied greatly, but for the most part there was only one wheel between the great wheel and escape wheel and sometimes not even that. The clocks generally needed winding every 15 hours and seldom went for 24. The wheels were of iron or (in smaller and finer work) steel although, as has been shown, De'Dondi was using brass in the early fourteenth century. The great wheel arbor was usually continued beyond its bearing hole in the framework to terminate in 3 or 4 pins, which operated as a 4-leaf pinion, engaging with a wheel on whose arbor was fixed the moving hand (which had generally supplanted the rotating dial during the fifteenth century). The striking train was situated behind the going train and had its own weight. In modern trains the clock usually prepares itself to strike a few minutes ahead of the hour, only waiting for the train to be released exactly at the hour. This is known as a warning piece and the mechanism is described in detail in chapter VIII. The primary object of a warning piece is to ensure that striking takes place precisely as the minute hand points to the hour, but before the adoption of minute hands this degree of precision was unnecessary and in many early clocks the striking was set going with one movement, without any warning preliminaries.

The bell was placed above the balance, being supported by four straps springing from each corner of the frame and meeting over the top of the bell. These, and the corner posts of the frame, were frequently decorated with crockets or similar gothic ornamentation.

It was quite usual to have an alarum mechanism as well as a striking train, the alarum being sounded by a crown wheel and verge with a hammer attached to its verge staff.

The framework itself was held together with pins or wedges, and screws were entirely unknown in clocks before 1550.

The controller took the form of either a foliot or a circular balance as previously described. It was located top and bottom by a potence, or bracket, and was usually suspended at the top by a thread which took the weight of the balance and so reduced friction in its bottom bearing. The driving weights consisted of bags, or cylindrical containers filled with lead shot.

With the foliot arrangement there were three ways of adjusting the rate of the clock:

(1) by altering the position of the weights hung on the foliot (moving them outwards made the clock lose).

(2) by altering the position of the verge-staff potences so as to vary the depth of engagement of the pallets with the escape wheel (a deep engagement meant a wider angle of swing for the balance and a slower rate).

(3) by varying the amount of shot in the driving weights.

With the plain circular balance the first method was, of course, not available. Both systems seem to have existed side by side and De'Dondi's clock had a circular balance in the early fourteenth century. The foliot did not remain popular long after 1500, but in the simple Black Forest clocks it survived into the eighteenth century and in Japan until the nineteenth century.

Such was the most popular form of domestic weight-driven clock in the early sixteenth century, and it continued to be made in considerable numbers until the end of the first quarter of the seventeenth century.

Occasionally the mechanism was protected from dust by brass-gilt plates, delicately engraved, which fitted or were pinned on to the structural framework, but such examples are more common in the second half of the sixteenth and early seventeenth century and will, therefore, be more appropriately considered in the next chapter. Usually, the open frame clocks were square on plan, with a pillar at each corner, but there are occasional variants, such as a triangular plan, or heptagonal as De'Dondi's. The size of open-frame gothic house clocks varies greatly.

PLATE 5

A typical house clock of the 1500 period. Overall height 19½ inches. Iron and steel movement; no screws. Four trains for hours, quarters, striking and alarum, each with its own weight. Note posted movement; foliot with movable weights for regulation; fixed chapter ring; early type of alarum similar to Plate 2.
(British Museum)

SPRING-DRIVEN CLOCKS

As long as clocks were weight-driven they could not be moved about at all easily. As they were also expensive, few households could afford more than one, and portability would therefore have been a valuable feature. This was achieved by the invention of the mainspring as an alternative motive power to weights.

It was no easy matter to make a coiled spring of sufficient power to drive a clock without constantly breaking, and it seems unlikely that this was successfully achieved before the last quarter of the fifteenth century. Steel is now the invariable material for mainsprings, but it is possible that the earliest springs were made of brass which would present less manufacturing problems and, as will be seen, perhaps the earliest surviving example is of brass.

Spring motive power possessed one grave shortcoming which must have become apparent at the outset. It is at its most powerful when fully wound and steadily declines as it unwinds. This is not important in a modern watch, where the balance is practically isochronous; but before the invention of the balance spring the rate of the clock reacted violently to the power exerted in driving it. Therefore, erratic timekeepers as were even the early weight-driven clocks, spring-driven clocks were even worse and some means had to be found of equalising the pull of the mainspring in its fully wound and unwound positions.

Two systems were found of doing this, known respectively as the stackfreed and the fusee. The former, developed in Germany, was a poor expedient which did not survive long into the seventeenth century; the fusee was a perfect remedy and survives in use in marine chronometers at the present day. The earliest known illustration of it is in one of the notebooks of Leonardo da Vinci, a little before 1500, so it may well have been invented by that universal genius.

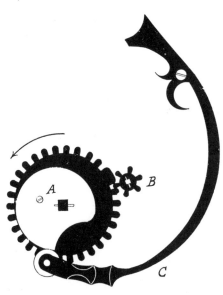

FIGURE 4. *Stackfreed. Camwheel A revolves once in the going period. Pinion B is pinned to the spring barrel arbor. The stackfreed C is a strong spring pressing against the cam, retarding its movement when the spring is fully wound and assisting it as the spring runs down. The shape of the cam varies considerably in different clocks and periods. The diagram is shown with the mainspring fully wound.*

Stackfreed

A wheel, geared to the spring barrel, and turning once in the period for which the clock would go without winding (usually 26 hours in the case of stackfreeds) has pinned and screwed to it a cam of the shape shown in FIG. 4. Pressing against the cam face is a small wheel carried at the free end of a strong spring anchored to the framework of the clock. The gear wheel carrying the stackfreed cam has two or three of its teeth left blank and un-cut. This serves as a stopwork to prevent over-winding. The cam is so cut that the spring, pressing against it acts as a brake when the mainspring is fully wound, and later helps it along when the mainspring is nearly unwound, thus roughly equalising the torque throughout the going period.

Fusee

This involves an additional wheel in the train, of which the arbor is in fact the 'fusee' which is of conical shape with its surface grooved, like a screw. A length of gut has one end fixed to the thick end of the fusee and is wound round the spring barrel to which the other end of the gut is attached. Also fitted to the fusee is a ratchet and click and a winding square. As the latter is turned, the gut is wound from the spring barrel on to the fusee. On the last turn of the fusee the gut comes in contact with a small hinged lever held in its path by a spring. As the gut is wound on the last turn of the fusee it pushes this little lever in front of it until the lever in turn obstructs a projection on the thin

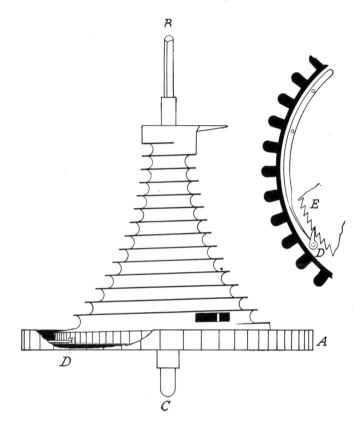

end of the fusee, which can then be rotated no further, and overwinding is prevented. While winding takes place the click rides over the ratchet previously mentioned, but as soon as the winding operation is complete the drive is transmitted through the ratchet to the train. The mainspring, being compressed, pulls the gut line back on to its barrel, off the fusee, thus providing the power to drive the clock. In the early stages it is winding the gut off the thin end of the fusee so that its mechanical advantage is low and the torque transmitted correspondingly weak; but as the day progresses it begins to unwind the gut off the thick end of the fusee so that the mechanical advantage is high, and the reduced power of the mainspring is duly compensated.

The fusee, in effect, affords a variable gear ratio, and its invention was indeed a flash of inspiration, fully worthy of the genius of Leonardo da Vinci.

The working of the stackfreed and fusee is more clearly shown by FIGS. 4 and 5.

Spring-clocks had wheel balances and the only easy method of regu-

FIGURE 5. *Fusee. Great wheel A drives the train and is a loose fit on the fusee arbor B C. A carries a click D engaging with the ring of ratchet teeth E on the fusee, by which it is driven. The fusee is driven by the mainspring via a gut wound round its spiral groove as explained in the text. During winding E is turned backwards and escapes past the click. The clock therefore stops during winding, the power being removed. The stop-work is not shown on this diagram but will be found on fig. 29.*

lating their rate was by altering the tension of the main spring. This was done by a click and ratchet on the spring barrel and this arrangement (or a worm and wheel) is invariably found on fusees in chronometers to the present day, although the balance now provides the effective means of regulation.

While it seems clear that the fusee was invented in Italy, and spring clocks probably originated from there, after 1500 Italy gradually fades out of the horological picture, and during the next 150 years the leaders are, first Germany and later France. No early spring clock of Italian origin survives.

Two early references to spring clocks nevertheless show that Italy was first in the field. The first (very recently discovered by Captain Antonio Simoni) is contained in a letter of Comino da Ponte-vico, an Engineer, dated 1482, which refers to a clock with 'a ribbon of tempered steel fastened in a brass barrel around which is wound a gut line . . . and . . . that line is placed there so that, being attached to the spring barrel, it has to pull the fusee'. The second reference is the preface to a sonnet written by Gaspare Visconti in 1493: 'There are made certain small portable clocks which, though with little mechanism, keep going, indicating the hours and the courses of many planets and the feast days, striking at the proper time. This sonnet is put in the mouth of a lover who, looking at one of these clocks, compares himself to it.'

But it is to Germany that we must turn for the further development of spring-clocks; Nuremburg seems to have been the principal centre of activity, and the name of Peter Henlein (1480–1542) emerges as its earliest exponent. Johannes Cocclaeus wrote of him in 1511 as follows: (using the

PLATE 6
(left and right)

The earliest known surviving spring-driven clock with the earliest known fusee, made by Jacob the Czech for Sigismund I, King of Poland, and dated 1525. Now the property and illustrated by permission of the London Society of Antiquaries. The functions of the astronomical dials is given on page 19. Overall diameter $9\frac{3}{4}$ inches. Note foliot balance and skeleton movement, typical of drum-shaped clocks in the first half of the sixteenth century.

name of Hele which can be identified as a corruption of Henlein) 'from day to day more ingenious discoveries are made; for Petrus Hele, a young man, makes things which astonish the most learned mathematicians, for he makes out of a small quantity of iron horologia devised with very many wheels, and these horologia, in any position and without any weights, both indicate and strike for 40 hours even when they are carried on the breast or in the purse.'

Two small clocks, probably of this period, exist on the continent though their present whereabouts is unknown. Up to 1939 one was in the National Museum in Munich. A third is owned by the Society of Antiquaries in London. The latter is signed 'Jacob Zech' (or Jacob the Czech) and is dated (on the spring barrel) 1525. As will be seen from plate 6, the clock is of drum shape.

It is unusually large, $9\frac{3}{4}$ inches in diameter by 5 inches high, and has a year wheel showing the position of the sun in the zodiac. There are two hour circles, the outer I–XII and I–XII and the inner 1–24. This latter has knobs, enabling it to be moved by hand, so that the time could be adjusted for countries such as Italy and Bohemia, which reckoned by a 24-hour day, starting at a time variable with the season. As in the case of later German watches, the 2's are in the form of z's. Within the band of the zodiac signs is a narrow band with BONUM, MEDIUM, MALUM under the signs. These indicate how propitious or unpropitious it is to start enterprises when the sun is in the related sign. The indications are deduced by the then important science of astrology. Within this band is a very narrow ring carrying the moon hand, which shows the age of the moon on the narrow ring of figures,

1 to 29½, on the outer edge of the central plate. This plate carries the sun pointer, and makes a re-volution in 369 days. The central hand shows mean time on the outer hour circle. There is a small bell inside the case on which a single blow is struck at every hour. The mainspring is of brass and so also is the escape wheel. The rest of the movement is of iron.

From the armorial bearings engraved on the clock, it is inferred that the clock was made for Sigismund I, King of Poland, to be presented to Bona Sforza whom he married in 1518.

Besides Peter Henlein and Jacob the Czech the only maker known of this early period is Caspar Werner, who was contemporary with Henlein and who is said to have 'devoted himself with especial industry to the making of watches which he brought into great popularity as the result of continual study and the introduction of various new inventions, though he injured his memory and health thereby'.

Spring clocks with vertical dials had posted movements, like the contemporary weight clocks, but their more characteristic development was on the lines of the Jacob Czech clock, when the train was contained entirely between two parallel plates, held at the correct distance from each other by pillars. (In actual fact, the Jacob Czech clock has only one complete plate, and the other is of skeleton form.)

WATCHES

From this starting-point, it was merely a matter of development before the mechanism could be reduced in size so as to be conveniently carried about on the person and Peter Henlein has generally been held to have been the first person to achieve this important objective. In another report he is described as 'a locksmith artist who gained renown through the small watchworks which he was one of the first to make in the form of the musk-balls at that time in use'. Italy's rival claim to priority has been mentioned above.

And in the Nuremburg archives for 1524, there is recorded a payment to Henlein of 15 florins for a gilt musk-apple with a watch.

The earliest watches appear to have been in one of two forms. One was of the sort just described as musk-ball, i.e. spherical in shape, and the other was a reduced form of the Jacob Czech clock, usually in a gilt case, engraved and pierced to allow the striking to be heard to advantage. The latter had hinged covers, that over the dial having holes to show each hour figure, while on the dial itself were knobs for feeling the time in the dark (with two knobs at the XII).

It is difficult to account for the simultaneous existence of two devices of such unequal merit as the fusee and stackfreed. The only disadvantages of the fusee were that it necessitated a considerable depth between plates and it introduced an extra wheel in the train, while the stackfreed watches usually ran for a longer period between windings than did the early fusee watches. It seems probable that the fusee was popular in some centres of manufacture and the stackfreed in others; the stack-freed is not found outside Germany.

So far we have spoken of clock and watch making in Germany from the time she took the lead from Italy; but France was little if at all behind her and these two countries were to remain horo-logically pre-eminent until the middle of the seventeenth century with France gradually going into the lead.

Blois was the first main centre of activity and Julien Coudray of Blois, clockmaker to Louis XII and François I, is the first we know of. His claim to have made watches is based on an order by

François I in 1518; 'Order to Jean Sapin, receiver general of Languedoil and Guyenne to pay to Julien Coudray clockmaker at Blois, the sum of 200 gold écus as payment for two fine daggers, their hilts containing two gilt horologes destined for the king's service.'

The idea that a watch could be made small enough to be fitted into the handle of a dagger at so early a date is surprising and these horologes may have been sundials; but it is at least fairly certain that watches were being made in France at this time, since Florimond Robertet, treasurer under three successive kings, left no less than 12 watches at his death, described by his widow as 'Twelve watches of which seven are striking and the other five silent, in cases of gold, silver and brass of different sizes; but of these I attach value only to the large one, merely of gilt copper, that my husband caused to be made, it shows all the stars and celestial signs and motions, which he understood perfectly.' In this inventory is the first known use of the word 'montre' as applied to a timepiece and specifically to one which could be worn on the person as opposed to all other types.

After Julien Coudray, five makers are known in Blois belonging to the first half of the sixteenth century, including Guillaume Coudray and Jehan du Jardin who were 'Horologers du Roi'.

This brings us to 1550. In the course of 250 years clocks developed from massive blacksmith's work into portable watches. It was a time of steady mechanical refinement rather than progress. Very few contemporary examples survive and the thread of development has been traced mainly through literary sources. From the collector's point of view the period is, therefore, virtually a blank. Yet it is impossible to appreciate what comes after unless at least this much of the pioneer period is known.

CHAPTER II

The age of decoration: clocks 1550–1657; watches 1550–1675

CHAPTER I ended at 1550 and Chapter II is to bring the story forward another century to the threshold of great events in horological history. Chapter III will recount the practical application of the pendulum to clocks, in 1657, and of the balance spring to watches, in 1675, and from then on accurate timekeeping, rather than external decoration, became the main preoccupation of the makers. It is for this reason that the present chapter carries the story forward to two different dates for clocks and watches respectively.

As has been shown, surviving examples of clocks made before 1550 are extremely rare and no watch can be dated with certainty at 1550 or earlier. From 1550 onwards specimens become increasingly common until by 1600 they are relatively plentiful. It is for this arbitrary reason alone that 1550 has been chosen as the dividing line between this present chapter and the last.

From the mechanical standpoint no important advance was made in the hundred-odd years from 1550 to 1657 now to be considered, and as the uncontrolled balance afforded inherently erratic timekeeping it was perhaps natural that makers should turn their attention increasingly to variety of external shapes and rich decoration.

CLOCKS 1550–1657

WEIGHT-DRIVEN CLOCKS

Weight-driven house clocks continued along essentially gothic lines and even as late as the first quarter of the seventeenth century examples may be found with open iron frames, iron trains, wheel balance and surmounted by a bell suspended from diagonally placed straps. Even traditional gothic ornamentation persisted in England with little concession to renaissance taste (and indeed, as may be traced architecturally, the gothic tradition never entirely died in England, and survived fitfully until the conscious 'Gothic Revival' of the eighteenth century).

Very rarely, the whole mechanism was completely enclosed in an enveloping metal case-work.

After 1600 weight-driven house clocks went out of fashion in Germany but in England they achieved great popularity. It is strange that when wall clocks went out of fashion in England, in the eighteenth century, they returned to popularity in other countries.

LANTERN CLOCKS

The type which became almost standard in England throughout the seventeenth century and continued throughout the first half of the eighteenth is generally known as the lantern clock. It has been said that the lantern clock has no ancestry but first appeared fully matured. It is, however, obvious that it is closely related to the gothic wall-clock, civilised and compressed, and encased with brass walls and doors. It is, indeed remarkable that so few transitional pieces remain but an undoubted example is that shown on plate 8. Here the gothic origin is clearly seen; the movement is all of steel as also are the corner pillars which are in the form of perpendicular-style gothic buttresses. Between these and behind the chapter ring are brass plates entirely enclosing the movement.

It was but a short step from this to the fully developed lantern clock which made its appearance about 1620. One of about this period by William Bowyer, one of the subscribers to the incorporation of the Clockmakers' Company, is illustrated on plate 9. The clock is of brass, the chapter ring,

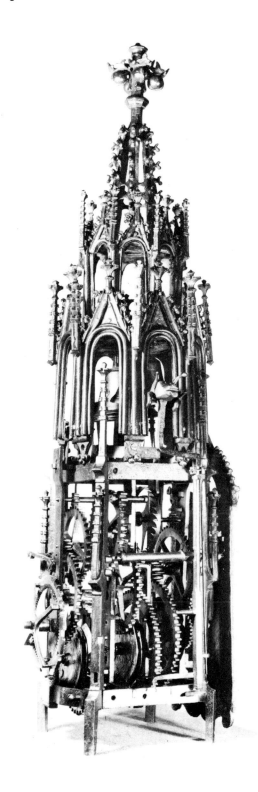

PLATE 7

German (Wurzburg) weight-driven house clock probably late fifteenth century. Entirely constructed of iron; one or two screws are later additions; going and striking trains. Three-quarter back view showing the back of the dial which is plain and has been repaired.
(Victoria and Albert Museum)

PLATE 8

Weight-driven house clock of the first quarter of the seventeenth century, exemplifying the transitional stage between the gothic house clock and the traditional English lantern clock. One of the brass side panels has been removed to show the steel posted movement with brass wheels. Note wheel balance beneath bell; going train in front of striking train; bar from front to back, level with 9.30 on the dial, which is the detent for letting off the strike; forged steel, diagonally-placed corner pillars with gothic detail; braided ropes running over spiked pulley. (British Museum)

which is slightly wider than the rest of the clock, being silvered. In the centre is the alarum dial, also silvered. The black-finished steel hand is pinned to its arbor, and has a tail (used for setting the alarum dial) almost as long as the indicator, which is finished off by a variant of the arrow-head which was almost universal throughout the sixteenth century. The barbs of the arrow-head have been curved outwards from the shaft and in later examples this was developed until each barb formed a complete circle, joining up once more with the shaft and forming a sort of figure eight. This is known, somewhat inappropriately, as the 'spade hand' and formed the basis for all the elegantly decorated hands of the late seventeenth century.

Minute hands are, at all periods, very rare on lantern clocks; in the period now under review they are unknown. The plate behind the chapter ring has shallow engraving of floral pattern. The side plates are hinged to the main framework as doors with simple turning latches. The makers name, when shown at all, is usually on the front plate, either inside the chapter ring or just below it. Occasionally it is on the bottom of the fret.

The buttress-shaped steel pillars of the gothic clock, calling for much skilled labour in their manufacture, have given way to easily made turned brass pillars, finished by small turned feet and tall finials. Top and bottom plates are rigidly attached to the four corner posts. Like the gothic clock, the bell is above the top plate, being hung from diagonal straps springing from the tops of the finials. The space between the top plate and the bell is filled by ornamental pierced frets of formal floral pattern.

The wheels are all of brass, much wider than contemporary steel wheels; the teeth of the great wheel are 3/16 inches wide. There is only one wheel between the great wheel and the crown wheel and all teeth are superbly cut although each tooth had to be filed individually; the tooth cutting machine did not come till about fifty years later. The wheels are pivoted in three narrow plates at front, back and in the centre of the clock, tongued into the top and bottom plates. In the gothic clock these were no more than pillars which gradually widened out until in contemporary spring-driven clocks they fill the full width of the clock. It is an essential feature of the lantern clock that the trains are behind each other, the going train at the front and the striking train at the back of the clock.

The inner pivot of the crown wheel is carried in a bridge-shaped potence riveted to the central plate, through which passes the verge. The balance is above the top plate, occupying almost the whole space inside the frets. The top pivot, no longer suspended from a thread, is supported by a potence screwed to the top plate inside the periphery of the balance which has only one spoke, and swings through an average arc of 80 degrees. The bottom potence of the verge is riveted to the vertical central plate.

There are no drums on to which the ropes were wound as in the case of the large turret clocks illustrated in the last chapter; instead, there are narrow pulleys with spikes in their grooves, connected to the going and striking train respectively by a ratchet and click. Over these were run a braided type of rope at one end of which were the weights. The other end terminated in a counter-weight which was pulled down to wind up the clock. All lantern clocks had this sort of winding and never a barrel and key-wind.

The use of chains instead of ropes dates from a considerably later period. Lantern clocks almost invariably run for thirty hours.

PLATE 9

One of the earliest surviving, fully developed English lantern clocks, by William Bowyer, circa 1620. Compare with transitional type in Plate 8 above and note similar arrangement of train but with turned brass (instead of forged steel) corner pillars with turned brass finials at top and bottom. Note also silvered chapter ring and alarum dial; arrow-shaped hand; shallow engraving on brass dial plate; pivot of alarum detent in dial plate above 11 o'clock; frets covering space between top plate and bell, concealing brass balance wheel.

(British Museum)

Two square bars can be seen in plate 9, about half-way up the side of the clock, extending from front to back and it is by arms at either end of these that the going train sets off the striking train at each hour.

For a detailed description of the operation of this and later striking mechanisms the reader is referred to chapter VIII.

The alarum crown wheel is bracketed on the outside of the back plate and requires its own small rope and weight to operate it. The single striking hammer arbor has pallets meshing with the alarum crown wheel. When, as happened to most of these early lantern clocks with wheel balances, they were later converted to pendulum, this external alarum mechanism was in the way of the pendulum and had to be removed. Evidence of its previous existence will generally be found in the form of a hole in the front plate, just outside the chapter ring, at about eleven o'clock, in which the alarum detent was pivoted. When there was no striking train, the alarum mechanism was then inside the clock, in the space which would otherwise have been occupied by the striking train.

PLATE 10

Square English table clock by David Ramsay, of early type with bell on top and dial above bell, circa 1600. (Victoria and Albert Museum)

This early lantern clock has been described in so much detail because it is typical of all later examples, and the many variations to be found are of a quite minor character. The size varies but a very usual average is six inches square and sixteen inches to the top of the finial above the bell. There are, however, a few larger ones and quite a number only three and a half to four inches wide. One very small example is only six inches high. In two examples in the Victoria and Albert Museum, London, nearly all the externally visible parts (except the bell and hand) are of silver.

In the last decade of the period covered by the present chapter floral or heraldic frets were largely superseded by an arrangement of two dolphins with intertwined tails, which achieved great popularity, and at the same time the chapter ring began to get wider and to over-sail the width of the clock by a greater extent. Clocks with widely overlapping chapter rings are sometimes called 'sheeps-head' from a fancied resemblance to the head-on view of a sheep.

But beyond the fact that any lantern clock which has, or has had a wheel balance may with certainty be dated prior to 1660, they are extremely difficult to date with any precision since early characteristics (such as the narrow chapter ring) may be found in quite late examples and vice versa.

SPRING-DRIVEN CLOCKS

Spring-driven clocks in the period under review are (in England at any rate) much more rare than the ubiquitous lantern clock but they nevertheless exist in great variety of form, mainly of German and French origin.

TABLE CLOCKS

The most usual form of early table clock was a circular drum, like the clock by Jacob Czech described and illustrated in the last chapter. From them developed square and hexagonal table clocks, with the dial above as in the drum type, generally belonging to the latter end of the sixteenth and to the seventeenth century, and nearly always having feet. Striking mechanism, which is not usual in the early drum clocks, becomes common. In the earlier clocks the bell was either between the plates, or else above the case, covered by an ornamental fret, with a small dial on top of it. In later clocks, the bell was mounted in a cover hinged to the bottom of the case.

In early drum clocks an alarum mechanism was often provided, which was quite separate from the clock proper, being arranged to stand on legs on the top cover when wanted for use. A detent descended from the case of the alarum movement into the path of the hand of the clock, and could be moved to any hour by turning the case. When the hand moved the detent the alarum was set off.

The cases are of brass gilt and the chapter rings are frequently silver. The movement is usually latched to the case. Of the shapes which follow the earliest drum type the square examples, which

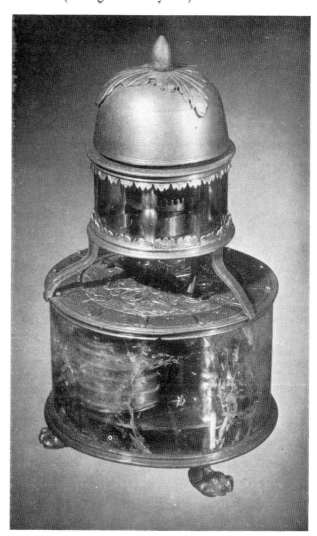

PLATE 11

Early type of spring-driven, drum-shaped table clock with separate detachable alarum mechanism on top of it. German, last quarter sixteenth century. Overall height 6 inches. Steel train. Note rock crystal sides to movement and alarum. Detent for alarum hanging down in path of the clock hand.
(British Museum)

tend to be the earlier, have four feet and the hexagonal type has three. The feet are usually turned but occasionally they are silver and carved in the form of grotesque feet or claws. Where the feet are silver the side panels are frequently also silver frets but otherwise they are usually glass or, in early examples, crystal. The balance, count wheel, winding squares and setting-up ratchets are below the bottom plate, being exposed to view when the bell frame, forming the bottom of the clock, is opened. The hammers are frequently carved in the form of grotesque animal heads. The movement and its layout is, in fact, practically identical with that of a large, contemporary clock-watch. The type (especially hexagonal) continued to be made until well into the eighteenth century, mainly in Germany.

MINIATURE TOWER OR TABERNACLE CLOCK

Another popular type, really descended from the gothic clock, was of miniature tower form, commonly three to four inches square and six to nine inches high. The layout of these clocks is identical with the English lantern clock except that instead of a pulley, rope and weight they have

PLATE 12

Hexagonal, spring-driven table clock by W. H. Gauer of Konigsburg, circa 1660. Note glass side panels; bottom view of clock with cover containing bell hinged open showing pierced cock and other ornamentation and engraved count-wheel. (British Museum)

PLATE 13

Miniature tower clock by Bartholemew Newsam. Late sixteenth century. Note early type of chapter ring and shallow engraving. As opposed to late examples (see Plate 14) the case is in one piece and slides bodily down over the movement, which is divided laterally, the going train above the striking train. The later typical examples are divided vertically, the going train in front and the striking train behind, as in Plate 14. (British Museum)

spring-barrel, fusee and gut for each train. In early examples the movement is entirely of steel; and brass wheels do not become common until the seventeenth century.

The steel frame is attached to a brass-gilt base and a similar plinth is attached to the top plate, above the balance. Four brass plates, gilt and engraved, enclose the clock, the two side pieces usually having short return uprights of architectural form so that the complete clock appears to have a pilaster at each corner. The bell is on top, but as close as possible to the top plate so that there is no place for the large frets of the lantern clock. It is either held by diagonal straps of varying shape, or a complete fret enveloping it entirely. The dial is at the front of the clock and the chapter ring, with Roman numerals, is either silvered or gilt. If the clock has an alarum mechanism the setting dial is inside the chapter ring, having arabic numerals and generally three holes in its surface in which to insert any pointed object for setting it. The going train is wound by a square engaged through a hole below the dial. If there is an alarum this has its own spring and hammer, placed at right angles to the main train, usually between the front and middle plate of the movement and wound through one of the side plates. The striking train is wound through the back plate which also usually has a dial numbered 1 to 12 in Arabic numerals, spaced at irregular intervals corresponding to those of the count wheel. The object of this dial was to see at a glance what the clock last struck. With the type of striking mechanism universal before 1675 the striking does not as a matter of course follow the hand, but always strikes the hours in succession. If therefore the striking train is allowed to run down while the clock is kept going such a dial is necessary to see what struck last before the striking spring ran down. An extension of the locking piece protrudes through the case and, after winding, may be let off by hand until the striking and going trains agree.

PLATE 14

German spring-driven, miniature tower or tabernacle clock. Overall height 8 inches, circa 1600. Iron and steel movement. Brass-gilt, engraved side plates with architectural treatment of corner pilasters. Note bell held by pierced fret with balance wheel beneath; twenty-four-hour dial; '2' shaped as 'Z' characteristic of German work at this period; alarum setter disc in centre of chapter ring; feeling knobs for telling time at night. One side plate has been removed to show the movement which has very early fusee chains with long links.

Such is the basic tower-type clock which was capable of many detail variations and, frequently, complications in the form of calendar and astronomical dials.

These clocks are by no means easy to date since their basic layout altered but little in the period under review. Steel movements may be found right up to the end of it but brass wheels begin to appear in the last quarter of the sixteenth century and even earlier in isolated examples. Moreover, it is not only common, but usual to find later replacements in brass, at any rate for the third and escape wheels of the going train, even when the original balance remains. When an early clock was converted to pendulum a considerable rearrangement was necessary as the escape wheel arbor had to be vertical instead of horizontal and this entailed the introduction of a contrate wheel as the third wheel in the train. Evidence of the conversion may be seen in the alterations to the top plate.

Guild-marks and makers initials may sometimes be found stamped small on the outside plates and it is the external appearance of these clocks which gives the best guide to their age. Although the Renaissance had become firmly established in Italy by the middle of the fifteenth century (indeed, the gothic style never came naturally to the sunny climate of Italy) it gained a tardy and less complete ascendency in the northern countries. Accordingly, gothic ornament is still predominant in German clocks of the sixteenth century and it is by the amount of Renaissance detail that they can best be dated. The engraving, very delicate at the beginning of the period, becomes increasingly coarse as the seventeenth century progresses.

Towards the end of the sixteenth century, a modified form of tabernacle clock appeared, with a large front for the dial and comparatively shallow. The superstructure covering the bell is then a rectangular dome, the dome being generally elaborately pierced and chiselled. In this type the trains are side by side and sometimes at right angles to the dial.

PILLAR CLOCKS

Lastly there is the type with a base carrying a pillar and a vertical dial on the pillar. The

PLATE 15

Small German pillar clock, mid-sixteenth century. The dials are in the box above the man's head. The movement and bell are in the base.

movement or striking train only is housed in the base, with connection to the dial through the pillar. Sometimes the pillar carries a turning globe with an hour band, the pointer being fixed either to the frame of the globe or carried by a figure standing on the base. The pillar in some examples takes the form of a crucifixion, with automata round the base.

Watches on pillar stands are fairly common and are distinguished from these pillar clocks by the base and pillar not housing any part of the mechanism. Most frequently, the stand is a later part made to hold the watch.

SPECIAL CLOCKS

There are many clocks which are isolated forms and belong to no particular type, but are often very elaborate and of considerable interest. The tabernacle clock reaches its acme of complexity in two very similar German clocks of about 1625. One is in the museum of the Clockmakers' Company at the London Guildhall, illustrated in Plate 17, and the other in the Kunsthistorische Museum in Vienna. The former is by Johann Schneider of Augsburg. It consists of an octagonal base of gilt metal, cast and chiselled, supporting by a group of boys and a dolphin, a cylindrical main clock. This is surmounted by a small rectangular alarum, with a canopy on pillars above it. Under the canopy is an automaton group of St. George and the dragon, and above is a figure in Roman dress. The dial of the main clock has, starting from the

PLATE 16

Silver parcel-gilt Crucifix clock. German. First quarter seventeenth century. Overall height 11 inches. Brass movement in base drives a revolving chapter ring at the top of cross. In the separate illustration showing the movement with bottom cover hinged open note stackfreed (in run-down position); count wheel with internally-cut gearing; foliot balance with bristle regulator operated by dial calibrated 1–8.
(British Museum)

PLATE 17

Pillar or pedestal astronomical clock by Johann Schneider of Augsburg, circa 1625. Overall height, 32 inches. The twenty-four-hour dial is surmounted by a square alarum movement with twelve-hour setter disk. On the back are calendar dials and countwheel dial. (The Worshipful Company of Clockmakers)

34

outside, a broad silver band on which a year calendar is engraved, with the Saint's name for each day. Then a narrow minutes ring. Then a silver hour ring for 24 hours. Then a silver band with shutters for showing the length of daylight. The centre is occupied by an astrolabe. A steel hand shows the minutes and gilt hands the hour and the age of the moon. On the back are six small dials which show the day of the week and of the month and the striking position for hours and quarters.

The British Museum has a clock standing about four feet high, made in 1589 by Isaac Habrecht, the maker of the second Strasburg clock. There is a tradition that it was made for Pope Sixtus V to imitate the Strasburg clock. It is illustrated in Plate 18. The large dial at the bottom is engraved with feast days, holy days and astronomical signs. The next storey has a dial for minutes and one for the hours, and two figures which move a scythe and an hour glass when the hour strikes. The top storey is occupied by groups of automaton figures, and the whole is surmounted by a cock which crows and flaps its wings after the chiming.

Another clock in the British Museum is in the form of a three-masted ship, 3′ 3″ high, made by Hanns Schlott of Augsburg in 1580, and said to have belonged to the Emperor Rudolph II. The dial is at the base of the middle mast, and behind it figures pass in procession before the Emperor, crowned and seated on a throne.

In the Grunes Gewolbe in Dresden is (or was) the famous rolling ball clock, sometimes called the Tower of Babel clock, made in 1602 by Hanns Schlottheim of Augsburg, Prague and Dresden,

PLATE 18 *(left and right)*

Large standing German clock made in 1589 by Isaac Habrecht, probably for Pope Sixtus V, in imitation of the Strasburg clock. Overall height about four feet. The operation of the various dials is set out on page 35. The removal of some of the side plates shows the layout of the movement in storeys. (British Museum)

for Christian II. An octagonal tower, about four feet high, has two galleries, a lantern above and a base with the clock dial. Between the two galleries is a spiral runway of 16 turns and, every minute, a crystal ball is released from the upper gallery and rolls round the spiral runway to the lower gallery. It is then raised up again by the clock mechanism. Eight automaton figures of musicians stand round the lower gallery and play their instruments while an organ plays inside the tower. Figures representing the Gods of the planets stand round the upper gallery, and Saturn strikes a bell every minute.

As opposed to these ornate clocks, the very plain one illustrated in Plate 19 is of great mechanical interest as its maker Hans Kiening evolved entirely his own substitute for the fusee or stackfreed. Geared to the great wheel is one revolving once in 24 hours, carrying a spiral-shaped cam against which presses a spring-tensioned follower, pivoted to the clock plate. The balance potence is carried on the far end of this lever, which has the effect that when the spring is fully wound the pallets are deeply meshed with the crown wheel, thus giving a large arc and slowing the clock, while the engagement becomes shallower as the spring runs down. This clock, dating from about 1590 is superbly made and in proper adjustment has shown itself capable of keeping time within a minute over a period of 24 hours, having gained a minute in the first 12 and lost it again in the second; a highly remarkable performance for a spring-driven pre-balance-spring timekeeper.

Rare, if not unique, is the large bracket clock illustrated in Plate 20. It is of particular interest as being of London make. The maker was N. Vallin by whom several very fine watches and clocks are known. The whole clock is of steel, with brass outside plates, which are pinned to the framework. The balance is some seven inches in diameter and the complete swing to and fro is at the exceptionally low speed of 15 per minute, affording timekeeping within an error of five minutes a day, which is unusually close for clocks prior to the introduction of the pendulum. There are separate trains, at right angles to the dial, for striking and chiming, the latter being an unusually lengthy performance on 13 bells at each quarter. This is executed by a pinned drum which is one of the oldest existing examples. The size of the clock is roughly eight inches square and extreme height twenty-two inches. It is dated 1598.

The description of a few such unique clocks is essential to make the historical picture of this period reasonably complete, but one is unlikely to come the way of the private collector; he can, however, well hope to possess a lantern or miniature tower type clock of the period, although probably converted to pendulum, from the original wheel balance. Even late examples of the iron gothic clocks are more common than might be expected, and in these the original balance is more often found to have survived, no doubt for the reason that by the time the pendulum was invented they were already considered too out of date to be worth converting.

TRAVELLING OR COACH CLOCKS

This classification covers a wide range of spring-driven timekeepers, made in the form of a watch, but too large to wear in the pocket. They were intended for travelling, and are three to five inches in diameter. Originally they had outer protective cases but these have seldom survived. They are discussed in greater detail in Chapter IV, to which period the great majority of surviving examples belong, but they are also found in the sixteenth and early seventeenth centuries and some especially fine specimens were made by Edward East.

PLATE 19

Bottom view of a table clock by Hans Kiening, last quarter sixteenth century, showing an alternative to stackfreed and fusee, in the form of automatically varied depthing of the escape wheel, explained on page 36. Note contrate wheel for winding and very high finish throughout.
(British Museum)

PLATE 20

Weight-driven English house clock by N. Vallin, dated 1598. Overall height 22 inches. In this back view the brass side panels have been removed to show the iron and steel posted movement. The balance wheel is hidden behind the narrow panel between the movement and the bell frame. This is the earliest known surviving musical clock and plays a tune on thirteen bells at each quarter.
Note three trains at right angles to the dial.
(British Museum)

WATCHES 1550–1675

The cases of all surviving sixteenth century watches are of gilt bronze. It is known from the Nürnberg archives and from the inventory of the effects of the French statesman, Robertet, quoted in the last chapter, that silver and gold were used for watch cases, but other inventories indicate that gilt bronze cases were the rule. The cost of a gold case would have been small compared with the

PLATE 21

Travelling or coach clock by Edward East. Third quarter seventeenth century. Diameter 4½ inches. The clock has a shaped leather outer travelling case not shown. The case is brass-gilt, pierced and engraved, with times of sunrise and sunset on back. The dial has hands indicating the date, hour and minutes (of which this is a very early example). The movement has four trains for going; hour bell in back cover; quarter bell under dial; alarum. On the movement, note anti-clockwise seconds dial between 'Edwardus' and 'East' (one of the first examples known); irregular shape and floreate pattern of balance cock, screwed to plate and located by pins (typical of third quarter seventeenth century). (British Museum)

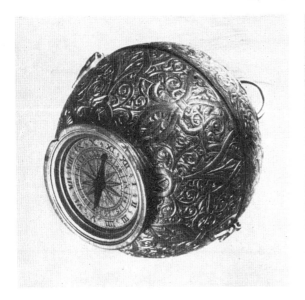

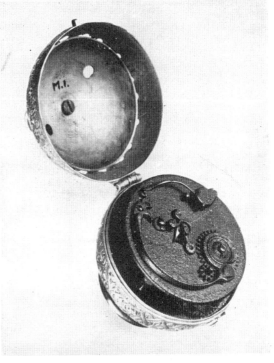

Small spherical German clock-watch, circa 1550, similar to the earliest spherical watches by Peter Henlein. The iron stackfreed movement is in two layers (striking and going trains). The mainspring has no containing barrel. The dial is at the opposite end to the pendant. The case is brass-gilt.
(Ashmolean Museum, Oxford)

PLATE 22

cost of the watch movement, and it is probable that the rare use of a precious metal is attributable to guild restrictions. As an instance, at Blois, the rights of the goldsmiths were guarded by a proviso that any gold or silver used by watchmakers had to be purchased from them and marked by them. For us, it is fortunate that the early watches were cased in a metal that was not worth melting down.

Throughout the period described in this chapter watches were suspended from a cord or chain worn round the neck, rather than in the pocket, and this practice is largely responsible for their great variety of shape and decoration. Only from 1625 onwards do unornamented watches start to become common (mainly English, doubtless in deference to the growing Puritan movement). After about 1660 the more exuberant shapes are confined to watches intended to be worn by women.

It is not known whether the first watches were spherical or drum-shaped. About six spherical watches survive, all of very early date and one at least, German, probably dates from the second quarter of the sixteenth century. The oldest dated French watch, by the celebrated Jacques de la Garde, made in 1551 is also spherical; but it is certain that the drum-shaped watch started nearly, if not quite as early as the spherical form and rapidly superseded it.

Prior to 1590, nearly all surviving watches are German and their characteristics differ so markedly from the French that the two schools, and the subsequent English which derived from them, are best considered separately in the first instance.

PLATE 23

German clock-watch with alarum; last quarter six-teenth century. Case brass-gilt, pierced and chiselled. Note twenty-four-hour dial with '2' shaped as 'Z' and feeling knobs for night use; stackfreed and foliot with bristle regulator. (Ashmolean Museum, Oxford)

40

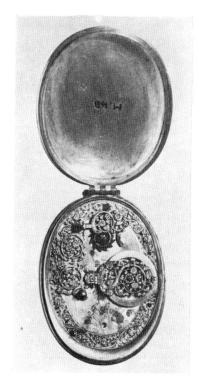

PLATE 24

Oval watch by Johann Bock of Frankfurt, circa 1630. Although German, the decoration of the movement is more in accordance with French and English style; the border is characteristically English. The brass-gilt case is chiselled and engraved. (Ashmolean Museum, Oxford)

EARLY WATCH-MAKING IN GERMANY

There are many table clocks without striking or alarum mechanism, but most of the sixteenth century German watches had either one or both. In consequence, the cases were pierced round the edge and on the bottom. The bell was usually fixed to the bottom of the case, and the movement was then hinged to the case and had to be turned out of it for winding. Occasionally, the bell was fixed to a hinged cover, and then the movement dropped into the case from above and was held in by a latch.

In the spherical form the pendant was opposite to the dial, which therefore hung downwards. The movement was in two layers, divided by a central plate. On the side nearest to the pendant was the striking train and bell; on the other was the going train and dial.

The dial in most cases had an outer ring of figures I-XII and an inner ring of figures 13 to 24 to suit the time-reckoning in Italy, Bohemia and south-western Germany. The cover then was pierced with two series of holes for the two rings; more rarely, there is one series of large holes.

The Arabic figure 2 in sixteenth century German watches was nearly always formed like a Z.

Many watches have the knobs at each hour which were provided on both watches and table clocks for feeling the time in the dark.

The part of the dial inside the chapter ring was usually engraved, a rose, or star-shaped pattern being the most usual form of decoration.

The dial plates were either of metal gilt or of silver, silver always being used when there was enamel decoration. Sometimes the hour figures were incised and filled with enamel.

The hand was always steel and carefully shaped. It was often clumsy, but it had to be strong enough to withstand being pushed round to set the watch to time. The ugly, flat, un-chiselled hands sometimes found on early watches are almost always later replacements.

As already described, the cover over the dial was pierced so that the time could be seen without opening it, and the rest of the outer case was also pierced, so that the striking could be heard to advantage. This piercing was executed in complex patterns, and enhanced by fine chiselling and engraving. Towards the end of the sixteenth century the amount and depth of the chiselling diminished and its place was increasingly taken by shallow engraving.

The earliest drum type of watch had a flat top, bottom and sides but by 1575 both the cover and edges were becoming rounded and by 1600 the edge usually had a band of almost semi-circular section all round it. Also soon after 1575 the octagonal and elongated octagonal forms became common though the circular form persisted. The flat-sided oval form was not common before 1600 and the rounded oval or 'puritan' watch did not appear until the seventeenth century.

The term 'Nuremburg Egg' is often applied quite indiscriminately to early German watches. It is in fact a quite meaningless term and is not met with prior to about 1730. It probably originated from a confusion between the words *Ueurlein* meaning a little clock and *Eyerlein* meaning a little egg.

German watch-making suffered severely during the Thirty Years War (1618–48) from which it never really recovered, and during this time it lost its supremacy to the vigorous French industry.

EARLY WATCH-MAKING IN FRANCE

As was shown in the last chapter, watchmaking in France goes back almost, if not quite as far as in Germany and there is considerable evidence to show that watches were being made at Blois as early as 1518. The industry at Blois came to considerable prosperity and importance during the sixteenth century and other centres grew up at Autun, Rouen, Paris, Lyons, Sedan, La Rochelle, Dijon and Grenoble.

The oldest known French watch is the one already mentioned, dated 1551, by Jacques de la Garde, in the Louvre, and there is another similar, but larger, by him, dated 1565, in the Maritime Museum, Greenwich, illustrated in Plate 25. The only sixteenth century French watch in the British Museum is one by Augustin Forfaict of Sedan, who died in 1587.

The Pierpont Morgan collection in the Metropolitan Museum of Art in New York has two watches of the last quarter of the sixteenth century, one by F. Vallier, father of Jean Vallier, the greatest maker of his time, and the other by Nicholas Gaillard, both of Lyons. Besides the spherical watch in the Louvre, and the large one in the Maritime Museum, and two or three in private collections, there is no French watch which can be assigned to a date before the last decade of the sixteenth century. None of these is of the circular drum type; two are spherical, another is in the form of a tulip, and the others are oval.

From 1590 onwards French watches are comparatively numerous. The most common form is an oval, with straight sides and moderately domed covers, and the case is generally of gilt metal, covered with engravings of scenes, figures and foliage patterns. Another common form is an elongated octagon. The covers are not pierced, as in German watches; piercing required for striking or alarum watches is confined to the sides. Dial plates are generally gilt with engraved silver chapter rings.

The surfaces pierced and chiselled in German watches are, in the French, engraved.

One of the finest watches of the period is by Jean Vallier of Lyons, in the British Musem. Its rather unattractive shape is redeemed by the exquisite engraving covering the whole case. The movement, which shows most beautiful workmanship and decoration, contains striking, alarum and calendar mechanisms which are all in perfect order.

Jean Vallier was a maker of great repute in Lyons, and all his watches have beautiful work, both in the decoration and movement. Thirteen are known, of which one is in the Victoria and Albert Museum, two in the Fitzwilliam Museum, Cambridge, and three in the Louvre. The first record of Jean Vallier in the Lyons archives is in 1596, and he died in 1649.

EARLY WATCH-MAKING IN ENGLAND

England was much behind Germany and France in producing watches. No English watch is known of a date before 1580 and only a short time before this is there any record of an English watchmaker. Queen Elizabeth

PLATE 25

Large spherical French clock-watch by Jacques de la Garde, circa 1550, about 4 inches in diameter. Brass wheels. Note long thin fusee typical of earliest spring-driven instruments; engraved spring barrels. (National Maritime Museum, Greenwich)

PLATE 26 *(left and right)*

French watch by Gribelin. First quarter seventeenth century. The dial records the hours, day of the week, date, phases of the moon and signs of the zodiac. The case is caste and finelly chiselled in high relief. The table of figures inside the cover gives times of sunrise and sunset. The flowing pattern of the pierced ornamentation of the top plate of the movement, with wheel balance, is typical of French work in the first half of the seventeenth century.
(Ashmolean Museum, Oxford)

possessed a number of watches, but it is more probable that they came from abroad than that they were the work of English makers of whom we have no record.

She had two clockmakers; Nicholar Urseau, who is mentioned in 1553, 1556 and 1572 and died in 1590, and Bartholomew Newsam, who was working as a clockmaker in 1568 and died in 1593. There is no record of Urseau as a watchmaker, but Bartholomew Newsam almost certainly made watches as well as the small table clocks of which examples survive. The Metropolitan Museum of Art has a large striking watch, four inches across, with a mark B x N, which is most probably by him. This has a German type of case, but a dial which is essentially French or English. Also Newsam's will mentions 'One cristall jewell with a watche in it, garnished with goulde'.

The English watch of the end of the sixteenth century appears to have been copied from both German and French types. The striking watch by Randolf Bull of London (working 1582–1617), in the Mallett Collection, at the Ashmolean Museum, Oxford, is a good example of the composite type. The case is typically German; the mechanism, with fuzee, cock and tangent screw set-up is French; the inner ring of hours, 13–24 on the dial belongs to Germany and has no meaning for England, but the two's are not formed as z's, and there are no feeling knobs.

Two English watches are known with pierced covers of the German type, one the watch just mentioned by Bartholomew Newsam, and the other a watch by Richard Crayle, who was born in

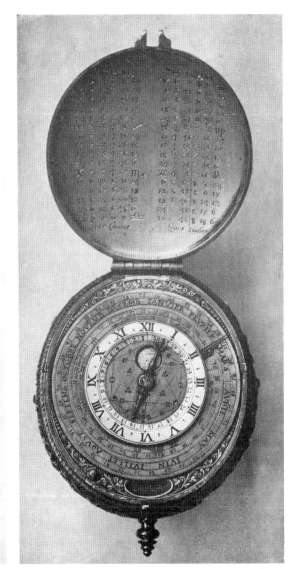

1600 and was a petitioner for the incorporation of the Clockmakers' Company in 1631. A Scottish example is by Heironymus Hamilthon dated 1595.

By contrast, a watch in the Webster Collection by François Nawe, or Francis Noway, who was known in London 1580–3, is of predominently French Type. The gilt metal case is of oval shape, finely engraved and the dial is similarly treated, with an arrow-shaped steel hand.

During the first quarter of the seventeenth century English watchmaking settled down into a style of its own and English workmanship rapidly improved until it could stand comparison with the best continental standard.

The most characteristic type all through the middle of the seventeenth century was a fairly small

PLATE 27

English clock-watch by Michael Nouwen, circa 1600. The case and dial are decorated with shallow chiselling and engraving. Note dial cover pierced for reading the time. On the movement note decorative border typical of early English work, but the S-shaped cock and foliot show German influence and the rest of the movement shows French influence. (Metropolitan Museum of Art, New York)

rounded oval watch, seldom as much as two inches long, now known as the 'Puritan Watch'. The silver case and dial plate are seldom engraved and the chapter ring is simply engraved with Roman numerals. This simplicity was doubtless partly in deference to puritan taste and it may be that such watches were worn in the pocket and not exposed. The movement, by contrast, is no less decorative than any other watch of the period.

In this connection some uncertainty exists. The first known pocket is in a garment dated about 1625, but until 1675 pockets were confined to breeches and were not therefore very suitable for carrying watches. Yet in hardly any seventeenth century portraits is a watch visibly worn. In about 1675 Charles II introduced the long waistcoat to fashion and from then on watches were worn in the pocket.

But these very plain watches must also be attributed to the English functional approach to horology which found its reward in the acknowledged supremacy of English watchmakers before the end of the seventeenth century.

PLATE 28

English alarum watch by Cornelius Mellin, first quarter seventeenth century. The case is pierced, caste and chiselled. The inside of the cover and the dial are finely engraved. The decoration of the top plate of the movement is in the French style. Note the fixing of the balance cock, which fits over and is pinned to a stud fixed to the watch plate. The decorated wheel (gilt over blued steel) is stop-work for alarum. (British Museum)

PLATE 29 (*above*)

'Puritan' watch by Edward East, mid-seventeenth century. The case, entirely without ornament, is typical of this specially English style. This example is unique in having a gold case.
(Ashmolean Museum, Oxford)

PLATE 30 (*right*)

Pair-case watch by William Snow of Marlborough. Third quarter seventeenth century. A rare and early example of English provincial work of very high quality and of the use of the pair-case. The outer case is covered with black leather decorated with silver pinwork. Note plain, loosely fitting, ring type pendant, typical of the second half seventeenth century; typically English, undecorated dial and hand. On the movement, note set-up, worm wheel regulator with blued-steel, decoratively pierced bearings; gilt cock with very early appearance of continuous border to foot and plate; cock-fixing by a screw although it is still located by fitting over a stud (see Plate 28). Note also early use of 'tulip' watch pillars.

49

PLATE 31

Pair-case watch by Edward Hampton, circa 1670–5. Outer case leather and silver pinwork. Silver, champlevé type dial with single hand and calendar ring. This must be one of the last English watches made without a balance spring.
(Ashmolean Museum, Oxford)

By the middle of the century the plain circular pair-case watch was becoming common, the inner case plain silver and the outer usually leathercovered and decorated with silver pinwork. The evolution of the pair-case is distinctly illogical. In the first place, highly decorated watches were provided with outer cases for their protection when not required for use or display. But when watches became more common, the inner case, as usually worn was quite plain and it was the outer case, reserved for special occasions, which was decorated. In such cases (generally at a later date than this chapter) there was yet a third outer case to protect the middle one. Out of these extremes developed the ordinary watch, in which both inner and outer cases were almost completely plain and the outer case only served to keep dust out of the winding holes and make the watch a good deal thicker than it had any need to be.

*   *   *   *

The characteristics of the three principal national styles of watchmaking will be further examined in the section at the end of this chapter devoted to mechanism, but having traced their general beginnings we may now turn to the wide range of shape and decoration which was current everywhere from about 1625 to 1675. Throughout the whole period watches continued to be execrable timekeepers and it was therefore natural that the main interest should centre upon their decoration. With the invention of the balance spring relatively accurate time-keeping became possible and, withdrawing finally into the pocket, watches became primarily utilitarian.

In the meantime, the half century from 1625 to 1675 was the great age of watch decoration.

WATCH-CASE DECORATION
Lapidary's work

Lapidary's work is found on watch cases in a great variety of forms, and mainly from 1600 to 1675. Rock crystal was the stone most commonly used, generally the clear crystal, but sometimes the rarer smoky variety.

The most usual form of crystal case has a crystal block hollowed out to take the movement; a gilt metal frame is

PLATE 32
(*above*)

Watch with case of rock crystal mounted in a metal frame, circa 1620.
(British Museum)

PLATE 33
(*left*)

Watch by Michael Nouwen, circa 1600. Case of smoke rock crystal without any frame. Gold dial with red and green champlevé enamel.
(British Museum)

fixed to the crystal and the movement with dial is hinged to the frame, while a separate piece of crystal, also held in a frame, is on the same hinge and forms the cover.

A very rare form is without the metal frames. A metal hinge with the pendant knob is rivetted on to one end of the crystal block and a metal catch on to the other end. The cover is a crystal plate slightly hollowed out, and this also has only the two small metal attachments of a hinge and a catch.

Five watches of this type are recorded, of which one is in the British Museum and two at the Louvre. Perhaps the finest is the watch by Michael Nouwen in the British Museum, in an octagonal smoky crystal case. The dial is of gold, with inlay of red and green enamel, and there is the very unusual feature of an enamelled gold plate on the top plate of the movement. The date of the watch is about 1600.

The Metropolitan Museum of Art in New York has an octagonal watch in a slightly smoky crystal case by Nicolas Bernard, of about 1620.

There are some striking watches with a bell under the dial and pierced edging covering the bell. The movement is attached to a plate below the bell and this is hinged to a crystal block covering the movement.

Probably the earliest watch in a crystal case, which must date from the sixteenth century, is in the Olivier collection. The case is a crystal barrel and the movement, much higher than it is wide, is pushed endwise into the barrel, the dial closing one end and the back plate the other end.

It is strange that a plain smooth crystal case is very rare. The crystal is always cut in facets or, very commonly, in lobes, or with a pattern of shallow cuts. The Wallace collection has one with engraving on the crystal, but this is extremely rare. The commonest forms are long octagonal cut in facets, and circular and oval cut in lobes. Crystal cross watches are not uncommon and every variety of form is found; the British Museum has a representative selection.

Chasing and repoussé work

These two decorative processes are similar in that the metal is not cut, but is formed by a hammer and punches. In chasing, the metal is worked on from the front, in repoussé from the back. In early examples the two forms were combined. This form of decoration became fashionable in the eighteenth century, but it is rare before the last quarter of the seventeenth.

A very perfect example, in the British Museum, is the cross watch by C. Tinelly of Aix of about 1635. The repoussé work is done on gold plates soldered on to gilt metal covers.

Chiselling

The earliest German watches were pierced and finely chiselled, but towards the end of the sixteenth century the extent and depth of chiselling decreased and the use of engraving began to take its place. Apart from this early period, the use of chiselling is rare except in quite low relief. The Fitzwilliam Museum has a watch with cast silver case and cast cover, and both back and front are chiselled in relief to show a battle scene and a group of figures. It is by Nicholas Cuisinier of Paris, and dates from about 1650.

There are many watches in cast silver cases, and all are chiselled, but the work here is no more than cleaning up the pattern of the casting to give a properly finished surface.

The finest example of cast and chiselled work is in the much earlier book watch probably by Hans Kiening, in the Mallett collection. Here there is chiselling of a floral pattern on the solid parts

PLATE 34
Framed crystal watch by Sermand of Geneva, circa 1660. The gilt frame is decorated in enamel and the dial is painted enamel. (British Museum)

53

PLATE 35

Silver outer case, caste and chiselled and engraved.
Mid-seventeenth century. (British Museum)

of the cast covers and also the chiselling of pierced work in thick plates to give it form. This pierced and chiselled work was brought to great perfection about the middle of the century. There are four examples all, curiously enough, on square watches, with a pierced plaque on a background of contrasting colour. One in the Louvre by Baltazar Martinot, of about 1675, has an openwork plaque of bright gold, pierced and chiselled in a floral pattern, on a backing of steel blued to a deep blue.

Another of about 1660 is similar; it is by F. L. Meybom of Paris and is in the Fitzwilliam Museum. A third watch in the British Museum has a silver plaque on a gilt case; the work is less fine but the pattern is attractive. It is by Johann Michael Kheller of about 1640. A fourth, an exceptionally fine watch, is constructed differently in having the back of gold, deeply champlevé to leave an ornamental pattern in relief. The champlevé background is guilloché and covered with translucent green enamel. It is by Nicolas Lemaindre of Blois of about 1650 and is in the Louvre. Lemaindre was born in 1600 and was clockmaker to Louis XIV and to the Duc d'Orléans. Three other watches by him are known.

Form watches

About the middle of the seventeenth century form watches became fashionable. Generally they were ugly and often the cases were of poor quality, but there are exceptions, especially in some of the earlier book watches. Several have been mentioned as examples of chiselled work, the skull watch by Johann Maurer and the dog watch by Jacques Joly.

A book watch with exceptionally fine work is that already mentioned, probably by Hans Kiening, of about 1575. The hour dial has figures I–XII and I–XII and an inner ring marked 1–24, this being rotatable to show the Italian day, which started at a time depending on sunset. In the centre is an alarum dial; unlike the modern alarum, this watch could be set to ring at a time more than 12 hours ahead. Above the hour dial is a meridian sundial with style missing. It shows ingenuity on the maker's part to have selected the one form of dial that could have been fitted into the narrow space available. On the inner side of the cover is a dial movable by hand, showing the relationship between the age of the moon and its phase, and a horizontal sundial with figures for four different latitudes.

A most unusual form watch is the silver sphere engraved with a map of the world, in the Staats Museum, Amsterdam. The movement is signed Henry Sebert, Strasbourg, a maker unknown by any record or by any other work. The workmanship, both of movement and of the engraving is of high quality.

Another form watch in a cast silver case is the tulip watch in the British Museum by Thomas

Sande, a maker unknown by any record. The case is chiselled in a chequer pattern, the sunk squares being filled with fine cross-hatching to give strong contrast with the polished raised squares. The watch belongs to the first quarter of the seventeenth century.

Enamel

Enamelling is a very old decorative process, which flourished in the East and then, as new processes were invented, found a home in Limoges.

Enamel is a glass composed of silica, red lead and potash; normally it is colourless and is then called 'flux' or *fondant*, but generally it is used coloured by the addition when fused of oxides of metals.

By varying the proportions of its constituents, its melting temperature can be varied. If the temperature be made low, giving a 'soft' enamel, the surface is liable to deteriorate from long exposure to the atmosphere. The 'hard' enamel with high melting point retains its original surface and colour indefinitely, but it has the disadvantage of cracking more readily, both from shocks and from temperature differences between the enamel and its metal backing. Also, it can be used only on metals of high melting point.

PLATE 36

'Form Watch' by Didier Lalemand, Paris, in the shape of a cross. Second quarter seventeenth century. Crystal case. The dial is an early example of enamel painting. (British Museum)

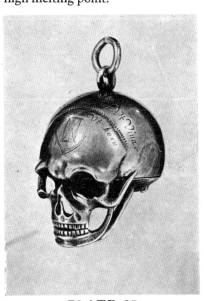

PLATE 37

'Form Watch' in the shape of a skull. Mid-seventeenth century. The jaw hinges open to reveal the dial.

In early enamels, cells were formed in the metal plate and were filled with enamel, each cell, generally with a single colour. In champlevé enamelling, the cells are formed by cutting away a thick metal plate with a graver, leaving walls of metal up to the level of the original surface. By varying the depth of the cells, gradations of colour could be obtained when translucent enamels were used. In cloisonné enamelling, the cells are formed by fixing thin strips of metal, nearly always gold, on to a plate, the edges of the strips being the outlines of the design. The strips are fixed to the plate or held in place by a thin layer of enamel on the plate.

However the cells are formed, they are filled with powdered enamel and the whole fired; the powder, on fusing shrinks, and several fillings and firings are needed to bring the enamel up to or just above the level of the plate or of the top edges of the cloisons. The enamel is then ground down to metal level and a shiny surface obtained either by polishing or by a short firing just enough to fuse the surface of the enamel.

Simple forms of champlevé enamelling are often found on the dials of German watches before and after 1600. In some the hour figures are sunk and filled with enamel, or a star or sun is formed in the centre of the dial and filled with translucent enamel.

The crystal watch already mentioned by Michael Nouwen has a dial with enamelling of this type, the sinks in the gold plate being filled with red and green enamels.

The most perfect example of cloisonné enamel is on the watch by Jacques Huon of Paris, in the Victoria and Albert Museum. Each flower is in a cell formed by a cloison which is so fine as to be hardly visible; the pistils and stems are the top edges of cloisons made thick enough to be visible. The shading on the individual flowers is done by the process of painting on enamel, to be described later. The watch, dating from about 1650, has an outer case of shagreen. Only one other watch by Huon is known, at Dresden.

An earlier watch made at Blois but unsigned, is also in the Victoria and Albert Museum. In this the cloisons are in a thick layer of translucent blue enamel and are filled with differently coloured enamels.

PLATE 38

Watch decorated in champlevé enamel,
circa 1660. Probably French.
(Victoria and Albert Museum)

Painting in enamel

Painting in enamel started at Limoges soon after 1500 and continued for a century, when it fell into decadence. Differently coloured and generally opaque enamels were applied to the metal plate without any cells or cloisons to separate the colours. It reached a remarkable degree of perfection about the middle of the sixteenth century, and was applied to plaques, reliquaries, book-covers and other objects considerably larger than watch-cases. To these it was unsuited, and no example of a watch with Limoges enamel is known in any European Museum. However the Pierpont Morgan collection, now in the Metropolitan Museum in New York, contains examples.

Enamel decoration without cells, forming patterns as opposed to scenes and figures, is fairly common in the first half of the seventeenth century. An exquisite example is the watch by Edward East in the Victoria and Albert Museum. The gold case has a smooth layer of turquoise-blue enamel and enamel is applied on this in small blobs or thin threads. Flowers are formed by specks of white enamel standing out in relief; the foliage is indicated by the process to be described later. The date is about 1650.

Another form of enamelling without cells is on pierced work. The Victoria and Albert Museum has an example, probably French, of a watch case with back and cover pierced and chiselled to form a pattern of flowers and foliage, and opaque and translucent enamels are applied to the pattern.

The watch by Louys Vautier of Blois in the British Museum has a similar, though more formal, pierced pattern laid over a layer of white enamel. The centre of the dial has a white ground with a pattern of flowers in cloisons. Vautier was born in 1591 and died in 1638. Another watch by him is in the Louvre.

Limoges enamellers used a device, especially in their decadence, to give brilliance. Translucent enamels were applied over *paillons*, of small bits of gold or silver foil cut to suit the pattern. These paillons are often seen in cloisonné and champlevé work.

A form of enamelling called *basse-taille* is a thin layer of translucent enamel over an engraved plate, the engraving being generally of a pattern. Early examples are not common, but the watch by Simon Hackett in the Victoria and Albert Museum has a broad band of orange enamel over a guilloche ground, consisting of a mass of little scoops cut by a round graver. Simon Hackett was three times master of the Clockmakers' Company from 1646 to 1659, but the enamelling on this watch is of poor quality for work of the best period.

Basse-taille enamel became very common towards the end of the eighteenth century and later, when engine-turning (also called *guilloche* in French) was a frequent form of decoration. The geometric patterns are most effective under the enamel layer.

Painting on enamel

This process was discovered by Jean Toutin, a goldsmith who was born in Chateaudun in 1578 and died in Paris in 1644. Felibien des Avaux wrote in 1676 that Toutin had made the invention in 1632, but there is a royal order for 'sept boistes d'or émaillées à figures' in 1630, and this is a more probable date in view of the extent to which the process had developed in Blois in 1635.

The process was ideal for watches because, in the hands of the great masters, scenes, figures and portraits could be painted with extraordinary delicacy. From the start, it became fashionable for miniature portraits and Jean Petitot, born in Geneva in 1607, and a pupil of Toutin or one of his followers, became renowned in France and England for his portraits in enamel.

PLATE 39

Watch by Edward East. Mid-seventeenth century. The case is pale blue enamel, decorated with painting in enamel, probably English work. (Victoria and Albert Museum)

Enamel, white or lightly tinted, was fused on to the metal plate in a uniform layer and given a matt surface. This layer was used as a ground for a miniature painting by brush-work, using oxides of metals as colours. The oxides were mixed with just enough powdered flux to make them vitrifiable, and they were made to adhere to the enamel ground by firing the plate until the surface was fused. The painting was then covered by a thin layer of transparent flux as a protection.

Paintings on enamel are rarely signed before 1675. No work by Jean Toutin is known, but watches enamelled by his sons Henri and Jean exist. Blois was the centre and the home of the best work. Later, the painting was done in other countries, but the art finally came to rest in Geneva where, about 1800, the output was very large. It is still the centre.

The Blois masters who painted on watches were: Isaac Gribelin, master before 1634; Dubie, said to have been one of the first taught by Toutin; Pierre Chartier, born 1618 and master in 1638, specialized in flowers; another flower painter was Christophe Morlière, born in Orleans in 1604 and, coming to Blois in 1628, acquired great renown in enamel work. He died in 1643. A watch in the Kunsthistorische Museum, Vienna, by Jacques Poëte of Blois has a most lovely painting of flowers on its back; since Morlière was a brother-in-law of Poëte the painting is attributed to him. A flower plaque in the Grune Gewolbe, Dresden, is attributed to Chartier. Nothing approaching these mid-seventeenth century flower paintings has ever been done since, and black and white reproductions give no idea of their beauty.

Robert Vauquer, born in 1625, son of the watchmaker and engraver Michel Vauquer, inherited Morlière's vogue and is said to have surpassed him in skill. The Louvre has two watches enamelled by him.

Interest in paintings on enamel is generally centred on watches with figure scenes or portraits. These are rare when perfection is sought, mainly because the period of the best work was so short. After 1650 there is a marked decline, though technical skill continued.

One of the finest examples known of the period 1635–40, in the British Museum, is by Blaise Foucher of Blois. He became master in 1631 and died in 1662. The enamel paintings are unsigned. They show four scenes from the legends of Theseus and Antiope and Hippolyta. A feature unknown in any other watch is that these scenes are repeated in miniature in six scenes on the curved edge, two of the scenes on the covers each being divided into two.

An equally fine specimen in the Victoria and Albert Museum is by Goullens of Paris, also with unsigned paintings.

A watch dating from the middle of the century, the end of the finest period, is by Nicolas Bernard of Paris, a signatory to the second series of statutes of the Corporation of Paris in 1646. It may be noted that the colours are brighter than those in the earlier watches. This watch is of the normal type with enamel paintings. The main figure scenes are on the outsides of the covers, while the insides and dial have landscape scenes, sometimes in monochrome. The two watches by Foucher and Goullens are quite exceptional in having scenes of equal importance on the insides as well as on the outsides of the case.

In the second half of the century a family of painters on enamel became famous, largely because they always signed their work. The first, Pierre Huaud, was a goldsmith in Geneva in 1635, who died in 1680. He painted on enamel, but no work of his is known. He had three sons, Pierre, Jean and Amy, born 1647, 1655 and 1657. The eldest was the best painter. He went to the Court of Brandenburg in 1685 and, after three years at Geneva, was appointed painter to the Elector in 1691 and died about 1698. The earliest known painting by him is 1679. He signed his work with various names, 'Huaut l'aisné', 'P. Huaud primogenitus', 'Pierre Huaud', 'Petrus Huaud major natus'. Watches painted by him are in the Louvre and the Musée d'Art de Genève.

Jean signed 'Huaud le puisné', and watches painted by him are in the British, Victoria and Albert and Cluny Museums. He worked mostly with his brother Amy, and the two were appointed painters to the Court of Prussia in 1686 and went to Berlin, returning to Geneva in 1700. Before 1686 they signed 'Les deux frères Huaut les jeunes'. After 1686, 'Les frères Huaud', with the addition of 'peintres de son A.E. a Berlin' or similar title. After 1700, the signature was 'Les frères Huaut' or 'Peter et Amicus Huaut' or 'Fratres Huault'. Examples of their work are found in all the principal Museums.

PLATE 40

Watch by Blaise Foucher, Blois. Mid-seventeenth century. The case is painted enamel. The movement is of the remarkably thin pattern usual with an enamel case. (British Museum)

Their technique was extremely good, but their colours are hard and inclined to be garish. In their figure scenes they liked to display the charms of robust women.

Other seventeenth century enamel painters who signed their work are:—Pierre Bordier of Geneva, master 1629, who enamelled a watch presented by the English Parliament to General Fairfax; Pierre Lignac, a pupil of the Toutins, born *ca.* 1624 and died 1684. He went to Sweden in 1645 and Stockholm has a watch enamelled by him. Jean André of Geneva, a pupil of the first Pierre Huaud, was born in 1646 and died 1714. The Claudius Cote collection has a watch signed by him. Camille André enamelled a watch by Tompion in the British Museum, and a watch by Gribelin, also in the British Museum, is enamelled by Jean Mussard of Geneva, born 1681 and died 1745. Finally, Jean Louis Durand of Geneva enamelled a watch in the Gelis collection.

Perhaps the earliest example of painting on enamel, of about 1630, is that on the dial of the crystal cross watch in the Mallet collection by Didier Lalemand of Paris. The painting of the emblems of the Passion is of the simplest character.

Painted enamel dials

The dials of watches decorated with paintings always have a painted scene in the centre, generally a scene of buildings and trees with small figures. Later, a figure scene is more common, as on the dial of the square watch by Pierre de Baufre of Paris, of about 1675. The hand is always gilt, with the centre engraved as a sunflower.

The hour band is almost always a white enamel band with black or dark figures, and it is surrounded by a narrow gilt engraved band.

Niello

In the process of niello, an alloy of silver, lead and copper, mixed with sulphides, is run into a champlevé plate in a molten state. The sulphides maintain a black surface on the silver alloy, and this contrasts well with the surrounding silver. It looks well when the silver is kept bright, but, in Museums, the silver is generally blackened and the contrast is lost.

Niello is rarely found on early watch cases. The niello watch by Edward Bysse, an original member of the Clockmaker's Company, in the British Museum, dates from about 1625.

Cases of amber and ivory

Any material other than metal or stone is very rare in a watch case, but examples in ivory and amber are known.

Outer cases

The natural result of decorating watches with works of art was the provision of a protective case. Sometimes it was a case to keep the watch in when not in use, treating the watch as a jewel to be brought out on ceremonial occasions but, in the second half of the seventeenth century, an outer case suitable for the watch when worn became common. It in turn was often decorated and, since materials could be used which were unsuited to watch cases themselves, the decoration also was quite different from that on the watch.

An early outer case is the plain silver case of the French watch with pierced and enamelled work in the Victoria and Albert Museum. A later outer case of the middle of the seventeenth century is on the enamelled watch with flowers and leaves in champlevé in the same Museum. This case is unusual in having two engraved scenes of Joseph and his brethren.

Outer cases of the latter half of the century and later were most frequently of leather studded with gold or silver and tortoise-shell with inlaid silver. Though enamelled watches generally had an outer case from the earliest times, these highly decorated outer cases were rare before 1675.

DIALS

In the plainer type of watch of the early part of the seventeenth century, the dial is generally a gilt metal plate with an hour ring engraved on it, or with a silver ring applied to it, and these simple dials are common on crystal watches. Less frequently a silver disc with hour ring engraved on it is applied to the dial plate.

The hour ring is nearly always a good deal smaller than the plate, and in the more decorative watches the surrounding space is filled with floral scrolls, often with a head or a reclining female figure. In cross watches, the arms frequently have engravings of the emblems of the Passion. Profane engravings are less common on cross watches. The centre of the dial, when engraved, generally has a scene with buildings or figures. Less often the floral scrolls outside the hour ring are continued inside it. In the more elaborate watches, with several dials on the plate, the whole plate is usually covered with engraving. In alarum watches, a pierced central disc on a blued steel ground is not uncommon.

In German watches, the circle of Arabic numbers tends to disappear after 1625, and the dial approaches the French type. Silver dials and engraving became more common.

Hour figures are stumpy, the IIII being as wide as high or wider. Almost always the half-hour is marked by a fleur-de-lys or a star or point. A mark at the quarters is not so common in French or English watches as in the earlier German watches.

Towards the middle of the century, the hour ring or disc tends to become larger, leaving only a narrow band for ornament. Sometimes this narrow space is occupied by a day of the month ring. The ring, with engraved figures, may turn, or it may be fixed, with a pointer on a narrow turning ring.

HANDS

Hands are always steel except in the enamelled watches. They have long tails and are well shaped and finished; there is a tendency to shorten the tail in the later watches. Hands of special forms are very rare; doves with white enamel and lizards with coloured enamels are known. Minute hands are very rare before 1675 but there are a few examples which possess even a seconds hand. These were doubtless intended for use by doctors. On the other hand, in watches with multiple dials and quarter-striking, there is frequently what amounts to a minute hand. A hand is fixed to the arbor of the quarter-striking wheel, which revolves once an hour, and its separate dial is marked with the four quarters, in Roman numerals.

PENDANTS

Early pendants are usually a plain round knob, occasionally decorated, with a loose-fitting ring. As watches were suspended from a cord worn round the neck the hole for a ring is from back to front, though the knob has so often become loose in the case that there is no back or front. About the middle of the century, the hole is sometimes from side to side and later this becomes more common.

The pendant with a pivoted loop starts about 1675 and later becomes the usual type.

WATCH GLASSES

Watches of the first quarter of the seventeenth century generally had a cover which had to be opened to read the time. Crystal covers were quite common, but not as a rule transparent enough to see the hand. It is doubtful when glass began to be used, because one cannot say that a glass on a watch belongs to the date of the watch. Glasses were made by blowing hollow spheres of glass and cutting circles from them, and early glasses looked rather bulbous. It is not uncommon in early watches with plain metal covers, to find a hole about the size of the hour ring cut in the cover and a glass fitted; this may have been done at a date much later than the date of the watch.

The earliest method of fixing a crystal or glass was by tags. Sometimes a separate ring was used with two sets of tags, one set being bent inwards to hold the crystal, while the other was bent outwards to hold the ring in the cover. The method of fixing by tags was used for a long time, till well beyond 1650, but before this, the alternative of splitting the bezel at the hinge became common. Towards the end of the century, the split bezel gave way to the modern method of holding the glass, in which the bezel has an undercut groove and the glass can just be sprung past the upper edge of the bezel and snaps into the undercut portion where it fits more freely. This method was introduced a little before 1675.

The great period of watch decoration ends at 1675 or soon after. Every form of decoration is found in it. Engraving, first of figure scenes and later confined to flowers and foliage, almost disappears in the eighteenth century, and lapidary's work becomes rare. Repoussé work, on the other hand becomes fashionable and reaches great perfection.

French and English watches are hardly distinguishable. It is probable that much of the decorative work on early English watches was done in France or by French artists in England.

WATCH MECHANISM

The early German watches are relatively thin and as has already been explained, even the very early spherical watches have fairly thin movements as the going and striking trains are situated on each side of a common centre plate. This thinness may have been responsible, in part at least, for the widespread use of the unsatisfactory stackfreed in German watches up to 1600 and it did not die out entirely until after 1650.

In the much later going barrel, the inner end of the mainspring is attached to the centre arbor to which also is fixed the click and stopwork. The outer end is then attached to the outside of the spring barrel, which is made integral with the great wheel. With the early stackfreeds the opposite method was employed, the outer end of the spring being attached to a fixed pillar held between the top and bottom plates and the drive was imparted to the centre arbor. There was, therefore, no spring barrel. Integral with the arbor was a ratchet wheel whose click was on the concentrically mounted great wheel, whereby the power was imparted to the train.

The arbor carrying the spring mounting served as a winding square and also on this square was a pinion geared to the stackfreed wheel so that one turn of the stackfreed went to about three and a half turns of the great wheel. Two or three teeth of the stackfreed wheel were left blank and this served as a stopwork. On the great wheel arbor was mounted another pinion geared to the wheel carrying the hand, so that the three and a half turns of the great wheel produced a little more than two rotations of the hand assuming, as was usual with stackfreeds, that the watch ran for about 26 hours.

There was, therefore, no quick and easy means of altering the set-up of the mainspring and, in the absence of a balance spring, some other means had to be found of regulating the rate of the watch. This was done by placing bristles in the path of the balance so as to limit its supplementary arc. The supplementary arc of any balance is that part of its swing after it has received its impulse (and in the case of a verge escapement it is the supplementary arc which accounts for the recoil). If the supplementary arc is limited by the bristle the rate will be made faster, so that, by mounting the bristle on a movable arm, the watch can be roughly regulated.

No French watches have a stackfreed but all early French watches are fitted with the fusee. In the spherical French watch by de la Garde, the greater part of the available space is taken up by the going train and the striking train is contained in a shallow frame under the dial. Only the spring for the strike is situated between the main plates. Even more normal-shaped French watches are much thicker than contemporary German types and they were thus able to accommodate a fusee. The greater width of spring produced much greater power from a given length of spring, but even so, the early fusee watches generally only ran for about 15 hours compared with the 26 hours running of a stackfreed. This is explained by the fusee watches generally having only a three-wheel train as against the almost universal four of the stackfreed. The early fusees are very thin and have a relatively slight taper. They also have a very large number of turns; anything up to 16 or 17. With a fusee the centre arbor of the spring barrel does not turn and the drive is transmitted via the outer end of the spring to the spring barrel. The winding square is on the fusee as also is the stopwork. The power is therefore cut off from the train and the watch stops during winding. This was later to be overcome by the provision of a maintaining power to drive the train during winding but with the erratic performance of pre-balance-spring watches this shortcoming of the fusee was more than outweighed by its advantages.

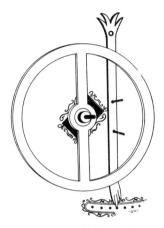

FIGURE 6. *Bristle regulator, as used on stackfreed watches.*

With this form of drive the initial tension of the mainspring can readily be varied and in a watch without a balance spring this immediately affects its rate. This method of regulation was invariably used in fusee watches prior to the introduction of the balance spring. In the earliest examples and up to about 1625, this was effected by a click and ratchet wheel on the arbor of the spring barrel but after this date a worm and wheel was increasingly employed, which enabled a much closer adjustment. The worm was on a long shaft mounted parallel to and outside of the top plate. One end of the shaft was squared to fit a key. Its two bearings were made of blued steel finely pierced and chiselled. Indicator dials became usual from 1625 onwards. Although unsatisfactory in that it upset the relationship of the power-curve of the spring to the torque-conversion factor of the fusee, the worm regulator was nevertheless more reliable than the bristle arrangement which is seldom found in conjunction with a fusee watch.

The earliest fusees were connected to the spring-barrel by catgut but fusee chains were introduced soon after 1600 and from about 1625 they became increasingly popular. By 1675 they were universal for watches, though gut remained in use in bracket clocks until the nineteenth century. The earliest chains, which are very rare, have much longer links than was usual from 1650 or 1660 onwards. Gut-driven fusees have rounded grooves and chain-driven fusees have squared grooves. Sometimes gut was later replaced by chain, and the fusee recut with squared grooves, but the holes in the barrel and fusee will show whether the chain is original.

The earliest German watches have a balance of dumb-bell shape (somewhat like the old foliot balance) which is more convenient than a wheel in conjunction with the bristle regulator. The wheel balance becomes more usual from 1575 onwards, usually in conjunction with a fusee but, like the stackfreed, the dumb-bell balance may be found as late as 1625.

French watches invariably, and English watches almost invariably, have balance wheels. The method of mounting the balance staff varied considerably. In the earliest German watches it was carried in undecorated, S-shaped cocks fixed to the top and bottom plates respectively (the bottom plate being cut away for the purpose). This made it possible to adjust the depthing of either top or bottom pallets more or less independently; but later in the sixteenth century, the bottom cock was given up and the staff pivoted direct into the bottom plate. The early escape wheels were of large diameter but they became smaller by the end of the sixteenth century and the bottom pivot of the balance staff was then carried in a bracket at the bottom of the contrate-wheel potence, which had always been riveted to the top plate.

The early German movements were all of steel but by 1575 steel was giving way to brass, especially for the plates, which could be cast whereas steel plates had to be laboriously hammered and filed to the correct thickness. Trains wholly of steel wore rapidly, though this was mitigated by hardening the pinions. Brass wheels and steel pinions wear far less rapidly, but even so, all-steel trains are found in German watches as late as 1625.

Early German movements have little decoration and those with steel plates virtually none. Steel wheels usually have four spokes and brass wheels three.

French watches are rarely found with steel trains and even the 1551 spherical watch has its movement entirely of brass.

Finely pierced and chiselled brass-gilt cocks are found soon after 1600. Nearly all cocks are screwed to the plate but in rare and early examples before the general use of screws, they were pinned to a post riveted to the plate.

The piercing of early French cocks is usually of spiral pattern and the part of the cock over the balance roughly circular. The early English cocks tend more to have a foliate pattern of piercing and the part over the balance to be oval in shape.

After 1650 the oval pattern tended more and more to become circular but the foot continued to have an irregular outline.

The top plates are not much decorated before 1650 but a band of engraving round the edge, or a wreath, is quite characteristic of English work. After 1650 pierced cock feet and regulator bearings spread over an increasingly large proportion of the entire plate. During the second and third quarters of the century the makers' signatures on the plate are mostly in a fine, tall bold script, that of Edward East being perhaps the best.

Even the earliest watches generally possess at least one screw. These screws have dome-shaped heads and the slots are V-shaped. The thread is coarse and irregular. In the case of stackfreed watches the stackfreed spring was attached to the plate by a screw and in the case of early fusee watches the click of the setting-up ratchet was usually pivoted on a screw.

Prior to 1650 the pillars between the plates are usually of plain baluster form, rivetted to the bottom plate, but the squared and tapered Egyptian form is found from 1625. From 1650 onwards a great variety of pillars is found and the tulip shape begins to become popular.

Also prior to 1650 it was usually necessary to swing the movement out of its case for winding, but thereafter, winding holes became usual, generally protected by shutters, which disappear again when the watch has a utilitarian pair-case.

Striking work underwent some development during the period of this chapter but this is dealt with in the chapter devoted to striking mechanism.

THE GUILDS

The period covered by this chapter saw the widespread establishment of clock and watch making as an industry and the corresponding formation of Guilds for their protection and control. The earliest clockmakers were blacksmiths, working in iron, but the smaller, spring-driven clocks and watches were all made by lock-smiths, accustomed to working in brass and steel. Nevertheless, the first English clock and watchmakers were all members of the Blacksmiths' Guild, until the London Clockmakers' Company was founded in 1631.

The earliest clockmakers' Guild known was founded at Annaberg, in Saxony, in 1543 but no example from Annaberg now exists. The pioneer Nuremburg makers were not formed into a guild until 1656, and even as late as 1629, a locksmith and gunsmith could work as a clockmaker, but not vice versa. Paris had a guild as early as 1544, but the better known Blois makers were not formed into a guild until 1597. The different guilds had various tests which an applicant had to pass to gain his mastership, and the requirement of the Nuremburg Rat, to be completed within one year, was as follows: 'Two timepieces, the first a standing piece, 6 inches high 4½ broad and 2½ deep in its iron case. Its movement of wheels and pinions to show good craftsmanship and to strike the four quarters and the hours; on one side it shall show the 24 hours of sun and moonshine during the day and night, indicating the quarters as well as the hours; on the other side shall be the calendar and the planets with the length of day. The other piece shall be of small size, such as one wears hanging at the neck; the movement shall strike up to 12 and have an alarm.'

CHAPTER III

Counting the minutes; the invention of the pendulum and balance spring

THE PENDULUM

THE present chapter covers perhaps the most important period in horological history. In the space of a quarter of a century accurate timekeeping became a possibility and to a very large extent it was actually achieved. In 1655 a clock did well to keep time to within five minutes a day; in 1675 its error might, under favourable circumstances, be only as many seconds. Similarly, watches were brought from an almost entirely unpredictable performance to within two or three minutes' accuracy a day or even less with reasonable luck.

The sudden advance was brought about by the application of the pendulum to clocks, and the balance spring to watches. The sequence of events leading up to these achievements is of such considerable interest and importance as to merit a chapter solely devoted to them. As will be shown, while there were many claimants to the invention both of the pendulum and balance spring, it was the Dutch astronomer, mathematician and horologist, Christian Huygens van Zulichem (1629–95) who first applied them in practical form to timekeepers sold to the public. Huygens himself never claimed the honour of 'inventing' either device, but was content to point out, with evident justice, that it was he who made them work.

There can be little doubt that the first person to envisage a pendulum was Leonardo da Vinci and that, moreover, applied to a verge escapement in exactly the form used by Huygens and all the successful early pendulum makers. There is, however, nothing to suggest that Leonardo ever made or caused such a clock to be made.

His drawings of pendulums belong to the period 1493–4 and appear in the Codice Atlantico and the Ravaisson-Mollien MSS. A horizontal escape wheel of normal verge pattern has a horizontal verge staff lying across it, to one end of which is attached a pendulum. Another sketch shows a vertical escape wheel and verge staff with a horizontal projection from its bottom end. No actual pendulum is shown and if one is in fact intended it would have to be in the form later made popular in Friesland clocks and described later in this chapter.

Leonardo da Vinci's claim to have invented the pendulum has received strong support in a published translation of selections from his note books, among which is the following:

"Cause an hour to be divided into 3,000 parts and this you will do by means of a clock by making the pendulum higher and heavier."

The passage of which this purports to be a translation is as follows:

66

"fa che unora sia δuj sa in 3,000 partj e cquesto faraj colloriolo allegerēdo o agravādo il cōtrapeso."

The literal translation of the latter part of the sentence is clearly: 'and this I should do by means of a clock by making the counterweight lighter or heavier.'

Since this is precisely the way of regulating a verge and foliot escapement without a balance spring, it seems that the translator had recourse to unnecessary ingenuity in a passage where a literal translation would have served.

Leonardo also invented a variant on the verge escapement and although it offers no apparent advantages it is of interest as being the prototype for many basically similar inventions in later centuries. There are two parallel escape wheels with pin-type teeth, those on one wheel staggered in relationship to those on the other. The balance staff lies between the two escape wheels and has two pallets projecting from opposite sides of the staff and at the same level. These pallets, of curved shape, are engaged alternately by the pin-teeth of the escape wheels.

The next contestant is the clockmaker Jost Bodeker who made a turret clock for the Osnabrück Dom in 1587. This had two alternative forms of escapement which could be engaged at will; one was a normal verge and foliot and the other a conical pendulum. The latter is in principle no more than a fly and involves no escapement whatever. Its claims to be a timekeeper rely on the pendulum being attached at its upper end to a vertical, revolving arbor driven by the train. The pendulum is thus swung in a circular path and its free end will tend to fly outwards as the speed increases. The further outward the pendulum is swung the more power is needed, and it was thus hoped that some measure of isochronism would be obtained. In fact, all efforts to apply a conical pendulum to timekeepers have proved abortive but Bodeker nevertheless made an important invention. Had he applied both escapements so as to act simultaneously, he might well have improved on the timekeeping of the verge and foliot alone.

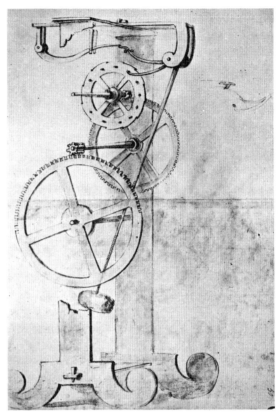

PLATE 41

Vicenzio Galileo's own drawing, made in 1641, of his Father's pendulum clock and escapement.
(Medicean Archives, Florence)

The famous astronomer Galileo Galilei discovered the isochronism of a swinging pendulum. He believed that the swing of any given pendulum occupied the same length of time whatever the arc traversed. In fact, wide arcs take slightly longer than small ones but this was not discovered until many years later by Huygens. In the meantime, Galileo used a simple pendulum for astronomical observation, kept swinging by an assistant who also counted the beats. Later, he proposed a not very practicable form of count wheel which is only of interest as involving the seed of the idea of the passing spring of a chronometer. A stylus projecting from the pendulum came in contact, at its centre point, with a bristle which, bending before the pendulum, moved the tooth of a vertical wheel of exactly similar type to a verge escape wheel. The bristle, in returning, rode over the sloping back of the tooth without moving the wheel and was thus ready to move the next tooth at the succeeding impulse from the pendulum.

However, he did not pursue this idea but turned his mind to the invention of an escapement which would not only count the beats of the pendulum but also keep it in motion; and this he succeeded in doing by a very neat device which is in reality a form of duplex escapement, the unlocking and impulse being effected quite separately from each other. The escape wheel has locking teeth in the same plane as the wheel, which are held by a pivoted detent of claw shape which engages the teeth. The impulse pallets are in the form of studs projecting vertically from the face of the escape wheel, exactly as in a duplex watch.

The pendulum is fixed to an arbor which also carries two horn-shaped arms, one in the plane of the detent and the other in the plane of the impulse pallets. At the end of its swing the unlocking arm lifts the detent and permits the escape wheel to advance whereby the impulse pallet engages with the impulse arm on the pendulum arbor. As the pendulum moves away under this impulse the locking detent falls on the next tooth in preparation for the next swing of the pendulum. This escapement is a great improvement on the verge in that the pendulum is free for the greater part of its travel and its only disadvantage lies in the fact that the unlocking and impulse take place at one end of the pendulum's arc and not at or near its vertical position, which is the ideal for good timekeeping. This could have been done without great difficulty by the application of a passing spring to the detent and, as has already been shown, Galileo had in fact also hit upon the idea of the passing spring in his abortive count-wheel. Had he combined the two he would have invented the chronometer well over a century before it actually arrived, and produced an exceedingly perfect timekeeper.

As it was, in 1641, being by then stricken with blindness, he imparted the idea to his son Vincenzio. A year later he died but Vincenzio took no steps to make the clock until 1649 in which year he, in turn, died, without having completed it. What were presumably the unfinished remains are listed in the inventory of the belongings of Vincenzio's widow, who died in 1669: 'An iron clock, unfinished, with pendulum, the first invention of Galileo.'

Thus, Galileo's important invention came to nothing and such few people as knew of it were apparently unable to appreciate its significance. It is fortunate indeed that Galileo's original drawing survives, in the Medicean Archives at Florence, and a reconstruction has been made for the London Science Museum where it is kept working.

The astronomer Johann Hevel, hearing of Galileo's discovery concerning the isochronism of pendulums, experimented with a pendulum and eventually achieved some measure of success just before Huygens put his clocks on the market. Hevel acclaimed Huygens' success, but no details of his own escapement are known.

It appears that after the death of Vincenzio Galilei, the unfinished model was seen by Prince Leopold de Medici, a keen and discerning horologist, who caused a copy to be made by his court clock-maker, Philip Treffler in 1656, a year before Huygens' first clock, although it was apparently not adjusted to the point of success until two or three years later.

These are the people who can be said with reasonable certainty to have anticipated Huygens in the invention of the pendulum. Others are known, but their claims cannot be substantiated; no doubt there were other experimenters and as soon as Huygens had made a commercial success of the pendulum clock many people were eager to claim the honour of having invented it; of whom Huygens, in a letter dated February 26th, 1660, remarked laconically 'C'est une chose estrange que personne devant moy n'ait parlé de ces horloges, et qu'a cette heure il s'en decouvre tant d'autre autheurs'.

So far as Huygens himself is concerned, the facts are as follows:

In 1657 he communicated his plan for a pendulum clock to Salomon (or Samuel) Coster, a skilful clock-maker at the Hague. He assigned his rights in the invention to Coster who submitted it to the States-General and was granted a patent (Octrooi) for twenty-one years from June 16th, 1657.

A pendulum clock either does, or did exist at the Rijksmuseum Amsterdam signed 'Samuel Coster— Haghe met privilege 1657'. It must therefore be among the first clocks made to Huygens' design. It is spring-driven, with a going barrel, and has a horizontal escape wheel of normal verge pattern. The verge staff terminates in a crutch through which passes the short pendulum, suspended from a thread between curved cheeks.

This clock differs from Huygens' own first sketch which introduces a gearing between the verge staff and the pendulum in order to reduce the arc traversed by the pendulum. In this machine the escape wheel is shown vertical as also, in consequence, is the verge staff. At the top of the latter is a pinion engaging with a contrate wheel which has a considerably greater number of teeth than the pinion. The contrate wheel arbor then carries the pendulum crutch and in view of the reduced arc, Huygens did not consider it necessary to place the curved cheeks on either side of the threads from which the pendulum is suspended.

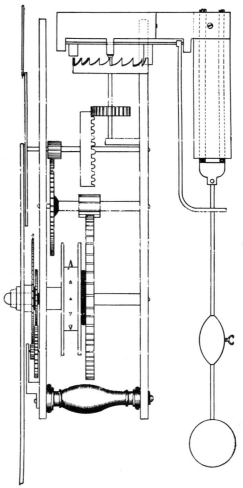

FIGURE 7. *Huygens' standard weight-driven clock, without gearing between verge and pendulum, but employing cycloidal cheeks, as drawn in his 'Horologium Oscillatorium' (1673).*

The first Coster clocks had 9¾ inch pendulums beating half seconds but Huygens evidently preferred the type shown in his sketch, as he was experimenting with it in 1658 in conjunction with a 39 inch pendulum beating seconds, again without the curved cheeks. During this year he also continued his experiments with the pendulum and although he had been aware from the outset that it was not truly isochronous (which the curved cheeks were supposed to counteract) it was not until then that he was able to discover the formula which determines its performance. This is, that the time occupied by the swing of a pendulum varies as the square root of the length of its arc, and inversely as the force of gravity. This irregularity is known as 'circular error'. He also discovered that if the weight of a pendulum can be made to follow a cycloidal path the pendulum will then be isochronous for all sizes of arc. A cycloid is the path traced out by a point on the circumference of a circle as that circle is rolled along a flat plane, and its shape is such that a pendulum following it must get shorter as it approaches the ends of its swing. Huygens discovered that this could be achieved with his thread-suspended pendulum by confining the thread between cheeks, also of cycloid shape. This he had anticipated empirically in the first clocks made by Coster, but the cheeks in that case were only curved and not truly cycloidal.

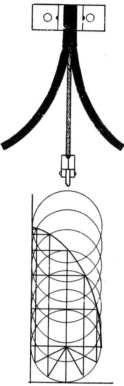

FIGURE 8. *Cycloidal cheeks used by Huggens' to correct circular error. The pendulum rod is suspended on a cord placed between two metal 'cheeks' curved in cycloidal shape. If a circular disc is rolled along a flat plane the path traced out by a point on its periphery is known as a 'cycloid'.*

He preferred the long pendulums without cheeks for normal timekeepers but valued his cycloidal arrangement in conjunction with his efforts to produce a sea-going timekeeper. In this he was unsuccessful, but his experiments will be described at greater length in a later chapter devoted to the marine chronometer, as well as his invention of the remontoire and maintaining power.

Huygens also used another means of applying a pendulum to the verge escapement, of a kind which may have been anticipated by Leonardo da Vinci, as stated at the beginning of this chapter. It consists of a vertical escape wheel, with a long horizontal arm projecting from the bottom end of the verge staff. This passes through a vertical slot formed about one third down the pendulum. Huygens seems to have evolved this arrangement for a large turret clock which he made for the church at Scheveningen but it became popular in the Zandaam and Friesland house clocks and persisted into the nineteenth century.

The first English clocks on Huygens' system were made by the firm of Fromanteel. This Dutch family had long been settled in England and the first Ahasuerus Fromanteel was an original member of the Clockmakers' Company in 1631. Less than three months after the grant of Coster's Dutch patent John Fromanteel was sent over to work under him, to learn how to construct the new pendulum clocks. Accordingly, the Fromanteel firm was able to advertise them for sale in England in the broadsheet 'Mercurius Politicus' of October 27th–November 3rd, and 'The Commonwealth Mercury' of November 28th, 1658. The Fromanteel's seem to have specialised in long-case clocks with short pendulums of which several examples still exist, and there are some spring-driven bracket clocks. The long-case clocks are, of course, weight-driven, go for eight days, and have bolt-and-shutter maintaining power. This is more fully described in the next chapter.

While Huygens gained such a long lead by evolving a commercially practicable application of the pendulum to timekeepers, he never seems to have realised that no serious advance could be made so long as the pendulum was constantly interfered with by the motive power, as is the case with the verge escapement. Thus, even had his correction of circular error been completely successful in its result Huygens would never have produced a really accurated timekeeper so long as he adhered to the verge escapement.

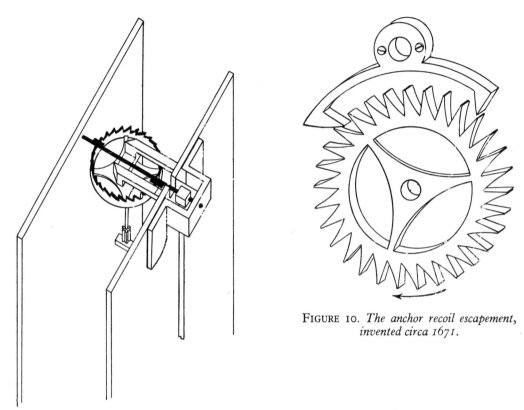

FIGURE 10. *The anchor recoil escapement, invented circa 1671.*

FIGURE 9. *The application of a pendulum to the verge escapement as effected in early English clocks. Note the integrally mounted pendulum rod in contrast to Huygens' cord suspension.*

It was at this point that England made the first of her many important contributions to the advancement of horology by the invention of the anchor escapement.

In this escapement the escape wheel is vertical but, unlike the crown wheel of the verge escapement, its teeth are in the same plane as the wheel. The actual teeth are much the same shape as those of a verge crown wheel but what are the backs of the teeth on a crown wheel now travel foremost and give the impulse to the pendulum. The pendulum arbor is above the escape wheel and mounted on it is an anchor-shaped contrivance which straddles some eight teeth of the escape wheel. At each end of the anchor are curved impulse pallets which engage with the curved faces of the teeth on the escape wheel. In actual fact, the pendulum is no more free from interference with an anchor escapement than with the verge, but the force of the interference is not so great. Furthermore, the anchor escapement enables the use of a long pendulum with a small arc, without recourse to the intermediate gearing which Huygens was forced to employ for this purpose. Like the verge, the anchor has a greater or less amount of recoil, according to the precise shape of the teeth and pallets, but some recoil is actually an advantage, as it provides a rough and ready compensation for variations in motive power. Another of its advantages over the verge is the important one of greatly reduced wear. It is still the escapement most generally used for pendulum clocks.

It is not known who invented the Anchor escapement but it seems certain that it was either the clockmaker William Clement or the famous architect, scientist and mathematician Robert Hooke.

Clement's claim to the honour rests on the strong factual evidence that he made the first known example, in a turret clock for King's College, Cambridge. After two centuries of service this clock was transferred to the London Science Museum where it is still kept working. It is stamped 'Gulielmus Clement Londini Fecit 1671'.

John Smith, in his 'Horological Disquisitions', published in 1694, wrote that several makers were engaged on eliminating the shortcomings of Huygens' verge clocks but 'that eminent and well-known artist Mr. William Clement had at last the good fortune to give it the finishing stroke, he being indeed the real contriver of the curious kind of long pendulum which is at this day so universally in use among us'.

It has nevertheless been observed that since Clement evinced no spark of inventive genius at any other time it is unreasonable to suppose that he would have been likely to evolve such a radically novel device as the anchor escapement. Nor was Clement himself at pains to claim the invention as his, and had he regarded it as such he would have been more likely to sign his Cambridge clock '— invenit et fecit', in the manner of that time.

Be that as it may, Clement must have the important credit for having made the oldest surviving clock with this excellent form of escapement.

Robert Hooke (1635–1703) was a universal genius, in an age of intellectual giants. He rose from obscurity to fame solely by his own brilliance and his mind ranged over the whole field of science and mathematics then known. He seldom interested himself in any subject without enriching it and, as will be seen, he made several important contributions to the advancement of horology.

Like Leonardo da Vinci before him, he was, however, inclined to throw out the germ of an invention and then lose interest in it, but if someone else then developed and perfected his idea he was prone to abrogate the whole credit to himself. He was, moreover, suspicious and secretive in his nature so that it is perhaps only to be expected that doubt and recrimination surrounded many of the inventions which he claimed as his own. His contemporary, Richard Waller, describes him as sharp and pale of feature, crooked and lean in body and 'he went stooping and fast—. He was of an active, restless, indefatigable Genius, and always slept little, seldom going to sleep till two, three or four a clock in the Morning. His temper was Melancholy, Mistrustful and Jealous, which more increased upon him with his years'. He was Curator of Experiments to the Royal Society up to the time of his death and also, latterly, its Secretary. It is known that he was experimenting with long pendulums as early as 1664 but no mention is made of the escapement; and as has been shown, Huygens was using a seconds pendulum as early as 1658 in conjunction with the verge escapement. And although Huygens used an intermediate gearing to secure a short arc, it is quite possible to use a long pendulum and verge escapement without this intermediary on the one hand, or an excessive arc on the other, as may be seen in the model working in the London Science Museum.

In 1669 Hooke was working on an even longer pendulum, 13 feet long, beating once in two seconds and swinging through an arc of only one degree. But here the escapement was definitely not an anchor since the point of the experiment was to show how such a pendulum could be kept in motion by a very small force, such as a watch train.

Unfortunately Hooke's own diaries, which are so informative concerning his later inventions, do not start until 1672, nor is there any mention of the anchor escapement in the Proceedings of the Royal Society. Yet so prominent was Hooke in all horological progress in this country that it is not unreasonable to suppose that he was at least initially responsible for the invention of the anchor escapement, even if Clement developed it to the point of perfection.

An important improvement which Hooke unquestionably invented was the spring suspension for pendulums, as he demonstrated it to the Royal Society in 1666. He substituted a short length of flat spring steel for Huygens' thread, wherefrom to suspend the pendulum. Its upper end terminated in a small block which rested on a bracket attached to the back plate, a slit being cut in the bracket just wide enough for the spring to pass through it. Tompion later developed this as a means of regulating clocks where there was no back door to the case. The spring was then pinned and screwed to a movable platform which could be raised or lowered from a dial and indicator at the front of the clock, thereby drawing the suspension spring up through the slit in the mounting bracket, and reducing or increasing the effective length of the pendulum. (A pinned and fixed anchorage was also used on the very earliest spring-suspended pendulums, but examples are exceedingly rare.)

Yet another invention of Hooke's was the tooth and wheel cutting machine, in 1672, without which English makers could hardly have risen to the unassailed pre-eminence which they attained in the last quarter of the seventeenth century. Previously, blanks were placed in the centre of a circular brass platform having engraved upon it three concentric circles, and radial lines corresponding to the various numbers of teeth in general use. An arm pivoted at the centre of the platform carried a hard point at its other extremity, by which the positions of the teeth were marked on the blanks. The spaces were then filed out by hand. Hooke contrived a circular file and made the platform moveable so that each part of the circumference of the wheel could be brought in turn within the action of the file or cutter.

Although nothing came of it until half a century later, Hooke was apparently the first to suggest using the different coefficients of expansion under heat, of brass and steel, as a means of compensating a pendulum against alterations in temperature, and this he proposed to do by making his pendulum in the shape of a Rhomboid, with its outline of steel and its longest diagonal of brass.

THE BALANCE SPRING

But by far Hooke's most important achievement in the field of horology was his invention of the balance spring as applied to watches, although here again, his own suspicious and secretive nature robbed him of the full credit, since it was once more Huygens who brought the invention to complete success, and put it on the market in a form which has survived, in all important particulars, to the present day.

It is certain that Hooke was experimenting with the balance spring before 1660. Derham described his first attempt as 'a tender straight spring one end whereof played backward and forward with the balance' and it seems that such a watch was given to Dr. Wilkins, afterwards Bishop of Chichester, in about 1661. This instrument presumably resembled a German watch by Smod of Geilsheiln, mentioned and illustrated in earlier editions of this book. This had a long straight bristle, fixed at one end to the watch, while the free end was confined between two pins standing up vertically from the rim of the balance. Thus, as the balance vibrated the bristle was flexed first to one side and then the other. Towards its fixed end it passed between the collets of a movable regulator by which means the effective length of the bristle could be altered at will. This watch, which had the appearance of belonging to the period 1650–60, seemed to be entirely in its original state, and not to have been modified in any way. Hooke may, therefore, even have been anticipated by this unknown German maker.

He amplified his theories in his Cutlerian lectures of 1664 and made further demonstrations to the Royal Society in 1668. He said he knew twenty different ways of applying a balance spring to watches but naïvely added that he withheld the best one till he might have gained some advantage by it. This he sought to do in partnership with some wealthy persons, but the terms they proposed being entirely unreasonable, Hooke refused to go on with them and the nature of his appliance was never made known. He also experimented with two balances geared together. In one such arrangement one pallet was on the staff of each and in another both were on one, the other being introduced only as a steadier. Hooke also experimented with the loadstone as a regulator.

There is no evidence that Hooke used the spiral spring in any of these contrivances and as will be seen later, there is everything to suggest that he did not. The only confirmatory suggestion comes from the purely hearsay report of Dr. Derham in his 'Artificial Clockmaker' published in 1696, in which he may well have been influenced by what Hooke would clearly wish to be thought.

In 1665 Sir Robert Moray wrote to Huygens, by then resident in Paris, describing such of his conclusions as Hooke had made public, to which Huygens replied that as long previously as 1660 the Duc de Roannais had taken him to the Clockmaker Martinot who was making a balance-spring watch to the designs of the Duke and Monsieur Pascal. But Huygens said he did not think their method practicable and himself already knew of a better. Clearly, then, other experimenters were in the field almost, if not quite as early as Hooke.

In 1668, Lorenzo Magalotti of the Florentine Academy, visited England and reported Hooke's work as follows: 'We also saw a pocket watch with a new pendulum invention. You might call it with a bridle, the time being regulated by a little spring of tempered wire which at one end is attached to the balance wheel, and at the other to the body of the watch.' This, again could be either a straight-line or spiral spring.

Huygens own experiments do not seem to have started until Hooke had already laid his aside, but by the end of 1674 he had brought them to a successful conclusion with the assistance of the French maker, Isaac Thuret, working to his instructions under pledge of secrecy. His watch consisted of what later came to be known as a Pirouette, described as follows by Dr. Derham '1. The Verge hath a Pinion instead of Pallets; and a Contrate-wheel runs therein, and drives it round more than one turn. 2. The pallets are on the Arbor of this Contrate-wheel. 3. Then followeth the Crown-wheel etc. 4. The ballance, instead of turning scarce quite round (as Dr. Hook's) doth turn several rounds every vibration'. Most of the earliest balance springs applied to a normal verge escapement, had only $1\frac{1}{2}$ or 2 turns, but Huygens had 4 or 5 and, as is usual with Pirouettes, beat very slowly.

In January 1675 he wrote to Oldenburg, Secretary to the Royal Society, who had on various occasions been of service to him, offering him the English rights in his new watch, whose nature he concealed in an anagram, as was usual at that time. Hooke had used the same device, his anagram concealing the words 'Ut tensio sic vis'. Huygens' epitome took the more cumbersome form of 'Axis circuli mobilis affixus in centro volutae ferreae'.

In February he obtained a provisional 'Privilège' from the French Academy of Science but its confirmation was obstructed by the Abbé Hautefeuille who had submitted a straight-line balance spring to the Academy in 1674, and Huygens did not bother to contest the point.

A few days later Hooke heard from Boyle that Huygens' watches were on the market and vehemently accused Oldenburg of confiding his secrets to Huygens. Whether or not Oldenburg had been indiscreet, Sir Robert Moray's correspondence with Huygens in 1665 shows that Huygens in any case had no need to plagiarise Hooke, and even at that date had his own ideas on the subject.

Boyle was apparently able to describe the nature of Huygens' watch to Hooke since in his diary for February 20th Hooke wrote 'Zulichem's spring not worth a farthing'—from which it may be concluded that, since Huygens' spring was spiral, Hooke's definitely was not.

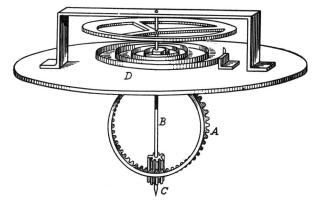

FIGURE 11. *A reproduction of Huygens' own sketch of a spiral balance spring. The verge (not shown) is attached to the contrate wheel A, below the plate. The balance staff B has a pinion C geared to A, whereby the balance wheel will swing through a much greater arc than in a normal verge watch. The balance spring, D, has four turns. The arrangement had been used by Huygens in pendulum clocks, and was revived in the eighteenth century in conjunction with the cylinder escapement and then known as a 'pirouette'.*

Hooke had met Thomas Tompion in 1674, when Tompion had constructed an exceedingly fine and complicated quadrant to Hooke's design, and he now ran to Tompion in a belated attempt to establish his own priority in the matter by the hasty construction of a balance-spring watch to his design. This watch may have had a spiral spring, but all the indications are to the contrary. Tompion had only been at work on this watch for a short time when, on March 8th, Hooke confided to him his 'way of fixing Double Springs to the inside of the Ballance wheel thus ⊛ '. The watch was finished on April 7th when Hooke, accompanied by Sir Jonas Moore and Tompion, showed it to Charles II. Its balance was covered by a pierced plate which bore the inscription 'Robt Hooke Inven 1658. T. Tompion fecit 1675'.

Apparently Oldenburg had already submitted the Huygens-Thuret watch to the King who verbally expressed his preference for the Hooke-Tompion and ordered one to be made for him. Tompion then took the watch away for final adjustment and the opposing faction next gained the King's ear, who threatened to grant his patent to Oldenburg unless Hooke's watch was placed in his hands without delay. The King's new watch was a different one to that made in such haste for Hooke, and from Hooke's diary it is apparent that the form of its balance spring was still the subject of much anxious experiment; for on April 13th 'Tryd perpendicular spiral spring at Tompions. Tryd double perpendicular spring did well' and on May 9th 'Tompion here about watch. The thrusting spring did best'. The meaning of neither is at all clear, any more than is Hooke's own sketch of the 'double springs' which, however, appears to have been an S-shaped spring attached at its outer ends to the rim of the balance with its centre passing through a slot in the balance staff (or it may equally well have been in two halves). If this is so it was no more than a balance wheel with spring-spokes, and since the springs would have to be fairly stiff to support the rim, their flexibility cannot have been great. Nor could there have been any means of regulation.

At last, on May 17th 'with Sir J. More to the King who Received the watch very kindly, it was locked up in his closet'. But in two days it was back again needing attention and remained with Tompion, in constant consultation with Hooke, until August 26th when it was finally returned to the King.

So far as the coveted patent was concerned, in the end the King did not grant one at all; to the great advantage of English horology.

Even after this, and as late as 1679, Hooke was still experimenting with different sorts of balance spring and chafed at Tompion's slowness in carrying out these experiments. Once, within the space of a fortnight (during which Christmas fell into the bargain) Tompion is, successively, 'a slug', 'a clownish churlish Dog' and 'a Rascall'. This however, was a not unusual condition among Hooke's acquaintance and he and Tompion seem to have remained on friendly terms until Hooke's death in 1703.

As against this evidence suggestive that Hooke did not use a spiral spring is the fact that soon after 1675 Tompion was making watches with a spiral spring, but without Huygens' superfluous pirouettes; and Graham stated that he had always understood from Tompion that he at any rate believed Hooke to have been the inventor of such watches. In the face of so much conflicting evidence it seems doubtful if the truth will ever be known. Probably Hooke and Huygens arrived at the spiral spring quite independently.

In conjunction with his balance-spring watches Tompion evolved the type of regulator which remained in general use until about 1800. The regulator collets were mounted on a segmental rack which followed the outer curve of the balance spring. This rack was geared to a wheel carrying a key square and indicator dial.

Hooke's tooth-cutting machine combined with his own unmatched skill soon enabled Tompion to turn out watches far surpassing those of any other country and capable of keeping time to a minute or two a day. With clocks incorporating the anchor escapement and long, 'Royal' pendulum (as it came to be called) able to perform within a few seconds a day, England found herself suddenly in a position of unassailable horological pre-eminence. After this spate of inventiveness her foremost makers applied themselves to consolidate their enviable position, for which they were considerably indebted to the inventive but irascible Dr. Hooke.

CHAPTER IV

English supremacy: circa 1660–1750

THIS chapter takes up the story from two different dates; 1657 for clocks and 1675 for watches. The former date marks the commercial application of pendulums to clocks and the latter, the successful addition of balance-springs to watches.

These two events opened up new vistas in horology and, for the first time, accurate timekeeping became a serious possibility. Although both achievements are attributable to the Dutchman, Huygens, it was in England that they received their most complete and rapid development so that by 1680 England had secured an unchallenged pre-eminence in the horological field; a pre-eminence which she was to enjoy for about a century. This rapid advance by English makers was due to several craftsmen of the highest ability, among whom Thomas Tompion was the acknowledged leader. He, and Abraham Louis Breguet working a century later, together enjoy a reputation accorded to no other makers; and although Tompion is now mostly remembered for his clocks, in his day it was, like Breguet, for his watches that he was most famed. Nor is this surprising, since he made about 5,500 watches and only about 650 clocks.

Clocks of the period covered by this chapter are those most sought after by the generality of collectors and it is, accordingly, the period which commands the highest prices. Nor is this without reason, for in case-work, sumptuousness was combined with sound proportions and good taste, while the movements have all the vigour and *joie de vivre* of a strong man rejoicing in his new-found strength. For the first time makers could take a pride in the performance of their products, and not only in their decorative finish, and this is apparent in every detail of craftsmanship and design. Particularly is this so up to about 1700 when the new technique was still being perfected. Afterwards, a measure of standardisation was reached and both clocks and watches lose the sense of experimental striving towards perfection which is so apparent and attractive in the earliest pendulum and balance-spring instruments.

As Tompion was the pioneer of British pre-eminence so, naturally, he was also the first to attain a standardised design for his clocks and watches, considerably before 1700. After about 1690 both his clocks and watches tend towards a less interesting uniformity and particularly is this true of his watches so that, except in performance, a 1700 Tompion may seem, superficially, uninteresting compared with examples by less famous, but nevertheless first-class makers.

After 1700, to find the vigour of individual craftsmanship one must look among the lesser men but, in general, it is before 1700 that the most striking individuality of craftsmanship and design is found.

Nowhere is this trend more apparent than in watches by Daniel Quare, of which his earliest are unsurpassed in their unmistakeable evidence of a craftsman's pride in his handiwork, while later examples decline into an uninspired uniformity.

After 1700, and for the next fifty years, development continued slowly upon the lines established in the pioneer years, yet with but few signs of decadence. George Graham assumed the mantle of his master Tompion, and his finest clocks can stand comparison with anything in the history of clock-making. His watches are, by contrast, uninspiring, although they are excellent technically. To him, also, are attributable the most important inventions of the first half of the eighteenth century, the modern type of cylinder escapement for watches and the dead-beat escapement and compensated mercurial pendulum for clocks.

Undoubtedly the antiquarian appeal of clocks of this period is enhanced by the fact that they are also practical timekeepers. To some extent, however, this has its drawbacks, since many a fine bracket clock has had its verge escapement converted in more or less recent times to anchor, in a vandalistic search for even better timekeeping. In point of fact, the verge and pendulum can keep time perfectly satisfactorily within the limits of reasonable domestic requirements, and accuracy to within two or three minutes a week is by no means exceptional.

The timekeeping properties of verge watches have been freely anathematised by people who have never taken the trouble to ascertain at first hand how they perform in the pocket. It can, however, be said that a good verge watch of 1700 or later (or earlier if a Tompion) in reasonable condition, will perform regularly to within a minute or two a day, at reasonably steady temperatures.

Many collectors are satisfied with a clock or watch if it is just capable of ticking, but for the collector to whom a clock or watch is something more than an inanimate object to put in a show-case, his enjoyment is enhanced by the knowledge that it is still capable of doing the job for which it was made, and as it was made. Not many people are now willing to wear so bulky an object as an early eighteenth century watch, but the collector who does so may find an added pride and pleasure in ordering his affairs by an instrument which has performed that office for eight or more generations of owners past, sharing so intimately in their day-to-day failures and successes.

From 1660 onwards for the next 170 years, the progress of English and French clocks (as opposed to watches) followed such different lines that they cannot easily be traced side by side. Accordingly, a separate chapter is devoted solely to French clocks during this period and, so far as clocks are concerned, this chapter deals almost exclusively with the English school. Its great length, in comparison with earlier chapters, is commensurate with the great number of clocks and watches of the period which survive, and with the amount of interest which they command.

ENGLISH CLOCKS 1657–1750

The invention of the pendulum profoundly influenced the appearance of clocks and the layout of their mechanism. The finer wheel work and more accurate performance of the pendulum clock made it desirable to protect the movement from dust, and as the metal cases previously universal would have become excessively heavy if made large enough to contain a complete movement and its pendulum, they were immediately and almost entirely superseded by wooden cases. Since the clock maker was not skilled in woodworking he had to look to the joiner to supply his cases and from 1657 onwards casemaking became a separate craft. The joiner-casemaker took his training and tradition from furniture makers and in consequence clock cases followed styles in furniture, but with a considerable time-lag. During the period covered by this chapter, the appearance of clocks was more highly stylised than at any other time.

The bracket clock and the long-case clock account for almost the whole output of English makers. Each type will be described separately, with sub-divisions into arbitrary periods. This method entails a certain amount of repetition but seems, on the whole, to be the most convenient arrangement. Before turning to the bracket and long-case clock there are some other forms which survived from the previous era and which should first be considered.

LANTERN CLOCKS

Lantern clocks may be said to have taken the pendulum in their stride and indeed, they continued to be made with the old wheel balance for a decade after the invention of the pendulum. Conversely, many old balance-wheel escapements were converted to pendulum and an unaltered balance-wheel escapement is now a very great rarity.

The two trains continued to be one behind the other, with the going train in front. The verge staff extended the full depth of the clock so that the pendulum swung behind the back plate of the striking train, having a round bob-weight.

Examples are found in which the pendulum swings in front of the dial, but these are continental.

A somewhat rare, and very decorative arrangement was to place the pendulum between the going and striking train. The pendulum weight was then made flat and generally shaped like an anchor so that in the course of its swing its tips protruded far beyond the confines of the case. To accommodate it the case was fitted with two segmental-shaped wings, made of brass like the rest of the case. The upper edges of these wings, being at an angle of about forty-five degrees to the vertical, were decorated with frets similar to those round the top of the case, and the fronts of the wings were fitted with glass so that the action of the pendulum was visible.

Lantern clocks continued to be weight driven, but towards the end of the century chains began to supplant ropes. Pendulum clocks only have one weight since their rate can be regulated by the

PLATE 42

'Wing-type' lantern clock by Ignatius Huggeford. Last quarter seventeenth century. The clock has an anchor-shaped pendulum, placed between the going and striking trains. The wing-shaped projections at each side of the clock are to allow for its swing. Note the alarum dial, also the weights suspended on chains instead of the earlier rope.

PLATE 43 *(left)*

Small 'Sheep's-Head' lantern clock by Thomas Tompion with verge and pendulum escapement, circa 1675. Note enlarged chapter ring which gives this type of lantern clock its name.

PLATE 44 *(below left, below, and right)*

German travelling or coach alarum clock by David Buschmann, circa 1680. Diameter 3⅜ inches. The case is silver-gilt 'Pierce à jour' and finely engraved. Note irregular shaped foot and table of balance cock and Barrow regulator, typical of earliest balance spring instruments. (British Museum)

pendulum. An advantage of this is that the single weight running over two pulleys affords maintaining power during winding.

Eight-day movements are exceedingly rare and thirty-hour trains continued to be almost universal.

Very rarely, quarter-striking examples are found, with a second bell, placed inside the larger.

Never an aristocratic clock, a single hour hand continued to suffice for the lantern, even when made by Tompion and the other great makers. When a minute hand exists it is almost certain to be a subsequent addition. Hands in general continued to be of simple spade form, but from 1675 onwards they became gradually more ornate. The wider chapter ring, sometimes known as the 'sheep's-head clock' came in towards the end of the seventeenth century.

Apart from these details the general appearance of the lantern clock continued almost unaltered, and examples are difficult to date. They were not generally made in London after 1700 but provincial makers were still producing them in the mid-eighteenth century, differing but little from examples of 150 years earlier.

TRAVELLING OR COACH CLOCKS

Clocks which are, in every respect, very large watches were widely used when travelling. They are usually three to five inches in diameter and thick in proportion, and originally had a protective outer case covered in tooled leather, which have seldom survived. They were of a size and shape convenient for packing and their watch-type pendant enabled them to be hung up on a convenient hook in coach or inn.

Early examples are almost universally clock-watches, striking the hour on a bell fitted in the back of the case. The count wheel, usually decorated with an engraved rose-pattern, was outside the back plate of the movement.

After the invention of rack striking and repeating mechanisms they were more usually made as repeaters, which are more suited to the bed-chamber than clock-watches; but the clock-watch variety continued to be made, generally with a let-off repeater. In either case the repeater is set off by pulling a cord or chain which emerges through the side of the case opposite the pendant. Later clock-watch examples sometimes have the complicated *grande-sonnerie* striking and quarter chiming mechanism.

As befits a travelling clock, they are almost always fitted with calendar and alarum mechanisms.

In early examples there is a date aperture but in later types (usually of the second half of the eighteenth century) the date is more usually indicated by a hand, the days of the month being marked between the hour and minute circles.

In early examples the alarum is set by a disc in the middle of the dial with hours marked I to XII. The hour at which the alarum is required to go off is set under the tail of the hour hand at the time of setting. In later examples a movable hand (usually geared to a key-square) is set to the hour on the dial at which the alarum is required to go off.

Early examples have silver champlevé dials and late examples have white enamel dials.

The dividing line between what have been described as 'early' and 'late' examples may be put at about the middle of the eighteenth century but for more precise dating they may be compared with the fashions in watch design, described in the second part of this chapter.

In this form they continued to be made throughout the eighteenth century but they are rare after 1800. Very late examples are sometimes set in a round wood frame so as more conveniently to hang flat against a wall. Other forms of travelling clock are occasionally found. One, which seems to have been particularly favoured by Quare, was in the form of a small bracket clock, the case, metal gilt, with its top fitted with a carrying ring and a ball and socket mounting. Quare specialised in portable clocks and barometers.

Tompion made one or at most two travelling clocks of a most rare and interesting type. They had the usual verge escapement but the controller is a balance wheel and spiral spring to which a pendulum may be coupled at will. A pin on the large vertical balance wheel fits through a slot in the pendulum and both move together; an interesting and perhaps unique combination. For use when travelling a system of levers holds the pendulum clear of the balance wheel. One example is dated (1693), a rare feature, and may have belonged to William III. The dial and plates measure only $4\frac{3}{4}$ by $5\frac{9}{16}$ inches. It also strikes and repeats the quarters on two bells. The workmanship throughout is superb, and the chapter rings are solid silver; a very rare feature after 1670.

TABLE CLOCKS

Clocks with horizontal dials, being designed to stand on a table, continued in undiminished popularity from the last period, and except for being fitted with a balance spring, their design altered in no important particular. The majority are of German origin and English examples are rare. They continued to be made until 1750 but later examples are very rare.

Eighteenth century specimens occasionally have a minute as well as an hour hand. Where there is a repeating mechanism it is usually of the let-off variety, actuated by a button. The cases, square or hexagonal, are always of brass gilt, but the mounts, chapter ring and feet may be silver. Table clocks sometimes have outer, wood or leather travelling cases.

Until the end of the seventeenth century German and Italian makers continued to produce the sixteenth century style of tabernacle clock with vertical dials, often of great complexity, but with the addition of a pendulum. Three or four trains are quite usual.

BRACKET CLOCKS

Introductory

The coach, table and lantern clocks were all survivals from the pre-pendulum era but the bracket and long-case clock did not exist prior to 1657.

The term 'bracket clock' clearly infers that such clocks always stood on brackets. Very often they did so, more particularly in France, and sometimes they were supplied with brackets to match them; but more often they had no fixed position and were frequently moved from one place to another. 'Spring-driven clocks' would be a more accurate definition, but the name 'bracket clock' has become such a well-understood generalisation that it will be used throughout this chapter.

The earliest pendulum clocks by Samuel Coster were spring driven. They had going barrels for going and striking trains, verge escapement, and bob pendulum suspended from a cord between curved cheeks.

Almost for the first time, the trains were placed side by side so that both could be key-wound through the dial. The cases were plain black, of rectangular shape, mostly with a pediment top. The rectangular dial opening was usually covered with velvet, with a plain silvered brass or gilt chapter ring and the maker's name on a separate gilt plaque. The hands were decoratively pierced and gilt. These clocks were almost certainly designed to hang, but nevertheless they sometimes had four small circular gilt feet.

The English bracket clock is found from 1658 onwards and so many examples exist that the trends of development may be followed very closely. It will be convenient to consider them in arbitrary periods; the first up to 1675 and then on in divisions of 25 years, up to the end of the chapter at 1750. All dates relate to London practice and provincial makers lagged anything up to 25 years behind them, according to their distance from the Capital, and the innate conservatism of themselves and their clients. In the earliest period specimens (especially spring-driven) by provincial makers are very rare. Exceptions to all dates can be discovered but those given are correct for the general trend. It is, of course, an essential feature of all bracket clocks that the trains are placed side by side and wound through the dial.

1657–75

The architectural type of bracket clock and weight-driven hooded wall-clock were fashionable for about fifteen years, from 1660 to 1675, although much simplified wall clocks, by provincial makers, with triangular or arched pediments, continued to be made until well into the eighteenth century.

The earliest examples had plain matted dial plates with a narrow silver or silvered chapter ring. An equally early type had the dial plate engraved all over with the newly-introduced tulip flower. Only very slightly later, and well within the 'architectural' period, came the beautiful Cherub spandrel, to fill the four triangular spaces outside the dial. In this type, the space inside the chapter ring is matted and the four triangular spaces are plain gilt. In each spandrel is placed an ornament in the form of a cherub's head flanked by his two wings arranged so as to fill the triangular space most neatly. Cast and chiselled, the earliest cherub spandrels are in very bold relief. The chiselling, in particular, is of the finest quality but even before the end of the seventeenth century a decadence set in which continued with only rare exceptions. The castings became progressively shallower and the chiselling more perfunctory until, in the second half of the eighteenth century, the castings were sometimes put onto the clock just as they came out of the mould. Spandrel ornaments are usually metal gilt, but the finest examples are of silver, which gives an exceedingly rich effect against the mercurial gilt of the dial plate.

Spandrel ornaments are fixed to the dial plate by a square-headed screw inserted from the back of the plate. They are therefore easily movable and interchangeable and the presence of an early cherub spandrel must not be taken as infallible evidence of early date.

Until 1675 the maker's name, mostly latinised, was usually engraved on the dial plate below the chapter ring. Only in one or two clocks of this period is the name found engraved in the centre of the dial plate.

Bracket clocks frequently had an alarum mechanism, in which case the setter or alarum dial took the form of a silver or silvered disc about two inches in diameter in the centre of the dial. Where there is no alarum the corresponding central space of the dial plate is sometimes engraved with a spiral or floral pattern but this is seldom found after 1675. Very rarely this centre ornament took the form of an applied silver or gilt fret and the dial plate is then usually plain gilt, not matted, or alternatively, velvet.

A calendar aperture is usual at any period.

PLATE 45

Bracket clock by Robert Seignior, circa 1670. Note architectural treament of case which is oak veneered with tortoiseshell, with ebony mouldings embellished with built-up, metal-gilt bases and capitals. There is a drawer in the plinth to hold the winding key. On the dial, note engraved rosette in centre, simple type of 'spade' hour hand; quarter-hour divisions on inside edge of chapter ring and minute divisions on outside edge with minute numerals inside the divisions; narrow chapter ring with IIII as wide as high; gilt cast and chiselled cherub's head spandrel ornaments; signature at base of dial. The back plate is engraved with the tulip pattern typical of second half of the 'architectural' period. Note the bob pendulum.

In later clocks it became customary to inscribe two or three concentric rings round the winding and calendar apertures. This was done partly to avoid the scratching of the dial plate by ill-directed assaults with a winding key. On the other hand, the existence of ringed apertures is not necessarily an indication of late date as they may have been added to cover up the disfiguration by scratches of an early dial. Ringed apertures were at no time universal.

The earliest clocks had their winding holes opposite the 10 and the 2 but after about 1670 the position of the winding holes on the dial is no indication of date.

Very early hour hands are of simple spade pattern. The minute hands have a plain pointer on the end of a small S-shaped section near the centre. All hands are of steel except with velvet dials. The more ornate type of hand, developed from 1680 onwards, very occasionally appeared before 1675, but when decorated hands are found on clocks made before 1675, they are likely to be replacements.

The chapter ring itself was narrow, so that the IIII is wider than it is high. Some very early examples consist of a thin silver ring on brass but the great majority are silvered brass. Silvering does not last indefinitely, and usually displays tarnished streaks after 50 years or less. The appearance of many early clocks is spoilt by discoloured chapter rings, which their owners refuse to have resilvered in the pious belief that the existing silvering is original. In fact, this is exceedingly rarely the case as if a clock has been in regular use it is more likely to have been resilvered half-a-dozen times.

On the inside edge of the chapter ring is a narrow ring of quarter-hour divisions against which the tip of the hour hand should register. On the outer edge is an almost equally narrow ring of minute divisions against which the tip of the minute hand should register. Towards the end of the eighteenth century makers became somewhat casual about the proper length of their clock-hands, but hands of incorrect length on an early clock are certainly not original.

Since people were not yet accustomed to clocks which would tell time to the minute, and probably found some difficulty in automatically relating the position of the two hands to each other, makers sometimes figured each separate minute from 0 to 60 but this is rarely found after 1675. It was, however, more usual to figure every fifth minute, and this remained invariable practice until 1775. What is, however, peculiar to this earliest period is that the minute figures are placed *inside* the confines of the minute divisions. This was necessary owing to the narrow width of the chapter ring, and as soon as this became wider, from 1675 onwards, the minute figures were put outside the divisions, where they could be made of a more legible size. Bracket clocks very rarely have seconds dials.

PLATE 46

Bracket clock by Thomas Tompion, circa 1675. Note panelled top typical of transition from architectural to bell top case; spiral-twist pillars with metal-gilt bases and capitals; bolt and shutter maintaining power; alarum setter disc. The case is olive wood and ebony.

A form of chapter ring used occasionally up to the end of the seventeenth century, but mostly, during this first period, is of skeleton form, the spaces between the hour figures being cut away. This fashion probably came from Holland, where a skeleton chapter ring looked particularly elegant against the background of velvet so often used to cover the dial plate.

As has already been said, the earliest wood cases followed the earlier metal fashion in being of architectural design. The dial opening is flanked by pillars with gilt corinthian capitals which support a triangular portico top. In the middle of the portico there is often a gilt escutcheon and it is generally topped by three gilt finials which balance the gilt feet on which the clock stands. Finials remained fashionable until the early nineteenth century.

Carrying handles are not found in conjunction with architectural cases, but from 1670 onwards there begins to appear the type of case with a carrying handle on top, which was to remain fashionable until the end of the eighteenth century. The pediment gave way to a dome-shaped top, at first very shallow (scarcely more than an inch and a half deep) but later to assume a variety of shapes and sizes. A variant only found in the earliest period is a plain chamfered panel, treatment, without a handle, and supported on spiral-twist pillars. It may really be regarded as the transitional style between the pediment and dome top. When a bracket clock has pillars at all four corners it will generally be found that there is a socket in the middle of the base with a spigot so that the clock could be turned to face in any direction. With the dome top, the corner pillars give way to a plain, flat door across the whole front of the clock. Metal escutcheons were often applied to the uprights of the door, one as an embellishment to the keyhole and the other to balance it. The top rail of the door was generally pierced in a fretwork pattern, backed with coloured silk, to facilitate the egress of sound when the clock struck.

The most popular wood was ebony veneered on oak, but kingwood, olivewood and lignum vitae were also used. Walnut did not come into general use for clock cases until after 1670.

The mechanism of spring-driven bracket clocks changed but little for a century after their introduction, and the verge escapement remained popular long after the anchor escapement had established itself in long-case clocks. Bracket clocks were designed to be carried about and the verge escapement, with its wide arc, is less sensitive than others to being stood slightly out of level.

As has been explained in the last chapter, the first Dutch pendulum clocks had their pendulums suspended from a thread and the pendulum rod passed through a fork attached

PLATE 47

Bell top bracket clock by Joseph Knibb, circa 1685, showing his conservatism in design exemplified by the shallow dome; engraved border round dial plate; every minute separately marked with numerals inside minute division; continued use of wood fret above door. Note also (typical of Knibb) false key-hole in right-hand escutcheon and use of IV instead of IIII indicating use of 'Roman' striking (see page 88); also skeleton chapter ring.

rigidly to the verge staff. In the first English examples the pendulum rod itself was rigidly attached at right angles to the verge staff. The front end of the verge staff was pivoted into the front plate but the back end was on a separate cock, usually on a knife-edge, but occasionally by means of a pivot only, in very early examples. These knife-edges were a source of trouble owing to rapid wear. In both English and Dutch types the clock was regulated by screwing the round pendulum bob up or down the rod, which was threaded for the purpose, and the bob had a core of wood which securely gripped the thread.

Nearly all bracket clocks before 1675 strike the hour, and sometimes the half hour, indicated by a single stroke on the bell or another bell. Quarter-striking is rare in this early period.

From the outset, nearly all bracket clocks were made to go for eight days (continental clocks with going barrels frequently go for two or three weeks) and makers found some difficulty in making a spring long and strong enough to provide striking power for so long. Joseph Knibb devised a means of economising in power, which is known as Roman Striking, since it is related to the Roman system of numerals. It requires two bells of different pitch. Anything represented by a Roman I is struck on the small bell, and V is indicated by one stroke on the large bell. Thus 4 o'clock is struck as • *, five as *, six as * •, and so forth. X is regarded as twice V so that XII, for example is heard as ** •• . In order to make his chapter ring consistent with the striking, Knibb used a IV instead of the IIII usual on clocks. Such a clock has a somewhat unbalanced appearance and explains why tradition has favoured the strictly incorrect IIII, which more nearly balances the equally heavy VIII. Clocks with Roman striking are rare and much valued by collectors.

Instead of the usual, dome-shaped bell commonly found in clocks of all periods, Knibb used a bell with almost parallel sides and an almost flat top, and a sharp angle where the two meet. The same shape was also used by Henry Jones.

Another unusual system is Dutch striking. When heard from another room, or too far from the clock to read the hands in a dimly lit apartment, a half-hour strike is not very helpful, and to overcome this the Dutch used two bells, large and small. The hour was struck on the large bell, and by way of indicating the half-hour, the next succeeding hour was struck on the small bell. In the next period, 1675 to 1700 this system was developed into the full *Grande-Sonnerie* striking.

Very occasionally, bracket clocks in this and succeeding periods were fitted with maintaining mechanism whereby the clock continued to go during winding. The method used was the 'bolt and shutter' whereby the winding holes were normally covered by a shutter which had to be moved to one side, by moving a bolt, before the winding square was accessible to the key. The bolt wound up a small subsidiary spring which kept the clock running for two or three minutes while the power was reversed during winding. However, maintaining mechanism was much more usual on weight than on spring-driven clocks, which were hardly accurate enough at this date to merit the refinement.

In the first spring-driven clocks the pillars between the plates were made of baluster shape, pinned behind the back plate. It was soon realised that it would be more sightly to rivet the pillars to the back plate and pin them between the front plate and the dial. This became the general rule from 1670 onwards, and the pillars became symmetrical to match. Good class makers used hinged latches instead of pins and this applies without exception to Tompion.

Although all but the very earliest bracket clocks had glazed back doors the back plates were practically never engraved, as later became almost universal. The only decoration imparted to them was the maker's name, boldly engraved. The locking plate for the striking, however, was behind the back plate and this was often engraved with a Tudor rose or similar pattern.

This first period has been described at great length because it struck out a new line which was to continue with relatively little change for more than a century. What has been described above will therefore be found to hold good in large measure for what follows, both for long-case and bracket clocks, and as each successive period comes under review, less and less will require to be said about it. In both clock and watchmaking, the period 1660 to 1700 was one of the very utmost activity and rapid development.

1675–1700

By 1675 the bracket clock had become established in all the essential characteristics which were to continue in production for more than a century. Architectural cases were not made after 1675, although the panel top and spiral-twist pillars were made for a further decade. The quarter century now under review was one of standardisation. The great makers had finished their period of experimentation by 1680 or 1685 and laid down the lines upon which their workmen could produce clocks in relatively large numbers. The touches of individual genius and experiment disappear from clock-making, leaving instead a very highly developed article wrought with an extremely high standard of craftsmanship. Nevertheless, with such a system established, the onset of decadence could not be long delayed; but little sign of it will be found before the turn of the century.

Makers such as Knibb and East, who favoured the refined proportions of the narrow chapter ring, continued for some time to place their minute numerals inside the minute divisions; but Tompion, whose outlook was primarily utilitarian, early developed a wider, if slightly less elegant ring, which permitted both larger hour and minute numerals. Tompion had been admitted to the Clockmakers' Company in 1671 and became acquainted with Hooke in 1674, and from that time onwards he rapidly became established as the leader of the horological world. Where he lead, others followed.

The wider chapter ring necessarily shortened the hour hand for which Tompion and others abandoned the simple spade and adopted instead a wider, more decorated shape, which enabled it, in a candle-lit room, more easily to be distinguished from the minute hand. There can be little doubt that all these developments were made in the interests of legibility, but they conspire to give the dials of late seventeenth century clocks a heaviness which is not so ele-

PLATE 48

Bell top walnut bracket clock by Joseph Knibb. A typical and perfect example of the 1680–90 decade.

gant as their immediate predecessors. And it is noticeable, as window areas increased and artificial lighting improved towards the end of the eighteenth century, that there was a return to a lighter style of dial treatment.

Another addition to the dial which became fashionable between 1690 and 1695 was a slit through which a bob, attached to the verge staff, was visible. This moved with the pendulum so that it could readily be seen whether the clock was going. If the clock stops, it should not be restarted by means of this 'false pendulum' which is not usually strong enough for the purpose.

Until about 1690 the cherub spandrel reigned almost supreme, but as early as 1680 Tompion had begun to introduce mechanical refinements which involved alterations to the standard dial.

It appears that as early as 1666 Hooke had devised a way of mounting the pendulum which was, in fact, a refinement of the Dutch system. But where Huygens had hung his pendulum on a thread, Hooke substituted for the thread a length of spring steel, which was in itself a substantial improvement, and paved the way to the anchor escapement and its long pendulum, which was too heavy to hang on a thread.

In this capacity it had appeared in all long-case clocks from the early seventies, but Tompion saw in it a means of overcoming the inconvenience of regulating bracket clocks by screwing the bob up and down the rod. Not only was the bob difficult to get at inside the case, but it involved turning the clock round to regulate it.

Tompion therefore mounted his pendulum on a spring which passed between fixed blocks placed somewhat below the mounting. Then, by mounting the spring anchorage on a moveable carriage the whole pendulum can be raised or lowered, thus altering the effective length of the pendulum below the blocks. The moveable carriage may be operated by a lever forming part of the dial so that the clock can be regulated without even moving it.

This lever Tompion placed in one spandrel of the dial and matched it in the opposite corner by a 'strike-silent' lever which enabled the striking to be put out of action when the clock was taken at night into the bed-chamber. Occasionally, Tompion filled the remaining two bottom spandrels with two further levers operating claws behind the back plate which, when brought together, held the pendulum immovable. This was a great convenience and safeguard when transporting the clock any distance, and was incorporated in cases without a back door.

PLATE 49

Bell top bracket clock by Thomas Tompion. This is his typical design of bedroom clock from 1685 onwards. Note pull repeat cord at side; glass side windows; chapter ring becoming wider with minute numerals outside minute divisions; woman's head spandrel ornaments; false pendulum aperture and bob; subsidiary dials for regulation and strike-silent, with signature on medallion between them.

With the spring-mounted pendulum Tompion substituted a flat, lenticular-shaped bob for the old round bob, thus saving a certain amount of depth in the case.

In the earliest examples, Tompion fitted the subsidiary dials precisely into the triangular spandrels, but later he slightly enlarged them so that there was a space between them, above the chapter ring. This provided a convenient place to inscribe a medallion with the maker's name, engraved much larger than was possible in the narrow strip below the dial to which it had previously been relegated. This added height in the clock was also a convenience where it had a complicated chiming mechanism on several bells.

This particularly applied to the rare and expensive clocks with *Grande-Sonnerie* striking which first appeared during this period.

In this system, after each quarter was struck it was followed by the last preceding hour, being thus a development of the Dutch striking mentioned in the last period. *Grande-Sonnerie* striking is not only complicated mechanically but requires a great deal of power to drive it, as the hour is repeated at each quarter.

A further improvement in striking mechanisms was also invented by Edward Barlow about 1676. Previously, with the count wheel, or locking plate then universal, the hours struck in succession regardless of the hands. With Dr. Barlow's 'rack and snail' the striking was positively locked to the hands so that the correct hour was bound to strike. Barlow shortly followed this by inventing the repeating mechanism, whereby, on moving a lever at any time the last hour and quarter are struck. The power for striking the hours in this form of repetition comes from the striking train, but if there is no striking mechanism (as is common in many of Tompion's bracket clocks, intended for bedrooms) the cord which is pulled to make the repeater work, winds up a spring which provides power to operate the strike was well as the quarters. This spring may be either spiral or straight-line and Tompion favoured the latter arrangement. Most seventeenth century repeaters give the quarters; half-quarter, five minute and minute repeaters followed in the eighteenth century though it seems that Hooke at any rate worked out a system for minute repeating.

PLATE 50

Engraved back plate of bracket clock by Joseph Windmills with decorative pierced pendulum cock, circa 1700. Note main-spring set-up ratchets, which are usually between front plate and dial.

Tompion and other leading makers arranged their repeaters with cords coming out on both sides of the clock so that they could be operated with equal convenience on whichever side of the bed the clock was standing.

Clocks are very occasionally found with lock plate striking and rack and snail repetition, and where there was no repeater the lock-plate remained popular for many years and was still made throughout the nineteenth century, especially in French and American clocks.

From 1675 onwards, and for the century following, back plates were engraved with varying degrees of complexity, and much ingenuity has been expended on drawing a variety of conclusions from this circumstance. It has been argued that back plates would not have been engraved if they were not intended to be seen, and that bracket clocks were therefore intended to be stood on a table in the middle of the room, or against a mirror. They may at times have been so placed, but the makers engraved their back plates from no such ulterior motive, but simply from pride and pleasure in their work, in just the same way as they applied expensive decorative frets to the back plates of their watches, which were never intended to be seen at all under normal circumstances.

FIGURE 12. *The 'tic-tac' escapement used by Tompion and others in bracket clocks circa 1670–80.*

PLATE 51

Basket top bracket clock by Fromanteel and Clark, circa 1690 ?. Note the exuberance of applied ornament. The case is oak veneered with tortoiseshell. The three winding-holes inside the chapter ring are for going, chiming and grande sonnerie striking. The alarum is wound by a square on the chapter ring between X and XI. The two upper subsidiary dials are for regulation, and strike-silent. The two lower dials are to lock the pendulum when moving the clock.

The earliest engraving was usually of the fashionable tulip, but in about 1690 this gave way to conventional patterns. Another form of decorating the back plate was an ornamental pierced cock attached to the back mounting of the verge staff, and at times these assumed extravagant proportions. They disappeared with the adoption of the spring-mounted pendulum to which they were not easily applicable.

Reverting to the casework, ebony remained by far the most popular wood, long after it had gone entirely out of fashion for long case clocks; but the other woods previously mentioned continued to appear. The use of walnut was exceedingly rare. Very occasionally, too, bracket clocks were made in metal gilt or silver gilt cases.

In about 1685 metal replaced wood for the fret above the door, and frets were also inserted in the sides of the clock, instead of glass. Metal frets were also applied to the sides and front of the shallow dome which was just beginning to appear in 1675, and in order to permit the free egress of sound the wood was cut away behind the frets. These metal embellishments sometimes covered the entire

PLATE 52

Double basket top bracket clock by John Hough, circa 1700. Note ringed winging holes.

PLATE 53

Night clock by Joseph Knibb, circa 1670. A lamp inside the clock shines through the apertures in the dial plate. The fixed roman numerals indicate the quarters, past which the arabic numerals move in succession. The time as illustrated is 7.38.
(British Museum)

dome; and when the whole of the structure is of pierced metal it becomes known as a 'basket top'. Before the end of the century this already sufficiently ornate arrangement had been capped by a second 'basket' on top of the first, known, appropriately enough, as a 'double basket'.

The less ostentatious wooden dome had nevertheless continued and developed by the end of the century into a moulding of ogee section, known as an inverted bell.

The plain, low, unornamented dome also remained popular and was principally favoured by Tompion, who clearly understood the difference between richness and gaudiness, and sedulously avoided mere vulgar ostentation in all his clocks.

Mechanically, apart from the application of the spring-suspended pendulum to the verge escapement in bracket clocks, the only development during this period was the 'tic-tac' escapement occasionally used by Tompion and others.

Its apparent purpose was to combine the wide arc of a verge with the advantages of the anchor

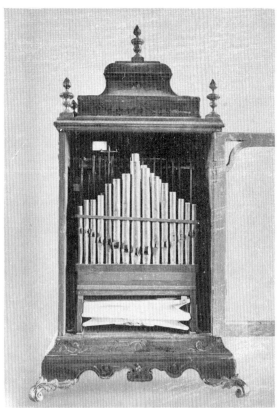 

PLATE 54

Organ-clock by Markwick Markham, made for the Turkish market, circa 1770. The case is red lacquer. Once every three hours the organ plays and ships move across the water-scape above the dial. The view of the back of the clock shows the organ, which has stopped pipes, tuned by their ears.

escapement and it is, in fact, little more than the pallets of an anchor brought so close together as to span only two or three teeth of the escape wheel. It is seldom found before 1675, nor after 1700. Perhaps its main interest lies in its similarity to the cylinder escapement for watches, as originated by Tompion and indeed, if Tompion had followed it more closely, so as to obtain a double instead of only a single impulse in one direction, his experiments with the cylinder escapement might have been more successful.

A form of bracket clock which first appeared soon after the pendulum and thereafter fitfully into the nineteenth century, was the 'Night Clock'. It had no hands but a revolving dial plate or some other arrangement with voided numerals. A light placed inside the clock shone through these cut-out numerals so that the time could be read although the room was in complete darkness. Such clocks were often fitted with a silent escapement, the pallets being formed of gut, held taut, while the escape wheel had symmetrical teeth, roughly conforming in shape to an equilateral triangle. The gut wore through at intervals but could be easily renewed.

PLATE 55

Inverted-bell-topped bracket clock by Tompion and Banger, circa 1705–10. Note strong general similarity to the earlier Tompion model, Plate 49, and continued simplicity despite the increasing fashion for ornament. The back plate is engraved with a conventional flowing pattern as against the tulip pattern fashionable until 25 years previously. Note (compared with Plate 45) the spring-suspended pendulum with regulation effected from the subsidiary dial on dial plate; lenticular pendulum bob; absence of count-wheel (owing to use of rack striking); operating levers for repeating mechanism. The oil sinks are a later modification.

The Turkish market

In about 1680 England began to develop a considerable export trade to Turkey. Early examples of export clocks are rare, but after about 1740 they become increasingly common (as also watches). They may therefore conveniently be considered between these two periods.

Turkish-market clocks were not generally made by the leading men but the principal exceptions are Christopher Gould (Clockmakers Company 1682. Died 1718) and Markwick Markham (*circa* 1725–80).

The cases were usually executed in lacquer or tortoiseshell, with brass or silver mounts. Hemispherical dome tops were also popular. The chapter rings, naturally, are engraved with Turkish numerals. Female heads and angel spandrels, such as would have offended religious susceptibilities, were tactfully avoided.

Musical and chiming movements, and clocks incorporating small organs which played (usually every three hours) were popular.

PLATE 56

Break-arch musical bracket clock (with ten bells) by Quare and Horseman, circa 1720. An early example of the use of the break-arch dial in bracket clocks. The subsidiary dial in the break-arch is for regulation.

1700–1725

By 1700 the bracket clock had reached its final development and for the next fifty years it continued to be made with little alteration.

Ebony and ebonised pear continued as the most popular woods, but with walnut and lacquer increasingly used. The inverted bell and the dome top both persisted, with a carrying handle on the top. Mouldings are generally similar to those of the preceding period, but less bold, and more fussy. Metal frets, however, continued to improve in execution and superb examples of side frets are found throughout the period.

Dials remained much as before and cherub spandrels continued to be used. The more fashionable design, however, was a small woman's head surrounded by a formal pattern. An important modification to the dial took place in about 1710, in the form of a break-arch top such as Tompion had introduced into longcase clocks fifteen years previously. When first introduced into bracket clocks this extension to the dial area usually contained a calendar or strike-silent dial. The makers name began more frequently to appear on the dial inside the chapter ring, or on the chapter ring itself.

When minute numerals were placed on a separate ring, outside the minute divisions, there was always a decoration at the half-quarters of this ring. This ornament went out of fashion by 1725.

Engraved back plates continued throughout the period.

Musical movements were introduced about 1715 but they were never usual during the first half of the century.

1725–1750

The same characteristics as before persist with remarkably little change in fashion.

The break-arch dial is almost universal and the woman's head generally disappears from the spandrel ornaments, which become flowing arabesques of varying merit. Nevertheless, the old cherub spandrels are occasionally found until the middle of the century.

Back plates continued to be engraved, though with less complex designs than before.

Lacquered cases continued to be popular up to 1750 but went out of fashion soon afterwards, except for the Turkish market.

The quarter and half-hour divisions inside the chapter ring gradually disappeared during this period and are rarely found afterwards. The minute divisions and numerals, however, continued as before.

An important development of the dial, which dates from the beginning of this period, although it did not become at all widely used until after 1750, was a round instead of a square window in the front door, thus obviating the need for spandrels. Curiously enough, in one of the earliest examples, by William Webster, the door itself has ornamented spandrels in exactly the same way as the dial would have had with a square window.

PLATE 57

Bracket clock by Perigal, circa 1760. Note continued fashion for inverted bell top and innovation of circular window for dial, eliminating spandrel ornaments; one-piece silvered dial plate and elimination of quarter and half-hour divisions. The serpentine minute hand may be slightly later.

The bezel was usually of brass and was fixed in the door. The arrangement whereby the front of the clock was fixed and only the bezel was hinged, did not arrive until towards the end of the century. In these early examples the glass is always flat. Behind such a glass the separate, super-imposed chapter ring was abandoned and a one-piece, silvered dial substituted for it. Such dials were engraved in much the same way as before, but there was only a single circle inside the hour numerals, and no half- or quarter-hour divisions. The fleur-de-lis ornaments between the hour numerals were also omitted. The maker's name is usually engraved in the centre of the dial. The cases of such clocks are always entirely plain, generally surmounted by an inverted bell (later to turn into the true bell) and handle. Ellicott particularly favoured clocks of this design (often without striking mechanism) and their excellent taste was at once a pointer to the future and a welcome change from the played-out designs which had done duty with such little change for 75 years, and were to continue in less degree for yet another fifty.

HANGING WALL CLOCKS

Hanging wall-clocks vary in type. Many examples are little more than thirty-hour lantern clocks with square dial-plates, in a wooden case; but there are fine eight-day examples with the trains arranged side by side and key-wound. These latter all belong to the period 1660–75 and have cases of architectural type similar to contemporary bracket clocks or the hoods of long-case clocks.

LONG-CASE CLOCKS

Introductory

With the advent of the pendulum, eight-day trains became usual. In the case of weight-driven clocks the heavier weights necessary for eight-day going imposed a severe strain on any wall bracket; but by placing the movement on a pedestal standing on the floor this strain was obviated. It seems probable that the long-case clock was invented in this way, while the enclosure of the weights, safe from interference, was an obvious additional advantage.

The earliest long-case clocks are all English and it seems reasonably certain that they are an English invention. They never became really popular on the continent.

It will be found convenient to consider the development of the long-case clock in arbitrary periods, as was done in the case of bracket clocks, and in the first period especially, much of what was said about bracket clocks applies equally to the long-case.

1659–1675

No wood long-case clock was made before 1659.

For the first twelve years all had the verge escapement and short pendulum, about $9\frac{1}{2}$ inches long, beating half-seconds. They were seldom if ever above six feet high and had dials 8 or $8\frac{1}{2}$ inches square. The dial openings are square and the design of the dial and hands follow precisely the form described in detail in the preceding section, dealing with bracket clocks, to which the reader is referred (pages 84 to 88). Clocks with a half-second pendulum practically never had a seconds dial. The bolt-and-shutter maintaining mechanism, on the other hand, is more commonly found on long-case than on bracket clocks.

The refinement of maintaining mechanism is only found in clocks of high quality (such as are all surviving examples of the earliest period) and it is often found to have been removed at a later period. After about 1720 it was rarely fitted at all, except to clocks of the 'Regulator' class designed solely as timekeepers. Certainly in the case of short-pendulum, verge escapement clocks, their timekeeping ability was not of such great accuracy as to make a few seconds occupied in winding the clock once a week a matter of any consequence. Huygens used a form of maintaining mechanism and the fashion was probably copied from him.

The cases are made of dark-coloured wood, generally ebony or lignum vitae veneered on oak.

They are in three sections; plinth, trunk and hood. The plinths are plain unpanelled and the doors have three panels, the top and bottom panels being almost equal in size, with a small square panel between them. The doors fit flush into the case, having no moulding to cover the division between case and door and act as a stop, as later became universal.

At the top of the trunk is a convex moulding, connecting it to the hood. These convex mouldings are found in practically all seventeenth century clocks. After about 1700 the mouldings are concave. In this first period convex mouldings are universal. The moulding between trunk and plinth is usually of ogee section.

The back of the trunk is continued upwards for the full height of the clock and the hood is attached to it by grooves. The hood itself has no door, so that to wind the clock it has to be slid upwards on these grooves. It is normally impossible to lift the hood which is locked by a catch. The catch has a spoon-shaped projection which extends downwards into the doorway opening, and it is held in position by the door when shut, so that

PLATE 58

Weight-driven wall clock by Edward East, circa 1665. Note architectural treatment of case with built-up corinthian capitals; engraved dial spandrels, typical of early pendulum clocks; bolt and shutter maintaining power; brass-gilt cannister containers for driving weights.

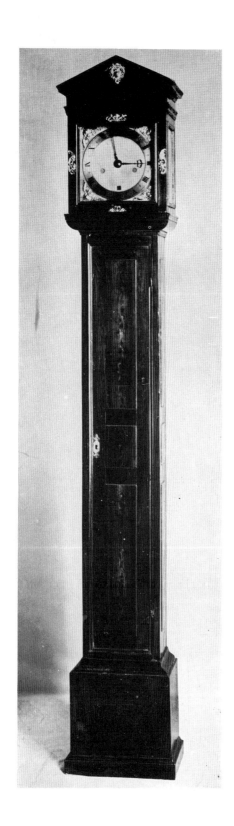

PLATE 59

The earliest type of English long-case clock, by Aha-suerus Fromanteel, circ 1660. Oak case, veneered with laburnum. Note 8 inch dial; architectural treatment of hood; convex moulding between trunk and hood; side windows same depth as front window (1660 decade only); three-panelled door fitting flush into case. The illustration of the movement shows the short, half-seconds 'bob' pendulum. The date wheel can be seen next to the dial plate. The Dutch pattern of hammers is found only in very early English pendulum clocks.
(British Museum)

100

when the latter is opened the catch is automatically released. Thus, so long as the door is kept locked it is impossible for anyone to tamper with the clock. When the hood has been raised clear of the dial it is again held by another catch and will stay in the raised position while the clock is wound or the hands set. The catch is released by hand to lower the hood.

Lift-up hoods are sometimes found to have been converted so as to have a door which opens forwards, as became usual after 1700.

The hood is of architectural form, like the contemporary bracket clock. The dial is flanked by three-quarter round pillars (usually responded by quarter round pillars at the back) with mercurial gilt corinthian capitals. The top is of triangular portico shape, sometimes with a gilt ornament in the tympanum. The side windows are the same depth as that in front of the dial, and this feature is only found in the first decade.

PLATE 60

The 8 inch dial of another early Fromanteel long-case clock, circa 1660. Note applied central pierced ornament; bolt and shutter maintaining power; cherub's head spandrels; simple 'spade' hour hand; quarter-hour divisions inside chapter ring; minute numerals inside minute divisions; signature at base of dial plate.

The short pendulum in conjunction with its verge escapement swings through an angle of about 50 degrees. A thirty-nine inch pendulum, beating seconds, and swinging through such an arc, could not be accommodated in a clock case.

By means of using very long pallets with rather shallow depthing, a thirty-nine inch pendulum can be made to operate with a ten to twelve degree arc in conjunction with a verge escapement, and this arrangement is found in eighteenth century French clocks; alternatively, a small arc can be achieved by interposing a reduction gearing between the verge staff and pendulum crutch, as was at any rate designed by Huygens. In point of fact, neither of these expedients was applied to the English long-case clock and it was not endowed with a long pendulum until after the invention of the anchor escapement in 1671, as was related in Chapter III. The long pendulum is so essential a part of the long-case clock that the short pendulum type which has just been described can hardly be said to be a true long-case clock at all, but more in the nature of a prototype. Nor did the architectural case long survive the invention of the anchor escapement, although there exists a clock by William Clement, made prior to 1675, with a 61-inch pendulum, beating $1\frac{1}{4}$ seconds, and an architectural case

PLATE 61 (*left*)

Long-case clock by George Harris showing operation of slide-up hood, usual prior to 1700. The spoon locking device is seen below the moulding at the top of the trunk. This clock, which is circa 1675, has the 61 inch, $1\frac{1}{4}$ seconds pendulum, and the front of the plinth is provided with a door to allow access to the pendulum bob for regulation.

PLATE 62 (*right centre*)

Long-case clock by Daniel Quare, circa 1675. A late example of the architectural style. Note engraved dial plate and single hand. Despite the use of a seconds pendulum and anchor escapement the clock goes only for 30 hours and the movement is similar in layout to a lantern clock. Provincial clocks of this kind are common up to about 1750, but examples such as this by a leading London maker are very rare.

PLATE 63 (*far right*)

Long-case clock by Thomas Tompion, circa 1675. An early example of a crested top. The case is olive wood with inlaid medallions of geometrical design. The somewhat unusual dial is ten inches square. The clock goes for a month and has complicated calendar work.
(British Museum)

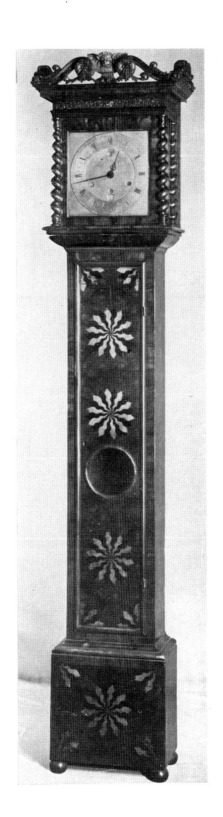

with 8-inch dial and portico top. It is, however, an exception and between 1670 and 1675, there was a rapid transition to a clock of bolder proportions, devoid of architectural inspiration, which laid the foundations of all subsequent development. Long pendulums before 1675 are, nevertheless, so rare, that it will be more convenient to discuss the type in the next chronological section.

Another very primitive type of long-case clock falls into no particular period, but was made by small provincial craftsmen at all times. This has a 30-hour movement with the trains one behind the other and is wound by pulling down the ropes or chains by hand, as with a lantern clock. These clocks usually have oak cases, square dials, brass chapter rings and only one hand. They are, in fact, no more than lantern clocks with a long pendulum, enclosed in a long case.

1675–1700

After 1675 it is rare to find a long-case clock with an eight-inch dial, and for the next twenty years, ten inches remained the most popular size. The overall height of the clock also grew to an average of nearly seven feet. The portico top disappeared completely by 1685. From 1675, examples are found with an open-work cresting and the view has been expressed that all flat-topped clocks originally had such a cresting, or a shallow dome. From the same date it is usual to find a band of fretwork, backed by coloured material, immediately above the dial opening.

The flat top, with or without cresting, is perhaps at once the simplest and best balanced finish to a long-case clock of moderate size; but the growing fashion for high rooms brought about a demand for clocks in proportion, and this led to a variety of mouldings which often seem to be piled on top of each other with no other object than of adding to the stature of the clock. The first signs of this movement may be found, as early as 1680, in a shallow dome such as appeared on bracket clocks at the same time. This was usually accompanied by finials of one sort or another; sometimes one at each corner and usually a third, on top of the dome. Apparently meaningless detail will often be found originally to have supported a finial which has since disappeared. The dome top developed and grew in size, but the meaningless superstructures which followed it belong to the next century. By 1700 dome-topped clocks were usually seven feet high overall.

As happened with the bracket clock, the plain corinthian columns and metal gilt capitals of the architectural case gave way to spiral-twist columns, either without capitals or with a narrow metal band at most.

The spiral-twist column remained fashionable on long-case clocks longer than on bracket clocks, but by 1690 it was generally replaced by a very slender, plain round column, which continued with little variation throughout the eighteenth century. Twist columns nevertheless appear occasionally until as late as 1715.

The lift-up hood remained in general use until 1700, even with clocks seven feet high.

With the advent of the ten-inch dial, the minute numerals were soon moved outside the minute divisions. They are placed at five-minute intervals and are of a much more legible size than before. Nevertheless numerals inside the division ring, occasionally with every minute numbered, may be found on ten-inch dials up to the end of the century. Quarter-hour divisions on the inside of the chapter ring remained universal.

From about 1690 it became increasingly usual to engrave the maker's name on the chapter ring, instead of below it, on the dial plate.

With the introduction of the long pendulum seconds dials became almost universal. At first made with as narrow a chapter ring and as long a hand as possible, they later became more heavy and clumsy in appearance. Seconds hands never had a tail during the seventeenth century.

To keep pace with the growing size of the clock case, the dial grew to eleven inches and twelve-inch dials began to appear about 1700, and winding holes began to be ringed somewhat earlier, although they never became universal and are not a reliable indication of date.

The cherub spandrel remained fashionable (in slightly elaborated form) but with the arrival of the twelve-inch dial a larger ornament became necessary. This took the form of two cherubs supporting a crown (perhaps a compliment to the joint monarchs) or a relatively small-sized woman's head surrounded by an arabesque pattern which could be of any desired shape or size.

Minute hands underwent no serious alteration, continuing as a straight pointer projecting from a small S-shaped section near the arbor. The spade type of hour hand is rarely found in long-case clocks after 1675 and gave way to a more complicated pierced pattern whose overall shape was of more pronouncedly pointed (and, accordingly, more legible) shape.

As was explained in Chapter I Solar time and Mean time rarely agree and since the sun provided the only means of setting a clock, it was important to know its variation from mean time at any moment. Printed tables were available for this purpose, but Tompion invented a most ingenious mechanism which showed automatically how many minutes solar time was in advance of or behind mean time. This took the form of a kidney-shaped cam which revolves once a year. A spring, or weight-loaded follower bears against the face of the cam and can be geared to a dial known as an 'Equation

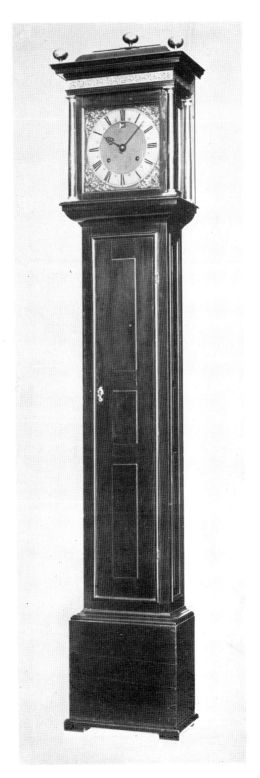

PLATE 64

Long-case clock by Joseph Knibb, circa 1685. Note combined use of ebony case with panelled door; also shallow dome top; 10 inch dial; month movement; roman striking; elaborated form of cherub's head spandrel.

PLATE 65 *(left, below, and right)*

Typical late seventeenth century long-case clock by Thomas Tompion. Walnut case with shallow dome top and convex mouldings to hood. Note 11 inch dial; satyre's head spandrel ornaments; minute numerals outside minute divisions and half-quarter ornaments between them; half-hour divisions inside chapter ring; plain minute hand with short curved section near the base; plain seconds hand without tail; calendar aperture; plain, unringed winding holes with bolt and shutter maintaining mechanism; Tompion's name at base of dial. On movement note long pendulum crutch typical of Tompion, and clip for holding hood in raised position.

106

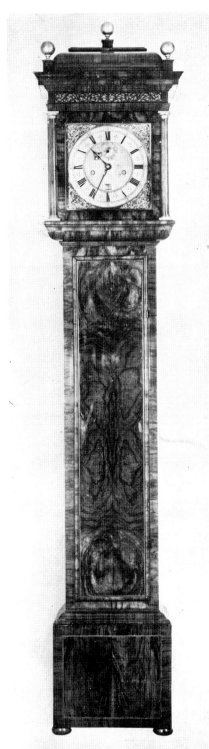

of Time Indicator'. This indicator may take a variety of forms; generally a moving quadrant showing the number of minutes 'late' or 'early'.

The oldest surviving and probably the first Equation clock was made by Tompion for William III in 1695 and it is engraved 'Tho: Tompion London Invent'. This clock still belongs to the Royal Family and owing to the great expense of equation clocks they were made only for the wealthiest clients and are correspondingly rare. Tompion always made his own equation mechanism, but other makers seem to have bought it ready-made from one Joseph Williamson, who worked mainly for Quare and specialised in equation-work. In this Royal clock the variations of solar time are shown by a moving annular ring outside the chapter ring so that mean and solar time may be read simultaneously off the minute hand.

Geared to the motion-work are other plates providing a complete year calendar. As these plates are above the chapter ring, Tompion was obliged to extend the normal square-shaped dial opening so as to accommodate them. He accordingly extended the dial opening upwards by means of a semi-circle whose diameter is a little more than one third that of the chapter ring. In this semi-circular space are arranged quadrant-shaped openings through which the calendar plates are visible.

Dials with the semi-circular extension are known as 'break-arch', the qualification 'break' indicating that the arch is of smaller diameter than the main dial. In the second quarter of the eighteenth century the break-arch became almost as wide as the main dial, but only in late and very complicated astronomical clocks does the break disappear altogether. But in one form or another, the break-arch became almost universal from 1720 onwards, if for no better reason than that it provided a functional reason for increasing the overall height of the clock.

With innate artistry Tompion seized upon the break-arch dial as a means of providing the hood itself with a top of new and exquisite shape. He emphasised the break-arch with a series of concentric mouldings terminating logically in a break-arch top to the hood itself. This he surmounted with a small square turret and ball finial. Most tall clocks have some element of clumsiness in their make-up, but in this Royal clock Tompion achieved a height of eight feet

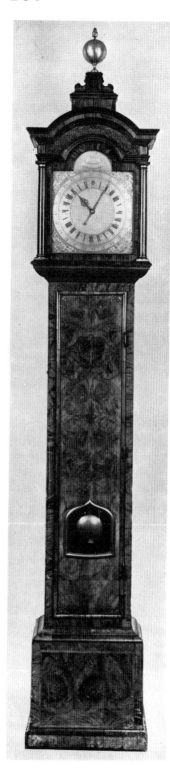

(7′ 3″ without finials) coupled with complete and faultless elegance. It goes for a year between windings and, like many year clocks, has a 24-hour dial. The minute hand, which is counter-balanced, revolves only once in two hours.

In the break-arch dial and hood Tompion set a fashion which did not become general until after 1720, for the square-shaped dial remained virtually universal throughout the seventeenth century.

No alteration in outline of the trunk and plinth took place during this period, but panels of inlaid decoration appeared from 1680 onwards. These consist of fairly bold floral or star-shaped patterns. In the floral variety the leaves are commonly stained green. Inlaid furniture in general, which came into the fashion at this time, reflects Dutch influence and it has been wrongly suggested that the earlier inlaid clock-cases were imported from Holland. Such an inconvenient and expensive arrangement seems most improbable, but undoubtedly there was a considerable influx of Dutch workmen into this country, who executed the inlay work in which native craftsmen were as yet unskilled. The inlay at first was invariably in panels and all-over inlay did not appear until after 1690. Lacquer began to be used towards the end of the period, but lacquered cases are rare before 1700.

The cases were mostly of olivewood or walnut, the latter gaining in popularity.

'Oyster' pattern was at all times popular, consisting of cross-cuts across the grain of the wood, generally laburnum. The use of ebony and ebonising almost entirely disappeared.

PLATE 66 (*left*)

Long-case clock made by Thomas Tompion, circa 1695 for William III and reproduced by gracious permission of Her Majesty Queen Elizabeth II. It goes for a year at one winding and has the first example of equation work and of a break-arch dial. Note the 24-hour dial and counterbalanced minute hand usual in year clocks.

PLATE 67 (*right*)

Long-case clock by Thomas Stones, circa 1700. Case decorated with 'all-over' marquetry of floral pattern. Note 12 inch dial with seconds dial and ringed winding holes; development of dome hood; concave moulding between trunk and hood, rare before 1700.

PLATE 68 (*far right*)

Long-case clock by Charles Clay, circa 1710. Case decorated with 'all-over' marquetry of arabesque design. Note inverted bell top surmounted by a short pillar which probably originally carried a third finial.

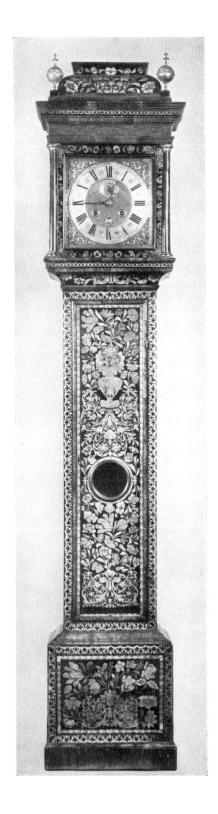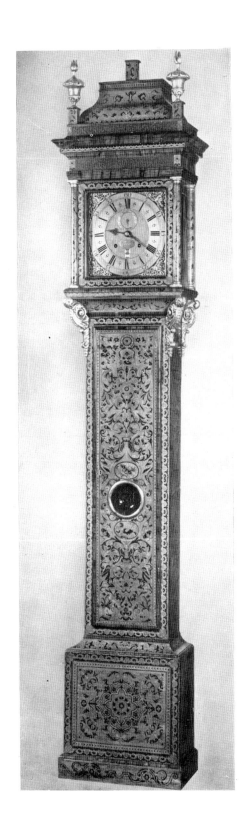

109

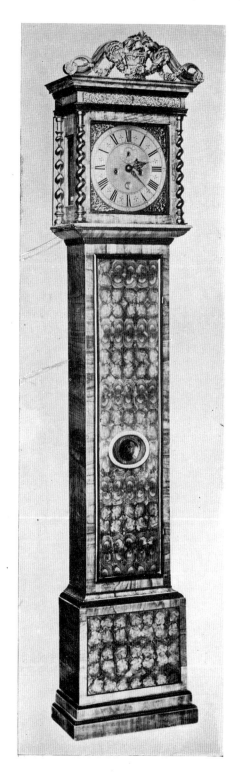

It is noteworthy that clocks by Tompion and his successor Graham are practically never inlaid. Like Breguet, a century later, Tompion's products are often exceedingly richly finished, but have a minimum of irrelevant ornament.

Doors remained universally square-topped. Pride in the new long pendulum was often displayed by a window in the door through which the pendulum could be seen swinging. It also showed if the clock had stopped.

The search for even better time-keeping led some makers, notably William Clement, to experiment with a pendulum 61 inches long, beating every $1\frac{1}{4}$ seconds. When these are used the window is not in the door but in the plinth, which has a hinged front. The ordinary 39-inch pendulum has a loosely fitting lenticular shaped bob. The end of the rod is threaded and has a nut with which the height of the bob and so the rate of the clock is regulated. As it is almost impossible to get at the bob of a 61-inch pendulum, buried in the plinth of the clock, the spring mounting of the pendulum was supplied with a micrometer adjustment. Another evidence of a 61-inch pendulum is that the seconds dial is divided into 48 instead of 60 divisions.

The 61-inch pendulum had gone out of fashion by 1700. Examples are in any case rare.

The movement underwent no notable alteration during this period. Except for month clocks, rack striking rapidly gained in popularity from the time of its invention in 1676.

The various forms of striking set out in the section on bracket clocks are all found in long-case clocks but repeaters are very rare.

An extremely rare variant of the typical long-case clock, which first appeared during this period, is the 'dwarf long-case', which is a complete miniature in perfect proportion, about 5 feet high, but containing a 39-inch pendulum.

PLATE 69

Long-case clock by Daniel Quare, circa 1700. Case inlaid with walnut and laburnum 'oyster' veneer. Note late use of cresting and convex moulding between trunk and hood; 12 inch dial.

1700–1725

No great changes took place during this period. Among provincial makers clocks six feet high, with ten-inch dials continued to be made, but the fashion was for something taller, and important clocks were between seven and eight feet six inches high, with eleven or twelve inch dials. Under such conditions the lift-up hood was impracticable and it is rarely found after 1700. Pull-forward hoods all have a door so that the door itself only has to be opened in order to operate the maintaining power, wind, and set the clock.

Now that the craft began to be practised fairly widely in the provinces, fashions long out-of-date in London continued to appear in provincial pieces. Thus the flat-topped, crested hood, with spiral-twist columns, so fashionable in the 1675–1700 period, may still occasionally be found as late as 1715.

A flat dome with three ball finials remains the most usual form of top but the inverted bell afforded a convenient means of increasing height and other makers piled up a meaningless superstructure of unrelated detail. The break-arch top did not become at all popular until quite at the end of the period, despite Tompion's example a quarter of a century earlier.

Three-quarter pillars remained universal and pierced frets begin to be found in the sides of the hood. Many clocks which now have plain glass in the sides of the hood may once have had pierced frets which have since been broken and otherwise disappeared.

The concave moulding between hood and trunk, and trunk and plinth, and concave mouldings generally, increasingly replaced convex mouldings.

The trunk door remained square-topped throughout the period.

Lacquer (which has a resin base and demands special skill in its application) and Japanning (which is a wider term and later came to include ordinary paint) remained popular throughout this period and the next, but apart

PLATE 70

Long-case clock by William Clement, circa 1685. Note crested hood; floral inlay in panels; window in plinth to show 61 inch, 1¼ seconds pendulum; 10 in. dial; cherub's head spandrel ornaments.

PLATE 71

Miniature long-case clock by Joseph Knibb, circa 1680. The clock, which has a full 39-inch pendulum, is only 5 feet 3 inches high overall, with a 7¾ inch dial. A full-size, long-case clock is shown beside it for comparison. It is by John Ebsworth, circa 1690. Note floral inlay in panels and unusual type of cresting. The disc in the centre of dial is for lunar work.

from this, walnut veneer was almost universal for clocks of any importance. 'All-over' inlay was popular and gradually deteriorated into the fussy style of seaweed marquetry during the first decade of the century. Oak is found only in country-made clocks.

Dials remained much as they had been in 1700 but with increasing use of the break-arch for housing subsidiary dials, such as equation, calendar, or strike-silent. Square-topped dials may also have subsidiary dials arranged in the same way as for bracket clocks, with the space between them decorated in a variety of ways. Elaborated cherub spandrels persist but the more adaptable arabesque pattern is usual with the larger sizes of dial. Winding holes are generally ringed, but Graham, in particular, never seems to have adopted this utilitarian but rather ugly fashion. Bolt-and-shutter maintaining power may be found throughout the period, but in diminishing popularity.

Seconds hands developed tails about 1710 to 1715. The hour and minute hands underwent little alteration but tended in general to become somewhat lighter.

The maker's name may appear almost anywhere on the dial—below the chapter ring; on it; on a cartouche inside it; or in the break-arch.

During this period and the next the dials of George Graham achieve a quite remarkable degree elegance, attributable to a slight lightening of all the details as against the dials of Tompion. In particular, he generally abandoned the half-hour ornament on the chapter ring and the ring on the inside edge of it had only half-hour and no quarter-hour divisions. His seconds dial was made as large as possible in diameter, with the ring itself very narrow, together with a long slender hand. Like Tompion's, Graham's cases are seldom decorated, but well proportioned.

To Graham also is attributable the only important mechanical improvement of this period, known as the dead-beat escapement.

PLATE 72

Long-case clock by James Markwick, circa 1735, decorated in blue lacquer. 13½ inch dial. Note break-arch dial and break-arch hood. Month movement and chiming on six bells.
(Victoria and Albert Museum)

In this escapement the pallets of the anchor have two quite distinct faces, an impulse face and a locking face. The locking faces are arcs of circles whose centre is the arbor of the anchor, so that when a tooth of the escape wheel rests on a locking face during the supplementary arc it undergoes no recoil and, apart from friction, no energy is imparted to the pendulum and none is taken from it. Much discussion took place as to the best radii for the impulse and locking faces, but the point is now realised to be unimportant.

The impulse arc is only about two degrees, so that the total arc may be very much less than in the case of an anchor escapement, which requires about eight degrees as usually laid out for a 39-inch pendulum. This is the maximum beyond which circular error begins to assume considerable proportions, but the dead-beat escapement will work with as little as two degrees, when circular error is insignificant.

FIGURE 13. *Graham's 'dead-beat' escapement.*

As was occasionally done by Tompion with the anchor escapement, the anchor in the dead-beat escapement was sometimes inverted, so as to lie below the escape wheel.

Graham's escapement remained the best for Regulators and long-case clocks of high quality, until Riefler's escapement, invented in 1893, in which impulse is imparted to the pendulum through the flexing of its suspension spring.

1725–1750

During the last period of this chapter the fashion for long-case clocks seems to have declined and relatively few examples have survived. The vast output of provincial long-cases belongs mostly to the second half of the century.

Walnut veneer, lacquer or japanning are almost universal for cases. Marquetry is rarely found after 1725 and lacquered or japanned cases are rare after 1750. Oak continues in country pieces. Mahogany cases before 1750 are exceedingly rare.

The door in the trunk departs, for the first time, from the plain rectangular shape. Break-arch hoods or dials are usually reflected by arch-topped doors, and doors with wavy edges, which will become general in the next chapter, begin to appear before 1750. The corners of the case also begin to be chamfered.

Hoods underwent certain modifications. The inverted bell gained in popularity as also did the break-arch top, generally in conjunction with a similar dial.

Broken pediments begin to appear in provincial clocks, representing a half-hearted return to the architectural cases of fifty years earlier. But the classical broken pediment soon gave way to a more baroque treatment with curvilinear 'horns'. Although this design appears in Chippendale's 'Directory' it never seems to have been used by London makers.

Dials became generally lighter in design, but the superimposed chapter ring remained universal until the middle of the century. The half-hour ornaments and quarter-hour division ring on the inside of the chapter ring almost completely disappeared. The half-quarter ornaments on the

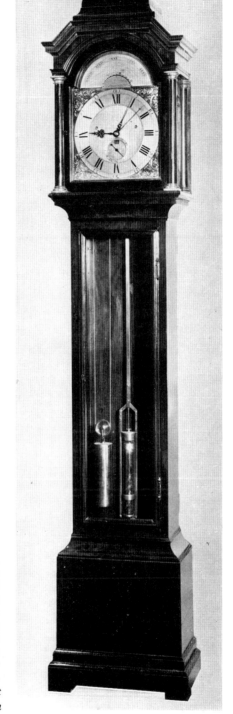

PLATE 73

Regulator type of long-case clock by George Graham, circa 1740. Mahogany case. 12-inch dial. The clock has equation work and in addition to the normal equation dial in the break-arch, the gilt minute hand always points to solar time, while the steel hand points to mean time. Month movement with Graham's dead-beat escapement. It is a time-piece and does not strike; the second winding square is for changing the calendar. Note glass door to trunk showing mercury-compensated pendulum; 12-inch dial with seconds dial and tail to seconds hand; bolt and shutter maintaining power (the shutters have been drawn in the detail view of the dial); break-arch dial with equation and calendar work; chapter ring without half-hour ornaments between the hour numerals; arabesque pattern silver spandrel ornaments. (British Museum)

115

minute circle are seldom found during this period. Minute numerals persisted and tended to become larger, while hands remained much as before. Maintaining power is practically never found.

Cherub spandrels persist in the square-topped dials of provincial clocks, but break-arch dials are all but universal in London-made clocks. The Spandrel designed round a woman's head no longer appears, and the usual pattern is a flowing arabesque of increasingly perfunctory design and execution.

In 1726 Graham brought to perfection experiments which, in conjunction with his dead-beat escapement, attained time keeping within a few seconds a month. Very high-class clocks were made for the first time with accuracy of timekeeping as their sole objective, and for this purpose no complication, such as striking mechanism, was permitted. Such clocks are called 'Regulators'.

The timekeeping of pendulum clocks is upset by changes in temperature which vary the length of the pendulum. Graham discovered that by shaping his pendulum rod in the form of a stirrup, and supporting on it a tall jar of mercury, the upward expansion of the mercury under heat could be arranged precisely to compensate the downward expansion of the pendulum. The distance from the top-fixing of the pendulum to the centre of gravity of the 'bob' thus remains constant.

In 1735 Harrison evolved an alternative form of compensation (primarily in conjunction with his efforts to produce an accurate sea-going timekeeper, to be described in the next chapter). Harrison observed that brass and steel have different co-efficients of expansion (a fact previously known to Hooke) and by arranging a series of such rods coupled together in pairs, he achieved a seconds-beating pendulum of almost perfect compensation. This device, known, from its appearance, as a 'gridiron' pendulum, rivalled Graham's mercury pendulum, and for 150 years one or the other formed an essential part of every regulator, and many high-class clocks. Both were eventually superseded by the series of nickel-steel alloys developed by Guillaume, which have virtually no co-efficient of expansion under heat and therefore need no compensation.

Ellicott produced a variant of the Harrison gridiron in which he avoided the multiple rods by using levers (contained in the pendulum bob) to multiply the different co-efficients of expansion of brass and steel. But it tended to operate in jerks and never became popular.

John Harrison and his brother James only made a very few long-case clocks, in which he coupled his gridiron with a most peculiar escapement of his own, called a 'grass-hopper' which also appeared in his first three marine timekeepers. Basically, the action of the grasshopper escapement is similar to that of the anchor recoil; it differs in that the pallets are pivoted to the anchor and spring tensioned. They were frequently made of lignum vitae and have a slight recoil. Thus, when a tooth on the escape wheel collects a pallet it draws it into engagement and no movement as between tooth and pallet is possible. The pallet therefore follows the tooth during recoil and impulse, being enabled to do so by its pivoted mounting. It is only released at the end of the impulse stroke by another tooth collecting the other pallet, and the immediate recoil thus separates the first-mentioned tooth and pallet. The spring tension then immediately returns the disengaged pallet to its normal position.

The crisp action of this escapement is fascinating to watch and leaves no doubt as to how it came by its name. It is extremely critical to adjust and few but Harrison have ever used it. It also requires a large arc to operate with certainty and a fine regulator by Harrison, now owned by the Royal Astronomical Society, has an arc of $12\frac{1}{2}$ degrees. This implies that small variations in arc would produce a serious circular error and this Harrison looked after by a remontoire to ensure that the motive power should be perfectly constant, and by the use of cycloidal cheeks for the pendulum mounting. It will be seen that the escapement avoids friction but only at the expense of a recoil and a wide arc, and it is not therefore a theoretically sound escapement. But it works extremely well and Harrison had a regulator with grasshopper escapement and gridiron pendulum which ran in his house for fourteen years without varying more than one second a month, while its error during the whole time was less than thirty seconds. Harrison's rugged individualism led him to some very unusual designs which owe little or nothing to his predecessors. His mechanical outlook must have been very similar to that of Ettore Bugatti, the great automobile designer of almost two centuries later. Bugatti's work defies most of the accepted canons but, like Harrison's, it works very well and in character these two great men must have had much in common.

While Graham went to great lengths to avoid recoil in his escapements, even at considerable cost

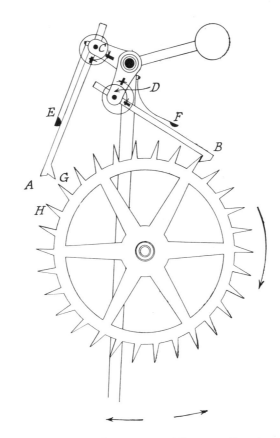

FIGURE 14. Harrison's 'Gridiron' pendulum. The five steel rods are black and the four brass rods are white.

FIGURE 15. Harrison's 'Grasshopper' escapement. The two pallets A and B are hinged to the pendulum arbor at C and D, being located by spiral springs assisted by recoil buffer springs E and F. The pendulum is shown at the extremity of its arc, pallet B having engaged the escape wheel and produced a recoil whereby A has ceased to be held on tooth G of escape wheel and swung clear of the path of G, under the influence of its spiral locating spring. The escape wheel will now impart impulse to B, carrying the pendulum towards the opposite end of its travel until tooth H engages with pallet A, recoil again takes place, B is disengaged and jumps clear, and so on.

in friction, Harrison was willing to accept a considerable recoil provided he could avoid friction by doing so. The secret of Harrison's horological successes lay in the avoidance of friction and the ensurance of constant motive power by the use of a remontoire. His work is further discussed in the next chapter.

A variant of Graham's dead-beat escapement was invented in 1741 by the French maker Amant, and is known as the 'pin-wheel' escapement. This, however, will be more appropriately described in Chapter VI dealing with French clocks.

Prior to 1750 regulator clocks did not differ in appearance from other long-case clocks, although their cases were usually plain in design. But in the second half of the century their casework developed a style of its own, of great simplicity and elegance.

George Graham died in 1751; for eighty years he and his master Thomas Tompion had dominated the horological world They lie buried together in Westminster Abbey. The lead was now gradually to pass to France while England was to take the lead in marine timekeepers.

WATCHES 1675–1750

The almost simultaneous introduction of waistcoats and balance springs had a profound effect on the appearance of watches.

The novel and rather intractable balance spring was not, at first, easily fitted to watches of small size, and good timekeeping, previously unobtainable from any size of watch, was now more readily obtained from a reasonably large one.

Large and heavy watches are not convenient or comfortable to have hanging about the person of their wearers, suspended from a cord or chain; but size and weight are not so objectionable when contained in a waistcoat pocket.

Moreover, when watches became primarily useful, as opposed to mainly decorative, and were in any case generally concealed from view in a pocket, there was not so much temptation to make them of fanciful shape and decoration.

WATCH CASES

The commonest watches (including many of the highest quality) have pair-cases in gold or silver, both of which are perfectly plain. The casemaker's initial is found on plain gold and silver cases, and where these do not tally in the two cases the outer is not original. In good class watches the number of the watch was repeated on the cases. Gold cases are 22 carat, and silver-gilt, brass gilt and Pinchbeck are all found. Pinchbeck, called after its inventor, is an amalgam of copper and zinc intended to imitate gold. Silver cases are very rarely hall-marked before about 1740. Earlier hall-marks on gold are fairly common.

Engraved work becomes increasingly rare and is usually shallow. It is mostly found on clock-watches and repeaters, in conjunction with pierced work. Landscape and figure scenes are never found except in miniature panels between pierced sections. Floral patterns, generally with birds and animals, continue, the pattern often being on a large scale with less conventional flowers. Heraldic medallions are also found. Cases in gold or silver filigree exist but they are very rare, and are all earlier than 1700.

Cast and chiselled work is seldom found after 1675, being replaced by repoussé work, which gives a lighter case of somewhat similar appearance.

PLATE 74

*Gold paircase watch by Daniel le Count, circa 1676. Cast and en-
graved outer case. Note irregular-shaped cock foot and Barrow
regulator found only in the earliest balance spring watches.*
(Ashmolean Museum. Oxford)

119

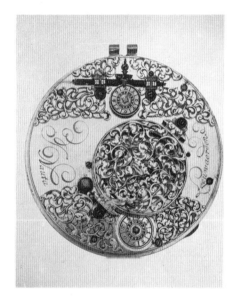

PLATE 75

Dutch pair-case watch by Jacobus Nauta. Late seventeenth century. Outer leather case with gold pinwork decoration. Note superb pierced decoration of movement and very thin calibre. Thin watches were also made by Quare and others but this is an an almost unique survival. (British Museum)

Repoussé work became increasingly common from 1715 onwards and from 1725 to 1750 it was the usual form of decoration. After 1750 it again declined and is rarely found after 1775.

An early form of repoussé work, found only in the last quarter of the seventeenth century, is in the form of flutes (usually wavy) radiating from a central foliage pattern.

In alarum, striking and repeating watches repoussé work is found combined with pierced and engraved panels, and the inner case is then only engraved and pierced.

Towards the middle of the century repoussé work tended to become increasingly deep and when it was too deep to be worked on one plate, a second plate was used for the highest relief, hard-soldered to the main plates.

PLATE 76

Gold pair-case repeater watch by Strigner with carnelians let into the outer case. Made for James II, circa 1687. Inner case has the Royal arms chiselled and engraved. (British Museum)

Outer cases were frequently made of leather or fish-skin and where the outer of a pair-case was repoussé there was sometimes a protective, third, outer case, with the back of glass.

Leather outer cases were generally studded with gold or silver pinwork. Shagreen and various sorts of fish and leather were used, often dyed green to imitate shagreen. Real shagreen is the skin of a shark or similar fish, but the imitation product is the skin of a horse or donkey, prepared by pressing hard round seeds into it until the skin becomes dry. It is then rubbed down to a level surface, polished, and stained green. Whereas other forms of skin are more usual in the first half of this chapter, in the latter part anything but shagreen is rarely found.

Another popular decoration for outer cases at the end of the seventeenth century was silver or gold pin-work or tortoise-shell inlaid with silver or gold. Grooves (according to the pattern) are cut in the tortoise-shell and the metal is inlaid in it, merely by pressure, when the shell is hot.

Painting on enamel continued to flourish with the Huaud brothers, mentioned in Chapter II, as the chief artists.

Apart from the forms of decoration mentioned above, other varieties are rare in the period of this chapter.

Cases of crystal or other stone are very unusual and stones, when used, are set in gold cases, as in the late seventeenth century examples in the Victoria and Albert and British Museums, with cornelians set in a chased gold framework.

In general, it may be said that the best decoration is found on watches made before 1700, and after 1725, work of the finest quality is rare. In France and Switzerland, repoussé work was less common than in England but enamel, on the other hand (mostly of little merit), was more popular.

DIALS AND HANDS

The dials of English and French watches differ radically. The champlevé engraved dial, which was the standard pattern in England throughout the whole of this chapter, was rarely used in France, where the rather clumsy arrangement of separate enamel plaques for each hour, mounted on a metal dial plate was the usual form.

Hands

Very rarely, watches with minute hands are found before 1675, but soon after the introduction of the balance spring the minute hand was universally adopted in England. The hands of English watches are generally of the pattern known as 'beetle' for the hour hand (being reminiscent of a stag beetle) and 'poker' (which is self-explanatory) for the minute hand. Occasionally, the hour hand is of the elegant 'tulip' pattern. Early steel hands are black and later examples, usually of more delicate design, are blued. Gold examples are found in conjunction with enamel dials. Pierced hands were more usual in France than England. French and German makers frequently continued to supply watches with only one hand until the end of the century and even later, long after two hands had been almost universally adopted in England.

Single-handed French watches had the winding square in the middle of the dial, projecting through the centre of the hand, and it was because of the convenience of this arrangement that the French makers retained the single hand until as late as 1725. The hand is moved to time by pushing it round with a finger.

Champlevé dials

The design of dials altered considerably with the introduction of the minute hand. With one hand, the chapter ring was generally wide, and inside the figures was a ring with quarter-hour divisions. With the introduction of the minute hand the chapter ring was narrowed from the outside so as to leave room for a ring giving minute-divisions, and outside this came a further set of twelve plaques marking the minutes, at five-minute intervals, in arabic numerals. The hour figures, in Roman numerals, were engraved on plaques standing up from a ground sunk by the graver; the engraved figures were filled with black wax which was put on hot. The ground was matt and the plaques and rings were polished. There was also usually a polished narrow lozenge between each pair of hour plaques.

In eighteenth century Dutch watches, the minutes ring was usually made in the form of twelve arches, the minute figures being inside each arch. This distinction is quite important as many Dutch watches are marked with the name of London makers.

The centre of the champlevé dial was a separate plate of metal, a little larger in diameter than the hole in the middle of the chapter ring, which lies on top of it. The middle portion usually carries the name and town of the maker, either on a repoussé plaque or an engraved ribbon. This was no

PLATE 77
*Watch by Peter Paulus of Amsterdam with case
painted in enamel on gold by the elder Huaud of
Geneva. Late seventeenth century.*
(British Museum)

123

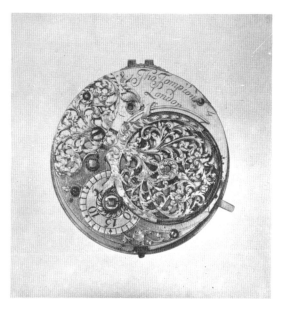

PLATE 78

Pair-case watch by Thomas Tompion, number 04, circa 1682. Note tendency for edge of cock foot to follow outer edge of plate; also circular table over balance wheel; early example of rack and pinion type of regulator with indicator; early use of subsidiary seconds dial; tulip hour hand. This is one of Tompion's earliest numbered watches. (British Museum)

PLATE 79

Pair-case watch by Demelai, marked 'London' but of typical Dutch design, circa 1740. Note dial with pierced centre ornament over background of blued steel (against which the hands are hardly visible). Note also, arcaded minute ring and bridge-type balance cock.
(British Museum)

124

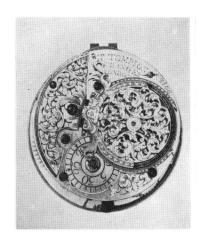

PLATE 80 (*top and bottom right*)

Gold pair-case watch by Tompion and Banger, number 3560, Hall-marked 1703. Typical watch of the period with champlevé type dial with separate centre section carrying maker's name. Note plain pointer minute hand and tulip hour hand; large cock foot with regular border extending all round to edge of plate; late use of square hinge to outside case and ring-type pendant.
(British Museum)

PLATE 81 (*top left and centre*)

Small French watch by Louis Ourry, circa 1675–80. Plain silver case. Very early balance spring movement with early example of going barrel. Note early enamel dial and early type of balance cock. (British Museum)

doubt convenient from a production point of view, as the same chapter ring would suit a large number of makers, each of whom then merely needed to have his individual centre plate.

Champlevé dials are made in gold or silver according to the material used for the cases. It is extremely rare for a gold dial to be used with a silver case, and vice versa, but both materials are found in leather and skin cases.

Enamel dials

The all-white enamel dial begins to appear by 1675 but except in conjunction with enamel cases it was not common in France or Switzerland before 1700, nor in England before 1725. The earliest examples have a somewhat dull and pitted surface, but after 1725 they are smooth and polished. In the best watches (notably those of Graham and Mudge) the enamel is sometimes laid on gold which helped to impart a particularly delicate lustre to the enamel.

PLATE 82

Gold pair-case repeater watch by Quare and Horseman, circa 1710.
Note pierced, cast and chiselled outer case with square hinge; stirrup-
type pendant with long repeater push-piece; early enamel dial;
'beetle and poker' hands; early example of solid, engraved cock foot;
jewel endstone to balance staff (probably original)
(British Museum)

On English enamel dials the hour and minute figures are painted (black) in much the same style as the champlevé dial, but there is only a single circle to mark the inside of the chapter ring, and no half-hour divisions etc. The maker's name never appears on enamel dials before 1750. The minute figures get steadily smaller and after 1770 they begin to disappear altogether, as also does the circle inside the chapter ring. A typical dial on French watches of about 1700 has large separate enamel plaques for the hour figures and either small plaques for the minute figures or an enamel band, mounted on a gilt-metal dial plate. After 1700 hour plaques were sometimes retained on a one-piece all-white dial by doming them or outlining them with a fine black line. The enamel plaque dial was

PLATE 83

Gold repoussé pair-case watch by George Graham, number 6574, circa 1750. Note solid engraved cock foot of the type always employed by Graham (the diamond endstone is missing); typical Graham enamel dial with polished steel centre-seconds hand; gold hour and minute hands not typical of Graham who usually used the beetle and poker as in Plate 82, and probably not original; curved ends to hinge in outer case typical of mid-eighteenth century; side view of movement showing escape wheel of the cylinder escapement. (British Museum)

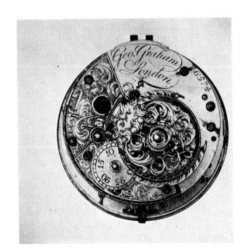

never used in England and it disappeared in France after 1725.

In French watches it became common to wind through the dial, the hole for the winding square being placed without regard to the hour figures or decoration. In single-handed French watches the winding-square is usually in the centre of the dial, protruding through the boss on which the hand is mounted.

PLATE 84

French 'Oignon' watch by Jean Rousseau, circa 1700. Brass-gilt case with deep chasing. Note dial plate of metal gilt, with separate enamel hour plaques; single hand with winding square protruding through centre of hand; solid engraved, bridge-type cock with aperture for false pendulum bob (the numbers visible through the pendulum aperture relate to the regulator); very deep movement. (British Museum)

128

PLATE 85

French 'Oignon' watch by Pascal Hubert, circa 1720. Note two hands of pierced decorative shape; one-piece dial of typical French design; pierced bridge cock; visible mechanism of rack and pinion regulator.
(British Museum)

Hour and minute indicators

It was many years after the introduction of the minute hand before people acquired the habit of telling the time by looking at the positions of the two hands on the dial, without having to examine the figures at which they were pointing. So it was thought to be quite convenient to have something pointing to an hour figure and something pointing to a minute figure, wherever on the dial these figures might be.

A great deal of ingenuity was shown in devising different methods of showing hours and minutes, and far more variety is found in watches than in clocks. For the most part, a particular device was confined to the inventor's watches, but there was one scheme that was so frequently used that it can be regarded as a type. This was the 'wandering hour figure' watch, introduced near the end of the century, and an example is shown in plate 86. The minutes are shown on a semi-circular slot in which the figure III is appearing through a hole in a dial plate rotating clockwise below the fixed dial plate once in two hours. When the hole with III showing reaches 60 minutes, another hole with IIII showing through it appears at 0 minutes and, in turn passes round the semi-circle to 60 minutes. The mechanism is quite simple. Two small discs are pivoted to the rotating dial plate below it. One has the even hours on it and the other the odd hours, the small discs being in positions such that one of the hours on each appears through one of the two diametrically opposite holes in the rotating dial plate. Each disc has six teeth and, after the hole has passed beyond the semi-circular slot, a fixed pin gives the disc one-sixth of a turn, to change the hour figure below the hole. Thus, when III disappears on the right, it is changed to V on its way to the left, and appears at 0 minutes on the left when IIII reaches 60 minutes on the right.

Another, even more popular form is known as the 'sun and moon' dial. It has a champlevé dial plate with outer minute circle, the five-minute figures being engraved on polished plaques; and a semi-circular band with hour figures VI to XII and again I to VI. Inside this and beneath the dial,

PLATE 86

'Wandering Hour' pair-case watch by Peter Garon, circa 1690. This system of recording the time is explained on page 129; the inner circle of figures are quarters; the moving segment is the hour; the outer circle is minutes. Note the royal cypher on the dial; outer case with fluted repoussé decoration.

is a disc rotating once in 24 hours below the dial, so that only half is visible. For the day-time hours there is a pointer with the sun on the disc to indicate the hour, and for the night-time a moon, the moon appearing at VI on the left when the sun is disappearing at VI on the right. These watches, therefore, have the unusual quality of showing whether it is day or night.

A quite different, less usual, but more practical scheme for showing hours and minutes with a single hand is on the watch illustrated on page 132. The small hour circle has hour figures I to VI, with arabic figures 7 to 12 superimposed on them. Outside is a band of minute figures showing 60 minutes in the space corresponding to each hour. The figures 20, 40, 60 are then repeated six times round the dial and there is a division for every 2 minutes. The hand, of course, revolves once in six hours.

About half a dozen watches exist with an even more ingenious system. The minute band has polished plaques with a figure for every five minutes, and a single hand indicates on this band. A very small central hour dial makes eleven-twelfths of a turn in an hour, and the minute hand also shows the hour on this dial. Watches of this type, with what is known as a differential dial, are so

PLATE 87

'Sun-and-Moon' pair-case watch by Edward Speakman, circa 1695. This system of recording the time is explained on page 130. The sun-and-moon dial is blued steel with the moon and stars let into it in silver and the sun in gold. The fixed dial plate is silver. The outer case is tortoise-shell inlaid with silver. Note the typical, loose-fitting, ring-type pendant seldom found after 1700.

rare that they do not merit an illustration here, but one is to be found on page 238, figure 374, of the sixth and also in earlier editions, of this book.

An inconvenient scheme, giving the minutes and their subdivisions great importance, is on the watch by Richard Street of about 1700 in the Guildhall Museum. The minute hand goes round in 15 minutes, so that the hour hand has to be read to a quarter of an hour.

These odd forms of hour and minute indicators are nearly all found in watches made between 1680 and 1700, they are rarely found in earlier or later examples.

PENDULUM WATCHES

For a short time before and after 1700, some makers of second rank adopted the thoroughly bad practice of so arranging the watch movement that the balance was immediately under the dial instead of being in its usual position over the top plate on the other side of the watch. It was by then recognised by the public that the pendulum had made a revolution in timekeeping for clocks, and there is little doubt that it was hoped that a little blob, swinging back and forth like a pendulum bob, would delude the ignorant into thinking that the watch was endowed with the virtues of a pendulum. It did have the practical merit of showing if the watch had stopped.

Dutch and some French makers adopted the little disc on the balance, almost as a standard form, in the eighteenth century, but they left the balance in its normal position, merely using a solid cock with a slot in which the disc could be seen swinging on opening the case. The solid part of the cock

PLATE 88

Watch by Daniel Quare with 'six-hour' dial (explained on page 130), circa 1680. Note the superimposing of the arabic numerals from 7 to 12 over the roman numerals I to VI. Note also the minute ring with two-minute calibrations; irregular-shaped cock foot typical of early balance spring period. The pendant is later.

was then engraved and sometimes bore a motto. To this practice there was no objection, because it left the balance in its easily accessible position.

PENDANTS

The pivoted loop becomes the most common form, but the small spherical knob with loose-fitting circular ring is found up to about 1700.

WATCH MECHANISM

The vigorous and individual character of craftsmanship and design so evident in watches for the first twenty years of the balance spring era extended even to the decorative features of the movement, which attained a degree of interest and elegance not reached before or since.

Pillars between the plates began to assume an importance and variety of shape which is helpful in dating a watch, and some of the more usual patterns are illustrated on this page.

In most of the early movements of a small size the pillars were round; the larger pillars were usually square, and often engraved; but one of the first obvious departure from the utilitarian forms in order to please the eye is shown in No. 1 of the engraving on page 134. This is known as the tulip pillar, and seems to have been introduced in deference to what may be called the tulip mania, which

PLATE 89

'Pendulum' watch by David Lesturgeon, circa 1705. Note the aperture in the dial showing the false pendulum bob; flat top plate of movement (carrying a cast and engraved portrait of Queen Anne) owing to the balance wheel being immediately behind the dial. (British Museum)

followed the introduction of tulip bulbs into England and led artists to incorporate the flower in almost every kind of decoration. For about twenty-five years from 1675 many of the finest watches were made with tulip pillars. In some instances the vertical division shown in the engraving was omitted. The square Egyptian pillar, No. 2, was introduced about 1700 and continued in use for many years, the central slit being often wider than the example, but always tapering to a point. A pillar of similar shape but more attenuated proportions is found from 1640. The plainer square pillar, No. 3, had also a long life, for it is met with in watches nearly two hundred and fifty years old, and also in specimens produced in the early part of the nineteenth century. No. 4 is a form favoured by Dutch and some English makers from about 1730 to 1770, and is occasionally seen applied to much later productions. Pillars like No. 5, dating from the first half of the eighteenth century, are more often seen in French and German watches than in English, and are often of silver. No. 6 is taken from a watch by Ellicott, the case of which has the hallmark of 1746, and the elegant outline is quite in accord with the popular taste at that time. No. 7 is a little later, and is taken from a watch by John Markham, a well-known maker for the Dutch market. During the period devoted to decorative pillars, repeaters and clock-watches, where space was an object, usually had plain round pillars, with small bodies and collars formed at top and bottom to afford a more secure bearing on the plates.

The balance spring provided improved facilities for regulation, the regulator consisting of two pins embracing the balance spring between them, and mounted on a segment moving on the same

FIGURE 16. Some typical watch pillars.

radius as the balance. In a very early and rare example, known as the Barrow regulator (see plate 44) this was fitted on a long threaded shaft, mounted on the top plate, and squared at one end to fit a key, similar to the old set-up regulator. Apart from this rarely-found arrangement the form used on nearly all English watches through the eighteenth century consists of a toothed wheel, geared to the regulator segment. This wheel is entirely concealed from view by pierced fretwork round it and a polished circular silver plate on top of it, with a central key-square. This plate has a ring with division marks and arbitrary numbers (either 1 to 6 or 5. 10. 15. 20. 25). A fixed pointer which is part of the fret, forms an index, and by turning the plate so that the numbers increase as they pass the index, the effective length of the balance spring is reduced and the watch goes faster; and vice versa. In most eighteenth century continental watches the regulator dial plate is fixed and a moving indicator hand is fixed to the square. Good verge watches are extremely sensitive to their regulators and if large movements of the regulator are necessary to produce a noticeable change of rate it is an almost sure sign that the watch will be a bad timekeeper. On two or three of the earliest balance spring watches, both set-up and hair spring regulators appear on the top plate; but as soon as the full potentialities of the balance spring were realised the set-up adjustment was put between the plates and was then only used by the maker and repairer to get the best relationship of mainspring torque to fusee. In French, and some nineteenth and late eighteenth century English watches, the set-up adjustment consists of a simple ratchet mounted between the back-plate and dial. In nineteenth century watches the set-up ratchet was frequently mounted on the top-plate.

The pierced fret and cock form one of the best guides to the date of a watch.

At first, both the foot of the cock and the part over the balance were of foliate pattern and irregular outline, but the latter rapidly assumed a completely circular shape with a rim, exactly covering the balance. The balance itself was larger than before owing to the need for a heavier balance with a balance spring, but a very large size (sometimes little less than the diameter of the plate itself) is a fairly sure sign of early date. The foot of the cock retained an irregular outline, not following the edge of the plate, for a longer period, but rarely after 1685. After this time it becomes of wedge shape, extending to the edge of the plate, and itself having well-defined edges.

The extent of the frets varies, but after 1695 it usually covers the whole of the plate except for one small triangular space between the cockfoot and balance, just large enough to engrave the maker's name, town and, usually, a number.

The name is usually written in cursive lettering.

The tall, bold style, such as was always used by Edward East is an early sign and and after 1690 the writing takes on a stereotyped, characterless appearance. Roman capitals, as an alternative to cursive lettering, also remained popular in France rather longer.

The pierced fretwork also changed in character. The foliate pattern popular in the pre-balance-spring era rapidly gave way to a flowing arabesque, and where the foliate pattern is found, between 1675 and 1695, it is usually of a rather small and fussy design, the pierced portions hardly more than a series of small holes. This kind of fret has an absolutely flat top surface, decorated with very shallow engraving. A more interesting arabesque pattern current during the same period is of very bold design, with fairly large voids. The design is strengthened by slight chiselling and fairly heavy engraving. After about 1695 this became the standard form of fret but the design became rather closer, and less vigorous in its curves, without chiselling. Curiously enough, after about 1730 a more open pattern, but with more flowing lines, frequently quite boldly chiselled, returned to fashion, and is found in provincial watches until the last quarter of the century.

After the first quarter of the century the cock foot was usually solid and engraved with a rather weak pattern, and the fretwork is uninteresting. The superbly made watches of George Graham have the most perfunctory and uninteresting decoration on the cock and top plate.

In all watches from about 1675 to 1740 the pattern on the part of the cock above the balance is symmetrical about a centre line drawn through the junction with the foot, but in later watches the design is more often asymmetrical.

Silver cocks are occasionally found but brass-gilt is almost universal.

Dust caps over the movement are very rarely found before 1715 and did not become at all popular until after 1725. Occasionally they are of silver but generally of brass-gilt.

French watches were quite differently decorated. The cock always completely spanned the (usually very large) balance in the form of a bridge with two opposite eyes and screw fixings. Apart from the cock, it is unusual to find any other form of decoration on the top plate of a French watch. The cock sometimes has in its centre a small piece of highly polished steel (usually of keyhole shape) which acts as an end bearing to the balance staff and is known as a coqueret.

French movements throughout this period are mostly very massive and this is reflected in the great size of their watches, generally known as 'oignons'. Some of these have an equally massive repeating train which may often be found to have survived better than the finer English workmanship in early watches.

A method of jewelling pivot holes was invented in 1704 by Facio de Duillier and P. and J. Debaufre but it is rarely found in watches before 1715. After about 1725, however, it is common to find a fairly large diamond endstone mounted in the cock. For nearly a century the art of jewelling remained an exclusively English secret.

The balance is always polished steel; brass balances only came much later in the century. It usually has three spokes, but where it is of very large size, so that the winding square has to emerge inside the rim of the wheel, two of the spokes are cranked to avoid the winding square. It is rare for the arc of a verge escapement balance to exceed 100°.

The balance spring is pinned to a brass collar which is a friction fit on the balance staff. Its outer end passes through a hole in a small stud (which may be rivetted to the plate or just a push fit into a hole in the plate), and is held in position by a pin, also pushed through the hole in the stud. This hole is usually round in section, causing some distortion in the spring, but Tompion and Graham always made the hole and pin square in section.

Early balance springs are soft and untempered, and very easily become distorted. It is important to see that they do not at any point touch the top plate or balance, and also that the shape of the outside curve roughly follows the course of the regulator segment. The earliest springs only had $1\frac{1}{2}$ to 2 turns, but by 1750, 4 to 5 turns had become more usual.

Modifications in the train followed upon the introduction of the balance spring. A watch without a balance spring requires more power to drive it than does one with the sprung balance. Accordingly, before its introduction, watches rarely had more than three wheels in the train, or went for more than fifteen hours. Some very early balance spring watches have a three-wheel train but nevertheless go for 26 or 28 hours, but this involves a fusee with a very large number of turns, up to 17, and the use of five-leaf pinions which cause a lot of friction, and are jerky in action and altogether undesirable.

The general introduction of minute hands followed immediately upon the improved timekeeping of balance spring watches. The employment of a minute hand involved an alteration in the layout of the train in that the second wheel, revolving once an hour, had to be in the centre of the watch, carrying the minute hand. In single handed watches the hand was driven by gearing under the dial from the great wheel, or fusee.

The use of three wheel trains is very rare after 1690 except by old-fashioned makers; four wheels, with six-leaf pinions are almost universal.

In the first flush of enthusiasm for the balance spring some pioneers, including Tompion, thought that they could discard the fusee and fitted their watches with going barrels. Such watches are extremely rare and in English work are certainly earlier than 1685. French makers re-introduced the going barrel in the eighteenth century and used it increasingly.

After about 1700 makers began to pay increased attention to lubrication. A drop of oil on a pivot hole tends to spread over the adjacent parts of the plate and dry up, but in about 1715 Sully discovered that by forming a small sink or basin round each pivot hole, the surface-tension of the oil, which makes it reluctant to go round a corner, tended to keep it within the confines of the sink, so that it lasted much longer. However, despite the apparent advantages of the arrangement it is rarely found in watches before 1750.

The inner end of the escape-wheel arbor is pivoted in the bracket which also carries the bottom pivot of the verge. The exact position of this wheel is very critical, both laterally and in its depthing, and the leading French horologist, Julien Le Roy, about 1740 introduced screw-adjusted sliding plates containing the pivot holes, whereby the escape wheel could be located to a nicety. The superb quality of Le Roy's work gave such a fillip to the whole of the industry in France that French clock and watch-making made rapid strides and, from 1725 onwards, increasingly threatened the English supremacy.

Clock-watches are common in the seventeenth century, with count wheels above the top plate, but after Quare succeeded in applying repeater mechanism to watches in about 1687, it rapidly ousted the clock-watch from popularity, although clock-watches of all periods continued to be made.

Prior to 1750 the repeating mechanism, actuated by pressing in the pendant, sounds the hour and quarters on a bell fixed to the back of the case and enveloping the movement. The hours are represented by one stroke each, and each quarter by a rapid double stroke. Half-quarter (giving the time to $7\frac{1}{2}$ minutes) and five-minute repeaters were developed prior to 1730 but are very rarely found in watches before 1750.

Very early repeaters had the defect that if the pendant was not pushed right home the time was

FIGURE 17. *Tompion's experimental watch escapement. Pins (shown as white circles on the ends of the black teeth of the escape wheel) alternately rest on the rounded back of the balance staff roller, and impart impulse to its flat (or slightly curved) face. Impulse is in one direction only.*

not struck correctly, but a device known as an 'all-or-nothing piece' was soon evolved whereby the repeating mechanism would not strike at all unless the pendant was pushed right home.

Later clock-watches with rack striking sometimes have an arrangement where, by pressing the pendant the rack is released and strikes the last hour, thus providing another form of repeater, provided the spring of the striking train has been wound.

Repeating watches were a great boon at a time when it was a considerable undertaking to obtain a light in the night and they still provide a very agreeable method of telling the time in the dark.

Until 1750 the verge escapement was most generally used but from 1725 onwards it was increasingly challenged by the cylinder escapement. This had been invented by Tompion in co-operation with Edward Booth and William Houghton, and patented in 1695, but its development does not seem to have been prosecuted by them with much energy, or success. No example by Tompion is known to have survived, but from a drawing in Rees' Encyclopoedia of 1813 it seems to have had more in common with the Virgule escapement (described in the next chapter) than with the cylinder as we now know it. The escape wheel only gave impulse on alternative beats and was probably subject to setting.

George Graham developed the Cylinder escapement and brought it to a considerable state of perfection by 1725 and after 1727 he never used anything else in his watches.

In the cylinder escapement, as opposed to the verge, the escape wheel lies in the same plane as the balance and for this reason it is often referred to as the 'horizontal escapement'.

The central part of the balance staff consists of half a cylinder. The escape wheel has short stalks standing up from its rim (13 in number in Graham's watches) and on top of each is a triangular-shaped tooth with the sharp point pointing in the direction of rotation. As the balance swings, a tooth falls on the outside of the cylinder and is held there until the hollow part of the cylinder comes round to it, whereupon the tooth enters the inside of the cylinder. It stays there while the balance completes its swing and returns to the point where the tooth can escape. Each edge of the cylinder is chamfered as also are the backs of the teeth of the escape wheel so that the latter impart impulse to the balance as they enter and leave the cylinder. The action is made clear by Fig. 18.

This escapement has the merit that the train interferes with the balance less than in the case of a verge, and is free from recoil. Owing to the amount of friction involved the cylinder has to be oiled,

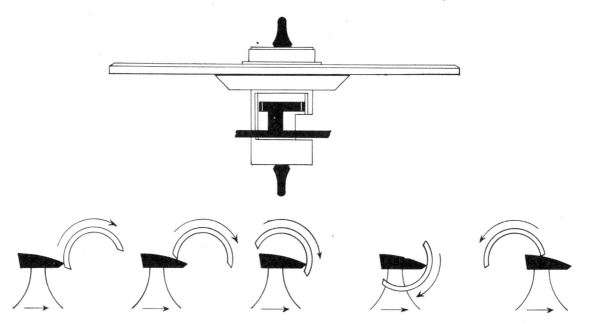

FIGURE 18. *Cylinder escapement. In the side view of the balance wheel and staff a segment of the escape wheel is shown in black with one of its teeth inside the cylinder. The sequence of events is shown by five drawings of the cylinder seen in plan. The middle drawing corresponds to the central plan view.*

and this in itself provides a rough-and-ready, but remarkably effective compensation. In cold weather the thickening of the oil provides extra friction and (with the short balance spring then used) slows the watch, thus largely counteracting a natural tendency to gain at low temperatures; and vice versa.

As made by Graham and his contemporaries up to 1750 the cylinder was made of steel and the escape wheel of brass and this provoked very rapid wear of the cylinder, especially on its edges. In early cylinder watches the cylinder is often found almost cut in half. This was a considerable disadvantage as against the verge, as also was the inherent delicacy of the cylinder, which is much more inclined to snap under shock than is the robust verge.

Both these drawbacks were considerably mitigated at later dates, as will be explained in a later chapter, and the cylinder remained a very popular escapement for 150 years from the time of its perfection by Graham. Nevertheless, the verge at its best is capable of giving almost if not quite as good a performance as an early cylinder and this, coupled with its greater robustness and ease of manufacture, accounted for the continued popularity of the verge long after the invention of the cylinder.

Owing to the periods when the escape wheel, resting against the cylinder, is held motionless, the cylinder escapement is said to belong to the family known as 'frictional rest escapements'. It was not, however, the first of these, being antedated by Peter Debaufre who evolved such an escapement in 1704.

This is known as the Debaufre, or 'Clubfoot' (because of the shape of the pallet) or 'chaff-cutter'

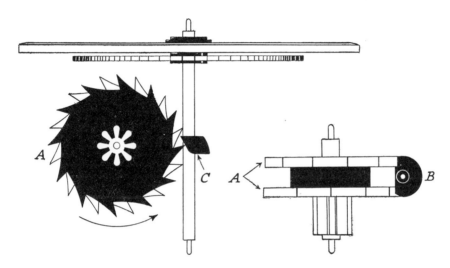

FIGURE 19. *Debaufre's escapement (also called the 'Ormskirk' or 'clubfoot') shown in side view and plan. A is the double escapewheel and B the pallet attached to the balance staff. In the side view a black tooth of the escape wheel is in process of imparting impulse to the impulse face of B. The locking face is marked C.*

(because of the shape of the escape wheel) or 'Ormskirk' (where it was largely made about 1800) escapement. It has two escape wheels, mounted on the same arbor, with teeth shaped like a circular saw or chaff-cutter. The balance staff passes between these two wheels and has a pallet in the form of a disc attached to it, semi-circular in plan and wedge-shaped in side elevation. The teeth of the escape wheels, which are staggered in relation to each other, alternately rest against the flat underside of the pallet and escape past its chamfered edge, giving impulse to the balance. The escapement gives results about as good as the cylinder, but is also subject to fairly rapid wear and imposes considerable end thrust on the balance staff. It has a noticeable resemblance to Leonardo da Vinci's escapement.

In 1722 the 'Rack Lever' escapement was invented by the Abbé d'Hautefeuille, being an application of Graham's dead-beat clock escapement to watches. The escape wheel and anchor are almost identical with the clock escapement but the anchor is pivoted at the point about which it rocks, and at the opposite end to the anchor is a toothed segment. This meshes with a pinion on the balance staff itself. Without such a gearing the balance would not swing through a wide enough arc to be effective, but by its means it may have as large an arc as desired. It is in fact similar, yet opposite to Huygen's device for obtaining a narrow-arc pendulum with the verge escapement.

The rack lever worked much better than it had any right to do, but was not popular until about 1800. Its main interest lies in its development into the detached lever escapement, as will be recounted in the next chapter.

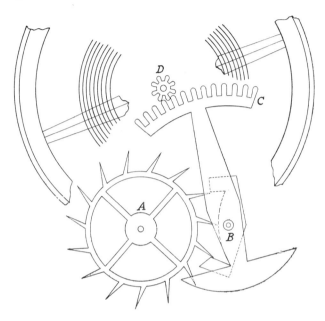

FIGURE 20. *Rack lever escapement invented by Hautefeuille. The escape wheel A and anchor B are almost identical with Graham's dead-beat anchor escapement. Attached to B is a segmental rack C which engages with D, a pinion on the balance staff. By means of this gearing the balance wheel is able to traverse an arc sometimes as much as two complete turns, as compared with the 10° or less of B.*

CHAPTER V

Counting the seconds: 1750–1830

INTRODUCTORY

THE evolution of the pendulum and the balance spring in the third quarter of the seventeenth century brought timekeeping from a matter of hours to an accuracy of minutes. The evolution of the Marine Chronometer in the third quarter of the eighteenth century further refined that accuracy from minutes to seconds, and stimulated makers to achieve a degree of exactness in pocket-watches never before dreamed of. So does this Chapter merit its title, even though the regulators of George Graham, described in the last chapter, had anticipated this extreme refinement of timekeeping, so far as the long case clock was concerned. Indeed, so perfect was the Graham regulator, with its deadbeat escapement and mercury-compensated pendulum, that little remained to be done in the advancement of pendulum clocks and the greatest interest throughout the period of this Chapter lies in its watches and marine chronometers.

The story of the chronometer is one of the most interesting in the whole history of horology, but it can only be traced here in the barest of outline. Nevertheless, the work of the half-dozen men who brought it from infancy to perfection, stands so much apart that it has been described here in a separate section of this chapter.

Earnshaw, the youngest of the six, died in 1829. The incomparable Breguet had died in 1823, and by the end of the first quarter of the nineteenth century the pocket watch had attained to a degree of elegance which has never, and a degree of accuracy which has hardly, been surpassed.

1830 also marks the end of the French Directoire and, virtually, the end of artistic clock-making in France, so that Chapter VI, devoted exclusively to French Clocks, also ends at this date.

It may therefore be said that a survey of this kind cannot be carried beyond 1830 with any particular advantage. This does not mean that an instrument made after 1830 is of no interest to the collector: throughout the nineteenth century superb regulators, in plain, well-proportioned cases continued to be made. The firms of Breguet and, in England, Jump, produced watches of the utmost elegance and refinement in the pure Breguet tradition, while Frodsham and others kept alive the English tradition in lever and chronometer watches which are now eagerly sought by collectors. But none of these had anything appreciable to say which had not been said by 1830.

It remained only for Phillips to formulate the science of the balance spring; for Guillaume to evolve the series of nickel-steel alloys; and for the Swiss industry to profit by these in producing factory-made watches whose accuracy equals or surpasses anything that the greatest craftsman of a century earlier could hope to achieve.

Turning to the twentieth century; in the realm of clocks, the Shortt free pendulum, with its electrically operated slave clock, brought timekeeping to within a fraction of a second a year, only to be surpassed by the Quartz-crystal clock. But these are not yet matters for the collector. It may be said without much fear of contradiction, that the artistic and mechanical development of timekeepers, made by individual craftsmen, had reached their final stage by 1830, and thereafter waged a losing battle against the engulfing tide of commercialism.

CLOCKS

As during the period of the last Chapter, so in this the evolution of French clocks pursued entirely different lines to the English trend. The reader must again be referred to Chapter VI for a description of French clocks.

The third quarter of the eighteenth century saw a sharp break with the traditional designs which had held sway for nearly a century. Nevertheless, the old continued to thrive alongside the new, and many a clock of the early nineteenth century might, on superficial inspection, be misdated by 70 or 80 years. From the middle of the nineteenth century, as also in France, there was a conscious revival of eighteenth century style, especially in the form of large and ornate musical clocks, and even today there is a fashion for miniature bracket clocks in metal or wood in the style of the late seventeenth century. The fashion set by Tompion and his contemporaries may therefore be said never quite to have died, but by 1750 the public had seen enough of it to be in a mood for something radically different.

SURVIVAL OF TRADITIONAL STYLES IN LONG-CASE AND BRACKET CLOCKS

Before considering the new fashions it will be as well to examine the minor alterations manifested during the declining years of the old.

Long-case clocks

Long-case clocks by London makers are very rare, except for the occasional complicated astronomical clock, and for the perfectly plain type of regulator; but they became popular in Lancashire and Yorkshire from about 1760 onwards. Before this date the use of mahogany cases is almost completely unknown, but thereafter it quickly became universal, except for the simplest clocks where oak continued to be used. Japanning or lacquering was rare after 1750 and had stopped entirely by 1760. At any rate until the last decade of the century the Northern provincial clocks are usually fairly plain and their general proportions follow mid-century London lines. Their hoods have corner columns and either a break-arch top or the broken pediment with curly horns, at times refined almost to the point of the true swan-neck. A new form of curved pediment top also appeared soon after 1760. The front and back are perfectly flat, but the front elevation is roughly bell-shaped, having two concave curves surmounted and joined together by a convex section. The flat front is usually decorated with shallow carving or fretwork with three ball finials at the top and corners.

Break-arch tops sometimes have a fringe of open fretwork and this pleasing finish is often found in the splendid American long-case clocks made by the Willard family of Massachusetts, around the turn of the century.

Long-case clocks: dials and hands

Dials may still have the matted plate and superimposed chapter ring, but the quarter-hour division ring becomes increasingly uncommon although minute numerals survive prominently. The

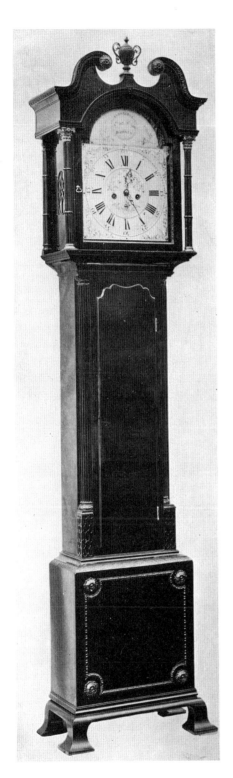

PLATE 90 (left)

Provincial long-case clock by Thomas Clare of Warrington, circa 1775. Note horn top; Battersea enamel break-arch dial; free-standing corner columns to hood; reeded quarter-columns to trunk; good general proportions.

PLATE 91 (right)

Long-case clock by Joseph Yorke Hatton, London, late eighteenth century. This type of hood first appeared soon after 1760, having a flat back and front, and being bell-shaped in section. Note traditional type of chapter ring with smooth silvered centre; interlaced skeleton hands; dial break-arch repeated by break-arch top to door; corner columns to hood and reeded quarter-columns to trunk.

pierced gilt spandrel ornament also continued. The early type of hour and minute hand continued but from 1770 there was an increasing use of wavy hands with arrow-head ends; centre-seconds hands were occasionally used from 1750 onwards. Another type of dial had a one-piece silvered dial plate with engraving, similar to that of the superimposed chapter ring, but never having quarter-hour divisions. From about 1775 iron dials, painted white, became very popular. The figures, usually in Roman, but occasionally in Arabic numerals, are painted black. The spandrels are painted in colours, usually with floral subjects but occasionally to represent the four Seasons or other fanciful subjects. In conjunction with the painted dial gilt hands were sometimes used, generally of skeleton form. The break-arch top might be filled with calendar or moon work, or with a tide indicator suited to the place in which the clock was to be sold; but simple automata, such as a rocking ship, or a windmill with revolving sail, became very popular, especially in conjunction with the painted dial. Equation work is rarely found; earlier equation clocks had to be altered when the modern calendar was brought into use in 1752.

Long-case clocks: hood and trunk

Hoods and trunks may have three-quarter, or even free-standing corner pillars, and the latter appear in the designs which Sheraton included in his *Cabinet-maker's & Upholsterer's Drawing Book*, published in parts between 1791 and 1794, although, as he states, the long-case clock was then no longer fashionable in London. Alternatively, the corners may be chamfered and, generally, fluted. Doors usually have break-arch tops. Plinths sometimes have a central raised panel.

PLATE 92

Provincial long-case clock by John Wyke of Liverpool. Late eighteenth century. Note survival of metal dial with applied chapter ring and spandrel ornaments; heavy proportions combining fine materials and workmanship with mixed and excessive ornamentation.

PLATE 93 (above)

Late survival of traditional style of bracket clock by Vulliamy; late eighteenth century. Note bell top; traditional dial with applied chapter ring retaining minute numerals but omitting half-hour marks and ornaments; applied spandrel ornaments; traditional type of hour hand similar to a century earlier, but later type serpentine minute hand. The eight-day, three train movement chimes at each quarter and plays a tune on bells at the hour. (British Museum)

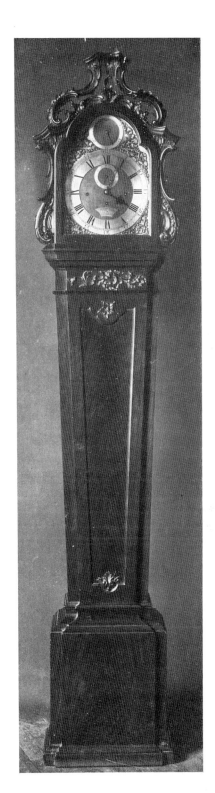

PLATE 94 (right)

Long-case clock by John Holmes, London, circa 1770. Note tapering trunk in the style advocated by Chippendale in his 'Director' as early as 1750; traditional type of dial very similar to those made by George Graham forty years earlier.

145

With the last decade of the century there was some return to inlaid decoration, in the Sheraton style, but in general, from 1790 onwards there was a deplorable decadence in the design of long-case clocks, especially those from the North-country. While superficially continuing along traditional lines, the proportions became increasingly clumsy, wide and squat. The newly fashionable Gothic taste was manifested by irrelevant detail, especially in the form of lancet-topped doors. Cases were also ornamented with quite irrelevant inlay of geometrical design which accentuated, instead of relieving the already ponderous proportions. It is therefore rare indeed to find a long-case clock of traditional type, later than 1800, which is worthy of consideration. Nevertheless, a few long-case clocks of good proportions and restrained decoration continued to be made by London makers, no doubt to special order by clients of conservative taste, throughout the first quarter of the nineteenth century.

The movements underwent no change or improvement beyond some popularity of musical trains, and the anchor escapement remained universal. Pendulums are not compensated except in regulators.

Bracket clocks

The old type of bracket clock continued with even less alteration than the long-case. Ebony or, more often ebonised cases with break-arch dials and inverted bell tops had side carrying handles or else a single handle on top. The true bell top is still found after 1750. Finials remained popular. Dials had matted plates, applied silvered chapter rings and pierced gilt spandrel ornaments. The break-arch dial may carry calendar work, strike-silent, or a plain raised boss with the maker's name.

The verge escapement remained in general use for bracket clocks up to 1800 after which it finally gave way to a form of anchor arranged to swing through a relatively wide arc. The engraving of back plates continued but is hardly ever found after 1800.

THE RISE OF NEW STYLES FOR LONG-CASE AND BRACKET CLOCKS

While these old fashions stayed so mortally long a-dying, others grew up around them and rapidly developed into such a startling multiplicity of shapes that, as in the case of French clocks, it is impossible to describe them all.

Long-case clocks

Owing to its being unfashionable in London the new style of long-case clock is rare, and this is regrettable since such few as were made are often of superbly elegant proportion.

In his *Director*, first published as early as 1754, Chippendale had shown long-case clocks with trunks tapering towards the bottom and a few of these very handsome clocks exist.

Chippendale's designs are, of course, in the rococo style, but with the classical revival which gained a rapid ascendancy from 1760 onwards and held sway for forty years, the tapering trunk was again pressed into service. These designs betray a considerable measure of French influence in that the part of the clock comprising the dial is quite sharply divided from the trunk, so as to give almost the appearance of a bracket clock standing on a pedestal. Such clocks, which are exceedingly rare, may take the form of a square top, generally surmounted by a flambeau or a classical urn, standing on the tapering base or therm; or else of a balloon clock on a similar base; or of a perfectly plain round dial placed with hardly any linking motif on top of a plain or fluted pillar.

Dials may be of the plain silvered and engraved variety, or a metal sheet painted with a white ground (from about 1775 onwards). Enamel dials are unusual in long-case clocks owing to the difficulty of making so large an enamel surface. Long-case clocks in this markedly classic style were mostly made between 1770 and 1790 but from 1750 onwards a more functional and enduring style was developed for the Regulator class of clock. Such clocks almost invariably have the Graham dead-beat escapement (very rarely the Harrison grass-hopper or the French pin-wheel) and either the gridiron or mercurial compensated pendulum. True regulators never have a striking train, or any other avoidable complication. The beginning of this style had been provided by Graham, in his simple but perfectly proportioned regulators, but in its final form, reached soon after 1760, it took on lines of even greater severity. The perfectly square dial opening and hood is reminiscent of the long-case clock of 1670–80 and the whole case has a minimum of decoration. The dials are almost always silvered, and in order to avoid motion-work with its extra friction, there was a return to the multiple dials which had been so popular in seventeenth century watches. Usually only the minute hand sweeps the full diameter of the dial. After 1810 it became customary for the whole of the door to be glazed and, a little later, for the hood to be completely arched, with only a narrow band of wood showing round the top of the dial. Thus the case-work was cut down to an irreducible minimum, yet even so, the total effect is completely satisfying because of its essentially functional character, and the extreme delicacy and fine craftsmanship displayed in the smallest details. Movements also underwent further refinement in the form of jewelled holes or friction rollers, and jewelled pallets. A high-numbered train is customary in the best work and pinions have twelve leaves or more. The movement plates and mounting for the pendulum need to be exceptionally strong and rigid. Such clocks were made by

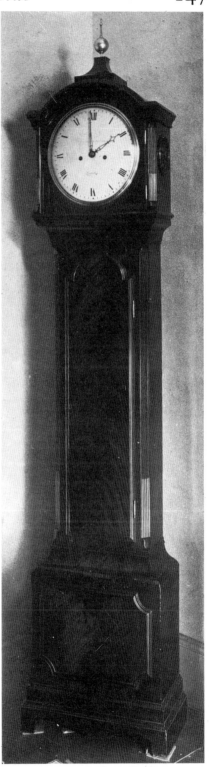

PLATE 95

Long-case clock by Dwerrihouse Carter and Co., early nineteenth century; a late example of the London-made long-case. Note painted dial without minute numerals; interlaced skeleton hands; circular window for dial; break-arch top to hood and door of trunk; chamfered and reeded corners to hood and trunk; good and refined proportions.

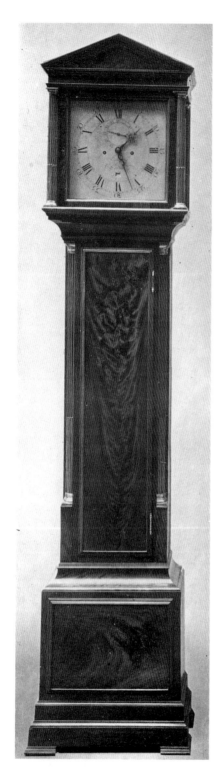

PLATE 96 (*above*)

Movement of regulator clock by Justin Vulliamy. Note the grass-hopper escapement with ivory pallets.

PLATE 97 (*left*)

Long-case clock by Justin Vulliamy, circa 1780. Note reversion to architectural style reminiscent of a century earlier; one-piece silvered and engraved dial.

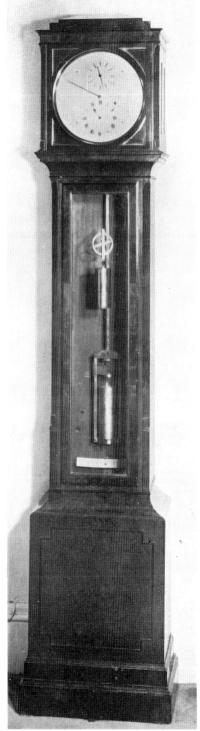

PLATE 98

Regulator clock by Barraud, London, circa 1820. The final simplification and refinement of the long-case. The eight-day movement and the pallets of the dead-beat escapement are jewelled. The train is high-numbered and the plates are very heavy and firmly mounted. Note also the multiple dials to avoid motion work and the mercury compensated pendulum.

149

clock-makers for use in their own shops; for observatories and similar scientific establishments; and they may also be found in the halls of Clubs and large houses as the master clock by which the other timepieces in the house were set. In this form they continued to be made throughout the nineteenth and into the twentieth century.

PLATE 99

Bracket clock by Reid of London, circa 1820. Note break-arch top; plain silvered dial without minute minerals; Breguet-type hands; round domed window mounted on very narrow hinge.

PLATE 100

Bracket clock by Wray of Birmingham, circa 1830. Note arch top case with complete lack of ornamentation and regulator type of dial. The movement has a half-seconds pendulum with the type of pin wheel escapement described on page 244, whereby the second hand moves only once a second.

Bracket clocks

A simplified form of bracket clock also appeared in about 1750 and some of the earliest examples are by Ellicott. A walnut, ebonised or mahogany case, with inverted or true bell top with a carrying handle, was shorn of all embellishments. The important innovation lay in the treatment of the dial, for the front window was no longer square or break-arch, but round, being limited to the exact size of the dial. The latter was silvered and engraved with Roman hour and Arabic minute numerals, exactly like the contemporary enamel watch dial. The hands were traditional. The glass was held in a round brass bezel, mounted in the plain wood front door of the clock. This form of bracket clock may be regarded as the transitional form between the traditional pattern and the many new forms which began to appear from 1760 onwards.

PLATE 101

Bracket clock by John Denne, London, circa 1820. Note panel top; enamel dial; pierced silver spandrel ornaments; ebonised case with brass inlay; brass feet, fish-scale frets to side doors.

The next break with tradition was the abandonment of the bell top and the substitution of a break-arch top, starting in about 1770. The earliest break-arch tops were fairly flat. If the radius of the break-arch differs from that of the dial there is a crescent shaped space above the dial opening and this and the spandrel spaces below the dial are generally filled with applied wood or metal frets. The feet are small and inconspicuous. The dials may be either silvered or enamel, and the circle inside the hour numerals began increasingly to be omitted. Minute numerals also began to shrink in preparation for their complete disappearance by the end of the century. Hands take on a variety of forms and may be either steel or, more rarely, gilt. One of the simplest and most effective is a plain tapering finger with a small spade point. An equally simple and effective treatment is the 'Breguet' hand with its voided circle and pointer. The pointer is usually solid but may also be voided. This is usually a late feature, rarely seen before 1800. Skeleton hands with interlacing curves, and wavy hands were also popular, but soon after 1810 makers seemed to loose their sureness of touch, and hands either too light, or too heavy for the rest of the clock, or just plain ugly, became increasingly common.

In about 1800 it became usual to make the front of the clock a fixed part of the case, allowing the brass bezel only to be opened. The glass in such cases is domed and the inner ring of the bezel is frequently engine turned. While logical enough, the arrangement has the disadvantage that it is only possible to provide a very short hinge for carrying the fairly heavy door.

Bracket clock cases

In 1810 the break-arch top had become more curved, with its radius almost half the width of the

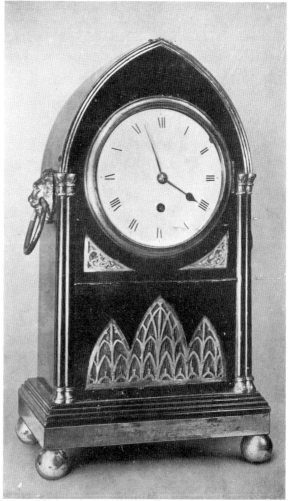

PLATE 102

Bracket clock by James Cowan, Edinburgh, circa 1780. Note reeded top; one-piece enamel dial retaining the Graham layout of marking, and refined edition of Graham hands.

PLATE 103

'Lancet' bracket clock, note gothic revival ornamentation, circa 1815.

case, so that it was only a short stop to omit the break and arrive at the completely arched top. Such clocks are usually very simple in design and ornamentation.

Another variant which appeared soon after 1800 is the chamfered panel top, reminiscent of the first break with the architectural pediment top in 1675. The chamfer may be gadrooned or reeded and is often surmounted by a gilt finial.

Also in the first decade of the nineteenth century appeared the lancet clock, being shaped like a lancet window, in deference to the gothic taste and in fact, all the different 'Tastes' of the basic regency style manifested themselves in the ornamentation or outline of clocks in the first quarter of the

PLATE 104

'Balloon' bracket clock by Peacock, London. Late eighteenth century.

PLATE 105

Tavern clock with lacquered trunk, the dial gold markings on black, circa 1760.

nineteenth century. From 1800 onwards brass inlay, common to all styles of regency furniture, was widely used on clocks, standing in excellent contrast to the rich colour of the mahogany or rosewood.

In entire contrast to all these forms was the balloon clock which first appeared in about 1760 and stayed in fashion until 1810. It was undoubtedly inspired by the typical Louis XV bracket clock with its arched top and slightly waisted sides. The typical balloon clock however, has a much more pronounced waist, and it was probably well-established long before it got its name, since the earliest hot-air balloons of the Montgolfier brothers, which these clocks resemble in silhouette, did not make their first ascents until 1784. Balloon clocks are usually quite plain with a panel of inlay below the dial. The larger varieties may, however, be fairly complicated, with some sort of reeded or similar top above the dial with a large gilt finial, and there is often a break where the dial runs into the curve of the base.

From about 1790 onwards, metal frets became almost standardised in the 'fish-scale' pattern and this may also fill the sunk panels in the front of the clock.

Particularly after 1800, many English clocks were made in conscious imitation of the French

PLATE 106

Travelling or coach clock by William Travers of London. Hall-marked 1787. Note outer case of green-dyed fish skin with silver engraved ornamentation; enamel dial with minute numerals; subsidiary dials for calendar and alarum; finely engraved top plate of movement with pierced, symmetrical ornamentation of table of cock; 4¾ inch diameter. (British Museum)

Louis XVI and Directoire styles. These, however, may more properly be regarded as French clocks and studied in the chapter which deals with them.

'Tavern' clocks

A quite different type of clock which is generally associated with the turn of the century, but actually covers a very much longer span, is the so-called 'Act of Parliament' clock. In 1797, William Pitt inadvisedly levied an annual tax varying from 2/6 to 10/– on all clocks and watches which so decreased the demand for them that inn-keepers took to providing cheap clocks in their establishments. They consist of a large wooden painted dial (usually black with gold painted numerals), two to two feet six inches in diameter, with a small drop case for the pendulum and weight, the clock being designed for hanging on a wall. As the offending Act was repealed only a year later it is obvious that only a relatively small proportion of the very large number of surviving 'Act of Parliament' clocks date from the year 1797–8. Most of them were, however, made during the period of the present Chapter, namely 1750–1830. 'Tavern' clock would be a more suitable name. For the most part they are very simply made, but fine examples with a considerable amount of decoration, such as might grace an assembly room, are occasionally found.

Travelling or coach-clocks

These continued to be made throughout the eighteenth century. They may have metal or enamel dials. A pull-repeat mechanism is very usual. Some of the last examples are mounted in a flat wooden frame suitable for hanging against a wall.

Wall clocks

In the beginning of the nineteenth century many fine hanging wall-clocks were made, in round or octagonal wooden cases; many of them for government offices. Except occasionally for brass inlay they are seldom decorated.

CLOCK MECHANISM

As has already been said, bracket clocks prior to 1800 usually had a verge escapement, but thereafter the anchor type became the more usual. A type of escapement developed about this time, and peculiar to bracket clocks, is known as 'semi-dead-beat'. The escape wheel and anchor look very much like an ordinary dead-beat but in fact the pallets have their locking faces cut so as to produce a slight recoil. A fairly wide arc is desirable in a bracket clock, which may not always stand exactly level, and this escapement has the advantage that the slight recoil counteracts any inequalities in torque and so preserves a fairly constant arc. Compensated pendulums and maintaining power are seldom found in bracket clocks, and repeating mechanism became increasingly rare after 1750.

Musical and organ-clocks became more popular during the last half of the eighteenth century, especially those designed for the Eastern market. A musical clock which also has a fairly protracted chime may well have as many as four trains, for going, chiming, striking and music. Three-train clocks are usually quarter-chime only. When musical they usually perform at three-hourly intervals only, and do not chime.

PLATE 107
Wall clock by Vulliamy, circa 1820, with wooden frame and simple spade hands.

There was little development of the clock escapement during the period covered by this chapter. There were, indeed, isolated inventions, but since they came to nothing they are only of theoretical interest and are not likely to concern the collector, for whom this book is primarily intended. As one example, to indicate the lines upon which people were thinking, a superb late eighteenth century bracket clock by Emery has what appears, at first sight, to be an ordinary dead-beat, pin-wheel escapement. Closer examination reveals that it is more nearly related to a chronometer, for the escape-wheel is locked, not upon the pallet, but upon a detent, which is only released by the pendulum in time for the escape wheel to deliver its impulse to the pallet. What appears to be the second pallet on the anchor is in fact no more than a safety precaution, and normally does not come into operation at all. The pendulum therefore only receives impulse in one direction, and is entirely free from locking friction.

The dead-beat pin-wheel escapement, invented by Amant about the middle of the century, is no more than a variant of Graham's dead-beat escapement. It was popular in France but never in England, and it is therefore illustrated and described in Chapter VI on French clocks. Also in Chapter VI are described the detached and remontoire escapements which the French used extensively in conjunction with pendulum clocks. Their theoretical advantages were not, however, attended by practical success and after the first quarter of the nineteenth century they were gradually discarded.

Gravity escapements

One such English escapement does, however, call for a more detailed description since it was the prototype for many regulator and turret clock escapements during the second half of the nineteenth century and afterwards. This is Mudge's gravity, or remontoire escapement, which is quite a different thing to a remontoire interposed at some point in the train. Mudge's escapement is of particular interest because of its close relationship to his more famous constant force or remontoire escapement which he employed in the remarkable marine chronometer described in the second half of this chapter.

It appears that Mudge invented this escapement a little before the constant force escapement of his marine timekeeper, which was completed in 1774. Another gravity escapement was devised by Alexander Cumming at about the same time.

The double three-legged gravity escapement devised by Lord Grimthorpe for the famous Westminster Clock, Big Ben, and used subsequently in so many turret clocks, is a direct descendant of Mudge's escapement and Lord Grimthorpe's assessment of it is therefore worth quoting, both because of its historical interest and because of its remarkable clarity. The passage is taken from his book (written when he was Sir Edmund Beckett) *Clocks, Watches and Bells*:

"A gravity or remontoire escapement is one in which the impulse is not given to the pendulum directly by the Clock-train and weight, but by some other small weight lifted up, or a small spring bent up, always through the same distance, by the Clock-train at every beat of the pendulum. And the great advantage of them is that the impulse is therefore constant; for the only consequence of a variation in the force of the Clock is that the remontoire weights are lifted either faster or slower, which does not signify to the pendulum, as the lifting is always done when the pendulum is out of the way. If this can be managed with certainty, and without exposing the pendulum to some material variation of friction in the work of unlocking the escapement, which it must perform, its motion and therefore its time must be absolutely constant, since there is nothing else to disturb it."

Lord Grimthorpe's description of Mudge's escapement may also be quoted:

"The pallets, *AC, BC*, are no longer fixed on one arbor, but on two, as close to the bend of the pendulum spring as possible. The acting faces are so shaped and placed that whenever the wheel moves from *B* towards *A* a tooth will lift one of them until it is stopped by the nib '*a*' or '*b*' at the end of each acting face. Here the pallet *A* has just been lifted and is holding the tooth that lifted it. As soon as the pendulum comes, moving to the right, it will evidently push that pallet out of the way by means of the fork-pin *P*, and so free the tooth, and the wheel will begin to turn, and the opposite tooth will immediately lift the pallet *B* till it likewise is stopped by *b*. The pendulum is all the time going on rising to the right and carries the right pallet with it as far as it likes to go; when it begins to fall the pallet falls with it, not only to the place where it was taken up, but to a lower place, corresponding to that of the left pallet in the picture: and the fall of the weight of the pallet from the place where it is taken up by the pendulum to the place where the pendulum leaves it, or the difference between its rise and fall with the pendulum, constitutes the impulse, and that difference is evidently constant, however far the pendulum may swing."

Mudge's escapement suffered from the defect that it was subject to complete or partial tripping, and despite the efforts of several subsequent inventors this practical weakness in a theoretically almost perfect escapement was eventually only overcome by Lord Grimthorpe in his cumbersome and violent but nevertheless highly successful double three-legged gravity escapement.

WATCHES

If this chapter can recount but little progress in clockmaking, its period of eighty years saw the greatest advance to be made in watches during the whole history of horology, except only the invention of the balance spring.

FIGURE 21. *Mudge's gravity, escapement, described on page 157.*

In 1750 the watch was in much the same state as had prevailed for the previous seventy years, and except for a relatively few cylinder watches by Graham or an occasional freak, the verge escapement reigned supreme. Pair cases with enamel or metal dials were all but universal.

In 1830 the cylinder escapement had almost entirely ousted the verge, and the highest grade watches had a duplex, lever or chronometer escapement with compensated balance; their accuracy of timekeeping had improved tenfold. The lever escapement had not yet established its supremacy for pocket watches but it was very shortly to do so. Pair-cases had almost entirely disappeared and the Breguet watch was completely modern in appearance, except that it was keywound. The keyless wind had, nevertheless, already been invented.

While English makers were responsible for most of the mechanical improvements, it was the French who evolved the modern watch, and in so doing, took back the leadership which the English so long held. The English instead gained a different supremacy in the commercial manufacture of marine chronometers and deck watches.

In no other period has the collector such a wide field of choice, nor a greater need for a keen discrimination between good and bad mechanism, and between artistic and trash ornament.

WATCH DIALS AND HANDS

Dials underwent very great changes. In 1750 the gold or silver dial was being made in exactly the same style as it had been for the past 75 years and it did not finally die out until about 1775. But even

PLATE 108

Watch by Martin, hall-marked 1778. Note revival of the use of multiple dials. In addition to a centre-seconds hand one of the subsidiary dials has a hand which revolves once in a second by quarter-seconds jumps. The back is translucent enamel over engine-turning and in the centre an oval cartouche of armorial bearings in painted enamel. (British Museum)

by 1750 the enamel dial was more fashionable. The average diameter of an English pocket watch had shrunk from 2 to 1¾ inches and the metal dial did not look so well in this smaller size. The enamel dials all followed the same pattern. Outermost were the minutes, in arabic numerals, at five minute intervals; next came a double circle with the minute divisions; next came the hours, in Roman numerals, and inside them another single circle. It was very unusual for the maker's name to appear on the enamel dial of an English watch before 1775 but examples do exist. In the highest quality watches the enamel was laid on gold. This kind of dial lasted until about 1790 by which time the figures had become smaller and lighter, especially the minute numerals, and the circle inside the hour numerals was generally omitted. After 1750 the same kind of dial is also found on French and Swiss watches, but with more complicated pierced gilt hands. On English watches the hands were almost universally 'beetle and poker', as they had been for many years previously, either in gold or blued steel.

Occasional examples have centre seconds hands, usually polished steel, and these impart a particularly elegant appearance to the watch.

PLATE 109

Swiss repeater watch, early nineteenth century. Note the small chapter ring flanked by gilt automata which strike mock bells when the watch is repeating.

PLATE 110

A type of cheap Swiss watch popular in the early nineteenth century, with painted dial and windmill automaton.

This typical mid-century English watch was fairly small in diameter, and about one inch thick, including its heavily domed glass, and this kind of dial and hands suited it to perfection. But with the French trend towards flatter and wider watches it was no longer really suitable. Large, heavy figures had made a bold effect on the old small dials, but the tendency in the last quarter of the century was to use light and delicate figures as a foil to the large unrelieved enamel surface. Minute figures disappeared, or at most, were very small, and at 15-minute intervals. Hour numerals were still sometimes in Roman numerals, but were usually arabic. As with clocks, there was a renewed interest in multiple dials, usually with centre seconds. Multiple-dial watches were also sometimes astronomical while Martin specialised in stop watches which, in addition to centre seconds, had a further subsidiary dial whereof the hand revolved once a second, being driven by a special wheel geared to the escape wheel. Like all eighteenth century watches, the stopwork stopped the entire watch.

From about 1800 watches, mostly Swiss or French are found in which the chapter ring only is enamel with the centre filled by an architectural scene with small figures in chased gold and silver. If the watch is a repeater, these figures may perform some action in time with the striking while occasionally some part of the background may be slid aside to reveal the enactment of a scene of questionable propriety.

In cheaper watches, the centre part of the dial may be painted with a simple scene which may have considerable charm. Sometimes this painting may cover the entire dial, the dial proper then occupying only a small circle in the middle, or even forming part of the actual picture, such as a clock dial on a tower. Simple automata may also be included, such as the sails of a windmill or figures passing across an opening. Such dials remained popular until the second quarter of the nineteenth century.

Dials in four-colour gold became popular in about 1800, after this form of decoration had been used in cases for some fifty years. It consists of gold mixed with other substances to give red, yellow, white and green tints. The dial, of one colour, is usually engine turned and separate skeleton Roman numerals of another colour are soldered on to it; a band of foliate ornamentation, outside the chapter ring, is in the other two colours. This form of dial is usually accompanied by heavy polished gold hands.

In about 1785 both the typical Continental and English enamel dial became standardised in a form which was to continue with little variation for a century or more. Both are innocent of minute numerals and have a band of minute divisions outside the hour numerals. In the English watch the hour numerals are Roman, fairly long, thin and delicate.

Seconds hands are by no means universal, and the practice of counter-sinking the seconds dial was unusual in English watches before 1860.

The hands are generally very simple; a plain pointer for the minute hand and a simple spade end for the hour, executed either in blued steel or gold.

Breguet's style

In the French cases, probably pioneered and certainly perfected by Breguet, the numerals are arabic, slightly sloping and giving almost the appearance of having been written on quite casually. Yet they are executed with such perfect artistry that the smallest alteration would upset the balance. The appropriate hands, invariably used by Breguet, are moon hands, almost invariably in steel (gold hands were only used with metal dials). Owing to the widespread faking of Breguet's watches, even in his own lifetime, he devised a form of 'secret' signature, in cursive lettering, with the number of the watch. On enamel dials it is placed just below the 12, and on metal dials on either side of the 12. It is believed to have been executed with a diamond-pointed pantagraph, after glazing, and can only be easily detected by looking slantwise across the dial towards the light. Not all Breguet watches have a secret signature but in such as do, it may be regarded as an infallible sign of authenticity. The secret signatures on silver dials have mostly disappeared when the chapter ring has been polished at some later date. This alternative fashion for gold or silver dials also appears to have been started and was certainly popularised by Breguet. The minute divisions are represented by a series

PLATE 111 *(right)*

Watch with four-colour gold case and dial. Early nineteenth century.

PLATE 112 *(above and right)*

Late-type English silver pair-case watch by C. Jenkins, hallmarked 1779. Note retention of beetle and poker hands and the arrangement of figures traditional throughout the earlier part of the eighteenth century, but omitting the concentric circles. On the movement pierced ornament is confined to the symmetrical pattern of the balance cock table.
(British Museum).

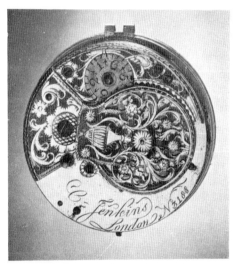

of dots and the hours are indicated by fairly short Roman numerals, engraved on a polished chapter ring and filled with wax. The space inside the chapter ring is engine turned with intercrossing lines so fine as more to suggest a silky sheen than any noticeable pattern.

Seconds dials are not usually found on Breguet's enamel dials but when they do exist he usually countersunk them by the process of grinding away the glaze. They are more usually found on his metal dials and are then always countersunk. Typical of his strictly functional approach to watchmaking, Breguet seldom bothered to bring his seconds dial opposite the 6 (like all other makers) but positioned it wherever was most suitable to the movement. It is this ability to make beautiful watches without any apparent striving after beauty that makes Breguet certainly the greatest horological *artist* of all time. To say, as many do, that he was the greatest *horologist* is almost certainly going too far, since although he delighted in solving complicated problems, and his workmanship is superb, in actual timekeeping only his tourbillons could rival the pocket chronometers of Arnold which antedated them by a quarter of a century.

Both English and Breguet styles had a flat lunette glass, the Breguet being the flatter of the two.

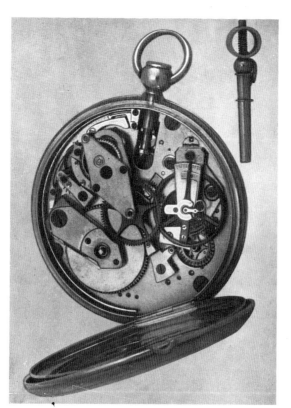 

This he achieved by having a relatively broad body to his case (usually flat-sided) with a bezel which is the narrowest possible ring in which a glass can be held. He frequently used natural rock crystal instead of glass, but the difference is most difficult to detect. The English had usually no visible body (or fixed part of the case) at all, or only a narrow rim, and a wide, curved bezel, thus perpetuating the lines of the obsolescent pair-case. Nearly all Breguet's watches are remarkably thin for their date and some are thin by any standard.

WATCH CASES

The English pair-case began to go out of fashion by 1775, when the French started the fashion towards thinner watches, but pair-cases continued to be made throughout the first half of the nineteenth century and in nineteenth-century examples it is quite difficult at first glance to distinguish between single and pair-cases. This is for the reason stated in the last paragraph, but also because the English makers continued to hinge their movements to the case so that it could be swung clear of it when the glass was opened. In fact, all they had really done was to preserve the pair-case, merely permanently fixing the two parts together, and combining in one the two dial openings. The practice of hinging the movement to the case continued in some high class English watches until about 1870.

The French early abandoned the pair-case and in fact had rarely used it at any time. To avoid

PLATE 113 *(left and right)*

Gold repeater watch by Breguet 1815. Note typical engine-turned gold dial and 'Breguet' hands; asymmetrical position of seconds dial; 'barley-corn' engine turning of case; movement with typical Breguet development of the Lepine calibre showing also repeating train, compensation curb and parachute; 'Breguet' or 'tipsy' ratchet winding key (incapable of winding backwards). Ruby cylinder escapement.
(British Museum)

having to open the movement in order to wind the watch they usually arranged for it to be wound through the dial, which considerably marred its appearance and subjected enamel dials to considerable risk of chipping. Breguet therefore adopted the preferable arrangement of having a quite separate flat-sided, annular body to the watch to which front and back bezels, consisting of narrow rings, were hinged. Glass or rock crystal was fitted into the front bezel and a corresponding plate of metal into the back bezel. The movement was rigidly fixed to the body which had a second, hinged, inside lid, or 'dome' at the back, with winding holes, thus corresponding to the fixed inside back of the English single case. Breguet thus arrived in one step at the modern form of watch case which has never subsequently varied. He usually made the inside dome of brass-gilt and only made it of gold in watches of 'ouvrage première classe'.

Turning to the types of case decoration, during this chapter many of the best watches have no decoration at all, but have cases of plain gold or silver, entirely unadorned. Painting on enamel continued until the end of the century but it does not compare with the exquisite work of the seventeenth century. There was a tendency to use rather dull colours under a thick, glassy glaze. The enamel painting, which had in earlier times covered the whole outside of the watch, tended now in continental watches to be confined to round or oval panels set in the gold case, whereof the visible gold portion was either repoussé or (in the case of clock-watches and repeaters) pierced and chased. A very beautiful form of enamel painted, characteristic of the Louis XVI period, consists of a figure scene painted in grisaille on an oval-shaped ground of opaque dark-coloured enamel.

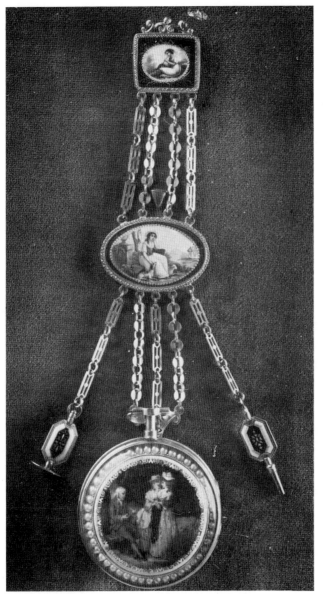

This oval is framed by a narrow band, usually of white enamel and gold, outside which is a field of transparent enamel. The edge of the case is often decorated with half-pearls or brilliants.

Yet another form of enamelling, seldom found before 1790, is transparent enamel over engine-turned gold, usually edged with pearls or brilliants, and this, at its best, gives a superb effect.

Champlevé enamel on silver or gold is unusual, but may be found at any time up to 1830.

Guilloche, or engine turning, began to be used as a means of watch decoration from 1770 onwards, but it is rare before 1790, after which it was widely used by Breguet. The simple barley-corn is at once the most effective and most usual pattern.

Repoussé work had reached its climax by 1750 but may be found in ever-deteriorating quality up to 1775 at latest.

Embossed and chiselled cases in four-colour gold may be found at any time from 1800 to 1830 and remained popular until as late as 1880. This form of decoration is sometimes found on continental watches as early as 1750. An attractive form of decoration found on cheaper English watches consisted of painting covered by a thin sheet of transparent horn.

PLATE 114
(*above*)

French watch, last quarter eighteenth century, decorated with painted enamel and pearls, with gold and enamel chatelaine. Reproduced by permission of the Syndics of the Fitzwilliam Museum, Cambridge.

PLATE 115
(*p. 165, above, two views*)

Gold watch by Jonas Crossley, Manchester, hall-marked 1796. The back decorated with grey translucent enamel over engine-turning, surrounded by a border of half-pearls.

(British Museum)

PLATE 116
(*p. 165, below, left*)

Gold pair-case watch by John Willats, hall-marked 1762. Deep repoussé in two layers (the limbs of the figures are actually free-standing). The case signed: Guitcoll.

(British Museum)

PLATE 117
(*p. 165, below, right*)

Pair-case watch decorated with painted horn. Early nineteenth century.

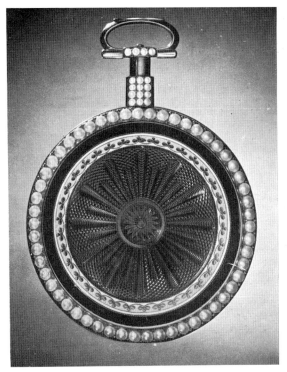

TURKISH AND CHINESE MARKET WATCHES

At the end of the eighteenth Century England enjoyed a flourishing export trade to Turkey and many export watches have either found their way back to England or else never left it. They have, of course, Turkish numerals, usually very ornate cases, as many as three or four, and are seldom of good quality.

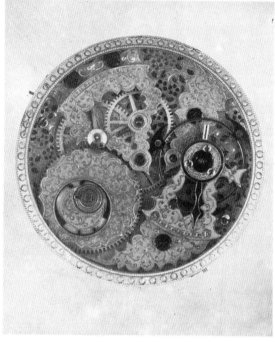

PLATE 118

English watch by George Charle for the Turkish market, circa 1800.

PLATE 119

Movement of Swiss watch for the Chinese market with Lepine-type calibre and each part intricately engraved. The escapement is the variant of duplex described on page 176.

England also had a considerable Chinese export trade, which was later captured by the Swiss.

Early Swiss examples were notable only for their gaudy finish in stones and enamel, but in the nineteenth century decoration of the movement gave the Chinese watch a character of its own, and a considerable number found their way to this country. A peculiarity of the Swiss make is that they were often made in pairs. The layout is with separate bridges, of curvilinear pattern, and either engraved or engine-turned. Steel parts are blued or polished and the inside cover is of glass so that the movement may be inspected without damage. The enamel dials nearly always had centre-seconds hands which move only once a second. This was achieved by a special form of duplex escapement which is described at the end of this chapter (page 176).

PENDANTS

Pendants in 1750 had pronouncedly stirrup-shaped bows but by the end of the century the stirrup had gradually changed into a flattened oval. Finally, under Breguet, there was a return to the plain circular ring which had been popular in the late seventeenth century. The pendant stems of repeaters were necessarily long, to allow of their being pushed in to operate the repeating mechanism, and this started a fashion towards the end of the century for all watches to have long thin pendants, regardless of whether or not they were repeaters.

However, in the early nineteenth century, to balance the large diameter watches which had then become fashionable, there was a tendency to use fairly wide, flat pendant stems or alternatively to use a short stem with a big spherical button. These paved the way for the early keyless-wind knurled buttons which had already appeared before 1830.

PLATE 120
Three typical early nineteenth century Swiss Form watches.

FORM WATCHES, ETC.

Form watches, which had not been at all widely made since 1675, returned to fashion for women's watches during the first quarter of the nineteenth century in a wide variety of shape and treatment.

A novel style of watch developed by Breguet is known as 'à tact'. An otherwise normal watch has a cover, with raised studs at each hour. It also has a strongly made hand or pointer which is not driven by the movement and does not normally turn. But when turned clockwise by the wearer it stops when the current hour is reached. 'à tact' watches are often known as blind men's watches, but the large number (many of them highly ornate) made by Breguet shows that this idea is mistaken. He intended them primarily as a simpler alternative to a repeater. Breguet was such a leader of fashion, and so fascinating are his watches, that many could be described with advantage, but there is no space to discuss his work further here. The reader may, however, study his work in detail in Sir David Salomon's book entirely devoted to the subject and entitled *Breguet*.

Breguet never made two watches alike, except for the series known as 'Souscription', which were subscribed for in advance and made in batches, several at a time. They were intended as the cheapest possible watch of the highest possible quality, and with this end in view Breguet even omitted a minute hand and relied on a long hour hand and a very large diameter ($2\frac{5}{16}$ inches) enamel dial from which the time can easily be read to two minutes. The case of a 'Souscription' may be plain silver or rarely gold, but the most typical and elegant have a plain silver body, and back, and gold bezels and pendant ring. The movements incorporate Breguet's usual features such as the ruby cylinder, compensation curb, parachute and going barrel. They are wound through the centre of the dial like the single-handed French 'oignon' of a century earlier. Even 'Souscriptions' have been faked and the secret signature should be looked for.

In general fashions, it will be seen that France took the lead after 1750 and although English watches retained their own character and supremacy in precision work, they tended increasingly to follow French fashions. The Swiss industry, which began during this period to assume proportions of some consequence, entirely followed French fashions.

WATCH MECHANISM

In 1750, almost without exception, watches had a verge or cylinder escapement. No form of temperature compensation had been devised that was applicable to watches. The full-plate movement made for thickness and indeed, little effort seems to have been made to produce a thin watch.

In 1830 the verge escapement still held the field for common watches and was to continue in diminishing use until 1880. In addition, two escapements, invented in the early eighteenth century and described in the last chapter, came into widespread use in England, at the end of the century, continuing until nearly the end of this chapter. These were the rack-lever, and the Debaufre, the former popularised by Litherland of Liverpool and the latter by several makers at Ormskirk, near Liverpool. But despite this conservatism the period saw a truly startling progress in the appearance and performance of pocket watches. It saw the invention of the lever escapement which is now universal for all watches, and the development by Breguet of the Lepine calibre to produce a thin watch of completely modern appearance.

The evolution of the marine chronometer was followed by the application of spring and pivoted detent escapements to watches, together with compensation curbs or bi-metallic compensation balances. The deep, isochronous helical balance spring could only be applied to very thick watches, but Breguet showed with his 'overcoil' how a flat spiral spring could be made isochronous and this spring is still used for watches of the highest grade.

Among many ingenious escapements two beside the lever and detent, or chronometer, attained considerable popularity; namely, the Virgule and the Duplex. The lever did not attain its undisputed superiority until about 1850.

All this inventive activity must now be examined more closely, in the following order: escapements; balance spring; compensation; layout and, finally a section devoted to Breguet's pioneer work.

Cylinder escapement

The most popular escapement throughout the whole period, for high-class watches, continued to be Graham's cylinder, despite the rapidity with which wear took place at the lips of the cylinder. This, however, was largely overcome by the use of a ruby cylinder in conjunction with a steel escape wheel. Although Breguet made numerous watches with lever (rarely chronometer or duplex) escapements, the great majority of his watches from 1800 onward have a ruby cylinder escapement with a steel escape wheel. As made by Breguet it seems almost completely immune from wear so that such watches perform as well today as when they were made.

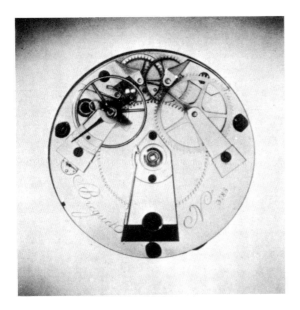

PLATE 121

Breguet 'Souscription' watch with one hand. 1818. The watch is wound by the square emerging through the centre of the hand, corresponding with the large central going barrel seen in the view of the movement. Note also the compensation curb and parachute. Ruby cylinder escapement. On the dial, note the form of signature almost invariably used by Breguet on enamel dials. The much enlarged view shows the 'secret' signature on the same dial, five times enlarged.

Breguet's cylinder had one unique quality which, however, will be more appropriately discussed shortly in the subsection of this chapter devoted entirely to his work. Although the ruby cylinder is always thought of particularly in connection with Breguet's name, he was anticipated by Ellicott and Arnold, and it was later used by most high-class makers.

Detent escapement

The detent or chronometer escapement is described in the section devoted to the marine chronometer. It was first applied to pocket watches by John Arnold who made numerous examples from about 1773 onwards, at first with pivoted and, after 1780, with spring detents.

Arnold was soon followed by Earnshaw and other leading chronometer makers and throughout this period the escapement may be found fitted to watches of the highest quality. They may have compensation curbs or bi-metallic balances; helical or spiral springs. Even after the final establishment of the lever escapement, the detent escapement continued to be fitted to high-class watches throughout the nineteenth century. The spring detent is not, however, really suited to pocket use as it seems more subject to position errors than a well-adjusted lever, (especially, examples with a heavy balance). If not expertly adjusted, or if subjected to sudden shocks, it is also prone to tripping or setting.

In addition to genuinely pocket-size chronometers, there were also 'deck watches'. They were supplied in a box like a ship's chronometer but are cased like an ordinary watch of very large size and, being no thicker than an old French oignon, may just be accommodated in a waistcoat pocket. Such use is not, however, advisable where the balance is so heavy that any sudden shock would put an undue strain on the balance staff pivots.

Virgule escapement

The virgule escapement is a direct development of the cylinder. It seems to have been devised initially by Jean-André Lepaute, but the form generally found was developed by Jean Antoine Lepine in about 1780, and enjoyed considerable popularity for a period of about 20 years. It is only found in French watches.

The escape wheel has teeth upstanding from its rim, but the part performing locking and impulse is a half-round, as opposed to the pointed teeth of the cylinder escapement.

The virgule, mounted on the balance staff, and so-called from its resemblance to a comma, consists of a very small cylinder with the exit lip extended into a long curved tail. On entering the cylindrical part of the virgule the tooth of the escape wheel imparts impulse to the balance as in the

PLATE 122 (*p. 171, above, two views*)

Silver pair-case watch by Thomas Earnshaw, hall-marked 1799, with spring detent escapement, compensated balance and helical balance spring, made for the Astronomer Royal, the Rev. Neville Maskeleyne and now owned by his descendant, Nigel Arnold-Forster, Esq.

PLATE 123 (*p. 171, below, two views*)

Gold watch by John Arnold, hall-marked 1780. Note Typical Arnold hands and dial; stirrup-type pendant; balance cock with engraved foot and narrow, pierced and engraved table; Arnold's 's' balance with solid steel rim and curved bi-metallic strips; helical balance spring. The escapement, originally a pivoted detent, was very early converted by Arnold to his spring detent.
(British Museum)

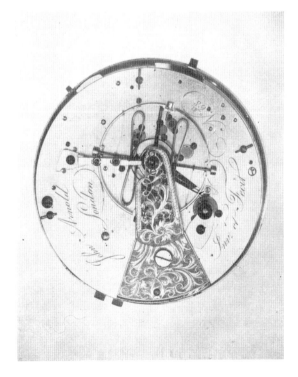

171

case of a cylinder but, owing to the very small diameter of the cylinder, this impulse is correspondingly feeble. Also owing to the small diameter of the cylinder, the two periods of frictional rest (on its inside and outside faces) involve much less friction than a normal cylinder escapement. Finally, on escaping from the cylinder, the escape wheel tooth slides along the curved tail to which it imparts a very brisk impulse.

This escapement has theoretical advantages over the cylinder, but has the more than counteracting disadvantages that practically all the impulse is only given in one direction; it does not hold oil as well as a cylinder; its performance deteriorates rapidly with the least wear; and it is very fragile

PLATE 124

Gold watch by James Ferguson Cole, hall-marked 1821. Note typical 1820 period English dial; superbly finished movement with Lepine type of calibre, compensated balance and Cole's patented pivoted detent escapement. (British Museum)

FIGURE 23 *(right). The Duplex escapement. The drawings numbered 1 to 4 show the sequence of events, and after these are perspective views of one pair of teeth on the escape wheel and of the balance staff. Impulse tooth A registers with impulse pallet B and locking tooth C registers with locking roller D. In the four plan views, (1) is the period of frictional rest, C being held against D. In (2) C registers with the slot in D and is about to escape. In (3) C has escaped (imparting a very small amount of impulse in so doing) and A now drops on B, imparting impulse. (4) shows the commencement of the next period of frictional rest.*

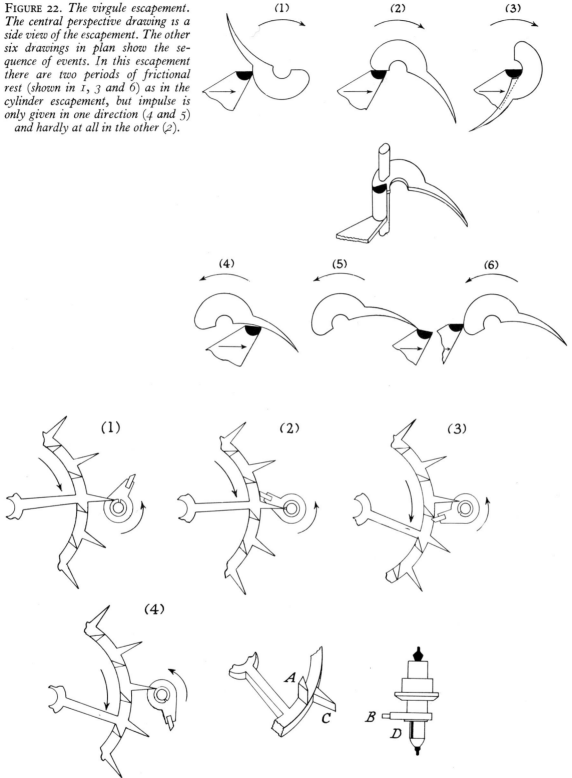

FIGURE 22. *The virgule escapement. The central perspective drawing is a side view of the escapement. The other six drawings in plan show the sequence of events. In this escapement there are two periods of frictional rest (shown in 1, 3 and 6) as in the cylinder escapement, but impulse is only given in one direction (4 and 5) and hardly at all in the other (2).*

(1)   (2)   (3)

(4)   (5)   (6)

(1)   (2)   (3)

(4)

A

C

B

D

and difficult to make. Its considerable popularity was therefore short-lived and examples are not particularly plentiful.

The original form as invented by Lepaute had teeth projecting alternatively from either side of the rim of the escape wheel and this arrangement was probably simultaneously invented by Pierre-Augustin Caron who later gave up watch-making and had a brilliant court and literary career as Beaumarchais. Caron's escapement had two virgules, one for each set of teeth, and is called a double

virgule. It was very difficult to make and surviving examples are so exceedingly rare that they can practically be discounted by a modern collector.

Duplex escapement

The duplex escapement is also related to the cylinder but it proved more successful than the virgule. It was even widely preferred to either the chronometer or the lever escapement for watches of the highest quality and when well executed it was, indeed, capable of an excellent performance. Various rather improbable escapements have been claimed as its prototypes but the form in which the duplex became widely used was first devised by Pierre Le Roy in about 1750. It was, however, in England that it was most widely used, from about 1790 to 1860.

The escape wheel has two separate sets of pointed teeth; on different planes; the longer set are for locking and the shorter for impulse.

The locking portion of the balance staff is a small ruby roller with a narrow notch or slice cut out of it. The locking teeth rest against the outside of the roller until the point of a tooth is able to enter the notch and so escape, imparting a very feeble impulse in so doing. On the return swing of the balance the notch passes the tooth with a barely audible click.

PLATE 125 (*left and right*)

The first lever watch ever made, constructed by Thomas Mudge in 1759–60 for George III and illustrated by gracious permission of Her Majesty Queen Elizabeth II. Note traditional 'Graham' type of centre-seconds dial; movement with solid balance wheel and bimetallic compensation curb.

Projecting from the balance staff, just above the roller, so as to register with the shorter teeth on the escape wheel, is a long arm which is the impulse pallet and in later examples the impulse face is jewelled. As the escapement unlocks, in the manner already described, the impulse tooth overtakes the impulse pallet and imparts impulse to the balance. The escapement thus fulfils the dual object of reducing the friction of the cylinder escapement, and of imparting impulse through a more advantageous leverage, but only in one direction. Nearly all examples have the two sets of teeth mounted on a single escape wheel, as shown in the illustration, but examples are occasionally found in continental watches with two quite separate wheels, one for each set of teeth, mounted on the same arbor.

The form of duplex escapement applied to the Chinese watches already mentioned has locking teeth with a two-pointed forked end. Thus, as the first point enters the notch in the roller and escapes the escape wheel only moves by a fractional amount since the second point is then locked on the roller. Thus, the escape wheel only escapes fully on alternate swings and impulse is given at the same interval. This undesirable arrangement was necessary so that the centre-seconds hand should only appear to move once a second.

Like the virgule, the duplex escapement suffers from the difficulty of making it well, and its considerable fragility when made. Its performance deteriorates rapidly with wear and becomes subject to setting, owing to the impulse being only in one direction. Nevertheless, there are well-made and well-maintained examples which are still giving a good performance after 150 years of constant use, and the duplex escapement was only driven at last out of use when makers had attained so much experience of the lever escapement that they could achieve a better performance, with less trouble, by its means.

Lever escapement

The lever escapement was strangely ignored for 80 years after its invention, and was not popular at any time within the period of this chapter, up to 1830. Surviving examples are therefore of great interest, for this escapement was eventually to drive all others from the field and is now universal in all watches and portable clocks.

The detached lever escapement was invented by the great English horologist Thomas Mudge and he appears to have completed the first example in a clock in 1754.

Mudge appears to have thought well enough of it to hint that it could out-perform Harrison's successful marine chronometer (No. 4) but he did not consider its advantages commensurate with the difficulties of making it. So far as marine chronometers were concerned, he fixed his hopes on his very complicated remontoire escapement, which never came up to his expectation, for the reasons explained in the section dealing with marine chronometers. So far as the lever escapement was concerned he wrote "I think, if well executed, it has great merit, and will in a pocket watch particularly, answer the purpose of time-keeping better than any other at present known; yet it has the disadvantage that it requires great delicacy in execution that you will find very few artists equal to, and fewer still that will give themselves the trouble to arrive at; which takes much from its merit. And as to the honour of the invention, I must confess I am not at all solicitous about it; whoever would rob me of it does me honour".

In view of this inauspicious start the first example in a watch, completed in 1770 is of the utmost interest and merits a fairly detailed description. It was made for George III and given by him to Queen Charlotte. It is still owned by the Royal Family, and is preserved at Windsor Castle.

All the elements of the lever escapement existed in the rack-lever escapement described in the last chapter, but Mudge had the flash of inspiration to see that the rack and pinion, which shackelled the balance wheel at all times to the anchor escapement, could be entirely dispensed with, leaving the truly detached lever escapement, in all essentials as we know it today. The details of the Mudge watch will better be appreciated if the principle of the modern lever escapement is first understood and this is shown in the accompanying illustration.

The escape wheel is engaged by an anchor with jewelled pallets *A* and *B* which have separate locking and impulse faces like a dead-beat pendulum escapement. As a safety measure, however, the locking faces are cut back at an angle of about 12° so as to draw them into engagement and prevent their being jerked out by any sudden shock. This is called the 'draw' and produces an imperceptible recoil. The lever *C* ends in a fork *D* which registers with an impulse pin *E* attached to roller *H* on the balance staff *F*. As the balance swings, *E* rides into the fork *D*, carrying the lever with it, and moving a pallet from the locking on to the impulse face. The fork then imparts impulse to the pin which then again swings clear of the fork leaving the anchor again locked on the escape wheel. During the remainder of its swing the balance is then entirely free until, on its return journey, it again engages with the escapement and repeats the operation in the opposite direction. As an additional precaution

FIGURE 24. *The modern lever escapement. The three plan views show the sequence of events from locking to impulse and re-lockings, described in greater detail in the text.*

to the 'draw' the lever carries a 'safety dart' or finger *G* which registers with a 'safety-roller' *H*, on the balance staff. This has a crescent-shaped recess through which the dart can only pass at the moment of unlocking, so that if the lever is jolted out of engagement prematurely it is stopped by the dart riding against the safety roller until the appropriate moment arrives. Excessive locking is prevented by the banking pins *I* and *K*.

The Queen's watch (as it has always been known) is outwardly a normal, fairly large, gold pair-case of the period with enamel dial, blued steel poker and beetle hands, and centre seconds. The overall diameter is $2\frac{7}{16}$ inches and the depth, including the glass, $1\frac{5}{16}$ inches.

The escape wheel is of very large diameter, nearly $\frac{3}{4}$ inch, and has 20 teeth, formed to a blunt point and with the impulse face exactly radial. The anchor is also very wide and embraces five teeth; the pallets are jewels. The balance staff only clears the escape wheel by a millimetre so that the lever lies almost exactly under one arm of the anchor. The whole assembly is thus unbalanced and a counterbalance weight was necessary to restore equilibrium. It is this alone which gives the lever an appearance markedly different from a modern watch. At the end of the lever are fixed two sapphire pallets, in different planes, one above the other, for unlocking and impulse. On the balance staff are two cam-shaped projections which register with the inside faces of these two sapphire pallets. This dual arrangement was replaced in subsequent watches, as in fig. 24 above, by a flat fork with a single

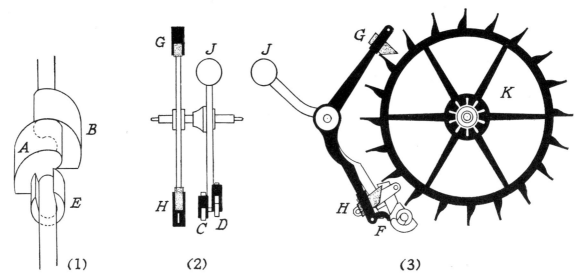

FIGURE 25. *Mudge's lever escapement.* (*1*) *is a perspective view of the balance staff.* (*2*) *is a side view of the lever and* (*3*) *shows the escape wheel, lever and balance staff in plan. A and B are the two pallets on the balance staff engaging with the impulse pallets C and D on the lever. E is the safety roller engaging with the safety dart F. G and H are the pallets* (*shown dotted*) *of the anchor. J is a counterbalance and K is the escape wheel.*

jewelled pin on the balance staff which, riding into the fork, first unlocks the lever and then receives its impulse. In the Mudge prototype one cam unlocked the escapement and the other received the impulse.'

In only one other respect does this beautiful mechanism differ from its modern counterpart. The locking faces of the pallets have no draw so that the lever could be jerked out of engagement at the wrong moment. On the other hand, the only consequence would be that the dart and safety roller would be brought into play and, in fact, many of Breguet's early lever watches have no draw and suffer no apparent inconvenience thereby.

The Queen's watch has, of course, a solid steel balance. It has, however, two balance springs, one above and one below the balance. That below has a little over three turns and has no provision for regulation. That above has four turns, and moveable curb-pins worked through leverage by a bimetallic strip, thus providing for changes of temperature. It was thus one of the first, if not absolutely the first pocket watch to be fitted with temperature compensation. The whole compensation apparatus is pivoted and may be turned for the purpose of regulating the watch.

The use of two balance springs working in opposition to each other achieved isochronism, and Mudge also applied two such springs to his special watches and marine timekeepers.

The Queen's watch seems to have given entire satisfaction, but owing to Mudge's subsequent pre-occupation with his marine timekeeper, he does not seem ever to have made another. He did, however, make two bracket clocks with the lever escapement, and balance wheel, which have survived, and a model of the escapement for his patron, Count Bruhl, which seems to have disappeared.

In 1782, however, Count Bruhl induced the London watch-maker, Josiah Emery, to make a watch from Mudge's model, and during the next decade Emery made about 32 lever watches for

PLATE 126

Gold watch by Josiah Emery 1792–3 with Lever escapement. Note the regulator-type of dial generally used by Emery and the bridge cock used on nearly all his lever and other high-quality watches. Also illustrated are a balance wheel, lever and escape wheel from a similar watch by Emery.
(British Museum)

179

wealthy clients. Contrary to the widely-held belief he never used 'draw', which was invented by Leroux in 1785 but used by no other eighteenth-century maker. In his escapement Emery followed Mudge but laid out with the escape-wheel arbor, the balance wheel arbor, and the pivot-point of the lever in line with each other; and this 'straight-line' layout has been used widely ever since. Other London makers of the lever escapement before 1800 were Leroux, Margetts, Pendleton, Perigal, Grant, Dutton and Taylor. Breguet was the first continental maker to use it, probably from 1787. The English makers (except Leroux, Taylor and later Ferguson Cole) all used pointed teeth for their escape wheels, inclined at slightly more of an angle than Mudge's, so that all the lift was on the pallets. They continued to use this arrangement as long as good quality lever watches were made in England up to about 1914. Breguet, on the other hand, introduced the club-shaped teeth now universally employed, in which the flat top of each tooth is cut at a slight angle so that the lift is divided between tooth and pallet. Breguet does not appear to have used draw until about 1814. The English makers after Emery abandoned the straight line layout and placed their lever tangentially to the escape wheel. It is probable that the English layout was first used by Leroux and it is found in a watch made by him in 1785.

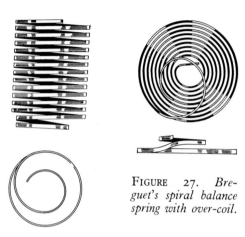

FIGURE 27. *Breguet's spiral balance spring with over-coil.*

FIGURE 26. *Arnold's helical balance spring with end-curves.*

After 1800 the lever escapement came increasingly into use but it did not attain acknowledged supremacy until considerably later than the end of this chapter in 1830. Any examples before this date are therefore worthy of consideration. Many inventors devised variations and complications of the lever escapement which, when found, are usually of technical and historical interest; but none of them prevailed, and the original design of Mudge has survived, subject only to the minor improvements mentioned in the foregoing paragraphs. Those who may wish to study the development of the lever and other escapements in greater detail are recommended to obtain *It's about Time* by P. M. Chamberlain, published by R. R. Smith of New York in 1941; republished in London 1971 (both unfortunately now somewhat rare).

Balance spring

A watch is no better than its balance spring. The first springs had less than two turns which rapidly grew to three, and this was sufficient for the 100 degree arc of a verge escapement. The greater amplitude of a cylinder escapement merited a further increase to five turns and the lever, which may have an arc of $1\frac{3}{4}$ turns, has ten at least. Nevertheless, Mudge, in his first lever used only three and four turns respectively for the two springs of his lever watch. The soft drawn wire which was universal up to 1770 gradually gave way to hardened and blued steel which was less susceptible to fatigue and rust. Nevertheless, Earnshaw used untempered metal for his springs and roughly counteracted their shortcomings by adjusting them so as to be fast in the short arcs.

The chronometer makers from Le Roy onwards had striven to attain isochronism in their balance springs and from 1776 Arnold devised and used various end curves which he had found by experiment to be isochronous. His pocket chronometers had helical springs but Earnshaw used helical or spiral indifferently. Arnold often used gold springs, which are non-magnetic and do not rust, but as against this they cannot be tempered, are heavy, and gold is a material of inferior elasticity.

The ordinary spiral spring is not isochronous, and if it were to be so in one particular position of the regulator, it would not be for any other. However, Breguet found that by giving the outer curve of a spiral spring an upward twist and then curving it inwards, anchoring it near the centre of

PLATE 127

Watch by Lepine with unusual numbering of the dial consisting of mixed arabic and roman numerals. The movement has the original type of Lepine's own calibre. Virgule escapement. Hall-marked 1789.
(British Museum)

the balance, it could be made isochronous, thus securing the benefits of isochronism with the convenience of a flat spiral spring. The 'Breguet overcoil' is almost universally used in the best modern watches. To obtain its full advantage it cannot be fitted with a regulator and therefore has to be carefully adjusted to time in the first place, after which a 'freesprung' watch (i.e. one without a regulator) can only be regulated by the timing screws at the ends of the cross bar of the balance wheel. In all this the pocket watch only followed the example of the marine chronometer and the question is dealt with again in that section.

Compensated balance

The chronometer makers also led the way in connection with temperature compensation, but watch-makers were quick to benefit by their researches, at first with compensation curbs and later with bi-metallic compensated balances. It is doubtful if any pocket watch before 1830 had auxiliary compensation, and no watch was by then sufficiently accurate to justify this extreme refinement. French makers have never employed it. It has been claimed that a lever pocket watch by Leroux, of 1785, has auxiliary compensation, but it seems far more likely that he was only concerned to limit the effects of centrifugal force on the thin bimetallic arms of his balance.

PLATE 128

Skeleton watch movement, late eighteenth century; really a variant of the Lepine calibre. (British Museum)

PLATE 129

Watch by J. R. Arnold with early keyless wind on the Prest pattern, circa 1820. Note the typical 1820 period hands and dial. The hands had to be set by a key. (British Museum)

All this has been superceded in the best modern watches which have an elinvar type balance spring and uncut invar balance wheel.

Lepine calibre

An important improvement of quite a different kind was invented in about 1770 by the French maker Antoine Lepine. Instead of containing the train of his watches between two circular plates, and the balance outside the top plate, supported at its upper end by a cock mounted on the plate, Lepine discarded the top plate altogether and employed separate cocks, mounted on the single plate, for the train, including the balance. Especially in conjunction with a going barrel the Lepine calibre enabled genuinely thin watches to be made for the first time; so thin, indeed, as to render the main-spring undesirably narrow. To mitigate this weakness some makers took the daring step of doing without a cock for the spring barrel which was supported solely by an arbor of exceptional thickness and strength.

The Lepine calibre was adopted enthusiastically by the French makers but the English refused to associate themselves with it, retaining their full-plate movements with fusee, and outside balance.

PLATE 130

View under dial of an early nineteenth century Swiss musical watch showing the wheel carrying the actuating pins and the 29 tuned metal strips which they twang.

PLATE 131

Breguet watch. 1812. Under-dial view showing calendar work and typical Breguet straight-line lever escapement.

Although, from the point of view of performance, they were right to retain the fusee, the demand for thin watches grew and French watches soon gained the fashionable pre-eminence. Even when, in the second half of the nineteenth century, English makers abandoned the full-plate, they still retained the centre and third wheels between the plates. The Lepine calibre or barred movement is now in universal use for all watches.

Winding mechanism

Various attempts at keyless winding had been made from 1800 onwards. The most popular form was known as 'pump-winding' in which a spring plunger on the rim of the watch body was moved in and out several times to wind the spring. The modern form of keyless wind, with a knurled nob on the end of the pendent had, however, been invented by Prest in 1820 although it was not to come into at all general use for another 50 years. Keyless winding is in any case difficult to combine with a fusee, and fusee watches as a whole continued to be key-wound long after the others.

Musical watches

Soon after 1800 the Swiss made a considerable number of musical watches. They are generally well made and cased in the Breguet style.

Breguet mechanisms

Last to be considered comes the remarkable list of innovations in watches brought about by the genius of Abraham-Louis Breguet, some of which have already been mentioned: his special form of ruby cylinder, parachute, the watch 'à tact', self-winding watch, or 'perpetuelle', tourbillon, overcoil, and many *ad hoc* inventions to meet the wishes of special clients in watches of unbelievable complexity and perfection of workmanship.

Breguet, who was of Swiss parentage, set up in business in Paris, probably in the early 1780s, where he continued until his death in 1823.

Except in very early watches and special watches he always used the Lepine Calibre with minor modifications, and generally divided his train on both sides of the plate. The part between the plate and the dial is not, therefore, ordinarily visible. Breguet's use of the Lepine calibre enabled him to endow his watches with their peculiarly modern external appearance.

Many of Breguet's earliest watches, starting probably in 1787, had the lever escapement, and were 'perpetuelles' or self-winding. Such watches contain a heavy pivoted weight (generally platinum) which rocks to and fro with the normal movements of the wearer, and winds the mainspring by a ratchet gear in the process. When the spring is fully wound a stop-work locks the weight. In order that the wearer may know how far his watch is wound at any moment, such watches usually have a subsidiary 'up-and-down' dial.

After about 1800 Breguet gave up making perpetuelles, except to special order, and it is probable that he found that, even with his standards of workmanship, he could not make them so as to operate with reliability over a long period. Also, once out of order, very few people could undertake a repair. Subsequent experiments were no more successful until, since about 1930, some of the best wristwatches have been successfully fitted with a durable self-winding apparatus.

Breguet's ruby cylinder has already been referred to. The usual defect of a ruby cylinder is that the balance staff, is so exceedingly fragile. Breguet overcame this weakness to some extent by making a plain, short steel balance staff, with the ruby cylinder fitted over the end of it, so as to over-sail the bearing of the bottom pivot. Thus, the cylinder and escape wheel are between the plate and the dial and cannot be seen except by removing the dial.

Breguet understood perfectly well the superiority of the lever or chronometer escapement, compensated balance and fusee, over the cylinder, compensation curb and going barrel; but he felt that the latter trio gave quite sufficiently good time-keeping for normal requirements, were more robust, and less vulnerable in the hands of moderately skilful repairers. His opinion in this was fully justified by the results achieved.

An idiosyncrasy found in many of Breguet's watches is a 'jumping-hour' hand, in which the hour hand only moves once an hour. At five minutes to this hour it starts to move, covering the equivalent of $2\frac{1}{2}$ minutes in the next five. It then jumps to the next hour and then remains stationary for the next 55 minutes. This arrangement avoids motion-work and, in repeaters, makes a surprise-piece un- necessary; but it is not really known why Breguet thought so highly of it.

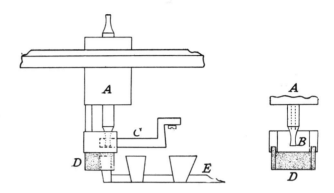

FIGURE 28. *Breguet's ruby cylinder escapement. The balance staff A is very substantial and its bottom pivot B is held in a slender potence C. The ruby cylinder (shown dotted) D is held in a downward extension of A, so that the cylinder and escape wheel E are entirely below the level of C.*

It is practically impossible to adjust a watch so that it will maintain an unaltered rate in all positions. Breguet overcame this in some of his finest watches by mounting the balance and escape wheel on a movable platform geared to the third wheel, so that the platform makes a complete revolution, usually once a minute. Thus, all position errors occur recurrently and so, for practical purposes, cancel each other out. A tourbillon watch may have a lever or detent escapement and some exceptional pocket watches are still made with it. It does, however, demand superlative standards of workmanship if it is to be justified by results.

The tourbillon was patented by Breguet in 1801 but a less exacting and equally effective variant was devised by Bonniksen of Coventry in 1894. This he called a 'karussel' in which the platform only revolves once in every $52\frac{1}{2}$ minutes.

An excellent device incorporated by Breguet in most of his watches after about 1793 is his 'Parachute'. This consists of mounting the end-stones of the balance staff on arms of spring steel, long enough to have considerable elasticity. If the watch is subjected to some extreme shock the Parachute will generally give sufficiently to save the balance-staff pivots from breaking.

If the overcoil balance spring has proved to be the only one of Breguet's inventions to survive in wide-spread use, his intangible influence on his contemporaries and successors is too great to assess. By the obvious 'rightness' of all his mechanism, coupled with its superb but unostentatious finish; the excellent performance and extreme durability of his watches; the perfect simplicity and proportion of his cases and dials, he set a standard for the modern watch which has never been surpassed.

During the whole of this period, the Swiss industry followed French fashions but Breguet's contemporary Frederic-Japy (1749–1812) showed a remarkable aptitude for devising machine tools. By their means he was able to manufacture watch parts in large numbers and laid the foundations for the accurately mass-produced watch which is now Switzerland's principal industry, and the source of most of the world's watches.

THE LONGITUDE STORY

EARLY EFFORTS

No aspect of horological history is more charged with human and technical interest than the development of the marine chronometer; moreover, it affords an excellent opening for the discriminating collector of moderate means.

As a ship sails north or south, the apparent altitude of the heavenly bodies in relation to it changes, so that the latitude of the ship may be accurately determined by their observation; the calculation of its longitude is not so simple. Various methods have been proposed, by observation of the heavenly bodies, but most of these methods are impracticable and none is satisfactory. Nevertheless, for centuries nothing better could be suggested, and so great was the need that Charles II established Greenwich Observatory for the main purpose of 'rectifying the tables of the motions of the heavens, and the places of the fixed stars, so as to find out the so-much desired longitude of places for perfecting the art of navigation'. Nevertheless, in the course of some half a century his purpose remained so far unfulfilled that in 1714 the Government passed an Act (anno 12. Anne Cap. 15) 'for providing a publick reward for such person or persons as shall discover the Longitude'.

The test for any proposed method or mechanism was a voyage from the British Isles to the West Indies and the rewards offered were £10,000 for accuracy within one degree; £15,000 if within 40', and £20,000 if within half a degree. Large rewards were also offered by other countries.

Despite so great an encouragement, and so generous the margin of error allowed, almost a further half-century was to elapse before any of the awards was made.

As a ship sails eastwards the rotation of the earth will cause the heavenly bodies to cross her meridian earlier; or if she sails westwards, later, than at her port of departure. As long ago as 1530 Gemma Frisius had pointed out that if a ship could carry an accurate timekeeper, for comparing standard time, with the local time for the ship as found by observation, the ship's longitude would at once be known. Since a minute of time corresponds to fifteen minutes of longitude, it follows that to determine a ship's longitude to within half a degree, at the end of a six week's voyage, her timekeeper must keep time within two minutes over the whole voyage (or within 3 seconds a day). Nor is such a margin of error any too small for practical requirements, since a minute of time represents a linear distance at the equator of nearly fifteen nautical miles.

Although such limits of timekeeping were just within the capabilities of the best clocks when the Longitude Act was passed, such clocks relied upon a long pendulum for their accuracy, and they would have been quite useless on a ship at sea. Nevertheless, it was by means of a timekeeper that the prize was eventually won, and then by a Yorkshire carpenter.

An epic of human endeavour lay behind this achievement, but over a century and a half were to pass before the story found a worthy narrator in the late Lieutenant-Commander Rupert T. Gould. R.N., F.R.G.S. In *The Marine Chronometer—its History and Development* he combined historical research, technical knowledge, skill in draughtsmanship, literary style, humour, and human understanding in a degree which make this book great literature in a sense far wider than its purely horological scope. This chapter could hardly be more than a précis of Gould's work—now unfortunately difficult and costly to obtain.[1] Since he wrote, little has been added to the subject, but in 1940 Editions Tardy produced an important work by a syndicate of French writers: *Pierre Le Roy et la Chronométrie*, which is particularly valuable for its many illustrations of Le Roy's wonderful timekeeper, described later in this chapter.

It was fitting that Huygens, who first made successful pendulum clocks and balance-spring watches, should also be the first to attempt the construction of a machine which would keep accurate time at sea.

As early as 1660 he produced a timekeeper for this purpose. It was spring-driven, and to secure an equality of driving power at all times Huygens employed, not a fusee, but a weight-operated remontoire. The purpose of this device is to segregate the train from the escapement as far as possible, and where the escapement is not detached, the interpolation of a remontoire between it and the train is almost a pre-requisite of good timekeeping. Accordingly, the succeeding century was to see many ingenious variants of Huygens' invention, but in the end, the detached chronometer escapement rendered it superfluous. Huygens evolved several forms of remontoire but in the simplest he drove his escape wheel by a small weight. Each time the escape wheel advanced and the weight dropped, it was immediately rewound by the train. In this way the escapement was assured of motive power as nearly constant as possible, and quite cut off from any irregularities in the operations of the mainspring and train. The escapement was, necessarily at that date, the verge and pendulum; but to mitigate the rocking of a ship Huygens gave his pendulum the widest possible base. It took the form of a wire, bent in the shape of an equilateral triangle with its apex downmost. The pendulum weight was attached to the apex and the two uppermost corners of the triangle were suspended from threads confined between cycloidal cheeks. A projection at right angles to the verge-staff terminated in a fork which straddled the horizontal leg of the pendulum and imparted motion to it.

The arrangement worked pretty well in reasonably calm waters, but was so utterly erratic on the open sea that Huygens abandoned his attempts to produce a marine timekeeper. Several later experimenters worked on basically similar lines, of whom Henry Sully showed the greatest ability, but all such efforts were foredoomed to failure. It was by means of the inherently more erratic, but less easily upset balance spring, and not the pendulum, that the problem was eventually solved.

One of the first serious attempts at a sufficiently accurate balance-spring timekeeper seems to have been made by George Graham and there exists by him what is, in effect, a very large cylinder watch (in a drum-shaped case) of superb workmanship and having a very sensitive regulator. It was evidently intended that the timekeeper should be rated on shore against a thermometer. At sea the timekeeper would be kept in company with a thermometer, and constantly regulated in accordance with previously ascertained ratings. The date of this instrument is not known, but Graham began making cylinder escapements in 1725 and died in 1751.

Four names stand pre-eminent among those who made practicable a seagoing timekeeper. Few men can have been responsible for so great a saving of life as has resulted from their prolonged and unwearied efforts. They are, John Harrison, Pierre Le Roy, John Arnold and Thomas Earnshaw.

To John Harrison fell the honour of completing, in 1759, the first successful marine timekeeper and one, moreover, which performed far more accurately than the Longitude Act required, and which was capable of being re-produced (although only at considerable expense). Nevertheless, only three instruments on this pattern were ever made (Harrison's nos. 4 and 5 and Kendall's no. 1. Kendall's nos. 2 and 3 differed radically from Harrison's model) and in all points except priority in

[1] It is understood that a new edition is in course of preparation.

time, the pioneer honours must be accorded to the Frenchman, Pierre Le Roy. In 1766, after experimentation almost as prolonged as Harrison's he produced a timekeeper which not only equalled Harrison's in performance, but possessed a detached escapement and compensated balance, neither of which formed part of Harrison's machine, but which form an essential part of every successful marine chronometer ever made, with only one exception. The two English horologists, John Arnold and Thomas Earnshaw, probably not benefitting appreciably by Le Roy's work, had by 1780 evolved a design which has remained the standard pattern for marine chronometers ever since. Bitter rivals, they accused each other of plagiarism and the absolute priority of idea has never been settled. Almost simultaneously the Frenchman, Ferdinand Berthoud, reached the same point, but the far greater significance of Arnold and Earnshaw lies, not so much in their inventions, as the use they put them to. For whereas Berthoud remained an experimenter all his life and rarely made two machines alike, Arnold and Earnshaw each set up an organisation for large scale production. In the space of 40 years they produced about 1000 chronometers at the relatively cheap price of about £40 each, as against the 70 made by Berthoud during the same period.

It is remarkable that although Earnshaw outlived Arnold by 30 years, the number of his chronometers which have survived is relatively small. It is certainly the case that, prior to 1790, he worked almost entirely for the trade, and that his name seldom appeared on instruments which he had made. In view of the large number of surviving chronometers by Arnold it seems likely that Earnshaw at no time equalled Arnold's rate of production.

Two other names, both English, Larcum Kendall and Thomas Mudge, complete this list of seven names who, between the fruitful years of 1760–80 decided the future of the marine chronometer. Kendall and Mudge followed in the steps of Harrison and although their work had individual success, it led to nothing.

The greatest, without question, are Harrison, Le Roy, Arnold and Earnshaw.

After this preliminary survey, the work of each may now be examined in greater detail, but for a complete study of the subject, Gould's book is necessary.

THE ENGLISH PIONEERS

John Harrison, 1693–1776

John Harrison was the son of a Yorkshire carpenter and was himself brought up to that trade. Early in life he took a great interest in horology and made several long-case clocks almost entirely of wood. His invention of the compensated gridiron pendulum has already been mentioned and he followed this by an equally ingenious device known as the 'grasshopper' escapement, whose operation may be understood from the illustration on page 117, FIG. 15. Although in no way detached, it has the great merit of involving so little friction that the pallets do not need to be oiled, and Harrison often made them of Lignum vitae. By 1726 he had completed two regulators, one of which did not vary by a second a month during fourteen years, while its total error never exceeded half a minute. Another regulator by Harrison, belonging to the Royal Astronomical Society, has also a remontoire wound every 30 seconds, and employs roller bearings, the rollers pivoted in a revolving cage.

By 1728 Harrison had worked out on paper the design of a marine timekeeper and this he took to London where he showed it to George Graham. Graham was so much impressed that he lent a substantial sum of money, traditionally £200, to Harrison, without interest or security. Harrison then returned to Yorkshire to make the clock which was completed by 1734–5.

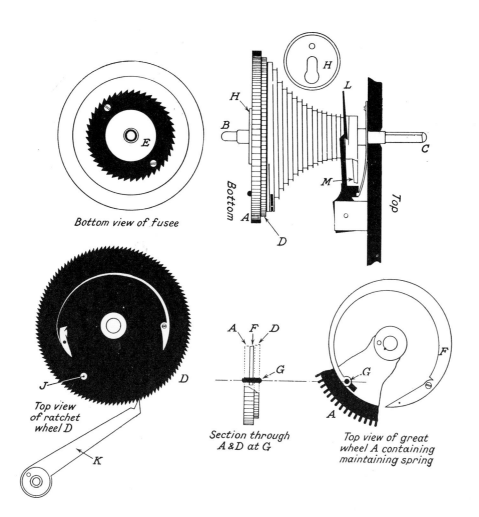

Bottom view of fusee

*Top view
of ratchet
wheel D*

*Section through
A & D at G*

*Top view of great
wheel A containing
maintaining spring*

FIGURE 29. *Harrison's maintaining-power mechanism. The operation of the fusee is as explained in Chapter I (see Fig. 5) the great wheel A being loosely mounted on the fusee arbor B C, but the ratchet wheel D, instead of being integral with the fusee is also loosely mounted on the arbor. Integral with the underside of the fusee is another ratchet wheel E whose teeth are cut in the opposite direction to those of D. Attached to D is a click (left white) which registers with the teeth of E. Attached to the top side of A is a spring F whose free end carries a pin G engaging with a slot also in the great wheel A, and when assembled, also with the hole J in ratchet wheel D (see sectional diagram). A and D are held in position on B C by a locating collet H. The action is as follows: In normal running the mainspring exerts pull on the fusee via the fusee chain. The fusee drives ratchet wheel D via the ratchet E on the fusee and the click on D. The drive is carried from D to A via the pin G. The spring F being weaker than the main spring is itself put under some tension in this process. As the whole assembly gradually turns the teeth of ratchet D escape one by one past a separate click K fixed to the plate. When winding the action is as follows: The fusee now being turned in the opposite direction to normal carries with it its integral ratchet wheel E whose teeth are able to escape past the click on ratchet wheel D. Unlike the earlier form of fusee (see Plate 5) D is unable to turn with the fusee, being held by its click K. The pull of the mainspring being removed from D, the spring F on D is now able to assert itself, and begins to dissipate the tension previously stored up in it, continuing to drive the great wheel and train. It is usually able to drive the timekeeper for three or four minutes, being more than enough to allow for winding to be completed. This diagram also shows the fusee stopwork. As the fusee chain reaches the last two turns of the spiral it engages with the hinged and spring-tensioned lever L and pushes it towards the top plate until L comes into the path of M, a nib forming part of the fusee. M comes up against L and further winding is thus prevented.*

189

It comprises two huge foliot balances, working in a vertical plane and in contrary motion, and connected together by wires running over brass arcs. These balances are controlled by four helical springs constantly in tension and to them are attached the first of any attempts to compensate a balance spring against the effects of heat and cold. This Harrison achieved by a variant of his 'grid-iron' principle, operating so as to vary the initial tension of the springs. The escapement is Harrison's 'grasshopper' and the train is quite normal, driven by two mainsprings driving a central fusee, incorporating maintaining power. As already stated, Huygens had long previously devised a maintaining power for weight-driven clocks, but Harrison's application of it to a spring and fusee is of interest as being the only one of his inventions to survive in use in all modern ship's chronometers and every other high-class watch employing a fusee. It is equally applicable to a weight-driven clock.

It will be remembered that all fusees transmit their drive to the Great wheel via a ratchet and click, to allow for winding, and this means that during winding the power is either removed from the train or reversed so that the escapement stands still or runs backwards. In Harrison's maintaining power a subsidiary spring is interposed between the fusee and the Great wheel. The inner end of this spring is attached to the Great wheel arbor and the outer end is attached to a wheel which may, for convenience, be called the 'maintaining wheel'. This wheel has a ratchet which only allows it to turn with the Great wheel and never against it. The maintaining wheel in its turn is driven through a ratchet by the fusee. It is, in fact, in exactly the same relationship to the fusee as is the Great wheel in watches where no maintaining power is fitted. When the fusee is being wound the maintaining wheel is prevented by its own ratchet from turning with it and the maintaining spring (which the mainspring normally keeps fully wound) takes over the duty of driving the clock. In this way, the timekeeper does not stop during winding and as soon as winding is completed the mainspring again takes up the drive via the fusee chain, fusee, maintaining wheel, maintaining spring, and great wheel, in that order. It also immediately restores the tension expended by the maintaining spring during winding. The operation of the mechanism is shown by FIG. 29. In the case of a weight-driven clock the fusee is replaced by the barrel.

Except for the escape wheel, all the wheels of Harrison's first clock are made of wood, the teeth of oak, being let into the wheel in groups of four, and the pinions are all of lantern pattern with lignum vitae rollers. Nearly all pivots are supported by friction wheels which had been invented by Henry Sully. In this arrangement, pivots do not revolve in holes in the plates, nor even in jewels, but between the rims of three or four wheels or segments. For the bearings of the foliot balances, Harrison used counterbalanced segments of more than ten-inch radius, held in place by spiral springs.

This cumbersome machine weighs about 72 lbs. and is about two feet wide and almost as high. The Board of Longitude (appointed under the Act of 1714) tried it on a voyage to Lisbon in 1736 when it acquitted itself favourably enough for the Board to advance Harrison £500 to make further experiments. Crude as it is, this was the first timekeeper which was capable of an accurate performance on shipboard and Commander Gould was of opinion that it might, with luck, have qualified for the £10,000 prize. One exceptional quality it does possess, in that it requires no lubrication whatever. Harrison next made a second machine which was a refined edition of his first, made all of metal, and incorporating a remontoire, wound 16 times an hour. It is even more cumbersome than the first, weighing 103 lbs. without its case and gimbals, and was finished by 1739. It was, however, not tried at sea as Harrison preferred to make a third machine on a yet further improved pattern which (for reasons not known) occupied him for the next 17 years, from 1740 to 1757. As before, it has two balances, but circular, and controlled by a single spiral spring, in place of the earlier helical springs. The compensation system is again novel, and of a type which remained popular in chronometers and good quality pocket watches until well into the nineteenth century, being known as a 'compensation curb'. Instead of the gridiron, Harrison rivetted two straight strips of brass and steel together. One end of the resulting bar is fixed rigidly to the clock and on the other are mounted two curb-pins between which pass the balance spring. The different coefficients of expansion of brass and steel cause the bar to bend one way in heat and the opposite way in cold and this shortens or lengthens the effective length of the balance spring. What Harrison could not overcome was that a spiral

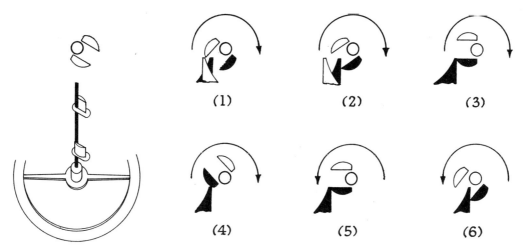

FIGURE 30. *The escapement of Harrison's marine timekeeper No. 4. On the left is a perspective view of the verge or balance staff and pallets, looking up from its bottom pivot towards the balance. The six plan views show the sequence of events. White pallet engages with white tooth and black pallet with black tooth. The direction of rotation of the balance staff is shown by arrows. In (1) white tooth has just delivered impulse to white pallet and escaped. In (2) black tooth has engaged with black pallet, but the balance continuing in the same direction under its own momentum produces recoil. In (3), the balance still continuing in the same direction, black tooth now passes the tip of black pallet and helps the balance towards the end of its arc by pressing against its curved back side in (4). During (4) the escape wheel therefore advances slightly, but as the balance swings back again a second recoil takes place (5), and only when the balance has returned, in (6) to the same position as (2), does the train finally reassert itself and black tooth imparts impulse to black pallet and so on.*

spring is not inherently isochronous and even when a spiral spring is isochronous, it is only so for a particular length, so that its isochronism is upset by a compensation curb such as Harrison's. Indeed, it was probably this curb which proved so troublesome and caused so long a delay in completing the machine. However, by 1757 Harrison reported to the Board that it was ready for trial, but desired to hold it back until he had finished a much smaller fourth timekeeper, and this was accomplished in 1759. By 1761 Harrison reported that its going equalled his third, and asked that the third and fourth should be tried together. However, by the time the expedition was ready to sail Harrison determined to send 'number 4' alone, and accordingly (he himself being by then 67 years old) his son William embarked on the 'Deptford' on November 18th 1761, bound for Jamaica with this remarkable instrument, superficially resembling any pair-case carriage clock of the period, and only $5\frac{1}{5}$ inches in overall diameter. Illustrations of the dial side, and of the movement, are shown in plate 132.

It incorporates a fusee with Harrison's maintaining power and on the fourth wheel is a very delicate and beautiful remontoire, operating every $7\frac{1}{2}$ seconds. The fourth wheel drives an ordinary verge-type escape wheel and the balance staff also closely resembles that of a verge watch. The pallets are, however, quite different, being made of diamond, very small, their impulse faces parallel to to each other and their backs rounded, of cycloidal contour.

PLATE 132
(left and right)

John Harrison's fourth time-keeper which won the £20,000 prize offered by Parliament for a means of ascertaining the longitude at sea. $5\frac{1}{5}$ inches diameter. Completed in 1759. (National Maritime Museum Greenwich)

The action of this escapement is most complex and entirely remarkable. It is best understood by reference to FIG. 30 and its caption.

The limit of banking is about 145° from the dead point, and as will be seen from the third diagram, this banking limit is of vital importance since if the balance were to advance by a very few degrees further the black tooth would escape past the back of the black pallet and the escape wheel would continue to race through until the remontoire spring was exhausted. As will be seen, the drop on the escapement is extremely small (.006 inches) and it accordingly runs very silently. Harrison stated that the train had only one eightieth as much control over this balance as had the train over an ordinary verge escapement. The balance wheel is of plain steel, $2\frac{1}{5}$ inches in diameter, making five beats a second, and the spring is tempered and polished steel, having slightly over three turns. It is fitted with a compensation curb basically similar to No. 3. Finding that the balance was not isochronous,

being slow in the short arcs, Harrison planted a cycloidal pin between the curb-pins and the spring anchorage which influenced the balance spring so as to mitigate this defect; but forced Harrison to abandon his ordinary regulator for bringing the watch to mean time.

The pivots are jewelled, as far as the third wheel, with ruby jewels and diamond end-stones.

Harrison had not been able to get the compensation exactly adjusted, to the extent that it gained

3 seconds a day at 42° F. But he said he was willing to stand by an average rate of one second a day gaining, which presumed an average temperature of 62° F.

So accurately did number 4 perform on its trial run that the longitude of Jamaica was determined by its means with an error of only 1¼′ as against the 30′ required by the Act to gain the £20,000 reward. Moreover, although the official trial ended at Jamaica, William Harrison and No. 4 returned in the *Merlin*, experiencing extremely rough weather, and its error, at the end of five months, was only 1 minute 53½ seconds, equal to 28½′ of longitude!

To comply with the Act Harrison still had to satisfy the Board that his invention was of practical application, and whereas they had previously given him valuable support and encouragement, they now opposed him by every means in their power. For ten years this wrangling continued, during which time Harrison, though nearing 80 years old, completed a fifth timekeeper, very similar in pattern to No. 4; and in the end he asked the King to test No. 5 in his own observatory at Kew, which George III graciously consented to do, and in a trial lasting ten weeks its total error on mean time was only 4½ seconds. So impressed was the King that he used his full influence on Harrison's behalf, to such effect that Parliament passed a private Act, in the teeth of the Board of Longitude, authorising payment to Harrison of the remainder of the £20,000 due to him.

Three years of life remained to him during which he seems to have been content to rest on his laurels, producing only a long and confused pamphlet of which only the following words are of technical interest: "and I can now boldly say, that if the Provision for Heat and Cold could properly be in the Ballance itself, as it is in my Pendulum, the watch (or my Longitude Time-keeper) would then perform to a few seconds in a year";

Harrison died on March 24th, 1776, and is buried at St. John's Church, Hampstead.

His first four timekeepers are kept on exhibition, and going (except when under repair), at the National Maritime Museum, Greenwich. No. 5 belongs to the Clockmakers' Company and forms part of their important collection at the London Guildhall. William Harrison made a sixth, simplified, instrument after his father's death, but its whereabouts (even if it still exists at all) are unknown. He died in 1815.

The followers of Harrison

To satisfy the Longitude Board of the general practicability of his timekeeper, Harrison had to dismantle and explain it to a technical committee among whom were two eminent clockmakers, Larcum Kendall and Thomas Mudge, and although each of them subsequently produced very successful timekeepers, their work had no permanent influence on the development of the marine chronometer.

Larcum Kendall (1721–1795)

Kendall was officially employed by the Board to make a duplicate of No. 4, for which they paid him £450. Harrison acknowledged the superiority of its workmanship to his own and it performed superbly on the second of Captain Cook's famous voyages, during which he circumnavigated the South Pole in the space of three years. It now lies beside No. 4 at Greenwich. Kendall afterwards made two further instruments of his own, much simpler than Harrison's No. 4 and omitting the remontoire, but their performance never approached that of No. 4, or Kendall's own copy of it. No. 2 was with Captain Bligh on the *Bounty* at the time of the famous mutiny, when it was carried off by the mutineers and only returned to England in 1843, after a chequered career. It is now in the Royal United Services Institution, Whitehall.

Thomas Mudge (1715–1794)

Mudge was a far more original thinker than Kendall and at the time he was called on to examine No. 4 he had already formed his own ideas for making a marine timekeeper. To avoid charges of plagiarism he set these down in a document which he sealed and deposited with the Royal Society. As recounted elsewhere, he had already (in 1759) invented the lever escapement, and it is strange that he did not persevere with it for his marine timekeeper. But he never seems to have rated it at its proper value and although he stated that it was capable of rivalling the performance of Harrison's No. 4, he nevertheless preferred to devote his efforts to a most intricate and ingenious escapement.

Where Harrison had put his remontoire between the fourth and escape wheel, Mudge used two remontoires and placed them between the escape wheel and the balance which is thus completely detached from the train, although it is practically never detached from the remontoires. These consist of two pivoted arms, mounted on coil springs and co-axial with the balance. The train is only concerned to wind up the coil springs of the remontoires (through $27°$) and there lock them. The balance staff is shaped as three sides of a rectangle, so as to avoid the remontoires, and from the two horizontal sides of the staff project vertical pins whose path lies in the path of the remontoire arms. Then, as the balance swings it picks up one of the remontoire arms and carries it along with itself to the end of its swing, whereupon the remontoire spring and arm assist it on its return swing, returning to the balance, not only the energy which the balance stored up in the remontoire spring, but, in addition, the $27°$ of tension previously stored up in the remontoire spring by the train. No sooner has the balance left one remontoire spring behind than it picks up the other one and starts the same procedure with it, and so the balance is kept in motion. The action is, in fact, a species of constant-force escapement. In conjunction with it Mudge used a variant of Harrison's compensation curb.

He made, in all, three of these instruments of which the first (an 8-day) was completed in 1774. One was reputedly lost at sea, one was purchased by the Dresden Museum and only one (the first) remains in this country, in the British Museum.

Mudge's son subsequently set up to manufacture timekeepers to the same pattern, and Mudge lived just long enough to see the first completed. About twenty were made in all, but their performance never approached that of the originals, and the extreme delicacy of the escapement evidently demanded all Mudge's artistry and skill to make it work successfully.

On the formula used in the early chronometer trials Mudge's timekeepers failed to beat the performance of Harrison's, so that Mudge died a somewhat disappointed man (in 1794). But Commander Gould subsequently re-analysed the performance of Mudge's first timekeeper in the light of the formula used from 1840 onwards, when he found that it produced a trial number of 11.73 (as against 124.4 for Harrison's No. 4) which was only surpassed, and then by a very narrow margin, in 1873, and would be highly creditable for any modern instrument.

THE FRENCH PIONEERS

Pierre Le Roy 1717–1785

Pierre Le Roy, famous son of a hardly less famous father, must be accounted among the foremost horologists of all time. He seems to have begun to interest himself in the problem of timekeeping at sea during the 1740's and in 1748 he presented l'Académie des Sciences a paper describing a more or less detached detent escapement of not very satisfactory design. There is no evidence that this design was ever put into effect, but the following passage in Le Roy's Memoire shows how deep an understanding he had, even at this early date, of the problems involved: "It seems to me that we ought to imitate the most experienced doctors. When nature works for the cure of their patients they take good care not to interfere with her; they content themselves with giving her a guiding hand to

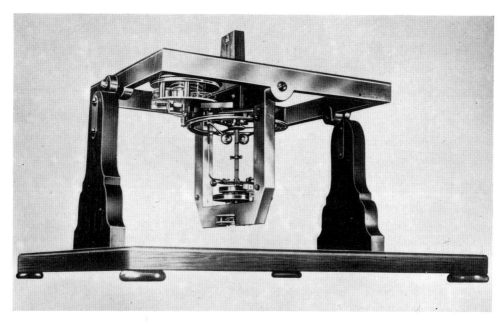

PLATE 133

Pierre Le Roy's marine timekeeper with detent escapement, complete in 1766. Note the double balance springs (at bottom of balance staff) and balance compensated by thermometers. Note also that the whole of the movement (top left-hand corner) takes up less space than the balance with its compensation which is about five inches in diameter. The wooden stand is modern. (Conservatoire des Arts et Métiers, Paris)

lead her in the required direction; they respect her and do not upset her with violent remedies of which the effect is nearly always mischievous. It is on this principle that I have tried to proceed in the construction of the escapement now to be described and which I propose to call my *detent escapement*."

Le Roy continued his experiments until 1766, when he was called upon to demonstrate to Louis XV his final achievement, which must be accounted one of the most beautiful mechanisms ever designed for timekeeping.

The action, which is illustrated in Fig. 31, is both simple and certain in operation. Both locking and impulse take place at the rim of the balance. The escape wheel takes the form of a very light, six-pointed star and the detent is pivoted. Apart from Le Roy's earlier experiments, this was the world's first detached escapement.

As has already been quoted, Harrison, writing in about 1774, had expressed the ideal of incorpor-

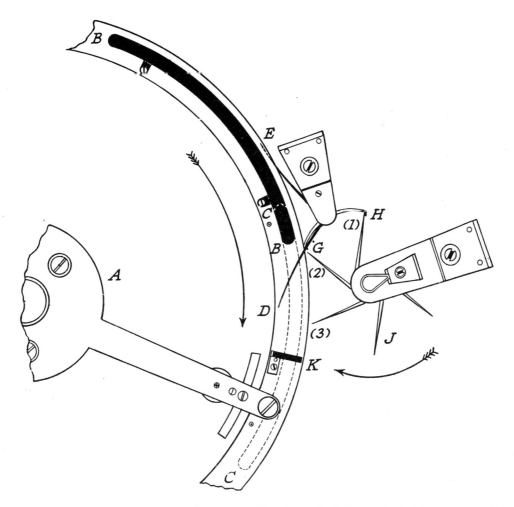

FIGURE 31. *Pierre Le Roy's detent escapement. The rim of the balance wheel A has segments B-B (shown in black) and C-C (shown dotted) projecting from its upper and lower sides. The pivoted detent has four arms in all, two of which, D and E (shown black) register with B-B and C-C. The other two G and H (shown white) register with the teeth (numbered 1, 2, 3) of the escape wheel J. K, is the impulse pallet, fixed to the rim of A. The action is as follows: The balance is shown about halfway through its clockwise swing and tooth (1) of J is locked on H. B-B is about to engage with D thus turning the detent and unlocking tooth (1) from H. The balance then continues uninterrupted to complete its swing. J being unlocked, starts to rotate but is locked again almost immediately by tooth (2) engaging with G. On the return swing of the balance, C-C engages with E, turning the detent and unlocking tooth (2) from G. Tooth (3) then imparts impulse to the balance via pallet K. H is once more in the path of the escape wheel and locks it on tooth (2) and so on.*

ating the compensation for heat and cold in the balance itself, which he had never been able to achieve. Had he but known it, this had already been done by Le Roy in 1766.

For his compensation Le Roy used a thermometer filled partly with alcohol and partly with mercury. The thermometer was so arranged that when the temperature was cold the mercury moved outwards towards the rim of the balance, thus slowing the machine, and vice versa. Later (in 1769) he was the first to make a bi-metallic compensation balance but he always preferred his thermometric balance, and with some justice, since it can be made free from the defect known as 'middle temperature'; error shortly to be described, which was inherent in all bimetallic balances for upwards of half a century after Le Roy's invention.

Le Roy used two spiral balance springs and experimentally discovered the length for which they were isochronous. He then adjusted for rate by timing screws on the balance itself.

The balance was suspended from a wire and its pivots ran between friction rollers. Accordingly, on account of its freedom from any degenerating lubricant, its isochronism, its theoretically perfect compensation, and its detached escapement the instrument had every quality to endow it with an excellent performance. And so confident of it was Le Roy that he took the minimum of trouble over the train in which the wheels ran in plain brass holes, there is no remontoire, and even no fusee, but only a plain going barrel. The chronometer ran for 38 hours. A weakness of the instrument was that the balance moved through an arc of barely 100 degrees.

Trial at sea showed that Le Roy's timekeeper just about equalled the superb performance of Harrison's No. 4 and he expressed the view that it was incapable of further improvement. Several seem to have been made but it is thought that only one survives, in the Conservatoire des Arts et Métiers at Paris. It and No. 4 are certainly the most famous marine chronometers in the world.

But whereas Harrison forced an inferior design to work superlatively well, Le Roy made a superlative design which would work as well with quite ordinary workmanship, and in so doing he set the stage for the next step in the development of the marine chronometer.

Ferdinand Berthoud 1729–1807

Berthoud was a prolific experimenter and writer in the early development of the marine chronometer and among his 70 products scarcely two are alike. He can show as good a claim as Arnold or Earnshaw to have invented the spring detent, but apart from this, and the general value of his experiments and writings, he left no permanent mark on the development of the marine chronometer.

ENGLISH DEVELOPMENT

John Arnold 1736–1799; Thomas Earnshaw 1749–1829

These two English horologists are best considered together, since their work so largely overlaps. Arnold, the elder, made his first chronometer in 1770. It incorporated a plain steel balance, spiral balance spring, compensation curb, detached escapement, and an unusual form of pivoted detent. It was not successful.

In 1773 he made a number of pocket chronometers with a more normal type of pivoted detent.

In 1776 he began to fit his instruments with compensated bi-metallic balances of which he evolved several patterns during the rest of his life, and with helical balance springs.

He was the first to use helical balance springs, frequently made of gold, and in 1782 he patented inward-curved terminals by which, purely empirically, he achieved isochronism.

PLATE 134

*Typical John Arnold Marine
Chronometer (number 26), circa
1790, showing his final type of
bimetallic balance wheel and helical balance and spring detent.
Arnold did not use gimbals.*
(British Museum)

In 1779 one of his pocket chronometers (No. 36 made in 1776) was worn over a period of 13 months during which time its total error was only 2 minutes 33 seconds and its daily rate never varied more than 2 seconds on consecutive days.

In 1780 he produced his final form of escapement with spring detent.

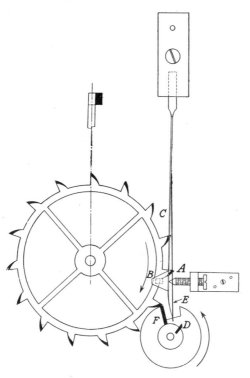

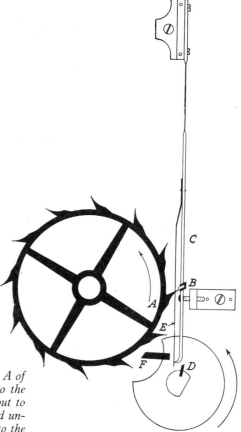

FIGURE 32. *Arnold's spring detent escapment. As drawn, tooth A of the escape wheel is locked on the locking pallet B attached to the detent C. The discharging pallet D on the balance staff is about to engage with the passing spring E thus deflecting the detent and unlocking the escape wheel which will thereupon impart impulse to the balance via impulse pallet F. C returns to its normal position and locks the next tooth of the escape wheel. On the return swing of the balance, D will deflect E away from C and so pass it without moving C. The teeth of the escape wheel have projections from the plane of the balance rim, shown black on the drawing, and a side view of one tooth is also shown separately.*

FIGURE 33. *Earnshaw's spring detent escapement. The action, and various parts, are as in Fig. 32 above, except that the escape wheel turns in the opposite direction and as drawn the passing action is about to take place.*

Thomas Earnshaw, 13 years younger than Arnold, started by working for John Brockbank and some time about 1780 he also evolved a spring detent escapement. Being unable to afford a patent he made an arrangement with one Wright, who, however, did not apply for a patent until 1783, by which time Arnold had produced his. The great similarity of the two designs is shown by the accompanying illustrations which also make clear the working of the spring detent. This in fact consists of two springs, one very much weaker than the other. The strong spring is fixed to the watch plate and on it is mounted the locking pallet. This spring does not quite extend into the path of the discharging

PLATE 135

Typical Thomas Earnshaw marine chronometer, circa 1800, showing his type of bimetallic balance wheel and helical balance spring. The escapement is spring detent. Note the mounting is gimbals.
(British Museum)

pallet on the balance staff. Fixed to the strong spring is one very much weaker, which does extend into the path of the discharging pallet. As the latter swings in an anticlockwise direction (as seen in the illustration) the pallet presses the weak, or 'passing' spring against the stronger spring, moving both and so unlocking the escape wheel, which imparts impulse to the impulse pallet. On its return swing the discharging pallet bends the passing spring away from the stronger spring, which is undisturbed. Thus, as in Le Roy's original design, impulse is only imparted to the balance on alternate beats.

Earnshaw hotly accused Brockbank of betraying his design to Arnold and the rights of the matter have never been established. In any case, Arnold and Earnshaw were always at loggerheads for one reason or another. Quite probably Earnshaw, Arnold and Berthoud all evolved the spring detent independently at about the same time. As opposed to the pivoted detent, its great advantage is that there is no pivot to be oiled.

Arnold's escape wheel has teeth of which the impulse faces are epicycloidal in shape, the object being that these should impart impulse as smoothly as possible; but Earnshaw used a pointed tooth which hit the pallet and did not remain in contact with it. Arnold's is, perhaps, the best in theory, but Earnshaw's design proved better in practice, and his has remained the standard chronometer escapement almost without alteration, up to the present time.

Earnshaw also invented the modern method of making bi-metallic balances, in which Arnold and Le Roy had previously shaped the two segmental strips independently, rivetted the two strips together, and screwed them to the cross-bar. Earnshaw ran molten brass onto the rim of a steel disk from which he then cut his balance, which was thus a perfectly homogeneous whole. The wheel was then turned to shape and the rim cut to allow the compensation to operate.

Although Earnshaw's escapement proved, in the long run, to be better than Arnold's, his methods of springing were inferior and he used an untempered spring, either spiral or helical. To make matters worse, on his pocket chronometers he as often as not used a compensation curb and a plain steel balance. As the non-isochronous, soft spring fatigued its rate progressively altered over a long period.

Therefore, it may be said that Arnold and Earnshaw share pretty equally the honours of having evolved the marine chronometer as we know it today. What is even more important is the fact that they produced them in considerable quantities at moderate prices. Each process was carried out by different, specialist workmen, and Earnshaw and Arnold themselves only carried out the final springing and adjustment.

Gradually the small band of pioneers was joined by others, but in the eighteenth century the number was small; notably, Barraud, Brockbank, Emery, Margetts, Haley, Jamison, Peto, Hardy and Pennington

Earnshaw, the youngest of the pioneers, lived on to the age of 80, and did not die until 1829, by which time the marine chronometer was practically commonplace.

LATER DEVELOPMENT OF THE MARINE CHRONOMETER

The only permanent improvements to the marine chronometer, since the time of Arnold and Earnshaw, have been in connection with springing, and compensation. Earnshaw's standard escapement has remained practically unaltered, although not for lack of people who tried to do better, including the incomparable Breguet, and Cole, Frodsham, Hardy, Ulrich, Pettavel, Leslie, Gowland,

Benoit, Riefler, Hillgren and many others whose inventions cannot here be described, for lack of space, and none of them has stood the test of time. Latterly, however, the lever escapement has begun to rival the detached chronometer escapement, especially in the hands of the eminent horologist, P. Ditisheim.

The bi-metallic balance of brass and steel has the inherent shortcoming that a graph of its compensation effect at different temperatures does not follow a straight line. Accordingly, it will only perform to any given rate at two particular temperatures. In the early nineteenth century many

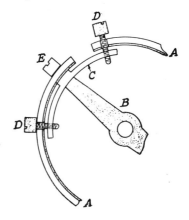

FIGURE 34. *Auxiliary compensation balance. The normal bimetallic rims A, A are attached to the cross-bar B. B also carries a segment C with screws D, D threaded into it. These screws pass through, but do not normally touch, the bimetallic rims, which are drilled for the purpose. By suitable adjustment of the screws their heads will limit the movement of the rims in extreme temperatures, thus mitigating middle temperature error. Screw E is nothing to do with the compensation, being merely the normal timing screw.*

attempts were made to counteract this failing and in general they have consisted of secondary bimetallic strips attached to the balance in a variety of ways and places. Some are continuous in action and some only come into operation outside certain temperatures.

The latter, although theoretically not so good, are more easily made, and robust, and have proved the most popular. Mercer's is illustrated as a typical example. Nevertheless, this shortcoming of the bimetallic balance encouraged various of the foremost horologists to persevere with the mercurial balance; notably E. T. Loseby, J. G. Ulrich and R. Gardner. But the extreme difficulty of making it and, particularly, of securing perfect equilibrium at all temperatures, has discouraged most others from seeking perfection in this direction.

More simple and successful has been the 'Integral' balance of Edouard Guillaume whose metallurgical researches have so greatly advanced the cause of horology.

The 'Integral' balance looks much the same as any other bi-metallic compensating balance, but the steel used is a special nickel alloy which, in conjunction with the brass, practically eliminates middle-temperature error.

Various materials have been used for balance springs, in which resistance to rust, magnetism, and fatigue are important considerations. Gold possesses these qualities but it is heavy and requires very powerful compensation. Glass is also an excellent material but although it is quite strong, a glass spring is very difficult to make. It requires very little compensation but tends to crystallise. Palladium springs were introduced in 1880. They are rustless and non-magnetic, and do not show such pronounced acceleration during their early life as do steel springs. As against this, palladium springs are not so elastic as steel and cannot be tempered.

Elinvar is an alloy composed of steel, nickel and chromium, developed for balance springs by E. Guillaume. It has virtually no change of elasticity in differing temperatures. 'Elinvar' is a variant of

'Invar', which is an alloy consisting of a fairly critical amount of nickel, roughly 36%, and in this proportion the alloy has virtually no co-efficient of expansion at varying temperatures. It is therefore probable that chronometers in future will increasingly employ a Guillaume type of balance spring and uncut balance.

Arnold experimentally produced an isochronous helical balance spring and Breguet did the same for a spiral spring by twisting the outside coil upwards, clear of the other coils, and curving it in again in the centre. Naturally, no truly isochronous balance spring can be fitted with a regulator and they are accordingly said to be 'free-sprung'. Their rate can only be adjusted by screws on the rim of the balance wheel itself, and these are fitted at the ends of the cross-bar where their adjustment will not interfere with the compensation. Other screws in the balance rim are for the purpose of adjusting the equilibrium and compensation characteristics of the balance.

Despite the early empirical achievements of Le Roy, Mudge, Arnold, Breguet and a few others in making isochronous balance springs, it was not until 1861 that M. Philips enunciated the properties of isochronism in mathematical terms, and pointed out that a pre-requisite to full isochronism is that the centre of gravity of the spring should always lie on the axis of the balance.

Truly can it be said that in no branch of horology has so much ingenuity and untiring experiment been devoted to the search for perfection, as in the construction of the marine chronometer.

CONCLUSION TO HISTORICAL SECTION

Between the planetarium clock of De'Dondi and the last masterpieces of Breguet lie five centuries of incessant striving towards perfection. Few other mechanisms in use today can show such a long unbroken sequence of development.

The Italians led the world during the fourteenth and fifteenth centuries, after which the lead was held by Germany and France for the next century and a half. This era marked the development of the watch and portable timekeeper, but saw little advance in accurate timekeeping.

In the third quarter of the seventeenth century the Dutchman Huygens evolved the pendulum and spiral balance spring and thus transformed the whole science of horology. But the continental makers failed to grasp the full implication of his work and it fell to the English, under the leadership of Tompion, to gain a pre-eminence in the new field of accurate timekeeping which they held for over a century and a half.

In the eighteenth century Graham brought the pendulum clock to a degree of accuracy beyond which further advance is of interest only to astronomers, and Mudge invented the lever escapement for watches. After the pioneer, but unfruitful work of Harrison and Le Roy, it was the English makers Arnold and Earnshaw who developed the marine chronometer virtually as it is known today, and English makers as a whole were concerned with the production of accurate pocket watches to the exclusion of other considerations.

In France, however, Breguet used the Lepine calibre to develop the modern watch, while conceding little to the English in accuracy of timekeeping, so that the French regained the lead which they had lost more than a century previously.

And finally, the Swiss Japy laid the foundations of the mass-produced watch which enables Switzerland to lead the world in horology over a century later.

By 1830 all the essentials of modern horology were in existence and this was the date logically chosen at which to end the seventh edition. Horological history since 1830 has seen the refinement and finally the decline of the British-made watch; and the development of mass-production in Switzerland and America. Precision time keeping has been brought to a very high level of perfection, both in watches and clocks. These developments are traced in the additional chapter which has been written for the eighth edition.

CHAPTER VI

French clocks 1660–1830

INTRODUCTORY

FRENCH and English pendulum clocks differ in almost every respect, and only after 1800 did the national styles again begin to merge. The great French styles are covered by the reigns of Louis XIV, XV and XVI and it is amazing to reflect that the first two Monarchs between them reigned for 130 years.

In all forms of French art, including clocks, dates are rarely mentioned, but only styles, associated with the reigns of the Kings. Unfortunately, the styles do not exactly fit the reigns.

The dates of the reigns are: Louis XIII 1610–43. Louis XIV 1643–1715. Regency 1715–23. Louis XV 1723–74. Louis XVI 1774–90. Directoire 1795–9. Empire 1800–30.

Before passing to a particular examination of clocks it may be found helpful to consider very briefly the trends of fashion through these various styles, and in this connection it is important to remember that the design of French clock cases is to be related far more closely to contemporary furniture-styles than was the case in England. In France, the furnishing of a room was treated in a far more 'unified' fashion.

The Louis XIV style really corresponds to the Baroque, both in form and in its sombrely splendid colouring, such as the black and gold of Boulle. This style begins to give way from about 1700 onwards to a lighter, gayer manner, sometimes known as Régence, but more properly described as early rococo. The natural colours of wood play a greater part and mounts begin to disregard the architectural form of the clock case. Under the influence of two designers (*not* executive artists) Meissonier and Pineau, the rococo style attains its apogee about 1730–5; all classical forms disappear, asymmetry is widely used, and vegetable and animal forms rather than architectural features comprise the main element of the decoration. Partly in reaction against the exaggerations of this rococo style, the return to classical forms begins about the middle of the century. This movement received great impetus from the interest aroused by the rediscovery and excavation of Pompeii and Herculaneum (the important excavations began in 1749); by the mid-1760's a fully developed classical style (the Louis XVI style) was in existence, corresponding roughly to the Adam style in England. There is increasing emphasis on the imitation of classical models throughout the rest of the century. There is no essential break in style between the Louis XVI and the Directoire and Empire styles, the main difference being a lowering of the standards of craftsmanship owing to the impoverishment of France during the Revolution and the Napoleonic wars. Such features as the use of Egyptian Sphinxes appear at least thirty years or more before Napoleon's Egyptian campaign. A definite break, however, occurs at the Restoration in 1815, when patronage finally passed from the aristocracy to the middle classes, giving rise to a riotous demand for 'styles' rather than style.

A marked difference in outlook between English and French clocks is that in England it is the maker of the movement who matters, and the name of the casemaker is never known, whereas in France the maker of the case is at least equally important, and after about 1750 his name is generally known. In that year orders were promulgated that members of the Guild of *Ébénistes* (roughly speaking, cabinet makers and carpenters) should stamp their names on their pieces. This did not apply to metal cases where the maker's name seldom appears, and when a famous name is stamped on a metal case, it is generally to be regarded with considerable suspicion.

The movements of French clocks are often of superb quality. Early examples display a refreshingly robust vigour; while the later influence of such men as the two Le Roys, Berthoud and Breguet, brought in an era of unsurpassed craftsmanship and ingenuity coupled with very high finish. The exuberant decoration, and sinuous and fanciful lines of most French clocks before Louis XVI seldom appear to advantage except in company with French furniture, and perhaps for this reason their considerable mechanical interest and merit has been somewhat undeservedly ignored by horological connoisseurs in England.

In about 1950 Editions Tardy published *La Pendule Française*, in five parts, covering the whole history of French clocks. The number of illustrations devoted to French clocks in the present book is necessarily limited and cannot hope to be fully representative. The reader wishing to become more fully acquainted with the many types of French clocks is therefore recommended to study them in the profusely illustrated *La Pendule Française*.

PLATE 136

Louis XIV mantel clock by Le Maire, circa 1670. The case is oak veneered with ebony and tortoise-shell with inlaid brass strips. 'Religieuse' clocks more frequently have fluted pilaster side panels to the door. Note the typical arched top, elaborate gilt hands and gilt chapter ring with all minutes marked, on a red velvet ground. The clock has going barrels, verge escapement and cycloidal cheeks.

LOUIS XIV 1643-1715

The reign of Louis XIII does not really concern us, for the purposes of this chapter, but the first type of French pendulum clock is called the 'Religieuse' and generally described as 'Louis XIII', although Louis himself had been dead for some 20 years before the first one appeared. In probable fact, the Religieuse is not of French origin at all, and took its inspiration from the first Dutch pendulum clocks of Samuel Coster, which it very closely resembles. It is an essentially architectural style, not unlike the earliest English bracket clocks, and it seems to have been designed sometimes to stand on its feet, and sometimes to hang on a wall.

The Religieuse clock has a rectangular frame with a pair of side pilasters on a plinth, supporting an arched or portico top. Between the pilasters is a glass in a narrow frame, generally rectangular, but in later examples sometimes arched. Behind the glass, either in the arch or right at the top of the

PLATE 137

Louis XIV mantel clock by Mazurier of Paris, late seventeenth century, typical of the transition from the 'Religieuse' proper to the fully developed Louis XIV style found after 1700. Note dome top; free-standing side columns; minute hand less elaborate than 'Religieuse'; boulle decoration; early appearance of small figures on top. The movement has three trains and is musical.

PLATE 138

Movement of typical Louis XIV mantel clock by Du Chesne, Paris. Note large going barrel; pierced steel decorative detent for the striking train; baluster pillars pinned through the back plate; regulator consisting of an arbor round which is wound the thread from which the pendulum is suspended.

rectangular frame, is an annular silver, gilt or pewter chapter ring and, below it, some form of gilt decoration, backed by black or plum-coloured velvet filling the whole space visible through the glass. The door generally includes the pilasters, but sometimes is only the frame between them. One-handed clocks are rare. The two hands are usually gilt, elaborately pierced.

The pilasters have acanthus capitals and are fluted, though the flutes may be only indicated by inlay. Twisted columns instead of pilasters are rare; also, very rare and only found in the earlier clocks, are plain uprights decorated with marqueterie in tortoise-shell.

Later clocks, probably not properly called Religieuses, have round columns instead of pilasters.

All available flat surfaces have marqueterie of brass or white metal and tortoise-shell, and three finials or vases are at the ends and centre of the arched top. It is rare to find cast and gilt corner pieces in the spandrels of the doors. Later clocks may have a basket top and no plinth, but these are transitional in style from the Religieuse to the Louis XIV style proper. Also in these transitional pieces the velvet 'dial plate' becomes curtailed, and the pendulum bob is seen swinging behind the ornament below the chapter ring. The framework of the case is generally walnut, with oak in the later clocks.

With the establishment of the Louis XIV style proper, about the middle of the reign, the decoration becomes more and more elaborate. The architectural shape of the Religieuse is given up. Side columns are turned sideways and are covered with ornamentation, and soon disappear. The arched top gives place to basket and inverted bell types, and these become narrower until they just provide a small platform for a gilt figure, generally large compared with the earlier finials or vases.

PLATE 139

Typical late Louis XIV mantel clock in the 'Grand Style'. Note arched top carrying a fairly large figure; also use of figures on base; enamel hour plaques on engraved gilt dial plate; undecorated minute hand; pendulum bob visible below dial plate; case veneered with tortoiseshell with applied gilt ornament.
(Wallace Collection, London)

The front of the clock is a framework with heavily carved arched top; ormolu figures and decorative pieces are applied at the upper corners, and gradually spread to almost every part that has space for them. Reaching the bottom corners, they give the clock a shape gradually widening to its base and, in later clocks, the frame itself is slightly waisted or curved outwards towards the base. What is known as the 'Grand Style' lasted up to the end of the seventeenth century and then merged into the 'Regency' with an increasing exuberance of applied ornament.

The typical Louis XIV dial has white enamel plaques for the hour figures on a dial plate of gilt repoussé metal. In watches, these did not appear before 1690, but they were used earlier on clocks. They accord with the Louis XIV clock, but are somewhat inelegant on a watch. Generally, there were no minute figures, but 5-minute enamel plaques are found and the engraving of every minute on a narrow gilt band is not uncommon.

Hands became simpler; the minute hand especially had little or no piercing.

This was the great period of marqueterie of tortoise-shell and brass or white metal, which was brought to perfection by Charles André Boulle, 1642–1732. As in all marqueterie, two sets of pieces were made together, by sawing superimposed sheets of shell and metal. By using a very fine saw, both sets could be used, to produce an inlay of metal in a shell ground, and an inlay of shell in a metal ground. The former, called the first part, was more prized than the latter, called the second or counterpart.

Boulle's sons continued their father's work and Boulle marquetry was used as a form of decoration on furniture throughout the eighteenth century. No one, however, achieved the perfection of craftsmanship and design evolved by Charles André Boulle himself.

The wood of the case on which the marqueterie sheet was laid was almost always oak, though it was nowhere visible externally, since the parts not covered by the Boulle decoration were veneered with ebony.

The bracket clocks were generally called mantel clocks by the French, *horloges de cheminée*, but so many were made with their own wall brackets, which followed the design and decoration of the clocks, that their use on brackets must have been as frequent as on mantels. Sometimes one finds a plinth evidently belonging to the clock, three to four inches high; the clock with its own feet stands on the base which again has its feet. These probably were intended for mantel clocks.

Then appeared a type of clock, found nowhere outside France, and at no other period, in which a bracket clock was provided with its own tall pedestal, giving the general appearance of a long-case clock, though the clock remained a spring-driven clock with short pendulum and verge escapement. These clocks appear at the end of the reign of Louis XIV and during the Regency period, that is, during the first quarter of the eighteenth century.

Real long-case clocks, with weights and seconds pendulums are rare until after 1700. France was far behind England in adopting the long-case clock, and it never achieved the popularity it had in England. It is probable that this was due to the French continuing to use the verge escapement when the English, except country makers, had quite given it up. With a verge escapement, the small arc of swing which a long-case imposes makes a seconds pendulum difficult, although not impossible to accommodate.

PLATE 140 (*opposite, left*)

Late Louis XIV spring-driven clock with its own pedestal; the movement by Minuel. Note increasingly curvilinear treatment and appearance of a slight waist; figure above arched top; tortoiseshell with brass inlay and applied gilt ornament. The whole is of particularly superb and rich quality.
(Wallace Collection, London)

PLATE 141 (*opposite, right*)

Louis XV long-case clock by Gudin, circa 1750. A late example of the bulging case, originally designed to take a wide-arc, long pendulum, but unnecessary in this instance, where the escapement is a Graham-type dead-beat. The clock has perpetual calendar and equation work. The signed case is by Duhamel.
(Conservatoire des Arts et Métiers, Paris)

211

The tall pedestals, bringing the clock dial above eye level, nearly always tapered downwards to a narrow base; a rectangular shape is rare. They are decorated with the same sumptuous profusion of marqueterie and ormolu as the clock itself. It was probably due to the tapering shape of these pedestals, that the long-case clock, when it did come in, was too narrow at pendulum bob level for an adequate swing of the pendulum and was given a bulge for the bob, which made the cases singularly inelegant. The long-case clock was called in France a *Régulateur*, or *Horloge de parquet*.

REGENCY 1715–1723

Returning to the bracket or mantel clock, always a favourite in France, the chief feature of the Regency style is the abolition of the straight line. The sides of the case, from the circular top, curved inwards to give the clock a waist and, from the waist, curved outwards again to the feet. These were often formed by figures or gilded castings applied to the corners of the case at the bottom, while between them, the bottom edge of the case carried a mass of ormolu ornament, all with curved outlines, generally merging into an elaborate figure group or plaque rising centrally up to the bottom of the dial.

The top of the case too became curved everywhere and most often supported a large figure. Symmetry remained in the shape and decoration of the case proper, but asymmetry appeared in the central and topmost figure groups.

Dials and hands did not alter to any great extent but the 'thirteen piece' dial appeared as a transition from the characteristic enamel plaque dial of Louis XIV to the one-piece enamel dial of Louis XV. The thirteen-piece dial consists of a central enamel plate, surrounded by twelve hour plaques.

LOUIS XV 1723–1774

The Regency style had displayed an increasingly naturalistic and lively spirit, in contrast to the dignified grandeur of the true Louis XIV. It prepared the way for the Louis XV style proper, which had developed by about 1730 and continued until 1750. This period is essentially rococo, but after 1750 the long trend towards extreme exuberance had spent itself and there was a gradual return to simplicity and straight lines, in preparation for the Louis XVI style which thus became established during the previous reign.

Bracket clocks from about 1725–35 had a more marked waist and, generally, developed a more graceful form, with less profuse ornamentation. This had a tendency towards asymmetry, but it was not aggressive. The straight line was still banished.

Then the wooden case for bracket clocks tended to give way to a bronze casting, generally a mass of curved forms with shell and foliage motifs. Symmetry of ornament gradually gave way to tormented shapes devoid of any pattern.

The casemaker acquired importance, and after 1750 wooden cases are almost invariably signed. Phillippe Caffiéri, 1714–1774, was, perhaps, the most famous caster and chiseller, and inclined more

PLATE 142 (*opposite*)

Mid-Louis XV mantel clock by C. Daillé with rococco bronze gilt, asymmetrical case with typical figures on top. The pendulum bob in the form of sun-rays is visible through the window below the dial. The base contains a musical box. (Wallace Collection, London)

213

PLATE 144 (*right*)

Louis XV clock by Jean Baptiste Baillon. Metal case with typical Caffieri elephant. The base contains a musical box.

towards symmetry, while Juste Aurèle Meissonier, 1675–1750, was the apostle of asymmetry. It needed an artist of the first rank to make cases of the latter types that were not repulsive.

In long-case clock cases the curves became more tortuous. A bulge for the pendulum bob, generally with spy-hole, was usual. Even when the clock was a real long-case clock with seconds pendulum, it was often given the appearance of a bracket clock on a pedestal; it is characteristic of the style that the naturally flat top of the part simulating a pedestal was nearly always curved.

The wooden cases of the long-case clocks and of the earlier bracket clocks were usually of oak covered with marqueterie of shell and metal or of coloured woods, but veneers of various decorative hard woods are not uncommon.

A decorative process which had first appeared in the reign of Louis XIV is the use of horn, both in place of shell in marqueterie, and as a base for painted subjects and decoration. The sheets of horn were attached to the oak case, but were first coloured on the back faces and

PLATE 143

Early Louis XV spring-driven clock by Prevost au Havre, typical of the Regency period, with thirteen-piece dial. (The fully developed thirteen-piece dial, however, was wholly enamel, with no metal mounts visible.)

215

216

PLATE 145 (*left*)

Louis XV clock by Julien Le Roy decorated with porcelain flowers and figures. Note completely asymmetrical design; one-piece dial; asymmetrical disposition of winding holes.

PLATE 146 (*right*)

Louis XV 'cartel' clock by Fieffé. Note all-metal, asymmetrical case containing a half-seconds pendulum.
(Wallace Collection, London)

PLATE 147 *(left)*

Long-case clock by Ferdinand Berthoud,
typical of the transition from Louis XV to
Louis XVI. Note the return to straight
lines and symmetry; also Harrison-type
gridiron pendulum. The dial at the top of
trunk is a barometer. The case is stamped
B. Lieutard (died 1780).
(Wallace Collection, London)

often painted with flower decoration. The tortuous panels or strips with horn covering were always in frames of cast ormolu work.

The other new form of decoration was *Vernis Martin*, which became very popular towards the middle of the century for furniture and clock cases. The importance of Vernis Martin was that it enabled the rococo decorators to introduce a wide range of colour into their work, and colour was one of the most important ingredients of rococo taste. It was the most successful of any European attempts to imitate oriental lacquer. Robert Martin, 1706–65 and his brother, who invented this process in about 1730, were appointed Vernisseurs to the King in 1733. Their lacquer was used for

PLATE 148 *(right)*

Louis XVI clock by Bouchard. Note the introduction of marble in the base with bronze decoration.

PLATE 149 *(left)*

Louis XVI Regulator by Le Paute, circa 1770. The case by Nicolas Petit. Pin-wheel escapement; gridiron pendulum; equation work. Note the brass-gilt decoration. (Conservatoire des Arts et Métiers, Paris)

both European and oriental style decorations. The oak case was generally covered with a veneer of pearwood, which has a much closer grain than oak and provided a better ground for the background colour of the lacquer.

Towards the end of the Louis XV period, clocks were often supported on animals or grotesque figures. Elephants were a speciality of the Caffiéris.

Porcelain, generally in combination with ormolu, came into use, sometimes as figures on the base, sometimes as flowers on a tree, with a clock face in the branches, and clocks of this type are greatly prized.

The Louis XV period brought in a type of clock which never found any favour in England – the Cartel or wall clock. The clock was set in a frame of cast and gilt bronze or of gilt carved wood, the frame being lengthened downwards to admit a half-seconds pendulum. At this time in France, highly carved and partially gilded panelling was the main feature of wall decoration. These panels were unsuitable for paintings, but the rococo forms of Cartel clocks and barometers blended admirably with their decoration.

The thirteen-piece dial remained fashionable until about the middle of the century when the dial makers succeeded in producing a large porcelain dial in one piece; the dial with separate plaques then quickly disappeared.

Hands, and especially the minute-hands, again became more elaborate. They were usually of steel, finely pierced and shaped.

LOUIS XVI 1774–1790

The reign of Louis XVI began in 1774, but the style may be regarded as covering most of the second half of the eighteenth century. It was the finest period of French clockmaking, both in design and craftsmanship. There was a return to symmetry and the straight line. Bronze work on a large scale continued for structural purposes, but ornamentation is mostly on quite a small scale.

In the last two decades there was a growing tendency towards a slavish copying of the antique which also characterised the immediately post-revolutionary 'Directoire' style.

Dials are smaller, and the clocks are generally mantel clocks and not bracket clocks. Perhaps the chief characteristic of the mantel clock is the use of white marble, with applied decoration of gilt bronze in the form of panels and mouldings. Sometimes the whole construction is of marble; sometimes a marble base supports a clock case constructed wholly of bronze. Cases are frequently executed in bronze, less commonly in marble and occasionally in biscuit porcelain. Wood continued in use for cases, especially in the provinces, and for long-case clocks.

The long-case clock is a far more graceful piece of furniture than it was in the previous period. There is a tendency towards a rather small dial, and the precision clock, corresponding to what in England is called a regulator, has, generally, a rectangular case of the same width from the top of the dial to the plinth, with a glass door; in spite of the completely plain outer form, these clocks often achieve great beauty.

Towards the end of the period, a type of mantel clock became common which may be called the 'column' clock. There are two side supports carrying a portico top and with the clock hung between them. The supports may be marble with appliqué bronze decoration, or each may be a pair of cylindrical columns or a pair of caryatides; or they may be bronze figures.

Perhaps the most graceful type of mantel clock is the lyre clock, appearing also near the end of the period. The frame of the lyre may be marble with bronze mounts, or it may be bronze; often enamel and diamenté decoration is added. The clock face is central in the lower circular space of the lyre, while the gridiron pendulum rises up to simulate the strings of the lyre. Sometimes the bob of the pendulum is a large ring, set with paste brilliants and brought forward to be in the plane of the clock face. Since the pendulum is above the clock mechanism it is the bob which connects with the escapement.

Throughout the second half of the eighteenth century clocks were frequently made with horizontal turning hour and minute rings. Most commonly the construction includes a marble or bronze-gilt vase or urn, standing on a marble base, with a snake pointing to the hour with its tongue, or a figure stretching up an arm and pointing with a finger. The appropriateness of the snake for this purpose is that it is an emblem of eternity, and hence a symbol of Time.

Dials are always of white enamel in a single piece. Sometimes they are annular, showing the

PLATE 150

Louis XVI clock by Robin. Note the typical arrangement of metal base, supporting side figures and urn on top; simple Breguet-type hands; use of less heavy numerals on the dial than formerly.
(Wallace Collection, London)

221

PLATE 151

Louis XVI clock by Tavernier, a popular type of marble case in which the movement is supported by two columns. The base is a large musical box. (Conservatoire des Arts et Métiers, Paris)

PLATE 152 (*right*)

Louis XVI 'Lyre' clock by Kinable. Note mock gridiron pendulum simulating the strings of the lyre; ring of paste brilliants forming part of the pendulum and encircling the dial; delicately painted signs of the zodiac outside the chapter ring, in the style of Coteau. The movement is below the pendulum. A very fine example of this favourite Louis XVI style. (Victoria and Albert Museum, London)

223

PLATE 153

Louis XVI 'Ring and Snake' vase clock. The ring-type chapter rings (for hours and minutes) rotate and the time is indicated by the head of the snake (symbol of eternity)

movement through the centre. Large minute figures remain later than they did in English clocks, and although there is a tendency for them to become small in later clocks, they are found very large right to the end of the period. Dials are nearly always clear, well designed and well executed. Towards the end of the period, certain dial painters (Coteau and Dubuisson were outstanding) achieved fame for really beautiful work, painting garlands of flowers for ordinary clocks, or signs of the zodiac in a ring of cartouches for calendar and astronomical clocks.

Among the graceful manifestations of the Louis XVI style was a return to something closely resembling the Religieuse. A glass front is flanked by slender columns supporting a break-arch top with a circular dial of simple design. The pendulum swings below the dial, visible through the glass front.

In contrast with this simplified style there was a simultaneous return to the Grand Style of Louis XIV, particularly as executed by Boulle, which had never gone out of fashion throughout the whole of the eighteenth century. These 'throw-backs' may be detected by the accuracy of the workmanship and general finish, and by the later style of the movement. The difference between Louis XVI and Louis XIV Boulle is in the bold character of the mounts on the former. But the two styles are often indistinguishable in this particular medium.

Hands on Louis XVI clocks are generally elaborate; indeed, the minute hand, often fairly plain under Louis XV, is generally as much decorated as the hour hand. Lattice-work designs were especially popular. Gilt brass is more usual than steel.

The pendulum bob, when visible, is highly decorated, most usually in the form of sunrays.

DIRECTOIRE 1795–1799

This style embraces the Revolution period and marks the transition from Louis XVI to Empire. It has no very well-defined characteristics beyond a general continuance of the neo-classic Louis

PLATE 154

Directoire 'Régulateur de Cheminée' by Lepaute. Note the severe simplicity of line.

PLATE 155

Empire clock with urn on top, reminiscent of the similar, but more ornate, Louis XVI clock in Plate 150. The movement by Julien Le Roy is earlier than the case which was made to house it.

XVI style; it is exemplified by some very grotesque and ugly clocks. The decorative motives of the clock cases are generally taken from ancient Greek art. In its progress towards the Empire, the period also produced some superb, quite plain bureau clocks. The Revolutionary influence is displayed by a certain number of decimal dials.

EMPIRE 1800–1830

This period, which continues up to the year selected as the terminating point of this book, comprises the Consulate (1799–1804), Napoléon I (1804–15), Louis XVIII (1815–24), and Charles X

PLATE 156

*Empire clock by Cronier. Marble and bronze case with figures; a development of the similar Louis XVI
style as in Plate 148.*

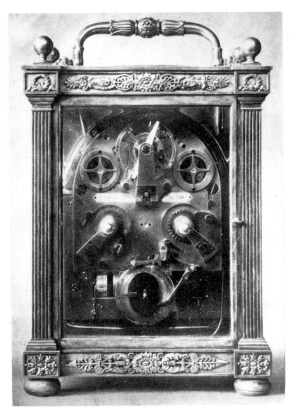 

PLATE 157

Empire travelling clock by Breguet, number 780. The case is gilt and the dial silver. The parts of the dial not polished are engine-turned. The clock is a repeater and incorporates equation work and perpetual calendar. The escapement is detent and tourbillon. Note Breguet's style of compensated bimetallic balance wheel.
(Ashmolean Museum, Oxford)

(1824–30). As with the contemporary English Regency, an overall 'Style' comprehended a considerable number of widely differing 'Tastes' (as, for example, the 'Greek', 'Gothic' and 'Egyptian' taste). Greek influence was perhaps stronger in France than in England, where its chief apostle was the oppressively scholarly Thomas Hope. Simultaneously, and no doubt as a sort of nostalgic recollection of the old régime, there was a quite widespread reproduction of the Louis XV and XVI styles, especially in Boulle.

The clock with columns continued for a time and some of the neatest clocks found are of this type. A favourite later type was a chariot or vehicle drawn by some animal, with a clock face in the wheel, where, the hands being indistinguishable from the spokes, it is practically impossible to read the time. But no combination of clock face with a group or structure could be too incongruous; for example, a vase, (bronze or porcelain), with a clock stuck in the side. A redeeming feature was the high craftsmanship of the decorative work. The figures and figure groups, although of fine execution, are far inferior to those of the Louis XVI period.

The materials used were bronze, gilt or with patina, marble of all kinds and colours, and porcelain.

Dials are smaller and often of gilt or silvered metal, though white enamel remains the most common. Hands are much more simple, and tend towards the plain steel moon hand which became very popular.

The very pinnacle of simple artistry was reached in the bureau clocks of Ferdinand Berthoud, Antide Janvier and Abraham-Louis Breguet. Using gilt or silver cases and dials, plain gold or steel moon hands, and the liberal application of engine-turning as the sole decoration, they achieved, by perfection of proportion and craftsmanship alone, a degree of elegance which has never been surpassed in the history of horology. Such refinement could not give complete satisfaction if it was only external, but it is, in fact, matched by even greater beauty and precision in the movements. Breguet made relatively few clocks, and very few pendulum clocks indeed. Many of Berthoud's also have balance-wheel escapements. Nor were other makers far behind, and Robin and the Le Roy firm, both names long-established in French horology, produced splendid examples. Breguet's greatest tour-de-force in this branch of horology was his 'Pendule Sympathique' which was designed and constructed in conjunction with what appears to be a normal Breguet pocket watch. This watch is fixed at night on to a bracket forming part of its parent clock which then sets it to time and moves the regulator by an amount proportional to its previous day's rate. The watch and clock are wound simultaneously by a single operation.

The simple style of long-case regulator, dating back in its inception to Louis XVI, continued with increased popularity and elegance. These mostly employ the Amant pin-wheel or Graham dead-beat escapement and Harrison gridiron pendulum.

After the Empire, French makers plunged with enthusiastic abandon into the wildest excesses of the Gothic revival and produced clocks whose repellence easily outdistances the worst that could be managed at the time in England. It was few beside the Breguet firm who could stem the tide and continue to produce clocks with the stamp of good breeding.

FRENCH PROVINCIAL CLOCKS

These appear to have received no systematic study and indeed, they are for the most part remarkably unattractive. Long-case clocks are found in many districts. The cases, usually of oak, are fairly plain, but their proportions are uncomfortable and suggest that the decision to put clockwork into them was fortuitous, and arrived at too late to make more than a bodged-up job of the business. Bracket clocks follow the styles of Paris, with less florid decoration, and attractive examples are found. Nevertheless, these gawky long-cases may house some splendid mechanism which repays the closest examination, with interesting local traditions. To take one example only, clocks from the Morbier district have an unique system of striking since, having struck the hour, they repeat the performance two minutes later. This is done by a form of rack striking with, necessarily, no warning mechanism. The rack itself is straight, being attached to a sliding rod which, being released only a second before the first stroke on the bell, falls by gravity on to the snail. The straight type of rack is also found in other provincial pieces.

MECHANISM

The general standard of workmanship under Louis XIV was inferior to that of the English makers,

but under Louis XV Julien Le Roy, first of the great
line of horologists, brought about a marked improvement which soon raised French horology once more to
a level at least comparable with the English.

The anchor escapement was never really popular in
France where the verge escapement survived longer than
in England, especially in long-case clocks. By the use of
very long pallets it was found possible to operate a
39-inch pendulum with an arc little wider than that
required for an anchor escapement. Such pendulums
usually have three or four hinges in the rod and may be
folded up for travelling. The carting about of large
quantities of furniture in eighteenth century France was
much more common than in England. Verge escapements in mantel clocks were sometimes of the silent
variety, with silk or gut 'pallets'.

The French seem to have experimented with variants
of the anchor escapement where, by making one of the
pallets separate from the pendulum crutch, the pendulum was given some small measure of freedom. The first
of these was devised by Thiout, but although they are
much illustrated in eighteenth-century horological
books, it is doubtful if any examples have survived, so
that they are not of much practical interest.

In 1741 Amant devised the first of the many dead-
beat, 'pin-wheel' escapements which have been so popular in France. In the form used by Amant the escape
wheel, of large diameter, has pins projecting from its rim
and these engage alternately with the two pallets of the
pendulum. Like Graham's escapement, the pallets thus
have two quite separate faces, for locking and impulse.
The appearance of this escapement is shown in FIG. 35.
A fault in the original design was that the drop of the
pins on the locking faces was necessarily excessive, but
this was later remedied by cutting away the back half of
each pin, leaving the acting portion of the pin D-
shaped.

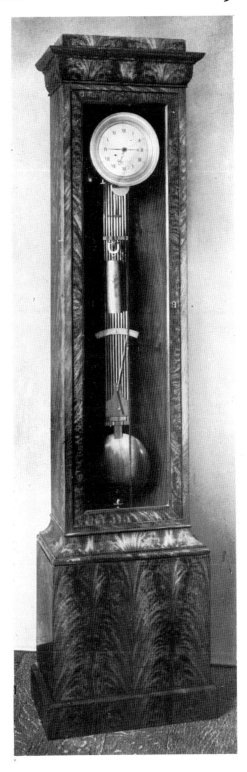

PLATE 158

*Empire regulator clock. Note typical extreme simplicity of line
and small dial; gridiron pendulum.*

Jean André Lepaute devised a modification of this escapement with the pins alternately on the two sides of the wheel. The supposed merit was that the locking faces were at the same radius. But only Lepaute seems to have used it and other makers produced a multiplicity of variations on the original theme by Amant.

During the second half of the eighteenth century French makers vied with each other in applying

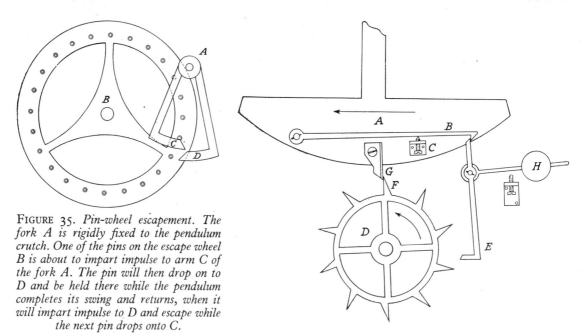

FIGURE 35. *Pin-wheel escapement. The fork A is rigidly fixed to the pendulum crutch. One of the pins on the escape wheel B is about to impart impulse to arm C of the fork A. The pin will then drop on to D and be held there while the pendulum completes its swing and returns, when it will impart impulse to D and escape while the next pin drops onto C.*

FIGURE 36. *Berthoud's detached pendulum escapement. Pendulum bob A carries a hinged claw B which normally rests by gravity against a stop C. When the pendulum swings from right to left, in the direction of the arrow, B collects detent E and carries it along with B whereupon the escape wheel D is unlocked and tooth F imparts impulse to the pendulum at G. Before the impulse is complete the claw B clears detent E which is returned to its previous position by a counterweight H and again locks the escapement immediately after the impulse stroke is complete. On the return swing of the pendulum the chamfered end of B rides over the similarly chamfered top of E without interference to either pendulum or escapement.*

a great variety of detached escapements to pendulum clocks. The first detached escapement had been invented by Pierre Le Roy in 1748 in the course of his evolution of a marine chronometer, but Ferdinand Berthoud was among the first to apply a detached escapement to a pendulum clock; this escapement of about 1760, illustrated in FIG. 36, is not only in all essentials a pivoted detent chronometer escapement, but the basis for all the variants which followed after. As with most of its successors, it was arranged for use in a 'Lyre' or similar clock where the movement is situated below the pendulum bob.

Several would-be refinements upon the Berthoud prototype incorporated a gravity-operated remontoire which was wound at each stroke by the escape wheel, and locked by the detent. It then imparted impulse to the pendulum. Yet despite the theoretical appeal of these detached and constant-force escapements they were not successful in practice, as applied to pendulum clocks, and they went out of fashion with the lyre-clock, in which they had a practical use.

Apart from these characteristically French escapements, French clocks as a whole have certain other mechanical features which differentiate them from their English contemporaries.

At no time were they as wedded to the fusee as were English makers; the going barrel was generally more popular. From about 1750 there was a pronounced trend towards lightness in all the parts, especially the pivots. The conservatism of the French in adhering to the verge escapement finds a parallel in their retention of the locking-plate mechanism for striking, long after rack striking had become almost universal in England. The French continued to use both systems impartially throughout the period of this chapter. They often arranged their trains so that the winding holes were asymmetrical in the dial. When there was only a going train its winding hole might be placed anywhere on the dial.

This chapter is devoted to clocks only, because the French watch developed along lines more closely related to other nationalities. The pioneer work of Pierre Le Roy and Ferdinand Berthoud on marine chronometers, and the evolution of the modern watch by Lepine and Breguet, are therefore described in the appropriate chapters elsewhere in this book.

CHAPTER VII

National styles

IN the five centuries of horology up to 1830 the lead has been taken, successively, by Italy, Germany, France, England and again France. Swiss supremacy was not established until after the period covered by this book.

These countries shaped the main thread of fashion and design, but others had national styles of their own which, while they had no widespread influence, are nevertheless in themselves artistic and interesting. The adequate study of each would require its own book, so that the present chapter can do no more than describe in barest outline the characteristics of the national schools; nor can more than the basic types be illustrated.

It is nevertheless hoped that this series of sketches, however inadequate, may serve as a general survey of the more important national styles.

It is noteworthy that, except for Switzerland, none of the countries in question has produced anything important or characteristic in the way of watches. It is in the manufacture of clocks only that they have excelled.

AMERICA

America cannot be said to have had a watchmaking industry before 1830. Most existing American watches were made after 1850. Thomas Harland had a business in Norwich, Connecticut, where he was reported to be making two hundred watches per annum soon after 1800, and Luther Goddard made about five hundred watches at Shrewsbury, Massachusetts, in the second decade of the nineteenth century. But these watches are not in themselves interesting and the chief interest in American horology before 1830 centres around their clocks.

The clockmaking industry in American had two quite distinct phases, divided fairly sharply by the year 1800. The eighteenth century was the time of individual craftsmen closely following English traditions; the early years of the nineteenth century saw the birth of American mass-production.

Clockmaking in eighteenth-century America must have been a precarious business because the population was so scattered; while the difficulty of obtaining brass enforced the general use of wooden movements, though a few early brass movements have survived. For these reasons it is remarkable what fine clocks were made by these lone craftsmen.

LONG-CASE CLOCKS

The individual craftsmen of the eighteenth century concentrated almost wholly upon long-case clocks which could be made with an absolute minimum of metal parts.

Possibly the earliest surviving example is by Abel Cottey, 1655–1711, who emigrated with William Penn and set up in Philadelphia in 1682, where he prospered considerably. This and other early clocks are perfectly plain, with flat-topped hoods and are indistinguishable from their English predecessors.

Break-arch dials and shallow dome tops with finials appeared in the second quarter of the eighteenth century. Apart from the finials, and wooden frets in the spandrel spaces of the hood, the cases continued to be without decoration. The metal spandrel ornaments of the dial correspond to the English 'woman's head' ornament, except that an urn takes the place of the head. A clock made in about 1740 by Samuel Bagnall of Boston has a break-arch hood closely following the line of the break-arch dial. The break-arch space of the dials may contain a strike-silent dial, calendar, moon-work, or a name plaque.

From about 1760 the curly horns of English provincial pattern appeared on the hood of American clocks and remained almost universal throughout the second half of the century. Dials passed through all the stages of development already described in connection with English clocks. The trunks remained almost entirely innocent of decoration except for a few very special clocks, and for an occasional raised panel on the door with a cockle-shell top, then fashionable and known as the 'Rhode Island Block Front' style. Simple band inlay appeared at about the turn of the century.

Free-standing corner pillars on the hood were fashionable from 1760 to 1820.

In about 1790 a type of hood began to appear which is rarely found in England. Hoods with a break-arch top had their outer edge decorated by a crest or band of irregular outline, colloquially known as 'Whales-tails'. Later this cresting became a little wider, and pierced, and

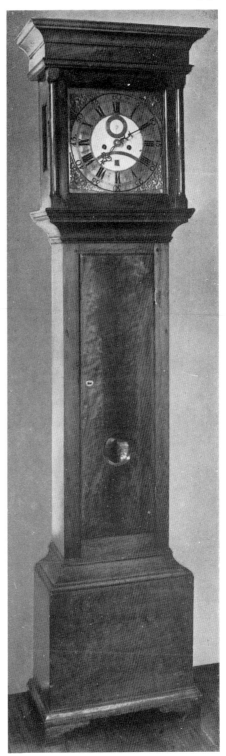

PLATE 159

Long-case clock by Benjamin Chandlee of Nottingham, Maryland, circa 1714. Typical of the earlier American long-case clocks showing strong English influence. Walnut case. Overall height 6 feet 9½ inches.

thus produced a very decorative and tasteful effect. Notable examples exist by Simon and Aaron Willard of Massachusetts, and other fine makers.

The movements of long-case clocks may be either thirty-hour or eight-day, according to whether they are made of wood or brass. Wooden movements have oak plates and either leaf or lantern pinions. Only the escape wheel is of brass. The locking plate is outside the plate and usually of very large size.

Miniature long-case clocks are less uncommon in America than in England and may well have provided the inspiration for the popular shelf-clock of the nineteenth century which, in its earliest form, is no more than a very small long-case clock in which the trunk and plinth have been compressed into one unit of about the same height as the hood.

SHELF CLOCKS

The shelf clock is a purely national style and at its best possesses considerable charm. It appears to have been introduced by the Willards. As described in the last paragraph, its earliest manifestation looks much like a small long-case clock in which the hood has joined up with the plinth to the complete exclusion of the trunk. The average overall height is two feet six inches.

A variant of this early form of shelf clock, with its two quite separate parts, has what is known as a 'Kidney dial'. The dial opening has a straight, or only slightly curved lower edge; a semicircular top outlining the dial circle; and slightly waisted sides.

The finest development of the shelf clock was introduced by Eli Terry in 1817 and is known as the 'Pillar and Scroll'. Apart from this innovation, Eli Terry (1772–1852) is an important person in American horology as he was the first man to produce cheap clocks in large quantities, first with wood and later with brass movements. The Pillar and Scroll Shelf Clock is not quite twice as high overall as it is wide. The fixed parts of the case consist of two slender pillars, one on each side; a narrow base with slight bracket feet connected by a series of scrolls of varying outline; and a top consisting, almost invariably, of a swan-neck pediment with three finials. The space between these pillars and scrolls is wholly occupied by a glazed door having a narrow, undecorated frame, with the window divided by a horizontal transome. The painted iron dial occupies the upper and larger division and the lower part has a simple painting of a landscape, or a conventional pattern, and an unpainted space through which the pendulum bob is visible. As made by Eli Terry and his early contemporaries the whole clock had a quality of unsophisticated gracefulness.

Later, the proportions became coarse and heavy and the swan-neck deteriorated into horns. In about 1825 the pillar and scroll clock began to lose popularity owing to the introduction of the 'Bronze and Looking-Glass Clock' by Chauncey Jerome. Jerome had worked for Terry and later developed quantity production into true mass production. It is recorded that in one year, about 1850, he made four hundred thousand clocks, but his business capacity did not rival his ability as a salesman and his undertaking eventually failed catastrophically. The bronze and looking-glass clock is a simplified pillar and scroll clock. The lower edge is a flat shelf; the top scroll is more simple and less graceful in outline; the pillars are thicker and have bronze mounts; and the painted landscape is replaced by a mirror. The bronze and looking-glass clock was not an improvement on the pillar and scroll clock.

After 1830 the bronze and looking-glass clock was superseded by the 'Ogee' and other even less graceful variants of the shelf clock.

PLATE 160 (*above*)

Pillar and Scroll shelf clock by Eli and Samuel Terry of Plymouth, Connecticut. A very fine and completely typical example. Note the side pillars, and scrolls top and bottom which give this type of clock its name; delicately painted and proportioned dial and hands, and painted panel below, through which the pendulum bob is visible.

PLATE 161 (*right*)

A fully developed American long-case clock by Thomas Harland, a prominent English-trained maker of Norwich, Connecticut, circa 1785. Note break-arch tops to door and hood, the latter with 'whalestails' cresting.

The shelf clock was weight-driven because of the difficulty of making springs. Early examples were mostly time-pieces but later clocks had striking trains. Wooden movements ran for thirty hours and continued to be made until about 1837. Brass movements ran for eight days.

WALL CLOCKS

The earliest American hanging wall-clocks are hooded thirty-hour movements with unenclosed weight and pendulum, known colloquially as 'Wag-on-Wall'.

The early Willard type of shelf clock was adapted as a wall-clock, but after it came what are unquestionably the most artistic clocks developed in America: the 'Banjo', 'Lyre' and 'Girandole'.

The Banjo clock was patented by Simon Willard in 1802 and may be accounted America's most important artistic contribution to horology, having a shape at once beautiful and functional. The dial has only a narrow metal frame and bezel for the glass (usually domed), and on top of it is a finial. Below the dial is a narrow trunk, slightly narrower at the top than at the bottom, down which the weight travels, with the pendulum rod in front of it. Below the trunk is a box-shaped base which houses the pendulum bob. Slender, curved, gilt metal ornaments provide a connecting motif for the three main parts of the clock, and the finest examples have a bracket-shaped pendant below the base. The whole, as executed by the Willards and other good makers, was most delicately and tastefully executed and perfectly proportioned. Banjo clocks are still made.

The 'Lyre' clock is simply a 'Banjo' in which the trunk is shaped like a lyre, usually with somewhat ponderous carving.

PLATE 162 (*left*)

Typical American wooden movement of a hanging wall clock by Gideon Roberts of Bristol, Connecticut. One of the earliest mass-produced examples, thirty-hour, circa 1790.

PLATE 163 (*p. 237, left*)

Eight-day Banjo clock by Aaron Willard of Boston, Massachusetts who invented this type in 1802. The example illustrated is circa 1810 and is unusual in possessing a striking train. Note the typical eagle finial, well-proportioned hands and dial and curved scrolls from dial to base. The weights lie behind the pendulum.

PLATE 164 (*p. 237, right*)

Lyre clock by John Sawin of Boston, Massachusetts, circa 1822. Note the typically heavy carving of the Lyre-shaped trunk.

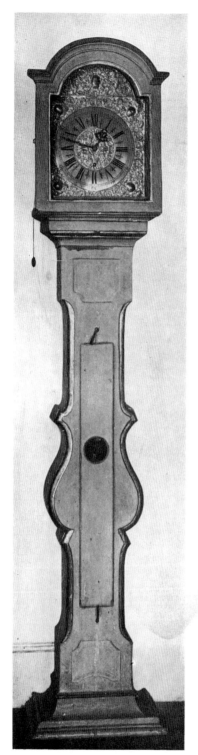

The 'Girandole' (much prized by American collectors) is a Banjo with a circular, instead of a rectangular base.

*   *   *

After 1830 the design of American clocks deteriorated and became coarse in exactly the same way as those of European countries. Subsequent interest centres around the development of mass-production methods which, by the middle of the century, constituted a serious threat to the cheap clocks exported from the Black Forest.

AUSTRIA

Prior to the invention of the pendulum, the Austrian centres (Vienna, Prague and Innsbruck) participated in the general south-European style. But when Germany lay prostrate after the disastrous Thirty Years' War (1618–48) Austria, as the seat of the Holy Roman Empire, made a more rapid recovery.

The first pendulum clocks, which are rare, have posted movements, and some of them have complicated astronomical trains with dials on all sides of the clock, superbly engraved. English influence, which was strong in Austrian work from 1680 to about 1780, may be displayed by cherub spandrels. Often the whole case was silvered with metal cresting concealing the bell or bells. As early as about 1680 a long pendulum might be combined with a verge escapement, the clock either standing on a bracket, or on a pillar case. In the latter form, the weights would be contained inside the pillar and the long pendulum, with its fairly wide arc, swung outside, and to the rear of the pillar.

PLATE 165 (*left*)

Austrian provincial long-case clock, circa 1730. The case is painted and the dial plate is gilt repoussé. Note the typical bulging lines. The month movement is of iron. The clock is a timepiece and has a pull-repeater. This type of provincial clock displays Styrian influence and is known as a 'Monastery Clock'.

PLATE 166 (*p. 239, left*)

Long-case clock by Jacob Bendele, Salzburg. Month timepiece movement, circa 1750. The typically shaped case is decorated in marquetry and the superlative gilt mounts are entirely executed in wood.
(The Austrian Museum of Applied Art)

PLATE 167 (*p. 239, right*)

Austrian hanging wall regulator by Marenzeller of Vienna, circa 1820. Note the typical pediment top and bracket case. The escapement is dead-beat. The month movement has quarter-striking and grande sonnerie and calendar work.

 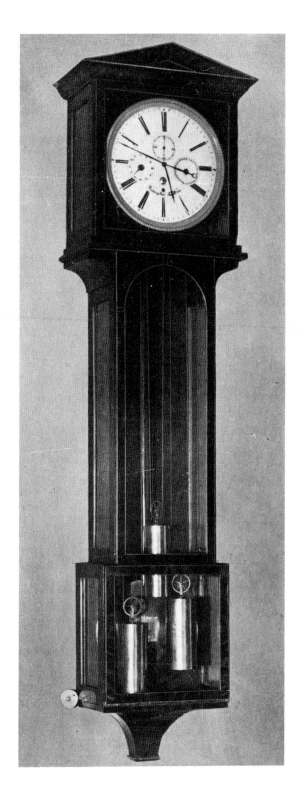

239

In the early eighteenth century clock cases mostly followed the English style, coupled with typical Austrian baroque ornamentation. In the south, however, long-case clocks began to develop the bulbous, provincial French style (described in Chapter VI) which was later to grow into a typical native style. Bold, appliqué, gilt mounts were popular, but unlike the French clocks, the Austrian mounts were often wood, instead of metal. The dials, by contrast, followed English styles, with separate metal chapter rings on a gilt plate; but while cherub spandrel ornaments are often found, the spandrel spaces may instead be engraved or enamelled. Ringed winding holes were popular. On the south-Austrian clocks the dial was repoussé.

In about 1780 a type of regulator clock began to become popular. This type generally has a plain, triangular portico top. Some of the best examples have an annular chapter ring with the escapement showing through the centre. The trunk and plinth are also glass fronted and the large pendulum bob swings in the base. The unusual feature of these clocks is that they are almost all designed to hang on a wall, and some examples have a bracket attachment under the base. The overall height is about four feet. Cheaper versions of these fine, late eighteenth and early nineteenth century regulators continued to be made throughout the whole of the nineteenth century. The pendulum rod might be either wood or a gridiron, and the dead-beat escapement was almost universally of the pin-wheel type. Good examples ran for a month or even a year.

Plate-shaped clocks were popular throughout the whole of the seventeenth century, and may be found as late as 1750. Following the Augsburg technique the later examples have a silver or pewter chapter ring, with richly repoussé centre, and the hand or hands generally have elaborately pierced ends. These clocks may hang, or stand on a small pedestal.

Pendulum bracket clocks were very popular from about 1680 and showed markedly English characteristics. Spiral-twist corner pillars were popular.

From about 1740 a national style in bracket clocks began to develop, being really a compromise between English and French influence. The case was ebony or ebonised, with bold ormolu mounts, coarsely engraved (or, alternatively, gilt wood appliqué). The top, usually an inverted bell, was surmounted by a gilt figure.

Dial openings had a break-arch top which often contained subsidiary astronomical dials or, in later examples, painted enamel plaques. The dial had at first a silver chapter ring on an engraved dial plate with applied, baroque spandrel ornaments. Where there was a pendulum slit in the dial the false bob was usually made of a paste brilliant. Later clocks had enamel dials, sometimes with superb flower paintings.

After 1780 came a great variety of bracket clocks displaying not only pronounced national character but also very considerable imaginativeness and charm. They are known as the 'Stockuhr' or 'Stutzuhr' (meaning a short clock). The most usual sort have a fairly standard layout, but with an infinite variety of application. Some, too, were obviously made for people of quite moderate means, with gilt wood mounts, while others are most richly executed. Basically, these clocks consist of a substantial base, about ten inches wide and roughly equal height, with a flat top. Above the base, and connected to it by a slender bracket, is the dial. The dial is further supported by flanking ornaments in ormolu, frequently using the dolphin motif. Above the dial stands a figure or an imperial eagle.

The base is usually of vaguely architectural form, often with alabaster pillars forming a colonnade. The pendulum bob may be visible behind these, or through an arch, usually backed by a mirror. The dial generally has an annular chapter ring with the gilt dial plate ornamented with ormolu and sometimes automata which perform at the hour.

These clocks exist in considerable numbers in Austria, and, if they were more widely disseminated, they would form a very charming species for a collector.

After 1800 came a further variety of styles, often of extravagantly fanciful design, such as a gothic ruin, which nevertheless contrive to remain artistically pleasing. Ormolu mounts, which had previously been heavy and coarsely engraved, now rivalled the French in their refinement and high

PLATE 168

Mid-Eighteenth Century Austrian (Bohemian) bracket clock by Joseph Graff of Prague. Note the typical gilt ornament of the case, surmounted by a figure; break-arch dial with subsidiary dials; mock pendulum bob in the form of a paste brilliant. This type is known as 'Chapel' because of its shape.

PLATE 169

'Stockuhr' or 'Stutzuhr'; a typical example of a widely diversified style very popular in Austria from 1815 to 1830. Note the colonnaded base with mirror back and visible pendulum, and movement on top. The birds are gilded wood and the smaller mounts are repoussé. The skeleton dial is typical of better-class Austrian clocks of this period.

PLATE 170

Austrian bracket clock, circa 1790, typical of the fanciful designs, popular at that time, corresponding to the 'Gothic ruin' of English landscape gardening. The case is ormolu. The glass is heavily domed.
(The Vienna Clock Museum)

PLATE 171

Bracket clock by Brendl of Vienna, 1813. Note the dolphin mounts, especially popular in Austria, and other mounts displaying the very high standards of ormolu achieved in Austria in the first quarter of the nineteenth century. Also typical is the annular chapter ring with the movement and subsidiary dials visible through the centre. The eight-day quarter - striking movement has recoil escapement. The small subsidiary dials attached to the hands are operated by gravity and give local time, phases of the moon, days of the week and month, and independent seconds. The overall height of this exceptionally fine clock is about 1 foot 6 inches.

finish. Simple pillar clocks of refined classical design, are also typical of this period, reflecting the French Empire style.

Travelling clocks of all kinds were popular at all times, mostly of very high quality. Early nineteenth-century examples have fine gilt cases.

In the beginning of the nineteenth century a miniature clock—almost a toy, achieved popularity and is now widely sought by continental and American collectors. It is called the 'Zappler' because of the very fast movement of its tiny pendulum (or pair of pendulums) in front of the dial. These clocks are one to two and a half inches high, in a great variety of shapes and materials. The escapement has usually a rudimentary form of cylinder.

From the mechanical standpoint, a high standard was generally prevalent. Before the invention of the pendulum, experiments were made in search of improved timekeeping and foremost among these early makers was the Swiss-born Jost Burgi, of Kassel and later Prague (died 1632) who invented a most ingenious form of cross-beat escapement with two cross-beating foliots, which attained an accuracy of time-keeping within a minute a day. They were the timekeepers used by Tycho Brahé for his astronomical observations and an unaltered specimen survives in the Danish National Museum at Copenhagen. Burgi also invented the remontoire, thus anticipating Huygens by some eighty years. He achieved standards of accuracy in tooth-cutting and general finish which were hardly surpassed for the next two hundred years.

Austrian makers were much attracted by complications in the form of perpetual calendars and equation work, and there were several churchmen who devoted much time to the study of these complicated mechanisms in which they achieved a very high standard of craftsmanship. Among these, David a San Cajetano (Ruetschmann) developed the differential gear in the course of his experiments.

Later characteristics of Austrian work, in the eighteenth century, are finely-engraved back plates, somewhat thick arbors, and a general preference for the going barrel. The pin-wheel escapement became popular for high-class work towards the end of the eighteenth century and a variant seldom found outside Austria combined a seconds hand moving once a second, with a half-second pendulum. A normal pin-wheel escapment has two arms, each with a dead face and an impulse face, which swing with the pendulum. In the Austrian variant there is only one such arm. Mounted on it is a small pivoted arm with a counterweight which, in its closed, or lowered position, registers with the impulse pallet and forms a continuation of its dead face. As each pin of the escape wheel drops, it falls on to the top face of this pivoted arm, carrying it to the lowered position. Thus obstructed, the pin passes the impulse face and is held on the dead face of the impulse pallet. The pivoted arm, thus released, is returned by its counterweight to its open position, and on the return swing of the pendulum the pin is able to escape and gives its impulse to the pendulum. Thus, the escape wheel only moves on alternative swings of the pendulum.

Austrian watches are often of high quality but display no markedly national characteristics.

THE BLACK FOREST

The clocks which came from the German 'Black Forest' constitute one of those backwaters, remote from the main stream of development. Their study makes a pleasant digression for the general student of horology, or an object for the specialist.

When the peasants of the Black Forest turned to clock-making in the middle of the seventeenth century, they used wood as being the material which they could obtain and which they were accustomed to work. They did so with the tools they already had, and used metal only when wood was completely unsuitable.

PLATE 172

Typical Black Forest wooden movement, circa 1740. All the parts are wood except the escape wheel and lantern pinions.

PLATE 173

Black Forest Clock, circa 1740. An early example of the fully enclosed movement, two hands, striking train and pendulum. Note the typical arrangement of the pendulum hanging in front of the water-colour-painted dial. The aperture above the XII may have contained an alternating sun and moon, now missing. Note also the archaic style of marking the quarters, the minute hand therefore being shorter than the hour hand.

The earliest European clocks of which we have any first-hand knowledge are the monumental iron machines of the late fourteenth century, with documentary evidence extending over a century earlier, but it is reasonable to suppose that these were preceded by experiments on a smaller scale, and in a more easily shaped material, such as wood. So it may well be that in the wooden clocks of the Black Forest we see a throw-back to the earliest mechanical clocks, of which we have no record. The oldest type, of the mid-seventeenth century, had a foliot balance, going train only, and one hand. All the parts are wooden except the verge, the metal pins which serve for teeth on the escape wheel, and the 'teeth' of the lantern pinions, although later examples have a normal crown-wheel made all of wood. The weight is stone. This primitive type continued unaltered for almost a century until, between 1730 and 1740, came the addition of striking mechanism, the pendulum and the cuckoo. Glass-blowing was another native industry, so it was natural that the bells should be made of glass, but the use of glass was fairly shortly superseded by metal.

The first pendulums were short, and swung in front of the dial, but despite their tardy adoption they did not at once oust the foliot, of which examples are found dating from as late as 1760, after the more adventurous people were already using the long pendulum and anchor escapement. The first cuckoos had a bird and a trap-door very much like those still made. The bird-call is, of course produced by two small organ pipes, tuned a minor third apart, and miniature bellows. Very few cuckoo clocks before about 1840 have survived. Brass wheels were popularised during the second half of the eighteenth century, although they were still mounted on wooden arbors, often decoratively turned, and pivoted in wooden plates with brass bushes. Brass arbors and plates did not become universal until well into the nineteenth century.

The first clocks had wooden dials, painted in water colours, and a single wooden hand; but about the middle of the eighteenth century came the (mis-called) 'Dutch' style, with a boxed movement, and an applied wooden dial plate with a painted arched top. The chapter ring was of convex section and the hands were brass. Variants were introduced during the nineteenth century, but the popular 'chalet' style did not appear until about 1850. Complicated clocks, with automata, or musical trains (organ or zither) or both are also occasionally to be found, with bold baroque ornamentation.

What had started as a home-handicraft in time became an industry, and during the summer, some members of a family would peddle the clocks which the family had made during the previous winter. Gradually an export trade developed, and the selling of the clocks became separated from their manufacture. Many were sold in England, where they even survived fierce competition from the cheap American clocks of the mid-nineteenth century.

HOLLAND

Holland may justly claim the two most important contributions to the science of horology throughout history. These are the development, by Christian Huygens, of the pendulum and the balance spring, to the point of practical utility and commercial success. The credit for the invention of these two vital components in every modern clock and watch has been widely claimed for many inventors, although Huygens never bothered to do so for himself. In any case, the point is only of academic interest, since there is no doubt that Huygens alone brought them to the point of general application, and therein lies Holland's greatest horological achievement.

But Dutch makers as a whole failed to take full advantage of Huygens' lead and both in the case of the pendulum and the balance spring it was the English who carried out the succeeding stages of refinement and accuracy in application.

Nevertheless, Dutch makers have produced certain types of clock which are peculiar to Holland.

Watches, bracket clocks, and long-case clocks were made in considerable numbers in Holland and a number of Dutch watchmakers also emigrated to England. But in the main none of these types attained a measure of individuality which merits their description as a national style. On the other hand, there was strong Dutch influence in English furniture and clock-case design at the end of the seventeenth century, especially in the form of inlay.

Before describing the true Dutch national styles it is desirable to say something about the striking arrangements which are common to all, and differ generally from English striking. Moreover, what is known in England as 'Dutch striking' is particularised in Holland as 'Double striking'.

Where there is only one bell the Dutch and English systems agree, except that in single-handed Friesland clocks the half-hour each side of one o'clock is not struck at all, to avoid confusion. In these clocks the striking is let off by a star-wheel and minute-hand clocks cannot easily use this arrangement. The full 'Double striking' employs two bells of markedly differing pitch. The hour is struck on the large bell. The first quarter is indicated by one stroke on the small bell. At the half-hour, the next succeeding hour is struck on the small bell. At the third quarter one blow is struck on the large bell. In Zaandam clocks the quarters are not operated by the striking train but by a cam on an intermediate wheel geared to the minute wheel. They therefore strike without any warning whatever which tends to have a very startling effect upon the unsuspecting. The same cam moves the tails of the hammers in and out of engagement so that the correct bell is used at the hour and half-hour respectively. Occasionally there is only one hammer in which case the whole hammer is pumped across from one bell to the other.

ZAANDAM CLOCKS

What are generally known as Zaandam clocks were in fact made throughout the whole of Zaanland, starting in about 1670 and continuing until the middle of the eighteenth century. They are, in effect, hooded, weight-driven wall-clocks. The clock rests on two angle-brackets fixed to a large wall-case of curvilinear outline which accommodates the pendulum. The clock case has four corner-pillars, usually spiral-twist, and the dial plate is frequently covered with velvet on which are mounted the metal

PLATE 174

Dutch long-case clock, circa 1780. Note typical shaped base supported on claw-and-ball feet; waisted door; painted landscape below the dial with windmill automaton, and ornamented hoodtop with three figure finials.

chapter ring and spandrel ornaments. There may be one or two hands, but sometimes there is only one hand for the main dial and a small subsidiary dial below with quarter-hour divisions only, its hand revolving once an hour (an arrangement common in early Italian clocks). The hood entirely encases the movement and is surmounted by brass frets at front and sides surmounted by the two bells which Zaandam clocks invariably possess. These bells are arranged with the smaller above the larger.

Zaandam clocks almost invariably have ropes for the weights, and very rarely chains. The weights are pear-shaped and the counterweights sometimes in the form of apples. Where there is an alarum train the same shaped weights are used in miniature.

The movement is of posted form, with the striking train behind the going train. Striking is always on the locking-plate system. The train is thirty hour. The wheels of the train have most delicately shaped spokes, always three in number, and bi-furcated at their outer end. It is also characteristic of Dutch clocks (and many watches) to have decoratively turned arbors.

The escapement is verge, with a vertical escape wheel, as though for a balance-wheel movement. The verge is therefore also vertical and has a rod or pin projecting horizontally from it with a vertical pin at its far end which passes through a flattened loop attached to the rod of the pendulum which can accordingly operate with a quite moderate arc. The pendulum is separately mounted in the case of the clock. This rather awkward arrangement was used by Huygens himself in an old turret clock at Scheveningen which he adapted to the pendulum.

FRIESLAND CLOCKS

Friesland clocks, which did not appear until the early eighteenth century, were probably in origin only a cheaper form of Zaandam clock; they are, nevertheless, highly decorative. They are also called 'Stoeltjesklok', because of the little stool on the bracket under the movement.

The movement has an iron back-cover and side doors of glass and the dial plate is of iron painted, usually, in a floral pattern surmounted by a landscape. A single hand was usual throughout the early part of the eighteenth century and sometimes there is a date indicator and phases of the moon. The wooden back plate of the clock is usually flanked by sawn-out wooden ornaments, generally mermaids. Surrounding the dial are boldly executed gilded leaden ornaments of which the upper one conceals the bell. Above all is a shaped canopy, usually with further cast lead decorations such as cupids and finials.

The movement is of lantern form with iron plates at top and bottom connected by boldly turned corner posts. As with the Zaandam clocks, the wheels are pivoted in three parallel brass plates. The wheels have plain spokes, three in number, except for the first wheel of the striking train which has four. Striking is nearly always by a locking plate and is more commonly on one bell than on two. Originally, all Friesland clocks had alarum trains. The alarum counter-weights are cone-shaped. The weights are always suspended on chains with links of 8 shape, twisted so that the two halves of the link are at right angles to each other.

The escapement and pendulum are arranged similarly to the Zaandam clock but the horizontal projection from the verge has no vertical pin, simply passing through a slot in the pendulum rod. This layout produces a wider arc than the Zaandam type and the pendulum swings clear of the case on each side. The train is thirty hour.

Friesland clocks are never signed and practically never dated.

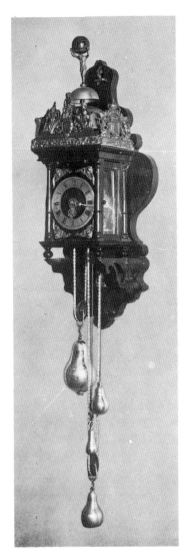

PLATE 175

Zaandam clock, circa 1740. Note hollow wall-case containing the pendulum; glass side doors to movement; chapter ring and cherub's head spandrel ornaments on black velvet ground; cast brass cresting partly concealing the two bells; polished brass pear-shaped weights and counterweights, for going and striking trains, supported on cords. In the close-up side view, note the posted movement; heavy brass wheels with bifurcated spokes; vertical verge.

STAARTKLOK

Another Friesland development was the more sophisticated Staartklok, first appearing after the middle of the eighteenth century. The movement is contained in a hood similar to that of a long-case clock. It is similarly arranged to the Stoeltjesklok but has an anchor escapement with a pendulum beating usually sixty-six or seventy-two per minute. Striking is more frequently on two bells, sometimes by a rack. The pendulum swings in a flat case against the wall with a widened bottom section to contain the bob, which is visible through an oval window. The weights hang on chains which pass in front of the pendulum case.

The dial often has calendar and moonwork, and moving automata.

Staartkloks were exported in quite large quantities in the nineteenth century but eventually failed to compete with the cheap German regulator. They are still made in Joure (Friesland) and are very common in Holland.

MINIATURE STOELTJESKLOK AND STAARTKLOK

Both these types are found in miniature form, with short pendulums swinging four beats per second. These usually have a horizontal escape wheel with the pendulum rod attached rigidly to the verge, in the normal English style. They were intended for use on ships and barges where they manage to keep going in reasonable time. In both forms they are called 'schippertje'.

AMSTERDAM CLOCKS

'Amsterdam' clocks were intended for fairly well-to-do people who either could not afford or accommodate a long-case clock. They are generally similar to the Staartklok but more finely executed. The case is made of oak, often veneered with walnut. The movement is arranged with the two trains side-by-side, the striking either by count-wheel or rack. The movement is thirty hour and the weights are usually suspended on rope and not chain.

Amsterdam clocks are considerably less common than the other Dutch national styles.

'DUTCH' CLOCKS

All-wooden clocks are often called 'Dutch' but they in fact emanated from the Black Forest and are described in that section of this chapter. The name may have come from 'Deutsch'.

JAPAN

In 1873 Japan adopted the European Calendar and system of timekeeping. Up to that date Japanese clocks were still being made with an uncontrolled foliot balance, just as it had been first used some six centuries earlier, and two centuries after it had been abandoned in all European countries. It therefore seems appropriate to consider Japanese clocks up to 1873, as an exception to the date of 1830 chosen as the finishing point for the rest of this book. Furthermore, owing to the

PLATE 176 (*p. 251, left*)

Friesland clock or Stoeltjesklok, circa 1820. Note the little stool on the bracket on which the clock stands, giving it its alternative Dutch name, also the typical painted dial and lead frets; pendulum attached to the backplate and the mermaid side-frets to the latter; brass-encased canister weight and smaller weight for alarum with conical counterweight, suspended on chain with 8-shaped links.

PLATE 177 (*p. 252, right*)

Staartklok, of a type made with little variation throughout the whole of the nineteenth century. Note the typical painted dial and break-arch hood with three figure finials; hollow wall-case containing the pendulum; brass canister weight and smaller alarum weight with conical counterweight, supported by chains.

conservatism of Japanese craftsmen, it is extremely difficult to date their clocks exactly within the two hundred and fifty years during which they were being made. After 1873 so many of the then outmoded clocks were exported as curiosities that they are now extremely rare in Japan, but fairly common in Europe and America.

The traditional Japanese Calendar was an extremely complicated affair and anyway there was more than one variety in current use. It would take too long to explain it here and readers are referred to *The Evolution of Clockwork* by Drummond Robertson (a work unfortunately now out of print and somewhat rare) which contains an exhaustive section on Japanese clocks.

The Japanese day was divided into two parts, by sunrise and sunset, the official time of each being altered twice monthly. Each part was divided into six parts from which it follows that the official 'day' and 'night', each with its six divisions, were constantly varying in their duration. To record this fluctuating state of affairs by a clock involved either a dial, on which the position of the division marks could be altered, or an escapement which changed its rate by an appropriate amount at sunset and sunrise. Both solutions were used by Japanese clockmakers.

Domestic clocks were restricted to the homes of the very rich. The common people relied on the Temple clock. The stroke of one, two or three on the Temple bell had a liturgical significance, and the lowest number which could be struck by the clock was therefore four. The 'hours' of day and night were struck in diminishing sequence, starting at nine and ending at four. Nine was struck at midday and midnight.

Clocks were probably introduced into Japan by missionaries or traders in the sixteenth century, but it was not until the early seventeenth century that native craftsmen began to make their own clocks, adapted to meet the peculiar exigencies of their system of recording time. The types which may be found have so many interesting variants that they cannot all be mentioned here, but (apart from special pieces) there are three basic types which may be described in some detail. In the first place, however, it is necessary to understand the mechanism common to all types.

Where the hand or other indicator moves at a steady speed, the dial or scale across which it moves must have adjustable division marks to record the unequal subdivisions of day and night. In these cases the movement itself follows closely on European practice and the earliest specimens have posted movements arranged very much like an English Lantern clock. The earliest type of all had a fixed dial plate, locking-plate striking, and a single going train with an uncontrolled foliot balance, so that the position of the foliot weights had to be altered by an appropriate amount at official sunset and sunrise; a most inconvenient arrangement.

Where the dial was arranged so that the spacing of the division marks could be varied at will, the whole problem was at once simplified. The movable divisions were a fairly stiff sliding fit in a circular groove, and were altered twice-monthly to record the six unequal divisions of the official day and night. A projecting pin was fixed to the back of each movable division and the whole circle revolved, the hand or indicator being fixed. As the dial rotated the pins in turn moved the lifting piece for the striking train and thus the necessary unequal intervals of striking were obtained through a conventional, equally divided locking plate. In this type of clock, of course, the going train maintained a (roughly) equal rate throughout the complete cycle.

An even more ingenious arrangement was evolved at the end of the seventeenth century, consisting of two quite separate verges and foliots, one for the day and one for the night. Between the verges were two escape wheels, joined back to back, on a single arbor. The bottom pivot of each verge was carried in a hinged potence. These movable potences registered with a cam-shaped arrangement which was moved twice a day (at sunset and sunrise) by the locking-plate wheel. The cam raised one verge so that its pallets did not register with their escape wheel, and lowered the other so that its pallets and escape wheel did register with each other. Each foliot had its regulating weights adjusted so as to give an appropriate rate for day or night for the current half month, so that as it was brought into action the rate of the clock immediately altered. Striking was then a simple

matter. Despite the advantages of this most ingenious plan, clocks with a single foliot continued to be made until well into the nineteenth century.

The foliots usually have between thirty and thirty-five notches, and sometimes have engraved graduations for ease of regulation. The arrangement of the trains varies greatly and the clocks usually need to be wound at least twice a day.

In addition to striking the six primary divisions of day and night (by strokes from nine to four as already described), the half-division was also struck, at first by a single stroke, but later, by two strokes for the half following an even-numbered division, or one stroke for the half following an odd-numbered division.

Alarum trains and calendar-work are found at any time after about 1700. Where there is an alarum train in a

PLATE 178

Weight-driven wall clock, eighteenth century. The oldest type of Japanese Clock, with a single escapement. Note typical decorative nut to bell; adjustable foliol weights for regulation; dial with fixed hand and rotating Chapter ring carrying movable 'hour' plaques for variable length of day and night. Note also posted movement. The case is brass. Overall height 7 inches.
(British Museum)

clock with a revolving chapter ring, the satisfactorily simple mediaeval system is adopted. Each division-mark had a hole in it and a peg was inserted in the appropriate division at which the alarum was required to operate. At the time appointed the peg reached and tripped a detent which released the alarum.

The train may be made of steel or brass, but except in a very broad way the material used is unreliable as an indication of age. Japanese clocks were very seldom signed or dated.

PLATE 180

Portable spring-driven clock with verge escapement, balance wheel and spring, outer case Shitân wood. The hand is fixed and the Chapter ring rotates carrying movable 'hour' plaques for day and night. Overall height 7 inches. Mid-nineteenth century.

(British Museum)

PLATE 179

A later variant of the weight driven wall clock, standing on its own base. Note the straight-sided bell and double foliot which operates alternately for day and night time; also the free-standing corner pillars to the clock proper, indicating a date not earlier than 1830. The Chapter ring is fixed and the hand rotates. The stand is carved and lacquered. These clocks vary greatly in size, this example being unusually small with an overall height of only 25 inches.

(British Museum)

The three main types of Japanese clock may now be considered individually.

(1) WEIGHT-DRIVEN WALL CLOCKS

This is the oldest type and was made continuously from the early seventeenth century until 1873. In general appearance it is not unlike a lantern clock, being encased by side plates, and having a bell on top. The plates are usually made of silvered copper and may be engraved. In early clocks the bell was round-topped and deep; later it became shallower and flat-topped. The bell was secured on its post by a sort of butterfly nut, made of coiled metal strip, or a turned nut.

After about 1830 a desire for increased decoration led to the construction of clocks with a complete top and bottom plate, with free-standing corner pillars of turned brass. The movement itself continued to be enclosed by detachable plates.

The size of this type of clock varies roughly between the same extremes as are found in English lantern clocks. They generally stood on a special stand in the form of a truncated cone, inside which were the weights; or on a special table usually with cabriole legs; or were suspended from a hook.

(2) PORTABLE SPRING-DRIVEN CLOCKS

These were introduced in about 1830 and have a case roughly conforming to an English bracket clock, but lighter and smaller. The sides are glazed, and the visible plates of the movement are elaborately engraved or pierced. The wooden casing is fairly lightly constructed and glued together. On top is a carrying-handle. The average height is eight or nine inches. Early examples have two uncontrolled balances but the majority have a wheel balance and balance spring. Having a constant rate they therefore have a dial with movable divisions. They have a peculiar form of count-wheel which, in addition to the usual deep notches, has a shallow serration for each blow to be struck. A gathering pallet turns the count-wheel by means of these serrations. The system is therefore a compromise between locking-plate and rack striking. Actual rack striking is very rare. The use of a pendulum was also most unusual.

(3) WEIGHT-DRIVEN PILLAR CLOCKS

·This is the cheapest kind of Japanese clock and was also introduced in about 1830. They are weight-driven and were designed to be attached to the central pillar of the house. They vary in height from one to four feet. The movement is contained in a glazed case at the top of the clock. The visible plates are decoratively engraved or pierced. The escapement may be by a single foliot, balance wheel, or (rarely) pendulum.

PLATE 181

Weight-driven pillar clock. The weight moves down inside the trunk, carrying the horizontal bar which indicates the time against the front plate of the trunk which is calibrated to serve as a 'dial'. The slanting lines, faintly visible in the illustration, indicate the variable 'hours' of day and night at the different seasons. The striking train forms the weight, being tripped by fixed detents in the trunk. The escapement is verge and balance wheel with balance spring. Overall height 19½ inches.
Mid-nineteenth century.
(British Museum)

The weight moves inside a narrow pillar and a pointer, attached to the weight, projects through a slit in the front of the pillar and serves to indicate the time. The division marks are located on a groove, in which they can be slid up and down according to the variable night and day.

This type of clock could not be adapted to strike until a most ingenious plan was hit upon. This was, to employ a spring-driven striking train and use it as the weight to drive the clock proper. The division marks then have pins projecting inside the pillar, and as the striking train descends it reaches each in turn, and the pin operates the lifting piece of the train.

The objection to this ingenious plan is that unless the clock is wound at exactly the same time each day, after the 'weight' has passed all the pins of the division marks, the sequence of the striking will be upset. Suffice it for this brief survey to say that various rather clumsy expedients were arrived at to overcome the difficulty. The clock having been wound in the usual way, the winding square for the spring of the striking train then came opposite a hole in the front plate through which it, in its turn, could be wound.

Enough has been said to show that Japanese clocks form a complete and quite distinct branch of horology, and there are many interesting variants within the main types which have here been briefly described.

SWITZERLAND

Switzerland has received little mention so far, for the reason that her makers did not develop any marked national style until after the close of this book in 1830. Before that date her influence, although considerable, was indirect. The leading men either emigrated – as the Vulliamy's and Emery, to England, while to France went makers of such foremost eminence, as Lepine, Berthoud and Breguet. Watches were being made in Geneva in the sixteenth century, but in the main they followed French styles, and by the end of the seventeenth century a Swiss-made 'oignon' may equal the quality of the best French, and after the Revocation of the Edict of Nantes in 1685 many Hugenots emigrated to Switzerland. But in the main, Swiss products were not intended to be of the best quality, and during the eighteenth century, a considerable number of cheap movements were exported to England, with the English type of cock and decoration. Among artists who continued working on their native soil, and yet attained a European reputation, were the famous Huaud family of enamel painters, in the seventeenth century, and Jaquet-Droz in the eighteenth.

Geneva was at first the centre of watch-making in Switzerland but by degrees the industry spread to other Cantons, some of which eventually rivalled the supremacy of Geneva. Switzerland has mostly concentrated on the manufacture of watches, as opposed to clocks.

By 1800 Switzerland was producing various types of watch with recognisable native characteristics, among which are those designed for export to Turkey and China. The Turkish market was captured from the English, and like the English examples, the watches are characterised by gaudily decorated cases, sometimes three or four to one watch. The Chinese watches were more characseristic, having sweep centre-seconds and a form of duplex escapement in which the seconds hand only appears to move once a second. This is achieved by having two points on the end of each tooth of the escape wheel. Both of these have to escape before the escape wheel can advance and impart impulse to the balance. The wheel (and therefore the seconds hand) does advance by an imperceptible amount as the first point of each tooth escapes, but the motion can hardly be detected, so that the hand only appears to advance once a second, on every other complete oscillation of the balance.

These watches, of large diameter, have enamel dials with ordinary roman numerals, gaudy enamel backs, and profusely engraved or enamelled cocks for each wheel of the movement, which is visible through a protecting glass dome on opening the back of the watch. Some are of high quality. They were often made in pairs.

Other Swiss specialities in the early nineteenth century were complicated watches, thin watches (which achieved unsurpassed slenderness by the middle of the century) and watches with annular, white enamel chapter rings, either with the movement showing in the centre, or fine gilt ornament. Repeating watches usually had automata in the form of small figures which appeared to strike a bell, or performed other movements, in time with the repetition. Switzerland also reintroduced form watches, after they had been out of fashion for more than a century.

But apart from these trivial novelties, it was during the first quarter of the nineteenth century that Switzerland was preparing herself for the world leadership in mass production which she attained later in the century. Fredéric Japy was the inventor of many of the machine tools which formed the basis of mass production and another pioneer was Favre-Jacot (1743–1817) who founded the Zenith factory. During this period Swiss makers gradually changed over from the full-plate movement, with verge escapement, to the Lepine calibre and cylinder escapement of the kind found almost universally in Swiss watches throughout the nineteenth century. Only in the twentieth century did Swiss makers learn to combine the extreme accuracy of performance, with mass production methods, for which their watches are now justly famous.

CHAPTER VIII

Alarum, striking, and repeating mechanisms

THE variety of striking and repeating mechanisms is wide. In this chapter only the basic types are described, to which the many variants are more or less closely related. The drawings are diagrammatic, being arranged for ease of comprehension rather than working accuracy.

Chiming mechanisms are similar in principle to striking gear and therefore are not separately described.

There are two quite distinct types of striking train. 'Locking-plate' or 'count-wheel' striking seems to have been invented in about 1330 and was universally employed until 1675, when the Reverend Edward Barlow (he changed his name from Booth) invented 'rack-striking', which gradually superseded the earlier type. Locking-plate striking has the defect that the hours are inevitably struck in sequence, so that if the hands are moved quickly through two or more hours without allowing the clock to strike at each; or if the striking train is allowed to run down before the going train; the hands and the strike will not agree and the strike must be let off by hand until it has caught up with the hands. With rack-striking, the strike automatically follows the hands.

Repeating mechanism is based on rack-striking, but instead of the clock or watch striking automatically, it only does so at will, by manually operating a lever. A repeater may tell only the hours, or, in addition either quarters, half-quarters, five minutes, or even individual minutes. The example chosen for illustration (because it is most easily understood from a drawing) is a quarter-repeating watch of late eighteenth century type.

Alarum mechanisms antedate any other form of striking. In the earliest monastic clocks, when the alarum warned the clock-keeper to awaken the brethren, there was no hand, but the whole dial-plate rotated. This had holes pierced through it at intervals and a peg was inserted in the appropriate hole according to the time next required for warning. As this hour was reached, the peg tripped a detent, which let off the striking weight and clanged a bell until the weight had run down. The less crude form of alarum illustrated in this chapter is that employed with little variation from the mid-sixteenth century until the present time.

Alarums are all set by turning the setter disc or hand in one direction only. Under no circumstances must the setter disc or hand be moved in the opposite direction past the hour hand of the clock or watch; nor should the hands be turned backwards so that the hour hand passes the setter hand.

Although there are clocks in which it is safe to do so, it is generally dangerous to move the hands of a striking clock backwards, and if this must be done, they should not be moved between warning-and striking. In some forms of rack-striking, heavy frictional loading of the going train takes place if the striking train is allowed to run down. If it is desired to silence such a clock it is usually wise to tie up the rack so that it is clear of the snail (of course, this is not necessary if the clock has a 'strike silent' lever).

The hands of Repeaters (provided they do not also strike or chime) may safely be turned backwards.

ALARUM

The example illustrated is a single handed, seventeenth-century alarum watch with separate setter disc. The dial is shown partly cut away, the back plate underneath it being shown black.

The setter disc A is a friction fit on the hour hand arbor.

Release-disc B is attached rigidly to A,

To set the alarum (whose spring must be separately wound) the disc A is turned (by rotating it with a pin inserted into one of the holes C provided for the purpose) clockwise until the required hour numeral is under the tail D of the hour hand.

A and B are then carried round with the hour hand until the slot E registers with the nose of the spring-tensioned detent G. Pin H is thus released and lets off the alarum-train (which is between the plates and is not shown).

FIGURE 37

As A and B continue to be rotated by the hand, G is lifted out of the slot E on its sloping face and the alarum-train is again locked.

COUNT-WHEEL OR LOCKING-PLATE STRIKING

The clock illustrated strikes hours only. Sequence of operations at one o'clock:

(1) At approach of hour, star-wheel under dial (shown inset) rigidly attached to hour hand arbor, lifts detent A.

(2) Warning detent B, attached to same arbor as A, raises hoop-wheel detent C via integrally mounted lever D, so as to clear hoop on hoop-wheel H.

(3) Train thus liberated begins to run but is stopped in about half a turn of the top wheel (driving the fly, or air-brake) when the pin E on this wheel reaches the detent at the end of B.

(4) Count-wheel detent F, on same arbor as C and D, has now risen but is not yet clear of slot in count-wheel G.

(5) A continues to be lifted by the star-wheel until the hour, when it clears the star-wheel tooth and drops, together with B.

(6) C also drops but is arrested by periphery of hoop. F is also now clear of slot in G.

(7) Train is now free to run and pin J on pin-wheel K raises hammer-tail L and, on clearing, the bell is struck once.

(8) On completion of one revolution of H, all cams return by gravity to normal position and train is again locked.

Sequence of operations at two o'clock and subsequent hours:

(1) As above up to and including (7).

(2) On completion of one revolution of H, the detents cannot return to normal or locked position as count-wheel G, driven by gearing from pin-wheel K, has now turned, and F drops on to its outer periphery; F carries C with it. The train therefore continues to run; H makes another revolution, another pin passes the hammer-tail L and the bell is again struck.

(3) When correct number of blows has been struck by successive pins on K, as permitted by the spacing of the slots in G, F drops into the next slot and the train is again locked as in (8) above.

Note. To produce a half-hour strike of one blow it is only necessary to provide a star-wheel of 24 points, and to make the slots in count-wheel G wide enough for F to drop back into the same slot after one blow at the half-hour.

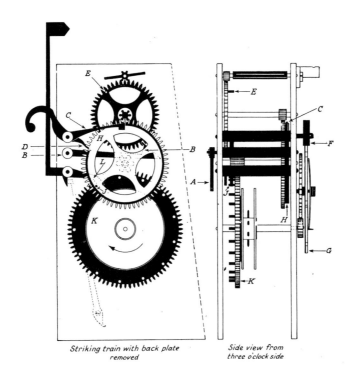

Striking train with back plate
removed

Side view from
three o'clock side

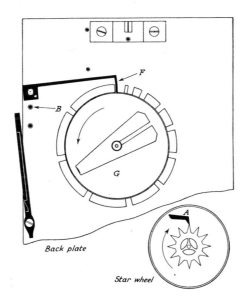

Back plate

Star wheel

FIGURE 38

261

RACK STRIKING

The clock illustrated strikes the hours, and one blow, on the same bell, at the half-hour. It is shown as shortly after 8.30. The whole of the rack mechanism (which takes the place of the count-wheel in the previous diagram) is under the dial and the rest of the striking train (pin-wheel, hammer, warning, fly, etc.) is between the plates. These are all the same in principle as in the count-wheel mechanism and are therefore not again illustrated or described.

Sequence of operations:

(1) Pin A lifts detent B which actuates warning through slot C in the front plate.
(2) Simultaneously pin D on detent B raises rack-detent E, allowing rack F to drop under spring-tension G until pin H on the integrally mounted rack-tail is stopped by step J of snail, on cam-wheel K.
(3) On hour, B clears A and drops, releasing warning so that train begins to run, and gathering pallet L (driven by train, through the plate) rotates anticlockwise about its arbor M.
(4) Nose of gathering pallet (shown nearest letter L) gathers one tooth of rack, so turning the rack clockwise until pin N (on E), riding up back of tooth, falls behind the tooth that has been gathered and locks it.
(5) The gathering operation continues until all teeth have been returned and gathering-pallet-tail P is locked against rack-pin Q. Striking is now complete, one blow on bell having been struck as each tooth is gathered. There are twelve teeth on F and the number to be gathered is determined by the drop of H on to K which is calibrated to give progressive striking.

Sequence of operations at half-hour:

(1) Pin T lifts detent B as before, but as T is nearer the centre of its wheel than the hour-pin A it does not lift B so far. It does, however, lift it just far enough for pin N on E to clear the first tooth on the rack, which is shorter than the others.
(2) Pin N then locks on second (full-length) tooth, and after warning on the half-hour, the train begins to run. The first tooth is gathered and the bell is struck once. The train is then locked as before.

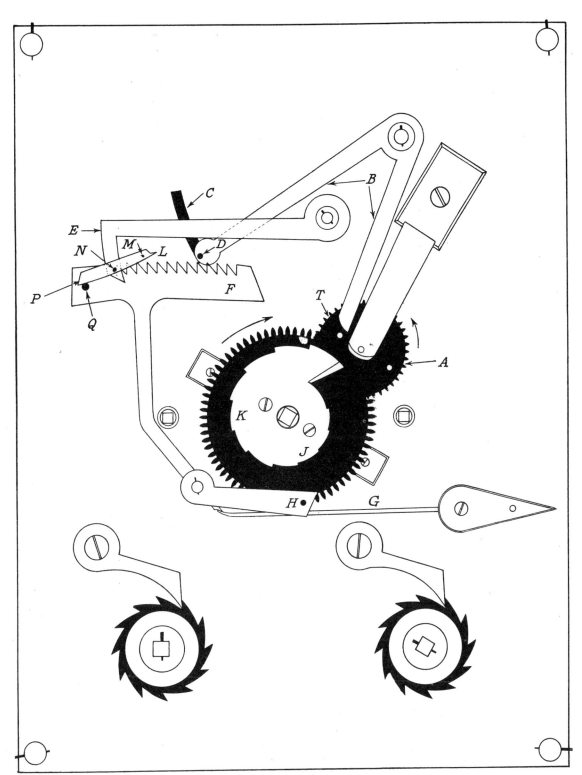

FIGURE 39

263

QUARTER REPEATER

The diagram is shown at the moment when the plunger A has been depressed but striking has not yet started. Before A was depressed, the nose D of the quarter rack C was held on the tail E of the all-or-nothing piece H. The time is about 1.35.

PREPARATORY SEQUENCE

As A is depressed, it moves push-piece B against hour-snail G which is mounted on a star-wheel which is moved forward once an hour by a pin (not shown) on the quarter rack M (but see also later under 'Surprise-piece').

The all-or-nothing piece H is pivoted at I and also carries the arbor of the hour-snail and star wheel at pivot K. As B presses against G it slightly displaces G and H, turning them about pivot I until H reaches stop J. This takes E clear of D and the quarter-snail C, driven by the spring L, moves up against the quarter-rack M, which goes round with the minute hand. Until the all-or-nothing piece has been dislodged, no striking can take place.

Also, as A and B are depressed, B pulls chain O which winds up a spiral repeater spring (not shown) attached to the quarter-rack gathering-pallet N.

Under the watch plate is the hour rack (not shown) pivoted on the same square as N and the spiral repeater spring, and operating striking hammer-pallet P.

STRIKING SEQUENCE

As soon as pressure is released from A, striking will commence as follows:

The extent to which the hour rack and its spring have been wound is decided by the distance B travels before being stopped against G. This is arranged so that, when the spring starts to unwind the repeating train, the hour rack strikes the correct number of blows via hammer-pallet P.

When the hours have been struck, the pallet N gathers the pin Q on C and returns the double-ended quarter rack to its original position. As it moves, the two racks strike (in this case, being between thirty and forty-five minutes past the hour) two ting-tangs via the hammer-pallets P and R. The two hammers are located by four springs, each marked Z.

When quarter striking is completed, D again clicks into position behind E so that C is held by H.

SURPRISE PIECE

The action of the surprise-piece S (shaded on the diagram) remains to be described. It comes into operation at the hour, to ensure correct striking just each side of the hour, when it is otherwise difficult to synchronise the hour and quarter snails. S is pivoted with M and is spring-tensioned in the position shown. The pin which moves the hour-rack star wheel is actually fixed below and on the surprise piece and not on the quarter snail itself. As this pin presses against the star wheel, the shaded portion is pushed back behind the edge of the quarter snail. As the pin clears the star wheel, the shaded portion flirts forward again under its own spring tension. Thus, the new hour and the nil quarters come into operation at exactly the same moment.

FIGURE 40

265

CHAPTER IX

Records of famous makers

IN this chapter are reproduced many of the notes collected by Mr. Britten concerning the lives and work of famous horologists, and included in earlier editions. The list was neither representative nor exhaustive, being confined mainly to English makers (the exceptions were Christian Huygens and Abraham Louis Breguet); but it contains much useful information not to be found elsewhere. Inclusion of notes of this kind of all the notable Clock and Watch-makers would have made it necessary to re-issue this book in two volumes, a course which has not been considered to be in the interests of the reader. The Editors have therefore been content to reproduce from previous editions, mostly verbatim, a number of facts about famous makers which would not otherwise be accessible in current print. The only additional lives included are those of Julien and Pierre le Roy, and Ferdinand Berthoud, because of their quite outstanding importance in the history of horology and the French industry. On the other hand, the fairly lengthy passages in previous editions devoted to the description of individual timepieces have here mostly been omitted as being of insufficient general interest to merit their retention, and this has involved leaving out several names of whom the record consisted of no more than a description of one or more examples of their work.

NICHOLAS CRATZER (or Kratzer), 'deviser of the King's horologies and astronomer' to Henry VIII, was a Bavarian, born in 1487, who, it is said, resided for thirty years in this country without being able to speak English. In the second part of the facsimiles of the National Manuscripts, photographed by Colonel Sir Henry James, there is a letter from Cuthbert Tunstal, Master of the Rolls (who was then in Germany) to Cardinal Wolsey. It is dated 12th October, 1520, and contains the following: "Please it your Grace to understand that here, in these parts, I met with a servant of the King's called Nicholas Craczer, a German, deviser of the King's horologes (who showed me how the King had licensed him to be absent for a season, and that he was ready to return into England), whom I desired to tarry until I might write to the King's Highness, to know his pleasure whether he would suffer him to be in company with me for a season, until the assembling of the electors were past." In a Book of Payments by the Treasurer of the Household from Candlemas-day, 29 Henry VIII, to Midsummer 33 Henry VIII, in the Arundel Manuscripts (No. 97), among the discharges of the former year (1538) is the entry, "Nicholas Cratzer, Astronomer, received five pounds as his quarter's wages."

There is no doubt that Holbein assisted Cratzer by designing cases and decoration for clocks and sun-dials. Horace Walpole purchased at Monsieur Mariette's sale a complicated piece of horology which embodied the conceptions of the two masters. On the summit was a clock driven by wheel work, below were fore and afternoon dials showing the time by shadows, and beneath these a clepsydra indicating the quarters of an hour on an exceedingly ingenious plan, the invention of which has been claimed for many subsequent horologists. It is mentioned by Bettinus, and in Plot's 'Oxfordshire' 1676, Christopher Wren is credited with having made for Sir Anthony Cope at Hanwell a Clepsydra on the same principle which is thus described: "moves by water and shows the hours by a new gilded sun for every hour, moving in a small hemisphere of wood, each carrying in their centres the number of some hour depicted black;

PLATE 182

Many tradesmen in the eighteenth century had printed cards advertising their wares. Most were conspicuous for their decorative treatment, but the example illustrated is of of special interest as showing the tools used in the Clock and Watch trade in the late eighteenth century.

PERKINS and SPENCER,

Clock, Watch-Makers and Tool-Sellers,

At Nº. 44, oppofite St. Sepulchres Church, Snow Hill,

L O N D O N.

MAKE, and Sell, at the Loweft Prices, all Sorts of Clocks, Repeating, Horizontal, Seconds, Skeleton, and Plain Watches, for Exportation or Country Trade.

Likewife Clock and Watch-makers Tools and Materials,

As Under.

DUCTH Brafs	Bolts	Side do.	Borax
English do.	Locking Springs	Cafe hammers	Shears
Flatted do.	Ballances	Finifhers Stakes	Hard wood Handles
Caft Brafs	Pillars	Watch holders	Soft wood, do.
Brafs wire	Studds	Blewing Tools	Winder Handles
Follower do.	Cafe Springs	Adjufting Tools	Clock Pinions
Dovetail, do.	Buttons	Pottance and Pillar Burn-	Clofe cafes
Pendulum Studd	Brufhes	ifhers	Pottance files
Ring wire	Gravers	Pivot Burnifhers	Pillar files
Blew Stones	Screw Keys	Oval do.	Crap files
Grey Stones	Broaches	Broaches in handles	3 Square files
Bohemia Stones	Sculpers	Bright board vices	Round files
Turkey oil Stones	Spitftickers	Black do.	Screw Head
Plantation oil Stones	Knife Tools	Turn Benches	Four fquare
Oil Stone Slips	Corn tongs	Ballance Tools	Barrel Hole files
Chip Boxes	Tweezers	Ballance and ⎰ in one	Endlefs fcrews, do.
Packing Boxes	Pinion Gauges	Pottance tools ⎱	Half Round
Iron wire	Hammers	Pottance Tools	Hollow Edge
Binding wire	Rivitting Preffes	Spring Tools	Ballance wheel
Clock Line	Bright watch hand Vices	Fuzee Engines	Peircing files
Catt Gutt	Black, do.	Ballance wheels Engines	Nicking
Clock Gutt	Bright Clock, do.	Flatt wheel do.	Equaling
Working Candlefticks	Black do.	Clock Engines	Rounding off
Working Lamps	Pinvices	Barrel do.	Pinion
Gold pendants	Sliding Tongs	Pivot Tools	Pivot
Silver, do	Dividers	Upright Tools	Shouldering
Mettal, do.	Wing Compaffes	Steel wire	Verge
Common Keys	Beam do.	Sheffield files	Warding
Turn'd Shanks, do.	Curb, do.	Emery	Superfine Pivot
Ground Glaffes	Watch Screw Plates	Putty	Banking
Common, do.	Clock do.	Pollifhing drops	Tinback
Main Springs	Nippers	Melting pots	Slitting
Pendulum Springs	Clock Plyars	Gilders tongs	Swing wheel
Pendulum Spring wire	Watch Plyars	Scratch Brufhes	Bottoming
Verges	Pendulum, do.	Magnifying glaffes	Rounding off with Points
Pinions	Frame faws	Enamel Plates	Holbert files
Contrait wheels	Peircing do.	Movements	Entering
Ballance wheels	Callipers	Motion wheels	Hand files
Pinion wire	Barr Callabers	Borax Boxes	Knife files
Verge wire	Do. with Barr and Index	Blow pipes	Saw edge
Click wire	Upright Cafe ftakes	Spelter Soder	Ballance arm

N. B. Moft Money given for Old Copper, Brafs Clipings and brafs Duft.

as suppose of one a clock, which ascending half way to the zenith half hour; whence descending half way towards the horizon, three quarters past one; and at the last absconding under it, then presently arises another gilded sun above the horizon at the other side of the arch, carrying in its centre the figure two; and so of the rest." The clepsydra for driving appears to have been in the form of a drum with divisions.

BARTHOLOMEW NEWSAM was one of the earliest English makers of portable clocks whose work survives. It is conjectured that he was a Yorkshireman, but he must have attained some position in London before 1568, for in that year he secured a thirty years' Crown lease of premises in the Strand, near Somerset House, where he resided till his death. In the British Museum is a very fine example of his skill, which proves Newsam to have been a master of the craft. This is a striking clock, in a case of brass, gilded and engraved, about $2\frac{1}{2}$ in. square and 4 in. high, exclusive of an ornamental domed and perforated top, which brings the total height to $6\frac{1}{2}$ in. The centre of the dial as far as the hour ring is below the surface of the case, so that on removing the base, the movement, together with the centre of the dial and hand, may be drawn out. The movement is arranged in storeys, there being three plates held in position by four corner posts. Above the top plate is a semi-circular bell; between the upper and middle plates is the going train, and between the middle and lower plates the striking train, the locking-plate occupying a position below the lowest plate. The arbors are placed vertically, and the winding holes are at the bottom of the case. The wheels are of steel or iron, the fusees very long, and with but little curve in their contour; they are connected with the barrels by means of catgut. The plates, posts, and barrels are of brass, the barrel covers of iron held in by a number of tenons around the edge. The hand is driven from the great wheel of the going part by a contrate wheel. The escapement is, of course, the verge. The workmanship, unusually fine for the period, is remarkably free from subsequent interference. There is a very small hinged door on each side of the case, giving, when open, a view of the fusees to estimate the period for winding. No screws are used in the construction of the movement, which is inscribed 'Bartilmewe Newsum'.

In the *Calendar of State Papers* of the time of Queen Elizabeth I is a record of a grant in 1572 to B.N. (who no doubt was Bartholomew Newsam) of the office of clockmaker to the Queen in reversion after the death or surrender of N.U. (probably Nicholas Urseau). In the same *Calendar* is a letter

dated 5th August, 1583, from Bartilmew Newsham to Sir Francis Walsyngham. This letter probably refers to a renewal of Newsam's lease, and it desires Sir Francis to favour the writer's petition to Her Majesty for the augmenting a certain term of years, wherein he had moved Sir Philip Sidney to speak for him. He was clock-keeper to the Queen prior to 1582, and on 4th June 1583, under Privy Seal was paid 32s. 8d. for 'mending of clocks during the past year'. Under the date 1590 is a grant to Bartholomew Newsham of the office of Clockmaker to the Queen, in place of Nicholas Urseau, deceased. Newsam appears then to have combined the offices of Clock-keeper and Clock-maker, which had previously been kept distinct.

His tenure of the double appointment was a brief one, for he died in 1593. By his will, dated in 1586, he bequeathed to his apprentice his 'seconde clock'; to John Newsam, clockmaker of York, his "best vice save one, a beckhorne to stand upon borde, a great fore hammer, and to (two) hand hammers, a grete longe beckhorne in my backe shoppe; and all the rest of my tooles I give unto Edward Newsom, my sonne, with condicion that he become a clockmaker as I am, yf not I will the foresaid tooles to be sold by my executors." He gave to a friend "a sonne dyall of copper gylte"; to another, "one cristall jewell with a watche in it, garnished with goulde;" to another "one watch gylte to shew the hower;" to another "a strickinge clocke, in a silken purse, and a sonne dyall to stande upon a post in his garden"; and to another, "a chamber clocke of fyve markes price."

John Newsam continued at York for some years. In 1593 he repaired the clock on Ousebridge in that city.

BULL. Rainulph or Randulph Bull appears to have been an English horologist of note. In the British Museum is a rather large oval watch by him, dated 1590. It has on a shield the arms of the owner and his name, 'W. Rowley.' Bull was also keeper of the Westminster great clock. In Devon's *Issues of the Exchequer* there is an entry under date 1617, 1st April; "By order, dated 29th March 1617. To Ranulph Bull, keeper of his Majesty's great clock, in his Majesty's palace at Westminster, the sum of £56 . 13 . 4d., in full satisfaction and discharge of and for divers sums by him disbursed for mending the said clock, in taking the same and other quarter clocks all in pieces, and repairing the same in the wheels, pulleys, hammers, weights, and in all other parts, and in new hanging, wiring, and cordings of the same clock, and other necessary reparations thereunto belonging, the charge whereof, with his own workmanship and travail therein, doth amount to the sum aforesaid. By writ dated 27th March 1617, £56 . 13 . 4d."

In an account of the household expenses of Prince Henry, in 1610, 'Emanuel' Bull, the 'clocke-keeper', is mentioned. '

DAVID RAMSAY. One of the earliest British watch-makers of particular renown was David Ramsay.

Among the Salting collection at the Victoria and Albert Museum is a very early watch by him in a small irregular octagonal case of gold and silver. It has hinged covers over the front and the back, and is decorated with engravings of the Annunciation and the Nativity.

In the British Museum is an oval watch of his make, with a gold case in the French style. The period assigned to this watch is 1600 to 1610. It is inscribed 'David Ramsay, Scotus, me fecit'.

There is an entry in the account of money expended by Sir David Murray, Kt., Keeper of the Privy Purse to Henry, Prince of Wales, who died in 1612. "Watches three bought of Mr. Ramsay the Clockmaker lxjli" (£61). In the same account, among the list of 'Guyftes and Rewardes', is the item, "Mr. Ramsay the clockmaker xjs' (11s.).

A splendid clock-watch with alarum by him, dating from about 1615, has the three-wheel train usual in early watches, and the fusee is cut for twelve turns, and the end of the great wheel arbor, which goes through the pillar plate, is fashioned into six pegs or leaves, identical with a lantern pinion in its action. These leaves work in a wheel pivoted into the centre of the pillar plate, having sixty teeth, and carrying the single hand of the watch. Thus ten turns of the fusee are equivalent to an entire circuit of the hand on the dial and so the watch would require to be wound twice a day. The ratchet wheel, which sets up the mainspring, is on the top plate, and the stop work is identical in principle with that in modern fusee watches. The stop for the alarum part is effected by a wheel and pinion, the wheel having a portion the size of two teeth left uncut, and which serves as a block to the pinion after it has been wound three turns. The wheels and pinions have a wonderfully smooth action, though they appear to be cut by hand rather roughly. On the margin of the top plate, in tiny characters, as if almost to escape observation, is engraved "David Ramsay invt Fecit", the 'et' having been obliterated. In the Victoria and Albert Museum is a superb square table clock, also by him.

The *Dictionary of National Biography* says David Ramsay belonged to the Ramsays of Dalhousie, and quotes Ramsay's son William to the effect that "when James I, succeeded to the crown of England he sent into France for my father, who was there, and made him page of the bedchamber and keeper of his Majesty's clocks and watches". In 1613, James gave David Ramsay a pension of £200 per annum, and in the same year a further pension of £50 per annum. In the grant he is styled 'Clockmaker Extraordinary'. In 1616 a warrant was signed to pay him £234 10s. for the purchase and repair of clocks and watches for the king. On 26th November 1618 he was appointed to the office of 'Chief Clockmaker' to his Majesty, with fees and allowances for workmanship. On 30th September 1622, he received £232 15s. for repairing clocks at Theobalds, Oatlands, and Westminster, and for making a chime of bells adjoining the clock at Theobalds.

In 1625 James I, his patron, died, but Ramsay appears to have retained his appointments, for on 25th January 1626 a warrant to pay to David Ramsay £150 for coins to be given by the king, Charles I, on the day of his coronation, was signed. Again "17th March 1627, is a warrant to David Ramsay, Page of the Bedchamber and Clockmaker, £441 3s. 4d. for work done for his late Majesty, and £358 16s. 8d. in lieu of diet and bouche of Court". In 1628, 13th July, a warrant was signed to pay him £415 for clocks and other necessaries delivered for the king's service.

Among the *State Papers*, Ann. Dom., 1653, are two receipts taken from the Jewel House at Whitehall soon after the death of Charles I. The first is as follows: "18 die Feb. 1649. Recd. one clocke with divers mocions, two globes, one case for a clocke, and a glassee, one Bullet Clocke, one clocke with five bells, and one other clocke, all which were lying at Whitehall late in the charge of David Ramsay." The second is merely a subsidiary receipt of the same date for "one other clocke in a Bow received from Ramsay".

Sir Walter Scott introduces Ramsay in *The Fortunes of Nigel*, as the keeper of a shop a few yards to the eastward of Temple Bar, and in a note to that novel he is described as "Constructor of Horologes to His most Sacred Majesty James I".

That Ramsay was the most celebrated watchmaker of the day may be inferred from the fact that, when the clock-makers obtained their charter of incorporation, he was therein appointed to the office of Master. He does not appear to have taken a very active part in the management of the company. During his absence in the country, Mr. Henry Archer was appointed Deputy Master. William Ramsay dedicated *Vox Stellarum* to his father in 1652, and in a postscript dated 1653 remarks, "from my study in my father's house in Holborn, within two doors of the 'Wounded Hart', near the King's Gate," and there David Ramsay probably died. The exact date of his death is uncertain, but it occurred about 1654, and though his age is not stated, he was then certainly very much past the meridian.

He is known to have been an inventor or schemer from the beginning of the century, and between 1618 and 1638 he took out no less than eight patents, none of which, however, seemed to be connected with horology; they related to raising water, draining mines, making saltpetre, separating gold and silver from the base metals, smelting iron, constructing furnaces of various kinds, dyeing fabrics, etc. He was a friend of James Lilley the astrologer, who, in his autobiography, relates that he accompanied Ramsay to Westminster at night to make some experiments with a view to discovering treasure by means of the divining rod.

THE CLOCKMAKERS' COMPANY. In 1627 a proposal to grant letters patent authorising French clockmakers to carry on their trade within the City appears to have occasioned an agitation among the London craftsmen in favour of incorporation as a trade guild. Prior to that date, individual freemen had been associated with one or other of the existing companies, that of the Blacksmiths having been most favoured. In 1630 a committee of clockmakers was formed, funds were raised to defray expenses, and petitions were addressed to the King, with the result that a charter was obtained from Charles I on the 22nd of August 1631.

In this document, "The Master, Wardens, and Fellowship of the Arts or Mystery of Clockmaking of the City of London" had very comprehensive powers for ruling and protecting the rights of the craft. They were entitled to make by-laws for the government of all persons using the trade in London, or within ten miles thereof, and for the regulation of the manner in which the trade should be carried on throughout the realm. And in order to prevent the public from being injured by persons "making, buying, selling, transporting, and importing any bad, deceitful, or insufficient clocks, watches, larums, sun-dials, boxes, or cases for the said trade", powers were given to the company "to enter with a constable or other officer any ships, vessels, warehouses, shops, or other places where they should suspect such bad and deceitful works to be made or kept, for the purpose of searching for them"; and, if entrance should be denied, they might effect it by force. Any such works as were faulty or deceitfully wrought they had power to seize and destroy, or cause them to be amended. Every member of the fellowship paid fourpence a quarter to meet the necessary expenses of these searches. In 1708 this quarterage produced over £28.

By the charter, David Ramsay was appointed to be the first master; Henry Archer, John Wellowe and Sampson Shelton were the first wardens; and James Vautrollier, John Smith, Francis Forman, John Harris, Richard Morgan, Samuel Lynaker, John Charlton, John Midnall, Simon Bartram, and Edward East, assistants of the said fellowship of the said art or mystery, and Thomas Copley, Clerk.

The charter also declared that future masters and wardens must be, or have been professed clock-makers, an important regulation, which certainly appears to have been contravened in late years. The right of search was exercised regularly till 1735, when it was abandoned.

On the incorporation of the Company, stringent by-laws were made regarding apprentices. No person was to take an apprentice without leave of the Master, and then to have but one, until he shall be called to bear the office of Master, Warden, or Assistant, and after that, not to exceed the number of two apprentices at any time whatsoever. But when his first apprentice had served five years, any member of the fellowship might take another, but not sooner, under a penalty of £10. And in the early history of the Company several of its members were brought to an account and fined for disobeying this regulation. Among them were several eminent members of the craft, including Thomas Loomes and Ahasuerus Fromanteel.

Then it was ordained that after an apprentice had served his time he should serve his master or some other member of the fellowship for two years as journeyman, and produce his 'masterpiece' of work before he was allowed to be a workmaster. This period of probation might, if the Company saw fit, be commuted to one year on payment of a fine.

Those craftsmen who had joined the Blacksmiths' and other Companies prior to the incorporation of the Clockmakers' were from time to time admitted as 'brothers' of the Clockmakers' Company.

As provided by the charter, the 'court' or directorate consists of the Master, three Wardens, and ten or more Assistants. The Assistants are chosen for life from among the freemen, and the usual, but not invariable, course is that the Assistants fill the higher offices in succession according to seniority; each one being elected first as Junior Warden, the next year as Renter, the next year as Senior Warden, and the following year as Master. After his retirement as Master, he resumes his seat as an ordinary member of the court.

In 1656 Ahasuerus Fromanteel and thirty-one other members complained to the court that, in spite of members having to pay 4d. a quarter, the meetings were held in taverns. They also objected to the presence of Frenchmen among the ruling body, and recounted other grievances. A counter-petition traversed the allegations, and asserted the confidence of the signatories in the management of the Company.

In 1671 the Company obtained the right to bear arms, and in that year letters patent were granted for this distinction. They recounted "that whereof at present Nicholas Coxeter is Master, Samuel Horne and Jeffery Bailey are Wardens, as also Edward East, the only persons now living of those mentioned in the said Letters Patents of Incorporation, John Nicasius, John Pennock, Edmond Gilpin, Jeremie Gregory, Thomas Taylor, Thomas Clayton, John Freeman, Evan Jones, Isaac Daniell, John Browne, Nicholas Payne, Richard Ames, and Benjamin Bell, are Assistants, and to the rest of the Fellowship and Company thereof, and to their successors for ever: the Armes, Crest, Supporters and Motto hereafter mentioned, vizt Sable, A Clock ye 4 Pillars therefore erected on four lyons, and on each capitall a globe with a Crosse, and in the middest an Imperial Crowne all Or, and for Their Crest upon an helmet Proper Mantled Gules Doubled Argent and Wreath of their Colours a Spheare Or, The Armes Supported by the Figures of a Naked Old man holding a Scithe and an Hour Glasse representing Time, and an Emporour in Roabes Crowned holding a Scepter, Their Motto—

TEMPVS RERVM IMPERATOR.

As in the margent they are all more lively depicted.

In 1677 Mr. George Deane, engraver, a member of the company, "having by the hands of Henry Jones presented to this court the Company's coat of arms engraved on a copper-plate fit to be used for tickets and divers other occasions of the company which was very well liked, this court did kindly accept it, and returned him thanks."

During the latter part of the seventeenth century the suitability of watch-making as a profession for women was recognised, and in 1715 the company sanctioned the taking of female apprentices. The names of several will be found in the list at the end of this book, where also is recorded the admission of a few female members of the company. The employment of female labour in watch work does not, however, seem to have made much progress in England till watch factories were established in quite recent years.

In 1781 it was decided to elect leading members of the trade as honorary freemen, even though not working in the City. This course, politic as it probably was, seems to indicate that at this period the prestige of the company in the horological world was insufficient to induce distinguished craftsmen to take up the freedom in the ordinary way.

The Company has never risen to the importance and comfort of possessing a hall of its own for meetings and other business. For brief periods during its history it had the use of a hall belonging to a more favoured guild, but most of its meetings were held in taverns, more than forty of these establishments having been so favoured. Its last meeting before the Great Fire of London was held on 20th August, at the Castle Tavern in Fleet Street; and the first meeting after, on 8th October 1666, at the Crown Tavern, in Smithfield. Later still, the Devil Tavern, near Temple Bar, was patronised.

Only a certain number of freemen from certain of the companies is permitted to take up the livery or freedom of the City, the whole matter being in the discretion of the Court of Aldermen. The claims of the Clockmakers' Company were not recognised in this respect till 1766, when it was allowed to select sixty of its members for the privilege; this number was upon petition, increased to one hundred and twenty in 1786, a still further increase to two hundred was sanctioned in 1810, and in 1826 the present limit of two hundred and fifty was reached.

No. 2 of the bye-laws provided "that every person of the said Fellowship chosen in the said Livery shall accept and take upon him to be of the said Livery, and shall within fourteen days after notice of such election take such oaths as by these ordinances shall be appointed for him".

The honour of election to the livery does not seem to have been always appreciated, for in 1813 "William Mansell, of Rosoman St., Clerkenwell, Watch casemaker, who was summoned to take the Livery on the 19th August 1812, again on 7th September 1812, and repeated on the 11th October last, was peremptorily summoned to be at this court, and being now in attendance for the first time, refused to take the Clothing, and the penalty of Fifteen Pounds being awarded against him for such refusal, he paid the sum in Court, and his Election to the Livery was thereupon discharged".

"William Welborne, of Leather Lane, Holborn, has been summoned to take the Livery in November 1811, and also in January, February and July 1812, but having failed so to do, was again summoned for that purpose to the last Quarter Court, when he attended and requested until this day, promising either to take the clothing or pay the penalty for refusal. He being now present and declining to take the same, the penalty of £15 was ordered to be enforced, which being paid in Court, his election to the Livery was likewise thereupon discharged".

The fine on taking up the livery was then fixed at £21.

As already stated, the company does not possess a hall of its own. Its business is transacted at the Guildhall, where, by permission of the Corporation, its library is kept and its remarkably fine museum of timekeepers displayed for public inspection. By arrangement with the Worshipful Company of Goldsmiths, its functions are held in the Goldsmiths' Hall.

FROMANTEEL, also spelt 'Fromantel' 'Fromantil', and 'Fromenteele'. Ahasuerus Fromanteel primus, of Dutch extraction, was a maker of steeple clocks at East Smithfield. In 1630 he was warned by the Blacksmiths' Company to bring in his certificate of seven years' service as apprentice. With this he complied, and was forthwith elected free of the company. On the incorporation of the clockmakers, he joined them. In 1656 he became restive under the somewhat inquisitorial proceedings of the court relating to his apprentices and the antecedents of his workmen, and for a long period in the history of the guild his name appears in petitions and other documents, expressing disapproval of the management of the company, or as being called to account for infraction of its rules, some of which, it must be confessed, could not fail to be exasperating to a man with an extensive business, as Fromanteel appears to have had.

A second Ahasuerus Fromanteel appears on the list as free of the Clockmakers' Company in 1655.

A third Ahasuerus Fromanteel was, in 1663, on completion of his apprenticeship with Simon Bartram, admitted as a member of the Clockmakers' Company.

In 1663 also, John Fromanteel, who had been apprenticed to Thomas Loomes, was admitted to the freedom.

Then Abraham, son of Ahasuerus Fromanteel, was elected in 1680.

In 1658 proceedings were taken against Ahasuerus Fromanteel and his son Louis for keeping more apprentices than the regulations of the company allowed, so that there was a fairly large family of the Fromanteels in the clock trade at that period, and most of them seem to have been connected in business.

In 1657 John went to Holland to learn the art of making pendulum clocks as recently invented by Huygens and made by Coster. On his return, the Fromanteels were the first to make pendulum clocks in England as they hastened to publicise in *Mercurius Politicus* for October 27th, and in the *Commonwealth Mercury* for November 25th 1658, in the following advertisement:

"There is lately a way found out for making of clocks that go exact and keep equaller time than any now made without this Regulator (examined and proved before His Highness the Lord Protector by such Doctors whose knowledge and learning is without exception) and are not subject to alter by change of weather, as others are, and may be made to go a week, a moneth, or a year, with once winding up, as well as those that are wound up every day, and keep time as well, and is very excellent for all House Clocks that go either with springs or weights; and also Steeple Clocks that are most subject to differ by change of weather. Made by Ahasuerus Fromanteel, who made the first that were in England. You may have them at his house on the Bankside, in Mosses Alley, Southwark, and at the sign of the Mermaid, in Lothbury, near Bartholomew lane end, London."

Under date 1st November 1660, Evelyn, in his Diary writes:

"I went with some of my relations to Court to shew them his Maj^ties cabinet and closset of rarities. . . Here I saw . . . amongst the clocks one that shew'd the rising and setting of the sun in Y^e Zodiaq, the sunn represented by a face and rais of gold upon an azure skie, observing Y^e diurnal and annual motion rising and setting behind, and landscape of hills, the work of our famous Fromantel."

Again, under date 1st April 1661, Evelyn records that he "dined with that great mathematician and virtuoso, Monsieur Zulichem (Huygens), inventor of the pendule clock'; and on 3rd May, "I return'd by Fromanteel's, the famous clockmaker, so see some pendules, Monsieur Zulichem being with us".

Mosses Alley, or Moses Alley, was a passage leading from the northern end of Bankside, Southwark, to Maid Lane.

The Mermaid in Lothbury was for over a century a noted shop for clocks. In 1650 Thomas Loomes, who was associated with the eldest Fromanteel in his attacks on the government of the Clockmakers' Company, and to whom John Fromanteel was apprenticed, resided there, and, after the time of Loomes, it was occupied by John Fromanteel.

EDWARD EAST, watchmaker to Charles I, was a true horologist and a worthy successor to

David Ramsay. He at one time lived in Pall Mall, near the tennis court, and attended the king when tennis and other games were being played in the Mall, his Majesty often providing one of East's watches as a prize. Edward East seems to have removed to Fleet Street, for it is related that at a later period the king's attendant, Mr. Herbert, failing in the punctual discharge of his duties in the morning, his Majesty provided him with a gold alarm watch, which was fetched from the king's watchmaker, Mr. East, in Fleet Street. He was in Fleet Street in 1635, and Lady Fanshawe, in her *Memoirs*, stated that when she came from France in the autumn of 1646 she lodged in Fleet Street at Mr. East's the watchmaker. The locality of a presumably still later residence is indicated by a reference to "Mr. East at the Sun, outside Temple Bar", in the *London Gazette*, January 22–26, 1690.

East made clocks and watches of all kinds including night clocks, with a revolving chapter ring and perforated numerals through which shone a lamp placed inside the clock. All his work attained a very high standard of accuracy and finish and is signed in a tall script lettering of great elegance.

Edward East was one of the ten original Assistants named in the charter of incorporation of the Clockmakers' Company, and at once took a leading part in its proceedings, and after serving in the subordinate capacities was elected Master in 1645, a post he again occupied in 1652. He was the only Treasurer ever appointed, and the creation of the office came about in a curious way. In 1647 the Renter Warden, Mr. Helden, refused to give the usual security for the stock of the company, and in this dilemma the office of Treasurer was created, Mr. East and Mr. Hacket being nominated thereto, and the former chosen.

On the death of Mr. East the office was allowed to lapse.

The dates of Edward East's birth and death are not known with certainty, and from the great span of years which the name covers it has been suggested that there were two men of the same name operating during the seventeenth century and further evidence of this may yet come to light. As against this there are the following facts in favour of one man attaining the great age of ninety-four. On August 22nd 1602, Edward, son of John East, was baptised at Southill in Bedfordshire (quite close to Tompion's birthplate). On March 27th, 1618, an "Edward East sonne of John East of Southill—" was apprenticed to Richard Rogers of the Goldsmiths' Company. In 1631 he was a founder member, and the most junior Assistant of the Clockmakers' Company. Edward East was successively appointed to Charles I and II and in 1671 he was described as the only surviving founder member of the Company. In 1693 an Edward East gave £100 to the Company "now in his lifetime" and on February 3rd, 1697, the Will was proved of "Edward East of the parish of Hampton in the County of Middlesex, Watchmaker and Citizen and Goldsmith of London".

This sequence of events is the result of research by Mr. H. Alan Lloyd.

JOHN and JOSEPH KNIBB. Several members of this family are known among the seventeenth century clockmakers. Samuel Knibb was admitted to the freedom of the Clockmakers' Company in 1663, Joseph in 1670, Peter in 1677, Edward in 1700 and Joseph junior in 1717.

The most famous of these is Joseph senior who had, in addition, a brother John who lived and worked in Oxford and so had no occasion to join the Clockmakers' Company.

Joseph Knibb was born in 1640 and moved to Oxford in 1667 where he appears, somewhat surprisingly, as the gardener of Trinity College. That he was nevertheless practising as a clockmaker is shown by protests from the Oxford smiths that, being no freeman of the city, he had yet set up shop within it. They accordingly demanded that he should "suddenly shutt down his windows and remove either to St. Clement's (from whence he came) or else to some other place out of the city liberties". It may have been to circumvent this situation that the college appointed him as its gardener. Anyway, by 1668 the opposition were placated and Joseph was admitted to the freedom of the city on paying a fine of £6 13s. 4d. and a 'leathern buckett'.

Associated with Joseph was his younger brother John and when Joseph moved to London, John stayed behind and continued in practice on his own in Oxford, where he became Mayor in 1700. His work is not generally the equal of Joseph's but evidently the brothers remained in fairly close collaboration, for there exists a bracket clock with Joseph's name on the back-plate, concealed by a contemporary engraved plate bearing the name of John, whose name is also engraved on the dial.

Joseph is noted for his fine work and particularly for the elegance of his clocks. He retained the old-fashioned, narrow chapter ring, with a long, simple, spade hour hand, after Tompion had set the fashion for a wider chapter and shorter, heavier, and more ornate hour hand. Knibb clocks on this account may sometimes be taken for an earlier date than is in fact the case. The hands of a Joseph Knibb are particularly elegant and sharply bevelled. He also employed the roman system of striking which is described on page 88 and has the merit over the ordinary system of conserving power. Clocks with roman striking may easily be recognised since they have a IV instead of the usual IIII.

Several night clocks by Knibb survive.

Joseph prospered in London and supplied clocks to Charles II.

In the *London Gazette*, July 9–12, 1688, "a striking watch, two gold cases engraven, a brass case over them, Joseph Knibb, maker, day of the month, pins to feel the hours," was advertised for, "information to be given to Mr. Jos. Knibb, at the Dial, in Fleet Street." There are other references to him, of which the following may be of interest:

"Lost on the 26th inst., near the Ferry Place, Putney, a gold Pendulum Chain Minute-watch, made by Joseph Knibb, of London, in a Shagreen case, studded, with a Gold Knob, and marked with 48 on the inside of the case. Whoever will give notice of it to Mr. Joseph Knibb, watchmaker, in Fleet Street, shall have 2 guineas and charges; or, if pawned or sold, their money again and a good gratuity" (*London Gazette*, April 30, May 4, 1691).

"Left in a coach or drop'd, the 12th inst., a Gold Out-Case of a striking watch, engraven. Whoever shall bring it to Joseph Knibb, clockmaker, at the Dyal, near Serjeants-Inn, in Fleet Street, shall receive 40s. reward" (*London Gazette*, January 11–14, 1691).

"At the Clock Dyal, in Suffolk Street, near Charing Cross, on Friday, the 23rd inst., will begin the sale of a great Parcel of very good Pendulum Clocks, some do go a year, some a quarter of a year, some a month, some a week, and some 30 hours; some are Table Clocks, some repeat themselves, and some, by pulling, repeat the hours and quarters; made and sold by Joseph Knibb, at his House at the Dyal, in Suffolk Street, aforementioned. There are also some watches to be then and there sold" (*London Gazette*, April 15–19, 1697).

Joseph retired at some time after this sale and moved to Hanslope, in Buckinghamshire, and a few clocks exist from this period, marked "Joseph Knibb of Hanslope" or "Joseph Knibb att Hanslop". They are not the equal of his London work and may possibly have been made for him by John who outlived him and proved his will on May 4th 1712.

CHRISTIAN HUYGENS. This distinguished mathematician and optician was born at the Hague in 1629. He was sometimes referred to as 'Zulichem' with which town he was connected.

Huygens occupies a similar place in horology to Hooke in that both were men of wide interests and attainments and who profoundly influenced the advancement of horology without themselves having any training or executive skill in the art.

In 1657 Huygens presented to the States of Holland a pendulum clock made to his design by the Dutch clockmaker Samuel Coster. Although Huygens was not, and never claimed to be the inventor of the pendulum, his instrument of 1657 was the first to take pendulum clocks out of the experimental stage into the realms of large-scale commercial production. In connection with pendulums he discovered circular error and the means of correcting it by cycloidal cheeks; he also invented a remontoire and a form of maintaining power.

He also attempted the construction of a pendulum—controlled marine timekeeper but being unsuccessful he turned to a watch with a spiral balance-spring and pirouette which he caused to be made for him by the French Court clock-maker Jacques Thuret in 1674–5. But in this he was also disappointed of his objective since he had no means of compensating temperature errors. Nevertheless, his watch does seem to have been the first successful balance-spring watch, although, again, he never bothered to claim it as such. The merits of his right to have done so are further discussed in Chapter III, where, and also in Chapter V, his other inventions are described in somewhat greater detail.

Being a Protestant, Huygens returned to Holland in 1685, following the Revocation of the Edict of Nantes. He died in 1695.

His portrait was painted by Netscher, among others, and engraved by G. Edelink.

DR. HOOKE. Robert Hooke was born in 1635 at Freshwater, Isle of Wight. After his father's death in 1648 he lived with Dr. Busby, headmaster of Westminster School. He entered Christ Church College, Oxford, in 1653, and there his genius soon attracted the notice of Dr. Ward, whom he frequently assisted in his astronomical operations. Dr. Ward introduced Hooke to the Hon. Robert Boyle, who engaged him as an assistant in his mechanical and philosophical works.

Hooke took part in and wrote upon all the scientific questions of his time. Sir Isaac Newton styled him 'The Considerer'. On the institution of the Royal Society he was elected a Fellow in 1663, was afterwards entrusted with the care of its Repository, and made Professor of Mechanics to that body. About the same period he was elected Professor of Geometry in Gresham College.

No portrait of Hooke is known but a lively word-picture is given in Aubrey's *Lives of Eminent Men*:

"He is of middling stature, somewhat crooked, pale faced, and his face but little belowe, but his head is lardge; his eie is full and popping, and not quick; a grey eie. He has a delicate head of haire, browne, and of an excellent moiste curle. He is and ever was very temperate and moderate in dyet, &c. As he is of prodigious inventive head, so he is a person of great vertue and goodness."

He discovered that the resilience of a spring is proportional to the angle through which it has been wound, and propounded the whole theory in the sentence, "Ut tensio sic vis," meaning that the force is proportionate to the tension. He proposed to patent his discovery in 1660, and, to quote his words, "Sir Robert Moray drew me up the form of a patent, the principal part whereof, viz., the description of the watch, is his own handwriting, which I have yet by me; the discouragement I met with in the progress of this affair made me desist for that time."

Derham describes the earliest of Hooke's essays in this direction as a "tender strait spring, one end whereof played backward and forward with the ballance". It is stated that several watches were made under Hooke's supervision at this period, and one of the first to which the balance spring was applied he is said to have presented to Dr. Wilkins, afterwards Bishop of Chester, about 1661.

It appears that Hooke then conceived it to be an advantage to have two balances coupled together, and had two double balance watches constructed. In the first, which had no balance spring, the escape wheel was placed in the centre of the movement with its teeth in a horizontal plane. There were two verges standing vertically on opposite sides of the wheel and connected with each other by means of toothed wheels of equal size; each verge had one pallet and carried a balance at its upper end, one balance overlapping the other.

In the second watch the verge escapement was arranged in the ordinary way, the balance being mounted on a verge with two pallets; on the verge was also a toothed wheel which engaged with another of the same size mounted on a stud, and the pipe of this wheel carried the second balance; the toothed wheels being of small size, one balance was placed a little higher than the other and overlapped it. Each balance was controlled by a balance-spring.

However, Hooke turned his attention to other matters, and in January 1675 Huygens addressed a letter to Henry Oldenburg, Secretary of the Royal Society, in which he described as his invention the application of a spring to control the balance in watches. This aroused the wrath of Hooke, who accused Oldenburg of having divulged the discovery in his correspondence with Huygens. Hooke enlisted the interest of Charles II, and in a lecture, entitled *Potentia Restitutiva &c.*, said "His Majesty was pleased to see the experiment that made out this theory tried at Whitehall, as also my spring watch".

In 1660, Hooke devised a pendulum timekeeper for ascertaining the longitude at sea. This was tried in 1662, and he subsequently proposed a compensation pendulum in the form of a rhomboid, the outline being of steel and the long horizontal diagonal of brass. This form, being wider than it was long, was considered to be impracticable. Troughton afterwards constructed a pendulum in which the rod was a series of small rhomboids arranged to compensate on Hooke's plan.

Hooke devised the first wheel-cutting engine about 1670. Prior to that time the operation of forming the teeth was tedious and imperfect, but by means of Hooke's engine the blanks were accurately marked and cut.

His investigations covered a very wide field of science, but his restless disposition rarely allowed him to pursue steadily any subject to a conclusion. No sooner was he satisfied of the feasibility of any project, than he left it, thus allowing others to perfect his inventions. On the death of Oldenburg, in 1677, he was appointed Secretary to the Royal Society, and, by an order of the Society, he was requested to give a full description of all the instruments which he had contrived, but ill-health prevented him from performing it. During the last year of his life he was almost helpless. He died at Gresham College, 3rd March 1703 and was buried at St. Helen's, Bishopsgate.

Hooke profoundly influenced the work of Tompion and this aspect of his life is discussed in the life of Tompion which follows.

The merits of his claim to have invented the anchor escapement and the spiral balance spring are further discussed in Chapter III. His diaries and many other works have been published (*Early Science in Oxford*, edited by R. T. Gunther).

EDWARD BARLOW (BOOTH). This talented man was born near Warrington in 1636. He was ordained in the English Church at Lisbon, and took the name of Barlow from his godfather, Ambrose Barlow, a Benedictine, who suffered at Lancaster for his religion. Edward Booth devoted considerable attention to horological instruments. He was undoubtedly the inventor of the rack striking work for clocks, from which followed the invention of repeating mechanism, first applied to clocks in about 1676. He also devised a repeating watch on the same principle, and made application to patent it in 1686. His claim was successfully opposed by Daniel Quare, who was backed by the Clockmakers' Company. The king, James II, tried both watches, and gave his preference to Quare's, which repeated the hours and quarters with one push from a pin near the pendant, whereas Barlow's watch was furnished with a pin on each side of the pendant and required two distinct operations to attain the same end.

Booth invented the precursor of the cylinder escapement, and patented it in conjunction with William Houghton and Thomas Tompion in 1695 (No. 344). The invention is described as a "ballance wheele either flatt or hollow, to worke within and crosse the centre of the verge or axis of the balance with a new sort of teeth made like tinterhooks to move the balance and the pallets of the axis or verge, one to be circular, concave and convex". He died in 1716.

THOMAS TOMPION was born at Ickwell Green, a hamlet of Northill, Bedfordshire in 1639. He was presumably brought up a blacksmith, like his father and grandfather before him, and the family forge still exists and bears a plaque commemorating its historic connection with England's most famous clockmaker, who did more than any other to establish her in that position of unassailed supremacy which her makers enjoyed at the close of the seventeenth century.

Tompion had a brother James and a sister Margaret, both younger than himself.

Some unknown chance decided him to leave the smithy and come to London and it is not even known to whom he was apprenticed. He became a brother in the Clockmakers' Company in 1671, and in 1674 moved to the premises in Water Lane at the sign of the Dial and Three Crowns, where he conducted an ever increasing business throughout his life. Water Lane is now called Whitefriars Street and Tompion's shop was at the Fleet Street corner. In the same year he met Dr. Robert Hooke and this may well have been the turning point in his career. He was at once commissioned to make an extremely accurate Quadrant, which he did to Hooke's entire satisfaction, and the year following, 1675, Hooke sought Tompion's help in establishing his prior invention of the spiral balance spring to Huygens'. This brought Tompion to the notice of Charles II and he rapidly rose to be the leading maker of his day without challenge. He made the first clocks for Greenwich Observatory in 1676. There can be little doubt that he owed much to Hooke, even if their friendship had its ups and downs (a state of affairs common to all Hooke's friends and acquaintances). For although Tompion was an ingenious craftsman of unsurpassed skill, he seems to have had little inventive genius, and it was here that he was so greatly helped by the famous physicist and mathematician. A direct result of his co-operation with Hooke was that he was the first English maker to apply the spiral balance spring to a watch and with so much success that

his watches were shortly in demand in France, although Huygens' own balance spring watches were already in production in Paris by the famous French maker Thuret. Two of Tompion's watches were bought by the Dauphin.

In 1695 Tompion collaborated with Booth and Houghton in patenting an escapement with an horizontal escape wheel which has been acclaimed as the forerunner of the cylinder. But in truth it is more closely related to the virgule, impulse only being given in one direction. No surviving example is known.

In the same year Tompion was joined by George Graham, then just out of his articles, and in the following year Graham married Elizabeth, Tompion's niece, the daughter of his brother James.

Also in 1695 Tompion (aided doubtless by Hooke) devised the first clock with equation work (showing the difference between solar and mean time). This superb timepiece which goes for a year, was supplied to William III and is still at Buckingham Palace.

From 1701 Tompion was in partnership with Edward Banger, previously his apprentice, and the husband of his niece, and pieces of this period are signed with their joint names. But whether Banger got in to debt, or for what other reason not now known, the partnership was broken up abruptly in 1707 or 1708, and circa 1711 Tompion took George Graham into partnership and so continued until the end of his life. Clocks or watches signed by Tompion and Graham are now very rare.

In 1703 Tompion was elected Master of the Clockmakers' Company.

Apart from his more famous special clocks, both bracket and long-case, Tompion early developed various more or less standard types which he produced with little variation, the most popular being an ebony bracket timepiece with repeating mechanism.

But although he is now thought of mainly as a clock-maker, in his lifetime it was for his watches that he was most renowned. For whereas he only made about six hundred and fifty clocks, at the rate of less than twenty a year, he produced in all about five thousand five hundred watches. For these he charged £11 in a silver case or £23 in gold, but a gold repeater cost the then tremendous sum of £70.

Some time between 1680 and 1685 Tompion started to number his products, being apparently the first maker to do so. His clocks go up to 542, but it has not so far been possible to attribute definite dates for the numbers (except on the general idea that he made eighteen or twenty clocks a year) since the only two of his clocks to be dated are not numbered. He started to number his watches at about the same time, stamping the number on the dial plate and engraving it on the top plate. From about 1700 onwards he also stamped the number under the balance cock. Gold watches can sometimes be dated by the hall-mark, but silver watches in Tompion's time were seldom hall-marked. Tompion had three series of watch numbers of which ordinary watches went up to about 4600. Repeaters and alarums each seem to have a separate series amounting in all to about 500. In special watches the number was prefixed by 0, of which there seem to have been about 1000, mostly fairly early. After Tompion's death, the same numbering was carried straight on by Graham, so that the series extends in all over nearly seventy-five years.

One of the boldest of Tompion's conceptions was a clock to strike the hours and quarters, driven by mainsprings and yet requiring to be wound but once a year. The clock was made for William III at a cost of £1,500, and was in his bedroom at Kensington Palace when he died. It was left by him to the Earl of Leicester, and now belongs to Lord Mostyn, in whose family it has been ever since. It is still in going order, and Lord Mostyn has the name of nearly every one who has wound it during the last hundred years. The total height to the top of the spear is 30 in.; the body or plinth below the dial is 10 in. in width, 7 in. in height, and 6 in. from front to back.

The case, of ebony with silver mounts, is a fine piece of work in one piece, forming really a hood or cover, for it slides down over the movement and rests on the metal feet.

The movement is in three portions; the lower part below the dial is attached to the heavy scroll feet, and contains the two mainspring barrels, the two fusees, and the larger driving wheels. The middle portion behind the dial contains the smaller wheels and pinions, while the verge escapement above is held separately, so that it may be easily detached. The pendulum, 6 in. long, is in front of the movement just behind the dial, and its action may be seen through the glazed door below the dial, which is removed when winding or regulation is needed. Regulation is effected by raising or lowering the chops which embrace the pendulum spring, very much in the way adopted for modern clocks; the sliding chops are actuated by a tangent wheel and screw, and there is on the front plate a micrometer index for noting the amount of adjustment made.

The hours are struck on a bell attached to the front plate, the ting-tang quarters being sounded on this and on a smaller bell, which surmounts the movement. On each side of the case is a pull-repeating arrangement.

During the building of St. Paul's, it was frequently reported that Tompion was to construct a wonderful clock for the cathedral; and in *The Affairs of the World*, published in October 1700, the following announcement appeared: "Mr. Tompion, the famous watchmaker in Fleet Street, is making a clock for St. Paul's Cathedral, which it is said will go one hundred years without winding up; will cost £3,000 or £4,000, and be far finer than the clock at Strasburg." Though this statement seems to have been unwarranted, it is quite possible he would have been entrusted with the construction of a timekeeper of some kind, but after unremitting application to his profession for more than thirty years, he was at this time, it may be assumed, just beginning to indulge in well-earned leisure; during the last years of his life he allowed himself considerable relaxation, and was absent from London for extended periods. In the course of his migrations he visited Bath, possibly to derive benefit from the healing properties of the hot mineral waters. In the Grand Pump-room there is a splendid example of Tompion's later work, which he presented to the city, as is thus recorded on a tablet adjacent to the timekeeper: "The Watch and Sun-dial was given by Mr. Thos. Tompion, of London, Clockmaker, Anno Dom. 1709." The dial is of brass, with ornamental corner pieces and silvered rings, the minute circle being 15 in. in diameter; the day of the month is shown through an aperture. On a high arch above is an equation index and scale, 0 being in the centre, and the variation to a maximum of fifteen minutes shown on each side; on the right, "Sun faster," and to the left, "Sun slower." The months and days are engraved on a silvered 10 in. circle, of which an arc is shown through an opening. The number of minutes shown by the index gives the difference between sun time and mean time; this 10 in. circle makes its annual circuit by means of an endless screw and pinion, worked from the dial wheel, which makes one revolution per hour. The index is kept in position by a small counterpoise with a pulley fitted to its arbor; the pulley is attached by a fine chain to a cranked arm, which rises and falls with the indentations and protuberances of a properly shaped plate or cam attached securely to the 10 in. circle.

The case is of solid unpolished oak, 9 ft. high to the top of the arched head which is surmounted by brass ball ornaments. The body of the case is 17 in. wide and about 6 in. narrower than the head and base, with a semicircular door 8 in. across and 5 ft. in length.

The clock is in a recess at the eastern end of the room, and it occupied a similar position in the old Pump-room, the erection of which was finished in 1706. As the recess is particularly suited for the reception of a clock, it may be conjectured that Tompion was in Bath when the old Pump-room was being built, and that the ever-vigilant 'Beau' Nash obtained from him a promise to present a timepiece when the building was completed.

The Royal Society possesses a paper in Hooke's handwriting, imperfect and undated, showing that Tompion and Hooke were in communication on the subject of the barometer, which is of interest as evidence of the estimation in which Tompion was held by Hooke. It occurs about the middle of a parchment-bound volume lettered 20 *Hooke's Papers*, and is headed *Aerostatick Instruments*. In it Hooke states that a form of his barometer, in which the height of the mercury was indicated by a column of water, "was tryed at Mr. Thomas Tompion's, a person deservedly famous for his excellent skill in making watches and clocks, and not less curious and dexterous in constructing and handworking of other nice mechanical instruments." A barometer by Tompion is at Hampton Court Palace.

The extent of Tompion's business may be judged from the fact that in the advertisements for the recovery of lost watches during the period he was in business, timekeepers of his make largely preponderate, and the following are a few quotations from such advertisements:

"Lost on Wednesday, 20th of this Instant September at night in or about St. James's, a Gold Pendulum watch of Mr. Tompion's making, having three motions, a shagreen case, a cipher on the Back Side, and marked within the Box 277, with a Gold Chain and three seals, viz. one Figure and two Heads. Whoever give notice thereof to Mr. Nott, a Bookseller in Pall Mall, or to Mr. Loman at the Lord Cavendish's House in St. James's Square, shall have 15 Guineas Reward" (*London Gazette*, September 22, 1682).

"Lost on Monday, the 25th Instant in the Fields betwixt Islington Church and Newington Green, a gold watch with a Shagreen Case, with a cipher studded in gold on the Bottom. Made by Thos. Tompion, London. Whoever brings the said watch to Mr. Robert Halstead, Goldsmith at the Crown in Fleet St. shall have three Guineas Reward" (*London Gazette*, January 25, 1685–6).

"Lost out of a gentleman's Pocket, the 19th past, betwixt Lyme St. end in Fenchurch St. and the end of the Minories, an indifferent small size gold pendulum watch, going without string or chain, showing the hours of the day, and day of the month, the name Tompion, in a shagreen case, pinned with a Cypher in the bottom of the case, wound up on the dial plate, at the hour of 12, a straight key with a Steel Nose. Whoever brings it to Mr. Tompion, Clockmaker, at Water Lane, and in Fleet St., shall have one guinea reward, or, if bought, their money again with reasonable profit" (*London Gazette*, November 10–13, 1690).

"Lost, the 3rd inst. between the Sun-Dial, in St. James Park, and Man's Coffee House, a silver Minute Pendulum watch, made by Tho. Tompion, in a Shagreen studded case, on the bottom of the inner case the number 458; with a gold Ring hanging upon the silver chain, with the Effigies of their Present Majesties" (*London Gazette*, March 3–7, 1691).

"Lost on the 24th instant, about Kingston-on Thames, a Gold Minute and Second Chain Pendulum watch, with a Stop, the hours seen through a hole in the Dial plate, and in a plain Shagreen Out-Case, the name Tho. Tompion, London, a number in the bottom of the Box, 0201. Whoever gives notice of it to Mr. Tho. Tompion, Clockmaker, at the corner of Water Lane, in Fleet St., shall have 3 guineas reward; or if bought already, your money again with reasonable profit" (*London Gazette*, June 25–29, 1691).

"Lost on the 23rd instant a Gold Pendulum Watch made by Thos. Tompion, Fleet Street, in a Shagreen Studded Case with a Steel Seal set in gold tied to it, bearing a Coat quartered with the arms of the Crown battoned; the Box numbered 422 and the maker's mark (II)" (*London Gazette*, July 23–27, 1691).

"Lost on the 21st instant from the Duke of Richmond's in St. James's Square, a gold striking watch with a Shagreen case studded round, with little holes between, having 3 links of plain gold chain, made by Thos. Tompion, in Fleet St. Whoever brings it to Mr. Compton, Goldsmith, in Duke St. near Lincoln's Inn Fields, shall have 6 Guineas" (*London Gazette*, February 21–23, 1694).

"Lost, some time in November last, at Oxon, a Gold Minute Pendulum watch in a plain gold case; the names on the upper peak, Tho. Tompion, Edwd. Banger, London; with this number, 3428, on the bottom of the Box within side, and likewise upon the upper plate. Whoever give notice of it (so it may be had again) to the Reverend Dr. King, of Christ Church College, at Oxon, or to Tho. Tompion, Clockmaker, at the Dial and Three Crowns, at the Corner of Water Lane, Fleet St. London, shall have three guineas reward; or if bought or pawned, your money again with reasonable profit" (*London Gazette*, December 4–7, 1704).

Tompion died on November 20th 1713 being aged seventy-four years, and was buried in Westminster Abbey.

Little is known of Tompion's domestic life, but he was a bachelor, and his portrait was painted by Sir Godfrey Kneller. There are many mezzotint engravings of this portrait by I. Smith. His will, executed on the 21st October 1713, was proved on the 27th November, in the same year, by George Graham, who was one of the executors. By this document he bequeathed to his nephew, Thomas Tompion, son of his brother James, his land and property at Northill, Bedfordshire, and the interest on £100. To his niece, Margaret Banger, wife of Edward Banger, clock-maker, and daughter of his late sister, Margaret Kent, he gave a life interest in £500, which at her death was to revert to Elizabeth Graham, wife of George Graham, daughter of his said brother James. Another daughter of his sister, Elizabeth Kent, is mentioned, and a cousin, Thomas Finch. George Graham and his wife were residuary legatees. Tho. Tompion, junr. was apprenticed to Charles Kemp in 1694 and admitted as a member to the Clockmakers' Company in 1702, presumably when he had completed his apprenticeship. He does not seem ever to have worked with his famous uncle and namesake. He was evidently a bad character as in 1720 he was committed to Newgate Prison for pickpocketing.

In 1724 he attended the funeral of Daniel Quare.

GEORGE GRAHAM. 'Honest George Graham,' was born in 1673 or 1674. He tramped to London at an early age, and in 1688 became apprenticed for seven years to Henry Aske, when he described himself as "George Graham, sonne of George Graham, late of ffordeland in the county of Cumberland, Husbandman, deceased". He was admitted a freeman of the Clockmakers' Company on completing his indentures in 1695, and immediately entered the service of Thomas Tompion, thus beginning a life-long friendship, severed only by the death of Tompion in 1713. In 1696 he married Tompion's niece Elizabeth. A few clocks and watches during the last years of Tompion's life, are signed "Tompion & Graham". The following announcement appeared in the *London Gazette* for 28th November to 1st December 1713: "George Graham, Nephew of the late Mr. Thomas Tompion, who lived with him upwards of seventeen years, and managed his trade for several years past, whose name was joined with Mr. Tompion's for some time before his death, and to whom he left all his stock and work, finished and unfinished, continues to carry on the said trade at the late Dwelling House of the said Mr. Tompion, at the sign of the Dial and Three Crowns, at the corner of Water Lane, in Fleet Street, London, where all persons may be accommodated as formerly."

In 1720 Graham relinquished Tompion's old premises, as will be seen by the appended official notification from the *London Gazette* of March 22–26th 1720: "George Graham, watchmaker, is removed from the corner of Water Lane, in Fleet Street, to the Dial and One Crown on the other side of the way, a little nearer Fleet Bridge, a new house next door to the Globe and Duke of Marlborough's Head Tavern." Here in the rooms over the shop Graham lived until his death. The little shop had two plain bow windows, with the doorway between them, and, with but little alteration in appearance, remained as a watch-maker's for many years. Graham was elected as a Fellow of the Royal Society in 1721 and chosen as a Member of the Council of that body in 1722. He contributed twenty-one papers on various subjects to the *Philosophical*

Transactions. Also in 1722 he became Master of the Clockmakers' Company.

After the expiration of Booth, Houghton, and Tompion's patent, Graham devoted some thought to the cylinder escapement, which in 1725 he modified to practically its present form, and after 1726 introduced it into all his watches. Securing to himself the monopoly of any of his discoveries was foreign to his disposition. The reputation which English horology acquired on the Continent during the eighteenth century was due in no small measure to Graham's candid treatment of his brethren in the art in other countries. In answer to inquiries, Julien Le Roy received from Graham one of his cylinder escapement watches in 1728, and the French horologist's generous avowal of its superiority is worthy of his acknowledged greatness.

He invented the dead-beat escapement in 1715 and the mercury pendulum in 1726, and the combination of these two produced a degree of accuracy in timekeeping which was only surpassed by Riefler a hundred and seventy years later.

Graham continued the serial numbers started by Tompion and he appears only to have made a hundred and seventy-four clocks of all types, numbered from 600 to 774. As against this he made nearly three thousand watches. No. 4369 is labelled "Tompion & Graham", which cannot therefore be later than 1713 and No. 6574, the highest number so far known, bears the hall mark for the year 1751, when Graham died. Like Tompion, Graham had a separate series for repeaters, ranging from No. 402, hall-marked for 1713, to No. 965. This must be about the last made, since No. 968 bears the name of Thomas Colley, Graham's successor and so, curiously enough, does No. 962, indicating some overlapping. It is noteworthy that Graham's repeaters are always smaller than his other watches, despite the extra mechanism involved. This may be attributed to the great cost of his repeaters, which could only be afforded by the wealthiest clients. His earliest, verge watches, have a pierced cock-foot, but he soon abandoned this for a very plain type of cock with a solid, engraved cock-foot. Some of his watches have a finely-shaped, polished steel centre-seconds hand and these also have stop-work (stopping the entire watch).

Graham's watches were much forged, even in his life-time, but this may generally be detected, since he not only marked the number in the usual place on the back-plate, together with his name, but also on the pillar-plate, under the dial, and on the under-side of the cock.

In addition to clocks and watches, Graham was equally famed for his scientific instruments, especially astronomical, and his continental reputation probably rested more on his astronomical than on his horological work.

Graham's mode of living was distinguished by its simplicity, honesty and generosity. An example of his generosity is the interest-free loan which he made to John Harrison, although both of them were working on the Longitude problem. His later years were chiefly occupied with astronomical work, which he carried on as the valued coadjutor of Halley and Bradley till his death. By his will, executed in 1747, he left to his wife one-half of his personal estate. He also bequeathed £20 to the Clockmakers' Company. He died on November 16th 1751, aged seventy seven. The grave of Tompion in Westminster Abbey, was opened to receive his pupil, and the exceptional honour of their interment in that place is the best testimony that can be adduced as to the estimation in which these eminent horologists were held.

The grave is at about one third of the length of the nave from its western end, and on the south side. The inscription on it is as follows:

"Here lies the body of MR. THO TOMPION who departed this life the 20th of November 1713 in the 75th year of his age. Also the body of George Graham of London watchmaker and F.R.S. whose curious inventions do honour to $\frac{e}{y}$ British genius whose accurate performances are $\frac{e}{y}$ standard of mechanic skill. He died $\frac{e}{y}$ XVI of November MDCCLI in the LXXVIII year of his age."

Immediately after Graham's death there was some competition to claim his goodwill. Only two days later the following notice appeared in the *General Advertiser*: "Thomas Mudge, watchmaker, apprentice to the late Mr. Graham, carries on business in the same manner as Mr. Graham did, at the sign of the Dial and One Crown, opposite the Bolt and Tun, in Fleet Street."

On December 3rd 1751 the *Public Advertiser* contained a rival announcement by the executors of Graham's will: "Samuel Barclay, Foreman and Executor to Mr. George Graham, clock and watchmaker, deceased, succeeds the said Mr. Graham in his business and shop at the Dial and Three Crowns next door to the Globe Tavern in Fleet Street; opposite Salisbury Court, in partnership with Mr. Thomas Colley, the other Executor. The customers may depend upon everything being executed to the same perfection as in the lifetime of Mr. Graham and on his principles, Mr. Barclay has served his apprenticeship to him, lived with him six and thirty years and had the sole conduct and inspection of his work these several years." This partnership did not last long as the *Public*

Advertiser for August 15th 1752 announced "Mr. Thomas Colley, successor to the late Mr. Graham, watchmaker in Fleet Street" and soon afterwards Colley was joined in partnership by John Preist, another of Graham's apprentices.

In view of the fact that Barclay inherited Graham's business it is puzzling that his address is given at the Dial and Three Crowns, which Graham had left in 1720; whereas Mudge's address is given as the Dial and One Crown which was Graham's address after 1720. The probable explanation is that at some time after 1720 Graham changed his sign back from one to three crowns. Graham's advertisement of 1720 and Barclay's of 1751 both give the address as being next to the Globe Inn although Graham refers to one crown and Barclay to three.

Graham's portrait was painted by T. Hudson and engraved by I. Faber. A second engraving was made by T. Ryley as late as 1820.

DANIEL QUARE. This worthy contemporary of Tompion was born in 1647.

About 1680 he produced repeating watches of his own design, and when the Rev. Edward Barlow, in 1686, sought to patent a repeating device, Quare, backed by the Clockmakers' Company, opposed the monopoly. The case was considered by the Privy Council on 2nd March 1687, and Barlow's application for a patent refused. In Quare's arrangement a single push on a pin projecting from the case near the pendant sufficed to sound the hour and the quarters, while Barlow's required a distinct action for each. The king, after a trial of both repeating watches, gave the preference to that of Quare, which fact was notified in the *Gazette*.

The Quare repeater watch in the Ashmolean Museum, Oxford is probably the one submitted to James II. In his subsequent repeaters the pendant is pushed in, instead of the separate pin as in this prototype.

By several writers Quare is credited with the invention of the concentric minute hand, but such indicators were in use long before his time, the hour hand being driven from the great wheel, and the minute hand from the centre arbor. Quare's improvement consisted in devising a mechanism so that the hour and minute hands should be actuated together. The earliest known form of this device is applied to a clock-watch, in which at first sight there appears to be motion work of the kind now in general use, but an important variation is apparent on examination. Both of the hands are driven direct from the great wheel. A wheel and pinion corresponding to the minute wheel and nut fit on to a squared arbor projecting from the great wheel. The cannon pinion runs loose on a stud in the centre of the watch, and on it is placed the hour wheel in the usual way. The wheel and pinion attached to the great wheel are of brass, and to allow the hands to be set they fit friction tight on to a steel boss, which has a square hole to correspond with the end of the great wheel arbor. Attached to the bottom face of the cannon pinion is a star wheel for releasing the striking work every hour. Under the arrangement in vogue before Quare's time, by which each hand was driven independently of the other, if the minute hand was set forward or backward, the hour hand would cease to correspond with it. As the cannon pinion was mounted on a stud there was no necessity of having the second wheel of the train in the centre of the movement, and so the going train was continued to one side of the centre, leaving the other side for the striking work. The one advantage of the present arrangement of motion work over Quare's is that the minute hand now follows the motion of the centre pinion without shake, but in Quare's plan the position of the minute hand was not so absolute on account of the backlash of the motion wheels.

In 1695 Quare obtained a patent for a portable weather glass, and several instruments made by him according to his specification are known to exist.

Quare was admitted as a brother of the Clockmakers' Company in 1671, and served as Master in 1708. During the latter part of his career he took into partnership Stephen Horseman, who had been apprenticed to him, and the business was carried on at the same address under the title of Quare and Horseman.

The following is a selection from the inquiries respecting Quare's timekeepers:

"Lost on 2nd instant, a silver pendulum watch. The name Daniel Quare, London; it had but six hours upon the dial-plate with six small cipher figures within every hour, the hand going round every six hours, which shows also the minutes between every hour. Whoever gives notice of it to Daniel Quare at The Kings Arms in Exchange Alley, London, shall have a guinea reward" (*London Gazette*, 25th March 1686).

"Lost between Firle and Shoram Ferry, in Sussex, a gold watch, made by D. Quare, in a black Shagreen Case with a 'Cypher J.C. Whoever brings it to Mr. Shelley, Goldsmith, in Panton Street, near the Haymarket, shall have 2 guineas reward" (*London Gazette*, 16th May 1691).

"Lost April 25, a Gold Minute Pendulum Clock, the name on upper plate D. Quare, London, 726 engraven on it, and a Shagrine case. Whoever gives notice of it to Daniel Quare, Clockmaker, at the King's Arms in Exchange Alley, shall have 3 guineas reward; or if already bought, their money returned again with content" (*London Gazette*, 26th May 1692).

"Lost on the road between Hungerford and Marl-borough, a Gold Repeating Watch, made by Quare and Horseman, with an old Gold Chain, and several seals hanging to it. Whosoever will bring them to Mr. Horseman, at Mr. Quare's, in Exchange Alley, shall have 20 guineas reward and no questions asked (*London Gazette*, 9th August 1718).

"Lost on the road between Newark and Tuxford, about 22 of June last, a Gold Watch, made by Quare in London, No. 4448, double cased and winds up on the dyal Plate. Whoever shall secure the watch if offered for sale, or send it or notice of it to Mr. Andrew Drummond, Goldsmith, by Charing Cross, shall receive 5 guineas reward" (*London Gazette*, 8th July 1732).

Quare seems to have liked watches with a six-hour dial, of the kind described in the first of the above quotations, as several examples by him have survived.

The books of the Society of Friends show that Daniel Quare was a trusted man among the Quakers, and that he at first refused the office of Clockmaker to George I because he objected to taking the oath of allegiance; the difficulty respecting the taking of an oath was, however, overcome, and freedom to enter the palace by the back stairs accorded to him. "The Yeoman of the Guard," he said, "lets me frequently go up without anybody for leave, as otherwise he would tho' persons of quality." He had one son, Jeremiah, who does not seem to have followed the craft, and three daughters. At the marriage of his daughter Elizabeth with Silvanus Bevan in 1715, among witnesses who signed the deed of settlement was the Duchess of Marlborough. Daniel Quare died at Croydon in 1724, and was buried in the Quakers' ground at Bunhill Fields, Finsbury.

After Quare's death, Horseman carried on under the name of the partnership until 1733 when he became bankrupt and the stock of the business was sold up.

ELLICOTT. The first John Ellicott, watchmaker, whose parents came to London from Bodmin, in Cornwall, was apprenticed to John Waters in 1687, admitted to the freedom of the Clockmakers' Company in 1696, elected on the Court of Assistants in 1726, and served as Warden from 1731 till his death in 1733. He resided in the parish of Allhallows, London Wall. He was an excellent craftsman and there exists one movement by him, dating from soon after 1700 of a very thin watch, measuring only $\frac{1}{5}$ inch between the plates. Such watches are now extremely rare, but a few are known to have been made by Quare. Another watch by him has a very early example of a centre seconds hand. He often concealed his name under the cock and balance. The most eminent watch and clockmaker of the family was his son John Ellicott, born in 1706, who established himself in business about

1728 at Sweeting's Alley, which was situated just where the statue of Rowland Hill now stands, near the Royal Exchange. After the fire which destroyed the old Royal Exchange in 1838, Sweeting's Alley was not rebuilt. He was elected a Fellow of the Royal Society in 1738, being recommended for that honour by Sir Hans Sloane, Bart., Martin Ffolkes, John Senex, the celebrated globe maker, and John Hadley, the astronomer. At the meetings of the Royal Society, he became acquainted with James Ferguson, who afterwards frequently visited Ellicott's private house, at St. John's Hackney, where an observatory was fitted up, and various scientific experiments were made.

Ellicott was the inventor of a compensation pendulum in which the bob rests on the longer ends of two levers, of which the shorter ends are depressed by the superior expansion of a brass bar attached to the pendulum rod. It tended to operate in jerks and was not widely used.

Ellicott's productions were distinguished by excellent workmanship. He paid great attention to the cylinder escapement, and did much to bring it into use. He appears to have adopted it only two or three years after its invention by Graham in 1726. In some of his later examples the cylinders were of ruby. His more costly watches were lavishly decorated, the cases in repoussé, and the dials enamelled on gold.

Ellicott was on the council of the Royal Society for three years, and read several papers before the Society. They included one on the *Influence which two Pendulum Clocks were observed to have on each other*. The ball of each pendulum weighed above 23 lbs.; the cases were placed sideways to each other, so near that the pendulums when at rest were little more than 2 ft. asunder. In less than two hours after they were set going, one of them, called No. 1, always stopped. As it had always kept going with great freedom before, the other regulator No. 2, was placed near it, Ellicott conceived its stopping must be owing to some influence that the motion of one of the pendulums had upon the other; and upon watching them narrowly the motion of No. 2 was found to increase as No. 1 diminished. At the time No. 1 stopped, No. 2 described an arc of 5°, being nearly 2° more than it would have done if the other had not been near it, and more than it moved in a short time after the other pendulum came to rest. On this he stopped the pendulum of No. 2, and set No. 1 going, the pendulum describing as large an arc as the case would admit, viz., about 5°; he presently found the pendulum of No. 2 begin to move, and the motion to increase gradually, till in seventeen minutes forty seconds it described an arc of

2° 10', at which the wheel discharging itself off the pallets, the regulator went, the arcs of the vibrations continued to increase till, as in the former experiment, the pendulum moved 5°, the motion of the pendulum of No. 1 gradually decreasing as the other increased, and in forty-five minutes it stopped. He then left the pendulum of No. 1 at rest, and set No. 2 going, making it also describe an arc of 5°; it continued to vibrate less and less till it described but about 3°, in which arc it continued to move; the pendulum of No. 1 seemed but little affected by the motion of No. 2. Ellicott's explanation was that, as the pendulums were very heavy, either of them set going communicated a slight motion to the case and in a lesser degree to whatever the case touched. Ellicott's experiment was useful as showing the necessity of fixing clocks with heavy pendulums to the wall of a building or other ponderous and unyielding structure.

John Ellicott seems to have used one series of numbers for his watches. An early number, 123, dates from 1728, at about the time he set up in Sweeting's Alley. The last known example bearing his name "Jno Ellicott London" is No. 4315 dating from 1760 after which the signature is "Ellicott" or, later "John Ellicott & Son". The series was continued after John's death, and in the Guildhall Museum is a watch of 1787 with the number 8319.

Ellicott designed several of our public clocks, amongst them that of the London Hospital, and was appointed Clockmaker to the King. He died suddenly in 1772, having dropped from his chair and instantly expired. John Ellicott was succeeded by his eldest son, Edward, who had been in partnership with him since about 1760. Edward Ellicott died at his residence in Great Queen Street, in 1791. The business was then carried on by his son Edward, who, after serving in the subordinate offices, was elected as Master of the Clockmakers' Company in 1834. Though brought up as a watchmaker he had but little liking for the business, and left the conduct of it in a great measure to others. From Edward Ellicott & Sons the title of the firm was altered to Ellicott & Taylor in 1811, and to Ellicott & Smith in 1830. After the destruction of Sweeting's Alley, Ellicott & Smith removed to 27, Lombard Street, and remained there till 1842.

There was a third John Ellicott admitted to the Freedom of the Clockmakers' Company by patrimony in 1792. He was the second son of the first Edward, but appears to have taken no part in the watch or clock making business. His grandson, Dr. Ellicott, was Bishop of Gloucester and Bristol.

Ellicott's portrait was painted by Sir Nathaniel Dance and engraved by Robert Dunkarton.

PINCHBECK. Among the celebrated clock and watch-makers of the eighteenth century must be reckoned Christopher Pinchbeck, known principally as the discoverer of an alloy of metals, called after him 'Pinchbeck', and as an inventor of 'Astronomico-Musical Clocks'. He resided at Clerkenwell in a turning out of St. John's Lane called Albion Place, which, prior to 1822, when it was rebuilt, was known as St. George's Court. From there he removed to Fleet Street, as is shown by the following advertisement which appeared in *Applebee's Weekly Journal* of 8th July 1721:

"Notice is hereby given to Noblemen, Gentlemen, and Others, that Chr. Pinchbeck, Inventor and Maker of the famous Astronomico-Musical Clocks, is removed from St. George's Court, St. John's Lane, to the sign of the Astronomico-Musical Clock in Fleet Street near the Leg Tavern. He maketh and selleth Watches of all sorts and Clocks, as well for the exact Indication of Time only, as Astronomical, for showing the various Motions and Phenomena of planets and fixed stars, solving at sight several astronomical problems, besides all this a variety of Musical performances, and that to the greatest Nicety of Time and Tune with the usual graces; together with a wonderful imitation of several songs and Voices of an Aviary of Birds so natural that any who saw not the Instrument would be persuaded that it were in Reality what it only represents. He makes Musical Automata or Instruments of themselves to play exceeding well on the Flute, Flaggelet or Organ, Setts of Country dances, Minuets, Jiggs, and the Opera Tunes, or the most perfect imitation of the Aviary of Birds above mentioned, fit for the Diversion of those in places where a Musician is not at Hand. He makes also Organs performing of themselves Psalm Tunes with two, three or more Voluntaries, very Convenient for Churches in remote Country Places where Organists cannot be had, or have sufficient Encouragement. And finally he mends Watches and Clocks in such sort that they will perform to an Exactness which possibly thro' a defect in finishing or other Accidents they formerly could not."

His reputation was world-wide, to judge from the appended extract from a letter of the period:

"Mr. P has finished a fine musical clock, said to be a most exquisite piece of workmanship, and worth about £1,500, wch is to be sent over to ye King of France (Louis XIV) and a fine organ to ye great Mogul, worth £300."

Pinchbeck exhibited his "astronomico-musical clocks", together with a variety of curious automata, at Bartholomew Fair, and the *Daily Journal* of 17th August 1729 announces that the Prince and Princess of Wales went to Bartholomew Fair to see his exhibition. Pinchbeck also attended Southwark Fair, and with Fawkes, a celebrated juggler and conjurer of that day, had a united 'show'.

Pinchbeck gold was much used for watch cases and the like. It is an alloy of three parts of zinc to four of copper; but its composition was jealously guarded by the inventor, as may be gathered from the following extract from a contemporary letter:

"Mr. Xtopher Pinchbeck had a curious secret of new-invented metal wch so naturally resembles gold (as not to be distinguished by the most experienced eye), in colour, smell, and ductibility. Ye secret is communicated to his son."

He died in 1732, at the age of sixty-two years, and was buried in St. Dunstan's Church, Fleet Street.

Christopher Pinchbeck's portrait was painted by Isaac Whood and engraved by I. Faber.

Edward Pinchbeck, second son of Christopher, who was born in 1713, succeeded his father in the business, as is evident from a "Caution to the Public", which he inserted in the *Daily Post* of 9th July 1733.

"To prevent for the future the gross imposition that is daily put upon the publick by a great number of shopkeepers, hawkers, and pedlars, in and about this town, Notice is hereby given, that the ingenious Mr. Edward Pinchbeck, at the Musical Cock, in Fleet Street, does not dispose of one grain of his curious metal, which so nearly resembles gold in colour, smell and ductility, to any person whatsoever; nor are the toys made of the said metal sold by any one person in England except himself." After recounting the various articles he makes from the alloy, the notice continues: "And in Particular watches, plain and chased in so curious a manner as not to be distinguished by the nicest eye from real gold, and which are highly necessary for gentlemen and ladies when they travel, with several other fine pieces of workmanship of any sort made by the best hands. The said Mr. Pinchbeck likewise makes astronomical and musical clocks; which new invented machines are so artfully contrived as to perform on several instruments great variety of musick composed by the most celebrated masters, with that exactitude, and in so beautiful a manner that scarce any hand can equal them. They likewise imitate the sweet harmony of birds to so great a perfection as not to be distinguished from nature itself. He also makes repeating and all other sorts of clocks and watches; particularly watches of a new invention, the mechanism of which is so simple, and the proportion so just, that come nearer truth than any others yet made."

Christopher Pinchbeck, eldest son of the first named Christopher, carried on a successful business as a clock and watch-maker in Cockspur Street, being described as Clockmaker to the King. In 1766 he is said to have bought from Ferdinand Berthoud, for George III, a pocket watch made with a compensation curb. In 1781 he was elected as an Honorary Freeman of the Clockmakers' Company. He died at Cockspur Street in 1783, aged seventy-three, and was buried at St. Martin's-in-the-Fields.

Christopher Pinchbeck the younger supplied a complicated astronomical clock to George III, in 1765, and a very similar one was sold to the king at about the same time by Eardley Norton. Both of these are still at Buckingham Palace.

JULIEN AND PIERRE LE ROY. The famous father and son, Julien and Pierre Le Roy, occupy much the same position in the history of French horology as do Thomas Tompion and John Harrison in England; for Julien raised French craftsmanship from a somewhat low ebb to a standard which rivalled the English school inspired by Tompion; and Pierre brought the marine chronometer to success at about the same time as did Harrison in England.

An earlier Julien Le Roy was a locksmith and he died in 1689 leaving a son Pierre, who was the first generation to turn to clockmaking, and practised in Tours. He in turn had two sons, both of whom were clockmakers. Pierre, the less noteworthy, moved to Paris and died in 1762.

Julien, the other son, rose to be the leading exponent of his day. He was born in 1686 and in 1699 was apprenticed to the Parisian maker Le Bon. Such was the excellence of his work that in 1739 he was appointed *Horloger du Roi* with lodgings at the Louvre.

He enjoyed a lifelong friendship with Sully and it was through Sully's introduction of English craftsmen into France that he was inspired to emulate their skill and so, by his example, the whole standard of French clockmaking. After the battle of Fontenoy, in 1745, Voltaire said to his son Pierre "Votre père et le Maréchal de Saxe ont vaincu l'Angleterre".

Julien perfected the oil-sinks invented by Sully, and in about 1725 invented the adjustable potence for the escape wheel of a verge escapement which is seen in almost all French verge watches in the second half of the eighteenth century. He made fine repeater watches and is said to have invented

wire gongs, instead of bells, upon which the time was repeated, thus paving the way for thin repeater watches. He seems also to have been the first to make dumb repeaters, in which the hammer strikes on a block fixed to the case, and also to have invented the use of a miniature anchor escapement, to regulate the speed of striking, instead of the friction train used in all early English repeaters.

In 1727 he asked Graham for an example of his new cylinder escapement, and himself frequently used it, acknowledging its superiority to the verge. (In this, however, he was not joined by his brilliant son, who disliked the cylinder because it needed lubricating. He claimed that if a cylinder watch was rated dry and then oiled, it showed an immediate gain of twelve minutes a day).

Julien Le Roy died on September 20th 1759. His portrait was painted by Perroneau and engraved by Moitté.

His son Pierre was born on November 24th 1717. He was of a retiring and shy disposition, and had indifferent health for much of his life. He married but had no children.

In 1748 he presented to the Academy of Sciences his "Mémoire contenant la description d'une montre de nouvelle construction", being an instrument for keeping time at sea. Although it does not appear ever to have been made, the design was historic as being the first detached escapement for which Le Roy invented the name 'éschappement à détente', which has been used in all countries ever since. The design was, nevertheless, far from perfect and Le Roy continued to devote most of his time to its improvement. In 1754 he published further designs for a marine timekeeper which he proposed to have a going time of only six hours, being wound every four, when the watch was changed, since "Il y a toujours dans un vaisseau beaucoup de gens qui n'ont rien à faire."

In 1766 he presented to Louis XV his final solution of the problem and his instrument which is preserved in the Musée des Arts et Métiers, at Paris, must be accounted as one of the most perfect and important in the whole history of horology. For in this timekeeper he incorporated, for the first time, the three essentials of all subsequent successful marine chronometers, namely, the detached detent escapement; the compensated balance; and the isochronous balance spring. The chronometer is described in further detail in Chapter V (see Plate 133 and FIG. 31).

Thus, although nothing can rob John Harrison of having been the first to produce a successful marine timekeeper, it was the only slightly later work of Le Roy which proved to be of the more lasting value.

It was tested on board the French ship *Aurore* and seems to have performed about as well as Harrison's No. 4, but it never underwent the searching tests of Harrison's Nos. 4 and no detailed record of its rate seems to have survived.

Soon afterwards Pierre Le Roy retired to his country house at Viry-sur-Orge where failing health and perhaps discouragement at lack of recognition, seems to have prevented him from doing any more creative work.

He had been appointed *Horloger du Roi* at the death of his father, but as has been shown, he himself did little commercial clockmaking, leaving the direction of the business to others while he devoted himself to the perfection of his marine chronometer.

He died on August 25th 1785 and the whereabouts of his tomb is unknown.

The firm of Le Roy continues in the production of fine work to the present day.

HENRY SULLY. This talented but unfortunate horologist was born in 1680, and apprenticed to Charles Gretton, of Fleet Street, in 1697. On the completion of his apprenticeship he travelled over the Continent, visiting Holland and Austria. In 1714 he published *Régle Artificielle du Tems* in Vienna. From Vienna he went to Paris with the Duke d'Aremberg, where he made the acquaintance of Julien Le Roy, Law, the noted Scottish speculator, and others. Le Roy at once recognised the genius of the young enthusiast who was imbued with ideas for perfecting timekeepers, and encouraged him to continue his researches. The following year, commissioned by Law, he journeyed to London and engaged sixty watch and clockmakers, who, with their families, were located at Versailles, where a factory was started. After two years of unremitting toil Sully was displaced from the directorate, but a little later, under the protection of the Duke de Noailles, another factory was established at St. Germain. Although this venture proved a failure, it nevertheless introduced to French makers a standard of workmanship superior to anything they had known and led to great advances in French horology, principally under the leadership of Julien Le Roy. Sully then returned to England, bringing his staff of workpeople with him, but the same ill fortune dogged his steps here, and in his extremity he returned to Paris, where for a time he existed by repairing watches. In 1721, when a little more prosperous, he turned his attention to the production of a marine timekeeper, and in 1724 presented it to the Academy of Sciences. This instrument has a modification of Debaufre's escapement, which

Sully devised for the purpose, and a vertical balance controlled by a weight. It carried cycloidal metal pieces, around which the upper end of a slender wire was wound, the lower end being attached to a lever with an adjustable weight, with the idea of keeping the vibrations of the balance isochronous. The pivots of the balance, instead of being in holes, were supported on the edges of large rollers, to diminish the friction, a device adopted afterwards by Mudge and others. In 1726 Sully published *Description abrégée d'une Horologe d'une Nouvelle Invention pour la Juste Mesure du Temps sur Mer*. When subjected to the tossing of the ocean, his timekeeper failed to yield the results anticipated from its performance on land. Though mortified by his failure, he again set himself to the solution of the problem. He had already made a marine watch with two balances geared together, as designed by Dr. Hooke, and now proceeded with a new timekeeper of different construction; but while engaged thereon he was seized with a serious illness, induced by over-application and worry, and succumbed to inflammation of the lungs in 1728.

Sully's enduring contribution to the science of horology was his invention of oil wells for retaining oil at the pivots. He at once communicated his idea to his friend Julien Le Roy who further perfected it in the form subsequently universally employed.

At the church of St. Sulpice, Paris a few days before his death, he had traced a meridian line on the pavement of the transept, and secured its permanence by inlaying a thin brass edge. He blocked up the south transept window except for a small hole in a metal plate at the upper part, through which the rays of the sun cast a luminous disc about $10\frac{1}{2}$ in. in diameter on the floor. The disc moves across the line which at noon bisects it. In this church he was buried, and a fine obelisk of white marble erected to his memory in the north transept, in a position that allowed the meridian line to be carried up the face of the monument. A laudatory inscription recounted his services to horology, but the greater part it was cut out by the revolutionaries of 1793, who possibly resented the suggestion that French watchmakers could be indebted to a foreigner.

In the Guildhall Museum is a timekeeper with Sully's curious vertical balance. It is in the form of a bracket clock with a walnut bell-top case, has a seconds hand above the centre of the dial, and shows the days of the month through a slit below the centre. It is inscribed "Henricus Sully, invenit et fecit (1724), Horloger to the Duke of Orleans".

JOHN HARRISON. was born at Foulby or Wragby near Pontefract, Yorkshire, in 1693. He was the son of a carpenter, which business he followed for several years. In 1700 the family removed to Barrow, in Lincolnshire. At a very early age John Harrison showed a great predilection for mechanical pursuits, and particularly directed his attention to the improvement of clocks.

In the Guildhall Museum, London, is a very early long-case clock by him, completed in 1715, in which all the wheels except the escape wheel are made of wood. A similar clock, of the same date, is in the Science Museum, London.

The offer, by Act of Parliament, of large sums for the production of a timekeeper sufficiently accurate to ascertain the longitude at sea, induced him to turn his attention to the subject. He devised a peculiar form of recoil escapement, and a pendulum in which the effects of heat and cold in lengthening and shortening the pendulum were neutralised by the use of two metals having different ratios of expansion. His escapement, is called the 'grasshopper', see FIG. 15, p. 117. The pallets of ebony, or other hard wood, are jointed to a bell-crank lever carried by the crutch; though free to move at the joints they are kept sufficiently near to position by springs. The teeth of the escape wheel alternately push the left-hand and pull the right-hand pallet, this action giving the necessary impulse to the pendulum. The chief merit is that, as there is no rubbing between the pallets and the wheel teeth, no lubrication is required at these contacts. However, the invention was rarely adopted by others, but his pendulum, known as the gridiron form of compensation was widely employed in England and abroad (see FIG. 14, p. 117). It is composed of nine parallel rods, five of steel and four of brass, the total length of each kind being nearly as 100 to 60, that being the ratio of expansion of the two metals.

In 1728 Harrison journeyed to London, taking with him his pendulum, his escapement, and drawings of his proposed timekeeper, hoping to obtain the approbation and aid of the Board of Longitude. Before being submitted to the notice of that body they were inspected by Graham, whose maturer judgment prompted him to advise Harrison first to make the timekeeper, and then ascertain, from its actual going, what claims it might have to further notice. Graham backed his advice by the practical help of a substantial loan, interest free.

Harrison continued plodding on in the country, repairing watches and clocks and making a variety of experiments till 1735; then, in his forty-second year, he came to London and took up his residence in Orange Street, Red Lion Square. He brought with him a timepiece he had invented and constructed. It was a cumbersome affair in a wooden frame, and had two balances. He obtained certificates of the excellence of this timekeeper from Halley, Graham and others. On their recommendation he was allowed, in 1736, to proceed with it to Lisbon in a King's ship, and was enabled to correct the ship's reckoning by 1° 30', actually 1° 27', the difference of longitude between the Start and the Lizard. In consequence, the error of the machine must have been almost negligible, say five miles at most.

It is of interest and importance to note that this machine, Harrison's No. 1, had a gridiron compensation for heat and cold, the first recorded instance of such a device being applied to a marine timekeeper—or, indeed, to any timekeeper fitted with a balance (or balances).

In consideration of this result, the Board of Longitude gave him £500 "to proceed with his improvements". In 1739 he finished another timekeeper, and afterwards a third, which was smaller and appeared to the members of the Royal Society to be more simple and less likely to be deranged than either of the preceding ones. In 1749 he received the gold medal which was annually awarded by the Royal Society to the most useful discovery, but he was still not satisfied with his productions. The experience gained by prolonged trial led him to abandon the heavy framing and wheels which characterised his earlier essays and to devise and construct his celebrated 'watch' which eventually won for him the coveted reward (see Plate 132, pp. 192 & 193, and FIG. 30, p. 191).

He spent some time in improving and correcting his fourth nautical timekeeper, and then applied to the Commissioners of the Board of Longitude for a trial according to the Act of Parliament. This, after much delay, was granted, and his son William was in his stead allowed to take a voyage to Jamaica. William Harrison embarked in the *Deptford*, at Portsmouth, on 18th November 1761. After eighteen days' navigation the vessel was supposed to be 13° 50' west of Portsmouth by ordinary calculations, but by the watch was 15° 19', and the timekeeper was at once condemned as useless. William Harrison, however, maintained that if Madeira were correctly marked on the chart, it would be seen on the following day; and in this he persisted so strongly that the Captain was induced to alter his course accordingly, and the island was discovered the next day. A contemporary points out that had the ship continued on her course she would not have sighted Madeira at all, and that her doing so "was a matter of relief to the ship's company, who were then in great scarcity of beer."

In like manner William Harrison was enabled by the watch to announce all the islands in the order in which they would fall in with them. When he arrived at Port Royal, after a voyage of sixty-one days, the chronometer, as we may now call it,★ was found to be about nine seconds slow. On 28th January 1762 he set sail from Jamaica on board the *Merlin*, after an absence of five months the error on returning to Portsmouth was 1 min. 53½ sec., or 28½′ of longitude at the Equator, equal to 18′ in the latitude of Portsmouth. This was much within the limit of the thirty miles prescribed by the Act of 1713; yet, several objections being raised, William Harrison was obliged to undertake a second voyage, the proof from the first not being considered sufficiently decisive by the Board, although they advanced £5,000 on account of the reward.

Accompanied by Dr. Maskelyne, as the representative of the Board, William Harrison embarked in the man-of-war *Tartar*, on 28th March 1764, and arrived in Barbados on the 13th May, when it was found the chronometer had gained forty-three seconds; he set out for the return journey on board the *New Elizabeth* on the 4th of June, and arrived at the Surrey Stairs on 18th July, when it was ascertained that, after allowing for the estimated rate of one second a day gaining, there was an excess of fifty-four seconds for the whole period of 156 days. The result of this second voyage was so satisfactory, that the Board unanimously declared Harrison had really exceeded all expectations and demands of the Act of Parliament, and he was paid a further advance of £5,000, with the condition that he explained the construction of his timekeeper. A sub-committee, consisting of Maskelyne, John Mitchell, Ludlam, Bird, Mudge, Mathews and Kendall, were appointed, and instructed to make themselves acquainted with the mechanism of the instrument. They reported themselves satisfied in 1765, but even then considerable delay occurred. Kendall was commissioned to make a duplicate of the chronometer, which appears to have taken three years to execute, for the date of Kendall's instrument is 1769. The final payment of £8,750 was made to Harrison in 1773, after the personal intervention of H.M. King George III, who afforded a private trial at the Kew Observatory to Harrison's No. 5, now in the Guildhall Museum. Its total error in 10 weeks was 4½ secs. only.

★ The late Mr. R. B. Prosser said the term chronometer appears to have been introduced by Loulie of Amsterdan in 1698 as descriptive of the instrument now known as a metronome. Jeremy Thacker was the first to apply it to a precision timekeeper in a pamphlet published in 1714.

Harrison's timekeeper is in the form of a large silver pair-case watch, with a centre seconds hand. Harrison had an aversion to gimbals and it reposed on a soft cushion; on its trial voyages it was carefully tended by William Harrison, who avoided position errors as far as possible by shifting the timekeeper to suit the lie of the ship. The timekeeper is described in some detail in Chapter V.

Besides the early clocks mentioned, there is a regulator of very superior workmanship and made circa 1750, in the possession of the Royal Astronomical Society. The whole affair is a mass of ingenious complications departing from the beaten track. Several of the contrivances embodied may be briefly summarised. The escapement is a variation of the 'grasshopper'. Cycloidal cheeks are provided for the pendulum, which vibrates through no less than 12° of arc. There is a double minute hand which goes round in two hours, being jumped forward at half-minute intervals by a remontoire which the escape wheel releases. The escape wheel has a hundred and twenty teeth, and as it makes but one turn in four minutes a four-finger seconds indicator is provided. The seconds dial is sunk, and each of the fingers in succession comes into sight and points to the seconds figures. The bearings of the great wheel run on rollers pivoted into rings and the other bearings are supported on the edges of large friction rollers. Altogether the cost of this timekeeper must have been enormous.

On Harrison's tomb near the south porch of Hampstead Church is the following inscription:

"In memory of Mr. John Harrison, late of Red Lion square, London, inventor of the timekeeper for ascertaining the longitude at sea. He was born at Foulby, in the county of York, and was the son of a builder at that place, who brought him up to the same profession. Before he attained the age of twenty-one, he without any instruction, employed himself in cleaning and repairing clocks and watches, and made a few of the former, chiefly of wood. At the age of twenty-five he employed his whole time in chronometrical improvements.

"He was the inventor of the gridiron pendulum and the method of preventing the effects of heat and cold upon timekeepers by two bars fixed together; he introduced the secondary spring to keep them going while winding up; and was the inventor of most (or all) the improvements in clocks and watches during his time. In the year 1735 his first timekeeper was sent to Lisbon, and in 1764 his then much-improved fourth timekeeper having been sent to Barbadoes the Commissioners of Longitude certified that it had determined the longitude within one-third of half a degree of a great circle, having not erred more than forty seconds in time. After sixty years' close application to the above pursuits, he departed this life on the 24th day of March 1776, aged eighty-three. This tombstone was put up many years after his death.''

Harrison's guiding principle in horology was the elimination of all avoidable friction and the securing of constant motive power. Although his form of maintaining power in watches is the only one of Harrison's inventions to have survived in use today in all fusee chronometers, the great value of his life's work lay in his being the first man to prove convincingly that it was practicable to calculate a ship's position at sea by means of a clock. It was his success which directly stimulated those other pioneers who, within fifteen years, brought the marine chronometer to the form in which it has been made ever since.

Apart from No. 5 which is in the Guildhall Museum, London, Harrison's first four marine timekeepers are normally on view at the National Maritime Museum at Greenwich, together with Kendall's No. 1, where one or more of them are kept going.

John Harrison had a brother James and it has been suggested that he owed much of his success to this brother's ingenuity. The extent of his indebtedness has, however, never been established.

After his death a sixth timekeeper was made by his son William, on the same lines as numbers 4 and 5, but its history and present whereabouts, if it survives, are unknown.

Harrison's portrait was painted by T. King and engraved by L. Tassaert.

THOMAS MUDGE, born at Exeter in 1715, was the son of a clergyman, who kept a school at Bideford, and subsequently attained considerable fame for his erudition while incumbent at St. Andrews, Plymouth. Young Mudge showed so great a taste for mechanics, with a particular inclination for horology, that his father placed him as an apprentice with Graham. Here he made rapid progress in his art, and on the completion of his indentures took a leading position in the establishment. He was admitted to the Freedom of the Clockmakers' Company in 1738, and called to the livery in 1766. At Graham's death, in 1751, Mudge inserted the following notice in the *Daily Advertiser* of 18th November 1751: "Thomas Mudge, watchmaker, apprentice to the late Mr. Graham, carries on the business in the same manner Mr. Graham did, at the sign of the 'Dial and One Crown' opposite the 'Bolt and Tun' in Fleet Street." Shortly after Mudge was established,

Ferdinand the Sixth, of Spain, ordered an equation watch from John Ellicott, who, in consequence of the difficulties presented by this unusual construction, had recourse to Mudge. Ferdinand was a lover of mechanical work, and hearing of this circumstance, sent an order direct to Mudge to construct for him any piece of horology which he thought the most curious, and to charge for it whatever he chose. In response Mudge constructed a watch which showed true and apparent time, struck the hours, and repeated not only the hours and quarters, but the minutes also; the watch was set in the top of a walking cane, with sliding shutters over the dials. The King set great store by this piece of workmanship, for which Mudge charged him 480 guineas. About 1755 he entered into partnership with William Dutton, another apprentice of Graham.

Mudge and Dutton made superb watches with a perfected form of Graham's cylinder escapement, and some with a ruby cylinder, but in 1759 Mudge made for George III what is perhaps the most historically important watch in the world, see Plate 125, pp. 174 & 175, and FIG. 25, p. 178. Not only was it the first pocket watch to have an automatic device for compensating changes in temperature, but it contained Mudge's invention of the lever escapement, which was eventually to attain complete supremacy in watches so that it is now the only escapement made. Yet so great were the difficulties of making it at first that Mudge would never make another and believed it could never be made a commercial success. Nor was another made until 1782, by Josiah Emery, who thereafter constructed about three a year and sold them at the then tremendous price of £150 each. George III gave the Mudge lever to his wife, Queen Caroline, and it is still in going order at Windsor Castle. It is described in some detail in Chapter V. Much contemporary correspondence exists concerning the watch which show that Mudge was well aware that it possessed imperfections in the form of position errors, imperfect isochronism and over-compensation for temperature changes. Nevertheless, he was able to say "I think it is the most perfect watch that can be worn in the pocket, that ever was made, and I should not be at all fearful of my character's suffering, if it was to undergo the same strict examination at the royal observatory, that Mr. Harrison's has undergone: for, from all the observations I have made upon it, compared with those published by Mr. Maskelyne of Mr. Harrison's, it appears to go better, rather than worse, and that not under one particular circumstance only, but under every different circumstance in which his was tried." Mudge elsewhere reports that over the period of a year during which he observed the going of the watch, the greatest variation in its daily rate was only five seconds, a record of which any twentieth century watch might well be proud.

Mudge made a model of the escapement for his patron Count Bruhl, which no longer exists and there are two bracket clocks known by him, with the lever escapement and a large balance wheel. It is said that in about 1784 he sold a second lever watch to a Colonel Johns, but its whereabouts are not known, and the story seems somewhat improbable as he had previously refused to make one for his patron and friend Count Bruhl.

In 1765 he published *Thoughts on the Means of Improving Watches, particularly those for Use at Sea*. From this time his attention was mainly directed to marine timekeepers, and in 1771, leaving the conduct of the Fleet Street business to Dutton, he quitted London, and went to reside at Plymouth, where he devoted himself to the construction of chronometers. The first one was sent to Greenwich Observatory in 1774, and afterwards to Baron Zach (who was astronomer to the Duke of Gotha), and lastly to Admiral Campbell, who took it a voyage to Newfoundland, when its performance was pronounced to be satisfactory. The Board of Longitude sent him £500, requesting him to continue his researches. Two other chronometers were sent to the Greenwich Observatory for trial in 1779.

Dr. Maskelyne and Mudge could not agree. Maskelyne, who was Astronomer Royal, carried the Board of Longitude with him. It was asserted that chronometers by Arnold performed better than those of Mudge. Arnold had not submitted his chronometers for the Government reward, and therefore Mudge objected to the comparison. On the petition of Mudge, the House of Commons, in 1791, appointed as a committee to investigate the performance of his chronometers consisted of the Bishop of St. David's, Mr. Atwood, Mr. De Luc, Mr. Ramsden, Mr. Edward Troughton, Mr. Holmes, Mr. Haley, and Mr. Howells, the last three being watchmakers of repute. After much bickering, Mudge, in 1793, was paid £2,500, in addition to £500 he had already received as encouragement, although the Board of Longitude dissented from this course.

The salient features of Mudge's marine timekeeper are described in Chapter V. Like his lever watch, it had two balance springs and a bimetallic compensation curb for temperature changes. But the remontoire escapement demanded even greater delicacy in construction than did his lever, and under the formula adopted by Maskelyne, it did not perform as well as the more robust and simple chronometer escapement of Arnold. Nevertheless, when the late Lt. Commdr. R. T. Gould, R.N., analysed its rate in accordance with the formula now used, it proved to have a trial number which was not rivalled nearly for a century and would even today not be discreditable. But owing to its extreme delicacy and complication it could never have been produced commercially.

Mudge was appointed Clockmaker to George III in 1776, which duty he fulfilled by proxy, and died at his son's house in Walworth on November 14th 1794.

After Mudge's migration to Plymouth, the Fleet Street business seems to have reverted entirely to William Dutton, although the title of Mudge & Dutton was retained till 1794.

Thomas Mudge, junr., who was an attorney at 3 Old Square, Lincoln's Inn, engaged Messrs. Howells, Pennington, Pendleton, and others to produce chronometers on his father's plan; but they were too costly, and not successful. By 1799 the younger Mudge sold eleven at 150 guineas each, which did not pay him. Of others in course of manufacture some were finished by his coadjutors, and some by Messrs. Barraud & Jamison.

Mudge's portrait was painted by Sir Nathaniel Dance and engraved by Chas. Townley.

JOHN ARNOLD. This famous horologist was born in 1736, at Bodmin, in Cornwall, where he was apprenticed to his father, a watchmaker. While a youth he left home, and after a stay of some time in Holland he determined to try his fortune in London. Arnold, by his own account, was for some time a gunsmith. He afterwards worked as a journeyman, but soon found an opportunity of establishing himself at Devereux Court, Fleet Street. One of his earliest acts here was to make an exceedingly small half-quarter repeating watch, which he had set in a ring, and presented to George III in June 1764. When it is stated that the whole movement measured but little more than $\frac{1}{3}$ inch across, his ability as a fine workman and his marvellous sense of touch will be appreciated. The escapement selected was a cylinder one, the cylinder, made of ruby and measuring $\frac{1}{54}$ in. in diameter, being the first made of that material. The King accepted the repeater, and presented its maker with 500 guineas as an acknowledgment of his surpassing skill.

According to the Annual Register for 1764, the whole of this repeater, composed of 120 parts, weighed, but 5 dwts. $7\frac{3}{4}$ gr., the following being the weight of the principal items: the movement, complete, is 2 dwts. $2\frac{1}{8}$ gr.; great wheel and fusee,

$2\frac{3}{4}$ gr.; second wheel and pinion, $\frac{3}{4}$ gr.; barrel and mainspring, $3\frac{1}{2}$ gr.; third wheel and pinion, $\frac{1}{9}$ gr.; fourth wheel and pinion, $\frac{1}{10}$ gr.; cylinder, wheel and pinion, $\frac{1}{16}$ gr.; balance-spring, cylinder and collet, $\frac{2}{3}$ gr.; the balance-spring $\frac{1}{300}$ gr.; the chain, $\frac{1}{2}$ gr.; barrel and mainspring, $1\frac{1}{4}$ gr.; great wheel and ratchet, 1 gr.; second wheel and pinion, $\frac{1}{7}$ gr.; third wheel and pinion, $\frac{1}{8}$ gr.; fourth wheel and pinion, $\frac{1}{9}$ gr.; fly wheel and pinion, $\frac{1}{17}$ gr.; fly pinion, $\frac{1}{20}$ gr.; hour hammer, $\frac{1}{3}$ gr.; quarter hammer, $\frac{1}{3}$ gr.; rack, chain and pulley, $1\frac{1}{3}$ gr.; quarter and half-quarter rack, $\frac{2}{3}$ gr.; the quarter and half-quarter snail and cannon pinion $\frac{2}{3}$ gr.; the all-or-nothing piece, $\frac{1}{2}$ gr.; two motion wheels, 1 gr.; steel dial-plate with gold figures, $3\frac{1}{2}$ gr.; the hour snail and star, $\frac{1}{2}$ and $\frac{1}{16}$ gr.

Arnold's achievement at once brought him into notice, and from that time his future success was assured.

It is said that the Empress of Russia offered Arnold 1,000 guineas for a duplicate of the repeater made for George III, but the offer was declined, not that Arnold doubted his ability to produce it, but because he desired the miniature royal timekeeper to remain unique.

Arnold now turned his attention seriously to the problem which was engaging the thoughts of leading horologists here and in France. John Harrison had already fulfilled the conditions laid down by the Board of Longitude, and thus practically secured the £20,000 offered by Parliament in 1714 for a timekeeper sufficiently exact to ascertain the longitude within certain limits. Mudge was already in the field, and seemed bent on adhering to the remontoire principle somewhat on Harrison's plan. But it was clear to other minds that a nearer approach to perfection might be obtained by a chronometer of altogether a different character to the one invented by Harrison.

The chronometer which Captain Cook took with him in the *Resolution* on his second voyage, in 1772, was Arnold's No. 3. Two other timekeepers of Arnold's were on board the *Adventure*. The two in the *Adventure* were earlier, and presumably Arnold's No. 1 and 2.

None of these performed at all satisfactorily, but in the next four years Arnold made great advances, devising a bimetallic compensation balance, an improved form of pivoted detent escapement, and his helical balance spring. These features he also incorporated in a number of pocket chronometers of which one, No. 36, was tested at Greenwich over a period of thirteen months, being worn in the pocket, during which time its total error was only 2 minutes 33 seconds, while its greatest variation in rate on any two consecutive days was 3 seconds.

Its greatest variation in rate in different positions was 4.2 seconds, a very remarkable achievement with the heavy balances then used.

In 1782 Arnold patented his truly isochronous helical balance spring with incurved ends and also his spring detent escapement at about the same time as Earnshaw did the same, and Earnshaw always insisted that his secret had been communicated to Arnold by John Brockbank to whom Earnshaw had shown it under a pledge of secrecy. The truth of the matter was never established, and the spring detent may have been arrived at independently, at about the same time by Earnshaw, Arnold & Berthoud.

In 1787 Arnold took his son, John Roger, into partnership, and from then on their instruments were signed "John Arnold & Son".

Some time after 1764 Arnold quitted Devereux Court for Adelphi Buildings, which is the address given in his patent specifications, and in an account of the going of a pocket chronometer, in 1781, it is stated to have been compared with the regulator at his house in the Adelphi. About 1785 he removed to 112 Cornhill where he carried on business until his death. Arnold & Son also had a chronometer manufactory at Chigwell in Essex.

In a book, *Certificates and Rates of Going*, which he published in 1791, he gives the price of his large marine chronometers as from 60 to 80 guineas; pocket chronometers, in gold cases, 120 guineas, and in silver 100 guineas; repeaters from 150 guineas for the best kind in gold, down to 25 guineas for the commonest, in silver cases.

The rival claims of Mudge, Arnold, and Earnshaw to the rewards offered for the best chronometer were submitted to a Select Committee of the House of Commons, assisted by a committee of experts, and eventually each was awarded £3,000; but a moiety of Arnold's portion was not paid till after his death, when it was received by his son. Arnold had not laid claim to the reward when depositing his chronometers at the Greenwich Observatory; but their good performance was made use of by Maskelyne as a reason why Mudge's claim should not be recognised.

Arnold told the committee he had then made upwards of 900 timekeepers, but never two alike, so long as he saw room for any possible improvements; adding, "I have twenty number ones."

Arnold's son John Roger was apprenticed in Paris to Breguet and there exists in the Ilbert collection, a Tourbillon chronometer in an engine-turned silver case, with square edges. The foot of the balance-cock is especially wide, and bears the following inscription: *Premier régulateur à tourbillon de Breguet réuni à un des premiers ouvrages d'Arnold. Hommage de Breguet à la mémoire révérée d'Arnold offerts à son fils. An 1808.*

John Arnold was admitted as a member of the Clockmakers' Company in 1783, and chosen on the livery 1796. He died at Well Hall, near Eltham, Kent, in 1799. His portrait was painted by R. Davy and engraved by S. E. Reid.

John Roger Arnold was admitted to the Clockmakers' Company in 1796, and became master in 1817. In 1820 he removed from Cornhill to 27 Cecil Street, and from thence, in 1830, to 84 Strand, where he entered into a partnership agreement for ten years with E. J. Dent, and during this period the business flourished; but immediately the term expired, Dent set up for himself at 82 Strand, carrying with him the confidence of most of the customers of the late firm. John R. Arnold continued at 84 Strand till 1843 when he died. It has been suggested that he inherited neither the horological ability nor the commercial aptitude of his father, and he was certainly much decried by Earnshaw who, however, had an axe to grind. But watches made by him after his father's death show no falling off in quality, while as to his commercial aptitude, he inherited an ample fortune from his father and so had no need to exert himself for a livelihood. Finally, with the early death of his son there was no farther incentive to remain in business.

THOMAS EARNSHAW. To Thomas Earnshaw, who was born at Ashton-under-Lyne in 1749, must be ascribed the merit of having devised the chronometer escapement and compensation balance almost precisely as they are now used.

That Earnshaw was a true horologist by intuition is evident. He is said to have been honest and straight-forward, but somewhat rugged in his manner. There are, however, but few details of his life to be obtained. He was apprenticed to a watchmaker when fourteen years of age, and seems to have come to London immediately on completion of his indentures. After working for some time as a finisher of verge and cylinder watches, he taught himself watch jewelling and then cylinder-escapement making, using ruby cylinders and steel wheels. He married early in life, and the necessity of providing for a family out of his earnings seems to have hampered him considerably in carrying out his projects.

To improve the chronometer escapement he, in 1781, conceived the idea of substituting a spring detent for the pivoted form as applied by Le Roy and other French artists. After showing the new method to John Brockbank, for whom he worked, he took it to Thomas Wright of the Poultry, another of his customers, and agreed that when a watch with the device was finished, Wright should patent it. But the latter kept the watch for a year to observe its going, and did not obtain the patent till 1783. In the meantime John Arnold had lodged a patent specification, claiming the same thing as his invention. To the end of his life Earnshaw lost no opportunity of declaring in emphatic language his belief that John Brockbank had divulged his plan to Arnold.

According to Earnshaw's account his own actions were always marked by trusting simplicity, though his confidence was continually betrayed. The patent cost Wright £100, and as all negotiations with Brockbank, Haley, Wm. Hughes, Best, and other leading watchmakers to purchase a share of it failed, watches with the new escapement were manufactured for various people on payment to Wright of a royalty of £1 each. The first dozen were not a success; the impulse roller being too small in relationship to the escape wheel, they were liable to stop. Earnshaw discovered the fault and with better proportions brought the new escapement into favour for pocket watches. The earlier ones were stamped ($^{Wright's}_{Patent}$) in small characters; a form of marking which was dropped after a few years.

Dr. Maskeleyne, the Astronomer Royal, having tried one of his watches in 1789, advised Earnshaw to apply to the Board of Longitude for permission to submit timekeepers for official trial at Greenwich Observatory. Five of his watches were tested there in 1791, and then he obtained an order for two chronometers, and these were deposited at the Observatory on 1st January 1798.

Although Earnshaw is generally recognised as meriting an equal share of praise with Arnold for making the marine chronometer a commercial proposition at an economic price, it is nevertheless remarkable that chronometers by him are now considerably more rare than those of Arnold, although Earnshaw outlived him by thirty years. Earnshaw's are remarkably small in size, even when compared with a modern instrument, but particularly by the side of Arnold's massive instruments. His earlier examples were very highly finished and it was suggested that they only owed their performance to this high quality. Whereupon Earnshaw took to leaving his chronometers "in the grey" and people then said his workmanship was entirely inferior.

Although marine chronometers by Earnshaw are now rarely found, there are many surviving examples of his pocket chronometers. Some of these have movements hinged into the case as was then usual, but many have the movement screwed into the case so that the escapement can only be seen by removing the whole movement. From his having devised the modern system of fusing together the brass and steel strips of a compensated balance wheel it might be expected that he would always have used a compensated balance in his pocket chronometers. In fact, however, he as often used a solid steel balance and a claw-like compensation curb of which the jaws opened as the temperature dropped. He also used spiral and helical balance springs with apparent impartiality. He seems to have sold his pocket chronometers very much more cheaply than Arnold, and in 1791 he submitted to Greenwich five pocket instruments, priced at £42 each, which out-performed four box chronometers which Arnold submitted at the same time. This compares remarkably with Arnold's cheapest pocket chronometer at £100, and Emery's price of £150 for his pocket lever watches.

In 1794 or 1795 Earnshaw succeeded to the business which had been carried on for some years by Wm. Hughes at 119, High Holborn one door east of the turning then known as King Street but now called Southampton Row. The shop referred to was pulled down when the thoroughfare was widened in 1901.

The committee of investigation appointed to consider the claims of chronometer improvers awarded Earnshaw £500 in 1801 on account of his inventions, and in 1803 a further £2,500 making his total reward £3,000. Rightly or wrongly, he was of the opinion that he was not well treated, and in 1808 issued *Longitude: An Appeal to the Public* declaring he was entitled to more pre-eminent recognition.

Earnshaw also made a small number of clocks. For the first one, a regulator, which was ordered by the Archbishop of Armagh, he was paid £150 and an additional £100 for going to Armagh to fix it.

He died at Chenies Street in 1829, but the business was carried on for some years by his son, first at the Holborn premises and afterwards at Fenchurch Street.

Earnshaw's portrait was painted by Sir Martin Archer Shee and engraved by Samuel Bellin.

FERDINAND BERTHOUD was born on March 19th 1729 at Placemont, in the Canton of Neuchâtel, Switzerland. Originally destined for the Church, he showed so much mechanical ability that he was allowed to start training as a watchmaker at the age of fourteen. In 1745, when he was sixteen, he moved to Paris, where he achieved early fame and was appointed *Horloger de la Marine* in 1762. In this capacity he carried out a great deal of experiment and produced in all about seventy marine timekeepers during his life. These showed a steady improvement, from very rudimentary designs at the first, to something closely resembling the standard spring-detent escapement, during the 1780's.

Berthoud was a very hard worker and produced many fine clocks and watches, often exhibiting considerable originality in design. Apart from his marine timekeepers he made many superb regulators and he also designed a form of detent escapement for application to pendulum clocks.

But apart from his fine practical work it is as a technical writer that he is mainly famous. The bulk of his writings is tremendous, the most important works being the *Essai sur l'Horlogerie* (1763); *Traité des Horloges Marines* (1773); and *Histoire de la Mesure du Temps* (1802).

He had many distinctions conferred upon him during his lifetime, including Fellow of the Royal Society; Membre de L'Institut, and Chevalier de la Légion d'Honneur.

He died at his home at Groslay Montmorency, on June 20th 1807, aged eighty years. An important collection of his marine timekeepers and chronometers may be seen at the Musée des Arts et Métiers, Paris, together with his bust.

He was succeeded by his nephew, Louis Berthoud (1750–1813) who also attained fame as a chronometer maker, and other members of the family also produced work of a very high quality.

ABRAHAM LOUIS BREGUET. The intense and abiding interest taken in the works of this, the predominant continental horologist of his period, may be traced to the great variety of his conceptions and the exactness with which they were carried out. He had the faculty of surrounding himself with assistants who were good mechanicians and able to embody his ideas to the best advantage. Clocks, chronometers, and watches of his make all bear the stamp of originality in some particular. A defect in construction had only to be pointed out or the whim of a customer revealed, when Breguet was ready with the requirement. The characteristics of his work are described in considerable detail in Chapter V.

Breguet's parents were of French Protestant origin, living in Neuchâtel, where he was born on January 10th 1747. In 1762 he was apprenticed to a watchmaker in Versailles and attended night classes at the College Mazarin under the Abbé Marie, who was so much impressed by his ability that he brought him to the notice of Louis XVI, himself a keen horologist.

It is not known at what date he set up on his own account, and he does not seem to have kept

PLATE 183

Eighteenth century 'watch paper'. Nearly all watchmakers had their own watch papers printed, and put them in the back of the pair-case of any watch which they had made or repaired. The paper served the purpose of a thin washer between the inner and outer case, preventing the two from rattling, or chafing against each other. Many examples, as the one of Vulliamy illustrated above, are in the form of equation of solar time table.

any books until 1787, since which date the records of the firm have been kept and preserved without intermission. In the same year he took into partnership the revolutionary clock-maker Gide who brought 50,000 livres in cash and an equal value in clocks. The partnership terminated in 1791. Beillard relates that Marat, who also came from Switzerland, and Breguet were intimately acquainted, and one night early in the Revolution when they met at a friend's house in the rue Greneta, the populace under the windows shouted, "Down with Marat." The situation becoming serious, Breguet dressed Marat up as an old woman and they left the house arm in arm. Some time after, when the guillotine was set up *en permanence*, Marat, finding Breguet was in danger, gave him a pass to Switzerland. Breguet took a post-chaise forthwith and reached Locle in safety.

Breguet later visited England where he was kindly received and lodged with the jewellers John Duval & Son. He returned to France in 1795. His workshop was at 51, Quai de l'Horloge, of which the number was changed in 1812 to 79. The firm also had a shop, latterly at 28 Place Vendôme. George Brown retired in 1970, when the business was taken over by the firm of Chaumet and conducted from their shop at 12 Place Vendôme.

Breguet and Arnold entertained a strong mutual admiration and Arnold's son, John Roger, was apprenticed to Breguet in Paris. After his father's death Breguet gave him a chonometer by Arnold to which he had added a tourbillon, and inscribed on the movement: *Premier régulateur à Tourbillon de Breguet réuni à un des premier ouvrages d'Arnold. Homage de Breguet à la mémoire révérée d'Arnold offert à son fils. An 1808.*

Breguet had a son Louis Antoine, born in 1776, who was sent to school in England, with the idea that he, in turn, should be apprenticed to Arnold; but this did not come about, as he returned to France, having found the "English way of life rude and violent".

Breguet took him into partnership in about 1807 after which watches were signed 'Breguet et fils' instead of merely 'Breguet'. In 1815 he was appointed 'horloger de la marine' and this also is an indication of date in pieces so signed.

When the seventh edition of this book was published, in 1956, so little was known about Breguet's chronology that no connection between dates and numbers had been established. The true position is now clearly understood. Breguet used, in all, three series of numbers. The first started in 1782 and continued apparently until 1788, just after the second series started. They all have a fractional number as well as the series number. Thus, a very early self-winding watch, belonging to the Worshipful Company of Clockmakers (to be seen in the City of London Guildhall) is numbered 8 10/83. This is taken to mean that it is Breguet's eighth watch and was finished in October 1783. All these watches are signed 'Breguet à Paris' which he continued until the mid-1790s but only in a handful of known watches subsequently. Most watches signed 'Breguet à Paris', of a manifestly later date, are 'fakes; but watches numbered up to about 300, so signed, are genuine. Many faked Breguets have very high numbers, and anything numbered 6,000 or over is certainly a fake. Most Breguet fakes are easily detected, but some are highly perfected copies of his work.

The second series started in 1787, following the partnership with Gide, and the first thirty-one were self-winding, or 'perpetuelles'. They were all quarter repeaters and nearly all have very light compensation balances and lever escapements. It was they, more than anything, that finally established his reputation. All had enamel dials, but nearly all were subsequently re-cased, and re-dialled in silver, by Breguet himself. An unaltered example, No 15, appears in the colour plates. This series ended at No 295 in 1793, apparently when the Gide partnership was wound up. The third series of numbers started in 1794 and continued until Breguet's death, at about No 4,000, and

subsequently by his son, probably until his death in 1833. There are anomalies, but it may be said that No 500 was reached by 1800, 2,000 by 1810 and 3,500 by 1820.

With increasing years Breguet became deaf; latterly completely so; but this never affected his kindly and cheerful disposition. He died suddenly on September 17th 1823, aged seventy-six. His portrait was painted more than once and several engravings were made of them. His bust was also made and reproduced.

Breguet left no writings though he was long known to have been collecting material for a magnum opus. At the time of his death he had confided these to Moinet, his secretary, for arrangement, after which no more was seen of them until 1848, when Moinet published an important horological work under his own name. It was recognised that this was based largely on Breguet's notes and on application by the Breguets to the Courts the notes were returned and still belong to the firm.

Breguet having died in harness in 1823, his son Louis Antoine retired in 1833 and died in 1858. His son Louis Clément François, 1804–83, had a son, again christened Louis Antoine who, although a capable horologist, failed to attain the ripe old age of the three previous generations and died in 1882 aged only thirty-one years. They had, however, anticipated that no further members of the family would come into the business and in 1870 took into partnership an Englishman Edward Brown who conducted the business until his death in 1895. He had two sons Edward and Henry, of whom Edward soon retired and Henry had a son, George Brown, who remained head of the firm until 1970.

Breguet had a world-wide reputation and *clientèle* in his life-time and exerted a tremendous influence on watchmaking throughout Europe. He had many famous pupils of whom the Dane Urban Jurgensen (1776–1830) was probably the most eminent. Several of these afterwards set up on their own, often producing watches almost or quite equal in merit to those of Breguet himself. These they were proud to sign with their own name coupled with the words *élève de Breguet*. Prominent among the *élèves* were Ingold, Kessels, Jurgensen, Winnerl, Oudin, Jacob, Firche, Laissieur, Fatton, Lopin and Renevier.

CHAPTER X

Developments since 1830

IMPROVEMENTS since 1830, in clocks and watches employing a mechanical escapement, have been mostly of a detailed nature. However, two radical advances have been made which were not foreseen until long after 1830 and which have had a great effect upon accurate timekeeping. These are, in watches, the development of metals for balance-wheels and balance-springs whose performance is almost unaffected by changes in temperature; and in clocks the development of a 'free' pendulum. (In a free-pendulum clock a fairly normal 'slave' clock does all the ordinary work, from which a second, 'free' pendulum receives its impulse and, in return, corrects any errors in the 'slave' clock.)

CLOCKS

Apart from the free-pendulum clock, which was of interest only to observatories, the advances in clockmaking have been small. The free-pendulum arrangement is theoretically compatible with a purely mechanical operation, but in its successful application the employment of an electric circuit to effect the interdependence of the two pendulums has been found essential. It was brought to its final perfection by W. H. Shortt in about 1924 using as a basis the commercially-produced Synchronome clock developed by F. Hope-Jones. Capable of accuracy within about one-hundredth of a second a year, the Shortt clocks have only been superseded at last by the quartz crystal clocks which are outside the scope of this book.

In domestic use the Graham regulator, with its dead-beat escapement and mercury-compensated pendulum, has continued to be the standard for precision timekeeping, and when well made, and provided the pallets are oiled about once every eighteen months, it answers all day-to-day requirements of accuracy. The need for a compensation pendulum has virtually disappeared by the development of the metal 'Invar' by Dr Charles-Edouard Guillaume. This compound has an almost nil coefficient of expansion, and will be discussed in more detail under 'Watches', later in the chapter.

Two other forms of escapement were developed which have been applied to a very small number of domestic clocks and are therefore of the greatest interest to technically-minded collectors.

The first of these is the gravity escapement clock as perfected by Lord Grimthorpe and made famous by its application to Big Ben. The gravity escapement had already been invented by Thomas Mudge in about 1770 (see Fig. 21 on page 157) but in its original form it was dangerously prone to tripping. Lord Grimthorpe devised, first his 'single three-leg' escapement, in about 1850, and finally his 'double three-leg' version as applied to Big Ben. In the latter form there are two co-axial escape wheels, each of three teeth, so that the wheel advances 60° at each unlocking. Also co-axial with the escape wheels is a fly which mitigates to some extent the naturally violent operation of the escapement and reduces the tendency to tripping, which is inherent in any gravity escapement. Dent made some splendid, very plain, domestic regulators in the 1850s, with either a single three- or four-leg gravity escapement, together with a zinc and steel gridiron pendulum, which will run for a large number of years without attention, to a very high level of accuracy.

The other notable advance was the free-pendulum regulator developed in 1891 by Dr Siegmund Riefler. Again, it is seldom found outside observatories, but although its operation is extremely finely poised and easily upset, it is compatible with domestic use, and gives very fine results. It comprises a dead-beat anchor, very much like a Graham, but instead of being connected rigidly to the pendulum via the crutch, it is fixed only to a rocking carriage from which hangs the suspension spring of the pendulum. The rocking of the carriage unlocks the train, which in turn imparts impulse to it, which is conveyed to the pendulum via the suspension spring, with sufficient force to keep it in motion through the very small arc that is required to keep the clock going. The escape wheel is in fact a double wheel of which one is responsible only for locking and unlocking, and the other imparts impulse.

Apart from these very rare escapements, and the Graham-type regulator which has been in continuous high-grade production, long-case clocks were already out of fashion by 1830 and have only been made subsequently in traditional style but of ever-decreasing quality and elegance. Very occasionally, long-case regulator clocks of simple lines, in good taste, may however be found to the end of the century, and even later, by makers such as Jump and Dent.

Bracket clocks also continued on traditional lines but with well-maintained standards of quality and taste. Vulliamy, in particular, continued to make bracket clocks of high quality, and restrained decoration, well past the middle of the nineteenth century; many of them for government offices. These might have a dead-beat, semi-dead-beat, or anchor escapement. Bracket clocks as now made are mostly of small size and fitted with a platform lever escapement. They are, in effect, carriage clocks in wooden cases. It is carriage, or travelling clocks that showed the most steady increase in popularity throughout the nineteenth century, that has continued to the present time, although for a different reason from that for which they were intended.

As its name indicates the carriage clock was designed originally for travelling use and its predecessor was the chaise clock; in effect a very large watch. This was an inconvenient arrangement as it had always to be hung from a hook, which might be all right in a carriage or chaise, but not in an hotel. The carriage clock was undoubtedly developed by Breguet, usually as a highly complicated and luxurious piece of equipment such as the one illustrated in Plate 157. It consists of a train or trains pivoted between vertical front and back plates, contained in an outer box-shaped case, consisting (usually) of glass sides and top framed in slender gilt-bronze pillars and bars. On top is a hinged carrying handle. The escapement sits on a horizontal platform at the top of the train, spanning the front and back plates, the drive from the train to the escape-wheel being via a contrate wheel. The escapement is usually a lever with a compensation balance, but in the cheaper specimens of the mid- or early nineteenth century it might be a cylinder, or a variety of debaufre known as the Garnier escapement, with a plain steel balance. English-made examples are fairly rare, and generally of very high quality, with fusees, and sometimes with a detent escapement and even a tourbillon. They are usually of relatively large size.

In the days before electric light and telephones, a traveller needed to be able to tell the time at

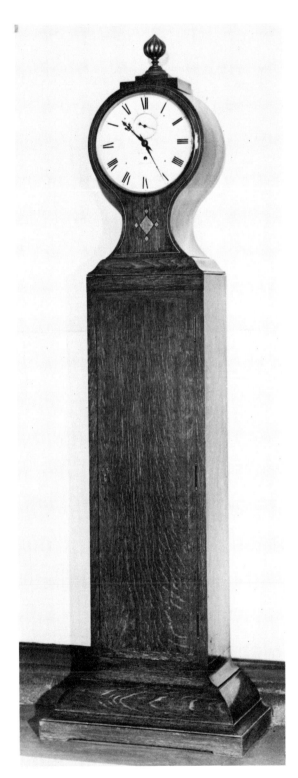

PLATE 184 (*left*)

Long-case regulator clock by Jump. Circa 1900. Long-case clocks of good mechanical quality, but in unduly ornate cases have continued to be made since 1830; also high-quality regulator clocks in plain cases. This clock is a very rare combination of a regulator movement with a case of restrained and elegant design. It was made for the Ecclesiastical Commissioners and now belongs to their successors the Church Commissioners for England.

PLATE 185 (*above*)

Bracket clock in the style of Vulliamy, and probably by him but unsigned. Mid-nineteenth century. British bracket clocks of good taste and simple, contemporary design, are rare after 1830. This clock was made for the Office of Woods, Forests and Land Revenues of the Crown, and now belongs to their successors, the Crown Estate Commissioners.

night, and to be woken up in time to catch his train or coach, so that fully equipped travelling clocks are repeaters and have an alarum. Hour-striking clocks repeat the hours only, but quarter repeating clocks usually give a choice of *grande-sonnerie* quarter striking; *petite-sonnerie*, or silence. Travelling clocks may also have varying degrees of calendar-work from days of the week up to perpetual calendar.

They were supplied originally in a leather-covered outer case.

In place of glass the sides may be of gilt-metal or painted porcelain.

A variant, originated by Breguet, was made of silver with an arch-top, following the outline of the dial. This type had a carrying chain in lieu of a handle. Fine examples were made by Jump and these had Breguet-type engine-turned silver dials. Nicole Nielson made a few exceedingly fine clocks of this type, with enamel dials, and a lever-tourbillon escapement.

Although travelling clocks are no longer a near-necessity of travel, they are still much sought after because of their small size, consistent with small modern rooms, and because they do not have to stand on an exactly level surface.

A few clocks, which are essentially carriage clocks, but contained in wooden cases with varying amounts of applied decoration, were made by Breguet, and subsequently by other makers up to the present day.

Something between a carriage and a bracket clock is the fairly common but ingenious 'Atmos' clock which has a heavy horizontal revolving pendulum or, more properly balance, with a very slow clock escapement. It is wound up by changes in temperature, it being stated that a change of 2°F will keep the clock running for forty-eight hours while when fully wound it will go for 100 days. They are made by the firm of Jaeger-le-Coultre.

Marine chronometers continue of high quality up to the modern instruments of Thomas Mercer. The more sophisticated specimens may have auxiliary compensation and many interesting varieties of balance wheel. Examples running for eight days are occasionally to be found.

WATCHES

If clockmakers since 1830 on the whole have shown a disappointing amount of initiative, watch-makers have displayed an almost compulsive inventiveness. To list and explain all the escapements devised during the second and third quarters of the nineteenth century would throw this book completely out of balance and indeed be quite alien to its purpose which is to follow the main lines of development throughout horological history. These escapements consist mostly of variations upon the lever escapement, but there have always been a few faithful huntsmen of that horological chimera, the constant-force escapement. The mechanically curious may study these elegant eccentricities in Chamberlain's *It's About Time* and Tardy's *La Montre – Les Echappements*.

By 1830 the verge escapement was giving way to the cylinder for cheap watches, and by 1840 the flow of cylinder escapements from Switzerland had almost certainly surpassed it. Nevertheless, verge watches were still made in considerable numbers in the last quarter of the century, and even into the present one, so that all told the verge escapement had a run of over 600 years without any variation of design. As is often found in mechanisms, simplicity, strength and reliability prove in the long run to be qualities valued above complication, delicacy and high performance.

In England, in 1830 the duplex and spring-detent escapements held the field for high-grade watches, and they continued in production until the end of the century. On the continent the lever already was in the lead, and to discover the reason for this difference it is necessary to look back into the eighteenth century.

The British undoubtedly were the pioneers of the lever escapement. Mudge invented it in 1754 and first incorporated it in a watch in 1769. Emery began production, at the rate of about three a year, from 1782. He was soon joined by Leroux, Perigal, Pendleton, Dutton, Grant, Margetts and Taylor (the last a mysterious and completely unrecorded maker, perhaps not quite of the eighteenth century, while of Margetts' lever watches none is known to survive). But by 1805 they had either died or come to the conclusion that the results did not justify the effort and skill involved, and it is doubtful if any example of the lever escapement was made in England between 1805 and 1815. Apparent specimens prove invariably to be later conversions. The workmanship of the pioneers was always of the very highest quality but it failed to live up to expectations, almost certainly because of its massiveness. It was also very expensive.

In 1815 the escapement was revived in two different forms by Edward Massey and George Savage. Savage's 'two-pin' escapement was the better but the less successful, or influential of the two. It consisted, in effect, of a single roller escapement with two, instead of one impulse pin and a very wide fork. What would be the safety crescent in a single-roller watch was a notch closely fitting the safety pin. The two 'impulse' pins in fact did little more than unlock the escapement while the 'safety' pin received most of the impulse. The intended merit of the escapement was that it unlocked on the line of centres. It worked well, but called for very accurate fitting, so that it never became popular, but it continued in limited production throughout the century.

Massey's escapement was a variant of the crank-roller escapement which the pioneers had evolved by about 1790, and it is often known as such, although incorrectly, because the impulse pin was neither cranked nor rollered, but a solid steel nib forming an integral part of the balance staff. Machined on each side of it was a vertical groove. The fork of the lever was simply a two-pronged fork with pointed ends which fitted into the two grooves just mentioned, and these constituted the safety action. The escapement thus was both simple and took up very little depth (although this quality seems never to have been exploited). Massey patented the escapement in 1815 and from that time it was widely used for the next thirty years or so, especially by the Liverpool and Prescot makers. This reintroduced the lever escapement to English makers, but in a cheap and simple form quite different from the difficult and complicated eighteenth-century designs. It was soon joined by the single-roller escapement that was to become the standard English escapement for the next hundred years. It was almost certainly invented by Breguet, who was using it in his tourbillons by 1810, but no English specimen is known from before 1820. Unlike the modern, double-roller escapement, illustrated in Fig. 24, it has only one roller which carries the impulse pin, and out of which is cut the crescent-shaped groove of the safety action. Although so long espoused by the British makers, it calls for more accurate workmanship than the double roller, and has a larger escapement arc. Despite this it attained a measure of popularity which fairly soon outstripped Massey's escapement, and the London makers, notably Earnshaw and J. R. Arnold, had taken it up for their second grade watches by the mid- or late 'twenties. Still however the lever escapement lacked a champion to restore to it the high esteem to which the eighteenth-century pioneers had raised it. The first man to do so was the almost unrecorded Thomas Cummins. About five watches by him are known of which the earliest is dated 1824 and all are from the 1820s. However, there is one similar watch by Charles Cummins, presumably a son or nephew, hall-marked as late as 1837. All are of the highest quality and massive elegance. The movements are full-plate and have Massey's escapement, but with a jewelled impulse stone. Some have resilient banking and all have fine compensation balances with helical springs; and regulator dials, either enamel or engine-turned gold. Thomas Cummins evidently thought so highly of their timekeeping abilities (and not without justice) that he turned most of them out with no motionwork nor any square by which the hands may be set. However, his influence, other than as a pointer, was probably slight and it was not until the early 'thirties that the

PLATE 186

Gold watch by Charles Cummins, hallmarked 1837. Massey's lever escapement with helical spring and compensation balance. Full-plate movement. The Cummins father and son championed the revival of the lever escapement for high-grade watches from 1825.

leading London makers began once more to espouse the lever escapement with any show of enthusiasm. Even then, this may well have been due to foreign influence. Indeed, the high grade London levers of this decade mostly bear little resemblance to the three-quarter-plate watches that were to become the British standard for the next hundred years. Probably a leading influence was Sylvain Mairet (1804–90) who worked in England from 1830–4 where he was a close friend of Ferguson Cole and made watches for Hunt & Roskell and B. L. Vulliamy. These have lever escapements with all the lift on the teeth of the escape wheel, as pioneered by Leroux and later used by Taylor. Watches made by Mairet are stamped with his initials, whatever the name on the dial. They usually have regulator dials with a large sector for a thermometer. One of his finest, which must be accounted as one of the most beautiful watches of all time, made for Hunt & Roskell, is illustrated in colour and from the fact that it is hall-marked 1846 it seems that his English connection lasted far longer than his three-year domicile on British soil.

Another London maker who showed a great diversity of talent was Charles Edward Viner. His work, always of very high quality, varied from verge-alarums, with his patent pendent alarum-setter, to duplex, detent and lever escapements. Some are 'à tact' and others minute repeaters. He employed key-wind and pump-wind and was an early exponent of the full keyless, and keyless

PLATE 187

Gold watch by Viner, hallmarked 1862. Lever escapement with compensation balance. Lepine calibre. Minute repeater. An early example of keyless wind and handsetting. The movement is probably of Swiss manufacture with English escapement.

hand-set operation. He seems to have had no standard ébauche, varying from full-plate to Lepine. Nothing seems to be known about his workshop, and it may be that he was only an English example of the merchant-watch-assemblers that were beginning to appear in Switzerland. But whatever the facts are, he is known to have enjoyed an aristocratic clientèle and certainly his watches are of great beauty and must have exercised an important influence in their day.

James Ferguson Cole (1798–1880) was another maker whose work combined considerable elegance with what appears at times to be an almost wilful diversity of mechanical inventiveness. Perhaps the best-known of his many escapements is the 'double rotary' invented in 1840. This had an auxiliary staff, geared up 2:1 from the balance staff, to prevent tripping.

The Vulliamy's, succeeded by Jump, made watches throughout the century very much in the

Breguet tradition, but probably it is Dent and Frodsham that produced the most consistently British and most consistently high-grade watches throughout the second half of the nineteenth, and first third of the twentieth centuries. They employed invariably the three-quarter plate layout, with either the lever or spring-detent escapement.

Frodsham's high-grade watch movements bear the letters A.D.FMSZ. If the letters in 'Frodsham' are numbered 1 to 8, the letters FMS represent the figures 185. The letter Z then arbitrarily represents 0 indicating that the series started in A.D. 1850.

But although the competition fell away rapidly after 1900, in the previous half-century Frodsham and Dent were by no means alone in producing high-grade watches, which display, pretty consistently, the restrained elegance of good breeding, coupled with fine workmanship and performance, that makes their ownership and use a very practical pleasure.

Although John Roger Arnold, with his foreman Thomas Prest, were pioneers of keyless winding in conjunction with a going barrel, the English preference for the fusee, and the difficulty of combining it with keyless winding, long delayed the widespread adoption of keyless winding in England. Barraud and Lund were among the pioneers of keyless-wound fusees, which work satisfactorily. A practical and simple variant was used by Dent who fitted a turnbuckle on the winding square in the back of the watch where it ordinarily lay flat and took up no additional thickness. For winding the back was opened, as for key-winding, when the turnbuckle could be brought into a vertical position and used to wind the watch. The hand-setter was a similar little star-shaped projection in the centre of the back. But keyless winding was not really universal in England until the end of the century.

So far as England was concerned, the next advance was a very important one, taking the escapement watch to the highest point of accuracy it is ever likely to reach; certainly in terms of ability to maintain a close and constant rate over a long period. This was the 'Karrusel' watch invented by Bahn Bonniksen of Coventry and patented in 1892. This had a revolving escapement, like Breguet's tourbillon, but more simply achieved, as it called for less precise workmanship, while in operation it is less violent than the ordinary minute tourbillon. In the karrusel the escapement is mounted upon the revolving carriage or platform, but is not concerned with its business. The fourth wheel is concentric with the carriage but not mounted upon it, so that the escape-wheel revolves round it. The fourth wheel pinion is driven by the third wheel in the ordinary way and the pinion of the third wheel drives the carriage, whose rate of revolution in the first model was $52\frac{1}{2}$ minutes. The carriage had no top bearing and ran dry in its guide. In a later model, introduced in 1903, the carriage had a top bearing and it was driven by a separate train from the centre wheel, to revolve in 39 minutes. Yet another variant, with a centre seconds hand, revolves in 34 minutes. The escapement is always a normal English lever. Karrusel watches dominated the Kew trials for many years after their introduction, but with the general decline in the English watch trade their production was discontinued in 1923. Bonniksen supplied his karrusels to several makers, or they were made under licence; notably Dent, Nicole Nielsen, Usher & Cole, and Rotherham & Son.

Almost concurrently with the karrusel there was an English revival of the one-minute lever tourbillon. Although these might bear the name of Smith, Dent, or Frodsham most of them were made by Nicole Nielson. They were, and are, capable of a magnificent performance, especially when fitted with a Guillaume balance. They were made up to the mid-1930s and are among the most sought-after watches today.

PLATE 188

Silver watch by Dent, hallmarked 1911. Thirty-five minute Karussel movement and lever escapement. Such watches achieved the highest level of accuracy for pocket-watches.

However, towards the outbreak of the Second World War it was apparent that the English high-grade watch-trade was on its way out. The writing had been on the wall for seventy years at least and Lord Grimthorpe had advised the British industry to go over to machine-production; but to no avail. John Harwood had patented a self-winding wrist-watch in 1924 but the industry failed to take advantage of this potential lead, and the self-winding wrist-watch failed to establish itself until after the Second World War, 170 years after its invention.

With the decay and disappearance of all the skilled trades it might be thought impossible that a high-grade watch could ever again be made in Britain, yet the impossible has happened. The making of one-minute detent tourbillons is once more undertaken by George Daniels of London, the first having been finished in 1969. Its construction meant that he personally had to make every part of the watch, except for the balance-spring and main-spring. This of course includes the case and the dial and, at the other extreme, even the screws. The watches are of superb appearance and performance and are eagerly sought by discriminating connoisseurs. One is illustrated in colour (see Plate III).

France seems to have done little to defend the pre-eminent position won for her by Breguet, although the firm, and one or two others, such as le Roy, continued to make high-grade watches.

While the British trade took a century a-dying, the future of watch making was being worked out in America and Switzerland. Initially, America took the lead in the all-important field of machine-production, while Switzerland concentrated upon the organisation of skilled labour. In the end, it is

PLATE 189

Movement and escapement of watch by George Daniels. Hallmarked 1969. For the dial see colour plate No. III. The one-minute tourbillon carries a pivoted detent escapement but later watches by Mr Daniels have spring detents. Every part of the watches except the balance springs and main springs are made by him. There are two going barrels. The temperature-compensated balance spring is coupled with an uncut balance.

Switzerland that has gained an almost undisputed lead in the production of watches of all grades, so it may be appropriate to consider first what happened in America.

American horological history, unhappily, consists for the most part of a tale of commercial failures. However, the first pioneer, Luther Goddard, did succeed. He set up his factory in 1809 and had completed 500 verge watches by the time he retired in 1817. Nothing is known of his methods, and it was not until 1838 that the next attempt was made by James & Henry Pitkin, who aimed at mass-production, but were in liquidation within three years. It was not until 1860 that Edward Howard (1812–1904), after several financial crises, finally succeeded in producing a commercially successful, American-made, mass-produced, precision watch. In their final form, they were constructed to a high level of mechanical finish and appearance.

Of later projects the Waltham company saw the greatest success, their famous 'Riverside Maximus' reaching a level of finish and general excellence that has never been exceeded; certainly in any sort of quantity production.

At the other end of the scale the attempt by the Waterbury Watch Company to produce a very cheap watch met with considerable, although not enduring success. The first model, produced in 1880, was really a sort of karrusel, since the whole movement revolved once an hour in the case. It had a crude form of duplex escapement and took an excessively long time to wind. It sold for $4. Types are lettered from A to W and a complete set is a much-desired possession among American collectors. After about 1890 a new model was introduced, which was not a success, and the company was taken over by the Ingersoll brothers who employed the factory to make watches selling for only $1. In its run of thirty years it produced no less than sixty million watches.

The final triumph of American mass-production came with the need in the Second World War to set up at very short notice the very large quantity production of high-precision marine chronometers and deck watches. This was met with the greatest possible success by the Hamilton Company and the techniques which they evolved in such a short time have been of value to the world industry ever since.

As opposed to these feats of machine-production, two highly individual artists stand out in the history of American watch making. They are Charles Fasoldt (1818–98) and Albert Potter (1830–1908). Potter made a considerable range of escapements but Fasoldt concentrated mainly on an escapement of his own which was midway between a lever and detent. But the work of both men is of the highest quality and specimens are eagerly sought in America.

Before turning to the Swiss industry as a whole it is perhaps convenient to describe briefly the Swiss Roskopf watch which was in many ways the precursor of the Ingersoll. The aim of George-Frédéric Roskopf (1813–89) was to produce a watch to sell to the poorest members of the community for 20 francs. This he succeeded in doing by eliminating every possible complication and refinement and using a very crude, pin-wheel lever escapement. Like Ingersoll it relied upon an enormously powerful spring to make it work. However, unlike the American watches, Roskopf had no means of setting up a factory specifically designed for the project. He had therefore to persuade the network of outworkers to employ techniques which were both new and displeasing to them. That he succeeded, and at the intended retail price, was therefore no mean achievement of diplomacy and organisation. The first watches were in production in 1867 and gained a bronze medal at the Universal Exhibition at Paris in 1868. This ensured success and it led to an export trade in very cheap watches from which Switzerland still benefits.

However, it is in the mass-production of medium to very high-grade watches that Switzerland now excels.

The first move towards this situation was in about 1780 when Frédéric Japy developed a range of specialised cutting tools and lathes, for making particular watch parts, and other tools for drilling, riveting, and similar tasks.

In 1820 Humbert and the Dariers set up a factory for the machine production of watch parts and although they succeeded in this, the ultimate goal of interchangeability eluded them. This was not achieved until about 1840, by G. A. Leschot, working for Vacheron & Constantin, at first by the somewhat cumbersome means of a very large pantograph. But by 1845 he had devised a successful complete range of machine tools.

Nevertheless, the full adoption of the factory system in Switzerland was long delayed. Even as

PLATE 190

*Gold watch by Waltham of Massachusetts. Club-tooth lever escapement. Gold train. Jewelled throughout. The
'Riverside Maximus' was the highest-grade quantity-produced watch to come out of America. First quarter of
the twentieth century. Property of Austin Niland.*

late as 1870 the majority of the 34,000 people employed in the industry were still outworkers producing an overall average of forty watches per head per annum. It was not until the present century
that the proportion of factory workers began to predominate.

Despite the successive advances of Japy, Humbert, Darier and Leschot, the Swiss industry had
a number of difficulties to contend with. As late as 1830 it was recognised that their watch trains
were of thoroughly bad quality and in the whole of Switzerland there was no one who could make a
balance-spring. Attempts to improve this state of affairs were made by public competition.

Concurrently, merchant-watchmakers were applying their organising ability, and commercial
enterprise, to assemble, in quantity, watches made up of the parts supplied by the outworkers, and
these men did much to build up the export trade which would provide the outlet for Switzerland's
ever-increasing production.

Up to 1850 and even later, the industry concentrated largely upon the cylinder escapement and
from 1840 succeeded in producing the very thin watches that were immediately in fashionable
demand.

Switzerland's horological influence upon England has always been considerable. The first batch
of émigrés arrived at the end of the seventeenth century following the revocation of the Edict of
Nantes and there was a further flow a century later, many of whom settled in and around Man-

chester where they were able to enhance greatly the prosperity of the already well-established Lancashire clock and watch industry. At the same time there came to London such top-class artists as Josiah Emery. Finally, their exhibits at the Great Exhibition of 1851 secured for them a vast export market in Britain.

It says much for Swiss industriousness and organising ability that even after the Americans had outstripped them in techniques of machine-production, the Swiss were still able to undercut their prices, quality for quality.

Against this emphasis on quantity production, some watches of the highest quality continued to be made in Switzerland, and watches by Audemars, Girard Perregaux, Jules Jürgensen and even many anonymous pieces, may equal the finest work of the French or British at the time. In particular, Neuchâtel was the principal producer of tourbillon watches during the second half of the nineteenth century and on until about 1960.

Another Swiss speciality has been the production of watches of extreme complication, by most of the leading firms, during the first half of the present century. They contain chronograph, perpetual calendar, equation of time and minute repeating mechanisms. They are, naturally, massive and not at all elegant, but as the ultimate in mechanical complication they make a strong appeal to some collectors.

Germany has not featured much in horology since the Thirty Years War, but an honourable nineteenth-century exception must be made in favour of the firm of Lange of Glaschutter, who produced watches and marine chronometers, both with the lever escapement, of consistently high quality.

It is at this point that we must return to the history of the lever escapement on the continent as opposed to its highly idiosyncratic career in England.

There exists a watch-movement, signed by Julien le Roy, containing a remarkable and obviously very early type of lever escapement, and the remains of a gridiron system of temperature of a kind that actually survives in a watch of 1764 by Ferdinand Berthoud. Julien le Roy died in 1753 which seems an impossibly early date for the escapement (which would thus antedate Mudge) but subsequent research has shown that Pierre le Roy continued frequently to use his father's signature long after his death. The indications are that the watch was made in about 1775, but even so, this makes it the second oldest lever escapement watch in the world.

Like Mudge, no one seems to have been particularly keen to follow le Roy's lead, and it was not until the mid-1780s that a crude version of the escapement, with a very slow train, was produced in Switzerland by Pouzzait. However, the true pioneer of the lever escapement on the continent, and as it is known today throughout the world, undoubtedly was Abraham-Louis Breguet. When he started to experiment with it is not clear, but almost certainly some time in the mid-1780s. In 1787 he made plans for his famous thirty 'perpetuelles' with lever escapement, and fifteen of these were in hand before production was discontinued on account of the French Revolution. As opposed to the contemporary English work, these early levers of Breguet are characterised by their extreme lightness. Like the London makers, Breguet did not use draw and seems to have adopted it only reluctantly and to the least possible extent about 1815. Except in his tourbillons, Breguet did not often use the lever escapement between about 1800 and 1815 (exactly the same period, curiously enough, as its discontinuance in England) but around 1815 he arrived at a double-roller escapement with divided lift, which was his final word on the subject and was, indeed, the lever escapement as we know it today, apart from the proportions of the lever. In his early watches Breguet used a lightened version of his friend John Arnold's compensation balance, together with Arnold's helical spring. Later he used a modern type of balance and a flat spring but with the famous 'Breguet overcoil', aimed at reducing side-pressures on the balance pivots and thus improving isochronism and the reduction of position errors.

In this form the lever escapement was taken up by continental makers for work of the highest class, but despite this start over the British, it did not come into widespread use until well after 1850.

It was John Arnold who first hit upon the idea of terminal end-curves for balance-springs in 1776 and Breguet who followed with his flat spring and overcoil; but the technique remained empirical. The object of end-curves is to bring the centre of gravity of the spring as near as possible to the centre of gravity of the balance, and while it was known that changes in the shape of the overcoil produced changes in isochronism, the theory producing these changes was not understood until a watchmaker named Jacob persuaded Professor Edouard Phillipps, a French mining engineer, to conduct a mathematical research into the subject. This work took him two years and in 1861 he produced his *Mémoire sur le Spiral Réglant des Chronomètres et des Montres*. Although this great work was entirely French in inspiration and execution, the Swiss were quickest to seize upon it and put its precepts into practical execution. Jules Grossmann was the pioneer executant in the subject and devoted the years 1868–1901 to producing his 'theory of timing'.

The greatest scientific advances in nineteenth-century watchmaking were in the field of metallurgy and the name of Charles-Edouard Guillaume (1861–1938) is pre-eminent. Although Swiss-born, he was employed as Director of the International Bureau of Weights and Measures at Sèvres. His great metallurgical researches were undertaken primarily for the advancement of the Swiss industry and first published in 1899 in the *Journal Suisse d'Horlogerie*. These were directed primarily to the elimination of middle-temperature error. In any of the bi-metallic compensation balances previously devised, a watch or chronometer could be made to keep time at two given temperatures, but between them it would gain, and outside them it would lose. Guillaume evolved a metal incorporating nickel-iron alloys which, when used instead of steel in a bi-metallic balance, virtually eliminated middle temperature errors. The 'integral' or Guillaume balance could not however be used economically in pocket watches, so the idea followed of developing a metal for balance-springs which was itself constant in all temperatures and thus would not need a compensation balance. Experiments were carried out by Guillaume with a Neuchâtel timer Paul Perret, with a considerable measure of success, but finally it was Guillaume, as the result of further calculation, who found that by adding exact quantities of chromium and carbon to his previous metal, he could produce a metal whose nature remained almost constant at all temperatures. His previous alloy he had named 'invar' and the new alloy he named 'élinvar', being a contraction of 'élasticité invariable'. Experiments carried out in 1913 confirmed the correctness of Guillaume's calculations. There existed thus a metal for balance-springs which did not need the assistance of a compensation balance, provided the balance itself remained invariable at different temperatures. The élinvar spring does in fact have a slight residual temperature error to counteract which Paul Ditisheim devised a small bi-metallic affix to the monometallic balance.

Even so, élinvar has its disadvantages; notably its extreme softness and considerable lack of elasticity. M. R. Straumann carried out subsequent researches to produce a metal of superior hard-

PLATE 191 (*left*)

Gold watch by S. Smith & Son. Hallmarked 1899. This watch possesses most of the possible complications including perpetual calendar, minute repeating, and split-seconds chronograph. Hardly anything is visible of the movement which is not therefore illustrated.

PLATE 192 (*below*)

Silver watch by Stopfer. Lever escapement with stop-watch movement. Mid-twentieth century.

ness and elasticity, and at least equally non-magnetic. This he succeeded in doing, primarily by the introduction of the metal beryllium, to produce an alloy which he called 'Nivarox', which may be regarded as the final stage in the production of the precision escapement watch.

★   ★   ★

If this chapter has seemed to be devoted to a history of people, firms, systems and experiments, rather than the history of styles followed in the rest of the book, this is because it is how horology since 1830 has developed. There has been no consistent evolution of styles, either nationally or internationally. As to decoration: following a trend which was apparent long before 1830, the watch had become a strictly utilitarian object and its elegance had to be inherent in its design, and not achieved by applied decoration.

Decorated watches there certainly have been since 1830, but because they violated this rule, they have (with the exception of women's wrist watches) been almost uniformly of a manifestly meretricious character.

The interest to a collector of watches since 1830 must be centred primarily upon their technical interest or excellence. If he observes this rule, he will find that they have elegance enough, into the bargain. By knowing the general history which has been told in this chapter, the collector will be reasonably equipped to recognise the provenance of any watch he comes across, and thus able to form a valid assessment of its merit or importance.

Colour Plates

Watch by Benjamin Hill, London. Verge escapement. Engraved silver dial. Rock-crystal case mounted in gilt brass, circa 1640.
(Victoria and Albert Museum)

Watch case of gold enamelled in transparent green over an engine-turned gold ground, surrounded by a border of half-pearls. The verge movement by Rundell and Bridge, London, early 19th century.
(Victoria and Albert Museum)

Watch case of gold, enamelled light blue. Possibly by a London artist trained at Blois. The verge escapement movement by Eduardus East, London, circa 1640. (For a picture of the outside of the case see colour plate No. III)
(Victoria and Albert Museum)

Watch case of gold covered all over with transparent champlevé enamel with flowers and foliage. The dial is similarly decorated. Mid-17th century. The movement is 18th century.
(Victoria and Albert Museum)

Watch case of gold, the back (shown in the plate) containing a panel of jasper. The sides contain six oval onyx panels. The remainder is enamelled blue, white and green, circa 1635. The movement is late 17th century.
(Victoria and Albert Museum)

Watch case of gold pierced with conventional floral designs, enamelled in red and green translucent colours and in opaque blue and white. The cover is enamelled thus on both inner and outer sides. Second quarter 17th century. Later movement and dial. The watch was given by Charles I to William Graham, 7th earl of Menteith.
(Victoria and Albert Museum)

Watch case of copper enamelled with floral sprays in panels reserved on a blue ground. English, circa 1780, apparently by an independent London artist. Verge escapement movement by R. Hampton, London No. 5008.
(Victoria and Albert Museum)

PLATE I

Watch case of gold enamelled white and transparent
blue, 1779, with matching chatelaine. The verge
escapement unsigned.
(Victoria and Albert Museum)

Watch by Breguet, Paris, No. 3452. Ruby cylinder
escapement. Plain balance with compensation curb.
Half-quarter repeater on a gong. Engine-turned
gold case. Engine-turned silver dial. 1822. With
Breguet short chain and key. Breguet's highest-grade
standardised product.

Watch by Hunt and Roskell, London, for whom
Sylvan Mairet made the lever escapement
movement. Gold case and engine-turned gold dial
with subsidiary dials for hours, minutes, seconds and
thermometer, 1846. This very thin watch may be
considered one of the most elegant products of
19th century horology.
(T. Camerer Cuss Collection)

London-made watch, the lever escapement, full-
plate movement unsigned. Compensation balance.
Gold case with decorative engraving. Engraved gold
dial with applied gold numerals, 1862.

Watch by Breguet, Paris, No. 15. Self-winding,
lever escapement movement with compensation
balance. Quarter repeater on a block. Plain gold
case and enamel dial. Started in 1787 and sold in
1793. This is one of the very few of Breguet's
famous first thirty 'perpetuelles' to remain in
completely original condition.

PLATE II

'Oignon' watch by Gloria à Rouen. Verge
escapement. Quarter repeater on a bell, circa 1700.
Engraved gold case and engraved gold dial with
separate enamel circles and chapters. It is very rare
for oignon watches to possess a gold case; nearly all
are gilt-metal or enamelled.

Silver-gilt watch case, finely engraved and pierced
with flowers. The verge escapement, clock-watch
movement is by Johannes Bayes, London, active
1646–1675. There is also an outer case of tortoise-
shell inlaid with a landscape of gold piqué.
(Victoria and Albert Museum)

Outer case of a watch by Markwick, London No. 288.
Verge escapement, circa 1700. Tortoise-shell piqué
with silver.
(Victoria and Albert Museum)

Watch case of gold, enamelled light blue, the edges
decorated with small flowers in relief. Possibly by a
London artist trained at Blois. The verge
escapement movement by Eduardus East, London,
circa 1640. (For a picture of the dial see colour
plate No I.)

Watch by George Daniels, London. Gold and silver
engine-turned case, hall-marked 1969. Silver
engine-turned dial with jump-hour hand on a sector.
For an illustration, and particulars of the
movement see plate No 191.

Watch by John Arnold, London, No. 17/67.
Pivoted detent escapement. 'S' compensation balance
and helical spring with terminal curves. Half-
quarter repeater on a block, circa 1780. Recased in
gold with skeleton dial in 1823.

PLATE III

APPENDIX I

Glossary of technical terms

This short glossary is provided for quick reference and contains only terms generally current in antiquarian horology, whose meaning is not self-apparent.
Terms which are also of general application to furniture, engineering or jewellery (e.g. 'marquetry' 'ratchet' or 'repoussé') are not included.

ACT OF PARLIAMENT CLOCK. In 1797–8 a tax was imposed on all timekeepers. So few people carried watches, owing to this tax, that many innkeepers installed wall-clocks in their public rooms. These clocks consist of a large wooden painted dial and a fairly narrow trunk, housing the weight and pendulum. An example is illustrated in PLATE 105. They take their name from the Act of Parliament which inaugurated the tax which, however, had so disastrous an effect on the industry that it was very soon repealed. Probably only a small proportion of these clocks was, therefore, made during the currency of the Act and they may more appropriately be described as 'Tavern Clocks'.

ALARUM. A mechanical warning device in a timekeeper which rings a bell at some pre-selected time. A typical specimen is illustrated in FIG. 37.

'ALL-OR-NOTHING' PIECE. In very early repeaters insufficient hours were repeated if the actuating lever was only partially depressed. The introduction of the 'All-or-nothing' piece ensured that the repeating train is only let off if the lever is fully depressed. Otherwise it does not operate at all.

ANCHOR ESCAPEMENT. The anchor escapement was invented in or before 1671 to enable the use of a long pendulum with a narrower arc than is readily practicable with the verge escapement. The pallets are placed on a pivoted bar which, with the pallets, somewhat resembles a ship's anchor. A drawing is in FIG. 10.

ARBOR. The horological term for the axle, shaft or spindle upon which the wheels of the clock or watch train are mounted.

ARC. The angle through which a pendulum or balance wheel swings.

AUTOMATA. This term covers the many mechical devices which may be driven by the striking or going train of a clock or watch. Examples are revolving windmill sails, ships tossing on the sea, and model men who strike the time on real or imitation bells. More elaborate examples are dancing figures, jugglers and the like.

AUXILIARY COMPENSATION. The subsidiary compensation sometimes fitted to a bimetallic balance wheel to overcome middle temperature error (q.v.).

BACK PLATE. The arbors of a clock train are held between two plates. The back plate is that further from the dial.

BALANCE. The timekeeping qualities of a timekeeper are derived from the to-and-fro swinging motion of a controller placed at the opposite end of the train to the mainspring or driving weight. When the controller takes the form of a wheel in equilibrium, it is known as the 'balance'.

BALANCE-COMPENSATED. See 'Compensation Balance'.

BALANCE SPRING (BREGUET). For balance springs generally see 'Balance Spring (Spiral)'. A plain spiral balance spring is not truly isochronous, i.e., will not take exactly the same time to swing through a wide arc as through a narrow one. Breguet discovered that a spiral spring could be made isochronous by bringing an extension of the outer coil in across the other coils and fixing it at a point as near as possible to its centre. The terminal curve may have various shapes whose theory was later formulated by Edouard Phillips. Also called an 'overcoil' spring (see FIG. 27).

BALANCE SPRING (HELICAL). For balance springs generally see 'balance spring (spiral)'. A plain spiral balance spring is not truly isochronous, i.e., it will not take exactly the same time to swing through a wide arc as through a narrow one. Arnold discovered that isochronism could be achieved by using a spring of helical shape (q.v.) with incurve ends of a shape arrived at by him empirically, but whose theory was later formulated by Edouard Phillips.

311

BALANCE SPRING (SPIRAL). Since about 1675 in all balance-controlled timekeepers, the inner end of a weak spiral spring is attached to the staff (or spindle) of the balance. The outer end is fixed to the plate of the timekeeper. The spring winds and unwinds as the balance swings and ensures much more accurate timekeeping than the uncontrolled balances which preceded its invention. Hooke enunciated the principle of the balance spring in the Latin phrase 'ut tensio sic vis' (the force of the spring depends on how much it has been wound up). Also called the 'hairspring'.

BALANCE STAFF. The staff, or arbor upon which the balance (q.v.) is mounted.

BALLOON CLOCK. A bracket clock in the shape of the hot-air balloons of the late eighteenth century.

An illustration is in PLATE 104.

BANJO CLOCK. A popular type of American Wall Clock, introduced by Simon Willard in 1802, and so called because its shape somewhat resembles a banjo.

An illustration is in PLATE 163.

BANKING PIN. In its simplest form, on verge watches, a pin protruding from the edge of the balance wheel, which registers with stops on the balance cock, thus preventing the balance from swinging too far if the watch is turned abruptly. In later escapements it takes other forms which fulfil the same object. In the lever escapement, banking pins are used to prevent the lever moving through more than its proper travel.

BARREL (GOING). In spring-driven timekeepers not incorporating a fusee, is the barrel upon which the Great Wheel is mounted, and which contains the mainspring.

BARREL (SPRING). The barrel containing the main-spring (see also 'going barrel' above).

BASCULE. In most timekeepers with the 'detent' or 'chronometer' (q.v.) escapement, the detent is mounted on a spring, with the object of avoiding the need for lubrication. It may, however, be made to pivot, in which case the detent is known as a 'bascule'.

BASKET TOP. A form of top to English bracket clocks popular in the last quarter of the seventeenth century has somewhat the shape of an inverted basket, formed of pierced silver or metal gilt. An example is illustrated in PLATE 51.

BEAT. The 'tick' of a clock or watch, caused by the teeth of the escape wheel striking the pallets of the escapement.

BEETLE HAND. The form of hour hand found on most English eighteenth century watches, so called from a fancied resemblance to the stag bettle. Usually found in company with a 'poker' minute hand (q.v.). An example is shown in PLATE 82.

BELL TOP. The most popular form of top to English bracket clocks in the late seventeenth century, so called because it is bell-shaped in section. An example is in PLATES 47, 48 and 49. See also 'Inverted bell'.

BEZEL. The metal rim in which a clock or watch-glass is fitted.

BI-METALLIC. The adjective applied to all forms of temperature compensation which rely for their operation on the flexing of a strip of metal formed by fusing or rivetting together two strips of metal (usually brass and steel) having different coefficients of expansion. Nearly all good-class watches have a bi-metallic balance, but before these were in general use, an automatic regulator was formed by a bi-metallic strip called a 'compensation curb' (q.v.).

BLIND MAN'S WATCH. See 'Tact'.

BOB. The weight at the end of any pendulum. More particularly a 'bob pendulum' is one with a round bob threaded onto the pendulum rod, and screwed up or down it to regulate the clock. These are only found on early bracket (and exceedingly early long-case) clocks with verge escapement and short pendulum. They were superseded by the lenticular-shaped bob which is made to slide up and down the rod by turning a small screw threaded on to the rod.

'BOLT AND SHUTTER'. A form of maintaining power (q.v.) originally incorporated in most long-case clocks prior to about 1715 to keep the clock going while being wound. The 'bolt' is a lever at the side of the movement which, being depressed, flexes a spring sufficient to keep the train going for a few minutes while the clock is wound. The 'shutters' are flaps, connected to the 'bolt', which normally close the winding holes in the dial. When the 'bolt' is operated the 'shutters' move aside to give access to the winding square. Their object was to make it impossible to wind the clock until the maintaining power had been brought into play. The bolt and shutter are often found to have been subsequently removed and were not generally used during the eighteenth century, except in Regulators (q.v.).

BOTTOM PLATE. In all watches before the introduction of the Lepine calibre, in about 1770, and in nearly all English watches, the wheels of the train are held between two plates. The bottom plate is the one furthest from the dial.

BOW. The metal ring or stirrup hinged or looped to the pendant (q.v.) of a watch whereby the watch may be attached to a chain, strap or fob.

BRACKET CLOCK. The generic name for all spring-driven clocks designed to stand on a table, shelf or bracket. Some authorities claim that most of such clocks should more correctly be described as 'table clocks', but the term 'bracket clock' is well established and understood.

BREAK-ARCH. An arched top to a clock where the outside diameter of the arch is less than the width of the hood. Alternatively, an arched top to a clock-dial where the inside diameter of the arch is less than the width of the dial-plate.

BREGUET BALANCE SPRING. See 'Balance Spring (Breguet)'.

BREGUET HAND. A form of hand much used by Breguet in which the shaft of the hand is very slightly tapered and the pointed head is carried on an annular ring at the end of the shaft. Also sometimes called a Moon hand.

An example is in PLATE 113.

BREGUET KEY. A form of watch key used by Breguet in which, by interposing a spring-tensioned ratchet and click in the shaft of the key, he ensured that the watch could not be damaged by being wound in the wrong direction. Also called a 'tipsy key'. An example is in PLATE 113.

BULLSEYE GLASS. A form of watch glass popular during the second half of the eighteenth century. Like earlier glasses it is a flattened dome in shape, but has a small circular flat ground in the centre, usually about half an inch in diameter.

CALIBRE. The type of design or layout of a movement, also its size.

CANNON PINION. The pinion which carries the minute hand. Its hollow arbor is a friction fit on the centre-wheel arbor thus allowing the hands to be set. It is part of the under-dial motion work (q.v.)

CARTEL CLOCK. A wall clock of French origin in which the dial is surrounded by rococo ormolu ornamentation.

CENTRE PINION. The pinion in the going train driven by the Great Wheel. It is usually in the centre of a watch, but is still so-called even when it is not central.

CENTRE SECONDS. A seconds hand pivoted at the centre of the dial, concentric with the hour and minute hands. Also called 'sweep centre seconds' because it sweeps the whole dial.

CHAISE-CLOCK. A portable time-keeper in the form of a very large watch, intended for use when travelling.

CHAPTER RING. That part of a dial on which the hours are marked. Prior to 1750 (and often later) it was separate ring, pinned to the dial plate.

CHRONOGRAPH. A watch which is also a stop-watch, in which the chronograph hand can be started, stopped and returned to zero without interfering with the going train.

CHRONOMETER. In antiquarian horology, a watch or portable clock with a detent escapement. (In modern parlance it includes any watch or clock which passed certain stringent observatory tests.)

CIRCULAR ERROR. A pendulum normally mounted and traversing the segment of a circle is not truly isochronous, i.e., it does not take the same length of time to swing through arcs of different amplitude. This shortcoming in a pendulum is known as 'circular error' (see also 'cycloidal cheeks').

CLEPSYDRA. A timekeeper regulated by the flow of a liquid.

CLICK. A spring-tensioned pawl holding up against the tension of the mainspring and enabling it to be wound. So called from the noise caused during winding by the teeth of the ratchet-wheel escaping past the click.

CLOCK-WATCH. A pocket watch which automatically strikes the hour (as opposed to a repeater q.v.). Also applied to Sedan Clocks (q.v.) which strike.

CLUB-FOOT VERGE. A form of dead-beat verge invented by Debaufre in 1704 or earlier. An illustration is in FIG. 19. See also 'Ormskirk Escapement' and 'Debaufre escapement'.

COCK. A bracket with one end attached to a plate of which the other end supports the pivot of a wheel. In all watches before about 1675, and English ones afterwards, only the balance wheel is so supported and the cock is finely pierced or engraved. In early French and many other continental watches the cock has two supports, completely spanning the balance wheel, and it is then known as a 'bridge cock'. In watches with the Lepine calibre (introduced about 1770) each wheel in the train has a separate cock.

COLLET. A brass ring, solid or split, used for fixing purposes, such as, securing the minute hand or the inner end of the balance spring to the balance staff. Also, the shoulder at the centre of a wheel by by which it is mounted upon its arbor.

COMPENSATION BALANCE. A balance wheel compensating the effects of heat and cold. Almost invariably this takes the form of a wheel with two spokes or arms to each of which is attached a bimetallic (q.v.) rim. This rim is in two parts, each attached at one end to one arm; the other, free end flexes inwards or outwards in heat or cold (respectively) thus counteracting the tendency of the watch to lose in heat and gain in cold.

COMPENSATION CURB. A device for compensating the effects of heat and cold in watches before the adoption of the compensation balance (q.v.). The regulator has one of its curb pins (q.v.) mounted on a bimetallic (q.v.) strip which moves its pin away from the other in cold, and towards it in heat, thus roughly compensating the tendency of the watch to gain in cold and lose in heat.

COMPENSATION PENDULUM. A pendulum compensating the effects of heat and cold. The two principal forms are the Graham mercurial pendulum and Harrison gridiron pendulum, in which the distance between the centre of gravity of the pendulum and its anchorage, remains constant at varying temperatures.

COMPLICATED WORK. Any mechanism not involved in timekeeping or striking, e.g., repeaters, chronographs, calendar and astronomical work.

CONSTANT FORCE ESCAPEMENT. An escapement in which impulse is given to the controller by a falling weight or a spring and is thus constant in force. The weight is raised, or the spring flexed by the going train after each impulse. See also 'remontoire escapement'.

CONTRATE WHEEL. A toothed wheel whose teeth are at right angles to the plane of the wheel. In horology, mostly used with the verge escapement being the wheel which drives the escape wheel pinion. Also used for the same purpose in carriage clocks, etc., having their escape wheel in the horizontal plane.

CONTROLLER. The part of a timekeeper, either the balance or pendulum, which controls its timekeeping.

COQUERET. A polished steel end-plate for the balance staff pivot, screwed to the cock, and used in continental watches before the introduction of jewelling from England. See also End-plate.

COUNT-WHEEL. A wheel in the striking train, with twelve slots cut in its periphery, at progressively widening intervals, in which a claw drops. At each hour the claw is lifted and the wheel revolves, the clock then strikes until the claw drops into the next slot. The clock therefore cannot avoid striking progressively, regardless of the position of the hands. The operation of this mechanism is shown in FIG. 38. Count wheel, or locking-plate striking was superseded by rack striking (q.v.).

CRESTING. Free-standing pierced ornament (in wood or metal) above a clock-case.

CROMWELLIAN CLOCK. Colloquial name for a Lantern Clock (q.v.).

CROWN-WHEEL ESCAPEMENT. Another name for the verge escapement, attributable to the resemblance of the escape wheel to a crown.

CRUTCH. In most pendulum clocks [except those with the verge escapement and bob pendulum (q.v.)] the pendulum is not directly attached to the escapement. It is loosely embraced by a claw called the crutch, on an arm attached to the anchor staff or arbor.

CURB PINS. The pins attached to the regulator of a watch, which embrace the outer curve of the balance spring. Also called the Index Pins.

CYCLOIDAL CHEEKS. An ordinary pendulum, traversing the segment of a circle is not truly isochronous (see 'Isochronism' and 'Circular Error') but if its bob can be made to travel in a cycloidal path it becomes isochronous. This was achieved by Huygens who suspended the pendulum on a thread held between two metal cheeks of cycloidal shape. In the anchor and dead-beat escapements (q.v.) the arc is too small for circular error to become a serious factor and no such counteraction is necessary.

CYLINDER ESCAPEMENT. The dead-beat watch escapement developed by Graham in 1726 as an improvement on the verge. A cylinder, with a segment cut away, is mounted as part of the balance staff. The escape wheel rotates in the same plane as the balance wheel. A number of pins project vertically from its rim. On the top of each pin is a flat, triangular, pointed tooth, pointing in the direction of rotation. The point of each tooth is successively held against the outside of the cylinder; gives impulse as it passes the lip; rests on the inside face of the cylinder; and again gives impulse as it escapes past the other lip. The escapement is illustrated in FIG. 18. It belongs to the family of 'Frictional Rest Escapements' (q.v.) and is also known as the 'Horizontal Escapement'.

DART. In the lever escapement (q.v.) the safety action is provided by the 'dart', being a dart-shaped projection on the end of the lever nearest the balance.

Lying in its path is a roller, on the balance staff which has a crescent-shaped piece cut out of it. The roller makes it impossible for the dart to cross the axis of the balance, except when the crescent registers with the dart, which happens at the moment of unlocking and impulse; this prevents the lever from being unlocked from the escape wheel by any sudden shock, and so getting out of phase with the cycle of operations.

DEAD-BEAT ESCAPEMENT. Any escapement in which there is no recoil (i.e., in which, at some stage in the cycle, the balance or pendulum drives the train backwards), e.g., Graham's escapement for clocks and cylinder escapement for watches.

DEBAUFRE ESCAPEMENT. A form of dead-beat verge escapement invented by Debaufre in 1704 or earlier. An illustration is in FIG. 19. See also Club Foot verge and Ormskirk Escapement.

DECK WATCH. A very large watch (usually rather too large for pocket wear) supplied with a box generally resembling a small marine chronometer, and used on ships for carrying the time from the Ship's Chronometer to other parts of the ship, for use when taking observations of the sun or stars.

DETACHED ESCAPEMENT. Any escapement in which the controller is free from interference by the train during a considerable part of its swing (e.g., the Lever and Detent escapements).

DETENT. Any locking device. Also, the name given to the Chronometer escapement where the escape wheel is locked on a spring-mounted or pivoted detent.

DIAL PLATE. The whole visible extent of the dial. In a clock with a square dial opening or window, it is the dial plate to which is fixed the chapter ring and spandrel ornaments.

DOME. The second cover revealed on opening the back of most watches (not pair-cases). Also the top of a clock.

DOUBLE ROLLER ESCAPEMENT. The highest quality of Lever escapement (q.v.) having separate rollers for 'safety' and 'impulse' introduced shortly before 1830.

DRAW. The imperceptible recoil action of the lever escapement provided to ensure that the lever is drawn into full engagement with the escape wheel, and to make it very difficult for the lever to be jolted out of engagement prematurely.

DROP. The free travel of the escape wheel after impulse and before locking again.

DRUM. In a weight-driven clock, the barrel on to which the gut or cord of the weight is wound.

DUMB REPEATER. A repeater in which the hammer strikes a fixed metal block, instead of a bell or gong.

DUPLEX ESCAPEMENT. A watch escapement combining the disadvantages of the cylinder and chronometer escapements. Locking is on the frictional rest principle, as in the cylinder, but impulse is in one direction only, delivered by separate impulse teeth to an impulse pallet projecting from the balance staff. The advantage over a cylinder is that the frictional rest takes place on a roller of much less diameter than the cylinder, while the impulse is delivered with a better mechanical advantage. The disadvantage is that it is very delicate, inefficient when wear has taken place, and prone to setting. At its best it can give excellent results and was generally preferred to the lever by English makers in the first half of the nineteenth century. An illustration is in FIG. 23.

DUST CAP. From about 1715 for the next hundred years many watches, mainly English, in which the movement was hinged to the case, had a dust-proof cap which fitted over the movement. They were made of brass-gilt or, rarely, silver.

DUTCH STRIKING. A system of striking on two bells. The hour is struck on the large bell. At the half hour the next succeeding hour is struck on the small bell. The quarter-hour may also be indicated by a stroke on one bell, and the three-quarter by one stroke on the other.

END-PLATE. A plate covering a pivot hole against which the end of the pivot works, thus taking the end thrust. See also Coqueret.

ENDSTONE. An end-plate made of a jewel.

EQUATION CLOCK. A clock showing the current difference between solar time and mean time.

ESCAPEMENT. The system by which the controller (balance or pendulum) of a timekeeper allows the train to 'escape' by equal amounts at regular intervals and thus accurately records the passage of time.

ESCAPE WHEEL. The last wheel in the going train of a timekeeper, which is alternately locked by and gives impulse to the controller (balance or pendulum).

FALSE PENDULUM. A non-functional attachment to a pendulum, showing as a slit through a slit in the dial. Also called a 'mock pendulum'.

FIVE-MINUTE REPEATER. A rare form of repeater which, in addition to the quarters, gives also each five minutes.

FLIRT. Any device designed to move or flick forward by jumps. Also the sprung lever which releases the chiming train in a chiming clock.

FLOATING HOUR DIAL. A form of watch dial used during the last quarter of the seventeenth century. The dial plate, which is mostly non-functional, contains a segmental slit about $\frac{1}{4}$ inch wide and one inch long, along one side of which are marked the minutes (usually in intervals of ten or fifteen) from 0 to 60. A revolving plate is seen through the slit, containing round holes exactly as far apart as the 0 and 60 minute marks. The hour numeral appears through one of these holes and the hole and hour numeral then pass across the segment in an hour, the position of the hole in the segment thus indicating the number of minutes elapsed. As the hole reaches 60 another hole, showing the next hour, appears at 0. An example is illustrated in PLATE 86. Also called 'Wandering Hour Dial'.

FLY. An air brake, usually in the form of a two-bladed paddle-wheel, placed at the end of the striking train of a clock to regulate the speed of striking.

FOLIOT. The first form of controller to be applied to an escapement clock, in conjunction with the verge escapement. It has two arms with an adjustable weight at the end of each for bringing the clock to time. The arms swing in a horizontal plane.

FORK. The fork-shaped end of the lever in a lever escapement into which the impulse pin on the balance staff fits, successively unlocking the escapement and receiving impulse.

FORM WATCH. A watch in the shape of some irrelevant object, such as a cross, skull, or flower-bud.

FOURTH WHEEL. The fourth wheel from the great wheel in the going train of a clock or watch. It is usually the wheel which carries the seconds hand and drives the escape wheel.

FRICTIONAL REST ESCAPEMENT. The generic name for dead-beat escapements, in which the escape wheel is locked by resting against some part of the controller. Friction takes place between the two during the supplementary arc.

FRICTION ROLLER. A friction roller is a species of roller bearing in which the rollers take the form of wheels, or segments of wheels, whose peripheries overlap. As a bearing for pivots it possesses the advantage of needing no lubrication.

FRONT PLATE. The arbors of a clock train are held between two plates. The front plate is that nearest to the dial.

FULL PLATE. The form of watch calibre in which all the wheels of the train are held between two plates.

FUSEE. A device credited to Leonardo da Vinci, whereby a spring-driven timekeeper automatically 'changes gear' as the spring runs down and so preserves a more or less constant torque on the train throughout its running time. When the spring is freshly wound, and exerting its maximum torque, it is made to pull a high ratio; and when the spring is nearly run down and at its weakest, it pulls a low ratio and thus the effective torque is kept equal. This is done by mounting on the Great wheel arbor a cone-shaped piece with a spiral track cut round it. This piece is the fusee. A length of gut or chain has one end fastened to the spring barrel and is wound round it. The other end is attached to the fusee at the end of the spiral track at the wide end of the cone. When the timekeeper is wound up, the gut or chain is wound off the spring barrel on to the fusee. A ratchet and click (q.v.) enable the fusee to be turned in this direction. When fully wound the spring starts to pull the gut or chain back on to its barrel as fast as the escapement will permit, the torque being transmitted to the train via the above mentioned ratchet and click.

An illustration is in FIG. 5. Alternatives to the fusee are the stackfreed and going barrel (q.v.). See also 'Reversed Fusee'.

GATHERING PALLET. Part of the striking

train in a clock fitted with rack striking. The gathering pallet is a small piece of metal shaped like a comma, mounted on an arbor which rotates once for each stroke on the bell or gong. At each rotation the pallet 'gathers' one tooth on the rack until all have been passed and the striking operation is completed. The same arrangement exists in repeaters.

GIMBALS. A form of universal joint used in ships chronometers whereby the chronometer always remains horizontal whatever the angle of the ship.

GRAHAM ESCAPEMENT. Graham invented two important and successful escapements; the dead-beat escapement for clocks and the cylinder escapement for watches. It is the former which is referred to as the 'Graham Escapement'. It is a variation of the earlier anchor escapement, from which it differs in having the teeth of the escape wheel, and the pallets on the anchor, cut so that there is no recoil at any part of the arc. It is thus a frictional rest escapement.

GRAHAM PENDULUM. Graham made a steel pendulum with a stirrup where is normally the bob. On this stirrup he mounted a jar full of mercury. As the pendulum rod got longer when heated, the mercury also expanded so that the height of the column of mercury in the jar increased. The length of the rod and the amount of mercury could be adjusted so that the distance between the anchorage of the pendulum, and its centre of gravity, remained constant at all temperatures, thus ensuring a constant rate from the clock.

GRANDE SONNERIE. A form of quarter-striking in which the hour last struck is also repeated at each quarter.

GRANDFATHER CLOCK. The colloquial name for a long-case clock.

GRANDMOTHER CLOCK. The colloquial name for a miniature long-case clock.

GRASSHOPPER ESCAPEMENT. A recoil escapement needing a very wide arc, used by John Harrison, but hardly anyone else. Its merit is that it needs no lubrication. Its name derives from the convulsive action of its hinged pallets, resembling a grasshopper. An illustration is in FIG. 15.

GRAVITY ESCAPEMENT. An escapement in which impulse is given to the pendulum by a falling weight and is thus constant in force. The weight is raised by the going train after each impulse. Also called a constant-force escapement. See also 'Remontoire escapement'.

GREAT WHEEL. The first wheel in the train, mounted either on the drum in a weight-driven clock, or, in a spring-driven timekeeper, on the going barrel, or on the fusee, according to which is used.

GRIDIRON PENDULUM. The pendulum invented by John Harrison to counteract the effects of heat and cold. A system of steel and brass rods is arranged so that the steel rods expand downwards and the brass rods upwards when heated. The effective length of the pendulum can therefore be made to remain constant at all temperatures.

HAIR SPRING. A colloquial name for the balance spring (q.v.).

HALF-CHRONOMETER. An escapement where the impulse is imparted to the controller direct by the escape wheel, but the locking of the escape wheel is effected by a lever.

HALF-PLATE. A watch calibre in which all the wheels of the train except the fourth wheel and escape wheel are held between plates. These two wheels (as also the balance wheel) have separate cocks.

HALF-QUARTER REPEATER. A form of repeater in which, besides the usual repeating of the quarters, a further single stroke indicates when $7\frac{1}{2}$ minutes or more of the next quarter have passed.

HALF-SECONDS PENDULUM. A pendulum 9·78 inches long, beating half-seconds.

HELICAL SPRING. A balance spring formed by winding a spring round a rod or cylinder. Almost universally used for marine chronometers. See also 'Balance spring' (helical).

HOOP WHEEL. A wheel in a count-wheel striking train, having a hoop fixed to it, which holds up the count wheel detent during striking.

HORIZONTAL ESCAPEMENT. An alternative name for the cylinder escapement (q.v.).

IMPULSE AND LOCKING. The two phases in the action of any dead-beat escapement. Impulse is the period during which the train imparts impulse to the balance or pendulum. During the rest of the time the train is locked.

IMPULSE PALLET. A pallet which receives impulse.

INVERTED BELL. A form of top to an English bracket clock popular throughout most of the eighteenth century. The curves of its outline are all the exact opposite to those of the bell-top which it gradually superseded. An example is in PLATE 55.

ISOCHRONISM. The ability of a balance or pendulum to traverse arcs of varying amplitude all in the same length of time.

JACK. A model figure which strikes or appears to strike the time on a bell. Jacks were particularly popular in mediaeval turret clocks and many examples survive in England and on the continent where they are called jacquemarts.

JUMP-HOUR. An hour hand which only moves once an hour, when it jumps forward. This arrangement was often used by Breguet in his repeater watches.

LANCET CLOCK. A form of bracket clock, popular in the early nineteenth century, whose shape resembled a gothic lancet window. An example is illustrated in PLATE 103.

LANTERN CLOCK. An English clock first appearing in about 1630; widely used throughout the seventeenth century and surviving throughout the first half of the eighteenth. A posted movement is held between top and bottom plates with corner pillars. The going train is in front of the striking train. Early examples have a balance controller, later examples have a pendulum. All are weight-driven. The movement is enclosed by detachable brass plates, to one of which is attached the chapter ring. Exceedingly few lantern clocks originally had two hands. On top is a single bell, surrounded by pierced cresting. The clock stood on a wall bracket. Examples are illustrated in PLATES 9 and 42.

LANTERN PINION. Probably the oldest form of pinion. Instead of the teeth or leaves of an ordinary pinion the lantern type has pins or 'trundles' fixed in two end-plates. In certain examples one of these end-plates was omitted.

LEAF OF PINION. In pinions other than lantern pinions the teeth are referred to as 'leaves'.

LEPAUTE ESCAPEMENT. A form of dead-beat clock escapement in which the teeth of the escape wheel are pins projecting at right angles to the plane of the wheel. It is thus called, although Lepine had an equally good claim to its invention. Also called the 'pin-wheel' escapement. An illustration is in FIG. 35.

LEPINE CALIBRE. The watch calibre devised by Lepine in about 1770 in which the movement has only one plate, to which are screwed a number of separate cocks, as many as one for each wheel.

LEVER ESCAPEMENT. The lever escapement is now universally used for all watches. It is the only watch escapement ever to have achieved popularity, in which impulse is not delivered to the balance wheel direct by the escape wheel, but through the agency of a lever. On one end of this lever is an anchor and pallets very much as in a Graham dead-beat clock escapement. At the other end of the lever is a fork. At each swing of the balance wheel, in either direction, a pin on the balance staff enters between the two prongs of the fork and carries the lever with it, thus unlocking the train. The train, being unlocked, imparts impulse to the lever which transfers it through the pin before-mentioned, to the balance and is then again locked, on the other pallet and the next tooth of the escape wheel. Thus, the balance is free from the train during the greater part of its swing. Excessive travel of the lever is prevented by banking pins. An additional safety action is provided by the safety dart (q.v.) and by the provision of 'draw' (q.v.). An illustration of the modern lever escapement and of the original form as invented in 1759 by Mudge, are in FIGS. 24 and 25 respectively. Also called the 'detached lever escapement'. See also 'Double Roller Escapement'.

LIFT. The angle of the impulse faces of the pallets of the lever escapement or of the dead-beat pendulum escapement.

LITHERLAND ESCAPEMENT. A form of rack-lever escapement (q.v.). So called because it was patented in 1791 and widely made by Litherland.

LOCKING AND IMPULSE. See Impulse and locking.

LOCKING PLATE. An alternative name for the Count wheel (q.v.).

LONG-CASE CLOCK. A clock driven by weights in which the movement stands on a hollow trunk containing the pendulum and weights. In its best known, English form, first appearing in about 1660, it consists of three well-defined parts; at the top, a hood, containing the movement and framing the dial; below the hood a trunk, narrower than the hood, and containing the pendulum and weights; and below the trunk a wider plinth or base, supporting the whole.

LUNETTE GLASS. A form of watch-glass, popularised by Breguet, which superseded the deep dome-shaped glasses popular previously. The lunette is three-centred in section, with a small radius for the curves at each side and a very much larger radius for the curve of the central portion. The lunette glass remained popular throughout the first half of the nineteenth century and even later and having then been superseded by the ugly flat crystal glass, it is now again fashionable. Also the window in the door of a long-case clock opposite the pendulum bob.

MAINSPRING. The spring which supplies the driving power in a spring-driven timekeeper.

MAINTAINING POWER. When any clock or watch (except one with a going barrel q.v.) is wound, the power is removed or even reversed so that the train either stops or runs backwards. 'Maintaining Power' is the name given to a number of devices which provide subsidiary driving power sufficient to keep the timekeeper going during the period of winding. The earliest form was 'bolt and shutter' (q.v.). The modern form was invented by John Harrison.

MARINE CHRONOMETER. A timekeeper specially designed to keep sufficiently accurate time on a sea-going ship for its longitude to be determined at any time. Strictly speaking it should have a detent escapement, but the term is generally taken to cover any timekeeper used for this purpose.

MATTING. The finely speckled metal surface used for the centre of clock and watch dials in the seventeenth and eighteenth centuries.

MEAN TIME. The time recorded by a clock; that is to say, all days and hours are of equal length. This is as opposed to Solar Time where all days are not of equal length.

MIDDLE TEMPERATURE ERROR. Bi-metallic temperature compensation (q.v.) for a balance-spring timekeeper is not perfectly regular in its behaviour, so that a watch with a bimetallic balance will only be accurate in its rate at two given temperatures. Its gaining rate between these two temperatures is known as Middle Temperature Error and may be corrected by a variety of secondary compensating devices.

MINIATURE TOWER CLOCK (see Tabernacle Clock).

MINUTE REPEATER. A repeater which records not only the hours and quarters but also the minutes.

MOCK PENDULUM (see False Pendulum).

MOON HAND. An alternative name for a Breguet hand. The shaft of the hand is very slightly tapered and the terminal point is carried on an annular ring, at the end of the shaft. An example is in PLATE 113.

MOTION WORK. The gearing between the hour hand and minute hand, mounted between the top or front plate and the dial.

MOVEMENT. What is commonly called 'the works'.

NUREMBURG EGG. A term mistakenly applied to early German watches.

OIGNON. The colloquial name applied to the large French watches of the late seventeenth and early eighteenth centuries.

OIL SINK. A small hollow, cut into the outside of a plate of a clock or watch, concentric with a pivot-hole, for the purpose of retaining oil.

ORMSKIRK. Watches made at Ormskirk (Lancashire) in the early nineteenth century with a variety of the Debaufre, or dead-beat verge, escapement (q.v.). The Ormskirk form has two parallel escape wheels, mounted on one arbor.

OVERCOIL. See 'Balance Spring-Breguet'.

PAIR-CASE. The form of case almost universal in English watches from 1650 to 1800 and also found in Continental watches. The movement is hinged in an ordinary case with a bezel and glass, which is contained in an entirely separate glass-less outer, or 'pair' case. The pair-case may be decorated with repoussé work, enamel painting, semi-precious stones, or it may be quite plain.

PALLET. The parts of an escapement (excluding cylinder and Duplex) which successively lock and/or receive impulse from the escape wheel.

PARACHUTE. Breguet's device for saving the balance staff pivots of a watch from damage by excessive shock. He mounted the bearings of the pivots in short arms of spring steel.

PASSING SPRING. The short spring mounted on the detent in a detent escapement. It enables the discharging pallet on the balance staff to pass the detent without disturbing it, while on the return spring it unlocks the escape wheel which can then impart impulse to the balance. The passing spring is generally made of gold and is thus sometimes known as the 'gold spring'. Its operation is shown by FIGS. 32 and 33. It is also used in detent escapements for pendulum clocks.

PEDIMENT TOP. An architectural style of top to a clock, in the form of a triangular pediment.

PENDANT. The shaft, or neck, fixed to the case of a watch, to which the bow (q.v.) is fitted. In key-less-wound watches the winding button is mounted on the end of the pendant.

PENDULUM. A shaft, pivoted or flexibly mounted at its upper end with a weight at its lower end, which is connected with the escapement of a clock and, being set swinging, successively unlocks and receives impulse from the escapement, controlling the rate of the clock by the periodicity of its swing.

PENDULUM BOB. The weight at the free end of the pendulum. It may be cylindrical, globular or lenticular in shape.

PENDULUM-COMPENSATED. A pendulum compensated so that its effective length remains constant at all temperatures. (Also refers to compensation for barometric pressure.)

PENDULUM CRUTCH. The arm on the end of a pallet arbor or verge which connects it to a separately mounted pendulum.

PENDULUM-HALF-SECONDS. A pendulum 9.78 inches long, beating half-seconds.

PENDULUM-SECONDS. A pendulum just over 39 inches long beating seconds.

PERPETUAL WATCH. A watch wound by the oscillation of a heavy weight, pivoted to the back plate, which moves to and fro with the normal movements of the wearer of the watch. Also called a 'self-winding watch'.

PINION. A small toothed wheel; the smaller of the two mounted upon one arbor in a clock or watch train, having often only six teeth, or 'leaves', but more in high-quality timekeepers.

PIN-WHEEL ESCAPEMENT. Any escapement in which locking and impulse is effected by pins mounted near the rim of the escape wheel, and at right-angles to the plane of the wheel (see also Lepaute Escapement). See FIG. 35.

PIROUETTE. A geared-up balance wheel which therefore swings through a very large arc, often two or more complete turns. It is usually coupled with a cylinder escapement, but Huygens' first balance-spring watch with verge escapement, had a pirouette.

PIVOT. The ends of an arbor (usually turned down to a reduced diameter) which are mounted in jewels or the plates of a clock or watch, and in which it revolves.

PIVOTED DETENT. The detent in a chronometer escapement is usually mounted on a spring, but it was sometimes pivoted and is then known as a 'pivoted detent' and the escapement is known as a 'pivoted detent escapement'. Also known as a 'bascule' (q.v.).

PLATE. The flat parallel plates of a clock or watch in which the wheels of the train are pivoted.

POKER HAND. The form of minute hand found on most late seventeenth and eighteenth century English watches, so called because of its resemblance to a poker. Usually found in company with a 'beetle' hour hand (q.v.). An example is in PLATE 82.

POSITION ERRORS. The changes in rate of a watch when held in different positions.

POSTED MOVEMENT. In early clocks (all sixteenth century and earlier) the wheels of the train are not pivoted in plates, but are arranged behind each other, being pivoted in quite narrow strips of metal located by top and bottom plates. These plates in turn are attached to four corner pillars or posts. Such clocks are said to have 'posted' movements.

POTENCE (OR POTANCE). A cock or bracket, fixed to the plate of a clock or watch and supporting one pivot of an arbor.

PULL-REPEATER. A repeater where the repeating mechanism is set in motion by pulling a cord.

PUMP-WIND. An early form of keyless winding for watches, where the pendant is moved (or 'pumped') in and out to wind the watch.

PURITAN WATCH. A plain undecorated watch of oval shape, particularly popular during the middle of the seventeenth century. An example is illustrated in PLATE 29.

QUARTER CHIME. A clock which strikes on more than two bells at each quarter.

QUARTER RACK. The rack in a quarter striking, chiming or repeating timekeeper which selects the correct performance at each successive quarter hour.

QUARTER REPEATER. A repeater which records the hours and quarters.

QUARTER STRIKE. A timekeeper which strikes the quarters on one or two bells (as opposed to a quarter chime which employs more than two).

RACK. In horology, a serated lever in the striking train which, being released by the going train, falls on the snail (q.v.) and thus selects the correct number of blows to be struck by the striking train.

RACK LEVER. A predecessor of the lever escapement invented by the Abbé Hautefeuille in 1722 but popularised by Litherland after 1791. An ordinary dead-beat anchor, as in a pendulum clock, is pivoted and has at its other end a toothed segment. This meshes with a pinion on the balance staff whereby the balance wheel is made to swing through a very large arc, usually two complete turns or more.

RACK STRIKING. The form of striking mechanism which employs a rack (q.v.) as opposed to a locking-plate or count-wheel (q.v.) to select the correct number of blows to be struck. Unlike Count-wheel striking, rack-striking depends solely on the position of the hour hand. The operation of this mechanism is shown in the drawing in FIG. 39.

RATE. The performance of a timekeeper. An accurate timekeeper is said to have a good rate and vice versa. Also, according to whether it gains or loses, it is said to have a gaining or losing rate.

RECOIL. The backward rotation of the escape wheel in a recoil escapement under the influence of the controller during its Supplementary arc (q.v.).

RECOIL ESCAPEMENT. An escapement [as opposed to a dead-beat (q.v.) or frictional rest (q.v.) escapement] in which recoil (q.v.) takes place.

REGULATOR. This term has two quite different meanings in horology, viz.: (1) The index arm on which are mounted pins embracing the balance spring near its fixed end. By moving the index, the effective length of the spring is lengthened or shortened and the timekeeper thus made to go slower or faster. (2) a pendulum clock designed solely for accurate timekeeping. It is devoid of all irrelevant complications or striking mechanism, is weight-driven, has a detached or dead-beat (never recoil) escapement and a compensated pendulum.

REMONTOIRE. A spring or weight, interposed between the main driving spring or weight and the escapement and which drives the escape wheel.

Being re-wound at frequent regular intervals its force is kept more constant than is possible in a timekeeper not possessing a remontoire. It was a prerequisite to accurate performance in any watch, etc., not fitted with an isochronous (q.v.) balance and was incorporated by Harrison in all his marine timekeepers except his first.

REMONTOIRE ESCAPEMENT. An escapement in which a remontoire spring (or springs) is interposed between the escape wheel and the balance. It is to this extent different from a remontoire, which is fitted between the driving power and the escape wheel. Mudge's marine timekeeper had a remontoire escapement. See also 'Constant Force Escapement'.

REPEATER. A timekeeper which strikes the last hour and (according to its type) divisions of an hour, only when the striking train is set in motion by moving a lever or pulling a cord. The operation of a typical repeating mechanism is illustrated by the drawing in FIG. 40.

REVERSED FUSEE. A form of fusee (q.v.) mostly used in eight-day spring-driven clocks, where, by crossing over the fusee chain, etc., the fusee and spring barrel rotate in opposite directions. The arrangement has the mechanical advantage of dividing the side loading on the fusee arbor.

ROLLER. The disk, fitted on the balance-staff of a lever or chronometer escapement, to which the impulse pin or pallet is attached. In a duplex escapement it is the cylindrical part of the balance staff which, having a slotted V cut in it, provides for frictional rest and unlocking.

ROMAN STRIKING. A rarely-found form of striking, mostly used by Knibb and devised to conserve power in the striking train. Striking takes place on two bells of different pitch. Every I on the dial is represented by a stroke on the smaller bell and every V by a stroke on the larger (and deeper-toned) bell. X is taken to be two V's. In clocks with Roman striking, four o'clock is indicated on the Chapter ring by IV instead of the otherwise universal IIII.

ROYAL PENDULUM. The name given to the first long pendulums (beating seconds or more), in conjunction with the anchor escapement, immediately after the invention of the latter in or before 1671.

RUBY CYLINDER. A cylinder escapement (q.v.) in which the cylinder is made of ruby, instead of steel.

SAFETY ROLLER. A disk fitted on the balance staff of a lever escapement with a crescent-shaped hollow cut out of its periphery. The safety roller lies in the path of the safety dart (q.v.) attached to the lever, which can thus only move across the axis of the balance when the dart registers with the crescent. The lever is thus prevented from moving (as the result of a sudden shock, etc.) except at the appropriate moment in the cycle of events.

SECONDS PENDULUM. A pendulum slightly more than 39 inches long, beating seconds.

SEDAN CLOCK. A clock in the form of a watch in a wood frame carried in Sedan chairs.

SELF-WINDING WATCH. Another name for a 'perpetual' watch (q.v.).

SEMI-DEAD-BEAT ESCAPEMENT. An escapement found mostly in high quality early nineteenth century bracket clocks with a half-seconds pendulum. The escape wheel and pallets look as though they belonged to a dead-beat escapement but are actually cut to give a slight recoil. This is designed to counteract irregularities in driving torque, which might produce variations in arc and thus promote circular error (q.v.). This is a material factor in bracket clocks which mostly employ a fairly wide arc. The escapement was intended to combine the advantages of the anchor and dead-beat escapements as applied to bracket clocks.

SETTING. When a watch stops through the balance coming to rest (generally because of a sudden turning movement by its wearer), even though partially wound, it is said to have 'set'.

SET-UP. The residual tension to which a mainspring is set when the watch or clock is fully run down.

SHEEP'S-HEAD CLOCK. A lantern clock with a Chapter ring much wider than the rest of the clock, so called from a fancied resemblance to the head-on view of a sheep.

SHELF CLOCK. A clock designed to stand on a shelf but particularly applied to a type of American Clock (see the section in Chapter VII on American Clocks) illustrated in PLATE 161.

SIDERIAL TIME. The time elapsing between two successive transits of a fixed star across the meridian. A siderial day is 3 minutes 56 seconds less than a mean solar day.

SIX-HOUR DIAL. A rare form of dial found in late seventeenth century watches. The dial has only one hand which revolves once in six hours. The hour divisions are thus sufficiently far apart to calibrate a division for every two minutes. The Chapter ring is marked in roman numerals from I to VI and then smaller, arabic numerals from 7 to 12 are superimposed on the roman numerals. Also commonly used in Italian clocks. An example is in PLATE 88.

SKELETON DIAL. A dial with a separate Chapter ring from which all the spare metal, except the actual edges of the ring and the numerals has been cut away.

SLIDE UP HOOD. The form of hood found almost universally in seventeenth century long-case clocks. The whole hood slides up on runners on the back board, and as the front of it does not open, it must be raised either to wind the clock or set the hands and, of course, to get at the movement. It is locked in its normal position by a 'spoon fitting' (q.v.) and held up by an automatic catch placed on the right-hand side of the back board of the clock case. See PLATE 61.

SNAIL. The part of the striking train in the rack strike layout, consisting of a stepped wheel, against which the rack, being released, comes to rest, thus selecting the number of blows to be struck.

SPADE HAND. The form of hand found on most English Clocks during the second and third quarters of the seventeenth century. The name seems to have little connection with the shape, which consists of a figure eight set across the axis of the hand near its pointer. An example is illustrated in PLATE 45. The term is also used, more appropriately, for the form of hour hand found on many early nineteenth century English watches (and late eighteenth century watches of Arnold) which does somewhat resemble a pointed, playing-card type of spade. An example is illustrated in PLATE 129.

SPANDREL. Where a dial opening is square, and the chapter ring is circular, the corner spaces are the spandrels.

SPOON-FITTING. The catch which locks the slide-up hood (q.v.) of a seventeenth century long-case clock in position. So-called because it is operated by a spoon-shaped handle which projects down into the door-way opening of the trunk. When the door is shut it presses against the spoon and locks the hood. The hands or works thus cannot be tampered with as long as the door of the trunk is locked.

SPRING BARREL. The barrel containing the main-spring.

SPRING DETENT. A detent mounted on a spring, generally applied to the spring detent escapement.

STACKFREED. An inferior alternative to the fusee, found in all sixteenth century German watches. Geared to the great wheel (which in this layout is fixed to the spring arbor) is a wheel rotating once in the going period. Mounted on the same arbor is a cam-shaped piece against which a follower is pressed by a strong tensioning spring. The contour of the cam is such that, when the mainspring is fully wound, the cam is working against the spring of the follower. When the Spring is nearly run down the follower assists the cam-wheel forward. By this means the torque of the mainspring is roughly equalised throughout the going period which, with a stackfreed watch, is usually 26 hours. See FIG. 4.

STAR-WHEEL. A star-shaped wheel used for lifting a detent, usually in connection with striking work, calendar work and similar mechanisms.

STEADY PINS. Pins in the under-side of a cock (q.v.), etc., which register with holes in the plate and so serve to locate the cock.

STOP WORK. A device which prevents overwinding.

STRAIGHT-LINE LEVER. A lever escapement in which the balance staff and the arbors of the lever and escape wheel are arranged in a straight line.

SUN AND MOON DIAL. A dial found on some late seventeenth century watches, in which, instead of an hour hand, the hour is indicated by a sun (from 6 a.m. to 6 p.m.) and by a moon (from 6 p.m. to 6 a.m.). The minute hand is of normal type. An example is in PLATE 87.

SUPPLEMENTARY ARC. The portion of the arc of a balance or pendulum after impulse has ceased.

SURPRISE PIECE. The part of a repeating train which ensures correct striking just before and after the hour, which otherwise tends to be somewhat erratic.

SUSPENSION SPRING. The spring on which a pendulum is suspended.

SWEEP SECONDS. A seconds hand mounted in the centre of the dial and sweeping the full area of the dial.

TABERNACLE or MINIATURE TOWER CLOCK. A small German domestic clock popular from *circa* 1580–1670 for which there seems to be no very satisfactory or universally accepted name. They are mostly of vaguely architectural form (see PLATES 13 and 14), to which the name 'Miniature Tower' seems appropriate. The more elaborate, less architectural shapes are generally known as 'Tabernacle clocks'.

TABLE CLOCK. Purists maintain that what is normally spoken of as an English 'bracket clock' should in fact be described as a 'table clock'. But in generally accepted parlance a 'table clock' is a small metal-cased clock of the late sixteenth to early eighteenth century. An example is illustrated in PLATES 10, 11 and 12.

TACT (or 'Montre à tact'). A speciality of Breguet, alternatively (but erroneously) known as a 'blind man's watch'. Usually in addition to an ordinary dial is another, of metal, with feeling knobs at each hour. A strong hand is fitted which is not connected with the movement; but when it is turned by hand in a clockwise direction it moves freely until it comes to the current time, where it stops against a resistance. It is thus an alternative to the more complicated repeater for telling the time in the dark. The loose-fitting hand will not stop the watch when worn in the pocket.

TAVERN CLOCK. The more correct name for what is generally known as an 'Act of Parliament Clock' (q.v.).

TEMPERATURE COMPENSATION. Any device for compensating the effects of fluctuations in temperature upon the rate of a timekeeper.

TERMINAL CURVE. The curves on the end coils of a helical (or similar) balance spring; or the incurve on the outer coil of a Breguet balance spring (q.v.) designed to secure isochronism (q.v.). An example is illustrated in FIG. 26.

THIRD WHEEL. The third wheel in the train away from the Great, or first wheel. Thirty-hour trains have four wheels in addition to the escape wheel and balance wheel.

THIRTEEN-PIECE DIAL. A form of dial found in mid-eighteenth century French clocks. The dial plate is completely covered by thirteen enamel plaques, one for each hour and one large circular plate for the centre of the dial. An example is illustrated in PLATE 143.

THREE-QUARTER PLATE. A watch calibre (q.v.) in which all wheels up to and including the fourth of the train are pivoted in plates, but the escape wheel and balance wheel have separate cocks.

TIC-TAC ESCAPEMENT. A rare escapement found in late seventeenth century bracket clocks. It is, in effect, an anchor escapement in which the anchor embraces only one and a half teeth. A drawing is in FIG. 12. Also found in cheap nineteenth century clocks.

TIMEPIECE. Any clock which does not strike or chime.

TIMING SCREWS. Screws in the rim of a balance wheel (q.v.) which have nothing to do with its compensation or poising and are solely concerned with adjusting its rate. They are therefore fitted at the ends of the cross-bar of the balance.

TIPSY KEY. See 'Breguet Key'.

TOP PLATE. The plate of a watch next to the dial.

TOURBILLON. Breguet's invention for neutralising vertical position errors (q.v.) in a watch. The balance wheel and escape wheel are mounted on a platform which revolves, usually once a minute, driven by the third wheel. Thus all vertical positions (and, therefore, position errors) are gone through successively and so neutralise each other. Later variants revolved more slowly (e.g., the Karrusel in $52\frac{1}{2}$ minutes).

TRAIN. The wheels and pinions of a timekeeper.

TRIAL NUMBER. The number on a Certificate indicating the standard attained by a timepiece submitted for trial at Greenwich Observatory. The lower the number the better is the category. On the formula now employed, Harrison's No. 4 obtained the number 124·4 Mudge's No. 1 obtained 11.73; Arnold's famous pocket chronometer No. 36 had 44.91. In the mid-nineteenth century the best figure each year was around 20. Mudge's No. 1 was not surpassed until 1873. Single figures were first obtained in 1882 (Kullberg, with 9.1) and are now regarded as commonplace and necessary.

TRIPPING. A fault to which the chronometer and duplex (and rare clock escapement's, such as Mudge's gravity) are subject, whereby, under abnormal conditions, the balance receives impulse twice in one vibration, because the escapement 'trips'. In consequence the seconds hand moves twice in one beat.

TRUNK. The thin, central portion of a long-case clock.

UP-AND-DOWN DIAL. A subsidiary dial indicating how far the main-spring is wound.

VERGE ESCAPEMENT. The earliest escapement applied to clocks, first known in the thirteenth century and made until the late nineteenth century. The balance staff, or verge, has two pallets, at 95°–100° to each other and registering with opposite sides of the escape wheel, which is of contrate formation and, from the shape of its teeth, is also known as the Crown wheel. The pallets escape alternately past the teeth of the escape wheel. A drawing is in FIG. 2.

VERGE STAFF. In a verge escapement the arbor upon which the balance, pendulum or crutch is mounted is the 'verge' or 'verge staff'.

VIRGULE ESCAPEMENT. A rare French watch escapement, similar in principle to the cylinder escapement. The cylinder is greatly reduced in size and is only concerned with locking. One lip is extended by a tail, giving this the appearance of a comma (or virgule in French) which receives impulse. Impulse is therefore imparted in one direction only (instead of both as in the cylinder). This escapement was in use during the second half of the eighteenth century. A drawing is in FIG. 22.

WALL-CLOCK. Any clock which hangs on a wall.

WANDERING HOUR DIAL. See 'Floating Hour Dial'.

WARNING. The preparatory operation of a striking train. This takes place a few minutes before striking is due. The train is momentarily released, and carries out all its preliminary motions, but is then instantly stopped again on the 'warning piece'. This in turn is released by the minute-hand wheel at the exact instant when striking should begin. A similar mechanism exists in chiming clocks. Early, one-handed clocks, sometimes have no warning mechanism.

WARNING PIECE. See 'Warning'.

WATCH CAP. See 'Dust Cap'.

WATCH COCK. See 'Cock'.

WATER CLOCK. See 'Clepsydra'.

WINDING Square. The square end of the arbor on which a key is placed for winding.

APPENDIX II

Hall-marks

THIS chapter is to be regarded only as a rudimentary guide to the dating of gold and silver articles. The standard text-book on the subject is *English Goldsmiths and their Marks* by Sir Charles J. Jackson (Macmillan & Co., Ltd., London).

These marks are stamped on gold or silver wares to signify that the metal has been tested by a chemical assay at one of the authorised assay offices, and found to be of the correct legal standard. There are at present assay offices at London, Birmingham, Sheffield, Chester, Edinburgh and Glasgow. Formerly there existed offices at other towns, for example, Newcastle, Exeter and York, and there is also one at Dublin, which prior to 1922 was a British office. Watch cases along with the majority of other wares must be hall-marked before they can be legally sold in this country. There are certain exemptions from compulsory hall-marking, such as silver articles weighing less than five pennyweights. Silver watch cases before about 1720 are, in fact, seldom hall-marked. The following marks normally appear on the article—the maker's mark, the town mark, the standard or quality mark and the date letter. These are reproduced here from designs kindly supplied by the Worshipful Company of Goldsmiths.

MAKER'S MARK

This consists of the maker's initials in a shield and is distinctive for the particular maker.

TOWN MARK

This indicates the assay office at which the article was tested. For London, the town mark is a leopard's head. This mark has been used continuously since 1300 when compulsory hall-marking was instituted by an Act of Edward I. The leopard's head was uncrowned between 1300 and 1478, crowned between 1478 and 1821 and has been uncrowned ever since:

Other offices have their own town marks, viz.,

Birmingham—an anchor

Sheffield—a crown for silver

—a York rose for gold

Chester—three wheat sheaves and a sword

Edinburgh—a castle

Glasgow—a tree, bird, bell, fish and ring (taken from city arms)

STANDARD MARK

This indicates the quality of the metal. There are two standards of silver, the Sterling and Britannia standards.

Sterling, which is the usual standard, is denoted by a lion passant in the case of the English offices.

At Glasgow a thistle and lion rampant are used and at Edinburgh a thistle alone.

The Britannia standard is denoted by a figure of Britannia, the leopard's head town mark in the case of London being replaced by a lion's head erased.

The Britannia standard was compulsory between the years 1697 and 1720 but is now only occasionally used. Sterling silver contains 92.5 per cent and Britannia silver 95.84 per cent of fine silver.

Prior to 1798 there was only one standard of gold, namely 22 carat. In 1798 an 18 carat standard was authorised and in 1854, 9, 15 and 12 carat standards. In 1932 the 15 and 12 carat standards were abolished and a 14 carat standard substituted. 22 carat gold had the same marks as silver until 1844 when a crown and the figure 22 were substituted for the lion passant. A crown and the figure 18 was authorised for the standard mark for 18 carat gold on its intro-duction in 1798. The standard mark for the lower standards of gold is the carat figure followed by the decimal equivalent. The standard marks at present used are therefore:

22 carat—a crown and the figure 22
18 carat—a crown and the figure 18
14 carat—Figure 14 and the decimal equivalent (.585)
9 carat—Figure 9 and the decimal equivalent (.375)

FOREIGN WARES

Prior to 1842 foreign made wares did not require to be hallmarked before being sold in this country. In 1842 such marking became compulsory and between this date and 1883 a capital 'F' was added in addition to the other marks and was used until 1904 when it was superseded by the sign of Phoebus. In 1906 a special set of marks was authorised to replace the marks used for British wares. Foreign hall-marks, especially French, are a complicated study of their own which it is impossible to describe here.

DUTY MARK

In 1784 a duty was imposed on silver plate and to signify that this had been paid, a mark showing the head of the reigning sovereign was added to the hall-mark. Watch cases were exempted from duty in 1798 but other wares were liable to plate duty until 1890 when it was finally abolished.

DATE LETTER

This gives the date that the article was tested. Each assay office has a different sequence of alphabets but it is possible to determine the date from a suitable reference book. The date letter is of immense use to collectors. A useful little work for quick reference is *British and Irish Silver Assay Office Marks 1544–1943 and Old Sheffield Plate Makers' Marks 1743–1860* by Frederick Bradbury, F.S.A. The following is a list of London date letters from 1678 to 1835.

a	1678	a	and	A	1716	a	1736	A	1576	a	1776	A	1796	a	1816
b	1679	b	1697	B	1717	b	1737	B	1757	b	1777	B	1797	b	1817
c	1680	c	1698	C	1718	c	1738	C	1758	C	1778	C	1798	c	1818
d	1681	s	1699	D	1719	d	1739	D	1759	d	1779	D	1799	d	1819
e	1682	e	1700	E	1720	e	1740	E	1760	e	1780	E	1800	e	1820
f	1683	ff	1701	F	1721	f	1741	f	1761	f	1781	F	1801	f	1821
g	1684	g	1702	G	1722	g	1742	G	1762	g	1782	G	1802	g	1822
h	1685	h	1703	H	1723	h	1743	h	1763	h	1783	H	1803	h	1823
i	1686	s	1704	I	1724	i	1744	J	1764	i	1784	I	1804	i	1824
k	1687	k	1705	K	1725	k	1745	k	1765	k	1785	K	1805	k	1825
l	1688	l	1706	L	1726	l	1746	L	1766	l	1786	L	1806	l	1826
m	1689	m	1707	M	1727	m	1747	M	1767	m	1787	M	1807	m	1827
n	1690	n	1708	N	1728	n	1748	Ω	1768	n	1788	N	1808	n	1828
o	1691	o	1709	O	1729	o	1749	O	1769	o	1789	O	1809	o	1829
p	1692	p	1710	P	1730	p	1750	p	1770	P	1790	P	1810	p	1830
q	1693	q	1711	Q	1731	q	1751	Q	1771	q	1791	Q	1811	q	1831
r	1694	r	1712	R	1732	r	1752	R	1772	r	1792	R	1812	r	1832
s	1695	s	1713	S	1733	s	1753	S	1793	s	1793	S	1813	s	1833
t	1696	t	1714	T	1734	t	1754	T	1774	t	1794	T	1814	t	1834
to March 27, 1697		s	1715	V	1735	u	1755	U	1775	u	1795	U	1815	u	1835

Note: A shield without points ☐ is also found, mostly on small articles, between 1776 and 1875.

APPENDIX III

Bibliography

Chosen in order to provide a wide conspexus of the subject for specialised study

ABBOTT, HENRY G. *The Watch Factories of America, Past and Present.* 8°. 145 pp. 9 pl. (Chicago, 1888).
  Describes the difficulties of early American Factories.
ALBRECHT, RUD. *Die räder Uhr.* 4°. 25 pp. 20 figs. 40 pl. (Rothenburg, [1906].)
  Several illustrations of Gothic clocks.
ALLEXANDRE, R. P. DOM JACQUES. *Traité Générale des Horloges.* 8°. 388 pp. 26 pl. (Paris, 1734.)
  Good illustrations of tools and mechanism with a general description; also a bibliography.
ANONYMOUS. *L'art de l'horlogerie enseigné en Trente Leçons par un Ancien Elève de Breguet.* 8°. 618 pp. 17 pl. (Paris 1827–35.)
  Historically interesting.
— [TAVAN]. *Description des Échappements les plus usités en horlogerie.* 4°. 52 pp. + 12 pl. Fol. (Geneva, 1831 and 1851.)
  Historically interesting.
ARNOLD, JOHN. *Certificates and Circumstances relative to the Going of his Chronometers.* 4°. 66 pp. (London, 1791.)
  Showing accuracy of time-keeping at that date.
ATKINS, CHARLES EDWARD. *Register of Apprentices.* Lge. 8°. 348 pp. 14 pl. (London, 1931).
  List of all apprentices in the Clockmakers' Company.
ATKINS, S. E. and OVERALL, W. H. *Some Account of the Clockmakers' Company.* Lge. 8°. 369 pp. 8 pl. (London, 1881.)
  A history of the company.
BAILLIE, G. H. *Watches: their History, Decoration and Mechanism.* Lge. 8°. 408 pp. 76 pl. Many coloured. (London, 1929.)
  A very good book with fullest details on watches.
— *Watchmakers and Clockmakers of the World.* Lge. 8°. 432 pp. (London, 1929.)
— Books on Horology. *Book Collectors' Quarterly*, April 1932. 8°. 14 pp. (London.)
  Short bibliography of all the historically important books.
— *Catalogue of the Library of The Clockmakers' Company in the Guildhall, London.* 8°. 82 pp. (London, 1931.)
  List of books which are available for reference.
— *Catalogue of the Museum of the Clockmakers' Company in the Guildhall, London.* 8°. 143 pp. (London, 1949.)
  List of a very fine collection of clocks and watches of great technical interest.
— *Watchmakers and Clockmakers of the World.* 8°. 413 pp. (London, 1947.)
  Largest list, containing 35,000 names.

— *Clocks and Watches: An Historical Bibliography.* 8°. 427 pp. 120 figs. (London, 1951.)
  Description of every publication up to 1800.
BALET, LÉO. *Führer durch die Uhrensammlung.* 8°. 108 pp. 84 ill. (Stuttgart, 1913.)
  A short history of horology based on the collection in Stuttgart Museum.
BASSERMANN-JORDAN, ERNST VON. *Die Geschichte der Räderuhr.* 4°. 112 pp. 36 ill. (Frankfurt, 1905 and 1906.)
  Good history of early clocks and watches.
— UHREN. *Bibliothek für Kunst-und Antiquitäten-Sammler.* 8°. 174 pp. 110 ill. (Berlin, 1914, 1920, 1922.)
  Handbook on clocks and watches from the earliest days including escapements.
— *Alte Uhren und ihre Meister.* 4°. 179 pp. 164 ill. (Leipzig, 1926.)
  General notes on horological subjects.
BECKETT-DENISON, EDM. LORD GRIMTHORPE. *A rudimentary Treatise on Clock and Watchmaking.* 8°. 280 pp. (London, 1850–68.)
— *A Rudimentary Treatise on Clocks and Watches and Bells.* 8th ed. 8°. 404 pp. 1 pl. ill. (London, 1903.)
  The standard book of this period.
BERNER, PAUL. *Historique du Réglage de Précision.* 8°. 20 pp. (Bienne, 1910.)
  Adjusting watches and clocks. Historical survey.
BERTHOUD, FERDINAND. *L'art de conduire et de régler les Pendules et les Montres.* 16°. 79 pp. 4 pl. for 1st ed. (Paris, 1759–1841.)
  Berthoud was a prolific writer. This is his first book and it was a standard work for many years.
— *Essai sur l'Horlogerie.* 2 vols. 4°. 477 and 452 pp. 38 pl. (Paris 1763 and 1786.)
  Interesting contemporary account.
— *Traité des Horloges Marines.* 4°. 590 pp. 27 pl. (Paris, 1773.)
  Early work on marine chronometers.
— *De la Mesure du Temps, ou Supplément au Traité des Horloge Marines et l'Essai sur l'Horlogerie.* 4°. 275 pp. 11 pl. (Paris, 1787.)
  A supplement to foregoing.
— *Traité des Montres a Longitude.* 4°. 230 pp. 3 pl. (Paris, 1792.)
  Additional and later information.
— *Histoire de la Mesure du Temps.* 4°. 2 vols. 373 and 447 pp. 23 pl. (Paris, 1802.)
  The standard history of this date.

BERTHOUD, LOUIS. *Entretiens sur l'Horlogerie à l'Usage de la Marine.* 16°. 127 pp. (Paris, 1812.)
Following on Ferdinand Berthoud's books.

BILFINGER, GUSTAV. *Die Mittelalterlichen Horen und die Modernen Stunden.* 8°. 279 pp. (Stuttgart, 1892.)
Explanation of the canonical hours and a history of the development of time measurement.

BION, NICOLAS. *Traité de la Construction et des principaux Usages des Instruments.* 2nd ed. (Paris, 1716.) Translated and augmented by Edmund Stone, entitled *The Construction and principal Uses of Instruments.* Fol. 332 pp. 30 pl. (London, 1723 and 1758.)
Full description with plate of a pendulum clock with cycloidal cheeks.

BOLTON, L. *Time Measurement.* 8°. 166 pp. 8 pl. 28 ill. (London, 1924.)
A good short general history and explanation of the calendar.

BRADBURY, FREDERICK. *British Assay Office Marks.* 16°. 80 pp. (London, 1922.)
Useful for hallmarks in watch cases. N.B.: The duty mark was omitted after 1797 when the 18 carat stamp was introduced.

BREGUET ET FILS. *Horlogerie pour l'Usage Civil.* 4°. 16 pp. 2 pl. 1 fig. (Paris, *c.* 1823.)
The catalogue for his shop.

BREGUET, A. L., *Le Centenaire de.* Special number of the *Journal Suisse de l'Horlogerie.* 40 pp. ill. (Neuchâtel, 1923.)
Interesting facts on his life and work.

— *Centenaire.* Exposition Galliéra. Sm. 8°. 45 pp. 16 pl. (Paris, 1923.)
Catalogue of the special exhibition of his work.

BRITISH CLOCKMAKERS' HERITAGE EXHIBITION. *Catalogue.* 8°. 93 pp. 32 pl. (London, 1952.)
Large and important exhibition at the Science Museum, London.

BRITTEN, F. J. *The Watch and Clockmakers' Handbook, Dictionary and Guide.* 8°. Latest ed. 552 pp. 492 figs. (London, *c.* 1870 to date.)
Useful guide for repairs.

— *Old English Clocks.* The Wetherfield Collection. Fol. 114 pp. 131 ill. (London, 1907.)
Well illustrated.

BUCKLEY, FRANCIS. *George Graham.* Lge. 8°. 6 pp. 1 pl. (Uppermill, 1929.) *John Ellicott.* Lge. 8°. 6 pp. 1 pl. (Uppermill, 1930.) *Daniel Quare.* Lge. 8°. 6 pp. 1 pl. (Uppermill, 1930.) The Tompion-Banger problem; short article, 1 page, in *The Practical Watch and Clockmaker,* April, 1933.
Important articles giving details on numbering etc., of watches.

CARRÉ, LOUIS. *A Guide to Old French Plate.* 8°. 26 + 270 pp. Many illustrations. (London, 1931.)
Useful for dating French watches.

Catalogues. See under owners' or authors' names.

CESCINSKY, HERBERT. *Old English Master Clockmakers.* 8°. 194 pp. 277 ill. (London, 1938.)
A representative collection of clocks by important makers.

CESCINSKY, H. and WEBSTER M. *English Domestic Clocks.* 4°. 354 pp. 407 ill. (London, 1913.)
A very good reference book for clocks.

CHAMBERLAIN, PAUL M. *Watches.* The Paul M. Chamberlain Collection at the Art Institute of Chicago. Lge. 8°. 58 pp. ill. Chicago, 1921.)
Very good drawings of escapements.

— *It's about Time.* Lge. 8°. 500 pp. 350 ill. (New York, 1941.)

First class treatise with fine drawings on the development of escapements.

CHANDLEE, E. E. *Six Quaker Clockmakers.* 4°. 260 pp. 163 ill. (Philadelphia, 1943.)
Finely produced by the Historical Society of Pennsylvania.

CHAPUIS, ALFRED. *Histoire de la Pendulerie Neuchâteloise.* 4°. 502 pp. 41 pl. 377 ill. (Neuchâtel, 1917.)
Full history of Neuchâtel clockmaking.

— *La Montre Chinoise.* 4°. 272 pp. 33 pl. 245 ill. (Neuchâtel, 1919.)
History of Swiss watches for export to the Orient.

— *Pendules Neuchâteloises, documents nouveaux.* 4°. 275 pp. 400 ill. (Neuchâtel, 1931.)
Well illustrated specimens of all periods.

— *Montres et Émaux de Genève.* 4°. 234 pp. 48 pl. many in colour. (Lausanne, 1944.) English translation, text only. (Geneva, 1945.)
Very fine illustrations of the Wilsdorf Collection.

— *L'Horlogerie. Une Tradition Helvétique.* 4°. 327 pp. 37 pl. Many figs. (Neuchâtel, 1948.)
Comprehensive history of watches and chronometry.

— *La Montre Automatique Ancienne.* 4°. 234 pp. 153 figs. (Neuchâtel, 1952.)
History of the self-winding watch.

CHAPUIS, A. and GÉLIS, E. *Le Monde des Automates.* 4°. 2 vols. 800 pp. 7 pl. 540 ill. (Paris, 1928.)
Historical and technical study of automata, some applied to horology.

CHAPUIS, A. and DROZ, Ed. *Les Automates.* 4°. 436 pp. 18 pl. 490 figs. (Neuchâtel, 1949.)
Companion volume to above.

CONSERVATOIRE NATIONAL DES ARTS ET METIERS. *Catalogue du Musée Horlogerie.* 8°. 330 pp. 99 figs. (Paris, 1949.)
Historical survey of horology.

— *Chefs d'Oeuvre de l'Horlogerie.* 8°. 20 ill. 576 items. (Paris, 1949.)
Catalogue of the special exhibition.

— *Les Conférences.* 4°. 390 pp. 541 ill. (Paris, 1950.)
Twelve lectures given during the Exhibition.

COX, JAMES. *A Descriptive Inventory of the Exquisite Pieces of Mechanism for Disposal by Way of Lottery.* Lge. 8°. 71 pp. (London, 1774.)

CUMMING, ALEXANDER. *The Elements of Clock and Watchwork adapted to Practice.* 4°. 198 pp. 16 pl. (London, 1766.)
The standard work of this period.

CUNYNGHAME, SIR HENRY HARDING. *Time and Clocks; a Description of Ancient and Modern Methods of Measuring Time.* 8°. 200 pp. 86 ill. (London, 1906 and 1909.)
A short general technical book.

CUSS, T. P. CAMERER. *The Story of Watches.* 8°. 172 pp. 160 ill. (London, 1952.)
A useful collectors' guide.

DE CARLE, DONALD. *Practical Watch Repairing.* 8°. 307 pp. 553 figs. (London, 1946.)
Useful for repairs.

— *Watchmakers' and Clockmakers' Encyclopaedic Dictionary.* 8°. 252 pp. Many figs. (London, 1950.)
Glossary with sketches for parts and tools.

— *Practical Clock Repairing.* 8°. 249 pp. 450 figs. (London, 1952.)
Useful for repairs.

DEFOSSEZ, LEO. *Les Savants du 17 ème Siècle et la Mesure du Temps.* 4°. 343 pp. 44 pl. 120 figs. (Lausanne, 1946.)
Well illustrated history of the seventeenth century.

DERHAM, WILLIAM, D.D., F.R.S. *The Artificial Clock-maker.* 12°. 132 pp. 2 pl. (London, 1696.) 5th and last ed. 12°. 160 pp. 3 pl. (London, 1759.)
　　The best known early English book.

DEVELLE, E. *Les Horlogers Blésoirs aux XVI et XVII Siècles.* 4°. 2 vols. 374 pp. 18 pl. (Blois, 1913.) 2nd ed. 4°. 2 vols. 460 pp. 30 pl. (Blois, 1917.)
　　Well illustrated history of this period.

DIDEROT ET D'ALEMBERT ENCYCLOPÉDIE. *Encyclopédie raisonné des Sciences.* 28 vols. Fol. Horological items in several volumes. First ed. 1751–72. Last ed. 1782–1832. 169 vols. of text. 159 vols. of plates. 4°.
　　Beautiful plates on details and tools.

DITISHEIM, PAUL. *John Harrison et la Chronomètre—250° anniversaire de l'observatoire de Greenwich.* 4°. 34 pp. 36 ill. (Paris-Neuchâtel, 1926.)
　　A good short history of the Observatory.

— *Le Spiral Réglant et le Balancier depuis Huygens jusqu'à nos jours.* 4°. 115 pp. 117 ill. (Lausanne, 1945.)
　　Historical survey by a technical expert.

DITISHEIM, P., LALLIER, R., REVERSHON, L. LE COMMANDANT VIVIELLE. *Pierre Le Roy et La Chronomètre.* 4°. 147 pp. 32 pl. 85 ill. (Paris, 1940.)
　　History of marine timekeepers.

DREPPARD, CARL W. *American Clocks & Clockmakers.* 8°. 312 pp. 75 pl. 400 ill. (Garden City, 1947.)
　　A useful well illustrated history.

DUBOIS, PIERRE. *Histoire de l'Horlogerie.* 4°. 408 pp. 42 pl. (Paris, 1849.)
　　A comparatively early history, not a very accurate one.

— *Collection Archéologique du Prince Soltykoff.* 4°. 214 pp. 20 pl. (Paris, 1858.)
　　Beautiful illustrations of sixteenth and seventeenth century clocks and watches.

EARNSHAW, THOMAS. *Longitude; an Appeal to the Public.* 8°. 332 pp. (London, 1808.)
　　Full description of his difficulties in obtaining an award.

EDWARDES, ERNEST L. *The Grandfather Clock.* 4°. 253 pp. 54 pl. 6 figs. 2nd ed. (Altrincham, 1952.)
　　History of the grandfather clock.

FERGUSON, JAMES, F.R.S. *Select Mechanical Exercises.* 8°. 334 pp. 9 pl. (London, 1773.) 4th ed. (London, 1822.)
　　Theoretical. Original clocks described.

FOX, C. A. O. *An Anthology of Clocks and Watches.* 8°. 68 pp. 14 pl. (Swansea, 1947.)
　　Collection of poetry on horology with pictures of clocks not illustrated elsewhere.

FRAUBERGER, HEINRICH. *N. P. Fraenkel's Uhrensammlung.* Fol. 73 pp. 44 pl. 65 figs. (Dusseldorf, 1913.)
　　A very well illustrated catalogue with full descriptions.

FRÉMONT, CHARLES. *Origine de l'Horloge à Poids.* 4°. 28 pp. 34 figs. (Paris, 1915.)
　　Original study of this subject.

GALLON, M. *Recueil de Machines et Inventions Approuvées par l'Academie Royale des Sciences.* Vols. 1–6. 1666–1734. (Paris, 1735.) Vol. 7, 1735–1754. 4°. (Paris, 1777.)
　　Fine engraved plates of interesting inventions.

GAZELEY, W. J., *Watch and Clock Making and Repairing.* 8°. 432 pp. 314 figs. (London, 1953.)
　　Practical book on repairs and use of tools.

GARNIER, PAUL. Collection of watches—see Migeon.

GEISSLER, J. G. *Der Uhrmacher oder Lehrbegriff der Uhrmacherkunst.* 4°. 1478 pp. 87 pl. (Leipzig, 1793–9.)
　　Long contemporary technical treatise.

GELCICH, EUGÈNE. *Geschichte der Uhrmacherkunst.* 5th ed. of Barfuss' History. 208 pp. and Folio atlas 9″ × 5½″. (Weimar, 1892.)
　　This edition gives a good history.

GELIS, EDOUARD. *L'Horlogerie ancienne, Histoire, Décor et Technique.* Sm. 4°. 255 pp. 110 pl. 12 in colour. (Paris, 1950.)
　　Decoration of watch cases well represented.

GLASGOW, DAVID. *Watch and Clockmaking.* 8°. 354 pp. 69 figs. 1st ed. (London, 1885.) 3rd ed. (London, 1897.)
　　Good technical book.

GORDON, G. F. C. *Clockmaking Past and Present.* 8°. 240 pp. 35 pl. 1st ed. London, 1925, 1928 and 1949.
　　General treatise on maintenance of old clocks.

GOULD, LT. CMDR. R. T. *The Marine Chronometer; its History and Development.* 8°. 303 pp. 40 pl. 85 figs. (London, 1923.) Another ed. to follow shortly.
　　The standard work on the marine chronometer.

GRAHAM, GEORGE. A contrivance to avoid the irregularities in a clock's motion occasioned by the action of heat and cold: In *Phil. Trans. of the Royal Society*, No. 392. (London, 1726.)
　　First description of the Mercury pendulum.

GRAHAM, R. P. HOWGRAVE. See Howgrave-Graham.

GREEN, F. H. *Old English Clocks.* 4°. 96 pp. 55 pl. (London, 1931.)
　　Well illustrated early masterpieces.

GRIMTHORPE. See Beckett-Denison.

GROLLIER. See Servière.

GROS, CHARLES. *Echappements d'Horloges et de Montres.* 8°. 263 pp. 277 ill. (Paris, 1913 and 1922.)
　　The standard work on the numerous escapements.

HARCOURT-SMITH, SIMON. *Catalogue of Clocks, Watches, etc., in the Museums.* 4°. 34 pp. 41 pl. (Peiping, 1933.)
　　Good illustrations of clocks exported to China in the eighteenth century.

HARRISON, JOHN. An Account of the Proceedings in order to the Discovery of the Longitude at Sea. 8°. 98 pp. (London, 1763 and 65.)

— Remarks on a pamphlet lately published by the Rev. Mr. Maskelyne. 8°. 34 pp. (London, 1767.)
　　Story of the £20,000 award for discovering the longitude. See also; Longitude, Board of.

HASWELL, J. ERIC. *Horology: the Science of Time Measurement and the Construction of Clocks, Watches and Chronometers.* 8°. 283 pp. 21 pl. 126 ill. (London, 1928 and 1937.)
　　A technical book on the science.

HATTON, THOMAS. *An Introduction to the Mechanical Part of Clock and Watchwork.* 8°. 400 pp. 18 pl. (London, 1773.)
　　References to contemporary watchmakers and their reputations.

HAVARD, HENRI. *Les Arts de l'Ameublement. L'Horlogerie.* 8°. 183 pp. 80 ill. (Paris 1892 and 1928.)
　　Short general history from the earliest date.

IHERING, DR. D. W. *The Lure of the Clock, an Account of the James Arthur Collection at New York.* 8°. 135 pp. 89 figs. (New York, 1932.)
　　Description of a comprehensive collection of clocks readily available for study.

HERITAGE EXHIBITION at the Science Museum. See British Clockmakers.

HOOPES, PENROSE R. *Connecticut Clockmakers of the 18th Century.* 4°. 187 pp. 57 figs. (Hartford, Conn., 1930.)
　　Local history of clocks.

HOSOKAWA, HANZO. 3 vols. one of which is devoted to clocks. 8°. 32 pp. 9 pl. 65 figs. (1796.)
　　Contemporary pictures of clocks.

HOWGRAVE-GRAHAM, R. P. Some clocks and Jacks, with notes on the history of horology. *Archaeologia*, vol. 77. 4°. 54 pp. 15 ill. (London, 1928.)
Details indicating the age of the early turret clocks.

HURCOMBE. See Wetherfield.

HÜSELER, KONRAD. *Katalog der Uhrensammlung Dr. Anton Feill.* Fol. 58 pp. 430 ill. 30 tab. (Hamburg, 1929.)
Well illustrated catalogue of a good collection.

HUYGENS, CHRISTIAAN. *Opera varia.* 4°. 776 pp. 58 pl. (Leiden, 1724.)
Contains all his treatises.

JAMES, ARTHUR E. *Chester County Clocks and their Makers.* 8°. 205 pp. 55 figs. (West Chester, U.S.A., 1947.)
Local history of clocks.

JAMES, EMILE. *Les Sonneries de Montres, Pendules et Horloges.* 12°. 94 pp. 60 figs. (Paris-Geneva, 1899; Bienne, 1927.)
Striking mechanisms.

JANVIER, ANTIDE. *Étrennes chronométriques, le Temps, ses Divisions, leurs Usages.* 16°. 306 pp. 2 pl. (Paris, 1810.) 2nd ed. *Manuel chronomètrique.* 16°. 304 pp. 3 pl. (Paris, 1815, 1821 and 1835.)
Contemporary horological data.

JAQUET, EUGÈNE and CHAPUIS, ALFRED. *Histoire et Technique de la Montre Suisse.* 4°. 270 pp. 188 pl. 30 figs. (Olten, 1945.)
Important work on Swiss watches.

JEROME, CHAUNCEY. *History of the American Clock Business.* 12°. 152 pp. (New Haven, 1860.)
Contemporary history.

JURGENSEN, URBAN. *Principes généraux de l'exacte Mesure du Temps.* Translated by his son L. U. J. 4°. 288 pp. 19 pl. (Copenhagen, 1805 and 1838.)
Contemporary technical work.

— *Mémoires sur l'Horlogerie exacte.* Translated by his son L. U. J. 4°. 64 pp. 5 pl. (Paris, 1832.)
Similar to above.

KAFTAN, RUDOLF. *Illustrierte Führer durch das Uhren Museum der Stadt Wien.* 8°. 112 pp. 88 figs. (Vienna, 1929.)
Vienna Horological Museum Catalogue.

LACROIX, PAUL. *Les Arts au Moyen Âge.* 4°. Horology 19 pp. 10 figs. (Paris, 1869.) English Translation. *The Arts in the Middle Ages.* 4°. 17 pp. 10 figs. (London, n.d.)
Historical survey.

LE PAUTE, JEAN ANDRÉ. *Traité d'Horlogerie.* 4°. 371 pp. 17 pl. (Paris, 1755.) 3rd ed. (1767.)
Contemporary standard work.

LE ROY, JULIEN. See Sully.

LE ROY, PIERRE. *Etrennes Chronométriques.* 16°. 195 pp. (Paris, 1760.)
Description of clocks and watches.

— *Mémoire sur la Meilleure Manière de Mesurer le Temps en Mer.* 8°. 60 pp. 6 pl. (Paris, 1770.) Translation into English, 1806.
First description of the detached escapement.

LEUTMANN, JOHANN GEORG. *Vollstandige Nachricht von den Uhren.* 8°. 2 pts. 300 pp. 42 pl. (Halle, 1717–21.) 3rd ed. 8°. 307 pp. 48 pl. (Magdeburg, 1732.)
Contemporary details of clock and watch manufacture.

LLOYD, H. ALAN. *Chats on old Clocks.* 8°. 186 pp. 74 pl. (London, 1951.)
A general history of clocks.

LONGITUDE, COMMISSIONERS OF. *The Principles of Mr. Harrison's Timekeeper.* 4°. 34 pp. 10 pl. (London, 1767.)

— *An Account of the going of Mr. Harrison's watch.* 4°. 84 pp. (London, 1767.)
Official description and performance of the timekeeper which won the award.

— *An Answer to a Pamphlet entitled a Narrative of Facts by Mr. Thomas Mudge.* 8°. 172 pp. (London, 1792.)
Part of the longitude controversy.

— *An Explanation of Timekeepers constructed by T. Earnshaw and J. Arnold.* 4°. 67 pp. 6 pl. (London, 1806.)
Description of the first two practical marine chronometers.

LÜSBERG, BERING. *Urmagere og Ure i Danmark.* 4°. 290 pp. 12 pl. (Copenhagen, 1908.)
The first book dealing with Danish horology.

MANDEY, VENTERUS and MOXON, JAMES. *Mechanick—powers or the Mystery of Nature and Art unvail'd.* 4°. 330 pp. 17 pl. (London, 1696 and 1709.)
Early treatise.

MARGUET, F. *Histoire de la Longitude à la Mer en France.* Lge. 8°. 240 pp. 33 figs. (Paris, 1917.)
A full history on this subject.

MARFELS COLLECTION of watches. See Williamson.

MARRYAT, H. *Watches. Henlein to Tompion.* 8°. 100 pp. 135 figs. (London, 1938.)
Detailed description of the earlier portion of his collection.

MASKELYNE. See LONGITUDE, COMMISSIONERS OF.

MAUNDER, E. WALTER. *The Royal Observatory, Greenwich.* 8°. 320 pp. figs. (London, 1900.)
History of the Observatory.

MIGEON, GASTON. *Collection of Paul Garnier au Musée du Louvre.* 12°. 112 pp. 48 pl. 60 ill. (Paris, 1917.)
Description of the famous collection.

MILHAM, WILLIS I. *Time and Timekeepers.* 8°. 628 pp. 338 figs. (New York, 1923 and 47.)
A good general book covering all aspects.

MODY, N. H. N. *A Collection of Japanese Clocks.* 4°. 14 + 27 pp. 135 pl. (London, 1932.)
A well illustrated catalogue of his collection.

MOINET, LOUIS. *Nouveau Traité Général Astronomique et Civil.* 8°. 2 vols. 444 and 544 pp. 52 pl. (Paris, 1848–77.)
Practical book and illustrations of Breguet watches.

MORPURGO, ENRICO. *Dizionario degli Orologiai Italiani.* 8°. 239 pp. no figs. (Rome, 1950.)
List of Italian makers.

MUDGE, THOMAS JUNIOR. *A Narrative of Facts relating to some Timekeepers.* 8°. 106 pp. (London, 1792.)

— *A Reply to the Answer of the Rev'd Dr. Maskelyne.* 8°. 172 pp. (London, 1792.)

— *A Description of the Timekeeper invented by the late Thomas Mudge.* 4°. 337 pp. 10 pl. (London, 1799.)
The three books illustrate Mudge's difficulties in obtaining the £3,000 award.

NUTTING, WALLACE. *The Clock Book.* Lge. 8°. 312 pp. 250 pl. (Framingham, 1924; New York, 1935.)
A good American reference book.

OTTEMA, NANNE. *De Uurwerkmakerskunst in Friesland.* 8°. 38 pp. 4 pl. (Leeuwarden, 1923.) Enlarged ed. 112 pp. 42 ill. (Assen, 1948.)
Friesland watch and clockmakers.

OVERTON, G. L. *Clocks and Watches.* 8°. 126 pp. ill. (London, 1922.)
A short history with technical details.

PALMER, BROOKS. *The Book of American Clocks.* 4°. 318 pp. 312 ill. (New York, 1950.)
Historic horology in America brought up to date. Well illustrated.

PALMER, BROOKS, (*Contd.*)
— *Romance of Time.* 8°. 96 pp. ill. (New York, 1954.)
    A short history of the development of the American clock and watch industry.
PATENT OFFICE, LONDON. *Abridgements of the (Patent) Specifications* 1661–1876. 3 vols. 12°. 426 pp.
    List of all English patents.
— *Subject List of Works on Horology.* 16°. 56 pp. (London, 1912.)
    Useful reference library.
PERIODICALS. See end.
PLANCHON, M. *L'Horloge, son Histoire rétrospective.* Sm. 4°. 264 pp. 107 ill. (Paris, [1898].) 2nd ed. 8°. 232 pp. 150 ill. (Paris, 1923.)
— *L'Évolution du mécanisme de l'horlogerie.* 8°. 47 pp. 25 figs. (Bourges, 1918.)
— *La Pendule de Paris.* 8°. 190 pp. 175 figs. (Paris, 1921.)
    A good series of historical books.
POPPE, J. H. M. *Ausführliche Geschicte der theoretisch-praktischen Uhrmacherkunst.* 8°. 564 pp. (Leipzig, 1801.)
    Best history of this date.
RAWLINGS, DR. A. L. *The Science of Clocks and Watches.* 8°. 303 pp. 96 figs. 2nd ed. (New York, 1948.)
    A good scientfic approach to the subject.
REES' CYCLOPAEDIA. Articles on Horology. 4°. Many plates. 45 vols. (London, 1819–20.)
    Good contemporary information on all branches.
REID, THOMAS. *Treatise on Clock and Watch Making.* 8°. 476 pp. 19 pl. 1st ed. (Edinburgh, 1826.) 8°. 482 pp. 19 pl. 7th ed. (Edinburgh, 1859.)
    The standard book of this period.
ROBERTSON, J. DRUMMOND. *The Evolution of Clockwork.* 8°. 374 pp. 101 ill. (London, 1931.)
    Excellent historical treatises on Japanese clocks.
ROBERTSON, W. B. and WALKER, F. *The Royal Clocks in Windsor Castle, etc.* 4°. 42 pp. 20 ill. (London, 1904.)
    Clocks from four royal palaces.
ROBLOT, CHARLES. *Collection de Cadrans de Montres (Exposition Universelle 1900).* 8°. 98 pp. Many ill. (Paris, 1900.)
    Useful reference for watch dials.
SALOMONS, SIR DAVID, BART. *Breguet.* 8°. 115 pp. 117 pl. (London, 1921.) *Supplement.* 8°. 12 pp. 18 pl. (London, 1921.) *Addenda.* 8°. 4 pp. 3 pl. (London, 1921.) French ed. 8°. 168 pp. 172 pl. (Paris, 1923.)
    A well illustrated description of watches, and a few clocks.
SARASIN, ERNEST. *Uhren Sammlung.* Auction Catalogue. 4°. 197 items. 32 fine plates. (Lucerne, 1948.)
    Important collection of early watches.
SAUNIER, CLAUDIUS. *Traité d'Horlogerie.* Lge. 8°. 840 pp. 21 pl. 1st ed. (Paris, 1869–89.) English Translation. Lge. 8°. 860 pp. 21 pl. (London, 1882 and 1951.)
    The standard practical book.
SCHMIDT, FRIEDRICH AUGUST. *Beitrag zur Zeitmesskunst.* 8°. 300 pp. 6 pl. (Leipzig, 1797.)
    Good description of manufacture at this date.
SERVIÈRE, N. GROLLIER DE. *Recueil des Ouvrages curieux.* 4°. 136 pp. 88 pl. (Lyons, 1719–33.) 3rd ed. 4°. 184 pp. 88 pl. (Paris, 1751.)
    Showing unusual clocks.
SIDENBLADH, ELIS. *Urmakare i Sverige under aldre Tider.* Enlarged ed. Fol. 256 pp. 129 pl. (Stockholm, 1947.)
    Historical treatise on Swedish horology.
SMITH, H. CLIFFORD. *Buckingham Palace.* Fol. 299 pp. 351 ill. (London, 1931.)
    Several illustrations of fine clocks.

SMITH, JOHN. *Horological Dialogues.* 12°. 134 pp. (London, 1675.)
— *Horological Disquisitions concerning the Nature of Time.* 12°. 92 pp. (London, 1694.) 2nd ed. (London, 1708.)
    First English books with descriptions of clocks and watches and how to keep them to time.
SMITH, JOHN. *Old Scottish Clockmakers.* Enlarged ed. 8°. 451 pp. 25 pl. (Edinburgh, 1921.)
    Full information on this subject.
SPITZER, S. *La Collection. Antiquité, Moyen Âge, Renaissance.* Vol. 5. Horloges et Montres. Fol. 37 pp. 37 figs. 8 pl. 1 col. (Paris, 1892.)
    Fine collection of early clocks and watches.
STERNFELD, JOSEPH. *List of Books and Booklets* 1920–48. 4°. 20 pp. (New York, 1949.)
    Useful list of modern books.
SULLY, HENRY. *Règle artificielle du tems.* 12°. 114 pp. 1 pl. (Vienna, 1714.) Another ed. (Paris, 1717.) Augmented ed. 12°. 457 pp. 5 pl. (Paris, 1737.)
    A famous horological book.
— *Description abrégée d'une Horloge d'une nòuvelle Invention.* 4°. 290 pp. 2 pl. (Paris, 1726.)
    Description of his famous marine time-keeper.
SUSSEX, DUKE OF. *Sale Catalogue (Christie's) of clocks and watches.* 4°. 13 pp. 137 lots. (London, 1843.)
    Details of a famous collection.
SWINBURNE, SIR JAMES, F.R.S. *The Mechanism of the Watch.* 8°. 88 pp. 62 ill. (London, 1950.)
    An approach to the subject from a rather different point of view.
SYMONDS, R. W., F.S.A. *Masterpieces of En lish Furniture and Clocks.* Fol. 172 pp. 138 pl. 8 col. (London, 1940.)
    Fine illustrations—well documented.
— *A Book of English Clocks* (King Penguin Series). 8°. 80 pp. 71 pl. 1st ed. 1947. 2nd ed. (London, 1951.)
    An admirable production.
— *Thomas Tompion. His Life and Work.* 4°. 320 pp. 4 col. 273 large ill. (London, 1951.)
    Magnificent production showing the mechanism behind the dial as well as the cases. Well documented.
— *Furniture Making.* 17th and 18th Century England. A chapter on clocks.
    To be published shortly.
TALLQVIST, PROF. HJ. *Urens och Urteknikens Historia.* 8°. 336 pp. 271 figs. (Stockholm, 1939.)
    General history.
TARDY, *Bibliographie Générale de la Mesure du Temps.* Lge. 8°. 353 pp. (Paris, 1947.)
    Complete list of all books and articles in all languages.
— *Lu Pendule Française des Origines à nos Jours.* Fol. 230 pp. 1175 ill. (Paris, 1948 50.)
    Good illustrations of French clocks including the mechanism.
— *Origine de la Mesure du Temps.* Fol. 120 pp. 110 ill. (Paris, 1950.)
— *La Montre:* 1ier Fascicule Les Eschappements à Recul—2ième Fascicule Les Eschappements a demi-Recul et à Repos—3ième Fascicule Libres à Ancre. Fol. 188 pp. 394 ill. (Paris, 1950–3.) *Les Echappements à Detente.* To follow.
    Well illustrated details of escapements.
TERRY, H. *American Clockmaking, its Early History and Present Extent.* 8°. 26 pp. (Waterbury, 1870.)
    Contemporary history of the industry.
THIOUT, ANTOINE. *Traité de l'Horlogerie mécanique et pratique.* 2 vols. 4°. 430 pp. 91 pl. 1st ed. 1741. 2nd ed. 1767.
    The standard work of this period.

THOMSON, ADAM. *Time and Timekeepers.* 12°. 207 pp. (London, 1842.)
    A good general book of the period.

TIC-TAC. *Les Coqs de Montres du Mont St. Michel et leur Classement Historique.* 12°. 50 ill. (Paris, 1900 and 1902.)
    Illustrations of some of the watch cocks in the museum.

ULLYETT, KENNETH. *In Quest of Clocks.* 8°. 264 pp. 82 pl. (London, 1950.)
    Embodying the author's experience in collecting.

UNGERER, ALFRED. *L'Horloge Astronomique de Strasbourg.* 8°. 40 pp. 12 ill. (Strasbourg, 1919–24.)
    Description of the most famous clock.

— *Les Horloges Astronomiques et Monumentales.* 4°. 516 pp. 458 ill. (Strasbourg, 1931.)
    The standard work on turret clocks of all ages.

USHER, JAMES WARD. *An Art Collector's Treasures.* Fol. 13 col. pl. of horology. (London, 1916.)
    Good coloured illustrations.

VIAL, EUGÈNE ET COTE, CLAUDIUS. *Les Horlogers Lyonnais de 1550 à 1650.* 4°. 256 pp. 12 pl. (Lyons, 1927.)
    Good history for this town. Well illustrated.

VIGNIAUX, P. *Horlogerie pratique, à l'Usage des Apprentis et des Amateurs.* 8°. 350 pp. 12 pl. (Toulouse, 1788.) 2nd ed. 8°. 442 pp. 14 pl. (Toulouse, 1802.)
    Practical treatise.

VOLLGRAFF, DR. J. A. *Christiaan Huygens. L'Horloge à Pendule de 1656 à 1666.* 4°. 238 pp. 1 pl. 79 ill. (La Haye, 1932.) Another ed. (1934.)
    All the works and correspondence of Huygens.

WARD, DR. F. A. B. *Time Measurement, Pt. I. Science Museum.* 8°. 56 pp. 11 pl. 2 figs. (London, 1947.) *Time Measurement, Pt. II. Science Museum.* 8°. 95 pp. 10 pl. (London, 1950.)
    Excellent handbooks on the history and the museum exhibits.

WENHAM, EDWARD. *Old Clocks for Modern Use.* 8°. 192 pp. 16 pl. 71 ill. (London, 1951.)
    Traces the evolution of clocks and their ornaments.

WETHERFIELD, D. A. F. *The Wetherfield Collection of 222 Clocks sold by W. E. Hurcomb.* 4°. 95 pp. 222 ill. (London, 1928.)
    Famous collection of English clocks. See Britten.

WILLIAMSON, DR. G. C. *Catalogue of the Pierpoint Morgan Collection of Watches.* Fol. 306 pp. 92 pl. (London, 1912.)
    Sumptuous book, beautifully illustrated.

WINS, ALPHONSE. *L'Horloge à travers les âges.* 8°. 343 pp. 163 ill. (Mons, 1924.)
    Useful history particularly of the early specimens.

WOOD, EDWARD J. *Curiosities of Clocks and Watches from the Earliest Times.* 8°. 443 pp. 1 pl. (London, 1866.)
    Interesting collection of references to horology.

ZERELLA E YCOAGA, DON MANUEL DE. *Tratado general y matematico de reloxeria.* Lge. 8°. 422 pp. 22 pl. (Madrid, 1789 and 91.)
    Well illustrated, original treatise.

PERIODICALS

American Horologist and Jeweller. Denver, 1941 to date.

Antiquarian Horology. London, 1953.

Bulletin of the National Association of Watch and Clock Collectors. Columbia, 1943 to date.

Clessidra. Rome, 1944 to date.

Deutcheuhrmacher Zeitung. Berlin, 1876–*c*.1944, afterwards Stuttgart, *c.* 1944 to date.

Horological Institute of America Journal. Indianapolis, 1946 to date.

Horological Journal. London, 1858 to date.

Horology. Los Angeles, 1934–41.

Journel Suisse D'Horlogerie. Lausanne, 1876 to date.

Neue Uhrmacher Zeitung. Ulm, 1946 to date.

Practical Watch and Clockmaker. London, 1928–39.

Revue Français des Bijoutiers-Horologers. Paris, 1939 to date.

Suisse Horlogère. English ed. Last 3 yrs. La Chaux-de-Fonds, French. 1886 to date.

Addenda to the Eighth Edition

Reprints and new editions:

BRITTEN, F. J. *Old Clocks and Watches and their Makers.* 6th ed. Demy 8°. 891 pp. 934 ill. (London, 1971.)

CHAMBERLAIN, P. *It's About Time.* Medium 8°. 490 pp. ill. (London, 1964.)

DIDEROT AND D'ALEMBERT. *Encyclopédie ou Dictionaire Raisonné Des Sciences, Des Arts et Métiers.* (Milan, 1971.)
    Facsimile reproduction of horological plates.

REES, ABRAHAM. *The Cyclopaedia; or Universal Dictionary of Arts, Sciences and Literature* (1819). 29 cm. 295 pp. ill. (Newton Abbot, 1971.)
    Facsimile reproduction of horological articles and plates. Historically valuable.

English translation:

JAQUET, E. and CHAPUIS, A. *The Swiss Watch.* Medium 4°. 272 pp. ill. (London, 1970.)
    See above for French original.

New books since 1956:

BEESON, C. F. C. *English Church Clocks 1280–1850.* Medium 8°. 130 pp. ill. (Chichester, 1971.)
    Many new facts.

CLUTTON, C. and DANIELS, G. *Watches.* Fol. 159 pp. ill. (London, 1965.)
    Complete and profusely illustrated history.

CUSS, T. P. C. *The Country Life Book of Watches.* 8°. 128 pp. 4 pl. (London, 1967.)
    Fairly short; useful.

DANIELS, G. *English and American Watches.* 4°. 127 pp. ill. (London, 1967.)
    Short but useful history.

EDEY, W. *French Clocks.* Demy 8°. 83 pp. ill. (London, 1967.)
    Short but most useful. Well illustrated.

HOWSE, D. and HUTCHINSON, B. *Clocks and Watches of Captain James Cook 1769–1969* Post 4°. 67 pp. ill. (London, 1971.)
    Many new facts concerning this pioneering era.

JAGGER, C. *Paul Philip Barraud. A Study of His Life and Successors in the Family Business, 1750–1929 etc.* Demy 4°. 170 pp. ill. (London, 1968.)
Useful eighteenth- and nineteenth-century history.

LEE, R. A. *The first twelve years of the English Pendulum Clock or the Fromanteel Family and their Contemporaries 1658–1670.* Fol. 68 pp. ill.
Although nominally only an exhibition catalogue, a most valuable historical essay, superbly illustrated.

LEOPOLD, J. *The Almanus Manuscript.* A4. 288 pp. ill. (London, 1971.)
An important contribution to the history of late fifteenth-century clockmaking.

LLOYD, H. A. *The Collectors' Dictionary of Clocks.* Royal 4°. 214 pp. ill. (London, 1964.)
Useful general reference. Well illustrated.

MERCER, V. *John Arnold & Son Chronometers 1762–1843.* Oct. 302 pp. ill. (London, 1972.)
Contains much new historical fact, especially of John Arnold's pioneer work.

Precision Timekeeping: Collected essays [various authors]. Oct. 117 pp. ill. (London, 1965.)
A most valuable symposium on the important 1760–90 period.

QUILL, H. *John Harrison: the man who found longitude, with a foreword by Sir Richard Woolley.* 23½ cm. 255 pp. ill. (London, 1967.)
Many new facts additional to those contained in Gould's *Marine Chronometer.*

TARDY. *Dictionaire des Horlogers Français.* (Paris, 1971.)

WARD, F. A. B. *Time Measurement.* Medium 8°. 62 pp. ill. (London, 1970.)
Catalogue of the important London Science Museum horological collection.

In the course of printing:

ALLIX, C. and BONNERT, P. *Carriage Clocks.*
The first comprehensive study of this important type of clock.

BRITTEN, F. J. *The Watch and Clockmakers' Handbook, Dictionary and Guide.*
Completely revised and enlarged.

COOLE, P. G. and NEWMANN, F. *The Orpheus Clocks.*
Deals with an important group of sixteenth-century table clocks.

DANIELS, G. *Breguet.*
To be the definitive work on this important maker.

FORMER CLOCK AND WATCH MAKERS

Former clock and watch makers

ABBIS, J., *37 Bishopsgate St. Within*, 1807.

ABBOTT, FRANCIS. *Manchester*; *3 Smithy Door*, 1825; afterwards at *50 Market St.*; watch paper, C.C., about 1840; wrote a book on the management of public clocks (n.d.), about 1838.

ABBOTT, JOHN. Admitted C.C. 1788; charged with making an agreement to go to St. Petersburg to work at clockmaking, and convicted at Hicks' Hall of the offence; known as a maker of long-case clocks, 1787–1800.

ABBOTT, PETER. C.C. 1719.

ABBOTT, PHILLIP. *London*. C.C. 1703.

ABBOTT, RICHARD. Apprenticed in 1668 to Helkiah Bedford; C.C.

ABBOTT, THOS. *41 Allen St.*, 1820–22.

ABBOTT, WM. Long-case clock marked 'Wm. Abbott Saroon, fecit,' about 1720.

ABBOTT, WM. *Prescot*, 1770.

ABDY, WILLIAM. Livery Goldsmiths' Company, *5 Oat Lane, Noble St.*, 1768–1817.

ABELING, WILLIAM. *7 Wynyatt St., Clerkenwell*, 1817; *36 Spencer St.*, 1835–42.

ABERLEY, JOSEPH. Apprenticed in 1664 to Isaac Sutton; C.C.

ABRAHAM, EBENEZER. *Olney*. Watch, 1773.

ABRAHAM, JOHN. *27 Steward St., Bishopsgate*, 1820–23.

ABRAHAMS, H. *21 Bevis Marks*, 1800–20.

ABSOLON, —. *London*. Long-case clock, about 1770.

ACAM, ROBERT. *London*. Apprenticed 1767, C.C. 1774–1824.

ACEY, PETER. *York*, f., 1656.

ACHARD, G. *Geneva*. Watch, about 1810.

ACHARD, GEORGE, ET FILS. *Geneva*. Watch, about 1780.

ACHER, —. *Paris*. 1740 master. Pierre François. *Paris*, master 1746.

ACHURCH, WM. Apprenticed in 1691 to Wm. Jacques, C.C.

ACKERS, WILLIAM. *St. Andrew's, Holborn*. Pair-case watch in V. & A., early part of eighteenth century; his bankruptcy noted *Lond. Gaz.*, 28th Oct. 1706.

ACKLAM, JOHN PHILIP. *423 Strand*, 1816; *138 Strand*, 1840.

ACOTT, WILLIAM. *London*. Apprenticed 1784, C.C. 1791–1824.

ACOTT, JOHN. *London*. Apprenticed 1791.

ACTON, ABRAHAM. Apprenticed in 1691 to Henry Montlow; C.C. 1700.

ACTON, ABRAHAM, son. *London*. C.C. 1738.

ACTON, JNO. *Clerkenwell*, C.C. 1677.

ACTON, THOMAS. *London*. C.C. 1677.

ADAM, A. Watch, Pierpont Morgan collection, signed 'Melchior Adam', balance-cock pinned on, about 1610.

ADAM, MELCHIOR (? Melchior Adam). *Paris*. Octagonal crystal-cased watch, Soltykoff collection, about 1585.

ADAMS, BRYANT FRANCIS. Succeeded Benj. Webb at *21 St. John's Sq., Clerkenwell*; master C.C. 1848; 1810–48.

ADAMS, C. & J. *10 King St.*, Cheapside, 1788.

ADAMS, CHARLES. *Drogheda*, 1820.

ADAMS, GEO. Apprenticed to Jos. Dudds, 1745; C.C. 1752; *60 Fleet Street.*, 1770; table timepiece, Guildhall Museum, about 1795.

ADAMS, GEORGE WILLIAM, son of Francis Bryant. *London*. Apprenticed 1822, C.C. 1829.

ADAMS, HY. *Church St., Hackney*. Fine long-case clock, about 1800; watch, h.m., 1808.

ADAMS, JNO. *Halesowen*, 1760.

ADAMS, JOHN. *1 Dove Court, Moorfields*, 1770–72.

ADAMS, JOHN. *31 Maiden Lane, Covent Garden*, 1790–94.

ADAMS, STEPHEN. *3 St. Anne's Lane*, 1774; Stephen & Son, 1788.

ADAMS, WILLIAM. *Boston, U.S.A.* 1809–25.

ADAMS, WILLIAM & SAMUEL A. EATON. *Boston, U.S.A.*, 1816–21.

ADAMSON, —. *Paris*. Clockmaker to the Royal Family, 1790.

ADAMSON, HUMFRY. Maker of a clock for Whitehall Chapel, 1682; bracket clock, about 1690; Wetherfield collection.

ADAMSON, JOHN. Admitted C.C. 1686; "A Gold Minute Watch, lately made by Mr. Adamson, over against the Blue Boar in Holborn" (*Lond. Gaz.*, 3rd March 1686).

ADAMSON, JOHN. *London*, C.C. 1813.

ADCOCK, WM. *London*. Bracket Clock about 1750.

ADDIS, GEORGE. *79 Cornhill*. 1786–94.

ADDIS, GEORGE CURSON. *3 Birchin Lane*, afterwards 47 *Lombard St.*; livery C.C. 1787; 1780–98.

ADDIS, WILLIAM. *Cannon St.*, afterwards at *3 Birchin Lane*. Son of Robert A., of Bristol; apprenticed to George Sims, 1738; admitted C.C. 1745, master 1764.

ADDISON, EDMUND. Apprenticed in 1678 to Joseph Ashby, C.C.

ADDISON, JNO. *York*, f.; 1789.

ADDISON, JOSH. *London*. Watch, 1770.

ADDISON, JOSH. *Lancaster*, 1817; f.; son of James Addison, *London*.

ADEANE, HENRY. Apprenticed to Rich. Scrivener in 1663; C.C. 1675.

ADEANE, HENRY. C.C. 1705.

ADKINS, THOS. *Shoe Lane*, 1735.

ADLINGTON, JOHN. *London*. l.C.C. 1806–17.

ADNEY, RICHARD. *Bull and Mouth St.*, 1770–76.

ADNEY, THOMAS. *London*. C.C. 1767.

AGAR, —. *York*. Several generations.

AGAR, CHARLES. f., 1779, settled at *Pontefract*.

AGAR, EDWARD. *New York*. 1761.

AGAR, JNO. f., 1760; died 1808; a fine regulator.

AGAR, JOHN. f., 1782, settled at *Malton*.

AGAR, SETH. f., 1743.

AGAR, THOS. *Bury*, 1820.

AGERON, FRANÇOIS. *Paris.* Master 1741–79. Two gold engraved watches. striking cal. clock Bernal sale.

AICKEN, GEO. *Cork.* Watch, 1780.

AICKEN, GEORGE, son. *London.* Apprenticed 1763, C.C. 1777.

AIGELDINGER, M. *Trälleborg* and *Malmö.* born 1772, died 1849.

AIKINSON, PEABODY. *Concord, U.S.A.* 1790.

AINGE, ALEXANDER. *London.* Apprenticed 1749, C.C. 1766–83.

AINSWORTH, GEORGE. *Warrington,* 1818.

AIREY, JNO. *Hexham,* about 1770.

AIRY, GEORGE BIDDELL. Astronomer-Royal, 1835–81; K.C.B., 1874; died 1892, aged 90; devoted much attention to the perfecting of timekeepers.

AISH, SIMON. *Sherborne.* Long-case lantern-movement clock, 10-inch dial, about 1690.

AITCHISON, ROBERT. *Edinburgh.* Apprenticed 1756, died 1790.

AITKEN, JOHN. *55 St. John's St., Clerkenwell.* Received in 1824 a prize of twenty guineas from the Society of Arts for a clock train remontoire; 1800–26.

AITKEN, JOHN. *Edinburgh.* Apprenticed 1750, died 1779.

AKCED, JNO. *London.* Watch, 1795.

AKERS, JAS. *Derby.* Watch, 1802.

ALAIS, MOISE. *Blois.* Master 1630, died 1682.

ALBERT, ISAAC. C.C. 1731.

ALBRECHT, MICHAEL GEORGE. Gold repeating watch in the V. & A., bearing the royal arms, outer case *repoussé,* about 1720.

ALCOCK, THOMAS. Petitioner for incorporation of C.C. 1630; warden 1646, did not become master.

ALCORNE, JAMES, son. *Edinburgh.* 1733–60.

ALCORNE, RICHARD. *Edinburgh.* Apprenticed 1694–1738.

ALDEN & ELDRIDGE. *Bristol, Conn.,* 1820.

ALDER, J. *London.* Bracket clock, about 1700.

ALDERHEAD, JNO. *114 Bishopsgate Within.* Livery Goldsmiths' Company 1775–94; card, "at the Ring and Pearl, Bishopsgate St., near the Southsea House."

ALDERMAN, EDWIN. *22 Barbican,* 1818–34; livery C.C. 1822.

ALDERSON, JOSIAH. *London.* Apprenticed 1749, C.C. 1758–61. Watch.

ALDRED, JNO. Apprenticed in 1686 to Hy. Reeve, C.C.

ALDRED, LEONARD. C.C. 1671.

ALDRIDGE, EDWARD. Striking and pull quarter repeating bracket clock, about 1710.

ALDRIDGE, JAMES. *11 Northumberland St., Strand,* 1816–30.

ALDRIDGE, JOHN. C.C. 1726.

ALDRIDGE, THOMAS. *London.* Apprenticed 1753, C.C. 1769.

ALDWORTH, SAMUEL. Brother C.C. 1697. A lantern clock, inscribed 'Saml. Aldworth, Oxon.,' about 1700; a bracket clock had under nameplate 'John Knibb, Oxon.'; 'Saml. Aldworth, Strand.'

ALEXANDER, ISAAC. *Nottingham.* Watch, about 1760.

ALEXANDER, JOHN. *Edinburgh.* Apprenticed 1667–1707.

ALEXANDER, ROBERT. *Leith.* Apprenticed 1764. Died 1830.

ALEXANDER, ROBT. *Edinburgh,* 1709.

ALEXANDER, WM. *10 Parliament St.,* 1828–40.

ALIBERT, F. *Paris.* Watch, 1800.

ALIMENIS. *v.* CAMPANUS.

ALISON, JOHN. *Montrose.* 1798–1822.

ALKER, JNO. *Wigan.* 1818.

ALKINS. *London,* about 1730.

ALLAM, ANDREW. *Grubb St.* Apprenticed in 1656 to Nicholas Coxeter; C.C. 1664; maker of lantern clocks.

ALLAM, MICHAEL. *London,* 1723.

ALLAM, ROBT. *Next St. Dunstan's Church, Fleet St.,* 1736–65.

ALLAM, WILLIAM. *Fleet St.,* 1770–80.

ALLAM & STACEY. *175 Fleet St.,* 1783.

ALLAMAND, JEAN MARC. *Geneva.* About 1770–98. Juré.

ALLAN, GEORGE. *9 New Bond St.* Hon. freeman C.C. 1781; 1760–83.

ALLAN, JOHN. *119 New Bond St.,* 1798–1800.

ALLAN & CLEMENTS. *119 New Bond St.,* 1785–94.

ALLAN & CAITHNESS. *119 New Bond St.,* 1800–04.

ALLARD (ALAR), JEAN CLAUDE. *Paris.* Master 1757–89.

ALLAWAY, JOHN. Apprenticed to Bernard Rainsford; C.C. 1695.

ALLBRIDGE, SAMUEL. *London.* Apprenticed 1786.

ALLEN, CHARLES. *London (Shoe Lane).* C.C. 1770–75.

ALLEN, CHARLES. *London.* Apprenticed 1747, C.C. 1763–69.

ALLEN, ELIAS. Brother C.C., master 1636; died 1654.

ALLEN, GEORGE. *London (Temple Bar).* C.C. 1771.

ALLEN, GEORGE. *Fleet St.* Liveryman C.C. 1776.

ALLEN, GEORGE. *14 Red Lion Passage, Holborn.* Watch paper, C.C. 1812–42.

ALLEN, JAS. Brother C.C. 1635.

ALLEN, JAMES. *76 New Gravel Lane.* An ingenious watchmaker to whom the Board of Longitude awarded £105 for engine dividing, 1790–1800.

ALLEN, JOHN. *London.* C.C. 1653.

ALLEN, JOHN. C.C. 1720.

ALLEN, JOHN. *London.* Apprenticed 1737, C.C. 1753.

ALLEN, JOHN. Watch-case maker, *Barbican;* convicted in the Mayor's Court for refusing to become a member of the C.C., although he was at the time free of the Goldsmith's Company, 1785–89; *Aldersgate St.,* 1794.

ALLEN, JOSEPH. *London (Christ's Hosp.).* Apprenticed 1773, C.C. 1781–1810.

ALLEN, NATHANIEL. Apprenticed in 1650 to Wm. Bowyer, C.C.

ALLEN, P. *Macclesfield,* 1770.

ALLEN, THOS. Apprenticed in 1663 to Robt. Whitwell, C.C.

ALLEN, THOS. *Deptford,* 1780.

ALLEN, THOMAS. *Buckingham.* About 1790 C.C.

ALLEN, WILLIAM. *London.* Apprenticed 1736, C.C. 1745–60.

ALLENBACH, JACOB. *Philadelphia,* 1825–40.

ALLÉOUD, PIERRE. *Geneva.* Born 1741–85.

ALLET, GEORGE. Apprenticed in 1683 to Solomon Bouquet, but turned over to Thos. Tompion; C.C. 1691; bracket clock, ebony case, Wetherfield collection, about 1705.

ALLEXANDRE, JACQUES. *Paris.* A priest who devoted much attention to timekeepers; published in 1734, 'Traité Général des Horloges.'

ALLIÉ, M. *Geneva.* Centre seconds repeating watch with calendar, about 1790, Horological School, Geneva.

ALLIER, . *Paris (Rue St. Antoine).* 1807–24.

ALLIEZ, BUCHELARD & TÉROND FILS. *Geneva.* Watch, about 1820.

ALLING, JAMES. *22 Red Lion St., Whitechapel.* 'Foreman to Mr. Hatton, London Bridge'; watch paper, C.C. 1838–42.

ALLING, RICHARD. Admitted C.C. 1722.

ALLINSON, GILBERT. *Sunderland,* 1775.

ALLINSON, WM. *Liverpool,* about 1765.

ALLKINS, —. *Horncastle.* Watch, 1785.

ALLMAN, ANDREW. *London.* 1656. C.C. 1664.

ALLMAN, W. *Prince's St., Storey's Gate, Westminster.* Card, B.M., 1798.

ALLPORT, —. *Birmingham.* Bracket clock, about 1770.

ALLPORT, SAM. 1790–1836.

ALLSOPP, JOHN. *London.* Apprenticed 1786, C.C. 1794. From *Quebec.* cf. ALSOPE.

ALLSOP, JOSHUA. *Northamptonshire.* Brother C.C. 1689; handsome long Oriental lacquer-cased clock belonging to the Blecker family, New York; long-case clock, richly inlaid, inscribed 'Josh. Alsope, East Smithfield,' about 1710.

ALLVEY, HY. *5 Old Sq.*, about 1795.

ALMOND, JOHN. C.C. 1671.

ALMOND, RALPH. Apprenticed to Oswald Durant in 1637; C.C. 1646, master 1678.

ALMOND, WILLIAM. *Lothbury.* Maker of a clock for Hall, Bishop of Exeter; C.C. 1633.

ALRIC FILS, *à Toulouse.* Repeating watch, virgule escapement, about 1810.

ALRICH (or ALRICHS), JACOB. Born 1775, died 1857.

ALRICH (or ALRICHS), JONAS. *Wilmington, Del.*, born 1759, died 1802.

ALRICH (or ALRICHS), JONAS & JACOB. *Wilmington, Del., U.S.A.* 1795. Firm dissolved 1797.

ALRICH (or ALRICHS) & McCLARY. *Wilmington.* 1810–13. Partnership of Jacob with Samuel McClary.

ALSOPE, see ALLSOP.

ALSOPE (ALSOP), JOSHUA. *London.* 1689, C.C.—about 1710. long-case clock. See ALLSOP.

ALSTON & LEWIS. *30 Bishopsgate St.*, 1820; Alston & Hallam, 1830–42.

ALT, JOHANN JAKOB. *Basle.* Born 1725, died 1812. Gross und Kleinuhrmacher.

ALVEY, SAMUEL. Apprenticed to Jas. Wood; admitted C.C. 1757.

AMABRIC, ABRAHAM. *Geneva*, 1760–80; barrel-shaped gold watch with *repoussé* ornament enamelled, Pierpont Morgan collection; dial apparently later signed Amabric Frères.

AMABRIC, AMI, son. *Geneva.* About 1800–42. Watch N.Y. Univ.

AMABRIC, FRÈRES. *Geneva*, 1793.

AMAN, J. *Lund.* Born 1786, died 1849.

AMAN, MATHIAS MAURITZ. *Köping* and *Stockholm.* Master 1770–86.

AMANT, 'maître horloger, Paris'; spoken of by Thiout in 1741; he invented the pin wheel escapement about 1749.

AMANT, ANNE HENRY. *Paris.* Master 1759, died 1773.

AMANT, FESTER. *Philadelphia.* 1793.

AMANT, JEAN (LE JEUNE). *Paris (Quai Pelletier).* Master 1755–89.

AMANT, JEAN LOUIS (L'AÎNÉ), son. *Paris (Faubourg St. Martin).* Master 1751–89.

AMARCK, NICLAS. *Stockholm.* 1751-99. Bracket clock.

AMBROSE, DAVID. C.C. 1669.

AMBROSE, EDWARD. Apprentice of Elias Voland, 1634. *London.* C.C. 1637.

AMES, RICHARD. Apprenticed in 1648 to Peter Closon; C.C. 1653; died in 1682, after election as master; clock by him with dolphin frets and bob pendulum working between going and striking; clock marked 'Richard Ames Neere St. Andrews Church in Holburne fecit'. In 1684 Robert Browne was apprenticed to Katherine Ames.

AMES, WILLIAM. Apprenticed to Richard in 1675; C.C. 1682.

AMIRAULT, LOUIS HENRY. *Paris.* Juré 1762.

AMONTONS, GUILLAUME. *Paris.* Born 1663, died 1705. Able mechanician. Published book on a water clock in 1695.

AMOURETTE. *À Marseille.* Watch, about 1650.

AMYOT, PETER. *Norwich.* Lantern clocks, about 1660.

AMYOT & BENNETT. *Brigg's Lane, Norwich*; in 1793 they issued a little book by J. Bennett on the management of a watch.

AMYOTT, PETER. *Norwich.* Watch, Nelthropp collection, about 1720.

AMYOTT, THOS. *London.* Watches, h.m., 1751–71; one, Nelthropp collection, about 1770.

ANDERSON, ALEX. *London.* Watch, 1770.

ANDERSON, ALEX. *Liverpool.* Watch, 1786.

ANDERSON, DAVID D. *Marietta, U.S.A.* 1821–24.

ANDERSON, GEO. Sued in 1777 by Cabrier for putting his name on five watches.

ANDERSON, HUGH. *London.* Apprenticed 1737, C.C. 1745–55. Movement maker.

ANDERSON, J. *London.* Watch, 1775.

ANDERSON, RICHARD. *Lancaster*, 1767, f.; also at *London* and *Preston.*

ANDERSON, RICHARD. *Preston.* Watch, 1778.

ANDERSON, ROBT. Apprenticed in 1691 to Thos. Tompion, C.C.

ANDERSON, SAMUEL THORNTON. *London.* Apprenticed 1783, C.C. 1801–11.

ANDERSON, SARAH. *London.* 1789 C.C.

ANDERSON, WILLIAM. *London.* C.C. 1649.

ANDERSON, WM. *Lancaster*, about 1770.

ANDERSON, WM. Apprenticed in 1646 to Simon Bartram.

ANDERSSON, NILS. *Malmö.* Born 1790, died 1871.

ANDERTON, JNO. *Little Wild St.* Repeating watch, about 1750.

ANDERTON, WM. *London.* Watch, h.m., 1767.

ANDRÉ, AUGUSTIN. *Paris.* 1764, master 1780.

ANDRÉ, CAMILLE. Prob. of Swiss family. About 1700. Enameller of watch by Tompion B.M.

ANDRÉ, JEAN. *Lyons.* Apprenticed 1600, master 1605–19.

ANDRÉ v. LANDER.

ANDRÉ, LOUIS. *La Rochelle.* 1758–90.

ANDRÉ, NOEL AUGUSTIN. *Paris.* Master 1771–89. Employed at the Manufacture d'Horlogerie.

ANDREW, J. *Dublin.* Apprenticed 1757–80. Watch.

ANDREW, J. *14 Queen St., Ratcliff Cross*, 1820.

ANDREWS, BENJ. *Bartholomew Lane*, 1725.

ANDREWS, ELIZA. *85 Cornhill*, 1790–1800.

ANDREWS, ISAAC. Apprenticed in 1674 to Edm. Fowell, C.C.

ANDREWS, JAMES. C.C. 1719.

ANDREWS, JOHN. *Leadenhall St.* Admitted C.C. 1688.

ANDREWS, NATHANIEL JAMES. *London (Grub St.).* C.C. 1772.

ANDREWS, RICHARD. C.C. 1703; watch 1730.

ANDREWS, ROBERT. Apprenticed in 1661 to Benj. Hill; C.C. 1709.

ANDREWS, ROBERT. *London.* Apprenticed 1695, C.C. 1710–44. Watch.

ANDREWS, THOS. Apprenticed in 1686 to Joshua Hutchin; C.C. 1705.

ANDREWS, THOS. *Steyning*, 1760.

ANDREWS, W. H. *Royston.* About 1790. C.C.

ANDREWS, WILLIAM. *Bishopsgate St.* C.C. 1719.

ANDREWS, WILLIAM. *London.* Apprenticed 1756, C.C. 1767–83.

ANDRIES (ANDRIESEN, ANDERS), JOHANNES KLAAS, *Grouw.* 1800–31.

ANGOILLE, JEAN. *Paris.* Master 1690, juré 1712. Watch.

ANGUS, GEO. *Aberdeen.* Long-case clock, about 1760.

ANICH, PETER. *Innsbruck.* Born 1723, died 1766. Astronomer and mathematician. Made fine astronomical clocks.

ANJOU, JEAN GUSTAVE. *Stockholm*. 1771–90. *Uppsala* in 1779. Watch.

ANNAT, NICHOLAS. Apprenticed in 1673 to Henry Jones, C.C.

ANNESS, WILLIAM. *102 Cheapside*, 1798–1820; livery, C.C. 1802.

ANNIN, M. *New York*, 1786.

ANNOTT, CHAS. Apprenticed in 1673 to Jas. Ellis, C.C.

ANNS, BENJAMIN. *Highworth*. 1770. C.

ANNS, JAMES. *Highworth*. Master 1777.

ANSART, PIERRE. *Paris*. Master 1767–89.

ANSELL, HY. *17 Colchester Sq., Savage Gardens*, 1830; *74 Lennan St.*, 1838.

ANSELL, (or ANSELME), RICHARD. Apprenticed to Jeffery Baily; C.C. 1680.

ANSELL, THOMAS. *Abingdon*. From 1780–about 1810.

ANSERMIER, JEAN RODOLPHE. *Chaux-de-Fonds*. 1799. Maître pendulier. Made musical movements.

ANSTEY, JNO. Apprenticed to George Nau in 1683.

ANTES, JNO. *London*. Apprenticed to Wm. Addis; pocket chronometer, G.M., h.m., 1787.

ANTHONY, —. Clockmaker to Henry VIII, 1529.

ANTHONY, JOHN. *Maidenhead*, 1790.

ANTHONY, WILLIAM. *55 Red Lion St., St. John's Sq., Clerkenwell*. A magnificent long oval watch by him, in a gold case, bearing the hall mark for 1796, had an oval dial; the hands were jointed, and automatically lengthened and shortened as they travelled around. Another example is an 8-day watch of similar shape, duplex escapement, movement beautifully engraved. He was reputed one of the most expert watchmakers of his day, and such specimens of his work as remain quite bear out this belief. He carried on a successful business in Red Lion St., St. John's Square, and most of his watches bore the inscription 'Wm. Anthony, St. John's Square'. At one time he was in good circumstances, and took an active part in founding the Watch and Clockmakers' Benevolent Institution in 1815, though he lived to be a recipient of its bounty.

ANTIS, JNO. *Fulneck, near Leeds*. Received in 1805 £21 from the Society of Arts for a clock escapement.

ANTOINE, —. *Rue Galande, Paris*, 1770.

ANTRAM, JOSEPH. *London*. Apprenticed to Chas. Gretton; C.C. 1706; long walnut-case clock, square dial, cherub corners, circles round winding holes, about 1700; watch, about 1720; "watch and clock maker to his Majesty".

ANVELIUS, DANIELI & SON. *Vienna*. Complicated astronomical clocks. About 1770.

APIOHN (UPJOHN), HENRY. Apprenticed in 1649 to Robert Whitwell, C.C.

APOLLINARIS, PHILLIP J. *Kremsminster, Austria*. Mystery clocks. About 1770.

APPERLEY, MARY, daughter. *London*. C.C. 1807.

APPERLEY, THOMAS. *London*. 1807 C.C.

APPLEBY, EDMUND. *London*. C.C. 1712. Watch.

APPLEBY, EDWARD. *London*. Watch, about 1700.

APPLEBY, JOHN JAMES. *London*. C.C. 1823.

APPLEBY, JOSHUA. *Bread St.* Apprenticed to Daniel Quare; C.C. 1719, master 1745.

APPLEBY, THOS. *Charing Cross*, 1800.

APPLEGARTH, THOMAS. Apprenticed in 1664 to Hugh Cooper; C.C. 1674.

APPLETON, JNO. *Liverpool*, 1818.

APPLEY, EDMUND. *Charing Cross*. Apprenticed to Jeffery Bailey 1670; C.C. 1677; small repeating bracket clock, black case basket top about 1680.

ARCHAMBO, JNO. *Prince's St., Leicester Fields*. Bracket clock in case, similar to Chippendale's design; mar-

quetry case clock, arch dial; *repoussé* case watch, hall mark 1730, and another watch of a later date; 1720–50.

ARCHDEKIN, MICHAEL. *Dublin*. 1769–1800. W.

ARCHER, EDWARD. C.C. 1711.

ARCHER, GEO. *Rochdale*, 1818.

ARCHER, HENRY. Subscribed £10 for incorporation of C.C. and was the first warden; 1630–49.

ARCHER, JOHN. Apprenticed in 1650 to Jas. Starnill; admitted C.C. 1660.

ARCHER, RICHARD SEWELL. *London*. C.C. 1758.

ARCHER, SAMUEL. *15 Leather Lane*, 1794; *33 Kirby St., Hatton Garden*, 1810; a prominent man in the trade. In 1820 he was treasurer to the Watch and Clockmakers' Benevolent Institution.

ARCHER, SAM. WM. *Hackney*, 1805–12.

ARCHER, THOMAS. *6 Long Lane, Smithfield*, 1814–20.

ARCHER, WALTER. Long-case clock, about 1715, at the Van Courtland Mansion, New York.

ARDIOT, —. *Paris*. 1772–1812.

ARGAND, J. L. *Place Dauphine, Paris*. 1770. Repeating watch 'Argand, Paris,' about 1770, Pierpont Morgan collection.

ARGAND, L'AÎNÉ. *Geneva*, about 1740.

ARIEL, JAMES. Watch-movement maker, *10 Wilderness Row*, 1815–20.

ARIEL, JOHN. *10 Percival St.*, 1822–39.

ARIEL, SAMUEL, brother. *London*. Apprenticed 1804, C.C. 1822, l.C.C. 1823.

ARIS, JNO., & CO. *Old Jewry*, 1794.

ARIS, JOHN. *London*. Apprenticed 1731, C.C. 1764-92. Shagreen case-maker.

ARIS, SAMUEL. *Leicester Fields*. Watch, 1750, Mr. Evan Roberts; long-case clock, about 1760.

ARLANDI, JOHN. Chain-maker for watches, *Red Rose St., Covent Garden*, 1680; C.C. 1682.

ARLAUD, ANTHOINE. Cruciform watch, Pierpont Morgan collection, late sixteenth century.

ARLAUD, BENJAMIN. Maker of a large silver repeating watch in the B.M., about 1680.

ARLAUD, FRANÇOIS. *Geneva*. Born 1720–76. Mém. to Soc. des Arts on a depth tool for crown wheel.

ARLAUD, HENRY. Fine calendar watch, Schloss collection, about 1630, silver case, back inscribed 'Richard Baille, at the Abbay'. This watch was probably English work. Another specimen of a rather later date was inscribed 'Arlaud, London.'

ARLOTT, THOS. *Sunderland*, 1780–91.

ARLUDE, CLAUDE. *Paris*. Juré 1692.

ARMAND, J. *Copenhagen*; born 1732, died 1819; a talented horologist.

ARMIGER, JOSEPH. *London*. C.C. 1688.

ARMITAGE, THOS. *Manchester*, 1815.

ARMITAGE, & CO. *88 Bishopsgate Within*, 1798.

ARMOUR, JOHN. *Kilmaurs*. 1780–1808.

ARMSTRONG, JOHN. C.C. 1724.

ARMSTRONG, THOS. *Manchester*, 1804–1820.

ARNAUD, ANTOINE. *Paris*. Master 1780–1812. 4-colour gold watch.

ARNOLD, CHARLES. *Eltham*. C.C. 1824.

ARNOLD, JOHN. *London*. Born 1736, C.C. 1783, died 1799. One of the most famous English makers. Had a chron. factory at *Chigwell*. Made rep. watch set in ring for George III in 1764. Invented helical balance spring for chrons. and a detent escapement similar to the modern chron. escapement. Also end curves for helical balance spring and several compensation balances (Patents No. 1113 of 1775 and No. 1328 of 1782). Was the principal chron. maker of his day.

ARNOLD, JOHN R., & DENT. *84 Strand*, 1830–40.

ARNOLD, JOHN ROGER. *Bank Buildings, 102 Cornhill*, 1804; *26 Cecil St.*, 1816–30.

ARNOLD, THOMAS. Apprenticed in 1687 to Nat. Chamberlaine, jun.; admitted C.C. 1703.

ARNOLD, THOMAS. *London (Fetter Lane)*. Apprenticed 1742, C.C. 1750–72. Watch.

ARNOLD, WM. *London*. Watch, 1790.

ARNOLD, & SON. *London*. 1787–99. Firm of John and his son J. Roger. Three pocket and a marine chron. G.M. Watch mt. with helical gold balance spring Ilbert coll. Regulator Weth. coll.

ARNOLTS, THOMAS. *Hamburg*, 1635. Pair-case silver watch signed 'Thomas Volffgang Arnolt, Hamburg', about 1680.

ARNOTT, RICHARD. *18 Red Cross St., Barbican*, 1810–25.

ARSANDAUX, LOUIS XV. mantel clock (Musée des Arts Decoratifs Paris).

ARTHAUD, LOUIS à *Lyon*; silver alarum watch, nicely pierced case, Schloss collection, about 1650. Born 1612, died 1662.

ARTHAULT, JACQUES ANDRÉ. *Paris*. Master 1756–89.

ARTHUR, WILLIAM. Apprenticed in 1669 to Nich. Coxeter; C.C. 1676; watch, 'Arthur à Paris', about 1720.

ARTUS, CLAUDE. *Paris*. Boule mantel clock early 18th century, Musée Carnavalet.

ARTUS, JEAN. *Paris*. Master 1757–89. "Un des plus renommés, est des plus à la mode pour les montres à répétition." Watch M.M.A.

ARWEN, WM. *Huddersfield*, about 1770.

ARZT, JOHANN MARTIN. *Munich*. Court C. 1752. Town C. 'Mechanicus' to the Bayerische Akad. der Wiss. 1773. Went to *Vienna* 1793. Died 1800. Very famous maker of automatic clocks.

ASBERG, G. J. *Söderköping*. 1820–35.

ASCOUGH, see AYSCOUGH.

ASH, —. Subscribed £2 for incorporation of C.C. 1630.

ASH, LAWRENCE. *Philadelphia*. 1762. Clocks and Watches.

ASH, RALPH. C.C. 1648.

ASH, ROBERT. *London (Cheapside)*. C.C. 1820–25.

ASHBOURNE, LEONARD. At the Sugar Loaf in *Paternoster Row*, next *Cheapside*. Inventor and maker of a clock lamp, 1731.

ASHBROOKE, JNO. Apprenticed to Zach. Mountford in 1686; C.C.

ASHBROOKE, THOS. Apprenticed to Cuthbert Lee in 1685; C.C.

ASHBY, JAMES. *Boston, U.S.A.* 1769.

ASHBY, JOSEPH. Apprenticed in 1663 to Matthew Crockford; C.C. 1674; Edmond Addison was apprenticed to him in 1678.

ASHENHEIM, JACOB. *Edinburgh*. 1818–38.

ASHFORD, RICHARD HENRY. *London*. Apprenticed 1820, C.C. 1827.

ASHLEY, CHAS. *London*. Watch, 1767.

ASHLEY, JAMES. *London*. Apprenticed 1755, C.C. 1763.

ASHLEY, JAS. Apprenticed in 1647 to Robert Smith, C.C.

ASHLEY, JNO. English watch, 1780.

ASHLEY, J. P. *99 Baches Row, City Rd.*, 1800.

ASHLEY & MANSER. *34 Rosoman St., Clerkenwell*, 1825–35, afterwards at *15 Garnault Place*.

ASHMAN, —. *462 Strand*, 1822.

ASHTON, JNO. Apprenticed in 1672 to Jno. Savile, C.C.

ASHTON, MILES. Apprenticed in 1663 to Benj. Wolverstone, C.C.

ASHTON, THOMAS. *London*. 1654 C.C.

ASHTON, THOS. Apprenticed 1687 to Thos. Bradford, C.C. Long-case clock, about 1710.

ASHTON, THOS. *Macclesfield*, 1760.

ASHTON, THOS. *Leek*, 1790.

ASHURST, JAMES. *Chorley*. Watch, 1777, died 1793.

ASHURST, WILLIAM. C.C. 1699.

ASHWELL, NICHOLAS. Apprenticed in 1640 to Robt. Grinkin; C.C. 1649.

ASKE, HENRY. Apprenticed in 1669 to Edward Norris; C.C. 1676; George Graham was apprenticed to him in 1688; 1676–96.

ASKELL, ELIZABETH. Apprenticed in 1734 to Elinor Mosely.

ASKWITH, JNO. *York*, f. 1740.

ASPINALL, HY. *Liverpool*, 1790–96.

ASPINALL, J. *Leicester*. Brass lantern clock about 1720.

ASPINWALL, JOHN. *Liverpool*. Long-case clock, about 1750.

ASPINWALL, JOSIAH. Brother C.C. 1675.

ASPINWALL, ROBERT. *Liverpool*. 1807–24 C.C. Watch.

ASPINWALL, SAMUEL. Clock-watch about 1655.

ASPINWALL, THOMAS. Small oval watch, about 1605.

ASPREY, WM. *4 Bruton St.*, 1820.

ASSELIN, FRANCIS (French), C.C. 1687. Bracket clock, case covered with tortoise-shell on a red ground, about 1690.

ASSELIN, STEPHEN. *London*. About 1700. Bracket clock Ilbert coll. Watch; another somewhat similar clock, inscribed 'Stephen Asselin'.

ASTLEY, ED. *Liverpool*, 1833.

ASTRÖM, NILS. *Hälsingborg*. Born 1784, died 1852.

ASTWOOD, JOSEPH. Apprenticed in 1659 to Ben. Bell, C.C

ATCHISON, ROBERT. Apprenticed to Robert Harding, 1753; C.C. 1760; 1760–1819.

ATFIELD, JAMES. *Brentford*, 1712.

ATHAUD, LOUIS à *Lyon*. Mid-seventeenth-century watch, V. & A., silver case pierced and engraved.

ATHERN, JNO. *Liverpool*. Long-case clock; above dial motto, "Time shows the way of life's decay", about 1780 (?).

ATHERTON, NATHAN, jun. *Philadelphia*. 1825. Watch.

ATIS, LEONARD. *London*. Lantern clock, about 1660.

ATKIN, ROBT. *Liverpool*, 1818. Also FRANCIS, same date.

ATKINS, —. *Eastbourne*. End eighteenth century. C.C.

ATKINS, FRANCIS. *35 Clement's Lane*; born 1730; apprenticed to Joshua Hassel 1746; C.C. 1759, master 1780; clerk 1785; died 1809.

ATKINS, GEORGE. Son of Francis, born 1767; *35 Clement's Lane*; warden C.C. 1809, afterwards clerk; died 1855.

ATKINS, IRENEUS. *Bristol, U.S.A.* 1830. Clock.

ATKINS, JONATHAN. Apprenticed in 1689 to Sam. Clay, C.C.

ATKINS, JOSEPH. Apprenticed to Robt. Fowler, 1654; C.C.

ATKINS, JOSHUA. *Chipping Norton*. Late eighteenth century. C.C.

ATKINS, ROBERT. *20 Salisbury St., Strand*, 1770–88; *Snow Hill*, 1800.

ATKINS, SAMUEL. *London (Temple Bar)*. Born 1697, died 1768. 'Eminent' clock and watches.

ATKINS, SAMUEL. *Palgrave Court, Temple Bar*, 1752–65.

ATKINS, SAMUEL, & SON. *Palgrave Court, Temple Bar*, 1759–63.

ATKINS W. *7 Upper Ashby St., Clerkenwell*, 1820.

ATKINS, W. *3 High St., Hoxton*, 1835.

ATKINS, WILLIAM. *71 High St., Poplar*, 1835–42.

ATKINS, WM. *Chipping-Norton*, 1780.

ATKINSON, JAMES. C.C. 1667, assistant 1697.

ATKINSON, JOSEPH. *London*. 1687 C.C.

ATKINSON, JOSEPH. *Gateshead*, 1770–90.

ATKINSON, MARY. *Baltimore, U.S.A.* 1802–07. Watches and Clocks.

ATKINSON, M. & A. *Baltimore, U.S.A.* 1804.

ATKINSON, RICHARD, 1785 f.

ATKINSON, THOMAS. *Lancaster,* 1767 f.

ATKINSON, WM. 1817 f.

ATLEE, HENRY. Apprenticed in 1662 to Charles Rogers; C.C. 1671.

ATLEE, ROGER. Apprenticed in 1664 to Job Betts, C.C.

ATMORE, —. *London.* 1735. Watch.

ATTEMSTETTER, DAVID. *Augsburg.* A celebrated enameller, died 1617.

ATTWELL, ROBT. *Brown's Lane, Spitalfields,* 1810–18.

ATTWELL, THOS. *London.* Clock, about 1750. —, near the Court House, Romford; watch paper, C.C., about 1790.

ATTWELL, WM. *11 Pitfield St.,* 1815–25.

ATTWOOD, GEO. Born 1746, died 1807; an eminent mathematician; studied watch work, and reported to Parliament on Mudge's timekeeper, 1793.

ATWOOD, GEO. *17 Leonard St., Shoreditch,* 1805–21.

ATWOOD, W. *Lewes.* Watch, 1774.

AUBER, DANIEL. *Whitefriars,* 1750.

AUBERT, DENIS. *Blois.* Master 1662–1703.

AUBERT, ESTIENNE. *Lyons.* 1661. Settled in *Paris* 1667 master 1685.

AUBERT, JEAN JACQUES. *Paris.* 1737. 'Horloger du Roi.' l'aîné. *Paris.* 1789–1824. Mantel clock, Mobilier National, Paris. Fine. cal. and centre seconds clock, Pal. de Fontainebleau.

AUCH, JAKOB. *Seeberg.* Born 1765. *Weimar,* 1798, died 1842. Court C. Published two books on horology. Large gold astronomical watch Schloss M. Berlin. Lever watch Furt. M.

AUDEBERT, —. *Paris (Rue Montagne Ste Geneviève).* 1807–25. See AUDIBERT.

AUDEBERT, D. *Amsterdam.* Long-case clock, about 1720.

AUDEMARS, BENJAMIN LOUIS. *La Vallée, Switzerland.* 1782–1840.

AUDIAUX, THOMAS. *Paris.* Juré 1752.

AUDIBERT, JEAN PIERRE. *Paris (Rue du Petit-Pont).* Master 1756–89. See AUDEBERT.

AUDIERNE, JEAN LOUIS. *Paris.* Master 1787–1813.

AUDLEY, JOS. Apprenticed to Thos. Tompion in 1683.

AUGHTON, R. *London.* Bracket clock, about 1720.

AUGIER, JEHAN. *Paris.* Maker of large watches, about 1650.

AULD. See REID & AULD.

AULD, WILLIAM. *Edinburgh.* 1795–1823. *v.* REID & AULD.

AULT, THOMAS. *34 Prince's St., Leicester Sq.,* 1820–25.

AUSENDER, GRENADS. *London.* C.C. 1812–17.

AUSSIN, —. French cruciform watch, Wallace collection, about 1650.

AUSTEN, —. *Cork.* 1740–60. Made three-wheel clock.

AUSTEN, AARON. *Bristol.* 1775–97.

AUSTEN, HENRY. *London.* Apprenticed 1700–20 C.C.

AUSTEN, JOHN. *Shoreditch.* C.C. 1711; bracket clock with square dial, pull-chime, black bell-top case, 1711 25.

AUSTEN, JOHN. *London.* C.C. 1712–25.

AUSTEN, RICHARD. *London.* C.C. 1769–1817.

AUSTEN, RICHARD, son of Richard. *London.* C.C. 1817.

AUSTIN, ISAAC. *Philadelphia,* 1785–1805.

AUSTIN & Co. *176 Oxford St.,* 1820.

AUTRAY, FRANÇOIS. *Paris,* 1737–50.

AVARD, JOSEPH. *Guernsey,* 1780.

AUZIÈRE, GEORGES. *Geneva,* 1770. *Ferney,* about 1790. *Besançon,* 1795. Died 1799. In 1795 was given a concession to start a factory at Besançon, which failed.

AUZIÈRE, JACQUES. *Geneva.* About 1770–89.

AVELINE, DANIEL. '7 Dials'; 1750–71.

AVELINE, RICHARD. *London.* l.C.C. 1766.

AVENALL (or AVENELL). A family well known as clock-makers in Hampshire for two centuries, 1640 onwards.

AVENALL (or AVENELL), EDWD. Apprenticed to Joseph Duke; C.C. 1706; bracket chiming clock, 'Avenell, London', about 1710.

AVENALL (or AVENELL), JNO, son of Edwd. C.C. 1735.

AVENALL (or AVENELL), RALPH. *Farnham.* Balance escapement clock, about 1640.

AVENALL (or AVENELL), THOMAS. *London.* 1700–10. C.C. 1705.

AVERY, —. *Boston, U.S.A.* 1726. Maker of clock in old North Church.

AVERY, AMOS. *Cheapside,* 1774.

AVERY, ANDREW. *London (Paul's Alley).* Apprenticed 1760, C.C. 1777–88.

AVERY, JOHN. *Preston, U.S.A.* 1732–94.

AVERY, JOSEPH, son. *London.* Apprenticed 1804, C.C. 1811.

AVERY, PHILIP. *Red Cross Sq.,* 1790–94.

AVICE, —. *Reims.* Watch, about 1723.

AXEBOROUGH, —. *Otley,* 1730.

AYERES, RICHARD. *London.* C.C. 1680.

AYLOSSE, ELIZABETH. Apprenticed in 1678 to Joane Wythe (widow), C.C.

AYLWARD JNO. *Guildford.* Lantern clock about 1695. Another about 1710 inscribed 'John Aylward, Braintford'.

AYMES. See AMES.

AYNSWORTH, J. *Westminster.* Maker of Lantern clocks 1645–80.

AYRES, BENNETT. *160 Fenchurch St.,* 1815–20.

AYRES, RICHARD. Apprenticed in 1670 to Hy. Jones; C.C. 1680.

AYRES, SAMUEL. Apprenticed in 1664 to Edwd. Norris, C.C.

AZEMARD, JACQUES. *Geneva.* About 1770–91. Watch.

BACCUET, —. Watch enamelled, painting, 'Roman Piety', on back, about 1690.

BACHAN, HENRY. *London.* Long-case clock, about 1770.

BACHELDER, EZRA. *Denvers, U.S.A.,* 1793–1840.

BACHHOFEN, HANS KONRAD. *Zürich.* Second half seventeenth century. Noted maker of pendulum clocks.

BACHMAN, JOHN. *Bachmanville, Lancaster, U.S.A.* Born 1798. Long-case casemaker; put his own name on clocks.

BACKHOUSE, JAMES. *Lancaster* 1726, died 1747. Watch.

BÄCKMAN, FREDRIK. *Göteborg.* Born 1754, died 1818. Bracket clock and watch.

BÄCKVALL, PAUL ERIC. *Stockholm.* 1810–35. Long-case clock and watch.

BACON, CHARLES. C.C. 1719.

BACON, JOHN. Brother C.C. 1639. —, "Paid Mr. Bacon, clockmaker, of Tewkesbury, for a clock and case, ye summe of six pounds and five shillings," 1708. ('Diary of Thos. Newnham.')

BACON, THOMAS. *Tewkesbury.* 1708–50. Watch V. & A.

BACON, THOMAS. *London.* Apprenticed 1780, C.C. 1791–1824.

BACOTT, PETER. *London,* about 1700.

BADDELEY, JOHN. *Tong.* About 1720–66, then *Albrighton* to 1780. Clocks and watches. Prob. two makers.

BADDELEY, PHINEAS. Apprenticed to Evan Jones 1652; C.C. 1661; long-case clock, signed 'Baddeley, Tong', about 1720; long-case clock, dead beat escapement, about 1750, signed 'Jno. Baddeley, Tong'.

BADGER, HY. Apprenticed 1672 to Jno. Harris, C.C.

BADGER, JOHN. Apprenticed to Brounker Watts, C.C. 1720.

BADILEY RICHARD. *London.* Long walnut-case clock, about 1730.

BADLEY, THOS. *Boston, U.S.A.*, 1712.
BADOLLET (several generations at *Geneva*).
BADOLLET, J. J. 1770.
BAFFERT à *Paris*. Clock, Jones collection, V. & A., about 1780.
BAGGS, SAMUEL. *3 South St., Grosvenor Sq.*, 1820-35.
BAGHIJN, ADRIAN VAN. *Amsterdam*. 1750. Maker of repute.
BAGLEY, THOMAS. *London*. C.C. 1658, died 1679.
BAGLEY, THOMAS. Apprenticed to Richard Morgan 1650; C.C. 1664.
BAGNALL, BENJ. *Boston, Mass*, about 1700.
BAGNALL, BENJ. *Charleston, U.S.A.*, 1740-60.
BAGNALL, BENJAMIN. *Philadelphia*. 1749-53. Watch.
BAGNALL, BENJAMIN. *Boston, U.S.A.* 1770-about 1800.
BAGNALL, JOHN. *Dudley*. 1762-91. Clocks and Watches. Also BAGNELL.
BAGNALL, SAMUEL, son of Benj. (1). *Charleston* and *Boston, U.S.A.* 1740-60. Long-case clock M.M.A.
BAGNALL, WILLIAM. *Boston, U.S.A.* Early eighteenth century. 8-day clocks.
BAGNELL, HENRY. *London* ((Bell Lane). Died 1783. C.C watch.
BAGNELL, HENRY, son. *London* (*Windsor St.* and *Bishopsgate St.*). Apprenticed 1783, C.C. 1795, l.C.C. 1802-17.
BAGNELL, HENRY, son. *London*. Apprenticed 1810.
BAGNELL, WILLIAM. C.C. 1719.
BAGSHAW, EDWD. Apprenticed in 1681 to Thos. Wheeler; C.C. 1691.
BAGSHAW, HY. *London*. Watch, 1820.
BAGSHAW, WILLIAM. C.C. 1722.
BAGWELL, RICHARD. *3 Queen St., Cheapside*, 1790-94.
BAILEY, CATHERINE. Watch-case maker, *22 Clerkenwell Green*, 1790-94.
BAILEY, CHAS. *London*, about 1805.
BAILEY, ED. *13 Oxford St.*, 1730.
BAILEY, JEFFERY. "At yͤ Turn Style in Holburn"; C.C. 1648, master 1674; maker of lantern clocks.
BAILEY, JEREMIAH. C.C. 1724.
BAILEY, JNO. *London*. Bracket clock, about 1730.
BAILEY, JNO. *Hanover, U.S.A.*, 1770-1815.
BAILEY, JNO. *London*. Watch in case of gilt metal decorated with machine engraving, about 1780 V. & A.; another watch, h.m., 1812.
BAILEY, JOHN. *Boston, U.S.A.* 1803-16. Watch.
BAILEY, WILLIAM. *Philadelphia*, 1820. Watches and clocks.
BAILLON, ALBERT. *Paris*. Watch, about 1695.
BAILLON, ESTIENNE. *Paris*. Watch, about 1750.
BAILLON, JEAN. *Rouen*. Master 1659, juré 1663-72.
BAILLON, JEAN BAPTISTE. *Paris*. Horloger de la Reine Marie Leczinska, 1751, later on horloger de la Reine Marie Antoinette; he did a large trade and was reputed to be the richest watchmaker in Europe; enamelled watch, V. & A., inscribed "J. B. Baillon, horlog. du Roy".
BAILLY. *Paris*. An eminent maker, 1750-75; clock on elephant's back, about 1760.
BAILLY, FILS, à *Paris*, about 1780. Watch, 'Bailly Paris', 1790.
BAIN, ALEXANDER, *Edinburgh*. Inventor of electric clocks, 1838-58.
BAINBRIDGE, GEORGE. *Dublin*. 1766-95. Watch.
BAINS, JNO. *Snaith*, 1770.
BAIRD, JOHN. *190 Strand*, 1770-83.
BAIRD, W. & J. *4 Hatton Garden*, 1810-30.
BAITSON, THOS. *Beverley*, 1822.
BAKER, —. *Hull*, 1760.
BAKER, BENJAMIN F. *Philadelphia*. 1825.

BAKER, BENJAMIN H. *Philadelphia*. 1824. Watch.
BAKER, EDWARD. *33 White Lion St.*, 1785-1805, afterwards at *Angel Terrace, Pentonville*. Duplex Watch, G.M., h.m., 1787.
BAKER, GEORGE. *Providence, U.S.A.* 1824.
BAKER, HENRY. *Town Malling*. Before 1768-84. Watch.
BAKER, HY. Hon. freeman C.C. 1781.
BAKER, JOHN. *5 King St., Covent Garden*; hon. freeman C.C. 1781; 1768-84.
BAKER, JOHN. *London* (*Rotherhithe Wall*). Apprenticed 1806, C.C. 1813.
BAKER, POINTER. *London*. Repeating watch, h.m., 1772.
BAKER, RICHARD. Brother C.C. 1685; pull quarter repeating bracket clock, Wetherfield collection, square ebony case, brass basket top, about 1680; 8-day clock, ebony marquetry case, square dial, cherub corners, no door to hood; also a similar clock in oak case, fine hands, 1685-1710. "A silver Minute Pendulum watch with a silver outcase and a coat-of-arms engraven on it (a Lyon Passant with three Cross Croslets, made by Richard Baker, London), lost in Dunghil Fields nigh Whitechapel Church" (*Lond. Gaz.*, March 3-6, 1689). "A silver watch with a shagreen case, with G. M. on it, and with Baker on the Dyal Plate" (*Lond. Gaz.*, April 15-18, 1685).
BAKER, RICHARD. C.C. 1726.
BAKER, THOS. *Gosport*. Watch, about 1740.
BAKER, WILLIAM. *London*. C.C. 1779. Watch.
BAKEWELL, —. Lantern clock, about 1700, inscribed 'Thomas Bakewell, on Tower Hill, fecit'.
BALCH, CHAS. H. 1787-1808.
BALCH, DANIEL. *Newburyport U.S.A.*, 1760-90.
BALCH, DANIEL, son. *Newburyport*. 1782-1818.
BALCH, THOS. H. Died 1819.
BALDWEIN, of *Marburg*. Active, 1563-8.
BALDWIN, ANTHONY. *Lancaster, U.S.A.*, 1810-30.
BALDWIN, CHRIS. Apprenticed 1656 to Jno. Freeman, C.C.
BALDWIN, GEO. *Sadsburyville*, 1808-32.
BALDWIN, HENRY SMITH. *London*. Apprenticed 1778, C.C. 1785.
BALDWIN, J. *Andover*, 1760.
BALDWIN, JABEZ. *Boston, U.S.A.* 1812.
BALDWIN, JEDEDIAH. *Hanover, U.S.A.* 1780.
BALDWIN, JNO. Apprenticed 1691 to Stephen Rayner, C.C.
BALDWIN, ROBT. Apprenticed 1682 to Thos. Virgoe, C.C.
BALDWIN, THOS. Apprenticed 1672 to Jno. Benson; C.C. 1685.
BALDWIN & JONES. *Boston, U.S.A.* 1812.
BALDWYN, THOMAS. C.C. 1706.
BALE, THOMAS. *London*. C.C. 1704.
BALE, THOMAS. C.C. 1724.
BALFOUR, JOSEPH. *London*. Apprenticed 1753, C.C. 1761.
BALL, EDWD. *32 Ironmonger Row*, 1794.
BALL, JNO. *Newport Pagnell*, 1760.
BALL, JOHN. C.C. 1637; fine long lacquer-case calendar clock about 1760, signed 'Wm. Ball, Biceter'.
BALL, SAM. *High-Wycombe*, 1786.
BALL, THOMAS. *London*. Apprenticed 1711, C.C. 1724.
BALL, VICTOR. 1630-50.
BALLANTYNE, WILLIAM. *Edinburgh*. 1778-1806.
BALLANTYNE, WM. *6 Cable St.*, 1815-20; *2 White Lion St., Goodman's Fields*, 1835; 1820-42.
BALLARD, JOHN. *London*. C.C. 1768.
BALLARD, WILLIAM. *London*. Apprenticed 1707, C.C. 1736.
BALLARD, WILLIAM, son of William. *London*. C.C. 1792. (*Fetter Lane*) 1799; (*Holborn*) 1808.

BALLARD, WILLIAM. *London.* C.C. 1813.

BALMER, THOS. *Liverpool*, 1833.

BALTAZAR, CADET (the younger), *Place Dauphine, Paris,* 1769; "clockmaker to Mesdames filles de Louis XV."

BALTAZAR, CHAS. *Paris.* About 1710.

BALTAZAR, LOUIS CHARLES. *Paris (Rue du Boule).* Master 1763–89.

BALTAZAR, MICHEL ANTOINE. *Paris.* Master 1744–69.

BALTAZAR, NOEL. *Paris.* About 1770.

BALTEAU à *Lyon.* Cruciform watch, Pierpont Morgan collection, about 1610.

BAMFIELD (BANFIELD), THOMAS. *London (St. John's St.)* Apprenticed 1762, C.C. 1773.

BANBURY, JOHN. C.C. 1685.

BANCE, MATTHEW. *Kintbury.* Watch dated 1775.

BANCROFT, WM. *Scarborough*, 1822.

BANGER, EDWARD. Apprenticed to Joseph Ashby for Thomas Tompion 1687; C.C. 1695.

BANGILONER, —. *London.* Clock-watch, about 1660.

BANISTER, THOM. *Norton.* Long-case clock, about 1765.

BANKES, WILLIAM. Apprenticed 1690 to Ben. Bell; C.C. 1698; on a large lantern clock, 'Wm. Bankes in Sheffield', date about 1680.

BANKS, JOHN. *Chester*, 1682.

BANKS, JOSEPH. *Philadelphia.* 1819. Watch.

BANKS, ROBERT. *London.* Apprenticed 1732, C.C. 1750–53.

BANKS, S. & W. *Leicester.* Chiming clock, about 1760.

BANNISTER, ANTHONY. C.C. 1715; watch with sun and moon indicator, signed 'Anthony Bannister', on dial 'Bannister, Liverpool', about 1705.

BANNISTER, JAMES. *14 Clerkenwell Close,* 1820–35; *32 Prince's St., Leicester Sq.,* 1810–42.

BANNISTER, THOMAS. *London,* about 1801.

BANNISTER, THOMAS & JAMES. *39 Kirby St., Hatton Garden,* 1825.

BANNISTER, WILLIAM. *Liverpool.* 1734–54. C. Also BANISTER.

BANSTEIN, JOHN. *Philadelphia*, 1791.

BANTING, WILLIAM. C.C. 1646.

BARACHIN, STEPHEN (French). C.C. 1687.

BARANCOURT, PIERRE MICHEL. *Paris.* Master 1779, juré 1783–89. Vase clock.

BARAT, PHILIPPE. *Paris.* Juré 1764.

BARBE, JOSEPH. *Paris.* 1777 master–1810.

BARBER, —. *Lincoln.* Wall clock on Smeaton-Franklin plan, about 1770.

BARBER, BENJAMIN. *21 Red Lion St., Clerkenwell,* 1788–94.

BARBER, CHARLES. *London.* Apprenticed 1786, C.C. 1796–1804.

BARBER, JAS. *York*, f. 1814.

BARBER, JONAS. *Ratcliffe Cross.* Brother C.C. 1682.

BARBER, JONAS. *Winster, Windermere.* Died 1720; long-case clock, 'J. Barber, Winster,' about 1750; watch, 'J. Barber, Winster,' 1755.

BARBER, JOSH. *168 Borough,* 1795–1817.

BARBER, THOS. *75 Lamb's Conduit St.,* 1810–17.

BARBER, WM. *30 Cornhill,* 1785–94.

BARBER & WHITWELL. *York*, 1818.

BARBERET, JACQUES.• *Paris.* Octagonal watch, Garnier collection; cruciform watch, about 1620; splendidly enamelled watch, about 1640.

BARBIER LE JEUNE. *sur le Pont Marie, Paris,* 1770.

BARCELET, MATHIEU. *Paris*, about 1570. A square table clock, with dome over.

BARCLAY, C. *London.* Watch, 1815.

BARCLAY, HUGH *Edinburgh,* 1727.

BARCLAY, JAMES. *7 Jamaica Terrace, Commercial Rd.,* 1820; James Pyott succeeded him in 1873.

BARCLAY, JOHN. *London (Bull Yd., Fan St.).* Apprenticed 1779. C.C. 1787–96.

BARCLEY, SAMUEL. *London.* Apprenticed 1715 to Geo. Graham, C.C. 1722–51. Was Graham's foreman and executor and succeeded him, entering into partnership with Thos. Colley. 'Barclay & Colley, Graham's Successors' on a long-case clock with ingenious mechanism for perpetual calendar, about 1760. See Colley.

BARCOLE, JOHN. Admitted C.C. 1648.

BARFORD, THOS. Apprenticed 1655 to Thos. Daniell, C.C.

BARGEAU, PETER. *London.* Long Oriental lacquer-case clock, 1740.

BARIDON, J. A. *Geneva.* About 1800. Died 1844. Several fine turret clocks.

BARIDON & FILS. *Geneva.* Gained a Prize in 1823 for a curious gravity regulator, Geneva Horological School.

BARIL, BERCHER. *29 Prince's St.,* near Mansion House, 1763–72.

BARIL, LEWIS. *Tokenhouse Yard,* 1754–59.

BARIN, JOHN. Livery C.C. 1776.

BARJON, JOHN. C.C. 1685.

BARKER, B. *New York*, 1786.

BARKER, BRYAN BLAKE, son. *London.* C.C. 1806.

BARKER, DAYE. *London.* Clock, about 1720, lantern movement, 7-inch dial arched.

BARKER, JOHN. *London.* Apprenticed 1806, C.C. 1813.

BARKER, THOS. *London.* Watches, 1792–1813.

BARKER, WILLIAM. C.C. 1632.

BARKER, WILLIAM. *Boston (Howe St.),* U.S.A. 1800–13.

BARKER, WILLIAM. *Boston (Town Dock),* U.S.A. 1806–25.

BARKER, WM. *Wigan*; about 1760.

BARKHAM, GEO. 1630–50; C.C.

BARKMAN. OLOF. *Jönköping.* 1774. Died about 1802. Gold watch.

BARLOW, —. Served as steward C.C. 1677.

BARLOW, BENJ. *Ashton* and *Oldham*, 1780–85.

BARLOW, (BOOTH) EDWARD. Invented the rack striking work and a forerunner of the cylinder escapement; born 1636, died 1716.

BARLOW, GEO. *Oldham.* Long-case clock, about 1790.

BARLOW, J. H., & Co. *7 Vere St.,* 1812–20.

BARLOW, JAS. *Oldham*, 1775.

BARLOW, JNO. *Oldham.* Long-case clock, 1780.

BARLOW, THOS. C.C. 1692.

BARLOW, W. *Ashton*, 1760.

BARNARD, JNO. Apprenticed 1675 to Francis Dinnis; C.C. 1682.

BARNARD, JNO. *36 Little Sutton St.,* 1817.

BARNARD, NICH. Apprenticed 1662 to Thos. Claxton, C.C.

BARNARD, PHIL. *London.* Long japanned case clock, about 1745.

BARNARD, RALPH. Apprenticed 1778 to Jno. Cotsworth, C.C.

BARNARD, ROBERT. *London.* Apprenticed 1726, C.C. 1740.

BARNARD, THOS. *72 Strand,* 1783–1823.

BARNARD, WM. *Newark,* 1760–80.

BARNARD & KIDDER. *72 Strand,* 1809–12.

BARNARD & SAVORY. 1786–99.

BARNARDISTON, JNO. *London.* Long-case clock, 1760

BARNES, GEO. Apprenticed 1693 to Josh. Allsopp, C.C.

BARNES, JNO. *Badger Row, Red Lion St.,* 1770–94.

BARNES, RI. *Worcester.* Oval watch, V. & A., about 1600; another, Schloss collection, about 1610.

BARNES, ROBERT. *Liverpool.* 1754. Went Birmingham 1775–78. Clocks and Watches.

BARNES, THOMAS. *Lichfield, U.S.A.* 1760–90.

BARNETT, J. "The corner of Shakespeare's walk, near Shadwell Church, Ratcliff Highway." card, about 1780.

BARNETT, JOHN. "At yᵉ Peacock in Lothebury"; apprenticed 1675 to Jno. Ebsworth; C.C. 1682; long marquetry case clock, ebonised dome top, 10-inch dial, Wetherfield collection. A very fine clock signed 'John Barnett, Londini, fecit'.

BARNHILL, ROBERT. *Philadelphia.* 1777. Watch.

BARNISH, JNO. A well-known maker of *Toad Lane, Rochdale,* who probably succeeded Wm., is traced till 1816.

BARNISH, WM. *Rochdale.* Died 1776.

BARNWELL, RICHARD. *London.* Apprenticed 1698, C.C. 1712, died 1719.

BARON, EDMD. Apprenticed 1692 to Thos. Feilder, C.C.

BARONA, RAFAEL. *Madrid.* Clockmaker to King of Spain and Director of the Royal Factory.

BARONEAU, LOUYS, *Paris.* Clockmaker to the Queen, 1760.

BARONNEAU, JOSEPH. *Paris.* 1681 master, juré 1690.

BARONNEAU, LOUYS. *Paris.* 1640–64. C. to the Queen. Watch, gold filigree and another silver alloy Blot-Garnier collection. Watch movement. G.M. Fine engraved watch Ilbert collection. Fine Boulle bracket clock Pal. de Pau, Paris.

BARR, —. *Bolton;* about 1790.

BARR, THOS. *Lewes.* Lantern clock, about 1700.

BARRACLOUGH, JOHN. *Haworth,* 1750. Afterwards at Thornton.

BARRAL, ABRAHAM. *Geneva.* About 1760–77.

BARRATT, P. *Strand,* 1785; *71 Swallow St.,* 1812; *83 New Bond St.,* 1830.

BARRAUD, —. *Paris.* 1809–55. Mantel clock, bronze by Ravrio, made for Napoléon, Pal. de l'Elysée. Clock Pal. de la légion d'honneur.

BARRAUD, FRANCIS & PAUL JNO. *Wine Office Court,* 1759–94; watch, h.m. 1756.

BARRAUD, FREDK. JOSEPH. Committee of C.C. 1813.

BARRAUD, HY. Presented a spoon to C.C. 1636.

BARRAUD, JAMES, brother of John. *London.* Apprenticed 1807, C.C. 1815, l.C.C. 1824.

BARRAUD, JOHN, son of Paul P. *London.* Apprenticed 1806, C.C. 1813, l.C.C. 1814.

BARRAUD, PAUL PHILIP. *86 Cornhill;* master C.C. 1810, 1811; 1796–1813.

BARRAUD & LUND. *41 Cornhill,* 1838–42.

BARRAUD & SONS. *85 Cornhill,* 1813–36; *41 Cornhill,* 1838.

BARRET, —. In the churchwardens' book at Halifax Parish Church in 1720 is "Paid Wm. Barrett for Clock work £0 9s. 0d."

BARRETT, DANIEL. *Chatham.* About 1800 C.C.

BARRETT, HENRY. Apprenticed to Chas. Gretton; admitted C.C. 1692.

BARRETT, HENRY WILLIAM. *24 Queen St., Bloomsbury,* 1815; *25 Museum St.,* 1820; *18 Plumtree St.,* 1835–42.

BARRETT, JOHN. *47 New Compton St.,* 1820.

BARRETT, JOSEPH. *Cheapside,* 1738. Clock watch, about 1760, inscribed 'Barrett, London'.

BARRETT, ROBERT, C.C. 1687.

BARRETT, SAMUEL. C.C. 1701.

BARRETT, SIMON. Apprenticed 1668 to Joseph Wells; C.C. 1678.

BARRETT, THOMAS. C.C. 1702.

BARRETT, THOS. *Lewes.* Known as a maker of lantern clocks; in 1690 he agreed to mend the town clock for twenty shillings. "Also hee to have four pounds yearly for ringing 'Gabriel' the Curfew Bell at four in the morning and eight at night."

BARRETT, THOS. *Canterbury,* 1700.

BARRIDGE, JNO. Apprenticed 1654 to Hugh Cooper, C.C.

BARRINGTON, URIAN. Apprenticed 1677 to Nat. Delander; C.C. 1684.

BARRON, JOHN. *Aberdeen.* Born 1765, died 1852. Watch.

BARROW, JAMES. See BROWN, ANDREW.

BARROW, JOHN. Apprenticed 1671 to Francis Ireland; C.C. 1681, master 1714.

BARROW, JOHN. *London.* C.C. 1704.

BARROW, NATHANIEL. Apprenticed to Job Betts 1653; C.C. 1660, master 1689; in the Guildhall Museum are an astronomical watch and a repeater by him; "A large silver chain watch, having two motions, the hour of the day, and the day of the month, with a black case studded with silver, lined with red sattin, and a silver chain to it, made by *Nathaniel Barrow,* in *London*" (*Lond. Gaz.,* July 26–30, 1677).

BARROW, SAMUEL. Apprenticed to Jno. Barrow 1688; C.C. 1696; "at the Spring Clock in East Smithfield, near Hermitage Bridge" (see Gatewood); 8-day long marquetry case clock, 'Samuel Barrow at the Hermitage', about 1705.

BARROW, SAMUEL. *Philadelphia.* From 1771. Previously in *London.* Said he worked for John Harrison.

BARROW, WILLIAM. Admitted C.C. 1709; Hatton, 1773, highly esteems the work of a watchmaker, named Barrow.

BARROW, WILLIAM JOHN. *London,* 1700 C.C.

BARROW, WM. *Lancashire.* Came to London before 1744; left London soon after 1746 (Ludlam).

BARRY, STANDISK. *Baltimore, U.S.A.* 1784–1804. Watch. v. JOSEPH RICE.

BARRY, WALLER, *Still Yard, Tower,* 1788–94.

BARTHOLOMEW, E. & G. *Bristol, U.S.A.* About 1820.

BARTHOLOMEW, JNO. C.C. 1675.

BARTHOLOMEW, JOSIAH. *25 Red Lion St., Clerkenwell.* Watch, B.M. He was a witness before the select committee of the House of Commons to inquire into the causes of the depressed state of the watch trade in 1817; 1800–42.

BARTHOP, —. *Isleworth.* Long-case clock, about 1780.

BARTLIFF, GEO. *York,* 1801. *Malton,* 1810.

BARTLIFF, ROBT. *Malton,* 1823.

BARTON, —. *Wainfleet.* About 1790 CC.

BARTON, JAMES. *London.* 1771. Son-in-law of John Harrison. Watch with engraved portrait of Harrison, Webster collection illuminated Baillie.

BARTON, JAMES. *194 Strand,* 1819–23.

BARTON, JAS. *Whitehaven.* Watch, 1751, Rochdale Museum.

BARTON, JOHN. *64 Red Lion St., Clerkenwell,* 1780–83.

BARTON, JOS. *Eccleston.* Long-case clock, about 1760.

BARTON, MATHIAS. *London.* About 1797, C.C. 1804.

BARTON, SAMUEL. Brother C.C. 1641.

BARTON, T. & J. *Market Pl., Manchester.* Watch, h.m., 1770.

BARTON, THOMAS. *Cheapside,* 1750–78; Earnshaw challenged him to a contest of work in 1776.

BARTON, THOMAS. *Manchester.* 1755, died 1791. In 1782 sold his business to RUNCORN. Watch.

BARTON, THOS. *7 Bermondsey Sq.,* 1799–1823; Thos. Mudge, jun., refers to Thos. Barton as 'eminently skilled'.

BARTON, WM. *London.* Large watch with Turkish numerals, on dial 'Markwick Markham, Wm. Carpenter', about 1780.

BARTRAM, SIMON. Petitioner for incorporation of C.C. and one of the first assistants, master 1646.

BARTRAM, WILLIAM. C.C.; 1684.

BARTRAM & AUSTIN. *109, 103 Oxford St.*; card, B.M., 1808.

BARTRAND. See BERTRAND.

BARTS, GEO. FRED. *Neards Court*, near *Soho Sq.*, 1775.

BARUGH, WILLIAM. C.C. 1715.

BARWELL, BARTHOLOMEW. *New York*. 1749–60. From Bath. Clock.

BARWELL, RICHARD. *London*. C.C. 1705. Watch.

BARWELL, WM. *Bath*. Bracket clock, about 1700; month long-case clocks, about 1720.

BARWICK, A. *Great Alie St.*, 1788–93.

BARWICK, H. & B. *35 Wapping*, 1794–96.

BARWICK, JAMES. *London*. Apprenticed 1790, C.C. 1798–1809.

BARWISE, JOHN. *29 St. Martin's Lane*, 1790; Weston & Jno., 1820–42; in 1841 John Barwise was associated with Alex. Bain in a patent for electric clocks, and in 1842–43 chairman of directors of the ill-fated British Watch Company.

BARWISE, LETT. *Cockermouth*, 1770.

BARWISE, NATHANAEL. *London*. Clock-watch, 1770.

BARWISE & SONS. *24 St. Martin's Lane*, 1819–23.

BASH, JAMES. *London*. C.C. 1729.

BASIL, JOHN. *76 St. Paul's Churchyard*, 1768.

BASIRE, JOHN. *London*. Apprenticed 1748, C.C. 1756, I.C.C. 1766–86.

BASKERVILLE, RICHARD. *London*. Clock in the sacristy of Bruges Cathedral, about 1750.

BASKERVILLE, THOS. *Bond St. Stables*, 1730.

BASNETT, WM. *1 Bond St.*, *Bath*, 1798.

BASS, GEORGE. Admitted C.C. 1722.

BASSEREAU, GUI. *Palais Royale, Paris*, 1780.

BASSET, CHAS. *58 Upper East Smithfield*, 1788–93; clock, Wm. Bassett, Mayfield, about 1790.

BASSET, GEO. FRANCIS. *Philadelphia*, 1797.

BASSET, JEAN, JACQUES, LOUIS. *York*, f., 1771.

BASSET, JOHN FRANCIS. *Philadelphia*. 1798. Watch.

BASSET, THOS. Apprenticed 1668 to Isaac Webb, C.C.

BASSETT, N. B. *Albany, U.S.A.* 1813.

BASSOT, —. *Paris*. 1750–1825. Clock ministère de la Guerre, Paris. Gold engraved cylinder watch.

BAST, T. *London*. Early eighteenth century–1756. Watches Huddersfield M. and Denham collection.

BATARD, JEAN ANDRÉ. *Geneva*. About 1770–91.

BATEMAN, —. Seventeenth-century oval watch, mentioned in vol. xxiii, *Archaeological Journal*. Nathaniel Bateman said to have worked for Delander in 1730.

BATEMAN, ANDREW. *5 Great Tower St.*, 1804–20.

BATEMAN, HY. *10 Bunhill Row*, 1780–85.

BATEMAN, NATHANIEL. Apprenticed to Nathaniel Delander; C.C. 1747–50.

BATEMAN, P. & A. *10 Bunhill Row*, 1798–1818.

BATEMAN, TERESA. *5 Great Tower St.*, 1820–30.

BATEMAN, WM. *108 Bunhill Row*, 1828–32.

BATES, ED. *London*. A good workman mentioned by Earnshaw, 1780–90.

BATES, JOHN. *Kettering*. 1768–1800 C.C. Watch.

BATES, JOSEPH. *White Alley, Holborn*. Admitted C.C. 1687.

BATES, T. P. *Liverpool*, 1780. Issued a token "works, Duke St., Retail, Exchange St."

BATES, THOMAS. C.C. 1684.

BATES, THOMAS. *Market Harboro'*. From 1783–about 1800 C.C. Watch.

BATESON, JOHN. *Boston, U.S.A.* 1720. Died 1727.

BATH, JAS. *Cirencester*. Clock, about 1775.

BATH, THOMAS. *London*. Apprenticed 1749, C.C. 1757–84. Watch.

BATT, WM. *Petersfield*, 1790.

BATTEN, EDWD. Apprenticed 1670 to Jno. Mark; C.C. 1677.

BATTEN, JOHN. Brother C.C. 1668.

BATTERSBEE, —. *Manchester*, 1770.

BATTERSON, HENRY. C.C. 1701.

BATTERSON, JAMES. *New York*, f., 1708–9; also at Boston, 'lately arrived from London'.

BATTERSON, R. Clock, long-case, lacquer decoration, about 1770.

BATTERSON, ROBERT. C.C. 1693.

BATTIE, JAS. *Sheffield*, 1770.

BATTIN, THOMAS. Apprenticed 1654 to Ed. Ward; C.C. 1661; a contrate second wheel of a 'dyal' taken from him, and judged by C.C. to be bad, 1658.

BATTINSON, JNO. *Burnley*, 1818.

BATTY, ANTHONY. *Wakefield*, 1750.

BATTY, EDWD. *Lancaster*, 1826, f.

BATTY, JNO. *Halifax*. Long-case clock, 1760.

BATTY, JNO. *Moorfields*, 1775.

BATTY, JNO. *Wakefield*. 1770.

BATTY, JOSEPH. *Halifax*. 1760–70.

BAUDET. *Paris*. Early nineteenth century gold enamel watch.

BAUDIN, —. *Paris (Rue des Petits Carreaux)*. 1807–25.

BAUDIT, PETER. *4 St. Martin's Lane*, 1790–94.

BAUDOIN, NICOLAS. *Paris*. 1675. Juré.

BAUER, CARL. *Amsterdam*. Cruciform watch, about 1650.

BAUFAY, B., & SON. *3 Bridgewater Sq.*, 1790–94.

BAUGH, VALENTINE. *Abingdon, U.S.A.*, 1820–30.

BAUGHAM, JOHN. *Bridgewater Sq.*, about 1745.

BAULDWIN. See BALDWIN.

BAUMANN, JOHANN JACOB, son of J. M. *Augsburg*. Comp. 1767, master about 1770–99.

BAUMANN, JOHANN MICHAEL. *Burgau*. About 1750–76.

BAUNE, GEORGE. *Bristol*. 1758. Died 1787. Watch.

BAUSSE, —. *Paris*. 1807–24.

BAUTE & MOYNIER. *Geneva*. Watch, about 1823.

BAUTTE, J. F. *Geneva*, 1820–25.

BAVIS, GEO. C.C. 1687.

BAWDYSON, ALLAINE. Clockmaker to Edward VI, 1550.

BAXTER, CHARLES. C.C. 1681.

BAXTER, MATT. *St. Neots*. Watch, 1723.

BAXTER, POINTER. *London*, 1772.

BAXTER, THOS. *Conderton*. Long-case clock, about 1790.

BAXTER, WM. C.C. about 1640.

BAXTER, WM. *London*. Watch, 1790.

BAYER, MARTIN. *Annaberg*. Juré 1605.

BAYES, BENJAMIN. Apprenticed to Jno Bayes 1661; C.C. 1675.

BAYES, JOHN. Brother C.C. 1647, warden 1658; maker of a watch given by Charles I to Mr. Worsley on his removal to Hirst Castle, November 1647; another example, a lantern clock, inscribed 'Johannes Bayes, Londini', date on fret 1643; watch, V. & A.

BAYFORD, GEORGE. *Upper Shadwell*.

BAYLE, THOMAS. C.C. 1703.

BAYLES, CHAS. *London*. Bracket clock, about 1760.

BAYLEY, BARNARD & SON. *3 Bridgewater Sq.*, 1800–05.

BAYLEY, BARNARD, son. *London*. Apprenticed 1777, C.C. 1784–95. Watches Ilbert collection.

BAYLEY, EDWARD. C.C. 1658. "A silver watch with a silver studded case engraven Edwardus Bayley, London" (*Lond. Gaz.*, December 19–22, 1687).

BAYLEY, EDWARD BRANSTON. *London*. Apprenticed 1728, C.C. 1738–65.

BAYLEY, GEO. *London*. Watch, 1750.

BAYLEY, JAMES. *London*. Apprenticed 1760, C.C. 1768.

BAYLEY, JNO. *Harrow*, 1725.

BAYLEY, JOHN. *Hanover, U.S.A.* 1770–1815.

BAYLEY, JOSIAH. *London.* Apprenticed 1770, C.C. 1778.

BAYLEY, RICHARD. *Cork.* About 1790 C.C.–1824.

BAYLEY, RICHARD. *12 Red Lion St., Clerkenwell,* 1807.

BAYLEY, SIMEON C. *Philadelphia,* 1794.

BAYLEY, THOMAS. Summoned to take up livery C.C. 1786.

BAYLEY, WILLIAM. Apprenticed 1654 to Ralph Ash; C.C. 1663.

BAYLEY & UPJOHN. *Red Lion St., Clerkenwell,* 1794.

BAYLIE. See BAILEY.

BAYLIS, J. *Tewkesbury.* Lantern clock, about 1700.

BAYLIS, WM. *Bristol,* 1842.

BAYLY, JOHN. C.C. 1700.

BAYLY, RICHARD. *Ashford.* Watch, 1770.

BAYSE, THOMAS. C.C. 1695.

BAZELEY, NATHANIEL. C.C. 1694.

BAZIN. *Paris.* About 1700.

BEACH, THOMAS. *Maiden Lane, Covent Garden,* 1765–70.

BEADLE, WM. Apprenticed 1667 to Wm. Raynes, C.C.

BEAKE, JOHN COVELL, son. *London.* Apprenticed 1745, C.C. 1752.

BEAKE, JONATHAN. *Savage Gardens,* 1725.

BEAL, MARTIN. *19 Gerrard St., Soho,* 1842.

BEALE. —. *Canton (China).* 1790–about 1810 in firm of COX & BEALE, then COX, BEALE & LAURENT, and then alone.

BEALE, CHAS. *London.* Watch, 1767.

BEALE, JAS. *38 Regent St.,* 1820–25.

BEALE, JNO. Apprenticed 1658 to Nich. Coxeter, C.C.

BEALE, JOSIAH. *Twickenham.* 1805–24. Watch.

BEALE, ROBERT. Apprenticed 1677 to Bernard Rainsford, C.C.

BEALE, WM. *London.* Watch, 1805.

BEARCOCK, JOHN. *Chatteris.* 1771–91. T.C.

BEARD, CHRIS. Apprenticed to Jas. Atkinson, 1670; C.C.

BEARD, DUNCAN. *Appoquinemonk, U.S.A.,* 1755–97.

BEARD, THOMAS. *London.* Apprenticed 1684, C.C. 1692.

BEARD, WM. Apprenticed 1667 to Jas. Ellis, C.C.

BEARD, WM. *Drury Lane,* 1812–17.

BEARE, JOHN. *Pilton,* 1780.

BEASLEY, JOHN. C.C. 1719.

BEASLEY, NAT. Apprenticed 1686 to Hy. Hammond, C.C.

BEASLEY, THOS. C.C. 1683.

'BEATSON, *32 Cornhill'*. McCabe's lowest grade full-plate watches, in silver cases, were so engraved.

BEAUCHAMP, R. *147 Holborn Hill,* 1819–23.

BEAUFORT, HENRI. *Paris.* Watch, revolutionary decimal time, about 1796.

BEAUMARCHAIS. See CARON.

BEAUMONT, —. Said to have made a clock at Caen in 1314.

BEAUMONT, JOSEPH. *Howden,* 1770.

BEAUMONT, PHILIP. Apprenticed 1689 to Wither Cheney, C.C.

BEAUPOIL, ISAC. *Amsterdam.* 1689. *Copenhagen,* 1713. Died 1737. From *Châtellerault.* Also BOPOEL and BOVEL.

BEAUVAIS, —. *Paris.* 1671.

BEAUVAIS, ANTHOINE. *Paris,* 1544.

BEAUVAIS, GUILLAUME. *Paris.* 1630–46. Sig. to Statuts of Paris corporation of 1646. Registered a private punch mark in 1630.

BEAUVAIS, PAUL. *London.* Watch, about 1730.

BEAUVAIS, SIMON. Admitted C.C. 1690; a celebrated maker; among his productions is a double-case verge, with a rack and pinion motion work, the hour hand travelling round the dial in twelve hours, but the minute hand travelling only from IX to III, in one hour, and, when arrived at the III, jumping back to the IX. The hand-setting is between III and IIII, and the centre of the dial and motion work are hidden by a small painting on ivory. There is in the B.M. a similar watch of a later period by a German maker; 1690-1730.

BEAUVARLET, JOSSE ADRIEN. *Paris.* Master 1763–89.

BEAVIN, HUGH. *34 Marylebone St., Golden Sq.,* 1800–30.

BEAVIS, JOHN. *Peartree St.,* 1789.

BECHTEL, HENRY. *Philadelphia.* 1817. Watch.

BECK, CHRISTOPHER. *Bell Alley.* Apprenticed to Francis Perigal; admitted C.C. 1761, livery 1787.

BECK, JAMES. *5 Sweeting's Alley, Cornhill,* 1815–23, see BENTLEY. Long-case clock about 1790, inscribed 'Thos. Beck, Bishampton'.

BECK, JOHN. *London.* Apprenticed 1673, C.C. 1681. Assistant to Daniel Quare. Also BECKE.

BECK, JOSEPH. C.C. 1701.

BECK, NICHOLAS. Apprenticed 1660 to Thos. Webb; C.C. 1669.

BECK, RICHARD. 'Near ye French Church,' C.C. 1653.

BECKET, FRANCIS. *Chester-le-Street,* 1770.

BECKETT, SIR E. See DENISON.

BECKETT, JNO. *23 Greenhill's Rents, Smithfield,* 1796–1803.

BECKETT, M. Long-case clock, about 1710.

BECKETT, THOMAS. *Bishop Auckland.* Born 1723, died 1803. Clocks and Watches.

BECKITT, MANN. *Durham,* 1780.

BECKITT, THOS. *Durham,* 1770.

BECKMAN, ANDERS. *Stockholm.* Comp. 1716, master 1721, died 1736.

BECKMAN, DANIEL. C.C. 1680. "A watch with a double case of Silver, with Minutes, Seconds and Hours, the name [Beckman] under the Crystal" (*Lond. Gaz.,* March 27–31, 1701).

BECKMAN, DANIEL. C.C. 1726.

BECKMAN, JOHN. C.C. 1695.

BECKNER, ABRAHAM. *Pope's Head Alley.* Admitted as a brother C.C. 1652, warden and died 1665; known as a maker of oval watches; 1650–65.

BECKWITH, WM. *Rotherhithe St.,* 1794.

BEDDEL. See BIDDLE.

BEDELL, JOSEPH. *London.* Apprenticed 1676, C.C. 1684.

BEDFORD, HELKIAH. In *Fleet St.* C.C. 1667; maker of lantern clocks; to him in 1668 was apprenticed Richard Abbott.

BEDFORD, ISAAC. *Dublin.* 1795–1824. Watch.

BEDFORD, SAM. Apprenticed 1691 to Joseph Windmills, C.C.

BEDFORD, WM. *London.* Watch, Nelthropp collection, about 1790.

BEECKMAN, JOHN. 'In the Pall Mall' basket top striking clock.

BEEFORTH, JNO. *York,* f., 1680.

BEEG, CHRISTIANA. C.C. 1698.

BEESLEY, ANN, daughter of John. *London.* C.C. 1769.

BEESLEY, JAS. *Manchester.* Long-case clock, about 1760; watch, 1787.

BEESLEY, JNO. *Dean St.,* 1725.

BEGGS, THOMAS. *Glasgow.* 1822–41.

BEGULAY, JNO. *Swanton, Norfolk.* Church clock at Ludham, 1676.

BEITELROCK, JOHANN. *Augsburg.* Master about 1736. Juré 1740–57. Watch movement.

BEITH, ROBERT. *Dublin.* 1795–1824.

BEKERS, —. *Paris.* 1807–25.

BELCHER, THOMAS. *London (Brownlow St.).* Apprenticed 1741, C.C. 1750–77.

BELHOMME, PIERRE JEAN BAPTISTE. *Paris.* Master 1755–1814.

BÉLIARD, DOMINIQUE. *Paris.* About 1700–36 master. Watch Gélis collection. Also BELLIARD.

BÉLIARD, FRANÇOIS. *Paris.* 1774. Master 1777, juré 1781–89. C. to Louis XV from 1781.

BÉLIARD, JULIEN ANTOINE (LE JEUNE), brother of P. F. *Paris.* 1779–1812. Master 1796, juré 1778.

BÉLIARD, PIERRE FRANÇOIS (l'aîné), son. *Paris.* Master 1774–89.

BELICHON, CLAUDE. *Lyons.* 1636–59.

BELK, WILLIAM. *Philadelphia.* 1796.

BELKNAP, EBENEZER. *Boston, U.S.A.* 1806–13. Watch.

BELKNAP, EBENEZER. *Boston, U.S.A.* 1818–25. C. Perhaps same as preceding.

BELKNAP, WILLIAM A. *Boston, U.S.A.* 1818. Watch.

BELL, BENJAMIN. Apprenticed to Thos. Claxton 1649; C.C. 1660, master 1682; maker of a large verge watch weighing over 8 oz. 1660–83. "Taken way by 4 Highwaymen in Maiden-head Ticket, A plain silver chain watch made by Benjamin Bell, the case lined with Red Satten, on the back of the case a Perpetual Almanack and little spikes placed at every Hour" (*Lond. Gaz.*, July 7–10, 1690).
"Lost on the 2nd inst., a gold watch with one motion, having a gold chain and a steel hook; made by Benjamin Bell. Whoever brings it to Mr. Sweetapple, a Goldsmith in Lombard Street, shall have 2 guineas reward" (*Lond. Gaz.*, May 4–7, 1691).
"Lost a silver watch with a black case studded with Silver, made by Benjamin Bell, with an Onyx Stone in a gold Ring tied to the watch in which is engraven the Head of King Charles the First. Whoever brings the said watch and seal to Mr. William Penrice, at the. Black-Boy in Gracechurch Street, shall have 2 guineas reward" (*Lond. Gaz.*, December 3–7, 1691).

BELL, BOUCHER. *London.* Apprenticed 1761, C.C. 1772.

BELL, DAVID. *Stirling.* 1801–50.

BELL, JAMES. *Cambusnethan.* 1770–90.

BELL, JNO. *New York*, 1734.

BELL, JNO. *Doncaster*, 1780.

BELL, JOHN. *London.* Apprenticed 1671–85 C.C.

BELL, JOHN. *Hexham.* About 1790–1827.

BELL, JOHN. C.C. 1719; 30-hour long-case clock, 'fecit 1751'.

BELL, JOHN. Musical clockmaker, *8 Elm St., Gray's Inn Lane*, 1835–40.

BELL, JOSEPH. C.C. 1691.

BELL, PETER. *Garstang*, 1770.

BELL, THOS. Apprenticed 1691 to Sam. Mather, C.C.

BELL, WILLIAM. *Cambusnethan.* 1790–1820.

BELL, WILLIAM. *Philadelphia.* 1805. Clocks and Watches.

BELL, WM. *2 Clement's Lane*, 1812–18.

BELLAMY, ADEY. *10 Poultry*, 1779–85.

BELLARD, FRANÇOIS. *Paris.* Horloger du Roy, 1783.

BELLARD, JOHN. C.C. 1674.

BELLE, T. French clock, about 1780.

BELLEFONTAINE, A. *59 Brewer St., Summers Town*, 1835.

BELLIARD, CHAS. *Pall Mall*, 1769–94.

BELLICHON, CLAUDE. *Lyons.* 1636–59.

BELLIN. See MOTT & BELLIN.

BELLING, JOHN. *Bodmin*, 1780, 1840.

BELLINGE, JAS. *Liverpool*, 1770.

BELLINGER, CH. Apprenticed 1686 to Jno. Bellinger, C.C.

BELLINGER, JAMES. *London.* 1731 C.C.

BELLINGER, JOHN. C.C. 1725.

BELLINGER, JOHN. *London.* About 1677, C.C. 1686–1721.

BELLINGER, RICHD. Apprenticed 1676 to Edwd. East; C.C. 1686.

BELLINGHURST, HENRY. *Aldersgate St.* Liveryman C.C. 1776; 1765–77.

BELLIS, JAS. *9 Pall Mall*, 1769–88.

BELLMAN, DANIEL. *Broughton, Lancs.*, 1818.

BELLUNE, PETER. 1730–50; C.C.

BELON, PIERRE. *Paris.* Clockmaker to the dowager Queen, 1649.

BELSON, THOS. 1630–50; C.C.

BELTZ, —. *Paris (Rue St. Denis).* 1807–25.

BELTZ, JEAN ADAM. *Paris.* Master 1785–89.

BENARD, F. *Paris.* Oval watch with sun-dial inside cover, about 1600 (sun-dial signed 'Chauvin'); Pierpont Morgan collection.

BENBOW, J. *Northwood, Salop.* Watch 1796.

BENBOW, THOMAS. *Newport (Salop).* 1778–about 1800.

BENBRICK, JAS. Apprenticed 1671 to Helkiah Bedford, C.C.

BENBRIDGE, THOS. Apprenticed to Robt. Starr 1669; C.C. 1683.

[BENDELE], JACOB. *Salzburg.* Master 1735, died 1772.

BENDELE, JOHANN MICHAEL. *Augsburg.* Born 1734, master 1763–86. In *Ansbach* 1772.

BENEDICT, S. W. *New York.* Early nineteenth century–1835. Watch N.Y. Univ.

BENEDICT BROTHERS. *New York.* Founded 1819.

BENFEY, B., & SON. *3 Bridgewater Sq.*, 1794.

BENGG, PAULUS. *Zug.* 1612, died 1642. Able maker. Crys. heart watch Blot-Garnier collection. Crucifix clock Zürich Landes-M.

BENGUEREL-DIT-JACOT, ABRAM. *Fontainemelon.* 1745–80. Maker of clocks with wooden wheels.

BENGUEREL-DIT-JACOT, DAVID. *Fontainemelon.* 1745–80. 'Maître horloger en bois.'

BENJAMIN, A. *Myrtle St., Hoxton*, 1835.

BENJAMIN, BARZILLAI. *New Haven, U.S.A.* 1823.

BENJAMIN, JOEL. *12 Bury St., St. Mary Axe*, 1820–35; J. Benjamin & Co., 1840.

BENJAMIN, M., *Bernard St., Commercial Rd.*, 1820; *77 Leman St.*, 1840–42.

BENN, ANTHONY. 1750; died when master C.C. 1763.

BENN, JNO. C.C. 1678.

BENN, ROBERT. *Fleet St.*; C.C. 1716.

BENN, THOMAS, brother. *London* and *Clifton.* C.C. 1764–86.

BENN, THOMAS, son of Robert. *London.* Apprenticed 1764, C.C. 1771, l.C.C. 1773.

BENN, THOS. Apprenticed 1660 to Ben. Hill, C.C.

BENNER, JOHANNES. 'Aug'; table clock, about 1680.

BENNETT, CHARLES. *London.* Apprenticed 1797. C.C. 1824.

BENNETT, GEORGE. *London.* Apprenticed 1697, C.C. 1702–22.

BENNETT, GEORGE. *London.* C.C. 1739.

BENNETT, J. *Bugg Lane, Norwich.* Watch, 1786.

BENNETT, JOHN. *Fleet St.* C.C. 1678.

BENNETT, JOHN. *London.* Apprenticed 1702, C.C. 1712–52.

BENNETT, JOHN. *Bristol.* C.C. 1712.

BENNETT, JOHN. *London.* C.C. 1733.

BENNETT, MANSELL. *Dial and 3 Crowns, Charing Cross.* C.C. 1685–99; fine marquetry long-case clock, V. & A., about 1695.

BENNETT, R. *159 Fleet St.*, 1817.

BENNETT, RICHARD. C.C. 1715.

BENNETT, SAMUEL. *London.* Apprenticed 1705, C.C. 1716–62.

BENNETT, SAMUEL. C.C. 1716.

BENNETT, SAMUEL. *London.* Apprenticed 1720, C.C. 1742–56. Watch.

BENNETT, THOMAS. Apprenticed 1667 to Henry Harper; movement of his condemned by C.C. 1677.

BENNETT, THOMAS. Apprenticed to Thos. Windmills; C.C. 1720; fine long-case clock in the Wetherfield collection, on the inside of the door directions for winding, and at the foot thereof 'Thos. Bennett, at the Dial in Exchange Alley, 1722'.

BENNETT, THOS. *Norwich.* Watch, 1795.

BENNETT, WILLIAM. C.C. 1607.

BENNETT, WILLIAM. *London.* Apprenticed 1675, C.C. 1692–1722.

BENNETT, WILLIAM. *London.* Apprenticed 1677, C.C. 1687–1702.

BENNETT, WILLIAM. *New St. Hill.* C.C. 1729.

BENNETT, WILLIAM. *Salisbury.* About 1790 C.C.

BENNIWORTH, T. & W. *St. Albans,* 1780.

BENOIT, J. E. Watch, apparently English, about 1780.

BENSLEY, J. Maker of a watch for the Duke of Sussex, 1790–1820.

BENSON, —. *Whitehaven.* Long-case clock, about 1760.

BENSON, JNO. Apprenticed 1652 to Jas. Starnell; C.C. 1669; long-case clock dated 1709.

BENSON, SAMUEL. C.C. 1700; watch, 1730.

BENSON & HIGGS. *London.* Bracket chiming clock, Sheraton case with lion-head handles, about 1790.

BENT, WM. *Chadwell St.,* 1820–44.

BENTELE, JACOBUS. *Salzburg.* Clock, Imperial collection, Vienna. Fine waisted long-case clock. Wooden gilt appliqué ornament. Died 1772.

BENTLEY, JOHN. *Thirsk,* 1770.

BENTLEY, JOHN. *5 Pope's Head Alley,* 1820; *Sweeting's Alley,* 1823; 'foreman to Jas. McCabe,' watch paper, C.C.

BENTLEY, SAM. *Kingsbridge.* Watch, 1790.

BENTLEY & BECK. 1815.

BENZ, LUDWIG. *Basle.* 1776–1850.

BERAIN, J. *Paris.* Designer and chaser of clock cases, 1655–1711.

BERARD, JEAN LOUIS GÉDÉON HIPPOLITE. *Geneva.* About 1770–91.

BERAUD, —. Oval watch, about 1600, signed 'A. Beraud à Bloys', Garnier collection.

BERAUD, HENRI. *Sedan,* 1565.

BERAUD, HY. Maker of a watch in the form of a shell, silver case enamelled, crystal over dial, about 1650; C.C., but date of election uncertain.

BERAUD, JAS. 1632.

BERAUD, RENE. *La Rochelle.* 1572, died a. 1615. C. to town in 1580.

BERAUD, STEPHEN. *London.* 1670 C.C.

BERAULT, JNO. Apprenticed 1691 to Thos. Jones, C.C.

BÉRAULT, ABEL. *Blois.* Master 1593. *Paris.* 1607. Died about 1620. Always signed 'BÉRAUD'.

BÉRAULT, JEAN, brother. *Blois.* Comp. 1626–49.

BERBETTE, LOUIS. *Chaux-de-Fonds.* 1781–1804. Calendar and musical clocks.

BERG, CLAES. *Stockholm.* 1762–82. Wall and four bracket clocks and watch.

BERG, F. L. *Augsburg.* Table clock, 1719.

BERG, JOHAN FREDRIK. *Stockholm.* 1823–46.

BERG, N. D. *Sala.* 1816–26.

BERG, NILS. *Stockholm.* Master 1751–90. Two bracket clocks in Nord Museum and National Museum Stockholm. Wall and two long-case clocks. Travelling clock and watch.

BERG, NILS. *Karlstad.* 1816–46.

BERGEAU (BERGEO), PETER. *London.* 1715–about 1770. Watch Denham collection.

BERGER, JEAN MARC. *Geneva.* About 1770–91.

BERGIER, ABRAHAM. *Lyons.* Master 1589. *Grenoble* and *Lyons,* 1597–1616. *Lyons,* 1624–42. Watch movement.

BERGIER, JEAN. *Grenoble.* 1648–69.

BERGIER, S. *Grenoble.* Watch, Marfels collection, about 1550.

BERGMAN, JOHAN. *Stockholm.* 1794–1815. Wall clock illuminated Sidenbladh.

BERGNER, CARL FREDRIK. *Stockholm.* 1763. Master 1766–78.

BERGSTENSSON, JOHAN ERIC. *Nyköping.* 1817. Died about 1832.

BERGUER, CHARLES. Musical clockmaker, *13 Richmond Buildings, Soho,* 1825.

BERGUER, FREDERICK. *201 High Holborn,* 1810; *135 High Holborn,* 1818–20.

BERGUER, JOHN. *44 Great Russell St., Bloomsbury,* 1810–20.

BERGUER, SAMUEL. *Chaux-de-Fonds.* 1749. Died 1777. C. Also BERGER.

BERKELEY, THOMAS. *London.* Apprenticed 1676, C.C., died about 1685.

BERKENHEAD, JOHN. *31 Gutter Lane,* 1783–94.

BERLING, —. *Uppsala.* 1787–1826. Probably same as following.

BERLING, CARL FREDRIK. *Göteborg,* 1815–18. *Stockholm,* 1836–40. *Visby,* 1845. Watch Nord. Museum by him or preceding.

BERNARD, DANIEL GASPARD. *Geneva.* About 1770–91.

BERNARD, JOSEPH. *Geneva.* About 1770–91.

BERNARD, NICHOLAS. *Paris.* Watch in case of rock crystal, primitive movement, balance-cock pinned on, about 1590, Pierpont Morgan collection; two watches, bearing the same name, V. & A., one about 1660 and the other about 1690.

BERNE, JEAN ZACHARIE. *Paris.* Master 1763–89.

BERNHARD (BERNHARDT), MARTIN. *Landsberg.* 1728–50.

BERNINCK, JAN. *Amsterdam.* Watch, B.M., a French enamelled inner case by G. Bouvier, outer *repoussé* case by H. Manley, about 1750.

BERQUEZ, FRANCIS. *17 Vere St.,* 1822; *6 Thayer St., Manchester Sq.,* 1825–35.

BERQUIN, URBAIN. *Paris.* Clock, 1680.

BERRAUD. See BARRAUD, also BERAUD.

BERRIDGE, JNO. *Boston.* Made a clock with compensated pendulum 1738 for Mr. Fotheringham, a Quaker of Holbeach.

BERRIDGE, ROBERT. *2 John St., Oxford St.,* 1790–95.

BERRIDGE, WILLIAM. *4 Holles St., Cavendish Sq.,* 1800–20, see BOWRA.

BERRIDGE, WM. *69 Oxford Rd.,* 1770–94.

BERRINGTON, —. *Bolton.* Watch, 1808.

BERRINGTON, JAS. *St. Helens, Lancs.,* 1818.

BERRINGTON, URIAH. Apprenticed to Nathaniel Delander; C.C. 1684.

BERRISFORD, EDWD. Apprenticed 1663 to Ben. Wolverstone, C.C.

BERROLLAS, JOSEPH ANTHONY. *Denmark St., St. Giles-in-the-Fields,* 1808; *Coppice Row, Clerkenwell,* 1810; afterwards *51 Wellington St., Goswell Rd.*; an ingenious watchmaker. In 1808 he patented a repeater somewhat similar to Elliott's, in 1810 a warning watch, in 1827 an alarm watch, also pumping keyless work; 1800–30.

BERRY, FRANCIS. *Hitchin.* Lantern clocks, about 1700.

BERRY, JAS. *Pontefract.* About 1740.

BERRY, JNO. *Manchester;* 1760.

BERRY, JOHN. *St. Clement's Lane.* Apprenticed 1674 to Richd. Pepys; C.C. 1688, master 1723; maker of a long-case clock at Merchant Taylor's Hall, arch dial, brass figures holding trumpets on top of case; 1688–1730. "Lost Nov. 14th, 1705, from a Gentlewoman's side between Honey Lane market and Great Eastcheap, A plain Gold Watch case. Whoever brings it to John Berry, watchmaker at the Dial in Clement's Lane, Dombard St., shall have 20s. reward for so doing" (*The Daily Courant*, 15th Nov., 1705).

BERRY, JOHN. *London.* Apprenticed 1684, C.C. 1692.

BERRY, JOHN. *London.* Apprenticed 1687, C.C. 1697.

BERRY, JOHN. *St. Clement's Lane.* C.C. 1728.

BERRY, SAMUEL. C.C. 1705.

BERRY, WM. *London.* Watch, 1815.

BERTHOUD, ABRAM HENRY. *Couvet.* 1778–1807. One of the foremost C. at Couvet.

BERTHOUD, FERDINAND. Born in Switzerland 1727; went to Paris when nineteen and settled there; died 1807; an eminent watchmaker, author of 'Essai sur l'Horlogerie', 'Traité des Horloges Marines', 'Histoire de la Mesure du Temps', and other works containing a mass of useful information concerning the history, theory, and practice of the horological art, dealing with Harrison's, Sully's, and le Roy's inventions, and, indeed, everything known in Berthoud's time. There are three clocks by him in the Wallace collection, one a splendid regulator in case of ebony with boldly chased mounts of gilt bronze; around the dial is a serpent with the head and tail meeting—an emblem of eternity. This clock is said to have been taken from the Tuileries in 1793, having been white-washed to hide its value.

BERTHOUD, ISAAC, brother. *Couvet, Fleurier* and *Paris.* 1749–98. Watches and Clocks.

BERTHOUD, JEAN HENRI, brother. *Paris.* 1742–92.

BERTHOUD, JONAS HENRI. *Couvet.* 1756. Died 1820. Made complex clocks.

BERTHOUD, LOUIS. *Paris.* Nephew of Ferdinand; died 1813.

BERTHOUD, PIERRE, brother. *Couvet.* 1740–67. Watches and Clocks.

BERTHOUD, PIERRE LOUIS, son of Pierre. *Paris.* Born 1754, died 1813. Successor to Ferdinand. C. to the Observatoire and the Bureau des Longitudes. Wrote 'Entretiens sur l'horlogerie'. Made many watches and clocks and about 150 chronometers. Used cylindrical balance springs in watches and conical balance springs in 1793. Pedometer winding centre seconds watch Ilbert collection.

BERTHOUD, FRÈRES. *Paris.* From 1813. Firm composed of Louis and Charles Auguste, sons of Pierre Louis. 'Horlogers de la Marine.'

BERTLES (BIRTLES), EDWARD. *Liverpool.* 1777–96. C.

BERTON, —. *Paris.* Late eighteenth century–1825. Cartel clock, Ministère de la Marine, Paris.

BERTRAM, WILLIAM. Died in 1732, when master C.C.

BERTRAND, CLAUDE JOSEPH. *Paris.* Juré 1771.

BERTRAND, JOSÈPHE. *Paris* (garde-visiteur), 1769.

BERTRAND, JOSEPH CHARLES (or CLAUDE) PAUL. *Paris.*

BERTRAND, MICHAND. 'Hor du Roy' (Francis I), 1515–47.

BERTRAND, PIERRE. *Lyons.* 1603–20. From *Geneva.*

BERTRAND, ROBERT. *2 Stewart St., Spitalfields,* 1790–94. A long-case clock signed 'Robert Bartrand, London', dating from about 1770.

BERWICK, ABNER. *Berwick, U.S.A.,* 1820.

BESCK, ZACKARIAS. *Stockholm.* 1697. Died 1727. Bracket and long-case clocks.

BESNARD, ANDRÉ. *Paris.* Master 1606. Juré 1616.

BEST, ROBERT. *5 White Lion Court, Birchin Lane.* A watch by him, V. & A., hall mark 1769; 1765–88.

BEST, ROBERT (formerly foreman to Brockbank). C.C. 1783–1820. Bankrupt 1796. *4 White Lion Court, Birchin Lane,* 1790; *4 Sweeting's Alley,* 1798; *1 Windsor Place, St. Paul's* 1810–20. He attested the value of Earnshaw's improvements in 1804.

BEST, T. At the Dial in *Lewes.* Card, B.M., 1780.

BEST, THOS. *3 Red Lion St., Clerkenwell.* Between 1770 and 1794 he made a large number of watches for the Dutch market; also known as a maker of musical clocks and watches.

BEST, THOS. *Newcastle.* Watch, 1785.

BESTWICK. In 1672 Jas. Dearmar was apprenticed to Katherine Bestwick, widow C.C.

BESTWICK, HENRY. C.C. 1686.

BETHELL, JNO. *Stowmarket.* Clock, about 1800.

BETHELL, R. *London.* Watch, 1760.

BETHELL, WILLIAM. *London.* C.C. 1770.

BETHNAN, ROBERT. *Paris.* Master 1767–89.

BETON, JNO. *London.* Watch, 1800.

BETSON, THOMAS. *London.* About 1740–80. Watch Chamb. collection.

BETTERTON, —. *London.* Watch, about 1780.

BETTINSON (or BETTISON), SOLOMON. *Newark,* 1776–92.

BETTS, JOB. C.C. 1656. "Stolen from Cheyne Rowe, of Walthamstowe, in Essex, Esq., a gold watch with a gold chain made by John Betts, with a silver Drinking Cup and other Plate. Whoever brings the said watch and chain or the watch only to Mr. Johnson, Jeweller, at the 3 Flower-de-Luces in Cheapside, shall have 20s. reward, and charges, or if pawned or sold their money again with content" (*Lond. Gaz.,* August 11–15, 1692).

BETTS, JOB. *London.* C.C. 1656–82.

BETTS, JOSEPH. *London.* 1706 C.C.

BETTS, SAMUEL. Back of Exchange; short train watch by him, about 1645. He was an early member of the C.C., and in 1656 attested the genuineness of Jas. Lello's masterpiece. In the Wetherfield collection is a 30-hour bracket clock by him; died before 1675 (see MARQUET). "Lost on the 8th Inst. betwixt Enfield and Wormley, on the rode to Warre a gold watch with a case and chain of gold, the Chrystall out, and the case lined with Pink-coloured Sattin, made by Mr. Betts in Lumbard Street. Whoever shall discover and return or cause it to be returned to Mr. Austin, Goldsmith at the Starre in Fenchurch St., shall have 40s. for his peynes" (*The Intelligencer,* 13th June, 1664).

BETTS, SAMUEL. Apprenticed to Samuel Davis for Job Betts 1675; C.C. 1682; calendar watch with revolving ring dials, to which a figure of Time points, in Dover Museum. In the G.M. is another specimen of his work: bracket clock, square dial, walnut case, Wetherfield collection, 1682–1700.

BETTS, SAMUEL. *London.* Apprenticed 1675, C.C. 1682–1700; bracket clock Wetherfield collection.

BEURLING. PETER HENRIC. *Stockholm.* Born 1763, died 1806. Had a large workshop, continued by widow till 1830 Watch Nord. Museum. Many wall clocks; bracket clock.

BEVAN, —. *London.* C.C. Died a. 1680.

DEVANS, WILLIAM. *Norristown, U.S.A.* 1816.

BEVENS, WILLIAM. *Philadelphia.* 1811–13.

BEVERIDGE, GEORGE. *Kettle.* 1799–1842.

BEVERLEY, JAS. Apprenticed 1683 to Robt. Doore; C.C.; bracket clock, about 1695; watch pendulum balance, about 1700, inscribed 'Ja. Beverly, London'.

BEVINGTON, J. *Bolton, Lancs.,* 1814.

BEWLEY, ERNEST. *London.* Long-case clock about 1740.

BEWLEY, GEORGE. *Whitecross St.* C.C. 1780.

BEYER, HANS. *Strasbourg.* 1587.

BEYER, JOHN *London.* C.C. 1769.

BEYSSAC, ANTOINE. *Rouen.* Master 1653–67. Introduced the pendulum at Rouen. "Ayant l'art et le secret de faire les mouvemens des horloges à pendule et y ayant très bien réussy à ceux de St. Ouen et Bonnes-

Nouvelles à Rouen." Repaired clock of Notre Dame, Dijon.

BEZAR, STEPHEN. Brother C.C. 1648.

BEZENCENET, ABRAM HENRI. *Boveresse.* Born 1774, died 1861. Made musical clocks and chronometers.

BEZENCENET, JEAN LOUIS. *Boveresse (Switzerland).* 1758-1776. C.

BIBLEY, JNO. *Corporation Row,* 1790-94.

BICKEL, FRANZ ANTON. *Augsburg.* Comp. about 1783-1800.

BICKERLO. See POOLE.

BICKERSTAFF, PETER. *Liverpool.* 1807-29. Watch.

BICKERSTAFF, WM. *Liverpool,* 1770.

BICKERTON, BENJAMIN. *14 Jewin St.,* 1795-1810.

BICKERTON, T. W. *14 Jewin St.,* 1816-20.

BICKLEY, THOMAS. *195 Ratcliff Highway,* 1790-94.

BICKLMANN, PHILIPP. *Linz, Austria.* About 1770.

BICKNELL, FRANCIS. Apprenticed to Job Betts 1653; C.C. 1665.

BICKNELL, JOSEPH & CO. *119 New Bond St.,* 1807-13.

BIDARD, —. Watch mentioned by Thiout, about 1730.

BIDAULT. *Paris.* A long succession of court clockmakers.

BIDAULT, AUGUSTIN FRANÇOIS, 1693.

BIDAULT, CLAUDE. 1628, lodged at the Louvre 1642.

BIDAULT, HENRI AUGUST. Succeeded his father at the Louvre 1652.

BIDDLE, JOSEPH. C.C. 1684.

BIDDLE, OWEN. *Pa.* Born 1737.

BIDERMAN, JEAN MARC ANDRÉ. *Geneva.* About 1770-91.

BIDLAKE, JAMES. *16 Sun St.,* 1798-1804. Livery C.C. 1816; *48 Chiswell St.,* 1816-20.

BIDLAKE, JAMES, & SON. *48 Chiswell St., Finsbury,* 1820-45.

BIDLAKE, JAMES. *London.* Apprenticed 1800-35. In partnership with following as J. & J. H. Bidlake.

BIDLAKE, JAMES HODGSON. *London (Chiswell St.).* Apprenticed 1801, C.C. 1809, l.C.C. 1818.

BIDLAKE, JAS. *31 Minories,* 1765-94.

BIDLAKE, THOMAS. *16 Sun St., Bishopsgate St.,* 1804-18; livery C.C. 1818.

BIDLES, THOMAS. *London.* Maker of bracket clocks, about 1760.

BIEGEL, HENRY W. *Philadelphia.* 1813.

BIELER à *Bienne.* Calendar watch, about 1790.

BIERFELDER, ERASMUS. *Steppach.* 1756-70.

BIESTA, JEAN. *Paris.* Master 1759-89.

BIGAUD. *Paris.* About 1750.

BIGG, BEN. Apprenticed 1678 to Robt. Cooke, C.C.

BIGGER, GILBERT. *Dublin.* 1783. *Baltimore, U.S.A.,* in partnership with Clarke for one year, then alone until 1807.

BIGGER, WILLIAM. *Baltimore.* 1802.

BIGGER & CLARKE. *Baltimore, U.S.A.* 1784. From *Dublin.* Clocks and watches.

BIGGS, RICHARD. *Salisbury, Romsey* and *London.* 1776 insolvent in London. Back in *London* about 1800. C.C.

BIGGS, ROGER. *5 Crescent, Jewin St.,* 1800.

BIGNEL, RICHARD. *London.* C.C. 1719.

BIGOT, —. *Rouen.* Juré 1777.

BILBEE, —. *London.* Long-case 30-hour clock, one hand, about 1710.

BILBIE. A well-known Somerset family of clockmakers. A lantern clock by Thomas Bilbie dating from about 1660; the fret in front shows the royal arms, and the side frets are of the dolphin pattern. Among other specimens are a long-case clock by Edward Bilbie, Chewstoke, about 1700; one of later date by Thos. Bilbie, Chewstoke; an 8-day long-case clock by William Bilbie, of the same place.

BILCLIFF (or BYCLIFF). *York.*

BILCLIFF, JNO. f., 1617-39.

BILCLIFF, ROBT. f., 1627-53.

BILLIE, JOHN. C.C. seized watches and movements by him 1687.

BILLINGE, WILLIAM. *Liverpool.* 1796-1824.

BILLINGER, JNO. C.C. 1637.

BILLINGHURST, ANTHONY. Apprenticed to Helkiah Bedford 1673; C.C.

BILLINGHURST, HENRY. *67 Aldersgate St.* Livery C.C. 1766; 1760-71.

BILLINGHURST, WM. Apprenticed to Thos. Fenn 1668; C.C.

BILLINGHURST, WM. Apprenticed 1694 to Sam Watson, C.C.

BILLINGTON, JOSEPH. *Chester.* 1670; C.

BILLINGTON, ROBERT. *London.* Apprenticed 1735 C.C. 1742-59.

BILLON, CHARLES. *Philadelphia.* 1802-19.

BILLON, & CO. *Philadelphia,* 1797.

BILLOP, WILLIAM. C.C. 1688.

BILLOW, CHARLES, & CO. *Boston, U.S.A.* 1796.

BINDLEY, —. Apprenticed 1674 to Rich. Pierce, C.C.

BINET, ABRAHAM GÉDÉON. *Geneva.* Born 1725, died 1800. Invented a wheelcutting machine.

BINÉTRUY, CHARLES. *Paris.* 1807-25.

BING, JOHN. *Ramsgate.* Died 1790 C.C.

BING, THOMAS. *London.* a. 1761-about 1785. Dutch type watch with Glasgow Art Galleries.

BINGHAM, THOS. Watch-chain maker, *3 Middle Row, Holborn,* 1769-81.

BINGHAM & BRICERLY. *Philadelphia,* 1778-99.

BINGLEY, GILES. Apprenticed 1692 to Edwd. Eyston, C.C. John Bingley, watchmaker, advertised for in *Lond. Gaz.,* 1st June, 1696.

BINGS, EDWARD. "Whereas there was stolen from the House of Mr. Thos. Dummer in Wellclose on Saturday night, between the hours of 9 and 11 o'clock, a Gold Pendulum Watch with a chain made by Mr. Edward Bings. You are desired to stop them and give notice to Mr. Thos. Beach, Goldsmith, at the Black-a-Moors Head in Cheapside, and you shall have 2 guineas Reward" (*Daily Courant,* 23rd Sept. 1706).

BINKS, —. *London.* Watch, G.M., about 1820.

BINKS, THOS. *Birmingham,* 1740.

BINLEY, J. W. *Ironmonger Row, Old St.,* 1790.

BINNS, —. *Halifax.* Clock 1720.

BINNS, GEORGE. *137 Strand,* 1832-38.

BINNY (BINNIE), DANIEL. *Edinburgh.* Apprenticed 1747-79. Succeeds his uncle And. Dickie in 1765.

BINNY (BINNIE) & GORDON. *Edinburgh.* 1774.

BION, NICOLAS. *Paris.* Born 1652, died 1733. Famous mathematical instrument maker, and published book on instruments in 1725.

BIRCH, RICHARD. *Bread St., Birmingham,* 1776-87.

BIRCH, THOMAS. Apprenticed to Thos. Mills 1649; C.C. 1658; Mr. John H. Baker has a lantern clock inscribed 'Thomas Birch in the longe walke Neere Christ Church Londini fecit'.

BIRCH, THOS. Apprenticed 1675 to Sam Clyatt; C.C. 1682.

BIRCHALL, GEORGE. *Warrington.* a. 1793-about 1820. Watch.

BIRCHALL, M. *Derby,* 1790.

BIRCHALL, WM. *5 St. James's Walk, Clerkenwell,* 1816; *5 Wellington St.,* 1834-42.

BIRCHALL, & SON. *Warrington,* 1770.

BIRD, EDWARD. *Bristol,* about 1810.

BIRD, EDWD. *London,* 1710.

BIRD, JACOB. *7 Cornhill*, 1783.

BIRD, JOHN. One of the examiners of Harrison's time-keeper 1765.

BIRD, JOHN. *Amersham*. About 1800 C.C.; from *London*.

BIRD, JOHN, & SON. *19 Bartlett's Buildings, Holborn*, 1822–25.

BIRD, LUKE. Apprenticed 1675 to Jas. Delander; C.C. 1682.

BIRD, LUKE. *London*. 1750 C.C.

BIRD, MICHAEL. Apprenticed to Ed. Gilpin in 1648; bracket clock inscribed 'Michael Bird, London'. On a 30-hour clock, one hand, about 1670, was inscribed 'Michael Bird, Oxon.'

BIRD, MICHAEL, son. Brother C.C. 1682–1713.

BIRD, NAT. C.C. 1693.

BIRD, RICH. Watch-chain maker, *Bartlett's Buildings*, 1794.

BIRD, THOS. *London*. Watch, h.m. 1753; 10 *Salisbury St., Strand*, 1816.

BIRD, WILLIAM. *London*. Apprenticed about 1726, C.C. about 1749.

BIRD, WILLIAM. *London*. 1785 C.C. Watch.

BIRD, WM. Apprenticed 1667 to Hy. Crump, C.C.

BIRD, SAMUEL JOSEPH. Watch-case maker (apprenticed to Jaspar Swindells), *Little Compton St.*; C.C. 1813.

BIRD & BRANSTOR. *30 Cheapside*, 1775.

BIRDWHISTELL, FRANCIS. C.C. 1687.

BIRDWHISTELL, ISAAC. C.C. 1692–1705. Watch.

BIRDWHISTELL, JOHN. C.C. 1718.

BIRDWHISTELL, THOMAS. C.C. 1693.

BIRGE, JOHN. *Bristol*, 1830–37.

BIRGE, MALLORY & CO. *Bristol, Conn.*, 1830.

BIRKHEAD, NICHOLAS. Removed from *King's Head, Holborn*, to *White Hart, Knightsbridge* (*Lond. Gaz.*, 29th May, 1st June, 1693).

BIRLEY, J. *Sheffield*. Curious watch, one hand, '1638' on metal dial in place of name, probably made sixty or seventy years after that date.

BIRNIE, LAURENCE, son. Apprenticed to his father, then *Philadelphia*, 1774.

BIRNIE, WILLIAM. *Templepatrick* and *Dublin*. About 1750–67. Also BIRNEY.

BISBEE, J. *Brunswick, U.S.A.*, 1798–1825.

BISHOP, JAMES GRIFFIN. *97 Fetter Lane*, 1816–24.

BISHOP, SAMUEL. *Portland St.*, 1769–94, hon. freeman of C.C. 1781.

BISHOP, SAMUEL. *London*. a. 1730. Watch.

BISHOP, THOMAS. *London*. Apprenticed 1808, C.C. 1816.

BISHOP, THOS. *Wych St.*, 1774; watch, date on movement 1810.

BISHOP, WILLIAM. *70 New Bond St.*, 1830.

BISHOP & BRADLEY. *Plymouth, U.S.A.* 1825–30.

BISOT, JACQUES. *Paris*. Clockmaker to the Duchesse d'Orléans, 1681.

BISSE, —. English alarum clock in gilt metal case, about 1620, V. & A., signed 'Edward Bisse Fecit' The dial is provided with projecting pins for feeling the time at night, see BYSSE.

BISSETT, JAS. (late Gibson). *12 Sweeting's Alley, Royal Exchange*, 1815–20.

BISSON, LOUIS PIERRE. *Paris*. Juré 1786–1809. Mantel clock, marble and ormolu.

BITTLESTON, JOHN. *207 High Holborn*, 1765–94; hon. freeman C.C. 1781. Example of his work—a very curious astronomical watch, with two elaborate enamel dials—one at the front, and one at the back—showing the hour and minute both sides, two centre seconds—one the usual long hand, the other having a small rotating enamel dial—day of the month, day of

the week, the month, moon's age, the tide, and a regulator, case pinchbeck, with a border each side of fine old paste in imitation of rubies and diamonds.

BIXLER, CHRISTIAN. *Easton, Pennsylvania, U.S.A.* Clock, about 1750.

BIXLER, CHRISTIAN. *Easton*, 1785–1830. A famous 8-day clock manufacturer.

BJÖRKDAHL, JON. DAN. *Västerds*. Born 1764, died 1810.

BJURMAN, ADOLPH FREDERIC. *Norrköping*. Born 1743, died 1812. Wall and bracket and travelling clock. Two watches.

BJURQVIST, HANS. *Göteborg*. Born 1750, died 1810.

BLACKBORROW, JAMES. Admitted C.C. 1711; died 1746, when warden.

BLACKBOURNE, WILLIAM. *Paternoster Row*, 1730.

BLACKBURN, ROBERT. *London*. C.C. 1720.

BLACKBURN, THOMAS. *London* (*Little Britain*). a. 1770. C.C. 1799, l.C.C. 1812. Watch.

BLACKBURN, WILLIAM. Summoned to take up livery C.C. 1786.

BLACKBURN, WILLIAM. *London* (*Shoe Lane*). C.C. 1768–75.

BLACKETER, PETER. *London*. C.C. 1786.

BLACKETT, JOHN. *London*. l.C.C. 1809–23.

BLACKMORE, JNO. Apprenticed 1689 to Ben. Bell, C.C.

BLACKWELL, J. *43 Plumber St., City Rd.*, 1820.

BLACKWELL, THOS. C.C. 1654.

BLAIN, JAQUES FRANÇOIS. *Geneva*. About 1770–91.

BLAINVILLE, —. *Rouen*. Calendar watch, about 1795.

BLAKE, CHAS. *14 Bishopsgate Within*, 1813.

BLAKE, JOHN. *Croydon*. 1767–84.

BLAKE, JONATHAN. *Fulham*. Watch, 1784.

BLAKE, WM. *Whitecross St.*, 1789–90.

BLAKEBOROUGH, HENRY. *Burnley*, 1818.

BLAKEWAY, CHARLES. *Albrighton*. 1774–95. Clocks and watches. "Wheels cut for clockmakers at 6d. per set and Dyal Plates engraved at 2s. 6d. each."

BLAKEY, WILLIAM.. *London*. Apprenticed 1701. *Paris*. 1774–55. Granted an exclusive privilege to make and sell pinion steel in France, promising to sell at one-third less than English steel. Wrote an account of springmaking published Amsterdam 1780.

BLANC (LE BLANC), —. *Paris* (*Rue des Vieux Augustins*). 1810–13.

BLANC (LE BLANC), FILS. *Paris* (*Palais Royal*). 1807–25.

BLANC (LE BLANC), JEAN. *Geneva*. Master about 1745–70.

BLANC (LE BLANC), LEWIS. *Philadelphia*. 1810. Watch.

BLANCHARD, ABRAHAM. *London*. Watch, 1730.

BLANCHARD, CHARLES. *Bartlett's Buildings, London*. Long-case clock, about 1750; chiming quarter bracket clock, square black case, strike-silent, bronze, handle on top, about 1760.

BLANCHARD, ROBT. Within *Temple Bar*, 1675.

BLANCHARD, WM. *Hull*, 1822.

BLANCHER, JAMES. *Attleborough*. a. 1774–91 Watch; long-case clock.

BLANCHETON, JEAN. *Lyons*. 1607. Died between 1629 and 1636. Octagonal silver watch Reichenberg Museum.

BLAND, —. *Howden* (*Yorks.*). About 1770–95. Watch.

BLATTER, PIERRE. *Chaux-de-Fonds*. 1779–1803. Clock.

BLAY, WILLIAM. *6 Princes St., Leicester Sq.*, 1825.

BLAYLOCK, JNO. *Carlisle*, 1830–42.

BLECKE (BLECHE or BLICK), FRANZ HENRIK. *Copenhagen*. Master 1740.

BLECKE (BLECHE or BLICK), JOHAN HEINRICH. *Copenhagen*. Comp. 1709, Master 1712–28. From *Westphalia*. Turret clock.

BLESSING, MARTIN. *Moscow*, 1809. *Furtwangen*, 1814. Born 1774, died 1847. Famous musical clock.

BLIN, JULIEN. *Paris*. Master 1775–89.

BLINKER, THOS. *London*, about 1745–70.

BLINKO, JOHN. *London*. Apprenticed 1811, C.C. 1819.

BLISS, AMBROSE. C.C. 1653; signed a petition in 1656.

BLISSETT, ISAAC. *70 Leadenhall St.*, 1823.

BLOCK, FRANCIS. Apprenticed 1689 to Jno. Bellinger, C.C.

BLONDELL, NICOLAS. *Paris*. Master 1743–89.

BLOUD, CH., à *Dieppe*, 1660.

BLUCK, W. *London*. 1779–about 1800. Dissolved partnership with James Young in 1779.

BLUMFIELD, JOHN. *Norwich*. 1782. Died 1815. C.C.

BLUNDELL, HENRY. Musical clock maker, *7 Red Lion St.*, 1830.

BLUNDELL, JNO. Apprenticed 1678 to Geo. Nau; C.C.

BLUNDELL, JOS. *Dublin*. Bracket clock, about 1770.

BLUNDELL, RICHARD. Threatened with prosecution by C.C. for exercising the art, not being admitted; he promised to take up his freedom at the next quarter court, 1682.

BLUNDELL, THOMAS. *Dublin*. 1733. Died 1775. Watch Belfast Museum.

BLUNDELL, THOMAS. *Dublin*. 1766–1824.

BLUNDELL, WILLIAM. C.C. 1715.

BLUNDY, CHARLES. *Charleston, U.S.A.* 1760. From *London*. Watch.

BLUNDY, JOSEPH. *21 St. John St., Clerkenwell*, 1781; *Brookes Market*, 1790.

BLUNT, MORRIS. 1630–50; C.C.

BOAD, THOS. Apprenticed 1684 to Robt. Nemes; C.C. 1692.

BOAD, THOMAS, son. *London*. C.C. 1744–72.

BOAK, SAMUEL. *Golden Spread Eagle, Without Aldgate*, 1692.

BOARDMAN, CHAUNCEY. *Bristol, Conn.*, 1815–38.

BOARDMAN & DUNBAR. *Bristol, U.S.A.* 1811.

BOARDMAN & WELLS. *Bristol, U.S.A.* 1815.

BOBINET, ABRAHAM. Cruciform watch in a case of crystal with a gilt and engraved cross, about 1630, probably French, Pierpont Morgan collection.

BOBINET, CHAS. (French) watch in circular crystal case, V. & A., about 1650, also (Salting collection) a cruciform watch in crystal and silver case; a circular watch by him in an agate case is in the Pierpont Morgan collection.

BOCK, JOHANN. *Frankfort*. Oval calendar watch, about 1620; Pierpont Morgan collection; clock, Vienna Treasury, about 1630; watch showing days of the month, about 1640.

BOCKEL, MATHYS. *Haarlem*. Oval watch, S.K.M., 1610.

BOCKELS, —. *Amsterdam*. In the Roskell collection was a handsome oval alarm watch by him, of large size, dating from about 1640; the inner case is of silver, and the outer one covered with fish skin; on the dial is inscribed 'Oliver Cromwell'.

BOCKELTS, —. Watch, B.M., about 1640.

BOCKELTS, JAN JANSS. Watch, Napier collection, 1620.

BOCKETT, RICHD. *London*. 1712.

BODDELL, JOSIAH. Apprenticed to Daniel Delander; admitted C.C. 1741.

BODDINGTON, JOHN. *London*. Apprenticed 1726, C.C. 1734.

BODDINGTON, JOHN. *London*. Apprenticed 1725.

BODDINGTON, WILLIAM. *London*. Apprenticed 1758.

BODDLE, JONAH. *London*. Apprenticed 1730, C.C. 1741.

BODE, WILLIAM. *Philadelphia*, 1797.

BODEKER, JOST. *Warburg*. 1587. Died probably after 1626. Made clock for Osnabrück Dom with foliot and, as alternative, a device which probably was a conical pendulum.

BODENHAM, EDWARD. Apprenticed to Brounker Watts; C.C. 1719.

BODHAM, STEPH. Apprenticed 1680 to Ed. Enys; C.C.

BODILY, ELIZABETH. C.C. 1692.

BODILY, N. *21 Butchers' Hall Lane, Newgate St.*, 1823.

BOECKETT, JAN JANSE. *Hague*. Oval watch, about 1610, stolen from the Horological Institute in 1873.

BOGARDUS, EVERARDUS. *New York*. f., 1698.

BOGNER, JOSEPH BENEDIKT. *Augsburg*. Master 1769–99.

BOGUET, F. *London*. Watch, 1640.

BOHEMUS, CASPAR. *Vienna*, late sixteenth century.

BOHM, MARCUS. *Augsburg*. Pendulum clock, about 1660.

BOIS-DE-CHESNE, JOHN FRANCIS. *Charleston, U.S.A.* 1750. From *London*; clocks and watches.

BOISSON, ETIENNE. *London*. Watch, 1700.

BOISSON, M. *London*. Watch, 1745.

BOISSON, MARC FRANÇOIS. *Geneva*. 1770–98 juré.

BOISLANDER, —. *Nancy*. Watch, about 1690.

BOISLANDON à *Metz*. Watch, about 1590, Horological School, Chaux de Fonds.

BOITEAU, S., à *L'Arcenal, Paris*. Watch, 1695.

BOLD, JNO. *Warrington*, 1770.

BOLD, T. *Warrington*. a. 1762, died 1795.

BOLLARD, RICHARD. *London*. Bracket clock, about 1770.

BOLTON, J. *Wigan*, about 1760; a finely made skeleton timepiece inscribed 'Bolton, London', dating from about 1800.

BOMAN, HANS. *Gäfle*. Master 1780, died a. 1805; watch.

BOMAN, ANDERS, son. *Gäfle*. 1808–25.

BOMMEL (POMMEL), JOHANN MELCHIOR, son. *Nürnberg*. Born 1644, died 1719; watch Feill collection.

BOMPARD, —., à *Paris*. Timepiece, G.M., about 1800.

BONBRUICT, JEAN, à *Blois*, 1650.

BONCHER, A. Musical watchmaker, *23 Frith St., Soho*, 1835.

BOND, —. *Boston, U.S.A.* It is claimed that in 1812, William Bond, the founder of this business, made the first marine chronometer produced wholly in the United States, and that, in default of a main-spring, he used a weight to drive it. Richard F. Bond in 1850 invented a remontoire, or spring governor, to be applied to a clock for ensuring continuous motion of an equatorial telescope.

BOND, CHARLES. *Boston, U.S.A.* 1825.

BOND, G. *London*. Watch, 1800.

BOND, THO. Apprenticed 1685 to Wither Cheney, C.C.

BOND, WILLIAM. *Boston, U.S.A.* 1793–1809. Wall clocks; made first American chronometer 1812. (See Bond.)

BOND, WILLIAM, & SON. *Boston, U.S.A.* 1813; the firm still exists as chronometer makers.

BONE, WM. *Essex*, about 1790.

BONET, JOSEPH. *London*. C.C. 1719.

BONEY, CALEB. A well-known Cornish clockmaker; died at Padstow 1827.

BONFANTI, JOSEPH. *305 Broadway, New York*. Advertised in 1823 "German clocks, some plain with music and some with moving figures, and French clocks, some with music, and will play different tunes".

BONFILS, DAVID. *Geneva*. About 1770–91.

BONFLEUR, ANDREW. *London*. C.C. 1804.

BONNER, CHARLES. Apprenticed to Nich. Clark 1650; C.C. 1658; watch, 1690, Evan Roberts collection; long-case marquetry clock, Wetherfield collection, about 1710.

BONNER, CHARLES. *London*. Apprenticed 1691–1715 C.C.

BONNER, CHARLES. *London*. Apprenticed 1693, C.C. 1705–17; long-case clock Wetherfield collection, signed 'Bonnor'.

BONNER, JASPER. C.C. 1704.

BONNER, JASPER, *London*. Apprenticed 1681, C.C. 1688.

BONNER, THOS. *Fair St., Southwark*, 1790–94.

BONNET, J. B. *Geneva*. Watch, about 1825.

BONNEY, THOMAS. *London (Horsleydown)* 1802–24.

BONNY, —. *London*. Maker of a repeater centre-seconds watch for the Duke of Sussex; 1790–1820.

BONUS, SIMON PETER. *London*. Apprenticed 1781, C.C. 1790–1808.

BONVALLET, LOUIS ANTOINE. *Paris*. Master 1756–1808.

BOOKER, NUGENT. *Dublin*. Long-case clock about 1750.

BOOKER, THOMAS. *London (Grub St.)*. Apprenticed 1752, C.C. 1759–75.

BOOLE, JONATHAN. Apprenticed 1676 to Sarah Payne, C.C.

BOOLE, THOS. *Reigate*. Watch, 1758.

BOONE, EDWARD. Apprenticed to Robert Dent, and came by several appointments to Thos. Tompion; admitted C.C. 1691.

BOOSEY, JOHN. *London (King St.)*. C.C. 1773–89.

BOOSEY, THOMAS, son. *London (Broad St.)*. Apprenticed 1782, C.C. 1792, l.C.C. 1812.

BOOT, GEORGE. *Manchester*. 1772–1814. Watch.

BOOT, JNO. Long marquetry case clock, inscribed 'John Boot, Sutton, Ashfield', dating from about 1710.

BOOT, JOHN & WILLIAM. 1725.

BOOT, JOHN. *Manchester*. 1775–94. Watch.

BOOTH, BEN. *London*. Watch, silver dial, red tortoiseshell case, *piqué*, inlaid landscape in silver, about 1780; Pierpont Morgan collection.

BOOTH, BENJ. *Pontefract*. Watch, 1738.

BOOTH, G., & SON. *Aberdeen*. 1820–46.

BOOTH, GEORGE. *Manchester*. 1758–88. Watch.

BOOTH, JAMES. *Rochester* and *London*. C.C. 1778, l.C.C. 1781, died 1822; watch movement.

BOOTH, JAS. *20 Little Tower Hill*, 1788–92.

BOOTH, JAS. BOWKER, *Manchester*. 1765.

BOOTH, JNO. *Manchester*. 1775.

BOOTH, JNO. *London*. Watch, 1780.

BOOTH, JNO. *Stalybridge*, 1818.

BOOTH, JOHN. *Wakefield*. a. 1765–97. Watch.

BOOTH, JOHN. *Aberdeen*. 1820–46.

BOOTH, JOSH. *Manchester*. 30-hour long-case clock, about 1700.

BOOTH, R. *Church Hill, Woolwich*, 1812–17.

BOOTH, RICHARD. *London (Alfred Ct.)*. Apprenticed 1773, C.C. 1785–1800.

BOOTH, RICHARD. *London*. Apprenticed 1795–1814 C.C.

BOOTH, WM. *Leeds*, 1828.

BOOTH, WILLIAM. *London*. C.C. 1790.

BOOTY, ALEXANDER. *London*, about 1764, C.C. 1776.

BOOTY, HENRY. *London*. Apprenticed 1760–1808; watch.

BOR, J. *Paris*. Fine clock in a square brass case, minutes shown on a small circle below the hour dial, minute hand driven from fusee; about 1590.

BORDENN, A. *Amsterdam*, about 1800–??

BORDIER, A. *Geneva*. Watch, Schloss collection, case beautifully enamelled, about 1785; watch in octagonal case, 'Leonard Bordier', V. & A., 1800. In the Paul Garnier collection is a watch signed 'Bordier, Paris, 1806'. It is in a square case of rock-crystal.

BORDIER, DENIS. Watch, crystal case, about 1630.

BORDIER, FRANÇOIS. *Geneva*, 1660–1722.

BORDIER, FRÈRES. *Geneva*, 1820–30, see also ROUX. Gold engraved watch set pearls; engraved apple watch; gold engraved watch V. & A.; gold engraved shell watch Stern. collection; two four-colour gold watches M.M.A.

BOREL, CÉLESTINE. *Boveresse*. About 1800–50.

BOREL, FRANÇOIS ANTOINE. *Couvet*. Born 1767, died 1827; maker of repute of turret and musical clocks and travelling clocks.

BOREL, HENRI SELIM. *Couvet*. Born 1792, died 1870.

BOREL, JACOB, *Couvet, Môtiers* and *Neuchâtel*. Apprenticed 1735, died 1779; many clocks.

BOREL, JEAN HENRI. *Couvet, Fontaines* and *London*. Apprenticed 1780–1821.

BOREL-JAQUET, ABRAM. *Côte Bertin*. Born 1731, died 1815; many clocks.

BORELLI, J. *8 Aldersgate St.*, 1790–95.

BORGIN, HENRY. *Without Bishopsgate*, issued a token bearing a dial and hands about 1677.

BORRELL, HENRY. *15 Wilderness Row*, 1795–1840; watch in finely enamelled cases, Turkish numerals, on dial 'Markwick Markham, Borrell, London', h.m., 1813.

BORRET, P. *5 Staining Lane, Wood St.*, 1805–16.

BORRETT, GEO. *Stowmarket*. Watch, G.M., about 1750.

BORRETT, M. M. *London*, about 1790.

BORROUGH, JNO. *Brampton*, 1770.

BORWICK, JNO. *Bartholomew Hospital*. Watch, 1785.

BOSCH, ULRICH. C.C. 1652.

BOSEN, —. *Paris*. Watch, 1806.

BOSLEY, CHAS. *Ratcliff Cross*. Succeeded Wm. Kipling; 1750–66; livery C.C.

BOSLEY, JOSEPH. *Leadenhall St.* C.C. 1725; *Clerkenwell Green*, 1730. In 1755 he obtained a patent for using in watches pinions with more teeth than usual. This involved an extra wheel and pinion, and the balance wheel turned the contrary way. Also for (secondly) a slide index for watches, which has no wheel, but turns upon a brass socket and points to an arc of a circle, with the word 'faster' at one end, and 'slower' at the other. Patent unsuccessfully opposed by C.C. 1725–63.

BOSSET, —. *Paris*. 1807–23.

BOSSET, J. JAQUE ANDRÉ. *La Neuveville*. 18c. watch G.M.

BOSSHARDT, J. J. *Basle*. Born 1749, died 1799; town C.; bracket clock Basle Museum; signed 'Bossardt Fils'.

BOSSHARDT, JOHANNES. *Basle*. Born 1718, died 1794; town C.

BOTLEY, ROBT. *Bletchingly*, 1740.

BOTTOMLEY, JNO. *Clayton*, about 1750.

BOTTRILL, EBENEZER. *Coventry*, about 1740.

BOTZMAYR, JOHANN SIMON. *Danzig*. Clock-watch, about 1740.

BOUCHAY, ABRM., 'from *London*'. Ebonised bracket clock about 1770.

BOUCHER, W. *4 Long Acre*, 1820.

BOUCHERET, JACOB. C.C. 1728.

BOUCHERET, JNO. *London*, 1750.

BOUCHET, JACOB. *London*. Apprenticed 1714, C.C. 1729.

BOUCHET, JEAN LOUIS. *Rue Saint Denis, Paris*. Clock-maker to the King 1769.

BOUDON, J. Octagonal watch inscribed 'J. Boudon à St. Flour', about 1600.

BOUDRY, GUSTAVUS. *64 Frith St., Soho*, 1826–42.

BOUFLER. See DE BOUFLER.

BOUGUET. See BOUQUET.

BOUHIER. Octagonal watches said to have been introduced by Bouhier à Lyon 1538.

BOUILLARD, PAUL. "At the Eagle and Pearl in Great Suffolk St., near the Haymarket"; card, Ponsonby collection, about 1775.

BOUILLON, NICOLAS. *Blois*. Comp. 1635, master 1636, died 1659.

BOUILLON v. BOILLON.

BOULANGER, DAVID. Apprenticed 1691 to Wm. Bertram, C.C.

BOULLE (BOULE, BUHL), ANDRÉ CHARLES. *Paris*. Born 1642, died 1732. Installed at Louvre as ébéniste to the King in 1673. Famous chaser and inlayer. Inlay of tortoise-shell and brass known by his name.

BOULT, —. *Bath*. Watch, 1760.

BOULT, JOSEPH, C.C. 1709.

BOULT, MICHAEL. *Cheapside*, 1738.

BOULTER, NOEL. Long-case chiming clock, about 1790.

BOULTON, JOB, at the 'Bolt and Tun', *Lombard St.*, had a gold and a silver watch, with other jewellery, stolen in 1683.

BOULTON, ROBT. *Wigan*, 1770.

BOULU, "éleve de Lepine horloger de l'impératrice, à Paris," about 1805.

BOUNEVAL. *Paris*. Late seventeenth century.

BOUQUET, DAVID. *London*. C.C. 1632; died 1665 (the books of the C.C. in 1676 and for some years after refer to Dorcas Bouquet, who was probably the widow of David) (see Knight, Thos. and Walkden, Thos.); maker of a watch in the B.M., fine case enamelled in relief and encrusted with jewels; another and earlier example, an oval watch with covers back and front; watch in a finely enamelled case, the movement clearly signed 'D. Bouguet, Londini', 1610–40. "Lost lately a steel watch, finely cut and the work of it made by Bouquet, in a black shagreen case. Whoever hath found the same, if they bring it to Mr. Michael Scrimpshire, Goldsmith, at the sign of the Golden Lyon in Fleet St., shall have 20s. reward" (*Lond. Gaz.*, Jan. 10, 1680).

"A Pocket Clock made some years since by Mr. Boguett of Black Fryars, Watchmaker, it hath two Silver Cases, the outmost plain, the other wrought; two Brass Keys, one of the usual form, the other forked for turning the hand of the Alarum, tied to a Silver Chain; it hath the day of the Month, Tides, age of the Moon, and some other motions; it strikes every hour" (*Lond. Gaz.*, March 3–7, 1689).

"Lost the 15 instant, between Rosse and Linton in Herefordshire, a watch with an alarum in a Silver Case, with a Silver Chain, the case lined with Crimson Satten, being an old piece; the name of the maker being exprest thus: *Daniel Bouquet, Londres*" (*Lond. Gaz.*, June 19–22, 1696).

BOUQUET, DAVID ALEXANDER. *London* (*Cannon St.*). Apprenticed 1786, C.C. 1793–1824.

BOUQUET, N. Calendar watch, Schloss collection, about 1700.

BOUQUET, NICOLAS. *Lyons*. 1647 master 1687. Watch; perhaps the same as Nicolas of Paris; fine calendar monstrance clock.

BOUQUET, SOLOMON. C.C. 1650; a celebrated maker 1650–70.

BOUQUET, SOLOMON. C.C. 1683; in the British Museum is a watch of his with highly engraved gold cases, 1680–1700.

BOUQUETT, DAVID. Apprenticed 1652 to Solomon Bouquett, C.C.; watch made for a member of the family of Sir Hugh Brown, of Newington Butts, is in the Fitzwilliam Museum, Cambridge.

BOURCHIER, W. *13 Broad St., Long Acre*, 1835.

BOURDIER, JEAN SIMON. *Paris*. Master 1787–1825; remontoire clock C.A. & M.; mantel clock Ministère de la Guerre, Paris; Singing bird.

BOURDILLON, AUGUSTIN. *Stockholm*. Born 1729, died 1799; a famous maker; gold engraved watch Stern. collection; 4 watch movements Nord. Museum; 2 gold watches National Museum Stockholm illuminated Sidenbladh; 3 travelling, 2 bracket and wall clock.

BOURDON, PIERRE. Master engraver of Paris; did much to advance the art of engraving as applied to clocks and watches. He published an essay on the subject in 1703.

BOURELIER, JOHN FRANCIS. *Arundel St., Strand*, 1769–83.

BOURGAUD, HUGUES. *Annonay* and *Lyons*. Master 1637–58.

BOURGEOIS, NICOLAS. *Grenoble*, 1656–1704.

BOURGET, JEAN PIERRE. *Lyons*. Master 1647–82.

BOURGHELL, J. *New York*, 1786.

BOURLET (BORLET), THÉODORE. *Lyons*. Master 1649–81; went to *Grenoble*.

BOURRET à *Paris*. Watch showing revolutionary, decimal, and ordinary time, about 1798.

BOURRIT, DANIEL. *Geneva*. Watch, 1775.

BOURRIT, J. D. *Geneva*. Late eighteenth century–about 1835; gold engraved watch M.M.A.

BOURSAULT, HELIE. *Chattellerault*, about 1680.

BOUSSOT DE VILLENEUVE, JACQUES. *Paris*. Master 1742–89.

BOUTEVILE, WM. HY. 1823.

BOUTEVILE & NORTON. *175 Aldersgate St.*, 1810–19.

BOUVET, GEO. *Coleman St.*, 1730.

BOUVIER, ÉTIENNE. *Lyons*. 1642–89. Master.

BOUVIER, FRÈRES. Watch with performing automata (Swiss), 1780.

BOUVIER, G. A well-known French painter of watch cases in enamel, about 1740.

BOVERICK, —. "To be seen at Mr. Boverick's, Watchmaker, at the dial, facing Old Round Court, near the New Exchange, in the Strand, at one shilling each person, the furniture of a dining-room in a cherrystone, a landau with horses complete, so minute as to be drawn along by a flea; 4-wheeled open chaise weighing so small, driven by flea also; a flea chained 200 links, padlock and key all weighing one-third of a grain; and steel sizzors so minute that six pairs could be wrapped in wing of fly, but cut large horse hair" (handbill 1745).

BOVET, ALPHONSE. *Fleurier*. Born 1788; *London*, 1815; died 1850; *v.* EDOUARD.

BOVET, EDOUARD. *Fleurier*. Born 1797; went *Canton*, 1818; *Fleurier*, 1826; *Besançon*, 1832; died 1849; in 1822 started with Alphonse a society for commerce in watches for China, which lasted till 1864.

BOVET, FRIDERIC. *Fleurier*. Began making watches for the Chinese market in 1830.

BOWDEN, JNO. *London*. Long-case clock, about 1740.

BOWEN, FRANCIS. Apprenticed to John Bowyer; brought his masterpiece on completion of his indentures, and was admitted C.C. 1654. Lantern clock inscribed 'Francis Bowen in Leaden Hall streete Londini'.

BOWEN, JOHN. C.C. 1709; clock with tidal record, about 1730, signed 'Bowen, Bristol'.

BOWEN, JOHN. *143 Long Acre*, 1807–10; *2 Tichborne St., Haymarket*, 1812–42 (Bowen & Holt 1814–18).

BOWEN, RICHARD. Apprenticed to Robt. Smith 1650; C.C. 1657. A 'Richard Bowen' was maker of a large silver watch with two cases, the outer one chased and engraved with a border of flowers and the figure of the king praying, and the words, "And what I sai to you I sai unto all, WATCH." It was said to have been given by Charles I while at Carisbrooke to Colonel Hammond, 1647.

BOWEN, RICHARD. Apprenticed to Richard Bowen 1670; C.C. 1678. In 1677 Jno. Bowen was apprenticed to Mary Bowen. "Lost, a watch in black shagreen studded case, with a glass in it, having only one Motion and Time pointing to the Hour on the Dial Plate, the spring being wound up without a key, and it opening contrary to all other watches, 'R Bowen, Londini, fecit,' on the back plate" (*Lond. Gaz.*, Jan. 10–13, 1686).

BOWEN, THOMAS. *6 Charing Cross*, 1797–1813; livery C.C. 1811.

BOWER, JNO. *London*. Large lantern clock, dolphin frets, about 1690.

BOWER, MICHAEL. *Philadelphia*, 1790–1800.

BOWER, PETER. *Redlynch*, 1760–80.

BOWER, WILLIAM. *Charleston, U.S.A.*, 1772. Clocks and watches.

BOWERS, WM. *Chesterfield*. Watch, 1807.

BOWLES, JNO. *Poole*, 1790.

BOWLEY, DEVEREUX. *54 Lombard St.* A well-known maker of repeating clocks; born 1696, died 1773; apprenticed to Wm. Tomlinson; C.C. 1718, master 1759; was a member of the Society of Friends, and bequeathed a large sum to their school in Clerkenwell, as well as £500 to the C.C.

BOWLEY, JNO. *London*. Watch, 1760.

BOWMAN, JAMES. Apprenticed to Daniel Delander; admitted C.C. 1743.

BOWMAN, JOSEPH. *New Holland, U.S.A.* About 1800.

BOWMAN, JOSEPH. *Lancaster, U.S.A.*, 1821–44.

BOWNE, SAMUEL. *New York*, 1751.

BOWRA, JOHN. *4 Holles St., Oxford St.*, 1820–28; "successor to W. Berridge"; watch paper, C.C.

BOWTELL, SAMUEL. C.C. 1681.

BOWTELL, WILLIAM. C.C. 1703.

BOWYER, JNO. Possibly successor to Wm., see BOWEN, F., & BOWER.

BOWYER, WM. A good maker; subscribed for incorporation of C.C.; in 1642 he presented to the C.C. a great chamber clock, in consideration of his being thereafter exempted from all office and service, as well as quarterage and other fees; 1623–42.

BOX, JOHN. *17 Ludgate St.*, 1775–86.

BOYCE, JAS. C.C. 1692; long marquetry case clock, square matted dial, circles round winding holes, silvered ring, angel and crown corners, about 1720.

BOYCE, JOHN. *London*, 1708 C.C.

BOYCE, THOS. Apprenticed 1687; C.C.

BOYD, THOMAS. *Philadelphia*, 1807. Watch.

BOYD & RICHARDS. *Philadelphia*, 1808. Watch.

BOYLE, RICHD. Apprenticed 1652 to Jno. Bayes; C.C. 1660.

BOYLE, WILLIAM. *11 Arundel St., Strand*, 1840–42.

BOYNTON, JAS. *Howden*, 1770.

BOYS, A., & DUDUICT, JACQUES. Makers of a large clock-watch, G.M., about 1700.

BOZEK, JOSEF. *Prague*. Born 1782, died 1835; able chronometer maker.

BRACE, RODNEY. *N. Bridgewater, U.S.A.* About 1830; wooden looking-glass clock illuminated Milham.

BRACEBRIDGE (& PEARCE, *Coppice Row*, 1800),

BRACEBRIDGE, EDWARD. *8 Red Lion St., Clerkenwell*, 1805–15. (Bracebridge & Sons, 1816–18).

BRACEBRIDGE, J. & E. C. *8 Red Lion St., Clerkenwell*, 1820–90; for a short time in 1865 they also had the shop 199 Bond St.

BRACEWELL, HUNTLEY. *Scarborough*, 1822.

BRACKLEY, GEORGE. C.C. 1677.

BRADDOCK, —. *Hayfield*. Clock, about 1760.

BRADEL, ANTONI. *Augsburg*, 1736. Master 1739–70; also BRADL.; signed 'A.B.'; very fine gold watch chiselled in high relief; watch in steel case with four-colour gold Feill collection.

BRADEL, NIKODEMUS. *Augsburg*. Master 1753–70; pair-case silver watch M.M.A. signed 'Bratel Nicodemus'.

BRADFORD, HY. *89 Bethnal Green Rd.*, 1820.

BRADFORD, J. *Liverpool*. Watch, 1816.

BRADFORD, ROBERT. *London*. A small watch by him, with fine gold dial, about 1700.

BRADFORD, THOMAS. C.C. 1680.

BRADFORD, THOMAS. C.C. 1692; watch, about 1700, Norman Shaw collection.

BRADFORD, THOMAS. *Strand*. Son of Robt.; watch G.M.; C.C. 1710–70.

BRADIN (or BRAEN), CASPAR. *Westminster Churchyard*. C.C. 1715.

BRADL, ANTHONY. *Augsburg*, 1680.

BRADLEY, BENJAMIN. Apprenticed to Langley Bradley; admitted C.C. 1728.

BRADLEY, HENRY. C.C. 1681.

BRADLEY, JOHN H., *3 Great Russell St., Bloomsbury*, 1842.

BRADLEY, L. & B. Made a clock for Bancroft's School, Mile End, the date on the bell being 1734; the clock was moved to Bancroft's new school at Woodford.

BRADLEY, LANGLEY. *Whitechapel*, afterwards in *Fenchurch St.* Apprenticed to Joseph Wise 1687; admitted C.C. 1695, master in 1726; maker of the St. Paul's and other turret clocks; long-case clock, Wetherfield collection. "Stolen out of Mr. Bradley's Shop, the 'Minute Dyall' in Fanchurch St., on the 8th Inst., a Gold minute watch in an engraven case," &c. (*Flying Post*, 8th Oct., 1698).

BRADLEY, THOS. *Ilkston*, 1760.

BRADSHAW, EDWD. *Puddle Dock Hill*. C.C. 1725.

BRADSHAW, HY. Apprenticed 1687 to Wm. Slough, C.C.; Thos. Reynolds was apprenticed to him in 1699.

BRADSHAW, JNO. Apprenticed 1651 to Lancelot Meredith, C.C. 1658.

BRADSHAW, JNO. *York*, f., 1762; at *Manchester* 1770.

BRADSHAW, JOHN. C.C. 1731.

BRADSHAW, RICHARD. *London*. Apprenticed 1713, C.C. 1725–39; watch G.M.

BRADSHAW, WM. *Liverpool*. Watch, 1810.

BRADSHAW & RYLEY. *Coventry*, 1760.

BRADSTREET, ROBERT. *Rochester*. Born 1737, died 1795; watch.

BRAEMAR, GERRETT, P. *Amsterdam*. Repeating watch, V. & A., about 1735.

BRAITHWAITE, GEORGE, son. *London*. C.C. 1797–99.

BRAITHWAITE, JOHN. *London*. Apprenticed 1760, C.C. 1768, died 1797.

BRAENE, CASPAR. *London*, 1729; C.C.

BRAFIELD, THOS. *London*. Long-case clock, about 1705.

BRAFIELD, WILLIAM. C.C. 1678; fined 5s. by C.C. in 1688 for making a bad watch-case.

BRAILLARD FILS. *Besançon*, 1680.

BRAITHWAITE, GEO. *Lombard St.*, 1738.

BRAITHWAITE & JONES. *Cockspur St.* A fine repeater, about 1800.

BRAMBLE, ELIZA. *9 Wells St., Oxford St.*, 1842.

BRAMBLE, JOSEPH. *407 Oxford St.*, 1804–35; clock, enamel dial, 'Joseph Bramble London', about 1805.

BRAMBLE, WM. & EDWD. *407 Oxford St.*, 1840.

BRAMBLEY, JOSEPH. *10 Maiden Lane, Wood St.* In 1797 founder and citizen; petitioned against being compelled to take up freedom in C.C. 1783–97.

BRAMER, GARRIT. *Amsterdam*. Clock-watch, about 1750.

BRAMER, PAULUS. *Amsterdam*. Watch, about 1700.

BRANCHU, JEAN FRANÇOIS. *Geneva*. Master a. 1750–70.

BRAND, ALEXANDER. *Edinburgh*, 1727; though not apprenticed in Edinburgh, he was by favour admitted to the Incorporation of Hammermen, and in return presented a clock to Magdalen Chapel, Cowgate, then the meeting-place of the Incorporation.

BRAND, BASIL. Apprenticed 1660 to Jno. Matchett, C.C.

BRAND, C. (see BRANDT). Musical watch maker to H.M., *22 Frith St.*, 1814–19.

BRAND, JAMES. *Edinburgh*, 1732–93.

BRAND & MATTHEY. *Philadelphia*, 1797.

BRANDER, JAMES. *Keith.* Born 1788, died 1835.

BRANDON, BENJAMIN. C.C. 1689.

BRANDRETH, JOSEPH. C.C. 1718. Long-case clock, 'Brandreth, Middlewich', about 1750.

BRANDRETH, OBADIAH. *Middleswich.* a. 1766–95; watch.

BRANDS & MATTHEY. *Philadelphia*, 1799.

BRANDT, ABRAM. *Neuchâtel* 1623–46; town clock.

BRANDT, AIMÉ. *Philadelphia*, 1817–31.

BRANDT, AIMÉ & CHARLES. *Philadelphia*, 1800–13; see preceding and two below.

BRANDT, CHAS. Musical watch maker, *74 New Compton St.*, 1815; *82 Theobald's Rd.*, 1820; *145 Regent St.*, 1825; *22 Upper Belgrave Place, Pimlico*, 1835.

BRANDT, DANIEL. Near *Chaux-de-Fonds.* Born 1718, died 1768.

BPANDT, JACOB. *Montbéliard*, 1693–1743 master.

BRANDT, JOACHIM. *Göteborg*, 1732–51; long-case clock Göteborg Museum.

BRANDT, JOACHIM. *Copenhagen.* Master 1777; master of Corporation, 1795–1800; watch Chamb. collection.

BRANDT, PIERRE. *Chaux-de-Fonds*, 1689–1727.

BRANDT, BROWN & LEWIS. *Philadelphia*, 1795; watch.

BRANDT & MATHEY. *Philadelphia*, 1795–99; watch.

BRANDT-DIT-GRIEURIN, DANIEL. *Switzerland.* Born 1718, died 1768.

BRANSTON & BIRD. *39 Cornhill*, 1775 (Thos. Branston, livery Glovers' Company).

BRANT, JOHN. *Stockholm*, 1730.

BRANT, RICHARD. Apprenticed to Sam Davis 1649; C.C.

BRANT, RICHD. Apprenticed 1692 to Jno Dickens; C.C. 1700.

BRANT, BROWN & LEWIS. *Philadelphia*, 1795.

BRASBRIDGE, JOSEPH. *98 Fleet St.*, 1794.

BRASBRIDGE & SON. *198 Fleet St.*, 1825.

BRASIER, AMABLE. *Philadelphia*, 1811.

BRASS, THOS. *London.* Long-case clock, about 1750; a bracket clock signed 'Thomas Brass, London', about 1760.

BRASSEUR, —. *Rue Bourg l'Abbé, Paris*, 1770.

BRATT, ANDRE. *Augsburg*, about 1740.

BRATTEL, JOHN. *London (Old St.).* Apprenticed 1751 C.C. 1761–70.

BRATTEL, LEWIS. *London.* C.C. 1787.

BRAY, JOHN. *London.* Apprenticed 1717, C.C. 1733.

BRAY, ROBERT. C.C. 1728.

BRAY, THOMAS. *St. Margaret's Churchyard*, 1798–1804; *8 Little Queen St., Westminster*, 1807–25.

BRAUN, JOHANN GEORG. *Augsburg*, 1712; left *Augsburg* 1735.

BRAYFIELD, JOHN. C.C. 1716.

BRAYFIELD, THOMAS. *London.* Apprenticed 1742, C.C. 1762.

BRAYFIELD, THOS. Apprenticed 1675 to Erasmus Micklewright; C.C. 1682.

BRAYFIELD, WILLIAM. Apprenticed to Thos. Williamson 1671; C.C. 1678. "Drop'd the 21st December in Little Weld St. or thereabout, a middle siz'd Silver Minute Pendulum watch, going Thirty hours, with a chain, in a silver case, the name 'William Brayfield, London'. Whoever brings it to Redmond Regard, Clockmaker, at the upper end of Russell St., near Drury Lane, shall have 40s. reward" (*London Gaz.*, January 25–28, 1691).

BRAYFIELD, WILLIAM. *London.* C.C. 1712.

BRAYLEY, JOSEPH. *6 Little Guildford St., Bernard St., Russell Sq.*, card, about 1810.

BRAZIER, AMABLE. *Philadelphia*, 1796–1825.

BRAZIER, JOHN. *London.* Apprenticed 1811, C.C. 1819.

BREACH, WILLIAM. *London.* Apprenticed 1763, C.C. 1773.

BREADY, C. L. *Philadelphia*, 1808; clock.

BREAKENRIG, ALEXANDER, *Edinburgh*, 1800–26.

BREAKENRIG, JOHN. *Edinburgh*, 1767–1800.

BREAKENRIG, ROBERT. *Edinburgh*, 1757–70; able maker; made clock with very early duplex escapement.

BREAKSPEAR & CO. *Oxford St.*, 1807.

BREAMES, LEONARD. C.C. 1633.

BREANI à *Paris.* Skeleton clock with Revolutionary Calendar.

BREAR, JAS. *Philadelphia*, 1793–99.

BREARLEY, —. *Spa Fields.* C.C. 1782.

BREARLEY, JAS. *Philadelphia*, 1797–1811.

BREBANT (or BREBENT), PETER. A regulator by Peter Brebant, London, about 1710; repeating watch, Peter Brebent, London, about 1690.

BRECKELL, RICHARD. *New York*, 1733; clock.

BRECKENRIDGE, ALEXANDER. *Edinburgh*, 1799–1848.

'BREGHTEL, J. H. C., *Hagae*,' signature on case of late-seventeenth-century clock, V. & A., see VAN DE BERGH.

BREGUET, ABRAHAM LOUIS. Born 1747, died 1823; a French watchmaker of rare attainments and inventive power; Berthoud, who was Breguet's senior by two years, ends a brief notice of his brilliant contemporary thus: "Il n'a rien publié."

BREGUET, LOUIS ANTOINE, son of the above. Retired 1833.

BREGUET, LOUIS ANTOINE, son. Born 1851, died 1882.

BREGUET, LOUIS, son and successor of L. A. Born 1804, died 1883; see BROWN, EDWD.

BREGUET ET FILS. *Paris*, 1807 to date; this firm was composed of Breguet, A. L., and his son, and later by his grandson and great-grandson, who brought in Edward Brown as successor, and he was succeeded by his sons Edward and Henry.

BREGUET ET NEVEU. *Paris*, about 1830; also BREGUET, NEVEU ET CIE; style of firm of BREGUET ET FILS for a short time.

BREIDENBAUCH, L. *Philadelphia*, 1807; watch.

BRENDL. *Vienna*, about 1810; bracket clocks in French style with skeleton movements.

BRENKELAAR, JAN. *Amsterdam*, early eighteenth century; pair-case watch and tortoiseshell watch Feill collection.

BRENNER, STEFFEN. *Copenhagen*, 1556–1602; court clock in 1563; with Johan Sibe made a magnificent astronomical clock; made silver table clock dated 1556, both in Rosenborg Castle.

BRENTWOOD, WM. *London.* Watch, 1775.

BRERETON, HENRY WILLIAM. *London.* Apprenticed 1780, C.C. 1791.

BREST, EDWD. *Prescot*, 1770.

BRETON, HENRY. Keeper of the Westminster clock 1413.

BRETONNEAU, AUGUST. *Paris.* A watch by him belonging to Earl Amhurst described in *Archaeological Journal*, vol. xvii, enamelled, Holy Family on one side, St. Catherine on the other, about 1680. In the Pierpont Morgan collection is a clock-watch by him of later date, with white enamel dial enclosing a gilt centre, silver case beautifully pierced with flowers and bird, a coat-of-arms on the back.

BRETT, JAS. Lantern clock, about 1695.

BRETT, T. *Portsmouth*, 1780.

BRETT, THOS. *London.* Bracket clock, about 1730.

BRETTON, JNO. *Milsom St., Bath*, 1798.

BREWER, EDWD. Apprenticed 1665 to Stafford Freeman, C.C.

BREWER, ISAAC. *Philadelphia*, 1813.

BREWER, J. *25 New Surrey St., Blackfriars*, 1810–15.

BREWER, JOHN. C.C. 1677.

BREWER, RICHARD. *Norwich.* Long-case clock, about 1720. Mr. Sheldon, *Leicester.*

BREWER, RICHD. *Lancaster*, 1783, f.

BREWER, THOS. *Preston*, 1818.

BREWER, WM. *Philadelphia*, 1785–91.

BREWER, WM. *Blackburn*, 1814–24.

BREWSTER & INGRAHAM. *Bristol, Conn.*, 1827–39.

BREWTON, ROBT. Apprenticed 1660 to Jno Archer, C.C.

BREYNTON, VAUGHAN. C.C. 1693.

BRIANSON, EDWARD. *London.* C.C. 1768.

BRICE, WM. *Sandwich.* Watch, 1784.

BRICERLY, —. *Philadelphia*, 1778–99; partner with Bingham.

BRICKELL, EDMUND. *London.* Clock, red lacquer case, about 1730.

BRICKENDEN, NAT. Apprenticed 1651 to Robt. Whitwell, C.C.

BRICKER, WM. *Hosier Lane*, 1730.

BRIDGDEN, HENRY. C.C. 1682.

BRIDGE, EDWD. *London.* Watch, 1802.

BRIDGE, RICHARD. *London.* Watch, 1748.

BRIDGE, THOS. *Wigan*, 1690–1720.

BRIDGE, THOS. *London.* Long-case clock, marquetry in panels, 'Thos. Bridge Londini fecit,' about 1695; another, arabesque marquetry, about 1700, Wetherfield collection.

BRIDGE, WM. C.C. 1674.

BRIDGEMAN, EDWD. Apprenticed 1655 to Jno. Matchett, *Russell St., Covent Garden*; C.C. 1662.

BRIDGEMAN, JAMES. *London (Church Row).* Apprenticed 1782, C.C. 1801–24.

BRIDGER, SAMUEL. Admitted C.C. 1703.

BRIDGES, HENRY. *Waltham Abbey*, 1730–41.

BRIDGES, ROBT. *London.* Watch, 1784.

BRIDGES, THOS. *London.* Long-case clock, bird and flower marquetry in panels, about 1700.

BRIEGEL, MARTIN. *Vienna.* Master about 1780–1811; restored Olmütz clock.

BRIGGS, JOHN. "A cutter of glasses for watches"; brother C.C. 1669; several generations of Briggs, clockmakers, in Gargrave and Skipton, Yorkshire.

BRIGGS, RICHARD. *London (Whitecross St.).* Apprenticed 1748; C.C. 1756–68.

BRIGHT, ISAAC. *Sheffield*, 1810.

BRIGHT, JNO. *72 Long Acre*, 1780–94.

BRIGHT, RICHD. *9 Foster Lane*, 1815–26, see UPJOHN.

BRIGHT & SONS. *Sheffield*, 1817–33.

BRIGHTBRIDGE, HENRY WILLIAM. *London.* Apprenticed 1779; C.C. 1790.

BRILLE, —. *Paris.* Clock, about 1750.

BRIMBLE, JOHN. *Bristol*, 1785–1801; watch.

BRIMBLE & ROUCKLIFFE. *Bridgwater*, 1770; their names are on the weathercock of St. Mary's Church, Bridgwater.

BRINCK, OLOF C. *Vasterås.* Master 1816–46; wall clock.

BRIND, WALTER. Livery Goldsmith's Company, *34 Foster Lane*, 1773–88.

BRINDEAU, —. *Paris*, about 1780–1823; signature on dial of mantel clock, Ministère de la Guerre, Paris.

BRINGHURST, JOSEPH. *Philadelphia*, 1813.

BRINKLEY, WILLIAM. *London.* Apprenticed 1756, C.C. 1766.

BRINKMAN, GEORGE. *12 Union St., Bishopsgate*, 1815–40.

BRINTZINGHOFFER, F. *Philadelphia*, 1804; watch.

BRISCARD, GILLES JEAN BAPTISTE. *Paris.* Master 1772–89.

BRISCOE, SAM. *London.* Watch, 1810.

BRISCOE, STAFFORD. At the "Three Kings and Golden Ball", *Cheapside*, 1738–59.

BRISCOE & MORRISON. 1768, see MORRISON, RICHD.

BRISSON, JEAN. *Paris.* 1675 master–1693.

BRISTOW, JNO. Apprenticed 1653 to Richd. Craille, C.C.

BRISTOW, TIM. Apprenticed 1691 to Vrian Berrington, C.C.

BRISTOW, WM. G. *6 Hoxton Fields*, 1790–1835; trunk dial, Guildhall, about 1800, inscribed 'Bristow, London'.

BRITTAINE, BOAZ. Apprenticed to Wm. Speakman 1670; C.C. 1679.

BRITTAINE, STEPHEN. C.C. 1692.

BRITTAINE, STEPHEN, son. *London.* Apprenticed 1720, C.C. 1728.

BRITTON, STEPHEN. C.C. 1728.

BROAD, JOHN. *Bodmin*, 1790–1820.

BROAD, R. *204 Bermondsey St.*, 1820.

BROAD, THOMAS. C.C. 1682.

BROAD, WM. *53 Leadenhall St.*, 1804–30.

BROADHEAD, BENJAMIN. C.C. 1709.

BROADLEY, JAS. *24 Wood St.*, 1772.

BROADWATER, HUGH. C.C. 1692.

BROADWOOD, —. *London.* Watch, 1795.

BROCK, BENJAMIN. *Bristol.* 1775–about 1794; C.C.; watch.

BROCK, JAMES. *Uxbridge*, 1750.

BROCK, W. *Charterhouse*, 1650.

BROCKBANK, ATKINS, & SON. *6 Cowper's Court*, 1840–42.

BROCKBANK, JOHN. Apprenticed to Joseph Hardin 1761; C.C. 1769, livery 1777; *7 Queen St., Cheapside*, card, Hodgkin collection; afterwards at *5 Cowper's Court, Cornhill.*

BROCKBANK, JOHN EDWARD, son of John. *London.* Apprenticed 1787, C.C. 1807.

BROCKBANK, JOHN, & MYLES. *6 Cowper's Court.* Myles was the son of Edward Brockbank, of Corners, in Cumberland, and was apprenticed to his brother John at *17 Old Jewry*, 1769; C.C. 1776; they were eminent chronometer makers; John died early in the nineteenth century, and Myles retired about 1808; they were succeeded by their nephews, John and Myles Brockbank, who for a few years carried on the business as John Brockbank & Company.

BROCKBANK, WILLIAM, brother. *London (Cooper's Ct., Cornhill).* Apprenticed 1794, C.C. 1807–18; succeeded to the firm of Brockbanks with his brother until 1814; Myles rejoined the firm between 1807 and 1814.

BROCKBANK & ATKINS. *6 Cowper's Court*, 1815–35.

BROCKBANK & GROVE. *6 Cowper's Court*, 1812–14.

BROCKBANKS. *London*, 1791–1835; three marine and four pocket chronometers and watch G.M.; one of the pocket chronometers is a repeating and an exceptionally fine watch; pocket chronometer M.P.S. Dresden. v. BROCKBANK.

BROCKE, SAMUEL. 1600–25; oval watch.

BROCKEDON, —. *Totnes*, about 1790.

BROCKETT, RICHD. *London.* Bracket clock, about 1750.

BROCKHURST, THOS. *Coventry.* Silver pair-case watch; clock, about 1720.

BROD (BRODT), JOHANN GEORG. *Augsburg.* Master 1755–92.

BRODERICK, CREASEY. *Boston*, 1791; clocks and watches.

BRODIE, HUGH. *London.* Apprenticed 1772, C.C. 1779–1811.

BRODIE, HUGH, son. *London (City Road).* C.C. 1811.

BRODON, NICOLAS. *Paris.* 1674 juré–1684.

BRODON, NICOLAS. *Paris.* Master 1744–75.

BRODON, PIERRE JOSEPH. *Paris.* Master 1772–89.

BROE, HENRIE. *London.* 1622–62 C.C. Alien.

BROGDEN, JAMES. At the Dial in *Aldersgate St.*; livery-man C.C. 1765–94.

BROGDEN, JAMES. *6 Bridgewater Sq.*, 1820–28.

BROGDEN, JOSEPH. *York*, f., 1774.

BROGDEN, ROBERT. *York*, f., 1713.

BROGDEN & GARLAND. 1830.

BROGDEN & MARRIOTT. *148 Aldersgate St.*, 1770–1804.

BROILLAT (BROLLIAT), HENRI. *Colombier*, 1791–1822.

BROMHALL, WOORSLEY. *London*. Apprenticed 1726, C.C. 1735.

BRONSON, JNO. *London*. Long-case and bracket clocks; 1760–80.

BROOK, EDMUND. C.C. 1709.

BROOK, GEORGE. C.C. 1681.

BROOK, JOHN. C.C. 1632.

BROOK, RICHARD, & SON. *Poultry*, 1795–1802; Richard Brook 1804–18; C.C. 1810.

BROOK, WILLIAM. *192 Upper Thames St.*, 1783–94.

BROOKER, NUGENT. *Dublin*. Watch, 1770.

BROOKER, RICHARD. C.C. 1694.

BROOKES, EDWARD. C.C. 1690.

BROOKES, GEORGE. *London*. Watch, 1700.

BROOKES, JNO. Apprenticed 1685 to Wm. Clement, C.C.

BROOKES, THOMAS. *London*. C.C. 1766–93.

BROOKHOUSE & TUNNICLIFF. *Derby*. Watch, Mr. H. Cook, on plate 'Brookhouse's Improved Rolling Lever'; the impulse pin was a pivoted roller such as Emery made, h.m., 1819.

BROOKS, JNO. Apprenticed 1693 to Mat. Crockford, jun., C.C.

BROOKS, JOHN. *115 Bunhill Row.* Liveryman C.C., 1786–88.

BROOKS, JOHN. *4 Bridgewater Sq.*, 1794–1813.

BROOKS, ROBERT. *London*. C.C. 1733.

BROOKS, THOMAS. Watch-case maker, *22 Golden Lane*, 1790–94.

BROOKS, THOMAS. *London*. Apprenticed 1729, C.C. 1738.

BROOKS, W. *14 Clerkenwell Green*, 1825.

BROOKS, WILLIAM. *Church Row, Aldgate*. Liveryman C.C. 1776; watch, 1790, 'Wm. Brooks, Pentonville'.

BROOKS, WILLIAM. *London (Old St.)*. C.C. 1760–87.

BROOKS, WILLIAM. *London*. Apprenticed 1777, C.C. 1787–1800.

BROOKSTED, JNO. Apprenticed 1671 to Jno. White, C.C.

BROOME, THOMAS. Admitted C.C. 1652.

BROOMHALL, CHAS. *41 Stanhope St.*, 1794.

BROON, NICH. *London*. Watch, about 1760, Rochdale Museum.

BROSS, JOHN. *106 Britannia St., City Rd.*, 1820–35.

BROSY, MICHAEL. *London*. Alarum watch, about 1640.

BROUGHAM, GEORGE. *Baltimore, U.S.A.*, 1774; from *London*; clocks and watches.

BROUGHT, HY. *Workington*, 1770.

BROUNNER, —. *Lucerne*. Watch, 1780.

BROWN, —. *65 Charing Cross*. Watch, 1804.

BROWN, ANDREW. *Edinburgh*. Apprenticed to Humphrey Mylne, made a freeman of the Incorporation of Hammermen in 1675, his essay being, "Ane knock with a watch luminary globe upon the dial"; died 1712.

"James Barrow, aged about twenty, of a low stature, a little pock-marked, speaks the English accent, had on when he went away a short flaxen coll-cut wig, in an ordinary habit, run away from his master the nine-teenth instant with a plain gold watch without a crystal (glass), with an enambiled dial. The enambling on the figure is broken off. A silver pendulum watch, made by William Young, at Charing Cross, London, with a shagreen case; the centre and balance wheels pierced. A plain silver watch and an oval brass watch and several other things. Whoever can secure the said youth, and give notice thereof to Captain Andrew Brown, watchmaker in Edinburgh, shall have two guineas reward" (*Edinburgh Gazette*, 1699). The title of 'Captain' refers to Brown's position in the Trained Band which was organised to defend the city.

BROWN, EDWD. An accomplished horologist, head of the house of Breguet, died at Paris, 1895; aged 66.

BROWN, GARVEN. *Boston, U.S.A.*, 1750–76; clock.

BROWN, GARVEN. *Boston*, 1789.

BROWN, GEO. Mahogany broken-arch bracket clock signed 'George Brown, Holbourn Hill', about 1790.

BROWN, GEO. *8 Great Sutton St.*, 1820.

BROWN, GEORGE. *Beverley*, 1770–91.

BROWN, GEORGE. *London*. C.C. 1773–81.

BROWN, HENRY. *Liverpool*, 1761–96; watch.

BROWN, HENRY. *London*. C.C. 1825.

BROWN, HENTON. *Borough*. Admitted C.C. 1726; master, 1753; livery, 1766; a maker of fine watches; *58 Lombard St.* in 1754.

BROWN, ISAAC. *Liverpool*, 1796–1818. Clock.

BROWN, J. *King St., Seven Dials.* An excellent cutter of clock-wheels on an engine designed by Hindley, 1770–1810.

BROWN, JAMES (*Croydon*). C.C. 1687.

BROWN, JAMES. *Elgin*, 1726–68.

BROWN, JAMES, son of Henton. *London*. Apprenticed 1735; l.C.C. 1766; master C.C. 1770; died 1781.

BROWN, JAMES. *London*. C.C. 1767.

BROWN, JAMES. *56 George St., Portman Sq.*, 1810–42.

BROWN, JAS. *Matlock*, 1770.

BROWN, JNO. *Edinburgh*, 1720.

BROWN, JOHN WM. *14 Cheapside*, 1760–83.

BROWN, JOHN. *76 St. Paul's Churchyard*, 1769–83.

BROWN, JOHN. *65 Charing Cross*, 1783–1810.

BROWN, JOHN. *London (118 Fleet St.).* Apprenticed 1766, C.C. 1773–95.

BROWN, JOHN. *London*. C.C. 1786.

BROWN, JOHN. *London*. Apprenticed 1793, C.C. 1807.

BROWN, JOHN. *Lancaster City, U.S.A.*, about 1800; long-case clocks.

BROWN, JONATHAN. *Lavington*. About 1710–15.

BROWN, JOSEPH. *Worcester*, 1766–96; clocks and watches.

BROWN, JOSHUA. *Liverpool*, 1734–73; clock.

BROWN, NATHANIEL. *Manchester*, 1750.

BROWN, NATHANIEL. *Whitefriars*. Livery-man C.C. 1776.

BROWN, PHILIP. *London*. Apprenticed 1680, C.C. 1688; also BROWNE.

BROWN, ROBERT. *London*. C.C. 1768.

BROWN, ROBERT. *London*. C.C. 1771.

BROWN, SAMUEL. *Edinburgh*, 1750–87 C.C.; son of John (1720–50); in partnership with George Skelton, 1784; watch.

BROWN, THOMAS. C.C. 1703.

BROWN, THOMAS. *Chester*, 1766–84; *Stockport*, 1795–1801.

BROWN, THOMAS. *Manchester*, 1820–36.

BROWN, THOMAS. *London*. Apprenticed 1738; C.C. 1747; l.C.C. and died 1767.

BROWN, THOS. *36 Bull Ring, Birmingham.* Watch, silver cock, h.m., 1761.

BROWN, THOS. *Chester*. Member of the Goldsmiths' Company, 1773.

BROWN, THOS. *14 Cheapside*, 1788–1800.

BROWN, WILLIAM. *N. Shields*, 1820–47.

BROWN, WILLIAM. *Philadelphia*, 1823–37; watch.

BROWN, WM. *40 Piccadilly*, 1800–10.

BROWNBILL. *Liverpool*.

BROWNBILL, HY. *Leeds*, 1780; he issued tokens of good design in 1793.

BROWNBILL, JAS. 1760.

BROWNBILL, JNO. 1780.

BROWNBILL, THOMAS. *Liverpool*, 1803–18; watch.

BROWNE, CHAS. Apprenticed 1692 to Thos. Brayfield, C.C.

BROWNE, JOHN. C.C. 1652; master 1681.

BROWNE, MATTHEW. C.C. 1633.

BROWNE, MOSES. Apprenticed 1687 to Robt. Nemes, C.C.

BROWNE, PHILIP. Apprenticed 1680 to Nich. Beck; C.C. 1688.

BROWNE, RANOCK. *London*. C.C. 1799; partner with John Perigal.

BROWNE, RICHARD. C.C. 1675; at yᵉ Green Dragon in Cheapside, on lantern clock, gallery frets, bob pendulum. "A watch having two motions, Richard Brown being engraved on it, in a studded case" (*Lond. Gaz.*, June 16–20, 1687).

BROWNE, RICHD. See PATERSON.

BROWNE, ROBT. Apprenticed 1684 to Katherine Ames, C.C.

BROWNE, THOS. Apprenticed 1653 to Richd. Beck; C.C. 1676.

BROWNE, WILLIAM. *London*. Apprenticed 1705, C.C. 1719–32.

BROWNING, ISAAC. *Penrith*, 1770.

BROWNING, JAS. Apprenticed to Thos. Platt, 1650; C.C.

BROWNLESS, GEORGE. *Staindrop (Darlington)*. Clock, about 1720; died 1799, aged 54.

BROWNLIE, ALEXANDER. *Edinburgh*, 1710–25.

BROWNSON, THOS. *London*. Watch, 1799.

BRUCE, —. *Cranbourne St., Leicester Sq.* Watch, 1830.

BRUCE, GEORGE. *London*. Long-case clock, about 1740.

BRUCE, JAMES. C.C. 1721.

BRUDER, IGNATZ. *Simonswald* and *Waldkirch*. Born 1780, died 1845; went to *Waldkirch* in 1834; a famous maker of automatic organs and musical clocks; wrote a book on them in 1829; known as 'Uhren-Nazi'.

BRUFF, JAMES. *New York*, 1766; clocks and watches.

BRUGERCIA, C. Musical snuff-box and clock maker, *13 Richmond Buildings, Dean St.*, 1820.

BRUGGER, JOHN. *Lynn*, 1815.

BRULEFUR, JEAN. *London*. Clock in fine marquetry case, V. & A., about 1690.

BRUMWELL, —. *Pall Mall*, about 1760.

BRUN, DANIEL. *Geneva*, about 1750–71.

BRUN, JACOB. *Copenhagen*, 1645–61.

BRUN, NICLAUS. *Basle*, 1550–71; also BRON.

BRUNETTE, SAMUEL. *13 Castle St., Bloomsbury*, 1814; *34 Gloucester St., Queen's Sq.*, 1825.

BRUNNER, KASPAR. Made a clock at Berne, 1557.

BRUNSLEY, WILLIAM. Apprenticed to Thos. Carrington, but turned over to Thos. Gray; admitted C.C. 1766. On reverse of a token 'William Brunsley'; at Lilly House, against Strand Bridge, his half-penny, on obverse a clock dial and hands.

BRUNTON, WALTER. *Edinburgh*, 1771–1808.

BRUNWIN, HENRY. *Whitecross St.*, 1770–85; watch, about 1780, stolen from Newington Free Library, engraved on the plate an eagle and a snail as a guide to regulation.

BRUTON, THOMAS. *London*. C.C. 1778–1811.

BRYAN, HENRY. *Strand*, 1768.

BRYAN, JNO. *3 Shadwell Dock*, 1790–94.

BRYAN, JOHN. *London (Aldersgate St.)*. Apprenticed 1727–73; C.C.; wall clock.

BRYAN, RICHARD. C.C. 1696.

BRYAN, ROBT. Apprenticed 1663 to Wm. Seabourne, C.C.

BRYAN, SAM. Apprenticed 1685 to Jas. Hassenins, C.C.

BRYAN, SAMUEL. *London*. Apprenticed 1718, C.C. 1765.

BRYAN, SAML. *104 Golden Lane*, 1755–94; japanned long-case clock, about 1760.

BRYAN, WILLIAM, son of Samuel (2). *London*. Apprenticed 1765; C.C. 1772.

BRYANT, FRANCIS. *London*, 1808 C.C.

BRYANT, GEO. Apprenticed 1657 to Wm. Smith, C.C.

BRYANT, JOHN. *Hertford*. Maker of good clocks, 1790–1829.

BRYANT, THOMAS. *London*. C.C. 1773, died 1815.

BRYANT & SON. *47 Threadneedle St.*, 1781.

BRYCE, CLEMENT. Apprenticed 1689 to Vere Martin, C.C.

BRYERS, ARTHUR. *Chester*, 1814–18.

BRYSON, ROBERT. *Edinburgh*. Born 1778, died 1852; F. Roy. Soc. Ed.; very fine maker; made sidereal clock for Edinburgh Observatory.

BUARDSELL, WILLIAM. *London*, C.C. 1771–75.

BUCHANAN, ARCH. *Dublin*. Long-case clock, about 1760.

BUCHANAN, JNO. *Ashton-under-Lyne*, 1818.

BUCK, —. *Chester*. Lantern clock about 1680.

BUCK, EDWARD. Exhibited his masterpiece, and was admitted C.C. 1632.

BUCK, RICHARD. *London*. Apprenticed 1718, C.C. 1725–37; bankrupt.

BUCKENHILL, EDWARD. C.C. 1687.

BUCKENHILL, JNO. Apprenticed 1664 to Wm. Thorogood, C.C. 1672.

BUCKINGHAM, JOSEPH. *Black-moor's Head and Dial, Minories*, 1690–1725; long-case clock with fine marquetry case, about 1700, inscribed 'Joseph Buckingham, London'. "Stolen from Mr. Richard Parke, in Pey Alley, Fanchurch St., a gold watch made by Jos. Buckingham" (*Lond. Gaz.*, July 13–16, 1691).

BUCKINGHAM, JOSEPH, JUNR. *Minories*, 1740–60.

BUCKLAND, JNO. Bracket clock, 1795.

BUCKLAND, THOMAS. *Greenwich*. a. 1775–about 1790 C.C.; watch.

BUCKLEY, G. *Hartshead*. Clock, about 1760.

BUCKLEY, JNO. *Ashton-under-Lyne*, 1818.

BUCKLEY, SAMUEL. *Philadelphia*, 1811; watch.

BUCKLIE, DAVID. *Bridgewater Sq.*, 1780–94; livery C.C. 1787.

BUCKMAN, GEORGE. *Baltimore, U.S.A.*, 1802; watch.

BUCKNALL, THOS. *Berkhampstead*. Watch, 1740.

BUCKNELL, BURSTEM. 1800.

BUCKNELL, WM. *10 Parliament St.*, 1816–28; succeeded by Wm. Alexander.

BUCKNER, PHILIP. Apprenticed 1658 to Nich. Coxeter; C.C. 1667.

BUCKNER, RICHARD, C.C. 1710.

BUCKSHER, J. *37 Three Colts St., Limehouse*, 1817.

BUCQUET, DAN. *56 Cannon St., Ratcliff*, 1812–20.

BUCQUET (BUCKQUIT), DAVID ALEXANDER. *London*. Apprenticed 1786, C.C. 1793–1824; also BOUQUET.

BUGDEN, —. *20 Brydges St., Covent Garden*. Watch paper, C.C., about 1800.

BUDGEN, THOS. *Croydon*, about 1740.

BUDGEN, WILLIAM. *Croydon* and *London*. 1750–1824; C.C.; watch.

BUFFET, JNO. *Colchester*. Watch, silver cock, 1735.

BUGNON, —. *Paris*. Repeating watch, 1780.

BUKINGHAM. See BUCKINGHAM.

BULCKE (BULKE), JACQUES DE. *London*, 1599; striking drum watch; two oval watches; employed to repair clocks "remayning in riche peeces of Plate within our Tower of London". Appears to have worked also in Paris.

BULET, D. *Geneva*, about 1750.

BULKDAY (BULKELEY), THOMAS. *London*. Apprenticed 1707, C.C. 1715–27.

BULL, EDMD. *Fleet St*, about 1610.

BULL, JAS. *124 Leadenhall St.*, 1813–18.

BULL, JNO. Apprenticed 1691 to Ben. Graves, C.C.

BULL, JOHN. Subscribed to incorporation of C.C. 1630; admitted 1632.

BULL, RAINULPH. Keeper of the "great clock in His Majesty's Palace of Westminster"; watch; British Museum, inscribed 'Randolph Bull' and dated 1590.

BULL, WM. *Stratford, Essex*, about 1770.

BULLBY, JOHN. C.C. 1632.

BULLIMORE, HY. Apprenticed 1687 to Jno. Fitter, C.C.

BULLINE, BEN. *London*. Watch, h.m., 1763; long-case clock, about 1770.

BULLINGFORD, BENJAMIN. *Liverpool*. Watch, about 1780.

BULLMAN, THOS. *Swan Alley*. Large marquetry case clock, twisted pillars, square dial, about 1690.

BULLOCK, CHRISTOPHER. *London*. Bracket clock, mahogany case, painted dial, about 1800.

BULLOCK, EDMUND. *Ellesmere*, about 1740. A well-known family of clockmakers in Somerset and Wiltshire.

BULLOCK, JAS. *Furnival's Inn Court*, 1790–94.

BULLOCK, THOS., son of Z. 1765–95.

BULLOCK, WILLIAM. *Bath*, 1795–1826; watch.

BULLOCK, WM. *Bradford*. A bracket clock, about 1740, of *Widcombe, Bath*.

BULLOCK, WM., son of Thos. Died 1846; succeeded by his nephew, Wm. Vokes.

BULLOCK, ZEPHANIAH, 1742.

BULMAN, JACOB. *Nuremberg*. Clockmaker, master of the Locksmiths' Guild, 1780–98.

BULSTROD, WM. Apprenticed 1671 to Henry Hester, C.C.

BULT, JAMES, & Co. *86 Cheapside*, 1815–25.

BULT, JAS. *London*. Watch, silver case with landscape painted on the back, Schloss collection, about 1780.

BULTRY, DAN. Apprenticed 1655 to Ralph Greatorex; C.C. 1663.

BUMSTEAD, ROBERT. In *Holborn*. C.C. 1707; fine pair-case *repoussé* repeater in leather case.

BUNCE, MATTHEW. C.C. 1698.

BUNCE, JAMES, son of Matthew. *London*. C.C. 1721.

BUNCH, NICH. *Bramshot*. 30-hour long-case clock, about 1730.

BUNNETT, WM. *London*. Watch, 1780.

BUNON, —. *Rue Coquillière, Paris*, 1770.

BUNTING, JOSH. Apprenticed in 1651 to Wm. Bunting for Thos. Wolverstone, C.C.

BUNTING, WILLIAM. *Pope's Head Alley, Cornhill*. Admitted C.C. 1646; watch in the British Museum, on the dial is inscribed, 'Ioanni Miltoni, 1631'.

BUNYAN, ROBERT. *London*, about 1780.

BUPERT, MICHEL. *Paris*. Clockmaker to the Duke of Orleans, 1641.

BURCH, WILLIAM. *Maidstone*, from 1795–1813; watch.

BURCHALL, THOS. *Nantwich*, 1760.

BURCHETT, JOHN. *London*. Apprenticed 1721, C.C. 1731–49.

BURCHETT, JOHN, son. *London*. Apprenticed 1743, C.C. 1751.

BURCHETT, PHILIP. *London*. C.C. 1705–15.

BURCKHARDT, J. C. *14 Northumberland St.*, *Strand*, 1816.

BURDETT, HENRY. *London*. Apprenticed 1723, C.C. 1734–37.

BURDITT, JOSEPH. *London*. C.C. 1805–10; also BURDETT.

BURDON, FRANCIS. *3 Hollen St.*, 1816.

BURGE, CALEB. Apprenticed 1682 to Simon Barrett.

BURGES, CHAS. *London*. Watch, about 1740.

BURGES, GEORG MATTHIAS. *Nürnberg*. Born 1750, died 1825.

BURGES, JNO. *London*, about 1720.

BURGES, THOS. *Gosport*, 1750–60.

BURGESS, —. *Old Bailey*, 1774.

BURGESS, —. *20 Cheapside*. Card, British Museum, 1782; "from T. Wright, watchmaker to the King", watch paper, about 1795.

BURGESS, ELIAS. *London*. Long marquetry case clock, 11-in. dial, Wetherfield collection, about 1700.

BURGESS, GEO. *10 Bishopsgate St. Without*, 1790. Watch.

BÜRGI, JOBST (De Burgi or Burgius). *Prague*. Born 1552, died 1632. A talented mechanician, who in 1602 was appointed clockmaker to Rudolph II. In the Vienna Treasury is a clock with a pendulum attributed to him. There are two oval dials of rock crystal framed with plates of smoky topaz. One dial shows the minutes and hours and the other the days of the week, as well as the age and phases of the moon. Striking work for the hours is behind one dial, and quarter-hour striking mechanism behind the other. The case, in the form of an obelisk, is of agate, adorned by three circlets of garnets.

He made a very advanced escapement comprising a cross-beat arrangement with two foliots.

BURGIS, CHARLES EDWARD. Apprenticed to James Clowes, 1678. Long-case clock, bird and flower marquetry in panels, 'Edwd. Burgis', about 1690; bracket clock, black bell-top case, back plate nicely engraved and inscribed, 'Edward Burgis, Londini, fecit', about 1720.

BURGIS, ELIAS. *London*. C.C. 1681; long-case clock, about 1700, Wetherfield collection.

BURGIS, JOHN. Subscribed to incorporation of C.C. 1630. 1632. Oval calendar watch, in Dover Museum, about 1625.

BURGIS, JOHN. *London*, 1680.

BURGIS, THOMAS. Apprenticed to Thomas Knifton, 1654.

BURGIS, WILLIAM. *London*, C.C. 1770.

BURKE, —. 1630–50; C.C.

BURKELOE, SAMUEL. *Philadelphia*, 1797.

BURKHARDT & BRANDT. *Chaux de Fonds*, 1810.

BURLEIGH, NINYAN. C.C. 1692. Bracket quarter clock, ebony case, finely engraved back plate, inscribed, 'Nin Burleigh, Durham', about 1730.

BURNAP, DANIEL. Maker of brass clock movements at *East Windsor, Connecticut, U.S.A.*, 1780–1800.

BURNET, JOHN. *Tarves*, 1810–46.

BURNET, THOMAS. *Bow*, 1700.

BURNETT, CHAS. *London*. Watch, 1760.

BURNETT, JNO. *Rosemary Lane*, 1822.

BURNETT, PHILIP. C.C. 1715.

BURNETT, RICHARD. C.C. 1705.

BURNS, HUGH. *Philadelphia, Dty.*, 1811.

BURNS, JAS. *76 Lisson Grove*, 1804–42.

BURNS, JOSEPH. *Walsall*, 1765–95; long-case clock.

BURNS, RICHARD. *Liverpool*, 1770. *Manchester*, 1777. Watch, Rochdale Museum.

BURPULL, JOHN. *Tooley St.*, 1720–50. A long-case clock dating from about 1735, appeared to be inscribed 'John Burpath, Tooley St., near London Bridge', and another signed John Burputt.

BURPUR. "Lost Oct. 29, about 11 of the clock, at the Queen's Head Ale House, a plain watch with a silver case made by one Burpur. Any person that shall see this watch offer'd to be sold or pawn'd are desired to send word to the Red Lyon behin'd the Royal Exchange, and they shall have a guinea reward" (*The Postman*, Nov. 1, 1705).

BURR, JAMES. *Bristol*, 1754–83.

BURRAGE, JOHN. *Annapolis, U.S.A.* Left in 1769, clocks and watches.

BURRILL, BOYS ERR. *Great Sutton St.*, 1805–20.

BURROWES, THOMAS. *Strasbourg, Lancaster, U.S.A.* Came U.S.A. from Ireland 1784–1810, then returned to Ireland. Back in U.S.A. 1822. Long-case clocks.

BURROWS, EDWD. *Fordham*, about 1740.

BURROWS, JOSEPH. Apprenticed to Wm. Addis; C.C. 1777; livery 1803.

BURROWS, JOSEPH. *London.* Apprenticed 1763, C.C. 1773, l.C.C. 1803, died 1816.

BURROWS, WILLIAM JAMES. *London (Barbican).* C.C. 1772–81.

BURTON, ABRAHAM. Apprenticed in 1650 to Richd. Masterton, C.C. 1657; watch, 1700.

BURTON, E. One-hand clock inscribed 'E. Burton, Kirby Kendall', body of case very narrow with side wings, about 1690.

BURTON, EMANUEL. *Kendal*, 1760–90.

BURTON, EMANUEL, JUN. *Kendal*, 1790–1828.

BURTON, JAS. *Whitehaven*, 1750–70.

BURTON, JAS. *Lincoln's Inn Gate, Carey St.*, 1806–20.

BURTON, JNO. Apprenticed 1672 to Richd. Warren, C.C.

BURTON, JOHN. *Blue Anchor Alley.* Livery-man C.C. 1776.

BURTON, ROGER. Apprenticed 1678 to Ch. Bonner, C.C.

BURTON, W. *Kendal*, 1780.

BURTON, WILLIAM. *London.* Repeating watch, about 1740; known also as a maker of spring clocks about 1760.

BURTON, WILLIAM, son of Wm. *London.* C.C. 1770.

BURRY (BURY or BURI), JAKOB. *Basle*, 1642–71.

BURRY (BURY or BURI), JAKOB, son. *Paris.* Born 1663, went Paris 1686, died 1722; watch Basle Museum; very fine crucifix of wood and silver with hour and moon dial on upper part and astronomical cylinder dials on ends of arms, Feill collection.

BURRY (BURY or BURI), LEONHARD. *Basle.* Born 1633, master 1669, died 1706; eminent maker, started watchmaking in Basle. Oval crystal watch Spitzer collection signed 'Bury'. Watch Gélis collection.

BURRY (BURY or BURI), LEONHARD, brother. *Basle.* Born 1672, master 1697, died 1730.

BURRY (BURY or BURI), LEONHARD, son. *Basle.* Born 1700, master 1730, died 1766.

BURSON, GEORGE. *London.* Apprenticed 1742, C.C. 1749.

BUSBY, NICH. 1630–50; C.C.

BUSCH, ABRAHAM. *Hamburg.* Watch, about 1710.

BUSCHBERG, CARL LUDWIG. *Berlin*, 1780–1805; clock.

BUSCHMAN, DAVID. *Augsburg.* Watch, Pierpont Morgan collection, about 1610; pretty floral balance-cock pinned on; another watch, Vienna Treasury, about 1620; large alarm watch in pierced brass case, Schloss collection, inscribed, 'David Buschman Augusta', about 1680; table clock, 'David Buschman Augsburg', semicircular dial with long light hand that jumps back, and three other dials; Norman Shaw collection.

BUSCHMAN, HANS. *Augsburg.* Astronomical clock by him, Vienna Treasury, about 1600.

BUSCHMAN, HANNS. Clock, 1690.

BUSCHMAN, JOHN (*German*). C.C. 1690.

BUSCHMAN, JOHN BAPTIST. C.C. 1725.

BUSCHMANN, CASPAR. *Augsburg.* Born 1512, died 1613; clock M.P.S. Dresden.

BUSCHMANN, CASPAR, son. *Augsburg*, 1590–1611; clock signed 'Casparus Buschman, Automarius in Augusta, 1611'.

BUSCHMANN, JOHANNES, brother. *Augsburg.* Master 1620–57; Guild of Watchmakers in 1657; watches and clocks in Palace of Grossen-Behringen in Saxe-

Coburg-Gotha, in Maximilian Museum in Augsburg and in K.H.M.

BUSCHMANN, JOHN BAPTIST WILLIAM, son. *London.* C.C. 1774; also BUSHMAN.

BUSH, GEORGE, son of Walter. *London.* C.C. 1813.

BUSH, GEORGE. *Easton, U.S.A.* 1812–37; clock.

BUSH, JAMES. C.C. 1729.

BUSH, JAMES. *104 High St., Shoreditch*, 1804–42.

BUSH, WALTER, son of James. *London.* C.C. 1770, died 1803.

BUSHELL, EDWARD. Apprenticed 1687 to Wm. Bennett, C.C.

BUSHELL, MATTHEW. *Arley (Cheshire)*, 1740. On long-case clock, about 1750, 'Matthew Bushell, Ashton.'

BUSHELL, SAMUEL. Apprenticed 1690 to Wither Chesney, C.C.

BUSHELL, TIMOTHY. His son John was in 1681 apprenticed to Wm. Lavell of the Cutlers' Company.

BUSHMAN, —. *Northwich*, 1790.

BUSHMAN, JNO. *Bolton*, 1814.

BUSHMAN, JNO. Watch, tulip pillars, revolving hour circle, about 1670. 'Jno. Bushmann, London,' calendar watch, about 1720.

BUSHMAN, JOHN. *London.* C.C. 1687–about 1710; watch showing hours and minutes in openings, V. & A. watches G.M., M.M.A. and Ilbert collection; lantern clock; repeating bracket clock Virginia Museum.

BUSHMAN, JOHN BAPTIST. Livery C.C. 1786.

BUSHMAN, WM. *Stratford, Essex.* Watch paper, C.C., about 1800.

BUSHNELLS, THOS. *At the Dial in East Smithfield*, 1692.

BUTCHER, GERSHAM, *London.* Apprenticed 1739, C.C. 1749.

BUTCHER, BENJAMIN. *London (Billingsgate).* C.C. 1781, l.C.C. 1812–20.

BUTCHER, BENJAMIN HENRY. *London.* C.C. 1813.

BUTCHER, HENRY. *London.* Apprenticed 1742, C.C. 1760–91.

BUTCHER, HENRY CHARLES, brother. *London.* C.C. 1818.

BUTCHER, WILLIAM, son. *London.* C.C. 1815, l.C.C. 1820.

BUTLER, JAS. *Bolton, Lancs.* Long-case clocks, about 1760–80.

BUTLER, JOHN. C.C. 1724.

BUTTER, JOSHUA. *36 New Bond St.*, 1804; *239 Oxford St.*, 1807.

BUTTERFIELD à *Paris.* Silver pocket sundial, about 1690.

BUTTERFIELD, JNO. *Todmorden*, 1770–1820.

BUTTERFIELD, THOS. *London.* Large-sized Parliament type of clock in japanned case, about 1790.

BUTTERBAY, JNO. *Horsham.* Lantern clock, about 1700.

BUTTERWORTH, —. Long-case clock, 'John Butterworth fecit', about 1725.

BUTTERWORTH, SAMUEL. *Rochdale*, 1760.

BUTTON & PUTLEY. *204 Boro'*, 1788. Card, British Museum.

BUXTON, HENRY. *Wolverhampton*, 1748–75. Long-case clock.

BUXTON, WILSON. *London.* Apprenticed 1726, C.C. 1733–37.

BUZ, JOHANNES. Octagonal striking calendar watch, in brass case, German, about 1640.

BYE, HENRY. Clockmaker to the City of Paris, 1413.

BYFIELD (BIFIELD, BIEFIELD, BEIFIELD, BEEFIELD, BEFFIELD), GEORGE. *London.* a. 1770–86. Watches Ilbert collection and N.Y. University.

BYRNE, JAMES. *Athlone*, 1820.

BYSSE, EDWARD. Curious watch, at the British Museum, about 1620; prohibited from working by C.C. 1632, but afterwards joined the Company. See also BISSE.

CABANEL, LOUIS. *Geneva*, about 1770–91.

CABANIS, JEAN PIERRE. *Geneva*, about 1760–82; from *Languedoc*.

CABOT, —. *Rouen*, about 1750.

CABRI, PAUL SALOMON. *Geneva*. About 1770–91.

CABRIER, CHARLES. *Broad St.* Admitted C.C. 1697. Clock, long marquetry case; 'Carolus Cabrier, Londini, fecit,' about 1690; in the British Museum is a very thick rounded repeater watch, period 1690.

CABRIER, CHARLES. *79 Broad St.* A celebrated maker; C.C. 1726; master 1757; *Pig St., Threadneedle St.*, in 1759.

CABRIER, CHARLES. C.C. by patrimony, 1756; in 1777 an action was tried in the King's Bench, Cabrier *v.* Anderson, the defendant having put on five watches the plaintiff's name, without his knowledge or consent; a verdict was given for the plaintiff with £100 damages. Specimens of Cabrier's work are in the Guildhall Museum; one of them is a bell repeating verge watch movement, with nicely wrought and pierced pillars having broad bases and caps. The Czar of Russia's collection in the Winter Palace, St. Petersburg, contained a prettily decorated repeating watch by him, h.m., 1752–53. It is suspended from a chatelaine which, like the watch, is ornamented with agate and sprays of diamonds.

CABRIER, CHARLES. *Stepney*. C.C. 1692.

CABRIER, FAVEY, & EXCHEQUER. *14 Wilderness Row*, 1794.

CABRIER, FAVEY & SON. 1798

CABRIER, JOHN, son of Chas. C.C. 1730.

CABRIER & LEEKY. *15 Basinghall St.*, 1781–1804.

CABRY, JEAN. *Grenoble*, 1624–45. Clockmaker to the Princess of Piedmont.

CACHARD, —. "Successeur de Charles Le Roy à Paris," about 1780.

CACHARD, GASPER. *13 Oxendon St.*, 1820, afterwards at *Henrietta St., Covent Garden*.

CADE, GEO. *Market Weighton*, 1820.

CADE, SIMON. Admitted C.C. 1688.

CADE & ROBINSON. *153 Leadenhall St.*, 1820–25; 8-day bracket clock, mahogany case, Wetherfield collection.

CADGELL, THOS. Apprenticed 1682 to Wm. Elmes, C.C.

CAESAR, DANIEL. Admitted C.C. 1703.

CAFFIERI, JACQUES. *Paris*, 1678–1755.

CAFFIERI, PHILIP. Born at *Rome* 1634, died at *Paris* 1716.

CAFFIERI, PHILIP, son of Jacques. 1714–74. Noted designers and makers of clock cases.

CAILLATE, A. *Geneva*, about 1725.

CAILLE, —. *London*, about 1770.

CAILLIATE, ABRAHAM. Watch, about 1610, Garnier collection; another about 1630, Pierpont Morgan collection.

CAILLIATE, BARTHOLOMEUS. *Copenhagen*. Master 1726, died 1761; master of Corporation.

CAILLOT, —. *Paris*, about 1790–1823; watch.

CAIRNS, JOHN. *Providence, U.S.A.*, 1788.

CAIRNS, RALPH, *Brampton*, 1833.

CAITHNESS, —. *New Bond St.* Verge watch, about 1750. See ALLAN & CAITHNESS.

CAJETANO, DAVID & SON. *Vienna*. Inventor about 1770 of differential gear; superb astronomical clocks.

CALAME, —. *Paris*, about 1790–1825; fine mantel clock.

CALAME-ROSSET, JEAN PIERRE. *Chaux-de-Fonds*. Born 1769, died 1833; clockmaker; many clocks.

CALBECK, JNO. Apprenticed 1672 to Jas. Field, C.C.

CALCOT, TOBIAS. Admitted C.C. 1664.

CALDER, JOHN. *Glasgow*, 1775–1816.

CALDERWOOD, ANDREW. *Philadelphia*, 1802–20; watch.

CALDERWOOD, THOMAS. *London*. Apprenticed 1717, C.C. 1724.

CALDERWOOD, THOMAS. C.C. 1724.

CALDWELL, —. *Appleton*. Clock, about 1770.

CALDWELL, JOHN. *Glasgow*, 1812.

CALDWELL, WILLIAM. *Glasgow*, 1820–37.

CALLAM, ALEXANDER. *74 Lower East Smithfield*. C.C. 1790–96.

CALLAM BROTHERS. *Castle St., Long Acre*. Celebrated makers of repeating mechanism, 1795–1825.

CALLEY, JOSEPH. *London*. Apprenticed 1744, C.C. 1752.

CALLIBER, JOHN. C.C. 1703.

CALLIBER, THOMAS. C.C. 1727.

CALLIN, G. P. *Geneva*, about 1650.

CALLIS, ROBERT. *London*. C.C. 1764.

CALLWOOD, JNO. *Liverpool*, 1770.

CALVERT, NICH. Apprenticed 1665 to Robt. Grinkin, C.C.

CAM, WILLIAM. C.C. 1686; lantern clock, inscription, 'William Cam, Londini fecit.'

CAMBRIDGE, JOHN. *London*, 1703 C.C.

CAMBRIDGE, SAMUEL. C.C. 1697.

CAMDEN, WILLIAM. *Plumtree Court, Shoe Lane*. C.C. 1708; a splendid long-case clock in a handsome mahogany inlaid case; repeating watch in pierced cases British Museum; watch reputed to have belonged to Charles XII of Sweden, silver case, handsomely chased silver dial, silver balance-cock, the movement altogether a very fine one, 1708–35.

CAMEEL, C. *Strasburg*. Octagonal watch, V. & A., about 1610.

CAMERER, ALEXANDER. *Dundee*. 1828–37. Watch.

CAMERER, ANDREW. 1788.

CAMERER, ANDREW, son of Andrew. 1815–about 1855.

CAMERER, JOSEPH. 1821.

CAMERER, LAWRENCE, 1788–1821.

CAMERER, A., & CO. 1799–1843.

CAMERER (ROPP & CO.). Wooden clockmakers, *2 Broad Street, London*, 1788–99.

CAMERON, D. *318 Strand*, 1820–25.

CAMILLE, ANDRÉ. Watch, British Museum, about 1675.

CAMPANUS, MATTHAEUS, DE ALIMENIS. *Rome*, 1661–78. A priest with mechanical tastes; author of two books, *Nuova invenzione d'orivoli giustissimi ad uso della navigazione*, 1672, and *Horologium solo naturae motu, atque ingenio dimetiens . . .*, *Amsterdam*, 1678. Shows an impracticable clock with two pendulums; became famous for his work in making telescope lenses.

CAMPANUS, PETRUS THOMAS. *Rome*, 1683. Night-light clock with moving hour figure in temple case, and crank connection to pendulum. Ilbert collection.

CAMPART, JNO. *Bishopsgate*, 1774.

CAMPBELL, ALEX. *393 Strand*, 1800–05.

CAMPBELL, CHARLES. *Philadelphia*, 1797.

CAMPBELL, CHAS. *Bo'ness*, about 1780.

CAMPBELL, COLIN. *Cherry Bank, Nr. Perth*. Watch, 1810.

CAMPBELL, ISAAC. *Philadelphia*, 1813–24.

CAMPBELL, JOHN. *3 Crowns, Strand*, 1691–1701.

CAMPBELL, JOHN. *Edinburgh*, 1799–1819.

CAMPBELL, NEIL. *Aylesbury*, 1725–60.

CAMPBELL, W. F. *60 Hatton Garden*, 1825–35.

CAMPBELL, WM. *Carlisle, U.S.A.*, 1765; *Philadelphia*, 1799.

CAMPE, THO. Apprenticed 1672 to Corn. Harbottle, C.C.

CAMPER, JAMES. *99 Bridge Rd., Lambeth*, 1800–40.

CAMPEY, JOSEPH. *York*, f. 1758.

CAMPLIN, JOSEPH. *Bristol*, 1794–1812.

CANBY, CHARLES. *Wilmington*, 1815–50.

CANCHE, JACQUES. *London*. Brother C.C. 1692; silver alarum watch, in the British Museum, plain silver cases, the outer one perforated.

CANN, JOHN, brother C.C. 1649.

CANN, JUDAH. Apprenticed to Jno. Cann, 1650.

CANNON, JOHN. *London.* Apprenticed 1715, C.C. 1723–32.

CANNON, JOSEPH. *London.* Long Chippendale case clock, day of week, day of month, age of moon, high tide, dead beat escapement, centre seconds, about 1790.

CANSON. See CAWSON.

CAPPER, MICHAEL. *Philadelphia*, 1779.

CAPPER, SAM. Apprenticed 1674 to Wm. Bridge, C.C.

CAPSTICK, THOS. *Knaresboro'*, 1745–85.

CARCEL, ALEXANDRE (le jeune). *Paris.* Master 1788–1825.

CARCEL, BERNARD GUILLAUME (l'âiné). *Paris.* Master 1778–1812.

CARD, EDMUND. Admitted C.C. 1679.

CARDINAUX. *Paris.* Louis XVI mantel clock, 1807–13.

CARELL, JOHN. *Philadelphia*, 1791–93.

CAREY, GEORGE. Admitted C.C. 1679.

CAREY, JAMES. *Brunswick, U.S.A.*, 1808–50.

CARELS, JOSEPH. *Philadelphia*, 1817; watch.

CAREY, THOMAS. Admitted C.C. 1705.

CARFOOT, CHAS. *32 Aldersgate St.*, 1814–25.

CARLETON, ROBT. Apprenticed 1687 to Joseph Bates, C.C.

CARLILL, JAS. B. *York*, f., 1801.

CARLOW, P. Maker of a watch for the Duke of Sussex, 1780–1800.

CARLTASSE, ABRAHAM. Watch, about 1650.

CARMICHAEL, JNO. *Greenock*, 1750.

CARNCEL, C. *Strassburg.* Maker of octagonal pillar timepiece in V. & A. about 1600.

CAROLAN, JAMES. *69 Red Lion St., Holborn*, 1816–25.

CAROLI, CHRISTIAN. Square table clock about 1625.

CARON, ANDREAS CHARLES, his son. An eminent watchmaker, *Paris.* Horloger of Louis XV, 1720–60.

CARON, DANIEL. *Lizy-sur-ourg, France.*

CARON, FRANCOIS MODESTE. *Paris.* Master 1770, juré 1788.

CARON, PETER AUGUSTE. *Paris.* Son of A. C.; he and Lepaute claimed the invention of an improved Virgule escapement, and in 1753 the Academy of Sciences decided the point in favour of Caron, who had by then, it is said, made a watch for the king and a very small one for Madame de Pompadour; a fine enamelled watch; he was an accomplished musician as well as a playwriter, and is better known, under the name of Beaumarchais, as the author of 'Le Barbier de Seville', and 'Le Mariage de Figaro', born in the *Rue St. Denis*, 1732, died 1799.

CAROVAGIUS, BERNHARD. *Paris*, 1550.

CARPENTER, THOMAS. *5 Islington Rd.* Summoned to take up livery C.C. 1786.

CARPENTER, THOS. C.C. 1767.

CARPENTER, WILLIAM. *10 St. Martin's Court.* Hon. freeman, C.C. 1781; *15 Frith St.*, 1793, *5 Haberdashers' Walk, Hoxton*, 1817; 1770–1817.

CARPENTER, WILLIAM. *London* (Soho), 1770–1805 C.C.; gilt musical automatic clock made for India, S.K.M., and two elaborate automatic musical clocks Peiping Museum by a Wm. Carpenter.

CARPENTER & SON. *4 Andrew St., Seven Dials*, 1785–90.

CARR, FRED. *18 Bridge St., Westminster*, 1822–25.

CARRE, DANIEL. Calendar watch, Nelthropp collection, about 1690.

CARRE, LOUIS DAVID. *Paris.* Master 1748, juré 1767, died 1779.

CARRELL, JOHN. *Philadelphia*, 1791.

CARRELL, JOHN & DANIEL. *Philadelphia*, 1785; clocks and watches.

CARRINGTON, GEO. Livery C.C. 1786.

CARRINGTON, GEORGE, brother. *London.* Apprenticed 1773, C.C. 1782.

CARRINGTON, HARRY CHARLES, son of Richard. *London.* Apprenticed 1785, C.C. 1791; went to *Basingstoke.*

CARRINGTON, JAMES. Posting office, 1730; warden C.C. 1767.

CARRINGTON, RICHD. *London.* Clock, about 1760; watch, 1765.

CARRINGTON, ROBERT. *Noble St.*, 1730, *22 Old Bethlem*, 1760; livery C.C. 1766.

CARRINGTON, ROBERT, son of Robert. *London.* Apprenticed 1758.

CARRINGTON, ROBERT, son of Robert (2). *London* (*Castle St.*). C.C. 1790.

CARRINGTON, THOMAS, brother. *London.* C.C. 1796.

CARRINGTON, THOS. *St. Paul's Churchyard*, 1730, afterwards *Bishopsgate St.*; liveryman C.C. 1766.

CARRINGTON & SON. *22 Old Bethlem*, 1794.

CARRON, SAMUEL. *London*, 1689. C.C.

CARSTENS, JOHN. *London.* C.C. 1707.

CARRUTHERS, GEO. *Blewett's Buildings, Chancery Lane*, 1789–94.

CARSWELL, J. *London.* Watch, 1770.

CARSWELL, JOHN. *London.* Apprenticed 1804, C.C. 1819.

CARSWELL, JOSEPH. *Hastings.* Long-case clocks about, 1760.

CARSWELL, WM. *58 Bishopsgate Within*, 1822–25.

CARTE, JOHN. C.C. 1695; a large thick watch by him, inscribed 'John Carte, in Garden Court, in the Middle Temple'; double sets of hour and minute numerals in relief on silver dial; hour hand rotates once in 24 hours, minute hand once in 12 hours. When Peter the Great was in England, he sold him a great geographical clock which told the time at any part of the world. "John Carte, watch maker from Coventry, and lately lived at the Dial and Crown near Essex St. in the Strand, is now removed to the corner of Lombard St." (*Flying Post*, Oct., 1696).

CARTER, —. *Bishop's Stortford*, about 1760–84; long-case clock; watch.

CARTER, EDMOND. *London.* Apprenticed 1732, C.C. 1740.

CARTER, EDMOND. *London.* Apprenticed 1739, C.C. 1749.

CARTER, FRANCIS. Apprenticed 1670 to Robt. Dingley, C.C.

CARTER, J. *57 Church St., Mile End*, 1804–20.

CARTER, JACOB. *Philadelphia*, 1806. Watch. See CARVER.

CARTER, JAS. *Hampstead.* Fine chiming long-case clock, about 1770.

CARTER, JNO. Apprenticed 1669 to Andrew Allum, C.C.

CARTER, JOHN. *Bartholomew Close.* C.C. 1728–72.

CARTER, JOHN, son of Wm. Carter. *Tooley St..* Apprenticed to Boys Err Burrill in 1819, *207 Tooley St.*, 1829–42; afterwards *61 Cornhill*; Lord Mayor, 1857; master C.C. 1856, 1859, 1864; died 1878.

CARTER, JOYCE. *London.* C.C. 1776.

CARTER, LEON AUGUSTUS. C.C. 1726.

CARTER, SAM. Apprenticed 1683 to Wm. Fuller, C.C.

CARTER, SAMUEL. *London.* Apprenticed 1747.

CARTER, THOMAS. C.C. 1659.

CARTER, THOMAS. *Bishop Auckland*, 1745; clocks and watches.

CARTER, THOMAS. *Philadelphia*, 1823. Watch.

CARTER, THOS. Apprenticed 1690 to Joanna May; C.C. 1699.

CARTER, WILLIAM. *Bermondsey St.*, 1760; *207 Tooley St.*, 1794.

CARTER, WILLIAM. *Philadelphia*, 1683. Died 1738; watch.

CARTER, WM. *Cambridge.* Watch, 1720.

CARTER, WM. *Ampthill.* Long-case clock about 1710. Curious short 'Grandfather' clock, inlaid case, gives age of moon, high water at London Bridge, solar time, &c., about 1750.

CARTER, WM., JUN. 1805–26.

CARTIER, GERMAIN. *Geneva*, about 1770–91.

CARTIER, JACQUES. Maker of a watch said to have belonged to Oliver Cromwell, 1635; another watch, 'Cartier, London', about 1680; watch, 'Cartier, Geneva' about 1810.

CARTWRIGHT, ANN. *45 New Bond St.*, 1783.

CARTWRIGHT, BENJ. *18 West Smithfield*, 1669–72.

CARTWRIGHT, GEO. C.C. 1706–12.

CARTWRIGHT, N. *Lombard St.* Watch with pierced silver pillars, in Guildhall Museum, about 1720.

CARTWRIGHT, THOMAS. Apprenticed to Christopher Gould, 1693. He lived "behind the Exchange"; watch by him in gold *repoussé* case, Schloss collection, inscribed 'Thos. Cartwright, watchmaker to the Prince', about 1715; another example in the Guildhall Museum is a watch with crystal cock, jewelled, 1700–30.

CARTWRIGHT, WM. C.C. 1713; long walnut case clock, about 1713, signed 'Benjamin Cartwright junior, London'.

CARUS. *Paris.* Clock-watch, V. & A., Paris hall mark for 1733–34; silver gilt case pierced and chased, outer case of tortoise-shell.

CARVER, ISAAC. C.C. 1667.

CARVER, JACOB. *Philadelphia*, 1797.

CARY, GEORGE. *London.* Apprenticed 1671, C.C. 1679–84. Also CAREY.

CARY, JAMES. *Brunswick, U.S.A.*, 1808–50; clock.

CASINGHURST, CHRISTOPHER. Apprenticed 1690 to Robt. Nemes, C.C.

CASPER, NATHANIEL. *13 Bury St., St. Mary Axe*, 1804–42.

CASS, GEORGE. *London.* Long-case clock, about 1790.

CASSINI, JACQUES. *Paris.* Born 1677, died 1756; devised a compensated pendulum, desc. in mem. pub. 1741.

CASSIWAY, CHAS. Apprenticed 1656 to Thos. Mills, C.C.

CASTAN, STEPHEN, & Co. *Philadelphia*, 1819.

CASSIN, JEAN FRANÇOIS. *Paris.* Master 1786, juré 1787.

CASTAGNET, JACQUES JOSEPH. *Paris.* Master 1776, juré 1780–89.

CASTANG, PHILIP. *London.* Watch, Nelthropp collection, 1777.

CASTE, J. *London.* Watch, about 1690.

CASTENS, JOHN. *London.* Apprenticed 1700, C.C. 1707.

CASTER, B. *London.* Watch, silver outer case embossed, about 1770.

CASTER, WM. Apprenticed 1690 to JOSHUA HUTCHIN, C.C.

CASTER, WM. *Ripon*, 1765.

CASTERTON, JAMES. *London.* Apprenticed 1794, C.C. 1803, l.C.C. 1812–15.

CASTLEFRANC, PETER. *40 Pall Mall*, 1769–83.

CASTON, JNO. *Kirkham*, 1765.

CASTON, WM. *Kirkham*, 1780.

CATCHPOOL. THOS. *113 Strand*, 1823.

CATCHPOOL, WM. *Fenchurch St.*, 1830–35.

CATER, —. Widow, *Moorfields*, 1671.

CATER, J. *London*, about 1780.

CATER, STEPHEN. *Charleston, U.S.A.*, 1744–48; clocks and watches.

CATHERALL, J. *Chester*, 1814.

CATHERWOOD, JOSEPH. *10 Bunhill Row*, 1775–1825.

CATHERWOOD, JOSEPH & WILLIAM. *2 Newcastle Place, Clerkenwell*, 1804–42.

CATHERWOOD, G. & R. *35 Kirby St., Hatton Garden*, 1809–30.

CATHRO, G. & R. *London*, 1802–25.

CATLEY, DAN. C.C. 1731, d. 1779 (Cattley).

CATLIN (a Quaker family of horologists at King's Lynn. Three Daniels died, 1770, 1812, and 1918). Bird cage clock, 4 in. by 3 in.; bob pendulum.

CATON, ROBT. *New St.*, 1730.

CATTELL, THOMAS. C.C. 1688. "Lost in Chancery Lane, a silver Minute Pendulum Watch, with a green and silver ribbond to the key, the watch made by Cattle, London" (*Lond. Gaz.*, January 19–23, 1692).

CATTELL, THOS. Apprenticed in 1691 to Thos. Cattell, C.C.

CATTELL, WILLIAM. *Fleet St.*, C.C. 1672; lantern clock, inscribed 'William Cattell, in Fleete Street, Londini', 1671–90.

CATTELL, WM. *York*, 1822.

CATTERALL, JNO. *Liverpool*, 1770.

CATTLE, JOHN, fecit 1633. Inscription under alarum disc of a lantern clock.

CATTLE, ROBT. *York*, f., 1807. Lord Mayor, 1841, died 1842.

CATTLE & BARBER. *York*, about 1790–1810.

CATTLIN, JAMES. *58 Great Marleybone St.*, 1804–42.

CATTON, RICHD. *Leadenhall St.* Duplex watch, h.m., 1818.

CAUL & DENNIS, *19 Plumtree St.*, 1816.

CAUSARD. Clock mounted on elephant, signed 'Causard Hor. du Royᵗ suivᵗ La Cour', date about 1760.

CAVE. See ROBINSON & CAVE.

CAVE, JAMES. *Liverpool*, 1800–29; watch.

CAVE, W. *York*, 1794.

CAVELL, NATANIEL. *Ipswich.* Clock, one hand, long-case of oak, about 1700.

CAVENDISH, RICHARD. Livery C.C. 1810.

CAVETON & CLARK. *Fetter Lane*, 1730. Clock, about 1760.

CAVIT, EBENEZER. *Bungay*, 1784; *Bedford*, 1785–1808; clocks and watches; partnership with Thos. Clare dissolved.

CAWDREY. See CORDEROY.

CAWDRON, GEO. Apprenticed 1675 to Jas. Graves; C.C. by patrimony, 1684.

CAWDWELL, THOMAS. *London.* Apprenticed 1733, C.C. 1742.

CAWKUTT, THOS. Apprenticed 1693 to Nat. Bird, C.C.

CAWLEY, ROBERT. *Chester.* Watch, 1719.

CAWLEY, ROBERT. *Chester*, 1762–97. watch; long-case clock Virginia Museum.

CAWLEY, WILLIAM. *London.* C.C. 1775.

CAWNE, ROBT. Apprenticed 1663 to Lionel Wythe; C.C. 1675.

CAWSON. *Liverpool* and *Lancaster*.

CAWSON, EDWD. 1790, f.

CAWSON, ELLEN. *Liverpool*, 1833.

CAWSON, JAS. 1779, f.; at Lancaster.

CAWSON, WM. 1817, f.

CAYGILL, C. *Askrigg.* Died 1792, aged 90.

CAYNE, ANDREW. *Without Bishopsgate*, 1696.

CAZARD, H. *Paris*, about 1750.

CECIL, CHARLES. *Philadelphia*, 1808; clock.

CEDERGRÉN, JOHAN FREDRIK. *Stockholm.* Born 1774, died 1839; two lever watches, bracket and wall clock Nord. Museum.

CEDERLUND, JONAS. *Stockholm.* Born 1768, d. 1857. Court clock; five bracket and wall clocks and three watches; clock in National Museum Stockholm illuminated Sidenbladh.

CELLAR, JNO. Wooden clockmaker, *4 Westgate St., Bath*, 1798.

CELLIER, —. *Lyons*, 1580–90.

CESAR, DANIEL. *London.* Apprenticed 1696, C.C. 1703.

CESON. *Londres.* On a watch with chain-repeating work, about 1710.

CETTI, JOSEPH. *London.* Watch, 1800.

CETTI & CO. *London.* Watch 1830.

CEXT, CATHARINE. Apprenticed to James Hubert and his wife, 1730.

CHABAND, HY. *9 Plumtree St., Bloomsbury*, 1816–25.

CHADD & RAGSDALE. *New Bond St.,* 1775.

CHADWELL, NAT. *London.* Long-case clock, ting-tang quarters, moon in arch.

CHADWICK, JAMES. *18 Great Bath St., Clerkenwell,* 1804–42.

CHADWICK, JNO. *36 Cornhill,* 1783–1813; *138 Holborn Hill,* 1817.

CHADWICK, JOHN. *Liverpool,* 1770.

CHADWICK, JOSEPH. *Boscowen, N.H., U.S.A.,* 1810–31.

CHADWICK, JOSEPH. *London.* C.C. 1815–40; watch.

CHADWICK, JOSHUA. *138 Holborn Hill,* 1820–55.

CHADWICK, WM. *London.* Watch, 1825.

CHALK, JAMES. *36 Bishopsgate St. Within,* 1798.

CHALK, JAMES. *London (New Road, Whitechapel).* C.C. 1810.

CHALKE, JAMES. *London.* C.C. 1796–1807.

CHALKLEN, *Canterbury.* Died 1766.

CHALLARD, WILLIAM. *London.* Apprenticed 1737 C.C. 1749.

CHALLONER, WILLIAM. *Skinner St.* Liveryman C.C. 1776.

CHALMERS, DAVID. *Edinburgh,* 1803–19.

CHALMERS, GEORGE. *1 Prince's St., Leicester Sq.,* 1783–88.

CHALMERS, GEORGE. *Dublin,* 1766–80; watch.

CHALMERS, WILLIAM. *London,* about 1768; watch.

CHALON, JEAN JAQUES. *Geneva,* about 1750–70.

CHALONS, LOUIS. *Paris.* Master 1757, juré 1786–89.

CHAMBERLAIN, C. *London.* Watch, 1800.

CHAMBERLAIN, DAN. Apprenticed 1660 to Thos. Chamberlain.

CHAMBERLAIN, JNO. *Hertford.* Long-case clock, about 1780.

CHAMBERLAIN, THOMAS. *Chelmsford.* In the British Museum is a watch by him, about 1630; calendar and striking watch, V. & A., with pierced case of silver-gilt, movement signed 'T. Chamberlain fecit'; oval watch, Cluny Museum, 'F. Chamberlin fecit'.

CHAMBERLAINE, —. *Mark Lane,* 1717.

CHAMBERLAINE, JOHN. *Bury.* C.C. 1687; watch with day of the month ring, British Museum, about 1670; lantern clocks, about 1700.

CHAMBERLAINE, JOSEPH. *Norwich.* "A little Gold Watch made by Joseph Chamberlain, of Norwich, with a plain Dial Plate in a plain black Shagreen Case" (*Lond. Gaz.,* March 15–19, 1687).

CHAMBERLAINE, NATHANIEL. Apprenticed 1650 to Ben. Hill; C.C. 1685; master 1717 "These are to give notice that Nathaniel Chamberlin, Watchmaker (who hath lived several years at *Chelmsford,* in *Essex*), for the better accommodation of his friends and customers, hath, at the request of divers of them, taken a Chamber at *Mr. John Rust's,* in *Angel Court,* in *Lombard Street,* where he doth intend, God willing, to attend the last Fortnight in every Term for the mending his own Work, and accommodating all persons that shall have occasion for New" (*Lond. Gaz.,* January 22–25, 1676–77).

CHAMBERLAINE, THOMAS. Apprenticed to Samuel Ross, and turned over to Henry Harper; C.C. 1687.

CHAMBERLAYNE, WEBB. *Salisbury,* 1790.

CHAMBERS, —. *56 Cornhill,* 1823.

CHAMBERS, EDWD. Apprenticed 1670 to Evan Jones, C.C.

CHAMBERS, GEORGE. *Gateshead,* 1775–95. Clocks and watches.

CHAMBERS, JAMES. *3 Squirrils, St. Dunstan's Church,* 1690.

CHAMBERS, JONATHAN. *London.* Long black and gold case clock, 10-in. dial, about 1690, Wetherfield collection.

CHAMBERS, ROBERT. *London.* Apprenticed 1711, C.C. 1734–58.

CHAMBLEY, JNO. *Wolverhampton,* 1780.

CHAMBON, JEAN. *Paris.* Master 1766–89; calendar watch Denham collection; watch with auxiliary decimal dial and two minute hands Ilbert collection.

CHAMBON, MATHIEU. *Paris.* 1750–master 1774.

CHAMPAGNIEU, CLAUDE. *Lyons.* Master 1627, died 1658; alloy watch British Museum; octagonal crys. watch Côte collection.

CHAMPION, CHARLES. *Paris.* Juré 1691.

CHAMPION, CHARLES. *Paris.* About 1770.

CHAMPION, DENIS. *Paris.* Clockmaker to the Duke of Orleans, 1669.

CHAMPION, GUILLAUME ET ISIDOR. *Paris.* Watch.

CHAMPION, ISIDORE. *Paris,* 1631. Registered a private punch mark; juré 1657; cross watch.

CHAMPION, JOHN. C.C. 1651–76.

CHAMPION, JOHN. *London.* C.C. 1640.

CHAMPION, JOHN. *London.* A watch by him in V. & A., outer case of shagreen, about 1770; watch, about the same date, pair cases, the outer one of agate, Chinese figures on dial, Pierpont Morgan collection; another, enamelled case, Schloss collection, about 1780.

CHAMPION, ROBERT. Lantern clock, 'Robert Champion, of Wells, fecit 1630'.

CHAMPOT, NICOLAS. *Paris.* Juré 1675.

CHANCE, B. *London.* Maker of a watch in the British Museum, about 1720.

CHANCE, W. & G. *London.* Watch, 1815.

CHANCELLOR, JNO. *81 Bishopsgate Without,* 1793.

CHANCELLOR & SON. *Sackville St., Dublin.* Well-known clockmakers, 1800–40; in 1811 Jno. Chancellor patented (No. 3,487) a musical clock.

CHANCEY, JAS. *London.* Watch, Nelthropp collection, 1741.

CHANDLEE, BENJAMIN. *Philadelphia,* 1710. Died 1747.

CHANDLEE, BENJAMIN. *Nottingham, Maryland, U.S.A.,* to 1710. *Wilmington,* died 1745. Clock.

CHANDLEE, BENJAMIN. *Chester Co. Penna.,* 1763. Watch.

CHANDLEE, JOHN. *Wilmington, U.S.A.,* 1795–1810.

CHANDLER, ABIEL. *Concord,* 1829–58.

CHANDLER, B. *Nottingham,* 1770.

CHANDLER, EDWARD. *London.* Apprenticed 1717, C.C. 1724–37, died a. 1742.

CHANDLER, GEORGE. Lantern clock, about 1680.

CHANDLER, ROBERT. *Martin's Court,* 1793; *8 Leicester Square,* 1815–25.

CHANDLER, TIMOTHY. *Concord, U.S.A.,* 1780–1840.

CHANDLER & SON. *London.* Watch, 1775.

CHANNELL, GEO. *London.* Watch, 1795.

CHANTLER, —. *London.* About 1750. Hatton speaks with admiration of his watches.

CHANVELL, JAMES. *London.* C.C. 1699.

CHAPEAU, PETER. *London.* Extra large repeating watch, cylinder escapement, three cases, inner pierced case silver, h.m., 1746, second case *repoussé* group portraying Æneas and Dido; outer case fish skin.

CHAPLIN, WILLIAM & THOMAS. *Bury St. Edmunds* from 1776–90. Clocks and watches. Wm. died 1799, Thos. continued to 1810.

CHAPMAN, B. *London*. Watch, 1765.

CHAPMAN, JNO. Apprenticed 1679 to Wm. Herbert, C.C.

CHAPMAN, JNO. "Opposite the Riding House in the Garrison, Sheerness," about 1780.

CHAPMAN, PETER. C.C., *St. Anne's Lane*, 1730.

CHAPMAN, SIMON. C.C. 1675.

CHAPMAN, THOS. Apprenticed 1648 to Ralph Ash, C.C.

CHAPMAN, THOS. *Bath*. Long-case musical clock, about 1760.

CHAPMAN, TITUS. Apprenticed 1683 to Thos. Williamson, C.C.

CHAPMAN, WILLIAM. *6 New Round Court, Strand*, 1790–94.

CHAPO, PHILIPPE AUGUSTE (le jeune). *Paris*, 1756–89.

CHAPO, PIERRE PHILIPPE (l'aîné). *Paris*. Master 1786–89.

CHAPO, VEUVE (of Ph. Aug.). *Paris*, 1789.

CHAPONNIÈRE, JEAN PIERRE FRANÇOIS. *Geneva*, about 1770–88.

CHAPPEL, ROBERT. C.C. 1720; maker of small size sheep's-head arch-dial clocks, 'Robert Chappel, London', on disc.

CHAPPEL, THOMAS. *Little Tower St.*, 1753–63.

CHAPPIUS, JUBILÉ. *Geneva*, 1800.

CHARAS, CHARLES SAMSON. C.C. 1692.

CHARBON, PIERRE. *Geneva*, about 1770–91.

CHARLAU (CHARLO, CHARLAY), PIERRE. *Copenhagen*. Born 1710 in the Hague. Came Copenhagen 1727, master 1740, died 1773. Court clock; gold engraved watch Rosenborg Castle.

CHARLE, GEORGE. Watch with Turkish numerals, h.m., 1794; *19 Wilderness Row*, 1804–42.

CHARLEPOSE, —. *London*. Gold repeating watch, silver cap engraved with the arms of Queen Anne, outer case set with lapis lazuli, rubies, and diamonds, about 1705.

CHARLES, ANTHONY. *London*. Black lacquer long-case clock, about 1740.

CHARLES, D. *Brompton, Kent*. Watch, 1798.

CHARLESTON, JNO. Apprenticed 1767 to Ed. Clough, C.C.; watch, 1685.

CHARLSON, P. *London*. Watch, h.m., 1764.

CHARLSTROM, WILLIAM. *Percival St.* Livery C.C. 1810; 1800–38.

CHARLTON, JNO. *Durham*, 1770.

CHARLTON, JOHN. One of the first assistants of the C.C.; master 1640.

CHARLTON, MATJONAH. Apprenticed to Geo. Graham; admitted C.C. 1728.

CHARMAN, PETER. *64 Piccadilly*, 1816–26.

CHARNOCK, JAS. Apprenticed 1693 to Thos. Wheeler, C.C.

CHARRINGTON, S. Died while master C.C., 1768.

CHARTIER, FRANCIS. *1 Angel Court, Throgmorton St.*, 1765–71.

CHARTIER, PHILIPPE DIT CHAMPMARQUÉ. *Blois*, 1664. Died 1694. Circular table clock.

CHARTIER, PIERRE. *Blois*. Excelled as a watch-case enameller, 1650–70.

CHARWELL, JAMES. *London*. Repeating watch, V. & A., outer case shagreen *piqué*, about 1740.

CHASE, TIMOTHY. *Belfast, U.S.A.*, 1826–40.

CHASSEREAU, EDWARD. *London*. C.C. 1803–14.

CHASSEREAU, ROBT. *4 Beech St., Barbican*, 1804–08.

CHASSEUR, —. *London*. Small timepiece with pendulum swinging in front, about 1700.

CHASTAIGNIER, PIERRE. *La Rochell*, 1695–1710.

CHASTELAIN (CHATELAIN), CLAUDE. *Lyons*. 1651 master, died 1671.

CHATBOURNE, JNO. Apprenticed 1677 to Jno. Bennett, C.C.

CHATER, ELIEZER. *10 Exchange Alley, Cornhill*. Master C.C. 1772; livery 1776.

CHATER, ELIEZER & JAMES. *3 Cherry Tree Court*, 1760–86; in 1785 Jas. C. patented (No. 1,785) a watch guard.

CHATER, JAMES. C.C. 1727.

CHATER, JAMES, & SON. *3 Cherry Tree Court, Aldersgate*, 1754–59.

CHATER, JAMES, son of James. *London*. Apprenticed 1746, C.C. 1753–85.

CHATER, JOHN. *London*. C.C. 1766.

CHATER, NATHANIEL. *London*. C.C. 1782.

CHATER, RICHD. *14 Cornhill*, 1787–1812.

CHATER, W. *134 Goswell St.*, 1804–42.

CHATER & LIVERMORE. *2 Exchange Alley*, 1790; *10 Bartholomew Lane*, 1794; *30 Tokenhouse Yard*, 1800.

CHATFIELD, —. "Lost on Saturday last, between Frith St., Sohoe, and Lumbard St., a Silver Minute Pendulum Watch in a tortoise shell case with a black ribon, engraved on the Dyal Plate (Chatfield, Londini). Whoever brings it to Mr. Clerkson at the King's Head, near the Pump in Chancery Lane, shall have 20s." (*Lond. Gaz.*, April 4, 1695).

CHATHAM, WM. *London*. Watch, 1782.

CHATIER, ISAAC. *1 Angel Court, Throgmorton St.*, 1768–88.

CHAUDOIR, LOUIS FRANÇOIS GUILLAUME. *Geneva*, about 1770–92.

CHAUDRON, J. *Philadelphia*, 1798. Watch.

CHAUDRON, P. *Philadelphia*, 1797. Watch.

CHAUDRON, S., & CO. *Philadelphia*, 1811.

CHAUDRON, SIMON. *Philadelphia*, 1799–1813.

CHAULTER. HATTON writing in 1773, esteems his work.

CHAUND, JOHN. *London*. Long-case clock, about 1760.

CHAUNES, —. *Paris*. Watch, 1620; small watch, 'Chaunes le jeune', about 1650.

CHAUVELL, JAMES D. *Old Broad St.* C.C. 1699; clock-watch, 1705; also a repeating watch in V. & A., about 1720; watch, 1714 signed 'James Chauvel, London'.

CHAUVIN. See BERNARD.

CHAWNER, THOS. *34 Ludgate Hill*, 1783–88.

CHEASBROUGH, AARON. Long-case clock, about 1705; Rev. W. B. Atherton.

CHEDEL, —. *Les Brenets*, 1735. Several makers of this name.

CHEENY, J. Clockmaker at *East Hartford, Connecticut, U.S.A.*, 1790.

CHEESEMAN, DANIEL. C.C. 1699.

CHEESMAN, R. *Horsmunden*. Lantern clock, about 1700.

CHEETHAM, J. *Leeds*. Long Sheraton case clock, about 1790.

CHELTENHAM, MICHAEL. C.C. 1712.

CHENEVIERE & DEONNA. *Geneva*, about 1880.

CHENEVIERE, URBAN. *Geneva*, 1760.

CHENEY, BENJAMIN & TIMOTHY. *East Hartford, Conn.*, 1745–81.

CHENEY, BENJAMIN. *Manchester, U.S.A.*, 1770–80.

CHENEY, TIMOTHY. *Manchester, U.S.A.* Born 1730, died 1795; clock.

CHENEY, WITHERS. Apprenticed 1646 to Elias Allen; admitted C.C. 1657; elected master 1695, but excused on making a contribution to the poor box.

CHERITON, GEO. Apprenticed 1685 to Jno. Buckenhill, C.C.

CHERRIL, EDWD. *6 Newcastle Pl.*, 1814.

CHERRIL, E. & SON. 1825–30.

CHERRINGTON, JOHN STANLEY. *London*. C.C. 1814–22; watch.

CHESNEAU, J, à *Orleans*. Watch, about 1610.

CHESNON, SALOMON. *Blois.* Born 1572, died a. 1634. Made clock for Marie de Médicis; two watches Louvre by him or his son; watch with sundial Blot-Garnier collection; watches Mallett and Miller collections.

CHESNON, SOLOMON. *Blois.* Maker of a very diminutive watch in the British Museum, with outer leather case, about 1640; another watch by him described in vol. xi., *Archaeological Journal*, had no hands; the hours indicated by an escutcheon engraved on a circular plate, which revolved within the hour circle. "Lost on Sunday, the eighth of this instant March, about 12 o'clock, between St. Paul's and St. Dunstan's Church, a French gold watch enameld with Flowers in a Case studded with gold studs made by Solomon Chesnon at Blois, tyed with a Pink-coloured Ribbon. Whoever shall bring the same watch to Major Pinkney's shop at the Three Squirrels over against the West End of St. Dunstan's Church in Fleet Street shall have fourty shillings" (*Lond. Gaz.*, March 12, 1673).

CHESSON, THOS. *Ludgate Hill*, 1754–59.

CHESTER, GEORGE, from *London*, opens a shop at the sign of the Dial, on the New Dock (advt., New York), 1757.

CHESTER, WM. *55 Shoreditch*, 1804–40.

CHETWOOD, JOHN. Apprenticed 1692 to Jno. Pilcher, C.C.

CHEUILLARD, BARTHÉLEMY, son. *Blois.* Apprenticed 1636–77.

CHEUILLARD, JEAN. *Blois.* Watch, Marfels collection, about 1620.

CHEVALIER, (& Co., *Geneva*. Watch, about 1750).

CHEVALIER AUX TUILERIES. *Paris.* Clockmaker to Louis XV; fine long-case clock, about 1760.

CHEVALIER, FRANÇOIS. *Lyons*, 1665–82.

CHEVALIER, NICOLAS, son. *Blois*, 1639–69.

CHEVALIER, ROBERT. *Blois.* Born 1584, died 1636; engraved watch Olivier collection.

CHEVALIER et cie. *Paris.* Many watches, 1760–90.

CHEVALIER & COCHET. *Paris* 1790–1805.

CHEYNE, WITHER. *London*, 1689–96. C.C.

CHILCOTT, JOHN. C.C. 1721.

CHILCOTT, RICHARD C.C. 1690; long-case clock, about 1700, inscribed 'Richard Chillcott, London'.

CHILD, HENRY, brother. C.C. 1642; died, while master 1664; a three-train 'ting tang' lantern clock by him, inscribed 'Henricus Childe, Londini'.

CHILD, HENRY. Apprenticed 1670 to Nich. Russell, Tower Royal, Budge Row, 1677–93. "Lost the 28 instant at Aldermary Church, or between that and the Tower Royal, a plain Gold Pendulum Watch, in a new Fashion Gold Grav'd case, name, Henry Child. It had a Tulip Hand, long freised hours, in the middle of the dial plate engraven with two Birds and Flowers; it was in a Gold Pinned Case" (*London. Gaz.*, May 25–29, 1693).

CHILD, JNO. Apprenticed to Thos. Taylor, C.C. 1769.

CHILD, JOHN. *Philadelphia*, 1813–25.

CHILD, RALPH. C.C. 1661.

CHILD, RICHARD. *Fleet St.* C.C. 1632; warden 1640–43; in 1638 the Blacksmiths' Company sued 'Child, the clockmaker', for breach of his oath.

CHILD, TRUE W. *Boston, U.S.A.*, 1825. Clock.

CHILTON, THOMAS. *London.* Apprenticed 1731, C.C. 1738–60; long-case clock Virginia Museum.

CHILTON, THOS. *London.* Lantern clock, with arch dial added about 1700.

CHINN, T. W. *Huddersfield.* Three-train bracket chiming clock, arch dial, walnut case, about 1720, Wetherfield collection.

CHIPP, ROBT. Apprenticed 1679 to Robt. Seignior, C.C.

CHIPPENDALE, GILBERT. *Halifax*, 1781.

CHISHOLM, ADAM. *Dumfries*, 1780–1821.

CHISMAN, GEORGE. *London*, C.C. 1772.

CHISMAN, TIMOTHY. Summoned to take up livery C.C. 1786; master 1803.

CHOLLET, JEAN BAPTISTE. *Philadelphia*, 1819.

CHOPHARD, SAUL. *Artillery Lane.* Apprenticed to David Hubert; admitted C.C. 1730.

CHOTARD, PAUL. *London.* Apprenticed 1720, C.C. 1742–47.

CHOUDENS. See DE CHOUDENS.

CHRISTIAN, JNO. *Aylsham.* Clock, about 1750.

CHRISTIE, GABRIEL. *Edinburgh.* Apprenticed 1736.

CHRISTIE, JAMES. *Perth*, 1820–43. Two of the same name.

CHRISTIE, WM. *22 Chancery Lane*, 1804–42.

CHRISTIN, —. *Paris*, 1770.

CHRISTMAS, JAS. Apprenticed 1682 to Thos. Birch, C.C.

CHUBB, JNO. *Ringwood, Hants*, 1785.

CHUR, GEORG MELCHIOR. *Munich*, 1717–51. a. 1717 in *Holland*, where he learnt to make long pendulum clocks.

CHURCHILL, CHAS. *London.* Centre-seconds watch, h.m., 1787.

CHURCHMAN, MICHAEL. C.C. 1694.

CLAGGET, THOMAS. *Newport, U.S.A.*, 1730–49; also WM., same date.

CLAIRAT (CLERAT), JEAN. *Neuchâtel*, 1647–68.

CLANFIELD, HENRY. *London.* Apprenticed 1699, C.C. 1707.

CLAPHAM, GEO. *Brigg*, 1770.

CLARBURG, JNO. Made a clock for York Minster in 1370.

CLARE, HENRY T. *15 Meredith St.*, 1804–42.

CLARE, PETER. *Manchester*, 1780–1818, a Quaker and watchmaker. Peter, son of the foregoing; born in Manchester in 1781, was a prominent figure there till he died in 1851.

CLARE, S. *Hatton* (near *Warrington*), 1770.

CLARE, THOS. *Warrington.* Long-case clock, Battersea enamel dial, Wetherfield collection, about 1790.

CLARIDGE, ROBERT. *London* (*Finchley*). Apprenticed 1794, C.C., 1802, l.C.C. and died 1812.

CLARK, —. *Lancaster.*

CLARK, AMBROSE. *Philadelphia* and *Baltimore*, 1784. v. Bigger & Clarke.

CLARK, ANTHONY. *Serjeants' Inn, Fleet St.*, 1763.

CLARK, BENJAMIN S. *Wilmington, U.S.A.*, 1737–50.

CLARK, BENJAMIN, son of Ephraim. *Philadelphia*, 1791–1848.

CLARK, BENJAMIN, EDWARD, EPHRAIM. *Philadelphia*, *Dty.*, 1797.

CLARK, BENJAMIN & ELLIS. *Philadelphia*, 1811.

CLARK, CORNELIUS. 1733, f.

CLARK, CURE. Watch, 1750.

CLARK, CURETON. *London.* Apprenticed 1735, C.C. 1747–52.

CLARK, DANIEL. *Waterbury*, 1815–20.

CLARK, DAVID. Watch-case maker, *58 Featherstone St.*, 1789–94.

CLARK, EDW. *56 Cornhill*, 1768–75.

CLARK, EDWD. *17 Middle Moorfields*, 1772.

CLARK, ELIZABETH. Apprenticed to the same, 1676.

CLARK, EPHRAIM. *Philadelphia.* 1780. Retired 1813; watch New York University.

CLARK, FRANCIS. *10 Jewin St.*, 1789–94.

CLARK (CLARKE), HUMPHREY. *London*, 1632 C.C.

CLARK, JAS. *Morpeth*, 1750.

CLARK, JESSE, W. & C. *Philadelphia*, 1811.

CLARK, JNO. *73 Mark Lane*, 1794–1823.

CLARK, JOHN STANFORD. *London*. Apprenticed 1686, C.C. 1696-1725; watch.

CLARK, JOSEPH. *London, 1750-75.*

CLARK, MARY. Apprenticed 1674 to Hy. Fevon and Christian his wife, C.C.

CLARK, NATHANIEL. *London (Shaftesbury Pl.).* C.C. 1782-99.

CLARK, RANDELL. *London.* C.C. 1778.

CLARK, RICHARD. *Charleston, U.S.A.,* 1767. From *London;* clocks and watches.

CLARK, RICHARD, son. *London (Spitalfields).* Apprenticed 1781, C.C. 1790, l.C.C. 1792.

CLARK, ROBERT. *Charleston, U.S.A.,* 1785. Clocks and watches and Mathematical Instrument maker.

CLARK, ROBERT. Clock and watch-spring maker, Providence Row, 1775-99; watch, Robert, London, 1780.

CLARK, ROBERT COWELL. *London.* Apprenticed 1756, C.C. 1774-1801; watch.

CLARK, STANFORD. London, C.C. 1696; watch, 1710.

CLARK, THEODORE CUTHBERT. *London (Clerkenwell).* 1804 C.C.

CLARK, THOMAS. C.C. 1720.

CLARK, THOMAS. *Ulverstone,* about 1770-95.

CLARK, THOS. 1767, f.

CLARK, THOS. *9 Goswell St.,* 1830-40.

CLARK, WILLIAM. *Morpeth,* 1784-1805 C.C.; clocks and watches.

CLARK, WILLIAM RICHARD. *London.* Apprenticed 1784, C.C. 1803-20.

CLARK, WM. *Kendal.* Clock, 1720.

CLARK, WM. *York,* f., 1758.

CLARK, WM. *26 Abingdon St.,* 1730. *Bishopsgate St.,* 1754-74; *Paternoster Row,* 1775.

CLARK, WM. *6 King St., Clerkenwell,* 1800.

CLARKE, —. *Richmond, Yorks,* 1814.

CLARKE, ANDREW. Apprenticed 1682 to Chris. Gould, C.C.

CLARKE, EDWARD. *9 Holborn,* 1768.

CLARKE, ELLIS. *Philadelphia,* 1813-48.

CLARKE, EPHRAIM & CHARLES. *Philadelphia,* 1808-11.

CLARKE, GEO. *Leadenhall St.,* 1725-40; the Earl of Macartney, our first Ambassador to China, mentioned as a prominent object in the palace of the Chinese Emperor at Pekin, a musical clock inscribed 'George Clarke, Clock and Watch Maker in Leadenhall Street, London'; a fine table clock by him in the Wetherfield collection.

CLARKE, GEORGE. *Whitechapel.* C.C. 1632.

CLARKE, HEMAN. *Plymouth Hollow, U.S.A.,* 1807. Apprenticed to Eli Terry.

CLARKE, HENRY. *London.* C.C. and l.C.C. 1812, w.C.C. 1825.

CLARKE, HUMPHREY. *Hertford.* C.C. 1668; lantern clock by him about 1700.

CLARKE, HY. Warden C.C. 1822-26.

CLARKE, JAS. *Paternoster Row,* 1768.

CLARKE, JAS. *52 Rahere St.,* 1778-1840.

CLARKE, JESSE. *Philadelphia,* 1809-14. Watch.

CLARKE, JNO. C.C. 1691.

CLARKE, JOHN. *Bristol.* Watch, British Museum, in an outer case of leather *piqué,* 1630-40.

CLARKE, JOHN. *Stamford.* C.C. 1696.

CLARKE, JOHN BASUL. *St. John's Lane,* liveryman C.C. 1776.

CLARKE, JOS. *Tuxford.* Watch, 1812.

CLARKE, RICHARD. *Cornhill,* C.C. 1720; calendar watch by him, dials back and front, 1745; Richard Clarke & Sons, *Cheapside,* 1815.

CLARKE, ROBT. *York,* f., 1807; settled at Hull.

CLARKE, SAM. Apprenticed 1687 to Jno. Martin, C.C.

CLARKE, THOMAS. Admitted C.C. 1709.

CLARKE, WILLIAM. C.C. 1654.

CLARKE, WILLIAM. *London.* C.C. 1819.

CLARKE, WILLIAM. *George Yard, Whitechapel,* 1769-72.

CLARKE, WM. Apprenticed 1688 to Thos. Clifton, C.C.; on the mantelpiece of the *Punch* Dining Hall at Bouverie St. is a small bracket clock inscribed 'Wm. Clarke Whitechaple', dating from about 1700.

CLARKE, WM. *87 Gt. Sutton St.,* 1804-20.

CLARKE & DUNSTER. *London.* Repeating watch, about 1705; repeating watch in silver cases, pierced, engraved and *repoussé,* early eighteenth century, V. & A.

CLARKE & HUTCHINSON. *Philadelphia.* 1813.

CLARKSON, H. *Stockport,* 1770.

CLARKSON, HEWITT. *Wolverhampton,* 1762-80; clocks and watches; from *London.*

CLARKSON, JNO. Apprenticed 1649 to Jno. Nicasius; C.C. 1657.

CLAUDE-MARIE, ABRAM LOUIS. *Fontaines,* 1787-1802. Able clockmaker.

CLAUSEAU, LOUIS. *Avignon,* 1676. Died 1732; clocks and watches; repaired clock of Sorgue; made clock for Caderousse.

CLAVERIE, DANIEL. *Paris,* 1674 juré. See CLAVIER.

CLAVIER, DANIEL. *Paris.* 1679 juré-1685. See CLAVERIE.

CLAXTON, RICHARD. *London.* Apprenticed 1638, C.C. 1646.

CLAXTON, THOMAS. C.C. 1646; signed petition against oppression of the Company in 1656; master 1670.

CLAY, B. *London.* Watch, h.m., 1770.

CLAY, CHARLES, *Flockton, Yorkshire,* petitioned Parliament for a patent in respect of a repeating and musical watch or clock, his invention; Mr. Quare produced a watch to answer the same end as Mr. Clay's; the Attorney-General reported in favour of Mr. Clay; C.C., however, opposed Mr. Clay, and after a tough fight, extending from Feb. 1716 to the latter part of 1717, the patent was not granted. He seems to have lived subsequently in the Strand. Complicated musical clocks.

CLAY, CHARLES. *Fenchurch S.* Watch in crystal case, V. & A., 1740; another example with chased outer-case, about 1750.

CLAY, SAMUEL. Apprenticed to Jeremy Gregory, 1680; C.C. 1687.

CLAY, THOMAS. *Chelmsford.* Lantern clocks, about 1650.

CLAY, WILLIAM. Brother C.C.; maker of a watch Cromwell presented to Col. Bagwell at the siege of Clonmel; also of a clock, inscribed 'William Clay, King's Street, Westminster'; watch of later date, G.M., 1645-80.

CLAY, WM. *London,* about 1750.

CLAYPOT, DENNIS. *York,* f., 1697.

CLAYTON, CALEB. *London.* Apprenticed 1725, C.C. 1734.

CLAYTON, CHAS. *London.* watches, 1805-20.

CLAYTON, DAVID. *London.* Apprenticed 1719, 1732 C.C., died 1772.

CLAYTON, JNO. *Prescot,* about 1745.

CLAYTON, JNO. *Marple,* 1765.

CLAYTON, JNO. *Blackburn,* 1770.

CLAYTON, JOHN. *Charleston, U.S.A.,* 1743. Previously *London* and *Jamaica.*

CLAYTON, MARTIN. *Manchester,* 1790-1820. C.C.; watch.

CLAYTON, RALPH. *Marple,* 1750.

CLAYTON, THOMAS. Admitted C.C. 1646: assistant, 1671.

CLEARE, WM. Apprenticed 1688 to Hy. Jones, C.C.

CLEEKE, HENRY. C.C. 1655.

CLEETER, WILLIAM. *London.* Apprenticed 1700, C.C. 1709.

CLEEVE, WILLIAM. Brother C.C. 1654.

CLEGG, —. *London.* Long-case clock, about 1790.

CLEGHORN, SAML. *65 Shoe Lane*, 1790.

CLEMENT, EDWARD. C.C. 1671; the inscription 'Edward Clement, Exon', on a lantern clock may apply to him.

CLEMENT, F. *Paris*, about 1690.

CLEMENT, WILLIAM. Brother C.C. 1677; master 1694. An eminent maker. The invention of the anchor escapement is variously claimed for him and Dr. Robert Hooke. The earliest known example is by him dated 1671, now in Science Museum, London. He specialised in long-case clocks with 60-inch pendulum with spring suspension and a vernier regulator. In 1684 William Clement, presumably his son, was apprenticed to him.

CLEMENT & SON. *Tring*, 1773. Watch, 'Clement, Tring', 1798.

CLÉMENT, CLAUDE. *Paris.* Master 1743, juré 1767–74.

CLÉMENT, PIERRE. *Blois.* Master 1647–73.

CLEMENTS, JNO. *London.* Watch, 1820; *214 Oxford St.*, 1840.

CLEMENTS, MOSES. *Broadway, New York*, 1747.

CLEMENTS, ROBT. C.C. 1686.

CLEMENTS, THOS. *Liverpool*, about 1790.

CLEMENTS, THOS. *London.* Maker of bracket clocks, about 1760.

CLEMSON, RICHD. Apprenticed 1661 to Thos. Claxton; C.C. 1673.

CLENCH, —. *Dublin.* Watch, 1797.

CLENT, GEO. Apprenticed 1684 to Jno. Barnett, C.C.

CLERK, JNO. *Bristol*, 1687.

CLERKE, DANL. *Amsterdam*, about 1720.

CLERKE, GEORGE. *3 Cherry Tree Court, Aldersgate St.* Summoned to take up livery C.C. 1786; 1780–1820.

CLERKE, GEO. *Cherry Tree Court*, son of the foregoing; livery C.C. 1810–42.

CLERKE, JNO. *Brentwood*, about 1780.

CLERKE, NATHANIEL. *London.* Watch, h.m., 1811.

CLEVELAND, HENRY. *London.* Apprenticed 1792, C.C. 1799.

CLEWES. See CLOWES.

CLIDESDALE, —. *Bell Yd., Temple Bar.* C.C. 1780.

CLIFF, JNO. *Royston*, about 1725.

CLIFF, WM. Apprenticed 1670 to Sam. Davis, C.C.

CLIFT, JONAS. *London.* C.C. 1808.

CLIFT, THOS. *Hull.* Long black lacquer case clock, about 1730.

CLIFTON, JOHN. *14 Fazakerley St., Liverpool*, 1785–90.

CLIFTON, THOMAS. Brother C.C. 1651.

CLIFTON, THOMAS. Apprenticed to Chas. Gretton; C.C. 1687.

CLINCH, GEORGE. *London.* Long japanned case clock, about 1730.

CLINCH, THOS. "At the sign of the Clock Case," *Long Alley, Moorfields*, 1730.

CLINTON, JAMES. *London.* Clock, 1790.

CLIVERDON, RICHARD, son of Thomas. *London.* Apprenticed 1732, C.C. 1762.

CLIVERDON, THOMAS. *Holborn.* C.C. 1722.

CLODION, MICHEL CLAUDE. Born at Nancy 1728, died at Paris 1814, celebrated artist and designer of clock cases.

CLOPTON, WM. Apprenticed 1655 to Onesiphorus Helden, C.C.

CLOSON, PETER, at *Holborn Bridge.* Subscribed to incorporation of C.C. 1630; three years senior warden, 1636–38; lantern clock with balance escapement,

inscription on fret, 'Peter Closon at London, fecit'. On another example is 'Peter Closon, at Holborne Bridge'. Another lantern clock inscribed 'Peter Closon, neare Holborn Bridge, fecit'.

CLOTEAU, PIERRE. *Paris.* 1746 juré.

CLOUD, RALPH. *Beaminster.* 1740, died 1764; clock.

CLOUGH, EDWARD. *Fetter Lane.* A watch of his make, with an outer case of leather *piqué*, in the British Museum, is inscribed, 'Mayor Johne Miller, his watche', 1630–40. "Stolen a silver watch in a black case, studded about the edges, and one studded flower at the back of it, having a minute motion and the figures of the hours and minutes twice over the plate, made by Edward Clough, near Gray's Inn Gate, in Holborn" (*Lond. Gaz.*, October 6–9, 1690).

CLOUGH, SAMUEL. *Boston, U.S.A.*, 1701.

CLOWES, B. *Liverpool.* Watch, 1795.

CLOWES, JAS. Brother C.C. 1670; long-case clock, about 1690.

CLOWES, JOHN. C.C. 1672; elected a warden, 1713, but unable to serve through ill-health; small square bracket-clock, bob pendulum, locking plate, cherub corners, inscribed, 'J. Clowes, Londini, fecit'; long-case clock inscribed, 'Jon. Clows, Russell St., Convent Garden'.

CLOWES, O. B. *Liverpool.* Watch, 1805.

CLOWES, RALPH. *London*, about 1700–05.

CLOWES, ROBT. *London.* Watch, 1812.

CLUER, OBADIAH. Apprenticed 1682 to Hy. Evans; C.C. 1709; long-case clock signed, 'Obed. Cluer', a man-of-war above the dial rocks with the swing of the pendulum; underneath are the words, 'The Royal Ann'.

CLUTER, WILLIAM. C.C. 1709.

CLUTTON & CO. *48 Rupert St.*, 1825.

CLYATT, ABRAHAM. C.C. 1680.

CLYATT, ABRAHAM, brother. *London.* C.C. 1708.

CLYATT, JOHN. C.C. 1708.

CLYATT, LEMUEL. *London.* Apprenticed 1703, C.C. 1712–23.

CLYATT, SAMUEL. C.C. 1672, *Bell Alley, Coleman St.*

CLYATT, SAMUEL. C.C. 1711.

CLYATT, SAMUEL, son of Samuel. *London.* C.C. 1702.

CLYATT, WILLIAM. C.C. 1709.

CLYMER, MARMADUKE. *Bristol*, 1785–1830. Watch.

COASTFIELD, JNO. Apprenticed 1682 to Robt. Starr, C.C.

COATS, ARCHIBALD. *Wigan*, about 1780.

COATS, JAMES. *London (Clerkenwell).* Apprenticed 1781, C.C. 1788–1822.

COATS, JOHN HARDWICK, son. *London.* Apprenticed 1813, C.C. 1822.

COATS, ROBERT. *Hamilton*, 1745–61.

COATS, THOS. *London.* Watch, 1780.

COATES, JAS. & R. *Wigan.* Watch, 1794.

COATES, JOHN. *London.* Bracket clock about 1740.

COATES, JOHN. *Cirencester*, 1778–1812.

COATES, W. & J. *Cirencester.* Watch, 1786.

COATES, WILLIAM. *Cirencester*, 1792–1812.

COBB, JOHN. Apprenticed to Andrew Yeatman; C.C. 1703.

COBB, WM. *York*, f., 1659.

COBBETT, GEORGE. *London.* Apprenticed 1802, C.C. 1810; watch.

COBHAM, JAMES. *London.* Apprenticed 1732, C.C. 1739–64.

COBHAM, JNO. *Barbican.* C.C. 1725; pendulum watch, 1750.

COBHAM, JOHN. *London.* Apprenticed 1729; C.C. 1737; died 1780; watch.

COBHAM, JOHN, son of John. *London.* C.C. 1790.

COBHAM, STOCKLEY, C.C., *Red Lion St., Clerkenwell*, 1730.

COCHARD, GEO. *10 Henrietta St., Covent Garden,* 1822–25.

COCHET, ALEXANDRE. *Grenoble*, 1672–1715.

COCHIN, D. A celebrated *repoussé* chaser of watch cases, 1735–70.

COCHIN, D. *Paris*. Watch, 1790.

COCHRAN, SAML. *291 Wapping*, 1760–94. Pair-cased watch, h.m., 1768.

COCHRAN, W. *266 Regent St.*, 1825.

COCK, CHAS. *Bow Lane*. Apprenticed to Thomas Reynolds; C.C. 1736.

COCK, CHAS. *Macclesfield*, 1760.

COCK, JNO. *London*. Long-case square dial clock, chiming on six bells, about 1700.

COCKERAM, JNO. *Downham*. Halifax clock, lacquer decoration, about 1750.

COCKERTON, JONAS. 1751–78.

COCKFORD, MATTHEW. C.C. 1693.

COCKS, SAM. *Worcester*, 1800.

COCKSHUTT, EDMUND. *Liverpool*, 1770.

COCKSHUTT, WILLIAM. *Liverpool*, 1790–1824. Watch.

COCKY, COCKEY, COKEY, COCKNEY. Several generations of Somerset clockmakers; clock, Wm. Cokey, *Wincanton*, about 1700; astronomical clock, dating from about 1780, by Edward Cockney. Edward Cockey made large astronomical clock for Queen Anne.

CODEVELLE, —. *Rue de Bussy, Paris*, 1770.

CODLING, W. *Sutton*. Clock, about 1795.

COEUR, EDME. *Paris*. Master 1759, juré 1787–89.

COGGS, JOHN. Against St. Clement's Church, 1690–1700.

COGNIAT, —. *Paris*. Watch, 1720.

COHEN, A. J. *Hamburg*, 1804–21.

COHEN, A. S. *9 Newcastle St., Whitechapel*, 1820.

COHEN, SAM JACOB. *3 Castle St., Whitechapel*, 1815.

COIGNET, ANTOINE. Began in 1665, and in 1667 finished the clock of the Pont Neuf, Paris, since known as 'l'horloge de la Samaritaine'.

COIGNET, JACQUES. *Paris*. 1676 master, juré 1691; watch G.M. by him or following.

COKE, WM. Apprenticed 1673 to Wm. Glazier; C.C. 1681.

COKER, EBENEZER. *Clerkenwell Close*, 1754–69.

COLAMBELL, ANTHONY. *Aldersgate St.* Liveryman C.C. 1776.

COLBERT, J. G. I. *Grafton St.*, 1825.

COLE, AQUILA. *London*. Apprenticed 1768, C.C. 1780.

COLE, BENJAMIN. *London*. C.C. 1733; pedometer British Museum.

COLE, DANIEL. Apprenticed to Geo. Graham; C.C. 1726.

COLE, EDWARD. *London*. Apprenticed 1715, C.C. 1721, died 1771.

COLE, I. B. *54 Barbican*, 1785.

COLE, JAMES FERGUSON. *Hans Pl., Chelsea*; then *Park St., Grosvenor Sq.*; then *9 Motcombe St., Belgrave Sq.*; born 1799, died at Tower House, Bexley Heath, 1880; an able watchmaker and expert springer; he devoted much attention to the lever escapement, of which he devised several forms, and was for some time a vice-president of the Horological Institute. From the exquisite quality of his work he has been described as 'The English Breguet'. His 'masterpiece', made when he was 21, in the Ilbert collection, has a compensated balance and pivoted detent escapement.

COLE, JOHN. *London*. Apprenticed 1722, C.C. 1729, died 1744.

COLE, JOHN. C.C. 1729; long-case clocks, 1729–60.

COLE, RICHARD. *Ipswich*. Apprenticed 1785–1822 C.C.; succeeded Basset; watch.

COLE, RICHARD STINTON. *Ipswich*. Watch by him in the Ipswich Museum. 1780.

COLE, THOS. *Lombard St.*, 1754–63.

COLE, WM. *Gutter Lane*, 1780–1805. Pedometer by him, British Museum.

COLEHEAD, RICHD. *Liverpool*, 1800.

COLEMAN, —. Clock, signed 'F. Francis Coleman, Ipswich, fecit, 1665'.

COLEMAN, FR. *Ipswich*. Watch, 1720.

COLEMAN, GEO. *London*. Bracket clock, about 1780.

COLEMAN, JOHN. *115 Newgate St.* Hon. freeman of C.C. 1781–84; 1768–83.

COLEMAN, SAMPSON. *London*. Watch, 1795.

COLEMAN, THOMAS. *6 Westmoreland St., St. Mary-le-bone*, maker of bracket clock, Chippendale style of case, 1810–42; livery C.C. 1813.

COLEMAN, WILLIAM. *Arthur St.*, 1790; *14 Strand*, 1794–99.

COLES, M. A. *25 Red Lion St.*, 1790.

COLEY, S. *London*. Watch finely enamelled royal blue, Schloss collection, 1795.

COLLADON, —. *Geneva*. watch, silver bridge, about 1765.

COLLADON & SONS. Watch, painting on dial, about 1785.

COLLARD, LEONARD. Apprenticed 1765 to Jno. Delander.

COLLES, CHRISTOPHER. Long-case clock, about 1700.

COLLET, AMY. *Blois*. Comp. 1619. Also COULET.

COLLET, THIMOTHÉE. *Rouen*. Master 1652, juré 1659; circular alloy calendar watch, British Museum; fine oval calendar watch Fränkel collection.

COLLETT, JOHN. *Royal Hospital Row, Chelsea*. Mahogany long-case clock, about 1780; watch, h.m., 1799.

COLLETT, THOS. *Acton*. Watch, about 1770.

COLLEY, JOSEPH. Apprenticed to James Harrison; C.C. 1752.

COLLEY, RICHARD. *London (Fleet St.)*. Died 1736; 'Eminent Watchmaker'.

COLLEY, THOS. *Fleet St.*, 1765–80; an exceedingly fine long-case clock, Wetherfield collection, inscribed 'Graham's successor Thos. Colley London'; see also BARKLEY & COLLEY.

COLLEY & PREIST. *London*, 1762. Successors to Thomas.

COLLIBER, JNO. Apprenticed 1690 to Wm. Slough, C.C.

COLLIBER, THOMAS, son, *London*. C.C. 1726–40.

COLLIER, ARCHIBALD. *9 New Bond St.*, 1790–1830.

COLLIER, BENJAMIN. A noted maker; C.C. 1693; 1693–1730 see COLLYER.

COLLIER, CHAS. *159 Sloane St.*, 1822.

COLLIER, DAVID. *Gatley*. Clock, about 1760.

COLLIER, JOHN. *London*. 1716 C.C.

COLLIER, JOHN. *Red Lion St., Clerkenwell*, 1770–85.

COLLIER, PETER. *Manchester*, 1784.

COLLIER, ROBT. C.C., *Gutter Lane*, 1730.

COLLIER, SAM. *Eccles*. Clock, about 1770.

COLLIER, THOS. *Chapel-en-le-Frith*, 1760.

COLLINGRIDGE, EDMUND. *27 Wilderness Row*. Livery C.C. 1810; 1793–1830.

COLLINGWOOD, MATTHEW. *Alnwick*, 1820–55.

COLLINGWOOD, SAMUEL JAMES. *8 Long Alley*. Livery C.C. 1786; 1766–94.

COLLINGWOOD, SAMUEL JOHN, son. *London*. Apprenticed 1747, C.C. 1759, l.C.C. 1787, died 1816.

COLLINGWOOD, ROBT. *Rochdale*, 1816.

COLLINGWOOD, THOMAS. *London*. Apprenticed 1724, C.C. 1734–66.

COLLINS, CLEMENT. C.C. 1705.

COLLINS, JNO. *Wattisfield*. Born 1750, died 1829.

COLLINS, JOHN. C.C. 1701; at the 'White Horse and Black Boy', *Great Old Bailey*, in 1705; see SHELTON, JOHN.

COLLINS, JOHN, son of John. *London*. Apprenticed 1716, C.C. 1726, repeating watch, silver case pierced, silver dial raised figures, about 1730.

COLLINS, PETER. Apprenticed 1679 to Jas. Atkinson; C.C. 1687.

COLLINS, RICHARD. *Margate*, 1798.

COLLINS, RICHARD BARRET. *London*. Apprenticed 1738, C.C. 1751; 'clocksmith'.

COLLINS, ROBT. Apprenticed 1646 to Ahasuerus Fromantil, C.C.

COLLINSON, JAS. *London*. Watch, 1770.

COLLIOT, FRANÇOIS. *Lyons*, 1699–1725.

COLLIS, CHAS. *London*. Watch, 1720.

COLLIS, RICHD. *Romford*, 1802–07.

COLLOMBY, ABRAHAM. *Geneva*. Watch, 1745; another with calendar. At the V. & A. in a calendar watch, about 1750, signed 'Abr. Collomby, London.'

COLLOMBY, HENRI. *Hüningen (Upper Alsace)*, 1680–1730; watch in enamelled case, V. & A., signed 'H. Collomby à Huninguen'.

COLLOMBY, HENRI. *Basle*, 1670; *Hüningen*, 1679–99. native of *Geneva*; maker of repute; watches V. & A., illuminated Baillie, National Museum, Munich and Mallett collection.

COLLOMBY, JACOB. *London*. Watch said to have belonged to Oliver Cromwell.

COLLOMBY, JAQUES. Watch, Pierpont Morgan collection, silver cases, outer one chased, about 1700.

COLLUM, A. *74 Lower East Smithfield*, 1800.

COLLYER, BENJ. *London*. Long green lacquer case clock, arch dial, about 1725, Wetherfield collection.

COLMAN, —. *Ipswich*. Watch, one hand, about 1685.

COLSON (? Colston), RICHD. Apprenticed 1637 to Jas. Vantrollier; C.C. 1646.

COLSTON, JNO. C.C. 1653.

COLSTON, RICHARD. Free of C.C. by patrimony, 1682; curious 24-day clock at Battle Abbey, Sussex; other examples of his work are a fine watch, with pierced contrate wheel, and a watch (inscribed 'Colston London'), with sun and moon pointers; long burr walnut case clock, 12-inch dial, Wetherfield collection; watch, about 1720, Pierpont Morgan collection.

COLYER. See COLLYER.

COMBAULT à *Paris*. Watch, about 1780.

COMBER, RICHARD. *Lewes*. Died 1824, aged 82; chiming clock, 1778; clock, Victoria Hospital, Lewes, about 1790.

COMBES, JOHN. *London*. Apprenticed 1772, C.C. 1779; watch movement, G.M.

COMBES, SIMON. Watch, 1780.

COMBRET, HUGUES, son. *Lyons*. Born 1596, died 1669; silver tulip watch Pal. du Cinquantenaire, Brussels.

COMBRET, JACQUES. *Blois*, 1630–47. Had relations with *Lyons*.

COMBRET, PIERRE. *Lyons*. Calendar watch 1613; watch in shell-shaped case, V. & A. about the same period; cruciform watch, about 1620, Pierpont Morgan collection.

COMBS, JOSEPH. C.C. 1720.

COMFORT, WILLIAM. Brother C.C. 1647; signed a petition in 1756.

COMLEY, THOS. *London*. Watch, G.M., about 1780.

COMPIGNÉ, DAVID. Bracket clock, about 1710, inscribed 'Compigne, Winton'; watch, 'Dav. Compigne, Winton', about 1750; good long-case clocks by him are to be met with in Hampshire.

COMPORT, EBENEZER. *Temple Bar*. C.C. 1728.

COMPORT, JOSEPH, son. *London*. Apprenticed 1750, C.C. 1767–75.

COMPTON, ADAM. C.C. 1716.

COMPTON, JOHN, E., JUN. *Winchester*, 1795 C.C.

COMPTON, WALTER. *Vere St.*, 1692.

COMTESSE, LOUIS. Watch-case maker, succeeded Peterman & Debois at *Soho*, 1810; afterwards at *East St., Lamb's Conduit St.*; see STRAM.

CONANT, ELIAS. *Bridgewater, U.S.A.*, 1776–1812; *Lynn*, 1812–15.

CONDEN, ROBERT. *51 Clerkenwell Close*, 1780–85.

CONDLIFF, JAMES. *Liverpool*, 1818–36.

CONDUITT, SAM. Apprenticed 1671 to Robt. Halstead, C.C.

CONDY, THOS. Apprenticed 1684 to Cornelius Jenkins; C.C. 1692.

CONGREVE, WILLIAM. *Garden Court, Temple, London*, and at *Woolwich*, 1808–23. Comptroller of Woolwich Laboratory; patented in 1808 a clock controlled by ball rolling down zig-zag path on tilting plane.

CONING, RICHARD. *Boston, U.S.A.*, 1796; clock.

CONNELLY, WM. *93 Piccadilly*, 1825.

CONNIGERVITS, WILLIAM. *London*. Apprenticed 1804, C.C. 1811.

CONNOLEY, M. *Dublin*. Watch, 1790.

CONNY, JOHN. *London*. Apprenticed 1630 under B.C., C.C. 1640.

CONQUEROR, PETER. *Berwick-on-Tweed*, 1806–27. Long-case clocks.

CONRAD & REIGER. German octagonal timepiece in S.K.M., about 1590.

CONSTABLE, W. & G. *Bunhill Row*, 1804; *27 Finsbury St.*, 1807.

CONSTABLE, WILLIAM. *Dundee*, 1806.

CONSTANTIN (or CONSTANTINE), —. *Geneva*. Heart-shaped watch, V. & A., about 1740.

CONSTANTIN (or CONSTATINE), FRANÇOIS. *Geneva*. Born 1787, died 1854; partner from 1819 in VACHERON & CONSTANTIN.

CONSTANTIN (or CONSTATINE), MOÏSE. *Geneva*. 1750–1800. Gold shield-shaped watch V. & A.; watch Chamb. collection; watch in form of melon.

CONSTANTIN (or CONSTATINE), PHILIP. *London*. Bracket clock, about 1710; long-case clock, about 1730.

CONSTANTIN (or CONSTATINE), VINCENT. *Dieppe*. Oval watch, about 1620.

CONSTANTINE, JOHN. *London*. C.C. 1716; long-case clock about 1720.

CONSTANTINE, PET. *33 Park St., Grosvenor Sq.* Card, British Museum, 1802.

CONTANDOIS. See LE CONTANDOIS.

CONTARD & CO. *Paris*. 15-day watch, 1831.

CONY, JOHN. Brother C.C. 1641.

CONYERS, RICHARD. C.C. 1689.

CONYERS, RICHARD, son. *London*. Apprenticed 1708, C.C. 1716–26.

CONYERS, THOS. *London*. Watch, about 1715.

COOK, EDWD. *210 Borough*, 1763–72.

COOK, JOHN. *22 Cheapside*, 1768; *24 Wood St.*, 1772–75.

COOK, JOHN. *London*. Apprenticed 1773, C.C. 1785.

COOK, JOSHUA. *Blue Anchor Alley*, 1793.

COOK, WM. *London*. Long-case clock, about 1700.

COOK, ZENAS. *Waterbury*, 1815–20.

COOKE, EDWD. Apprenticed 1687 to Wm. Kenning.

COOKE, G. E., *5 Jewin St.*, 1822.

COOKE, JOB. *London*. Apprenticed 1743, C.C. 1750.

COOKE, JOHN. Apprenticed to Isaac Law, 1641; C.C. 1649; hexagonal watch in case of rock crystal set in enamelled gold, Wallace collection, about 1660.

COOKE, JOHN. Apprenticed to Wm. Dobb, 1655; C.C. 1662; fine long-case clock, marquetry case, about 1680.

COOKE, JOHN. *London.* Apprenticed 1700, C.C. 1713–18.

COOKE, JOHN. *London (Aylesbury St.).* Apprenticed 1759, C.C. 1775–86.

COOKE, JOHN. *22 Cheapside.* Livery Goldsmiths' Company, 1765–77.

COOKE. JOSEPH. C.C. 1715.

COOKE, LEWIS. f., of York, 1614; petitioner for incorporation of C.C. 1630–32.

COOKE, ROBERT. C.C. 1667.

COOKE, ROBERT. *7 Star Alley, Fenchurch St.*, 1804–10.

COOKE, THOMAS. *London.* C.C. 1669–1702; long-case clock.

COOKE, WILLIAM. C.C. 1681.

COOKE, WILLIAM. C.C. 1708.

COOKE & GURNEY. *Foster Lane*, 1754–59.

COOLEY, HY. *London.* Long Sheraton-case clock, about 1805.

COOMBES, FISHER. Admitted C.C. 1728.

COOMBES, JAMES. *London.* C.C. 1719.

COOMBES, JAS. *10 Mitchell St., St. Luke's*, 1815; *3 Clerkenwell Green*, 1825.

COOMBES, JOSEPH. *London.* Apprenticed 1712, C.C. 1720.

COOMBES, WM. Apprenticed 1689 to Isaac Lowndes, C.C.

COOPER, BENJ. *Brownlow St.*, 1775.

COOPER, E. *Wynyatt St.*, 1820.

COOPER, EDWARD. Clock-case maker, *91 Sutton St.*, 1789–94.

COOPER, EDWD. *London.* Watch about 1730.

COOPER, GEO. *London.* Mahogany long-case clock, about 1760.

COOPER, HUGH. C.C. 1653.

COOPER, JAS. Apprenticed 1693 to Wm. Boad, C.C.

COOPER, JOHN. *London.* Apprenticed 1802, C.C. 1813.

COOPER, JON. *Cardiff.* Watch, pendulum balance showing through dial, minute hand only, blued steel rotating hour disc showing through curved slit in the lower half of the dial, silver medallion over top plate, with finely chased female head and military trophies, about 1700.

COOPER, JOS. *Whitchurch*, 1765.

COOPER, STEPHEN. Apprenticed 1675 to Thos. Morgan, C.C.

COOPER, THOMAS. *1 King St., Little Tower Hill*, 1800.

COOPER, THOMAS. *London.* Apprenticed 1789, C.C. 1798.

COOPER, THOS. *Newport.* Watch, 1796.

COOPER, WILLIAM. *44 Red Lion St.*, 1816; *12 Gee St.*, 1820–42.

COOPER, WILLIAM. *Hamilton*, 1808–24.

COOPER, WM. *8 Old Bailey*, 1804.

COOPER, WM. *Derby*, 1770.

COOPER & SON. *Derby.* Watch, 1786.

COOTE, THOS. *Dublin.* Bracket clock in pear-wood case, about 1750.

COOTH, JNO. *London.* Watch, 1720.

COPE, CHAS. JNO. *38 Berners St.*, 1800–30; he was a man of some note, and attested the value of Earnshaw's improvements in 1804.

COPE, PETER. Brother C.C. 1638.

COPELAND, ALEXANDER. *113 Leadenhall St.*, 1800–15. Livery C.C. 1810.

COPESTAKE, HY. *8 New Bridge St.*, 1793.

COPPER, REG. A. Watch; on plate over balance, 'Geo. Virtue his watch. From Berne, — 1750'.

COPPING, GEO. Apprenticed to Richard, 1654.

COPPING, RICHD. About 1640; C.C.

COPPINGE, —. Long-case clock, 'Richard Coppinge, at St. Edmund's Bury in Suffolke', about 1720.

COPPLESTONE, WM. Apprenticed 1683 to Wm. Robinson, C.C.

CORBET, NATHANIEL. Maker of a silver watch with studded case, frosted dial plate (*Lond. Gaz.*, Sept, 21–25, 1693).

CORBETT, —. *Hadleigh.* Watch, G.M., about 1780.

CORBETT, J. *42 Clerkenwell Close*, 1825.

CORBIGNY, —. French watch, 1700.

CORBITT, —. *10 Short's Bdgs.*, 1835.

CORBITT, BEN. Apprenticed 1682 to Thos. Snelling, C.C.

CORDEROY, PHIL. Apprenticed 1672 to Robt. Seignior; C.C. 1679.

CORDEROY, THOS. Apprenticed 1663 to Nicholas Coxeter; C.C. 1670.

CORDEROY, WALTER. Apprenticed 1692 to Thos. Taylor.

CORDING, CHAS. *118 Minories*, 1822–25.

CORDING, JNO. *232 Strand*, 1812–30.

CORDING, JOSH. *21 Holborn Hill*, 1817–25.

CORDING, THOMAS. *38 Aldgate*, 1822–30.

CORDINGLEY, THOS. *Leeds*, 1829.

CORDON, RICHARD. C.C. 1729.

CORDREY. See CORDEROY.

CORDWELL, ROBT. C.C. 1646.

CORGEE, ARTHUR. *Philadelphia*, 1823. Clock.

CORGHEY, JOHN. *Fleet St.*, 1754–59.

CORKER, D. *18 Langley Place, Commercial Rd.*, 1820–42.

CORMIER, PIERRE. In 1481 a sum of four livres tournois was paid to Pierre Cormier, locksmith, for making a clock case and doing sundry other work for Louis XI for his Château at Plessis-du-Parc.

CORNELIUS, JACOB. *London.* Small diamond-shaped spring timepiece, catgut line, about 1620; C.C., but date of election uncertain.

CORNIQUET, PHILIPPE JACQUES. *Paris.* Master 1785–1813; astronomical and calendar clock; mantel clock Pal. de l'Élysée.

CORNISH, MICHAEL. C.C. 1661.

CORNISH, WM. Apprenticed 1659 to Robt. Hanslapp, C.C.

CORNWALL, DANIEL. *Billericay, Essex.* 'Act of Parliament' clock, about 1798.

CORNWALL, DAUL. *London.* Small silver watch, about 1750.

CORNWALL, HY. *London.* Watch, 1790; another, 1800.

CORNWALLIS, WILLIAM. *London.* Watch, silver case, enamelled dial, with Hope and a ship, about 1800.

CORP, WM. *84 Aldersgate St.*, 1835.

CORRALL, FRA. *Lutterworth*, 1740.

CORRALL, THOMAS LISSIER. *Lutterworth.* a. 1756–95; watch.

CORRIE, PHILIP. *Langholme.* Long-case clock, about 1770–1817.

CORTAULD, SAMUEL. *Cornhill, opposite Royal Exchange*, 1759–63.

CORTAULD, P. & COWLES. *21 Cornhill*, 1768–75.

COSBEY, ROBERT. At *ye Diall, Rood Lane.* C.C. 1653–79.

COSENS, NATHANIEL. *Bristol*, 1781–97; clock.

COSENS, NICHOLAS. Hour glass maker, *York*, f., 1638.

COSMAN, PHILIP. *Amsterdam.* Watch, about 1790.

COSSE, JAMES. *Cornhill.* Watch, 1720.

COSSON, S. *St. George's East*, 1835.

COSTA, J. H. Timepiece of gold, signed 'Inventé et executé par Jh. Costa Amateur d'Horlogerie à Marseille', Turkish numerals, Wallace collection, about 1790.

COSTEN, ADAM. *Kirkham.* Died 1788, aged 77; long-case clock, about 1760; on another clock, about 1770, 'Adam Costen Kirkham'.

COSTEN, WILLIAM, son of above. Died 1831, aged 71.

COSTER, ROBERT. C.C. 1655.

COSTER, SAMUEL. *The Hague*. Maker of Huygens' first pendulum clocks; died 1659.

COSTER, THOMAS. *London*. Apprenticed 1756, C.C. 1764.

COSTER, WILLIAM. Admitted C.C. 1660.

COSTONTIN, VINCENT. *Dieppe*. Watch, Schloss collection, about 1660.

COTEAU, JEAN. *Sèvres*. Born about 1739, died after 1810; painter on enamel; dials in Mobilier Nat., Carnavalet Museum and Dijon Museum.

COTHER, WILLIAM. Brother C.C. 1668.

COTSWORTH, JNO. C.C. 1669; Edwd. Crouch was apprenticed to him in 1691; long-case month clock, about 1730, signed 'John Cotsworth, London'.

COTTEL, JOHN. Lantern clock, inscribed, 'John Cottel, fecit 1653'.

COTTER, EBENEZER. *13 Goldsmith Ct., Wood St.*, 1775.

COTTEREL, JOHN. C.C. 1721.

COTTEREL, WILLIAM. C.C. 1694.

COTTEY, ABLE. *Philadelphia*. Master about 1690–1710; watch.

COTTON, FRANCIS. *90 Shoreditch*, 1822.

COTTON, JOHN. *London*. C.C. 1695; watch, sun and moon hours, about 1710.

COTTON, JOHN, & SON. Watch, about 1715.

COTTON, JOHN. Admitted C.C. 1718.

COTTON, WM. London. Watch, 1740.

COTTONBELT, JOHN. *Wild St.*, C.C. 1729.

COUCHE, CHARLES. C.C. 1727.

COUCHON à *Paris*. Fine Boulle clock, Wallace collection, about 1690.

COULDRAY, GUILLAUME. *Blois*, 1532–47. Clockmaker to Francis I; clockmaker to town of Blois; made clock for St. Martin Vendôme, 1533.

COULDRAY, JULIAN. *Paris*, 1529.

COULDRAY, WILLIAM. Clockmaker to Henry II, 1550.

COULIN FRÈRES. *Geneva*. Watch 1780.

COULIN, JACQUES, and AMI BRY. *Paris* and *Geneva*, 1784–1800. Gold engraved watch V. & A. repeating automatic watch Marryat collection; fine 3-case gold engraved watch.

COULON, —. *Geneva*, 1780.

COULON, CHARLES. *Panton St.* Watch, 1762; *Prince's St., Leicester Fields*, 1765–68.

COULSON, CHARLES. *Soho*, 1769.

COULSON, HENRY. *Penzance*, about 1790 C.C.

COULSON, ROBERT. *Whiskin St.*, 1800–38; livery C.C. 1810.

COULSON, SAML. *16 North Audley St.*, 1825.

COULSON, WILLIAM. *N. Shields*, 1811–27. Long-case clocks.

COULSON, WILLIAM. *London*. Apprenticed 1805, C.C. 1814.

COULTON, FRANCIS. C.C. 1690.

COULTON, JNO. *York*, 1780.

COULTON, RICHD. Apprenticed 1641 to Morris Blunt, C.C.

COULTON, WM. *York*, f., 1701. Long-case clock, about 1740.

COUPÉ EDWARD. *Paris*. Clockmaker to the King, 1683.

COUPÉ, ELIZABETH. 'Horlogeuse du Roy' on watch, about 1700.

COUPÉ, JACQUES. *Paris*. Clockmaker to the King, 1680; watch, enamelled case and dial, about 1670, name-plate engraved 'James Coupé, London'; underneath on the plate of the watch was inscribed 'Marc Grangier'.

COUPPEY, JEAN ANDRÉ. *Paris*. Master 1764; went to *Vienna* 1773; clockmaker to the King and the city of Paris; several astronomical clocks.

COUPSON, ACHILLE LOUIS. *Paris*. Master 1737, died a. 1789; He, or the following, was mentioned by L. Berthoud as eminent; a watch with straight spring was approved by the Acad. des Sciences, in 1764.

COURT, HENRY. *London*. l.C.C. 1822.

COURT, ISAAC. *Henley-in-Arden* and *Solihull*, 1743–1801. Alarm attachment for watch.

COURT, JEAN. *Grenoble*, 1743–69.

COURTER, WM. *Ruthin*, 1780.

COURTNEY, JOHN. *London*. C.C. 1768.

COURTOIS, —. *Rue Saint-Jacques, Paris*. Clockmaker to Louis XV. 1750–72.

COURVOISIER a *Paris*. Fine ormolu wall clock, about 1780; many watches bear this signature; others signed 'Courvoisier Frères'; see also ROBERT and COURVOISIER.

COURVOISIER, FREDK. ALEX. *Chaux de Fonds*, born 1799, died 1854.

COURVOISIER, LOUIS. *Chaux-de-Fonds*. Born 1758, died 1832. Maker of great repute.

COURVOISIER & HOURIET. *Le Locle*, about 1775–1804. Partnership of David Courvoisier and Jacques Frédéric Houriet; very fine long-case and astronomical clocks; watch New York University.

COUSENS, R. W. *6 York St. East, Commercial Rd.*, 1835.

COUSENS, THOS. Pendant maker, *Bunhill Row*, 1793.

COUSIN, JOSEPH SIMON. *Paris*. Master 1778, juré 1782–89.

COUSINS, WM. *13 Finsbury Place*, 1814–18; see COZENS.

COUTA, G. *12 Blenheim St., Oxford St.*, 1822–25.

COUTOIS, JHA. *London*. Watch, Pierpont Morgan collection, about 1780.

COUTTS, JAMES. *Perth*, 1800–48.

COVELL, JOHN. *London*. 1764 C.C.

COVELL, RICHD. Apprenticed 1671 to Chris. Maynard, C.C.

COVENTRY, CARR. Apprenticed 1649 to Sam. Davis; C.C. 1657.

COVERDALL, DAN. Apprenticed 1683 to Thos. Rudkin, C.C.

COVIES, *Wakefield*, 1780.

COVIGNY de *Paris*. Watch, about 1700.

COWAN, JAMES. *Edinburgh*. Apprenticed to Archibald Straiton 1744; on completion of his indentures he went for a short time to Paris, and worked under Julien Le Roy; watch, Schloss collection, engraved Jas. Cowan, Edinburgh, gold *repoussé* case, about 1765; bracket clock, about 1770, Wetherfield collection; died 1781; see REID, THOS.

COWARD, WILLIAM. Apprenticed to John Fromanteel; C.C. 1681.

COWARD, WM. *Lancaster*, 1797–1830.

COWARD & Co. *Cornhill*. Centre seconds watch, 1780.

COWARD & JEFFERYS. *149 Fleet St.*, 1783.

COWDERY, GEO. *6 King St., Holborn*, 1817.

COWDEROY, JOHN. *London*. C.C. 1826.

COWDEROY, R. F., Fine watch, Hawkins collection, about 1750.

COWDEROY, WILLIAM. *London*. Apprenticed 1811, C.C. 1820.

COWELL, JOHN. *97 Royal Exchange*, 1763–1800.

COWELL JOHN. *London* (*Pope's Head Alley, Cornhill*). Apprenticed 1752, C.C. 1759, l.C.C. 1781–99; cylinder watch G.M.; gold watch Denham collection.

COWELL, JOHN or JOSEPH. *London*. Apprenticed 1737.

COWELL, JOHN FLOWER. *London*. Apprenticed 1724, C.C. 1734–75.

COWEN, H. *3 Sidney's Alley, Leicester Sq.*, 1800.

COWIE, JNO. *8 Aldermanbury Postern*, 1814–18.

COWLAND, JAMES. *52 London*. Wall-bracket clock, about 1830.

COWLES, GEO. & CO. *30 Cornhill*, 1780–90.

COWLEY, ROBT. *Chester*. Member of the Goldsmiths' Company, 1773.

COWLING, EDWD. *Richmond, Yorks*, 1823.

COWLING, RICHD. *London*. Watch, 1820.

COWPE, EDWARD. Brother C.C. 1687.

COWPE, JAMES. C.C. 1654.

COWPER, —. *London*. Watch, 1800.

COWTA, GEO, *12 Blenheim St., Oxford S.*, 1817.

COWTAN, JOHN MACMILVAN. *London*. C.C. 1825.

COX, BENJAMIN. *London*. Apprenticed 1726, C.C. 1734.

COX, BENJAMIN. *Philadelphia*. 1811–13.

COX, JAMES. *103 Shoe Lane*. A clever mechanician, who opened at Spring Gardens a museum of quaint clocks, singing birds, and costly mechanical toys. There were fifty-six pieces in the collection, and the charge for admission was half-a-guinea each person; a regulation providing for the presence of but few visitors at one time was, needless to say, quite unnecessary; in the British Museum is a large centre seconds elaborate watch by him, suited for the Oriental market, 1760–88.

COX, JAS. & SON. 1789–1800.

COX, JASON. *Long Acre*, 1745–60.

COX, ROBT. N. *Pickering, Yorks*, 1822–40.

COX, SAMUEL. *Long Acre*, 1770.

COX, THOMAS. C.C. 1708.

COX, THOMAS. *Thornbury*. Died 1784; watch; called 'very eminent'.

COX, WILLIAM. *London*. C.C. 1636.

COX, WM. *70 Cox Court, Little Britain*, 1763–72.

COX & WATSON. *23 Aldersgate St.*, 1780–85.

COXALL, SAMUEL, "from London, late apprentice and now successor to Mr. Thos. Kefford, at the Dial in Fore St., Royston", advertisement inside long-case clock, about 1750.

COXETER, JOHN. Master C.C. 1661–63.

COXETER, NICHOLAS. Apprenticed to JNO. Pennock 1638; C.C. 1646; master 1671, 1677; a celebrated maker; lantern clock, inscription, 'Nicholas Coxeter, neare Gold Smiths' Hall Londini fecit'; clock, Wetherfield collection, small narrow long-case with olive and laburnum veneer with stars inlaid.

COXETER, THOS. C.C. 1673.

COXETER, WM. Apprenticed to Nich. Coxeter 1647; C.C. 1654.

COZENS, JOSEPH B. *Philadelphia*, 1817–25.

COZENS, JOSIAH B. *Philadelphia*, 1819–24. Watch.

COZENS, WILLIAM. *3 Wilderness Row*, 1804–10; *13 Finsbury Place*, 1822–25. A prominent man in the trade; died 1842.

COZENS, WILLIAM & SON. *10 Bunhill Row*, 1822–42. Afterwards Cozens, Matthews & Thorpe.

CRABB, JAS. *Sarum*, 1780–95.

CRADOCK, E. *13 Charlotte Terrace, Lambeth*, 1835.

CRAGG, ISAAC. *London*. C.C. 1815–24; watch.

CRAGG, JAS. *Lancaster*, 1779, f.

CRAGG, JOHN. *London*. Apprenticed 1780, C.C. 1788–1811.

CRAGG, RICHARD. C.C. 1660.

CRAGG, SAM. Apprenticed 1690 to Jno. Northcott, C.C.

CRAGG, THOMAS. *Horsham*, about 1785. C.C.

CRAIG, CHAS. *Dublin*. Cylinder repeating watch, 1780.

CRAIG, JOHN. *Newcastle-on-Tyne*, 1790–1820.

CRAMBER, R. P. *London*. Watch, 1810.

CRAMPERN, JOHN. *Newark*. Long-case clock, about 1775; died 1794.

CRAMPERN, WM. *Newark*. Died 1770.

CRAMPTON, EDWD. *Newark*, 1780.

CRANAGE, JOSEPH. 1818.

CRANAGE, THOMAS STOKES. *Liverpool*, 1790–1836. Watch.

CRANBROOKE, GEO. *London*. Watch, 1770.

CRANE, THOS. Apprenticed 1682 to Thos. Hollis, C.C.

CRANFIELD, HENRY. C.C. 1706.

CRANMER, CHAS. *London*. Watch, 1800.

CRATHORNE, JNO. *Maidstone*, about 1750.

CRATZER (or KRATZER), NICHOLAS. Clockmaker to Henry VIII, 1538.

CRAVEN, THOMAS. Brother C.C. 1688.

CRAWFORD, ALEX. *Scarboro'*, 1770.

CRAWFORD, ALEX, jun. *Scarboro'*, 1822.

CRAWLEY, ABRAHAM. *Boston, U.S.A.*, 1816 C.

CRAWLEY, J. *London*. Watch, 1785.

CRAWLEY, THOMAS. C.C. 1660.

CRAWLEY, WILLIAM. Apprenticed to James Harrison; admitted C.C. 1756.

CRAWSHAW, ANDREW. *Rotherham*, 1810–28. Verge watch, pump-winding, Chamb. collection; see CRANSHAW.

CRAWSHAW, JAS. *Rotherham*, about 1740.

CRAWSHAW, THOS. *Rotherham*, 1770.

CRAWSHAW, THOS. *Retford*. Died about 1814.

CRAWSHAW, WM. *Washborough* (near *Barnsley*). 30-hour clock, about 1720.

CRAYFORD, FRANCIS. *London*. Apprenticed 1710, C.C. 1718.

CRAYLE, RICHARD. Member of the Blacksmiths' Company, petitioner for incorporation of C.C., 1610–55.

CRAYLE, WILLIAM. *Fleet St.* Afterwards at the Black Boy in the Strand; watch by him, British Museum, about 1660. "Lost a plain gold watch made by William Crealy, in a black shagreen case with gilt pins. If any can give notice to one of the King's Trumpeters next doore to the Kirk House near Charing Cross, they shall upon delivery thereof have five pounds for their peyns" (*The Intelligencer*, Jan. 11, 1663). "Lost on the 13 inst., a Gold Watch enamelled, the outside case seal-skin studded with gold; in the back-side of it was the history of St. Paul's Conversion, with small character *Saul, Saul, quid me persequeris?* And on the Dial part was the stoning of Stephen, with Lanskip round about; and in the inside of the back, a Damask Rose exactly enamelled, the Key fastened with a black Ribon. Whoever gives notice of it to Mr. William Crayle, a watchmaker at the Black Boy in the Strand, near the Savoy, shall have 3l. reward" (*Lond. Gaz.*, July 13–17, 1676). "Lost on Wednesday, the 2nd Inst., at night, in Kings St., near Southampton Fields, a Gold Watch with a Pink coloured Sattin Ribon to it, the case studded with a Heart darted and the watch made by Mr. Crayle in the Strand, and St. George and the Dragon engraven on the Dyal Plate. Whoever brings it to Mr. Norman Nelson, Stationer, at Grays Inn Gate, shall have 40s. reward" (*Lond. Gaz.*, 3rd June, 1680). "Lost on the 22 inst., between St. Andrews Church in Holborn and the further end of Grays Inn Road, a gold watch with the outer case studded, with Mr. William Craile's name engraved on the bottom plate of the said watch. Whoever gives notice of the said watch to Mr. John Wheatley, at the 3 Cups in Hatton Street, shall have two guineas reward" (*Lond. Gaz.*, March 20–24, 1690).

CRAYTON, WM. *London*. Watch, 1770.

CREAK, WILLIAM. *Cornhill* and *Bunhill Row*. Watch, G.M., 1740–68.

CREASER, THOS. *York*, f., 1815–22.

CREED, ROBT. Apprenticed 1689 to Thos. Tompion; C.C. 1699.

CREED, THOMAS. Brother C.C. 1668.

CREED, THOMAS. Brother C.C. 1674.

CREEDE, JOHN. C.C. 1727.

CREEKE, HENRY. A suit by C.C. for using clockmakers' trade contrary to the statute, compromised by Creeke promising to present to C.C. a new house clock and alarum, and 20s., 1654.

CRESPE, FRANÇOIS. *Geneva.* "Essai sur les Montres à répétition," 1804.

CRESSENER, A. M. *Red Lion Square.* Long inlaid case clock, about 1725.

CRESSENT, CHARLES. *Paris.* Maker of clock cases (1720-60), two examples, Wallace Collection.

CRESSNER, ROBERT. *London.* Maker of lantern bracket clocks, 1690-1730.

CRESWELL, JOSEPH. *Corner of Adelphia, Strand,* 1775.

CREUZÉ. Francis Creuzé, a Huguenot, settled in London, carried on business in the Parish of St. Peter le Poor; resided at Clapton; died in 1758, aged 64, and was buried in the old Churchyard at Hackney. His sons, FRANCIS and JOHN, carried on business at Broad St., City. Francis, born 1726, died 1809, and was buried at Leyton, Essex. John, born 1737, died 1823, at Stoke-next-Guildford.

CRIBB, WILLIAM. *58 Theobald's Rd.,* 1816-22; *17 Southampton Row,* 1829. A chronometer maker who succeeded Birchall & Appleton, formerly Molyneux; died 1876.

CRIPPLE, WILLIAM, brother. *London.* C.C. 1750-54.

CRIPPLE, WM. C.C. 1702.

CRIPPS, JOHN. St. Thomas Apostle, 1758-63.

CRIPPS, JOHN & FRANCILLON. *43 Friday St.,* 1769; *24 Norfolk St., Strand,* 1793.

CRISP, JOHN. *22 Old Jewry,* 1783.

CRISP, NICHOLAS. *Bow Churchyard,* 1754-59.

CRISP, WM. Wrentham, 1790.

CRISTOFF, —. Fine travelling watch, signed 'Jo. Cristoff, Kerizer'.

CRITCHLEY, ROBERT. *Liverpool,* 1805-29. Watch.

CRITCHLEY, WM. *Liverpool,* 1810-29.

CROCKFORD, MATTHEW. C.C. 1659; lantern clock, engraved on the fret 'At the Royall Exchang.'

CROCKFORD, MATTHEW, son. *London.* C.C. 1693-1718.

CROFT, JOHN. C.C. 1665.

CROFT, ROBERT. *Plymouth Dock,* about 1790 C.C.

CROFTS, RICHARD. *At the Bear in Foster Lane, right against Goldsmiths' Hall.* "A gold watch by Goulon à Paris, the inside a landscape, a studded case, lost near St. Martin's, to be taken to him if found" (*Lond. Gaz.,* March 25-29, 1675).

CROFTS, THOMAS, sen. *Newbury,* about 1790 C.C.

CROKER, JAMES. C.C. 1716.

CROKER, WM. *34 Great Alie St.,* 1842.

CROLEE, JAM. *London.* Clock, about 1730.

CROLEE, NATT. *London.* Watch, 1775.

CROLET à *Paris.* Late-seventeenth-century watch in engraved brass case, V. & A.

CROME, ROBT. Apprenticed 1644 to Sampson Shelton, C.C.

CROMEY, WM. *Bristol,* 1842.

CROMPTON, ADAM. *London.* C.C. 1716.

CROMPTON, ANDREW. *London.* Apprenticed 1695.

CRONHIORT, CARL GUSTAF. *Aby.* Born 1694, died 1774; C. from 1742.

CRONIER, J. B. F. *Paris,* about 1790. Watch, G.M.; clock, Wallace collection; bracket clock.

CROOKE, BENJ. *Church St., Hackney,* 1802-08.

CROOKE, ISAAC. Apprenticed 1675 to Nicholas Russell.

CROOKE, PETER. C.C. 1724.

CROOKE, SAMPSON. Apprenticed 1661 to Sam. Horne; C.C. 1668.

CROSBEY, JOSEPH. *London (Dorrington St.).* C.C. 1770-97.

CROSBEY, R. Long-case clock, about 1690, inscribed 'Robert Crosbey, in King Street near the Sqr'.

CROSFIELD, JOHN JOHNSON. *London.* C.C. 1794.

CROSMIER (? CRONIER), —. *Paris.* 1790.

CROSS, EDWARD. *Blewitt's Buildings, Fetter Lane,* 1780-94.

CROSS, JAMES. *Fetter Lane.* Liveryman C.C. 1776.

CROSS, JAS. Apprenticed 1687 to Jno. Browne, C.C.

CROSS, JNO. *Liverpool,* 1770.

CROSS, JOHN. *131 Old St.,* 1804; *35 Cursitor St.,* 1823.

CROSSLANDS, JAMES, son. *London.* C.C. 1818.

CROSSLANDS, JOHN HAYWOOD. *London (Hoxton),* Apprenticed 1773, C.C. 1785-1818.

CROSSLEY, HUMPHREY, also HENRY. *Manchester,* 1818.

CROSSLEY, JAMES. *London.* Maker of lantern clocks, about 1710.

CROSSLEY, JAS. *King's Ct., Bunhill Row,* 1814-18.

CROSSLEY, JOHN B. *London,* 1820-50 C.C.

CROSSLEY, RICHD. *14 Giltspur St.,* 1800-25.

CROSTHWAITE, JNO. *Dublin.* A good maker mentioned by Earnshaw, 1760-95.

CROUCH, EDWARD. Apprenticed 1682 to Jno. Cotsworth; C.C. 1691; master 1719; in 1697 his address was 'Under St. Dunstan's Church in Fleet St.', see WESTOBY.

CROUCH, GEORGE. C.C. 1668.

CROUCH, ROBERT. C.C. 1722.

CROUCH, JOHN. *Knightsbridge,* 1761.

CROUCHER, JOSEPH (associated with J. G. Ulrich). *27 Cornhill,* 1825. Livery C.C. 1828; *Swithin's Lane,* 1838.

CROUDHILL, THOMAS. *19 Bedford St., Bedford Row,* 1790-94.

CROUIN, JEAN. *Blois,* 1669-87. Also CROÎN and CROYN.

CROW, GEORGE. *Wilmington, U.S.A.,* 1740-70.

CROW, JOHN. 1770-98.

CROW, THOS. 1770-1824.

CROW, NAT. Apprenticed 1654 to Wm. Petty; C.C. 1661.

CROWFORD, G. *London.* Watch, 1768.

CROWLEY, JOHN. *Philadelphia.* 1805-25.

CROWTHER, WM. *London.* Watch, 1805.

CRUCIFEX, JOHN. Brother C.C. 1712; maker of sheep's-head brass clock, with arch dial, bought in Holland, and of a similar one at Stirling Castle.

CRUCIFEX, ROBERT. *Sweeting's Alley.* Brother C.C. 1689; blacket clock, about 1700; long-case clock, about 1725.

CRUCIFEX, ROBERT. *London.* C.C. 1745.

CRUICKSHANKS, GEORGE. *Elgin,* 1820-37.

CRUICKSHANKS, ROBERT. *17 Old Jewry,* 1772-75.

CRUMP, HENRY. Admitted C.C. 1667.

CRUMP, RICHARD. Apprenticed 1749, C.C. 1757.

CRUMP, THOMAS. *London.* C.C. 1793.

CRUMP, THOS. *Liverpool,* 1770.

CRUMPTON, WILKINSON. *London.* Apprenticed 1749, C.C. 1756, died 1821; gold watch Denham collection.

CRUTTENDEN, THOMAS. Apprenticed to John Fromanteel; C.C. 1677; f. of York, 1680; died 1698.

CSACHER, C. *Prague.* Watch, 1750.

CUBLEY, THOS. *54 Crawford St.,* 1820; *Homer St., New Rd., Marylebone,* 1830.

CUDWORTH, BENJAMIN. *London.* Apprenticed 1769, C.C. 1779-1802.

CUDWORTH, WILLIAM. *London.* C.C. 1769.

CUE, WILLIAM. *London.* Apprenticed 1679, C.C. 1691.

CUENDEL, SAMUEL. *52 Red Lion St., Clerkenwell,* 1815.

CUFF, BROADHURST. *204 Regent St.,* 1823.

CUFF, JAMES. *London.* C.C. 1699; a fine marquetry long-case clock by him, dating from about 1700-05.

CUFF, JAS. *70 St. Paul's Churchyard,* 1823.

CUFF, JNO. *138 New Bond St.*, and *106 Regent St.*, 1823.

CUFF, JOHN. C.C. 1718.

CUFF, WM. *Shepton Mallet.* Long-case clock, Bishop's Palace, Wells, about 1720; his name is also on the sundial in the palace grounds.

CUFFORD, FRANCIS. C.C. 1718.

CULLIFORD, J. *Bristol*, 1680–1700.

CULLUM, A. *Lower East Smithfield*, 1789–94.

CULPER, JOHANN. *Brieg*, 1677–1746. Travelling clock Damiano collection. Also KULPER.

CULVER, J. *Woodbridge*, 1730–41.

CUMMING, ALEXANDER, F.R.S. Born at Edinburgh, about 1732, died at Pentonville, 1814; a celebrated chronometer and clock-maker, who first suggested curved teeth for the cylinder escape wheel; he published in 1766 *The Element of Clock and Watch Work*; elected hon. freeman of the C.C. in 1781; he carried on business at the *Dial and 3 Crowns* in *New Bond St.*, 1777; resided at *12 Clifford St.* till 1794, then he kept a shop in Fleet St., which after his death was occupied by his nephew, John Grant; among the fine and curious clocks at Buckingham Palace is one by Alexander Cumming, made for George III, which registers the height of the barometer every day throughout the year; he had £2,000 for the clock, and £200 a year for looking after it; in the Wetherfield collection are a bracket clock, and a long mahogany-case clock with marquetry decoration, dating from about 1790.

CUMMING, ALEX. *Inverary.* Watch, 1775.

CUMMING, JOHN. 'At the Dial', *202 Oxford St.*, 1816–42. See PANCHAUD & CUMMING.

CUMMING, W. *M. Bond St.*, 1756–64.

CUMMINS, THOMAS. *Stockton (Durham)*, about 1790 C.C.

CUMMINS, THOMAS. *London.* C.C. 1806–20.

CUMMINGS, G. *London.* Watch, 1805.

CUMMINGS, T. *London.* Watch, 1802.

CUMMINGS, WILLIAM. *Roxbury, U.S.A.*, 1820–30.

CUNDEE, STEPHEN. *London.* Apprenticed 1744, C.C. 1751–91.

CUNDEE, STEPHEN, son. *London.* Apprenticed 1785, C.C. 1797–1822.

CUNINGHAME, JAMES. *Haddington*, about 1776.

CUNNINGHAM, —. *London.* Silver watch, enamelled dial with Arabic numerals, about 1790.

CUNNINGHAM, HUGH. *Dublin*, 1770.

CUNNINGHAM, W. & A. *Edinburgh*, 1790–1845.

CUPER. Watch, about 1590, signed 'Pierre Cuper à Blois', Garnier collection.

CUPER, BARTHÉLEMY. *Blois*, 1555–1611.

CUPER, BARTHÉLEMY, son of Paul (1). *Blois.* Master 1613, died 1638; clockmaker to the Queen; circular silver watch Petit Palais.

CUPER, JAMES BOYD. Clock, about 1700.

CUPER, JOSIAS (French). Blacksmiths' Company and C.C. 1627–34.

CUPER, LOUIS. C.C. 1632.

CUPER, MICHEL, son of Paul (1). *Blois.* Master 1613, died 1634; clockmaker to S.A.R. Gaston d'Orléans; octagonal silver watch Spitzer collection.

CUPER, PAUL, son. *Blois*, 1582–1618. Commissaire of the king's artillery; watch Louvre; circular alloy clock M.A.A.; crystal watch without frames, dated 1634, by him or Pierre; circular table clock by him or preceding, both Stern. collection.

CUPER, PAUL (2), son of Paul (1). *Blois*, 1603. Died 1622; clockmaker to the King and commissaire of his artillery.

CUPER, SIMON (2), brother. *Blois.* Born 1656–95; watch movement Glasgow Art Galleries probably by him.

CUPER, SIMON (3), son. *Blois.* Born 1696, master 1720.

CURRENT, JNO. *London.* Watch, 1770.

CURSON, GEORGE. Livery C.C. 1756.

CURTEEN, WILLIAM. *London.* C.C. 1766; watch movement.

CURTIS, ELISHA. *London (Southwark).* Apprenticed 1752, C.C. 1766–74.

CURTIS, JAS. *London.* Watch, 1810.

CURTIS, JOHN. C.C. 1671.

CURTIS, JOSEPH. *Chew Magna*, 1720.

CURTIS, LEMUEL. *Concord* and *Burlington, U.S.A.* Born 1790, died 1857; banjo clock, illuminated Milham.

CURTIS, SOLOMON. *Philadelphia*, 1793.

CURTIS, WILLIAM. *Exeter*, 1790–1827.

CUSIN, A. Clock-watch, Pierpont Morgan collection, signed 'A. Cusin à Corbigny', about 1700.

CUSIN, ABRAHAM. *Nevers.* Early seventeenth century; fine engraved silver octagonal watch, said to have been given to Charles I by Henrietta Maria; oval watch movement, Ilbert collection.

CUSIN, CHARLES. Born at Autun, in Burgundy, settled in Geneva, where it is said he introduced watch manufacturing, about 1587; cruciform watch, about 1600, signed 'J. Cusin', Pierpont Morgan collection.

CUSIN, NOEL. *Autun.* A watch by him, dated 1627.

CUSIN, NOEL, son. *Autun.* Born a. 1585, died 1656; square table clock Louvre, 1622.

CUSINS, THOMAS. *London.* Apprenticed 1725, C.C. 1735–39.

CUSTANS, STEPHEN, & CO. *Philadelphia*, 1819. Watch.

CUTBUSH, EDWD. *Maidstone.* Long-case clock, about 1705.

CUTBUSH, JNO. *Maidstone.* Long-case clock at Welbeck Abbey, dating probably from about 1700; at the top of the door of the case is an index hand pointing to the following, arranged in short lines to suit the width of the door down which the words are cut in relief: "Master, Behold me Here I stand, To tell ye hour at thy command, What is thy will 'tis my delight, To serve thee well by daye and night, Master be wise and learn from me, To serve thy God as I serve thee."

CUTBUSH, R. *Maidstone*, 1723.

CUTHBERT, AMARIAH. C.C. 1694.

CUTHBERT, J. *27 Piccadilly*, 1790–94.

CUTLER, GEO. Apprenticed 1692 to W. Jacques, C.C.

CUTLER, JOHN. *Albany City, U.S.A.*, 1822. Watch.

CUTLOVE, JOHN. *Harlestone, Norfolk.* Long-case clock, moving ship, about 1760.

CUTMORE, JNO. Watch, h.m., 1819; *6 St. Ann's Lane*, 1846–58.

CUTTING, CHRISTOPHER. C.C. 1694.

DADSWELL, JOHN. *Burwash*, 1700–20. Maker of lantern clocks.

DAFT, THOMAS. *New York*, 1786.

DAGLISH, JOSEPH. *Alnwick*, 1770.

DAGONEAU, PHILIBERT. *Grenoble*, 1629–1700. Fine *repoussé* watch with hour figures I to VI and 7 to 12 over them, Webster collection, illuminated Baillie.

DAHLSTRÖM, ISRAEL. *Stockholm.* Born 1762, died 1829; clock in cabinet National Museum Stockholm.

DAILLÉ. Fine ormolu three-part clock, Wallace collection, signed 'Daillé horloger de Madame La Dauphine', about 1750.

DAKIN, JAMES. *Boston, U.S.A.*, 1796. Watch.

DAKING, RICHD. *Halested.* Watch, 1780.

DALBY, JOHN. *105 New Bond St.*, 1783–1804.

DALE, ROGER. *Baynes Row*, 1774.

DALEMAIGE, JEHAN. *Paris*. Clockmaker to the Duchess of Orleans, 1401.

DALGLEISH, J. *Edinburgh*. Long-case clock, about 1750.

DALGLEISH, LAURENCE. *Edinburgh*, 1771–1821 C.C.

DALLAS, JAMES. Maker of a pocket chronometer for the Duke of Sussex, 1800–20.

DALLINGTON, WILLIAM. *London*. Maker of a watch, silver case and dial, day of the month, circle, about 1680.

DALRYMPLE, JOHN. *Dublin*, 1795–1824. Watch.

DALTON, JAC. *London*. Watch, 1720.

DALTON, JAMES. Watch movement maker, *Red Lion St.*, 1790; *12 Bunhill Row*, 1810; *27 Percival St.*, 1815–20.

DALTON, JNO. *27 Percival St.*, 1816–22.

DALTON, JNO. *York*, f., 1830.

DALTON, JOHN. *London* (*Clerkenwell*). C.C. 1777, l.C.C. 1788–1828; watch.

DAMANT, SAML. *Ipswich*. Watch, 1800.

D'AMI-GOUGE, —. *Paris*, 1789. Clockmaker to Louis XVI.

DAMMANT, BARN. *Colchester*. Long-case clock, about 1700; watch, 1715; lantern clock, square dial, about 1725; removed to London, 1735.

DAMPER, W. *Tunbridge Wells*, 1810.

DANA, PAYTON & NATHANIEL. *Providence, U.S.A.*, 1800.

DANBECK, ABRAHAM. *Augsburg*. Born 1649, died 1734; famous automata maker.

DANBECK, CHRISTOPH THEODOR. *Augsburg*. Born 1689, died 1749; famous automata maker.

DANCER. See TOLKIEN.

DANE, ROBERT. *72 Long Acre*, 1807.

DANE, THOS. *133 Oxford St.*, 1790–1817; *Regent St., N.*, 1823.

DANELL, JOSEPH. *214 Oxford St.*, 1822–30.

DANIEL à *Paris*. Watch, about 1650.

DANIEL, H. & J. *Liverpool*, 1825.

DANIEL, PHINEAS. *Bristol*, 1785–1800.

DANIEL, ROBERT. C.C. 1708.

DANIEL, STEPHEN. Brother C.C. 1698.

DANIEL, THOMAS. *20 Foster Lane*, 1783.

DANIELL, EDWARD. Brother C.C. 1647.

DANIELL, HY. Apprenticed 1646 to Hy. Kent, C.C.

DANIELL, ISAAC. C.C. 1648; warden 1674; did not become master.

DANIELL, THOS. C.C. 1656.

DANIELL, THOS. *Kirkham*, 1770.

DANIELL, WILLIAM. C.C. 1632.

DANIELS, *London*. Watch, 1820.

DANNENBERGER, JOHANN PETER. *Berlin*, 1769–88. Clock.

DANNES, ROBERT. *Clerkenwell*. Liveryman C.C. 1776; 1766–80.

D'ANNONE, NIKLAUS. *Basle*. Master 1678, died 1703; very able maker; made clock for Louis XIV for Versailles; astronomical clock Basle Historical Museum.

DANTEL, JOHANNES. *Augsburg*, 1772–88. Automatic wooden clocks.

DANTON, ROBERT. *London*. Apprenticed 1670, C.C. 1678.

DARBY, JAS. *London*. Watch, 1770.

DARBY, JOHN. *51 Gee St.*, 1820–42.

DARBYSHIRE, —. *Wakefield*. Centre seconds watch, 1785.

DARE & PEACOCK, *103 Minories*, 1770–72.

DARGENT, JAMES. C.C. 1700–05.

DARIER, DAVID. *Geneva*. Born 1770, died 1829; started machine production of hands in 1801, and in 1823 promoted the Geneva school of horology.

DARIFORD, —. Maker of fine *repoussé* gold pair-case watch, gold dial, with calendar, about 1735.

DARLE, THOMAS. *London*, about 1769.

DARLING, DARLOT. *Paris*. Decimal clock with Revolutionary calendar 1795.

DARLING, ROBERT. *Fenchurch St.* Sheriff of London, and knighted in 1766; on the court of C.C. 1766.

DARLING, ROBERT. *Edinburgh*, 1788–1825.

DARLING, WM. f. of York, 1829.

DARLING & WOOD. *York*, 1810.

DARLOW, THOS. Apprenticed 1685 to Geo. Deane; C.C. 1692.

DARNLEY, MATTHIAS. *London*. Apprenticed 1735, C.C. 1759–71.

DARNO, D. *London*. Watch, about 1750.

DARRELL, FRANCIS. Apprenticed 1693 to Thos. Speakman, C.C.

DARRELL, JOSEPH. *214 Oxford St.*, 1812–15.

DARROW, ELIJAH. *Bristol, Conn.*, 1822–30.

DARTNALL (DARWELL), THOMAS. *London*. Apprenticed 1701, C.C. 1713.

DARVELL, EDWD. *64 Watling St.*, 1775–94.

DARVELL (or DARWELL), ROBERT. Apprenticed to John Ellicott, C.C. 1708.

DARVILL, GEO. *London*. Watch, G.M., 1766.

DARWIN, E. *London*. Watch, 1770.

DASHPER, FREDERICK. *10 Pierpont Row, Islington*, 1820–46. To him was apprenticed Egbert Storer.

DASYPODIUS, CONRAD. Born 1531; supervised second Strassburg clock, 1571; died 1601.

DAUTEL, —. *Paris*, 1784–1825. Mantel clock Ministère de la Guerre, Paris.

DAUTHIAU. *Paris*. Clockmaker to the King of France, 1735–56.

DAVENPORT, JAS. *London*. Watch, 1780.

DAVENPORT, JAS. *Macclesfield*. Watch, 1790.

DAVENPORT, SAM. *15 Lime St.*, 1788.

DAVENPORT, WM. Apprenticed 1669 to Robt. Smith, C.C.

DAVENPORT, WILLIAM. *London*. Apprenticed 1695, C.C. 1706.

DAVERILL, JNO. C.C. 1636.

DAVID, FRATER, à *S. Cajetano*. *Vienna*. Born 1726, d. 1796; part maker of very complex astronomical clock at Zwettl, Austria.

DAVIDSON, C. *London*. Watch, h.m., 1802.

DAVIDSON, J. *12 Red Lion St., Clerkenwell*, 1814–17.

DAVIE, CHRISTOPHER. *Linlithgow*, 1783–1832.

DAVIE, JOHN. *Linlithgow*, 1753–84.

DAVIES, JENKIN. *London*. Long-case clock, 1770.

DAVIES, JOHN. *153 Leadenhall St.*, 1788.

DAVIES, RICHARD. *85 New Bond St.*, 1790–1800.

DAVIES, ROBERT. *85 Gracechurch St.*, 1788–94.

DAVIES, SIMON. *London*. Apprenticed 1748, C.C. 1757.

DAVIES, TIMOTHY. *Clifford St., Broad St.*, 1783; *15 New Bond St.*, 1793.

DAVIES, T. & H. *39 Brewer St., Golden Sq.*, 1800.

DAVIES, WM. *Chester*. Watch, 1784.

DAVIS, ANDREW. Apprenticed 1679 to Robt. Nemes, C.C.; fine marquetry long-case clock, Wetherfield collection, about 1720.

DAVIS, BENJAMIN. C.C. 1678; fine long marquetry-case clock.

DAVIS, CHARLES. *London*. Apprenticed 1746, C.C. 1753–56.

DAVIS, DAVID. *28 Bury St., St. Mary Axe*, 1830–42; several generations of Davis have carried on business in Great Yarmouth since 1700.

DAVIS, GEORGE. C.C. 1720.

DAVIS, I. Probably the son of John Davis, of Windsor, made the clock at Colnbrook Church, Bucks., 1746.

DAVIS, JAMES. *London*. Apprenticed 1722, C.C. 1732–42.

DAVIS, JAMES. *London*. Apprenticed 1796, C.C. 1803.
DAVIS, JAS. *Ratcliff Highway*, about 1705.
DAVIS, JEFFRY. C.C. 1690.
DAVIS, JEREMIAH. *London*. Apprenticed 1719–35 C.C.
DAVIS, JOHN. Brother C.C. 1653.
DAVIS, JOHN. *Windsor*. Walnut long-case clock with pendulum beating 1¼ sec., about 1678, the front of the base formed a door to get at the pendulum for regulation, and contained a bull's-eye of glass through which the bob could be seen; clock in the Curfew Tower, Windsor Castle, made by him in 1689.
DAVIS, JOHN. Apprenticed to Daniel Quare, admitted C.C. 1697.
DAVIS, JOHN. *Lamb's Conduit St.*, 1769.
DAVIS, JOHN. *New Holland*, 1802–05.
DAVIS, JOHN. *London*. Apprenticed 1804, C.C. 1818.
DAVIS, JOSEPH. *London*. Lacquer long-case clock, V. & A., about 1740.
DAVIS, SAM., JUNR. C.C. 1673.
DAVIS, SAML. *Pittsburgh, Dty.*, 1815.
DAVIS, SAMUEL, at *yᵉ Golden Ball in Lothbury*, C.C. 1647–82.
DAVIS, THEOPHILUS. *London*. Apprenticed 1736, C.C. 1764–60.
DAVIS, THOMAS. C.C. 1674.
DAVIS, THOMAS. C.C. 1726; watch, Newington Free Library, 1740.
DAVIS, THOMAS. *London (Hoxton)*. Apprenticed 1749, C.C. 1757–75.
DAVIS, TOBIAS. C.C. 1653.
DAVIS, WILLIAM. C.C. 1699.
DAVIS, WILLIAM. *London*. C.C. 1774.
DAVIS, WM. *Boston, U.S.A.*, 1683.
DAVIS, WM. *Lancaster*, 1761, f.
DAVIS, WM. *124 Newgate St.*, 1810–23.
DAVIS & BENNETT. *London*. Watch 1795.
DAVIS, PALMER & CO. *Boston, U.S.A.* Early nineteenth century.
DAVISON, C. *London*. Watch, 1820.
DAVISON, JNO. *London*, 1786.
DAVISON, WILLIAM. C.C. 1686.
DAVY, ROBT. *Hoveton*. Clock, about 1770; watch, about the same date, signed 'Robt. Davy, Aldeburgh'.
DAW, JOSH. *39 Cheapside*, 1822.
DAWKES, JOHN. Admitted C.C. 1770.
DAWSON, JNO. C.C. 1688; long-case clock, bird and flower marquetry in panels, 11-in. dial, domed hood, about 1700.
DAWSON, JOHN. *Holborn Bridge*, 1763.
DAWSON, JONAS. *Philadelphia*, 1813–24.
DAWSON, MATTHEW. *Haddington*, 1798–1843.
DAWSON, ROBERT, of *Alford*. C.C. 1678.
DAWSON, THOMAS. Petitioner for incorporation of C.C. 1630; transferred from the Imbroderers' Co. to C.C. 1636.
DAWSON, WM. Apprenticed 1659 to Ben Wolverston, C.C.
DAWSON, WM. *London*. Watch, 1778; another, 1805.
DAY, EDMUND. C.C. 1692; long marquetry case month clock, Wetherfield collection, about 1700; bracket clock showing day of the month, and in an oak case veneered with tortoise-shell; 1692–1720.
DAY, ISAAC. C.C. 1678.
DAY, ISRAEL. *Baltimore, U.S.A.*, 1802–07. Watches & clocks.
DAY, JACOB. Apprenticed 1693 to Isaac Day, C.C.
DAY, JNO. *Wakefield*, 1770.
DAY, JOHN. *London*. Apprenticed 1766; C.C. 1775–1812; watch New York University.

DAY, RICHD. *14 Drury Lane*, 1780–94.
DAY, THOMAS. C.C. 1691.
DAY, WILLIAM ARCHER. *London (Cornhill)*. C.C. 1820.
DEACLE, JOANA. Apprenticed 1672 to Eliza, widow of Thos. Webb, C.C.
DEACON, JOHN. *London*. Apprenticed 1773, C.C. 1781.
DEACON, JOSEPH. *27 Rosoman St.*, 1814–18.
DEACON, S. (Rev.). Maker of Lutterworth clock, 1790.
DEACON, SAMUEL. *Barton-in-the-Beans, Leicestershire*.
DEACON, WILLIAM ARCHER. *London*. Apprenticed 1803, C.C. 1820.
DEALTRY, THOMAS. *85 Cornhill*, 1783.
DEAN, DEODADUS. *80 Minories*, 1793–1804.
DEAN, GEORGE. Engraver, admitted to C.C. 1671; in 1677 he presented to the Court, through Mr. Henry Jones, a plate with the coat of arms.
DEAN, THOS. *Old Jewry*, 1810; *1 Swithin's Lane*, 1820–42.
DEANE, PHINEAS. *London*. Apprenticed 1723, C.C. 1734–42.
DEANE, PHINEAS, son of Phineas. *London*. C.C. 1766.
DEANE, THOMAS. *London*. C.C. 1734–37. Also DEAN.
DEARD, J. *Corner of Dover St., Piccadilly*, 1775.
DEARMAR, ABRAHAM. Apprenticed 1692 to Thos. East, C.C.
DEARMAR, JNO. Apprenticed 1672 to Katherine Bestwick, widow, C.C. 1680.
DEARMAR, JOHN. *London*. Apprenticed 1721, C.C. 1735.
DEATH, ISAAC. *Maldon*. Watch, 1790.
DEAVES, RICHARD. *Whitechurch*. Long-case clock, about 1770.
DE BAGHYN, ADRIAN. *Amsterdam*, 1710–50. Watch, silver dial with pierced centre, silver cases, the outer one *repoussé*, said to have belonged to the first Duke of Marlborough.
DEBARY, DOMINIQUE. *Geneva*. Born 1671, died 1736; in *Hüningen* and *Basle* about 1702.
DEBAUFRE, JAMES. *Church St., Soho*, admitted C.C. 1712; gold watch, V. & A., h.m., 1723; another example, large silver watch with day of the month circle; 1712–50.
DEBAUFRE, PETER. *Church St., Soho*. Admitted C.C. 1689. The Debaufres were an exceedingly clever French family of horologists, probably driven over here by the revocation of the Edict of Nantes. Peter and Jacob were associated with Facio in the patent he obtained in 1704 for watch jewelling. Peter Debaufre also invented a dead-beat or 'club-footed' verge escapement, in which there were two escape wheels, having between them a truncated cone formed of diamond, and cut away at the side to form an impulse plane acted on by the wheels alternately. Sir Isaac Newton had a watch so made, and spoke favourably of its performance. Sully modified it by using two pallets and one wheel. Under the title of the club-footed verge, each kind was used for watches by Garratt, of Ormskirk, and also by Houghton, of the same place. More recently the two-wheel form has been revived for French carriage clocks; alarum watch, about 1710, inscribed '"Pie," De Baufre, Inglese, Roma', 1686–1720.
DE BEAULIEU. A fine striking alarum and calendar watch, signed 'C. De Beaulieu a Basl', about 1640.
DE BELLE, J. F. *Paris*. Watch, about 1780.
DEBELLE, R. *Paris*, 1790.
DEBENHAM, —. *Melford*. Lantern clock, about 1690.
DEBOIS. See DESBOIS, also DUBOIS.
DEBOMBOURG, JEAN, son. *Lyons*. Born about 1634, died 1694 master.
DEBOMBOURG, PIERRE. *Lyons*. About 1633–61 master.
DEBOMBOURG, PIERRE, brother. *Lyons*. 1656–83 master.

DE BON, JACQUE. *Paris.* Clockmaker to the Duke of Orleans, 1776.

DE BOUFLER, ANDREW. *London.* Completed his apprenticeship 1769.

DEBRY, THEODORE. A famous French chaser of watch cases, 1590–1630.

DEBURGE. *Paris.* Watch, about 1590.

DEBURGES, JACOB. *Blois.* 1591–1643. Of English origin.

DEBURGES. JACOB. *Paris,* 1668–93. Alloy watch.

DE CAUX, LUCAS. *Norwich.* Pendulum watch, 1700.

DECELE, SAM. *Norwich.* Lantern clock, about 1710.

DE CHARMES, DAVID. Admitted C.C. 1692; plain silver pair-case repeater, rich cock and pillars, 'Des Charmes, London', inscribed on enamel dial, 1692–1740.

DE CHARMES, J. Bracket clock, 1740. A David De Charmes was buried in Fulham churchyard in 1783.

DE CHARMES, SIMONE (French). *Warwick St., Charing Cross;* came here through the revocation of the Edict of Nantes; built Grove Hall, Hammersmith, in 1730; his son David lived there; admitted as a brother C.C. 1691; 1688–1730. "Lost between Convent Garden and Leicester fields, on Wednesday, Nov. 14th, a silver Watch with a silver Chain, a steel Chain Diamond Cut, &c. Whoever brings the said Watch to Mr. S. de Charmes, Watchmaker, at his House the Sign of the Clock, the corner of Warwick St., Charing Cross, shall have 2 guineas Reward" (*The Daily Courant*, Nov. 16, 1705).

DÉCHEOLY à *Caen,* 1730–40. Example at V. & A.

DE CHOUDENS. Watchmakers in France and Switzerland from the end of the seventeenth to the end of the eighteenth century. Also ESQUIVILLON et. alarum watches.

DE COMBE. *Amye.* Louis XIII watch.

DECKA, JOHN. Apprenticed to Wm. Addis; C.C. 1757; maker of an 8-day long-case clock, mahogany case, inlaid with marquetry; 1757–90.

DECKA & MARSH. *Broad St., Ratcliff Highway,* 1790–1800.

DECLAIR, CLAUDE, à *Lyons.* Cruciform watch, about 1610.

DE CLAREBURG. See CLARBURG.

DECLE, J. H., PÈRE. *Paris* (garde-visiteur, 1769).

DECLE, JACQUES CHARLES. *Paris,* 1748. Juré 1754–60.

DE COLOGNY. *Geneva,* about 1770.

DECOVIGUY, —. *Paris.* Watch, 1710.

DE CRÛE. *Geneva,* about 1775.

DEE, WILLIAM. *Blackfriars.* C.C. 1729.

DEEME, HENRY. *Honiton.* Clock, 1760.

DE FÉALINS, JEHAN. Clock for Rouen, 1389.

DEFINOD (DELPHINOU, DE FINAULX), LOUIS. *Lyons.* Master 1633–60.

DE FOBIS (DE FOBYS), PIERRE. *Lyons.* Born about 1507–75; watch.

DE FOIGNY, JOSEPH. *Lyons,* 1691. Juré in 1708; from *Geneva;* watch Geneva Museum.

DE FONTAINE, L. *18 Wilsted St., Somers Town,* 1835.

DE FONTAYNE, JAMES. *London.* About 1735.

DEFORGES, —, à *Dijon.* Watch, 1700.

DEFOUR FOB ET CIE. Fine gold repeater, probably French, about 1780.

DEGAN, MATHEW. Watch, Vienna Treasury, oval brass case, about 1630.

DE GRÈGES, ANTOINE. *Rouen,* 1606–25. Founder member of Rouen corporation.

DE HANDIS. See HANDIS.

DE HECK, GERHART. Engraved a watch said to have belonged to James I.

DE HEMANT, CHARLES NICOLAS. *Paris.* Master 1750–89.

DE JERSEY. *Westminster.* Maker of long-case clocks, about 1810.

DE KABORS à *Geneva.* Clock-watch, about 1725.

DELABERE. *London.* Watch, about 1730.

DE LA CHANA, DAN. C.C. 1687.

DE LA CHAUSSÉE, FILS. *Rue Galande, Paris,* 1770.

DE LACOR, J. N. *Geneva.* Watch, about 1790.

DE LA CORBIÈRE à *Nismes,* 1790.

DE LA FONDS. Watch-spring maker, *44 Salisbury Court, Fleet St.,* 1790.

DE LA FONS, HENRY PETER BURNING. *London.* Apprenticed 1807, C.C. 1814.

DE LA FONS, JAMES. *Royal Exchange,* and *66 Threadneedle St.,* 1790–95.

DE LA FONS, JOHN. *Pinner's Court, Old Broad St.,* 1790–94.

DE LA FONS, JOHN. *66 Threadneedle St.,* 1800; corner of Bartholomew Lane, 1810; 25 *St. Swithin's Lane,* 1815; received 30 guineas from the Society of Arts in 1801 for a remontoire; in 1805 he patented (No. 2,893) a marine alarum chronometer.

DELAFOSSE, JEAN CHARLES. *Paris.* Late eighteenth century–1825; mantel clock Ministère de la Marine, Paris.

DELAFOSSE, SAMUEL (French). Brother C.C. 1692.

DE LA GARDE. Spherical striking watch, signed 'Jacques De la Garde, Bloys, 1551', G.M., and another the Louvre, Paris.

DE LA GARDE, ABRAHAM, son of Jacques. *Paris,* 1591; *Blois,* 1600; *Paris,* 1621. Clockmaker to the Dowager Queen, Catherine de Médicis, in 1588, and to the King in 1591; elected juré of the corporation of Paris, 1611; oval silver watch Webster collection.

DE LA GARDE, JEAN, son. *Blois,* 1580–1621. 'Horloger du Monsieur frère du roi' (duc d'Anjou).

DE LA GARDETTE, LOUIS MATHIEU. *Paris.* Master 1767–89.

DE LA HIRE, PHILIPPE. *Paris.* Born 1640, died 1718; professor of mathematics; used a zigzag spring attached to one arm of the balance; wrote on epicycloids for wheel teeth and published many articles on clocks and watches in the Mém. de l'Acad. R. des Sciences.

DELAINE, —. 'South Work'; clock, about 1720.

DELAMARE, LOUIS. *Paris,* about 1775.

DELAMARE, MARC. *Paris,* about 1720.

DE LANCE, JAS. *Frome,* 1720–35. Musical 30-hour long-case clock.

DELANDE, PIERRE, à *Paris.* Octagonal watch, about 1600, Pierpont Morgan collection.

DELANDER, DANIEL. Apprenticed 1692 to Chas. Halstead; C.C. 1699. According to the *Spectator,* D. Delander in 1712 moved from Devereux Court to a house between the two Temple Gates; he had been servant to Mr. Tompion. Gilt framed hanging 8-day timepiece and a fine thirteen-month clock with equation work; at Child's Bank in Fleet Street is a long trunk mural timepiece in a japanned case by him; other examples of his work are a silver-gilt clock-watch and a watch in silver pair cases, notable as being an early application of a jewel to the centre of the balance-cock, both in the Pierpont Morgan collection. "Lost some time since a large jewel watch, the box and case in one, it winds up on the dial plate and has a steel plate inlaid with gold to make it go faster and slower made by Dan Quare; whoever brings it to Dan Delander, watchmaker within Temple Bar, shall have 10*l* reward and no question asked, where all sorts of repeating jewel watches and other are made and sold" (*Lond. Gaz.,* October 5–9, 1714). 1699–1721.

DELANDER, JOHN. Case-maker, admitted C.C. 1675; *Salisbury Court*, 1730. "Lost on Monday, August 2, between Fleet Street and the Old Bailey, a gold watch box not finished, in a brass case. Whoever gives notice of it to Mr. John Delander, watch-case maker, over against St. Clement's Church, shall have 10s. reward" (*Lond. Gaz.*, August 5–9, 1675).

DELANDER, JOHN. *Salisbury Court*. Apprenticed to Nathaniel; C.C. 1705.

DELANDER, JOHN. *London*. C.C. 1675–87.

DELANDER, JOHN. Apprenticed to Richard Conyers, C.C. 1744.

DELANDER, NATHANIEL. Brother C.C. 1668; assistant 1689.

DELANDER, NATHANIEL. *Fleet St., near Temple Bar*, son of Daniel Delander, C.C. 1721; master 1747.

DELANDER, R. Oval watch, about 1610.

DE LANDRE, PETER. Brother C.C. 1641.

DELANDRE, JAMES. Brother C.C. 1668.

DE LA PLACE, —. *Rouen*. 1763 master, juré 1779; put ¼ str. to clock of St. Martin du Pont.

DELAPLAINE, JAS. K. f., *New York*, 1786.

DE LA PLANCHE, ÉTIENNE. *Geneva*. Apprenticed 1705; died a. 1770.

DE LA PLANCHE, JEAN LAZARE, son. *Geneva*. About 1740–70.

DE LA PORTE, C. H. *Delft*, 1720.

DE LA RUELLE, ANDRÉ. *Paris* (*Rue St. Martin*). Master 1762–89.

DE LA SALLE, JAS. THOS. *18 Cannon St.*, 1810–42. Livery C.C. 1826.

DE LA SALLE, THOMAS. *Brookers Row, Moorfields*, 1780; *42 St. Catherine's, Tower Hill*, 1800–18.

DELAUNAY. *Paris*. Large bracket clock, inlaid with tortoise-shell and brass, about 1760.

DELAUNCE, JAMES. Brother C.C. 1650.

DE LAUNDRE. See DE LANDRE.

DELAUNEY, NICOLAS. *Paris*. Juré 1734.

DELAUNEY, PETER. *68 New Bond St.*, 1822–25.

DELAVERSPERRE, WM. Brother C.C. 1650.

DELAVILLE, JAS. Apprenticed 1662 to Evan Jones, C.C

DE LA VOIPIÈRE, —. *Rouen*. Juré 1774–79.

DE LAWNCE, PETER. *London*. C.C. 1650.

DELEAMONT, ÉTIENNE. *Geneva*, about 1770–91.

DELEIDERIÈRE, JEAN LOUIS. *Geneva*, about 1770–91.

DE LESPINASSE, *Paris*. Very fine pair of obelisks, veneered with lapis lazuli, Wallace collection; on one a clock, over the dial a female figure holding a fan through a diminutive hole in which the light passes and at noon crosses a vertical meridian line; on the companion obelisk is mounted a barometer.

DE LISLE. *Brussels*. Second half seventeenth century enamel watch. *Paris*. First half eighteenth century, watch.

DELISLE & MORICAND. Watch so signed, about 1760, Mr. Willard H. Wheeler.

DELL, JAMES. *London*. Apprenticed 1761, C.C. 1768.

DELLE, JOHANN NIKOLAUS. *Augsburg*. Master 1732, juré 1736–57, died a. 1769; gold *repoussé* watch Schloss Museum, Berlin.

DELLESSER, ELLIS. *Liverpool*, 1818.

DELLUNG, PAUL. Apprenticed 1659 to Paul Lovell, C.C.

DELMAR, EDWARD. *London*. C.C. 1821.

DELOLME, NICHOLAS. *London*, 1770–96.

DE LORME. *Paris* 1720–40. Alarum watch, with inscription, 'From Admiral Lord Nelson to Post Captain Jonas Rose', silver pillars.

DE LORME, JEAN FRANÇOIS. *Geneva*, about 1770–91.

DE LORME, JEAN PHILIPPE. *Paris*. Juré 1736.

DELUNÉSY. Finely decorated clock, Wallace collection, about 1770.

DELUNÉSY, —, à *Paris*. Clock presented by the municipality of Lyons to the Duc de Mortemar, governor of that city, gilt case finely chased by Gouthière and dated 1771, now in the Wallace collection.

DEL VALLE, VINCENT. *Gibralter*. Watch, 1780.

DE MANIÈRE à *Paris*. Clock about 1750, M. Spitzer. See also MANIÈRE.

DE MASSO, MICHEL. *Lyons*, 1654 master, died 1691.

DEMAZA, GEORGE. *95 Strand*, 1825.

DEMELAIS, —. *London*. Watch, Dutch style, 1750.

DEMESMAY, —. *La Brévine*, 1815–30. Clock.

DEMOLE, —. *Geneva*. Watch, about 1780, M. J. Rambal.

DEMOLLES, ANTOINE. *Geneva*, about 1770–91.

DE MOYLYM, JOHN. Keeper of the Dulwich College clock in 1553.

DEMONCHANIN, PIERRE. *Paris*. Master 1746–69.

DEMPSTER, ANTHONY. *York*, 1822.

DEMPSTER, MARK ANTHONY. *York*, f., 1829–34.

DEMSTER, ROGER. *London*, about 1790.

DENCH, WILLIAM. *London*. Apprenticed 1811, C.C. 1835.

DENHAM, CHARLES. *Durham*, 1820–40.

DENHAM, GEO. *London*. Watch, about 1785.

DENIAU, CLAUDE. *Blois*. Master 1639–64.

DENISART, JEAN PIERRE. *Paris*. Master 1770–89.

DENISON, EDMUND BECKETT. Born 1816; elected President of the British Horological Institute, 1868; succeeded his father as a baronet, taking the title of Sir Edmund Beckett in 1874; called to the House of Lords under the title of Baron Grimthorpe, 1886; died 1905; designer if the Westminster clock; see DENT, E. J., and DENT, F.

DENIZAVE, —. *London*. Watch, 1802.

DENHAM, GEORGE FREDERICK. *London*. Apprenticed 1813, C.C. 1821; watch.

DENMAN, GEO. *24 Greek St., Soho*, 1820; *39 Newgate St.*, 1823.

DENN, BASIL. *Tooley St.*, 1776.

DENNE, JOHN. *28 Lamb's Conduit St.*, 1820–23.

DENNETT, JAS. *St. Helens, Lancs.*, 1818.

DENNIS, D. *54 New Bond St.*, 1816.

DENNIS, FRANCIS. Brother C.C. 1673.

DENNIS, PETER. C.C. 1712.

DENNIS, THOS. Apprenticed 1672 to Jas. Wightman, C.C.

DENODON, ABRAHAM. *Blois*. Master 1617–42.

DENODON, MICHEL. *Blois*. Master 1585–1623.

DENT, EDMD. Case maker, C.C. 1730.

DENT, EDWARD JOHN. Born 1790, died 1853; was apprenticed to a tallow chandler, but disliking that business induced Richard Rippon, in whose house he lived, to instruct him in making repeating mechanism; he worked as a finisher of repeating watches till 1830, when he joined J. R. Arnold in partnership, at *84 Strand*; during the ten years they were together the business was greatly extended, chiefly through the energy and ability of Dent, who, when the partnership expired, established himself at *82 Strand*, afterwards removing to No. 61; he also took Desgrange's shop at *33 Cockspur St.*, and another inside the Royal Exchange near the entrance to 'Lloyds'; he married the widow of Richard Rippon, whose sons, Frederick and Richard, took the name of Dent; he turned his attention to the compensation of chronometers, and secured the confidence of Professor Airy, the Astronomer-Royal. When the Royal Exchange was rebuilt, Dent, on Airy's recommendation, was selected to provide the large clock; for this work Dent equipped a suitable workshop in the Savoy and made an excellent clock, which was fixed in the tower of the Exchange in 1844. In the same year Vulliamy was commissioned to prepare a plan for the great clock of the Houses of Parliament. Dent asked to be allowed to compete for the making of the clock, but objected to having anything to do with Vulliamy's plans; he said he would be willing to follow instructions of the Astronomer-Royal, as he had done with the Exchange clock. The Commissioners applied to Airy, and on his advice plans and estimates were obtained from Vulliamy, Dent and Whitehurst of Derby. In May 1847 Airy reported and recommended Dent for the work. In 1851 Lord Seymour, Chief Commissioner, asked Edmund Beckett Denison, a barrister who had taken an interest in horology, to act as referee with the Astronomer-Royal, and in February 1852 a contract was signed with Dent to make the clock, he to do everything ordered by the referees who described in a general way what was required. Airy went abroad for a time about March 1852, giving Denison power to act for him. E. J. Dent died in March 1853. The businesses in the Strand and Royal Exchange were taken over by Frederick Dent, and the one in Cockspur St. by Richard.

DENT, FREDERICK, stepson of E. J. Dent, *61 Strand.* Died 1860. The initial proceedings in connection with the Westminster clock have been related under the head of Dent, E. J. Frederick had but little liking for clock work, and as the Astronomer-Royal in November 1853 resigned the office of joint referee, which he had held in conjunction with E. B. Denison, the superintendence of the making of the Westminster clock movement was left entirely to Denison. Dent's contract did not include the dials, and hands, which were designed by the architect, Mr. (afterwards Sir Charles) Barry, nor the provision or fixing of the bells. The clock was set going in May 1859. On the frame of the movement is the inscription, '*This clock was made in the year of our Lord 1854 by Frederick Dent of the Strand and Royal Exchange, clockmaker to the Queen, from the design of Edmund Beckett Denison, Q.C. Fixed here 1859.*' Vulliamy had many influential friends, and what with their opposition at every stage and the incidental difficulties of the work, any less determined man than Denison would have thrown up the matter in disgust. He prepared a specification for the bell founders in February 1855. The first hour bell, weighing nearly 16 tons, cast in August 1856, became cracked and useless; the second bell, weighing 13 tons 11 cwt., was tried with the four quarter bells in June 1858, but shortly after the clock was started a fissure was noticed, and in October 1859 the striking was stopped. Then for a short time the hour was struck on the largest of the quarter bells, but afterwards the hour bell was turned round so as to present a different surface to the hammer, and has ever since performed its office satisfactorily. The first set of hands, with their counterpoises, weighed 2¼ tons and proved to be too heavy for the clock to drive. The hour indicators were retained but the minute hands rejected in favour of lighter ones made of copper and tubular, and so the clock was not really finished till 1860. All's well that ends well, and the splendid time-keeper at Westminster, of which the nation may be proud, remains as an appropriate tribute to the ability and dogged perseverance of E. B. Denison (Lord Grimthorpe). Some particulars of the mechanism are given in the *Watch and Clock Makers' Handbook*. The hour bell was named 'Big Ben' in

honour of Sir Benjamin Hall (Lord Llanover), who, as Commissioner of Works in 1856, gave the order for it to be cast.

DENT, ROBERT. *London.* C.C. 1681; watch, 1710. Canon Greenwell has a long-case clock marked on dial 'Dent London, 1746'.

DENT, ROBERT. *Lincoln.* Early eighteenth century–1795; watch.

DENT, WILLIAM. C.C. 1674.

DENTON, ISAAC. *London*, about 1790.

DENTON, JOSEPH. *Hull.* Long-case clock, about 1760, Mr. Thos. Boynton.

DENTON, ROBERT. *Oxford.* Long-case clock, about 1750, Mr. H. Clark.

DENTON, SAM. *High St., Oxford*, 1780.

DENTON, WM. *Oxford.* Watch, 1764.

DENTON, WM. *Poultry*, 1816–20.

DEPREE (or DUPREE), ELIE. C.C. 1634.

DE PRESLES, JEAN. *Paris*, 1544.

DERBY, ARON. Apprenticed 1687 to Wm. Garfoot, C.C.

DERHAM, WILLIAM. Born 1657, died, and buried in Upminster, in 1735; a clergyman and Canon of Windsor, author of *The Artificial Clock-maker*, published in 1696; second edition in 1700; third in 1714; fourth and last in 1734. He appears to have been acquainted with and assisted by Hooke, Tompion, and Langley Bradley.

DE RIBAUCOURT, ANDRÉ (ALEXANDRE). *Paris.* Master 1770–89; dead-beat escapement C.A. & M.

DERIMO, LEWIS. *London*, 1711 C.C.

DERMERE, ABRAHAM. C.C. 1703.

DERNE, LOUIS. *Nancy.* Watch, British Museum, about 1640.

DEROCHE (or DEROCHES), FRAS. *Geneva.* Watch, Wallace collection, about 1720; enamelled watch, about 1750; watch signed 'Frs de Roches & Fils', about 1760; another 'Derocher Geneva', 1775; clock, 'De Roque à Paris', about 1770, M. Spitzer Derrick.

DE ROUVROY, JEAN. In 1446 he acquired the title of clock-smith and horloger of the town of Amiens.

DERRICK, WILLIAM. *London.* Apprenticed 1769, C.C. 1777–93; bankrupt. Also DIRRICK.

DERWOOD, W. M. *London.* Watch, h.m., 1780; another, 1805.

DE SAINT-JEAN, JEAN BAPTISTE. *Paris.* Master 1760–89; picture automatic clock C.A. & M.

DE ST. LEU, DANIEL. *London*, 1753–97. Succeeded by RIVERS & SON, watchmaker to the Queen in 1765; fine engraved watch, repeating watch, and pair-case gold striking watch G.M.; watch, set of diamonds, London Museum; repeating cylinder watch Denham collection; very fine bracket clock in silver case for Spanish Court.

DE SAINT-MARTIN, ANTOINE. *Paris.* Juré 1737.

DE SAINT-MARTIN, FRANÇOIS *Pierre. Paris.* Master 1770–89.

DE SAINT-MARTIN, JEAN JOSEPH. *Paris.* Master 1781.

DE SAINT, PAUL, DENIS. *Geneva*, 1573–1623. Refugee from *Lyons.*

DE SALLE à *Caen.* Watch, about 1720.

DESARTS, —, ET CIE. *Geneva.* Watch, 1780.

DESASSARS, ABRAHAM. C.C. 1682.

DESAUX, FRANÇOIS. *Geneva*, about 1750–73.

DESBOIS. Several generations of this family have carried on business in the neighbourhood of Holborn.

DESBOIS, DANIEL. Apprenticed to John Johnson, whom he succeeded at *9 Gray's Inn Passage*; died 1848, aged 75.

DESBOIS, JACOB. *London.* C.C. 1730. Also DEBOIS.

DESBOIS & WHEELER. *9 Gray's Inn Passage.* A watch by them is in the Guildhall Museum; 1803–35.

DESBOROUGH, CHRISTOPHER. C.C. 1665.

DESBROW, ELIZABETH. Apprenticed 1676 to Hy. Jevon and Christian his wife; C.C.

DESBROW, ROBERT. C.C. 1704.

DESCHAMPS, ANDRÉ. *Paris (Place Baudoyer).* Master 1788–1825; two clocks C.A. & M. by him or preceding.

DESCHAMPS, ÉTIENNE. *Paris.* Master 1764–89.

DESCHAMPS, JEAN. *Paris.* Master 1776–89.

DESCOMBATS, JEAN JACQUES. *Geneva,* about 1775–91.

DESESSART (DESESSARS, DESESAR), ABRAHAM. *London.* C.C. 1682, died 1739; watch.

DESESSART (DESESSARS, DESESAR), JAMES. *London.* Apprenticed 1698, C.C. 1707.

DESFLÈCHES, JACQUES. *Lyons.* Apprenticed 1668, master 1681–1707; also a caster of bells.

DESFLÈCHES, JÉRÔME. *Lyons,* 1693 master–1715.

DES GRANGES, PETER. Successor to Recordon, *33 Cockspur St.,* 1816–42. See DENT.

DESHAIS, MATTHEW. *London.* Bracket clocks, 1690–1710.

DESHAYES, PIERRE. *Rouen,* 1642–63. Made clock for St. Laurent, Rouen.

DESMARAIS, PETER. *St. Martin's Court,* 1794.

DESMEE à *Paris.* Watch, enamelled dial, Schloss collection, about 1750.

DESMORE, T. *11 Clerkenwell Green,* 1830.

DESONNAZ, JEAN. *Geneva,* about 1750–72.

DESTACHES, JNO. C.C. 1660.

DE ST. LEU, DANIEL. A good maker; was watchmaker to George III. In 1753 his establishment in *Cloak Lane* was called 'The Golden Head'; later it was *17 Cloak Lane.* He afterwards removed to *38 Cornhill,* and was succeeded about 1790 by Rivers & Son.

DESTOUCHE à *Middelbourg.* Watch, about 1800.

DÉTAPÉ, —. *Paris,* 1807–25. Temple clock, Palais de Pau, Paris.

DETHAU, MATTHEW. *London,* about 1720.

DEUTKE, JØRGEN. *Copenhagen,* 1645–61.

DEVALL, JNO. Apprenticed 1670 to Andrew Pryme; C.C. 1677.

DE VALS, HANS. *Madrid,* 1533–about 1580. Clockmaker to Philip II of Spain; clock with lamp, Spitzer sale.

DE VASSALIEU, HUMBERT. *Lyons,* 1523–57.

DEVERE, FREDERICK. *7 Angel Court, Throgmorton St.,* 1769–75.

DEVERELL, JNO. *London.* Watch, 1780.

DEVERELL, JOHN. *Boston,* 1789.

DE VICK, HENRY. About 1364 he made a turret clock for Charles V of France.

DE VILLE, ESTIENNE SIMON. *Paris.* Master 1767, juré 1784–89.

DE VILLENEUVE, —. *Rue de l'Arbre Sec, Paris,* 1770.

DEVIS, JOHN. *Gloucester St., Bloomsbury,* 1764, after *76 Lamb's Conduit St.* Hon. freeman C.C. 1764–83.

DEVIS, WILLIAM. *Fleet St.,* 1750–65.

DEWE, JNO. *Gravel Lane, Southwark.* C.C. 1730.

DE WELKE, CHRISTIAN. One of the signatories to the petition of incorporation of C.C. In the eighteenth century an oval watch by him was found in a field near Kettering; 1620–30.

DEXTER, M. *London.* Watch movement, G.M., about 1790.

DEY, LAURENT. *Paris.* Master 1744; watch movement with silver pillars and cock.

DEY, NICOLAS LAURENT, son. *Paris.* Master 1765–89.

DEYKIN, HENRY, son. *Worcester,* 1751–88. Watch. Also DEAKIN.

DEYKIN, THOMAS. Long-case clock, signed 'Thos. Deykin, in Worcester, fecit', beautiful inlaid case, birds and flowers, about 1700; 30-hour long-case square dial clock, inscribed 'Henry Deykin, Worcester', about 1710.

DIBON, JAMES. *London.* Apprenticed 1706, C.C. 1713–25.

DICHOUS à *Paris.* Clock, about 1785.

DICKENS, JOHN. C.C. 1688.

DICKENS, JOHN. *Bath,* 1755–about 1800. Clocks and watches; watch.

DICKENSON, RICHD. *London.* Watch, 1710.

DICKER, THOS. *Reading,* 1810.

DICKERSON, DANIEL. *Framlingham.* a. 1767–90; watch; long-case clock.

DICKERSON, DANL. *Yarmouth,* about 1750.

DICKIE, ANDREW. *Edinburgh.* Repeating watch in V. & A., h.m., 1735.

DICKIE, ANDREW. *London.* Long-case clock, 1765.

DICKIE, ANDREW. *Stirling,* 1723–39. Watch movement, G.M.

DICKINSON, —. *Boston,* about 1790 C.C.

DICKINSON, JOHN. *London.* Apprenticed 1768, C.C. 1790.

DICKINSON, JOHN. *Philadelphia,* 1823–25.

DICKINSON, RD. *Liverpool.* Watch, 1715.

DICKINSON, ROBERT. *York.* f. 1810–16.

DICKINSON, THOS. *Lancaster.* f., 1817–20.

DICKMAN, JOHN. *Leith,* 1800–50.

DIEBOLD, JOHANN. *Augsburg.* Master 1741–70.

DIEBOLDER, BALTAZAR, brother. *Basle.* Master 1578–1605.

DIEBOLDER, HANS, son of Michel. *Basle,* 1598. Died 1634.

DIEU, R., à *Paris.* Oval watch, no screws, about 1590; another, later, Newington Free Library.

DIGBY, CHARLES. *London.* Repeating watch, 1760.

DIGHTON, WM. Apprenticed 1687 to Sam. Rosse, C.C.

DIKE, JOSEPH. *London,* 1701 C.C.

DIKE, NATHANIEL. C.C. 1663.

DILGER, MICHAEL. *Neukirch* and *St. Märgen,* 1750–70. One of the first to make cuckoo clocks; wall clock Furt. M.

DILGER, SIMON. *Schollenbach.* Born 1672. In 1720 was one of the first to start clockmaking in the Schwarzwald.

DILKER, LEONHARD. *Thumenberg.* Born 1536, died 1603.

DILLINGTON, —. *London.* Watch, about 1750.

DIMIER, JEAN ANTOINE. *Geneva.* Born 1795, died 1863.

DIMSDALE, JOHN. *London.* Apprenticed 1758, C.C. 1766.

DIMSDALE, WILLIAM. *London.* Apprenticed 1789.

DIMUND, JOHN. *London.* C.C. 1786.

DINGLEY, ROBERT. *George Yard, Lombard St.* Apprenticed 1661 to Lionel Wythe; C.C. 1668; inlaid long-cased clock, about 1700; gold watch, hour-hand only, case with *appliqué* gold flowers, enamelled.

DINGLEY, ROBERT. *Bishopsgate St.,* corner of *Great St. Helen's,* 1728–40.

DINGWALL & BAILLIAM, *9 St. James St.,* 1813.

DINIZARD, —. *Paris,* 1790.

DINNIS, FRANCIS. Engraver; C.C. 1666.

DINNOTT, ROBT. *London.* Watch, 1795.

DINOCHEAU, MICHEL. *Blois.* Master 1670–91.

DISSMORE, RICHD. *York,* 1818.

DISTIN, JNO. *Totnes,* 1750.

DISTURNELL, PHILIP. *London.* Apprenticed 1759, C.C. 1769.

DISTURNELL, WILLIAM. *London.* Apprenticed 1750, C.C. 1759–63.

DITCHFIELD, RICHD. C.C. 1677.

DIVERNOIS, —. *Rue Dauphine, Paris,* 1770.

DIX, JOSEPH. *Philadelphia*, 1769. Watch.

DIXON, EDWARD. *London*. Apprenticed 1748, C.C. 1757.

DIXON, GEORGE JAMES. *London*. Apprenticed 1809, C.C. 1816.

DIXON, JAMES, son of John. *London*. C.C. 1789, l.C.C. 1791.

DIXON, JOHN. *London*. Apprenticed 1748, C.C. 1756.

DIXON, WM. Apprenticed 1686 to Dan. Beckman, C.C.

DOBB, WILLIAM. Brother C.C. 1646.

DOBBIE, ANDREW. *Glasgow*, 1820–48.

DOBBIE, GEORGE. *Falkirk*, 1821–50.

DOBBIE, WILLIAM. *Falkirk*, 1821–45. Clockmaker to the Queen; watch.

DOBBINGS, WM. *Leeds*, 1830.

DOBREE, ELISHA. *London*. watch, h.m., 1761.

DOBREE, JOHN. *3 Charing Cross*, 1815; *69 Charlotte St., Oxford St.*, 1823.

DOBSON, ARL. *London*. Watch with finely enamelled case in the British Museum; another example is an oval watch at V. & A., inscribed 'This watch was a present from yᵉ King to the Countess of Monteith, 1675'.

DOBSON, ARLANDER. *London*. Pull repeating bracket clock, about 1740; watch, 1765.

DOBSON, CHARLES, *Coldbath Fields*. Livery C.C. 1776.

DOBSON, FRANK. *Gt. Driffield*, 1822.

DOBSON, GEO. *Leeds*, 1829.

DOBSON, JOHN. *London*. Apprenticed 1698, C.C. 1714–44.

DOBSON, THOMAS. *London* (*Rosamon St.*). Apprenticed 1738, C.C. 1746–87.

DOBSON, THOS. *Red Lion St., Holborn*. C.C. 1730.

DOBSON, WILLIAM. Brother C.C. 1670; large lantern clock, about 1680, inscribed 'William Dobson, in High Holbourne, Londini, fecit'.

DOCKWRAY & NORMAN. *16 Princes St., Leicester Sq.*, 1815–19.

DOD, RICHARD. *London*. Long-case clocks, 1695–1720.

DODDINGTON, JNO. Apprenticed 1685 to Ben Wright, C.C.

DODDS, JOSEPH. *London* (*Aldersgate St.*). C.C. 1794, l.C.C. 1795, died 1817. a. 1793 partner with John Troutbeck.

DODDS, JOSEPH, son. *London*. Apprenticed 1807, C.C. 1814.

DODEMARE, L. *Caen*, 1770.

DODSON, JNO. Apprenticed 1655 to Isaac Law, C.C.

DODSWORTH, JOHN. Brother C.C. 1648.

DOIG, ALEXANDER. *Musselburgh*, 1814–36.

DOLLEY, JOHN, son. *London*. l.C.C. 1804.

DOLLEY, THOMAS. *London* (*Quakers Bdg.*). C.C. 1772–92.

DOLLEY, THOS. Master C.C. 1808.

DOLTON, JOHN. *London*. Apprenticed 1773, C.C. 1784.

DOMINIC, FREDERICK. *Philadelphia*, 1768–74.

DOMVILE, NATHANIEL. *Stockport*, 1820–42.

DONAC, —. *London*. Inscription on a watch, gold cases, outer one *repoussé*, h.m., 1807.

DONALD, JOHN. *London*. C.C. 1771.

DONDI, JOHN de Maker of a famous clock with wheels and balance and complicated astronomical work; C. 1350.

DONE, WILLIAM. *Manchester*. an 1778–95. Watches and clocks.

DONISTHORPE, GEO. *85 High St., Birmingham*, 1770. Died 1802.

DONNE, ANTHONY. *Red Lion St., Holborn*. C.C. 1730.

DONNE, ROBERT. *Lamb's Conduit St.*, 1763–94.

DOOLITTLE, ISAAC. *New Haven*, 1785–1810.

DOORE, ROBT. C.C. 1671.

DOOREY, JOHN, son. *London* (*Tooley St.*). C.C. 1790–1812.

DOOREY, JOHN GEORGE. *London*. C.C. 1816.

DOOREY, THOMAS. *London*. Apprenticed 1758, C.C. 1766, died 1790.

DORE, THOMAS. *London*. Apprenticed 1753, C.C. 1765.

DORER, ROBT. *Paris*, about 1760.

DORIA, ANTONIO. *Venice*, 1795–1827. Keeper of clock of S. Marco and repaired it 1820.

DORIGNY, ROBERT. Clockmaker to the Duke of Orleans, 1397.

DORMER, JAMES. *London* (*Whitecross St.*). Apprenticed 1735, C.C. 1742–55.

DORMER, P. *London*. Watch, 1800.

DORMES. *London*. Watch, about 1760.

DORRELL, FRANCIS. *Honeysuckle Court, Grub St.* Known as a maker of long-case clocks; C.C. 1702.

DORRELL, FRANCIS. C.C. 1755.

DORRELL, JOHN, son. *London* (*St. Giles, Cripplegate*). Apprenticed 1725, C.C. 1732.

DORRELL, WILLIAM. *Bridgwater Sq.* Summoned to the livery C.C. 1786; restored Cripplegate Church clock, and made it to strike the hours on the tenor bell, in 1797.

DORSETT, WM. *London*. Watch, 1790.

DOSSETT, GREGORY. C.C. 1662.

DOTY, JOHN F. *Albany, U.S.A.*, 1813–22 watch.

DOUD, JAMES. An oval metal watch by James Doud, dating from about 1600.

DOUFFNER, FRANS SAVERY. *Stockholm*, 1785–1819. Wooden clock.

DOUGHTY, JNO. *York*, f., 1772.

DOUGHTY, THOS. *Charles St., Somers Town*. Invented a compensation pendulum, 1811.

DOUGHTY, TOBIAS. C.C. 1696.

DOUGHTY, WM. P. *10 Great Ormond St.*, 1816–20.

DOUGLAS, ALEX. *18 Cross St., Hatton Garden*, 1810–18.

DOUGLAS, J. *London*. Watch, 1745.

DOUGLAS, JNO. *52 Red Lion St.*, 1816.

DOUGLAS, ROBT. *Bolton*, 1775.

DOUGLAS, ROBERT. *Liverpool*, 1781–1824. Watch. See DUGLASS.

DOUGLAS, SAM. *Liverpool*, 1818; also ROBT., same date.

DOUGLAS, WALTER. *Dollar*. Long-case clock, four season corners to dial, about 1790.

DOUGLASS, JOHN. *New Haven*, 1800–20.

DOULL, JAMES. *Philadelphia*, 1825–49.

DOUTY, HENRICK. *Philadelphia*, 1774.

DOUW, SIMON. *Rotterdam*. Contested Huygens' patent 1658.

DOVE, ARTHUR. Apprenticed to Wm. Clay; C.C. 1659.

DOVE, ARTHUR. "Gold Watch taken by Highwaymen with a gold Chain and a gold studded case made by Arthur Dove, of St. Martin's", &c. (*Lond. Gaz.*, Sept. 8, 1681).

DOVE, HENRY. C.C. 1667.

DOVER, R. *Westgate St., Bath*, 1770.

DOVER, ROBERT. *London*. C.C. 1671.

DOVEY, RICHARD. *6 Craven Buildings, Drury Lane*, 1765–70.

DOW, JAMES. Watch-case maker, *15 St. James's Buildings, Clerkenwell*, 1820.

DOW, ROBERT. *Clerkenwell Close*, 1790; *72 Long Lane*, 1810–35.

DOW, ROGER. *Vere St.*, 1780–85.

DOWDNEY, BURROWS. *Philadelphia*, 1768.

DOWIG, GEORGE. *Baltimore*, 1784. Watch.

DOWNES, ARTHUR. *Charleston, U.S.A.*, 1765–68.

DOWNES, CHRIS. C.C. 1632.

DOWNES, JERE. Apprenticed 1688 to Jas. Jackson, C.C.

DOWNES, JNO. *Shoe Lane*. C.C. 1725.

DOWNES, JOE. *London.* Watch, h.m., 1774.
DOWNES, JOHN, son. *London (Norman St.).* Apprenticed 1732, C.C. 1746, died 1774.
DOWNES, JOSEPH. *Coventry,* 1817.
DOWNES, ROBT. *Clerkenwell Close,* 1793.
DOWNES, ROBT. *Long Acre,* 1798–1818.
DOWNES, VALENTINE. *Louth,* 1790.
DOWNEY, JAMES. *Philadelphia.* Early nineteenth century. Watch New York University.
DOWNIE, WILL. *Edinburgh,* 1770.
DOWNING, JNO. *Liverpool,* 1770.
DOWNING, SAMUEL. *Liverpool,* 1767. Died 1788; watch.
DOWNINGE, HUMFREY. Apprenticed to Mr. Grinkin, free of Barber Surgeons; Blacksmiths' Company in 1637 applied to have him disfranchised.
DOWNS, BENJ. *Mansfield,* 1790.
DOWSE, GABRIEL. Apprenticed 1649 to Wm. Godbed, C.C.
DOWSETT, CHARLES. *Margate.* Master 1799 C.C.
DOWSETT, JEREMIAH. C.C. 1708.
DOWSON, —. *Bath.* Watch, 1760.
DOWSON, JOHN. *77 Holborn Bridge* and *Field Court, Gray's Inn.* Watch, skeleton movement, h.m., 1764; a later specimen, G.M.
DOWSON & PEENE. *Gray's Inn,* 1800.
DRABBLE, J. *London.* Bracket clocks, 1710–20.
DRACQUE, J. *Nerac.* Watch, silver case in the form of a fleur-de-lis, about 1620, Garnier collection.
DRAKE, J. *London.* Watch, 1760.
DRAKE, JOHN. *Fleet St.* Action by Blacksmiths' Company to disfranchise him 1633; C.C. fined him £10 for binding his apprentice to the Blacksmiths' Company 16—; signed a petition to C.C. 1656; a round silver watch, with plain outer case, silver dial, and steel hand, British Museum; 1630–59.
DRAKEFORD, EDWD. *Congleton,* 1818; also JNO., same place and date.
DRAPER, JAMES. C.C. 1712.
DRAPER, JOHN. C.C. 1703; a long-case clock by Jno. Draper, *Maldon,* about 1720.
DRAPER, JOHN. *London (Gt. Sutton St.).* C.C. 1787, livery C.C. 1794.
DRAPER, SIMON. Apprenticed 1688 to Sam. Drosade, C.C.
DRAPER, WILLIAM. *Maldon.* Lantern clock, about 1760.
DRAYCOTT, FRANCIS. C.C. 1678.
DRAYSEY, JOHN. *London.* Apprenticed 1778, C.C. 1795–1813.
DRAYTON, T. *Chardstock.* Eighteenth century.
DREIJER, HERMAN. *Stockholm.* Master 1709–49; court clock; fine watch.
DRESCHER, JNO. *Hull,* 1822.
DREW, EDWARD. C.C. 1692.
DREW, JOHN. C.C. 1684; long-case clock, about 1695, inscribed 'John Drew, Johnson Court in Fleet St'.
DRILLS, JNO. *London,* 1780.
DROESHOUT, JOHN. *London.* C.C. 1632.
DROSADE, SAMUEL. C.C. 1675; watch by him, British Museum, about 1680; another, with sun and moon hour indicators, about 1690.
DROSHUTE, JOHN. C.C. 1632.
DROUOT, JEUNE. *Paris (Place Maubert),* 1807–24.
DROUYNOT, P. Large striking watch signed 'Pierre Drouynot à Poitiers', about 1610.
DROYER, NICHOLAS. *Hamburg.* Watch first half eighteenth century.
DROZ, ABRAHAM. *Chaux-de-Fonds.* Apprenticed 1711–50.
DROZ, CHARLES A. 1819.

DROZ, HENRY LOUIS, son of Pierre Jacquet. Born 1752, died 1791; excelled, if possible, his father as an ingenious mechanician; he journeyed to England, France, and Spain; was condemned to death at Madrid by the Inquisition as a necromancer, and saved by the Bishop of Toledo.
DROZ, HUMBERT. *Philadelphia,* 1797.
DROZ, HUMBERT A. L. *Philadelphia,* 1811.
DROZ, JEAN JACQUES. *Hüningen,* 1720–44. From *Chaux-de-Fonds.*
DROZ, JEAN PIERRE. *Basle, Paris, La Ferrière* and *Chaux-de-Fonds.* Born 1686, died 1764; a very fine clock; numerous complex long-case and bracket clocks in museums at Chaux-de-Fonds, Le Locle and Neuchâtel.
DROZ, PIERRE JACQUET. Born at Chaux de Fonds 1721, died at Bienne 1790; a clever mechanician; he made a curious clock for the King of Spain; his sons, Henri Louis (born 1752) and Daniel, also good watchmakers in Chaux de Fonds; Humbert Droz settled in Philadelphia in the latter part of the eighteenth century.
DROZ & LESCHOT. Clock, about 1795, signed 'Pierre Droz & Leschot'.
DROZ & SONS, 1811.
DROZ-DIT-BUSSET, ADAM, son. *Chaux-de-Fonds,* 1700–39. Many clocks.
DROZ-DIT-BUSSET, PIERRE FRÉDÉRIC, son. *Chaux-de-Fonds.* Born 1723–70; also at *Val-de-Travers; Berlin* in 1770.
DROZTE, JEUNE. *Rouen.* Watch, 1799.
DRUMMOND, FRANCIS. Apprenticed 1767 to Sam Davis the elder; C.C.
DRUMMOND, THOS. *Liverpool,* 1818.
DRURY, DRU. *32 Strand,* 1770–85; card, "Dru; Drury, Goldsmith to Her Majesty, in the Strand, successor to Nath. Jeffreys". There seems to have been an earlier D. Drury. Clock, long-case inlaid in front, oyster-shell veneers on sides, spiral pillars to hood, which has no door, dial signed 'D. Drury, London', dating from about 1705.
DRURY, J. F., *19 Clerkenwell Green,* 1810.
DRURY, JAMES. C.C. 1694, master 1728, clerk 1731; died 1740.
DRURY, JAMES. *Banbury, Oxon.,* 1780–1800.
DRURY, JAMES, son of John. *London (Clerkenwell).* Apprenticed 1741, C.C. 1751, died 1811.
DRURY, JOHN. *Red Lion St., Clerkenwell.* C.C. 1720.
DRURY, JOHN PETER. *London.* C.C. 1811.
DRURY, WM. *32 Strand,* 1800–25.
DRUYER, CHARLES PIERRE. *Paris.* Master 1785–1810.
DRYER, SAM. *London.* Single-case watch by him, about 1674; another specimen, silver dial, about 1690.
DRYSDALE, WALTER SCOTT. *Edinburgh,* 1812–29.
DRYSDALE, WILLIAM. *Edinburgh,* 1786. Died 1823.
DRYSDALE, WILLIAM. *Dunbar,* 1791. Died 1839.
DRYSDALE, WM. *Philadelphia,* 1819–51.
DUAIME, PIERRE. *Geneva,* about 1770–91.
DUBANT à *Grenoble.* Watch, about 1690.
DUBARE, —. *Neuchâtel,* about 1660–1708. From *Geneva.*
DUBBAR, HUGH. Apprenticed 1648 to Jno. Freeman, C.C.
DUBIE, J. *Paris.* Court goldsmith who resided in the Louvre, excelled in fine enamelled watch-cases, 1640–50.
DUBOIS (or DEBOIS), FREDERIC WM. *Neuchâtel.* Born 1811, died 1869.
DUBOIS (or DEBOIS), G. Small pillar clock, Wallace collection, signed 'Gm. Dubois, in Paris', about 1770.
DUBOIS (or DEBOIS), JACOB. Apprenticed to David Hubert; C.C. 1730.

DUBOIS (or DEBOIS), PHILIPPE. *Le Locle*. Born 1738, died 1808. About 1770 exported wooden clocks into Germany.

DUBOIS (or DEBOIS), Et Fils. Watch, with modification of Debaufre's escapement, bought in Hanover by George IV., G.M., about 1770; watch, Wallace collection, about 1785.

DUBOULE, JEAN BAPTISTE. Lion-shaped watch, about 1600; watch in nut-shaped case, Wallace collection, about 1620.

DUBOULE, SAMUEL ABRAHAM. *Geneva*, about 1750–75.

DUBUC, aîné. *Paris*, about 1780–1819. Clockmaker. Supplied American market; mantel clock, Palais de l'Élysée.

DUBUISSON, —. *Paris*. His signature on many good clock dials, period Louis XVI.

DUC, —. Alarum watch, signed 'Dominique Duc à Loche', about 1570.

DUCASTEL, ISAAC. Admitted C.C. 1703.

DUCHEMIN, Dr. Horloger, *Rouen*, 1570.

DUCHEN. In the British Museum is a watch by him, in a chased case by D. Cochin, 1730.

DUCHÊNE, LS. & FILS. *Geneva*. watch in gold egg-shaped case, V. & A., about 1785.

DUCHÉNE, LUIGI (LOUS or LS.), et Fils. *Geneva*. 1790–1820. Gold spherical watch V. & A.; watches with automatic F.W.M. and Fränkel collection; Lyre watch; 4-colour gold watches Carnegie Museum and M.M.A.; egg-shaped watch.

DUCHESNE, CLAUDE, in *Long Acre* (of *Paris*). C.C. 1693; square full-repeating bracket clock, inscription on back plate, 'Claudius du Chesne, in Long Aker'; long-case clock in lacquer case, Agence de Commerce Etranger Ltd.; John Wesley's long-case clock by him, arch dial, age of the moon, walnut case, is still preserved in the Wesley Museum, City Rd. In the Green Vaulted Chambers of the Treasury at Dresden is a pair of long-cased clocks in walnut cases signed 'Claudius du Chesne, Londini, fecit'; they stand about 12 ft. high; the dials show the phases of the moon, the months, and days of the month, which are written in French; both clocks chime and play tunes before striking the hour; on the dial of one is a list in Dutch of the tunes played, and the repertory of the other consists of 'Air Polonais No. 1', 'Air Polonais No. 2', 'Air Italien, and 'The King enjoys his own'. Fine bracket clock; 1690–1720.

DUCHESNE, FRANÇOIS HOUET. *Paris*, 1726. Juré 1735–41. One of the principal Paris makers; watch British Museum; two watches Fränkel collection.

DUCHESNE, JOHANNES. *Amsterdam*. Fine clock, about 1750.

DUCIMEN, JACOP, *Amsterdam*. Large oval watch, Pierpont Morgan collection, about 1625.

DUCK, H. *London*, about 1720.

DUCKWORTH, R. *Halifax*, about 1670.

DU CLAIR, CLAUDE. *Lyons*. Master 1625, died 1649; crystal cross watch Côte collection; illuminated Vial & Côte.

DU CLAIR-VALLIER, JEAN BAPTISTE. *Lyons*. Born about 1636, master 1652, died 1699. Grandson of Jean Vallier.

DU CLÉRON, CLAUDE. *Lyons*. 1593 master, died 1637. Maker of repute, watch M.M.A.; illuminated Vial & Côte.

DUCOMMUN, A. L. *Philadelphia*, 1797–1820.

DUCOMMUN, ABRAHAM, et Cie. *Philadelphia*. Early nineteenth century. Lever watch Gélis collection.

DUCOMMUN, AIMÉ, son. *Chaux-de-Fonds*. Born 1760, died 1811. Regulators.

DUCOMMUN, J. P. *London*, 1756. Watch, jasper case, Stern collection.

DUCOMMUN, HENRI. *Chaux-de-Fonds*. Born 1798, died 1826. Several Louis XVI clocks.

DUCOMMUN, HENRY. *Philadelphia*, 1819–50.

DUCOMMUN, JEAN FRÉDÉRIC. *Chaux-de-Fonds*, 1757–85. Clock.

DUCOMMUN, JEAN JACQUES. *Chaux-de-Fonds*, 1723–50. Clock.

DUCOMMUN, JEAN PIERRE. *Chaux-de-Fonds*, 1740–1804. Repeating and musical clocks.

DUCOMMUN, JONAS FRÉDÉRIC. *Chaux-de-Fonds*. Born 1727, died 1798. Clock.

DUCOMMUN, JONAS PIERRE. *Chaux-de-Fonds*. Born 1743, died 1816. Very able maker; numerous signed clocks. Also at *Le Locle*.

DUCOMMUN-DIT-BOUDRY, ABRAM. *Chaux-de-Fronds*, 1680. Died 1729. Made very complex automatic clock.

DUCOMMUN-DIT-BOUDRY, ABRAM, son of Abram. *Chaux-de-Fonds* and *Les Brenets*. Born 1700, died 1755.

DUCOMMUN-DIT-BOUDRY, DANIEL. *Chaux-de-Fonds*, 1774. Died about 1779. Clock.

DUCOMMUN-DIT-BOUDRY, DAVID, brother. *Chaux-de-Fonds* and *Yverdon*. Born 1682, died 1762.

DUCOMMUN-DIT-BOUDRY, FRÉDÉRIC. *Madrid*, 1756–58.

DUCOMMUN-DIT-BOUDRY, FRÉDÉRIC. *Chaux-de-Fonds*, 1761–74. Clock.

DUCOMMUN-DIT-BOUDRY, FRANÇOIS. *Chaux-de-Fonds*. Born 1763, died 1839. A famous maker; several planetary movements in Neuchâtel and Chaux-de-Fonds Museum.

DUCOMMUN-DIT-BOUDRY, JEAN PIERRE. *Chaux-de-Fonds*. Born 1690, died 1762. Long-case clock.

DUCOMMUN-DIT-BOUDRY, PHILIPPE, son of David. *Yverdon*, 1720–49.

DUCOMMUN-DIT-BOUDRY, PIERRE. *Chaux-de-Fonds*, *Yverdon*, *Neuchâtel* and *Lausanne*. Born 1680, died 1760. Reputed maker of turret and complicated clocks; made clocks for Yverdon and Payerne; long-case clock Vieux-Vevey Museum.

DUCOMMUN-DIT-PETITJEAN, JONAS PIERRE. *Chaux-de-Fonds*. Born 1725, died 1794.

DUCOMMUN-DIT-TINNON, ABRAM LOUIS, son of Daniel. *Chaux-de-Fonds*. Born 1721, died 1819. Turret clock.

DUCOMMUN-DIT-TINNON, DANIEL. *Chaux-de-Fonds*, 1716–66. Turret and house clockmaker of repute.

DUCOMMUN-DIT-TINNON, DANIEL, brother. *Chaux-de-Fonds*, 1772. Turret clock.

DUCOMMUN-DIT-TINNON, FERDINAND. *Chaux-de-Fonds*. 1753. Clock.

DUCOMMUN-DIT-TINNON, FRÉDÉRIC, brother. *Chaux-de-Fonds*, 1739–about 1790. Turret clock.

DUCOMMUN-DIT-TINNON, JEAN PIERRE, brother. *Chaux-de-Fonds*, 1739–49. Clock.

DUCOMMUN-DIT-VERRON, ABRAM LOUIS. *Chaux-de-Fonds*. v. DUCOMMUN-dit-VERRON FRÈRES, but worked alone in 1745.

DUCOMMUN-DIT-VERRON, AMI. *Chaux-de-Fonds*. 1806–29. Fine clock.

DUCOMMUN-DIT-VERRON, CHARLES. *Chaux-de-Fonds*. v. DUCOMMUN-dit-VERRON FRÈRES.

DUCOMMUN-DIT-VERRON, DAVID. *Chaux-de-Fonds*. 1718. Maker of carillons for clocks.

DUCOMMUN-DIT-VERRON, FRÈRES. *Chaux-de-Fonds*. 1750–89. A very important firm of the three men above; many clocks.

DUCOMMUN-DIT-VERRON, JEAN JACQUES. *Chaux-de-Fonds*. Born 1756, died 1811. Clock.

DUCOMMUN-DIT-VERRON, JONAS PIERRE. *Chaux-de-Fonds.* Born 1727, died 1787.

DU COTY (DU COSTY), —. *Paris*, about 1750 master

DU COTY (DU COSTY), NICOLAS GARCIL. *Paris.* Master 1758–89.

DUDDELL, THOS. *106 Holborn Hill*, 1817–23.

DUDDS, JOSEPH. *Coleman St.*, 1730. Geo. Adams apprenticed to him in 1745; livery C.C. 1766. In the Czar of Russia's collection at the Winter Palace, St. Petersburg, was a watch by him. It has a case of faceted crystal and is suspended from a chatelaine, see STEPHENS.

DUDSON, SIMON. *Tower St.* C.C. 1654.

DUDUICT, DANIEL, brother. *Blois* and *Paris.* Master 1604, died 1636. In *Paris*, 1628–34. Engraved watch British Museum.

DUDUICT, JACQUES. *Blois*, 1560–90.

DUET, PIERRE. *Paris.* Fine enamelled watch, Pierpont Morgan collection, about 1740.

DUFALGA, PPE. *Geneva.* Watch, about 1775.

DUFF, JAMES. *Edinburgh*, 1758–74.

DUFF, JAMES. *London.* C.C. 1819. Watch.

DUFFETT, JNO. *Bristol.* Long-case tidal clock, 'High Water at Bristol Key', about 1780.

DUFFIELD, EDWARD. *Philadelphia*, 1741–80.

DUFFNER, ANTON. *Furtwangen.* Born 1752, died 1832. Musical clockmaker of repute; musical clock Furt. Museum.

DUFOUR, —. *Geneva.* Alarm watch, about 1800.

DUFOUR, ABRAHAM. Watch, leather case, ornamented with silver, Schloss collection, about 1630. A curious and well-made watch dating from about 1710 signed 'Isac Dufour'. The collection of the Czar of Russia in the Winter Palace, St. Petersburg, contained a repeating watch signed 'Dufour, London'; the outer case is cut out of a solid piece of lapis-lazuli carved with scrolls in the Louis XV style, and set with a large spray of very fine diamonds; it is suspended from a chatelaine with decoration of the same character.

DUFOUR, HENRI. *Blois*, 1662. Died 1689. Watch.

DUFOUR, L. *Geneva.* About 1770–1800. Engraved watch, set pearls and diamonds, F.W.M.; large alarum watch Denham collection.

DUFOUR & CERET. Associated with Voltaire at Ferney, 1770, see LEPINE.

DUGARD, THOS. *34 Red Lion St., Clerkenwell*, 1812–19.

DUGDALE, RICHD. *12 Broad St.*, 1800–05; *39 Great Marlborough St.*, 1817.

DUGUET, JEHAN. *Paris*, 1606 juré.

DUHAMEL, PIERRE. *Blois.* A small watch by him with enamelled dial in plain gold case, black shagreen outer case studded with gold; cruciform watch by him, Ecole d'Horlogerie, *Geneva*.

DUHAMEL, PIERRE. *Paris* and *Geneva*, about 1650–86. Engraved watch illuminated Baillie; probably the preceding.

DU HAMEL à *Paris.* Mid-seventeenth century watch in enamelled gold case, V. & A.

DU HAMEL, ISAAC. Long-case clock, Canon Greenwell, watch, G.M., about 1785.

DUKE, JOHN. *Fleet St.* Watch, British Museum, 1650.

DUKE, JOSEPH. Apprenticed 1666 to Jas. Markwick; C.C. 1682.

DUKE, JOSEPH. *London.* C.C. 1671.

DUKE, JOSEPH. C.C. 1728.

DUKE, NAT. Apprenticed 1656 to Thos. Wheeler; C.C. 1663.

DULIN, W. T. *10 Cornhill*, 1816–30.

DUMBELL, JOSEPH. *Liverpool*, 1800–29. Watch.

DUMBELL, JOSH. *Prescott*, 1816, see DUNBILL.

DUMBELL, THOS. *Rochdale*, 1818.

DUMESNIL, ANTHONY. *Boston, U.S.A.*, 1796–1807. Watch.

DUMONT FRÈRES. *Besançon.* Watch, silver cock, one hand, Schloss collection, 1735.

DUMVILE, NAT. *Stockport*, 1820–33.

DUN, HENRY. *London.* C.C. 1677.

DUNBALL, RICHARD. *London.* Apprenticed 1786, C.C. 1793, l.C.C. 1812–15.

DUNBAR, BUTLER. *Bristol, Conn.*, 1830.

DUNBAR, GEO. *London.* Watch, 1770.

DUNBILL, JOSH. *Prescot.* Watch, h.m., 1820.

DUNCAN, GEO. *London.* Watch, 1737.

DUNCAN, JAS. Watch, h.m., 1775, Mr. William Ranken; *98 Chancery Lane*, 1800–10; *44 St. James's St.*, 1815–25; *33 Old Bond St.*, 1825–30.

DUNCAN, ROBT. *London.* Watch, 1790; fine lancet-case clock, 'Duncan London', about 1800.

DUNCARTON, ROBT. *London.* Watch, 1765.

DUNCOMBE, RICHARD. *London.* Master C.C. 1798.

DUNDAS, JAS. *Edinburgh.* Apprenticed to Andrew Brown in 1710.

DUNHEIM, ANDREW. *New York*, 1775.

DUNKERLY, 1770.

DUNKLEY, BENJ. *London.* Long-case clock, japanned case with rococo figure subjects painted on door and base; plays seven tunes; on each side of the usual date a wedge-shaped opening showing month and day of week; moon in arch, about 1760.

DUNKLEY, JOHN. *88 Bethnal Green Rd.*, 1825–35.

DUNLOP, ANDREW. C.C. 1701–32 known as a maker of watches and long-case clocks; turret clock, Hawley House, Blackwater, Hants, dated on movement 1716; made earliest known five minute repeater, Ilbert collection, about 1725.

DUNLOP, CONYERS. *Spring Gardens, Charing Cross.* C.C. 1733, master 1758, died 1779.

DUNN, ANTHONY. C.C. 1719.

DUNN, BENJ. Apprenticed 1691 to Thos. Gibbs; C.C.

DUNN, CHARLES. *London (Fleet Mkt.).* C.C. 1773–96.

DUNN, HENRY. C.C. 1677.

DUNN, JNO. *Hull*, 1822.

DÜNNEBIER, EHRENFRIED. *Dresden.* Master 1703, died 1736. Pair-case watch, Ilbert collection.

DUNOD, CLAUDIO. *Munich*, 1679–96. Court clock.

DUNSTER, ROGER. A repeating watch by him in delicately pierced and chased gold case; hands and thumbpiece set with diamonds; gold outer case chased with allegorical figures; pierced border chased with scrolls, about 1700.

DUNSTON, PAUL. Apprenticed 1687 to Simon Chapman, C.C.

DUNTNELL, DANL. *131 Oxford St.*, 1783.

DU PERON, C., à *Lyon.* Oval watch, brass case with rock-crystal cover, Pierpont Morgan collection, about 1600.

DUPIN, PAUL. *London.* Fine repeating watch in gold pair cases, Schloss collection, about 1710; also bracket clock in red shell case, about 1720; repeating watch, G.M., three cases, inner case engraved and pierced, enclosed in a richly chased one by Moser, outer case of leather *piqué*, h.m., 1739; in the British Museum is a repeating watch by him inscribed 'Dr. Samuel Johnson 1767'.

DUPLOCK, CHAS. *129 Borough*, 1790–1815.

DUPLOCK & WIGGINS, 1816–30.

DUPONCHEL, GUILLAUME. *Paris.* Juré 1739–45.

DUPONS, EDWD. *London.* Watch, 1785.

DUPONT à *Castres.* Watch, British Museum, about 1650.

DUPONT, CHAS. *Cockspur St.*, 1798–1800.

DUPONT, J. P. *Rotterdam*, about 1750.

DUPONT, PAUL. *27 Ivy Lane, Newgate St.* Watch, G.M., case finely worked in *repoussé* by Moser, 1759–72; clock, 'Dupont late Emerys', not later than 1780.

DUPONT, PETER. *London*. Long-case clock in raised ornament Oriental lacquer case at the Armoury-Museum, Government House, Malta, about 1725; another clock inscribed 'Peter Dupont, St. John's, London'.

DUPONT, SAMUEL. *Paris*, 1755. Clockmaker to the King; made clock dials of painted glass to imitate enamel; method approved by Acad. R. des Sciences; cartel clock.

DUPPA, CHAS. Apprenticed 1646 to Wm. Clay, C.C.

DUPPA, JAMES. *15 Aldgate Within*, 1765–70.

DUPRÉ. *Paris*. Watch, about 1730.

DUPREE, ELIAS, a Dutchman, who worked for Edwd. East in 1635; he had then been in London about twenty years.

DUPUY, JACQUES. *Paris*. Went to *Neuchâtel* 1688. Died 1696. Watch Ilbert collection marked Neuchâtel.

DUPUY, JNO. 1770.

DUPUY, ODRAN. *Philadelphia*, 1735.

DURADE, ABEL. Watch, bridge over balance with enamelled portrait, Dutch style, about 1770, Pierpont Morgan collection.

DURAND, —. Octagonal watch, Garnier collection, about 1585, signed 'P. Durand à Rouen'; watch, P. Durand, London, 1790.

DURAND, JEAN. *Rouen*. Juré 1649. Also DURANT. Fine gold watch engraved flowers.

DURAND, PIERRE. *Paris*. Master 1772–89; silver watch Fränkel collection.

DURANT, J. L. A watch in British Museum, finely enamelled case, about 1690.

DURANT, OSWALD. Petitioner for incorporation of C.C.; admitted as brother in 1632; warden in 1645; did not become master; Ralph Almond apprenticed to him in 1637; 1630–45.

DURANT, P. *Rouen*, about 1590–about 1610. Octagonal watch Louvre; oval engraved watch; cast silver shell watch Ilbert collection.

DURDENT, ANDREW. C.C. 1662.

DURFALGA. *Paris*, 1790.

DURHAM, STEPHEN. *London*. Apprenticed 1716.

DURHAM, WILLIAM. *Edinburgh*. Apprenticed 1809–50.

DURKS, RINSE. *Grouw*, 1750. Died 1787. Bracket clock Friesch Museum.

DURN, —. *Paris*. Watch, 1690.

DURRANT, RICHD. *36 Museum St.*, 1820–42.

DURTNALL, DANIELL. *131 Oxford St.*, 1780–1805.

DURU, —. *Paris*, 1650–about 1700. Alarum watch Denham collection.

DURU, GUILLAUME. *Blois*. Comp. 1642.

DURWARD, JNO. Watch paper dated 1816. 'John Durward, 6 Leith Street, New Edinburgh.'

DURWARD, JOSEPH. *Edinburgh*, 1775–1819.

DUSEIGNEUR, PIERRE. *Geneva*, about 1750.

DUTCH, STEPHEN. *Boston, U.S.A.*, 1800–18. Watch.

DUTENS, GEO. *London*. Small watch in case of bloodstone, diamond push piece, silver cock over balance, about 1750.

DUTENS, PETER. *Leicester Sq.*, 1759–65.

DUTERTRE, JEAN BAPTISTE. *Paris*, 1750–80. Inventor of an escapement with two balances; repeating watch, 'Dutertre Paris', about 1750, Pierpont Morgan collection.

DUTERTRE, NICOLAS CHARLES, brother. *Paris*. Born 1715, master 1739, juré 1775, died 1793. His equation clock desc. in Gallon, 'Machines et Inventions', Vol. VII.

DU THUILLAY, —. *Hull*. Watch in large medallion frame, V. & A., frame signed 'J. S. Meyer, Zerbst, 1788'.

DUTTON, EDMUND. *London*. Apprenticed 1737, C.C. 1744.

DUTTON, GUY. Quarter clock, Shandon collection, about 1760.

DUTTON, JNO. *Liverpool*, 1770.

DUTTON, JNO. *Liverpool*, 1818.

DUTTON, MATTHEW, son of William. *London (Fleet St.)*. Apprenticed 1771, C.C. 1779, m.C.C. 1800–25. v. THOMAS.

DUTTON, MATTHEW & THOMAS. *148 Fleet St.* Matthew Dutton, son of and apprenticed to William Dutton; admitted C.C. 1779, assistant 1793, livery 1785, master 1800; Thomas Dutton, also apprenticed to William, admitted C.C. 1791, livery 1796; long mahogany-case clock inscribed 'Matthew and Thomas Dutton', about 1795, Wetherfield collection.

DUTTON, MATTHEW. *148 Fleet St.*, 1819–42; he returned to Church St., Stoke Newington, and died about 1843.

DUTTON, MATTHEW, son of Matthew. *London*. Apprenticed 1799, C.C. 1815.

DUTTON, THOMAS. *London*. Apprenticed 1776, C.C. 1791, livery C.C. 1796–99. Partner with Matthew.

DUTTON, THOMAS. *Bath*, about 1790 C.C.

DUTTON, WILLIAM. Apprentice of Graham, and afterwards partner with Mudge, *148 Fleet St.* C.C. 1746, liveryman 1766; 1746–94.

DUTTON & SONS. 1810–18.

DUVAL, FRANCIS & JOHN. *Warnford Court, Throgmorton St.*, 1755–65.

DUVAL, FREDERIC. *Paris*, 1780, à *Paris*. Fine clock, about 1810.

DUVAL, GABRIEL. *Paris*, 1675 master, juré 1684. Probably same as Gabriel De Val.

DUVAL, J. B. *Paris*. Juré 1613. Engraved watch F.W.M. by him or Gabriel.

DUVAL, JOHN. C.C. 1677.

DUVIVIER L'AÎSÉ. *Paris*, about 1740.

DUVIVIER, ET QUEENCL. *Rouen*, about 1775.

DU VIVIER, FRANÇOIS. *Rouen*, 1759–64. Double virgule watch movement Ilbert collection.

DUWALL, AXEL JOHAN DIEDRIC. *Sala*. Born 1787, died 1847.

DWERRIHOUSE, THOS. *Garston*. Watch, h.m., 1774.

DWERRYHOUSE, JOHN. *23 Charles St., Berkeley Sq.*, 1770–1805; hon. freeman C.C. 1781.

DWERRYHOUSE, OGSTON & CO. *27 Davies St., Berkeley Sq.*, 1835–42.

DWERRYHOUSE & BELL. *131 Mount St.*, 1840.

DWERRYHOUSE & CARTER. *30 Charles St., Berkeley Sq.*, 1809–18; *27 Davies St.*, 1823. Bracket clock, Wetherfield collection, about 1810; bracket clock, Dwerryhouse, Carter & Son, Berkeley Sq., about 1820.

DYDE, THOMAS. *London*. Lantern clocks and watches, 1640–70. He was free of the C.C., but date of election uncertain.

DYER, JOSEPH. *Addle St.*, 1735–40.

DYER & NEWMAN. *9 Lombard St.*, 1768–72.

DYKE, —. *Exchange Alley*, 1685.

DYMOND, JOHN. Watch-case maker, *Windmill Court, Smithfield*, 1790.

DYSON, HUMPHREY. *Manchester*, 1818.

DYSON, JOHN. Admitted C.C. 1694.

EADEN, RICHD. *London*. Watch, 1800.

EADY, WM. *14 West St., Smithfield*, 1800–18.

EAGLE, JOHN. C.C. 1690; long-case clock, about 1700, Wetherfield collection.

EAGLE, NATH. *London.* Metal-case watch, outer case tortoise-shell, about 1776.

EAGLETON, CHRISTOPHER. Apprenticed to Charles Halstead 1683. In the G.M. is a watch by him, silver case, silver dial, outer case tortoise-shell *piqué*; 1690–1710.

EAMES, JACOB, also THOS. *Bath,* 1850.

EAMES & BARNARD. *9 Ave Maria Lane,* 1816.

EARLE, EDWARD. *London.* Apprenticed 1750, C.C. 1757.

EARLE, THOS. Admitted C.C. 1720.

EARLES, —, (or ERYLES). Subscribed to incorporation of C.C. 1630.

EARLES, JNO. *London,* 1700–15.

EARNSHAW, EDWD. *Stockport.* An ingenious clock and watch maker, his shop was said to be a "regular Noah's Ark of mechanical nicknacs"; he was a friend of Jas. Ferguson, 1740–70.

EARNSHAW, LAWRENCE. A clever watchmaker; born at *Mottram,* near *Longendale, Cheshire,* 1705, died in 1767, aged 62 years; a monument was erected to his memory by public subscription in 1868.

EARNSHAW, THOMAS. *119 High Holborn,* born 1749, died 1829. Famous maker of marine chronometers from 1780 onwards.

EARNSHAW, THOMAS, JUNR. *87 Fenchurch St.,* 1825–42.

EAST, EDWARD. *Pall Mall,* 1632; *Fleet St.* later; one of the first assistants of C.C.

EAST, EDWARD. Apprenticed to R. Lyon and turned over to Saml. Clyatt; admitted C.C. 1696.

EAST, EDWARD, JUNR. Apprenticed to Thomas East; admitted C.C. 1710.

EAST, EDWARD. Apprenticed to Joseph Pomroy; freeman C.C. 1743.

EAST, JAMES. *London.* Clockmaker to the Queen in 1662; clockmaker to both Charles I and II, 1602–97?

EAST, JERE. Apprenticed 1653 to Jas. Seabourne, C.C.

EAST, JEREMY. Admitted as a brother C.C. 1640; maker of a small hexagonal watch, balance-cock pinned on, plate inscribed 'Jeremie East, Londini', crystal case, about 1600; also a small oval watch, plain silver dial, one hand, about 1610.

EAST, JOHN, son of Edmund. *London.* C.C. 1757.

EAST, JOHN, brother. *London (Cannon St.).* C.C. 1765.

EAST, JORDON, son of Edward East C.C. 1720.

EAST, PETER. C.C. 1692.

EAST, THOMAS. C.C. 1677.

EASTERLEY, JOHN. *New Holland,* 1825–40.

EASTLAND, THOMAS. *London.* Maker of repeating watches, about 1750.

EASTMAN, of *U.S.A.*

EASTMAN, ABEL B. *Haverhill,* 1816–21.

EASTMAN, ROBERT. *Brunswick,* 1805–08.

EASTMAN & CARY. *Brunswick,* 1808.

EASTON, EDWARD. *London.* Apprenticed 1700, C.C. 1788.

EASTWICK, ADRIAN. *102 Aldersgate St.,* 1770–85.

EASTWOOD, WM. *Burnley,* 1748–70.

EATON, J. *London.* Watch, 1790.

EAVE, JOHN. *8 Oxford St.,* 1790.

EAYRE, EBERT ISAAC. *Steyr, Austria,* about 1620. Crucifix clocks.

EAYRE, JOSH. *St. Neots.* Watch, 1770.

EAYRE, THOS. *Kettering.*

EBBEN, WM. *37 Islington Green,* 1816–42.

EBBERMAN, JOHN. *Lancaster, U.S.A.,* 1780–1820.

EBBS, JNO. *Dublin.* Clock about 1770.

EBERMAN, JACOB, brother. *Lancaster City,* 1773–1837. Long-case clocks.

EBHER, ISAAC. *Steyer.* 1617–mid seventeenth century. Wood and silver crucifix clock Feill collection. Stackfreed striking watch Ilbert collection.

EBSWORTH, CHRISTOPHER. C.C. 1670.

EBSWORTH, JOHN. A good clockmaker; C.C. 1665, master 1697.

ECKEGREN, DANIEL. *Copenhagen.* Master 1821; master of Corporation 1842–46.

ECLES, HY. Apprenticed 1654 to Tobias Davis, C.C.

ECLIPSE, JNO. *London.* Watch, 1798.

EDEN, JOHN. *London.* Apprenticed 1749, C.C. 1759.

EDEN, RALPH. *Liverpool,* 1770.

EDEN, WILLIAM. Admitted C.C. 1726.

EDENBURY, JOHN. *London.* Apprenticed 1783, C.C. 1791–1802.

EDEY, RICHARD. *London.* Apprenticed 1700, C.C. 1716; insolvent 1720. Also EDY.

EDGECOMBE, JOHN. *Market Street, Bristol,* 1750–1800.

EDGECOMBE, NATHANIEL. *Market Street, Bristol,* 1800–45.

EDGECOMBE, THOS. *St. Stephen's,* 1780.

EDGECOMBE & NICHOLS. *Bristol,* 1710.

EDINGTON, —. *24 N. Audley St.,* 1815.

EDINGTON, JNO. *10 Portland St.,* 1816.

EDKINS, JAMES. *2 High St., Kensington,* 1830–42.

EDLEY, WM. *London.* Watch, 1748.

EDLIN, GEORGE. *6 Aldgate Within.* Livery C.C. 1800–13.

EDLIN, JOHN. Apprenticed to Robert Webster; admitted C.C. 1687.

EDLYNE, EDGAR. *London.* Apprenticed 1740, C.C. 1747–51. Bracket clock.

EDLYNE, EDGAR. *Nevill Alley, Fetter Lane.* C.C. 1710–30; verge bracket clock, engraved back.

EDMONDS, B. *Liverpool,* 1778–1829. Watch.

EDMONDS, CHAS. Apprenticed to Thos. Taylor; C.C. 1772.

EDMONDS, D. *Liverpool.* Watch, 1810.

EDMONDS, ELIZA. Apprenticed 1679 to Hy. Fevon and Christina his wife, C.C.

EDMONDS, JAMES. *Charleston, U.S.A.,* 1745. From *London.* Clocks and Watches.

EDMONDS, JNO. *14 Strand,* 1820–30.

EDMONDS & WEST. *14 Strand,* 1779–1810.

EDMONDSON, JNO. Apprenticed 1660 to Hugh Cooper, C.C.

EDMONDSON, JNO. *Liverpool,* 1770.

EDMUNDS, WM. *London.* Watch, painted outer case, Schloss collection, about 1785.

EDRIDGE, WILLIAM. *London.* Apprenticed 1793, C.C. 1802.

EDSON, JONAH. *Bridgewater, U.S.A.,* 1815–30.

EDWARDS, ADAM. *London.* Watch, about 1768.

EDWARDS, CHARLES. *London.* 1775 C.C.–1811.

EDWARDS, D. *Liverpool,* 1790.

EDWARDS, GEORGE. *London.* Apprenticed 1756, C.C. 1763.

EDWARDS, GEORGE. *London.* C.C. 1792–1813.

EDWARDS, ISAAC. C.C. 1719.

EDWARDS, JAMES. *Stourbridge,* 1790.

EDWARDS, JAMES. *180 Fleet St.,* 1790–94.

EDWARDS, JAMES. *London (Goswell St.).* C.C. 1808–19.

EDWARDS, JAS. *Commercial Rd.,* 1814–35; watch marked 'near the West India Docks'.

EDWARDS, JAS. *93 Wood St., Cheapside,* 1820–25.

EDWARDS, JNO. *Norwich,* 1770.

EDWARDS, JOHN. *Annapolis, U.S.A.,* 1735. Watch.

EDWARDS, JOHN (3). *London.* Apprenticed 1760, C.C. 1775–77.

EDWARDS, JOSEPH. Apprenticed 1655 to Jno. Nicacious, C.C.

EDWARDS, NICH. Apprenticed 1687 to Robt. Dingley, C.C.

EDWARDS, ROBT. *Great Sutton St.,* 1820–25.

EDWARDS, T. *London*. Watch, h.m., 1766.

EDWARDS, THOS. Apprenticed 1680 to Robt. Player, C.C.

EDWARDS, THOS. *Epping*, 1720.

EDWARDS, WILLIAM. *4 Holborn*. Livery Blacksmiths' Company; 1764-83; gold *repoussé* watch; 109 *Cheapside*, 1790-94.

EDWARDS, WM. JNO. *Coleman St.*, 1783.

EDWARDS, WM. *26 New Bond St.*, 1800.

EFFINGTON, JOHN. Admitted C.C. 1702.

EGERSLEY, JAS. Apprenticed 1660 to Wm. Godbed, C.C.

EGLETON, CHRISTOPHER. Apprenticed to Charles Halstead in 1683, admitted C.C. 1695.

EICHSTET, JOHANN. *Elburg*. Hexagonal table clock, about 1635.

EICKSTEL, JOHAN. *Germany*, about 1600. Table clock; tower clock Feill collection.

EIFFE, JAMES SWEETMAN. Born 1800, died 1880; a clever chronometer maker, who for some time carried on business at *48 Lombard St.*; he invented a compensation balance very similar to that patented by Molyneux, see FLETCHER, JNO.

EISELÉ, W. A. *Brussels*. Oval watch Pierpont Morgan collection, about 1760.

EISEN, HEINRICH. *Nuremberg*, 1510.

EKEBECK, SVEN. *Linköping*, 1754-73. Long-case clock Nord Museum.

EKEROTH, JAKOB. *Stockholm*. Comp. 1751, master 1755, died 1766. Fine watchmaker; four watches, one in National Museum, Stockholm, illuminated Sidenbladh.

ELCHINGER, HANS CONRAD. *Amsterdam*. Watch, the dial engraved with representation of a pedlar crossing a brook, 1620.

ELDRED, DODSON. *London*. Apprenticed 1753, C.C. 1782.

ELDRIDGE, JOHN. Admitted C.C. 1677; long-case clock inscribed 'John Eldridge, Alresford', about 1730.

ELEY, JAMES. *11 Fenchurch St.*, 1770-85.

ELFES, BENJAMIN. *London*. Apprenticed 1666, C.C. 1674.

ELFES, THOS. Apprenticed 1671 to Geo. Hambleton, C.C.

ELFSTRÖM, PETTER. *Lovisa*, 1763-88. Watches and wall clocks.

ELIASON, DANIEL. *18 Leman St., Goodman Fields*, 1785-90.

ELISHA CALEB. *Duke St., St. James's*. Bracket clock, about 1810, *3 Marlyebone St., Golden Sq.*, 1820; *175 Piccadilly*, 1835; *8 New Bond St.*, 1842.

ELKES, JAMES. *London*. Apprenticed 1787, C.C. 1819.

ELKINS, CHAS. Apprenticed 1677 to Dan. Le Count, C.C.

ELKINS, WILLIAM. Apprenticed to John Ellicott; C.C. 1710; assistant 1730; large bracket clock at the India Office, 'Windmills and Elkins', about 1725.

ELLAM, THOS. *Runcorn*, 1833.

ELLED, —. *London*, 1780.

ELLESTON, ROBT. *Lancaster*, 1721, f.

ELLICOTT, ANDREW. *Baltimore, U.S.A.*, 1778-80. Clock.

ELLICOTT, EDWARD, son of John (2). *London (R. Exchange)*, 1758, died 1791. Watchmaker to the King; large-case Virginia Museum.

ELLICOTT, EDWARD, son of Edw. *London*. C.C. 1795, m.C.C. and died 1835.

ELLICOTT, EDWARD & SON. *17 Sweeting's Alley, Cornhill*, 1783-1810.

ELLICOTT, JEREMIAH. *London*, 1708 C.C.

ELLICOTT, JOHN. C.C. 1696; apprenticed to John Waters, 1687, *All Hallows, London Wall*, 1696-1733.

ELLICOTT, JOHN. *17 Sweeting's Alley, Cornhill*, an eminent maker; born 1706, died 1772.

ELLICOTT, JOHN. *London*. C.C. 1782-95. Watch.

ELLICOTT, JOHN & SONS. *17 Sweeting's Rents*, 1769-88.

ELLICOTT, JOSEPH. *Bucks County, Pa. and Baltimore*. Born 1732; went *Baltimore* 1775, died 1780. Planetarium and musical long-case clock playing 24 tunes in Philadelphia.

ELLICOTT & SMITH. *17 Sweeting's Alley, Cornhill*, 1830; *27 Lombard St.*, 1839-42.

ELLICOTT & TAYLOR. *Sweeting's Alley, Cornhill*, 1811-30.

ELLIOT, WM. *Whitby*, 1770.

ELLIOT, —. *Nottingham*, 1795.

ELLIOTT, HENRY. Brother C.C. 1688.

ELLIOTT, HENRY, son. *London*. Apprenticed 1704, C.C. 1720.

ELLIOTT, JAS. *Oxford St.*, 1780-1800.

ELLIOTT, JNO. Apprenticed 1681 to Jno. Goode, C.C.

ELLIOTT, JOHN MOSELEY. *Aylesbury St., Clerkenwell*. Patented a repeater in 1804 (No. 2,759).

ELLIOTT, JOSH. *Berkhamsted*. Musical clock, about 1750.

ELLIOTT, THOMAS. *London*. Apprenticed 1744, C.C. 1751.

ELLIOTT, THOS. *Greenwich*. Long-case clock, about 1740.

ELLIOTT, WM. *London*. Watch, h.m., 1787.

ELLIOTT & SON. *119 Oxford St.*, 1805.

ELLIS, DAVID. *2 John St., Oxford Rd.*, 1817.

ELLIS, GRIFFITH (successor to Mr. Newton). *29 Little Moorefields*, 1780.

ELLIS, HENRY. *Exeter*, 1810.

ELLIS, JACOB. *York*, f. 1636.

ELLIS, JAMES. C.C. 1667.

ELLIS, JOHN. *Little Old Bailey*. C.C. 1726.

ELLIS, JOHN. *London (Old Broad St.)*. C.C. 1817, l.C.C. 1822.

ELLIS, PAUL. Brother C.C. 1682.

ELLIS, RICHARD. *Westminster*. Apprenticed 1673 to Geo. Deane; C.C. 1683; bracket quarter clock, about 1730.

ELLIS, RICHARD. *London*. Apprenticed 1818, C.C. 1825.

ELLIS, RICHARD. *London*. C.C. 1777.

ELLIS, THOMAS. C.C. 1682.

ELLIS & COLLINS. *52 Strand*, 1804.

ELLISON, CALEB. Apprenticed 1691 to Sam. Vernon, C.C.

ELLISON, THOS. *York*, f. 1826.

ELLISTON, ROBERT. *Orange St.*, 1770; *12 Charles St., Covent Garden*, 1790-1820. His son, Robt. Wm. Elliston, a celebrated actor, was born at Orange St., 7th April, 1774.

ELLWOOD, JAMES. *London*. C.C. 1734.

ELLWOOD, JOHN. C.C. 1702; long marquetry case clock, square dial, 1702-25.

ELLWOOD, JOHN. *London (Whitefriars)*. C.C. 1702, 1734; long-case clock; watch.

ELLWOOD, MARTIN. Brother C.C. 1687; a watch by him in the Guildhall Museum, silver dial, curious tortoiseshell case inlaid with silver, 1680-1700.

ELLY, JAS. *52 Rathbone Place*, 1816.

ELMES, JOSEPH. Apprenticed 1673 to Wm. Elmes, C.C.

ELMES, RICHARD. Apprenticed to Edward Banger, admitted C.C. 1708; worked for Webster in 1730.

ELMES, RICHARD, son of Richard. *London*. C.C. 1747.

ELMES, WILLIAM. Brother C.C. 1667.

ELSGOOD, WM. *Norwich*. Clock, about 1770.

ELSON, DAVID. Brother C.C. 1646.

ELSWORTH, DAVID. *Windsor, U.S.A.*, 1780-1800.

ELTON, JOHN. C.C. 1675.

ELTON, THOS. C.C. 1677.

ELVINS, WILLIAM. *Baltimore, U.S.A.*, 1799-1802. Watches and clocks.

ELY, JAMES. *8 Soho Sq.*, 1825.

EMAN, JNO. Apprenticed 1669 to Isaac Daniell, C.C.

EMANUEL, JOEL. *Bevis Marks*, 1812–17.

EMANUEL, LEWIS & SON. *36 Swan St., Minories*, 1820–42.

EMANUEL BROTHERS. *1 Bevis Marks*, 1830.

EMBLEY, ROBERT ELLIS. *London.* Apprenticed 1798, C.C. 1812.

EMBRFE, EFFINGHAM. *New York*, Dec. 1785.

EMEREY, RICHARD. *London.* Apprenticed 1753, C.C. 1763.

EMERSON. Lantern clock, signed 'Richd. Emerson, fecit', about 1690.

EMERY, JOSIAH. An eminent Swiss watchmaker, who settled here and carried on business at 33 *Cockspur St., Charing Cross.* Hon. freeman C.C. 1781; an 8-day watch by him with extra wheel in the train, about 1780; another example is a watch in the Guildhall Museum, ruby cylinder, helical balance-spring, compensation curb; a bracket clock by him in an ebony case, dating from about 1790, is in the Wetherfield collection; chiefly famous for his lever escapement watches of which he made upwards of 30 between 1782 and about 1795. He was the first after Mudge to use this escapement. 1770–1805 (succeeded by Recordon).

EMMERTON, WILLIAM. *Wootton-under-Edge.* 1779; died 1793. His son opened a shop in *Woburn*, but died 1794.

ENDERLIN, —. *Basle.* Maker of equation clocks, 1715–60.

ENDERLIN, ABRAHAM, son of Wilhelm. *Basle.* Born 1719. Went to *Strasbourg* 1763.

ENDERLIN, HANS GEORGE, brother. *Basle.* Born 1678, died 1754. Clockmaker to the town from 1736; turret and house clock; watch Basle Museum with engraving on cock.

ENDERLIN, HANS JAKOB. *Basle.* Born 1707, died 1732.

ENDERLIN, HANS JOHANN JAKOB, brother. *Basle.* Born 1675, died 1736. Clockmaker to the town; turret clock made for Hässingen (Alsace) in Basle Museum; turret and house clock.

ENDERLIN, JAKOB. *Basle.* Born 1628; *Breslau*, 1648; *Basle*, 1658; died 1699. Turret and house clock.

ENDERLIN, JOHANN HEINRICH, son. *Basle.* Born 1672, died 1716.

ENDERLIN, REINHARD, brother. *Basle.* Born 1721, died 1755. Turret and house clocks.

ENDERLIN, WILLIAM ANDREAS, son of Jakob. *Basle.* Born 1681, died 1733. Watches Basle Museum with engravings on cocks.

ENDT, THEOBALD. *Philadelphia*, 1742. Clocks.

ENEN, WM. Apprenticed 1687 to Thos. Wise, C.C.

ENGALL, ABRAHAM. Brother C.C. 1648.

ENGAZ, —. *Paris.* Handsome clock, about 1790.

ENGEL, DAVID GUILLAUME. *Douanne Gléresse, Chaux-de-Fonds.* Born 1737, died 1800. Many musical and other clocks.

ENGELBRECHTEN, EDUARD. *Stockholm.* 1815–46. Two wall clocks and bracket clock.

ENGELSCHALK (ENGELSHALKH), BENEDICT. *Thorn*, about 1600. Octagonal crystal watch.

ENGELSCHALK (ENGELSHALKH), GEORG KONRAD IGNATZ, son. *Würzburg.* Apprenticed 1739, master 1754–94. Watch.

ENGELSCHALK (ENGELSHALKH), JOHANN. *Prague*, about 1650–1700. Maker of repute; silver watch; hexagonal table clock Fränkel collection.

ENGLAND, JNO. Apprenticed 1692 to Thos. Taylor, C.C.

ENGLOIS, GEO. Apprenticed 1648 to Ed. Ward, C.C.

ENGUERRANT, JACQUES. *Blois.* Master 1594–1639.

ENGUI, F. *London.* Gold watch, h.m., 1748.

ENOCK, EZRA. *London*, and later at *Sibford.* A Quaker, 1827.

ENON, CHAS. Apprenticed 1666 to Jere. East, C.C.

ENQVIST, JONAS. *Norrköping.* Born 1758, died 1802. Watch movement, Nord Museum.

ENT, JOHN. *New York*, 1758; *Philadelphia*, 1763. Died 1794.

ENTWISLE, LAURENCE. Apprenticed 1638 to Thos. Place, C.C.

ENYS, EDMUND. C.C. 1684.

ENYS, EDWARD. C.C. 1658.

ENYS, EDWARD, son. *London.* C.C. 1684–89.

EPPNER, WILHELM. *Chaux-de-Fonds*, about 1810–75. Very able maker.

ERB, ALBRECHT. *Vienna*, 1628–1714. Cross-shaped watch, case enamelled white, with bevelled cover of rock crystal; plate clocks with *repoussé* decoration.

ERBURY, HENRY. C.C. 1650.

ERHARDT, J. C. Watch, British Museum, about 1700.

ERIC (ERICK), WILLIAM. *London.* C.C. 1730–69. Watch.

ERICKE, ROBERT. *Maiden Lane*, C.C. 1719.

ERICKE, WILLIAM. C.C. 1730; watch by him with extra wheel in the train, the minute hand travelling once round the dial in two hours.

ERNST, JERG. *Germany*, about 1620. Oval watch, British Museum; octagonal crystal watch M.P.S. Dresden.

ERNST, JOSEPH IGNATIUS. *Augsburg.* Master 1756–86.

ERNST, PETER. *Växjö.* Born 1714. *Stockholm*, 1753. died 1784; well-known maker; many clocks and watches; examples in Nord. Museum and Berzelius Museum; astronomical clock Vetenskap Observatory; nine examples illuminated Sidenbladh.

ERVIN. See IRVINE.

ERYLES, See EARLES.

ESPLIN, —. *Wigan*, 1790.

ESQUIVILLON. Several watches, ranging from 1710 to 1774. Esquivillon & De Choudens; melon-shaped gold enamelled watch; watch with gold outer case set round with pastes, portrait in enamel of a lady on the back, also set in paste; these two examples are in the Pierpont Morgan collection, and date from about 1765. Esquivillon Frères & De Choudens, *Paris*; watch, *repoussé* outer case, about 1774. 'Esquivillon et Cie', watch, probably Swiss, enamelled case, about 1770.

ESSEN, —. *Paris*, 1790.

ESSEX, JOSEPH. *Boston, U.S.A.*, 1712.

ESSEX, ROBT. *223 Strand*, 1823.

ESTER (ESTHER), ESTIENNE. Prob. France, about 1630. Crystal sphere watch with signs of zodiac on dial, Spitzer collection; silver alarm watch, British Museum; engraved watch, Ilbert collection.

ESTER (ESTHER), HENRY (French). A watch resembling a pelican, V. & A.; another (British Museum) in the shape of a fleur-de-lis; another example of his work is a watch in the Vienna Treasury, the case is circular, worked à jour representing foliage and enamelled in different colours, on the dial of enamelled gold are the signs of the zodiac, 1630–60.

ESTER (ESTHER), J. Tulip watch, about 1680.

ESTERBROOK, —. *Theobald's Rd.*, 1830–70.

ESTERLIE, JOHN. *New Holland, U.S.A.*, 1812–30. German; long-case clocks.

ESTON, EDWARD. C.C. 1708.

ETCHINGER, HANS. *Amsterdam.* Watch, British Museum, about 1650.

ETHERINGTON, GEORGE. *Fleet St.*, C.C. 1684; master 1709; choice bracket pendulum clock of his make; also a long-case clock. "A Gold Minute Watch with a green Shagreen case, with gold studs, made by George Etherington" (*Lond. Gaz.*, Dec. 25, 1689). "George Etherington, Watchmaker, is Removed from the Dial in Fleet St to the Dial over against the New Church in the Strand, London, where all sorts of Jewel Watches and others are made and sold" (*Lond. Gaz.*, October 5–9, 1714). Of York: THOS., f., 1684; THOS., f., 1727; THOS., f., 1740; WM., f., 1788.

ETTRY, ABRAM. *Vlissingen.* Bracket clock, about 1740.

ETTRY, JOEL. Long-case 30-hour clock, about 1790.

ETTY, MARMADUKE. C.C. 1716.

EUSTACE, RICHD. Apprenticed 1687 to Withers Cheney, C.C.

EVA, RICHARD. *Falmouth*, 1775; curious long-case chiming and tidal clock, about 1780, planetarium in arch, with comet, signed 'Eva Falmouth'.

EVANS, DAVID. *Baltimore*, 1770–73.

EVANS, DAVID. See HIGGS & EVANS.

EVANS, DYMOKE. C.C. 1800.

EVANS, GEO. Apprenticed 1692 to Geo. Rant, C.C.

EVANS, HENRY. Apprenticed to Thomas Bagley for Thomas Trippet, C.C. 1682.

EVANS, JAMES. *London.* Apprenticed 1735, C.C. 1749–81. Partner with R. and Peter Higgs.

EVANS, JAMES. *7 Sweeting's Alley*, 1770–1800; Evans, Thomas, of *Swithin Alley*, son of James Evans, C.C. 1788; James, son of Thomas, was admitted in 1811; many timekeepers of good quality bear the names of some member of this family, which had a considerable connection in Spain and the Spanish markets; clocks dating from the latter part of the eighteenth century, signed 'Diego Evans, London', or 'Diego Evans, Bolsa Real, Londres' (James Evans, Royal Exchange, London), are to be met with; Higgs & Evans, both of Swithin, or 'Sweeting's' Alley, seem to have been associated in partnership from about 1780, or 1785, although the name of Evans appears independently after that date, see HIGGS & EVANS.

EVANS, JAMES, son of Thos. *London (Sweetings Alley).* C.C. 1811–24.

EVANS, JAMES. C.C. 1816.

EVANS, JAMES WILLIAM. *London.* C.C. 1816.

EVANS, JNO. *Shrewsbury*, 1770.

EVANS, PRYCE. *Shrewsbury.* Watch, 1789.

EVANS, ROBERT. *Halstead.* 30-hour clock, one hand, about 1740.

EVANS, S., and WILLIAM FURNISS. *New Castle County, U.S.A.*, about 1740. Long-case clock.

EVANS, SAMUEL. C.C. 1822.

EVANS, THOMAS. Apprenticed to Samuel David, C.C. 1673.

EVANS, THOMAS. Apprenticed to Jane Barker, widow of Richard Barker, C.C. 1718.

EVANS, THOMAS. Apprenticed to George Cartwright, Royal Exchange; C.C. 1720; watch, 1749.

EVANS, THOMAS. *London.* C.C. 1751.

EVANS, THOMAS. *New York*, 1766.

EVANS, THOMAS. Apprenticed to William Haward, and turned over to Josiah Alderson, C.C. 1769.

EVANS, THOMAS, son of Jas. *London (Sweetings Alley).* C.C. 1788–93.

EVANS, THOMAS SIMPSON. *London.* C.C. 1813–17.

EVANS, W. *Dublin.* Watch, 1802.

EVANS, WILLIAM. *23 Aldgate Without*, 1775.

EVE, JOHN. *19 New North St., Red Lion Sq.*, 1842.

EVENS, ROBT. *Halstead.* Lantern clock, about 1710.

EVERELL, JOHN, "by ye new church in ye Strand"; maker of a verge watch, square pillars, outer case of tortoise-shell, 1730–60.

EVERETT, JNO. *London.* Watch, 1770.

EVERS, CHAS. *Coventry*, 1818.

EVERS, PETER. *Chester.* 1814–18.

EVETT, ROBERT. *London.* C.C. 1636.

EVILL. Two or three generations of clockmakers in Bath.

EVILL, JAMES. About 1750.

EVILL, WILLIAM. *Union St.*, about 1800.

EWBANK, GEO. *Ellam*, 1770.

EWEN, JOHN. *Aberdeen*, about 1800.

EWER, JNO. Apprenticed 1687 to Luke Bird; maker of long-case and bracket chime clocks. See EYRE.

EWETT, ROBT. C.C. 1636.

EXCHAGNET, LOUIS. *Wilderness Row*, 1790.

EXELBY, JAMES. *St. John's Lane.* C.C. 1718; a good watchmaker, quoted by Hatton, known also as a maker of long-case clocks; 1718–50.

EYRE, JOHN. C.C. 1703.

EYRE, RICHD. Apprenticed 1637 to Oswald Durant, C.C.

EYRE, ROBERT. *London.* 1703 C.C.

EYRE, WILLIAM. *London.* C.C. 1821.

EYRIER, ESPRIT. *Avignon*, 1725–53. Made elaborate automatic clock.

EYSTON, EDWARD. C.C. 1659.

EYSTON, THOMAS. *London.* C.C. 1651–53.

EZEKIAL, —. *Exon.* Watch, h.m., 1794.

FABER, G. *Paris*, 1620.

FABER, JOSEPH. Apprenticed 1678 to Edwd. Whitfield, C.C.

FACCINI, BERNARDO. *Venice* and *Piacenza*, 1725. Made a complex planisphere clock for the Duchessa di Parma, now in the Vatican, desc. Hor. Jl. 1941; the clock was designed by Montanari. *v.* ANITO.

FACIO, NICHOLAS. Born at *Basle*, 1664; died in *Worcester*, 1753; introduced watch jewelling (patent No. 371, May 1704).

FAGE, EDWARD. Admitted C.C. 1667.

FAGG, JOHN. *Queen St., Margate.* Watch, h.m., 1781; lever alarum watch, 1821.

FAHLBORG, JOHAN FREDRIK. *Vasa (Finland)* and *Uppsala.* Born 1770, died about 1800.

FAIRBAIRN, ANDREW. *Edinburgh*, 1807–34. Long-case clocks; succeeded by J. Robertson.

FAIRCLOUGH, EDWD. *Liverpool.* Watch, about 1795, with the pedometer self-winding device patented by Recordon in 1790.

FAIRCLOUGH, HENRY. *Liverpool*, 1773–96. Watch.

FAIRCLOUGH, RICHARD. *Liverpool*, 1770.

FAIRCLOUGH, THOS. C.C. 1660.

FAIREY, JOHN. *22 Ratcliff Highway*, 1810–42.

FAIREY, RICHARD. *150 Tooley St.*, 1814–42.

FAIRFAX, WM. Apprenticed 1685 to Jno. Warner, C.C.

FAIRHURST, JOHN. *Liverpool*, 1824–36.

FAIRMAN, JOHN. *London.* Apprenticed 1738, C.C. 1769.

FAIRMAN, THOMAS HENRY. *London.* Apprenticed 1776, C.C. 1794, died 1799.

FALES, G. S. 1827.

FALES, JAMES. *New Bedford*, 1810–20.

FALKE, J. H. *Leipzig.* Watch, about 1780.

FALKENGREN, CARL. *Ystad*, 1783. Died 1795.

FALKNER, EDWD. Apprenticed 1692 to Cornelius Herbert, C.C.; quarter clock, about 1740.

FALKNER, JOHN. *153 Newman St., Oxford St.*, 1824–28.

FALKS, ROBERT. C.C. 1720–25.

FALLERY, DANIEL PIERRE. *Geneva*, about 1750–71.

FALLOW, MATTHEW. *Liverpool*, 1814.

FALLOW, MATTHEW & CO. *Manchester*, 1820, also J. FALLOW & CO., same date.

FARD, PIERRE. *Blois.* Very small watch, about 1670.

FARDOIL, JACQUES, son. *Blois.* Master 1664–94.

FARDOIL, PIERRE. *Blois.* Alarum watch, about 1680, M. Gélis; watch, 'Peter Fardoil, London', h.m., 1700.

FARDON, JNO. *Dedington*, 1800.

FAREWELL, JOHN. Apprenticed to Isaac Nicholls, and turned over to Charles Gretton, C.C. 1697.

FARFLER, STEPHAN. *Nürnberg* and *Altdorf*. Born 1633, died 1689. Made clocks of wood, bone and metal, and added chimes to Altdorf clock; made a device for turning a sand-glass at regular intervals.

FARGE, JEAN BAPTISTE. *Paris*. Juré 1738.

FARIS (FARRIS), HYRAM, brother. *Annapolis*. Born 1769, died 1800.

FARIS (FARRIS), WILLIAM. *London*. Died 1728.

FARIS (FARRIS), WILLIAM, son. *Annapolis*, 1757. Died 1804; from *Philadelphia*; long-case musical clock; month clocks.

FARIS (FARRIS), WILLIAM, son. *Annapolis*. Born 1762–88; *Norfolk, Va*, 1792–95; *Edinton* (*N. Carolina*), 1797.

FARMBROUGH, EDWARD. *London*. C.C. 1687.

FARMER, G. W. *32 Tavistock St.*, 1822–30.

FARMER, JAS. Apprenticed 1661 to Ralph Almond, C.C.

FARMER, JNO. C.C. 1657.

FARMER, LEONARD. Received £37 in 1617 for a clock and chimes and "twoe dyalls, and for a barrel and pricking thereof", from the churchwardens of St. Margaret's, Westminster.

FARMER, RICHARD. C.C. 1683.

FARMER, RICHARD. *Abingdon*, 1688 C.C.

FARMER, THOMAS. C.C. 1647.

FARMER, THOMAS. C.C. 1653; in the St. Margaret's, Westminster, churchwardens' accounts for 1658 appears "Item to Mr. Farmer for making of the new diall on the westward of the church, as by his bill appeareth, 14*l*. 10*s*."; also, "Item to Mr. Farmer for a new diall at the west end of the church on the church-yard side, 7*l*."; 1653–60.

FARMER, THOMAS. Brother C.C. 1689.

FARMER, THOS. Stockton, 1770.

FARMER, WILLIAM. *20 Hanover St.*, 1800.

FARNBOROUGH, RICHD. Apprenticed 1685 to Wm. Newton, C.C.

FARNWORTH, GEORGE. *London*. Apprenticed 1789, C.C. 1797.

FARNWORTH, JOSEPH. *Nottingham*, 1784–1815. Clocks and watches.

FARQUHARSON, GEO. *66 Strand*, 1775; *421 Strand*, 1780; *8 Exchange Alley*, 1793.

FARR, DAVID. *London*, 1662.

FARR, GEORGE. *London*. Apprenticed 1703.

FARR, JOHN C. *Philadelphia*, 1831.

FARR, JOHN. *Bristol*, about 1790, C.C.-1801. Watch.

FARR, JOHN and STEPHEN. ———. 1815–18. Watch.

FARR, THOMAS. *Bristol*, 1820–30. Fine verge watch G.M. Ruby cylinder watch, Ilbert collection.

FARRAR, CHARLES. *Pomfret*, 1790.

FARRAR, JONATHAN. Long-case clock, about 1720.

FARRAR, JOSHUA. *Brighouse*, 1750.

FARREND, V. *48 Cheapside*, 1825.

FARRER, ABRAHAM, JUNR. *Pontefract*, 1760.

FARRER, BENJ., also JNO. 1790; and JOSHUA, 1800–34.

FARRER, SAMUEL. *York*, f., 1625.

FARRER, THOS. *London*. Long-case clock, about 1770.

FARRER, WILLIAM. *Pontefract*. 1-day long-case clocks, about 1730.

FARRINGTON, THOMAS. *Bristol*, 1819–52. Clock.

FARROW, ——. *London*. a. 1747. Watch.

FARROW, JOHN. *London*, 1817. C.C. 1820–24.

FARRETT, RICHARD. C.C. 1670.

FATIO, L. U. Geneva, died 1887.

FATTON, FREDERICK LOUIS. *New Bond St.* Independent centre seconds watch marked 'Fatton élève de Breguet patent, London, No. 16'; in 1822 he patented an astronomical clock and watch (No. 4,645); many fine travelling clocks and good watches in the Breguet style of about the same period signed 'Fatton, Paris'; patented an ink-recording chronograph.

FAULKNER, EDWARD. Master C.C. 1734; 1710–35.

FAULKNER, WILLIAM. 1770–88; livery C.C. 1787.

FAULKNER, WILLIAM, son. *London* (*Shoe Lane*). Apprenticed 1788, C.C. 1796, died 1814.

FAULKS, ROBERT. *London*. Apprenticed 1712, C.C. 1723.

FAURE, CLAUDE. *Avignon*, 1676–1709. Fitted pendulum to clock on Hôtel de Ville. See FAVRE.

FAUX, JOHN. *Worship St., Moorfields*, 1780–85.

FAVEY, ALBERT FRANCIS. *London*. C.C. 1804.

FAVEY, FRANCIS. *12 Wilderness Row*, 1785–90.

FAVEY & SON. *5 Corporation Row*, 1804.

FAVRE (FAURE), ELÉAZAR. *Lyons*, 1678 master–1717 juré.

FAVRE (FAURE), FRANÇOIS. *Lyons*, 1648–59. From *Bourg-en-Bresse*. 'Très expert et adroit.'

FAVRE (FAURE), ISAAC. *Valangin* and *Neuchâtel*. Born 1750, died 1816; maker of repute.

FAVRE, ——. *London*. Watch, about 1750.

FAVRE, HENRIQUE. *Londres*. Bracket clock, about 1730.

FAVRE, HENRY. *London*. Watch, the Edward Devotion House, Brookline; bracket clock, about 1730.

FAVRE, HENRY. *27 Pall Mall*, 1800–18.

FAVRE, JOHN JAMES. *Philadelphia*, 1797.

FAVRE-BULLE, FRÉDÉRIC LOUIS. *Le Locle*. Born 1770, died 1849; one of the most eminent makers of the Neuchâtel district; duplex watch Science Museum.

FAWCETT WILLIAM. *Liverpool*. Long-case clock, about 1730.

FAWCETT, WM. Apprenticed 1638 to David Bouquett, C.C.

FAYRER, JAS. Clockmaker and wheel cutter, *35 White Lion St.*, Pentonville, 1810; in 1819 he was at *40 White Lion St.*, and was awarded by the Society of Arts the silver Isis medal for a sidereal regulator with a three-wheel train.

FAYRER, THOS. *Lancaster*, 1744, f.

FAZAKERLEY, THOS. "at the Dial and Crown in St. John's St., near Hicks' Hall, London"; clock, 1780.

FAZY, JEAN. Gold enamelled watch, V. & A. (French), about 1750. See TERROT.

FAZY, JOHN. *7 Red Lion Court, Fleet St.*, 1780–85.

FAZY, MARC CONRAD. *Moscow*. Born 1740. Clockmaker to the Russian court; started with Jean a factory at *Moscow* in 1765.

FAZY, THÉODORE MICHEL. *Moscow*. Born 1773; jeweller to the Czar.

FEALINS. See DE FEALINS.

FEARN, JOHN GEO. *114 Strand*, 1800; *73 Strand*, 1813; *18 Cornhill*, 1814; *22 Regent St.*, 1840; among the effects of Charles Kean sold at his decease was a gold duplex watch, gold dial with raised polished numerals, serpent hands, hall mark 1816, movement inscribed 'J. G. Fearn, 73 Strand'.

FEARNLEY, PETER. *Wigan*, 1780–1816.

FEARON, DANIEL. *Fetter Lane*. Liveryman C.C. 1776.

FEARON & STACEY. *Poultry*, 1780.

FEATHERSTONE, WILLIAM. *Newcastle-on-Tyne*, 1766–95. Watch.

FEATLEY, GEORGE. *London*. Apprentice 1803, C.C. 1811.

FEAU, NICHOLAS. Sixteenth-century table clock, inscribed 'Nicolas Feau à Mercelle'.

FEBUCE. See LE FEBUCE.

FEDERSPIEL, PETER. *Augsburg*. Juré 1742; town clock.

FEILDER, THOMAS. C.C. 1689; master 1715; 1689–1716.

FELL, ABRAHAM. *Ulverston*, 1740–70; he made a new style for the church sun-dial in 1763.

FELL, JAS. *Lancaster*, 1767.
FELL, JOHN. C.C. 1727.
FELL, WILLIAM. C.C. 1705.
FELMORE, E. *London*. Watch, 1778.
FELTER, THOMAS. C.C. 1709.
FELTON, GEORGE. *Bridgnorth*. Long-case clock, about 1780.
FÉMÉRETTE, ANTOINE. 'horloger de Louis XIII' (1610–43).
FENESTRE, PETER. *London*. Apprenticed 1722, C.C. 1732.
FENLEATER (FINLEATER), ALEXANDER. *Baltimore, U.S.A.*, 1807. Watch.
FENN, DANIEL & SAMUEL. *105 Newgate St.* D. Fenn, master C.C. 1766; 1760–1804.
FENN, DANIEL. *London (Warwick Lane* and later *Newgate St.*). Apprenticed 1725, C.C. 1737, m.C.C. 1766–1804.
FENN, DANIEL, son. *London*. C.C. 1767, m.C.C. 1791.
FENN, ISAAC. *Oxford Road*, 1770.
FENN, JOSEPH. *London*. C.C. 1777; died a. 1822.
FENN, ROBERT. *Westminster*. C.C. 1687. Long marquetry case clock, Wetherfield collection, about 1690.
FENN, SAMUEL & SONS. *105 Newgate St.* S. Fenn, master C.C. 1793; 1806–15.
FENN, SAMUEL. *London*. C.C. 1767, m.C.C. 1793, died 1821.
FENN, THOS. Apprenticed 1647 to Thos. Claxton; C.C. 1657.
FENNELL, JOHN. *London*. Apprenticed 1669, C.C. 1679.
FENNELL, RICHD. C.C. 1679; bracket clock, arch dial, bell-top shape with handle; also a long mahogany case clock inscribed 'R. Fennell, Kensington'.
FENNEY, —. *Liverpool*. Clock, about 1770.
FENTON, EDWARD. *London*. Apprenticed 1731, C.C. 1739.
FENTON, JAS. *York*, f., 1740.
FENTON, JOHN. Apprenticed to Thos. Taylor; C.C. 1662.
FENTON, WM. *Newcastle*, 1780.
FENTON, WM. *London*. Watch, h.m., 1784.
FERÉ, ADRIEN. *Paris*, about 1680.
FERGUSON, JAMES. Born 1710, died and buried in Marylebone churchyard, 1776; astronomer and mechanician.
FERGUSON, WM. *Alnwick*. Long-case clock, about 1770.
FERLITTE, GAUTIER. *Geneva*, 1599–1633.
FERMENT, JOHN. C.C. 1679; Wood mentions a square pedestal watch by Ferment, 1670–90.
FERMENT, PAUL. *London*. Watch, about 1745.
FERMENT, PHILIP. *London*, 1689–1701 C.C.
FERNAL, JNO. *Wrexham*, 1770.
FERRIN, A. *Rue Dauphine, Paris*, 1770.
FERON, JNO. *Lewes*. Watch, 1780.
FERRAR, JOHN. *London*. C.C. 1693–1705. See FERRERS.
FERRERS, JNO. *London*. Long-case clock, about 1700.
FERREY, JAS. *London*. Clock, about 1770.
FERRIER, ANTOINE. *Paris*. Lodged at the Louvre, 1607.
FERRIER, LAURENT. *Avignon*, 1590–1630. Town clock.
FERRIER, THORNTON. *Hull*, 1822.
FERRIER, WILLIAM, son of Antoine, whom he succeeded in 1622.
FERRIÈRE, ABRAHAM. *Geneva*, about 1770–88.
FERRIS, BENJAMIN, C. & W. *Philadelphia*, 1811.
FERRIS, TIBA. *Wilmington, U.S.A.*, 1812–50.
FERRIS, ZIBA, brother. *Wilmington, U.S.A.* Born 1786, died 1875.
FERRON, ABRAHAM. *St. Anne's Churchyard.* C.C. 1730.
FERRON, JOHN. *London*. C.C. 1692.
FERRON, LEWIS. *London*. Long marquetry case clock, pull chime quarters, angel and crown corners, about 1720.

FERRON, LEWIS. *London*. Watch, 1750.
FERRON, MICHAEL, son of Abraham. *London*. Apprenticed 1753, C.C. 1769, l.C.C. 1786.
FERRON, MICHAEL. *London*, 1793 l.C.C. *Gt. Missenden*, 1821.
FERROT, PHILIPPE. *Paris*, 1775–1800. Gold repeating watch.
FERRY, BERNARD, 'horloger de Henri III' (1574–89).
FERTBOUER, PHILIPP. *Vienna*. Died 1820; fine regulators and equation work.
FERTEAU (FESTEAU, and see FETTEAU), FRANÇOIS BONAVENTURE, l'aîné, son. *Paris (Rue St. Martin).* Master 1779, juré 1788; keeper of Bastille clock.
FERTEAU (FESTEAU, and see FETTEAU), JEAN LOUIS, brother. *Paris (Rue aux Ours).* Master 1783–1812; lyre clock.
FERTEAU (FESTEAU, and see FETTEAU), SIMÉON FRANÇOIS. *Paris (Rue de Montmorency).* Master 1750–89.
FESSLER, JOHN. *Frederickstown, U.S.A.*, 1782–1840.
FÉTIL, PIERRE. *Orléans*. Born 1753–1814; maker of repute; published in 1802 *La Théorie de l'horlogerie réduite en tableaux.*
FETTER, NICHOLAS. C.C. 1632.
FETTERS, HENRY. *East Smithfield*. Free Blacksmiths', 1630; C.C. 1653.
FETTERS, RICHD. C.C. about 1640.
FEURER (FEIRER), JOHANN BAPTIST. *Augsburg.* Comp. 1761, master 1768–95.
FEVER, HY. *Pall Mall*. Watch, about 1750. See FAVRE.
FEVON, HY. C.C. 1674.
FEWELLER (FEWLER). *Liverpool*, 1761–81.
FEYMEL, ANDREAS. Table clock, about 1680.
FIACRE, CLEMENT. *Paris*. Watch, 1700.
FICHTER, ANDREAS. *Dresden*. Master 1681–1700; silver watch, Fränkel collection.
FIDGETT, WILLIAM. C.C. 1789; *Dockhead, Bermondsey*; and *3 Bell Court, Fenchurch St.*, 1780–1825.
FIDLER, —. Made an orrery for Dr. Pearson, 1805.
FIDLEY, GEO. See FINDLEY.
FIEFFÉ, JEAN CLAUDE. *Paris*. Master 1757–89.
FIEFFÉ, JEAN JACQUE, PÈRE. *Rue de la Vieille Draperie, Paris* (garde-visiteur), 1769.
FIELD, DANIEL. *21 Red Lion St., Clerkenwell*, 1798.
FIELD, GEO. *London*. Watch, 1800.
FIELD, JAMES. *Hertford*. Long-case clocks, about 1800.
FIELD, JAS. C.C. 1672.
FIELD, T. W. *Aylesbury*. Watch, 1790.
FIELD, THOS. *2 Bond St., Bath*, 1795–99.
FIELD, WM. *London*. C.C. 1744; watch, 1750.
FIELD & SON. *Aylesbury*, 1770.
FIELDER, THOMAS. Apprenticed 1678 to Withers Cheney; C.C. 1687.
FIELDHOUSE, B. *Leinster*. Clock, about 1740.
FIELDSHAW, JAMES. *Leeds*, 1770–87. Watch, Ilbert collection.
FIERVILLE, —. *Caen*. Watch, 1770.
FILBER, JOHN. *Lancaster, U.S.A.*, 1810–25.
FILON, —. *Paris*, 1790.
FINCH, JACOB. Apprenticed 1686 to Isaac Carver, C.C.
FINCH, JOHN. C.C. 1675, master 1706 "A gold minute pendulum watch, with a chain and a large gold engraved case, made by John Finch, of London, about £20 value, was put to be mended to a watchmaker in Bristol who is since gone" (*Lond. Gaz.*, June 16–19, 1706).
FINCH, N. *London*. Apprenticed 1682, C.C. 1691.
FINCH, RICHARD. *London*. Apprenticed 1725, C.C. 1733–62.
FINCH, ROBERT. C.C. 1691.

FINCH, SIMON. C.C. 1706.

FINCH, THOMAS. Brother C.C. 1676–1706, possibly a cousin of T. Tompion.

FINCH, WILLIAM. *Kingston.* C.C. 1691; maker of long-case clocks, 1691–1720.

FINCH, WM. *Halifax.* Watch, 1759.

FINCHETT, ARNOLD. *Cheapside.* A water clock by him in British Museum, 1735.

FINDBOW, CHAS. *London.* Long-case clock, about 1780.

FINDLEY, J. *5 Duke St.,* 1820.

FINE, ORONCE. *Paris.* Professor of mathematics and designer of clocks; born 1494, died 1555.

FINELLY, —. *Aix.* Watch in the form of a pectoral cross, about 1560.

FINER, JNO. Apprenticed 1688 to Hy. Merryman, C.C.

FINER, JOHN. *5 Hatton Garden,* 1791–1800.

FINER, THOMAS & NOWLAND. *5 Hatton Garden,* 1800–05; *48 High Holborn,* 1808–23.

FINLEY, JOHN. *Baltimore, U.S.A.,* 1754. Clock.

FINLOW, ZACH. *London,* 1780.

FINNEY, JOHN. *Charleston, U.S.A.,* 1754. Clocks and watches.

FINNEY, JOSEPH. *Liverpool,* 1770–96. Long-case musical clock and watch.

FINNEY, JOSH. *Liverpool.* Long-case clock, about 1750; clock-watch, about 1760.

FINNEY, PICTON, in his 'Memorials of Liverpool', says, "Mr. Joseph Finney, a clock and watch maker in Thomas St., designed an octagonal chapel about 1763."

FINNEY, THOS. *Liverpool.* Curious watch, 1735.

FINNIE, HENRY. Admitted C.C. 1728.

FISCHER, JOHANN BENJAMIN. *Dresden,* 1780. Court clock; granted permit to start a factory in Grossenhain; ring watch Grüne Gewölbe.

FISCHER, KONRAD MICHAEL. *Onolzbach,* 1742–72. Court clock.

FISH, HENRY. *4 Sweeting's Alley, Royal Exchange.* Black bell-top case bracket clock, inscription on arch 'Henry Fish, Royall Exchange', probably son of Henry Poisson; 1730–75.

FISH, JOHN. Apprenticed to his mother, Mary, wife of William Fish; C.C. 1766.

FISH, ROBERT HOWARD. *London (Dean St. and Greek St.).* C.C. 1813–24.

FISH, SAM., "at the Golden Lion, St. John St., Smithfield", 1775. Bracket clock.

FISH, WILLIAM. 1737.

FISHER, —. *97 Portland Place, Edgeware Rd.* Bracket clock, about 1810.

FISHER, CHAS. Apprenticed 1679 to Thos. Player, C.C.

FISHER, DAN. *Bunhill Row,* 1769–72.

FISHER, DANIEL & SON. *9 Worship St., Finsbury,* 1790–1804.

FISHER, EBENEZER. C.C. 1725.

FISHER, HY. *Preston,* 1775.

FISHER, ISAAC. *3 Cockspur St.,* 1804–23.

FISHER, JNO. *Preston.* Long-case clock, about 1750, with the inscription 'Dum Spectus Frigis'.

FISHER, JOHN. *London.* Apprenticed 1746, C.C. 1763.

FISHER, JOHN. *York, Pa., U.S.A.,* 1790. Clock.

FISHER, JOSEPH. *2 Leicester Sq.* Livery Cutlers' Company 1773–1815.

FISHER, REBECKAH. Apprenticed to George Taylor and Lucy, his wife, 1715.

FISHER, RICHARD. *Liverpool,* 1790–1836. Watch.

FISHWATER, JOHN. C.C. 1726.

FISTER, AMON. *Philadelphia, U.S.A.,* 1794. Watch.

FITE, JOHN. *Baltimore, U.S.A.,* 1807–17.

FITREE, SAMUEL. *Whitecross St.,* 1790.

FITTER, JOHN. *Battersea.* C.C. 1685; splendid watch by him, 1665; Wood mentions a gold enamelled watch by Fitter, 1660–1700.

FITTER, THOMAS. *London (Clerkenwell Gr.).* C.C. 1710–37.

FITTER, THOMAZON. *37 St. John's Sq., Clerkenwell,* 1759–83. Watch, h.m., 1759.

FITTON, CHAS. Apprenticed 1667 to Sam. Horne; C.C. 1674.

FITTON, DAN. Apprenticed 1675 to Jno. Bartholomew, C.C.

FITTON, THOS. Apprenticed 1638 to Thos. Laud, C.C.

FITZJAMES, THOS. Apprenticed 1648 to Jno. Walters, C.C.

FITZWATER, HENRY. *London.* Apprenticed 1719–34 C.C.

FIX, JOSEPH. *Reading, U.S.A.,* 1820–40.

FLACK, G. *9 Princess St., Drury Lane,* 1820.

FLADGATE (& WILDER, *Conduit St., Hanover Sq.,* 1765), JOHN. *Conduit St., Hanover Sq.* Hon. Freeman C.C. 1781. In the British Museum is a small clock by him, brass dial with arch cherub corners.

FLAMENVILLE, —. *Paris,* 1727. Devised a modified verge escapement.

FLAMEYER, B. *London.* Small watch, silver pair cases, outer one curiously engraved, h.m., 1765.

FLANT (FLANC), JEHAN. *Geneva* and *La Rochelle.* Apprenticed 1584, died 1616; Clockmaker to the town of La Rochelle from 1599; fine astronomical watch British Museum; illuminated Baillie, with calendar starting 1610; watches Louvre and Gélis collection.

FLASHMAN, GEORGE. *18 Fleet St.,* 1790–1815 (succeeded by Jno. Tunnell).

FLAUT, —. Large watch, British Museum, about 1620.

FLAVCK, THOMAS. Watch, about 1650.

FLEET, JAMES. *London.* Apprenticed 1776, C.C. 1813.

FLEETWOOD, JOHN. *Dorrington St., Clerkenwell.* Born 1748, died 1812.

FLEETWOOD, ROBERT. *Featherstone Buildings, Holborn,* 1760; *13 Abchurch Lane,* 1776. Liveryman Goldsmith's Company, died 1789; Robt. Fleetwood & Co. till 1792.

FLEMING, ANDREW. C.C. 1725.

FLEMING, CURTIS. Opposite *Shadwell Church.* Livery C.C. 1774.

FLEMING, DAVID. *36 Shadwell High St.,* 1817.

FLEMING, JAMES. *Liverpool,* 1790–1829. Watch.

FLEMMING, WM. *105 Whitechapel,* 1815–19.

FLETCHER, BAZIL. Apprenticed 1692 to Thos. Wise, C.C.

FLETCHER, CECILIA. *Rotherham,* 1780.

FLETCHER, DANIEL. Brother C.C. 1646; in 1653 Richd. Roberts was apprenticed to Eliza Fletcher.

FLETCHER, EDWARD. C.C. 1697.

FLETCHER, GEO. *Dewsbury,* 1770.

FLETCHER, JAS. *Rotherham,* 1818.

FLETCHER, JNO. Apprenticed 1654 to Jno. Saville, C.C.

FLETCHER, JNO. *Barnsley,* 1750.

FLETCHER, JNO. *Ripponden,* 1760.

FLETCHER, JNO. *Holbeck.* Clock, about 1760.

FLETCHER, JOHN. *London.* Apprenticed 1727, C.C. 1744.

FLETCHER, ROBERT. *Chester,* 1784–1820. Long-case clock illuminated Cec. & Web; watch.

FLETCHER, ROBERT GRAHAM. *Edinburgh,* 1825–51.

FLETCHER, ROBT. *Chester,* 1814–34.

FLETCHER, THOMAS, in *St. Martin's*; admitted C.C. 1676; threatened with prosecution by C.C. for undue taking of apprentices 1682.

FLETCHER, THOMAS. *Newcastle-on-Tyne,* 1801–50. Clocks and watches.

FLETCHER, THOS. *Leeds,* 1829.

FLETCHER, TOBIAS. *Barnsley,* 1790.

FLETCHER, WIDDON. Ant. Freeman was apprenticed to him in 1653; C.C.

FLETCHER, WILLIAM. *Leeds,* 1770.

FLEUREAU, ESAYE. *London.* Wetherfield collection a long-case clock by him, dating from about 1710. It embodies a fine specimen of arabesque marquetry, which is continued on the moulding supporting the hood, over the base and round the sides of the case.

FLEURET, DONAT JEAN. *Geneva,* about 1760–87.

FLEUTRY, —. *Paris,* 1788.

FLEURY, JEAN (JACQUES) FRANÇOIS. *Paris.* Master 1759–89.

FLEXNEY, HY. Apprenticed 1657 to Gower Langford, C.C.

FLIGHT, BLAIR. *Kinross,* 1775–99.

FLING, DANIEL. *Philadelphia,* 1811.

FLOCKHART, ANDREW. *5 King St., Covent Garden,* 1814–35.

FLODEN, WILLIAM. *20 Skinner St.,* and *Coburg St., Clerkenwell,* 1835.

FLOOD, HUMPHREY. Received £220 for a clock "covered with gold and set with rubies and diamonds, delivered to his Majesty's use" (James I), 1607–17.

FLOOK, J. *Strand, London.* Bracket clocks, about 1750.

FLOURNOY, HENRY. 1690.

FLOURNOY, P. *Paris,* about 1740.

FLOWARD, WM. *London.* Watch, 1790.

FLOWER, GEO. Apprenticed 1670 to Jas. Atkinson; C.C. 1682; watch, about 1700.

FLOWER, HENRY. *Philadelphia,* 1753.

FLOWER, JNO. *Fenchurch St.,* C.C. 1725–30.

FLOWER, JOHN. *London.* Apprenticed 1724, C.C. 1734.

FLOWER, THOMAS. C.C. 1730; pendulum watch, Schloss collection, fine dial, about 1740.

FLOWER & MAINWARING. *London.* Watch, 1818.

FLOWERS, EDWARD. *Rolls Buildings, Fetter Lane.* Watch, beautiful outer case, set with pearls, h.m., 1783; 1769–84.

FLOYD, THOMAS. *Charleston, U.S.A.,* 1767. Clock.

FLOYD, WM. Apprenticed 1660 to Richd. Lyons, C.C.

FLY, JOSEPH. *London.* Calendar watch, Schloss collection, about 1770; another, about 1780.

FODEN, T. *Congleton.* Clock, about 1770.

FOGG, HUGH. *Near Exeter Change, Strand,* 1765–70.

FOGG, JOHN. *London.* Apprenticed 1727, C.C. 1735.

FOGG, JOHN. *London.* Apprenticed 1750, C.C. 1759.

FOGG, JOHN. *Liverpool,* 1807–29. Watch.

FOGGO, JAMES. *London.* Clock, about 1760.

FOL, J. *Paris,* 1770–87. Watchmaker to the King of Poland; maker of 8-day watches. His son was clockmaker to Louis XVI.

FOLE, ROBERT. C.C. 1667.

FOLKARD, JAS. *124 Great Surrey St.,* 1823.

FOLLETT, RICHD. Apprenticed 1653 to Thos. Wolverstone, C.C.

FOLMAR, ANDREW. *New York,* 1805. Watch.

FONNEREAU, PIERRE. *La Rochelle.* Master 1672, died about 1710; gold engraved watch.

FONNEREAU, ZACHARIE. *La Rochelle.* Apprenticed 1618–26 at *Lyons;* at *La Rochelle* from 1641; died a. 1683; octagonal crystal watch V. & A.; silver octagonal watch Côte collection; two crystal cross watches Petit Pal., Paris; circular silver watches Mallett, Ilbert, Gélis and Dutuit collections.

FONTAC, —. *London.* Watch, 1796.

FONTAINE, ABRAHAM. *Geneva.* Born 1721–68.

FONTAINE, JAQUES FRANÇOIS, son of Abraham. *Geneva,* about 1760–91.

FONTAINE, JOHN. *London.* Apprenticed 1748, C.C. 1759.

FONTANE, JOHN & MOSES. *London.* Half-quarter silver repeating watch, about 1790.

FOOTE, WILLIAM. Admitted C.C. 1726.

FORBES, EDWARD. *Liverpool,* 1803–29. Watch.

FORD, —. *31 Gracechurch St.,* 1820.

FORD, GEORGE. *Lancaster City, U.S.A.,* 1811. Died 1842; English; long-case clocks.

FORD, HY. Apprenticed 1647 to David Parry, C.C.

FORD, JNO. *Arundel,* 1750.

FORD, JOHN, son of Thomas. *London.* C.C. 1752.

FORD, JOHN. *London.* Apprenticed 1785, C.C. 1800.

FORD, ROBT. Apprenticed 1652 to Richd. Record, C.C.

FORD, SOUTHERLAND. *Charleston, U.S.A.,* 1741. Clocks and watches.

FORD, THOMAS. C.C. 1724.

FORD, WILLIAM. C.C. 1770.

FORD, WILLIAM. *London.* Apprenticed 1692–1701 C.C.

FORCHIER, JOHN. *London,* 1694.

FORDE, JNO. *Oxon.,* 1750.

FORDERER, JOHN. *Birmingham,* 1775–95. Watch, Birmingham Museum.

FORDHAM, JNO. *Dunmow.* Large lantern clock, about 1680.

FORDHAM, JOSEPH. *Bocking,* 1700. Fine long-case clock by Thos. Fordham, Braintree, Essex, about 1730.

FORDHAM, THOMAS. C.C. 1687.

FOREMAN, FRANCIS. *St. Paul's Gate.* Petitioner to Charles I for incorporation of C.C. and one of the first assistants; lantern clock, about 1620; 1620–49.

FOREMAN, MICHAEL. Livery, C.C. 1810.

FORESTER, J. *Union St., Bishopsgate.* Card, Hodgkin collection, about 1810.

FORESTIER, JOSEPH. *Geneva.* Watch, 1810.

FORFAICT (FORFAIT or FORFECT), AUGUSTIN. *Sedan.* Died 1587; watch in British Museum; one of the earliest known French watches illuminated Baillie.

FORFAICT (FORFAIT or FORFECT), ISAAC, brother. *Sedan,* 1585. Watches Cluny Museum and Blot-Garnier collection.

FORFAICT (FORFAIT or FORFECT), JACOB, son of Augustin FORFAICT. *Sedan,* 1582–1637. Fine maker; octagonal watch Louvre; Oval engraved watch, Ilbert collection.

FORFAICT (FORFAIT or FORFECT), NICOLAS. *Paris,* 1606–13. Juré; watches M.M.A. and Gélis collection.

FORFAICT, N. *Paris.* Maker of an octagonal watch presented to John Knox by Mary, Queen of Scots, which is now in the British Museum; oval watch, about 1590, Pierpont Morgan collection.

FORFARD, AUGUSTIN. *Sedan.* Oval watch, about 1650.

FORFAX, ISAAC. *Sedan.* Oval watch, Schloss collection, about 1605.

FORGAT, —. "A round brass clock, the Box well gilt and pearced all over, in a leather Case, the name *Forgat*" (*Lond. Gaz.,* March 29 April 1, 1680).

FORMANT, PHILIP. C.C. 1687.

FORREST, JOSEPH. C.C. 1692.

FORREST, MATT. Apprenticed 1672 to Jno. Lowe C.C.

FORREY, CHRISTIAN. *Lampeter & Lancaster Co., Pa., U.S.A.,* 1773. Watch.

FORSMAN, ERIK. *Linköping.* Born 1755, died 1815. Also FORSSMAN.

FORSELL, MICHAEL. *Stockholm,* 1770. Died 1780; year clock. Also FORSEL.

FORSTER, CLEMENT. C.C. 1682.

FORSTER, EDWARD. *Carlisle,* 1750–1813. Long-case clocks.

FORSTER, JACOB. Apprenticed 1690 to Jno. F., C.C.

FORSTER, JOHN. Apprenticed 1680 to D. Quare; C.C. 1689.

FORSTER, JOHN. C.C. 1726.

FORSTER, JOHN. *Carlisle*, 1810.

FORSTER, JOSEPH. *London*. C.C. 1815.

FORSTER, WILLIAM. Brother C.C. 1681.

FORSTER, WILLIAM. *London*. C.C. 1660. Also FOSTER.

FORSTER (FERSTER), JOHANN ANDREAS. *Vienna*. Master 1753; silver pair-case repeating watch.

FORSYTH, JAMES. *Albion Buildings, Bartholomew Close*, 1790–1800.

FORTE, JOHN. C.C. 1672.

FORTFART, ISAAC. *Sedan*, 1585.

FORTIER. See STOLLEWERCK.

FORTIN, AUGUSTE, PÈRE. *Rue de la Harpe, Paris*. Garde-visiteur 1769.

FORTIN, JEAN. *Paris*. Juré 1768.

FORTIN, MICHEL, same date.

FORTIN, MICHEL. *Paris*. Master 1743, juré 1762.

FOSS (? FOX), THOMAS. *131 Strand*. Maker of 8-bell chime clock, brass dial, with strike-silent, silvered circles at top; 1780–95.

FOSSARD, PIERRE. *Paris* (*Rue St. Antoine*). Master 1771–1825.

FOSTER, ISAAC. *1 Bartlett Passage*, 1788.

FOSTER, J. BENJ. *22 Cursitor St.*, 1817.

FOSTER, JOHN. *London*. Apprenticed 1693, C.C. 1726–38.

FOSTER, JOHN. *London* (*Aldersgate St.*). Apprenticed 1744, C.C. 1756–69.

FOSTER, JOSEPH. *Exchange Alley*. C.C. 1691.

FOSTER, JOSEPH. *London*. Apprenticed 1728–39 C.C.

FOSTER, NATHANIEL. *Newburyport*, 1818–28.

FOSTER, S. *Birchin Lane*. Watch, bloodstone and gold case, Hawkins collection, about 1780.

FOSTER, WILLIAM. *Manchester*, about 1780–1809. Long-case clock F.W.M.

FOSTER, WM. *Marnham*. 30-hour clock, about 1740.

FOTHERGAILE, JAS. Apprenticed 1661 to Ralph Almond, C.C.

FOTTER, WM. C.C. 1660.

FOUBERT, THÉODORE. *Blois*. Apprenticed 1621–41.

FOUCH, WM. *Goswell St.*, 1775.

FOUCHER, B. *Blois*, 1630. The Comte de Lambilly has a watch signed 'Blaise Foucher A Blois'.

FOUCHER, BLAISE. *Blois*, 1660–98.

FOUCHER, PAUL. *Paris*. Born 1811, died 1882. Fine maker of chronographs; published books on cylinder escapement and on wheel teeth.

FOULCON, BENJ. *London*, about 1780.

FOULD, HUMPHREY. Apprenticed 1646 to John Willowe, C.C.

FOULGER, SAMUEL. *London*. Apprenticed 1764, C.C. 1778.

FOULGER, SAMUEL, son. *London* (*Ratcliffe Highway*). livery C.C. 1812–19.

FOULKES, DAVID. Apprenticed 1671 to Peter Southworth, C.C.

FOULKES, ROBERT. *London*, 1737 C.C.

FOUQUET, CLAUDE. *Blois*, 1615–37.

FOUQUET, PIERRE. *Lyons*, 1645 master–1667.

FOWELL, EDMUND. C.C. 1670.

FOWELL, J. & N. *Boston, U.S.A.*, 1800–10.

FOWKES, GABRIEL. *Dartford*. Long Oriental lacquer-case clock, with picture in centre of door, arch dial, engraved silver centre, flower and scroll corners, about 1750; bracket clock, about 1780.

FOWLDS, ALLAN. *Kilmarnock*. Born 1719, died 1799. *v.* FOWLES.

FOWLDS, ANDREW. *9 St. John's Sq.*, 1790–94.

FOWLE, EDWARD. *London*. C.C. 1670.

FOWLE, JOHN. *Westerham*. 30-hour clock, about 1780.

FOWLE, JOHN. *Boston, U.S.A.*, 1805–13. Watch.

FOWLE, NATHANIEL. *Boston, U.S.A.*, 1803. Watch.

FOWLE, THOS. *East Grinstead*, about 1700. Several generations after till 1842.

FOWLER, ABRAHAM. *Amersham*, about 1760.

FOWLER, D. *London*. Lantern clock, about 1690.

FOWLER, GEO. 1819; afterwards at *Doncaster*.

FOWLER, ROBERT. 1810, settled at Leeds.

FOWLER, ROBT. C.C. about 1650.

FOWLER, ROBT. *Leeds*, 1829.

FOWLER, THOS. *London*. Watch, 1782. F. of York.

FOWLER, WM. *London*. Watch, 1780.

FOWLES, ALLEN. *Kilmarnock*. Said to have made a watch for Robert Burns in 1771.

FOWLS, AND. *London*. Watch, about 1780, case decorated with pearls.

FOX, CHARLES. C.C. 1662; lantern clock, inscribed 'Charles Fox, at the Fox, Lothbury, Londini, fecit', about 1670; also a stumpy bracket clock by him.

FOX, HUDSON. *Beverley*, 1822.

FOX, ISAAC. *39 Minories*, 1772; *7 Great Prescot c.*, 1782–94.

FOX, JOSEPH. *London*. Apprenticed 1763, C.C. 1770.

FOX, MORDECAI. C.C. 1689.

FOX, THOMAS. *131 Strand*, 1790. See FOSS.

FOX & SON. *7 Magdalen Buildings, Prescot St.*, 1788.

FOY. A Louis XIV chiming clock in Boulle work case, marked 'T. Foy La Roux à Paris'.

FOY, HENRY JNO. *London*. Clock about 1790.

FOY, JAS. *Taunton*, about 1770.

FRAIL, THOS. *92 Edgeware Rd.*, 1814–18.

FRAINCOMME, —. *London*. Watch, 1778.

FRAMBOROUGH, EDWARD. Admitted C.C. 1689.

FRAME, —. *Warrington*. Long-case clock about 1770.

FRAMES, GEORGE. *Gateshead*, 1811–33. Long-case clocks.

FRANCE, —. *Warrington*, about 1720.

FRANCESCHI, LOUIS. *Turin*, first half eighteenth century.

FRANCILLON, ERNEST. *Longines, Switzerland*. Did much to advance the duplicating system of watchmaking; died 1900.

FRANCIS, BALMER. *St. Bartholomew's*. C.C. 1731.

FRANCIS, BASIL & ALEXANDER. *Baltimore*, 1766.

FRANCIS, WILLIAM. *15 King St., Clerkenwell*. Livery C.C. 1810.

FRANCIS & VUILLE. *Baltimore, U.S.A.*, 1766. Clocks and watches.

FRANCIYCIFS, JOH. *Dresden*. Clock-watch, about 1740.

FRANCK, THOS. Crystal-cased watch, about 1580.

FRANCOIS, ANTOINE. *Paris*. Master 1766–89; very fine vase clock.

FRANCOIS, MARC AUGUSTE JULES. *Geneva*, about 1770–91.

FRANKCOM, —. *7 Quiet St., Bath*.

FRANKCOM, CHAS. 1795–1807.

FRANKCOM & MOWAT. 1835, afterwards Alex. Mowat.

FRANKLIN, BENJAMIN. *Philadelphia* and *London*. Born 1706, died 1790. Celebrated physicist; made clocks with three wheels and two pinions; desc. of a clock in Nicholson's Operative Mechanic, 1825.

FRANKLIN, JOSEPH. Apprenticed 1679 to Hy. Harper, C.C.; tall oak double-dome case clock at Innholders' Hall, signed on convex disc in arch of dial 'Josephus, Franklin, London', about 1720.

FRANKLIN, THOS. Apprenticed 1692 to Ben. Merriman, C.C.

FRANKLIN, WILLIAM. C.C. 1712.

FRANKLIN, WILLIAM. C.C. 1731.

FRANKLIN, WILLIAM. C.C. 1810.

FRANKSCOM, GEORGE. *London*. Apprenticed 1787, C.C. 1801.

FRASER, JOHN. Apprenticed 1681 to Edwd. Eyston, C.C.

FRASER, WILLIAM. *Lincoln, Lancaster, U.S.A.* Born 1801, died 1877; long-case clocks.

FRASER, WILLIAM. *Philadelphia, U.S.A.*, 1825.

FRAUDÉ, JACQUES. *Blois*, 1552–98. 'Orlogeulx.'

FRAUDÉ, PIERRE. *Blois*, 1636. Died 1672.

FRAY, JAMES. *London*. Apprenticed 1726, C.C. 1733–37.

FRAZER, —. *Bond St.*, 1788.

FREARSON, JOHN. C.C. 1689.

FREDMAN, ANDREAS ANDERSSON. *Stockholm*, 1705. Master 1712, died 1737; travelling clock Nord. Museum.

FREDMAN, JOHAN, son. *Stockholm*. Born 1712, master 1736, died 1767; court clock, 1745; long-case clock illuminated Sidenbladh; two bracket clocks.

FREE, A. *Blackburn*. Long-case clock, 1770.

FREE, JNO. *Oxon*. Watch, about 1700.

FREEBODY, JNO. Apprenticed 1671 to Jno. Sweetby, C.C.

FREEMAN, ANTHONY. Apprenticed 1653 to Widdon Fletcher, C.C.

FREEMAN, HENRY. *London*. Apprenticed 1807, C.C. 1814.

FREEMAN, ISAAC. *London*. C.C. 1733.

FREEMAN, JAMES. C.C. 1719.

FREEMAN, JAMES. *London*. C.C. 1767.

FREEMAN, JAS. *St. Botolph, Bishopsgate*. Apprenticed to John Watford, and turned over to Francis Robinson; C.C. 1736; in 1769 he patented a stop watch (No. 946).

FREEMAN, JOHN. C.C. 1646, assistant 1671; died 1680.

FREEMAN, JOHN. *London*. C.C. 1772.

FREEMAN, STAFFORD. Apprenticed 1656 to Wm. North; C.C. 1663.

FREEMAN, THOMAS. C.C. 1698.

FREESTONE, THOS. *Bury*, 1765.

FREETHY, JNO. Apprenticed 1672 to Chas. Rogers, C.C.

FREMIN, A. *France*, about 1600. Gold engraved watch, crystal cover, Spitzer collection; 8-lobed crystal watch, Webster collection, illuminated Baillie.

FRÉMON, PIERRE. *Blois*. Comp. 1627.

FRÉMY, JEAN (JULIEN) NICOLAS. *Paris*. Master 1742–89.

FRENCH, EDWARDS. *London*. C.C. 1782, l.C.C. 1811, died 1822; watch G.M.

FRENCH, JAMES. *17 Castle St., Holborn*, and *21 Tavistock St.*, 1810.

FRENCH, JAMES MOORE. *15 Sweeting's Alley*, 1808–38; *18 Cornhill*, 1839–42. Livery C.C. 1810. See also MITCHELL & FRENCH.

FRENCH, JAMES ORMSBY. *Baltimore, U.S.A.*, 1771. From *Dublin*; clocks and watches.

FRENCH, JAS. *Bristol*, 1844.

FRENCH, JOHN. *21 Tavistock St.*, 1783–88; *Mile End*, 1800.

FRENCH, THOS. *Norwich*, 1770.

FRENCHAM, JAMES. C.C. 1698.

FRESHFIELD, FREDERICK, brother. *London*. Apprenticed 1803, C.C. 1815, livery C.C. 1816. Also FRANCIS.

FRESHFIELD, JAMES, JUNR. C.C. by redemption 1744; letter as to non-payment of quarterage, 1796; centre seconds watch, about 1800.

FRESHFIELD, JAMES WILLIAM, son of the foregoing. C.C. 1801.

FRESHFIELD, JAS. Watch-case coverer, *19 Smithfield*.

FREULER, HANS JAKOB. *Basle*, 1719–58. Watch.

FREY, LORENZ. *St. Märgen*, 1680. Said to have been the first clockmaker in the Schwarzwald. v. HENNINGER and KREUZ.

FRIE, GEORGE. *Zittau*, about 1745. Court clock; bracket clock.

FRIPPETT, JOHN. C.C. 1665–70.

FRISBY, JNO. *5 Duke St., Grosvenor Sq.*, 1816–25.

FRISQUET, PETER. *30 Lothbury*, 1768–75.

FRITH, EDWARD. *London*. Apprenticed 1714, C.C. 1738.

FRODSHAM, CHARLES, brother. *London (Finsbury Pavement* and *Strand)*. Born 1810, C.C. 1854, m.C.C. 1855; after 1843 the firm was Arnold & Frodsham; a very able maker and writer.

FRODSHAM, CHARLES, son and apprentice of W. J. Frodsham, born 1810, died 1871; a skilful and successful watchmaker, *7 Finsbury Pavement*, 1842; afterwards succeeded J. R. Arnold at *84 Strand*; he conducted many experiments with a view of elucidating the principles underlying the action of the compensation balance and the balance-spring, and wrote several papers on technical subjects; he was for some time a vice-president of the Horological Institute; admitted C.C. 1845, master 1855–62. The present firm of Charles Frodsham are clockmakers to Queen Elizabeth II.

FRODSHAM, GEORGE, who succeeded him.

FRODSHAM, HENRY, who settled in Liverpool.

FRODSHAM, HENRY JOHN, who died 1848, and GEORGE EDWARD, who succeeded him.

FRODSHAM, JOHN and CHARLES.

FRODSHAM, JOHN. Born 1785, grandson of Wm (1); he entered into partnership with one Baker in 1809, and, under the style of Frodsham & Baker, continued the business at *Kingsgate St.* till about 1823, and afterwards at *31 Gracechurch St.*; elected to the livery of the C.C. in 1830, died in 1849; he had two sons associated with him in the business.

FRODSHAM, WILLIAM. *Kingsgate St., Red Lion Sq.* Born 1728; hon. freeman C.C. 1781; Earnshaw claimed to have taught him watch jewelling; he attested the value of Earnshaw's improvements in 1804; died 1807. For some years from 1790 the business was carried on in conjunction with his eldest son, William, under the title of William Frodsham & Son; the younger William predeceased his father, and the elder William bequeathed the business in Kingsgate St. to his grandson, John Frodsham.

FRODSHAM, WILLIAM JAMES, F.R.S., born 1778; grandson of the first-named William; eldest son of William and Alice Frodsham (Alice being the grand-daughter of John Harrison, famous as the inventor of the marine timepiece; he entered into partnership with William Parkinson, and commenced business in 1801 in *Change Alley*; admitted C.C. 1802, master 1836 and 1837; died 1850, bequeathing £1,000 to the C.C., to be known as the Parkinson and Frodsham Charity; he had brought up four sons to the trade.

FRODSHAM, WILLIAM & SON. *London*, 1790. Firm of William (1) and his son; gold lever watch Denham collection; watch signed 'Wm. Frodsham, jun'.

FROISSARD, —. *Geneva*, about 1800.

FROIDEVAUX, FRANÇOIS JOSEPH. *Chaux-de-Fonds* and *Berne*. Apprenticed 1774–1812; repeating alarum watch Chamb. collection; bracket clock.

FROMANTEEL. A large and famous family of Dutch clockmakers working in England. They made the first pendulum clocks in England, in 1658.

FROMANTEEL, ABRAHAM, son and apprentice of Ahasuerus Fromanteel; C.C. 1680; refused to serve as steward 1701.

FROMANTEEL, AHASUERUS. *East Smithfield*. Blacksmiths' Company 1630; C.C. 1632; 1630–50.

FROMANTEEL, AHASUERUS. *Moses Alley, Bankside*. C.C. 1655.

FROMANTEEL, AHASUERUS. *London*. Apprenticed 1654, C.C. 1663–85. A very famous maker; was the first to make pendulum clocks in England in collaboration with HUYGENS; the earliest dated 1658 is in the Prestige collection; long-case clock G.M.; bracket clock, illuminated Cec. & Web.

FROMANTEEL, AHASUERUS. Apprenticed 1679 to Jno. F., C.C.

FROMANTEEL, DAN. Apprenticed 1661 to A. F., Sen., C.C.

FROMANTEEL, JOHN. Ye Mermaid at Lothbury; apprenticed to Thomas Loomes; 1663–80; one of John Fromanteel's long-case clocks at the Dutch Church, Austin Friars, was dated 1679.

FROMANTEEL & CLARKE. *London*. Watches, from about 1680; long marquetry case month clock, domed hood with gilt figures on top, 12-in. dial, strikes the quarters, about 1710.

FRÖSELL, ANDERS. *Stockholm*, 1817–35. Bracket clock.

FRÖSELL, JOHN. *London (Clerkenwell)*. Apprenticed 1799, C.C. 1809, l.C.C. 1816.

FROST, —. *Exeter*. Put Lovelace's clock in order in 1833.

FROTHERINGHAM, SAMUEL. *Holbeach*. A Quaker, died 1745.

FROWDE, JNO. Apprenticed 1646 to Hy. Wansey; C.C. 1658.

FRY, SAMUEL. *Dublin*, about 1810. Watch movement, Ilbert collection.

FRY, WILLIAM. *London (Phillip Lane)*. Apprenticed 1779, C.C. 1786–1807.

FRYER, JOHN, f., of *York*, 1812, then at *Pocklington*.

FRYER, MOSES. *York*, 1822.

FRYER, WILLIAM, f., of *York*, 1809. Settled at *Pocklington*.

FRYETT, S. *130 Whitecross St.*, 1823.

FUERSTENFELDTER (FUERSTEN-FEL-DER), BENEDIKT. *Friedberg*. Late sixteenth century and early seventeenth century; watch and hexagonal table clock V. & A.; hexagonal minute repeating table clock Webster collection; striking repeating travelling clock Fränkel collection.

FUETER, —. *Berne*, about 1740.

FULKENER, EDWARD. C.C. 1702.

FULLER, CRISPIN. *Monkwell St.*, 1817.

FULLER, SAMUEL. *64 Red Lion St., Clerkenwell*, 1800–40; gave evidence in 1817 before a committee of the House of Commons on the distress among watchmakers in Clerkenwell.

FULLER, WILLIAM. C.C. 1675.

FULLWELL, HY. Apprenticed 1649 to Hy. Child, C.C.

FURET. Clock, Wallace collection, about 1740, signed 'Furet l'aîné à Paris'.

FURET, JACQUES LOUIS. *Paris*. Master 1763–89.

FURET, JEAN BAPTISTE ANDRÉ. *Paris*. Master 1743–89; clockmaker to Louis XVI; mantel clock Louvre.

FURNACE, GEO. *Dublin*. Watch, 1781.

FURNESS, —. *Monkwearmouth*, 1802.

FURNESS, JOHN. *9 Cross St., Hatton Garden*, 1830.

FURNESS, JOSEPH. *Uppingham*, 1784.

FURNESSE, JOSEPH. *Monkwearmouth*, 1770.

FURNESSE, THOMAS. Near *Three Compasses, Gravel Lane*, 1701.

FURNIFULL, RICHARD. C.C. 1722.

FYRBACH, CLAUS HENRIKSEN. *Copenhagen*. Master 1731, died 1743; turret clock.

GABRIER, CHARLES. *London*. This name on clocks and watches 1705–20 may possibly be fictitious. See CABRIER.

GADSBY, —. *Leicester*, 1770.

GADSDON, WM. *London*. Long-case clock, about 1750.

GAGNEBIN, DAN. *Chaux-de-Fonds*, about 1750.

GAILL, MATTHEIS. Large German watch, V. & A., about 1670.

GAILLARD, NICOLAS. *Lyons*, 1555. Died 1602; oval watch signed 'N. Galliard' M.M.A.

GAILLARD, PIERRE. *Geneva*, about 1770–91.

GALABIN, JOHN. *London*, 1761.

GALBRAITH, PATRICK. *Philadelphia*, 1797–1811.

GALE, JAMES. *64 Cannon St.*, 1783–89.

GALE, JOHN. *5 Red Lion Court, Spitalfields*, 1790–1829; *Lamb St.*, 1800–42.

GALEMIN. Watch, Pierpont Morgan collection, signed 'J. Galemin Autin', about 1620.

GALILEI, GALILEO. *Pisa, Florence* and *Padua*. Born 1564, died 1642. Celebrated physicist and astronomer; discovered the approximate law of the pendulum; described its application to a clock in a private letter in 1641; model in Science Museum.

GALILEI, VINCENZO, son. Began to have a clock made after his father's design in 1649, by Domenico Balestri; but died before its completion.

GALLAND, ANTOINE GABRIEL. *Paris*. Master 1778–1807.

GALLANDE (GALLONDE), LOUIS CHARLES. *Paris*. Master 1737–75; devised an anchor escapement and a centre-seconds clock desc. in Mem. de l'Acad. des Sciences, 1740; regulator C.A. & M.

GALLER, JAKOB. *Danzig*. Born 1688–1720.

GALLHANS, GABRIEL. Watch, Pierpont Morgan collection, about 1740.

GALLIMORE, JOSEPH. *Manchester*, 1775.

GALLMAYR, JOSEPH. *Munich*, 1727. Died 1790. A remarkable mechanic who made 52 automatic and clocks for the Bavarian Court; a celestial globe with clockwork in Fugger Museum, Augsburg; made a pedometer winding watch before 1776; repaired automatic clock of Munich in 1749.

GALLOT (GALOT), AUGUSTIN. *Paris*. Master 1758–89.

GALLOTT, ISAAC. Apprenticed in 1655 to Thos. Weekes, C.C.

GALLOWAY, CHRISTOPHER. Clock in a gateway to the Kremlin, Moscow, 1626.

GALLOWAY, JNO. Apprenticed in 1683 to Wm. Foster, C.C.

GALLOWAY, WALTER. *Kilbirnie*, 1780.

THE GALLOWAYS were well known in Leeds.

GALT, PETER. *Baltimore, U.S.A.*, 1802. Watch.

GALT, SAMUEL. *Williamsburg, U.S.A.*, 1751.

GAMARD, ANTOINE SIMON. *Paris*. Master 1740–49; clockmaker to Louis XV.

GAMBEY, LOUIS HENRY. *Paris*. Master 1788–1825; finished clock begun by Noblet for Auxerre.

GAMBLE, HENRY. *Pudsey*. Died 1780; 'Eminent' clockmaker.

GAMBLE, THOMAS. *London*. Apprenticed 1651, C.C. 1657.

GAMMAGE, T. Musical clockmaker, *6 Bridgwater Sq.*, 1823; *8 Wood St., Goswell Rd.*, 1835.

GAMMON, JNO. *London*. Lantern clock inscribed 'John Gammon, Londini, fecit', about 1670; silver watch, about 1680, J. Drummond Robertson collection.

GAMMON, JNO. *Lambeth*. Watch, 1725; another, 1760.

GAMMON, THOMAS. *Hereford*, 1774. Died 1786; C.C.; watch, Ilbert collection.

GAMMON, WILLIAM, son of William. *London* and *Birmingham*. Apprenticed 1795, C.C. 1814; watch; long-case clock.

GAMOD, G. *Paris*. Watch, about 1660; another watch signed 'G. Gamos, Paris'.

GANDO, NICOLAS. *France* or *Switzerland*, about 1670. See GANDOUZ *v.* GRANDO. Calendar watch, National Museum, Munich; square silver engraved watch V. & A.

GANDY, S. *Cockermouth.* Long-case clock, inscribed 'LIDDL Wm. and Mary, 1768'.

GANERAL, AUG. *7 Baker St., Clerkenwell*, 1835.

GANOT, NICOLAS. *Paris*, 1675 juré.

GANTHONY, RICHARD. *27 Cannon St.*, 1803; *49 Lombard St.*, 1807; *83 Cheapside*, 1825; master C.C. 1828–29.

GANTHONY, RICHARD, brother. *London.* Apprenticed 1813; C.C. 1820, died 1825.

GANY, THOMAS. C.C. 1699.

GARANDEAU (GARAUDRAN), —. *Paris*, 1579–1600. See GAVANDEAU. Clockmaker to the Queen; sig. to Statuts of Paris corporation, 1600; engraved watch Blot-Garnier collection; oval watch with émail en resille sur verre, Petit Palais, Paris.

GARBET, GABRIEL BENOÎT. *Paris.* Master 1770–89.

GARBETT, JERE. Apprenticed to Conyers Dunlop, turned over to Arthur Downes; admitted C.C. 1768.

GARBRAND, JNO. Apprenticed 1654 to Thos. Loomes, C.C.

GARD, HENRY. *Exeter.* Clock, 1770.

GARD, WILLIAM. *Exeter*, about 1790 C.C.; long-case clock.

GARDE, JAS. *London.* Bracket timepiece, square black case, minute circle within hour circle, about 1700.

GARDEN, PHILIP. *St. Paul's Churchyard*, 1759.

GARDEN, WILLIAM. C.C. 1712.

GARDENER, AMBROSE. *London*, 1698 C.C.

GARDENER, HENRY. *36 Norton Folgate*, 1794–1804.

GARDENER, HENRY. *London.* C.C. 1814.

GARDENER, JOHN. C.C. 1682.

GARDENER, JOSEPH. *Lancaster*, 1767, f.

GARDENER, OBADIAH. *London* (*Fleet St.*). Apprenticed 1700, C.C. 1712–27.

GARDENER, WILLIAM. *London.* Apprenticed 1764, C.C. 1771.

GARDINER, HENRY. *Rolls Buildings, Fetter Lane*, 1759–60.

GARDINER, JOHN. *Croydon.* C.C. 1687.

GARDNER, JNO. *Hull*, 1822.

GARDNER, JOHN. *London.* Apprenticed 1735, C.C. 1747–52; watch movement.

GARDNER, JOHN. *Annetwell Street, Carlisle*, 1820.

GARDNER, JOSEPH. *Lancaster*, 1767, f.

GARDNER, JOSEPH. *London.* C.C. 1769.

GARDNER, MARGARET. *London*, 1692 C.C.

GARDNER, T. *London.* Watch, 1762.

GARDNER, THOMAS. C.C. 1689. Long-case clock; another in the Wetherfield collection, a three-train chiming clock, arch dial, burr walnut case, about 1710.

GARDNER, THOS. *London.* Bracket clock, plain mahogany case, about 1790.

GARDNER, W. K., *Bridlington*, 1822.

GARDNER, WILLIAM. *London.* Apprenticed 1716, C.C. 1735.

GARDNER, WILLIAM. *Sandwich.* Walnut long-case clock, about 1760.

GARDNER, WILLIAM OBADIAH. C.C. 1711.

GARFOOT, WILLIAM. C.C. 1680.

GARLAND, JOHN. *Barbican.* Liveryman C.C. 1776; 1766–98.

GARLE, RICHD. Apprenticed in 1682 to Joseph Windmills, C.C.

GARLE, THOMAS. *London.* Apprenticed 1706, C.C. 1720–44.

GARLE, THOMAS, son. *London.* C.C. 1747; m.C.C. 1769–76.

GARMENT, MICHAEL. *London.* Apprenticed 1756, C.C. 1768.

GARNAULT, J. *Moscow*, about 1725. Watches Ilbert and Fränkel collections.

GARNAULT, JACOBUS. *The Hague*, about 1695. Watch movement, Ilbert collection. Probably the same as the preceding.

GARNE, T. *London.* Bracket clock, about 1680.

GARNEGY, CHAS. *55 King St., Soho*, 1817.

GARNER, THOS. *London.* Watch, 1770.

GARNET, W. *London.* Watch, 1766.

GARNETT, JNO. ANTHONY. Apprenticed in 1672 to Chas. Gretton, C.C.; he settled in France.

GARNETT, WM. *London*, about 1680.

GARNHAM, ABEL. *1 Lincoln's Inn Fields*, 1816.

GARNIER. Watch, about 1700, 'F. Garnier à Paris'.

GARON, PETER. *London.* C.C. 1694; watch, British Museum, with day of the month circle; curious watch with one hand; long-case chiming clock with ten changes in the hour; his bankruptcy noted (*Lond. Gaz.*, Oct. 31, 1706).

GARRANDOL, —. French hexagonal watch, crystal case, Wallace collection, signed 'Garrandol à Verdun', about 1640.

GARRARD, R. J. & S. *31 Panton St.*, 1822–42.

GARRARD, R. S. & Co. *London.* Watch, case set with rubies, 1780.

GARRARD, ROBT. *31 Panton St., Haymarket*, 1815–18. See WICKES, WM.

GARRAT, HUGH. *Ormskirk.* Maker of watches with Debaufre's dead-beat escapement, 1775–1800.

GARRAWAY, C. *Queen St., Westminster*, 1820.

GARRET, FERDINANDO. English watch in the form of a Tudor rose, about 1600.

GARRET, HUGH. See GARRAT.

GARRETT, CHARLES. C.C. 1690.

GARRETT, CHARLES. Admitted C.C. 1720.

GARRETT, PHILIP. *Philadelphia*, 1819.

GARRETT, WILLIAM. *188 Wapping*, 1804–15.

GARRIGUES, ANTOINE. *Paris.* Master 1782–1812.

GARRITT, THOS. *London.* Watch, 1790.

GARRON. See GARON.

GARRON, VINCENT. *Paris*, 1764 master-1771; gold engraved watch Stern. collection.

GARROT, JNO. *Warrington*, 1770.

GARTH, JOHN. *Aylesbury St., Clerkenwell*, 1750–55.

GARTHWAITE, JNO. *Colne, Lancs.*, 1818.

GARTLY, JNO. *Aberdeen*, 1810.

GARTNER (GERTNER), ANDREAS. *Dresden*, 1727. Geographical clock with 360 dials, M.P.S. Dresden.

GASCOIGNE, RICHD. Apprenticed in 1676 to Sam. Gascoigne, C.C.

GASCOIGNE, SAMUEL. C.C. 1676; "Lost, between Ludgate and Lothbury, on the 8th instant, a pendulum watch in a tortoise-shell Case, with a steel Chain and 2 Swiffles; made by Samuel Gascoigne" (*Lond. Gaz.*, July 14–18, 1692).

GASCOIGNE, WM. *Newark.* Active 1646–74; Owen, son of Wm. born 1647, died 1719; Wm. son of Owen; active until 1740.

GASDON, WILLIAM. *London.* Apprenticed 1700, C.C. 1712–24; watch Ilbert collection.

GASKELL, THOS. *Knutsford*, 1760.

GASKIN, JNO. *Dublin.* Watch, 1780.

GASS, DAVID & Co. *42 Oxford St.*, 1810–23.

GASS, WILLIAM. *London.* Apprenticed 1740, C.C. 1749, died 1806; watch.

GATE, ARCHER. Apprenticed in 1674 to Jas. Ellis, C.C.

GATE, THOS. *Carlisle*, 1770.

GATES, FRANCIS. *London.* Watch, 1795.

GATEWOOD. "Lost on 26 July 1705 a silver minute Pendulum Watch on the upper plate Gatewood and on the dyal Plate, Gatewood, London. Whoever has taken it up if they will bring it to Sam. Barrow, Clockmaker at the Sign of the Spring Clock in East Smithfield near Hermitage Bridge, shall have 20s. reward" (*The Postman*, July 31, 1705).

GATFORD, WM. *Uxbridge.* Watch, 1759.

GATHERCOLE, JOHN. *London.* Maker of a bracket clock, silvered arch dial, about 1780.

GATLAND, JOHN. *Cuckfield*, 1740.

GATTY, THOS. *Bodmin*, 1790–1820.

GATWARD, JOS. (from *London*). *Sevenoaks*, 1780.

GATWARD, THOS. Apprenticed in 1693 to Dan Rose, C.C.

GAUDRON (GAUDERON), ANTOINE. *Paris*, 1675 master, juré 1689.

GAUDRON, P. *Paris.* Clock and watch maker of repute, 1690–1730; spoken of as an authority by Thiout and by Lepaute; watch, leather case *piqué* with gold, wind in centre of dial, about 1720.

GAUDY, J. A. *Geneva*, about 1780.

GAULIN, ANTOINE. *Paris.* Master 1788–1825.

GAULTIER (GAUTRIER), PIERRE LAURENT. *Paris*, 1767 master–1789.

GAUNT, JOHN. *2 Bridgewater Gardens*, 1825–42.

GAUNT, JOSEPH. Apprenticed to James Wood, and turned over to Francis Rooker, and afterwards to Samuel Allvey, admitted C.C. 1761.

GAUNT, THOMAS, brother. *London.* C.C. 1815; watch.

GAUTHIER, ANTOINE. *Blois.* Master 1646, died 1670.

GAUTHIER, PIERRE. *Paris.* Enamelled watch, Pierpont Morgan collection, about 1710.

GAUTRIN, P. L. *Paris.* 1737–99; in 1799 petitioned for an award for a watch with only one wheel, stating that he had sold one 15 years before to 'Louis Capet'; a seconds watch by him approved by the Acad. des Sci.

GAUTSCHY, JAS. *London.* Watch, apparently Swiss, about 1785.

GAVELL, BENJAMIN. *London.* Apprenticed 1753, C.C. 1761.

GAVELLE, —. *Paris.* Clock, 1820.

GAVELLE, JAMES (alien). C.C. 1683; clock with square dial, boy and crown corners, 'James Gavelle, Londini, fecit', on circle; 1683–1700.

GAVELLE, JEAN JACQUES. *Paris (Rue de la Huchette).* Master 1753, juré 1778–89.

GAVELLE, JNO. *Moorfields.* Long-case clock, about 1705.

GAVELLE, PIERRE (l'aîné), son of Jean Jacques. *Paris (Rue St. Denis).* Master 1771, juré 1785–89; mantel clock.

GAY. SEE GUY.

GAZE, JAMES. *Primrose St., Bishopsgate*, 1782.

GAZE, SAMUEL B. Son and successor of James, a well-known clockmaker, *26 Princes St., Spitalfields*, 1814–59.

GAZUET, JÉRÔME. Admitted C.C. 1682; lantern clock, about 1700; long-case clock, at Belem, Lisbon, signed J., Gazuet, St. John's, London', about 1710.

GEBHARDT, HEINRICH. *Strasbourg*, 1631. Died about 1662; silver alloy watch British Museum; crystal fleur de lys watch Marryat collection.

GEDDES, CHARLES. *London, Boston, U.S.A., New York* from 1760. *Halifax, Nova Scotia.* Born 1749, died 1810.

GEDDES, JAMES. *Edinburgh.* Apprenticed 1728, died 1755.

GEDDY, JAMES. *Williamsburg (Baltimore, U.S.A.)*, 1774.

GEGENREINER, F. Z. *Augsburg*, about 1720.

GEGYE, RENE. *Charleston, U.S.A.*, 1740. Clocks and watches.

GEIST, THOMAS NARCISSUS. *Augsburg.* Apprenticed about 1778, comp. 1783, master 1793.

GELDARTE, JNO. *York*, f., 1674.

GELL. *York.*

GELL, JNO. f., 1634–63.

GELLS, THOMAS. Admitted C.C. 1720.

GEMBS, MELCHOIR. *Basle.* Master 1600–25; from *Württemberg.*

GENSPACHER, FR. BERNARDUS. *Kaisheim.* Born 1723, died 1794; from *Verona*; bracket clock Feill coll.

GENT, JOSEPH. *Walsall*, 1818.

GEORGE, ANDREW. Apprenticed in 1649 to Peter Delaundre, C.C.

GEORGE, LOUIS. *Berlin*, 1769–96. Clockmaker to the King; watch. Also GEORGES.

GEORGE, RICHARD. C.C. 1681.

GERARD, —. *Paris (Rue du Coq St. Honoré)*, 1807–25.

GERARD, J. B. *Quai des Grands Augustins, Paris* (gardevisiteur), 1769.

GERING, DANIEL. *Stockholm.* Master 1749, died 1797.

GERNON, BERNARD. Apprenticed to Solomon Wagson, of Bristol; admitted C.C. 1659.

GERONST, ALEX. *Coventry St., London.* Bracket clock, about 1730, seen at the Hague.

GERRARD, JOHN. *London.* Bracket clock, about 1725; verge watch, h.m., 1740.

GERVAS, THOS. *Epworth.* Clock, about 1770.

GEWOLL, GREGORY, SENR. *London*, 1730.

GIB, B. *Rotterdam.* Watch, Nelthropp collection, about 1720.

GIB, WILLIAM. *Rotterdam.* Two pendulum watches, G.M., about 1710; watch, silver cock, about 1725; fine long-case chiming clock.

GIBBARD, THOMAS. *Quakers' Buildings*, 1780–85.

GIBBONS (GIBBINS), BENJAMIN. *London.* C.C. 1721; watch.

GIBBONS (GIBBINS), HARRY. *London (Bermondsey St.).* Apprenticed 1809, C.C. 1826.

GIBBONS (GIBBINS), RICHARD. *London.* Apprenticed 1723, C.C. 1730–37.

GIBBONS (GIBBINS), THOMAS. *Philadelphia*, 1751. From *London.*

GIBBONS, BENJAMIN. C.C. 1750; died 1769.

GIBBONS, EDWARD. *New St.* C.C. 1730.

GIBBONS, JOHN. *6 King St., Clerkenwell*, 1810–23; *64 Hatton Garden*, 1836–42; livery C.C. 1811.

GIBBONS, JOSHUA. *45 White St., Borough*, 1810–18.

GIBBS, JAS. *Whitefriars.* C.C. 1725.

GIBBS, JNO. *11 Castle St., Aldersgate*, 1815–19.

GIBBS, JOHN. *London.* 1714 C.C.

GIBBS, JOHN. *London.* Apprenticed 1713, C.C. 1721–34.

GIBBS, JOHN. *London.* Apprenticed 1723, C.C. 1736.

GIBBS, JOSEPH. *London*, 1710 C.C.

GIBBS, JOSHUA. Apprenticed in 1689 to Thos. Gibbs, C.C.

GIBBS, RICHARD. *London (Fish St. Hill).* C.C. 1815, livery C.C. 1818.

GIBBS, RICHD. *London*, 1760. Long-case clock, said to be signed 'Pick Gibbs', is probably by him, and signed 'Rich. Gibbs'.

GIBBS, SOLOMON. *London.* Apprenticed 1708, C.C. 1716–35.

GIBBS, STEPHEN. *Milford Lane.* C.C. 1728; watch, 1750.

GIBBS, THOMAS. Apprenticed 1672 to Hy. Hester; admitted C.C. 1681; master 1711.

GIBBS, THOMAS. *11 Nichol Sq., Aldersgate St.*, 1825.

GIBBS, WALTER. Admitted C.C. 1648.

GIBBS, WILLIAM. *Moorfields.* C.C. 1707–30; pair-case verge watch, *repoussé* case, about 1720.

GIBSON, —. *Newcastle*, about 1750.

GIBSON, BENJ. Apprenticed 1654 to Richd. Masterton, C.C.

GIBSON, EDWARD. Livery C.C. 1787; master 1802; 1780–1803.

GIBSON, G. *Thetford*, about 1690.

GIBSON, JAMES. Brother C.C. 1669.

GIBSON, JNO. *Beith*. Curious geographical clock, 1761.

GIBSON, JNO. *Royal Exchange*. C.C. 1800–10; succeeded by Jas. Bissett.

GIBSON, JOHN. *Edinburgh*. Apprenticed 1758–80; long-case musical clock.

GIBSON, JOHN (? JAS.). *Whalebone Court, Lothbury*, 1761–1813.

GIBSON, JOHN. *Jedburgh*. Long-case clock, about 1770.

GIBSON, JOHN. *Alnwick*. a. 1781–1827; watch.

GIBSON, JOHN. *London (Sweetings Alley)*. C.C. 1806.

GIBSON, MARY. At the *Dial and Crown, Newgate St.* Dealer in all sorts of clock and watch makers' tools and materials, and for nearly twenty years the first in the business; having acquired a good fortune with a fair character, she retired from business in 1757 (Ludlam).

GIBSON, ROBERT. *Ecclefechan*, 1710. Died 1778; long-case clock.

GIBSON, WM. *Barnard Castle*, 1770.

GIBSON & FAUST. *5 Charlotte St., Rathbone Place*, 1800.

GIDE, XAVIER. *Paris*. Master 1762–89; watch, Meissen porcelain case, British Museum.

GIDEON, ROBERT. Admitted C.C. 1691.

GIEBICKE, FRIEDRICH WILHELM. *Augsburg*. Master 1747–70; from *Berlin*.

GIERS, A. *Borås*, 1825–46. Wall and bracket clocks.

GIFFIN, EDWARD BURR. *London (Holborn)*. Apprenticed 1758, C.C. 1766–78.

GIFFIN, GEORGE. *London*. Apprenticed 1733; C.C. 1740.

GIFFIN, THOS. *London*, 1820.

GIFFORD, THOMAS. Apprenticed to Robert Seignior, and turned to Robert Webster, admitted C.C. 1692.

GIL, WM. *Rotterdam*. Watches, 1770–90; watch, about 1780, signed 'Gill l'aîné'. See GIB, also GILL.

GILBARD, THOS. Watch-case maker, *Clerkenwell Green*, 1793.

GILBERT, —. *Chichester*. Long-case clock, about 1800.

GILBERT, AUSTIN. C.C. 1661.

GILBERT, CHARLES. C.C. 1700, à *Paris*; watch, about 1780.

GILBERT, DAVIS, M.P. *Tredrea (Cornwall)*. C.C. 1823.

GILBERT, EDWARD. *Chichester*, about 1790 C.C.

GILBERT, JOSEPH. Apprenticed in 1682 to Thos. Fenn, C.C.

GILBERT, PHILIP. *20 Cockspur St.*, 1807; *5 St. James's Sq.*, 1830. See GREEN.

GILBERT, RICHD. Apprenticed in 1664 to Thos. Hancorne, C.C.

GILBERT, THOMAS, son of William. *London*. C.C. 1733–36.

GILBERT, THOS. Apprenticed 1656 to Robt. Custer, C.C.

GILBERT, WILLIAM. C.C. 1695.

GILBERT, WILLIAM. *London*. Apprenticed 1747, C.C. 1767.

GILBERT, WILLIAM. *Gosport*, 1795 C.C.; watch; long-case clock.

GILBERTSON, JNO. *Ripon*, 1770.

GILDCHRIST (or GILCHRIST), ARCHIBALD. C.C. 1729.

GILDCHRIST (or GILCHRIST), STERLING. *Lombard St.*, 1755–65.

GILKES, GEO. Apprenticed in 1693 to Richd. Watts, C.C.

GILKES, JNO. Shipston, on plate of watch, Mary Gilkes on dial, hall-mark, 1766.

GILKES, RICHARD. *Devizes*. A Quaker, died 1822.

GILKES, RICHD. Apprenticed in 1678 to Wm. Hancorne; C.C. 1686.

GILL, CALEB. *Hingham, U.S.A.*, 1785.

GILL, DANIEL. *Rye*, 1790.

GILL, JOHN. C.C. 1707.

GILL, JOHN. *Gracechurch St.*, 1753–65.

GILL, LEAVITT. *Hingham, U.S.A.*, 1785.

GILL, THOMAS. *Birmingham*, 1748–66. From *Liverpool*.

GILL, WM. *Maidstone*. Lantern clock, about 1770.

GILL, WM. *Rotterdam*. Watch, 1794.

GILLE, —. *Paris*, 1769.

GILLE, l'aîné. *Paris*, about 1760–90. Many clocks, one Louvre, bronze by St. Germain; watch in engraved steel and gold.

GILLE, GUILLAUME JEAN, fils. *Paris (Rue St. Denis)*. Master, 1765–86.

GILLEPSY, CHAS. *Dublin*. Watch, 1796.

GILLESPEY, CHARLES. *Dublin*, 1747. Died 1771; watch movement.

GILLETT, CHA. EDW. *Manchester*. 30-hour one-hand clock, about 1740.

GILLETT, CHAS. ED. *Manchester*. Died 1819, aged 74.

GILLETT, EDWD., & SON. *Manchester*, 1775.

GILLETT & HEALY. *Manchester*, 1800.

GILLIER, C. *Berne*. Maker of an oval watch, about 1650.

GILLIES, ROBT. *Beith*, 1780.

GILLMORE. Lantern clock, inscribed 'Jno. Gillmore, Battel', about 1700.

GILPIN, EDMUND. Petitioner for incorporation of C.C.; a watch by him mentioned in *Archaeological Journal*, vol. XXII; oval watch, about 1620, Whitcombe Greene collection.

GIMBLET, JNO., JUNR., & VALE. *106 Snow Hill, Birmingham*, 1770.

GIMLINGHAM, JOHN. *London*. Apprenticed 1764, C.C. 1772–94.

GINGNER, ANTHONY (French). Admitted as a brother C.C. 1687.

GINN, WILLIAM. *London*. Freeman C.C. 1699–1723.

GIOX, —. *Paris*. Enamelled watch, 1780.

GIRARD, J. *London*. Watch, 1700.

GIRARD, MARC. *Blois*. Oval Watch, Soltykoff collection, about 1590; watch signed 'M. Girard, Bloy', in case of rock crystal, about 1580, Pierpont Morgan collection.

GIRARD, MARC. *Paris*. Oval chased watch-case of silver-gilt and rock crystal, about 1600.

GIRARD, MARC, son. *Blois*, 1652–99. Gold engraved watch M.M.A.

GIRARD, THÉODORE, son. *Blois*. Born 1596, comp. 1619, died 1680; engraved watch set stones, Ilbert collection.

GIRARDIER, L'AÎNÉ. *Geneva*, 1780–1805.

GIRAUD, BENOÎT. *Paris*. Master 1774–89.

GIRAUD, CHRISTOPHE. *Geneva*, 1814.

GIRGL, ANDREAS. *Munich*. Court C. 1713, died 1739.

GIROD, BENJ. *London*. Repeating watch, 1775.

GIROD, GASPER. An astronomical watch by him in British Museum, about 1610.

GIROD, JAMES (French). Watch, about 1660, signed 'Jacques Girod à Copet', admitted C.C. 1692; bracket clock, about 1700, inscribed 'James Girod, London'.

GIROUD, JEAN PIERRE. *Les Brenets*, 1766–85. Able maker.

GIROUST, à *Paris*. Fine clock, about 1790.

GIROUST, ALEXANDER. *Coventry St.*, 1760. Clock.

GIROUX, ANDRÉ FRANÇOIS. *Paris*. Master 1767–89.

GISCARD, WILLIAM. *Ely*. Born 1749, died 1812; clocks and watches.

GITEAU. *Etève de Breguet, Paris*. Watch, 1790.

GITTER, JNO. Apprenticed in 1683 to Nat. Pyne, C.C.

GLADSTONE, JOHN. *Biggar*. Born 1772, died 1851.

GLADSTONE, THOMAS. C.C. 1703.

GLAESNER. *Lyons*. Clock, about 1775.

GLAESNER & PRUD'HOMME. *Lyon*. Repeating watch, about 1780.

GLANVILLE, DAVID. *Waterford*, 1775–1824. Watch N.Y. University.

GLANVILLE, RICHARD. *Strand*, 1775.

GLASCO, THOMAS. *Dublin*. a. 1756–80; watch.

GLASE, THOS. *Bridgnorth*. Watch, 1790.

GLASGO, PHIL. & SON. *Dublin*. Pull repeating bracket clock, about 1720; watch, 1770.

GLASS, ALEXANDER. *306 High Holborn*, 1783.

GLASSUP, THOS. *London*. Bracket clock, about 1755; another, about 1780.

GLAVE, JOHN. *London*. Apprenticed 1768, C.C. 1782–1814.

GLAZEBROOK, JNO. *Mansfield*, 1780.

GLAZIER, WILLIAM. C.C. 1666; to him Simon Lamb was apprenticed in 1669.

GLEAVE, JOHN. *Liverpool*, 1805–29. Watch.

GLEAVE, MATTHEW. Watch by him, G.M., 1700.

GLEETER, —. *London*. Watch, about 1740.

GLENC, JOSEPH. *Prag*. Watch, about 1710.

GLENNY, GEORGE, son of Joseph (1). *London (Waterloo Pl.)*. Apprenticed 1807, C.C. 1819.

GLENNY, JOSEPH. Watch-case maker, *20 Red Lion St., Clerkenwell*. Livery C.C. 1810.

GLORIA, JACQUES. *Rouen*, 1696. Juré 1701–04; watch, Denham collection; calendar watch with balance spring Gélis collection; repeating watch movement, Ilbert collection; pendulum watch, 1697.

GLOSSOP, ROBT. *London*. Watch, 1815.

GLOVER, BOYER. *Leadenhall St*. C.C. 1740; died while serving as senior warden, 1768.

GLOVER, DANIEL. C.C. 1699.

GLOVER, J. *Manchester*. Watch, about 1820,

GLOVER, JAMES. *London*. Apprenticed 1751, C.C. 1764.

GLOVER, JOHN. *London*. C.C. 1700–20; watch, Ilbert collection.

GLOVER, JOHN, son of John. *London*. C.C. 1731.

GLOVER, RALPH. *Hyde Park Corner*. Watch, about 1770.

GLOVER, RICHARD. C.C. 1703.

GLOVER, RICHARD. *London*. Born 1676, master 1698; comp. watch.

GLOVER, SAMUEL. C.C. 1694.

GLOVER, SAMUEL. *London*, 1772–1811 C.C.

GLOVER, STEPHEN. *London (Petticoat Lane)*. C.C. 1792, livery C.C. 1795–1811.

GLOVER, THOMAS. *Drogheda*. Apprenticed 1820.

GLOVER, THOMAS. *London*. Apprenticed 1732, C.C. 1746–63.

GLOVER, THOMAS. *London*. Apprenticed 1755, C.C. 1767.

GLOVER, THOS. *New St*. C.C. 1700.

GLOVER, WILLIAM. *Boston, U.S.A.*, 1818–25. Watch.

GLUCK, ADAM. Watch by him in British Museum in a case of bloodstone, 1650–60.

GLYD, JAS. *Westminster*. Watch, h.m., 1771.

GLYNN, RICHARD. C.C. 1705.

GOBELS, JAN. *Bloemgracht (Flower Canal), Amsterdam*, 1767. A fine long-case clock with kettle base and marquetry decoration, shows moon, tides, day of the month, day of the week, and astronomical signs.

GOBERT, MATT. *London*. Watch, 1760.

GOBERT, PETER (French). Admitted C.C. 1687.

GOBERT, PHILIPPE. *Paris*. 1675 juré.

GOBRECHT, CHRISTIAN. *Baltimore*, 1820.

GODBED, MATT. Apprenticed in 1657 to Hy. Kent, C.C.

GODBED, WILLIAM. Apprenticed 1638 to Thos. Reeve, admitted C.C. 1646; watch, inscribed 'Guliemus Godbed, Lombert Street, Londini', octagonal case; another at the British Museum; signed a petition to C.C. 1656.

GODDARD, BEN. Apprenticed 1691 to Isaac Goddard; C.C. 1701; long-case clock by him in the Mosque of Achmet, Constantinople.

GODDARD, CHRISTOPHER. *London (Little Britain)*, 1729. C.C. 1756–61; bankrupt; bracket clock; watch.

GODDARD, EDWARD. *London (Helmet Row)*, 1780. C.C. 1787–99.

GODDARD, FRANCIS. *49 Oxford St.*, 1792; *8 Rathbone Place*, 1794–1825.

GODDARD, GEORGE S. *Boston, U.S.A.*, 1816–25. Watch.

GODDARD, ISAAC. Apprenticed 1675 to Thos. Grimes, C.C. 1684; long-case clock, Museum, Brunswick, inscribed 'Isaac Goddard, Londini'.

GODDARD, JOHN. *Houndsditch (from Paris)*. Described as a Papist who resided with and worked for Isaac Sunes in Houndsditch, 1615–18.

GODDARD, JOHN, brother. *London, China* and *London*. C.C. 1758–72; bankrupt.

GODDARD, LUTHER. *Shrewsbury, Mass*. Between 1809 and 1817 he manufactured watches.

GODDARD, NICHOLAS. *Newark*. Maker of lantern clocks; died 1741.

GODDARD, REYMOND. 1600.

GODDARD, STEPHEN. C.C. 1727; long-case clock, about 1740.

GODDARD, T. *28 Pitfield St.*, 1814; *20 New Gloucester St., Hoxton*, 1835. Of U.S.A.

GODDARD, THOS. Apprenticed 1638 to Richd. Child, C.C.

GODDARD, THOS. Apprenticed 1685 to Jno. Stanley, C.C.

GODDARD, WILLIAM. *London (Shoreditch)*. Apprenticed 1792, C.C. 1800.

GODDEN, THOMAS. *London*. Apprenticed 1771, C.C. 1779–96.

GODEAU. See LESTOURGEON.

GODEMAR, ANTOINE. *Geneva*, about 1770–1800. Associated with Moïse Pouzait; taught in the first school of horology in 1788.

GODEMAR, FRÈRES. *Geneva*. Virgule watch, about 1810; Gélis collection. See also POUZAIT.

GODFREY, GEORGE. *22 Charterhouse St.*, 1835.

GODFREY, HENRY. C.C. 1685; "A pretty large-sized Pendulum-watch in a Tortoiseshell Case; it shews the Hours and Minutes with a Sun and Moon Dial Plate, made by Henry Godfrey, London" (*Lond. Gaz.*, Oct. 7–10, 1700).

GODFREY, JNO. Apprenticed in 1682 to Jas. Hatchman, C.C.

GODFREY, WM. *Winterton*, 1773; succeeded by his son Wm. See TATE, THOS.

GODLYMAN, PETER. *Hurley*. Clock, brass dial, lantern movement, about 1700.

GODON. Clock, about 1750, signed 'A. L. Godon, R. de Camera de S.M.C.'

GODON, —. *Paris*, 1780–90. Appointed horloger to the Court of Spain in 1786; splendid clock in vase-shaped case of Sèvres porcelain, painted with birds in a medallion, and mounted with handles formed as caryatid figures, dating from about 1785.

GODWIN, JAS. *304 High Holborn*, 1801–42.

GODWIN, JOHN. *161 Strand*. See GOODWIN.

GOFF, THOS. *8 Rosoman St.*, 1793.

GOLD, CHRISTOPHER. *London*. Watch, British Museum, gold *repoussé* case, about 1760.

GOLD, JOHN. *118 Fleet St.*, 1806–19.
GOLD, RICH. *London*. Watch, h.m., 1772.
GOLDING, J. *55 Cornhill*, 1775.
GOLDNEY, THOS. *4 St. James's St.*, 1815–25.
GOLDSBOROUGH, GEO. *Scarborough*, 1775.
GOLDSMITH, JOHN. C.C. 1681.
GOLDSMITH, JOHN. C.C. 1720.
GOLDSMITH, THOS. Apprenticed in 1683 to Wm. Brafield; C.C. 1692.
GOLDSMITH, WILLIAM. C.C. 1719.
GOLDSWORTHY, E. *Chelsea*, 1820.
GOLLEDGE, RICHARD. *Stratford*, 1820.
GOLLING, ANDREAS. *Augsburg*, 1712 master–1746. Died a. 1755; *Vienna, Gratz, Prague* and *Breslau*; silver watch Feill collection; table clock.
GOLLING, MALTHIAS. *Munich*. Court clock 1739, died 1772.
GOLLING, ANSELM BENEDIKT. *Augsburg*. Master about 1770, juré 1776–93; striking repeating travelling clock Feill collection.
GOLLING, JOHANN GEORG. *Augsburg*. Master 1748–70.
GOLLING, JOH. SIMPERT. *Fürth*, about 1750. Went *Augsburg* 1789; died about 1800.
GOM, DANIEL. *Lyons*. Master 1629–70; from *Pomerania*; clockmaker to the town; made clock for Hôtel de Ville 1651; circular cast silver watch Fränkel collection; crystal cross watch Lemberg Museum.
GOM, DAVID. *Lyons*. Maker of a watch cased in jacinths, about 1650.
GOMPS, —. Hexagonal watch, silver case, signed 'Gomp à Armstrand, 1586'.
GONDOUX, JNO. *London*. Watch, 1780.
GONON (GONNON), BERTRAND. *Thiers*, 1637 master; *Lyons*, 1638–65; crystal cross watch Côte collection, illuminated Vial & Côte.
GOOCH (& HARPER, *12 Red Lion St., Clerkenwell*, 1810–13).
GOOCH, ALBERT. *13 Red Lion St., Clerkenwell*, 1816–25.
GOOCH, H. *25 Coppice Row, Clerkenwell*, 1830.
GOOCH, JNO. *25 Banner St.*, 1814–18.
GOOCH, JOHN. *London* (*Gt. Arthur St.*). C.C. 1779–90.
GOOCH, WM. *Bunhill Row*, 1825.
GOOD, JOHN. Author of *The Art of Shadows; or, Universal Dialling*, 2nd ed., London, 1711; C.C. 1678.
GOOD, JOHN. *305 High Holborn*, 1780–94.
GOOD, SAVIL. *London* (*Little Carter La.*). C.C. 1767.
GOODALL, CHAS. *26 Bridges St., Covent Garden*, 1793–1818.
GOODALL, GEO. *Micklefield*. Long-case clock, square dial, about 1720.
GOODALL, GEORGE. *Tadcaster*, 1800.
GOODALL, JAS. *London*. Watch, 1779.
GOODCHILD, JOHN. C.C. 1726.
GOODE, CHARLES. Brother C.C. 1686; bracket quarter clock and also very fine long marquetry case clock, about 1690, Wetherfield collection.
GOODERE, EPHRAIM. *Worcester*. Master 1782–1796 C.C.; watch.
GOODFELLOW, WILLIAM. *Philadelphia*, 1797.
GOODFELLOW, WILLIAM RICHARD. *London*. Apprenticed 1810, C.C. 1817.
GOOODFELLOW, WM. *378 Oxford St.*, 1793.
GOODFRIEND, JOHN. *London*. Bracket clock, about 1750.
GOODHALL, GEO. *Aberford*, 1775.
GOODHALL, WILLIAM. *London*. Apprenticed 1751, C.C. 1765–72.
GOODHUGH, R. & B. *2 Welbeck St., Cavendish Sq.*, 1825–35.

GOODHUGH, WILLIAM. *126 Regent St.*, 1825.
GOODING, HENRY. *Boston, U.S.A.*, 1810–25. Watch.
GOODING, JOSIAH. *Bristol, R.I., U.S.A.* 1788–mid-nineteenth century. Also *Dighton, Mass.*
GOODLAD, RICHARD. Admitted as a brother C.C. 1689.
GOODLIN, PETER. Admitted C.C. 1637.
GOODMAN, GEO. *London*, 1771. Fine repeating watch, Pierpont Morgan collection; watch in case of red agate, about 1780. Pierpont Morgan collection; another watch, about 1785.
GOODMAN, H. N. *London*. Watch, 1820.
GOODMAN, THOMAS. *Charleston, U.S.A.*, 1733. From *London*; watch.
GOODMAN, THOS. *London*. Watch, about 1760.
GOODMAN, TIMOTHY. *Towcester*. Lantern clock, about 1680.
GOODRICH, SIMON. Received a reward from the Society of Arts in 1799 for an improved escapement.
GOODRICH, WM. Apprenticed in 1689 to Amos Winch, C.C.
GOODWIN, JOHN. *70 Strand*, 1770–1800.
GOODWIN, SAMUEL. *Philadelphia*, 1820. Watch.
GOODWIN, WILLIAM. *Nottingham*. From 1789–1818; clocks and watches.
GOODWIN, WM. Apprenticed in 1675 to Jno. Harris, C.C.; lantern clock, about 1700, inscribed 'Wm. Goodwin, Stowmarket'; watch, about 1720.
GOODYEAR, JOHN. *Shoe Lane*. C.C. 1722.
GOODYEAR, JOSEPH. *Shoe Lane*. C.C. 1732.
GOODYER, JOSEPH. *London*. C.C. 1789.
GOORE, THOMAS. *London*. Apprenticed 1705, C.C. 1716.
GORDON, ALEX. *Dublin*. Watch, about 1750.
GORDON, ALEX. *336 Strand*, 1815–19.
GORDON, GEORGE. *Perth*. Apprenticed 1795 -1810.
GORDON, HUGH. *Aberdeen*, 1748–90, pair-case gold watch.
GORDON, JAMES. *Perth*, 1771–96.
GORDON, JAS. *Beith*, 1780.
GORDON, JAS. *London*. Watch, 1842.
GORDON, JOHN. *Black Spread Eagle, Ludgate St.* C.C. 1698; bracket clock, black case, arch dial inscribed 'John Gordon, London', on oval silvered plate, 1698–1712.
GORDON, JOHN. *Edinburgh*. Apprenticed 1747–99.
GORDON, PATRICK. *Edinburgh*, 1705–17.
GORDON, ROBERT. *Edinburgh*. An eminent maker; admitted freeman of the Incorporation of Hammermen in 1703, afterwards 'boxmaster' or treasurer; was also captain of the trained band for protecting the city; a chiming clock by him in the Bank of Scotland; 1703–30.
GORDON, THOMAS. *Edinburgh*. Apprenticed 1688, died 1743; an eminent maker; long-case clock illuminated J. Smith; watch movement, Roy. Museum, Edinburgh.
GORDON, THOMAS, 'from London'. Opposite the Merchants' Coffee House, New York, 1759.
GORDON, THOMAS. *New York*, 1758–71. From *London*.
GORDON, THOS. *Edinburgh*, 1703, f. Long-case clock, arabesque marquetry, about 1710.
GORDON, WILLIAM. *Lauder*. Apprenticed 1780–1805.
GORDON, WILLIAM. *15 Cross St., Islington*, 1794–1805.
GORDON & FLETCHER. *Dublin*. Watch, 1795.
GORE, WM. *Dublin*. Watch, 1770.
GORET, JEAN. *Rue Courture Ste. Catherine, Paris*. Garde-visiteur, 1769.
GORET, LOUIS. *Paris*. Master 1754, juré 1770–89.
GORGAS, JACOB. *Ephrata, Lancaster, U.S.A.* Came from *Germany*, about 1760, died 1829; well-known maker of long-case clocks.

GORGAS, SOLOMON, son. *Ephrata*, about 1780. Long-case clock.

GORHAM, JAMES. *High St., Kensington*, 1815–42.

GORSUCH, THOS. *Salop.* Watch, 1720.

GOSLER, THOS. *51 Fore St.*, 1815–19.

GOSLING, JOSEPH. *55 Cornhill*, 1775–85.

GOSLING, RICHARD. Apprenticed in 1649 to Thomas Claxton, C.C.

GOSLING, RICHARD & SON. *55 Cornhill*, 1765–75.

GOSLING, ROBERT. *160 Fenchurch St.*, 1770–85.

GOSSE, JEREMIAH. C.C. 1667.

GOSSE, JNO. Apprenticed in 1662 to Richard Scrivener, C.C.

GOSSELIN, J. PH. *Rue St. Honoré, Paris.* Clock, about 1760; garde-visiteur, 1769.

GOSSOIN. In 1667 he constructed the clock at Val de Grace, for which he received 3,000 livres.

GOSTAGE, SAM. *Birkenhead*, 1833.

GOSTLING, WILLIAM. *Diss.* From 1774–91 C.C.; long-case clock; watch.

GÖTHE, JOHANN ANDREAS. *Dünster* and *Frankfurt a. M.* Born 1733, died 1788; long-case clock Goethe House, Frankfurt.

GOTOBED, R. *Eton*, about 1790 C.C. Watch.

GOUBERT, JAMES. Admitted C.C. 1690.

GOUGH, WM. *Devizes.* Watch, 1720, in each of the pillars a niche containing a silver statuette.

GOUGH, WM. *London.* Watch, 1745, also curious touch watch, G.M., about 1760 in this a push piece at the pendant drove a rod against a snail pivoted to the plate, and turned by a pin in the cannon pinion.

GOUGY, PIERRE FREDERICK. *Tavistock St., Westminster.* Bracket clock at Windsor Castle, about 1830.

GOUJON, JEAN. *Paris.* Cruciform watches, about 1590.

GOUJON, PETER. *London.* Watch, 1735.

GOUJON, SAMUEL. *42 Newgate St.* Master C.C. 1760; 1752–94.

GOUJON, SAMUEL, son. *London.* C.C. 1793, l.C.C. 1802–13.

GOUJON, STEPHEN. *Seven Dials.* C.C. 1725.

GOULARD, JEAN DIT MARTINOT. *Paris*, 1663. Died 1692; clockmaker to Louis XIV in 1663.

GOULARD, JÉRÔME, son. *Paris*, 1692–1702. Clockmaker to Louis XIV.

GOULD, ABEL. C.C. 1683. "Lost on the 28th inst., a gold watch with two movements, having a black filagreen case studded like shells, made by Abel Gould" (*Lond. Gaz.*, March 26–30, 1691).

GOULD, CHESTER. *Red Lion St., Clerkenwell.* He patented in 1803 (No. 2,706) a nautical time glass, 1780–1803.

GOULD, CHRISTOPHER. C.C. 1682; in the Wetherfield collection are long-case clocks by him: one with bolt shutter maintaining power, 10½-in. dial, in marquetry case with finely carved pediment, about 1685; another, exceedingly small, repeats the quarters on five bells, burr walnut case with domed hood, about 1690; watch, Pierpont Morgan collection, about 1700. "Supposed to be drop'd in a Hackney coach on the 4th inst., a gold watch in a black shagreen case, made by C. Gold, the word 'Friendship' graved on the Movement" (*Lond. Gaz.*, March 18–21, 1694).

GOULD, JAMES. *London*, 1699 C.C.

GOULD, THOS. *London.* Watch, 1780.

GOULLONS, à *Paris.* Watch by him in Guildhall Museum, short train, escape wheel of 17, handsome enamelled case, 1⅛ in. in diameter, and ½ in. thick, about 1660, see Crofts à Marseille; fine enamelled watch, about 1670.

GOURDAIN à *Paris.* Watch, about 1720, Mons. E. Gélis.

GOURDIN (GOURDAIN), NICHOLAS. *Paris*, 1740. Juré 1747; devised a dead beat escapement desc. in Gallon, *Machines et Inventions*, Vol. 7; experimented on curve of balance spring; fine cartel clock, bronze by Ch. Cressent, Pal. de Justice, Paris.

GOURLAY, ALEX. *London.* Watch, 1785.

GOUT, RALPH. *6 Norman St., Old St.*, 1770–1800; *122 Birchin Lane*, 1815. He patented in 1799 (No. 2,351) apparatus for recording the paces made by man or horse, also an application of the invention for recording the revolutions made by the wheels of a carriage; bracket clock, mahogany case, silvered dial, engraved with festoons, etc., quarters chimed on eight bells, see Recordon.

GOUTHIÈRE, P. *Paris.* Celebrated chaser and gilder of clock cases; from 1740.

GOVETT, GEORGE. *Philadelphia*, 1811–19.

GOW, WM. *London.* Watch, h.m., 1787.

GOWERTH, JOHN. *Oxford*, 1701.

GOWLAND, CLEMENT. *Sunderland*, 1775.

GRACE, EDWARD. *London (Swan Alley).* C.C. 1773–86.

GRACE, THOS. *London.* Bracket clock, about 1720.

GRACE, WM. *Cronton.* Sun and moon watches, about 1695.

GRADELLE, —. *London.* Watch, Schloss collection, about 1740.

GRAET, PHILIP. *Lintz.* Fine travelling watch, about 1695.

GRAF, JOHANN PAULUS. *Munich*, 1756. Court clockmaker 1772; died 1778; fine maker; several clocks Munich Residenz.

GRAFF, JOSEPH. *Prague*, 1687–1762. Fine astronomical clocks and equation work.

GRAHAM, D. *London.* Watch, 1798.

GRAHAM, GEORGE. 'Honest George Graham', a most eminent clock and watchmaker; C.C. 1695, master 1722; died 1751, aged 77.

GRAHAM, GEORGE. *Cockermouth*, 1820–47. Watch.

GRAHAM, JAMES. *85 Piccadilly*, 1800–05.

GRAHAM, THOMAS. *Bellingham*, 1785.

GRAHAM, WILLIAM. At the *Dial in Lombard St.* A good maker; fine repeating watch, V. & A., 1724; long-case clock, Wm. Graham, London, about 1730.

GRAHAM, WILLIAM. *Bellingham*, 1785.

GRAINGER, —. *Holborn Hill.* Watch, 1830.

GRAINGER, RICHARD. Apprenticed in 1685 to Francis Munden, C.C.

GRAMOT, G. *Paris.* Watch in enamelled case, Pierpont Morgan collection.

GRAN, —. *Fleet St.* Watch, h.m., 1776.

GRAND, JOHN. *3 Cockspur St.*, 1780–1800. See FISHER, ISAAC.

GRANDEAU, —. Oval watch, about 1590, signed 'Grandeau à Paris', Garnier collection.

GRANDIN, JNO. *2 Macclesfield St., Soho*, 1815–19.

GRANDJEAN, DAVID HENRY. *Locle.* Died 1845.

GRANDPERRIN (GRANDPERIN), —. *Paris (Rue St. Honoré)*, 1807–25. Watch New York University.

GRANGER, JEAN. *Paris.* 1678 master–1685.

GRANGER, RICHARD. C.C. 1695.

GRANGIER (French), about 1650.

GRANT, EDWARD. *London (Long Acre).* C.C. 1769–96.

GRANT, JOHN. *75 Fleet St.* Apprenticed to Alexander Cumming, whose nephew he was; hon. freeman C.C. 1781; warden 1810, when he died; several specimens of his work are in the Guildhall Museum.

GRANT, JOHN. *75 Fleet St.*, son of the preceding, and an equally celebrated maker; C.C. 1817, master five times 1838–67.

GRANT, JOHN. *Glasgow*, 1818–41.

GRANT, RICHARD. *London*. Bracket clock, 1760.
GRANT, WILLIAM. *London*. C.C. 1660.
GRANT, WM. *London*. Watch, 1740.
GRANTHAM, J. *London*, 1750–70.
GRAPE, JOHN. *London*. Watch, G.M., 1737.
GRAPE, RICHARD. Apprenticed in 1685 to Jno. Wheeler, C.C.
GRAPE, THOMAS. *London*. C.C. 1721.
GRATREX, EDWARD. *Birmingham*. Long-case clock, about 1750.
GRATREX, ROBERT. *London*. Apprenticed 1784, C.C. 1791–1815.
GRAUPNER, J. G. Clock, Green Vaulted Chambers, Dresden, about 1700.
GRAUPNER, JOHANN GOTTLIEB. *Dresden*. Master 1716–39; table clock Schloss Museum, Berlin; pair-case silver travelling clock Feill collection.
GRAUPNER, PAUL GOTTFRIED. *Augsburg*. Master 1726, juré 1735–53; died a. 1757; wall clock.
GRAVE, GEO. *271 Whitechapel Rd.*, 1815–42.
GRAVE, JOSEPH. Apprenticed in 1687 to Joseph Williamson, C.C.
GRAVELL (& TOLKEIN, successors of Eardley Norton). *49 St. John St.*, 1790–1820. In 1817 they made a new clock for Winchester Town Hall.
GRAVELL, WILLIAM. *London* (*W. Smithfield*). 1810 C.C.
GRAVES, BENJAMIN. C.C. 1716, master 1705, clerk 1719; died 1731; Wm. Neighbour apprenticed to him, 1678.
GRAVES, JAS. C.C. 1675.
GRAVES, WM. *York*, f., 1730.
GRAY, ADAM. *17 Berkeley St., Clerkenwell*, 1788–1812.
GRAY, ALEXANDER. *Elgin*, 1754–74.
GRAY, BENJAMIN. *Pall Mall*. Clockmaker to George II; in the G.M. is a gold repeating watch by him, which was made for Sir Peter Somes in 1732; extra large long-case clock, with dead-beat escapement, about 1730, Wetherfield collection, 1720–60.
GRAY, JAMES. *Edinburgh*. Apprenticed 1765–1806; clock C.A.
GRAY, JAMES. *Perth*, 1777–1807. GREY.
GRAY, JAMES. *Edinburgh*. Long mahogany case clock, Sheraton style, about 1790, Wetherfield collection.
GRAY, JAMES, son of James. *Edinburgh*, 1805–36. Long-case clock Wetherfield collection, by him or his father.
GRAY, JAS. *London*. Watch, 1756.
GRAY, JNO. Apprenticed in 1680 to Jno. Westoby, C.C.; long-case clock, 'John Gray in Johnson's Court, Londini, fecit', about 1705.
GRAY, JNO. *68 Leadenhall St.* Apprenticed to Thos. Hardy; C.C. 1769; watch by him, G.M., 1769–1817.
GRAY, JOS. *Durham*. Watch, 1777.
GRAY, ROBERT & WILLIAM. *13 New Bond St.*, 1793; William, 1800–28.
GRAY, T. J. & G. *25 Strand*, 1800–05.
GRAY, THOMAS. *25 Strand*, 1780; *42 Sackville St.*, 1793.
GRAY, TIMOTHY. Brother C.C. 1633.
GRAY, WILLIAM. Apprenticed in 1691 to Peter Lodowick, C.C.; watch, about 1730, inscribed 'Wm. Gray, Bond St., London'.
GRAY & CONSTABLE. *Sackville St.* Makers of a thin verge watch decorated with enamel and jewels, G.M., about 1780.
GRAY & VULLIAMY. *Pall Mall*, 1746–60.
GRAYE, —. Subscribed £2 10s. for incorporation of C.C. 1630.
GRAYHAM, CHAS. *London*. Watch, 1810.
GRAYHAM, TIMOTHY. *Workington*, 1770.
GRAYHURST, B. *London*. Watch, 1778.
GRAYHURST, P. & M. *65 Strand*, 1785–1800.

GRAYHURST & HARVEY. *65 Strand*, 1810–30.
GRAYSON, WM. *Henley-on-Thames*, 1826.
GREATOREX, HENRY. C.C. 1711; in the *Postman*, 1710, is an advertisement for a silver pendulum watch, lost in White Conduit Fields, for which Mr. Greatorex at Bushby's Folly offers a guinea reward, 1710–11.
GREATOREX, RALPH. C.C. 1653.
GREAVES, ROBERT. *Macclesfield*, 1770.
GREAVES, S. *Mansfield*, 1770.
GREAVES, SAMUEL. *London*. Marquetry long-case clock, square dial, about 1720.
GREAVES, THOS. *92 High St., Birmingham*, 1770.
GREAVES, WM. *Newcastle*, 1760.
GREAVES, WM. *York*, died 1796.
GREAVES (GRIEVE), —. *Bedale*, about 1770–95. Clocks and watches.
GREAVES (GRIEVE), JOHN. *Birmingham*. Born 1684, died 1771; watch.
GREAVES (GRIEVE), THOMAS. *Newcastle-on-Tyne*, 1778–1820.
GRÉBAN, ALPHONSE. *France*. End sixteenth century; clockmaker to Henri IV; circ. striking table clock, Garnier collection.
GRÉBAUVAL, GAMALIEL. *Rouen*. Master 1608, master-1617; founder member of Rouen corporation.
GRÉBAUVAL, HIÉROSME (JÉRÔME). *Rouen*, 1614. Juré 1652–55; oval watches British Museum and Louvre; founder member of Rouen corporation.
GRÉBAUVAL, PIERRE. *Rouen*. 1617 master–1652; watch Louvre; founder member of Rouen corporation.
GREBAUVEL, HIÉROSME. *Lyons*. Oval watch, Soltykoff collection, about 1595.
GREBAUVAL, JÉRÔME. Watch, British Museum, about 1600.
GREBAUVAL, ROBERT. *Rouen*. Fine octagonal watch, G.M., about 1620.
GREBAY, PHILLIPE, à *Londres*. Watch, about 1610.
GREBAY, PHILLIPE. *Paris*. Alarm watch, V. & A., about 1670.
GREBLIN. See GRIBELIN.
GREBERT, PIERRE MARIE. *Paris*. Master 1787–1813; mantel clock, Château de la Malmaison.
GREEN, ABRAHAM. *London*. Watch, 1804.
GREEN, EDWARD. *London* (*Albemarle St.*), 1792–1800. C.C.
GREEN, EDWD. Apprenticed in 1682 to Thos. Davis, C.C.
GREEN, EDWD. *10 King's Stairs, Rotherhithe*. Watch for the Turkish market, Schloss collection, about 1790.
GREEN, FRANCIS. *London*. 1812 C.C.
GREEN, GEO. Apprenticed in 1661 to Matt. Crockford, C.C.
GREEN, GEO. *Leicester*, 1775.
GREEN, GEORGE SMITH, "an eccentric watchmaker of Oxford, with a turn for literature", died 1762.
GREEN, JAMES. *Morefields*. C.C. 1664; lantern clock with handsomely chased dial.
GREEN, JAMES. *5 Fenchurch St.* Calendar watch, pinchbeck, set with garnets; Ludlam, in 1755, refers to him as a watchmaker and seller of tools; master C.C. 1784; *8 Philpot Lane*, 1794.
GREEN, JAMES. *London*. Apprenticed 1736, C.C. 1747, livery C.C. 1770–77. Also GREENE.
GREEN, JAMES. *Nantwich*, about 1760. died 1782; succeeded by his daughter; gold engraved watch Fränkel collection.
GREEN, JAMES. *Easingwold*, about 1770–90.
GREEN, JNO. *London*. Sheepshead lantern clock, about 1700.
GREEN, JNO. *St. Martin's Court*, 1750–70.

GREEN, JOHN. *Philadelphia*, 1794.

GREEN, JOHN. *Boston, U.S.A.*, 1796. Watch.

GREEN, JOSEPH. C.C. 1723; long-case clock signed 'Jos. Green, North Shields', about 1730. Bracket clock, about 1750.

GREEN, JOSEPH, tools. *129 Whitecross St.*, 1793.

GREEN, MARGARET. *St. Martin's Court, Leicester Sq.*, 1765–71.

GREEN, NAT. Apprenticed in 1688 to Dan Beckman, C.C.

GREEN, NATHANIEL. *London*. C.C. 1695. GREENE, Probably the preceding.

GREEN, PETER. *Liverpool*, about 1695.

GREEN, RICHD. *Richmond, Yorks*, 1760.

GREEN, ROBERT. *Edinburgh*, 1781–1834.

GREEN, ROBT. *Lancaster*, 1767, f.

GREEN, ROBT. *London*. Watch, 1798.

GREEN, SAMUEL. *112 Bunhill Row*, 1788–1800.

GREEN, SAMUEL. *Boston, U.S.A.*, 1820. Watch.

GREEN, SAMUEL. *London (St. James's St.; Bunhill Row in 1795)*. Apprenticed 1754, C.C. 1772, l.C.C. 1787–1817.

GREEN, THOMAS. *Liverpool*, 1781–1800.

GREEN, THOMAS. *Bristol*, 1781–1801. Watch. Of GREEN & BARRY.

GREEN, WILLIAM. *London*. C.C. 1815, l.C.C. 1824.

GREEN, WILLIAM. *London*. Apprenticed 1785, C.C. 1798.

GREEN & ALDRIDGE. *62 St. Martin's-le-Grand*, 1765–85; Henry Green, livery Clothworkers' Company.

GREEN & BARRY. *Bristol*, 1792–1813. Watch.

GREEN & BENTLEY. Makers of a very complicated long-case musical and astronomical clock, about 1790.

GREEN, WARD & GREEN. *1 Ludgate St.*, 1800; *20 Cockspur St., Pall Mall*, 1817–38.

GREEN & WARD. *1 Ludgate St.*, 1793.

GREENALL, WILLIAM. *Liverpool*, 1811–29.

GREENAWAY, GEO. *Bath*, 1798.

GREENAWAY, RICHARD. *Whitecross St.* C.C. 1718.

GREENAWAY, WM. *Cripplegate*. C.C. 1730.

GREENE, JAMES. Apprenticed to Henry Jones; C.C. 1685.

GREENE, JOHN. C.C. 1711.

GREENFIELD, WILLIAM RICHARD. *London*. Apprenticed 1807, C.C. 1814.

GREENHILL, NAT. Apprenticed in 1674 to Edwd. Clough, C.C.

GREENHILL, RICHARD. Freeman of the City of Canterbury by redemption, 1676; long-case clock.

GREENHILL, SAMUEL. *Canterbury*. Apprenticed to Richard, his father, 1707.

GREENSILL, EDWD. *34 Strand*, 1793.

GREENSILL, JOSEPH. *36 Strand*, 1775–1800.

GREENWAY, JOHN. *London*. Apprenticed 1753–62 C.C.

GREENWAY, JOSEPH. *London*. Apprenticed 1737, C.C. 1747–62.

GREENWAY, RICARD. *London*. Apprenticed 1736, C.C. 1745.

GREENWAY, RICHARD. *London*. Apprenticed 1705, C.C. 1718–27, died a. 1737.

GREENWAY, WILLIAM. *London*. Apprenticed 1732, C.C. 1748.

GREENWOOD, G. *12 Hanway St.*, 1817.

GREER, JOHN. *Carlisle, U.S.A.* Died 1774; clocks and watches.

GREGG, FRANCIS. Apprenticed to John Clowes, 1691; in the Wetherfield collection is a long-case clock with a remarkably fine dial having a revolving equation of time calendar showing through an aperture below the centre; above the centre is the inscription, 'Fran. Gregg, Covent Garden'. "Francis Gregg, watchmaker, is removed from the Dial in Russell Street, Covent Garden, to the Dial in St. James St. over against the Palace Gates" (*Lond. Gaz.*, October 11–23,

1714). In the G.M. is a repeating watch by him with silver cap, 1698–1715.

GREGG, RD. *London*, about 1730.

GREGG, WM. *London*. Watch, 1796.

GRÉGOIRE, P., à *Blois*. Striking watch about 1620.

GRÉGOIRE, JEAN. *Blois*, 1626. Died about 1664; watches British Museum and Gélis collection; travelling striking clocks, Petit Palais and Blot-Garnier collection; watch, engraved dial, Carnegie Museum.

GRÉGOIRE, JEAN, son. *Blois*, 1651. Died 1668.

GRÉGOIRE, LAURENT. *Grenoble*, 1573–1611.

GREGORY, JAMES. *London*. Apprenticed 1650, C.C. 1657.

GREGORY, JAS. *Ormskirk*. Watch, Debaufre escapement, Guildhall Museum, about 1765.

GREGORY, JEREMIE, at yᵉ *Royal Exchange*. Early oval watch by him, Stamford Institution; C.C. 1652, master 1665, 1676; died 1685; a good maker of lantern clocks and watches; in *Mercurius Publicus*, 7th May 1663, is advertised a gold watch lost. "Give notice to Mr. Gregory, watch maker, near the Castle Tavern in Cornhill." In the *Lond. Gaz.*, Oct. 13, 1678, he advertises for Nestor Holmes, aged 18, a runaway apprentice. "A silver watch with a String, made by Jeremiah Gregory, showing the days of the month, the Box engraven with the King's Picture in the bottom" (*Lond. Gaz.*, March 29, 1680). A lantern clock, inscribed 'Jeremie Gregorie at the Royal Exchange'.

GREGORY, JEREMIAH. C.C. 1694.

GREGORY, JNO. *Upton Magna*, 1760.

GREGORY, JOHN. *London (Houndsditch, Basinghall St.*, in 1779)*. Apprenticed 1764, C.C. 1771–76.

GREGORY, ROBERT. C.C. 1678.

GREGORY, THOMAS. *London*. C.C. 1673.

GREGORY, THOMAS. C.C. by redemption 1671.

GREGSBY, EDWD. Clock, 1685.

GREGSON, JNO. *Lancaster*, 1818.

GREGSON, JOHN. Watchmaker to the Prince of Wales, *36 Bruton St., Hanover Sq.*, 1794–1800.

GREGSON, PHILIP. Apprenticed in 1663 to Ahasuerus Fromanteel, junr., C.C.

GREGSON, PIERRE. *Paris*. Horloger du Roy; watch, case finely enamelled, medallion with figure painting in centre, surrounded by a border of royal blue, 1780–90; watch, about 1795, signed Gregson à Geneva.

GREGSON & JEFFERSON. *36 Bruton St.*, 1800–05.

GREIG, DAVID. *Perth*, 1810–37.

GREIG, JAMES. *Perth*. Apprenticed 1765–1800.

GREMONT (GREMOUD), MICHEL (or NICOLAS) ANTOINE. *Paris (Creteil)*. Master 1765–89.

GRÉMY, MICHEL, son. *Blois*. Master 1664–90.

GRENDON, HENRY, at yᵉ *Exchange*. Admitted C.C. 1640; watch, V. & A., about 1610; another watch inscribed 'Henry Grendon at Exchange, Fecit', not later than 1630, Pierpont Morgan collection.

GRENNELL, RICHARD. Maker of a fine long-case clock, about 1750.

GRESSE, PIERRE. *Geneva*, about 1770–91.

GRETTON, CHAS. *The Ship, Fleet St.* Apprenticed to Lionel Wythe in 1662; C.C. 1672–1733; master 1700; an eminent maker; to him was apprenticed in 1697 the celebrated Henry Sully; in the Wetherfield collection were a lantern clock, a bracket clock repeating the quarters on six bells, and three long-case clocks by Chas. Gretton. "Lost the 24th Instant, a Gold Pendulum watch in a gold Fillegreen case, with a plain shagreen case over it, the name Charles Gretton, London, with a round Pendulum Spring, a steel chain, and Tulip Pillars, the Dial Plate straight, and a small long Hand to show the Hour. Whoever gives notice of it to Mr. Charles Gretton, Watch Maker in Fleet Street, shall have two guineas reward" (*Lond. Gaz.*, March 2, 1683). "Lost or taken away the 13th Instant at night out of a Gentleman's Pocket, a gold watch, with a gold chain to it, the case studded with gold, of Mr. Gretton's making, watchmaker living in Fleet St. over against Sergeants Inn Gate. Whoever brings the aforesaid watch to Mr. Fowles, goldsmith, at the Black Lyon in Fleet Street, shall have five guineas reward" (*Lond. Gaz.*, Jan. 18, 1685-6). "Taken away the 2nd Instant at night by two Highwaymen, a large silver watch by Charles Gretton, London. If the said watch be offered to be sold, Pawned, &c., you are desired to stop the watch and Party, and give notice to Mr. Charles Gretton at the Ship in Fleet Street, and you shall have a guinea reward" (*Lond. Gaz.*, Sept. 20, 1697).

GRETTON, WILLIAM, of *Black Fryers*. Maker of a lantern clock, balance escapement, dolphin frets, about 1665.

GREVILLE, JNO. Apprenticed in 1675 to Jere. Gregory, C.C.

GREY, JOHN. *68 Leadenhall St.*, 1823-30.

GREY, JOSEPH. *Durham*, 1765.

GRIBELIN, ABRAHAM. *Blois*. In the British Museum is a watch by him, dated 1600; another, V. & A., 1614; afterwards at Paris; clockmaker to the King, 1631.

GRIBELIN, N. *Paris*. Watch by him, British Museum, case finely enamelled by Muisard, about 1700; late-seventeenth-century French watch, in brass case, signed 'Gribelin à Paris', V. & A.

GRIBELIN, NICHOLAS. *Paris*. Square watch, about 1600, Pierpont Morgan collection; very small oval watch in crystal case, with enamelled gold mounting, early seventeenth century.

GRIBELIN, SIMON. *Blois*, 1588. Master 1593-1633; table clock Gélis collection.

GRIBELIN, SIMON. C.C. 1686.

GRICE, JOB. *Lancaster*, 1797-1830.

GRICE, THOMAS. 1675.

GRICE, WM. Apprenticed in 1687 to Mordecai Fox, C.C.

GRIDIN (or GREDIN). *Paris*. Watch, Pierpont Morgan collection, about 1750.

GRIELL, SAM. Apprenticed in 1648 to Peter Bellune, C.C.

GRIFFEN, HENRY. *New York*, 1805. Watch.

GRIFFIN, FRANCIS. *25 Gloucester St., Clerkenwell*, 1820-42.

GRIFFIN, GEORGE. *London*. Apprenticed 1733, C.C. 1740-62.

GRIFFIN, GEORGE. *London*. C.C. 1769.

GRIFFIN, JOHN. *Noble St.* C.C. 1720.

GRIFFIN, JOHN. *London* (*Cripplegate*). Apprenticed 1713, C.C. 1720-34.

GRIFFIN & ADAMS. *76 Strand*, 1800-23.

GRIFFING, THOMAS. *London*. Apprenticed 1751, C.C. 1758.

GRIFFIS, PAUL. *Birmingham*. Watch, 1782.

GRIFFITH, EDWARD. *Charleston, U.S.A.*, 1796. Watch.

GRIFFITH, EDWARD. *London* (*Hatton Gdn.* and later *Holborn*). Apprenticed 1789, C.C. 1802, l.C.C. 1810-25.

GRIFFITH, JAS. C.C. 1667.

GRIFFITH, R. *Denbigh*. Watch, 1830.

GRIFFITH, RICHARD. *London*. Long-case clock, 1790.

GRIFFITH, ROBT. *London*. C.C. 1706; watch, 1725.

GRIFFITH, THOMAS or GEORGE. *London*. Apprenticed 1712, C.C. 1720.

GRIFFITH, WILLIAM. *London*. Apprenticed 1732, C.C. 1744.

GRIFFITH, WM. *Shoe Lane*. C.C. 1720.

GRIFFITHS, EDWARD. *River St., Islington*. Livery C.C. 1810.

GRIGG, JNO. Apprenticed in 1684 to Edwd. Hunt, C.C.

GRIGGS, RICHD. C.C. about 1660.

GRIGNION, DANIEL. *London*. Born 1684, died 1763; native of France; in England from 1688; his watch No. 396 was lost in 1726.

GRIGNION, DANIEL & THOMAS. Fine repeating watch with beautifully enamelled case, about 1730; another bears the hall mark for 1748; a clock is inscribed 'Dan. and Tho. Grignion from the late Mr. Quare'. 'Thos. and Danl. Grignion, finisher to the late Mr. Danl. Quare, at the King's Arms and Dial in Russel Street, Covent Garden'.

GRIGNION, PIERRE. *Paris*. Master 1770-89.

GRIGNION, THOMAS, son. *London*. Born 1713, died 1784; watch V. & A.; pair-case silver watch and cylinder repeating watch G.M.; improved the cylinder escapement.

GRIGNION, THOMAS. *7 Great Russell St., Covent Garden*. A watch by him with a *repoussé* case in V. & A.; small travelling clock dated 1780; died 1784, aged 71.

GRIGNION, THOS. *7 Great Russell St., Covent Garden* 1800-25.

GRIGNION & SON. *Russell St., Covent Garden*, 1775. Spring clock with peculiar dead-beat escapement, G.M.

GRILLIAT, —. In 1729 had a project for stamping dial-plates for watches, discouraged by C.C. as being detrimental to engravers.

GRIMADELL, —. *Holbeach*, 1760.

GRIMADELL, PETER. *Stamford*, 1770.

GRIMALDE, PETER. *431 Strand*. A celebrated chronometer maker, 1800-10.

GRIMALDE & JOHNSON. *431 Strand*, 1815-25. See ANTHONY, WM.

GRIMAR à *Ath*. Clock, about 1730.

GRIMES, EDWD. Apprenticed 1640 to Elias Allen, C.C.

GRIMES, THOMAS. C.C. 1671.

GRIMES, WILLIAM. C.C. 1682; long-case clock, Dutch marquetry, about 1700.

GRIMLEY, WILLIAM. C.C. 1694.

GRIMSHAW, JNO. *Liverpool*, 1814.

GRIMSTEAD, THOMAS. *St. Paul's Churchyard*, 1753-63.

GRINDLEY, WILLIAM. *32 Crown St., Moorfield*, 1820.

GRINDON, HENRY. *London*. 1633 C.C.

GRINDON, W. *7 Tabernacle Walk*, 1820-30.

GRINKIN, EDMUND. *The Hague*, 1650-80. Silver watch with gold engraved decoration Mallett collection.

GRINKIN, EDWD. Petition C.C. 1656.

GRINKIN, ROBERT. C.C. 1632, master 1648, 1654; died 1660.

GRITTING, JNO. *London*. Long-case clock, about 1750.

GRIVET, JEAN PIERRE. *Geneva*, about 1770-91.

GRIZELL, JOHN. C.C. 1687.

GRO, WM. *Rotterdam*. Watch, about 1770.

GROCOT, THOS. *Liverpool*. A watch by him with Manx crest on cock, 1780.

GROLLIER DE SERVIÈRE, NICHOLAS. Born at Lyons in 1593; maker of many curious clocks and automata; died, aged 93.

GRÖNSTRAND, ANDERS. *Stockholm*. Comp. 1751-73.

GROS, P. *Paris*, 1780.

GROSE, ANTHONY. C.C. 1658.

GROSE, RICHARD. C.C. 1632.

GROSS, PHILIP. *12 Panton St.*, 1817.

GROSSER, FR. ADAM. *Fürth*. Died 1803.

GROSSER, JOH. JACOB. *Augsburg*, about 1750 comp.-1764; went *Fürth* 1768; died 1829.

GROSSOEUVRE, GASPARD. *Rouen*, 1558-77.

GROSVENOR & JONES. *85 Wardour St.*, 1815.

GROTZ, ISAAC. *Easton, U.S.A.*, 1810–35.

GROUNDS, JONATHAN. *London.* Watch, about 1690.

GROUNET, S. *Amiens*, 1650.

GROUT, WILLIAM. C.C. 1660.

GROVE, GEORGE. *95 Wood St., Cheapside.* C.C. 1715.

GROVE, GEORGE. *London (Bishopsgate St.).* C.C. 1787–91.

GROVE, GEORGE. *London (Wood St.)*, 1809. l.C.C. 1812, died 1814.

GROVE, JOHN. *London (Shoreditch).* C.C. 1766, died 1802.

GROVE, RICHARD. *93 Wood St.* Livery C.C. 1786; 1770–1817.

GROVE, THOMAS. C.C. 1715.

GROVE, W. R. Partner with Myles Brockbank; C.C. 1811–15.

GROVE, WILLIAM. *London.* C.C. 1802.

GROVE, WM. Watch, 1781.

GROVER & Co. *10 Greek St.*, 1817.

GROVES, GEORGE. *105 Bishopsgate St.*, 1790–95.

GROVES, THOMAS. *Birmingham*, 1770–97.

GRUBER, HANS. *Nuremberg.* Clockmaker and master of the Locksmiths' Guild in 1552; died 1597.

GRUBER, MICHEL. *Nuremberg*, 1600.

GRUET, A. A Swiss, reputed inventor of fusee chain, 1664, but earlier examples exist.

GRUNDEL, PETER. *Stockholm*, 1586–94. Apprenticed in *Hamburg*, then *Nürnberg*; came *Sweden* 1586; court clock.

GRUNDLER, JOHANN NEPOMUK. *Augsburg.* Master 1757, died 1790.

GRUNDSTRÖM, JOHAN GUSTAF. *Stockholm*, 1820–46.

GRUNDY, J. *Whalley*, 1760.

GRUSELL, MATHIAS. *Lögdö* and *Lagfors.* Born 1730, died 1792.

GRUSELL, MATS MATSSON. *Stjärnsund.* Born 1679, died 1766.

GUARDSELL, —. *London.* Long-case clock, about 1770.

GUAY. See LE GUAY.

GUDGEON, JNO. *Bury.* Watch, 1794.

GUENOUX. *Paris*, 1764–89. Bracket clock.

GUDIN, JACQUES JÉRÔME. *Quai des Orfévres, Paris*, 1769 Clock by him at Windsor Castle, about 1770.

GUEPIN, JNO. Apprenticed 1687 to David Minuel, C.C.; bracket chiming clock inscribed 'Peter Guepin', about 1750.

GUERIMAN, G. *London.* Watch, about 1720.

GUERINT, SÉBASTIEN FRANÇOIS. *Geneva* and *London.* Born 1791, died 1870; invention of engine-turning wrongly attributed to him; engine-turning was practised in 1670, though not on watches.

GUÉRLIN, JEAN PAUL. *Berlin.* Early nineteenth century; a clever maker specializing in very thin cylinder watches.

GUEST, GEO. *Aston*, 1760.

GUEST, GEORGIUS. 30-hour long-case clock, about 1690.

GUEST, JNO. *64 Fleet Market*, 1816.

GUEX. *Paris.* Watch, 1790.

GUIBET L'AÎNÉ à *Paris.* Clock, Jones collection, V. & A., about 1790.

GUIDON & Co. *Paris*, 1795.

GUIGNARD, JACQUES. *Blois.* Apprenticed 1635, master 1643–56.

GUIGUER, —. *Amsterdam.* Mid-eighteenth century; watch Denham collection.

GUIGUER, ANTHONY. *London.* C.C. 1687; 8-day watch.

GUILE, JOHN. *Philadelphia*, 1819–24.

GUILLEMOT, —. *London*, about 1810.

GUILLIN *la Charité.* Watch, about 1690.

GUILLIN (GUILIN, GWILLIN), ELY. *London.* C.C. 1647.

GUILLON, ANTOINE. *Nantes*, 1621. Died 1649.

GUILMETIN, —. *Paris*, 1867. Invented clocks which swung and acted as their own pendulums.

GUINAND, GUILLAUME. *Lyons*, 1670–86.

GUINAND, PIERRE. *Fontaines*, 1787–1802. Very able clockmaker.

GUISE, SAMUEL. *London (Wapping).* Apprenticed 1791, C.C. 1799–1807.

GUISE, THOMAS. *London.* Apprenticed 1807, l.C.C. 1815.

GULLIFORD, JOHN. *Bristol*, 1740.

GULLOCK, PHILIP. *31 Minories*, 1790–95.

GUNARD-DIT-VENDÔME, MICHEL. *Rouen.* 1720–62 from *Alisay.* Repaired town clock and clock of St. Laurent.

GUNSTON, JOHN. *London.* Bracket clock, about 1750.

GUNTER, HILDESLEY. Apprenticed in 1693 to Jno. Eagle, C.C.

GUNTER, R. *Queen St., May Fair*, 1790–95.

GURDEN, BENJ. 1794.

GURDEN, BENJAMIN & SON. *144 Wood St.*, 1775.

GURNEY, EZEKIAL. Apprenticed in 1692 to Edwd. Speakman, C.C.

GUSTERMANN, MARTIN. *Linz, Austria*, about 1685.

GUT, CHRISTIAN. *Augsburg.* Master 1727, juré 1742.

GUTCH, JOHN. C.C. 1673.

GUTHERIDGE, WILLIAM. C.C. 1728.

GUTHRIE, N. *Glasgow.* Clock, about 1770.

GUTKAES, JOHN CHRIST. FRIED. *Dresden.* Master 1815, died 1845; court clock, 1842; pocket chronometer, Fränkel collection.

GUTTIERRE, MANUEL. *Siguenza*, 1711.

GUTTRIDGE, JOSEPH. *London.* Apprenticed 1761, C.C. 1768.

GUY, CHARLES. C.C. 1714.

GUY, HENRY. *London.* Apprenticed 1695, C.C. 1702–41.

GUY, HENRY, son of Henry. *London.* Apprenticed 1722, 1736.

GUY, JAMES. *London (Bloomsbury).* C.C. 1778–1830.

GUY, JNO. *Liverpool*, 1770.

GUY, SAMUEL. Apprenticed in 1692 to Jno. Andrews, C.C.; fine long-case clock, decorated with Oriental lacquer work, about 1730; another clock by him belongs now to Mr. Wm. Craig, Detroit, U.S.A.

GUYDAMONS à *Paris.* Clock, about 1750.

GUYE, ABRAM. *Côte aux Feés*, 1710.

GUYE, DAVID, son. *Môtiers*, 1731–62. Clock.

GUYE, DAVID HENRI, son. *Verrières*, 1755–66. Watches and clocks.

GUYE, JEAN PIERRE, brother. *Verrières*, 1755–75. Clockmaker of repute.

GUYE, PIERRE. *Fleurier*, 1691–1765.

GUYE, PIERRE, son of Pierre. *Verrières*, 1711. Died 1743.

GUYERD, —. *Paris.* Watch, 1812.

GWILLIM, ELI. Brother C.C. 1647.

GWINNELL, J. *34 London Rd.*, 1812–15.

GYOTT, ABRAHAM. C.C. 1648.

GYOTT, ABRAHAM. Apprenticed in 1648 to Abraham Gyott, C.C.

GYBERG, JON. *Kristianstad.* Born 1760, died 1809.

GYBERG, LARS. *Åmål.* Born 1768, died 1846.

GYBERG, PEHR. *Lund.* Born 1756, died 1818.

GUYENET, DAVID HENRI. *Couvet*, 1745–77. Clock.

HAACK, ERNST DAVID FRIEDRICH. *Berlin*, 1785–1840. Clock.

HAAKMA, SICCO. *Leeuwarden*, 1765–80. Long-case clock.

HAAKMA, SIKKE ARENTS. *Leeuwarden*, 1732–60. Town clock.

HAAS, DAVID SIGMUND. *Augsburg.* Born 1685, died 1742; famous maker; clock presented by Maria Theresa to Prince Josias zu Coburg-Saalfeld, Gotha Museum.

HABEL. Watch, gold case in the form of a mandoline, enamelled white and blue, signed 'Joh. George. Habel à Güngs', about 1790; Pierpont Morgan collection.

HÄBERL, JOHANN PAULUS. *Augsburg.* Master about 1770, juré 1776–95. ½¼ repeating watch.

HABERT, DAVID. *Strand.* C.C. 1730.

HABERT, JAMES. C.C. 1682.

HABRECHT. In 1571 the mechanical construction of the Strassburg clock was entrusted to ISAAC HABRECHT, a clockmaker of *Schaffhausen, Switzerland*, and his younger brother JOSIAS; before this work was begun Josias migrated to Cologne, having been summoned by the Elector to make a clock for the castle of Kayserswerth. He died in 1620, aged 78.

HABRECHT, ABRAHAM (1), son of Isaac. *Strasbourg.* Born 1578, died about 1636.

HABRECHT, ABRAHAM (2), son of Isaac (1). *Strasbourg* and *Ratisbonne.* Born 1608, died 1686; maker of a musical and automatic clock in the Hotel de Ville, Ratisbonne, illuminated 'Les Habrecht', and a clock on the Brücktor.

HABRECHT, ABRAHAM (3), son of Isaac (3). *Strasbourg.* Born 1654, died 1728; very fine table clock, Strasbourg Museum, illuminated 'Les Habrecht'.

HABRECHT, ABRAHAM (4), son of Abraham (3). *Strasbourg.* Born 1693, died 1732.

HABRECHT, DANIEL (2), brother. *Strasbourg.* Born 1616, died 1684; tulip and skull watches, illuminated 'Les Habrecht'; silver skull watch Feill collection; stand clock.

HABRECHT, DANIEL (3), son of Daniel (2). *Strasbourg.* Born 1651, died about 1695; table clock Stuttgart Museum, illuminated 'Les Habrecht'.

HABRECHT, HANS, son. *Zürich.* Born 1540, died about 1594; clockmaker to the town.

HABRECHT, ISAAC (3), brother. *Strasbourg.* Born 1611, died 1686; 'Münster-Uhrmacher'; crucifix clock Strasbourg Museum, two madonna clocks, one in National Museum, Munich, and a hanging clock, all illuminated 'Les Habrecht'.

HABRECHT, ISAAC (4), son of Abraham (2). *Ratisbonne.* Born 1641, died 1667; turret clock.

HABRECHT, JOHANNES, son of Abraham (2). *Ratisbonne.* Born 1655, died 1701.

HABRECHT, MICHAEL ISAAC HABRECHT restored the Strassburg clock in 1669, and JACQUES S. made a further restoration in 1732. Skull watch by DANIEL HABRECHT, about 1630.

HACK, GRACE. Apprenticed in 1692 to Jas. Jenkins, C.C.

HACKETT, SIMON. *Royal Exchange.* C.C. 1632; master 1646–60, watch with movement 1 in. diameter. Case ornamented in high relief, and enclosed in an outer case of shagreen; movement exceedingly rough, and on the top plate, partly hidden by the balance-cock, an inscription, 'Simon Hackett, of the Royall Exchannge, fecit'; in the V. & A. are an alarum watch by him, in a pierced and engraved silver case, and one in an enamelled case; watch, about 1635, in enamelled case, Pierpont Morgan collection.

HACKINGS, JOHN. Successor to Henry Haines. Ludlam in 1759 wrote, "has worked for me constantly since midsummer, 1753; all my best tools were made by him; whatever has been done by him may be depended on."

HACKNEY, THOS. *London.* Chime clock, 8 bells, about 1740.

HADDACK, WM. *14 New Bridge St., Bath*, 1798–1800.

HADEN, THOS. Clock, about 1720.

HADLEY, HUMFREY. Received in 1708 £16 from the churchwardens of Aston, near Birmingham, for a new clock.

HADWEN, —. *Kendal.* Clock, about 1710.

HADWEN, ISAAC. *Liverpool*, 1754–81. Long-case clock.

HAEHNEL, C. H. *London.* Repeating watch, decorated with portraits of Joseph II and his family; Pierpont Morgan collection, about 1780; there is no hall mark in the case.

HAEHNEL, CHR. HEINRICH, son. *Fürth.* Born 1695, died 1754; bracket clock with cycloidal cheeks.

HAGELTHORN, J. P. *Ängelholm.* Born 1798, died 1852.

HAGEMANN, GOTTLIEB. *Schwerin.* Born 1792, died 1894.

HAGER, JOHAN GEORG. *Neüs.* Clock-watch, about 1725.

HAGER, WOLFGANG. *Wolfenbüttel.* Born 1643, died 1705; court mechanician and clockmaker; large watch.

HAGER & WOLFFENBUTEL. Watch by them, about 1730, mentioned by Thiout.

HAGGER, JAMES. *Grove Hall Lane.* Square bracket clock, Japanese case, cherub corners to dial, pull repeater, style about 1700.

HAGUE, JAS. *London.* Watch, 1760.

HAHN, ANDREAS, LEONHARD. *Nürnberg*, 1790–1810; watch Stuttgart Museum.

HAHN, CHRISTIAN, GOTTFRIED, brother. Born 1769; *Stuttgart* to 1795, later *Berlin*, and in 1798 *Philadelphia*; court mechanician in *Berlin*; watch Stuttgart Museum.

HAHN, CHRISTOPH MATTHÄUS, son of P. M. Born 1676, died 1833; *Echterdingen* and *Stuttgart*; court mechanician at Stuttgart 1790; watches and astronomical clocks; fine silver calendar watch.

HAHN, E. S. GOTTFRIED. *Echterdingn.* 1749–1801; assistant to P. M. Hahn.

HAHN, GEBRÜDER (CHRISTOPH and CHRISTIAN; also J. GEORG and CHRISTIAN). *Stuttgart*, 1791; watches.

HAHN, GEORG DAVID POLYKARP. *Kornwestheim.* Born 1747, died 1814; assistant to P. M. Hahn; night-light clock dated 1776.

HAHN, GOTTLIEB, brother. *Echterdingen*, about 1780; assistant to his father, P. M.

HAHN, JOHANN GEORG, brother. *Stuttgart.* Born about 1770, died 1813; court mechanician about 1806.

HAHN, MATHIAS. *Stuttgart.* Designer of clocks; born 1739.

HAILES, SAMUEL. *London.* Apprenticed 1730.

HAILES, THOMAS. *London (Huggin La.).* Apprenticed 1769, C.C. 1778.

HAINES, FRANCIS. Admitted C.C. 1706.

HAINES, HY. "an excellent workman"; worked for Ludlam from 1747 to 1753, when he was succeeded by John Hackings.

HAINES, JAMES. *London (Hackney Rd.).* Apprenticed 1780, C.C. 1793–1808.

HAINES, ROBERT. *Oxford*, 1775.

HAINKS, JOHN. *London.* Apprenticed 1728, C.C. 1750–64.

HAIRL, JNO. *Horselydown*, 1817.

HALAICHER, MATHIAS. *Augsburg.* Watch, about 1650.

HALE. *81 Cheapside*, 1800–05.

HALE, JAMES, son. *London.* Apprenticed 1816, C.C. 1834.

HALE, THOMAS. *London (Old St.).* Apprenticed 1798, C.C. 1815.

HALE, WILLIAM. *London.* C.C. 1769.

HALEY, SAM. Apprenticed in 1657 to Jno. Hillersden, C.C.

HALEY, THOS. *Norwich*, 1750; London, 1781.

HALEY, CHARLES. *7 Wigmore St.* A celebrated maker, hon. freeman C.C. 1781; patentee of a remontoire escapement for chronometers 1796 (No. 2,132). He was one of the experts appointed by the select committee of the House of Commons to report on Mudge's chronometers in 1793; 1770–1800.

HALEY & MILNER. *7 Wigmore St.*, 1800–15.

HALFORD, ROBT. *3 Old Orchard St., St. Luke's*, 1823.

HALIFAX, JOHN. *London*, 1759. Watch inscribed 'G. Washington to Gilbert Mortier de Lafayette, Lord Cornwallis's Capitulation, Yorktown, December 17th, 1781'.

HALIFAX, SAM. JOSEPH. *London*. Watch, silver cock and name-plate, 1775; watch, 'Halifax London', Fitz-william Museum, Cambridge.

HALKED, THOMAS. C.C. 1702.

HALKSWORTH, WILLIAM. *58 Fleet St.*, 1840–42.

HALL, ASA. *Boston, U.S.A.*, 1806. Watch.

HALL, CHARLES. *162 Fleet St.*, 1817; *118 Chancery Lane*, 1820.

HALL, CHRISTIAN. *Lititz, Lancaster, U.S.A.* Born 1775, died 1848; German; Long-case clocks.

HALL, CHRISTOPHER. Apprenticed in 1646 to Simon Bartram; C.C. 1655.

HALL, EDWD. C.C. 1710.

HALL, GEORGE. *London*. Apprenticed 1702, C.C. 1710.

HALL, JAMES, from *Westminster*, settled in Philadelphia about 1768.

HALL, JNO. BAPTIST. Apprenticed in 1669 to Edward Clough, C.C.; long-case clock, square dial, inscribed 'John Hall, London', about 1700.

HALL, JNO. *Beverley*, 1770.

HALL, JOHN. *Philadelphia*, 1802–25.

HALL, JOSEPH. *Birmingham*, 1781–1806. Clocks and watches.

HALL, JOSEPH. Apprenticed in 1684 to Edwd. Norris, C.C.; a lantern clock, inscribed 'Jos. Hall, London', dating from about 1700.

HALL, MARTIN. *Yarmouth*, 1780.

HALL, NATHANIEL. *London (Bishopsgate St.).* Apprenticed 1784; C.C. 1792–1811.

HALL, PETER. C.C. 1648.

HALL, RALPH. C.C. 1683.

HALL, THOS. Apprenticed in 1675 to Geo. Hambleton, C.C.; timepiece, 'Thos. Hall, London', about 1700.

HALL, THOS. *Rumsey*, 1760.

HALL, THOS. *Runcorn*. Watch, 1763.

HALL, WM. Apprenticed in 1680 to Cornelius Herbert, C.C.; long-case clock, about 1720, inscribed 'Wm. Hall, Woodborrow'.

HALL, WM. *39 Gee St.*, 1814–19.

HALL, WM. *93 High St., Marylebone*, 1815–19.

HALLEICHER (HALEICHER, HALAICHER), HANS OTTO, (JOHANN OTH). *Augsburg*, about 1670. Crystal cross watch Spitzer collection; automatic table clock British Museum; automatic clock Gotha Museum; clock worked by rolling sphere, M.P.S. Dresden; hexagonal table clock Ilbert collection.

HALLEWAY, —. *London*. Clock-watch, about 1685.

HALLEY, WM. Apprenticed in 1663 to Thos. Battin, C.C.

HALLIER, —. *London*, about 1800.

HALLIFAX, JOHN. *London (Old Bailey)*, 1730–55. Long-case and bracket clocks; musical striking and chiming bracket clock, illustrated Cec. & Web; watch.

HALLIFAX, JOHN. *Fleet St.* Maker of chime clocks; his bankruptcy noted *Lond. Gaz.*, June 14–17, 1740; a fine musical clock with automatic figures.

HALLIFAX, JOHN. *Barnsley*. On his tombstone in St. Mary's Churchyard, Barnsley, is the following: "In memory of Mr. John Halifax of this town, whose abilities and virtue few in these times have attained. His art and industry were such that his numerous inventions will be a lasting monument of his merit. He departed this life Sept. 25, 1750." A fine long-case

by him is at Wentworth House, the seat of Earl Fitz-william. His second son, Thomas, came to London, and carried on business as a goldsmith, became a partner in the bank of Glyn & Hallifax (afterwards Glyn, Mills & Co.), was Lord Mayor of London in 1776, knighted in 1778, sat in Parliament as member for Aylesbury in 1784, and died in 1789.

HALLIWELL, JOHN. *Warrington*, 1790–1820. Clock.

HALLIWELL, WM. *Chorley*, 1765; *York*, 1814.

HALLOWAY, WM. *Blackburn*, 1776.

HALLOWS, JONATHAN. *Liverpool*, 1818.

HALLSMAN, WM. *London*. Watch, 1790.

HALSALL, EDWARD. *Bristol*, 1825–30. Chronometers, watches and clocks.

HALLUS, *alias* LINUS FRANCISCUS. Author of *Explicatio Horlogii in Horto Regis. London*, a. 1659.

HALLY, THOS. *London*. Bracket clock, about 1660. Watch, 1675.

HALSEY, GEO. C.C. 1687.

HALSEY, JNO. *Norwich*, 1725.

HALSEY, JOHN. *London*. Apprenticed 1733, C.C. 1766.

HALSTEAD, CHARLES. C.C. 1677.

HALSTEAD, GEORGE, brother. *London*. C.C. 1710.

HALSTEAD, JOHN. C.C. 1698; long-case clock, arabesque marquetry.

HALSTEAD, MAUD. *London*. C.C. 1786.

HALSTEAD, RICHARD. C.C. 1669.

HALSTEAD, WILLIAM. C.C. 1715.

HALSTED, ROBERT. *Fleet St.* Bad watch movement seized by C.C. 1662; admitted C.C. 1668; master 1699.

HAM, JNO. Apprenticed in 1673 to Geo. Stevens, C.C.

HAM, JOHN. *47 Skinner St., Snow Hill*, 1820; *126 Newgate St.*, 1835–42. Livery C.C., 1821.

HAMBLETON, GEORGE. C.C. 1669.

HAMDEN, JNO. Apprenticed in 1638 to Jno. Charlton, C.C.

HAMEL, CLÉMENT. *Rouen*, 1596–1617. Founder member of Rouen corporation.

HAMERSLEY, WILLIAM. *London*. Apprenticed 1805, C.C. 1813.

HAMERTON, CHARLES. *London*. Apprenticed 1761, C.C. 1768.

HAMES, JNO. *9 Chandos St.*, 1835.

HAMILTON, GEO. Apprenticed in 1690 to Nathaniel Delander, C.C.

HAMILTON, JAS. *London*. Watch, 1800.

HAMILTON, JOHN. *Glasgow*. Bracket clock, about 1780.

HAMILTON, RICHARD. C.C. 1712.

HAMILTON, ROBERT. *London*. Apprenticed 1768, C.C. 1775.

HAMILTON, THE REV. DR. ROBERT. *London*. C.C. 1786, master C.C. 1792–1825.

HAMLEN, GEORGE. *Augusta, Me.*, 1795–1820.

HAMLET, THOS. *1 and 2 Prince's St., Soho*. In partnership with Francis Lambert, 1800; subsequently carried on business by himself; maker of a gold horizontal watch for the Duke of Sussex; 1795–1832.

HAMLEY. *Newcastle St., Strand*. Bracket clocks, about 1790.

HAMLEY, J. O., *1 Warwick Place, Bedford Row*, 1800–10; *24 Red Lion St., Holborn*, 1816–40.

HAMLEY, J. O., & SON. *284 Holborn*, 1810–16.

HAMLEY, O. JAS. *23 Duke St., St. James's Sq.*, 1815–18.

HAMLIN, RICHARD. *London*. Bad watch of his seized by C.C. 1676.

HAMLYN, THOS. Apprenticed in 1638 to J. Bisse, C.C.

HAMMERS, JNO. *London*. Long-case clock, about 1715.

HAMMOND, ANTHONY. Apprenticed in 1681 to Jno. North, C.C.

HAMMOND, HY. C.C. 1680.

HAMMOND, THOS. C. *York*, f., 1825.

HAMMOND & Co. *45 St. Martin's-le-Grand*, 1768.

HAMNSTEDT, P. *Stockholm*. Born 1767, died 1805.

HAMPSON. *Warrington*. Lantern clock, about 1700; long-case clock, 'Robert Hampson, Warrington', about 1730. *Wrexham*. Long-case clock, about 1720.

HAMPSON, ROBERT. *Manchester*, 1823–30.

HAMPSON, THOMAS. *Wrexham*, 1728. Died 1755; clocks.

HAMPSON & THELWALL. *Manchester*, 1812–23.

HAMPTON, EDWARD. *London*, about 1680. Watch, Mallett collection, illustrated Baillie.

HAMPTON, JOSEPH. Long-case clock, about 1700.

HAMPTON, RD. *London*. Watch, 1782.

HANBURY, JNO. Apprenticed 1664 to Hy. Jones, C.C.

HANCOCK, ANTHONY. *Otley*, 1822.

HANCOCK, EDWARD. *London*, about 1680. Watch, Mallett collection, illustrated Baillie.

HANCOCK, J. *Yeovil*. Long-case clock, about 1800.

HANCOCK, JEREMIAH. *Gloucester*, 1769–95. Watch.

HANCORNE, JAS. Apprenticed in 1675 to Philip Buckner, C.C.

HANCORNE, THOMAS. C.C. 1658; elected warden, 1683, but excused on paying a fine.

HANCORNE, WILLIAM. C.C. 1676.

HANDCOCK, —. *Yeovil*, 1773.

HANDE, THOMAS. In the British Museum is an oval tulip-shaped watch by Thos. Hande, about 1700.

HANDISIDE, GEO. *London*. Repeating bracket clock, about 1720.

HANDLEY (& MOORE, apprentices of Jno. Thwaites, *39 Clerkenwell Close*, 1798; a specimen of their work British Museum; G. Handley died 1824). See MOORE, JNO. & SONS.

HANDLEY, JNO. *Runcorn*, 1833.

HANDS, TIM. *London*. Watch, Guildhall Museum, about 1750; another, 1765.

HANDSCOMB, E. *Woburn*, 1780–90.

HANET, JOHN & GEORGE. *Porter St., Leicester Fields*, 1768; a specimen of their work British Museum.

HANET, N. *Paris*, 1680. Silver watch Horstmann collection; silver watch Gélis collection, mark of 1672–80, with balance spring.

HANET, NICHOLAS. *The Hague* and *Paris*. Clock the Louvre second half eighteenth century.

HANET, S. *London*. Long-case clock, about 1725.

HANKINS, JOHN. *Clapton*. a. 1774–about 1800; watch.

HANKS, BENJAMIN. *Litchfield, Conn., U.S.A.*, patentee of self-winding clock with air vanes, 1783.

HANNE. See MARCH.

HANNET, SAMUEL STEPHEN. *London*. Long-case clocks, about 1780.

HANNINGTON, WM. *London*. Watch, 1800.

HANRIOT, —. *Paris* and *Mâcon*, 1816–36. Award from Soc. Arts for an escapement.

HANSARD, WILLIAM. Watch-spring maker, *6 King's Head Court, Holborn*, 1790.

HANSEL, JAMES. *Philadelphia*, 1819–25.

HANSLAPP, ROBERT. Apprenticed to Edward East; C.C. 1653.

HANSLAPP, WILLIAM. C.C. 1603.

HANSON, GEO. Apprenticed in 1688 to Jno. Clowes, C.C.

HANSON, GEORGE. *Windsor*. Watch, 1791.

HANSON, WM. *Windsor*, 1820.

HANSSON, JEPPE. *Stockholm*. Comp. 1770. *Laholm*, 1778. Died a. 1785.

HANUSH, —. Maker of a clock for Prague Town Hall, about 1497.

HANWELL, ZACHARIAH. C.C. 1694; fine marquetry long-case clock, straight pillars, square dial, cherub corners, 'Z. Hanwell, Londini', on circle.

HAPPACK, —. *London*. Repeating watch, about 1760.

HARBEN, THOS. *Lewes*, 1740–70. Long-case clock, inscribed 'In the Cliff, Lewis'. One-hand clock of rather earlier date.

HARBERT. See HERBERT.

HARBOTTLE, CORNELIUS. C.C. 1667.

HARBUD, JAMES. *London (Cow Cross)*. Apprenticed 1756, C.C. 1767–1805.

HARBUD, JEREMIAH. Watch-movement maker, *2 Green Terrace*, 1810–38; livery C.C. 1812.

HARCOURTE, —. Maker or repairer of clocks, near Westminster Abbey, 1469.

HARDE, NICOLAS. *Paris*, 1674 juré.

HARDEL, LOUIS MICHEL. *Paris*. Master 1753, juré 1769–86.

HARDEMAN, SAMUEL. *Bridge and Canterbury*. In partnership with Wm. Nash 1762–94 and then alone; watch.

HARDEN, CHAS. *120 Fleet St.*, 1816–25.

HARDIE & CHRISTIE. *Manchester*, 1818.

HARDIN, JOS. *St. John's Lane*, 1730, afterwards at *Old Jewry*. Livery C.C. 1766.

HARDING, FRANCIS. C.C. 1687; clock, about 1700, inscribed 'Francis Harding, Portsmouth'.

HARDING, JNO. *Portsmouth*, 1780. Long-case clock with rotating hour dial.

HARDING, JNO. *Abingdon*. Watch, 1782.

HARDING, JOHN. C.C. 1685.

HARDING, JOHN. C.C. 1721.

HARDING, ROBERT. *London*, 1753.

HARDING, SAM. *131 Oxford St.*, 1816–23.

HARDING, THOMAS & CO. *43 Minories*, 1760–1800.

HARDING, WM. *London*. Watch for the Dutch market, finely embossed outer case, 1769.

HARDING & CO. *26 Great Winchester St.*, 1817.

HARDMAN, JACOB. *London*. Apprenticed 1714, C.C. 1720–45. Also HEARDMAN.

HARDMAN, JOHN GERARD. *Liverpool*, 1748–73. Watch.

HARDSTAFF, ZACH. Apprenticed in 1655 to Jno. Samon, C.C.

HARDWIDGE, WM. *52 Wapping*, 1823.

HARDY, EDWD. *Hull*, 1770.

HARDY, FRANÇOIS EDME. *Paris*. Master 1743–89.

HARDY, HORACE, brother. *London*. C.C. 1774–1805.

HARDY, JNO. *Morpeth*, 1775.

HARDY, JOHN. *Smithfield*, 1730, afterwards *8 Bridgewater Sq.* Livery C.C. 1766.

HARDY, JOHN. *Preston*, 1802–21. Clocks and watches.

HARDY, JONATHAN, son of John. *London*. Apprenticed 1766, C.C. 1774.

HARDY, JOSEPH. *26 Clement's Lane, Lombard St.*, 1800.

HARDY, RICHD. *Newark*, 1805.

HARDY, ROBT. C.C. 1776; watch G.M., h.m., 1803.

HARDY, ROBERT. *London*. C.C. 1802.

HARDY, SAMUEL, son of John. *London (Somerset St., Aldgate)*. C.C. 1778–1805.

HARDY, THOMAS. *London (Rosamonds Row)*. Apprenticed 1760, C.C. 1767–89; watch New York University.

HARDY, THOMAS. Watch-case maker, *14 Rosoman St., Clerkenwell*, 1780–1820.

HARDY, THOS., & SON. *Newark*, 1840.

HARDY, WILLIAM. *28 Coppice Row, Coldbath Sq., Clerkenwell*. A chronometer and clock maker of repute; he devised a compensation balance and an escapement for clocks for which he in 1820 received from the Society of Arts the gold medal and fifty guineas, 1800–30.

HARDY, WILLIAM. *Charleston, U.S.A.,* 1773. From *London.* Clocks and watches.

HARDY, WILLIAM. *London.* l.C.C. 1796.

HARE, ALEXANDER. *17 Grenville St., Hatton Garden.* Hon. freeman C.C. 1781; maker of a finely enamelled watch, h.m., 1782; a verge metal watch by him in the Guildhall Museum; 1770–1815.

HAREL. *Paris,* 1811–25. Lyre-shaped clock.

HARFORD. Lantern clock inscribed 'John Harford in Bath, 1658'.

HARFORD, —. *South Parade, Bath,* 1770.

HARGRAVES (or HARGREAVES), THOMAS. *Settle,* 1770.

HARGRAVES (or HARGREAVES), WM. *Settle,* 1710–30.

HARGROVES, WM. Apprenticed 1688 to Isaac Carver, C.C.

HARIMAN (HARRIMAN, HARRYMAN), JOHN. *Workington.* About 1770–1811; Long-case clock; watch.

HARLAND, HY. Apprenticed in 1647 to W. Godbed and put to Peter de Laundre; C.C. 1654.

HARLAND, T. *Norwich, Conn., U.S.A.,* 1750–90?; to him was apprenticed Ely Terry in 1786.

HARLAND, THOMAS. *New York,* 1805.

HARLEY, WM. *Salop.* Fine clock, 1760. Reid mentions Harley, of London, maker of ruby cylinders, about 1785, working with Mallet, a watch jeweller there.

HARLOCK, JAMES. *7 Horseferry Rd., Westminster,* 1842.

HARLOW, SAMUEL. *Ashbourne, Derby,* in 1789 patented (No. 1,708) the Breguet or tipsy watch-key, in which the upper and lower portions are connected by means of a ratchet clutch kept in gear by a spring, so that the upper part will turn the lower part in the proper direction for winding, but if the upper part is turned in the opposite direction, the ratchet clutch slips without moving or straining the lower part of the key. In 1813 he published *The Clockmakers' Guide to Practical Clockwork.* He there described himself as clockmaker and brassfounder, Summer Hill, Birmingham, but mentions that his book may be obtained at his house in *Ashbourne* and also of Walker & Sons, *49 Red Lion St., Clerkenwell.*

HARMAN, GEORGE. *High Wycombe.* Maker of the chimes of Cripplegate Church, 1792.

HARMAN, JNO. Apprenticed in 1681 to Thos. Jenkins, C.C.; lantern clock, 'Jno. Harman, Horsham', Mr. J. H. Mercer.

HARMAN, JOHN. 'Watchmaker and astrologer', of *Bloomsbury,* 1753.

HARMAR, JAS. *London.* Watch, 1690.

HARMER, JASPAR. Near *Smithfield Bars.* Cited by C.C. for exercising the art of clockmaker without having served seven years, 1685.

HARMWOOD, JOHN. *London.* Apprenticed 1731, C.C. 1739.

HARNS, GEO. *Old Jewry,* 1808–10.

HAROLD, RICHARD. C.C. 1690.

HARPER, HENRY. *Cornhill.* Apprenticed 1657 to Humphrey Pierce; C.C. 1664, assistant 1682; watch by him in silver case, Schloss collection, said to have belonged to Cromwell's daughter Bridget; the arms of the Protector incorporated with the royal arms are engraved on the case; in 1688 at the Mayor's Court some watch or pocket clock chains of steel belonging to him, and seized by C.C., were declared to be insufficient, and broken; he was the maker of a long-case month clock, presented to the Ironmongers' Company by John Woolfe, about 1689; a very similar clock at the Balls Hut Inn, Walberton, was sold by auction in 1910; a gold watch by him mentioned in *Lond. Gaz.,* Jan. 11, 1691; in the Guildhall Museum is a watch movement signed 'Harper, London'; it has tulip pillars, and dates from about 1680.

HARPER, JOHN. *1 Pear Tree St., Goswell St.,* 1810; *16 St. John St.,* 1815; *78 Goswell Rd.,* 1825.

HARPER, RICHARD. *Shrewsbury,* 1766. Died 1791; 'eminent watchmaker'.

HARPER, THOMAS, son of John Harper, of *St. Giles-in-the-Fields.* Apprenticed to Theophilus Davys, C.C. 1760; long-case clock, about 1770.

HARPER, THOMAS. Apprenticed to Henry Taylor, C.C. 1771.

HARPER, THOS. *207 Fleet St.,* 1800–30.

HARPER & SON. *Salop.* Clock, about 1775.

HARPLETT, CORNELIUS. Apprenticed in 1659 to Davis Mell, C.C.

HARRACHE, THOS. *Pall Mall,* 1765–75.

HARRINGTON, JOHN. *London.* Apprenticed 1733, C.C. 1740.

HARRIS, ANTHONY. C.C. 1683; lantern clocks by him; also a fine long Oriental lacquer case clock, goes seven weeks.

HARRIS, CHARLES, son of John. *London.* Apprenticed 1687, C.C. 1695.

HARRIS, CHARLES. Apprenticed to Robert Webster, C.C. 1695.

HARRIS, CHRISTOPHER. *Lombard St.* Admitted C.C. 1695; 1695–1720.

HARRIS, CHRISTOPHER. *London (Grays Inn and later Leadenhall St.).* Apprenticed 1721, C.C. 1729–45; watch.

HARRIS, CHRISTOPHER. *London (Old Jewry).* C.C. 1782–1823; watch G.M.

HARRIS, CLEMENT. *76 Cornhill,* 1822–42. C.C. 1816; Livery 1825; chronometer, Guildhall Museum, signed 'Harris, late Hatton and Harris'.

HARRIS, EBENEZER. Apprenticed in 1682 to Ben Bell, C.C.

HARRIS, E. *Warrington.* Watch, 1790.

HARRIS, FRANCIS WM. C.C. 1702.

HARRIS, GEO. Apprenticed 1668 to Thos. Long; C.C. 1674.

HARRIS, GEO. *Fritwell,* 1710–30.

HARRIS, HENRY. *Barbican.* C.C. 1711; watch, silver dial, 1711–20.

HARRIS, HENRY, brother. *London.* C.C. 1752.

HARRIS, HENRY. *6 Curtain Rd.,* 1815–25.

HARRIS, JACOB. Apprenticed in 1646 to David Bouquett, C.C.

HARRIS, JAMES. *London.* Apprenticed 1753, C.C. 1762.

HARRIS, JAS. *8 Parliament St.,* 1820.

HARRIS, JEFFREY. 'Ting-tang' pull repeating bracket clock, inscribed 'Jeffrey Harris, London', about 1700.

HARRIS, JOHN. *London.* Apprenticed 1717, C.C. 1737.

HARRIS, JOHN, son of William Aaron. *London.* Apprenticed 1761, C.C. 1772.

HARRIS, JOHN, son of John. *London.* C.C. 1766.

HARRIS, JOHN. Apprenticed to Robert Poole, *27 Old Jewry.* C.C. 1795–1808.

HARRIS, JOSEPH. At the *Dial and Cup,* just above ye *Upper Court House, Maidstone,* about 1770; card, Hodgkin collection.

HARRIS, JOHN. One of the first assistants C.C. 1631; master 1641.

HARRIS, JOHN. C.C. 1677.

HARRIS, JOHN. C.C. 1690; long-case clock, Wetherfield collection, about 1700.

HARRIS, JOHN. *Holborn Bridge.* C.C. 1659; master 1688.

HARRIS, L. *Brown Lane, Spitalfields,* 1810.

HARRIS, MATTHEW. *Bath,* 1800–19. Watch.

HARRIS, MATTHIAS. *8 Horse St., Bath,* 1798.

HARRIS, RICHARD. Said to have been the maker of a clock for St. Paul's Church, Covent Garden, in 1641.

HARRIS, RICHD. Apprenticed in 1693 to Thos. Brafield, C.C.

HARRIS, ROBERT. *London.* Apprenticed 1741, C.C. 1750.

HARRIS, RICHARD. *27 Old Jewry*, 1790–1810.

HARRIS, SAML. C.C. 1802.

HARRIS, SAML. *London.* C.C. 1787; long-case clock, about 1790.

HARRIS, SAMUEL, son of James. *London.* C.C. 1787.

HARRIS, SAMUEL. C.C. 1708.

HARRIS, SOLOMON. Apprenticed 1805, C.C. 1823.

HARRIS, THOMAS. In ye Strand. Good lantern clock, inscribed 'Thomas Harris, in ye Strand', about 1680.

HARRIS, THOMAS. *London.* Apprenticed 1720, C.C. 1733–60.

HARRIS, THOS. *St. Sepulchre's.* In 1770 he patented (No. 965) a rotating dial.

HARRIS, WILLIAM. *London (Goswell St.).* C.C. 1781–90.

HARRIS, WILLIAM. *London.* C.C. 1804; l.C.C. 1806–25.

HARRIS, WILLIAM. *Temple Bar.* Liveryman C.C. 1776.

HARRIS, WILLIAM. *27 Goswell St.* Apprenticed to Joseph Robinson, C.C. 1796; master 1830–32.

HARRIS, WM. *Chippenham.* Clock, about 1770.

HARRISON, ANTHONY. *Birchin Lane.* Apprenticed in 1693 to Joana May, widow; C.C. 1701; in 1721 appeared an advertisement respecting a small gold watch made by Anthony Harrison, and lost between Leadenhall and 'Spittelfields' markets; the finder was offered nine guineas reward, and no questions asked, if the watch were restored to Mr. John Chadwell, goldsmith, Castle Alley, Birchin Lane, 1701–20.

HARRISON, EDWD. *Warrington*, 1776. Centre seconds watch, 1795.

HARRISON, GEORGE. Apprenticed 1689 to Johana May, widow; turned over to Thomas Tompion, C.C. 1698.

HARRISON, JAMES. *Barrow.* Brother of the preceding; long-case clock by him in the G.M., 1720–50.

HARRISON, JAMES. *London.* Apprenticed 1720, C.C. 1737–51.

HARRISON, JAMES. Apprenticed to James Freeman, C.C. 1776

HARRISON, JAMES. *Waterbury, Conn., U.S.A.* Founder of the Connecticut wooden clock industry, 1790–1830.

HARRISON, JAMES. *Boston, U.S.A.*, 1816–18. Clock.

HARRISON, JAMES. *Barton-on-Humber* and *Hull.* A grandson of John Harrison and a clockmaker of some celebrity, made a fine clock for Christ Church, Hull; a clock by him in Filey Church had a detached escapement, an invention for which the Society of Arts awarded him a silver medal and £10, 1810–30.

HARRISON, JAS. *Grub St.*, C.C. 1730.

HARRISON, JOHN. *Newcastle.* Bracket clock, about 1765.

HARRISON, JOHN. Born 1693; died in *Red Lion Sq.*, and buried in Hampstead churchyard in 1776. The winner of the £20,000 prize for ascertaining the Longitude.

HARRISON, RALPH. *London.* Apprenticed 1742, C.C. 1751–60. In the firm of Fosset & Harrison.

HARRISON, ROBERT. *London* Apprenticed 1749, C.C. 1757.

HARRISON, THOMAS. *London.* Apprenticed 1776, C.C. 1786.

HARRISON, THOMAS. *London.* l.C.C. 1812, died 1820; cylinder movement, G.M.

HARRISON, THOS. *Liverpool*, 1770. Clock, Thos. & Finnie Harrison, Liverpool, about 1780.

HARRISON, THOS. *68 Fetter Lane*, 1795–1804.

HARRISON, THOS. *Regent St.* Watch, with hare and snail indicator, 1810.

HARRISON, WILLIAM. C.C. 1699.

HARRISON, WILLIAM, son of John. *London (Holborn).* Apprenticed 1752, C.C. 1763, died 1816. Fellow of the Royal Society; assisted his father in construction of Nos. 4 and 5, and took charge of the trial of No. 4; No. 5 is signed 'John Harrison & Son'.

HARRISON, WILLIAM. *London (Salisbury St.* and later *Chandos St.).* C.C. 1766–81; cylinder travelling clock and cylinder watch, about 1800, Ilbert collection, by him or Wm. below.

HARRISON, WILLIAM. *London.* 1815 C.C.

HARRISON, WILLIAM HART. *Chepstow*, 1822–48.

HARRISON, WM. *48 Fetter Lane*, 1780–94.

HARROCKS. *Lancaster.*

HARROCKS, JNO. 1783, f.

HARROCKS, JOSHUA. 1748, f.; made a church clock in 1759.

HARRYS (HARRIS), THOMAS. *Water Lane.* Maker of the celebrated clock with figures on the front of Old St. Dunstan's Church, Fleet St, 1671.

HARSCH, JOHANN MICHAEL. *Berlin*, 1785–1836.

HARSHELL, D. *12 Bevis Marks*, 1830.

HART, —. *Nottingham*, about 1790 C.C.

HART, AARON. *Westminster*, 1790.

HART, ALPHA. *Goshen, New York*, 1820. Wooden clock.

HART, EDWARD. *London.* Apprenticed 1766, C.C. 1773.

HART, HENRY. C.C. 1720.

HART, JACOB. *Hull*, 1822.

HART, JOHN. C.C. 1720.

HART, JOHN & ROBERT. *Glasgow*, 1821. Made clock dials illuminated by gas which was turned on and off by the clock.

HART, NOE. C.C. 1695.

HART, S. & M. *52 Prescot St., Goodman's Fields*, 1804–18.

HART & HARVEY. *5 King's St., Finsbury*, 1825.

HARTEL, PHILIPP. *Burghausen.* Apprenticed 1742–85; Kleinuhrmacher.

HARTICH, JOHANN WOLFGANG. *Augsburg.* Master 1712–70 juré.

HARTFORD, JNO. C.C. 1632.

HARTLEY, —. *New St., Shoe Lane.* Cited by the C.C. for trading in watches and clocks without having served seven years in the trade, 1680.

HARTLEY, JEREMY. *Norwich.* Fine bracket clock, about 1715.

HARTLEY, JNO. *George Court, Red Lion St.*, 1790–94.

HARTLEY, THOS. *Snaith*, 1770.

HARTMAN, JOHN GEORGE. Watchmaker to the University of Halle, 1756.

HARTMAN, PAUL. *Vienna*, 1764–1803.

HARTMAN, THOMAS. *Augsburg* and *Wald*, 1729 comp.–1746.

HARTWELL, FRANCIS. Apprenticed in 1678 to Dan. Stevens, C.C.

HARVEY, —. *Brentwood.* a. 1763; watch.

HARVEY, —. *Richmond, Yorks.* Watch, 1814.

HARVEY, ALEXANDER. C.C. 1726; in 1730 he worked for Clark, *Leadenhall St.*

HARVEY, B. *Weymouth*, 1770.

HARVEY, ELEANOR, widow. *Brentwood*, 1772.

HARVEY, JAMES. *Abergavenny*, 1777–95. From London; clocks and watches.

HARVEY, JNO. Apprenticed in 1691 to Philip Corderoy, C.C.

HARVEY, JOHN. *Weymouth*, 1760–91. Clocks and watches.

HARVEY, JOHN. *16 Fenchurch St.*, a Quaker, 1798–1809; *3 Falcon St.*, 1815; 1798–1818.

HARVEY, SAMUEL. C.C. 1696.

HARVEY, THOS. *York*, f., 1808.

HARVEY & CO. *2 King's St., Finsbury*, 1830.

HARWARD, ROBERT. C.C. 1730.
HARWOOD, JAS. Churchwardens' book, Halifax Parish Church, "1714 paid James Harwood for clock mending £1 12s. 6d."; again, "1721, paid James Harwood for mending the clock, 10s."
HARWOOD, LAURENCE. '*Acorn*', *Belle Sauvage Yard*. Died 1716.
HARWOOD, TAYLOR. *Cambridge*. 1791 C.C.
HASIUS. See HASSENIUS.
HASIUS, ISAAC. *Haarlem*. Late seventeenth century. Gold watch engraved by Huaud le puisné, Blot-Garnier collection; watch, sun and moon hour indicators, Stads Museum, Amsterdam.
HASIUS, JACOB. *Amsterdam*. 1682–about 1725. Watches Stads Museum, Amsterdam and Denham collection; long-case clock, Ilbert collection.
HASLAM. Watch signed 'John Haslam, Cheshire', 1810.
HASLER, HANS LEO. *Nürnberg*, 1564–1612. Made clock-watches.
HASLEWOOD, ROGER. *53 Salisbury Court*, 1772.
HASLUCK, JACOB. *St. John St., London*. Watch, with sun and moon hour indicator, about 1695, Pierpont Morgan collection.
HASSELL, JOSHUA. *Carter Lane*. C.C. 1730. See ATKINS, F.
HASSENIUS, JACOBUS. *London*, about 1710.
HASSENIUS, JAMES (alien). Admitted C.C. 1682; a long-case clock inscribed 'J. Hasius, Amsterdam', possibly by him.
HASTINGS, DAVID. *Alnwick*, 1770.
HASWELL, ALEX. *10 Clifford St., New Bond St.*, 1780–94.
HATCH, GEORGE. *Hatfield*, about 1690 C.C.
HATCH, JOHN. Admitted C.C. 1693.
HATCHMAN, JAMES. C.C. 1680.
HATFIELD, DAVID. *Bosworth*. Watch, h.m., 1737.
HATFIELD, HALLOWS. *London*. Apprenticed 1791, C.C. 1805–22.
HATHAWAY, WILLIAM. *London*. Apprenticed 1726, C.C. 1735.
HATHORNTHWAITE. *Lancaster*.
HATHORNTHWAITE, JNO. 1744, f., long-case clock, 'Peter Hathornthwaite, Kirby Lonsdale', about 1750.
HATHORNTHWAITE, PETER. 1703.
HATTON, CHRISTOPHER. Apprenticed to George Margetts, and turned over to James Hatton; C.C. 1815.
HATTON, GEO. C. *Lancaster*, 1826, f.
HATTON, JAMES. *4 St. Michael's Alley*. Apprenticed to Geo. Margetts; C.C. 1799; livery 1810; 1799–1812.
HATTON, JNO. C.C. about 1650.
HATTON, JOSEPH YORKE. *40 Tooley St.* Apprenticed to Newman Peachey, and turned over to John Chancellor; C.C. 1796; livery 1810; St. Magnus, London Bridge, 1830; many watches inscribed 'Yorke Hatton, Thames St'.
HATTON, PETER. *Stafford*, 1735.
HATTON, SAM. *Rose St., Soho*, 1775.
HATTON, THOMAS. *Lombard St.* Watchmaker, and author of *Introduction to the Mechanical Part of Clock and Watch Work*, published 1773; 1760–74; watch, 'Thos. Hatton, Preston', 1776.
HATTON & HARRIS. *4 St. Michael's Alley, Cornhill*, 1816–20. See HARRIS, CLEMENT.
HAUCHAR, J. D. *Paris, élève de Breguet*. Watch, about 1830.
HAUCK, ANTOINE. *Bamberg*. Repeating watch, about 1690.
HAUGHTON, ANN. *London*. 1784 C.C.
HAUGHTON, GEO. *London*, about 1760. Long-case chiming clock.
HAUGHTON, JAMES. *London*. C.C. 1770–84.

HAUGHTON, RICHARD. *London*. Apprenticed 1682, C.C. 1690–1707.
HAUGHTON, WILLIAM. *London*. Apprenticed 1737, C.C. 1746–1777.
HAUGHTON, WM. C.C.; in 1703 he worked for Heardman.
HAUKSBEE, JOHN. *London*. Apprenticed 1695, C.C. 1709. v. HAWKESBEE.
HAUSER, EDUARD. *Lenzkirch*. Born 1825, died 1900; developed clockmaking in the Schwarzwald and founded Lenzkirch factory.
HAUTEFEUILLE, JOHN (The Abbé). *Paris*. Born 1647, died 1724. He is said to have invented, about 1722, the rack lever escapement which was patented in England by Peter Litherland in 1791. Huygens, endeavouring to obtain a French patent for the balance-spring, was successfully opposed by the Abbé, who claimed to be the prior inventor of it.
HAUTON, JOHN. *London*. 1716 C.C.
HAUTSCH, GOTTFRIED, son. *Nürnberg*, 1662–92. Made automata.
HAVELLAND, WILLIAM THOMAS. *London*. Apprenticed 1783, C.C. 1792.
HAVELLAND & STEPHENS. *32 Aldgate High St.*, 1794.
HAVEN, ROBT. C.C. 1657.
HAVEN, THOS. C.C. 1652.
HAWES, JOHN. *31 New Bond St.*, 1775.
HAWKES, SUSAN. Apprenticed in 1683 to Sam. Davis and Mary, his wife, C.C.
HAWKESBEE, BENJAMIN. C.C. 1709.
HAWKESWORTH, JOHN. C.C. 1709.
HAWKINS. Pretty lantern clock, about 1650, inscribed 'Ambrose Hawkins Je Wells, ffecit'.
HAWKINS, GEO. Apprenticed in 1688 to Ben. Wright, C.C.
HAWKINS, JAMES. C.C. 1730.
HAWKINS, MARK. *Bury St. Edmunds*, 1710.
HAWKINS, MARKE. *Bury St. Edmunds*, 1670.
HAWKINS, RICHD. Apprenticed in 1677 to Wm. Fuller, C.C.
HAWKINS, THOMAS. *London*. Apprenticed 1703, C.C. 1711.
HAWKINS, THOMAS or GEORGE. *London*. Apprenticed 1765, C.C. 1772.
HAWKINS, THOMAS. C.C. *6 Castle Alley, Cornhill*, 1777–1816.
HAWKINS, WM. Apprenticed in 1676 to Francis Dinnis; C.C. 1684; fine lacquer long-case clock, about 1740, signed 'Wm. Hawkins, St. Edmund's Bury', about 1730, Wetherfield collection.
HAWKINS, WM. *Bury St. Edmunds*, 1735.
HAWKSEY, ENOCH. *Nantwich*. Watch, 1787.
HAWLEY, —. *120 Fleet St.* Card, Hodgkin collection, about 1830.
HAWLEY, HENRY. *London*. 1680 C.C.
HAWLEY, J. T., & Co. *London*, 1795–1825. Watchmaker to the King; bracket clock.
HAWLEY, THOMAS & Co. *75 Strand*. 'Watchmaker to His Majesty', 1760–1828.
HAWTHORN, D. *Darlington*, about 1705.
HAWTHORN, JOHN. *Newcastle-on-Tyne*, 1755. Died 1779; many watches. Also HAWTHORNTHWAITE and HAY-THORNTHWAITE.
HAWTHORNE, FERGUSON & Co. *London*. Watch, 1808.
HAWTING, JNO. *Holywell, Oxford*, 1770–80.
HAWTON, SAM. Apprenticed in 1690 to Jno. Wise, junr., C.C.
HAWXHURST, NATHANIEL. *New York*, 1786.
HAY, ALEXANDER. *Edinburgh*. 1718.
HAY, ELIZABETH. *York*, 1822.

HAY, GEO. *York*, f., 1808.
HAY, JOHN. *London*, 1770. Watch.
HAY, PETER. *20 Davis St., Berkeley Sq.*, 1805–40.
HAY, THOMAS. *Kelso*, 1778–1814. Also HOY.
HAY, WILLIAM. *London.* C.C. 1774.
HAYD, CHRISTIAN. *Olmütz*, 1687–90. Repaired town clock.
HAYD, RICHARD. *London.* Apprenticed 1714, C.C. 1733–45.
HAYD, SAMUEL. *Boston, U.S.A.*, 1796–1809. Watch.
HAYD, WILLIAM. *London.* Apprenticed 1731, C.C. 1746–54.
HAYDEN, JOHN. *Deptford.* Long-case clock, about 1710.
HAYDEN, WILLIAM. C.C.; *Noble St.*, 1717.
HAYDON, EDWARD. *London.* C.C. 1818.
HAYDON, JOHN. *London.* Apprenticed 1771, C.C. 1790.
HAYDON, JOHN. *London (Cheapside).* C.C. 1784, l.C.C. 1790–1804.
HAYDON, WILLIAM. *Croydon.* C.C. 1687.
HAYES, EDMOND. C.C. 1682.
HAYES, JAS. Apprenticed in 1693 to Harris, C.C.
HAYES, JNO. Apprenticed in 1676 to Jas. Wolverstone, C.C.
HAYES, WALTER. C.C. 1654; master 1680.
HAYES, WM. Apprenticed in 1686 to Daniel Le Count, C.C.
HAYES, WM. *Warrington.* Watch, 1782.
HAYLE, —. Watch, in fritillary shaped case of silver, beautifully engraved dial, movement inscribed 'Thomas Hayle (or possibly Hople) in Popeshead Alley', about 1650.
HAYLER, WILLIAM. *Chatham.* a. 1769–early nineteenth century. Long-case clock; watch.
HAYLEY, WILLIAM. *30 Great Marylebone St.*, 1788–93.
HAYNES, F. *London.* Pendulum watch, about 1708. See HAINES, FRANCIS.
HAYNES, JOHN. C.C. 1676.
HAYNES, WILLIAM. *London.* Apprenticed 1731, C.C. 1741.
HAYNES, WM. Apprenticed in 1680 to Thos. Williamson, C.C.
HAYNES & KENTISH. *18 Cornhill*, 1804–18.
HAYS, MICHAEL SOLOMON. *New York*, f. 1769.
HAYTER, WM. Apprenticed in 1685 to Jno. Parker, C.C.
HAYTON, F. *London.* Watch, 1760.
HAYWARD, JOHN. *22 Bush Lane, Cannon St.*, 1820.
HAYWARD, ROBERT. *Bermondsey*, 1815–35.
HAYWARD, WILLIAM. *Union Ct., Holborn.* C.C. 1720.
HAYWOOD, PETER. *Crediton, Devon.* In 1766 he patented (No. 836) a calendar ring.
HEAD, THOMAS CARTWRIGHT. Apprenticed to Christopher Gould in 1693.
HEADACHE, THOMAS. *London.* Apprenticed 1776, C.C. 1784.
HEADDING, RICHARD WILLIAM. *London.* Apprenticed 1804, l.C.C. 1812, died 1821.
HEADWORTH, P. *46 St. John's St.*, 1815–42.
HEADY, GEORGE. Apprenticed to Dan. Quare 1675; admitted C.C. 1682.
HEALEY, JNO. *Manchester*, 1818. Also THOS, same date.
HEAP, RICHARD. *5 King St., Covent Garden*, 1800–04; *39 Maiden Lane*, 1815–25.
HEAPH, JNO. *Stockport*, 1770.
HEARDMAN, JACOB. *Plum-tree Court.* C.C. 1720.
HEARDMAN, JACOB. *London.* C.C. 1746.
HEARDMAN, JOHN, son. *London.* Apprenticed 1735, C.C. 1749.
HEARDMAN, JOSEPH. *Plum-tree Court.* C.C. 1730–35.
HEARNE, —. *London*, 1630. Subscribed for incorporation of C.C.

HEARN, HEN. *London.* Watch, 1775.
HEARN, JOSEPH. Apprenticed in 1690 to Cornelius Jenkins, C.C.
HEATH, BEN. Apprenticed in 1661 to Chas. Rogers, C.C.
HEATH, J. *London.* Watch, h.m., 1770.
HEATH, THOMAS. *London.* Apprenticed 1748, C.C. 1762; universal ring dial Old Ashmolean Museum.
HEATHCOTE, EDWARD. *London.* Apprenticed 1725, C.C. 1733.
HEATHCOTE, TIMOTHY. C.C. 1698.
HEATHER, WILLIAM. *London.* 1701 C.C.
HEBB, JOHN. *London.* Apprenticed 1728, C.C. 1736.
HEBDITCH. Accounts of Bristol Cathedral, 1630, by favour of Mr. Edwin P. Morgan. "Item, Paide to Richard Hebditch for making ye Horloge at ye lower end of ye Cathedrall church, with divers and sundry motions in ye sume of £13 6s. 8d."
HEBERT, ANTHONY. 'Moorefields, nere London', 1670; a long-case clock so inscribed which strikes the hour twice; bracket clock, about 1690, inscribed, 'Anthony Hebert in Porter Street'. Anthony Hebert, *7 Dials.* C.C. 1725.
HEBERT, HENRY. *London.* C.C. 1734.
HEBERT, J. *Brightelmston*, about 1716.
HEBERT, JAMES. *London.* C.C. 1682; watch.
HEBERT, JNO. *Isleworth*, 1770.
HEBERT, MARY. *London.* C.C. 1795.
HEBRAT, JEAN. *Brussels*, 1640.
HECK. See DE HECK.
HECKEL, FRANCESCO, à *Fridberg*, 1730.
HECKLE, A. *Liverpool*, 1818.
HECKSTETTER, JOSEPH. C.C. 1694.
HEDENQUIST, PETER. *Uppsala.* Born 1740, died 1796.
HEDGE, NATHANIEL. *Colchester.* Lantern clocks, about 1740; also a fine long-case clock, about 1780.
HEDGE, NATHANIEL, JUN. *Colchester.* From 1765–90. Watches.
HEDGE & BANISTER. *Colchester.* Known as makers of long-case and other clocks, about 1800; watch by them, 1808.
HEDGER, GEORGE. *48 Great Sutton St.*, 1822–35; *10 St. John's Row, St. Luke's*, 1842.
HEDGER, W. *London.* Watch, 1790.
HEDGES, JOHN. *4 St. James's Walk, Clerkenwell*, 1800.
HEDIGER, J. *Zug.* First half seventeenth century; watch Louvre; oval crystal watch, Feill collection. Also HELIGER.
HEDSTRÖM, EPHRAIM. *Stockholm.* Born 1775, died 1816; two wall and three bracket clocks, one Nord. Museum; gold cylinder watch.
HEELEY & BURT. *Deptford.* Long-case clock, 1780.
HEERMAN, JOHN (Dutch). C.C. 1691.
HEIDMARK, P. *London.* Watch, 1780.
HEIJMAN, JOHAN FREDRICK. *Stockholm.* Master 1742, died 1778; court clock.
HEILIG, JACOB. *Philadelphia*, 1770–1824.
HEILIG, JOHN. *Germantown*, 1824–30.
HEINTZELMAN, JOHN CONRAD. *Manheim, Lancaster, U.S.A.* Born 1766, died 1796; long-case clocks.
HELDEN, CORNELIUS. Apprenticed in 1686 to Dan. Delander, C.C.
HELDEN, ONESIPHORUS. C.C. 1632; warden, 1648; did not become master.
HELE, PETER. *Nuremberg.* Died 1540. See HENLEIN.
HELIGER, J. *Zug.* Crystal case watch, about 1590.
HELLAM, JAMES. Apprenticed to Daniel Steevens, and turned over to Evan Jones, and afterwards to Henry Jones; C.C. 1690.
HELLIER, WM. *London.* Watch, 1740.

HELLIWELL, —. *Warrington.* Clock, about 1770.
HELLIWELL, WM. *Leeds,* 1829.
HELME, —. *London,* 1700.
HELME, THOS. *Ormskirk.* Repaired town clock, 1770.
HELLMERS, PETER HERMAN. *Hamburg,* 1804–21.
HELYE, F. BAPTISTE. *Paris.* Clock, about 1780.
HEMING, ARTIS. *Shadwell.* Liveryman C.C. 1776.
HEMING, ED. *Bicester,* about 1705. Clock inscribed 'Ed. Heming, Bisiter'.
HEMING, GEO. *151 New Bond St.,* 1793.
HEMING, THOMAS. *Piccadilly,* 1763; *131 New Bond St.,* 1769–75.
HEMING & CRAWNER. *New Bond St.,* 1780–90.
HEMINGWAY, JNO. *Manchester,* 1818.
HEMLETT, J. *London.* Watch, 1810.
HEMMEN, EDWARD. *London.* Watch, about 1710; another, h.m., 1760.
HEMMING, CHAS. Apprenticed in 1678 to Jas. Wolverstone, C.C.
HEMMING, HEN. *London.* Watch, 1780.
HENCHE, ULDRICH. Payment to him of £100 for a clock 'in manner of a branch', made by him and set up at *Whitehall,* 1605.
HENDERSON, JAMES. *Dublin,* 1795–1824.
HENDERSON, JOHN. *London.* 1662 C.C.
HENDERSON, JOHN. *Edinburgh.* Apprenticed 1795–1808; watch to the King.
HENDERSON, JOHN. *13 Broad St., Exchange,* 1775; *21 Cornhill,* 1783–1800.
HENDERSON, R. T. *St. Martin's Court,* 1800.
HENDERSON, ROBERT. *Scarborough.* A Quaker, died 1756, aged 78; long-case clock, about 1715, Sir Theodore Fry.
HENDERSON, ROBERT. *St. Martin's Court,* 1772; *18 Bridgewater Sq.,* 1800–05; chiming bracket clock; names of tunes engraved in the arch of the dial, 'March from Scipio, Sukey Bids Me, Miss Fox's Minuet'.
HENDERSON, ROBT. *Edinburgh.* Watch, V. & A., about 1750.
HENDERSON, THOS. *Hull,* 1770.
HENDRICK, JNO. & PETER. *Liverpool,* 1818.
HENDRICK, JOHN. *Liverpool,* 1790–1814.
HENDRICKS, AARON. *Devonshire St.,* 1760–68.
HENDRIE, JA. *Wigton,* 1770.
HENEY, RICHARD. Apprenticed in 1646 to Isaac Law, C.C.
HENGGELER, ANTOINE. *Chaux-de-Fonds,* 1784–1803; clock.
HENGGELER, CHRISTIAN. *Chaux-de-Fonds,* 1813–40; clock.
HENING (? HEMING), JOSH. Long-case clock, about 1780.
HENKELS, H. *Amsterdam.* Watch, 1780.
HENKELS, JEAN. *Amsterdam.* Watch, 1730.
HENLEIN, PETER. *Nürnberg.* Born about 1479, died 1542; master locksmith in 1509. At his death called 'vrmacher'. The first man known to have made a watch, about 1510. The Raths of Nürnberg ordered several watches from him between 1521 and 1525. Cocclaeus calls him Hele and Dopplmayr Heinlein, but in the Nürnberg Archives he is always referred to as Henlein.
HENLEY, J. *London.* Watch, 1810.
HENLEY, THOS. *London.* Watch, 1829.
HENNER, JOHAN. *Würtzburg.* Died 1756; early eighteenth century watch, V. & A.
HENNETT & SON. *16 Foster Lane,* 1772.
HENNINGER, SIMON. *St. Georgen,* end of seventeenth century. Said to have been the first clockmaker in the Schwarzwald. *v.* FREY.

HENNINGTON, WM. *London.* Watch, 1765.
HENNON, WILLIAM. *C.C.* 1674.
HENRIOT à *Geneva.* Watch in case of tinted gold, V. & A about 1785.
HENRY, —. *Falmouth,* about 1790 C.C.
HENRY, AUTIN à *Paris.* Clock-watch, about 1740.
HENRY, CLAUDE. *Lyons.* Apprenticed 1595, master 1610–23; died a. 1628; oval silver watch, Spitzer collection; watch, Fränkel collection.
HENRY, PETER. *London.* Watch, 1780.
HENRY, PIERRE. *Paris (Quai de l'Horloge).* Born 1744, died 1806; clockmaker to the King; nephew of J. A. Lepaute and in his business. When J. B. Lepaute retired in 1789, worked with Pierre Basile Lepaute, retiring in 1798. His son Augustin Michel established himself as Henry Neveu Lepaute. *v.* LEPAUTE.
HENRY, S. *59 Lower Brook St.,* 1810.
HENRY, S. *70 Leman St.,* 1830.
HENRY, W. & S. *44 Taylor's Buildings, Islington,* 1804.
HENSHAW, JOHN. *C.C.* 1696.
HENSHAW, WALTER. *C.C.* 1669; master 1695.
HENSON, WILLIAM. *London.* Apprenticed 1799, C.C. 1807.
HEPTON, FREDERICK. *Philadelphia,* 1785.
HEPTON, JNO. 1823–40.
HEPTON, THOS. *Northallerton,* 1770.
HEPTON, WILLIAM. *Northallerton,* 1777–1858. Watch.
HERANT BROTHERS & SON. *Berlin.* Enamelled watch, V. & A., about 1680.
HERBAULT, L. FR. *Rue St. Honoré, Paris.* Garde-visiteur, 1769.
HERBERT, CORNELIUS. *London Bridge,* 1670–1720.
HERBERT, CORNELIUS. *London Bridge.* Apprenticed to the above C. H., 1690; C.C. 1700; master 1727; in the vestry of St. Lawrence, Jewry was a long-case clock by him, dated 1721, and among the church papers is a receipt as follows: "Received from the church for the clock the sum of eight pounds. Cornelius Herbert"; a fine marquetry long-case clock by him was in the Wetherfield collection.
HERBERT, CORNELIUS. Apprenticed to his father, Cornelius; C.C. 1735.
HERBERT, EDWARD. *C.C.* 1664.
HERBERT, EDWARD. *Old Bailey,* C.C. 1710–30.
HERBERT, EVAN. *C.C.* 1691.
HERBERT, HENRY. *C.C.* 1713.
HERBERT, JAS. *London.* Repeating watch, 1740.
HERBERT, JNO. Apprenticed in 1672 to Nich. Payne; C.C. 1682.
HERBERT, MORGAN. Clock-watch, 1690.
HERBERT, THOMAS. *Whitehall.* C.C. 1676; red tortoiseshell bracket clock, about 1690, Wetherfield collection.
HERBERT, WM. Apprenticed 1663 to Hy. Child; C.C. 1671; watch without a balance-spring, about 1675.
HERBIER, P. *Grenoble,* early seventeenth century.
HERBSTREIT (HERBSTRIETH, HEBSTREIT), JAKOB. *Hinterzarten (Schwarzwald),* 1730–60.
HERBSTREIT (HERBSTRIETH, HEBSTREIT), JAKOB, son. *Hinterzarten* and *Neukirch,* 1770. Died 1801. The Black Forest type of small hanging clock was first made by him; called 'Jockele-Uhren' after him.
HERMAN, DOM JOSEPH. *Gruyère.* Born 1752, died 1820. Monk who made clock with ingenious automata, illuminated M. des Aut.
HERMANT, A. J. *Paris,* 1809–25.
HERNE, EDWD. Apprenticed in 1680 to Cornelius Jenkins, C.C.

HERON, ERSKINE. *Edinburgh.* Apprenticed 1752; *Charleston, U.S.A.,* 1765. Clocks and watches.

HERON, ISAAC. *New York,* 1769–80, f., 1769. Watch by him belonging to Philip Livingston, signer of American Declaration of Independence in 1776, now in the museum of the 'Sons of the Revolution', New York.

HERON, WM. *Newtown Ards,* 1784.

HERRING, JOSEPH. Free C.C. by redemption, 1770.

HERRING (HERREN), JOSHUA. *38 Cornhill.* Known as a maker of bracket clocks, 1753–75.

HERRING, RICHD. *Newark,* 1805–20.

HERSANT, PIERRE. *Blois.* Master 1638; *Paris,* 1639; died *Blois,* 1662.

HERTFORD. See HARTFORD.

HERTHAM, T. S. *London.* Watch, 1795.

HERVÉ. Fine clock, Wallace collection, signed 'Hervé à Paris', about 1740.

HERWICK, NICHOLAS. *Cheapside,* 1580.

HERZOG, JOHANN JAKOB. *Basle.* Born 1650, apprenticed 1662, died 1708.

HESS, L. *Zurich.* Watch, about 1760.

HESSEN, A. *Paris.* Enamel watch, about 1775.

HESSICHTI DIONISTUS. Book-shaped watch, 1627.

HESTER, HENRY. C.C. 1670.

HESTER, HENRY, JUNR. C.C. 1687. "Lost in Whitehall, on Sunday the 26th past, a Gold Watch with a plain Outside Case, made by — Hester, of Westminster, with a ribbon tied to it of Changeable Purple and Gold, and upon that two Seals, the one an Onyx with a Head cut in it, set with small Diamonds; and the other Seal a Stone set with rubies. Whoever brings the said Watch, &c., to Mr. Snagg, Goldsmith, in Lombard St., shall have 5 guineas reward" (*Lond. Gaz.,* July 30, Aug. 3, 1691).

HESTER, HENRY. *London.* C.C. 1671, died 1717.

HETTICH, C. *Lynn,* 1825.

HEURTAULT, DANIEL. *Lyons.* 1626 comp.

HEUSS, GEORGE. *Nuremberg,* 1509–60. He made a clock with automatic figures.

HEWARD, JNO. Apprenticed in 1686 to Jno. Miller, C.C.

HEWES, —. *London,* 1630. Subscribed for incorporation of C.C. *v.* HUE.

HEWISON, CHAS. *London.* Watch, 1800.

HEWITT (HEWETT), ALEXANDER. *London.* Apprenticed 1685. C.C.

HEWITT, ALEXANDER. *London.* C.C. 1725. Watch, 1730.

HEWITT, BENJAMIN. C.C. 1724.

HEWITT, GEO. *Marlboro',* 1720–30.

HEWITT, JAS. *Sunderland,* 1760.

HEWITT, JOHN. *London.* 1724 C.C.

HEWITT, THOMAS. *12 Upper Ashby St.,* and *10 King St., Tower Hill.* A chronometer maker who devised different forms of compensation balances; was a director of the British Watch Company; born 1799, died 1867.

HEWITT, WILLIAM. *London (Tooley St.),* 1765. C.C. 1771–85.

HEWKLEY, JAMES SNELLING, brother. *London.* Apprenticed 1776, C.C. 1788–1820.

HEWKLEY, JOHN, brother. *London (Alfred Court).* Apprenticed 1762, C.C. 1775, died 1819.

HEWKLEY, JOHN. C.C. 1732.

HEWKLEY, SQUIRE. *London (Jewin St.).* Apprenticed 1733, C.C. 1741–78.

HEWKLEY, SQUIRE, son. *London (Red Cross St.).* C.C. 1764, died 1782.

HEWLETT. *Bristol.* Long-case clocks.

HEWLETT, ISAAC, about 1750.

HEWLETT, ISAAC and JOSHUA, about 1780.

HEWLITT, G. *Foxley,* 1780.

HEWSON, JNO. Apprenticed in 1683 to Jno. Sellars, C.C.

HEYDEN, CHRISTIAN. *Nürnberg.* Born 1526, died 1576. Clockmaker and mathematician; celestial globe clock and sun- and moon-dial M.P.S. Dresden. Dial Old Ashmolean Museum; made an astronomical clock and several others for Maximilian II ang worked for the Dresden Court.

HEYDON, SAML. *London.* Watch, 1757.

HEYER, F. M. *Amsterdam.* Watch, 1775.

HEYLIN, ISAAC. *London.* Apprenticed 1786, C.C. 1795.

HEYWOOD, —. *London.* 1630. Subscriber to incorporation of C.C.

HEYWOOD, WILLIAM. *12 King St., Covent Garden,* 1807–10; *35 Goodge St.,* 1815–42.

HEYWORTH, JOHN. *218 Tottenham Court Rd.,* 1823.

HIBBEN, ANDREW. *Charleston, U.S.A.,* 1765. Clocks and watches.

HICCOX, JNO. Apprenticed in 1650 to Nicholas Ashwell; admitted C.C. 1657; repeating watch, inscribed 'Jno. Hiccox, London', about 1710.

HICK, MATTHEW. *York,* f., 1812. Died 1834.

HICKMAN, EDWD. *High St., Oxford,* 1818–20.

HICKMAN, JOSEPH. *20 Bridgewater Sq.,* 1779.

HICKMAN, WM. *89 Borough,* 1816–25.

HICKS, CHAS. *112 Whitechapel,* 1810–15.

HICKS, JAS. *112 Whitechapel,* 1804–15.

HICKS, JOHN. C.C. 1694.

HICKS, SAMUEL. *London,* about 1780.

HICKS, THOMAS. C.C. 1664. "Lost Sept. 21, betwixt Ingerstone and Rumford, a watch with a silver-pinned Case, showing the day of the month, the hour of the day, made by *Thomas Hicks, Londini,* with a blue taffety ribon fastened to the key thereof. Whoever will give notice thereof to Mr. Christopher Maynard, watchmaker at the Royal Exchange, London, shall have 40s. reward" (*Lond. Gaz.,* Sept. 23–27, 1675).

HICKS, THOMAS. C.C. 1666.

HICKS, WILLETT. *New York,* 1790.

HICKSON, THOMAS. C.C. 1690.

HIGGINS, BANGER. Apprenticed to Edward Banger, and turned over to William Wilde; C.C. 1724.

HIGGINS, THOMAS, son. *London.* Apprenticed 1755, C.C. 1764.

HIGGINS, THOMAS. *London.* C.C. 1790.

HIGGINSON, —. *Kirby St.,* 1782.

HIGGINSON, GEO. *East India House,* C.C. 1730.

HIGGINSON, HENRY. C.C. 1662.

HIGGINSON, JOHN. *27 Strand,* 1780; *38 Southampton St., Strand,* 1798–1815.

HIGGINSON, JOHN. *London.* 1698 C.C.

HIGGINSON, JOHN. *London,* 1785–1824. Succeeded by Wilson; watch.

HIGGINSON, RICHARD. *Fazakerley.* Watch, 1743.

HIGGINSON, SAMUEL. C.C. 1697. Hatton speaks of the splendid polish of the work of Higginson Brothers, watch finishers.

HIGGNETT, JNO. *London.* Watch, 1725.

HIGGS, JNO. C.C. 1688.

HIGGS, JOHN. Apprenticed to Robert Robinson, C.C. 1661.

HIGGS, RICHARD. *London.* 1730 C.C.

HIGGS, ROBERT. Apprenticed to Richard Blundell C.C. 1714; a small bracket clock by him, finely engraved back plate, two bells, coming hour struck on smaller one, pull for repeating hour.

HIGGS, ROBERT & PETER. *7 Sweeting's Alley,* 1740–69. Peter Higgs was apprenticed to Robert, C.C. 1740, and became master in 1767.

HIGGS, ROBERT. *London.* Long-case clock, about 1750; half-quarter repeating watch, 1785.

HIGGS, THOMAS. C.C. 1716.

HIGGS & EVANS. *7 Sweeting's Alley*, 1780–1822; a verge watch movement by them, with curious pillars, in the Guildhall Museum; clocks inscribed, 'Higgs y Diego Evans', for Spanish markets.

HIGHAM, THOMAS. *London.* Apprenticed 1796, C.C. 1803–24; watch.

HIGHFIELD, JOSIAH. *55 Rosoman St.*, 1790–94.

HIGHFIELD, WILLIAM. *Liverpool*, 1761. Later *Wrexham* and *Oswestry*, 1778. Watch.

HIGHMORE, EDWD. C.C. 1687.

HIGHMORE, JACOB. *52 Aldersgate St.*, 1790–94.

HIGHMORE, LANCASTER. Apprenticed in 1685 to Jno. Fitter, C.C.

HIGHTEM, THOMAS. *London.* Apprenticed 1796, C.C 1803.

HIGMAN, JACOB. *London.* C.C. 1788–1801.

HIGNAR (HICNAR), JEAN. *Copenhagen.* Born 1695 in *France*; 1750 in *Copenhagen.* Died 1762.

HIGNETT, JOHN. *London.* a. 1751; watch.

HIGNETT, RICHARD. *London.* Apprenticed 1795, C.C. 1805.

HIGON, PIERRE. *Place du Palais-Royal, Paris.* Garde-visiteur, 1769.

HILDEBRANDT, J. C. 1730.

HILDEBURN, SAMUEL. *Philadelphia*, 1811.

HILDEBURN & WOODWORTH. *Philadelphia*, 1819.

HILDERSON, JOHN. *London.* 1657. Lantern and bracket clocks.

HILDEYARD, THOMAS. *Rotherwas (Hereford)* and *Liége.* Born 1690, died 1747; devised modified verge escapement for clock at Liége, which was described in a book published in Liége 1726 and in London 1727.

HILL, ABEL. *Petworth*, 1730.

HILL, BENJAMIN. C.C. 1641; master 1657; in the British Museum are specimens of his work, one a small circular watch in a blue steel case, with exceedingly handsome covering of filigree gold; another plainer with outer case of shagreen; in the V. & A. is a watch by him in a case of rock crystal; he died 1670. "Lost a gold watch made by Benjamin Hill in a black case studded with gold, with a double chain, and the key on a single chain with a knob of steel upon it. Whoever gives notice of it to Mr. Ambrose Mead, at the Bird-in-Hand, Fleet St., shall be rewarded" (*The Newes*, April 27, 1665).

HILL, CHAS. *3 Charing Cross*, 1793–95.

HILL, D. *Reading, U.S.A.*, 1820–40.

HILL, EDWARD. C.C. 1698.

HILL, FRANCIS. C.C. 1679.

HILL, FRANCIS. *London.* Apprenticed 1664, C.C. 1672.

HILL, GEO. *Lambourn*, about 1770.

HILL, JAS. *5 Ball Alley, Lombard St.*, 1793–1810..

HILL, JNO. *King St., Covent Garden.* Long-case clock, about 1700.

HILL, JNO. *Prescot*, 1775.

HILL, JOHN. Petitioner for incorporation of C.C. 1630.

HILL, JOHN, son of Benjamin. *London.* C.C. 1670.

HILL, JOHN. *Seven Dials.* C.C. 1705–30.

HILL, JOHN. *Fleet St.* C.C. 1731–70.

HILL, JOHN *15 James St., Covent Garden*, 1820.

HILL, LEONARD. *61 Fleet St.*, 1817–23.

HILL, MATT. *Devonshire St., London*, about 1790.

HILL, ROBERT. *Stafford.* C.C. 1795; clocks and watches.

HILL, SAM. *Sheffield.* Maker of good clocks, 1770–1814.

HILL, SAMPSON, C. *9 Ball Alley, Lombard St.*

HILL, THOMAS. *London.* C.C. 1632.

HILL, THOMAS. *Fleet St.*, 1680–90. His name was engraved, in conjunction with that of Henry Harper, on a long-case clock in possession of the Ironmongers' Company; on the clock is the further inscription, 'The gift of John Woolfe, member of the Company'. 'Thos. Hill, over against Chancery Lane, Fleet St.', card, Ponsonby collection. He was a liveryman of the Ironmongers' Company.

HILL, THOMAS. *London.* C.C. 1783.

HILL, THOMAS. *London.* C.C. 1789.

HILL, THOMAS. *Aldersgate St.*, 1777–86. Thomas Hill was the maker of a gold verge watch, embossed case, said to have belonged to Captain Cook.

HILL, WM. Apprenticed in 1682 to Sam Clyatt, C.C.

HILL, WM. *Walsingham.* Long-case clock, about 1713, Mr. Geo. F. Glenny.

HILLCOAT, WILLIAM. *33 Queen St., Cheapside*, 1790–94.

HILLERSDEN, JNO. C.C. 1656.

HILLERY, JNO. Apprenticed in 1681 to Richard Farrett, C.C.

HILLIAR, RICHARD. *London.* Apprenticed 1723, C.C. 1740.

HILLIARD, G. *35 Queen St., Cheapside*, 1820.

HILLIARD, JAMES. *Charleston, U.S.A.*, 1738. Clocks and watches.

HILLIER, GEORGE. *London (Cheapside).* C.C. 1807–20.

HILLIER, JAMES. Watch-glass maker, *12 Church St., Spitalfields*, 1790–1810.

HILLIER, WILLIAM. C.C. 1679.

HILLIER, WILLIAM. *London (Aldersgate).* Apprenticed 1762, C.C. 1769, died 1807.

HILLINGS, BERNARD. C.C. 1652.

HILLIUS, MARTIN. *Dresden.* Master 1668; one of the first four members of the clockmakers' guild; watch and plate clock, set stones, M.P.S., Dresden.

HILLMAN, WM. *Plymouth Dock*, 1770.

HILLRICH, JOHANN. *Pestteine.* Regulator, Buda-Pesth Museum, about 1800.

HILLS. *Fleet St.*, 1774.

HILLS, JOHN. *London.* Apprenticed 1712, C.C. 1728.

HILLS, RALPH. *Sunderland*, about 1775. He was apprenticed to David Paterson, who was apprenticed to Jno. Ogden.

HILSON, THOS. Apprenticed in 1674 to Jno. Mark, C.C.

HILTON, EMANUEL. *Portsmouth.* Long-case clock, about 1790.

HILTON, JOHN. Apprenticed to Wm. Moraley but turned over to Thos. Tompion, admitted C.C. 1698.

HIMELE, JAS. *New York*, 1786.

HIND, PARIS. Watch jeweller, *26 Spa Rd.*, 1790–94.

HINDE, JOHN. *London.* 1680 C.C.

HINDLEY, HENRY. *York*, f., 1731. Died 1770; a clever clock and watch maker; watch by him in V. & A., London, h.m., 1766; made a clock for York Minster in 1750; also several others with pendulums 56 ft. long; is credited with having invented the screw-cutting lathe about 1740; about the same date he devised an improved wheel-cutting engine. See BROWN, J.

HINDLEY, JOSEPH. *York*, f., 1754. Made a clock for Holy Trinity Church, Hull, in 1772.

HINDLEY, I. Hanging clock, about 1710, signed 'Hindley, York', oak case.

HINE, JOHN. *68 Red Lion St., Clerkenwell*, 1790–94.

HINE, THOS. *Fleet St.*, 1760–74.

HINEMORE, GEORGE, son. *London.* C.C. 1771–85.

HINEMORE, JOHN. *London.* Apprenticed 1733, C.C. 1741–71; died a. 1777.

HINEMORE, JOHN, brother. *London.* C.C. 1777.

HINKS, WM. *Southampton.* Lantern clock, about 1700.

HINKSMAN, J. *Madeley*. Clock, about 1770.

HIMMERS, ROBERT. *Edinburgh*. Watch, about 1800.

HINTON, J. *91 Boro'*, 1815–20; *20 Tabernacle Row, Finsbury*, 1835.

HINTZCH, JACOB HANS. *Göteborg*. Born 1627, died 1697. Also HINSCH.

HINZE, ULRICH. *Brunswick*, 1594. From *Wolfenbüttel*. *Halberstadt* in 1600. The first watch in Brunswick.

HIORNE, JAS. *Snow Hill*. C.C. 1730.

HIORNE, JOHN. *Bartholomew Close*. C.C. 1707, master 1744.

HIORNE, WILLIAM, son. *London*. C.C. 1741.

HIRST. *Bury St. Edmunds*.

HIRST, ISAAC. 1740.

HIRST, JOHN. 1760.

HIRST, SAM. *Leeds*, 1770–95.

HISLOP, ADAM. *Biggar*. Born 1753, died 1827.

HISLOP, JOHN. *Peebles*. Born 1780, died 1856.

HISLOP, RICHARD. *Rosoman St., Clerkenwell*, 1775–1803.

HISLOP, RICHARD, son of the above. *53 Rosoman St.*, 1804–42.

HISLOP, WILLIAM, younger son of the first-named Richard, *15 Rosoman St.*, 1820; *96 St. John St. Rd.*, 1835–72; was some time hon. sec. and an active member of the governing body of the Horological Institute; died in 1876.

HITCHCOCK, JOHN. *London*. Apprenticed 1697, C.C. 1718–22.

HITCHEN, JOHN. *Queen St.* C.C. 1720; watch, 1740.

HITCHENS, JOSEPH. *Brown's Buildings, St. Mary Axe*, 1779–94.

HITCHMAN, NICHOLAS. Apprenticed in 1677 to Richard Ames, C.C.

HOADLEY, CALVIN. Associated with Eli Terry at *Plymouth, Connecticut*, in the production of American clocks during the early part of the nineteenth century.

HOADLEY, SAMUEL and LUTHER. *Winsted, U.S.A.*, 1807. With Riley Whiting, made wooden clocks.

HOADLEY, SILAS. *Greystone, U.S.A.* Born 1786, died 1870; in firm of Terry, Thomas & Hoadley, 1809; Thomas & Hoadley, 1810–13, and then alone till 1849.

HOBART, GABRIEL. *York*, f., 1750.

HOBBINS, —. *Freckenham, Worcester*, 1820.

HOBBS, ALLIN. *London*. Apprenticed 1727, C.C. 1734–44.

HOBBS, JAMES. *Lambeth*, 1830.

HOBBS, JAS. *142 Great Tower St.*, 1830.

HOBERG, ANDERS. *Stockholm*. Born 1766, died 1834; verge and cylinder watches, one Nord. Museum.

HOBLER, FRAS. *Porter St., Newport Market*, 1793.

HOBLER, PAUL. *Porter St., Newport Market*. Hon. freeman C.C. 1781; 1770–90.

HOBSON, JOHN. Petitioner for incorporation of C.C. 1630.

HOCHICORN, ISAAC. C.C. 1728.

HOCHNADEL. Small repeating bracket clock, about 1700, inscribed 'Pietro Hochnadel, Venezzia'.

HOCKER, JOHN. *Reading*. Apprenticed to John Martin, and turned over to Edward Josslin; C.C. 1729; lantern clock, about 1730.

HOCKER, JOHN. *London*. Apprenticed 1714, C.C. 1729–40.

HOCKER, JOS. *Basingstoke*. 30-hour clock, about 1740.

HOCKERS, G. *Ephrata, Lancaster, U.S.A.*, 1750. Tower clock for Ephrata cloister.

HOCKSON, JNO. *London*. Watch, 1700.

HODDLE, JNO. *Pye Corner*. C.C. 1705–30.

HODDLE, JOHN. *Reading*. Maker of lantern clocks, 1688.

HODGE, H. *London*. Watch, 1795.

HODGES, FREDK. *Dublin*. Rack lever watch, about 1806.

HODGES, JAMES. *London*. Long mahogany inlaid Sheraton style case clock, Wetherfield collection, about 1800.

HODGES, JNO. *227 High Holborn*. Card, British Museum, 1780.

HODGES, NATHANIEL. 'In Wine Office Courte, Fleet Street'. C.C. 1681; bracket clock, small square dial, ebony case with brass basket top, about 1685, Wetherfield collection; another specimen, about 1700.

HODGES, SAMUEL. *London*. C.C. 1770.

HODGES, THOS. *Antigua*, 1780.

HODGES, WILLIAM. C.C. 1719.

HODGINSON, SARAH. C.C. 1700.

HODGSON, HY. *Lancaster*, 1816 f.

HODGSON, JNO. *Skipton*, 1720.

HODGSON, MARCUS. *York*, f., 1676. Watch, inscribed 'Mark Hodgson, Eboraci', 1710.

HODGSON, THOMAS. *Durham*, 1820–47.

HODGSON, WM. *Philadelphia*, 1785.

HODIERNE, JNO. Apprenticed in 1638 to Platt, C.C.

HODSOLL, WILLIAM. *31 Primrose St., Bishopsgate*, 1800–08.

HODSON, GEO. *Bolton*, 1765.

HODSON, JNO. Apprenticed in 1666 to Thos. Rotherham, C.C.

HODSON, WM. *Bolton*, 1780.

HOFF, FRIEDRICH KARL. *Frankfurt-a.-M.* Born 1730, died 1795; made clock for Goethe's father; town clock.

HOFF, GEORGE. *Lancaster City, U.S.A.* Born about 1740 in *Germany*; went to *U.S.A.* 1765; died 1816; good watch and clock maker; many long-case clocks.

HOFFMAN, M. Octagonal watch, Marfels collection, signed 'Melchior Hoffman, Augsburg', about 1600.

HOFFNER, HY. *Philadelphia*, 1791.

HOGAN, J. Watch movement maker, *6 Badgers Yard, St. John St.*, 1808–20.

HÖGBERG, LARS JACOBSSON. *Malmö*, 1775–95. Watch movement Nord. Museum.

HOGLATE, JOHN. *London*. C.C. 1734.

HOGUET à *Paris*. Eighteenth century clock so signed.

HOGUET, AUGUSTUS. *Philadelphia*, 1819–25.

HÖHEER, JOHAN CHRISTOPH. Clock, green vaulted chambers, Dresden, about 1680.

HOLBORN, ROBT. *Sheffield*, 1770.

HOLBOROUGH, THOS. *Ipswich*, 1715.

HOLBROOK, HY. *Liverpool*, 1770.

HOLDCROFT, HY. Apprenticed in 1678 to Chas. Halstead, C.C.

HOLDER, HENRY. *London*. Watch, brass inner, enamelled outer case, 1760.

HOLDS, CHAS. *Silver Dials, St. Bartholomew Close*, 1793.

HOLDWAY, GEORGE. *305 Strand*, 1779.

HOLE, HENRY. *11 Lisle St., Leicester Sq.*, 1810; *12 Kingsgate St.*, 1817–23.

HOLEYARD, SAMUEL. C.C. 1705.

HOLGATE, W. *Wigan*, 1770.

HOLIDAY, SAMUEL. *London*. Apprenticed 1753, C.C. 1765.

HOLLAND, GABRIEL. *Coventry*. Bracket clock, about 1750.

HOLLAND, GEORGE. Petitioner for incorporation of C.C. 1630–55.

HOLLAND, HENRY. Probably apprenticed in 1657 to Walter Gibbs, C.C.; a bracket clock by him, strikes the hours but has only one barrel; black case.

HOLLAND, JAMES. *Bury (Lancs.)*, 1770.

HOLLAND, JOHN. *5 Bishopsgate Without*. Livery Goldsmiths' Company, 1765–77.

HOLLAND, LEWIS. Apprenticed in 1691 to Thos. Birch, C.C.

HOLLAND, LEWIS. C.C. 1699.

HOLLAND, REUBEN. *London.* Bracket clock, about 1780.

HOLLAND, ROBERT. *London.* Bracket clock, about 1740

HOLLAND, THOMAS. C.C. 1632; master 1656.

HOLLAND, THOMAS. *London.* C.C. 1659–67.

HOLLAND, THOS. *167 Fleet St.,* 1815–18.

HOLLAND, WM. *Chester,* 1814–18.

HOLLIDAIE, EDWD. *London.* C.C. 1650–56; signed petition in its favour, 1656.

HOLLIER, JOHN. *Newington, Surrey.* a. 1742, died 1769; watch.

HOLLIER, JONATHAN. *Skinner St.* Liveryman C.C. 1776.

HOLLINGSHEAD, J. *Olney,* 1790.

HOLLINSHEAD, JACOB. *Salem,* 1771.

HOLLINSHEAD, MORGAN. *Morris Town (Philadelphia),* 1775. Clocks and watches.

HOLLIS, THOS. Apprenticed in 1649 to Jas. Seabourne; C.C. 1656.

HOLLISONE, ALEX. *Liverpool.* Watch, 1795; another watch, 'Alex. Hollisone, London'.

HOLLIWELL, WM. *Liverpool.* Clock, about 1750.

HOLLIWELL & SON. *Derby,* 1780.

HOLLOWAY, —. Brass clock, signed 'William Holloway, at Stroud', 1669.

HOLLOWAY, ARTHUR. *London.* Apprenticed 1697–1712 C.C.

HOLLOWAY, EDWARD. C.C. 1650.

HOLLOWAY, RICHARD. Apprenticed in 1675 to Cornelius Herbert, C.C.

HOLLOWAY, ROBERT. C.C. 1632.

HOLLOWAY, THOS. *Winton,* 1740.

HOLLOWAY, WILLIAM. *Cullem St.* C.C. 1697.

HOLLYAR, SAM. Apprenticed in 1693 to Jno. Barrow, C.C.; clock, about 1710.

HOLM, J. P. *Halmstad,* 1824–40. Wall clocks.

HOLM, JNO. *Lancaster,* 1783.

HOLMAN, —. *Lewes,* 1787–1814. C.C. Watch.

HOLMAN. See KEMP and HOLMAN.

HOLMDEN, JOHN. Musical clockmaker, *18 St. James' Walk,* 1806; *50 King St., Goswell Rd.,* 1840. Livery C.C. 1807.

HOLME, JOHN. *Cockermouth.* Freeman of *Lancaster,* 1783.

HOLME, LAWRENCE. *Liverpool,* about 1820.

HOLMES, EDWARD. *9 Foster Lane, Cheapside.* 1773–94.

HOLMES, JOHN. Apprenticed to Peter Miller; C.C. 1697.

HOLMES, JOHN. *156 Strand,* near *Somerset House.* He seems to have been one among the leading mechanicians, and when the turret clock at Greenwich Hospital was destroyed by fire in 1779 was given the order for a new one, in connection with the design of which he sought the advice of Smeaton and Ludlam; a gold watch by him is in the Fitzwilliam Museum, Cambridge; it belonged to William Pitt, and bears the Pitt crest, a heron holding an anchor in the right claw; the Wetherfield collection contained two long mahogany-case clocks of his manufacture, one a particularly choice example of Chippendale dating from about 1770, and another about twenty years later; he was one of the experts appointed by the select committee of the House of Commons in 1791 to report on Mudge's timekeepers. George Yonge succeeded him in 1798.

HOLMES, MATTHEW STEEL. *10 Shoemakers' Row, Blackfriars,* 1820–42. Livery C.C. 1825.

HOLMES, NESTOR. Apprenticed in 1674 to Jere. Gregory, C.C.; he ran away from his apprenticeship.

HOLMES, RICHD. HY. *Hull,* 1822.

HOLMES, ROBERT. *Dublin.* Long-case clock, about 1776.

HOLMES, SAML. *Liverpool.* Watch, 1758.

HOLMES, THOS. Apprenticed in 1686 to Peter Miller; C.C.

HOLMES, THOS. *Cheadle,* 1735.

HOLMES, WM. *12 Clerkenwell Green,* 1783.

HOLMES, WM. *156 Strand,* 1810–12.

HOLMGREN, JACOB. *Stockholm,* 1811–35. Bracket clock.

HOLOWAY, JO. *Newberry.* Watch, with sun and moon hour indicators, 1680.

HOLROYD, JNO. *Wakefield,* 1775–1814.

HOLROYD, T. *Huddersfield,* 1810–14.

HOLT, JOHN. *Rochdale,* 1818.

HOLT, MATTHEW. *Wigan,* 1775.

HOLT, MATTHEW. *Coventry,* 1818.

HOLT, MATTHEW. *Wigan,* 1775. Died 1805; watch, Denham collection.

HOLT, RICHARD. *Newark,* 1804–42.

HOLT, T. *Wakefield,* 1814.

HOLT, THOS. *Lancaster,* 1747, f.

HOLT, VALENTINE, 1818–21.

HOLT, WM. 1767, f.

HOLTHAM, GEO. *London.* Watch, 1720.

HÖLTZEL (HÖLZEL), MICHAEL. *Cologne,* 1797–1813.

HOLTZMAN, JOHANNIS, in *Wien.* In the Schloss collection is a watch invented by him about 1775, in which the dial is raised much above the movement, the hands being driven through a tube.

HOLZAPFEL, MARTIN. *Hannstetten.* Came to *Augsburg* 1733–51; back in *Hannstetten* 1756.

HONE, RT. *London.* Watch, 1750.

HONEYBONE, R. *Fairford,* about 1690–1814 C.C.

HONEYBONE, THOMAS. *Old Brentford,* 1830–40.

HONEYCHURCH, SAML. *Cheapside.* Long-case clock, about 1770.

HONTON, RICHD. *Oversley-Green, Warwick,* about 1790.

HOOD, JAS. *London.* Watch, 1805.

HOOGENDIJK, ADRIAAN. *Rotterdam,* 1625–about 1650. Large watch M.M.A; watch movement, Stern. collection; travelling clock.

HOOKE, A. Silver-gilt watch, Fellows collection at the British Museum, inscribed 'A. Hook, 1661'.

HOOKE, JOHN. C.C. 1698.

HOOKE, ROBERT. Born 1635, died 1703; invented the balance-spring for watches and perhaps the anchor escapement for clocks.

HOOKER, JAS. *22 Five Fields Row, Chelsea.* Card, British Museum, 1791.

HOOKER, JOHN. *London.* C.C. 1698, died 1751; watch.

HOOKER, THOS. *London.* Long-case clock, about 1780.

HOOLE, S. *London,* 1770. Clock hands.

HOOPER, GILES. *London (Greville St.).* Apprenticed 1749, C.C. 1758–72.

HOOPER, HENRY. *39 Cheapside,* 1792.

HOOPER, JNO. *Winton.* Clock, about 1760.

HOPCRAFT, DAVID. *London.* C.C. 1734.

HOPE, CHAS. *London,* 1820.

HOPE, EDWARD. *Bridge St., Strand,* 1775; *97 Oxford St.,* 1783–85.

HOPE, GEO. *London.* Watch, 1825.

HOPE, PETER. *Liverpool.* Pair-case watch, h.m., 1795, Evan Roberts collection.

HOPE, WM. Watch, h.m., 1767.

HOPETOWN, WM. *London.* Watch, 1822.

HOPGOOD, T. B. *202 Bishopsgate Without,* 1807–23. Afterwards Hopgood & Salmon.

HOPKINS, A. B. *32 Aldgate,* 1823.

HOPKINS, ASA. *Northfield, U.S.A.,* 1820.

HOPKINS, EDWD. *48 King St., Soho,* 1817. A long-case timepiece, corner figures representing seasons, signed 'Edwd. Hopkins, Bradford', about 1800.

HOPKINS, JOHN. C.C. 1641.

HOPKINS, JOHN. *Fleet St.,* 1753–56.

HOPKINS, RICHARD THOMAS. *London (Foster La)*. C.C. 1769, livery C.C. 1802; watch V. & A.

HOPKINS, THOMAS. *London (Oat Lane)*. Apprenticed 1738, C.C. 1746–69.

HOPKINS, THOS. *Maiden Lane*. C.C. 1730.

HOPKINS, WILLIAM. *London*. Apprenticed 1742, C.C. 1751–59.

HOPLE. See HAYLE.

HOPPER, E. *Stockport*, 1770.

HOPPERTON. Long-case clock, 'Emmanuel Hopperton, Leeds', about 1760.

HOPPERTON, SAML. *Leeds*, 1770.

HOPPING, JAMES. *London*. Apprenticed 1774, C.C. 1781–88.

HOPPS, GEORGE. *London*. Apprenticed 1789, C.C. 1798, livery C.C. 1812.

HOPTON, ANTHONY and MATTHEW. *Edinburgh*, 1799–1817. Wooden clocks.

HOPTON, JOHN, son of Anthony. *Edinburgh*, 1817–50. Wooden clocks.

HORLE, URBAN. *Mainz*, early seventeenth century.

HORN, JOHANN MARTIN. *Augsburg*. Master 1750–86.

HORNBLOWER, THOMAS. *London*. C.C. 1772.

HORNBLOWER, WILLIAM. C.C. 1713; long-case clock, Japanese decoration, arch dial, style about 1740.

HORNBLOWER, WILLIAM H. (possibly a son of William) was beadle of C.C. 1779.

HORNBY, —. *London*. Watch, 1825.

HORNBY, GEO. *Liverpool*, 1765.

HORNBY, GERARD, *Liverpool*, 1780.

HORNBY, HY. *Liverpool*, 1818.

HORNBY, JNO. *Liverpool*, 1790.

HORNBY, RICHD. *Pool Lane, Liverpool*, 1810–30.

HORNE, EDWARD. *London*. Apprenticed 1696, C.C. 1704–33.

HORNE, GEORGE HENRY. C.C. 1718.

HORNE, HENRY. *London Bridge*. Master C.C. 1730–68.

HORNE, HENRY. *London*. Apprenticed 1813, C.C. 1820.

HORNE, JOHN. *London*. Apprenticed 1772, C.C. 1788.

HORNE, SAMUEL. C.C. 1654; master 1672–73.

HÖRNING, SVEN PETER. *Stockholm*, 1785–1805. Two bracket clocks.

HORNSBY, GERRARD. *Liverpool*, 1817.

HORNSBY, ROBERT. Apprenticed to William Harris; admitted C.C. 1788.

HORNSEY, THOS. E. *York*, f., 1826.

HORSEMAN, STEPHEN. Was apprenticed to Daniel Quare 1702, admitted C.C. 1709; Quare, prior to his death, took Horseman into partnership.

HORSFALL, WM. *Bradford, Yorks*, 1830.

HORSLEY, BEN. Apprenticed in 1693 to William Watson, C.C.

HORSLEY, CORNELIUS. *York*. A Quaker, f., 1656.

HORSNAILE, GEO. *Warfield*. One-hand clock, about 1730.

HORWOOD, CHARLES. *Bristol*, 1770–85.

HORWOOD, MOSES. *Bristol*, son of Charles, 1774.

HORTLANDER, HANS. *Pitea*, 1816–35.

HORY (ORY, HOURY), ANDRÉ. *Paris*, about 1700–about 1750. Fine Boulle-work bracket clock Pal. de Pau, Paris; watch with 6-hour dial Gélis collection; repeating watch, Ilbert collection.

HOSKINS, DANL. Clock, about 1630.

HOSKINS, JOSEPH. *London*. C.C. 1819.

HOSKINS & BIRD. *11 St. John's Sq., Clerkenwell*, 1822–30.

HOSMER, —. *Tonbridge*, about 1790 C.C. Watch.

HOTHAM, HY. Apprenticed in 1665 to Jno. Pennock; C.C. 1673.

HOUBLIN L'AÎNÉ. *Rue Montague, St. Geneviève, Paris*. garde-visiteur, 1769.

HOUDIN, JACQUES FRANÇOIS, son. *Paris*. Born 1783, died 1860; eminent maker; worked for Breguet; made clock for C.A. & M.

HOUDIN, ROBERT. *Paris*, 1820–30.

HOUDIN, ROBERT, son. *Paris*, early nineteenth century–1863. Published *L'art de connaître et de régler les montres et les pendules*.

HOUGH, JNO. *Knutsford*, 1740.

HOUGH, JNO. *Warrington*. Clock, about 1760.

HOUGHMAN, CHARLES. *Aldersgate St.* C.C. 1770–80.

HOUGHTON, JAMES. *198 Tooley St.*, 1790–94.

HOUGHTON, JAMES. *Ormskirk*. Assistant of William Garrat, and afterwards maker of watches with Debaufre's dead-beat escapement, with two escape wheels as modified by Sully, known in Lanarkshire as the clubfooted verge, 1800–20.

HOUGHTON, JOHN. *Chorley*, about 1770–95.

HOUGHTON, RICHARD. C.C. 1690.

HOUGHTON, THOMAS. *Chorley*, 1780–1840. Clubfooted verge watch Chamb. collection.

HOUGHTON, THOS. *Chorley*, 1780–1840.

HOUGHTON, WILLIAM. —. 1695. Patented with Edw. Booth an escapement with "a new sort of teeth made like tinterhooks".

HOUILLERE, JONATHAN. *London*, 1725–63. Watch.

HOULBROOK, HENRY. *Liverpool*, 1781–1814. Watch.

HOULHERE, —. 'Jona Houlhere at the sign of the spring clock in Broad St., London', about 1760.

HOULLGATT, W. Oval watch, V. & A., inscribed 'W. Houllgatt, att Ipswich', about 1640.

HOULTON, —. *Orange Grove, Bath*, 1770.

HOUNSON, THOMAS. *London*. Apprenticed 1738, C.C. 1746.

HOURIET, JACQUES FRÉDÉRIC. *Locle*. Born 1743, died 1830; clever horologist and maker of spherical balance-springs.

HOURY (HORY, ORY, OURY, OURRY), JEAN. *Paris*. Master 1777–89.

HOURY (HORY, ORY, OURY, OURRY), LOUIS. *Paris*. 1675 m., juré 1693; Boulle bracket clock; watch about 1680 with balance spring, Ilbert collection.

HOUSE, J. *Gray's Inn Lane*. Pair-case silver verge; sun and moon watch, 1700.

HOUSE, MATT. *Cork Lane*. C.C. 1730.

HOUSE, ROBERT. *32 Upper Moorfields*, 1790.

HOUSMAN, JACOB. *Lancaster*, 1732, f.

HOUSTON, S. *Dublin*. Watch, 1799.

HOVENSCHIÖLD, JOACHIM. *Stockholm*, 1767. Died 1800; many watches, two Nord. Museum; bracket and wall clocks.

HOVENSCHIÖLD, JOACHIM, brother. *Stockholm*. 1784–1820.

HOVENSCHIÖLD, JOHAN ERIC, son. *Stockholm*. Born 1782, died 1832; table clock.

HOW, BENJAMIN. C.C. 1691.

HOW, JOHN. *London*. Apprenticed 1796, C.C. 1811.

HOW, MATTHEW. *London*. Apprenticed 1730, C.C. 1747–53.

HOW, SAMUEL. *London*. Apprenticed 1727, C.C. 1735.

HOW, THOS. Apprenticed in 1670 to Isaac Romien, but turned over to Nat. Delander; C.C. 1677.

HOW, WILLIAM. C.C. 1667; elected assistant but excused, 1697.

HOW & MASTERTON. *White Hart Court, Gracechurch St.*, 1750–60.

HOWARD, —, at the *Ring and Pearl, New Round Court, Strand*, 1770.

HOWARD, EDWD. *5 Kirby St., Hatton Garden*, 1775–1804.

HOWARD, H. & M. *London*. Watch, steel index disc, 1792.

HOWARD, JOHN. C.C. 1694.

HOWARD, JOHN JARVIS. *68 Aldersgate St.*, 1790–94.

HOWARD, RICHARD. Apprenticed to Daniel Delander; C.C. 1718; long-case clock, arch dial, inscribed 'Richard Howard, New Brentford'.

HOWARD, THOMAS. *Philadelphia*, 1789–91.

HOWARD, WHARTON, son of Edward. *London (Hoxton and Shoreditch)*. Apprenticed 1780, C.C. 1787–1816; watch.

HOWARD, WM. Repaired the clock at Exeter Cathedral, 1760.

HOWARD, WM. *London*. Watch, h.m., 1777.

HOWARTH, JA. *Blackburn*, 1770.

HOWDEN, JAMES. *Edinburgh*, 1781–1842. Long-case clock.

HOWE, EPHRAIM. Apprenticed to Graham, C.C. 1729.

HOWE, JNO. *Alresford*, 1800.

HOWE, SAMUEL. C.C. 1712.

HOWELL, BENJAMIN. C.C. 1699.

HOWELL, DAN. C.C. 1637.

HOWELL, GEO. *London*. Watch, 1785.

HOWELL, JOHN. *Bull's Head Court, Newgate St.* C.C. 1724–30.

HOWELL, JOSEPH. *Golden Sq.* C.C. 1721.

HOWELL, STEPHEN. *London*. Watch 1770.

HOWELL, WM. *Bristol*. A long-case clock by him, dating from about 1770, shows 'High Water at Bristol Key'.

HOWELLS, WILLIAM. *Kennington*. Apprenticed to Thos. Sheafe; C.C. 1780; one of the experts appointed by the select committee of the House of Commons to examine Mudge's timekeepers.

HOWELLS, WILLIAM. *Bristol*, 1762–96. In 1796 entered into partnership with P. P. Barraud and G. Jamison of Portsea to make Timekeepers on the principle of Mr. Mudge.

HOWELLS, WILLIAM HENRY. Apprenticed to William Howells; admitted C.C. 1820.

HOWELLS & PENNINGTON. *London*, 1790. Employed by Mudge's son to make chronometers to his father's design; remontoire chronometer, G.M.

HOWES, JESSE JOHN. *London*. Apprenticed 1797, C.C. 1805. Also HOWSE.

HOWES, JNO. C.C. 1672.

HOWES, JOHN, son of William. *London*. l.C.C. 1780–1819.

HOWES, JOS. *Fleet St.*, 1760–75.

HOWES, S. *Downham.* Clock, about 1770.

HOWES, THOS. *London*. Clock, about 1680.

HOWES, WILLIAM. *London*. 1793 l.C.C. Possibly same as William above.

HOWES, WM. *Temple Bar*. C.C. 1730.

HOWLETT, JNO., son of the above. Migrated from *London* to *Bath*; his son afterwards carried on business at Calne.

HOWLETT, JOHN. *London*. Known as a maker of good watches, about 1750; a specimen in a gold *repoussé* case, Schloss collection, about 1770.

HOWLETT, STEPHEN. Apprenticed in 1657 to Peter Bellune, C.C.

HOWLETT, WILLIAM. *Coventry*, 1754–84. Partner in Vale, Howlett & Carr

HOWS, THOS. *The Sun, Pope's Head Alley*. Admitted C.C. 1632; known as a maker of watches, 1630–40.

HOWSE, CHARLES. *5 Great Tower St.* Watch, 1768, master C.C. 1787; 1768–94.

HOWSE, JESSE JOHN. *London*. Apprenticed 1797, C.C. 1805. Also HOWES.

HOWSE, JOHN. *Croyden*. C.C. 1687.

HOWSE, JOHN. Admitted C.C. 1706.

HOWSE, JOSEPH. 1698.

HOWSE, MATTHEW. *London*. C.C. 1730.

HOWSE, WILLIAM. *13 Fleet St.* C.C. 1731; master 1777; 1731–80.

HOWSON, JOHN. Admitted C.C. 1699.

HOYLE, HY. C.C. 1677.

HOYLE, WM. *Bolton-le-Moors*, 1818.

HOYSS, LEOPOLD. *Bamberg*, 1713. Died 1797; a clockmaker of great repute; made clocks with two pendulums swinging in opposite directions.

HOYT, GEORGE R. *Albany City, U.S.A.*, 1823.

HOYT, HENRY. *New York*, early nineteenth century.

HUART (HUAU), ALEXIS LOUIS MATHIEU. *Paris*. Master 1758–89.

HUAUD (HUAUT), AMY, brother. *Geneva*. Born 1657, died 1729. *v.* LES FRÈRES, below.

HUAUD (HUAUT), JEAN PIERRE, brother. *Geneva*. Born 1655, died 1723; signed 'Huaud le puisné'; watch illuminated Baillie; watches British Museum, V. and A., Cluny Museum, Garnier and Olivier collections. *v.* LES FRÈRES, below.

HUAUD (HUAUT), LES FRÈRES (JEAN, PIERRE and AMY). *Geneva*, 1682. Appointed painters to the Court of Prussia, 1686, and went to *Berlin*; returned *Geneva*, 1700; signed a. 1686, 'Les deux frères Huaut les jeunes'; signed after 1686, 'Les Frères Huaud', or 'Les deux frères Huaud', with the addition of 'peintres de son A. E. à Berlin', 'p.d. V. A. fct à Berlin'; signed after 1700, 'Les frères Huaut', or 'Les deux frères Huaut', or 'Peter et Amicus Huaut'; also signed 'Fratres Huault'. The name is spelt Huaud or Huaut and sometimes Huault. Watches British Museum, V. and A., Louvre, K.H.M., M.M.A., Hohenzollern Museum, Berlin, Königliche Museum, Berlin, Musée Condé, Musée de Dijon, Vienna Treasury.

HUAUD (HUAUT), PIERRE, son. *Geneva*. Born 1647; went *Germany*, Court of Brandenberg, 1685; *Geneva*, 1686; returned *Germany*, 1689; appointed painter to Elector, 1691; died about 1698. The best enamel painter of the three brothers. Several signed paintings; earliest known 1679; signed 'Huaud l'aisné' or 'P. Huaud primo-genitus' or 'P. Huaud P.G.' or 'Huaud l'aîné de Genève' or 'Pierre Huaud' or 'Petrus Huaud major natus'; watches Louvre, Musée d'art et d'histoire de Genève, Hohenzollern Museum, Berlin, and Olivier collection.

HUBBARD, JOHN. C.C. 1722.

HUBERT, DAVID. *Strand*. Admitted C.C. 1714, master 1743; repeating watch, silver case engraved and pierced, enamel dial, Roman hour numerals, Arabic figures outside for minutes, the plate covered with engraving, and inscribed 'Dav. Hubert, London'; a repeating watch by him sounds the minutes, and is therefore an early specimen of the kind; another specimen of his work is a bracket clock repeating the quarters on six bells by pulling a cord, which winds up the quarter repeating train, brass arched dial, strike-silent, day of the month, verge escapement; 1714–48.

HUBERT, ESTIENNE. *Rouen*, about 1620. Shell watch, crystal covers, Mallet collection, illuminated Baillie.

HUBERT, ESTIENNE. *Rouen*. Maker of a watch said to have belonged to Mary, Queen of Scots; in 1657 John Smith was fined 10s. for putting the name of Estinne Hubert on a watch; alarum watch in pierced and engraved silver case with inscription, 'Estinne Hubert à Rouen', V. & A., about 1610; watch, Pierpont Morgan collection, of about the same date. "Lost upon New-year's-day, above stairs in Whitehall, a gold watch with a plain shapen case; the watch was made at Rouen, maker's name Hubert. Whoever brings it to her Royal Highness the Princess of Denmark's porter at the Cockpit, shall have two guineas reward" (*Lond. Gaz.*, Jan. 2, 1689).

HUBERT, ESTINNE L'AÎNÉ. *Amsterdam.* Repeating watch, about 1690; watch, about 1710, 'B. Hubert, à la Rochelle'.

HUBERT, JACQUES. *Rouen,* 1663–77.

HUBERT, JACQUES. *Rouen.* Master 1694, juré 1696.

HUBERT, JAMES. Charlotte Hubert was apprenticed to him and Elizabeth his wife in 1725; and in 1730 Catherine Cext was also apprenticed to them.

HUBERT, JEAN. *Rouen.* Oval silver watch, about 1650; Buhl case bracket clock, about 1670; verge escapement, brass dial arched, silvered circle inscribed 'Jean Hubert'; below is a figure of Time with scythe, under which is the inscription, 'Solem Audet Dicere Falsum'; in the Pierpont Morgan collection is a watch, signed 'Jean Hubert, Rouen, au Grd. Monarque'; it has Turkish numerals, and dates from about 1680; watch, about 1795, inscribed 'P. Hubert l'aîné à Toulouse'.

HUBERT, JEAN LE JEUNE. *Rouen.* 1652 master, juré 1701; gold watch, Mallett collection.

HUBERT, NOEL. *Rouen.* Oval watch, V. & A., about 1620.

HUBERT, OLIVER, his son. C.C. 1749.

HUBERT, PASCAL. *Rouen.* Master 1649, juré 1697–about 1735; sun and moon watch, Ilbert collection.

HUBERT, PASCAL LE JEUNE. *Rouen.* Enamel watch; 1749.

HUBERT, PIERRE, son of Nicolas. *Rouen.* Master 1654, juré 1655.

HUBERT, TIMOTHÉE. Oval watch, signed 'Timothée Hubert à Rouen', in crystal case, about 1600, Pierpont Morgan collection; melon-shaped watch, Ashmolean Museum, silver case, richly chased dial, about 1650.

HUBNER, J. *Vienna.* Gold watch, Fitzwilliam Museum, eighteenth century (?).

HUCHASON, JAMES. *London.* C.C. 1718.

HUCHASON, RICHARD. C.C. 1702.

HUDLESTON, CHAS. Apprenticed in 1673 to Hy. Harper, C.C.; letter from L. Hudleston, to Mr. Keats, surgeon in Parliament St., 40th Oct. 1773, relating to a watch made by him for Miss Walter, Bury Hill, near Dorking; the price of the watch was 80 guineas, including enamelling, gold hands, and shagreen cases:

"As to the inside I can speak with more confidence, as there is not a single article but what is in part or altogether the work of my own hands; and this is one reason why I cannot dispatch a watch as expeditiously as others who trust to the work of other men's hands without making use of their own. To alter its going the silver plate in the inside should be moved by the little end of the key, bringing a higher figure towards the index in the cap to make it go faster and *vice-versa.* Moving the plate from one division to another will alter the watch's going about 2 minutes per day." ("MSS. of the Earl of Verulam.")

HUDSON, JNO. Apprenticed in 1684 to Chas. Halstead, C.C.

HUDSON, JNO. *Nottingham.* Watch, 1780.

HUDSON, JOHN. *St. Martin's Churchyard,* 1780–85.

HUDSON, RICHARD. " from Fleet St. at Grahams Head in Leadenhall St." 1770.

HUDSON, T. *Cheapside,* near the *Hen Cross, Nottingham,* about 1790.

HUES, PETER. *London.* 1652 C.C. See HUE.

HUES, PIERRY (PETER). C.C. 1632.

HUES, THOS. Apprenticed 1662 to Jno. Pennock, C.C.

HUET, FRANÇOIS. *Paris.* Master 1767–91; published *Dissertation sur l'horlogerie'. Paris,* 1791.

HUGES, JNO. *Maidstone.* Lantern clock, about 1710.

HUGGEFORD, IGNATIUS. Brother C.C. 1671; a watch by him played a prominent part in respect of the petition of Facio and Debaufre for extension of their watch jewel patent, 1671–1705.

HUGGEFORD, PETER. Apprenticed to Ignatius Huggeford, 1686, C.C.

HUGGINS, J. *Macclesfield,* 1810–15; *London,* about 1830.

HUGHES, H. *Caernarvon.* Watch, 1806.

HUGHES, HUGH. Long-case clock, about 1750.

HUGHES, JOHN. C.C. 1703, long-case clock, about 1710, signed 'John Hughs, London'.

HUGHES, JOHN. *94 Minories,* 1800.

HUGHES, MORRIS. Apprenticed in 1691 to Hy. Hammond. C.C.

HUGHES, RICHARD. *Carnarvon,* 1730–48.

HUGHES, S. *Gracechurch St.,* 1774.

HUGHES, THOMAS. *25 Broad St. Buildings.* Master C.C. 1765; first liveryman 1776; 1750–83.

HUGHES, THOMAS. *Broad St. Buildings.* C.C. 1712–35.

HUGHES, THOS., JUNR. *London,* about 1790.

HUGHES, WILLIAM. *119 High Holborn.* Hon. freeman C.C. 1781; centre seconds watch by him in the Guildhall Museum; four of Earnshaw's watches with his name thereon were deposited for trial at Greenwich Observatory in 1791; small enamelled watch, Schloss collection, about 1790; there was a fine travelling watch by him in the Summer Palace, Pekin; 7 in. in diameter, chimes on six bells and sets in motion mechanical figures, 1766–94. He was succeeded by Thos. Earnshaw.

HUGOT (HUGAULT), GILLES (GUILLAUME) NICOLAS. *Paris.* Master 1765–89.

HUGUELET, ABRAM. *Chaux-de-Fonds,* 1794–1822. Clock.

HUGUENAIL, CHARLES T., *Philadelphia,* 1799.

HUGUENIN, ABRAM, brother and partner. *Chaux-de-Fonds,* with London branch. Born 1702, died 1795; very able maker; clockmaker to the King of Prussia; many clocks.

HUGUENIN, ABRAM LOUIS, son of Moïse. *Neuchâtel.* Born 1733; went to *Berlin* in 1765 as Director of the royal clock factory at Berlin; on its failure in 1770, went to *Courtelary* and in 1775 to *Porrentruy; Rastatt* in 1778 as clockmaker to the Markgrave of Baden; at *Bienne* in 1792 and *Berlin* in 1804; died 1804.

HUGUENIN, AIMÉ. *Liverpool,* 1820.

HUGUENIN, CHARLES F. *Philadelphia,* 1795.

HUGUENIN, DAVID GUILLAUME. *La Brévine.* Born 1765, died 1841; watches and clocks.

HUGUENIN, FRÉDÉRIC LOUIS, son of L. Frédéric. *Chaux-de-Fonds,* 1764–1800. Several clocks.

HUGUENIN, HENRI CHARLES. *Chaux-de-Fonds,* 1772–84. Worked on the Jaquet-Droz automata.

HUGUENIN, ISAAC. *La Brévine.* Apprenticed 1785–1820; gold repeating cylinder watch.

HUGUENIN, JEAN PIERRE. *Chaux-de-Fonds.* Born 1718–86; several clocks.

HUGUENIN, LOUIS FRÉDÉRIC, son of Abram (3). *Chaux-de-Fonds.* Born 1713, died 1758; clockmaker to the King of Prussia; several clocks.

HUGUENIN, MOÏSE. *Chaux-de-Fonds,* 1727. Died about 1750; clockmaker to the King of Prussia.

HULBERT, WILLIAM. *Castle Green, Bristol,* 1708.

HULIER, WM. Apprenticed in 1669 to Thos. Creed; C.C. 1679.

HULL, HY. Apprenticed to Geo. Graham, C.C. 1738; a cylinder escapement maker, who worked for Ellicott and other celebrated manufacturers.

HULL, JNO. *York,* 1822.

HULL, PHILIP. Apprenticed in 1693 to Wm. Young, C.C.

HULME, JAS. *11 Bow St.,* 1817.

HULME, PETER. *Preston,* 1814.

HULST, JACOB. Admitted C.C. 1645.

HULTERSTROM, JOHAN FREDRIC. *Linköping.* Born 1797, died 1845.

HULTMAN, ANDERS. *Örebro.* Born 1756, died 1815.

HULTON, JOHN. Admitted C.C. 1724.

HUMBER, THOS. *London.* Long-case clock, about 1790.

HUMBERT, JOSEPH. *Paris*, 1789. *Geneva* and *Le Locle*, 1794. Started with Borel and Poterat the first watch factory in Geneva; it failed, and was taken over by the Republic; about 1800 made singing birds.

HUMBERT-DROZ, ISAÎE (ISAAC). *Paris.* Master 1776–89. HUMBERT.

HUMBERT-DROZ, JOSEPH. *Chaux-de-Fonds*, 1730–66. Able clock and watchmaker.

HUME, BENJ. Apprenticed in 1691 to Jno. Barnett, C.C.

HUME, CHAS. *London*, watch, 1830.

HUMFREY, NICHOLAS. Apprenticed in 1689 to Thos. Wheeler, C.C.

HUMFREYS, WM. Apprenticed in 1692 to Nat. Higginson, C.C.

HUMFUREY, W. H. *17 Great Surrey St.*, 1830–35.

HUMMEL, MATTHÄUS. *Waldau* and *Glashütte*, 1740–80. Made watches all of boxwood; one of the first to make ·cuckoo clocks; two wall clocks Furt. Museum.

HUMPHREYS, SAMUEL. *Fore St.* C.C. 1728.

HUMPHREYS, T. *Barnard Castle, Yorks.* Watch paper, about 1780.

HUMPHREYS, WM. Watch, about 1760.

HUMPHREYS, WM. *Barnard Castle.* Long-case clock, 1829, referred to by Dickens.

HUMPHRIES, J. *London.* Mantel clock, about 1750.

HUMPHRIES, THOMAS. *London.* C.C. 1815.

HUMPHRYS, WILLIAM. C.C. 1699.

HUNSDON, EDWD. *Chelmsford*, 1750.

HUNSDON, WILLIAM. *London.* C.C. 1768.

HUNSTMAN (HUNTSMAN), BENJAMIN. *Doncaster.* Born 1704, died 1774; turret clocks; improved steel-making and introduced 'Huntsman' steel; watch, Ashmolean Museum.

HUNT, —. Long-case clock, square dial, cherub corners, inscribed 'Rich: Hunt, Bristoll', about 1700.

HUNT, —. *Yarmouth.* About 1790 C.C.

HUNT, ABRAHAM. *Yarmouth.* Master 1788–95 C.C.

HUNT, EDWARD. Apprenticed to Thos. Williamson; C.C. 1684; watch movement with tulip pillars, in the Guildhall Museum. "Lost the 17 past, out of Mrs. Man's Lodgings in Sohoe, a gold minute pendulum watch, with a gold-studded case, the inward box marked E.H. and a coronet, made by Edw. Hunt" (*Lond. Gaz.*, September 15, 1692).

HUNT, GEO. *Bristol*, 1844.

HUNT, HENRY. *Salisbury*, about 1760–about 1800. Bracket clock and watch.

HUNT, HIRAM. *Robbinston, Maine, U.S.A.*; was said to have been the original 'Sam Slick' of Haliburton; he died at an advanced age in 1886.

HUNT, JAMES. C.C. 1708.

HUNT, JAS. *5 King St., Cheapside*, 1772.

HUNT, JOHN. C.C. 1671.

HUNT, JOHN. *London.* Apprenticed 1685, C.C. 1699.

HUNT, ROBT. Apprenticed in 1611 to Lawrence Sindrey, C.C.

HUNT, WILLIAM. *Ludgate St.*, 1753–56.

HUNTER, J. *Clapham.* Watch, 1815.

HUNTER, JNO. *Bristol*, about 1760.

HUNTER, JNO. *Bridlington*, 1770.

HUNTER, JNO. *Bridlington*, 1822.

HUNTER, JOHN. *Bristol*, about 1760–97. Long-case clock. Watches.

HUNTER, JOHN. *Clapham*, 1799–1815. Watch.

HUNTER, PETER. *Edinburgh*, 1794–1822.

HUNTER, ROBERT. *London (Little Britain).* C.C. 1801.

HUNTER, THOMAS. *43 Lombard St.*, 1754; *156 Fenchurch St.*, 1763. Liveryman C.C. 1768; 1754–94.

HUNTER, THOMAS, JUNR. *156 Fenchurch St.*, 1781–1800.

HUNTER, THOMAS. *54 Goswell Road*, 1788–94.

HUNTER, THOMAS. *Liverpool (Harrington St.)*, 1781–96. Watch.

HUNTER, THOS. *Liverpool*, 1780.

HUNTER, WILLIAM. *Dunfermline*, 1820–46.

HUNTER, WILLIAM. *51 Lombard St.* Livery Goldsmiths' Company, 1766–94.

HUNTER, WM. *156 Fenchurch St.*, 1804.

HUNTER & SON. *156 Fenchurch St.*, 1810–17.

HUNTSMAN, BEN. *Sheffield.* Born 1704, died 1776.

HUNZIKER, —. *Paris*, 1807–25. Gold engraved watch, set pearls, Fränkel collection.

HUON, JACQUES. *Paris.* Splendidly enamelled watch, V. & A., about 1650.

HÜPPE, SIGMUND. *Breslau*, comp. 1745; *Augsburg*, 1763.

HURLEY, ISAAC. *Red Lion St., Clerkenwell.* C.C. 1730–80.

HURLEY, JACOB. *London.* Apprenticed 1758, C.C. 1765.

HURLEY, JOSEPH. *Bristol* and *Bedminster*, 1775. Died 1793.

HURST, ARTHUR. *Ashford.* Lantern clock, about 1690.

HURST, ISAAC. C.C. 1677.

HURST, JOHN. *London.* Apprenticed 1764, C.C. 1771, livery C.C. 1792.

HURST, STEPHEN. *Liverpool.* Watch, 1807.

HURT, HENRY. *Ludgate Hill.* C.C. 1730–56.

HURT, NOE. Apprenticed in 1686 to Joseph Biddle, C.C.

HURTIN & BURGI. *Bound Brook, New Jersey, U.S.A.*, May 1766.

HUSBAND, DAVID. *Kirkcaldy*, 1820–37. Long-case clock.

HUSBAND, THOMAS. *Hull*, 1760–80. Long-case clock.

HUSSAM, CHAS. Apprenticed in 1672 to Jas. Wolverton, C.C.

HUSSEY, JOSEPH. Admitted C.C. 1685.

HUTCHIN, FRANCIS. *London.* 1685 C.C.

HUTCHIN, JAMES. C.C. 1697.

HUTCHIN, JOHN. C.C. 1703.

HUTCHIN, JOSEPH. C.C. 1703.

HUTCHINS, ABEL (also LEVI). *Concord, U.S.A.*, 1785–1818.

HUTCHIN, JOSHUA. C.C. 1682; in the British Museum is a watch by him, handsome silver dial with a semi-circular slit above the centre, through which appears blue sky, the sun in the day and the moon at night, pointing to the hour; a long-case clock by him, case of walnut with fine geometrical marquetry; 1670–1705.

HUTCHINSON, —. *Worksop.* Clock, 1710–20.

HUTCHINSON, —. *Retford.* Clock, 1720.

HUTCHINSON, ANTHONY. *Leeds.* Clock, about 1700.

HUTCHINSON, EDWD. *London.* Watch, about 1750.

HUTCHINSON, JNO. *Burnley*, 1780–1818.

HUTCHINSON, JNO. *London.* Watch, 1825.

HUTCHINSON, JOHN. Petitioned Parliament to grant a longer period than usually covered by a patent for his improved watch, which would be wound without an aperture in the case; successfully opposed by C.C., Mr. Charles Goode producing to the committee of the House of Commons a watch made fourteen years previously, which Mr. Hutchinson confessed was made as his; 1712.

HUTCHINSON, JOHN. *Newcastle-on-Tyne*, about 1800–17. Watch movement, Blackgate Museum, Newcastle.

HUTCHINSON, RICHARD. C.C. 1702–36.

HUTCHINSON, WM. Apprenticed in 1688 to Geo. Ethrington, C.C.

HUTIN, JAQUES FRANÇOIS. *Geneva*, about 1770–91. From *Dardagny*.

HUTTLEY, JOHN. *London (Clerkenwell)*. Apprenticed 1769, C.C. 1788–1802.

HUTTON, BARRETT. *London*. Apprenticed 1719, C.C. 1727–78.

HUTTON, JOHN. Chronometer maker, *Commercial Rd., E*, 1830; *Mark Lane*, 1830–68.

HUTTON, JOHN. *London*. Apprenticed 1716, C.C. 1724–27.

HUTTON, JOS. *London*. Watch, 1750.

HUTTON, JOSEPH. *London*, mid-eighteenth century. Watch movement.

HUTTON, PATRICK. *83 Cannon St.*, 1790.

HUTTON, RICHD. Apprenticed in 1691 to Thos. Brafield, C.C.

HUTTON, THOS. *London*. Mentioned by Earnshaw, 1776.

HUTTON, WILLIAM. *London (Gt. New St.)*. Apprenticed 1754, C.C. 1762–99.

HUX, THOS. *London*. Watch, 1825.

HUYGENS, CHRISTIAN. Born 1629, died 1695. He devised the first successful pendulum clock and balance-spring watch.

HYAMS, WOOLF. *Portsea*. Watch, 1815.

HYATT, JNO. *Chester*, 1818.

HYDE, EDWARD, *London*. Apprenticed 1731, C.C. 1741–44.

HYDE, JAMES. *38 Gutter Lane*, 1783.

HYDE, JNO. Apprenticed in 1637 to Simon Hackett, C.C.

HYDE, THOMAS. *33 Gutter Lane*, 1773–94.

HYDE, THOS. Apprenticed in 1691 to Hy. Harper, C.C.

HYETT, NICHOLAS. Apprenticed in 1648 to Richd. Morgan, and put to Robt. Rothwood, C.C.

HYLAND, JNO. *London*. Watch, 1770.

HYLLIUS, MARTINUS. *Dresden*, 1677–97. Watch with pendulum on verge, in cardan suspension in a silver spherical case; wall clock set stones; both in M.P.S. Dresden.

HYMAN, S. Watch, signed 'S. Hyman, Dock', 1811.

HYNAM, ROBERT. *4 Clement's Lane*. Hatton says, "the much improving Mr. Hynam makes his watches without collars to his pendants"; liveryman C.C. 1769–90.

HYNAM, ROBT. Horloger *de la Cour, St. Petersburg*. Quarter clock, about 1750; he probably went from London, for he was on the livery of the Joiners' Company till 1776, when his address was given as 'Russia'. In the Czar of Russia's collection, at the Winter Palace, St. Petersburg, was a small watch by him entirely covered with brilliants; it is suspended from a chatelaine of seven chains set with diamonds which also carries a watch key, a small seal of agate, and an enamelled acorn.

HYON à *Paris*. On a watch, V. & A., about 1740.

IBEL, THOMAS. Watch-spring maker, *Featherstone St.*, 1790.

IDELOT. Fine Boulle work clock and bracket, inscribed 'Idelot à Paris', about 1710.

IGNELL, ANDERS. *Stockholm*, 1811. Died 1827. Also INGELL.

IGOIN, PIERRE. *Paris*. Juré 1748.

IGOU, PIERRE. *Paris*. Juré 1789.

IHLSTRÖM, LARS. *Stockholm*. Born 1743, died 1790; bracket clock.

ILBURY, —, son. *London, Fleurier* and *Canton*. About 1805–43.

ILBURY, WM. *Goswell St.*, 1780; afterwards at *Duncan Terrace*, died 1839; a well-known manufacturer of fine enamelled and other watches for the Chinese market; a watch dating from about 1800, signed 'Ilbury, Paris', the case finely decorated with pearls.

ILES, THOMAS. *London*. Long-case clock, about 1790.

ILLIG, MORITZ FRIEDRICH. *Darmstadt*. Born 1777, died 1845; eminent maker; three-wheeled clock, showing hours, minutes and seconds, Darmstadt Museum; also striking repeating table clock and watch.

ILLMER, ANDREAS. *Innsbruck*. Maker to Archduke Ferdinand, 1566.

IMISON, —. *London*. Watch, h.m., 1786.

IMISON, JNO. *Manchester*. Clock, about 1770.

IMBERT, JEAN GABRIEL L'AÎNÉ. *Paris*. 1772 master–1789; porcelain clock Munich Residenz; mantel clock Pal. de Fontainebleau.

IMLAH, PETER. *London*. C.C. 1786; watch.

INGELMARK, JÖNS. *Stockholm*. Born 1759, died 1834.

INGERHAM, THOS. Apprenticed in 1686 to Alex. Warfield, C.C.

INGERSOLL, DANIEL, tertius. *Boston, U.S.A.*, 1798–1800. Watch.

INGERSOLL, DANIEL, G. *Boston, U.S.A.*, 1800–10.

INGLISH, DAVID. *Manchester*, 1818.

INGLISH, JAS. *36 Watling St.*, 1790.

INGOLD, PIERRE FREDERICK. Born at Bienne 1787; a clever mechanician, who devised machinery for duplicating parts of watches. He visited Paris about 1817, and worked for Breguet; started business for himself in Paris 1830; came to London 1840. In 1842 and 1843 he took out various patents for protecting the tools to be used by the British Watch Company; visited New York in 1845; afterwards returned to Switzerland and devoted himself to the manufacture of the 'Ingold Fraise', a serrated cylindrical cutter for shaping wheel teeth; he died 1878.

INGRAM, JOHN. *Spalding*, 1770.

INGRAM, THOMAS. C.C. 1695.

INGRAM, WILLIAM. C.C. 1730.

INKPEN, JOHN. *Horsham*. Long-case clocks, about 1770.

INMAN, JAS. *Colne, Lancs.*, 1818; *Stockport*, 1833; and at *Burnley*.

INNES, R. *London*. Watch, 1760.

INWOOD, S. *London*. Watch, green leather case *piqué*, about 1700.

ION, JOHN, son of Jos. *London*. Apprenticed 1803, C.C. 1811.

ION, JOSEPH, son. *London (Nightingale Lane)*. Apprenticed 1766, C.C. 1777, died a. 1803.

IRELAND, ANT. *Mile End*. Long-case clock, about 1770.

IRELAND, FRANCIS. C.C. 1668.

IRELAND, HENRY. *Lothbury*. C.C. 1654; maker of lantern clocks, 1650–75.

IRELAND, JOHN. *21 Maiden Lane*, 1779.

IRELAND, JOHN. *London*. Apprenticed 1660, C.C. 1668.

IRISH, JAMES. *Steyning* and *Brighton*. Apprenticed 1780–1800; watch movement.

IRISH, JOSEPH. *Portsmouth*, about 1790–1820 C.C. Clocks and watches.

IRONS, THOS. *Alcester*, about 1790.

IRONSIDE & BELCHER. *Lombard St.*, 1737–40.

IRVIN, JEAN. *32 Kirby St., Hatton Garden*, 1825.

IRVINE, ALEXANDER. *Edinburgh*, 1690. Died 1717.

IRVING, ALEXANDER. C.C. 1695; long-case clock, about 1700, signed 'Alexander Irving, Londini, fecit'; another, inscribed 'Alex. Ervin, London'.

IRVING, J. *Blackburn*, 1770.

ISAAC, DANIEL. Assistant C.C. 1670; 1660–70.

ISAAC, R. *Narberth*, about 1790 C.C.

ISAAC, SUTTON. Apprenticed in 1655 to Jno. Samon; C.C. 1662.

ISAACS, LEVY. *57 Mansell St.*, 1769–83.

ISAACS, RALPH. *Liverpool*, 1814–29. Watch.

ISELIN, BASILIUS. *Basle*. Born 1691, died 1731.
ISRAEL, JOHN. *180 Whitechapel*, 1783.
ISRAELS, JSH. *London*, about 1775.
IVE, FRANCIS. C.C. 1634.
IVE, G. H. *10 Finsbury Place*, 1825. Also at *17 Cornhill*, 1826–42.
IVE, THOMAS. *London*. C.C. 1634.
IVERY, JOHN. Repairer of the clock of St. Margaret's, Westminster, 1548.
IVES, FRANCIS. C.C. 1709.
IVES, JNO. Apprenticed in 1693 to Jno. Benson, C.C.
IVES, JOSEPH. *Bristol, Conn.*, 1811–25.
IVES, LAWSON. 1827–36.
IVES, ZACHARIA. C.C. 1682; 30-hour clock, hour hand only, inscribed 'Zac. Ives, fecit for Thos. Sclater, Gentl'.
IVISON, JNO. *Carlisle*, 1810.
IVORY, JAS. *Dundee*, 1760–90.
IVORY, THOS., son of Jas. 1795–1810.
IZOD, WILLIAM. Admitted C.C. 1649.

JACCARD, J. *60 Red Lion St., Clerkenwell*, 1820–22.
JACCARD, Jos. *London Bridge*, 1680.
JACKLE, JOHANNES, son. *Schwenningen*. Born 1808, died 1875; Schwarzwald clocks.
JACKLE, JOSEPH. *Schwenningen*. Born 1774, died 1851; Schwarzwald clocks.
JACKMAN, JOSEPH. Large verge watch movement in the G.M., inscribed 'Jos. Jakeman, on London Bridge', about 1690.
JACKS, JAMES. *Montego Bay (Jamaica)*, 1777; *Charleston, U.S.A.*, 1784. Clocks and watches.
JACKSON, DAVID. Apprenticed in 1684 to Luke Bird, C.C.
JACKSON, EDWARD. C.C. 1669.
JACKSON, EDWARD. *Newington, Surrey*. Apprenticed in 1672 to Robert Wilkins; C.C. 1680.
JACKSON, EDWD. *York*, 1818.
JACKSON, EDWARD. *London (E. Smithfield)*. Apprenticed 1783, C.C. 1790–1808.
JACKSON, GEO. *82 Charlotte St., Rathbone Place*, 1815–25.
JACKSON, HENRY. *29 St. Martin's Lane*, 1790–4.
JACKSON, ISAAC. *Wylam, Northumberland*. Born 1796, died 1862; a good mechanician; clock by him with three-legged gravity escapement, at Stephenson's factory, Newcastle.
JACKSON, ISAAC. *145 St. John's St.*, 1804.
JACKSON, JACOB. *Bristol*, 1798–1818. a. 1798 DANIEL & JACKSON. Watch.
JACKSON, JAMES. *London*. Apprenticed 1760, C.C. 1767.
JACKSON, JAMES. C.C. 1689.
JACKSON, JNO. *Lancaster*, 1820.
JACKSON, JOHN. C.C. 1682.
JACKSON, JOHN. *37 Basinghall St.*, 1759–74.
JACKSON, JOHN. *2 Bridgewater Sq.* Livery C.C. 1776, master 1796; 1760–1800.
JACKSON, JOHN, JUNR. *Bridgewater Sq.* Master C.C. 1822; 1800–30.
JACKSON, JOHN. *London*. Apprenticed 1753, C.C. 1778.
JACKSON, JOHN, JUN. *London*. C.C. 1779, l.C.C. 1783–87.
JACKSON, JOHN. *London*. Apprenticed 1799, C.C. 1806.
JACKSON, JOHN. *London*. C.C. 1824; watch.
JACKSON, JOSEPH. C.C. 1646.
JACKSON, JOSEPH H. *Philadelphia*, 1802–10.
JACKSON, JOSEPH. *London*. Apprenticed 1737, C.C. 1746.
JACKSON, JOSEPH. *London*. C.C. 1797.
JACKSON, MARTIN. C.C. 1697; master 1721; maker of a bell-top ebony case, pull-repeater clock, brass arch dial, 1697–1721.

JACKSON, MATTHEW, son of Matthew. *London*. Apprenticed 1723, C.C. 1730–36; lantern clock.
JACKSON, OWEN. *Cranbrook* and *Tenterden*, 1767–83. In 1796 in partnership with his son John at *Tenterden*; watch.
JACKSON, RANDAL, *8 Chapel Row, Spa Fields*, 1780.
JACKSON, RICHARD. C.C. 1632.
JACKSON, SAMPSON. Apprenticed in 1656 to Joseph Jackson, C.C.
JACKSON, STEPHEN. *London*. C.C. 1819.
JACKSON, THOMAS. C.C. 1688.
JACKSON, THOMAS. *52 Upper East Smithfield*, 1790; *53 Red Lion St., Clerkenwell*, 1810.
JACKSON, THOS. *Preston*, 1760.
JACKSON, WILLIAM. *Old Broad St.*, afterwards *Tower St.*, 1730–76; bracket clock by him in walnut case, about 1750, Wetherfield collection; known also as a maker of long-case clocks; liveryman C.C. 1776.
JACKSON, WILLIAM. *London*. Apprenticed 1728, C.C. 1736.
JACKSON, WILLIAM. *London*. Apprenticed 1732, C.C. 1739.
JACKSON, WM. *Frodsham*, f., of Lancaster, 1810.
JACKSON, WM. W. *Frodsham*, 1817, f., of Lancaster.
JACKSON, WM. *31 Cowcross St.*, 1820.
JACOB, BENJAMIN. C.C. 1706.
JACOB, BENJAMIN. C.C. 1718.
JACOB, CHARLES & ABRAHAM CLAUDE. *Annapolis, U.S.A.*, 1773–75. From *London*; watch.
JACOB, DAN. *57 Margaret St.*, 1817.
JACOB, DENNIS. *Cockspur St.*, 1775–1800.
JACOB, JEAN AIMÉ. *Paris*. Born 1793, died 1871; able maker; established a precision clock factory at *S. Nicholas d'Aliermont*; made one-year regulators, chronometers and chronographs.
JACOBS, CONRAD. *Leewarden*. Watch, about 1610.
JACOBS, E. *86 York St., Westminster*, 1820; *25 Bevis Marks*, 1825–35.
JACOBS, JEAN. *Harlem*. Octagonal watch, dated 1560.
JACOBS, JUDAH. *Whitecross St.*, 1769; *1 Little Mitre Court, Fenchurch St.*, 1771. A bracket clock by him, brass and silvered dial, mahogany case.
JACOPIN, ABRAM. *Chaux-de-Fonds*, 1727–50.
JACOPIN, GUILLAUME. *Fontaines*, 1791–1826. Several clocks.
JACOT, CHARLES EDOUARD. *Le Locle*, 1830. Said to have devised the Chinese duplex escapement; 1830; watch.
JACOT, GUILLAUME. *Fontaines*, 1791–1826.
JACQUES. See JAQUES.
JACQUES, CHARLES. *Chichester*, 1780–95. Clocks and watches; from *London*.
JACQUES, FRANÇOIS ÉTIENNE. *Paris*. Master 1746–75.
JADWIN, ROBT. Apprenticed in 1647 to Wm. North, C.C.
JAGGAR, EDWARD. *Fleet St.* C.C. 1702–30.
JAKEMAN, —. See JACKMAN.
JAMES, FRANCIS. C.C. 1662.
JAMES, GEORGE. *London*. C.C. 1771.
JAMES, J. *London*. Long-case clock, 1770.
JAMES, JOHN. Apprenticed to Thomas Loomes; C.C. 1661.
JAMES, JOSEPH. C.C. 1689; long-case clock, one hand, about 1700, signed 'Benj: James, Shaston' (Shaftesbury).
JAMES, MONAGHAN. Apprenticed in 1692 to Chas. Goode, C.C.
JAMES, W. *Bath*. Watch, 1796.
JACQUET, —. *London*, about 1720. Watch M.M.A. Also JAQUET.
JACQUET, JOSEPH. *Paris*. Master 1735, died 1797.

JÄGER, JOHANN GEORG. *Augsburg*. Master 1768–95.
JAGGERS, JOHN. *London* (*Westminster*). Apprenticed 1822, C.C. 1829.
JALOUX, FRANÇOIS. *Besançon*, 1551–75.
JAMESON, GEORGE. *Portsea*, about 1810.
JAMISON, GEORGE. *33 Charing Cross*, 1800–05. In conjunction with Howells & Barraud he completed chronometers on Mudge's plan; he also attested the value of Earnshaw's improvements in 1804; afterwards he carried on business at *High St., Portsmouth*.
JAMISON, WM. *Dublin*. Watch, 1809.
JAMMETT, T. Admitted C.C. 1704.
JANAWAY, JNO. *114 Cheapside*, 1815.
JANAWAY. WM. Apprenticed in 1675 to Jno. Saville, C.C.
JANNOT, ANDRÉ. *Geneva*, about 1755–71.
JANVIER, ANTIDE. Born 1751 at *St. Claude* in the *Jura*, settled in *Besançon*, and became an authority on horological construction; migrated to Paris and repaired Passemant's clock for the first Consul. His 'Essai sur les Horloges' was published at Paris in 1811; died 1835.
JANVIER, ANTOINE, LE JEUNE. *Paris* (*Rue Dauphine*). Master 1772–1815.
JANVIER, CHARLES. *Blois*. Apprenticed 1621–47.
JANVIER, CLAUDE ÉTIENNE. *St. Claude*, 1750–69.
JANVIER, JÉRÉMIE, L'AÎNÉ. *Paris* (*Rue St. Honoré*). Master 1770–89.
JANVIER, JOSEPH, brother. *St. Claude* and *Paris*. Born 1754, died 1820; went to *Paris* with his brother and returned *St. Claude* 1790.
JAPY, ADOLPHE. *Beaucourt*. Born 1813, died 1897.
JAPY, FRÉDÉRIC. *Beaucourt, France*. Born 1749, died 1813; in 1799 he patented a series of machines for producing parts of watches by unskilled labour; this appears to be the first attempt to manufacture watches on the factory system.
JAQUES, ROBERT. *London*. Apprenticed 1717–31 C.C. Also JACQUES.
JAQUES, WILLIAM. Apprenticed in 1679 to Jno. Wright, and turned over to Nathaniel Delander; C.C. 1687; master 1716; Wm. Achurch apprenticed to him in 1691.
JAQUET, P. Watch, inscribed 'Jacquet, London', silver dial and cock, brass cases, inner one beautifully engraved and pierced, Pierpont Morgan collection, about 1705; another watch of later date, inscribed 'Peter Jaquet, London'.
JAQUET-DROZ, HENRI LOUIS, son. *Chaux-de-Fonds, Nancy* and *Geneva*, with branch in *London*. Born 1752, died 1791; worked with his father; associated with J. F. Leschot at Geneva from 1784; London branch in charge of Henri Maillardet from 1775; celebrated clock, watch and automaton maker; made many watches for China, signed J‡D and, after 1784, J.L.-G; carillon watch with five bells; many watches in Swiss collections; several singing birds and automaton, illuminated M. des Aut.
JAQUET-DROZ, PIERRE. *Basle, Neuchâtel, Paris, Geneva* and *Madrid*. Born 1721, died 1790; celebrated clockmaker and mechanician; made a number of famous automata bought by Ferdinand VI of Spain; made clock winding by the difference in expansion of two metals in 1755; two long-case clocks École d'horlogerie, Geneva; the automata 'Le Berger' and a musical clock exist in Madrid Pal.; fine clocks Kunst und Gewerbe Museum, Vienna, and École d'Horlogerie, Chaux-de-Fonds; gold engraved cylinder musical watch with barrel and five bells Wilsdorf collection.

JARDIN, JOHN. *Bartholomew Close*. One of the witnesses to the will of Christopher Pinchbeck the younger in 1780; admitted hon. freeman C.C. 1781; repeating watch in shagreen case, about 1750; 1750–81.
JARDINE, JOHN. *Glasgow*, 1765. Died 1801.
JARLE, JEAN ANTOINE. *Paris*. Master 1765–89; mantel clock.
JARMAN, JOHN. C.C. 1728.
JARMAN, JOHN B. *25 Strand*, 1815–23.
JARMAN & CO. *33 St. James's St.*, 1825.
JAROSSAY, —. *Paris*, 1788.
JARRATT, WM. *London*, about 1760. Long-case clock.
JARRETT, BARNARD. *City Rd.* Livery C.C. 1786–1820.
JARRETT, GEORGE LEWIS. *London*. Apprenticed 1781, C.C. 1788.
JARRETT, JOHN WM. Livery C.C. 1786–1816.
JARRETT, RICHARD. C.C. 1670; master 1685; watch, Schloss collection, about 1665.
JARRETT, RICHD. C.C. 1632.
JARRETT, WILLIAM. *London*. 1806 C.C.
JARVIS, GEORGE. C.C. 1728.
JARVIS, JOHN. *Aldersgate St.*, 1775–94.
JARVIS, JOHN. *London* (*Quaker's Bdgs.*). Apprenticed 1754, C.C. 1762–90.
JARVIS, JOSEPH. Apprenticed in 1670 to Bart. Powell, C.C.
JARVIS, SAML. *Birmingham*, 1710.
JAWLETT, JOHN. *Bridgewater*, about 1750.
JAYNE, JOHN. *London*. C.C. 1687.
JEANIN, A. *28 Cranbourne St.*, 1842.
JEANMAIRET. See MAIRET.
JEANNERET, CHARLES FRANÇOIS. *Chaux-de-Fonds* and *Val de Travers*, 1779–87.
JEANNERET, HENRI FERDINAND. *Couvet*, 1809–30.
JEANRICHARD, ABRAM. *La Sagne* and *Morat*, 1707–34.
JEANRICHARD-DIT-BRESSEL, DANIEL. *La Sagne* and *Le Locle*. Born 1665, died 1741; went to *Le Locle* about 1700; one of the pioneers of horology in the Neuchâtel district; his five sons started a factory where many watches were made; watch Le Locle Museum.
JEANRICHARD-DIT-BRESSEL, FRANÇOIS JULIEN. *La Sagne*. Born 1796, died 1879.
JEEVES. Fine Chippendale long-case clock, Gillespie's School, Edinburgh, inscribed 'Anthony Jeeves, musical clock maker from Oxford', about 1770; the name 'Daniel Davidson' in arch of dial.
JEFFERIES, JOHN. C.C. 1639.
JEFFERSON, JNO. *Gt. Driffield*, 1822.
JEFFERSON, REED & WALTON. *38 Fetter Lane*, 1820–25.
JEFFERSON, SAMUEL. *35 Bruton St.*, 1805 42.
JEFFERSON & SON. *38 Fetter Lane*, 1815.
JEFFERY, THOMAS & JONES. *Cockspur St., Charing Cross*, 1769–94.
JEFFERY, WILLIAM KNIGHT. C.C. 1712.
JEFFERYS, G. *86 New Bond St.*, 1800.
JEFFERYS, GEO. *Chatham*. Long-case clock, 1790.
JEFFERYS, HENRY. *96 Fleet St.*, 1793; *49 Salisbury Sq.*, 1798–1804.
JEFFERYS, ISAAC. *London*. Apprenticed 1760, C.C. 1767.
JEFFERYS, ISAAC. *London*. C.C. 1787. (JEFFERIES.)
JEFFERYS, JOHN. *London*. Apprenticed 1717, C.C. 1726. (JEFFERY.)
JEFFERYS, JOHN. *London*. Apprenticed 1734–42 C.C.
JEFFERYS, JOHN. *London*. C.C. 1814. (JEFFREYS.)
JEFFERYS, NATHANIEL. *22 Queen St., Mayfair*, 1768–1804.
JEFFERYS, NATHANIEL. *Strand*, 1771. See DRURY DRU.
JEFFERYS, NATHANIEL, JUNR. *70 Piccadilly*, 1780–94.
JEFFERYS, SAM. *Chancery Lane*, 1780.

JEFFERYS, THOMAS. *Cockspur St.*, 1771.

JEFFERYS & GILBERT. *Cockspur St.*, 1800.

JEFFERYS & HAM. *49 Salisbury Sq.*, *Fleet St.*, 1810–15; *46 Skinner St.*, 1825.

JEFFERYS & JONES. *London*, about 1800.

JEFFREYS, JOHN. *Holborn*, C.C. 1726; to him was apprenticed Larcum Kendall in 1735.

JEFFREYS & JONES. Thin watch, about 1794.

JEFFS, BENJAMIN. C.C. 1702.

JEFFS, JAMES. *London*. C.C. 1700.

JEFFS, JOHN. Apprenticed to Jeffery Bayly, and turned over to John Walter; admitted C.C. 1697.

JEKYLL, JONATHAN. *London*. Apprenticed 1724, C.C. 1742.

JELF, WILLIAM. C.C. 1717.

JELLISON, ROBERT. *London*. Apprenticed 1725, C.C. 1736–44.

JELLY (JELLES), THOMAS. *London*. Apprenticed 1701, C.C. 1720.

JEMMETT, THOMAS. *London*. Apprenticed 1697, C.C. 1704–16.

JEMMETT, THOMAS. *London*. Apprenticed 1793, C.C. 1803.

JENKINS, CORNELIUS. C.C. 1678.

JENKINS, HENRY. *68 Aldersgate St.* Maker of curious astronomical and other clocks, 1756–83.

JENKINS, HENRY. *Cheapside*, 1774. Long-case clock, mahogany Chippendale case, about 1780.

JENKINS, HERMAN. *Albany, U.S.A.*, 1817–23.

JENKINS, JAMES. C.C. 1692; fine month clock, arch dial, about 1710.

JENKINS, JOHN. *London*. Apprenticed 1695–1704 C.C.

JENKINS, THOMAS. C.C. 1678.

JENKINS, WILLIAM. *London (E. Smithfield)*. C.C. 1771–1780.

JENKINSON, J. *Sandwith*. Watch, 1770.

JENNENS, J. C. *London*. Chiming bracket clock, about 1790.

JENNINGS, CHARLES. C.C. 1725.

JENNINGS, EMANUEL. Apprenticed 1682 to Jno. Colston, C.C.

JENNINGS, ROBERT. C.C. 1703.

JENNINGS, THOMAS. C.C. 1721.

JEPPS, WILLIAM. *London*. C.C. 1772.

JÉQUIER, JEAN JACQUES. *Fleurier* and *Lausanne*, 1730–early nineteenth century. Gold engraved watch, Fränkel collection; automatic watches.

JERNEGAN, EDWARD. *Great Russell St.*, 1737–40; *Featherstone Buildings*, 1750–59.

JEROME, CHAUNCEY. Pupil of Eli Terry; maker of American clocks, born at *Canaan, Litchfield Co.*, 1793; with his brother, Noble Jerome, he began business at *Bristol, Conn.*; in 1842 he shipped clocks to England, which the Customs authorities seized and paid for, believing they were undervalued. Shortly afterwards he started the Jerome Manufacturing Co., at *New Haven, Conn.*

JEROME, NOBLE, brother. *Bristol, U.S.A.*, 1824–40. Period of partnership with Jerome.

JERRAD, HENRY. *Hinton*. Clock, about 1770.

JERSEY, FRANCIS. Bracket clock, about 1760.

JERVIS, FRANCIS. Apprenticed in 1656 to Ralph Greatorex, C.C.

JESSOP, JOSIAS. *38 Southampton St.*, *Covent Garden*, 1781–90.

JEUBI, JOSIAS. *Paris*. Watch, about 1630.

JEVON, HENRY. C.C. 1673.

JEVON, MARY. C.C. 1706.

JEW, JAMES. *London*. C.C. 1814.

JEYES, JAMES. *London*. Apprenticed 1745, C.C. 1753.

JEYES, SAM. Apprenticed in 1670 to Philip Smith, C.C.

JOB, W. *London*. Watch, 1795.

JODIN, PIERRE. Born at *Geneva* 1715, died 1761; author of *Les Echappemens à repos à ceux échappemens à recul*, published in 1754.

JOHANN. Clock at *Mainz*, about 1820, signed 'Nicolas Alexius Johann à Mayance'.

JOHN, HANS. *Königsberg*. Maker of a curious watch, British Museum., having attached a small wheel-lock pistol, supposed to have been used as an alarum, about 1650.

JOHNS, THOS. *London*, about 1700.

JOHNSON, ADDISON. *Wolcottville, U.S.A.*, 1825.

JOHNSON, BENJ. *London*. Long-case clock, about 1690.

JOHNSON, C. *7 Sweeting's Alley*, 1820–23.

JOHNSON, CORNELIUS. C.C. 1694.

JOHNSON, CHARLES JACOCK. Apprenticed to Robert Higgs; C.C. 1750.

JOHNSON, CALEB. *Boston, U.S.A.*, 1803–06. Watch.

JOHNSON, CHAUNCEY. *Albany, U.S.A.*, 1823. Watch.

JOHNSON, CHRISTOPHER. *Knaresborough*, 1775.

JOHNSON, GEORGE. C.C. 1649.

JOHNSON, ISAAC. C.C. 1705; watch by him, 1720.

JOHNSON, ISAAC. C.C. 1723.

JOHNSON, J. & W. *19 Cross St., Hatton Garden*, 1825.

JOHNSON, J. F. *Dublin*. Watch, 1812.

JOHNSON, JAMES. Apprenticed to James Delaunder; C.C. 1706.

JOHNSON, JAMES. *Liverpool*, 1768–1821. Watch. Also JOHNSTON.

JOHNSON, JAMES. *New Rd., St. George's East*, 1790–94.

JOHNSON, JEREMIAH. *London (Deptford)*. Apprenticed 1770–1808.

JOHNSON, JEREMY. *Exchange Alley*. Apprenticed in 1660 to Abraham Beckner; C.C. 1668–90; in the British Museum is a small watch of his make in an irregular octagonal-shaped case with a faceted crystal over the dial, about 1650.

JOHNSON, JNO. & THOS., also JAMES. *Prescott*, 1770.

JOHNSON, JNO. *Walton*. Clock, about 1770.

JOHNSON, JNO. C.C. 1678.

JOHNSON, JOHN. *3 Flower de Luces, Cheapside*. C.C. 1680. See BETTS, JOB.

JOHNSON, JOHN. *Morpeth*. Born about 1710, died about 1778; watch; from *Berwick*. Also JOHNSTON.

JOHNSON, JOHN. *Charleston, U.S.A.*, 1763. Previously *London* and *Havana*. Watch.

JOHNSON, JOHN. C.C. 1701.

JOHNSON, JOHN. *Fleet Lane*, 1701.

JOHNSON, JOHN. *Halesworth* and *Yarmouth*, 1770. Died 1789; watch; long-case clock.

JOHNSON, JOHN. *London*. Apprenticed 1766, C.C. 1775.

JOHNSON, JOHN. *9 Gray's Inn Passage*, 1770–99. Balloon bracket clock, round enamelled dial, case and bracket of ebony with brass mountings, about 1790, Wetherfield collection.

JOHNSON, JOHN. *Elm St., Gray's Inn Lane*, 1790–1835.

JOHNSON, JOSEPH. *Dudley*, 1760–95. Clock; long-case musical clock and watch.

JOHNSON, JOSEPH. *Liverpool*, 1796–1830.

JOHNSON, LEOND. *19 Bartlett's Buildings*, 1825.

JOHNSON, MICHAEL. *Barnard Castle*. C.C. 1687; watch, about 1720.

JOHNSON, PETER. *Mitcham*. Watch, 1790.

JOHNSON, RICHARD. *Ripon*, 1770.

JOHNSON, RICHD. *18 Francis St., Bedford Sq.*, 1815–20.

JOHNSON, ROBERT. *Edinburgh*. Apprenticed to Andrew Brown in 1696; watch, signed 'R. Johnson, Wooltown', 1720.

JOHNSON, ROGER. Petitioner for incorporation of C.C. 1630.

JOHNSON, ROLAND. *Liverpool*, 1766.

JOHNSON, R. & J. *Liverpool*, 1781–1800. Watch.

JOHNSON, THOMAS. *London*, about 1680–1705. Two long-case clocks, one with 1¼ secs. pendulum, illuminated Cec. & Web.

JOHNSON, THOMAS. *London*. Apprenticed 1692, C.C. 1700; long-case clock inscribed 'Tho. Johnson Ratcliff Cross'.

JOHNSON, THOMAS. *London*. Apprenticed 1707, C.C. 1714–25; bankrupt.

JOHNSON, THOMAS. *Richmond*. C.C. 1713; watch, V. & A., about 1745.

JOHNSON, THOMAS. *9 Grey's Inn Passage*, about 1730.

JOHNSON, THOMAS. *London*. Apprenticed 1760.

JOHNSON, WILLIAM. Apprenticed to Dan. Quare in 1690; C.C. 1702; bracket clock, bell-top ebony case, with handle, brass dial, bob pendulum style, 1725, strike-silent.

JOHNSON, WILLIAM. *London*. Apprenticed 1734, C.C. 1741; watch.

JOHNSON, WILLIAM. *50 Strand*, 1825–42. Diminutive bracket clock, about 1825.

JOHNSON, WM., f., of *York*, 1665–1713.

JOHNSON, WM. *Flixon*. Clock, about 1700.

JOHNSON & CO. *London*. Repeating watch, 1830.

JOHNSTON, G. *7 Queen St., Northampton Sq.*, 1835.

JOHNSTON & BRECIANS. *London*. Watch, h.m., 1816.

JOHNSTONE, —. *Mitcham*, about 1800 C.C.

JOHNSTONE, JOHN. *London*. Apprenticed 1750, C.C. 1769; watch.

JOHNSTONE, JOHN. *Charleston, U.S.A.*, 1764. Apprenticed in *London*. Watch.

JOHNSTONE, JOHN. *Ayr*. Born 1755, died 1829.

JOHNSTONE, ROBERT. *Philadelphia*, 1825.

JOHNSTOUN, JAMES. *London*. Apprenticed 1698, C.C. 1706.

JOLE, ROBT. C.C. 1667.

JOLE, THOS. Apprenticed 1680 to Robt. Fole, C.C.

JOLLY, DAN. Apprenticed in 1637 to Jno. Droshute, C.C.

JOLLY, FRANÇOIS. 1790.

JOLLY, J. Watchmaker to the Paris Town Hall in 1550; worked also for Catherine de Medici; a watch by J. Jolly; skull watch (Soltykoff collection) by Jacques Jolly, about 1580; two watches by Joshua Jolly, Vienna Treasury, splendidly enamelled cases and dials, about 1670; a magnificent Louis XIV bracket clock, inscribed 'I Jolly à Paris'.

JOLLY, JOSEPH. *11 Dean St., Fetter Lane*, 1790–94.

JOLY (JOLLY), JOHN. *London*. Apprenticed 1732, C.C. 1739.

JOLY (JOLLY), JOHN. *London (Old Jewry)*. Apprenticed 1767, C.C. 1777–94.

JOLY (JOLLY), JOSIAS. *Paris*. Master 1609–40; watches British Museum, Louvre illuminated Baillie, Olivier collection; two watches with engraved flowers K.H.M.; all signatures have 'Paris'.

JOLY, JACQUES. *London*. In the British Museum is a watch by him, 1620–30; watch, signed 'Geo. Joly à Mondont'; on dial, 'Joly le Cadet', about 1765.

JON, J. *London*. Lantern clock, arch dial, about 1730.

JON, JOHN, son of Joseph. *London*. Apprenticed 1803, C.C. 1811, I.C.C. 1812.

JON, JOSEPH. *London*. Apprenticed 1 66, C.C. 1777–97, died a. 1803.

JONAS, SAML. *Exon*. Watch, 1783.

JONES, BENJ. Apprenticed in 1676 to Richd. Halstead, C.C.

JONES, CHAS. Apprenticed in 1663 to Walter Gibbs, C.C.

JONES, DAN. Apprenticed in 1672 to Edwd. Wilson, C.C.

JONES, DAVID. *Llangadog*, about 1770–1810. Bracket clock.

JONES, DAVID. *Merthyr Tydvil*. Born 1763–1835; striking clock.

JONES, DAVID. C.C. 1687.

JONES, EDWD. Apprenticed in 1686 to Wm. Bartram, C.C.

JONES, EVAN. C.C. 1648; signed petition 1656, assistant 1671.

JONES, EZEKIEL. *Boston, U.S.A.*, 1813–25. Watch.

JONES, FRANCIS. *London*. C.C. 1817, I.C.C. 1824.

JONES, GEORGE. *Wilmington, U.S.A.* Born 1782, died 1867; long-case clock.

JONES, GEORGE. *London*. Apprenticed 1809, C.C. 1820.

JONES, HENRY. *Inner Temple Gate*. Apprenticed in 1654 to Edward East; C.C. 1663; master 1691; an eminent maker. "Lost on 29th instant in Lincolns Inn fields, one silver striking watch with the day of the month in a steel case studded and garnished with silver made by Mr. Jones in the Inner Temple Lane, watchmaker. Whoever can give notice hereof and bring the said watch to Mr. Humphry Davis at the Duke's Head in Lincolns Inn Fields or to Mr. Jones aforesaid shall have 40s. reward" (*Lond. Gaz.*, 27 Jan., 1675–76).

JONES, HENRY. Apprenticed in 1668 to Chas. Bonner, C.C.

JONES, HENRY. Apprenticed in 1690 to Hy. Jones, his father; C.C. 1698.

JONES, HENRY. C.C. 1697–98.

JONES, J. *Chalford, Stroud*. Maker of Chalford Church clock.

JONES, JAMES. *65 Banner St.*, 1795–1810.

JONES, JAMES. *Brecon*. a. 1767–94; watch; clock National Museum, Cardiff.

JONES, JAS. Apprenticed in 1687 to Philip Thacke, C.C.

JONES, JENKIN. *61 St. James's St.*, 1775–83.

JONES, JNO. *London*. Repeating watch, 1775.

JONES, JNO. *Chester*, 1814–28.

JONES, JOHN. *Chester*, 1730. Died 1764; watch.

JONES, JOHN. *London*. Apprenticed 1743, C.C. 1756.

JONES, JOHN. C.C. 1716.

JONES, JOHN. Master C.C. 1762; 1748–63.

JONES, JOHN. *338 Strand*, 1821. Succeeded by his son, John Jones.

JONES, JOHN. *Bethesda*, 1803–79. Long-case clock.

JONES, JONATHAN. Apprenticed to Robert Smith, and turned over to Nathaniel De Launder; C.C. 1687.

JONES, JOSEPH. *London*. Apprenticed 1774, C.C. 1786.

JONES, MARMADUKE. Apprenticed in 1652 to Evan Jones, C.C.

JONES, OWEN. *Little George St., Minories*. Livery C.C. 1786; 1780–94.

JONES, RICHD. *London*. Long-case clock, about 1700.

JONES, ROBERT. *49 Little Bartholomew Close*, 1800.

JONES, ROBERT. *Ruthin*. Watch, 1819.

JONES, SAM. Apprenticed in 1688 to Edmund Massey, C.C.

JONES, SAM. *78 Cheapside*, 1820–25.

JONES, SAML. *Bath*. Watch, 1769.

JONES, SAMUEL. *London*. Apprenticed 1752, C.C. 1761.

JONES, SAMUEL. *Kingston, Jamaica*. 1795–1830 C.C.; clocks and watches.

JONES, THOMAS WM. C.C. 1679; very small watch by him, Schloss collection, gold dial, raised figures, outer case leather *piqué*; another stud underneath plate; watch, 'Thos. Jones, London', about 1680.

JONES, THOMAS. *Liverpool*, 1810–29.

JONES, VALENTINE. C.C. 1704.

JONES, WILLIAM. *London*. Apprenticed 1752, C.C. 1759.

JONES, WILLIAM. *London*. Apprenticed 1760, C.C. 1768.

JONES, WILLIAM. C.C. 1663.

JONES, WILLIAM. *27 Barbican*. Livery C.C. 1786; *31 Little Moorfields*, 1810; 1780–1810.

JONES, WILLIAM. *Criccieth* and *Pwllheli*. Born 1778, died 1861; long-case clock.

JONES, WILLIAM HENRY. *London*. C.C. 1811.

JONES, WM. Apprenticed in 1682 to Henry Jones, C.C.

JONES, WM. *White Cross St.*, 1810–15.

JONES & GRANT. *123 New Bond St.*, 1815–18.

JONNEREAU. See GOUNOUILHOU.

JONSTON, ROBT. *Cumber.* Clock, about 1770.

JORDAN, AARON. *London*, 1790.

JORDAN, JAS. *Chatham*, 1710.

JORDAN, JNO. *Bristol*. Watch, silver cock, about 1720; long-case clock, about 1730.

JORDAN, THOS. *Stadhampton, Oxon.*, 1780.

JORDAN, TIMOTHY. *40 Snow Hill*, 1770–80.

JOSELIN (or JOSSLIN), EDWD. Apprenticed in 1690 to Jas. Wolverston, C.C.; John Hocker served him as apprentice in 1728.

JOSEPHSON, —. *London*. Many watches, Dutch style, 1760–90.

JOSEPHSON, JOHN. *London*. a. 1751–81; watches New York University and Denham and Feill collections and Oldham Museum; pair agate caskets with watches, Peiping Museum.

JOSLYN, JAMES. *New Haven*, 1798–1820.

JOUARD, L. *Paris*. Garde-visiteur, 1769.

JOURDAIN, A. *6 Wheeler St., Spitalfields*, 1790–94.

JOURDAIN, WILLIAM. Apprenticed in 1646 to Robt. Smith, C.C.; timepiece with crown wheel escapement, short pendulum with pear-shaped bob, and 8-in. silvered dial; through a short circular slit in the upper part of the dial is shown a small silvered star, which vibrates with the pendulum, about 1680; clock by him, German oak case, dial Dutch style; watch, about 1690.

JOUVEL (JOVEL DIT MOUCHE), CLAUDE. *Grenoble*, 1663–82.

JOVAT, —. *London*. Calendar watch, about 1700.

JOYCE, CONWAY. *London (Lombard St.).* C.C. 1810–37; watch.

JOYCE, GEORGE. C.C. 1692.

JOYCE, JNO. *Ellesmere*, 1698.

JOYCE, JOHN. *Ruthin*, 1791–1822. Clocks and watches.

JOYCE, S. & C. *London (Lombard St.).* 1790–1825. Gold 8-day watch Denham collection; fine gold engraved musical watch, Feill collection.

JOYCE, SAMUEL, & Co. *38 Lombard St.*, 1790–1842.

JOYCE, STEPHEN. *Moor St., Soho*, 1769.

JOYNE, JNO. Apprenticed in 1660 to Jno. Smith, C.C. 1687.

JOYNE, JNO. *St. Germain, Paris*. Watch, British Museum, square case, crystal cover, 1690–1710.

JUDSON, THOMAS. Sent a letter to C.C. relative to watches seized. 1790.

JUHAN, A. *Dortrecht.* Watch, 1776.

JUILLARD, ADAM LOUIS. *Cortébert.* Born 1790, died 1830.

JULER, JNO. *N. Walsham*, 1770.

JULIAN, GREGORY. C.C. 1664.

JULLION, FRANCIS. *London*. Long-case clock, about 1780.

JULLION, JOHN. *Brentford*, 1730.

JULLION & SON. *New Brentford*, 1771. Watch, 'J. Julien, Brentford', 1792.

JULLIOTT, SOLOMON. *London*. Verge watch by him in the Guildhall Museum, date on mainspring, 1738.

JUMP, RICHARD THOS. Inventor of the proportionate gauge called a sector, which is used chiefly for wheels and pinions; joined B. L. Vulliamy in 1812.

JUNG, HERMAN. A clever Swiss horologist who settled in *Clerkenwell*; assassinated 1901.

JÜRGENSEN, JOERGEN. *Copenhagen.* Died 1811.

JÜRGENSEN, JULES FREDERIK. Another son of Urban, was born in 1808 at *Locle* during a short sojourn of his parents there in 1808; on attaining manhood he returned to Locle where he founded a business: his watches were highly esteemed in America; he died in 1877.

JÜRGENSEN, LOUIS URBAN. *Copenhagen.* Eldest son and successor of Urban; born 1806, died 1867.

JÜRGENSEN, URBAN. *Copenhagen*, son of the foregoing. Born 1776, died 1830; an eminent maker; author of *The Higher Horological Art* and *Principes de la Mesure du Temps*; Jürgensen was associated with the leading men of his day; he experimented with compensation balances made of brass and platinum, and strongly advocated the use of gold springs for marine chronometers; he made many excellent chronometers for the Danish navy, and very successful metallic thermometers.

JUST, LEONARD. *St. John's Sq.* 1790–1825; maker of watches for the Chinese market. City Rd., 1830–42; he made watches with movements wholly of steel, except the jewels and the bushes for the larger pivot holes, which were of gold; they were chiefly for the Chinese market; the pinion leaves wore into ruts quicker than if working with brass wheels.

JUSTIS & COMP. *Well Yard, St. Bartholomew's Hospital*, 1769.

K. Watch; tambourine case of brass, stackfreed, foliot balance, signed 'A.K.', about 1570, Pierpont Morgan collection; octagonal watch, about the same date, marked 'M.K.'

KANGIESSER, S. *24 Southampton St., Strand*, 1816–25.

KANNS, JOHN. C.C. 1712.

KATER, CAPTAIN HENRY, R. S. Conducted experiments for determining the length of the seconds pendulum in the latitude of London, 1817.

KAUFMANN, FRIEDRICH, son of Gottfried. *Germany*. Born 1785, died 1866; musical clockwork.

KAUFMANN, GOTTFRIED. Born 1751 near *Chemnitz*; died 1818; *Frankfurt-a.-M.*; musical clockwork; watch signed 'Johann Gottfried Kaufmann a Dresde', Ilbert collection perhaps by him.

KAUS, JAMES or JOHN. *London*. Apprenticed 1703, C.C. 1712.

KAY, DAVID. *Dundee*. Made a clock for St. Mary's Church in 1554.

KAY, JNO. *London*. Long-case chime clock, about 1750.

KAYE, JOHN. *Liverpool*, 1773–1811. Clock.

KAYE, WILLIAM. *Liverpool*, 1781–1804. Clock.

KEAL, WM. *London*. Watch, 1799.

KEANDLER, CHAS. *Jermyn St.*, 1793.

KEAT, JOSEPH (? Kent). *19 Cock Hill, Ratcliff*, 1810.

KEATE, ROBT. *Wallingford*, 1780.

KEATES, WM. *135 Fleet St.*, 1783–1800.

KEATING, A. *114 Strand*, 1796–1815.

KECKER, JEAN ABRAM. *Chaux-de-Fonds*, 1778–1800. Clock.

KEDDON (or KEDDEN), DANIEL. *Little Britain.* C.C. 1717; fine japanned long-case clock, about 1730; watch, about 1740.

KEDDON (or KEDDEN), JOSHUA, son. *London.* C.C. 1751.

KEEL, CHARLES. *London*. Apprenticed 1810, C.C. 1818.

KEELEY, THOMAS. *London.* Apprenticed 1761, C.C. 1784–1803.

KEELY, W. Gilder, *Orange Court, Clement's Lane*, 1790–94.

KEENE, JOSEPH. *London.* Apprenticed 1748, C.C. 1756.

KEEYS, JEREMIAH. *London.* Watch, 1800.

KEFFORD, THOMAS. *Royston.* Lantern clock, about 1710; long Oriental lacquer case clock, about 1730.

KEHLHOFF, FREDERICK. *St. George-the-Martyr, Southwark.* Patented in 1764 (No. 819) a centre-seconds going-barrel watch, with stackfreed and remontoire.

KEITH, ROBERT. *Forfar*, 1819–37.

KELHAM, JOSEPH. *London.* C.C. 1766.

KELHAM, MATHIAS, near *Vintners' Hall.* C.C. 1730.

KELHAM, ROBERT. *London.* C.C. 1769–75; watch.

KELHAM, ROBERT. *Chelmsford*, 1775–94. Watch.

KELL, JNO. C.C., about 1650.

KELLET, —. *Bredbury.* Long-case clock, about 1770; at top of the arch is the motto, 'Time feasts on all terrestrial things'.

KELLET, THOS. Fined by C.C. for defective watch, 1635.

KELLEY, ALLAN. *Sandwich, U.S.A.*, 1810–30.

KELLEY, DAVID. *Philadelphia*, 1808–13. Watch.

KELLO, SIMON. Apprenticed to John Higgs and turned over to Jos. Jackman; C.C. 1723.

KELLS, EDWD. *Shepley*, 1770.

KELLY, EZRA. *New Bedford, U.S.A.* Born 1798, died 1895; watch and maker of oils for clocks and watches.

KELLY, JOHN. *Liverpool*, 1813–29. Gold watch.

KELLY, RICHARD. *Devereux Court, Strand.* Long Chippendale case clock, about 1790.

KELME, —. *London.* Small timepiece on a horse, in the Massey-Mainwaring collection, 1670.

KELTON, SIMON. C.C. 1723.

KELVEY, ROBERT. *Gainsborough*, 1772, retired 1796. Watch.

KEMBER, JOS. SHAW. Watch, 1776.

KEMBLE, J. T., *Knightsbridge*, 1817.

KEMBLE, WILLIAM. *New York*, 1786.

KEMM, SAMUEL. *London.* Apprenticed 1753, C.C. 1763, died 1810.

KEMP, —. *Lewes.* Watch, 1760.

KEMP, CHARLES. Apprenticed to Prettyman Sergeant, and turned over to Charles Gretton; C.C. 1688; Thos. Tompion, junr., apprenticed to him in 1694.

KEMP, JAMES. *London.* C.C. 1780–1804.

KEMP, JAMES. *London (Peckham)*, 1799. l.C.C. 1812, died 1822.

KEMP, JOSEPH. *Curtain Rd.*, 1790.

KEMP, RICHARD. C.C. 1701.

KEMP, WILLIAM. Livery C.C. 1786.

KEMP, WILLIAM. *Lewes.* a. 1756–84; watch.

KEMP, WILLIAM HENRY, son. *London.* CC. 1808.

KEMP & HOLMAN. *Lewes.* Watch, 1782.

KEMPS, ANTHONY, 1650.

KEMPS, MATTHEW, son of Anthony. C.C. 1670.

KENDALL, —. *17 St. John's Sq.*, 1790–94.

KENDALL, LARCUM. Born at *Chalbury, Oxford*, 1721; apprenticed in London to John Jeffreys, 1735; *20 Wood St., Cheapside*, 1750; *Furnival's Inn Court*, 1765, when he was one of the judges appointed to report on Harrison's timekeeper; in 1766 he agreed to make a duplicate for the Commissioners of Longitude; the date on this instrument is 1769; it is at Greenwich Maritime Museum. He died in 1795.

KENDRICK, JOHN. C.C. 1719.

KENDRICK, JOHN. C.C. 1726.

KENDRICK, ROGER. *London.* Apprenticed 1742, C.C. 1752.

KENDRICK, WM. *36 Lombard St.*, 1772.

KENEY, VINCENT. Received £19 16s. 8d. from Henry VIII for 'xj clocks and dialls', 1530.

KENFIELD, RICHD. *Winton.* Fine long-case clock, about 1740.

KENNEDY, JAS. *London.* Fine duplex watch, 1813.

KENNEDY, JOHN. *Maybole*, 1820–37.

KENNEDY, PATRICK. *Philadelphia*, 1797.

KENNEDY, PATRICK. *Dublin*, 1795–1824. Watch.

KENNEDY, ROGER. *Dublin*, 1795–1824. Watch.

KENNEDY, THOS. *Wigan.* Watch, 1759.

KENNING, EDWIN. *London.* Lantern clock, about 1705.

KENNING, WM. C.C. 1684.

KENNON, WM. Apprenticed in 1656 to Job Betts; C.C. 1674.

KENT, —. *Monmouth.* Watch, 1799.

KENT, HENRY. *Westminster.* C.C. 1646.

KENT, HENRY, son of John. *Saffron Walden.* Born 1809, died 1874.

KENT, JAS. *Manchester*, 1759.

KENT, JNO. *Manchester*, 1770.

KENT, JOHN. *19 Broad St., Ratcliff*, 1817–35.

KENT, JOHN. *Saffron Walden.* Master about 1764–90.

KENT, JOHN, son of John. *Saffron Walden.* Born about 1765, died 1850; long-case clocks.

KENT, JOHN. *Monmouth*, about 1800–30. Watch.

KENT, JOSEPH. *19 Cock Hill, Ratcliff*, 1806–17.

KENT, WM. Apprenticed in 1681 to Sam. Marchant, C.C.

KENTISH, JOHN. *Pope's Head Alley*, 1758–61.

KENTISH, JOHN, & HAYNES. *18 Cornhill*, 1769–88. Watch, skeleton movement about 1800, signed 'John Kentish, junr'.

KENTON, JOSEPH. Admitted C.C. 1686.

KENYON, CLAYTON. *Liverpool*, 1805–21. Watch.

KENYON, RICHARD. *Manchester*, 1796–1813. Clock.

KERBY, BENJAMIN. *Bristol*, about 1800. C.C. 1830.

KERBY, FRAS. *St. Helier.* Long-case clock, about 1810.

KERBY, THOMAS F. *London.* Clocks, about 1760.

KERMON, WILLIAM. *London.* 1682 C.C.

KERNER & PAFF. *245 Water St., New York*, 1796. 'Musical clocks with figures, and cuckoo clocks' (advt. New York).

KERSHAW, GEORGE. *Tyler's Court, Carnaby Market*, 1780–94.

KERSILL, WILLIAM. *21 Aldersgate St.*, 1775.

KESSBORER, JOHAN. *Ulm (South Germany).* Watch in engraved silver case, second half of seventeenth century, V. & A.; clock, 1650.

KESSELS, HEINRICH JOHANNES. *Altona.* A celebrated maker of astronomical clocks; died 1849.

KESSLER, JOHN, JUN. *Philadelphia*, 1806–08.

KETTERER, FRANZ ANTON. *Schönwald.* Born 1676–1750; first maker of cuckoo clocks, and one of the first to start clockmaking in the Schwarzwald; cuckoo clock, Furt. Museum.

KETTLE, G. *London.* Watch, 1795.

KEWELL, THOS. Apprenticed in 1685 to Richd. Colston, C.C.

KEY, JNO. *Warrington*, 1770.

KEYES, MARKHAM. Apprenticed in 1653 to Jere. Gregory, C.C.

KEYMES, JOSEPH. Apprenticed in 1673 to Dan. Stevens, C.C.

KEYTE, RD. *Whitney*, 1770.

KIBLICH, MATTHEW. *Presburg.* Watch by him, Vienna Treasury, oval white enamel case ornamented with flowers, bezel encrusted with brilliants and emeralds, about 1716.

KIDD, GILBERT. *Malton*, 1760–80.

KIDD, JNO. Apprenticed in 1656 to Job Betts, C.C.

KIDDER, JOHN. *6 Strand*, 1816–23.

KIDSON, WM. *York*, f., 1614.

KIENING, HANS. *Füssen* (*Bavaria*), 1578. Astronomical clock in painted wood case K.H.M.; very fine book watch, Mallet collection, probably by him, illustrated Baillie. Another Ilbert collection.

KIHLBERG, JOHAN ABRAHAM. *Stockholm*. Born 1783, died 1853; cylinder watch, two mantel clocks and musical boxes.

KILBEY, F. *Cheltenham*. Died 1911.

KILGOUR, PATRICK. *Aberdeen*, 1672–92. Made town clock.

KILGOUR, WILLIAM. *Glithnow*, 1775. Died 1837.

KILLINGWORTH, JNO. *200 Brick Lane, Spitalfields*, 1815–18.

KILMINSTER, HENRY. C.C. 1677.

KIMBALL, JOHN, JUN. *Boston, U.S.A.*, 1823.

KINABLE, —. *Paris*, about 1780–1825. Very fine lyre clock, V. & A.

KINABLE, —. *Paris*, 1786. Lyre clock.

KING, HENRY. *Lincoln's Inn*, C.C. 1720; watch, gold *repoussé* case, Schloss collection, h.m., 1786.

KING, HENRY TUDOR, son of Henry. *London*. Apprenticed 1736, C.C. 1754.

KING, ISAAC. *Moorfields*, 1730.

KING, JAMES FREDERICK. *London* (*Bridgewater Sq.*). Apprenticed 1796, C.C. 1808.

KING, JOHN. C.C. 1729.

KING, JOHN. *Gough Sq.*, 1758–61.

KING, JOHN. *London*. C.C. 1715.

KING, JOHN. *London*. Apprenticed 1744, C.C. 1753.

KING, JONATHAN. C.C. 1689.

KING, NEHIMIAH. Lantern clock, dated 1693.

KING, PETER. *Long Acre*. C.C. 1715; a long-case clock by him in a fine marquetry case.

KING, R. *Scarborough*, 1808.

KING, THOMAS. C.C. 1669; marquetry long-case square dial clock, 1669–90.

KING, THOMAS. *Alnwick*, 1773.

KING, THOMAS. *London*. Apprenticed 1692, C.C. 1699.

KING, THOMAS. *London*. Apprenticed 1783, C.C. 1827.

KING, THOMAS WILLIAM. *London*. Apprenticed 1792, C.C. 1802–40.

KING, THOMAS & BENJAMIN. *82 Upper East Smithfield*, 1802–25.

KING, W. *34 High Holborn*, 1822–30.

KING, WILLIAM. In 'Birching Lane, watchmaker', admitted a freeman of the Cutlers' Company in 1707.

KING, WILLIAM. *London*. Apprenticed 1707, C.C. 1720.

KING, WILLIAM JOHN. *Monkwell St.* C.C. 1720; in the British Museum is a watch by him with *repoussé* case, 1730; another example, a repeating watch, 1745.

KING, WM. JNO. *Berkley Court, Clerkenwell*, 1780.

KINGERLEY, JNO. *Manchester*, 1810.

KINGMAN, JAS. *104 Leadenhall St.* Livery Goldsmiths' Co. 1774–83.

KINGSMILL, GEORGE. C.C. 1667.

KINGSNORTH, JNO. Apprenticed in 1688 to Thos. Stubbs, C.C.

KINKEAD, JAMES. *Philadelphia*, 1774. Clocks and watches.

KINKEAD, JOSEPH. *Christiana, Del., U.S.A.*, 1781. Master 1820.

KINNER, ANDREW. *London*. 1718 C.C.

KINNING, JOHN. C.C. 1701; watch, encased in glass, British Museum, 1700–30.

KINTZING, PETER. *Neuwied*. Born 1746, died 1816; clock; made the piano-playing automaton in C.A. & M. illuminated M. des Aut.; long-case clock Schloss Museum, Berlin; made movements for several clocks for the case maker David Röntgen.

KIPLING, WILLIAM. *Broad St.*, near *Ratcliff Cross*. Oak long-case clock, square dial, about 1710; watch with sun and moon hour indicators; another watch, h.m., 1730; another example, bracket clock, brass arched dial, strike-silent, day of month, elaborately inlaid case of hard wood, prolongation of pendulum seen through arc slot in dial; brought from the Emperor's Summer Palace at Peking, 1860; had then crown escapement, and was a 'pull repeater' with eight very sweet bells; engraved back plate, 1705–37. A clock by him with Turkish numerals and corner pieces on the dial in the form of a crescent. 'Wm. and John Kipling, London', on clocks about 1750.

KIPPIS, GEO. Apprenticed in 1687 to Chris. Gould, C.C.

KIRBY, CHARLES. *London*. Watch, 1795.

KIRBY, COLLINS. *London*. Apprenticed 1750, C.C. 1758.

KIRBY, ROBERT. C.C. 1722.

KIRBY, ROBERT. *London*. Apprenticed 1726, C.C. 1741.

KIRCHEL, BENNO JOSEPH. *Dresden*. Master 1811, died 1858.

KIRK, JOHN. C.C. 1677.

KIRK, JOSEPH. *Nottingham*. Long-case clock, about 1750.

KIRK, WM. *Stockport*, 1760.

KIRK, WM. *Manchester*, 1770.

KIRKPATRICK, MARTIN. *Dublin*, 1720. Died 1769.

KIRKWOOD, ALEXANDER. *Charleston, U.S.A.*, 1768. Clocks and watches.

KIRKWOOD, JOHN. *Charleston, U.S.A.*, 1761. Clocks and watches.

KIRKWOOD, THOMAS. *London*, 1680 C.C.

KIRNIER & KLEYSER. *14 Oxford St.* Card, British Museum, 1791.

KIRTON, JOHN. Apprenticed to Daniel Quare; C.C. 1705.

KISSAR, SAMUEL. C.C. 1712.

KITCHEN (or KITCHING), JNO. *Nantwich*, 1775.

KITCHEN & LLOYD. *Nantwich*. Long-case clock, about 1790.

KITCHING, JOSHUA. *14 Dover St., Piccadilly*, 1816–23.

KJEDING, OLOF. *Landskrona*. Born 1724, died 1805; long-case clock. Also KIEDING.

KLEIN, GOTFRED HENRIK. *Copenhagen*. Master 1741; Master of Corporation 1761–66.

KLEIN, JOHANN. *Prague*, 1687–1762. Fine astronomical clocks and equation work.

KLEIN, JOHANN HEINRICH. *Copenhagen*, 1703–28. From *Silesia*; table clock in ivory case, Rosenborg Castle; repeating watch.

KJELLSTRÖM, SVEN CHRISTOPHER. *Göteborg*. Born 1797, died 1839.

KLEBUST, LUX. *Basle*, 1648–60. Kleinuhrmacher.

KLEEMEYER, CHRISTIAN ERNST. *Berlin*, 1766–85. Clock; table clock.

KLENTSCHI, CHARLES FRÉDÉRIC. *Chaux-de-Fonds*. Born 1774, died 1854; a very able watch and clockmaker.

KLEY. A musical clock which plays every hour dating from about 1750, and inscribed 'John Kley, London'. It was brought from Amsterdam.

KLEYSER, GEORGE, & Co. Wooden clockmakers, *3 Little Tower Hill*, 1790–94.

KLEYSER, JNO. Wooden clockmaker, *191 High Holborn*, 1790–94.

KLEYSER, T. & J. *191 High Holborn*, 1810–30.

KLOCH, P. *Amsterdam*. Enamelled watch, about 1700.

KNAPP, PETER. *Karlshamn*, 1750–73.

KNAPP, WILLIAM. *Annapolis, U.S.A.*, 1764–67. Watch.

KNAUER, LEO. *Augsburg*. Master 1750–86.

KNAUSS, JOHANN LOUIS. *Darmstadt*, about 1730–70. Court clock; gold engraved watch; magnificent musical automatic clock, with silver mounts, known as the Maria Theresa clock, dated 1745; also bracket musical automatic clock, both Hofburg, Vienna; watch New York University.

KNAUSS *v.* VON KNAUSS.

KNEESHAW, ROBT. *Stokesley*, 1822.

KNELLER, JOHANN MICHAEL. Watch, British Museum, square brass case with silver filigree overlay, 1630–40.

KNIBB, ED. Apprenticed in 1693 to Joseph Knibb, C.C.

KNIBB, JOHN. *Oxon*. Verge watch movement, with curiously wrought pillars, G.M., style 1690; long-case clock, about 1695; in the Wetherfield collection a bracket repeating timepiece by him.

KNIBB, JOSEPH. *Oxon.* and *London*. C.C. 1670; a fine miniature timepiece by this maker.

KNIBB, PETER. C.C. 1677.

KNIBB, SAMUEL. C.C. on redemption 1663.

KNIFTON, THOMAS, at Yᵉ Cross Keys in *Lothebury*, 1640–57. Fine lantern clock by him. He was probably succeeded by John Ebsworth.

KNIGHT, —. *West Marden*, about 1790.

KNIGHT, BENJAMIN. *New St., Dockhead*, 1790.

KNIGHT, C. *Dunmow*, 1780.

KNIGHT, CHARLES. *Flower-de-luce, Great Russell St.* C.C. 1685–97.

KNIGHT, GEORGE. *London.* Apprenticed 1770, C.C. 1780.

KNIGHT, H. *Stafford*, about 1790 C.C. Watch.

KNIGHT, HENRY. C.C. 1723.

KNIGHT, JOHN. *6 Carpenters' Buildings, London Wall*, 1768.

KNIGHT, MICHAEL. Apprenticed to Lionel Wythe and turned over to Thos. Tompion, C.C. 1681; fine long-case clock, bird and flower marquetry, about 1690.

KNIGHT, RICHARD. *London.* Apprenticed 1674, C.C. 1682–95.

KNIGHT, RICHARD. C.C. 1682.

KNIGHT, THOS. Apprenticed in 1686 to Dorcas Bouquett.

KNIGHT, W. *Thaxted*, 1760.

KNIGHT, WILLIAM. *Bristol*, 1813–30. Watch.

KNIGHT, WM. *West Marden*, about 1750.

KNIP, GERRIT. *Amsterdam*, mid-eighteenth century-about 1780. Fine long-case clock; repeating watch, Ilbert collection.

KNOLLYS, FRANCIS. Apprenticed in 1669 to Jno. Harris, C.C.

KNOOP, JOHAN CHRISTIAN. *Stockholm*, 1769–85. Long-case clock illuminated Sidenbladh; wall clock.

KNOTT, ROBT. Apprenticed in 1682 to Clement Forster, C.C.

KNOTTESFORD, JNO. Apprenticed in 1680 to Wm. Knottesford; C.C.; month chiming clock in fine marquetry long case, Wetherfield collection, about 1700, inscribed 'John Knotsford, London'.

KNOTTESFORD, WILLIAM. Apprenticed to Hy. Child; C.C. 1663; master 1693; bracket clock, about 1680, with seconds dial and maintaining power; walnut case with spiral ebony columns as seen on hoods of long-case clocks; circular silver watch, British Museum, also a repeater in V. & A., h.m., 1684, and a large clock-watch, G.M.

KNOWLES, ANDREW. *Epsom*, 1730.

KNOWLES, JOSEPH. *Epsom*. Watch, 1760.

KNOWLES, ROBERT. *Liverpool*, 1800–29. Watch.

KNOWLES, WM. *Dublin*, 1780.

KNOX, ALEX. *Berwick*, 1770.

KNOX, JAMES. *Paisley*, 1820–36.

KNOX, JOHN. *Belfast*, 1729–83. John, nephew of the preceding to whom he was apprenticed, started business in Larne, and on the death of his uncle succeeded him in High St., Belfast; engraved a portrait of Washington for a watch paper; retired 1816. See NEILL, R.

KNOX, JOHN. *Larne*, 1769–83. A fine long-case clock-maker.

KNOX, ROBERT. *Paisley*, 1820–37.

KNOX, WM. *Paisley*, 1780.

KNÜPFER, GOTTLIEB FRIEDRICH. *Dresden*. Born 1724, died 1773 master.

KÖBERLE (COEBERLE), WILHELM. *Eichstätt*, 1680–1715. Striking travelling clock V. & A.; table clock, with canopy; watch, Fränkel collection; travelling clock M.P.S., Dresden; hexagonal clock with temple canopy, Stern. collection.

KÖBERLE, WILHELMUS. *Eijstet (Eichstadt, South Germany)*. Early clock-watch in case of gilt brass, pierced and engraved, V. & A.

KOCK, JACOB. *Stockholm*. Watch, 1740.

KOCH, JOHANN. *Cöllen*. Alarum calendar watch, about 1630.

KOCK, PETER. *Harlem*. Watch, 1780.

KOHLER (KÖHLER), JOHANN GOTTFRIED. *Dresden*, 1745–1800. Observatory clocks.

KOLB, ANDREAS. *Strasbourg*, 1744.

KOLBE, FRIEDRICH AUGUST. *Dresden*. Born 1754, master 1791, died 1838.

KOPPAUN, CHRISTOF. German square table clock, V. & A., signed and dated 1582.

KOSTER, DIRK. *Amsterdam*. Watch with sun and moon indicators, G.M., about 1695.

KOSTER, SAMUEL *v.* COSTER.

KOSTER, WM. *Amsterdam*, about 1700.

KOTTE, JACOB. Antique watch, Shandon collection, about 1630.

KOVER, —. *London*. Handsome watch, gold *repoussé* case, about 1720.

KRAMPE, JOHAN GEORG. *Basle*. Born 1729, master 1764, died 1790.

KRANZ, KASPAR. *Kitzingen-am-Main*. Born 1743, master 1794, died 1824; bracket clock.

KRAPP, JOSEPH. *Mannheim; Munich*, 1777. Court clock 1788–1803; table clock, Bay. National Museum.

KRATZENSTEIN, GEORG. *Copenhagen* and *Petersburg*. Wrote articles in Journal of the Academy of Petersburg on heat expansion as driving power for clocks and chronometers about 1756 and 1751; in 1780 finished a talking head.

KRATZER. See CRATZER.

KREBS, MATTHÄUS. *Villingen*, about 1750–80. Wall clocks Furt. Museum.

KREISBEUTEL (GREISBEUTEL, GREISSBÜTTEL), HANS. *Cassel*. Burgher in 1591; in 1602 repaired the Rathaus clock.

KREISBEUTEL (GREISBEUTEL, GREISSBÜTTEL), MARTIN, son. *Cassel*, 1631–59.

KREITT-MAYER, JOHANN. About 1645; watch ascribed to Bruce.

KREIZER, CONRAD. Watch in the form of a cross, Vienna Treasury, case of crystal, dial of silver, dial of gold, with instruments of the Passion engraved thereon, about 1600; octagonal watch, V. & A., about 1600.

KRENCKEL, PETER. *Eüchstet* (or *Füchstet*). Alarm table clock, V. & A., about 1700.

KRIEDEL, J. G. *Bautzen*, mid-eighteenth century. Repeating carriage watch.

KROESE, J. P. *Amsterdam*. Watch, fine enamel painting of Cleopatra; about 1770.

KRUTMEIJER, NILS J. *Malmö*. Born 1770, died 1847.

KÜLPER, JOHANN. *Brieg*, 1677–1746. Watch in snuff-box; repeating striking watch M.P.S., Dresden; travelling clock. Also CULPER.

KUMLING, CARL ADOLPH. *Hudiksvall*, 1803–46.

KYFFIN, EDWARD. Apprenticed in 1682 to Jno. Brown, C.C.

KYHL, HENRIK. *Copenhagen*. Master 1818; Master of Corporation 1832–36.

KYNING, JOHN. *London*. Apprenticed 1693, C.C. 1701–11.

KYNVYN, JONAS. Maker of a clock belonging to the Earl of Essex, 1593.

LABÉ (L'ABBÉ), CLAUDE. *Stuttgart*. Born 1671, died 1717; court clock; watch, Uhren Museum, Vienna.

LABHARD, JOHANN. *Cassel*, 1738–95. Swiss; designed clock for Observatory.

LABORNE, CHRISTOPHER. *Gt. Driffield*. Died 1831.

LABRU, —. *London*. Hexagonal table clock, about 1680.

LACEY, CHAS. *12 Ludgate St.*, 1783.

LACEY, PAUL. *Bristol*, 1780.

LACEY, WILLIAM. *London*. C.C. 1750.

LACON, PETER. *London*. Watch, 1785.

LACOUR, DANIEL. *New St., Covent Garden*, 1825.

LACY, JOHN. *London*. Apprenticed 1714, C.C. 1722–50.

LACY, SOLOMON. *London*. Apprenticed 1700.

LA CROIX, —. *Rue Denis, Paris*. Handsome clock, about 1790.

LA CROIX, —. *Geneva*. Watch, 1814.

LADD, J. *35 Cornhill*, 1823.

LADD, SAM. C.C. 1709.

LADONEAU, JEAN. *Paris*. Clockmaker to Louis XIV, 1680.

LAFONS. See DE LAFONS.

LAFOSSE, WM. *32 Old Broad St.*, 1738–94.

LAGERSTRAND, ERIC. *Uppsala*. Born 1783, died 1833. Watch.

LAGERSTRAND, NIKL. *Hälsingfors*. Born 1795, died 1849.

LAGIS (LAGISSE), PIERRE DIDIER. *Geneva*. Died 1679; went to *Ispahan* and became clockmaker to the Shah; gold engraved watches G.M. and Ilbert and Gélis collections; watch, Bernal sale.

LAGOE, JNO. Apprenticed in 1671 to Richd. Halstead, C.C.

LÄHNE, C. H. *Leipzig*, late eighteenth century–1800. Died a. 1814; gold engraved watch M.P.S., Dresden; maker of repute.

LAIDLAW, THOMAS. *16 Salisbury Sq.*, 1770–94. Hon. Freeman C.C. 1781.

LAINÉ, —. *Paris*. Miniature alarm clock 1790.

L'AINGE, —. *82 Cheapside*, 1842.

LAINY, DAVID. Watch in the Guildhall Museum, about 1670.

LAINY, JOHN. C.C. 1720.

LAISNE, SIBELIN. *Neuchâtel*, about 1750.

LAKE, BRYAN. C.C. 1674; 30–hour clock, bob pendulum, 'J. Lake, 1723'.

LAKE, ROBERT. *London (Enfield)*. C.C. 1770–1808.

LAKE, THOS. *Taunton*, 1770.

LALLEMAND (LALLEMAN, LALEMENT), —. *Paris*, 1790–1813. Cylinder repeating watch movement; C.A. & M.

LALLEMAND (LALLEMAN, LALEMENT), DIDIER. *Lyons*, 1672; *Paris*, 1686. Made a clockwork astronomical globe, described in *Phil. Trans.* Vol. XII, Oxford, 1683.

LALLEMAND (LALLEMAN, LALEMENT), HENRY. *Autun*, about 1630. Died 1670.

LALLEMAND (LALLEMAN, LALEMENT), LOUIS. *Blois*. Master 1667–1718; made turret clock at Blois.

LAMB (or LAMBE). Several generations beginning with Thomas Lambe, 1630; in 1704 it was reported to the C.C. that among other well-known makers the name of Lamb had been engraved on watches by persons in Amsterdam, which watches were sold as of English make.

LAMB (or LAMBE), ABRAHAM. Apprenticed in 1651 to Wm. Petit, C.C.

LAMB (or LAMBE), BENJ. *21 St. John's Sq.*, 1760–79.

LAMB (or LAMBE), EDMUND. *London*. C.C. 1676.

LAMB (or LAMBE), JAMES. *London (Christopher's Alley)*. Apprenticed 1751, C.C. 1759–83.

LAMB (or LAMBE), JAMES. *London*. Apprenticed 1775, C.C. 1798.

LAMB (or LAMBE), JNO. *Henrietta St.*, C.C. 1714.

LAMB (or LAMBE), JNO. *13 Red Lion St., Clerkenwell*, 1822–52.

LAMB (or LAMBE), LUKE. Apprenticed in 1683 to Johnson Weekes, C.C.

LAMB (or LAMBE), SIMON. Apprenticed 1669 to Wm. Glazier, C.C.; long-case clock, about 1700, inscribed 'Simon Lamb, Rochester'.

LAMB (or LAMBE), THOS. *Union St., Spitalfields*, 1790.

LAMB (or LAMBE) & WEBB. *21 St. John's Sq., Clerkenwell*, 1780–95.

LAMBDEN, RICHD. Apprenticed in 1685 to Joseph Hussey, C.C.

LAMBE, EDWARD. C.C. 1675; long-case clock, about 1690.

LAMBE, JOHN. *29 Fetter Lane*, 1774–1800.

LAMBE, THOMAS. C.C. 1632.

LAMBELL, SAMUEL. *Northampton*, 1750.

LAMBERT, —. *Besançon*. French enamelled watch, about 1780.

LAMBERT, EDWARD. *London*. C.C. 1767.

LAMBERT, EDWARD. *London (Bridgewater Sq.)*. C.C. 1773–87.

LAMBERT, FRANCIS. Partner with Hamlet in 1800; afterwards started business at *12 Coventry St.*, and subsequently entered into partnership with Rawlings at the same address.

LAMBERT, HARRY. *London*. C.C. 1821.

LAMBERT, JAS. *London*. Watch, 1760.

LAMBERT, JNO. *London*. A long-case square dial clock by him, the movement dated 1703.

LAMBERT, JOHN. *2 Tichborne St.*, 1775–1810.

LAMBERT, NICHOLAS. *London*, 1750–70. Long-case clock; chiming clock by him on the mantelpiece of the vestry of Lady Huntingdon's Chapel, Bath, with the inscription, 'This clock is the property of the Church at the Vineyards, Bath, given by the Countess of Huntingdon for the use of the minister for the time being.'

LAMBERT, PIERRE. *Abbeville*. Watch, about 1680.

LAMBERT, WM. *Cannon St.* C.C. 1730.

LAMIONE, A. *Philadelphia*, 1811.

LAMPE, JOHN. *Henrietta St.* Admitted C.C. 1713; Chippendale long-case clock, large hood and gallery round the top, inscription on disc, 'John Lampe, London'; 1713–65.

LAMPE, JOHN. *Baltimore, U.S.A.*, 1780. From *Annapolis;* watch.

LAMPLOUGH, JNO. *Bridlington*, 1822.

LAMPORT, D. *Bow St., Bloomsbury*. Watch, h.m., 1810.

LAMUDE, JNO. *Chard*, about 1740.

LAMUDE, PETER. Apprenticed in 1684 to Nat. Delander, C.C.

LAMUDE, REU. *Chard*. Watch, 1760.

LANCASTER, FRANCIS. *London*. A good workman, 1790–1800.

LANCASTER, NICHOLAS. Apprenticed in 1679 to Stafford Freeman, C.C.

LANCASTER, RICHARD. Apprenticed in 1677 to Thos. Hollis, C.C.

LANCASTER, RICHARD. Apprenticed in 1684 to Hy. Merriman, C.C.

LANDECK (LANDTECK), JOHANN CARL, son. *Nürnberg.* Born 1636, died 1712; went to *Amsterdam, Rotterdam, Copenhagen, Holstein.* At *Nürnberg* 1662, and in 1663 was town clockmaker; first to make pendulum clocks in Nürnberg; clock for Rothenburg-a.-d.-T.; bracket clock.

LANDECK (LANDTECK), JOHANN CASPAR, son of W. J. M. *Nürnberg.* Born 1752, died 1822; watch Stuttgart Museum.

LANDECK (LANDTECK), WOLFGANG JACOB MATHÄUS, brother. *Weimar.* Born 1715, died 1794; court clockmaker.

LANDIFIELD, THOMAS. *London.* C.C. 1772; retired 1777; watch.

LANDLEN, THOS. *16 Salisbury Court,* 1794.

LANDRE, L. *Brussels,* about 1650.

LANDRE, MICHEL. *Blois* and *Rennes.* Master 1605, died 1623; went *Rennes* 1610.

LANDRE, P. *Brussels,* 1700.

LANDRE, PIERRE. *Blois.* Skull watch, Pierpont Morgan collection, about 1630.

LANDRE, PIERRE, son. *Blois.* Born 1627, died 1679. Also ANDRÉ.

LANDRE, SALOMON, son. *Blois.* Master 1672, died a. 1691. Also ANDRÉ.

LANE, HENRY. *Bristol.* Long-case clock, tidal time in arch, and above, 'High Water at Bristol Key'; about 1780.

LANE, JNO. Apprenticed in 1679 to Sam. Vernon, C.C.

LANE, JOHN. *Fetter Lane,* about 1785.

LANE, JOSIAH. *London.* Apprenticed 1729, C.C. 1736.

LANE, W. *Calstone.* Long-case chiming clock, about 1750.

LANE, WRIGHT. *London.* 1687 C.C.

LANGCROFT, RICHARD. C.C. 1718.

LANGLANDS, JOHN. *Newcastle,* 1816.

L'ANGE, A. *51 Cornhill,* 1835.

LANGENBUCHER, CASPAR. *Augsburg,* early seventeenth century. A very able maker; clock, Brunswick Museum.

LANGFORD, ELLIS. Apprenticed in 1663 to Gowen Langford; C.C. 1672.

LANGFORD, GOWEN. C.C. 1652.

LANGFORD, THOS. Hon. freeman, C.C. 1781; long-case clock, 'Langford, Southampton', about 1780, *White Horse Hotel,* Romsey; broken arch bracket clock, enamel dial, about 1795.

LANGFORD, WM. *Ludlow,* 1770.

LANGHAM, WILLIAM. *London.* C.C. 1751.

LANGHORNE, THOMAS. *Threadneedle St.* Liveryman C.C. 1776.

LANGLEY, CORNELIUS. C.C. 1706.

LANGLEY, THOMAS. C.C. 1664.

LANGLOIS, CHARLES FRANÇOIS. *Paris,* 1730. Died 1757; watch National Museum, Prague.

LANGRISH, I. *Oldham,* 1770.

LANGTON, JAS. *Founders' Ct., Lothbury,* 1776.

LANGWITH, JAS. *York,* f., 1722.

LANGWITH, SAM. *York,* 1770.

LANSON, J. *Bradford.* Long-case clock, about 1750.

LANY, JOHN. *London.* C.C. 1720.

LANZ, NICHOLAUS. *Innsbruck,* 1566. Maker to the Archduke Ferdinand.

LARRARD, THOS. *Hull,* 1814–40.

LARCAY, L. *Paris.* An eminent horologist, 1725–35; he is spoken of by Thiout as Larsé.

LA PIERRE, BENNET. *Baltimore, U.S.A.,* 1802. Watches and clocks.

LARESCHE, H. *Paris,* 1807–27. Wrote a mem. on the lubrication of pivots, Rouen, 1827; many fine clocks; silver repeating watch, painted dial.

LARESCHE, JACQUES ANTOINE. *Besançon.* Born 1700, died 1782; several very fine bracket clocks.

LARGE, JONATHAN. *London.* Long-case clocks, about 1790.

LARKIN, ED. *Winchester,* 1681.

LARMETT, ABRAHAM. C.C., about 1650.

LAROCH, JOHN. *18 High St., Bloomsbury,* 1815–25.

LARPENT, ISAAC. *Copenhagen.* Born 1711, master 1745, died 1769; started watch factory at *Röskilde* with Joergen Jürgenson; watches F.W.M. and Chamb. collection; pair-case watch dated 1747, Feill collection.

LASARUS, ABRAHAM. *Gun Yard,* 1760–65.

LASHBROOK, HENRY. C.C. 1715.

LASHBROOK, JNO. Apprenticed in 1655 to Wm. Pettitt, C.C.

LASHBROOK, THOS. Apprenticed in 1693 to Richd. Conyers, C.C.

LASOFFE, WILLIAM. *52 Old Broad St.,* 1765–70.

LASSEL, —. *Toxteth Park, Liverpool.* Long-case clock, 'Lassel, Park', about 1735.

LASSEL, THURSTAN. Long-case clock, about 1775.

LASSEL, WILLIAM. Several long-case clocks, 1740–70.

LASSETER, WILLIAM. *Arundel.* Maker of long-case clocks, about 1770.

LAST, W. R. *Yarmouth.* Watch, 1810.

LATHAM, HY. Apprenticed in 1655 to Humfrey Downing, C.C.

LATHAM, JAS. *Preston,* 1814.

LATHAM, JOHN. C.C. 1700 watch with gold *repoussé* case, V. & A., 1720; in the Church of the Capucino, Cadiz, is a long-case clock by him; the Plough Inn, Cadsdean, Princes Risborough, Bucks., has another in a mahogany case, inscribed 'John Latham, London'.

LATHAM, T. *London.* Watch, 1795.

LATHAM, WM. *Macclesfield,* 1775.

LATIMER, JAS. *Philadelphia,* 1819.

LATOUR, RENÉ. Admitted C.C. 1730.

LAUCH, JOHANN FRIEDRICH. *Vienna,* about 1695–1740. Published designs for bracket clocks.

LAUD, THOS. In 1638 Thos. Fitton was apprenticed to him; C.C.

LAUGHTON, WILLIAM. *London.* C.C. 1683–94.

LAUNAY, DAVID F. Watchmaker, *9 Warren St., New York,* 1801, "has a high finished clock which decorated the library of the late King of France, made by Charles Berthand, of the Royal Academy; its original price 5,000 livres; to be sold for 500 dollars."

LAUNDY, JNO. Apprenticed in 1692 to Thos. Walford, C.C.

LAURENCE, HENRY. *London.* Apprenticed 1691, C.C. 1704–25. Also LAWRENCE.

LAURENT, FÉLIX. *Canton, China,* 1787–about 1800. Firm of Cox, Beale & Laurent from 1792.

LAURENT, PETER. *London.* Apprenticed 1700.

LAURIER, FRANÇOIS. *Blois,* 1654. Died 1663; watch movement British Museum; circular engraved watch Lincoln Museum.

LAURIERE, J. *62 St. James's St.,* 1822–30.

LAUTIER. *Bath.* See VIGNE.

LAUTIER, BENJAMIN. *Bath,* about 1790–1848 C.C. Watch New York University.

LAVER, BENJAMIN. *4 Bruton St., Berkeley Sq.*, 1790–1800.

LAVESPEARE, WM. C.C., about 1650.

LAW, ISAAC. Forbidden to work by C.C. in 1632, afterwards made free of the Company.

LAW, JERE. *Rochdale*, 1780.

LAW, JOHN. *London*. Apprenticed 1760, C.C. 1768.

LAW, JOHN. *Aberdeen*, about 1790 C.C.

LAW, JOHN. *Edinburgh*. Born 1770, died 1842.

LAW, SILVESTER. Apprenticed in 1689 to Richard Baker, C.C.

LAW, THOMAS. *27 Thomas St., Southwark*, 1790–94.

LAW, TIMOTHY. Apprenticed in 1690 to Wm. Cart, C.C.

LAW, WILLIAM. *Linlithgow*, 1820–37.

LAWELL, PAUL. C.C. 1653.

LAWLEY, ALVIS. *Bath*, 1826.

LAWRENCE, —. *Bath*, 1763.

LAWRENCE, BENJAMIN. *London (Shoe Lane)*. C.C. 1779–96.

LAWRENCE, HARRY, son of Benjamin. *London (Shoe Lane)*. Apprenticed 1789, C.C. 1796–1809.

LAWRENCE, HENRY. 1770.

LAWRENCE, HY. Apprenticed in 1691 to Richd. Colston, C.C. *Lancaster*.

LAWRENCE, JNO. 1761, f.

LAURENCE, RICHARD. *Bath*, 1757. Died 1773; skeleton silver watch G.M. Born 1729. Apprenticed 1744 to John Taylor, Bath.

LAWRENCE, THOS. *London*. Watch, 1772.

LAWRENCE, W. *Thame*, 1765.

LAWRENCE, WM. 1785, f., *Bristol*.

LAWRENCE, WM. 1780.

LAWRIE, C. A. *Carlisle*. Clock, about 1770.

LAWRIERE, JNO. *13 St. James's St., Pall Mall*, 1815–19.

LAWSON, JNO. *Bradford*, 1750.

LAWSON, JNO. *London*. Watch, 1763.

LAWSON, JNO. *Warrington*, 1818.

LAWSON, JOHN EDWD. *58 Bishopsgate Within*, 1800–25. Livery C.C. 1812.

LAWSON, RAMSAY. *Wigan*, 1770.

LAWSON, SAM. *Keighley*, 1740.

LAWSON, THOS. *Keighley*, 1765.

LAWSON, W. *Keighley*, 1810–14.

LAWSON, WILLIAM. *Todmorden*, about 1820.

LAWSON, WM. *Newton-le-Willows*, 1770.

LAWSON, WM. *Keighley*, 1780. Long-case clock bearing the inscription:—

> 'So glide the hours, So wears the day,
> These moments measure life away.'

LAWTON, THOS. *London*. Watch, 1820.

LAXTON, THOMAS. C.C. 1642.

LAXTON, THOMAS. C.C. 1653.

LAYBOURN, CHRISTOPHER, *Driffield*, 1770.

LAYFIELD, ROBT. *Lancaster*, 1785, f.

LAYTON, FRANCIS. C.C. 1726.

LAYTON, JOHN. C.C. 1653.

LAYTON, THOMAS. *Dean St.* Liveryman C.C. 1776; *82 Wardour St.*, 1794–1823.

LAYTON, WILLIAM. *London*, 1703 C.C. Also LAUGHTON.

LAYTON, WILLIAM, son. *London*. Apprenticed 1703, C.C. 1710.

LAZARE, —, a Serbian. Made a clock for Moscow, 1404.

LAZARUS, H. *112 Upper East Smithfield*, 1815.

LAZARUS, J. *15 Carter St., Houndsditch*, 1825; *39 Minories*, 1830.

LAZENBY, R. *Knightsbridge*. On a small clock with sunk seconds and day of the month circles, about 1770.

LAZENBY, WM. *Paradise Row, Chelsea*. Card, British Museum, 1784.

LEA, SAMUEL. *London*. Clock in the Wetherfield collection, about 1720.

LEA, THOMAS. *Old Jewry*. Livery C.C. 1766; master 1782; 1760–83.

LEACH, BENJ. *Winchester*. Watch, 1790; long-case clocks by him are much esteemed in Hampshire; in 1803 he submitted an estimate of seven guineas to repair the Winchester Town Hall clock, and substitute a long pendulum for the short one then existing.

LEACH, CALEB. *Plymouth, U.S.A.*, 1776–90.

LEACH, CHAS. *59 King William St., London Bridge*, 1820–30.

LEACH, JNO. *Kirkham*, 1816.

LEACH, THOS. *Lombard St.*, 1753–60.

LEACH, WILLIAM. *London*. Apprenticed 1740, C.C. 1749. Also LEECH.

LEADBEATER, CHAS. *Wigan*, 1820.

LEADBEATER, PETER. *Congleton*, 1818–34.

LEADBETTER, WILLIAM. *Cross Keys Court, Little Britain*, 1785–94.

LEAF, JOHN. *London*. C.C. 1785.

LEAH, SAMUEL HENRY. *29 Bath St., City Rd.*, 1823–42.

LEAKE, FAITH. Apprenticed to John White, but served Daniel Quare; C.C. 1685.

LEAKE, GEORGE. Apprenticed to John Wright, C.C. 1693.

LEATHWAITE, GEO. *Ulverstone*, 1770.

LÉAUTIER, PAUL. *Paris*. Master 1767–89; watch, New York University; travelling clock, Gélis collection.

LEAVENWORTH, MARK, also WM. *Waterbury, Conn.*, 1810–30.

LEAVENWORTH, WILLIAM. *Waterbury, U.S.A.*, 1810–15. Failed, and started with his son at *Albany*.

LEAVENWORTH & SON. *Albany, U.S.A.*, 1817–23. Clock.

LEAVER, NAT. Apprenticed in 1679 to John Wright, senr., C.C.; bracket clock, about 1730, inscribed 'Leaver, London'.

LEAVER, WM. *45 Great Sutton St.*, 1822–30.

LE BLOND, JEAN NICOLAS. *Paris (Rue St. Paul)*. Master 1777–1810.

LE BLOND, P. Watch, signed 'Le Blond', in rock crystal case, about 1600.

LE BLOND, PIERRE. *Paris (Rue St. Honoré)*. Master 1767–89.

LE BLOND, ROBT. *Artillery Lane, Stewart St.* Livery Blacksmiths' Company, 1770; watch, 1770; bracket clock, 1790.

LE BLOND-DU-QUINTAUX, NICOLAS. *Paris (Rue de la Vieille Boucherie)*. Master 1770–89.

LE BON, ALEX. *Paris*. Maker of equation clocks, 1727–30; clock, Jones collection, V. & A., about 1770, inscribed 'Le Bon a Paris'.

LE BRUN, JEAN. *Paris*, 1609. Juré.

LE CAMU, —. *Paris*, 1787–1807.

LE CAS, PAUL. *Paris*. Juré 1693.

LÉCHAUD, ANTOINE, son. *Geneva*. Born 1812, died 1875; worked with G. A. Leschot, and devised a very successful lever calibre.

LÉCHOPIÉ, ADAM. *Paris*. Master 1758, juré 1772–89. Table clock Blot-Garnier collection; mantel clock Louvre.

LECKIE, ANDREW. Watch, 1780.

LECKIE, T. *Newcastle-on-Tyne*. a. 1759. Watch.

LE CLERC (LE CLER, LECLERCQ), JEAN. *Blois*. Master 1604–32.

LE CLERC. *Paris*. Bracket clock, about 1630.

LE CLERK, DANIEL. *Paris*. Watch, Pierpont Morgan collection, about 1630.

LE COEUR, —. *Paris*, 1783–1808. Gold engraved watch V. & A.

LECOMTE (LECOUNT), DANIEL. Brother C.C. 1676. "Taken from Mr. Robert Murrel, on the 5th inst., by Foot Pads, near Newington, a Pendulum Watch made by Daniel Lecount" (*Lond. Gaz.*, Aug. 4–8, 1692). A clock by him with long case, finely inlaid; clock-watch, Turkish numerals, silver-gilt pierced case, Pierpont Morgan collection.

LECOMTE (LECOUNT), J. R. *60 Dean St., Soho*, 1763–83.

LECOMTE (LECOUNT), JAMES. C.C. 1687. "Stolen a silver watch, made by Mr. Le Count" (*Lond. Gaz.*, Feb. 15–18, 1691).

LE CONTANDOIS, NICOLAS. *Paris*, 1554.

LECOULTRE, ANTOINE. *La Vallée, Switzerland*, 1825.

LECOUNT, PETER. Livery C.C. 1810; *36 Pitfield St.*, 1823.

LEDART, RICHARD, in *Strassburg*. Watch, about 1620.

LE DESVÉ, LOUIS. *Rouen*, 1726–50.

LEDEUR, R. *London*. Hexagonal table clock, about 1600; small octagonal watch, rock crystal case, signed 'R. Ledeur', Pierpont Morgan collection.

LEDGARD, JOSEPH. *Newcastle-on-Tyne*, 1707–32. Watch movement, V. & A.

LEDIEU, JAS. *Soho*, 1817.

LEDOUX, PIERRE. *Paris*, about 1720–50 master. Vernis Martin bracket clock.

LEDOUX, PIERRE FRANÇOIS. *Paris* (*Rue St. André des Arcs*). Master 1758–89.

LEDRU, WM. *London*, 1795.

LEE, CHRISTOPHER. Apprenticed in 1691 to Wm. Young, C.C.

LEE, CUTHBERT. C.C. 1676; long-case month clock, about 1710, signed 'Cuthbert Lee, Jewen St'.

LEE, EZEKIEL. Apprenticed 1668 to Jeffrey Baily, C.C., lantern clock, about 1700.

LEE, GEORGE. *Lombard St.*, 1737–40.

LEE, ISAAC. *10 Devonshire Buildings, Great Dover St.*, 1840–42.

LEE, JAMES. *London*. Apprenticed 1790, C.C. 1797.

LEE, JOHN. C.C. 1719.

LEE, JOHN. *31 Noble St., Forster Lane*, 1800–04.

LEE, JOHN. *London*. Apprenticed 1703, C.C. 1737.

LEE, JOHN. *London*. Apprenticed 1719, C.C. 1737.

LEE, JOHN. *London*. Apprenticed 1734, C.C. 1745.

LEE, JOHN. *Cookham*. Apprenticed 1759–about 1800 C.C.

LEE, NICHOLAS. *Liverpool*, 1796–1811. Watch.

LEE, ROGER. *Leicester*. Watch by him, about 1700, Leicester Museum.

LEE, SAMUEL. C.C. 1694; long-case clock, arch dial, burr walnut case with black carved mouldings, Wetherfield collection, about 1720.

LEE, SARAH. *London*. C.C. 1756.

LEE, THOMAS. Apprenticed to Francis Robinson, C.C. 1730.

LEE, UNDERWOOD. Apprenticed in 1688 to Edwd. Staunton, C.C.

LEE, WILLIAM. *Charleston, U.S.A.*, 1768. Clocks and watches.

LEEDS, W. H. *20 Wilderness Row*, 1817.

LEEK, JOHN. *London*. Apprenticed 1753, C.C. 1760–69.

LEEKEY, GABRIEL. *15 Basinghall St.*, 1755–78.

LEEKEY, GABRIEL. Probably son of the foregoing, C.C. 1778–1815.

LEEKEY, GEORGE. *London*. C.C. 1778–1815.

LEEKEY, SAMSON. Watch, about 1805.

LEEMING, EDWARD. Watch-case maker, *8 Little Britain*, 1790–94.

LEEMING, EDWD. Livery C.C. 1787.

LEES, JNO. *Middleton*, 1818.

LEES, JONATHAN. *Bury*, 1770.

LEES, SAM. *Ashton-under-Lyne*, 1818.

LEES, THOMAS. *Bury*, 1790–1816.

LEES, THOMAS. *Drury Lane*, 1821–32.

LEES, WM. *Haslingdon*, 1816.

LE FAUCHEUR, ALEXANDRE. *Paris*. Horloger to Louis XV in 1746; his son Jean Ignace succeeded him in 1773.

LE FAUCHEUR, JEAN JACQUES IGNACE, son. *Paris*, 1773–89. Clockmaker to Louis XVI.

LE FEBUCE, CHARLES (French). Admitted C.C. 1687.

LE FEBURE, E. *Rouen*. Watch, about 1660.

LEFEBURY, CHAS. C.C. 1687.

LEFEBURY, DAN. Apprenticed in 1686 to Dan Lecompte, C.C.

LEFEBVRE, —. *Paris* (*Rue St. Honoré*), 1807–25. Succeeded J. F. Debelle.

LEFEBVRE, ÉLIE. *Rouen*. Master 1653, juré 1660–1709; keeper of cathedral clock; watch.

LEFEBVRE, PIERRE. *Paris*, 1736–56.

LEFEBVRE, TH. *Rue St. Louis, Paris*. Garde-visiteur, 1769.

LEFFERTS (CHAS.) & HALL. *Philadelphia*, 1819.

LEFFIN, THOMAS. C.C. 1720.

LEFOSSE, WM. *52 Old Broad St.*, 1769–72.

LEFOUNT, MARGARET SARAH. *London*. C.C. 1810.

LEFROY, GEORGE. *Wisbech*, about 1785.

LEG, JNO. *London*. A good workman, taught by Earnshaw, 1780.

LEGEIPS, JOHN. *London*. In the British Museum a very large repeating watch with silver case decorated in *repoussé*, 1720–30.

LEGER à *Paris*. Watch, about 1780.

LEGER, CLAUDE. *La Rochelle*, 1668–1701.

LEGG, JOHN. C.C. 1724; watch, signed 'John Legg Blechingly', 1787.

LE GAIGNEUR, JEAN. Master clockmaker in Paris. Received in 1639 the sum of 1,500 francs for a clock for the Château de Saint-Germain-en-Laye.

LE GRAND, FRANCIS. C.C. 1647.

LE GRAND, JAMES. C.C. 1641.

LE GRAND, JAMES. *London*. Apprenticed 1656–64 C.C.

LE GRAND, SIMON. *Paris*. Clockmaker to the King, 1657.

LEGRAND, JAMES, JUNR. C.C. 1664.

LEGRANDE, —. *Rouen*, 1552.

LE GROS, P. J. *1 Upper Crown St., Westminster*. Bracket clock, about 1800. In 1817 Philip Gross carried on business at *12 Panton St., Haymarket*.

LE GUAY. Fine Boulle clock with bracket inscribed 'Guillaume Le Guay, à Paris, au Louvre', about 1750.

LEGUESSE, L. J. About 1720.

LEHNER, ANSELM BENEDIKT. *Augsburg*. Master 1741, died about 1759.

LEHR, SEBASTIAN. Clockmaker to the city of Nuremberg; died 1556.

LE HURAY, NICHOLAS. *Guernsey*, about 1780; *Philadelphia*, 1811–25. Long-case clock.

LE HURAY, NICH. *Philadelphia*, 1819.

LEICESTER, JAS. *Drury Lane*. Pull repeating clock with visible pendulum, about 1710. Black lacquer long-case clock, inscribed 'Ye Strand, London'.

LEIF, G. T. *Sheffield*, 1821.

LEIGH, THOMAS. C.C. 1730.

LEIGH, WM. *71 Oxford St.*, 1792.

LEIGHTON, —. *Warrington*. Clock, about 1770.

LEIGNES, CHARLES PETER. *Northumberland St., Strand*, 1790–94.

LEINBACH, ELIAS and JOHN. *Reamstown, Lancaster, U.S.A.* 1788–1810. Long-case clocks.

LEJEUNE, JEAN BAPTISTE. *Paris*. Enamelled watch, about 1780.

LELLO, JAMES. Apprenticed in 1647 to Thos. Alcock; C.C. in 1656, on producing his masterpiece with his name, its genuineness being attested by Samuel Betts.

LE LOUTRE, F. 'horloger du Roy, Paris', 1754–80.

LEMAINDRE, NICHOLAS. *Blois*. Large alarum watch in pierced and engraved brass gilt case, V. & A 1620–30.

LEMAINDRE, NICOLAS, nephew. *Blois*. Born 1600–60. *Paris* for 15 years a. 1652; clockmaker to duc d'Orléans 1624; to Louis XIV 1646; exceptionally fine crystal watch with engraved crystal covers and gold engraved frame and dial plate Wallace collection; square watch Louvre illuminated Baillie; watch, Basle Museum; engraved watch, Gotha Museum; gold engraved watch, Gélis collection.

LEMAINDRE, NICOLAS, brother. —, 1653–1704.

LEMAIRE à *Blois*. Hexagonal watch, rock crystal case, Wallace collection, about 1610.

LE. MAIRE.. *Paris*. Watches and religieuse clock, about 1690.

LE MAIRE, JEAN PIERRE. *Copenhagen*. Master 1774; Master of Corporation 1787.

LEMAITRE, PAUL. Watch tool maker, *28 Grafton St.*, 1790–1810.

LEMAN, THOS. *London*. Watch, 1738.

LEMAND, —. *Blois*, about 1580.

LEMANN, JOHAN. *Wien*. Clock, about 1800.

LE MAZURIER, —. *Rue de la Comédie-Française, Paris*. Garde-visiteur, 1769.

LE MIRE, CHARLES. *Paris*. 1675 master–1699.

LEMIST, WILLIAM K. *Dorchester, U.S.A.*, 1812. Died 1820.

LEMMON, EDWD. *London*. Watch, 1790.

LE MOINE. *Paris*, 1776–89.

LE MOINE, A. *Philadelphia*, 1813. Watch.

LE MONNIÈRE, STEPHEN. *London*. C.C. 1712–19. Also LIMONIÈRE.

LE MONTJOYE. *Paris*. Clock, Wallace collection, about 1770.

LEMUDE, REUBEN. Long-case clock, about 1715.

LE NEPVEU, NICOLAS ANTOINE. *Paris*. Master 1773–89.

LENHAM, WM. *London*. Watches, 1815–25.

LENK, EGIDIUS. *Augsburg*. Master about 1780–99; striking alarum and repeating travelling clock, Ilbert collection.

LENKER, ELIAS. *Nuremberg*. Celebrated silver clock-case maker, died 1591.

LENNAN, JAMES. *London*. C.C. 1789.

LENNEP, JOHANN HARTMANN. *Cassel*. Born 1685, died 1755; Kleinuhrmacher and Mechaniker.

LENOIR à *Rennes*. Watch winding from the centre of the dial, G.M., about 1700.

LE NOIR, BAPTISTE. *Paris*. Alarm watch, brass case, pierced and chased, about 1760. Pierpont Morgan collection.

LE NOIR, ÉTIENNE. *Paris*, about 1740. A famous maker; watch G.M.; watch Fränkel collection winding at centre of dial; clock with ormolu work by CAFFIERI; two cartel clocks Pal. du Luxembourg; bracket clock National Museum Stockholm.

LE NOIR, JEAN BAPTISTE AUGUSTIN. *Paris (Rue de l'Arbre Sec.)*. Master 1764–89, alarum watch M.M.A.

LE NOIR, MARIE TOUSSAINT. Fils cadets, *Place du Pont St. Michel, Paris*. Garde-visiteur in 1769. Eight watch and clock makers of that name at about the same period, Etienne Le Noir being the most celebrated.

LE NOIR, PIERRE ÉTIENNE. *Paris (Quai des Orfèvres)*. Master 1743–89.

LENS, CHARLES, son of Wm. *London*. C.C. 1750.

LENS, WILLIAM. C.C. 1711.

LENORMAND, LOUIS FRANÇOIS. *Paris*. Juré 1754.

LENTZ, GEORGE K. *Philadelphia*, 1825.

LENWOOD, SAM. Apprenticed in 1655 to Thos. Claxton, C.C.

LEPAUTE, AUGUSTIN MICHEL HENRY, son of Pierre Henry. In business as 'Henry Neveu Lepaute' and, in 1854, changed his name to Lepaute. *Paris*. Born 1800, died 1885; clockmaker to Louis Philippe and Napoleon III; made clocks on Palais de Justice, Paris, and the Bourse, Marseilles.

LEPAUTE, JEAN ANDRÉ. Born at *Montmedi*, 1709, attained considerable eminence as a clockmaker in Paris; was appointed 'horloger du Roy'. He improved the pin-wheel escapement of Amant by putting pins on both sides of the wheel. Lepaute constructed several fine turret clocks and clocks for the Louvre at Paris, wound by means of an air current and fan, a method re-invented recently. He made many curious timepieces (equation, one-wheel clocks, &c.), and was the author of an excellent 'Traité d'Horlogerie' (Paris, 1760), revised and augmented, says Moinet, by the celebrated Lalande. In the second edition of this work appears Lalande's treatise on 'perfect pitching'. In the Jones collection at V. & A. is a fine clock in case of Vincennes porcelain and ormolu with the date letter for 1754 and signed 'Lepaute de Belle fontaine à Paris'. Twelve-month timepiece by him at Windsor Castle; there are four clocks by him in the Wallace collection.

LEPAUTE, JEAN BAPTISTE (LE JEUNE), brother. *Paris (Place du Palais Royal)*. Born 1727, died 1802; clockmaker to the King; in partnership with Jean André, and when he retired in 1774 took into partnership his nephews Pierre Henry and Pierre Basile Lepaute; retired 1789.

LEPAUTE, JEAN JOSEPH, grand-nephew of J. A. *Paris (Rue St. Honoré)*. Born 1768, died 1846; joined Pierre Basile in 1798; clockmaker to Napoleon I; made clocks for Pal. de Fontainebleau and the Château de St. Cloud; many fine house clocks.

LEPAUTE, PIERRE MICHEL, son. *Paris*, 1803. Died 1849. In his father's firm. Two regulators C.A. & M.; gold $\frac{1}{2}$ $\frac{1}{4}$ repeating duplex watch G.M.; made clock for the Bourse.

LEPINE, JEAN. "There is lately arriv'd in this city, Monsieur de l'Epine, Engineer and Machinist of the late King of France, who has brought over with him a piece of ingenuity, which is an Opera by Machines, that had been seen by his Majesty, by their Royal Highnesses the Princesses, likewise by a great number of persons of quality of this kingdom, with their general applause and satisfaction. And being to make but a short stay here, he invites the curious to come and see the said machine, giving no other explication of the same, only that there are symphonies, musick-master, whistler, drawing of the curtain, changes of scenes, thunder and lightings, &c., and what surprises the more, is, that all is performed without any body's touching it. To be seen from Ten in the morning to Ten at night, at the Mews Chocolate House near Charing Cross, up one pair of stairs, Price Half a Crown" (*Daily Post*, Feb. 1720). This is of interest, because the Lepine referred to was probably the father of John Antoine, a watchmaker of remarkable attainments who is referred to below.

LEPINE, JEAN ANTOINE was born at *Gex*, in *France*, in 1720, and is said to have been apprenticed to one Decrose of Grand Sacconex, Switzerland; at the age of 24 he went to Paris and worked for A. C. Caron; afterwards he established a reputation, and became watchmaker to Louis XV; about 1770 he introduced bars for carrying the upper pivots of a watch train instead of a top plate, rearranged the movement, dispensed with the fusee, used the cylinder escapement, and a mainspring barrel arbor supported at one end only. Forty or fifty watchmakers having been exiled from Geneva, Voltaire, it is said, engaged Lepine to establish a watch factory at Ferney, about a league from Geneva. Voltaire for a time ensured its success by persuading political friends to buy the watches, but after a few years the artisans returned to Geneva. Whatever part Lepine may have taken in advising Voltaire, it appears that he never left Paris, where he died in 1814; watch by him in 1810 marked 'horloger de l'impératrice', at the Geneva Horological School. The business was continued by his grand-nephew.

LEPLASTRIER, ISAAC. *17 King William St., Strand*, 1828; *21 Holles St., Cavendish Sq.*,1840–42. Livery C.C. 1829.

LEPLASTRIER, ISAAC. *London (Mark Lane)*. C.C. 1813–20. chronometers and watches.

LEPLASTRIER, JOHN. *138 Upper Shadwell*, 1790; *125 Minories*, 1815.

LEPLASTRIER, LOUIS. *142 High St., Shadwell*, 1804–15.

LEPLASTRIER & SON. *142 High St., Shadwell*, 1820–28.

LEPPINGWELL, JAMES. *London*. Apprenticed 1752, C.C. 1769–74.

LEPTROPE, —. *London*. Long-case clock, about 1740.

LE QUEUX. See PIERRE.

LEQUIN, —. *Geneva*, 1730–50.

LEROLLES. Fine ormolu-cased clock signed 'Lerolles Frères', about 1760.

LEROUX, ALEXANDER. C.C. 1706.

LEROUX, CHARLES DAVID. *Paris*, 1587–1635.

LEROUX, J. F. *Rue Guenegaud, Paris*. Maker of repeating watches, 1770–89.

LEROUX, JNO. *London*. Watch, 1710.

LEROUX, JNO. *8 Charing Cross*. Hon. freeman, C.C. 1781; there is a fine watch by him in the Guildhall Museum; 1750–1800. See RIGBY, JAS.

LEROUX, ROBERT, SON. *London*. Apprenticed 1707, C.C. 1745.

LEROW, LEWIS. *Boston, U.S.A.*, 1813–25. Watch.

LE ROY. "Lost a Gold Watch, made in Paris, not so broad as a shilling, in a case of black leather with gold nailes, on the 11th instant, about 11 at night, betwixt King Street, Westminster and Convent Garding. Whoever gives notice to Mr. Le Roy at the signe of the Pearle of Venice, in St. James Street, Convent Garding, shall have three pounds for his pains" (*Mercurius Publicus*, 8th Jan., 1662). This is interesting as showing that one of the French family of Le Roy resided here before the time of the distinguished Parisian member, Julien.

LE ROY, ABRAHAM. *Lancaster City, U.S.A.*, 1756–65. Swiss.

LE ROY, BASILE CHARLES. *Paris (Palais Royal)*. Master 1788–1825; clockmaker to Napoleon, Mme. Mère, the King of Westphalia, the Princess Pauline and the duc de Bourbon; two mantel clocks Ministère de la Guerre, Paris.

LE ROY, CHAS. *Paris*. 1765, succeeded by Cachard; clock, about 1808, signed 'Leroy & Fils'.

LE ROY, ÉTIENNE AUGUSTIN. *Paris (Rue St. Denis)*. Master 1758–89.

LE ROY, JEAN BAPTISTE SAMSON. *Paris (Rue Dauphine)*. Master 1753–89; clock.

LE ROY, JEAN JOSEPH. *Paris (Rue St. Martin)*. Master 1742–89.

LE ROY, JULIEN. *Paris*. A scientific watchmaker, born 1686, died 1759; he devised a form of repeating mechanism much used in French watches, and substituted springs for the bell in use before; fine long-case clock at Windsor Castle; two fine watches by him, Wallace collection, and one in the Pierpont Morgan collection.

LE ROY, PIERRE. Eldest son and successor of Julien Le Roy, born 1717, died 1785, the most eminent of French horologists; among his conceptions was a form of duplex escapement and an escapement on which the present chronometer escapement is founded; in 1766 he exhibited a chronometer having a compensation balance composed of mercurial thermometer tubes, a plan afterwards adopted by Loseby.

LE ROY, PIERRE. *Paris (Rue St. Martin)*, 1765–89.

LESAGE, AUGUSTUS. *Cockspur St.*, 1775; *St. James's, Haymarket*, 1788.

LE SCHEGS, ABRAHAM. *Amsterdam*, 1730.

LESCHOT, FRÉDÉRIC. *Chaux-de-Fonds*, 1733–67. Died a. 1786; clock.

LESCHOT, JEAN FREDERICK. Apprenticed in *Geneva* to P. J. Droz in 1784.

LESCOT, PIERRE. *Paris*. Cruciform watches about 1588.

LE SEYNE (LE SENNE), JEAN. *Paris*, 1600–about 1635. Sig. to Statuts of Paris corporation; fine striking alarum calendar travelling clock.

LESLIE, JAS. *6 Maiden Lane, Covent Garden*, 1784–88. Seconds and calendar watch, Schloss collection, about 1786; *5 Parliament St.*, 1790–94; *35 Oxford St.*; card, British Museum, 1799.

LESLIE, ROBT. *Philadelphia*, 1788–91.

LESLIE, ROBERT. *Merlin Place, Clerkenwell*. Patentee of pumping keyless work (No. 1,920); 1793.

LESLIE & PRICE. *Philadelphia*, 1799.

LESSER, T. *Paris*. Enamelled watch, V. & A., about 1770.

LESSWARE, —. *Dublin*. Large trunk-dial timepiece, about 1800.

LESTER, —. *Lombard St.*, 1774.

LESTER, RBEORT. *Philadelphia*,1791–98.

LESTER, TOHMAS. C.C. 1697.

LESTOURGEON, DAVID. *Rouen*. Master 1660. *London*, 1681.

LESTOURGEON, DAVID, in the Register of the French church, Spitalfields, for 1689, he is mentioned as a witness respecting David, the son of François Godeau, orlogeur; brother C.C. 1698; watch, sun and moon hour indicator, Schloss collection, dated 1696; another watch with finely pierced cock and pillars; curious pendulum watch, Pierpont Morgan collection; on the movement is a medallion portrait of William III and the date 1702; inlaid long-case clock, flat top, about 1715; a specimen of his work is also in the G.M.; 1690–1731.

LESTOURGEON, DAVID. C.C. 1721–51.

LESTOURGEON, THOMAS. *49 High Holborn*. Maker of long-case clocks, 1760–75.

LESTRANGE, ANTHONY. *Dublin*, 1795–1824. Watch.

L'ESTRANGE, DAVID. C.C. 1697.

LETALL, JAMES. *London*. Apprenticed 1754, C.C. 1777.

LETWITCH, WILLIAM. *42 Lombard St.* 1769–72.

LEUDL, JOHAN. Maker of a skull watch, about 1630.

LEUKERT, JOHANN GOTTLIEB. *Dresden*. Master 1752, died 1795; from *Schweidnitz*; watch, engraved jasper case, M.P.S. Dresden.

LEUMAS, J. & L. *London.* Watch, 1828.

LEUPOLD, JAKOB. *Schwarzwald.* Born 1674, died 1737; devised a wheel-cutting machine for Schwarzwald clocks, desc. in 'Theatrum Machinarum', Leipzig, 1724, which also contains methods of winding up clock weights and methods of making and hardening spiral springs and cutting fuzees.

LEUTIER, PIERRE. *Paris.* Timekeeper mounted on the back of a finely moulded bull of Dresden china, about 1750.

LE VACHER, ANDRÉ LOUIS, L'AÎNÉ. *Paris.* Master 1759–89.

LE VACHER, JACQUES JEAN, LE CADET. *Paris.* Master 1759–89.

LE VACHER, JEAN LOUIS. *Paris.* Master 1759–74.

LEVASSEUR, FIRMIN. *Frith St., Soho,* 1825–56.

LEVELY, GEORGE. *Baltimore, U.S.A.,* 1774. From *Philadelphia.* Clocks and watches.

LEVENS, JOHN. *Shoemakers' Row, Blackfriars,* 1790–94.

LEVER, BEN. *3 Bruton St.,* 1792.

LEVER, THOMAS. *London.* Apprenticed 1761, C.C. 1785.

LEVET, HUGUES. *Lyons.* Master 1591–1621, died a. 1627; entrusted with the re-making of the automatic clock of St. Jean, and secured the assistance of Nicholas Lippius.

LEVI, ISAAC. *Philadelphia,* 1780. Watch.

LEVIN, LEWIN. *63 Prescot St.,* 1804; *51 Mansell St.,* 1815; *123 Leadenhall St.,* 1830.

LEVIN, MOSES. *7 Cook's Court, Carey St.,* 1790–94.

LEVINS, JOHN. *London (Blackfriars).* Apprenticed 1752, C.C. 1761–65.

LEVITT, —. Sometime partner with Tobias, whose nephew he was.

LEVITT, JNO. Apprenticed in 1681 to Robert Williamson, C.C.

LEVY, A. *17 Camomile St.,* 1825–35.

LEVY, B. *High St., Whitechapel,* 1820.

LEVY, HYAM. *121 Whitechapel High St.,* 1775–85.

LEVY, J. *Coventry St., Haymarket,* 1815.

LEVY, J. & SON. *49 Tooley St.,* 1820.

LEVY, JONAS. *13 Bevis Marks.* Admitted free of the C.C. by redemption, being the first Jew, 1831, 1820–42.

LEVY, JONAS. *18 Somerset St.,* 1800; *135 Whitechapel,* 1810; *38 Minories,* 1820.

LEVY, JOSEPH. *New Round Court, Strand ,*1780–85.

LEVY, LYON. *121 Whitechapel High St.,* 1780–85.

LEVY, M. & CO. *19 Maiden Lane, Covent Garden,* 1790.

LEVY, MICHAEL. *Hull,* 1770.

LEVY, MICHAEL & ISAAC. *Baltimore, U.S.A.,* 1785. From *London. v.* MICHAEL below.

LEVY, MICHAEL. *Philadelphia,* 1802–17. Watch. Also LEVI. *v.* MICHAEL & ISAAC.

LEVY, PHILIP. *30 Jewry St., Aldgate,* 1798–1803.

LEVY, S. *19 Crutched Friars,* 1830.

LEVY & CO. *408 Strand,* 1825.

LEWIN, WILLIAM. C.C. 1731.

LEWIS, AMBROSE. C.C. 1725.

LEWIS, DAVID. *Egham.* About 1800 C.C.

LEWIS, E. *London.* Small watch, about 1590.

LEWIS, JOHN. *London.* Apprenticed 1697, C.C. 1705–12.

LEWIS, JOHN. *Llanidloes,* 1736–1801. Long-case clocks.

LEWIS, JOSEPH. *38 Foster Lane,* 1783.

LEWIS, JOSEPH. *London.* Apprenticed 1756, C.C. 1768.

LEWIS, LEVI. *Bristol, U.S.A.,* 1810–15. Wooden clocks.

LEWIS, T. *London.* Watch, 1776.

LEWIS, WILLIAM. *London (Clerkenwell).* Apprenticed 1783, C.C. 1796–1810.

LEWIS & ALSTON. *30 Bishopsgate Within,* 1815–25.

LEY, JNO. K. *London,* about 1760.

LEY, WILLIAM. *London.* Apprenticed 1700, C.C. 1712.

LEWVY, MOE. *Bristol,* 1795–1830. Watch.

LEXANDER, ERIC. *Uppsala* and *Viksta.* Born 1727, died 1806.

LEYLAND, THOS. *Prescot,* 1816.

LHUILLIER, JACQUES. *Paris,* 1769–89.

LIBIS, ANDREAS. *Augsburg.* Comp. 1752, master 1764–92. From *Alsace.*

LIDDEL, CHAS. *Stockton,* 1770.

LIDDELL, JOSEPH. *Old Swinford, Worcester,* 1760.

LIDDIARD, THOMAS. *54 St. Paul's Churchyard,* 1775–83.

LIDDLE, JNO. *Morpeth,* 1770.

LIEF, GEO. *Sheffield,* 1814.

LIENGME, —. *Cormoret,* 1800–33. Was in Le Locle about 1805–10; the only maker in Cormoret.

LIETUYT, JOHN, from *Delft,* 1368.

LIEUTAUD, HONORÉ. *Marseille.* Watch, about 1750.

LIEUTAUD, JEAN JOSEPH. *Paris.* Master 1764–89; gold engraved repeating cylinder watch, set diamonds, F.W.M.; mantel clock, Petit Palais, Paris.

LIGHT, BEN. Apprenticed in 1687 to Geo. Cawdren, C.C.

LIGHT, JNO. *Lit. Old Baily,* C.C. 1730.

LIGHT, JOHN. C.C. 1648.

LIGHT, JOHN. *London.* Apprenticed 1736, C.C. 1744–59.

LIGHTBODY, JOHN. *Lanark,* 1799–1837.

LIGHTFOOT, PETER, a monk, who may have made clocks and automata, fourteenth century.

LIKE, GEORGE. *29 Butcher's Row,* 1785–94.

LILLIOTT, RICHARD. *London.* Apprenticed 1733, C.C. 1740.

LILLY, —. *Smithfield Bars,* 1775.

LILLY, EDWARD. *London.* Apprenticed 1748, C.C. 1762.

LIMEBURNER, JOHN. *Philadelphia,* 1791.

LIMMARD, —. *54 St. Paul's Churchyard,* 1796.

LIMONIERE, STEPHEN. C.C. 1712.

LIMPARD, JOHN. A watch by him in the British Museum, about 1620.

LINAKER, HENRY. *Liverpool,* 1796–1829.

LINAKER, SAMUEL. Oval watch, Pierpont Morgan collection, about 1610.

LINAKER, SAMUEL. Was named in the Charter of the Clockmakers' Company to be one of the assistants.

LINCK, PAUL. *Falun,* 1816–35.

LINCKE, JOHAN JAKOB. *Copenhagen.* Master 1741; master of Corporation 1766–72.

LINCOLN, —. *London.* Bracket clock, about 1790.

LIND, JOHN. *Philadelphia,* 1791–99.

LIND, NICH. *4 Norman St., Old St.,* 1780–95; watch, silver cock.

LIND, WILLIAM. Apprenticed to William Harris, admitted C.C. 1796.

LINDD, HY. *Farnham.* Lantern clock, about 1700.

LINDESEY (or LINDSAY), GEORGE. Watchmaker to George III; a verge movement by him in the Guildhall Museum; died 1776. A three-train long-case clock in the Wetherfield collection, signed 'Geo. Lindsay sert to the Prince of Wales London'. Fine long-case clock with dead-beat escapement, about 1770. On his watch papers, 'G. Lindsay, watch maker to His Majesty and Her Royal Highness the Princess Dowager of Wales, at the Dial in the Strand".

LINDGREN, ERIK. *Stockholm.* Apprenticed 1715, master 1725, died 1741.

LINDGREN, ERIK. *Stockholm.* Born 1729, master 1754, died 1786; court clock; gold watch; two watch movements Nord. Museum; three wall clocks, two illuminated Sidenbladh, one Nord. Museum; bracket clock illuminated Sidenbladh; watch F.W.M.; gold engraved watch, National Museum, Stockholm.

LINDLEY, —. *10 St. Martin's Court, Old St.,* 1810.

LINDMAN, JÖNS. *Harg.* 1708–74; turret clocks at Harg and Kristineholm; two long-case clocks.

LINDSEY, JOHN. *69 Banner St.*, 1825.

LINDSEY, WM. *London.* Watch, G.M., about 1780.

LINDSTROM, —. *London.* Bracket clock, strikes the hours with but one barrel, about 1800.

LINDQVIST, JOHAN. *Stockholm.* Apprenticed about 1750 to Julien Le Roy; master 1754, died 1779; court clock-maker; nine gold and silver watches, three in Nord. Museum and illuminated Sidenbladh; bracket and wall clocks.

LINFORD, —. *Clapham*, about 1790 C.C.

LINFORD, HY. Apprenticed in 1691 to Edwd. Orton, C.C.

LINFORD, THOMAS. *London.* Watch, 1626.

LINGFORD, JNO. *Nottingham.* Watch, 1798.

LINLEY, THOMAS. *London.* Apprenticed 1740, C.C. 1748–64.

LINLEY, THOS. *Leather Lane*, C.C. 1732.

LINNET, JOHN. *9 Cursitor St.*, 1815–25.

LINNEY, JOHN. Watch-case maker and liner, *Featherstone St.*, 1790.

LINTER, THOMAS. *London.* Apprenticed 1728, C.C. 1737–1754.

LIPP, NICHOLAS. *Basle.* Maker of a remarkable clock at Lyons, 1598.

LIPPYUS. See LIPP.

LIPSCOMB, BENJ. *London.* Maker of long-case clocks, about 1760.

LIPSY, DAN. *136 Old St.*, 1817.

LIPTROT, WM. *London.* Watch, about 1780.

LISTER, —. *Lombard St.*, 1770.

LISTER, JOHN. *London.* Apprenticed 1731, C.C. 1746.

LISTER, JOHN. *Noble St.* C.C. 1730.

LISTER, JOSEPH. *Halifax.* Died 1805.

LISTER, SAM. *Bolton*, 1770.

LISTER, THOS. *Luddenden, Yorkshire.* Born 1718, died 1779.

LISTER, THOS. *Halifax*, son of the above Thos., born 1745, died 1814; a good maker; in 1774 he contracted to make, for £60, Halifax Church clock; in 1801 he made to the order of Dr. Birkbeck, for the Anderson College, Glasgow, an orrery which had been designed by Joseph Priestly, of Bradford; in 1802 he made for Illingworth Church a clock having a pendulum 30 ft. long, vibrating twenty times a minute.

LISTER, WILLIAM. Long-case clock, about 1750, inscribed 'William Lister, Midgley', bearing in the motto, 'No Time for Sin'; long-case clock of slightly later date, signed 'Wm. Lister, Keighley'; another, about 1770, signed 'Wm. Lister, Halifax'.

LISTER, WILLIAM. *Newcastle-on-Tyne*, 1820.

LITHERLAND, PETER. *Liverpool.* Patentee of the rack lever escapement (No. 1,830), Oct. 1791; and in 1792 (No. 1,889) of (1) a watch to beat once a second and (2), a compensation curb, and (3) mechanism to wind watches by means of an external lever. Under the title of Peter Litherland & Co. he carried on a successful business for some years. A watch so named belonged to Col. Benjamin Tallmadge, an intimate friend of Washington, and is now in the museum of 'Sons of the Revolution', New York. 1800–1816 his patent lever watches were made in large numbers by Litherland, Whiteside & Co., first at Ranelagh St., and afterwards at Church St. In 1816 the firm became Litherland, Davies & Co. and then Davies & Co. Other members of the family were JOHN and then RICHARD Litherland at Brownlow Hill. Richard in 1817 patented (No. 4,103) a modification of the chronometer escapement and also a compensation curb.

LITTLE, JOHN. *London.* Apprenticed 1726, C.C. 1733.

LITTLE, JOSEPH. *179 Strand*, 1800.

LITTLE, PETER. *Baltimore, U.S.A.*, 1799–1807. Watches and clocks.

LITTLEMORE, WHITESTONE. Apprenticed to Thos. Gibbs, but turned over to Thos. Tompion; admitted C.C. 1698.

LITTLEJOHN, JAMES. *London*, about 1750; *Charleston, U.S.A.* from 1761. Clocks and watches.

LITTLETON, JAS. *London.* Repeating watch, 1773.

LITTLETON, THOMAS. *London (Gt. Arthur St.).* Apprenticed 1752, C.C. 1769–74.

LITTLEWORT, GEORGE. *34 Cannon St.* Maker of watches for the use of the guards of the Royal Mail coaches, 1816–32.

LIVERMORE, EDWARD. *30 Tokenhouse Yard, Lothbury*, and *3 Cross St., Islington*, 1798–1810.

LIVERMORE, EZRA. *London.* Apprenticed 1765, C.C. 1773, died a. 1821.

LIVERMORE, EZRA, son of EZRA. *London.* C.C. 1821.

LIVESAY, —. *Bolton, Lancashire.* Lantern clock, about 1700.

LIVESAY, JNO. *Bolton.* Long-case clock, about 1730.

LIVINGSTONE, J. *London.* Watch, 1785.

LIVY. See LEVY.

LLOYD, —. At the 'Dial', *21 Aldersgate St.* Card, British Museum, 1790.

LLOYD, CHARLES. Apprenticed to Thos. Tompion; C.C. 1691.

LLOYD, DAVID. C.C. 1677.

LLOYD, EDWD. C.C. 1670.

LLOYD, EDWARD. *London.* Apprenticed 1741, C.C. 1763–76.

LLOYD, J. *Brecon.* Watch, 1802.

LLOYD, JAMES. C.C. 1700.

LLOYD, JAMES. *Sheep Pens, Smithfield.* C.C. 1722.

LLOYD, JOHN. *128 Minories*, 1785. Card, British Museum.

LLOYD, JOHN. *21 Aldgate Within*, 1790–94.

LLOYD, JOSEPH. C.C. 1673.

LLOYD, JOSEPH. *Wigan*, 1816.

LLOYD, LEWIS. Apprenticed C.C. 1673.

LLOYD, NAT. Apprenticed C.C. 1673.

LLOYD, PHILIP. *Bristol.* Long-case clock, about 1770.

LLOYD, RICHARD. C.C. 1681.

LLOYD, ROBERT. *London.* C.C. 1770.

LLOYD THOMAS, son of James. *London.* Apprenticed 1721, C.C. 1733.

LLOYD, WILLIAM. *Pye Corner.* C.C. 1668.

LLOYD, WILLIAM. *London.* Apprenticed 1658, C.C. 1671.

LLOYD, WILLIAM, brother. *London.* C.C. 1740–65.

LLOYD, WILLIAM. *London.* C.C. 1760.

LLOYD, WILLIAM JOHN. *London.* C.C. 1825.

LLOYD & NORTHLEIGH. *London.* Watch, 1785.

LOCHARD, JOHN. C.C. 1655; thick round silver watch, gut to fusee, engraved dial, serrated trident hand, inscribed 'John Lochard, fecit', 1655–70.

LOCHARD, ROBERT. Apprenticed in 1647 to JNO. Matchell; C.C. 1655.

LOCK, JAS. *New Westgate Buildings, Bath*, 1790–1800, afterwards at *11 Quiet St.* Long-case clock, about 1795.

LOCKHART, ROBERT. *Portsmouth Point*, about 1790 C.C.

LOCKIN, WM. Apprenticed in 1687 to Isaac Goddard, C.C.

LOCKWOOD, BENJ. *Swaffham, Norfolk.* Long-case clock, about 1740; watch, 1765.

LOCKWOOD, DAVID. Long-case clock, about 1730.

LOCKWOOD, JOSHUA. *Charleston, U.S.A.* From 1757–81.

LOCKWOOD, ROBT. Apprenticed in 1647 to Edward Taylor, C.C.

LODDINGTON, ISAAC. 'The Dial', *Tavistock St., Covent Garden*. Anna Maria Shaw was apprenticed to him and to Elizabeth his wife, 1733; 1719–34.

LODE, —. *London*. Pocket chronometer, about 1802.

LODERER, JOHANN EUSEBIUS. *Augsburg*. Master about 1770–76, died a. 1793.

LODGE, THOS. *London*. "Ordered that the Master should give directions to the Clerk to deliver the clock to Mr. Thomas Lodge to be cleaned" (*Minutes of the Cutlers' Company*, 1st October, 1713); maker also of a long-case clock, about 1730.

LODOWICK, PETER. Admitted C.C. 1689.

LÖFBERG, SIMON PETER. *Uppsala*. Born 1777, died 1810; two watches.

LOFT, WILLIAM. *London* (*Goodman's Fields*). Apprenticed 1747, C.C. 1759–73.

LOFTUSS, THOS. *Wisbech*. Lantern clock, about 1720.

LOGAN, ADAM. *New York*, 1805. Watch.

LOGG, M. *Vienna*, about 1725.

LOGGEN, JOHANNES. *Amsterdam*. Fine calendar watch, Schloss collection, sun and moon hour indicators, about 1680.

LOGIE, ROBERT. *Edinburgh*. Apprenticed 1784–1827.

LOMAS, JAS. *Blackburn*, 1770.

LOMAS, JNO. *Sheffield*, 1814.

LOMAX, GEORGE. *Brecon*, about 1730–55. Long-case clock; watch movement, National Museum, Cardiff.

LOMAX, SAM. *Blackburn*, 1780.

LOMBARD, —. *Chaux-de-Fonds*, 1781–1804.

LOMBARD, NATHANIEL & DANIEL. *Boston, U.S.A.*, 1825. Watch.

LOMBART, F., à *Paris*. Watch, about 1590.

LONDON, JNO. *Bristol*. Lantern clock, about 1690.

LONG, HENRY. *200 High Holborn*, 1770–80.

LONG, JNO. *Nottingham*. Clock-watch, about 1692.

LONG, JOHN. C.C. 1677.

LONG, JOHN. C.C. 1698.

LONG, THOMAS. C.C. 1653.

LONG, JOSEPH AMBROSE. *London*. C.C. 1774.

LONG, THOMAS. Hon. freeman C.C., 1781; 1760–81.

LONGCRAFT (LONGCROFT), RICHARD. *London*. Apprenticed 1698, C.C. 1718.

LONGHURST, —. *Chatham*, about 1790 C.C.

LONGHURST, RICHARD. *Steyning*. a. 1777–95 C.C.; watch.

LÖNNGREN, JOHAN. *Marstrand*, 1793–1820.

LONGLAND, FRANCIS. Apprenticed in 1671 to Bert. Powell, C.C.

LONGLAND, JOHN. Brother C.C. 1677. A long-case clock by him, William III period, inscribed 'Johannis Longland, Londini, fecit'; case, oak, with walnut veneer.

LONGLAND, THOMAS. *London*. 30-hour long-case clock, about 1725.

LOOMES, THOMAS, at yᵉ *Mermaid* in *Lothebury*. Apprenticed to Jno. Selwood, brother C.C. 1649; a celebrated maker. Example, a small lantern clock, inscription, 'Thomas Loomes, at yᵉ Mermayd in Lothebury, fecit, 1674'; 1630–74.

LOOR, THOS. *Amsterdam*. Watch, 1715.

LOOSLEY, JOHN. *London*. C.C. 1781–99.

LOPIN. *Pans*. Elève de Breguet.

LORD, JOSEPH. Apprenticed in 1684 to Jonathan Puller, C.C.

LORD, RICHARD. C.C. 1632.

LORD & GODARD. *Rutland, U.S.A.*, 1797–1830.

LORIMER, DAVID. *17 Shoreditch*, 1805–18. Afterwards Lorimer & Edwards.

LORIMER, ISAAC. *London*. Long-case clock, about 1740.

LORIMER, JAS. *London*. Musical long-case clock, about 1780.

LORIMER, WILLIAM. *24 Crown St., Finsbury*, 1830; *93 Wood St., Cheapside*, 1835–40.

LORIMIER, FRANÇOIS LOUIS, son of J. Jacques. *Fontaines, Geneva* and *Paris*, 1782–1810; at *Besançon* about 1805.

LORIMIER, LES FRÈRES (DAVID FRANÇOIS and JEAN JACQUES). *Fontaines* and *Paris*, 1760–1805.

LORION, JACQUES. *Blois*. Master 1670, died a. 1696.

LORY, CLAUDE, L'AÎNÉ. *Paris* (*Rue de Berry*). Master 1767–89. See LORRY. Made and repaired clocks at Châteaux de St. Germain, des Gobelins, de la Savonnerie, des Capucines, Meudon, Marly, de la Ste. Chapelle and de Vincennes.

LORY, MARC ANTOINE. *Paris*. Master 1742.

LOSEBY, EDWARD. *Shiffnal*. Long-case clock, about 1790.

LOSEBY, EDWARD THOMAS. Apprenticed to Rotherhams, of *Coventry*, afterwards at *Gerrard St., Islington*. Inventor of a compensation balance, which acted by the expansion and contraction of mercury in a curved glass tube fixed at each end of the laminated rim, which was shorter than usual (Patent 1,011, Dec. 1852); he was successful at the Greenwich chronometer trials, but feeling aggrieved at what he considered to be inadequate appreciation on the part of the Admiralty, he retired in dudgeon to Leicester; for the Market Hall, at Coventry, he made a remarkably fine clock, which may be called the standard timekeeper of the place. He died in 1890.

LOSSIER, —. *London*. Watch, 1770.

LOUARTH, JASPER. C.C. 1641.

LOUBET, FELIX, au *St. Esprit*. French table clock in gilt brass case, engraved with the four seasons, after Etienne Delaune, second half of the sixteenth century, V. & A.

LOUCHET, —. *Boulogne*. Watch, 1815.

LOUDAN, WM. *149 Great Surrey St.*, 1822; *228 Black-friars Rd.*, 1840–42.

LOUGH, HUGH. *Penrith*, 1740–91.

LOUGH, ROBERT. *Penrith*, 1770.

LOUGH, THOS. Apprenticed in 1680 to Geo. Tomlinson, C.C.

LOUGHTON, WILLIAM. C.C. 1683.

LOUMAND, LORENS. *Copenhagen*, 1689. Died 1728.

LOUNDE (LOWNDES), JONATHAN, in *Pall Mall*, C.C. 1680; steward 1696; a celebrated maker. Square black basket-top bracket-clock, Wetherfield collection, about 1685; walnut inlaid long-case clock, about 1695; bracket-clock belonging to the Long Island Historical Society of New York, about 1700; fine long panelled marquetry case, domed hood clock, 11-in. dial, Wetherfield collection, about 1700; another 12-in. dial, about 1710.

"Lost in St. James Chappel on Sunday the 17 February a gold pendulum minute watch, going with a chain the maker Lowndes in Pall Mall London: it hath two gold cases, the out case graved with a cypher and an earl coronet over it: Whoever can bring the said watch to Jonathan Lowndes at the Dial in Pall Mall shall have 3 guineas for their trouble" (*Lond. Gaz.*, 18th February, 1683–84).

"Lost on the 19 past, from a gentlewoman's side, a gold pendulum watch with 2 gold cases, the outer case engraved; made by J. Lowndes, in Pall Mall, London. Whoever brings it to Mr. Lowndes, at the Dyal, in Pall Mall, shall have three guineas reward; or, if bought, their money again with content" (*Lond. Gaz.*, Oct., 1–5, 1691).

"Lost on the 10 instant, in a Hackney Coach,

between Covent Garden and Jermyn St., a Gold Pendulum Watch, the maker's name Lowndes, the Chrystal crack'd; with 2 Steel Seals tyed to it, the Coat of Arms, 10 Crosses and a Baron's Coronet, and a small Famble (*sic*), made up of 2 little Diamonds and 4 or 5 Rubies. Whoever brings them to Sir Francis Child, Goldsmith, within Temple Bar, shall have 2 guineas reward" (*Lond. Gaz.*, Nov. 16–19, 1691).

LOUNDES, CHARLES. *Pall Mall.* Apprenticed in 1674 to Thos. Player; C.C. 1682; long-case clock; also a striking and repeating basket-top bracket clock.

LOUNDES, ISAAC. *Pall Mall Court.* C.C. 1682; long clock, Wetherfield collection, panelled marquetry case with domed hood, 12-in. dial, about 1705; long walnut case month clock, about 1710.

LOUNDES, JONATHAN. *Pall Mall Court*, about 1685–95.

LOUNDES, WM. Apprenticed in 1690 to Charles Loundes, C.C.

LOUTEAU, PIERRE. *Lyons*, 1604. Master 1607–28; crystal cross watch M.M.A.; watches Gélis collection and Spitzer sale; fine engraved cross watch Marryat collection.

LOVATT, —. *Newcastle.* Long-case clock, about 1780.

LOVE, CHRISTOPHER. *6 Old Bond St.*, 1816–25.

LOVE, JAS. *23 Aldgate*, 1770–90. Enamelled watch, V. & A.

LOVE, JOHN. *Baltimore, U.S.A.*, 1802. Watch.

LOVEJOY, JOHN. *London.* Apprenticed 1732, C.C. 1741.

LOVEJOY, PETER. *London (Finsbury Sq.).* Apprenticed 1787, C.C. 1794–1810.

LOVELACE, JACOB. *Exeter.* Died 1755, age 60; maker of a famous clock.

LOVELAND, J. *London.* Watch, 1770.

LOVELES, W. *14 Charles St.*, *Hoxton*, 1796.

LOVELL, GEORGE. *London.* 1793 livery C.C.

LOVELL, NATHAN. Apprenticed in 1655 to Jno. Samon, C.C.

LOVELL, PAUL. Subscribed to incorporation of C.C. in 1630; in 1654 Mr. Paul Lovell the elder did deliver to the renter warden one silver bowl in full of all demands due to the Company.

LOVELL, PAUL. Apprenticed to Paul Lovell in 1646; C.C. 1653.

LOVETT, JONATHAN. Apprenticed in 1692 to Hy. Pigott, C.C.

LOVETT, WILLIAM. C.C. 1702; watch, about 1710.

LOW, ALEXANDER. *Errol*, 1815–37.

LOW, JNO. C.C. 1672.

LOW, JOHN. *London.* C.C. 1692.

LOWDEN, JAS. *Edinburgh.* Watch, about 1760.

LOWDEN, THOS. *London.* Watch, 1768.

LOWE, —. *Dartford*, about 1790 C.C.

LOWE, EDWD. *London.* Watch, 1793.

LOWE, JNO. *19 Lower Smith St.*, *Northampton Sq.*, 1802–18.

LOWE, JOSEPH. *London.* C.C. 1709–30.

LOWE, RICHARD. *Ware*, about 1800 C.C.

LOWE, THOS. *Dartford.* Watch, hare and snail indicator, 1818.

LOWELL (LOVELL), PAUL. *London.* B.C. 1628–54, died a. 1672; subscribed for incorporation of C.C.; 'High German'.

LOWENS, DAVID. *Philadelphia*, 1785.

LOWRIE, EBENEZER, son. *London (Clerkenwell).* Apprenticed 1814, C.C. 1825.

LOWRIE, J. C. *London.* Watch, 1800.

LOWRY, MORGAN. *Holborn*, 1700; *Leeds*, 1760. Long-case twelve-month clock, about 1730. Morgan Lowry was sergeant-at-mace for the borough of Leeds till 1755.

LOZANO, THOS. *London.* Watch, 1700; bracket clocks, 1700–15.

LUCAS, EDWARD. C.C. 1727.

LUCAS, HENRY. C.C. 1731.

LUCAS, JOHN. *Pear Tree St.*, 1800–10.

LUCAS, RICHARD. *London.* Apprenticed 1765, C.C. 1772–97. Watch.

LUCAS, RICHARD. *London.* 1802–08 C.C.

LUCAS, WILLIAM. C.C. 1669; watch, apparently English, V. & A., about 1690, inscribed 'Lucas Amsterdam', in a finely enamelled case, signed 'Huaud l'aisne pinxit a Geneue'.

LUCAS, WM. *London.* Fine chiming clock, inlaid mahogany case, about 1800.

LUCIE, JOHN. C.C. 1663.

LUDFORD, RALPH. Apprenticed in 1656 to Wm. Almond, C.C.

LUDLAM, WILLIAM. Professor of Mathematics at Cambridge, regarded as an authority on horology; one of the judges of Harrison's chronometer, 1765. He corresponded with John Holmes in 1779.

LUDLOW, BENJ. *Gt. Yarmouth*, 1760.

LUDLOW, SAMUEL. C.C. 1706.

LUDWIG, JOHN. *Philadelphia*, 1791.

LUEB, MICHAEL. Apprenticed in 1655 to Isaac Daniel, C.C.

LUGG, JASPER, 'of Glocester, fecit'. Miniature lantern clock, with pendulum shaped like an anchor, about 1690.

LUITPRAND, a monk of *Chartres*, who at the end of the eighth century resuscitated the art of glass blowing, is said to have also invented the sand glass.

LUKE, WILLIAM. Shagreen and morocco case-maker, *147 Aldersgate St.*, 1810.

LUKINS, ISAAC. *Philadelphia*, 1790–1828.

LULLIN, PAUL. Watch without hands, French or Swiss, about 1700.

LUM, JOSEPH. *Spitalfields*, 1700.

LUMB, JOHN. *16 Southampton Buildings*, 1790–74.

LUMB, JOS. *London*, 1760.

LUMBER, HENRY. *Bristol*, 1797–1812. Watch.

LUMBER, JAMES. *Chester*, 1762–95. Watch.

LUMBLEY, G., JUNR. Watch, 1760.

LUMLEY, GEO. *Bury.* Watch, 1780.

LUMLEY, MARY, widow. *Bury St. Edmunds.* Born 1724, died 1800; 'eminent watchmaker'.

LUMPKIN, ROBERT. *Bishops Stortford*, 1730.

LUMPKIN, THOMAS. C.C. 1694; maker of a walnut marquetry long-case clock, centre engraved; over day of month circle G. R. and three crowns; 1694–1715.

LUMSDEN, GEORGE. *Pittenweem*, 1818–49.

LUMSDEN, JAS. *Aberdeen*, 1770.

LUMSDEN, JOHN. *Aberdeen*, 1735–57.

LUNAN, CHARLES. *Aberdeen*, 1760–1816.

LUNDBERG, JOH. *Norrköping.* Born 1770, died 1811.

LUNDBERG, JOHAN ERIC. *Hedemora*, 1802–40.

LUNDBERG, JOHAN GUSTAF. *Stockholm*, 1822–64.

LUNDIE, JOHN. *Dundee*, 1809–37.

LUNDIE, WILLIAM. *Inverurie.* Born 1743, died 1816.

LUNDSTEDT, ANDERS. *Stockholm*, 1786–1820. Silver cylinder watch; wall and bracket clock illuminated Sidenbladh.

LUNDSTEDT, CARL OTTO. *Stockholm*, 1822–45.

LUNDSTRÖM, JOHAN ERIC. *Stockholm*, 1810. Died 1827; two watches Nord. Museum.

LUNDVIK, OLOF. *Uppsala.* Born 1781, died 1820.

LUNGDELIUS, OLOF. *Örebro.* Born 1724, died 1791.

LUNOD, H. *Geneva*, 1799.

LUNTLEY, THOS. Apprenticed in 1684 to Wm. Dobson, C.C.

LUPTON, GEO. *Altrincham*, 1780.

LUPTON, JNO. *Altrincham*, 1825.

LUPTON, WM. *York*, f., 1645. Died 1680.

LUPTON, WM. *York*, f., 1681.

LUPTON & GILLAM. *23 St. Martin's Lane*, 1825.

LURASCO, FRÈRES. *Amsterdam*, late eighteenth century. Gold enamel watch.

LUSHBROOK, —. Admitted C.C. 1701.

LUTTMAN, WILLIAM. C.C. 1720.

LUTWICHE, THOS. WM. *Forgate St., Worcester.* Card, British Museum, 1794.

LUTWICHE, WM. *Fenchurch St.* Livery Embroiderers' Company, 1775.

LUTZ, JEAN CELANIS. *Geneva.* Born 1800; introduced superior balance-springs at a low price, 1847; died 1863.

LYDDIATT, THOS. *London.* Watch with sun and moon hour indicator, clock, 1695.

LYE, WILLIAM. *London*, 1716 C.C.

LYFORD, RICHARD. *London.* C.C. 1779.

LYMAN, —. *London.* Watch, 1810.

LYNAKER, SAMUEL. One of the first assistants of the C.C. 1630–49.

LYNAM, PHILIP. Apprenticed in 1682 to Jno. Harris, C.C.

LYNAM & BULL, 'at the Golden Salmon, 36 New Bond St.', card Ponsonby collection, about 1785.

LYNAM & WARWICK. *76 Strand*, 1793.

LYNCH, ROBERT. Admitted C.C. 1670.

LYNCH, JOHN. *Baltimore, U.S.A.*, 1802–32. Clock.

LYNDON, G. *30 Gerrard St., Soho*, 1825–30.

LYNE, JOHN. *London.* Apprenticed 1747, C.C. 1769.

LYNE, WILLIAM. C.C. 1703.

LYON, ANDREW. *Port Glasgow*, 1783–99.

LYON, CRAVEN. *Bridlington*, 1822.

LYON, GABRIEL. *London.* Apprenticed 1737, C.C. 1745.

LYON, JOHN. *Warrington*, 1685 C.C.

LYON, MATTHEW. *Lanark*, 1770.

LYON, THOS. GEO. *St. Martin's-le-Grand*, 1793.

LYNES, HENRY JOHN. *London (St. Giles, Cripplegate).* Apprenticed 1775, C.C. 1792–98.

LYNES, THOMAS. *London.* Apprenticed 1700, C.C. 1721–26.

LYONS, RICHARD. Apprenticed in 1649 to Wm. Almond; C.C. 1656; master 1683; calendar watch by him, Shandon collection 1670–84. Fine long-case clock, about 1690; case of figured walnut veneered on oak, 6 ft. 8 in. high; twisted columns at corners of hood, bases and caps carved in Corinthian style with acanthus foliage; dial 10 in. square.

LYSLE (LISLE), BENJAMIN. *Rotterdam*, about 1640–58. Circular cast silver watch V. & A.; watch British Museum.

LYSNEY, SEBASTIAN. Clockmaker to Edward VI, 1548.

MABB, WM. Apprenticed C.C. 1688.

MABERLEY, JOHN. *Red Lion St., Clerkenwell.* Master C.C. 1738. The springs of Harrison's chronometer were made by Maberley in 1755.

MABILLE, CHAS. *Paris.* Fine repeating watch, about 1785.

MACAIRE, ANTOINE. *Paris.* Watch, silver *repoussé* case, 1770; watch, about 1775.

MACAIRE, F. *London*, 1732. Handsome alarum watch.

MACAIRE, LOUIS BENJAMIN. *Geneva*, 1689–1733.

MACARA, ROBERT. *Dunfermline*, 1796–1820.

MACBETH, DANIEL. *Glasgow*, 1818–46.

McCABE. This house was much esteemed for fine watches and clocks, especially in India. JAMES McCABE was from a watch and clock making family in Belfast. He came to London at the latter part of the eighteenth century, and was at *11 Bell's Buildings, Fleet St.*, in 1778; *34 King St., Cheapside*, in 1783; *8 King St., Cheapside*, in 1788; *97 Cornhill Royal Exchange* in 1804. He was hon. freeman C.C. 1781; livery 1786; warden 1811, when he died, and was succeeded by his son JAMES, who was apprenticed to Reid & Auld, and admitted to the C.C. in 1822. The business was carried on as McCabe & Son, *99 Cornhill*, till 1820; McCabe & Strahan, 1825–26; J. McCabe, *97 Cornhill*, till 1838, when the Royal Exchange was destroyed by fire; then J. McCabe, *32 Cornhill*. ROBERT JEREMY McCABE, nephew of James, who succeeded his uncle at *32 Cornhill*, retired in 1883, when he closed the shop, declining all offers to purchase the business. He died in 1902, aged 67. McCabe's best watches were engraved 'James McCabe', the second grade 'McCabe', and the lowest quality 'Beatson'. Specialised in duplex escapement.

McCABE, JAMES, son of James. *London (Cornhill).* C.C. 1822–38.

McCABE, JOHN. *Baltimore, U.S.A.*, 1774. From *Dublin*; clocks and watches.

McCABE, ROBERT, son of James. *London.* C.C. 1821–24.

McCABE, THOMAS, son of James. *London.* C.C. 1815–19.

McCABE, WM. *Newry.* Watch, 1798.

McCARDIE, JAMES. *Strabane*, 1820.

McCARTHY, JAS. *47 Holborn*, 1798.

MACDONALD, JOHN. *Inverness.* Watch, about 1780.

MACDONALD, JOSEPH. *Liverpool*, 1770.

MACDONALD, PETER. *Inverness*, 1780–1801 C.C.

McCLARY, SAMUEL. *Wilmington, U.S.A.* Born 1788, died 1859; long-case clocks.

McCLURE, JOHN. *Boston, U.S.A.*, 1823–25.

McCOLLIN, THOMAS. *Philadelphia*, 1825.

McDANIEL, WILLIAM H. *Philadelphia*, 1819–25.

MacDOWALL, CHAS. & JOSEPH. 'Helix lever and horological machine manufacturers', *Vicar Lane, Leeds*, 1830.

MacDOWALL, JAS. *Philadelphia*, 1797–1825.

MACE, BARTHELMY à *Blois.* Enamel watch, about 1660.

MACE, LAWRENCE. *Drapers' Court, Aldermanbury*, C.C. 1742–50; to him was apprenticed Wm. Plumley, 1749.

MACE, MICHEL. *Paris.* Juré 1736; watch Besançon Museum.

McELWEE, JAMES. *Philadelphia*, 1813.

MACFARLANE, JOHN. *Boston, U.S.A.*, 1800–10.

MACFARLANE, PETER. *London.* Watch, 1801.

McGRAW, DONALD. *Annapolis, U.S.A.*, 1767. Watch; from *Edinburgh.*

MACGREGOR, J. *14 Charterhouse St.*, 1830.

MACHAM, SAMUEL. *London.* Long-case clock, about 1710; repeating bracket clock, about 1720.

McHARG, ALEXANDER. *Albany, U.S.A.*, 1817–1823. Watch.

McILHENNEY, JOSEPH E. *Philadelphia*, 1820–25. Watch.

MACKARSIE, G. *14 Great Queen St.*, 1820.

MACKARTHY, JAMES. *47 Holborn*, 1790.

MACKAY, CRAFTS. *London.* Apprenticed 1770, C.C. 1781.

MACKAY, CRAFTS. *Boston, U.S.A.*, 1789. Probably same as above

MACKDONALD, PETER. *New Compton St.*, 1790–94.

McKEEN, HENRY. *Philadelphia*, 1823.

MACKENZIE, COLIN. *London*, 1784–91; *Inverness*, 1800.

MACKIE, GEO. & SON. *54 City Rd.*, 1822–25.

MACKIE, JAMES. *Banner St., Bunhill Row*, 1810–35.

McLachlan, Hugh, son of Jno. *17 Upper East Smithfield*, 1810–42.
McLachlan, Jno. C.C. 1791.
Maclaren, James. *Glasgow*, 1779.
Maclaren, James. *Kingston, Jamaica*, about 1790 C.C.
Maclean, Andrew. *Edinburgh.* Apprenticed 1783–1812.
Maclean, George. *Edinburgh*, 1776.
Maclean, John. *Dublin*, 1780. Watch.
Maclennan, Kenneth. *May's Buildings, St. Martin's Lane*, 1778–1825. In 1801 he made a planetarium for the Royal Institution.
Maclennan, R. & W. *9 Great May's Buildings, St. Martin's Lane*, 1815–25.
McColgan, John. *Londonderry*, 1820.
McCormack, Andres. *Dundalk*, 1820.
McDowall, James. *Sligo*, 1820.
McMaster, Maxwell. *Dublin*, 1820.
McMaster, Wm. Jno. *26 Bartlett's Buildings*, 1814–19.
McNab, J. *Perth*, about 1816.
McPhail, C. *14 Regent's St., Pall Mall*, 1830.
Macpherson, Normand. *London.* Long-case musical clock, about 1790.
MacQueen, Alexander. *Edinburgh*, Apprenticed 1788–1834.
Macune, Thomas, son. *London.* Apprenticed 1769, C.C. 1783; watch.
Macure, Thomas. Musical clockmaker, *7 Great New St., Gough Sq.*, 1788.
MacWhinnie, Robert. *Ayr*, 1820–38.
Macy, Benjamin. C.C. 1712.
Madden, Thos. Apprenticed in 1647 to Wm. Rogers, C.C.
Maddison, Joseph. *London.* C.C. 1780, died 1821.
Maddock, L. *London.* Watch, 1787.
Maddock, Randle. *Leek.* Long-case clocks, about 1760.
Maddock, Thos. *Leek.* Long-case clock about 1725.
Maddox, Edwd. *London.* Centre-seconds watch, h.m., 1769.
Madelainy, —. *Paris.* Curious watch, about 1690; the movement, suspended on a gymbal ring and controlled by a short pendulum, was inserted in a spherical case rather less than 2 in. in diameter.
Maffid, P. *Monmouth.* Watch, 1798.
Maggs, William. Claimed to be successor to D. Quare, 1724–30.
Maginie, Samuel. *Duke's Row, Pimlico*, and *9 Prince's St., Westminster*, 1835.
Magitot, —, *Rue Saint Dominique, Paris*, 1770.
Magnen, Michel. *Paris.* Master 1770–89.
Magnette, Frédéric Elie. *Geneva*, about 1760–87.
Magniac, Francis. *St. John's Sq., Clerkenwell.* Manufacturer of complicated clocks and automata. 1770–1814; made for the Emperor of China two musical clocks with figures of soldiers, musicians, birds, and beasts put into motion by the mechanism; was Colonel in command of the Clerkenwell Volunteers, who were organised in 1797 and disbanded in 1814.
Magnin, J. S. *London.* Watch, 1760.
Magnus, N. *7 James Court, St. Martin's Lane*, 1823.
Magson, John. *Essex St.* In the Hawkins collection was a repeating watch by him, in pierced and finely engraved gold case, second case chased with classical figures and scrolls, in outer case of shagreen, about 1700; long-case clock, about 1720, signed 'John Magston, Essex St., London'.
Mahve, Matthew. *Philadelphia*, 1761. Watch finisher from *London*.
Mailand, Henri. *Paris.* Master 1764–89.

Maillardet, —. *Geneva*, early nineteenth century. Four-colour gold watch M.M.A.
Maillardet, —. *Val de Ruz (Neuchâtel).* Early nineteenth century; watch.
Maillardet, Henri, brother. *Fontaines* and *London.* Born 1745; 1768 in *Berlin* with Jean David; 1784–about 1815 in *London*, where he managed the branch of Jaquet-Droz & Leschot; worked on his own account after the death of Jaquet-Droz in 1791, and later with Philipstral, with whom he exhibited a number of automata; watches signed 'Henri Maillardet, London', and singing birds, for which he devised the single whistle with moving piston.
Maillardet, Henri Louis, son of J. D. *Chaux-de-Fonds.* Born 1790, died 1842; several clocks.
Maillardet, Jacques Rodolphe. *Fontaines.* Born 1743, died 1828; clockmaker; made watches for China.
Maillardet, Jean. *Fontaines*, 1662. Repaired clock at Corcelles.
Maillardet, Jean David, brother. *Chaux-de-Fonds* and *Fontaines.* Born 1748, died 1834; famous clockmaker and mechanician; made many remarkable automata; also watches for China.
Maillardet, Jean Daniel, son of J. R. *Fontaines* and *London.* Born 1768, died 1851.
Maillardet, Julien Auguste, brother. *Chaux-de-Fonds* and *Fontaines.* Born 1779, died 1852; very clever clockmaker and mechanician.
Maillardet, Père et Fils. *Fontaines.* Firm of Jean David and J. Auguste; two 'Magician' automatic clocks, M. d'Horlogerie, Chaux-de-Fonds.
Maillardet, Victor, son of J. D. *Fontaines* and *London.* Born 1775; *London* in 1792.
Maillett, Hy. *16 Bartlett's Buildings*, 1790–94.
Mainglair à *Geneva.* Watch, about 1795.
Mainwaring, —. *Terrace Walk, Bath*, 1770
Mainwaring, Thos. Apprenticed in 1686 to Jeffrey Staines, C.C.
Maire, —. *Nancy.* Horloger de la Reine; watch, about 1730.
Mairet, Sylvain. Born 1805, died 1890; a clever Swiss watchmaker; lived in London 1831–34, manufacturing chiefly for B. L. Vulliamy; returned to Switzerland and settled in *Locle*; inventor of keyless mechanism for watches with two barrels.
Mairon, Jean Baptiste. *Paris*, 1695–1751. Table clock Damiano collection.
Maisonneuve, Benjamin. *Craven St., Strand*, 1769–72.
Major, Nat. Apprenticed in 1686 to Thos. Player, C.C.
Major, Les. *Neuchâtel*, 1664–1723. Keepers of the Neuchâtel clocks.
Makepiece, Robt. *6 Serle St., Lincoln's Inn*, 1775–88. Afterwards Makepiece & Walford.
Malden, Samuel. *Rainham, Essex.* Maker of lantern clocks, about 1725.
Malet, Jean. *Paris*, 1764–90. Clock; engraved striking watch.
Malleson, Thos. *62 Cornhill*, 1769–83.
Mallet, Louis. *Paris*, end eighteenth century–1824. Clockmaker to duc d'Orléans; gold engraved watches Lincoln Museum and M.P.S., Dresden; gold engraved watch set pearls and stones Feill collection.
Mallet, Peter. *London.* Long marquetry case clock, about 1695, 'Horloger duc d'Orleans'; repeating watch, about 1790.
Mallet, Pierre Henry. *Paris.* Master 1757–89.
Mallett, —. A Devonshire family of clockmakers.
Mallett, Stephen. Apprenticed in 1689 to John Trubshaw, C.C.

MALLEY, JOHN. *Lancaster*, 1825.

MALLEY, TIMOTHY. *Lancaster*, 1825.

MALLINGLEY, ROBT. *135 Goswell Rd.*, 1709–93.

MALLOT, SAMUEL. *Blois*, 1733–40.

MALLOT, SAMUEL. *Paris*, 1675 master.

MALPAS, J. *91 Wood St.*, 1753–75.

MALTBY, H. D. *York*, 1814–22.

MALTBY, HENRY. *York*, f., 1812.

MALM, PETTER. *Stockholm*. Born 1744, master 1766, died 1796; bracket clock Nord. Museum; two watches.

MÄLZEL, LEONHARD. *Munich* and *Vienna*. Born 1776, died 1855; invented the metronome; mechanician to the Austrian Court; made a talking head and a trombone-playing automata.

MAN, JONATHAN. *Retford*, 1770.

MANASIERE, —. *Smithfield*, 1774–82.

MANBY, EDWD. *London*. Watch, 1828.

MANBY, JNO. *Skipton*, 1833.

MANCEAU (MANOREAU), JEAN. *Lyons*. Apprenticed 1591–1606; *Paris*, 1606–07. Died 1629 at *Lyons*; clockmaker to the Queen.

MANCHESTER, JOHN. C.C. 1700.

MANGEANT, —. *Rue de Pourtour-Saint-Gervais, Paris*, 1770.

MANGIE, EDWD. *York*, f., 1659.

MANGMEISTER, VITUS. *Augsburg*, 1753. Master 1756; in 1770 went to *Nürnberg*.

MANIÈRE, —. *Paris*. Louis XVI clock.

MANIÈRE, CHARLES GUILLAUME. *Paris*. Master 1778–1810; also bronze worker; clock, Windsor Castle; Lyre and mantel clock, Pal. de Fontainebleau; clock with turning rings on globe, Mobilier Nat. Paris.

MANING, RICHARD. *Ipswich, U.S.A.*, 1748–60.

MANLEY, —. *Norwich*. Lantern clock, about 1680.

MANLEY, DAN. Apprenticed in 1650 to Ed. Gilpin; C.C. 1660.

MANLEY, DANIEL. Watch by him, *Lond. Gaz.*, Sept. 21–25, 1693.

MANLEY, H. *Repoussé* watch cases; 1695–1730; fine specimen V. & A., signed 'H. Manly, Fec'.

MANLEY, JOHN. *Chatham*, a. 1782–about 1790 C.C. Watch.

MANN, FRANCIS. *London*. Apprenticed 1756, C.C. 1768.

MANN, JNO. *Kentish Town*. Long-case clock, about 1770.

MANN, JOSEPH. Apprenticed in 1687 to Thos. Davis, C.C.

MANN, JOSH. *London*. Watch, 1782.

MANN, PERCIVAL. *Lincoln's Inn Fields*, 1780; *Charlotte St., Oxford St.*, 1790–94.

MANN, THEO. Apprenticed in 1693 to Jas. Boyce, C.C.

MANN & MUDDELL. *114 Leadenhall St.*, 1830.

MANNING & EDMONDS. *Strand*. Watch, 1780.

MANROSS, ELISHA. *Bristol, Conn.*, 1827–40.

MANSELL, EDWARD. *London*. C.C. 1769.

MANSELL, WILLIAM. Watch-case maker; 1800, *Rosoman St., Clerkenwell*; fined £15 by C.C. in 1813 for refusing to take up the livery; *26 Spencer St.*, 1826.

MANSER, ROBERT. *Clerkenwell*, 1780, afterwards Ashley & Manser.

MANSFIELD, JNO. *London*. Clock, about 1750.

MANSFIELD, WILLIAM. *London*. Apprenticed 1791, C.C. 1800–05.

MANTIR, G. *71 Snow Hill*, 1830.

MANTS, —. *London*. Watch, 1760.

MANUFACTURE ROYALE DE FERNEY. *Ferney*, 1770. Managed by Dufour et Ceret; watch movement, Ilbert collection.

MANWARING, THOMAS. C.C. 1694.

MARA, FRANCIS. *London*. Apprenticed 1756, C.C. 1768–76; watch.

MARCH. "Lost from a gentleman about the 14th Instant, but he knows not how, a silver minute Pendulum Watch, the name William March, London. Anyone that will bring it to Mr. Hanne, Goldsmith, at the Bunch of Grapes in the Strand, near York Buildings, shall have a guinea reward" (*Daily Courant*, Feb. 19, 1705).

MARCHAND, —. *Geneva*, about 1725.

MARCHAND, AMEDÉE. *Geneva*. Master about 1695–1726; watches Horstmann and Gélis collections and Geneva Museum; clock.

MARCHAND, FILS à *Paris*. Watch, about 1790.

MARCHANT, —. *Prince's St., Leicester Fields*, nephew of — Archambo, 1750.

MARCHANT, ANDREW. *London*. Watch, 1760.

MARCHANT, M. *350 Oxford St.*, 1823.

MARCHANT, R. *20 Mortimer St.*, 1823.

MARCHANT, RICHD. Apprenticed in 1664 to Jere. Gregory, C.C.

MARCHANT, SAMUEL. C.C. 1689; warden, 1704; did not serve as master.

MARCHANT, SAMUEL. *London*. Apprenticed 1670, C.C. 1677.

MARCHANT, SAMUEL. *London*. Apprenticed 1692, C.C. 1700.

MARCHANT, WILLIAM. *255 High Holborn*, 1775–83.

MARCHE, —. *Rouen*. Watch, 1730.

MARCHET, RICHARD. *Fulwood Rents, Holborn*, 1790–94.

MARCHINVILLE, MORIN. Probably *Paris*, about 1685–about 1725; watch engraved Les Frères Huaud; pair-case striking watch G.M.; watch, Ilbert collection.

MARDER, JOSEPH. *London*. Apprenticed 1759, C.C. 1767; watch.

MARDUIT, ISAAC. C.C. 1724.

MARE, CHARLES. *Paris*, 1777–78.

MARÉ, J. LOUIS. *Geneva*. Enamelled watch, Marfels collection, about 1790.

MARELIUS, NILS. *Stockholm*. Born 1707, died 1791.

MARESCHAL, HUGUES. *Lyons*, 1636–1707.

MARESCHAL, JACQUES. *Lyons*. Master 1654, died 1679.

MARGAN & SHERBAN. *6 Strand*, 1793.

MARGARY, THOS. *4 Walbrook*, 1790.

MARGETTS, GEORGE. *21 King St., Cheapside*, 1785; *3 Cheapside*, 1804. A celebrated maker, C.C. 1779, livery 1799; an early maker of lever watches; a very complicated astronomical watch, British Museum.

MARGETTS & HATTON. *London*, 1805–11. Marine chronometer.

MARGOT, GREEN. *Pall Mall*, 1700.

MARGOTIN à *Paris*. Bracket clock with Boulle decoration, about 1770.

MARGOTIN, CLÉMENT. *Blois*, 1734–76. Oval engraved watch with compass and dial M.P.S. Dresden.

MARGOTIN, PIERRE. *Paris*. Juré 1681; watch Glasgow Art Galleries; clock.

MARIE, CHARLES FRANÇOIS. *Paris*. Master 1759–89; elected master without essay on the ground of his having married one of the 100 orphan girls of the Hôpital de la Miséricorde.

MARIE, DAVID. *St. Martin's-in-the-Fields*. In 1762 he patented (No. 771) a form of going barrel.

MARILIC à *Rouen*. Watch, British Museum, about 1680.

MARINOT. See MARTINOT.

MARISTON, ROBT. Apprenticed in 1649 to O. Helden, C.C.

MARK, JNO. C.C. 1667.

MARKS, ISAAC. *Chippenham*, 1730. Retired 1790.

MARKS, SOLOMON. *Cardiff*, 1822–75.

MARKHAM, JOHN. *London*. Maker of watches for the Dutch market, 1760–85. Also GEORGE.

MARKHAM, MARKWICK. Behind the *Royal Exchange*. From the number of watches and clocks bearing his name and having Turkish hour numerals, it may be assumed that he did a large business with the Turkish market; there are two watches by him in V. & A.; two in the G.M. In the Pierpont Morgan collection are several examples; in the Czar of Russia's collection at the Winter Palace, St. Petersburg, was a large repeater watch in a pierced gold case with *repoussé* decoration; it is attached to a chatelaine. There exist many watches dating from the end of the eighteenth century, and inscribed Markwick Markham together with the name of another maker added, *e.g.*, 'Markwick Markham, Perigal'; 'Markwick Markham, Recordon'; this may possibly have been done by arrangement with Markham's representatives after his death, and seems to show that he left a good reputation, 1720–60.

MARKHAM, ROBERT. Behind the *Exchange*, 1736–40.

MARKS, SAML. *Cowbridge*. Clock, about 1770.

MARKWICK, JAMES. *Royal Exchange*. Apprenticed to Edmund Gilpin; C.C. 1666–98; in the Wetherfield collection is a bracket clock signed 'Jacobus Markwick London', dating from about 1680. See MARQUET.

"Dropt the 3rd instant between the Cross Keys in Holborn, and the Temple Gate, a Gold Pendulum Minute Watch made by Jacobus Markwick, London. Whoever brings it to Mr. Wilkinson at the Black Boy against St. Dunstan's Church, in Fleet Street, shall have 3*l* reward" (*Lond. Gaz.*, July 6–9, 1691).

MARKWICK, JAMES. C.C. 1692; master 1720; several watches by him in the British Museum; one, in very large silver cases, is inscribed, 'Made for F.B., M.D.', another, a clock-watch of a slightly later period; long marquetry case clock, 'Markwick Londini', about 1695.

MARKWICK, MARKHAM. *London*, about 1725–about 1805. See preceding. Specialized in clocks and watches for Turkey; lacquer long-case clock, illuminated Cec. and Web.; watches in V. & A., G.M., M.M.A., K.H.M. and Fränkel collection.; watches are found with this name and that of another maker added, *e.g.*, 'Markwick Markham, Perigal' in British Museum., G.M., M.M.A., Feill and Fränkel collections; 'Markwick Markham, Story' and 'Markwick Markham, Borrell' in London Museum; 'Markwick Markham, Roger', Denham collection; Markwick Markham Recordon, gold engraved striking watch. Watches with the name Story are known to 1780, with Borrell to 1813 and with Perigal to 1825.

MARKWITH, JAMES. *London*. 1699 C.C. Perhaps MARKWICK.

MARLACK, WHITE C. *New York*, f., 1769; afterwards WM.

MARQUET, —. (MARKWICK?). "That divers Watches and Pocket Clocks which were Mr. Samuel *Betts*, deceased, are to be sold at his late shop, now the shop of Mr. Marquet, watchmaker, on the backside of the Royal Exchange" (*Lond. Gaz.*, Feb. 28, March 2, 1675).

MARQUET, JACOB. *Augsburg*, 1567.

MARR, FRÈRES à *Geneva*. Watch, about 1795.

MARR, JAS. C.C.; about 1650.

MARR, WILLIAM. *London* (*Moorfields* and *Bishopsgate St.*). Apprenticed 1752, C.C. 1769–75.

MARRIOTT, JOHN. C.C. 1715.

MARRIOTT, W. *10 Fetter Lane*, about 1760.

MARRIOTT, JOHN. Musical clock maker, *10 Fleet Lane*, 1780; *175 Fleet St.*, 1790. Master C.C. 1799, died 1824; bracket clock, ebony case with brass mountings, enamel dial, about 1780. Wetherfield collection, *148 Aldersgate St.*, 1806–10.

MARRIOTT, WM. & J. *27 Fenchurch St.*, 1823–30.

MARRIS, CHAS. *Hull*, 1822.

MARSDEN, JOHN. C.C. 1698; master 1731.

MARSDEN, JOSH. *Gainsboro'*. Long-case clock with motto, 'The Moon Do's Best Appear' 'When ye Air is most Clear', about 1760.

MARSDEN, SAMUEL. *4 Leathersellers' Buildings*, 1820.

MARSH, ANTHONY, 'at yᵉ dial opposite Bank of England.' C.C. 1724.

MARSH, JACOB. *78 Lombard St.*, 1754–68.

MARSH, JAMES & SAMUEL. *79 Broad St., Ratcliffe*, 1790–1810.

MARSH, JNO. Apprenticed in 1676 to Thos. Parker, C.C.

MARSH, JONATHAN. *London*. Apprenticed in 1691 to Richard Symonds, C.C.; long-case clock, about 1720.

MARSH, JOSEPH, son of Samuel (1). *London*. Apprenticed 1804, C.C. 1814.

MARSH, RICHD. *Ipswich*, 1770.

MARSH, ROBERT JOHN. *London* (*Bunhill Row*). Apprenticed 1785, C.C. 1795–1810; watch engraver.

MARSH, SAM. *79 Broad St., Ratcliffe*, 1793–1818.

MARSH, SAMUEL. *London* (*Ratcliffe Cross, Stepney* and *Limehouse*). Apprenticed 1761, C.C. 1770–1820; partner with John Decka; rack lever watch, Ilbert collection.

MARSH, SAMUEL. *London*. Apprenticed 1791, C.C. 1804.

MARSH, THOMAS, son of Anthony. *London*. Apprenticed 1770–1811; watch with his escapement S.M.S.K., patented in 1811.

MARSH, THOS. *King St., Clerkenwell*. In 1811 he patented (No. 3,488) an escapement.

MARSH, WILLIAM. *London*. Apprenticed 1773, C.C. 1787–91.

MARSH, WILLIAM. *London* (*Nicholas Lane*). Livery C.C. 1811; long-case clock.

MARSH, WM. B. *London*. Handsome long-case clock, about 1800.

MARSHALL, BENJAMIN. C.C. 1680.

MARSHALL, CHRIS. Appointed in 1701 to uphold the clock and chimes of Halifax Church in succession to Sam. Ogden.

MARSHALL, FRANCIS. *Durham*, 1770.

MARSHALL, GEO. *New St.* C.C. 1734.

MARSHALL, JNO. *London*. Probably about 1780.

MARSHALL, JOHN. *Rainbow Coffee House, Cornhill*. Apprenticed to Sam. Rouk, but turned over to D. Quare; C.C. 1689; long panelled marquetry case clock, hood with spiral pillars, 12-in. dial, about 1705, Wetherfield collection. "Lost out of a gentleman's pocket on the 2nd inst., a silver minute watch in a studded shagreen case. John Marshall, watchmaker, at the Rainbow Coffee House in Cornhill, near Birchin Lane" (*Lond. Gaz.*, March 12, 1693–94).

MARSHALL, JOHN. *Newark*. Long-case calendar clocks, about 1730.

MARSHALL, MATTHEW. C.C. 1689.

MARSHALL, RICHD. 1751.

MARSHALL, SAMUEL. *New St.* C.C. 1718, died 1750.

MARSHALL, THOS. *Lincoln*. Watch, 1790.

MARSHALL, WILLIAM, son. *London*. Apprenticed 1719, C.C. 1733–40.

MARSHALL, WM. *Newark*. Died 1770.

MARSHALL, WM. *3 Corporation Lane*, 1816; *6 Percival St.*, 1830–35.

MARSHINVILLE FRÈRES. Repeating watch, about 1750.

MARSTER, W. J. *26 Bartlett's Buildings, Holborn*, 1825.

MARSTON, JNO. His movement seized by C.C. 1661.

MARSTON, THOS, about 1705.

MARSTON, WILLIAM. C.C. 1669.

MARTIN, ABRAHAM. Engraver, C.C. 1682.

MARTIN, BENJAMIN. *Newton Head, Fleet St.*, "a friend of Jas. Ferguson"; maker of a curious table clock; born at Chichester 1704, died 1782.

MARTIN, EDMUND. *44 Queen St., Cheapside.* Apprenticed to William Howells, C.C. 1795.

MARTIN, EDWD. Apprenticed in 1662 to Jno. Nicasius C.C.; pair case watch, Dutch style, Fitzwilliam Museum, Cambridge.

MARTIN, FRANCIS. Apprenticed 1683 to Jno. Wells, C.C.

MARTIN, G. *13 Church Lane, Whitechapel.*

MARTIN, J. F. *26 High St., Marylebone*, 1810.

MARTIN, JEREMIAH. Apprenticed to Wm. Dent and turned over to Thos. Tompion; C.C. 1687.

MARTIN, JNO. Apprenticed C.C. 1684; bracket clock repeating quarters on six bells, marquetry case with domed top, Wetherfield collection, about 1700.

MARTIN, JNO. *Spalding*, 1773. Long-Sheraton case clock, signed 'Jos. Martin, Kippen', about 1790.

MARTIN, JOHANN *Augsburg*. Born 1642, died 1720; alarum watch, Denham collection; astronomical clock, National Museum, Munich; several sundials.

MARTIN, JOHN. *London.* Apprenticed 1705, C.C. 1714.

MARTIN, JOHN. *White Gate Alley.* Admitted C.C. 1679; threatened in 1682 with prosecution by C.C. for undue taking of apprentices.

MARTIN, JOHN. *16 Brownlow St., Bedford Row*, 1763–69.

MARTIN, JOHN. *Eton Bridge*, 1809. Long-case clock, about 1820.

MARTIN, JONATHAN. *London.* Watch, *repoussé* case, hall-mark, 1759.

MARTIN, RICHARD. *Northampton.* Maker of lantern clocks, about 1695.

MARTIN, ROBERT. *Glasgow* and *Grahamston*, 1782–99.

MARTIN, SAMUEL. *Dublin*, 1790.

MARTIN, SAMUEL. *New York*, 1805.

MARTIN, ST. à *Paris*. Repeating watch, about 1750.

MARTIN, T. G. *Dublin*, 1771.

MARTIN, THOMAS. *Wigan*, about 1680. Died 1716; one-hand watch movement with outer circle divided into 144, Ilbert collection.

MARTIN, THOMAS. *Dublin*, 1780–95. Watch.

MARTIN, THOMAS. *Baltimore, U.S.A.*, 1764. From *Philadelphia.* Watch.

MARTIN, THOMAS. *Royal Exchange.* Apprenticed in 1692 to Jere. Martin; C.C. 1699; diminutive bracket clock, about 1705.

MARTIN, THOMAS, son of Thomas Martin, citizen and poulterer, being by trade a clockmaker, C.C. 1771; a good maker; mentioned by Earnshaw, *27 Cornhill*, 1778–81; *St. Michael's Alley*, 1788–94; pocket-chronometer, G.M., h.m., 1780.

MARTIN, WILLIAM. *London.* Apprenticed 1685, C.C. 1702; long-case clock.

MARTIN, WILLIAM. *London.* Apprenticed 1699, C.C. 1710.

MARTIN, WILLIAM. *Liverpool*, 1795–1829. Watch.

MARTIN, WILLIAM. *Bristol.* Lantern and bracket clocks, 1700–30.

MARTIN, WILLIAM. C.C. 1709.

MARTIN, WILLIAM. Apprenticed to John Uffington; C.C. 1751.

MARTIN, WILLIAM. *75 King St., Westminster*, 1810–40.

MARTIN, YOUNG. *Dublin*, 1780–95. Watch.

MARTIN, ZACHARIE. Clockmaker to Louis XIV, 1674.

MARTIN & SAMUEL. *9 Bow*, 1817.

MARTINEAU, JOSEPH. *St. Martin's Court*, 1750–60. Bracket clock, engraved 'Josh. Martineau, senior'; maker also of gold *repoussé* watches; repeating watch, Pierpont Morgan collection, about 1760.

MARTINEAU, JOSEPH. *65 Red Lion St., Clerkenwell*, 1790–94.

MARTINIQUE à *Paris.* Clock in vase-shaped case of white statuary marble with side figures of nymphs of chased ormolu, about 1790.

MARTINOT, B. *Rouen.* Specimen at British Museum, about 1680.

MARTINOT, BALTHAZAR. *Paris.* Horloger to Louis XIII, 1637. "A four-square Gold Watch, made at Paris by Monsieur Martinot. Whoever can give notice of it to Mr. East, watchmaker, at Charing Cross, or else to the porter of Madam Gwinn's House in Pall Mall, shall have 20s. reward" (*Lond. Gaz.*, June 4–7, 1677).

MARTINOT, BALTHAZAR. *Rouen.* Master 1649, juré 1659. Probably same as Balthazar of Paris.

MARTINOT, BALTAZAR. *Paris.* Watch, 1714; Boulle-work clock, Jones collection, V. & A. about 1725.

MARTINOT, BARNABY. *Farringdon Within*, 1618.

MARTINOT, GILBERT. *Paris.* Clockmaker to Henry III, 1572; first of a long succession of Court clockmakers. DENIS succeeded in 1611; ZACHARIE in 1637; GILLE in 1662; JEAN in 1686; LOUIS HENRY in 1688; HENRI, nephew of Jean and son of Gille, succeeded his father at the Louvre in 1670; JÉRÔME in 1695; JACQUES in 1718; JEAN in 1727; CLAUDE in 1729.

MARTINOT, JÉRÔME. *Paris.* 'Horloger du Roy'; fine astronomical and calendar clock by him in the Paris Observatory, described by Thiout in 1741; clock, in case of ormolu, supported by a bronze elephant, Jones collection, V. & A., about 1760; the case is inscribed 'fecit par Caffieri'.

MARTINOT, M. *Avignon.* A watch by him, G.M., about 1700; presented an armillary sphere to the King of France in 1701.

MARX, PHILIPP. *Cologne*, 1797–1813.

MASCARONE, GIO. BATT. Padlock-shaped watch, about 1635.

MASEY, THOMAS. Mended St. Mary's clock, Oxon., 1550.

MASON, —. *Bedford.* Watch 1763.

MASON, EDWARD. *London*, a. 1775. Watch.

MASON, HENRY. C.C. 1715.

MASON, J. & E. *Worcester*, about 1790.

MASON, J. LADSON. *London.* Watch, 1780.

MASON, JNO. *Bristol.* Made a clock for the church of Alderly to the order of Sir Matthew Hale, 1673.

MASON, JOHN. C.C. 1712; lantern clock, square dial, cherub corners, bob pendulum, 1712–20.

MASON, JOHN. C.C. 1718; long-case clocks, 1718–30.

MASON, JOHN. *3 Helmet Row*, 1816–20; *1 Jubilee St., Mile End*, 1840.

MASON, RICHARD. C.C. 1632.

MASON, RICHARD. *St. Albans*, a. 1777–95 C.C. Watch.

MASON, ROBERT. *11 Strand.* In 1790 he sent a letter to the Clockmakers' Co. respecting watches seized on his premises.

MASON, ROBT. Apprenticed in 1658 to Peter Bellune, C.C.

MASON, SAMUEL. C.C. 1712.

MASON, SAMUEL. *Philadelphia*, 1820–25.

MASON, THOMAS. *Bawtrey*, about 1770–93; long-case clock.

MASON, WILLIAM. C.C. 1688. Several generations of Mason in Yorkshire: TIMOTHY, *Gainsborough*, 1695; then JOHN, *Doncaster*; long lacquer case clock by him, about 1740; then JOHN at *Bawtry*; THOMAS at *Bawtry*; TIMOTHY at *Chesterfield*, watch, h.m., 1795; then JOHN, apprenticed to Timothy at *Chesterfield*, began business at *Rotherham* in 1801.

MASON, WILLIAM. Near *East Lane, Rotherhithe Wall*, 1760–69; *Dockhead, Southwark*, 1781–83.

MASON, WM. *Bexley*. Watch, 1768.

MASON & HUDSON. *Strand*, 1772.

MASQUERIER, LEWIS. *12 Coventry St.*, 1780–85.

MASQUERIER, WM. *Gerrard St., Soho*, 1790–94.

MASQUERIER & PERIGAL. *Coventry St.*, 1775.

MASSE, JAMES. *Broad St.*, 1753–60.

MASSET, PETER. Long marquetry case clock, about 1700 (? MALLET, PETER).

MASSEY, BENJ. *116 Leadenhall St.*, 1810–26.

MASSEY, C. *40 Bridge Rd., Lambeth*, 1823–35.

MASSEY, EDMUND. C.C. 1682.

MASSEY, EDWARD. *Hanley, Staffs.*, 1804.

MASSEY, EDWARD. *London, Coventry* in 1814. Born 1772, died 1852; a well-known maker; invented the crank-roller lever escapement, and patented a pump-winding; watch with his escapement Chamb. collection; watch beating seconds, Marryat collection; watch with seconds hand turning once in 2½ seconds, Ilbert collection; Pub. arts. in Trans. Soc. Arts, Vol 21 and Phil. Mag. 1804 on clocks.

MASSEY, EDWARD. *Newcastle-under-Lyme*, 1778–95. Clocks and watches.

MASSEY, JOHN. *89 Strand*, and *40 Bridge Rd., Lambeth*, 1810–35.

MASSEY, PAUL. *Coventry St.* Long-case clock, revolving months, date dial, about 1760. A long-case clock, dated 1725, inscribed 'Jon Massey, Dundalke'.

MASSINGHAM, J. *Fakenham*. Bracket repeating clock, about 1770.

MASSON, DENIS. *Paris*. Clock, Jones collection, V. & A., about 1760.

MASSON, R. AIMÉ. *London*. Watch, Evan Roberts collection, about 1700.

MASSY, HENRY, son. *London (Charles St.)*. C.C. 1692–1745; fine watch G.M.; repeating watch S.M.S.K.; watch Denham collection; repeating watch Feill collection, about 1720; long-case and bracket clocks illuminated Cec. & Web.

MASSY, JACOB. *Leicester Fields*. C.C. 1715; maker of a black arch bracket clock, 1715–25.

MASSY, NICHOLAS. *Blois*. Master 1623. Died between 1646 and 1658; maker of repute.

MASSY, NICHOLAS. A French refugee, brother C.C. 1682; in the Pierpont Morgan collection is a small watch, signed 'Nicholas Massy à Blois', balance-cock pinned on, gold case with outer case of leather *piqué* with gold, about 1660; in the same collection is a silver alarum watch, signed 'Massy, London'; this dates from about 1690; no minute hand, pair cases, pierced, the outer one of particularly fine design and workmanship, has on the back a cypher, C.B., reversed. "Lost the 17 instant, between the Haymarket and Temple Bar, a new Silver Pendulum Watch made by Nich. Massy, with a tortoise-shell studded case, the studs wrought, and the case lined with red sattin; and 2 seals" (*Lond. Gaz.*, Nov. 24–28, 1692); 1690–1712.

MASSY, NICHOLAS, son of the foregoing Nicholas, *Cranbourne St.*, near *Leicester Fields*. C.C. 1693; striking watch, Schloss collection, royal arms and motto *Semper Eadem* on the movement; a watch move-ment by him, with an index on top of the cock, is in the Guildhall Museum.

MASSY, PAUL. *Coventry St.* Long Oriental lacquer case musical clock, tunes as engraved on the dial, 'Grannadears' March', 'The Happy Clown'; shows also days of the week and month, and signs of the zodiac, about 1740.

MASTER, W. HENSHAW. *London*, 1689 C.C.

MASTER, W. J. *26 Bartlett's Buildings*, 1823.

MASTERMAN, J. *White Hart Court, Gracechurch St.*, 1769–73. Masterman & Springhall, 1793.

MASTERS, —. *Wade's Passage, Bath*, 1770.

MASTERS, JAMES. *52 Strand*. Card, British Museum, 1803; livery C.C. 1810; after much negotiation he was in 1812 transferred to the Goldsmiths' Company on payment of £30 to C.C.

MASTERS, JNO. *London*. Watch, single case, about 1735.

MASTERS, JNO. *Bristol*, about 1780.

MASTERS, JOHN. *Dartmouth*, 1810.

MASTERS, RICHARD. Transferred from Clothiers to C.C. 1636.

MASTERS, WILLIAM. C.C. 1701.

MASTERSON, JNO. Apprenticed in 1648 to Richd. Masterson, C.C.

MASTERSON, RICHARD. Early watch signed 'Ri Masterson at the dyall at Mooregate', balance-cock pinned on about 1610, Pierpont Morgan collection; afterwards at the Royal Exchange; subscribed to the incorporation of C.C. in 1630; C.C. 1633; master 1642; died 1653; in the G.M. is an oval watch by him, cockle-shell case, plain silver dial, hour-hand only, catgut.

MASTON, D. *London*. Watch, 1795–1820.

MASTON, RICHARD. Apprenticed in 1649 to Wm. North, C.C.

MASTON, THOS. *Bawtry*, 1775.

MATCHETT, GEO. Apprenticed in 1651 to Wm. Petty, C.C.

MATCHETT, JOHN. *Covent Garden*. C.C. 1648; signed a petition against the Company's oppression, 1656; assistant, 1670; suspended, as well known to be a Popish recusant, 1678. "Lost on the 11th inst. about Lincoln's-Inn-Fields or Covent Garden, a silver watch ingraven with several Figures, made by John Machett, a studded case with silver Pins" (*Lond. Gaz.*, June 12–15, 1676). "Lost on Thursday, the 3rd instant, between eight and nine in the evening, in the Pall Mall, a gold watch with a silver-gilt chain, and a little cabinet key linked to it, made by John Matchet in Convent Garden. Whoever brings it to Mr. Mawson, Goldsmith, at the Golden Hind in Fleet Street, over against St. Dunstan's Church, shall have five pounds reward" (*Lond. Gaz.*, June 1680).

MATHAM, ROBT. *66 Newgate St.*, 1783.

MATHER, D. Watch with skeleton movement, about 1820.

MATHER, SAMUEL. C.C. 1691.

MATHERS, ADAM. *Coleraine*, 1820.

MATHEW, FRANCIS. C.C. 1656.

MATHEWS, W. & C. S. *128 Minories*, 1817.

MATHEWS, WILLIAM. *27 Fleet St.* Apprenticed to Charles Tolley, and turned over to John Smith; C.C. 1731; assistant and livery, 1766; one of the examiners of Harrison's timekeeper in 1765; watch, 1800, signed 'Matthews, Leighton Buzzard'.

MATHEWS, WILLIAM. *London*. Apprenticed 1736, C.C. 1744–68.

MATHEWSON (MATTHEWSON), ANDREW. *Kilconquhar*, 1795–1830.

MATHEWSON (MATTHEWSON), JOHN. *Anstruther*, 1755.

MATHEY, LEWIS. *Philadelphia*, 1797.

MATHIESON, PETER. *Copenhagen*. Master 1724; Master of Corporation 1758; died 1769; long-case clock illuminated Liisberg.

MATHIEU, C. *Paris*, 1780.

MATHIEU, EDME, LE JEUNE. *Paris*. Master 1769–89.

MATHISON, —. *London*, 1750.

MATLACK, W. C. f., of New York, 1769.

MATLACK, WHITE & WILLIAM. *Philadelphia*, 1780.

MATTHEW, JOHN. C.C. 1731; long oak-case clock, with day of the month circle, about 1740.

MATTHEWS, J. *Leighton*. Long-case clock, about 1810, Mr. Wm. Norman.

MATTHEWS, THOS. *London*. Clock with figure of Time working backward and forward; motto, 'Tempus Fugit', dated 1702.

MATTHEWS, WM. 1765; watch paper 'opposite St. Dunstan's Church, Fleet St., late apprentice to Mr. Graham'.

MATTHEY, FRÉDÉRIC. *Chaux-de-Fonds*, 1750. Died 1767; clock.

MATTHEY, JEAN JACQUES, son of Isaac. *La Brévine*, 1740–67. Turret and house clocks; several small clocks.

MATTHEY-CLAUDET, ABRAM. *La Brévine*,1796–1821. clock.

MATTHEY-DORET, ABRAM. *La Brévine, Donaueschingen* and •*Besançon*. Apprenticed 1786–1819; clock; silver medal at Paris Exhibition of 1819.

MATTHEY-DUPRAT, DAVID HENRI. *La Brévine*, 1807–24. Clock.

MATTHEY-DUPRAT, ISAAC HENRI. *Chaux-de-Fonds*, 1801. Clock.

MATTHEY-GUENET, PIERRE. *La Brévine*, about 1700–40. Made clock for La Brévine.

MATTISON, THOS. *62 Cornhill*, 1793.

MATTOCKS, JOHN. *St. Bride's Lane*. Livery C.C. 1786.

MATTOCKS, JOHN. *London*. Apprenticed 1738, C.C. 1747.

MAUBERT, PETER. Apprenticed in 1679 to David Meggret, C.C.

MAUD, HALSTEAD. *London*. Apprenticed 1767, C.C. 1786–94; watch-cap and spring maker.

MAUDE, BENJAMIN. *53 St. Martin's-le-Grand*, 1770–94.

MAUDE, EDWARD. *14 St. Paul's Churchyard*, 1793–98.

MAUDS, B. E. *Daventry*, 1780.

MAUDSLEY, G. *Wakefield*, 1770.

MAUDUIT, ISAAC. *London*. Apprenticed 1717, C.C. 1724.

MAUPAS, CHARLES. *Blois*, 1644. Died 1668.

MAUPAS, DANIEL, brother. *Blois*. Apprenticed 1615, comp. at *Lyons*, 1619; *Autun*, 1625; *Blois* to 1653.

MAURER, JOHANN, in *Fiessna*. In the British Museum is a small skull-watch by him, 1650–60.

MAURIS. Signature on chased watch case, about 1760.

MAURIS, HENRI. *Geneva*, about 1775–about 1810. Watch.

MAUS, JACOB. *Trenton, U.S.A.*, 1780–84. Clocks and watches.

MAVOR, JNO. Apprenticed in 1637 to Jas. Allen, C.C.

MAWEIS (possibly MAURIS), —. Chased watch case, about 1770–80.

MAWKES, J. *Derby*. Watch, 1794.

MAWKES, T. *Belper*. Long-case clock, about 1710.

MAWLEY, H. Watch, 1705.

MAWLEY, ROBT. *London*. An all-brass bracket timepiece with alarum by this maker, dating from about 1695, case plain except the sides, which are decorated with a Cupid's head with radiating bars; bracket clock, about 1725.

MAWMAN, GEO. *Beverley*, 1822.

MAWSON. See MATCHETT.

MAWTASS, NICHOLAS. *London*. C.C. 1768.

MAXWELL, A. *Philadelphia*, 1805–11. Clock.

MAXWELL, ROBERT. *London*. C.C. 1778.

MAY, BOYS ERR. *London (Bridgewater Sq.)*. Apprenticed 1746, C.C. 1753, died 1796.

MAY, DAVID. *Prescot*, 1770.

MAY, EDWD. *Henley*. Long-case clock, lantern movement, about 1680.

MAY, EDWD. *Witney*. Long-case clock, about 1725, no minute divisions on outer circle.

MAY, FREDERICK. *Dublin*, 1770–96. Watch.

MAY, GEO. C.C. 1754. "A large quantity of gold and silver watches, with a time piece, and some other curious things of value, were found in the gully hole at Holborn bridge, by the workmen, in cleaning it. These things had been taken some days before from the house of Mr. May, watchm'ker, in Bridgewater square; and were returned on the payment of 10 guineas, promis'd by advzt. for the recovy. of them" (*Gent.'s Mag.*, Aug. 24, 1765).

MAY, JOHN. *Southampton*, 1773. Died 1791. Clocks and watches.

MAY, JOHN. *Dublin*, 1820.

MAY, JOHN (Dutch). C.C. 1692; watch, about 1710; Pierpont Morgan collection.

MAY, JOHN. *Witney*. Long-case clock, about 1700.

MAY, SAMUEL. *London*. Apprenticed 1800, C.C. 1810.

MAY, WILLIAM. C.C. 1679.

MAY & SON. *Dublin*, 1798.

MAYBON, E. *St. Germain*. Watch, British Museum, about 1670.

MAYER, J. *Innsbruck*, 1590. Maker to the Archduke Ferdinand.

MAYERS, JNO. *Richmond*, 1770.

MAYET, FRANÇOIS PIERRE IGNAGE. *Paris*. Master 1770–89.

MAYET, PIERRE CLAUDE. *Morbier*, 1687–1729. Made clocks for St. Just d'Arbois in 1687, the Ursules de Nozeroy in 1699 and St. Anatoile de Salins in 1729.

MAYET, PIERRE FRANÇOIS, son. *Morbier*, 1729–63. With his son made clock for Bourg-en-Bresse in 1733.

MAYFIELD, EDWARD. *London (Little Minories)*. Apprenticed 1784, C.C. 1798, livery C.C. and died 1812.

MAYFIELD, JOHN. *London*. Apprenticed 1768.

MAYHEW, HEN. *Parham*. Lantern clock, say, 1690.

MAYHEW, WM. *Woodbridge*. A well-known Suffolk maker of 'Act of Parliament' and long-case clocks. A notice of his death with a eulogium of his virtues appeared in the *Ipswich Journal* of Jan. 29, 1791. Fine tall clocks in lacquer cases by this maker.

MAYLAND, THOMAS. C.C. 1698.

MAYNARD, —. *Long Melford*. He made the church clock there about 1650; lantern clock.

MAYNARD, CHAS. *St. Martin's-le-Grand*, 1774.

MAYNARD, CHRISTOPHER. *Royal Exchange*. Apprenticed to Hackett, C.C. 1667. See HICKS.

MAYNARD, GEO. Apprenticed in 1692 to Chris. Maynard. C.C.; f. of New York, 1702.

MAYNARD, GEO. *Metford*. Watch, 1767.

MAYNARD, GEORGE. *New York*, 1702–25.

MAYNE, —. *111 Union St., Stonehouse*. Watch paper, about 1790.

MAYO, —. *Coventry*, about 1780–90.

MAYO, JOSEPH. *Craven St., Strand*, 1769–72.

MAYO, THOMAS. *Hereford*, 1760.

MAYO, WM. Apprenticed in 1676 to Robt. Cawne, C.C.

MAYR, J. At Buckingham Palace is an astronomical clock dating from 1680, signed 'Jacob Mayr Junger, Augsburg', square case covered with turtle-shell, adorned with silver scrolls and bands; four dials; died 1714.

MAYR, JACOB. *Augsburg*. 1720 master–about 1750; clock Grüne Gewölbe, Dresden; watch Feill collection probably by him.

MAYR, JOHANN HANS GEORG. *Munich*, about 1650. Died 1684; court clock maker 1663–71; square table clock, Spitzer collection; astronomical table clock, tortoiseshell and silver with armillary sphere National Museum, Munich; magnificent astronomical musical clock K.H.M., Vienna; small striking alarum bracket clock, M.P.S., Dresden.

MAYR, JOHANN PETER. *Augsburg*. Master about 1740, juré 1745–58; silver repoussé watch; gold onyx watch; gold and porcelain watch, Fränkel collection; silver repeating watch Feill collection; repeating travelling clock, Ilbert collection. Also MEYR.

MAYRIUM, JOHANN GEORG. *Munich*. Spherical clock about 1690.

MAYSMOR, HUMPHREY. *London*. 1692 C.C. Also MAYSMAR.

MAYSMORE, WM. *Wrexham*, about 1720.

MAYSON, JOHN. C.C. 1704.

MAYSON, MCCABE & STRACHAN. *London*, 1822.

MAYSTRE, JEAN JACQUES. *Geneva*, about 1775–1791.

MAZURIER, ANTOINE. *Paris*. Watch, case enamelled by H. Toutin, about 1670.

MAZURIER (LEMASURIER), JACQUES. *Paris*. 1738 master, juré 1750–89; presented a clock with seconds pendulum to Louis XV; in 1754 made a clock with one wheel in going and one in striking train, described in Mém. de l'Acad. des. Sci. 1755.

MAZURIER (LEMASURIER), JEAN (or JACQUES) DENIS. *Paris*. Master 1774–89.

MAZZEL, COR. *Bolney*. Watch, 1740.

MAZZOLENI, GIUSEPPE. *Padua. Venice* from 1551; died 1577; keeper of clock of S. Marco.

MEAD, ABRAHAM. *London*, 1840–1919.

MEAD, BENJAMIN. *Casline, Me.*, 1800–10.

MEAD, R. *Lancaster*, 1760.

MEADE, GARRETT. C.C. 1703.

MEADER, J. W. *London*. Died 1915.

MEADES, THOMAS. C.C. 1687.

MEADOWS, WM. *London*. Watch, 1760.

MEAK, JOHN. Musical clock and watch maker, *7 Worship St.*, 1825.

MEAKIN, WILLIAM. *Dublin*, 1697.

MEAN, WILLIAM. *London (Albemarle St.)*. C.C. 1789, livery C.C. 1813; watch.

MEANLEY, —. *London*. Pair-case verge watch, with an engraving on the back representing the Queen of Sheba before Solomon; about 1770.

MEARS, ISAAC. Apprenticed in 1661 to Robt. Whitwell, C.C.

MEARS, JNO. Watch engraver, *18 Cloth Fair*, 1790–94.

MEARS, JNO. *York*, 1822.

MEARS, JOSIAS. *Dublin*. Long-case clock, about 1760, Sir Theodore Fry.

MEASURE, A. *420 Strand*, 1815–20.

MEBERT, ISAAC. C.C., about 1660.

MEDCALF, CUTHBERT. *Liverpool*, 1777–1805. Watch.

MEDCALF, WM. *Liverpool*, 1770.

MEDHURST, RICHARD. *Croydon*. C.C. 1687.

MEDOX, MICHEL. *Moscow*, 1776–93. Made musical automatic clock in Kremlin Museum for Catherine II.

MEEBERRY, ELIZABETH. Apprenticed in 1680 to Edwd. Norris and his wife, C.C.

MEEK, JNO. Musical clock and watch maker, *7 Worship St.*, 1812–18.

MEEKING, THOMAS. *Dublin*, 1682. Died 1709.

MEEKS, EDWARD, JUNR. *114 Maiden Lane, New York*, 1796; "has eight-day clocks and chiming time pieces" (advt.).

MÉGEVAND, LAURENT. *Le Locle* and *Besançon*. Born 1754, died 1814; went Besançon in 1790 and started the watch industry there in 1793, under the Government.

MEGROS, FRÉDÉRIC. *Luthy (Vevey)*. 1783–98 master.

MEHRER, JOHANN FERDINAND. *Augsburg*. Table clock, about 1670.

MEIFIELD, JAMES. *London*. C.C. 1818.

MEIFIELD, WILLIAM, son. *London*. Apprenticed 1818, C.C. 1825.

MEIGH, MOSES. C.C. 1712.

MELCHIOR. See ADAM.

MELL, DAVID. C.C. 1655. Cornelius Harplett was apprenticed to him through the C.C. in 1659; fine lantern clock, inscribed 'Davis Mell in Crutched Fryers, Londini', about 1675; John Aubrey's *Miscellanies* mentions "Mr. Davys Mell (the famous Violinist and Clock-maker)". He was Bandmaster to Charles II.

MELLET, JEAN SAMUEL. *Moudon*. 1762 master–1798. *Vevy* from 1762.

MELLIN, CORNELIUS. *London*, 1622. Alien; oval gilt watch.

MELLIN, GUI. *Blackfriars*. Maker of an oval watch in the British Museum, glass over the dial, 1600–20.

MELLY FRÈRES. *Paris*. Watch, 1780.

MELROSE, JAMES. *34 Nicolson St., Edinburgh*. Watch paper endorsed 'July 9, 1827, Captain Smith'.

MELVILL, ROBERT. *Stirling*, 1736–67.

MELVILLE, JAS. Watch-case maker, *13 Spencer St.*, 1816.

MELVILLE, JOHN. Hon. freeman C.C. 1781.

MELVILLE & STODDART. *61 Red Lion St., Clerkenwell*, 1804–10.

MEMEIS, ROBT. *Margaret St., Wilmington Sq.* Clock, about 1820.

MEMES, JAMES. *Berwick-on-Tweed*, about 1770–1811. Watch.

MEMESS, ROBERT. *London*, 1817. C.C. 1825.

MENDHAM, S. Received a silver medal from the Society of Arts in 1807 for a remontoire.

MENDS, JAMES. *Philadelphia*, 1795; afterwards BENJ.

MENESSIE, ELISHA. *Aldersgate St.*, 1790–95.

MENIALL, JAMES (French). Threatened with persecution by C.C. for exercising the art, not being admitted, paid costs, and was admitted forthwith, 1682.

MENS, BENJAMIN. *Philadelphia*, 1796.

MENU, DANIEL. *Geneva*. Born 1734–69.

MENU, SIMON. *Paris*. 1685 master.

MENZIES, J. *Philadelphia*, 1811–16.

MERCATOR. Evelyn's 'Diary', 28th Aug., 1666, "To the Royal Society where one Mercator, an excellent mathematician, produced his rare clock and new motions to perform the equations, and Mr. Rooke" (evidently should be Hooke) "his new pendulum".

MERCER BROTHERS. *Coventry*, about 1770–90.

MERCER, EDWD. Apprenticed in 1690 to Cuthbert Lee, C.C.

MERCER, JNO. *Liverpool*, 1818.

MERCER, JOHN. *Hythe*. Maker of long-case clocks, 1720.

MERCER, JOHN. *Manchester*, about 1800.

MERCHANT, SAMUEL. Admitted C.C. 1677; assistant 1698.

MERCHIE (MURCHI, MARKIE), JOHAN. *Copenhagen*, 1695–1717. Swiss; turret clock; made existing clock for Our Saviour's Church, Christianshavn, illuminated Liisberg.

MERCIER, —. *London*. Watch, 1725.

MERCIER, —. *Paris*. Watch, 1750, Sd Geneva; watch 1845.

MERCIER, LOUIS. *Geneva*, about 1690.

MÉRÉAUX, JEAN CHARLES. *Paris*. Master 1671–89.

MEREDITH, JNO. *Carlisle*, about 1740.
MEREDITH, JNO. *London*. Watch, gold box, h.m., 1758, outer case *repoussé*.
MEREDITH, JOHN. C.C. 1664.
MEREDITH, LANCELOT. C.C. 1637; signed a petition against the tyranny of the Company, 1656.
MEREDITH, WM. *Chepstow*. Fine long-case clock, about 1775.
MERFIELD, JAMES. *London*. C.C. 1818.
MERFIELD, WILLIAM. *London*. Apprenticed 1818, C.C. 1825.
MÉRIÉNNE, JEAN RENÉ. *Geneva*, about 1775–92. Awarded prize for watch by Soc. des Arts.
MERIGEOT, JOHN. Livery C.C. 1766.
MERISON, JAS. *Anderston*. Clock, inscribed 'Dial made for Robt. Liddal'.
MERITON, SAMUEL. Livery Turners' Company, *18 Foster Lane, Cheapside*, 1763–1800.
MERLIN, JOSEPH. Mechanical genius; born 1735 at *Huys*, near *Liège*. Arrived in England in 1760. Soon after this became principal mechanic at Cox's Museum, which he left in 1773; was an expert designer of engines, mathematicial instruments, and a watch and clock maker. He constructed a curious dial or regulator which was wound by the room door opening; died 1803.
MERMILLIOD, GUILLAUME. *Paris*. Master 1777–1825.
MERMILLON FRÈRES ET CIE. Swiss watch, 1780.
MERMOD FRÈRES. *Sainte Croix*, 1815–89. Makers of musical mechanism; devised repeating work operated by going train mainspring.
MERNY, CHARLES. *Spitalfields*. Liveryman C.C. 1776.
MERRA, PIERRE MARTIN. *Paris*. Master 1773–89. Vase clock Bernal sale.
MERRELL, JNO. *London*. Watch, enamelled case, 1790.
MERRIAM, SILAS. *Connecticut, U.S.A.*, 1790.
MERRILL, CHARLES. *London (Moorfields)*. Apprenticed 1748, C.C. 1757–96.
MERRILL, CHARLES, son of Chas. *London (Pudding Lane, Cumberland St.* and *Richmond)*. C.C. 1782, livery C.C. 1810.
MERRILL, JAMES, son. *London (Richmond)*. C.C. 1797.
MERRILL, JOHN. *London*. Apprenticed 1767, C.C. 1777.
MERRIMAN, TITUS. 1830.
MERRIMAN, TITUS and BUTLER. *Bristol, U.S.A.*, 1810–15. Wooden wall clocks.
MERRIMAN & DUNBAR. *Bristol, Conn.*, 1810.
MERRITT, CHARLES. *London*. 1808 C.C., livery C.C. 1810.
MERRY, CHARLES. *London*. Long-case clock, about 1740; livery C.C. 1766; master 1768.
MERRY, EDWARD. *London*. C.C. 1749.
MERRY, F. *Philadelphia*, 1799.
MERRY, JAMES OWEN, son of Charles. *London*. C.C. 1771.
MERRYMAN, BENJAMIN. C.C. 1682; clock-watch mounted as a sedan chair timekeeper; tulip pillars, about 1695, inscribed 'Benj. Merriman, London'.
MERRYMAN, HENRY. C.C. 1674.
MERRYMAN, JOHN. *London*. Apprenticed 1697, C.C. 1711.
MERRYMAN, THOS. Apprenticed in 1692 to Ben. Merryman, C.C.
MERTON & CO. *Liverpool*. Watch, 1792.
MERTTINS, GEORGE. *Cornhill*. Goldsmith and watchmaker, succeeded to the business of his father; C.C. 1688; master, 1713; knighted, 1713; Lord Mayor, 1724; died 1727.
MERZ (MÄRTZ), JOHANN ANTON. *Augsburg*, 1756–85.
MERZ (MÄRTZ), JOSEPH. *Augsburg*. Comp. 1784, master 1802.

MESNIEL, JAMES (French). C.C. 1682.
MESNIER, CLAUDE. *Paris*. Clockmaker to the Duke d'Anjou, 1655.
MESTAGER, HENRY. C.C. 1713.
(MESTAYER?), —, son. *London*. C.C. 1744; repeating watch.
MESTREGENT, FRANÇOIS. *Besançon*, 1685. Died 1722; called to Besançon to make clock for Monastère du Refuge.
MESURE, ANTHONY. *8 Craven Buildings, Drury Lane*, 1810; *420 Strand*, 1814–23.
METCALF, EDWD. Apprenticed in 1684 to Richd. Blundell, C.C.
METCALF, GEORGE MARMADUKE. *Round Court, St. Martin's-le-Grand*. Admitted C.C. 1781; livery 1786; *122 Newgate St.*, 1794–1825.
METCALF, JOHN. *Liverpool*, 1790–1818. Watch.
METCALF, JOSH. *146 Oxford St.*, 1816–42.
METCALFE, MARK. *Askrigg*. Died 1776, aged 89.
METCALFE & NICHOLL. *Halifax*, 1780.
METHEM, ROBT. *66 Newgate St.*, 1775.
MEURON, —. *Paris*. Watches, 1770–90.
MEURON & CO. *Paris*, about 1798. Watch signed 'Meuron, Silliman & Co., Chaux de Fonds', about 1770.
MEUSNIER (MEUNIER), CLAUDE FRANÇOIS. *Paris*. Master 1781–1812; clock.
MEYBOM, F. *Paris*, 1650.
MEYE, DIET. *Basle*. Watch, about 1750.
MEYER, —. *Paris*. Watch, 1780.
MEYER, —. *Paris*, seventeenth century. Circular silver engraved watch, Spitzer collection.
MEYER, APPOLLINARIS. *Basle*, 1583–1610.
MEYER, DIETRICH, son of Jakob. *Basle*. Born 1745, died 1807; watch movement signed 'Diet. Meye', M.M.A.; two watches, Basle Museum.
MEYER, FRANÇOIS. *Paris*. 1771 master–1789; gold engraved watch.
MEYER, JACQUES. *Basle*, about 1760.
MEYER, JAKOB. *Basle*. Born 1677, died 1737.
MEYERS, JOHN. *Frederickstown, Md., U.S.A.*, 1793–1825.
MEYLAN, F. & A. *Geneva*. Watch, 1820.
MEYLAN, PHILIPPE SAMUEL. *Brassus* and *Geneva*. Born 1770–1829; eminent maker of automata and complex watches; first to make musical watches with reeds and disc and later with barrel; invented the ring alarum with pin to prick finger; went to *Geneva* in 1811; in firm with L. Audemars and Isaac Daniel Piguet, 1811–28.
MEYNADIER, PHILIPPE. *Geneva*, about 1780–early nineteenth century. Gold engraved lyre watch and two gold engraved watches M.M.A.
MEYRAT, JEAN FRANÇOIS. *St. Imier*, 1781. Died 1800; started an important business, continued by his widow and daughter.
MEYRAT, JEAN PIERRE. *Courtelary*. Born 1738.
MEYRICK, WM. THOS. Meyrick, son of Wm. Meyrick, watchmaker, deceased, late of St. Andrews, Holborn, apprenticed to Jno. Williams, citizen and author, minutes of Cutlers' Company, 1803.
MICABIUS, JOHN. C.C. ordered him to be sued for failing to pay a promised contribution towards incorporation, 1632.
MICHAEL, D. & SONS. *Swansea*. Watch, 1801.
MICHAUD, DANIEL. *28 Greek Street*, 1794.
MICHAUD, P. *Paris*, about 1750. Repeating watch, signed 'Vve. Michaud, Paris', about 1750, Pierpont Morgan collection.
MICHEL, EDWARD ECCOTT. *London*. Apprenticed 1813, C.C. 1831.

MICHEL, JACQUES. *Paris.* Lantern clock, about 1650.

MICHEL, JEAN. *Paris,* 1770–99. Petitioned for an award for improvements in clocks without success.

MICHEL, JOHN. *London.* 1753 C.C.; probably same as MITCHELL.

MICHELEZ, ELÈVE, de Breguet. Equation clock, about 1828.

MICHELIN, SAML., à *Langres.* Splendid travelling watch, about 1680.

MICHELL, GEO. *Bristol, Conn.,* 1827–37.

MICHELL, JAM. *London.* Long-case clock, marquetry flowers in vase, about 1710.

MICHELL, JO. *Chardstock.* Lantern clocks, about 1700.

MICHELLS, —. *63 St. Mary Axe,* 1830.

MICHINALE, WILLIAM. *London.* Apprenticed 1693 C.C. 1702–16. Also MICHINALLE.

MICHOD, ABRAM LOUIS. *Vevey.* Apprenticed 1727, master 1742, died a. 1773.

MICHOD, JEAN BAPTISTE. *Vevey* and *Berne.* Apprenticed 1730–70 master; took over Ador's factory at Berne in 1762 and moved it to Vevey; watch movement.

MICKLEWRIGHT, —. C.C. 1708.

MICKLEWRIGHT, ERASMUS. C.C. 1673.

MIDDLECOATS, WM. *Newington, Surrey.* Bracket clock, about 1730.

MIDDLEMISS, ROBT. *Hull,* 1822.

MIDDLETON, THOMAS. *London.* Apprenticed 1718–81 C.C.

MIDDLETON, TIMOTHY. Apprenticed in 1680 to Robt. Dingley; C.C. 1687.

MIDGLEY, RICHD. *Halifax,* 1720–40. Many long-case clocks.

MIDNALL, JOHN, in *Fleet St.* One of the first assistants C.C.; maker of a small oval watch said to have belonged to Oliver Cromwell, British Museum; small oval watch, Pierpont Morgan collection; pretty balance-cock pinned on, about 1620; another watch by him of rather later date, in silver cases, outer case engraved with flowers.

MIDWINTER, JNO. *London.* Watch, h.m., 1763.

MIDWINTER, THOMAS. *London (Bridgewater Gdns.).* C.C. 1774–1810.

MIDWINTER, WILLIAM. *London.* C.C. 1774–94.

MIEGE à *Genève.* Watch, G.M., about 1750.

MILBORNE, JOHN. Admitted C.C. 1698.

MILDE, G. W. *Östersund,* 1820–46.

MILES, —. *Stroud.* Clock, lantern movement, square brass dial, about 1700.

MILES, —. *Lowley.* Chiming clock incorporated with mahogany bureau, about 1750.

MILES, G. *Guildford St., Boro',* 1830.

MILES, JOHN. *Stroud,* 1775–95. Watch; repaired Westbury Church clock.

MILES, SEPTIMUS. *32 Ludgate St.,* 1794. Livery C.C. 1810; *8 Little Carter Lane, Doctors' Commons,* 1825–42.

MILES, STEPHEN. *Kidderminster,* 1753–72. Clocks and watches.

MILES, THOMAS. *London (St. James' Walk, Clerkenwell).* C.C. 1768–99.

MILES & MORGAN. *32 Ludgate St.,* 1790–94.

MILFIELD, D. *London.* Watch, 1790.

MILLAR, RICHARD. *Edinburgh,* 1814. Died 1860.

MILLAR, THOMAS. *Philadelphia,* 1819–25.

MILL, DAVID. See MELL.

MILL, JOHN. *Montrose,* 1750–55.

MILLARD, D., à *Paris.* Alarum watch with enamelled d'lia pierced and engraved silver case, late seventeenth century, V. & A.

MILLENET, ANDRÉ. *Geneva.* Master about 1735–62.

MILLENET, DANIEL. Clock-watch with alarm, about 1630.

MILLENET, JACOB. *Geneva,* about 1755–74.

MILLER, —. *Lurgan, Ireland.* Maker of a curious clock in which the hour was uttered by a human figure, as appears from the journal of the Rev. John Wesley, in a clear articulate voice, 1762.

MILLER, AARON. *Elizabethtown, New Jersey, U.S.A.,* 1747.

MILLER, ABRAHAM. *Easton, U.S.A.,* 1810–30.

MILLER, CHAS. *Aldgate Within,* 1816–25.

MILLER, EDWARD, son of Peter. *London.* C.C. 1724–55.

MILLER, FRED. *38 Greek St.* Card, British Museum, 1797.

MILLER, GEO. *Gateshead,* 1770.

MILLER, JAMES. *Port Glasgow,* 1820–38.

MILLER, JOHN. C.C. 1674; lantern clock, dolphin frets, inscribed 'John Miller, Showe Lane'; Fromanteel in 1665 speaks of one Miller as taking many apprentices.

MILLER, JOSEPH. C.C. 1728; Jas. Wood apprenticed to him in 1738.

MILLER, PETER. C.C. 1681.

MILLER, RALPH. C.C. 1697.

MILLER, THOS. *London.* Maker of a pair-case watch, outer case tortoise-shell, painted dial, h.m., 1764; another, Dutch style, 1780.

MILLER, WM. JAS. *Ludgate St.,* 1760.

MILLER, WILLIAM. *London.* Apprenticed 1735, C.C. 1743–46.

MILLERET, W. Extra small watch, gold case, enamelled with a rose.

MILLET, WILLIAM. C.C. 1714.

MILLETT, EDWARD. C.C. 1680.

MILLETT, THOMAS. *London.* Apprenticed 1695–1734 C.C.

MILLIG, MICHAEL. *Southwark,* 1734.

MILLIGAN, ANDREW. *Ayr.* a. 1769–1801. Watch.

MILLINGTON, JOHN. *London.* a. 1756–72. Watch.

MILLINGTON, THOMAS. *31 Gutter Lane, Cheapside,* 1760–69; watch, brass cases, outer one *repoussé* and gilt.

MILLINGTON, THOMAS. *33 Wapping,* 1790.

MILLINGTON & LANCASHIRE. *London.* Watch, 1768; watch, signed 'Millington Salop', 1780.

MILLION, WILLIAM. *Blackfriars.* C.C. 1671.

MILLIS, MICHAEL. *London.* Apprenticed 1727, C.C. 1736–52.

MILLÖG, MARK ANTON. *Vienna.* Court clockmaker working in English style, died 1728.

MILLON, DANIEL. *London.* C.C. 1712–31.

MILLOT, P. 'Horloger du Roy, rue du Bac, Paris', 1764–72.

MILLS, —. *Gloucester.* Long-case clock, about 1780.

MILLS, DANIEL. *London.* C.C. 1796.

MILLS, EDWARD. *Liverpool,* 1796–1829.

MILLS, GEORGE. Long-case clock, 'George Mills, de Sunderland, fecit', about 1710.

MILLS, GEORGE. *141 Goswell St.,* 1825.

MILLS, JERE. Apprenticed in 1676 to Jno. Miller, C.C.

MILLS, RALPH. Apprenticed to Charles Gretton, and turned over to Cuthbert Lee; C.C. 1697.

MILLS, RICHARD. *Edinburgh.* Apprenticed to Humphrey Mylne; made a freeman of the Incorporation, 1678; his essay being, 'Ane clock watch and luminary, with the further addition of a lock and key'; declined the office of 'box-master' or treasurer in 1703; died 1705; lantern clock, signed 'Humphrey Mills, Edinburgh, 1685'. "Stolen out of a house near the West Port on the 19th, a gold watch with a steel chain and a sha-green case. Whoever can bring the said watch to Richard Mills, watchmaker in Edinburgh, shall have two guineas reward" (*Edinburgh Gazette,* 1695).

MILLS, ROBERT. *141 Ratcliff Highway*, 1790–94.

MILLS, ROBERT. *London.* Apprenticed 1809, C.C. 1838.

MILLS, THOMAS, in *Shoe Lane.* C.C. 1652; maker of lantern clock with dolphin frets; another example, inscribed 'Tho. Mills, Soe Lane, Londini', 1648–60.

MILLS, THOMAS. *London.* Watch, h.m., 1762.

MILLS, THOMAS & SON. *26 Red Lion St., Clerkenwell*, 1812–18; *91 Bishopsgate Without*, 1823.

MILLS, WM., same address, 1809–18.

MILNE, ALEXANDER. *Aberdeen*, 1820–37.

MILNE, GEORGE. *Edinburgh*, 1725–54.

MILNE, HUMPHREY. *Edinburgh*, 1660. Died 1692; a fine maker; lantern and long-case clock; lantern clock Glasgow Art Galleries. Also MILLS and MYLNE.

MILNE, JAMES. *St. Ninians*, 1761–84.

MILNE, RICHARD. *Edinburgh.* Apprenticed 1661, died 1710.

MILNER, HENRY. *7 Vere St., Oxford St.*, 1815.

MILNER, THOMAS. *London.* Long-case clocks, some inscribed 'Thomas Millner', 1740–70.

MILNER, THOMAS, son of THOMAS. *London.* Apprenticed 1754, C.C. 1763–72.

MILTON, G. D. *29 Marylebone St., Golden Sq.* Card, British Museum, 1802.

MILTON, THOMAS. *London.* Apprenticed 1767, C.C. 1777–1804.

MILWARD, —. *Hammersmith*, about 1790. C.C. 1824.

MILWARD, GEO. *2 Little Brook St.*, 1806–15.

MILWARD, WILLIAM. *London*, 1729. Watch case maker.

MIMESS, R. *Woolwich*, 1816.

MINCHIN, J. *Moreton-in-Marsh*, 1799–1821, afterwards at *Stow-on-the-Wold.*

MINCHINALE, WILLIAM. C.C. 1701.

MINCHINER, SAML. *London*, Long-case clock, about 1810.

MINET, —. *Paris*, 1807–25. Mantel clock.

MINOCHE, JULLIEN. *Paris.* Juré 1681.

MINOT, JULLIEN. *Paris.* Juré 1673.

MINSHULL, WM. Apprenticed in 1666 to Nicholas Reeves, C.C.

MINTEN, JNO. *London.* Watch, 1760.

MINUEL, DAVID. Admitted C.C. 1683.

MIRFIELD, ROBERT. *London* and, later, *Dublin.* C.C. 1749–64.

MIROIR, J. A large pull-repeating travelling clock-watch in silver case, outer case of leather with silver mountings, dating from about 1740, signed 'Miroir, London'; a very similar watch of apparently rather earlier date, inscribed 'J. Miroir, Augspurg'; another travelling watch dating from about 1760, inscribed 'J. Miroir, London'.

MIROLI, DENIS. *Geneva.* Watch, about 1720, M. C. Sivan.

MISKIN, WILLIAM SCAMMELL. *London.* C.C. 1819.

MISON, JERE. C.C. 1698.

MISPLACE, R. *Searle St., Lincoln's Inn Fields*, 1775–88.

MITCHELL, ALEXANDER. *Glasgow*, 1820.

MITCHELL, ARTHUR. *Dorchester.* Born 1701, died 1761; clock; in partnership with Mariane Viet.

MITCHELL, BARWISE. *Cockermouth*, 1820.

MITCHELL, CHAS. *84 Tower Hill.* Watch, 1822.

MITCHELL, GEORGE, & ROLLIN ATKINS. *Bristol, U.S.A.*, 1825–37. Looking-glass clocks.

MITCHELL, HY., f. of *New York*, 1787.

MITCHELL, JAMES EDWARD. *London.* Apprenticed 1819, C.C. 1829.

MITCHELL, JNO. *6 Cornhill*, 1817.

MITCHELL, JOHN. *St. James's St.* Apprenticed to Jno. Earles, C.C. 1712.

MITCHELL, JOSEPH. Apprenticed in 1674 to Nat Delander, C.C.

MITCHELL, MYLES. C.C. 1640.

MITCHELL, PHINEAS and MOSES WHITNEY. *Boston, U.S.A.*, 1813–21. Watch.

MITCHELL, PHINEAS. *Boston, U.S.A.*, 1822–25. Watch.

MITCHELL, ROBERT. Livery C.C. 1766.

MITCHELL, SAMUEL. *St. James's St.* Repeating watch, about 1745; another, h.m., 1776.

MITCHELL, T. & W. *Glasgow.* Watch, 1820.

MITCHELL, WILLIAM. *Richmond.* Watch, 1804.

MITCHELL, WILLIAM. *London.* a. 1744; watch.

MITCHELL, WILLIAM. *Glasgow*, 1798–1838. Partner in above firm.

MITCHELL & FRENCH. *5 Clerkenwell Close*, 1825.

MITCHELL & SON. *Glasgow*, 1830.

MITCHELL & VIET. *6 Cornhill*, 1768.

MITCHELSON, ALEXANDER. *45 Michael's Alley, Cornhill*, 1769–72.

MITCHELSON, JAS. *Throgmorton St.*, 1753–56.

MITCHELSON, WALTER. *3 Helmet Row*, 1780–1880.

MITFORD, JOHN. Apprenticed to Sir George Mertins, of *Cornhill*, whose daughter he married in 1714, when he was nineteen years old. £200 stock of the Exchange Assurance Association standing in his name, which, with interest, had accumulated to £6,600 in 1883, was then ordered by Mr. Justice Williams to be paid to his nearest relatives.

MITFORD, JOHN. *London.* Apprenticed 1703, C.C. 1710–16.

MITFORD, JOHN. *London.* C.C. 1717–58.

MITFORD, ROBERT. *London.* C.C. 1738, livery C.C. 1766 died a. 1775.

MITFORD, ROBERT, son. *London.* C.C. 1773–78.

MITTEN, FRANCIS. *Chichester.* 30-hour long-case clock, about 1750.

MITZELL, —. *London.* Pendulum watch, Schloss collection, about 1700.

M'KOWN, J. *Colerain*, 1820.

MODEVEG, D. *Malmö*, 1793–1826. Wall clocks.

MODEVEG, ELIAS. *Hälsingborg*, 1773–1824.

MODEVEG, JOACHIM CARL. *Malmö*, 1750. Died about 1787.

MOFFAT, ALEXANDER. *Musselburgh*, 1790–1831.

MOGINIE, SAMUEL. *1 Prince Row, Pimlico*, 1820–42.

MOHLER, JACOB. *Baltimore, U.S.A*, late eighteenth century. Clocks and watches.

MOILLIET, A. & CO. *Geneva.* Watch, 1790.

MOILLIET, DAN. *Geneva.* Watch, 1780.

MOINET, LOUIS. Born at *Bourges* 1768; died 1853. Author of 'Nouveau Traité Général Astronomique et Civil d'Horlogerie Théorique et Pratique'; *Paris*, 1843.

MOISAN, GUILLAUME. *Blois.* Master 1606, died 1645.

MOLE, JAMES. *Birmingham.* Long-case clock, about 1760.

MOLENS, CHARLES. C.C. 1709.

MOLINEUX, THOS. *Rochdale*, 1770.

MOLINEUX, WM. *Rochdale*, 1818.

MOLLARD, JACQUES. *Grenoble*, 1693–1717.

MOLLESON, THOS. *62 Cornhill*, 1788–1810.

MÖLLINGER, CHRISTIAN. *Berlin*, 1754–1826. Complex astronomical clock; astronomical and musical clock, Schloss Museum, Berlin; published description of a clock in the Akademie, showing true and mean time, Berlin, 1787, and 'Kleiner Uhrenkatechismus', Berlin, 1817.

MOLLISON, CHARLES. *Edinburgh*, 1770–87.

MOLTON, EDWARD. *London.* Apprenticed 1766, C.C. 1773, died 1802. Also MOULTON.

MOLTON, WILLIAM, son. *London.* C.C. 1802.

MOLYNEUX, WILLIAM. *Sligo*, 1820.

MOLYNS (MOLINS, MOLLINS), CHARLES. *London*. Apprenticed 1696, C.C. 1709–37; bankrupt.

MONCAS, JNO. *Liverpool*, 1818–36.

MONCRIEF, JNO. Apprenticed in 1688 to Jno. Bellard, C.C.

MONDAY, FRANCIS. *London*. C.C. 1653. Also MUNDEN.

MONDAY, JOSEPH. *London*. Apprenticed 1647, C.C. 1654–61.

MONGIN, DAVID. *Charleston, U.S.A.*, 1743–47. Watch.

MONGINOT, —. *Paris*, about 1680–1720. Clockmaker to the Court of Versailles.

MONK. Small sheep's-head clock, signed 'William Monk Barwick St. John', about 1730.

MONK, EDWD. *171 Fleet St.*, 1793. See MONKS.

MONKES, GEO. *Prescot*, 1770.

MONKHOUSE, JAS. *Carlisle*, 1768.

MONKHOUSE, JOHN. *London*. On dial of clock by Vullin, British Museum, about 1770.

MONKHOUSE, JOHN. *High Row, Darlington*, 1820. Died 1840.

MONKHOUSE, THOMAS. *Duke St.*, fecit, anno 1759. Inscription on the barrel of a fine 8-day long-case clock with high numbered train, end pieces, and all the repeating work pivoted with cocks; on the dial the name Curteen, 1759.

MONKHOUSE & SON. *Carlisle*, 1785–1810.

MONKS, CHAS. *Prescott*, 1812. Also GEO., same date.

MONNÉE, —. *Vienna*. Tulip-shaped watch, Pierpont Morgan collection, about 1770.

MONNIER, JOHN. *38 Southampton St., Strand*, 1812–28.

MONNOT, JEAN LOUIS, L'AÎNÉ. *Paris*. Master 1770–89.

MONRO, GEORGE. *Edinburgh*. Watch, about 1730.

MONTAGU, JNO. Apprenticed in 1641 to Jno. Midnall, C.C.

MONTAGU, T. *London*, about 1760. Watch, pinchbeck inner and shagreen outer case.

MONTANDON, ABRAM. *Chaux-de-Fonds*, 1780–97. Clock.

MONTANDON-JACOT, HENRI FRANÇOIS. *Le Locle*, 1764–1850. Clock.

MONTGOMERY, JOHN. *London*, 1726–49.

MONTGOMERY, ROBT. *New York*, 1786.

MONTJOYE, LOUIS. *Paris*. Master 1748–89.

MONTLOW, CONON. Apprenticed 1691 to Richd. Harold, C.C.

MONTLOW, HENRY. Apprenticed in 1678 to Richard Browne, C.C. 1685; Abraham Acton apprenticed to him in 1691; fine long-case clock, about 1695, inscribed 'Henricus Montlow, Londini—fecit'; another long-case clock, named 'Mowtlow'.

MONTLOW, HENRY. Apprenticed to John Delander; C.C. 1715.

MONTLOW, HENRY, son. *London*. C.C. 1749.

MONTMAIN, PIERRE. *Lyons*. Born about 1576, died 1666 master. Also MONTMAIN-BLACHON.

MONTMAIN, PIERRE. *Lyons*. Born 1612, died 1684. Also MONTMAIN-PEYRETIER & LE JEUNE.

MOODY, CHARLES. *45 Rupert St., Piccadilly*, 1815–25.

MOODY, DAVID. C.C. 1649; gave a silver dish in 1651.

MOOLINGER, HENRY. *Philadelphia*, 1794.

MOON, CHRISTOPHER. *4 Lower Holborn*, 1810. Watch, Schloss collection.

MOON, THOS. *London*. A '¼ wall clock' by him offered in the *Collectors' Circular*.

MOON, WILLIAM. *4 Lower Holborn*, 1815–42. Livery C.C. 1820.

MOON & CO. *4 Holborn Bars*, 1790.

MOORAN, ANDREW. *London*. Maker of clocks, about 1760. See MORAN.

MOORE, —. *Salisbury*. Long-case clock, Wetherfield collection, about 1780.

MOORE, AMBROSE. *Dublin*, 1780–95. Watch.

MOORE, DANIEL. C.C. 1697.

MOORE, E. T. *37 Clement's Lane*, 1823; *8 Prospect Pl., Kingsland*, 1835.

MOORE, EDMUND THOMAS. *London* (*Lombard St.* and *Kingsland Rd.*). Apprenticed 1772, C.C. 1781–1835.

MOORE, EDWARD. *Oxon.*, 1760.

MOORE, EDWARD. *London*. Apprenticed 1723, C.C. 1732.

MOORE, EDWD. *London*. Lantern clock, 1680.

MOORE, F. *37 Gracechurch St.* 1770–75.

MOORE, FRANCIS. *Ferry Bridge*. Long-case clock, about 1775.

MOORE, JNO. *Warminster*, 1780. Long-case clock, about 1800, Mr. C. B. Oliver.

MOORE, JNO. Formerly partner with Handley, *Clerkenwell Close*, then Jno. Moore & Sons; 1824–42.

MOORE, JOHN. *London*. Apprenticed 1736, C.C. 1742.

MOORE, JOHN. *118 Fleet St.*, 1769–75.

MOORE, JOSEPH. C.C. 1690.

MOORE, PATRICK. *15 Sweeting's Alley*, 1806–10.

MOORE, PETER. *London* (*Sweetings Alley*). a. 1756–1811; watches G.M. and Horstmann collection.

MOORE, PETER. M.P. *London*. C.C. 1823.

MOORE, ROBT. *Stoney St.* Long-case clock, about 1770.

MOORE, ROBT. Apprenticed in 1662 to Sam. Davis, C.C.

MOORE, T. *London*. Watch, 1763.

MOORE, THOS. *Ipswich*. The Wetherfield collection contains a striking and repeating bracket clock by him in an ebonised case, dating from about 1720; there are six bells on which the pull-repeating quarters are sounded. An attractive long-case musical and calendar clock chimes the quarters on four bells and plays one of seven tunes every hour, in the arch of the dial is an orchestra of eight moving figures; at Long Melford Church is a fine long trunk dial by him, the case with lacquer decoration. "Whereas Thos. Moore, clock and watchmaker in Ipswich, have for many years observ'd the misfortunes which very frequently happen to pocket-watches of all sorts—viz., by sometimes coming into unskilful hands, &c., and often into the hands of servants (in absence of the owners thereof) they, endeavouring to wind up the watch, have turned the wrong way, and by so doing, they have broke the work (and the like often happens when Juice of Grape Predominate). Therefore this to give notice. That the above Thos. Moore have now made up several curious Silver and Gold Watches (and will continue to do so) so curiously contriv'd, that let the watch be wound up which way they please, either to right or left, they cannot fail of winding up the watch, with more safety than if wound but one and the common way, and are to be sold at very reasonable price. Any person or persons may have the freedom to seeing any of the said watches at his house in Ipswich aforesaid" (Ipswich Newspaper, 1729). At the Horological Institute is a fusee of one of Moore's watches; the device was described by Thiout in 1741, some years after Moore's advertisement appeared.

MOORE, WILLIAM. *London*. Apprenticed 1749, C.C. 1759.

MOORE, WM. Apprenticed in 1693 to Ben Johnson, C.C.; C.C. 1701; fine long-case clock with large seconds circle in the arch of the dial, about 1715.

MOORE, WM. *55 Paternoster Row*, 1775–88; *5 Ludgate St.*, 1793. Watch, about 1790, silver case with crystal back showing the movement, Pierpont Morgan collection.

MOORE & EDWARDS. *4 Holborn*, 1793.

MOORE & GEARING, *55 Paternoster Row*, 1783.

MOORE & STARKEY, *89 St. Martin's Lane*, 1823.

MOORHOUSE, —. *Knaresborough*, about 1825.

MOQUIN, CHRISTIEN. *Geneva*, about 1775–91.

MORALEY, WM. Apprenticed in 1680 to Hy. Child; turned over to Philip Corderoy, and afterwards to Thos. Tompion; C.C. 1688.

MORALEY, WM. *London*, 1828.

MORAN, ANDREW. *Earl St.*, *St. Giles*. This name appears on the disc at the top of an arch-dial 8-day case clock at the Crown, Harlesden, where it is stated to have been since 1740.

MORAND, ANTOINE. *Pont-de-Vaux* and *Lyons*. Born 1674, died 1757; clockmaker to Louis XIV; made clock for Pont-de-Vaux in 1730; magnificent musical automatic clock Versailles.

MORCOMBE, JNO. Made the town clock for Hartland, Devonshire, in 1622–23; 'new made' it 1657–58; the latter entry from the accounts refers, it is suggested, to a conversion from balance to pendulum.

MORE, B. *London*. Watch, 1760.

MORE, JEAN LOUIS. *Geneva*. Watch, about 1810.

MORÉ, JEAN LOUIS. *Geneva*, late eighteenth century–1829. Gold engraved watch, set pearls; musical repeating watch.

MORÉ, JEAN PIERRE. *Geneva*, 1755–71.

MORECAND & CO. *Paris*, 1800.

MORECOCK, DANIEL. *Birmingham*, 1785–1801. Watch.

MOREHOUSE, W. *London*. Watch, 1807.

MOREL, JEAN SAMUEL. *Geneva*, about 1775–91.

MOREL, JOSEPH AIMÉ, son of J. B. *Sail-sous-Couzan*. Master 1789, died 1837.

MOREL, P. *Geneva*. Watch, 1780.

MORELAND, JOHN. Apprenticed to John Pike, C.C. 1738.

MORELAND, JOHN. *London*. Apprenticed 1747, C.C. 1766.

MORELAND, THOS. *Chester*. Watch, 1726.

MORELAND, THOS. *Chester*, 1810–42.

MORELL, JAS. Apprenticed in 1676 to Michael Rose, C.C.

MORET, NICHOLAS. *Paris*, 1544.

MOREY, S. *London*. Lantern clock, 1700.

MORGAN, CHARLES. *London*. Apprenticed 1734–43 C.C.

MORGAN, EDWARD. *London*. Apprenticed 1703, C.C. 1735; died a. 1654. In *Southwark* 1724; in *Clerkenwell* 1752; in *Holborn* 1754.

MORGAN, HY. C.C. 1677.

MORGAN, JOHN. C.C. 1703; long-case clock, inscribed 'John Morgan, Chancery Lane, London'. A Minute of the Court of the Cutlers' Company of the 30th October 1710 runs as follows:—"A peticōn was read of Anthʸ Russell praying to have liberty to prosecute one John Morgan (a watchmaker for fitting up joyneing and selling Swords altho' he served noe apprenticeship to that trade) in the name of this Corporacōn."

MORGAN, JOHN. *Bristol (Broad Ware)*, 1775–1815. Watch.

MORGAN, JOHN. *London*. Apprenticed 1783, C.C. 1790.

MORGAN, JUDE. C.C. 1654.

MORGAN, RICHARD. Petitioner to Charles I for incorporation of C.C. and one of the first assistants, 1629–49.

MORGAN, ROBERT. C.C. 1637.

MORGAN, THOMAS. C.C. 1658.

MORGAN, THOMAS. *Edinburgh*. Apprenticed 1767–1803.

MORGAN, THOMAS. *Bristol*, 1787. Died 1838.

MORGAN, THOS. *Baltimore, Md.*, 1774.

MORGAN, THOS. *Philadelphia*, 1779–93.

MORGAN, WILLIAM. *Southwark*, 1696.

MORGAN, WILLIAM. *London*. Apprenticed 1650, C.C. 1658.

MORGAN, WILLIAM. *London*. Apprenticed 1695, C.C. 1704.

MORGAN, WM. *London*. Watch, 1810.

MORGAN & MILES. *32 Ludgate St.*, 1790.

MORICAND & CO. *Geneva*. Watch, 1780.

MORICAND & DE GRANGE. *Geneva*, 1800–2n. Fine gold engraved very thin verge watch, Chamb. collection; gold engraved watch, M.M.A.

MORICE, DAVID. *London (Fenchurch St.)*. C.C. 1796, livery C.C., 1810–19; watch.

MORICE, DAVID, & SON. *15 Fenchurch St.*, 1804–23; *86 Cornhill*, 1826–36; a gold watch, h.m., 1816, 'D. & W. Morice, Fenchurch St.'; another watch, 1823, 'Fenchurch St. and Cornhill'.

MORICE, GEO. Apprenticed in 1653 to Thos. Eyston, C.C.

MORIER (MORI), G. S. *Vevey*, 1750–66 comp.

MORIFFET, R. & C. *22 Denmark St.*, *Soho*, 1783.

MORIN-MARCHINVILLE, LUC. *Switzerland*. Born 1659, died 1739; alarm watch.

MORIZOT à *Paris*. Watch, about 1824.

MORLAND, —. *17 Red Cross St.*, 1790–94.

MORLAND, JNO. *Smithfield*. C.C. 1734.

MORLAND, WM. *Red Cross St.*, 1780–85.

MORLEY, ROBERT. Hursley church clock, 1808.

MORLEY, ROBT. *York*, f., 1732.

MORLEY, WILLIAM. *London*. Apprenticed 1694, C.C. 1703–08.

MORLEY, WM. Apprenticed in 1691 to Jno. Willoughby, C.C.

MORLIERE, —. Born at *Orleans*. Excelled as a watch-case enameller at Blois, about 1650.

MORNAND, I. *Paris*. Thick alarum watch, hour numerals on enamel plaques, single case covered with leather *piqué*, about 1690.

MORPETH, THOS. *Hexham*, 1725–70.

MORREL, BENJ. *Boscowen, U.S.A.*, 1816–45.

MORRELL, JNO. *Whitby*, 1822–33.

MORRETON, —. *London*. Watch, about 1775.

MORRIS, EDWD. C.C. 1672; assistant 1677.

MORRIS, HENRY. *82 Fleet St.*, 1733–75.

MORRIS, JOHN. C.C. 1799.

MORRIS, JOHN. *Haverfordwest*. 1795 C.C.; long-case clock and watch. Also MAURICE.

MORRIS, T. *68 Bell Dock, Wapping*, 1794.

MORRIS, WM. *King's Head Court, Fetter Lane*, 1780.

MORRISET & LUKIN. *22 Denmark St.*, *St. Giles*, 1793.

MORRISON, RICHD. *15 Cheapside*, 1769–83. "Richard Morrison at his old shop [No. 15] the Three Kings and Golden Ball opposite Foster Lane, in Cheapside, successor to Mr. Stafford Briscoe", card.

MORRITT, WILLIAM. *London*. Apprenticed 1752, C.C. 1769–74.

MORRITT & LEE. *93 High Holborn*, 1816.

MORSE & MOSELY. *Albany, U.S.A.*, 1823. Watch.

MORSON (& STEPHENSON, *98 Fleet St.*, 1760–72).

MORSON, RICHARD. *12 Ludgate St.*, 1775.

MORT, JOHN. *London*. Apprenticed 1738, C.C. 1762.

MORT, RICHD. Apprenticed C.C. 1693.

MORTIMER, —. *Dartmouth*. Watch, 1825.

MORTIMOR, CHAS. *London*. Watch, 1824.

MORTON, SAMUEL. *210 Borough*, 1775.

MORTON & MILROY, 1800.

MOSBRUCKER à *Saverne*, about 1750.

MOSE, JAS. *Litchfield*. Long-case clock, about 1760.

MOSELY, LEWIS. *Liverpool*, 1770.

MOSELY, ROBERT. *London*. C.C. 1818; watch.

MOSELY, WILLIAM. C.C. 1680.

MOSER, ERHARD, son. *Schaffhausen*. Born 1760, died 1820; clockmaker to the town.

MOSER, GEORGE MICHAEL. Born at *Schaffhausen* in 1707; came to England, and in 1768 was appointed keeper of the Royal Academy; died 1783; fine *repoussé* work by him on watch-cases; he was also of repute as an enameller.

MOSER, HENRI, son of Erhard. *St. Petersburg and Schaffhausen*. Born 1805; went to *St. Petersburg* 1827 and to *Schaffhausen* 1848. Died 1874.

MOSER, JOHANNES. *Schaffhausen*. Born 1731, died 1820; town clock; clockmaker to the town.

MOSES, EPHRAIM. *135 Whitechapel*, 1790.

MOSES, SELEGMAN. *London*. Long-case clock, about 1775.

MOSLEY, ELINOR. Elizabeth Askel was bound apprentice to her in 1734; C.C. 1726–34.

MOSLEY, JNO. *Penistone*, 1790.

MOSLEY, MARTIN. *28 Goulston Sq.*, 1804; *6 Bevis Marks*, 1815–35.

MOSLEY, ROBERT, & SON. *113 Fetter Lane*, 1822–42.

MOSS, JOHN. *106 Holborn Hill*, 1825.

MOSS, THOMAS. *24 Ludgate St.*, 1775. Livery C.C. 1786; died 1827.

MOSS, THOS. *Frodsham*. Long-case clock, about 1740; a bell-top bracket clock by him in mahogany case strikes on three bells and repeats the quarters; also a long-case clock made in 1776 or 1778 showing days of the month, age and phases of the moon, and time of high water.

MOTEL, JEAN FRANÇOIS HENRI. *Paris*. Born 1786, died 1859; Horloger de la Marine; eminent maker of chronometers and observatory clocks; used Houriet's spherical spring, and devised cylindrical spring with conical ends; one of the first to employ heart cams in chronographs; succeeded by Dumas; marine chronometer, Ilbert collection.

MOTLEY, RICHARD. *Wapping*. C.C. 1682; long Oriental lacquer case clock, strike-silent, about 1720; long-case clock, ship worked by pendulum, mahogany case; on trade bill inside the case 'Richard Motley at the Hand & Buckle near King Edward Stairs, Wapping'.

MOTT (or MOTH), HY. Apprenticed in 1655 to Jno. Palfrey, C.C.; watch, about 1665, inscribed 'Henricus Mott in Drury Lane'.

MOTT (or MOTH), THOS. Apprenticed in 1648 to Jere. Gregory; C.C. 1656.

MOTT (or MOTH), WILLIAM. *91 Bishopsgate Without*, 1830; *55 Cheapside*, 1835.

MOTT (or MOTH) & BELLIN. *91 Bishopsgate Without*, 1815.

MOTTEUX, SAMUEL. C.C. 1697.

MOTTRAM, JOHN. *Warden Court, Clerkenwell Close*, 1780–94. Large musical clock by him in splendid case designed apparently for some Eastern potentate.

MOUCHOTTE, NICOLAS. *Avignon*, 1742–78. Town clock; made clocks for Orange and Caderousse.

MOUDE (MONDE), DAVID. *London*, 1662 C.C.

MOULDING, S. *London*. Watch, h.m., 1818.

MOULE, JAS. *London*. Long-case clock, about 1785.

MOULE, JNO. Apprenticed in 1679 to Richd. Jarret, C.C.

MOULINIÉ ET BAUTTE. *Geneva*, about 1795–1810.

MOULINIE & CO. *Geneva*. Watch, 1820.

MOULTON, EDWARD. *London*. 1780–1802 C.C.

MOULTON, EDWARD, son. *London*. C.C. 1802.

MOULTON, HENRY. C.C. 1685.

MOULTON, SAML. *210 Borough*, 1788–1800.

MOULTON, THOMAS. *London (Orchard St.)*. Apprenticed 1788, C.C. 1796–1814.

MOUNT, EDWARD. *London (Coleman St.)*. C.C. 1731.

MOUNT, WILLIAM. C.C. 1692.

MOUNTFORD, JOHN. *London*. Long-case arabesque marquetry clock, about 1705.

MOUNTFORD, THOS. *St. Albans*, 1715.

MOUNTFORD, ZACHARIAH. *St. Albans*. Admitted C.C. 1684; "Mountford for mending my master's watch 0 2 0" (*MSS., Earl of Verulam*, 1696); long-case clock, about 1700.

MOUNTLOW. See MONTLOW.

MOURGUE, PETER. *Charleston, U.S.A.*, 1735. Watch.

MOUSLEY, ARTHUR. Apprenticed 1671 to Jere. Johnson, C.C.

MOWBRAY, WM. *Doncaster*, 1770.

MOWLTON, CONAN. C.C. 1700.

MOWLTON, HENRY. C.C. 1715.

MOWRAY, ANTHONY. *London*. C.C. 1766–70.

MOWTLOW. See MONTLOW.

MOXON, J. Skeleton clock at Buckingham Palace, about 1820, inscribed 'Invented by William Congreve Esq., J. Moxon fecit'.

MOXON, JOSH. *Bradford*. Watch, 1780.

MOY, MATT. Apprenticed in 1661 to Ben Hill, C.C.

MOYNIER. *Geneva*. Watch, 1790.

MOYNIER ET FILS. *Geneva*. Watch, 1830.

MOYSANT, JEHAN. *Blois* about 1630. Watch, case finely painted in enamel; skull watch.

MOYSSET a *Toulouse*. Watch, about 1760. Gélis collection.

MOYSER, THOS. Apprenticed in 1653 to Wm. Godbed, C.C.

MOYSSET à *Toulouse*. Watch, about 1760. Mons. E. Gélis.

MOZE, HENRY. *Shadd Thames*. Clock, about 1740; watch, 1760.

MUCKARSIE, GEORGE JAMES. *47 High Holborn*, 1794. Livery C.C. 1824.

MUCKARSIE (MACKARSIE), JAMES. *London (Holborn)*. C.C. 1784, died 1801.

MUCKLE (MUKLE), BENEDIKT. *Furtwangen* and *Neukirch*. Born 1771, died 1857; musical clock of repute; musical clock, Furt. Museum.

MUDDLE, THOS. *Rotherfield*. Lantern clocks, 1700–10.

MUDGE, JNO. *London*. Long-case clock, about 1800, Wetherfield collection; regulator, about 1830.

MUDGE, THOMAS. *Fleet St.* A celebrated maker; born 1715, died 1794.

MUDGE & DUTTON. *148 Fleet St.*, 1759–90. Reid mentions an equation clock they made for General Clerk. Many fine cylinder watches by them exist. The partnership continued until Mudge's death.

MUGNIER, C. Horloger du Roy, *Paris*. Artistic watches, Breguet style, about 1820.

MUIRHEAD, JAMES *Glasgow*, 1817–41. Watchmaker to the Queen; duplex centre seconds movement, Ilbert collection.

MUKLÉ, ANTHON. *Stockholm*, 1784–1815. Wooden clock; long-case clock; cuckoo clock Nord. Museum.

MULFORD, JOHN. *Cursitor's Alley*. Died while warden C.C. 1748.

MULFORD, JOHN. *London*. C.C. 1716–29.

MULFORD, JOHN, son. *London*. Apprenticed 1736, C.C. 1748–54.

MULFORD, WM. Apprenticed in 1682 to Jno. Norcott, C.C.

MULGRAVE, GEO. *London*. Watch, 1800.

MULLER, ANDREAS. Clock, Soltykoff collection, about 1570.

MULLER, ANDREAS. *Dresden*, 1638. Died 1653; court clock; clock M.M.A.

MULLER, CHRISTOPH. *Augsburg*. Clock, about 1660.

MULLER, GEORG. *Basle*, 1763; *Paris*, 1793–95. Kleinuhrmacher.

MULLER, JOHAN CONRAD. Clock, about 1705.

MULLER, JOHANN HEINRICH. *Cassel*, 1672. Died 1738; court clock; dial Old Ashmolean Museum.

MULLIKEN, SAMUEL. *Newburyport, U.S.A.*, 1740–56; then JONATHAN, then SAML., at *Salem*.

MULLINEUX, THOS. Apprenticed in 1693 to Edwd. Boone, C.C.

MUNCASTER, *Lancaster*: THOS., 1797–1830; WM., 1806, f.; JNO., 1806, f.

MUNCASTER, JNO. *Ulverstone*, 1818.

MUNCASTER, JOHN. *Stricklandgate, Kendal*, 1820.

MUNCASTER, WILLIAM. *Whitehaven*, 1820.

MUNDAY, THOS. Apprenticed in 1688 to Jno. Benson; C.C. 1692.

MUNDAY, WILLIAM. *London*. Apprenticed 1740, C.C. 1747.

MUNDAY, WM. C.C., in 1734 he worked for Marshall.

MUNDEN, FRANCIS. C.C. 1653.

MUNDEN, FRANCIS. *London*. Apprenticed 1663, C.C. 1670.

MUNKERSON, DAVID. *Edinburgh*. Apprenticed to Paul Romieu the younger and admitted a free 'knock-maker' in 1712, his essay being a watch movement.

MUNGER, A. *Auburn, U.S.A.*, 1825.

MUNIER, PHILIPPE FRANÇOIS. *Geneva*, about 1775–91.

MUNRO, JOHN. *Charleston, U.S.A.*, 1785. Previously *Edinburgh* and *London*.

MUNRO, NATHANIEL. *Boston, U.S.A.*, about 1810.

MUNROE, WM. *Edinburgh*. Long-case clock with dead-beat escapement, about 1800.

MUNROE & WHITNEY. *Concord, Mass.*, 1805–25.

MUNSLOW, JOHN. *London*. Apprenticed 1792, C.C. 1799.

MURDOCH, JAMES, & SON. *Ayr*, 1820–50.

MURGATROYD, FREDERICK. *London*. Apprenticed 1809, C.C. 1821.

MURGATROYD, GEORGE. *London*, 1710. Watch.

MURPHY, JAMES. *Boston, U.S.A.*, 1803–06. Watch.

MURPHY, JOHN. *Northampton*, 1775.

MURPHY, P. *Dublin*. Watch, 1797.

MURRAY, DAVID. *Edinburgh*. Born 1755, died 1832.

MURRAY, JAMES. A celebrated chronometer and watch maker who carried on business at Cornhill from about 1814; livery C.C. 1817; one Strahan seems to have been in partnership with him at *19 Sweeting's Alley*, from about 1816 till about 1825. James Weddell, in his "Voyage towards the South Pole in 1822–4", stated: "Of chronometers I had one of eight days, No. 820, made by Jas. Murry; one of two days by Murry and Strachan, No. 403; one of twenty-four hours, also made by Murry; and they all performed sufficiently well to recommend the makers for their very improved mechanism in this important art." After the Royal Exchange was destroyed by fire in 1838 James Murray carried on a successful business at 30 *Cornhill*; he was succeeded by his two sons JAMES and JOHN.

MURRAY, T. *London*. Watch, Schloss collection, about 1780.

MURRAY, WM. *Edinburgh*, 1712.

MUSGRAVE, G. *Taunton*, 1770.

MUSGROVE, RICHARD. *London*. C.C. 1818.

MUSHIN (MUSHAM), JOHN. *London*. C.C. 1768.

MUSKET, JNO. *Prescot*, 1770.

MUSSARD, DANIEL (*Genevese*). C.C. 1686.

MUSGRAVE, RICHARD. *Wigton*, 1800–42.

MUSSON, F. *Paris*, 1782–95.

MUSTON & GATH. *Bristol*, 1796–1844.

MUT, GERARD. *Frankfort*. Watch, Vienna Treasury, with train wheels quadrangular and pentagonal, about 1670.

MUYTER, JAN DE. *Haarlem*, 1755–82; *Amsterdam*, 1785.

MYDDLETON. See MIDDLETON.

MYERS, HY. *164 Ratcliff Highway*, 1804.

MYERS, JOHN, f. of York, 1778; in *London* at *255 Borough* till 1804; long-case clock by him, V. & A.

MYERS, JOHN. *255 High Holborn*, 1790.

MYERS, MOSES. *152 Regent St.*, 1830.

MYLNE, HUMPHREY. *Edinburgh*. Admitted as a locksmith and knockmaker 1647; made a clock for Magdalen Chapel, Cowgate, the meeting-place of the Incorporation of Hammermen, in 1666, died about 1690.

MYNUEL, —. *Paris*. Clock, V. & A., 1700; another, Wallace collection.

MYRMECIDES, —. *Paris*, about 1530. Thought by Dubois to be the inventor of cruciform watches.

MYSON, JEREMIAH. C.C. 1698–1708.

NADAULD, W. R. *White Hart Court, Lombard St.*, 1819–33.

NADAULD, WM. *129 Houndsditch*, 1804–20.

NAGEL, ADRIEN. *Vienna*. A fine maker; made first pendulum clock for Town Hall; died 1710 aged 86.

NAISH, JAS. *London*. Clock, about 1770.

NAIZON, FRANCIS. *42 Poultry*, 1780–85.

NANGLE, NATHANIEL. *Bristol*, 1761. Died 1793. Watch.

NANTA, J. *Leuswarden*, about 1680.

NAPTON, WM. Apprenticed in 1688 to Edwd. Engs, senr., C.C.

NARDIN, ULYSSE. *Neuchâtel*. Born 1823, died 1876.

NARNEY, JOSEPH. *Charleston, U.S.A.*, 1753–61. Watch.

NASH, GEORGE, brother. *London*. Apprenticed 1794, C.C. 1810; watch.

NASH, HENRY RICHARD. *London*. Apprenticed 1803, C.C. 1826.

NASH, JNO. C.C. 1667.

NASH, SAMUEL. *11 Broadway, Blackfriars*, 1790–94.

NASH, THOMAS. C.C. 1717; clock, 'Tho. Nash, Salop', about 1770.

NASH, THOMAS, son of Thomas. *London (Jewin St.)*. C.C. 1768.

NASH, WILLIAM. *Bridge (Canterbury)*, 1762. Died 1794; watch movement, Ilbert collection.

NASH, WILLIAM STRUDWICK, son of Samuel. *London*. Apprenticed 1789, C.C. 1810; watch.

NASH, WM. Oval watch, metal case, about 1605.

NASH, WM. Apprenticed in 1663 to Thos. Birch, C.C.

NATHAN, HENRY. *Ratcliff Highway;* C.C. 1673; maker of long-case clocks, 1673–1700.

NAU, GEORGE. C.C. 1675.

NAU, RICHARD. C.C. 1661.

NAUDEY, FRANCIS. *59 Dean St., Soho*, 1842.

NAUTA, GYSBARTUS J. *Leeuwarden*, 1718. Died a. 1757; long-case clock.

NAUTA, JACOBUS. *Leeuwarden*, 1685. Maker of repute; table clock; fine pair-case gold engraved watch, Ilbert collection.

NAWE, FRANÇOIS, 'at London'. Watch, late sixteenth century.

NAYLOR, CHARLES. *Liverpool*, about 1770.

NAYLOR, J. Astronomical clock by 'Ion Naylor, near Namptwich, Cheshire', about 1725; another astronomical clock by him is at the Cluny Museum, Paris.

NAZE, JEAN. *Lyons*. Apprenticed about 1545, died 1581; maker of repute; hexagonal table clock Petit Palais, and square table clock. *v.* JEAN.

NEALE, JOHN. *Leadenhall St.*, 1743–59. In 1744 he obtained a patent for a 'Quadrantal planetarian'.

NEALE, MICHAEL. *London*. Apprenticed 1810, C.C. 1825.

NEALE, THOS. Apprenticed in 1655 to Joseph Quash, C.C.

NEAT, J. *40 Duke St., Manchester Sq.*, 1817.
NEATE, WM. *3 Sweeting's Alley*, 1817.
NEEDHAM, BENJAMIN. C.C. 1709.
NEEDHAM, CHARLES. *55 Piccadilly*, 1825.
NEEDHAM, GEORGE, son of James. *London*. C.C. 1790.
NEEDHAM, JAMES. *London* (*Lambeth Hill*). Apprenticed 1735, C.C. 1746–73.
NEEDHAM, JAS. *Fleet Lane*. C.C. 1734.
NEEDHAM, JNO. Apprenticed in 1691 to Richd. Parsons, C.C.
NEEDHAM, ROBT. *56 Piccadilly*, 1793.
NEEDHAM, THOMAS. *London*. Apprenticed 1745, C.C. 1756.
NEGUS, WILLIAM. *London*. Apprenticed 1780; C.C. 1787, died 1807.
NEIGHBOUR, WILLIAM. C.C. 1685, apprenticed to Ahasuerus Fromanteel, junr., and turned over to Benjamin Graves.
NEILD, J. *4 Upper Thames St.*, 1788.
NEILD, JAMES. *4 St. James St.*, 1755–94.
NEILL, JOHN. *Glasgow*, 1627–49.
NEILL, ROBERT. *High St., Belfast*. Succeeded John Knox in 1816.
NEISER, AUGUSTINE. *Philadelphia*, 1739–80.
NELMES, ROBERT. *21 Whiskin St.*, 1827.
NELMES, ROBERT. *London*. C.C. 1717.
NELSON, H. *London*. Watch, 1799.
NELSON, JAMES. Apprenticed to Oswald Durant, 1638; admitted C.C. 1645; maker of an astronomical watch in Guildhall Museum.
NELSON, JOHN. Apprenticed to Daniel Stevens and turned over to Daniel Quare; C.C. 1697.
NELSON, ROBERT. C.C. 1698.
NELSON, THOMAS. *London*. Apprenticed 1764, C.C. 1779.
NELSON, WM. *Liverpool*, 1775.
NEMES, JOHN. *Queen St.* C.C. 1724.
NEMES, ROBERT, son. *London*. Apprenticed 1702, C.C. 1717–45.
NEMES, ROBT. Apprenticed to Bart. Powell 1669; C.C. 1667.
NERIAULT, JEAN AUGUSTE. *Paris*. Juré 1748.
NERRY, JNO. *London*. A watch by him, Guildhall Museum, about 1730.
NESBITT, GEORGE. *Sunderland*, 1820.
NETHERWOOD, JOB. Apprenticed in 1686 to Clem Forster, C.C.
NETTER, ROBT. Apprenticed in 1681 Jno. Winn, C.C.
NETTMAN, DIETRICH HEINRICH. *Cassel*, 1767–84. Court clock; clock, Cassel Landes Museum.
NEUÉ, HEN. *Strand*, about 1740
NEUMANN, PETER. *Prague*, about 1688. Early pillar type long-case pendulum clocks.
NEUREN, D. (also spelt Neveren and Neweren). *London*. Maker of verge watches, 1760–90.
NEUWERS, MICHAEL. Made a clock for the Earl of Shrewsbury, 1599. See NOUWEN.
NEVE, HENRY. *Strand*, about 1700–05.
NEVE, JOHN, 'in ye Strand'. Basket top bracket clock, about 1680.
NEVE (NEUE), HENRY. *London* (*Strand*), about 1700–52. Bracket clock, illuminated Cec. & Web.; gold *repoussé* watch.
NEVILL, GEO. Apprenticed in 1653 to Wm. Comfort, C.C.
NEVILL, JOHN. *London* (*Clerkenwell*). Apprenticed 1774, C.C. 1783–1812.
NEVILL, THOMAS, son. *Bristol*, 1781–1818.
NEVILLE, J. *London*. Watch, about 1704.
NÉVIR, GEORG. *Berlin*, 1763. Died about 1815.

NEWAD, W. *London*. Watch, 1760.
NEWBALD, JAMES, f., *York*, 1830.
NEWBERRY, JAMES. *Annapolis, U.S.A.*, 1748. Watch.
NEWBERRY, JAMES W. *Philadelphia*, 1819–25.
NEWBROUGH, JEREMIAH. *Grays Inn*. Maker of long-case clocks, 1700–10.
NEWBY, JAS. *Kendal*, 1785.
NEWBY, JOHN. *3 Judd St.*, 1825.
NEWBY, WM. *Kendal* 1770.
NEWCOMB, JOSEPH. Livery C.C. 1810.
NEWELL, JNO. Apprenticed in 1681 to Robt. Doore, C.C.
NEWELL, THOMAS. *Sheffield, U.S.A.*, 1809–20.
NEWELL, WILLIAM. Livery C.C. 1810.
NEWELL, WILLIAM. *London*. Apprenticed 1747, C.C. 1754.
NEWLAND, AB. *London*. Watches, 1813–25.
NEWLOVE, JNO. *York*, f., 1823–30.
NEWMAN, CHARLES. *London*. Apprenticed 1783, C.C. 1794.
NEWMAN, EDWARD. *London*, about 1820.
NEWMAN, JOHN. *49 Lombard St.*, 1775–83.
NEWMAN, JOHN. *17 Piccadilly*, 1804–25. Livery C.C. 1810.
NEWMAN, JOHN ADDISON. *London* (*Bartholomew Close*). C.C. 1790, livery C.C. 1808, died 1820.
NEWMAN, JOSEPH. *30 Great Alie St.*, 1790.
NEWMAN, NAT. Apprenticed in 1694 to Hy. Merryman, C.C.; *Broad St.* in 1734.
NEWMAN, RICHARD. *Lynn*. Watch, shagreen case, about 1750.
NEWMAN, ROBERT. *London*. Clock, 1700.
NEWMAN, ROBERT. *London* (*Clerkenwell*). Apprenticed 1792, C.C. 1800.
NEWMAN, THOMAS. *London*. Apprenticed 1705, C.C. 1713.
NEWMAN, THOMAS. *London*. Apprenticed 1782, C.C. 1790.
NEWNHAM, NATHANIEL. C.C. 1703.
NEWSAM, BARTHOLOMEW. *Strand*. Appointed in 1572, clockmaker to Queen Elizabeth, in succession to Nicholas Urseau.
NEWSAM, JNO. *York*, f., 1568–98.
NEWSHAM, RICHARD. *Liverpool*. Calendar watch, 1791.
NEWSHAM, WM. *Clerkenwell Close*, 1765–93.
NEWSOM, THOS. *London*. Watch, 1828.
NEWSON, JNO. *Basinghall*. C.C. 1734.
NEWSON, JOHN. *London*. Apprenticed 1796, C.C. 1805–14.
NEWSTEAD, CHRIS. *York*, f., 1797.
NEWTON, GEORGE, *London*, about 1680.
NEWTON, HERBERT. Apprenticed in 1663 to Thos. Wheeler, C.C.
NEWTON, JAS. *Red Lyon Street, London*, 1760.
NEWTON, JNO. *10 Great Ormond St.*, 1788–1815.
NEWTON, JOHN. *London*. C.C. 1732.
NEWTON, JOHN. *76 Lamb's Conduit St.*, 1788–1810.
NEWTON, JONATHAN. *London* (*Red Lion St., Clerkenwell*). C.C. 1784.
NEWTON, RICHARD. *London*. Apprenticed 1684, C.C. 1695–1706.
NEWTON, THOMAS. *London*. 1664 C.C.
NEWTON, THOMAS. *Fenchurch St.*, 1753–56.
NEWTON, WILLIAM. *East Smithfield*. C.C. 1685.
NIBLETT, HENRY JOSEPH. *London*. C.C. 1825. Watch.
NICASIUS, JOHN. C.C. 1632; several times fined for abuse and disrespect, and in 1679 was suspended from being assistant; master 1653–55. Octagonal watch, G.M., inscribed 'Nicasius, London'.
NICHOL, ISAAC. C.C. 1681.

NICHOLAS, —. Lantern clock, inscribed 'David Nicholas, fecit', about 1680.

NICHOLAS, BENJ. Apprenticed in 1682 to Thos. Taylor (Holborn), C.C.

NICHOLAS, C. *London*, about 1700–05.

NICHOLAS, JOHN. *Daventry*. Timepiece with carriage-spring for driving, about 1820.

NICHOLAS, W. *158 Tooley St.*, 1825.

NICHOLAS, WILLIAM. *Birmingham*, 1785–1825. Watch, New York University; long-case clocks.

NICHOLLS, GEORGE. *New York*, f., 1728–50.

NICHOLLS, JOHN. Clock-case maker, *6 Red Lion St., Clerkenwell*, 1804–10.

NICHOLLS, JOHN. *London*. C.C. 1771–88.

NICHOLLS, ROGER. C.C. 1667.

NICHOLLS, THOMAS. C.C. 1707.

NICHOLLS & HARRIS. *Canterbury*, 1815.

NICHOLS, PETER. *Newport. I. of W.*, 1783.

NICHOLS, THOMAS. Apprenticed to Edward East; C.C. 1720.

NICHOLS, THOMAS. *London*. Apprenticed 1766, C.C. 1781–99.

NICHOLSON, J. *Whitehaven*, 1775.

NICHOLSON, JAMES. *London*. Apprenticed 1726, C.C. 1733–37.

NICHOLSON, JNO. *Durham*, 1770.

NICHOLSON, JOHN. *53 Cornhill*, 1816–30.

NICHOLSON, RICHD. C.C.; worked for Dudds in 1734.

NICKALS, ISAAC. *Wells*. Splendid long-case chiming clock, with lacquer decoration, phases of the moon and time of high water in arch, about 1740, Wetherfield collection.

NICKISSON, S. *Lower Ashby St.*, 1815–40; *33 Northampton Sq.*, 1842.

NICKLIN, WILLIAM. *Birmingham*, 1755–74. Long-case clock and watch.

NICOD, DENIS JOSEPH. *Paris*. Master 1770–89.

NICOL, JAS. *Edinburgh*. Long-case clock, about 1740.

NICOLE, JOHN. Keeper of the great clock within the Palace of Westminster in 1371, his wages being sixpence a day.

NICOLET, JACOB LOUIS. Settled in *St. Imier* 1770; made nearly all the parts of his watches, and when he had completed three, rode on horseback to Chaux de Fonds to sell them.

NICOLET, JACOB PIERRE. *Geneva*, about 1775–91.

NICOLET, JOSEPH MARCE. *Philadelphia*. 1797.

NICOLET, MARIE JOSEPH. *Paris*. Master 1784–92. *Philadelphia*, 1793–99; gold engraved watch signed at Paris.

NICOLL, JOHN. *117 Great Portland St.*, 1814–42.

NICOLL, WM. *117 Great Portland St.*, 1790–1835.

NICOLL, WM. JUNR. *London*. about 1825.

NIEDERMEYER, FRANZ JACOB. *Salzburg*. Master 1708–about 1730; pair-case silver and tortoise-shell watch, Feill collection.

NIEDERMEYER, JOHANN CHRISTOP. *Salzburg*. Died 1711.

NIGHTINGALE, JNO. Apprenticed C.C. 1655.

NIGHTINGALE, WM. *Red Lion St.* Liveryman C.C. 1776–94.

NILOE, HANS (Dutch). Maker of a musical clock for James I. In August 1609 Sir Julius Caesar writes to the Clerks of the Signet to the effect that Niloe is pressing for the £300 due to him for the clock.

NIVIANNE, JEAN AUGUSTE. *Paris*. Juré 1743.

NIXON, JOHN. *New York*, 1773. Called himself 'Musical, Repeating and Plain Clock and Watch-Maker, Periodical Titivator, the only regular Watch-Maker (Not of the London Company though)'. *v.* SIMNET.

NIXON, THOS. Oval watch, G.M., about 1605.

NOADES, J. *Strang*, 1775.

NOAKES, JAMES. *London (Houndsditch)*. C.C. 1789, livery C.C. 1794, died 1818; pair-case gold *repoussé* watch, Carnegie Museum.

NOAKES, JAMES. *London (Stoke Newington)*. C.C. 1796–1804.

NOAKES, JAS. Watch movement maker, *34 Charterhouse St.*, 1776–94; livery C.C. 1776.

NOAKES, JAS. *126 Houndsditch*, 1800; *24 Bishopsgate St. Within*, 1810–18.

NOAKES, WILLIAM. *London*. C.C. 1783.

NOAKES (& NYDLER, *129 Houndsditch*, 1790–94).

NOBLE, C. *211 Strand*, 1830.

NOBLE, JAS. *Lancaster*, 1733; f.

NOBLE, JOHN. *London*. 30-hour long-case clock, about 1690.

NOBLE, PHINEAS. Apprenticed in 1693 to Edwd. Whitfield, C.C.

NOBLE, WM. *London Bridge*. Long-case clocks, about 1760.

NOBLE, WM. *2 Cow Cross St.*, 1804.

NOBLE & HARRISON. *35 Fetter Lane*, 1816–25.

NOBSON, JOHN. Apprenticed to Daniel Quare; C.C. 1697.

NODES, JOHN. *Strand*, 1770–75.

NODES, WILLIAM. *126 New Bond St.* In 1790 he wrote to C.C. respecting watches seized on his premises; 1783–94.

NOEL, AYMÉ. Maker of a watch, British Museum, crystal case, dial and outer case of silver, about 1620.

NOEL, SAML. *London*. Watch, Schloss collection, about 1800.

NOHRMAN, ERIC. *Stockholm*. Master 1763. *Norrköping*, 1773. Died 1780; five watches and three travelling clocks, one in Nord. Museum.

NOIR, —. *Paris*. Watch, about 1770.

NOISY, —. *Paris*. Clockmaker to Louis XV, 1750.

NOKES. See NOAKES.

NOLDA, J. A. *London*. Watch, about 1740.

NOLEN, SPENCER. *Boston, U.S.A.*, 1813. Clock.

NOLLORTH, CHAS. *Yarmouth*, 1775.

NOLSON, JNO. Apprenticed in 1689 to Jno. Pilcher, C.C.

NOON, —. Seller of lamp clocks at the White Hart, in the Poultry, 1731.

NOON, JNO. Apprenticed in 1655 to Francis Munden, C.C.

NOON, W. *Ashby-de-la-Zouch*. Good long-case clocks, from about 1800.

NORBERG, DANIEL. *Stockholm* and *Sundsvall*. Comp. 1766–94.

NORCELL, JNO. *London*. Clock-watch, 1681.

NORCOTT, JOHN. C.C. 1681. "Lost on my Lord Mayor's Day, a middle-size Gold Pendulum and Minute Watch, with an engraven Out-case, having a scarlet French Ribon flower'd with Gold and black, the Inner-Case scraped on the backside with a Touch-stone; the name John Norcott. Whoever brings it to Shuttleworth's Coffee House at Charing Cross, shall have 5 Guineas Reward" (1691).

NORGATE, JOHN. C.C. 1712.

NORDAHL, JOHAN. *Skara*. Born 1710, died 1784; turret and other clocks. *v.* NOHRDAL.

NORDBERG, JOHAN. *Lilla Malma*. Born 1730, master 1766, died 1807; long-case lacquer clock.

NORDLUND, ERIC. *Östersund*, 1819–35.

NORDMAN, OLOF. *Stockholm*. Born 1717, died 1782.

NORDSTÉEN, PETER. *Petersburg*, 1760; *Stockholm*, 1764; *Moscow*, about 1785. Watch movement, Ilbert collection.

NORDTSEN, PET. *Abo.* Born 1740, died 1807.

NORDVALL, ERIC. *Sundsvall.* Born 1756, died 1808.

NORLING, JOHAN. *Stockholm.* Born 1747, master 1777, died 1799; court clock.

NORMAN, CHAS. *London.* Watch, 1820.

NORMAN, JAMES. *Poole.* A Quaker, died 1789, aged 74.

NORMAN, RALPH. *Dorsetshire.* A Quaker, died 1730; long-case clock.

NORMAN, SAMUEL. *50 and 51 Prince's St., Leicester Sq.,* 1825.

NORMAND, FRANÇOIS. *Paris.* 1749 master; watch.

NORMAND, LOUIS FRANÇOIS. *Paris.* 1789–1814 juré.

NORRBY, JAKOB. *Visby.* Born 1798l died 1883.

NORRIE, DAVID. *Leith*, 1787–1811.

NORRIS, CHARLES. C.C. 1687.

NORRIS, CHAS. *18 Gracechurch St.*, 1763–94.

NORRIS, CHAS., JUNR. *22 Cheapside*, 1795.

NORRIS, DAV. *London.* Long-case clock, about 1750.

NORRIS, EDWARD, at the *Cross Keys* in *Bethlem.* Apprenticed in 1650 to Wm. Selwood; C.C. 1658; master 1686; full-size lantern clock, balance escapement, dolphin frets, inscribed 'Edward Norris, at the Cross Keys in Bethlem, Londini'.

NORRIS, EDWARD, son of Edward. *London.* Apprenticed 1694, C.C. 1702.

NORRIS, HENRY. *Liverpool*, 1814–29. Watch.

NORRIS, JOSEPH. C.C. 1670.

NORRIS, JOSEPH. *Amsterdam.* Watch, about 1690.

NORRIS, PATRICK. *Liverpool*, 1765.

NORRIS, WM. *Birmingham*, 1770.

NORRIS, WM. *Liverpool*, 1785.

NORSELL, PETER. *Visby.* Born 1728, died 1789; long-case clock and watch.

NORRY, N. *Gisors.* Small clock-watch, about 1620.

NORTH, FREDK. *2 Old Compton St.*, 1816.

NORTH, JOHN. C.C. 1650.

NORTH, JOHN. *Silver St.*, C.C. 1720.

NORTH, L., f. of York, 1623.

NORTH, RICHARD. *Driffield*, 1770.

NORTH, RICHD. *44 Lombard St.*, 1772–1800.

NORTH, THOMAS. *Drogheda*, 1820.

NORTH, WILLIAM. Admitted C.C. 1639; maker of an oval watch; silver case, British Museum, 1620–64.

NORTH, WM. *White Hart Yard, Drury Lane*, 1790.

NORTH, WM. *York*, f., 1816.

NORTHAM, G. Musical clockmaker, *Tabernacle Sq., Finsbury*, 1825.

NORTHAM, J. *46 Greek St.*, 1817.

NORTHAM, SAMUEL. *London.* 1809 C.C.

NORTHAM, SIMON. *London.* Apprenticed 1794, C.C. 1802.

NORTHAM & SON. *49 Greek St., Soho*, 1825.

NORTHCOTE, JNO. C.C. 1681.

NORTHCOTE, SAMUEL. Son of a Plymouth watchmaker, and elder brother of James Northcote, the artist, was sent to London to Mudge to be instructed in watchmaking in 1766; a watch by him inscribed 'Samuel Northcote, Plymouth', about 1780.

NORTHEN, RICHD. *Hull*, 1780–1822.

NORTHEY, J. *Bethlem Court.* Watch, 1784.

NORTHEY, J. *Spitalfields.* Watch, 1794.

NORTHEY, JOHN. *181 Brick Lane, Spitalfields*, 1790–94.

NORTHGRAVES, DENTON. *Hull*, 1822.

NORTON, EARDLEY. *49 St. John St., Clerkenwell.* A well-known maker of musical and astronomical clocks and watches, 1760–94; in 1771 he patented (No. 987) "a clock which strikes the hours and parts upon a principle entirely new; and a watch which repeats the hours and parts, so concisely contrived and disposed as to admit of being conveniently contained not only in a watch but also in its appendage, such as a key, seal, or trinket." In Buckingham Palace is an astronomical clock with four dials he made for George III; a splendid four-train, repeating, and musical clock is 28 in. high, chimes the quarters on eight bells, and plays on sixteen bells one of eleven tunes every three hours. A fine musical clock was specially made for the Empress Catherine. They were succeeded by Gravell & Tolkein.

NORTON, EDWARD. *Warwick*, 1640–about 1700. Clock with 48 instead of 60 divisions on hour circle; watch.

NORTON, GRAHAM. Clock, about 1790.

NORTON, JOHN. *London.* Apprenticed 1766, C.C. 1770.

NORTON, S. *Market Row, Yarmouth*, 1788.

NORTON, SAMUEL. *Fish St. Hill.* liveryman C.C. 1776; 1770–80.

NORTON, THOMAS. C.C. 1720.

NORTON, THOMAS. *Philadelphia*, 1811.

NORTON, W. D. *London.* Watch, about 1820.

NORTON, YELDAYE. *London.* Bracket clock about 1780, so named, seen at the Hague; the name is a curious jumble of 'Eardley Norton', a well-known maker of the period.

NOT, JEAN JACQUES. *Geneva*, about 1775–91.

NOTTLE, JOHN. *Okehampton*, 1770, later *Holdsworthy*.

NOTYAP. See PAYTON.

NOURISSON, GUILLAUME. Reconstructed the Lyons clock in 1660.

NOURSE, ANTOINE, brother. *Lyons.* Born about 1629, died 1715; town clock with his brother.

NOURSE, CLAUDE, son. *Lyons.* Born 1738.

NOURSE, GUILLAUME, son of Guillaume. *Lyons.* Born 1660–1731; town clock in 1706.

NOURSE, GUILLAUME, son of Guillaume (2). *Lyons.* Master 1699–1716.

NOURSE, JEAN BAPTISTE, son of Guillaume (2). Born 1705; town clock in 1731.

NOURSE, PIERRE, brother. *Lyons.* Born 1670, died 1708.

NOURSE, THOMAS, brother. *London (Hoxton).* Apprenticed 1772, C.C. 1784, died 1801.

NOURSE, THOMAS. *22 Beach Lane.* Apprenticed to Edward Avenell; C.C. 1740; livery 1766.

NOURSE, WILLIAM, son. *London.* Apprenticed 1767, C.C. 1774.

NOURRY, JEAN, son of Pierre (1). *Lyons.* Born about 1637–84.

NOURRY, PIERRE. *Lyons.* Born about 1587, died 1677; bracket clock by him or Jean.

NOURRY, PIERRE. *Paris.* Clockmaker to Louis XIV, 1650.

NOUWEN, MICHAEL. *London*, 1590–1613.

NOWLAND, THOMAS. *Philadelphia*, 1806–08. Watch.

NOYTOLON, CHRISTOPHE. *Lyons.* Born 1558, died 1607; Clock with armillary sphere Côte collection, illuminated Vial & Côte.

NOYTOLON, CHRISTOPHE, brother. *Lyons.* Born 1589–1626; died a. 1654.

NOYTOLON, PIERRE, son. *Lyons.* Born 1588–1630; died a. 1646; clock.

NUER, JEAN. 'A. Saintes'; oval watch, about 1600.

NURSE, JOHN. C.C. 1718.

NUTSFORD, WM. *Whitehaven*, 1833.

NYBERG, JOHAN. *Stockholm.* Born 1713, died 1768; long-case lacquer clock.

NYBERG, JOHAN. *Stockholm.* Born 1740, died 1801; bracket and long-case and four wall clocks.

NYLANDER, GUSTAF. *Stockholm.* Born 1707, died 1751; three long-case and two bracket clocks.

NYMAN, JOHAN ISRAEL. *Stockholm.* Born 1726, master 1753, died 1780; watch.

OAKES, JNO. *Oldham*, 1818–32.
OAKES, JOHN. *4 Grub St.*, 1775–80.
OAKES, RICHARD. Shagreen case maker, *86 Snow Hill*, 1775.
OAKEY, JNO. Apprenticed in 1685 to Wm. Dent, C.C.
OAKLEY, WILLIAM, son of William. *London.* Apprenticed 1769, C.C. 1776.
OAKLEY, WM. *39 High St.*, St. Giles, 1804–20.
OAKMAN, JAMES. *London.* Apprenticed 1793.
OAKMAN, THOMAS. *London.* Apprenticed 1798, C.C. 1809.
OATWAY, JOHN. *Torrington*, 1797.
OBERKIRCHER, JOACHIM. *Vienna.* Fine pillar type long-case pendulum clocks; clock in St. Stephen's Cathedral; died 1716.
OCLEE, JAMES. *Ramsgate*, about 1790 C.C.
OFARD, —. Enamelled watch, 'Ofard a Gex', about 1675.
OFFINGTON, SAMUEL. *London.* Apprenticed 1732, C.C. 1740.
OGBORN, SAMUEL. *London.* C.C. 1698–1722; watch.
OGDEN, BEN. *Darlington*, about 1740.
OGDEN, J. *Alnwick*, 1820.
OGDEN, JNO. *Bow Brigg, Yorkshire.* Long-case clock, 1681. A lantern clock, crown wheel escapement, bob pendulum, by SAM. OGDEN, a son of Isaac Ogden, of Sowerby; he was born in 1669 and baptized at Halifax Parish Church; there are numerous entries in the accounts of Halifax Parish Church between 1693 and 1700 of payments to him in respect of the clock; he probably died in 1701, for in that year Chris. Marshall was appointed to succeed him in upholding the clock and chime for 20s. per annum. There was a JAMES OGDEN at Water Green in Soyland, who died in 1715. Two brothers, SAMUEL and THOMAS OGDEN, each carried on business at Ripponden; they were nephews of JOHN OGDEN and Quakers; experiencing trouble with the Church party at Ripponden they shifted, Samuel to Newcastle and Thomas to Halifax, where he carried on business in Crown St.; in the Churchwardens' accounts at the Parish Church, Halifax, is the following: "1725 Tho. Ogden for mending the chimes, 3s."; he died in 1769, and by his will he left his engines, tools, implements of his trade as watchmaker, and stock to John Knight, "he paying for the gold case prepared for an eight days watch of his own making" JOHN OGDEN, son of John Ogden, of Bowbridge Hall, was born 1704 and lived at Sunderland. JANE OGDEN, widow of John Ogden, of Sunderland.
OGDEN, THOMAS. C.C. 1659.
OGSTON & BELL. *Davies St.* Patented a watch with two barrels in 1826 (No. 5,314).
O'HARA, CHARLES. *Philadelphia*, 1799.
OHLSSON, ÅKE. *Lund.* Born 1724, died 1819.
OHLSSON, OLOF, son. *Lund.* Born 1773, died 1844.
OHLSSON, PER, brother. *Lund.* Born 1776, died 1852.
ÖHMAN, ERIC PETTERSSON. *Stockholm.* Master 1759–78; court clock; made musical clock playing on strings and pipes; wall and three travelling clocks; watch movement, Nord. Museum.
OKEHAM, EDWARD. Admitted C.C. 1632.
OKES, THOS. *Oldham*, 1818.
OKESHOT, ROBT. Apprenticed in 1664 to Ralph Greatorex, C.C.
OLDBERG, OLOF. *Stockholm*, 1769–80. Long-case clock.
OLDHAM, JOSEPH. *Liverpool*, 1818.

OLDHAM, THOS and SAML. *Coventry*, 1765–75.
OLDIS, JOHN. *Dorchester*, 1760–80. Watches, Dorchester Museum.
OLIN, JACQUES CHARLES. *Paris.* 1776 master, juré 1778–89.
OLIPHANT, ROBERT. *London.* 1790 C.C., livery C.C. 1811, died 1818. See OLLIPHANT.
OLIVER, —. *Cambridge*, 1780–95.
OLIVER, BERNARD. *Geneva*, about 1750–70.
OLIVER, GRIFFITH. *Philadelphia*, 1785–93.
OLIVER, HENRY, brother. *Geneva*, about 1750–70.
OLIVER, JOHN. *Manchester*, early eighteenth century-1749, when he sold his stock.
OLIVER, JOHN. *Charleston, U.S.A.*, 1764. From *London*; watch.
OLIVER, JOHN, JUNR. *Charleston, U.S.A.*, 1765. From *London*; watch.
OLIVER, SAM. *London.* Watch, 1725.
OLIVER, THOMAS. *17 Fleet St.*, 1780; *2 Brook St., Hanover Sq.*, 1790–1800.
OLLEY & CLARK. *Poplar*, 1817.
OLLIPHANT, ROBERT. *London.* C.C. 1776. See OLIPHANT.
OLLIVANT & MORTON. *Manchester*, 1818.
OLLIVE, THOMAS. *Tenterden* and *Cranbrook.* Master 1777–95; watch.
OLTRAMARE, ESTINNE. Large watch in enamelled case, about 1610. Pierpont Morgan collection.
OLTRAMARE, JAQUES. *Bordeaux*, 1777–about 1800. Watch, virgule escapement and jump secs. with independent train, Chamb. collection.
OLTRAMARE, PIERRE FRANÇOIS, son. *La Rochelle.* Born 1777, died 1851.
OOSTERWIJCK, SEVERIJN. *The Hague.* Worked for Huygens after death of Coster, 1659.
OOSTERWYK, ABRAHAM. *Middleburgh.* Month long clock, Wetherfield collection, repeating on small bell at the half-hour the time struck at the previous hour, 12-in. dial, fine marquetry case, with domed hood, about 1710.
ORAM, MORRIS. Apprenticed in 1684 to Richard George, C.C.
ORANGE, —. *Versailles.* Watch, about 1780.
ORCHARD, ROBERT. *London.* Apprenticed 1794; C.C. 1801.
ORDSON, WILLIAM. In the Guildhall Museum is a verge watch by him, square pillars, enamel dial, the hours represented by letters forming the name 'James Newman', about 1720.
ORE, THOMAS. *Wolverhampton* and *Tong*, 1763–79; then *Birmingham* to 1788. Clock in Birmingham cathedral; long-case clocks and watch.
OREL, THOS. *London.* Watch, 1770.
ORFORD, ROBT. *71 Oxford St.*, 1795–1810.
ORME, JNO. *Lancaster*, 1712, f.
ORME, THOS. *Oldham*, 1818.
ORMOND, DAVID. *Westminster.* Long-case clock, square dial, about 1710.
ORPWOOD, GEO. *58 Bishopsgate Within*, 1810–42.
ORPWOOD, RICHARD. *7 Worship St., Finsbury*, about 1800.
ORPWOOD, WM. *Ipswich.* Clock, about 1790.
ORR, THOMAS. *Philadelphia*, 1811.
ORRELL, JNO. *Preston*, 1818.
ORTELLI, A. *Oxford.* Watch, about 1790.
ORTON, EDWARD. C.C. 1687.
ORTON, JNO. *Manchester*, 1818.
OSBORN, WILLIAM. C.C. 1700.
OSBORNE, T. *Birmingham.* On clocks, 1800–42.
OSBORNE, THOMAS. *London (Ironmonger Row).* C.C. 1767.

OSBORNE & MOLYNEUX. *Dublin*, 1820.

OSGOOD, JOHN. *Boston, U.S.A.*, 1823. Watch.

OSMAN, RICHARD. *London (Southwark)*. Apprenticed 1793, C.C. 1812, livery C.C. 1817.

OSMOND, HY. Apprenticed in 1681 to Sam. Gascoigne, C.C.

OSMOND, JAMES. *London (Whitecross St. and Union St.)*. C.C. 1774–99.

OSMOND, JAS. Apprenticed in 1681 to Jas. Clowes, C.C.

OSWALD, ROBERT. *Market Place, Durham*, 1820–60.

OTHENIN-GIRARD, ABRAHAM. *Chaux-de-Fonds*, 1743–78. Made elaborately ornamented clocks.

OTLEY, THOMAS. *55 Piccadilly*, 1823.

OTTERGREN, DANIEL. *Ystrad*, 1816–46. Watch.

OUDIN, CHARLES. *Rue Vivienne, Paris*. Pupil of Breguet; maker of fine watches, and inventor of a form of keyless work, 1807–25.

OUGHTRED, BENJAMIN. C.C. 1639.

OUGHTRED, WILLIAM. Author of several books on mathematics, including *Clavis Mathematicæ*, Oxford, 1677; Derham speaks of him with admiration.

OURRY, LOUIS. *Paris*, about 1740.

OUTHWAITE, THOS. & CO. *Liverpool*, 1818.

OVERALL, HENRY. *Dover*, 1778–95. Watch.

OVERALL, HENRY. *Daventry*, 1780.

OVERBURY, HY. Apprenticed in 1687 to Thos. Overbury, C.C.; pendulum watch, Nelthropp collection, signed 'Henry Overbury, Rotterdam', about 1705; repeating watch, 1718, signed 'Henry Overbury, Overschie'.

OVERBURY, THOMAS. Brother C.C. 1688.

OVERZEE, GERRARD. *Isleworth* (naturalised). Brother C.C. 1678; maker of lantern and other clocks, 1670–90.

OVERZEE, TIMOTHY. Apprenticed in 1693 to Thos. Whitehead, C.C.

OVINGHAM, —. Watch, h.m., 1819.

OWEN, BEN. *London*. Completed his apprenticeship 1694; maker of long-case clocks, 1694–1740.

OWEN, GRIFFITH. *Philadelphia*, 1811; then JNO.

OWEN, HUMPHREY. *Carnaervon*, 1790.

OWEN, J. S. *Swansea*, 1800.

OWEN, JOHN. *Llanrwst*. Clock, about 1780.

OWEN, JOHN. *Philadelphia*, 1819. Clock.

OWEN, JOSEPH. *10 Helmet Row*, 1800; *243 St. Margaret's Hill*, 1810.

OWEN, RICHD. *London*. Watch, 1830.

OWEN, THOMAS. *London*. Apprentice 1771, C.C. 1789.

OWEN, WATKIN. *Llanrwst*, 1770.

OWEN, WILLIAM. *Cheapside*, 1737–40.

OWEN, WILLIAM. *London (Limehouse)*. C.C. 1775.

OWSTON, MICHAEL. *Scarboro'*, 1822.

OXLEY, JOSEPH, a Quaker, died 1775.

OYENS, PETER. *London*. Long-case clock, about 1730.

OYSTER, DANIEL. *Reading, U.S.A.*, 1820–40.

PACE, JNO. *19 Cock Hill, Ratcliffe*, 1790–94.

PACE, JOHN. *Bury St. Edmunds*, a Quaker. Patented in 1833 (No. 6,506) a night time-piece.

PACE, THOMAS, at the *Crown* in *Fleet St.* Maker of several small-sized lantern clocks, originally with balances, 1630–60.

PACE, THOMAS. *128 Whitechapel*. A well-known maker of bracket and long-case clocks, 1788–1840; watch by him, 1800.

PACK, RICHARD. C.C. 1712.

PACKER, JNO. *Tingewick*, 1780.

PACKER, WM. *Buckingham*. Watch, 1795.

PADBURY. *Dorset* and *Hampshire*: ANDREW, 1730–75; THOS, 1800; JNO., 1825.

PAGARS, DAN. *44 St. Martin's Lane*, 1793.

PAGE, HENRY. *Jewin St.*, C.C. 1713.

PAGE, ISAAC. *Chippenham*, 1760–74.

PAGE, ISAAC. *Cheltenham*. About 1790 C.C.; long-case clock.

PAGE, JNO. *Ipswich*. Long-case month timepiece, about 1750; bracket clock, crown wheel escapement, having the acting parts of catgut, about 1770.

PAGE, JOHN. *129 Strand*, 1775–90; *8 Hind Court, Fleet St.*, 1794.

PAGE, JOSEPH. Apprenticed to Jeffery Bailey; C.C. 1683.

PAGE, LUKE. Apprenticed in 1683 to Ben. Marshall, C.C.

PAGE, THOS. *Norwich*. Watch, about 1750.

PAGE, WM. *17 Liquorpond St.*, 1815–18.

PAGET, AMBROSE. C.C. 1728.

PAGNES, WILLIAM. *Butcher's Row, East Smithfield*. Lantern clocks, about 1690.

PAILLARD, ANTOINE. *Paris*. Master 1776, juré 1782–89.

PAILLARD, BAPTISTE. Watch, 1760.

PAILLARD, FRÈRES (PIERRE ANTOINE and CLAUDE ANTOINE, sons). *Besançon*, 1735–about 1770. Watch and several fine bracket clocks, Vuillemot Museum, Besançon.

PAILLARD, JEAN JAQUES. *Geneva*, about 1775–92.

PAIN, BENJ. Apprenticed 1672 to Wm. Watmore, C.C.

PAIN, DAVID. *London*. Watch, gold-chased case, about 1735; bracket chime clock, about 1740.

PAIN, JOHN TERRILL. *London*. C.C. 1768.

PAIN, PETER. *London*. C.C. 1729.

PAIN, THOMAS. Long-case clocks, about 1760.

PAIN, WILLIAM. C.C. 1729; 8-day clock, brass dial, 'William Pain, Darlington'.

PAIN, WM. *Trowbridge*. Long-case clock, about 1790.

PAINE, EDMOND. *London*. Watch, 1711.

PAINE, FRANCIS. *London (Mile End)*. Apprenticed 1752, C.C. 1770; watch. Also PAYNE.

PAINE, JOHN P. *39 High St., St. Giles's*. Received in 1826 a silver medal from the Society of Arts for a method of illuminating dials, 1826–40.

PAINE, WM. *Trowbridge*, about 1785.

PAIRAS, CHARLES. *Blois*. Two octagonal watches by him, V. & A., about 1605; on one in the Salting collection the name was spelt Perras.

PALAY, LOUIS. *Geneva*, about 1750–71.

PALFREY, JOHN. C.C. 1654.

PALLIER, —. Locksmith, of *Valence*. In 1451 contracted with the town of Montelimart for a public clock.

PALLISER, JNO. *Thirsk*, 1822.

PALLISONE, JNO. *London*. Watch, 1792.

PALMER, B. *21 King St., Covent Garden*, 1830.

PALMER, HY. Apprenticed 1693 to Josiah Ridley, C.C.

PALMER, JNO. Apprenticed in 1647 to Hy. Ireland, C.C.

PALMER, JNO. Apprenticed 1692 to Alex. Warfield, C.C.

PALMER, JOHN. *London*. Apprenticed 1761, C.C. 1769.

PALMER, JOHN. *Philadelphia*, 1795.

PALMER, JOHN. *59 Great Marylebone St.*, 1825–35.

PALMER, JOSEPH. *112 Whitechapel*, 1814–18.

PALMER, JOSEPH GUNN. *London (London Wall* and *Whitechapel)*. Apprenticed 1801, C.C. 1809–25.

PALMER, ROBERT. Liveryman C.C. 1776.

PALMER, SAMUEL RICHD. Gold watch-case maker, *2 Red Lion St.*, 1790–1810.

PALMER, THOMAS. *London (St. John St.* and later *Fetter Lane)*, 1737–62. Watch.

PALMER, THOMAS. *Fetter Lane*. Liveryman C.C. 1776.

PALMER, THOMAS. *132 Lower Holborn*, 1783–1810.

PALMER, THOS. *Sheffield*, 1740.

PALMER, THOS. *Sheffield*, 1800.

PALMER, WILLIAM. *Shoe Lane*. Liveryman C.C. 1776.

PAMER, EDWARD. *London*. Watch, 1802; another, 1826.

PAMPHILLON, WILLIAM. C.C. 1725.

PANCHARD, ABEL. *Oxford St.*, 1765–80.

PANCHAUD, DAVID. *202 Oxford St.*, 1790–1825. Livery C.C. 1802.

PANCHAUD & CUMMING. *202 Oxford St.*, 1806–10.

PANCK, RALPH. Apprenticed C.C. 1677.

PANIER (PANIÉ, PANNIER), JACQUES CHARLES. *Paris (Rue de la Verrerie)*. 1759 juré–1789; repeating watch.

PANIER, JOSSUÉ. *Paris*. Clock, V. & A., 1725; also a watch of earlier date, signed 'Iosve Panier à Paris'.

PANIER (PANIÉ, PANNIER), SAMUEL. *Paris*. 1678 juré.

PANNELL, JOSHUA. *Northallerton*, 1770.

PANNELL, ROBT. Apprenticed in 1653 to Paul Lowell, senr., C.C.

PANTHER, B. *London*. Watch, 1785.

PANTIN, JEAN. *Paris*, 1544.

PANTIN, LEWIS. *45 Fleet St.*, 1770–75; *62 St. Martin's-le-Grand*, 1800.

PANTIN, NICH. Apprenticed in 1651 to Downing, C.C.

PANTIN, ROBT. Apprenticed in 1674 to Wm. Robinson, C.C.

PAPAVOINE, ISAAC (French). *Duke's Court*. Admitted C.C. 1687; maker of long-case clocks, 1680–1710; a fine bracket clock by him, basket top, claw feet; long-case clock, Wetherfield collection.

PAPILLON, JEAN FRANÇOIS. *Geneva*, about 1770–91.

PAPIN, HENRI. *Blois*. Apprenticed 1604, died 1658.

PAPON, LEONARD. Watch, British Museum, about 1620.

PAPWORTH, JOHN. C.C. 1688.

PARADISE, JOHN. C.C. 1718.

PARADISE, JOHN. *13 Newcastle St., Strand*, 1823.

PARBURY. This name on a very fine *repoussé* gold watch case; a watch by Jno. Latham, h.m., 1719, enclosed in a choice *repoussé* case signed Parbury.

PARE, THOS. *London*. Clock, long marquetry case, about 1700.

PARIA, S. Clock, about 1780.

PARIS, —. *Nyon*. 1751 juré.

PARIS, CHARLES. *Pekin*. Born 1738–93; clocks and a writing automaton.

PARIS, JACQUES LOUIS. *Paris*. 1738 master; retired 1790.

PARIS, JAMES. *London*. Apprenticed 1768, C.C. 1778–1814.

PARIS, M. *Rennes*. Watch, British Museum, about 1620.

PARISH, SIMON. C.C. 1723.

PARK, JAMES. *Preston*, 1818.

PARK, JNO. Apprenticed in 1659 to Jno. Bayes, C.C.

PARK, NICHOLAS. C.C. 1641.

PARK, SETH. *Park Town, Pa.*, 1790.

PARKE, BENJAMIN. *London*. Apprenticed 1728, C.C. 1735.

PARKE, JOHN. *London*. Apprenticed 1724, C.C. 1733. PARK.

PARKE, JOSEPH. *Liverpool*, 1734–66. Clock, Liverpool Museum. PARKS.

PARKE, SOLOMON. *Philadelphia*, 1791–1811.

PARKER, CUTHBERT. Apprenticed in 1659 to Wm. Petty, C.C.

PARKER, DANIEL, 'in Fleete St., London'; marquetry long-case month clock, 1¼ seconds pendulum, about 1690, Wetherfield collection.

PARKER, GEO. *Ulverstone*, 1818.

PARKER, HARRY, of *Well St.*, in the *City of London*, watchmaker, is mentioned in the number of the Cutlers' Company for 1788.

PARKER, ISAAC. *Philadelphia*, 1819–25.

PARKER, JAS. *Cambridge*. Watch, 1770.

PARKER, JOHN. C.C. 1674; John Pinson was his apprentice in 1677.

PARKER, JOHN. *Cateaton St.* C.C. 1678.

PARKER, JOHN. Apprenticed to James Delander, C.C. 1706.

PARKER, JOHN. *55 St. Paul's Churchyard*, 1769–75.

PARKER, JOHN. *London*. Apprenticed 1739, C.C. 1747–about 1775.

PARKER, JOHN. *High St., Marylebone*, 1793; *2 Rathbone Pl.*, 1804.

PARKER, MATTHEW. *Dunfermline*, 1786–1830. Musical calendar clock.

PARKER, RICHARD. *London*. Mid-eighteenth century; watch, tortoiseshell outer case.

PARKER, ROBERT. *London*. Apprenticed 1659–76 C.C.

PARKER, ROBERT. Apprenticed to J. Markwick; admitted C.C. 1698.

PARKER, THOMAS, 'in St. Ann's Lane, neere Aldersgate fecit', inscribed on a lantern clock; apprenticed to Wm. Almond in 1658; C.C. 1669.

PARKER, THOMAS. *Philadelphia*, 1797–1811.

PARKER, THOMAS, & Co. *Philadelphia*, 1817–19.

PARKER, THOS. *Dublin*. Watch, 1709; a fine bracket clock, about 1710.

PARKER, THOS. *Warrington*. Watch, 1786.

PARKER, THOS. *37 Berners St.* Watch, h.m., 1786; 1786–1817.

PARKER, THOS. *15 Wilderness Row*, 1788.

PARKER, WILLIAM. *London*. Apprenticed 1703, C.C. 1710; watch.

PARKER, WILLIAM. *London*. Apprenticed 1774, C.C. 1782.

PARKER, WILLIAM. *Philadelphia*, 1823.

PARKER & BIRKETTS. *16 Prince's St.*, 1804.

PARKER & WAKELIN. *Panton St.*, 1760–75.

PARKES (& KING, watch, about 1750).

PARKES, JNO. *Old Change*, 1800.

PARKHOUSE, JAMES. *London*. Apprenticed 1716, C.C. 1734–38.

PARKHOUSE, ROGER. *Richmond, Yorks.*, 1730.

PARKHOUSE, WILLIAM, son. *London*. Apprenticed 1751, C.C. 1763–91.

PARKHOUSE, WILLIAM, son. *London*. C.C. 1791.

PARKHURST, MICHAEL. Apprenticed in 1683 to Jno. Bellard, C.C.

PARKINSON, EDWD. *Settle*, 1775.

PARKINSON, FRANCIS. *London*. Watch, 1788.

PARKINSON, JAMES. *4 Cross St., Goswell Rd.*, 1820.

PARKINSON, MATTHEW. *London*. Apprenticed 1712, C.C. 1719.

PARKINSON, ROBT. C.C. 1637.

PARKINSON, ROBT. *Lancaster*, 1732, f.

PARKINSON, THOS. *Bury*, 1814.

PARKINSON, WILLIAM. *Lancaster*, about 1770, died 1799.

PARKINSON, WM. *Lancaster*, 1708, f.

PARKINSON, WM. *Lancaster*, 1789, f. Clock, 'Parkinson, Richmond', about 1730.

PARKINSON, WM. & FRODSHAM. *4 Change Alley*, 1801–42. Wm. Parkinson and W. J. Frodsham, both admitted C.C. 1802.

PARKWICK, JAS. Assistant C.C. 1698.

PARMELEE, EBENEZER. *Guildford, Conn., U.S.A.*, 1706–41. In 1706 made a wooden turret clock for the church, said to be the first public clock in U.S.A.

PARMIER, JOHN PETER. *Philadelphia*, 1793.

PARNELL, THOMAS. *High St., Bow*, 1815–42.

PARNELL, THOMAS. *Canterbury*. Master 1785–1801; clocks and watches.

PARNHAM, THOMAS. *London*. Apprenticed 1746, C.C. 1758.

PARQUOT, P. *London*. Watch, 1706.

PARR, EDWARD. Apprenticed to Jas. Plumbly, *16 New Cavendish St.*, 1824.

PARR, JNO. Apprenticed in 1692 to Jno. Herbert, C.C.

PARR, JOHN. *Liverpool*, 1805–29.

PARR, THOS. *27 Cheapside*, 1735–75.

PARR, WILLIAM. *20 Strand*. Watches by him from 1790–1808; in 1804 he published a 'Treatise on Pocket Watches'.

PARR, WILLIAM. *Liverpool*, 1781–1810. Clock.

PARRAT, HY. Apprenticed 1678 to Jno. Finch, C.C.

PARRAT, JNO. Apprenticed 1691 to Chas. Knight, C.C.

PARRAT, SAM. *Bridge Row*. C.C. 1736.

PARRAULT, THOS. Apprenticed in 1667 to Ed. Whitfield, C.C.

PARROTT, THOMAS. *London*. C.C. 1702.

PARRY, DAVID, at *Fleet Bridge*. Very small silver watch, Ashmolean Museum, about 1630; brother C.C. 1646; Hy. Ford was apprenticed to him through the C.C. in 1647.

PARRY, FRANCIS. Apprenticed in 1646 to Thos. Laud, C.C.

PARRY, JOHN I. *Philadelphia*, 1796–1825.

PARRY, JONATHAN. Apprenticed in 1659 to Richd. Lyons, C.C.

PARSON, SAMUEL. *London*. Apprenticed 1762, C.C. 1770.

PARSONS, GEO. *Goswell St.* Watch, h.m., 1778.

PARSONS, JOHN. Admitted C.C. 1696.

PARSONS, JOHN. *8 St. Martin's Court*, 1775.

PARSONS, RICHARD. Apprenticed in 1682 to Isaac Day; admitted C.C. 1690; known as a maker of bracket and other clocks at *54 Goswell St.*, 1690–1730.

PARSONS & HORNE. *Castle St., Holborn*, 1825.

PARTEN, WILLIAM. C.C. 1720.

PARTER, FRANCIS. C.C. 1730.

PARTER, WILLIAM. C.C. 1692.

PARTINGTON, C. F. Author of *Clock and Watchmakers' Complete Guide*, 1826.

PARTINGTON, J. *High St., Marylebone*, 1790.

PARTINGTON, PULESTON. *Chester*, 1671–88. Watch.

PARTINGTON, WILLIAM. *53 Paddington St.*, 1815–42.

PARTON, WILLIAM. *Sunderland*, 1820.

PARTON, WILLIAM. *London*. Apprenticed 1712, C.C. 1720, died a. 1757.

PARTRIDGE, JOSEPH. *Bartholomew Close*, 1760–63.

PARTRIDGE, WALTER. *London*. Long-case clock, Hampton Court, about 1700.

PARTRIDGE, WM. C.C. 1640.

PASCAL, CLAUDE, à *la Hage*, on a splendidly decorated watch, about 1650; he worked for Coster and, after Coster's death in 1659, for Huggius.

PASCALL, JAS. *18 Wilderness Row*, 1820.

PASHLER, EDWD. *Bishopsgate St.*, 1774. Large ebonised case, bracket clock, tunes at the hour.

PASHLER, JNO. *London*, 1755. Long-case clock, about 1760.

PASQUIER, —. Horloger du Roy. In 1773 made a hunting watch for 1,200 livres for the Comte d'Artois as a wedding present. This Prince, brother of Louis XVI, became Charles X. See also PIERRE.

PASSANINE, HY. Apprenticed C.C. 1646.

PASSEMONT, ADMIRAL. Designer of equation and astronomical clocks, 1720–50.

PASSEVANT, WM. *10 Red Lion Passage*, 1793.

PASTEUR, JACQUES. *Geneva*, about 1780.

PATCHING, ELISHA. C.C. 1728.

PATENOSTE, JEAN. *Geneva*, about 1775–92.

PATERSON, JAMES. *Banff*. Born 1757, died 1829.

PATERSON, JAMES. *Edinburgh*. Apprenticed 1789–1825.

PATMORE, PETER. *Ludgate Hill*. C.C. 1813.

PATRICK, EDWD. *London*. Long-case clocks, 1690–1710.

PATRICK, JOHN. C.C. 1712.

PATRICK, MILES. *Greenwich*. Cylinder watch, 1790.

PATRICK, THOMAS. *London* (*Haberdashers Sq.* and *Moorfields*). Apprenticed 1756, C.C. 1765–78.

PATRICK, THOS. *Market Weighton*, 1775.

PATRON, DANIEL. *Paris*. Born 1723, died 1792. Gold engraved watch.

PATRON, J. *Geneva*, 1760–80. Watch, globular gold enamelled case, Pierpont Morgan collection.

PATRY, ALEX. *Geneva*. Watch, 1790.

PATTEE, THOMAS. *Mile End Rd.* Livery C.C. 1810.

PATTENSON, ROBERT. *London*. Apprenticed 1661, C.C. 1688.

PATTISON, JOHN. *Halifax*, 1780–1801.

PATTISON, ROBERT. *London*. Apprenticed 1661, C.C. 1668.

PATTISON, ROBERT. Apprenticed in 1676 to Thos. Tompion; C.C. 1688.

PATTON, ABRAHAM. *Philadelphia*, 1799. Also DAVID, then PATTON & JONES.

PATTRU, —. Watch, British Museum, about 1620.

PATY, WM. *London*. Watch movement, G.M., about 1760.

PAUL, NOWELL. Alien, threatened with prosecution for working as clockmaker within the liberties of C.C. 1668.

PAUL, THOMAS. Apprenticed to John Fromanteel; C.C. 1670.

PAUL, WILLIAM. *London*. Apprenticed 1759, C.C. 1766.

PAULE, PHILIP. *15 Cleveland St., Fitzroy Sq.*, 1810–23.

PAULET, JNO. C.C. Watch, V. & A., 1703; another of about the same date, marked 'I. Paulet Without Temple Bar'; long arabesque marquetry case clock, Wetherfield collection, about 1705; travelling clock, about 1710; repeating watch, 1728; in 1730 he worked for Ellicott.

PAULI, WILHELM. *Stockholm*, 1795–1810. Watch, bracket and wall clocks.

PAULIN, LEWIS. *45 Fleet St.*, 1772.

PAULUS, PIETER. *Amsterdam*. Enamelled watch, 'Roman Piety', by Huaud, about 1710.

PAXTON, JNO. *St. Neots*. Long-case musical clock, ten tunes; movement said to be by Mudge, about 1770; watch, 'Jno. Puxton, St Neots', h.m., 1790, probably by him.

PAY, C. *London*. Repeating watch, 1730.

PAY, JAS. *London*. Watch, 1750.

PAYN, JOHN. *Southwold*. A smith, received 6s. 8d. for a new clock from the churchwardens of Walberswick, Suffolk, 1495.

PAYNE, —. *Hadleigh*, about 1720.

PAYNE, GEO. Apprenticed 1687 to Jere. Johnson, C.C.

PAYNE, H. & JOHN. *44 Cheapside*, 1753–75.

PAYNE, J. *17 Foster Lane*, 1794; *18 St. Ann's Lane, Aldersgate*, 1800–25.

PAYNE, LAWRENCE. *New York*, 1732–55, f., 1732.

PAYNE, NICHOLAS. Apprenticed in 1641 to Wm. Daniel; C.C. 1648; was assistant C.C. in 1671; in 1676 Jonathan Boole was apprenticed to Sarah Payne.

PAYNE, RICHARD, brother. *London*. C.C. 1755–62; watch signed 'Richard Payne Junior'.

PAYNE, RICHD. *Carthusian St.* C.C. 1730; watch, 1765.

PAYNE, ROBT. *Waltham*, 1813.

PAYNE, SOUTHERN. *Bridgewater Sq.* Livery C.C. 1766, master 1778.

PAYNE, WM. *East Smithfield*, about 1618.

PAYNE, WM. *62 South Moulton St.*, 1816; *39 High St., Bloomsbury*, 1825; *163 New Bond St.*, 1830–50.

PAYRAS (PAIRAS, PEIRAS, PERRAS, PEZAR, PEZAS, PLAIRAS), CHARLES. *Blois*, 1597. Died 1616; octagonal watch, V. & A.; watch, Louvre.

PAYRAS (PAIRAS, PEIRAS, PERRAS, PEZAR, PEZAS, PLAIRAS), PASQUIER. *Blois*, 1594. Died 1632; watch, Louvre; oval watch with fine engraving, Mallet collection, illuminated Develle; octagonal gilt watch with very fine pierced and chiselled covers, Arts Museum, Prague.

PAYRAS (PAIRAS, PEIRAS, PERRAS, PEZAR, PEZAS, PLAIRAS), SALOMON, son of Charles. *Blois*. Born 1605, died 1684; fine painted engraved watch by him or his son, Stern. collection.

PAYRAS (PAIRAS, PEIRAS, PERRAS, PEZAR, PEZAS, PLAIRAS), SALOMON, son. *Blois*. Master 1657–97.

PAYTON, WM. Watch-case maker, *3 Addle St., Wood St.*, 1790–94; a watch inscribed 'Notyap, London', probably by him.

PEACHEY, JOHN, brother. *London (New St. Hill)*. Apprenticed 1747, C.C. 1755–68.

PEACHEY, JOSEPH. 1759.

PEACHEY, NEWMAN. *12 Dean St.* Livery C.C. 1766; 1760–78.

PEACHEY, WILLIAM. *New St.* C.C. 1727.

PEACHEY, WILLIAM, brother. *London.* C.C. 1754–59.

PEACOCK, —. *Richmond*, 1814.

PEACOCK, FRANCIS. *London.* a. 1776; watch.

PEACOCK, GEO., 'at the Dial behind the Royal Exchange', 1765; *4 Sweeting's Alley*, 1778–81.

PEACOCK, GEORGE. *65 Threadneedle St.*, 1769–75.

PEACOCK, JOHN. *Penrith*, 1820.

PEACOCK, SAMUEL. *30 Old Exchange*, 1793.

PEACOCK, WM. *York*, f., 1789–1832.

PEALE, CHARLES WILSON. *Annapolis, U.S.A.*, 1764. Clocks and watches.

PEARCE, ADAM. C.C. 1664.

PEARCE, HENRY. *London.* Apprenticed 1739, C.C. 1749.

PEARCE, J. *Stratford-on-Avon.* Watch, h.m., 1825.

PEARCE, JNO. *Newgate St.*, 1753–60; Pearce & Newton, 1760–63.

PEARCE, SAMUEL. *Honiton*, 1760.

PEARCE, WILLIAM. Livery C.C. 1787; master 1804.

PEARKES, F. *15 St. Martins Court*, 1823.

PEARNE, WM. *11 Leicester Sq.*, 1793.

PEARSALL & EMBREE. *New York*, 1781–86.

PEARSE, JNO. *Tavistock*, 1760.

PEARSE, JOHN. *Newgate St.*, 1753–60.

PEARSON, JAMES. *London.* Watch, about 1790.

PEARSON, JOSEPH. *New York*, 1773–75. Watch.

PEARSON, MARY. *31 Fleet St.*, 1772–75.

PEARSON, SAM. *Halifax*, 1790.

PEARSON, THOMAS. *Newcastle-on-Tyne*, 1778–1827. Clocks and watches.

PEARSON, THOMAS. *New York*, 1773. Watch.

PEARSON, THOS. *Berwick*, 1765.

PEARSON, WILLIAM. *New York*, 1768–75. Clocks and watches.

PEARSON, WM. *Blackburn*, 1775.

PEARSON & GREY. *George Town (S. Carolina)*, 1768. Clocks and watches.

PEARSON & PRICE. *11 Great Sutton St.*, 1830.

PEARSON, THE REV. W., LL.D., F.R.S. *East Sheen*, 1811; *South Kilworth, Leicestershire*, 1821; author of the splendid treatise on horology which appeared in Rees' *Cyclopædia*, published in 1791 and revised in 1819; died 1847, aged 80.

PEAT, JNO. *Darlington*, 1760.

PEATLING, THOMAS. C.C. 1682.

PECK, EDSON C. *Derby, U.S.A.*, 1827.

PECK, ELIJAH. *Boston, U.S.A.*, 1789. Watch.

PECK, GEORGE. C.C. 1725.

PECK, GEORGE, son. *London.* C.C. 1755, died a. 1792.

PECK, GEORGE, brother. *London.* C.C. 1800.

PECK, MOSES. *Boston, U.S.A.*, 1789–1800. Watch.

PECK, WM. *Keysoe.* Long-case clock, fine Oriental lacquer decoration, about 1750.

PECKETT, JOHN. C.C. 1691.

PECKHAM, HENRY. *Bermondsey.* Patented in 1798 (No. 2,280) the application of a compass to a watch.

PECKOVER, RICHARD. *London (Change Alley* in 1735, *R. Exchange* in 1751). Apprenticed 1700–54; probably took over Quare & Horseman's business in 1733. The Nos. of watches signed by him are known from 6480 to 7377, the series apparently continuing from Quare & Horseman's; repeating watch movement, G.M.; watch M.M.A. with Turkish figures; small bracket clock, Wetherby collection; gilt metal case bracket clock, Prestige collection.

PEDDIE, JAMES. *Stirling*, 1801–50.

PEERS, BENJ. Long-case clock, about 1790.

PEERS, JNO. Apprenticed 1676 to Rob Cosby, C.C. Chester; a noted family of clockmakers from about 1745–1840.

PEFFINHAUS. Oval watch, signed 'Wilhel Peffinhauss', Pierpont Morgan collection, about 1620.

PEFFINHAUS, PHILIPP HEINRICH. *Augsburg.* Master 1683; silver table clock, engraved and set stones, K.H.M.; pair-case repeating silver watch; Dial, British Museum.

PEFIDANT, JEAN N. *Paris*, 1782–89.

PEIRAS. Oval watch, 1590, Garnier collection, signed 'Pasquier Peiras, Blois'; another also in the Garnier collection, about the same date, signed 'Charles Peiras, Bloys'.

PEIRSON, WM. *Kirby Moorside*, 1770.

PELLETER, SOLOMON. *14 Broad St.*, 1775.

PELLETIER, —. *Paris.* Clock, about 1810.

PELLETIER, JACQUES. *Paris.* 1736 master–1789; clockmaker to Louis XVI.

PELLITIER (LE PELLETIER), PETER. *London.* Apprenticed 1729, C.C. 1736.

PELOUX, ANTOINE. *Geneva*, about 1770–91.

PEMBERTON (SAMUEL), SON & MITCHELL. *Birmingham*, 1818.

PENARD, ISAAC. Skull watch, about 1630.

PENDLETON, RICHARD. *London.* a. 1780–1808. Worked for Mudge junr., about 1795 and previously for Emery. Later made fine lever watches on his own account, similar to Emery. Two of these are in the Ilbert collection.

PENFOLD, JOSHUA. C.C. 1695.

PENFOLD, MILES. *115 Newgate St.*, 1769–75.

PENKETHMAN, THOMAS. C.C. 1692.

PENLINGTON, THOS. *Sheffield*, 1770–1814.

PENN, JOHN. *London (Barbican).* Apprenticed 1756, C.C. 1764–76.

PENN, RICHD. *London.* Watch, 1780.

PENN, THOMAS, son of Thomas. *London.* Apprenticed 1769, C.C. 1776.

PENNINGTON, CHRISTOPHER. *Kendal.* Watch, 1780.

PENNINGTON, JOHN, also JOSEPH. *Liverpool*, 1818.

PENNINGTON, ROBERT. Chronometer maker, *Camberwell.* Invented an imporved form of sector, 1780–1816. Worked for Mudge junr.

PENNINGTON, ROBERT & SON. *11 Portland Row, Camberwell*, 1832–42. John Pennington, the son referred to, afterwards succeeded Grohe, at *Wigmore St.*

PENNOCK, JOHN. *Lothbury.* C.C 1638, master 1660; gave a fine house clock of his own make to the Company in 1652; on a lantern clock by him, dating from about 1640, is the address 'Within Bishopsgate'; another lantern clock by him with dial, engraved 'at Petty France Gate in yᵉ Moorfields'.

PENNY, CHARLES. *Bristol,* 1781–1801. Watch.

PENNY, CHARLES. *Bristol,* 1781–1801. Clocks and watches.

PENNY, GEORGE. *Wells (Somerset),* late eighteenth century.

PENNY, JOHN. *London (Aldersgate St.).* Apprenticed 1763, C.C. 1770, livery C.C. 1790, died 1818.

PENNY, JOHN. *Portsea (Hants),* about 1790 C.C.

PENNY, JOHN. *London.* Apprenticed 1787, C.C. 1804, livery C.C. 1813.

PENNY, RICHARDS. *London.* Watches, 1695–1715. "Deliver'd to a carter in Whitechapel to be carried to Mr. Pearson's, at the Warren by Sir Henry Hicks, an old bob clock with John Webster's name on it, which clock was not brought thither. If any persons give notice of this clock to R. Penny of Whitechappel clock maker so as it may be had again shall receive 5s. as a reward" (*The Post Man,* Aug. 28, 1705).

PENTON, CHARLES. *Upper Moorfields,* 1760–75.

PEPIN, —. *Rue de la Coutellerie, Paris,* 1770.

PEPPER, JAS. *Biggleswade,* 1770.

PEPPER, JNO. Apprenticed 1684 to Geo. Ethrington, C.C.

PEPPER, SAM. Apprenticed in 1655 to Thos. Mills, C.C.

PEPPER, THOMAS. *5 George St., St. Martin's.* Livery C.C. 1787; 1776–94.

PEPPIN, SAM. *22 Greville St., Hatton Garden,* 1517.

PEPYS, JOHN. Apprenticed in 1672 to Jno. Harris; C.C. 1680, master 1707; watch by him, British Museum; long-case month clock, 11-in. dial, burr elm case, Wetherfield collection, about 1705; other examples are occasionally met with, 1680–1708.

PEPYS, JOHN, JUNR. *Fleet St.* C.C. 1715, master 1739. "Lost on Saturday night last a gold repeating watch in chased case with an enamel dial plate, the maker's name John Pepys, London, No. 3,470. Whoever brings the same to Mr. John Pepys, at the 'Crown and Sceptre', in Fleet St., shall have twenty guineas reward and no questions" (*Public Advertiser,* April 10, 1744).

PEPYS, PETER. Apprenticed 1680 to Richard Pepys, C.C.

PEPYS, RICHARD. C.C. 1674.

PEPYS, WILLIAM. C.C. 1723.

PERCHARD, MATTHEW. *Cannon St.,* 1753–59.

PERCHARD, PETER. *15 Abchurch Lane,* 1760–62.

PERCHE (PORCHER), —. *Paris,* 1807–25.

PERCIVAL, JNO. *Woolwich.* Clock, 1790.

PERCIVAL, M. *Woolwich,* 1817.

PERCIVAL, N. *36 Old Bond St.,* 1798–1800.

PERCIVAL, THOS. *36 Old Bond St.,* 1804.

PERCIVAL, WILLIAM CHENNEL. *London.* Apprenticed 1814, C.C. 1822.

PERDRA, WM. *London.* Watch, 1805.

PERES, MARK. C.C. 1680; large lantern clock with two bells, about 1700, inscribed 'Marcos Pères', London.

PEREY, ÉTIENNE LOUIS HENRI. *Geneva,* about 1775–92.

PERGAUD, LOUIS CHARLES. *Geneva,* about 1770–91.

PERIER, H. *London.* Watch, about 1730. See PERRIER.

PERIGAL, FRANCIS. *9 Threadneedle St., Royal Exchange.* The first of a family of able horologists; excellent watches and clocks of their make are to be met with; C.C. 1741, master 1756.

PERIGAL, FRANCIS. C.C. 1756, master 1775.

PERIGAL, FRANCIS. Watchmaker to the King, *37 New Bond St.* Hon. f. C.C. 1781; watch, V. & A., signed 'Francis Perigal, Bond St., watchmaker to His Majesty', h.m., 1786; 1770–94.

PERIGAL, FRANCIS, JUNR. *Royal Exchange.* Apprenticed to his father 1778; C.C. 1786; livery 1787. See FRANCIS PERIGAL & SON, below.

PERIGAL, FRANCIS & SON. *9 Royal Exchange* (Francis S. Perigal, junr., master C.C. 1806), 1790–1808.

PERIGAL, JNO. *55 Prince's Street, Soho,* 1810.

PERIGAL, JOHN. *12 Coventry St., Haymarket*; hon. f. C.C. 1781; 1770–1800.

PERIGAL, THOS. *London.* Watch, 1812.

PERIGAL & BROWNE. *11 Coventry St., Piccadilly,* 1794–1800.

PERIGAL & DUTERRAU. 'Watchmakers to His Majesty', *62 New Bond St.,* 1810–40.

PERINOT, ABRAHAM. Known as a maker of long-case clocks, about 1780.

PERINS, JOHN. *193 Strand,* 1750–94.

PÉRISCEL, PIERRE. *Lyons.* Master 1623–65 master.

PÉRISCEL, VINCENT, son. *Lyons.* Born 1624–59. *Geneva,* 1668.

PERISSE, JAQUES LAURENT. *Geneva,* about 1755–72.

PERKIN, R. *55 Tooley St.,* 1790.

PERKINS, EYLUM, of 'Rederiffe, the end of Love Lane'. Apprenticed in 1670 to Jas. Atkinson; in 1682 he was threatened with prosecution by C.C. for exercising the art, not being admitted; he promised to take up his freedom at the next quarterly court.

PERKINS, JAMES. C.C. 1730.

PERKINS, JNO. Apprenticed in 1661 to Sam. Horne, C.C.

PERKINS, THOMAS. *Philadelphia,* 1778–99.

PERKINS, THOMAS. *Evesham,* 1757. Died 1785; long-case clock; watch.

PERKINS, THOMAS. *Pittsburg, U.S.A.,* 1815.

PERKINS, VINEYARD. *53 Dorset St., Salisbury Sq.,* 1793.

PERKINS & SPENCER. *44 Snow Hill,* 1765–75.

PERNELL, T. *London.* 30 hour long-case clock, about 1730.

PEROT, PASQUE. *London.* 1664 C.C.

PERPIGNAN, PETER. *Philadelphia,* 1819–23. Watch.

PERRACHE, —. 'Fournisseur du Roy', *Paris.* In 1752 made a clock with a balance-spring going a fortnight.

PERRAS. See PAIRAS.

PERRAULT, C. Contrived a clock driven by water and controlled by a pendulum; died 1688.

PERRELET, ABRAM LOUIS. *Neuchâtel.* Born 1729, died 1826.

PERRELET, ABRAM LOUIS, son of A. L. *Chaux de-Fonds,* 1760–97. Turret clock.

PERRELET, ABRAM ROBERT. *Le Locle,* about 1750–66. Watch and tool-maker.

PERRELET, LOUIS FRÉDÉRIC, grandson of Abram Louis. Born at *Locle* in 1781, migrated to *Paris* and worked for Breguet; died 1854.

PERRENOUD, F. *192 Brick Lane, Whitechapel,* 1810.

PERRENOUD, FRÉDÉRIC LOUIS. *Ponts-de-Martel* and *La Brévine,* 1761–1801.

PERRET, JEAN JACQUES HENRI. *La Brévine.* 1772–1816; clock.

PERRET, THEODORE. 'Gentil Horloger de sa Majesté le Roy de Prusse, au Locle'; balloon clock, about 1750.

PERRET-DIT-TORNARE, ABRAM. *Le Locle, La Sagne* and *Neuchâtel,* 1630–72. Made church clock at Le Locle.

PERRET-GENTIL, JEAN JACQUES. *Le Locle,* 1750–75. 'Expert horloger en pendules'. Several clocks. *v.* PERRET.

PERRET-GENTIL, MOÏSE. *Chaux-de-Fonds*, 1749–69. Clock.

PERRET-GENTIL, PIERRE. *Le Locle*. First half eighteenth century. Watch.

PERRET-GENTIL, THÉODORE. *Le Locle*. Apprenticed 1748; clockmaker to the King of Prussia; several clocks.

PERRET-JEANNERET, DAVID. *La Brévine*, 1774–1807. Clock.

PERRET-JEANNERET, ISAAC HENRI, brother. *La Brévine, Le Locle* and *Couvet*. Born 1794, died 1873; fine maker; several clocks.

PERRET-JEANNERET, JULES FRÉDÉRIC, brother. *La Brévine*. 1783–1826; a fine clock.

PERRET-JEANNERET, PHINÉE, nephew. *La Brévine, Le Locle* and *Chaux-de-Fonds*. Born 1777, died 1851; a fine maker of clocks and regulators.

PERRIER, PETER. Apprenticed to Jas. Lello in 1660, C.C.; silver watch, the back plate covered with representation of Crucifixion, about 1680.

PERRIN, C. *Paris*, 1780.

PERRIN, JEAN. *Paris*, 1807–24.

PERRING, H. *179 Great Surrey St.*, 1830.

PERRINGHAM, FRANCIS. Back of Exchange, 1790.

PERRON, —. *Geneva*. In 1798 he introduced a lever escapement with round pins as pallets.

PERRON, L. *Besançon*. Born 1779, died 1836; a very fine maker of watches and clocks; designed in 1798 the pin-lever escapement with pin pallets; published 1834 *Essai de l'histoire abregée de l'horlogerie*; in 1819 made the first chronometer in Besançon.

PERRON, RICHD. *7 Worship St.*, 1790–94.

PERRY, HENRY. C.C. 1691.

PERRY, JOHN, son. *London*. C.C. 1691–1725.

PERRY, JOHN ADDINGTON, son of Peter. *London*. Apprenticed 1798, C.C. 1807, master C.C. 1850.

PERRY, JOSEPH. *London*. Apprenticed 1787, C.C. 1814.

PERRY, MARVIN. *New York*, f., 1769.

PERRY, MERVIN. Advertisement, New York paper, 1766, "Mervin Perry repeating and plain watchmaker from London where he has improved himself under the most eminent and capital artists in those branches, has opened shop in Hanover Square at the sign of the Dial. He mends and repairs musical, repeating, quarterly, chime, silent pull and common weight clocks."

PERRY, PETER. *London (Rosemary Lane)*. Apprenticed 1754, C.C. 1763–71.

PERRY, PETER, son of Peter. *London (Aldgate)*. Apprenticed 1777, C.C. 1784, livery C.C. 1812. Watch.

PERRY, RICHD. Apprenticed in 1656 to Sam Davis, C.C.

PERRY, THOMAS. *New York*, f., 1750.

PERRY, THOMAS & MERVIN. *New York*, 1767. Watch; partnership of Thomas with his son Mervin.

PERRY, THOS. *Dock St., New York*, 1749. "Thomas Perry, watchmaker from London, makes and cleans all sorts of clocks and watches. He will import, if bespoke good warranted clocks at £14 they paying freight and insurance, and clocks without cases for £10" (Advt., New York, 1756).

PERRY, THOS. *London*. Watch, about 1790.

PERSIGNY, PIERRE. *Paris*. Circular box-shaped watch of white metal, separate dials for hours and minutes, about 1680, Pierpont Morgan collection.

PESCHEL, ADAM FRIEDRICH. *Dresden*. Born 1711, died 1785 master.

PESCHEL, CARL AUGUST. *Dresden*. Born 1750, died 1812 master.

PESCHEL, JOHANN FRIEDRICH. *Dresden*. Master 1787, died 1831.

PESCHOT (PÉCHOT), —. *Paris (Rue neuve St. Eustache)*, 1807–24.

PESCHOT (PÉCHOT), JEUNE. *Paris (Rue St. Honoré)*, 1810–25.

PETCH, JNO. T. *Huddersfield*, 1833.

PETERKIN, JOHN. *25 Cleveland St.*, 1810–40.

PETERMAN & DEBOIS. Watch-case makers, *Bateman's Buildings, Soho Sq.*, 1800–10.

PETERS, ANDRÉ JAQUES ÉTIENNE. *Geneva*, about 1750–71.

PETERS, EDWD. *Sheffield*, 1770–1814.

PETERSEN, JOHANN G. *Hamburg*, 1801–21.

PETIT, FRANÇOIS. *Paris (Rue St. Denis)*. Master 1768–89.

PETIT, GUILLAUME. Petitioner for incorporation of C.C. 1630; Abraham Lamb was apprenticed to him in 1651; gave a silver bowl to the Company in 1656.

PETIT, GUILLAUME. *Rouen*, 1559. Died 1578; clockmaker to Charles IX in 1573.

PETIT, JEAN BAPTISTE. *Paris (Quai des Orfèvres)*. Master 1781–1825.

PETITPIERRE, DAVID, son. *Môtiers, Neuchâtel* and *Couvet*. Apprenticed 1735, died 1771; clock.

PETITPIERRE, HENRI. *Couvet*, about 1770; *Geneva*, 1780. died 1825; invented many improvements in watch-making tools.

PETITPIERRE, JEAN HENRI. *Couvet*, 1741–56. 'Très expert horloger'; many fine clocks.

PETITPIERRE, LOUIS. *Couvet*, 1794; *Neuchâtel*, 1800–30. Clock.

PETITPIERRE, PIERRE DAVID. *Couvet*, 1775–98. Clock.

PETITPIERRE-BOY-DE-LA-TOUR, CHARLES HENRY, son. *Pekin, Macao, Manilla* and *Batavia*. Born 1769; in 1792 went to *Pekin* with Lord Macartney's mission in charge of the clocks and automata taken as presents.

PETITPIERRE-BOY-DE-LA-TOUR, PIERRE DAVID. *Couvet*, 1769–76. Clock.

PETO, —. *London*. Spoken of by Earnshaw as a capital workman, 1780–1800. Invented a cross-detent escapement.

PETRE, JAMES. *London*. Apprenticed 1763, C.C. 1770.

PÉTREMAND, ABRAM, son. *Neuchâtel*, 1684. Died 1747; turret and other clocks; made clock for the Tour de Diesse in 1715.

PÉTREMAND, JACOB. *Neuchâtel*, 1680–1700.

PETRI, JOHANN HEINRICH. *Basle*. Apprenticed 1686, master 1689–1701; a watch by J. H. Petri of *Heidelberg* Denham collection.

PETTER, CHRISTOPHER. C.C. 1730.

PETTERSSON, JOHAN GABR. *Göteborg*. Born 1788, died 1851; long-case clock.

PETTIGREW (PETTYGREW), JOHN. *Edinburgh*, 1780–1804. Watch.

PETTY, —. *Richmond, Yorks*, 1812.

PETTY, WILLIAM. C.C. 1646.

PEW, EDWARD PHILLIPS. *London*. Apprenticed 1735, C.C. 1778; watch.

PEW, RICHARD GRIFFITH, son. *London*. Apprenticed 1766.

PEWTRESS, THOMAS. *Gracechurch St.*, 1753–56.

PEYTLESS, J. *Boston*, 1796. Clocks and watches. PEATLING.

PEYTLING, THOMAS. *London*. Apprenticed 1675, C.C. 1682.

PEYTON, RICHARD. *Gloucester*. In the composing room of the *Gloucester Journal* is a long-case clock by him, which belonged to Robert Raikes, who founded the journal in 1722 and died in 1757.

PEYTON, RICHARD or RICHARDSON. *Gloucester*, 1743. Died 1774; succeeded by Theophilus James; pair-case gold watch.

PEYTON, ROBERT. *Gloucester*. a. 1740. Watch.

PEYTON, THOMAS. *London*. Apprenticed 1777.

PEZIERES, DOMINIQUE. *Paris*, 1737–57.

PFAFF, JEREMAS. *Augsburg*. Fine table clock by him, which is provided with an alarum, and repeats the hours and quarters. There are, besides the barrel and fusee for the going part, four barrels, four hammers, and three bells, the largest bell serving for the hour and for the alarm; inscribed 'Jereme Pfaff, Augsburg', about 1680.

PFALTY, JOHN WILLIAM. *Baltimore, U.S.A.*, 1802. Watches and clocks.

PFLUGER, —. *Soleure*. Several of this name were town clockmakers from 1600–1850.

PHAREZ, JOHN. *London*. Apprenticed 1767, C.C. 1774.

PHEILPS, FRANCIS. *London*. Watch, about 1750.

PHELIPPSON, J. *London*. Watch, h.m., 1735.

PHELISOT, C. *Dijon*. Crystal case watch, about 1560.

PHELP, JOHN. *Brighton*, about 1790 C.C.

PHILIBERT, A. French clock, about 1785.

PHILIP, —. *Brighton*, about 1760.

PHILIP, JOSHUA E. *Brighton*, about 1790 C.C.

PHILIP, ROBERT. Musical clockmaker, *6 New Court, St. John St.*, 1779–88 (Robert Philip on some watches).

PHILLESSON, ISAAC. *London*. Qurater chime bracket clock, about 1740. See RIMBAULT.

PHILLIP, WILLIAM. *Edinburgh*. Apprenticed 1796–1846. Also PHILIP.

PHILLIPS, —. *Birkenhead*. Long-case clock, about 1770.

PHILLIPS, CHARLES THOMAS. *Kingston*. Apprenticed 1798, C.C. 1819.

PHILLIPS, JAMES THOMAS. *London*. C.C. 1772.

PHILLIPS, JOEL. *35 Norton Folgate*, 1820.

PHILLIPS, JOHN. *Coldbath Fields*, 1817; *91 Goswell St.*, 1835.

PHILLIPS, JONAS. *London*. Apprenticed 1750, C.C. 1771, died 1797.

PHILLIPS, JOSEPH, f. of New York, 1713–35.

PHILLIPS, PHILIP. *10 St. John's Sq.* C.C. 1790–1800.

PHILLIPS, SAM. Apprenticed 1671 to Nat. Chamberlain, C.C.

PHILLIPS, SAM. *Oswestry*, 1780.

PHILLIPS, W. *Ludlow*. Watch, 1782.

PHILLIPS, WILLIAM, son of Jonas. *London* (*Aldersgate St.*). C.C. 1797–1805.

PHILLIPSON, THOS. *London*. Watch, 1815.

PHIPPS, JAMES. *40 Gutter Lane*, 1783.

PHITHIAN & GARNET. *Lancashire*. Toolmakers, about 1720, quoted by Hatton.

PHYFE, DUNCAN. *New York*, 1768–1854. Case-maker; long-case clock case M.M.A.

PHYLANDER, SYLVANUS. Pair-case silver calendar watch, h.m., 1772.

PICARD, —. *Autun*, 1666–87. In charge of cathedral clock

PICCARD, JEAN —. Born 1620, died 1682; first observed in 1666 the variation of period of a pendulum with temperature.

PICHON, —. *Cherbourg*. Watch, 1790.

PICHON, ANDRÉ. *Lyons*. Master 1637–58; watch.

PICKER (PICKEN), JOHN. *Edinburgh*. Apprenticed 1796–1850.

PICKERING, JAMES. *Dublin*, 1737. Died 1771; watch.

PICKERING, JNO. Apprenticed 1686 to Richd. Knight, C.C.

PICKERING, JOSEPH. *Philadelphia*, 1817–25.

PICKETT, —. *Marlboro'*. Fine clock, long Sheraton style of case, plays a dance tune every three hours, when a curtain rises in the arch of the dial, a couple appear dancing, while other figures pass in procession, about 1780.

PICKETT, JOHN. *London*. 1693 C.C.

PICKETT, JOHN. *Marlborough*. 1790–95 C.C.; long-case clock dial.

PICKETT, WILLIAM. *32 Ludgate Hill*, 1768–72. Succeeded Thead & Pickett.

PICKETT & RUNDELL. *32 Ludgate Hill*, 1775–83. Afterwards Rundell & Bridge.

PICKMAN, WM. *57 Dean St.*, Soho, 1816–25; *6 Albany St.*, 1835.

PICKNETT, JOSEPH. *London*. C.C. 1771.

PIDE, DAVID. Watch, 1740.

PIDGEON, THOS. Apprenticed in 1660 to Jno. Bayes, C.C.

PIERCE, ADAM. Apprenticed to Edward East; C.C. 1664.

PIERCE, HUMPHREY. Apprenticed in 1646 to Robt. Smith; C.C. 1653.

PIERCE, JNO. Apprenticed in 1680 to Geo. Tipping, C.C.

PIERCE, RICHD. Apprenticed in 1646 to Thos. Reeve; C.C. 1657. In 1678 Jno. Papworth was apprenticed to Sarah Pierce.

PIERCE, THOMAS. *Bristol*, 1739. Died 1793.

PIERCE, ZACHARIAS. *London*. Apprenticed 1770, C.C. 1788.

PIERRE, LE QUEUX. Clockmaker to the Duke of Orleans, 1396.

PIERRE, PASQUIER. C.C. 1648.

PIERRET, MATHEW. *Philadelphia*, 1795.

PIGG, ROBT. Apprenticed in 1674 to Jno. White, C.C.

PIGOTT, HENRY. C.C. 1687.

PIGOTT, MRS., daughter of Joseph Kirk. *Nottingham*, 1736. Died 1786; watch.

PIGUET. See PIQUET.

PIGUET, ISAAC DANIEL. *Geneva*. Born 1775, died 1841; one of the finest makers of complex watches.

PIGUET ET MEYLAN. *Geneva*, 1811–28. Firm with Philippe Samuel Meylan. Very fine makers; often signed 'PM'.

PIKE & GREEN. *48 Bunhill Row*, 1806; *Bartholomew Sq.*, 1820–30.

PILKINGTON, J. *Woolwich*, 1815.

PILKINGTON, R. J. *London*. Bracket clock, about 1760.

PILKINGTON, THOMAS. *Dublin*, 1795–1824.

PILLING, JNO. *Boothfield*, 1800.

PILLON, —. *Paris*. Watch, about 1720.

PILON, GERMAIN. *Paris*. Cruciform watches, about 1590.

PILSON, ABRAHAM. *Plymouth*. Watch, about 1700.

PINARD, PAUL. *2 New St.*, Covent Garden, 1775.

PINCHBECK, CHRISTOPHER. *Clerkenwell* and *Fleet St.* A clever maker of musical clocks and of watches; inventor of pinchbeck alloy; 1670–1732.

PINCHBECK, CHRISTOPHER, son of the above-named Christopher, *Cockspur St.*; died 1783, aged 73.

PINCHBECK, EDWARD. *Fleet St.* Son and successor of the above; 1732 66.

PINDAR, JOSEPH. Apprenticed in 1692 to Geo. Halsey, C.C.

PINE, PHILIP. *20 Aldgate*, 1779–82. Card, British Museum.

PINELL, WILLIAM. *London*. Apprenticed 1723, C.C. 1735.

PINET, NICOLAS & GABRIEL. *L'Isle* and *Avignon*, 1703–25. Made clock for Flassan and re-repaired Avignon clock; town clockmaker of Avignon.

PINFOLD, THOMAS. *Banbury*, 1760. See PENFOLD.

PINGO, JNO. Apprenticed to Rob Thompson, C.C. 1684.

PINHORNE, —. *Portsea*. Quarter clock, about 1800.

PINK, J. *London*. Watch, h.m., 1767.

PINKART, JNO. Apprenticed in 1663 to Joseph Quash, C.C.

PINKERTON, JOHN. *Haddington*, 1804–50. Watch.

PINKSTON (PINGSTON), CHARLES. *London*, 1726–44. Watch.

PINNIVELL, WILLIAM. *London*. Apprenticed 1723, C.C. 1735.

PINON, —. Horologer du Roy and des Princes, 1765–70. There is a curious memorandum from an account for work done for the Comte d'Artois (subsequently Charles X): "For repairing a movement of a clock in the Prince's apartment, renew, in fine bronze, the female figure on the clock case which the Prince amused himself in scratching with a knife from one end to the other with the object of cleaning it, renewing the cock and other accessories; total, livres, 2,068."

PONSON, RICHD. *London.* Watch, 1810.

PONTEM, JAS. *London*, 1780.

POOL, J. C. *St. Anne's Lane*, 1654.

POOLE, GEO. C.C. 1654; made a clock for the Mayor of Kendal as a gift to that town. On the dial was the motto, "Time runneth. Your work is before you".

POOLE, GEORGE. *88 Bartholomew Close*, 1783–85.

POOLE, JAMES. *London.* C.C. 1778.

POOLE, JNO. Near *Norfolk St., Strand.* C.C.; arch top bracket clock, about 1712.

POOLE, JOHN. *36 Charles St., City Rd.*, 1822; *7 Brunswick Terrace, Commercial Rd.*, 1835–40.

POOLE, MATTHEW. *London.* Apprenticed 1786, C.C. 1794.

POOLE, ROBERT. *Aldersgate St.* Livery C.C. 1766; master 1781; 1760–81.

POOLE, ROBERT. *Pershore.* 1793 C.C.

POOLE, WILLIAM. *London.* C.C. 1777.

POOLE & BICKERLO. *88 Bartholomew Close*, 1769–75.

POOLS, EDMONDE. Admitted C.C. 1722.

POPE, JOSEPH. *Boston, U.S.A.*, 1788–1803. Watch.

POPE, NICH. Apprenticed 1678 to Gerard Overzee, C.C.

POPE, THOS. *Wharton's Court, Holborn*, 1793.

POPE, ROBERT. *Boston, U.S.A.*, 1786.

POPPE, JNO. HY. *Göttingen*, 1797.

POPPLEWELL, JNO. *Bridlington*, 1770.

PORTAL, ABRAHAM, & GEARING. *34 Ludgate Hill*, 1769–75.

PORTAL & COYLE. *Ludgate Hill*, 1760–63.

PORTE, FRANÇOIS. *Rouen*, 1740–56. Repaired clock of St. Laurent.

PORTER, A. *Oakingham.* About 1790 C.C.–early nineteenth century.

PORTER, FRANCIS. *London.* Apprenticed 1717, C.C. 1730–44.

PORTER, FRANCIS CRUMPTON. *London.* Apprenticed 1778.

PORTER, GEORGE. *Coventry*, 1727–53. Watch; Mayor of Coventry.

PORTER, JOHN. *London.* C.C. 1779.

PORTER, MARK. *Oakingham.* a. 1775–95. See MARK below.

PORTER, MATT. Apprenticed 1682 to Thos. Taylor, Strand; C.C.

PORTER, ROBT. Apprenticed in 1687 to Jno. Cotsworth, C.C.

PORTER, SAMUEL, son. *London.* Apprenticed 1743, C.C. 1756.

PORTER, SEBASTIAN. Apprenticed in 1680 to Jef. Bailey, C.C.

PORTER, WILLIAM. *Penrich.* a. 1771; watch.

PORTER, WILLIAM. *London (Hosier Lane).* C.C. 1771–83.

PORTER, WILLIAM. *Tutbury*, 1795. Clocks and watches.

PORTER, WILLIAM. *Williamstown, Mass., U.S.A.*, 1800. Joined with Daniel Clark and Zenas Cook in 1810 at *Waterbury*; the firm failed about 1815; long-case clock, illuminated Milham.

PORTEOUS, ROBT. *Manchester*, 1818.

PORTHOUSE, GEO. *Penrith*, 1790–1810. Long mahogany case clock with dial inscribed 'Matt. & Catherine Fairless 1771'. 'Wm. Porthouse, Penrith.' The Matt. Fairless referred to was a colliery proprietor; he was murdered for the money with which he was going to pay the men at the pit.

PORTHOUSE, WM. *Penrith.* Clock in carved long-case, on dial a tablet inscribed 'Thos. and Ann Harrison, 1749'.

PORTHOUSE, WM. *Barnard Castle*, 1760.

PORTSMOUTH, JNO. Apprenticed in 1660 to Isaac Puzzy, C.C.

POST, RICHARD. *London.* C.C. 1771.

POST, WILLIAM. *42 Fish St. Hill.* Watch, 1760; long-case clock, 'William Post, London Bridge'; liveryman C.C. 1776.

PÖSTDORFFER, JOHANN. *Dresden*, about 1600–40. Came to *Dresden* from *Prague* about 1600; octagonal crystal watch Grünes Gewölbe, Dresden; watch M.M.A.; oval watch signed 'Johann Poestd'.

POTHEUST à *Paris.* Watch, about 1750.

POTIER, MICHEL. *Paris*, 1544.

POTTER, CHRISTOPHER. *Shoe Lane.* C.C. 1730.

POTTER, EPHRAIM. *Concord, U.S.A.*, 1775–90.

POTTER, FRANCIS. *London.* C.C. 1730.

POTTER, GEORGE. Watchmaker, and Mayor of Coventry, 1727.

POTTER, HARRY. *5 Well St., Aldersgate*, 1755. Master C.C. 1795, and again in 1812, when he died before the expiration of his year of office.

POTTER, HARRY, JUNIOR. *London.* w.C.C. 1792, m.C.C. 1812, died 1813.

POTTER, JAMES. Livery C.C. 1810.

POTTER, THOS. *Gainsboro'*, 1795.

POTTER, WILLIAM. *London.* Apprenticed 1731, C.C. 1738.

POTTINGER, JNO. *6 Bells Buildings, Salisbury St.*, 1793.

POTTS, JNO. *Partrington*, 1775.

POTTS, JNO. *Redcar*, 1823.

POTTS, JOSHUA, *York*, f., 1810–33. Maker of musical clocks.

POTTS, THOMAS. *London (St. James' St.).* Apprenticed 1713–51 C.C.; watch.

POUCHET de *Claremont.* Oval watch, about 1650, British Museum.

POUCHOULIN, J. L. *Geneva*, 1750.

POUILLY, —. *Rue Dauphine, Paris*, 1690.

POULAIN, GILLES. *Blois.* Master 1666–82.

POULSON, THOS. *London.* Watch, 1815.

POULSON, WILLIAM. *London.* Apprenticed 1786, C.C. 1801.

POUND, ISAAC. *Charleston, U.S.A.* From 1746; clocks and watches.

POUND, JNO. Apprenticed 1673 to Joseph Wincoek, C.C.

POUZAIT & GODEMAR. *Geneva*, about 1780–1800. Watch with virgule escapement; made Lepine cylinder watches with sweep seconds, example in Feill collection.

POUZIT, MOISE. *Geneva.* A clever watchmaker; made centre seconds watches; did much to popularise the lever escapement and executed a large model of it in 1786; watch, virgule escapement, signed 'Pouzait & Godemar Frères', about 1780.

POW. See POY.

POWELL, BARTHOLOMEW. C.C. 1668.

POWELL, EDWARD. *London.* Apprenticed 1753, C.C. 1777.

POWELL, EDWARD. *Bristol*, 1795–1818. Watch.

POWELL, H. *56 St. Paul's Churchyard*, 1793.

POWELL, JAMES. *7 Prince's St., Leicester Sq.*, 1828–35.

POWELL, JNO. Apprenticed in 1665 to Isaac Daniel, C.C.

POWELL, ROBERT. *Chelsea.* C.C. 1710.

POWELL, WILLIAM. *London.* Apprenticed 1752, C.C. 1763.

POWER, ANNE. *London.* Apprenticed 1714, C.C. 1722.

POWER, THOS. Lantern clock inscribed 'Tho Power de Wellingborou Hoc Fabricavit', about 1700; also a basket-top bracket clock, inscribed 'Thos. Power, Wellingbrow'.

POWERS, THOS. *St. Albans*, 1798.

POWIS, ROBT. *36 Rosoman St.*, 1806–23.

POWLEY, —. *Asby, Westmorland*, 1730.

POWLEY, ROBT. *Appleby*, 1770.

POWNALL, NAT. Apprenticed in 1649 to Wm. Izod, C.C.

POWRIE, HENRY. *Edinburgh* and *Glasgow*, 1822–37.

POY, GODFREY. *78 Mortimer St.*, 1775–95.

POY, GODFRIE. A choice, small pull-repeating and alarum clock by him, said to have been made for George II when Prince of Wales. Gilt case, with military emblems over the arched top surmounted by a handle; silvered dial, in the arch strike-silent plate marked 'Schlaat, Nit schla'; engraved back plate; bell at the bottom of the movement. Also maker of a very fine quarter repeater watch, inner case pierced and *repoussé*, h.m., 1729, outer case shagreen; another of his productions is a black, pull-chime bracket clock; in the collection of the Czar of Russia at the Winter Palace, St. Petersburg, was a repeating watch by him, the outer case set with emeralds and diamonds; it is attached to a chatelaine which is also decorated with precious stones; 1718–50.

POZZI, A. *Wooton Bassett*. Watch, 1840.

PRAEFELT, JOHN. *Philadelphia*, 1797.

PRATT. Of *Askrigg*, 1790. He was apprenticed to C. Caygill, and had two sons, JAS. and WM., who were in partnership till 1830. Wm. continued till 1841.

PREDDY, WM. *Langport*, 1780.

PREIST, WM. Corner of *Lad Lane, Wood St.*, 1763.

PRENTICE (PRENTIS), PHILIP. *London*. Apprenticed 1742, C.C. 1749.

PRENTIS, DANIEL. *25 Charterhouse Lane*, 1788–96.

PRENTIS, JOHN, same address, 1817.

PRENTIS & SON. *25 Charterhouse Lane*, 1804–07.

PRESBURY, WM. *Coventry*, 1780.

PRESBURY & SON. *9 New St., Covent Garden*, 1804.

PREST, —. *Fleet St.* See PRIEST.

PREST, THOMAS. *Chigwell, Essex*. Patentee of keyless action for watches (No. 4,501), 1820; he was foreman to J. R. Arnold; died 1855.

PRESTBURY, CHAS. *9 New St., Covent Garden*, 1793.

PRESTICOTT, PETER. *New Rents, St. Martin's-le-Grand*, 1790–94.

PRESTIGE, BARTHOLOMEW. C.C. 1703.

PRESTON, EDWARD. C.C. 1721.

PRESTON, EDWARD. *London*. Apprenticed 1713, C.C. 1721.

PRESTON, ROBERT. *Liverpool*, 1781. In 1783 also in *Chester*; 1796 bankrupt; watch.

PRESTON, TOBIAS. Apprenticed in 1640 to Christopher Vernon, C.C.

PRESTON, WM. *Lancaster*, 1818.

PRESTWOOD, JOSEPH. C.C. 1703; maker of long-case clocks, 1703–20.

PRETTY, JOHN. *London (Deptford)*. Apprenticed 1796, C.C. 1807.

PREUDHOMME, L. B. *Paris*, 1780.

PRÉVOST, JOSEPH. *Blois*. Master 1667–79. Also PRÉVAULT, PROVOST and PROUVOST.

PRÉVOST, PIERRE. *Blois*, 1629–51. Also PRÉVOT and PROUVOST.

PREVOST, L. N. *London*. Watch, 1750.

PREVOST, NI. *London*. Year clock, about 1710; watch, 1730.

PRICE, CHAS. Apprenticed 1680 to Geo. Stevens, C.C.

PRICE, DAVID. *London*. C.C. 1770.

PRICE, EDWARD. *Liverpool*, 1777–96. Watch.

PRICE, FRANCIS. *London*. Apprenticed 1774, C.C. 1786, livery C.C. 1787–93.

PRICE, GEORGE. *St. Martin's Churchyard*, 1788; *89 Oxford St.*, 1793–1806.

PRICE, ISAAC. *Philadelphia*, 1797.

PRICE, J. *Deptford*. Watch, 1796.

PRICE, JNO. Apprenticed in 1678 to R. Nemes, C.C.

PRICE, JOHN. *London*. Apprenticed 1731, C.C. 1744.

PRICE, JOSEPH. *Baltimore*, 1799.

PRICE, PHILIP. *Philadelphia*, 1817–25.

PRICE, RICHARD. *London*. C.C. 1772.

PRICE, W. *17 Maiden Lane, Wood St.*, 1825.

PRICE, WILLIAM. *Pembroke*, 1791–1830. Watch; long-case clock.

PRIDDITH, JOHN. C.C. 1639.

PRIDDITH, THOMAS. *London*. C.C. 1639.

PRIDEAUX, EDMUND. *31 Hatton Garden*, 1780–94.

PRIDGRIN, W. *Hull*. Watch, 1797.

PRIDGRIN, WM. *York, f.,* 1778.

PRIDHAM, LEWIS. *Sandford*. Long-case clock, about 1710.

PRIDHAM, WILLIAM. *Great Alie St., Goodman's Fields*, 1760–63.

PRIEST, —. *Fleet St.*, 1765–75.

PRIEST, —. *Bugg Lane, Norwich*. Watch, 1796.

PRIEST, GEORGE. *Norwich*, 1796–1854. Watch.

PRIEST, JNO. *Aldersgate*. C.C. 1730.

PRIEST, JOHN. Apprenticed to George Graham, C.C. 1746.

PRIEST, THOS. *St. John's Lane*. C.C. 1729.

PRIEST, W. & JAMES. *30 White Cross St.*, 1768–72.

PRIEST, WILLIAM. *Bristol*, 1772–93. Watch. See PREIST.

PRIESTMAN, JOSEPH. Apprenticed to Henry Jones, C.C. 1703.

PRIESTMAN, M. *19 Prince's St., Leicester Sq.*, 1817.

PRIGG, JOHN. *Bethlehem*. Livery C.C. 1776.

PRIGG, MATT. *London*. Watch, 1750.

PRIGG & ANSELL. Clock and watch spring maker, *Middle Moore Fields*, 1781–94.

PRIGGIN, JNO. Apprenticed in 1646 to Elias Allen, C.C.

PRIGGIN, WM. *Hull*. A Mahogany long-case clock about 1770, brass and silvered dial, 13-in. in diameter, shows the phases of the moon, time of high water, and days of the month.

PRIGNAN, JEAN. *Paris*. Master 1778–1812.

PRIME, ABRAHAM. Apprenticed in 1665 to Andrew Prime, C.C. 1672.

PRIME, ANDREW. C.C. 1647, long-case clock, V. & A.

PRINCE, RICHARD. C.C. 1680.

PRINCE, THOS. Apprenticed in 1674 to Jno. Bellard, C.C.

PRINGLE, ADAM. *Edinburgh*, 1800.

PRINGLE, GEORGE. *Edinburgh*. Apprenticed 1793–1822.

PRINGLE, THOS. *Dalkeith*, 1810–43.

PRINT, RICHARD. C.C. 1698.

PRINTZ, PEHR. *Stockholm*, 1769–80. Court clock; published in 1769 *Försök Til en Historisk Beskrifning Om Wägg och Byxsäcks-Uhr*; long-case bracket and wall clocks and three watches.

PRIOR, EDWARD. Also a maker for the Turkish market contemporaneously with the last-named George, carried on business in *Clerkenwell* at first alone, and afterwards in partnership with Wm. Chambers; a long-case clock by Edward Prior is in the Mosque of Achmet, Constantinople; watch, 'Edward Prior, London', Turkish numerals, about 1800.

PRIOR, GEORGE. *31 Prescot St., Goodman's Fields*, 1765–88; *Rosomond's Row*, 1794; *5 George Yard, Lombard St.*, 1798–1810.

PRIOR, GEORGE, son of John, of *Otley* and *Leeds*. In 1809 he received from the Society of Arts a silver medal and 25 guineas for a clock escapement, and in 1811, 20 guineas for a remontoire escapement; in 1818 he patented (No. 4,214) a remontoire; in the Yorkshire Directory for 1822 he is described as of Woodhouse Lane, Leeds, but he afterwards removed to City Rd., London, and became reputed as a maker of watches for the Turkish market.

PRIOR, HY. *Leeds*, 1818.

PRIOR, JOHN. *Nessfield*, near *Skipton-in-Craven, Yorkshire*. Born 1747; received the following rewards from the Society of Arts: 1798, 30 guineas for detached escapement; 1803, 30 guineas for improved striking work; 1805, silver medal and 20 guineas for an alarum; 1811, silver medal and 10 guineas for striking work; 1817, silver Isis medal and 2 guineas for striking work; 1820, large silver medal and 20 guineas for striking work.

PRIOR, WM. *82 Minories*, 1793.

PRITCHARD, GEO. *Madelywood*. Watch, 1802.

PRITCHARD, PHIL., JUNR. C.C. about 1650.

PRITCHFORD, ZACHARIAH. Apprenticed 1674 to Ed. Eyston, C.C.

PROCTOR, WILLIAM. *New York, f.,* 1737–60; then CARDAN.

PROCTOR, WM. Apprenticed to John Brockbank; admitted C.C. 1797; livery 1810.

PROSSER, EDWD. Apprenticed in 1655 to Robert Lochard, C.C.

PROSSER, JOHN. *61 Piccadilly*, 1822–30.

PROSSER, WILLIAM. *Strand*, 1769–72.

PROVAUX, —. *Charleston, U.S.A.*, from 1775. Watch.

PRYME. See PRIME.

PUCKRIDGE, CHARLES. *Goldsmiths' St., Shoe Lane*, 1788–94.

PUCKRIDGE, CHARLES, son of Charles. *London*. C.C. 1808–24.

PUCKRIDGE, J. *73 Snow Hill*, 1716–40.

PUCKRIDGE, JOHN. *72 Snow Hill*, 1790–1818; livery C.C. 1814.

PUGH, BENJ. Watch gilder, *34 Jewin St.*, 1790–94.

PUGH, ELLIS. *Cockspur St.*, 1775–94.

PUGH, JOHN SANKEY. *London*. C.C. 1808.

PUIGUER, —. *London*. Watch, about 1780.

PULBROOK, JOSEPH ZACHARIAH. *London*. C.C. 1822.

PULLAN, BEN. *Bradford*, 1710–35.

PULLAN, BENJAMIN. *Leeds*. a. 1767, died 1787; watch.

PULLEN, DAVID. *Coleman St.*, C.C. 1730.

PULLEN, DAVID, son. *London*. Apprenticed 1763, C.C. 1773.

PULLEN, JAS. Apprenticed C.C. 1669.

PULLER, JONATHAN. Apprenticed 1676 to Nich. Coxeter; C.C. 1683, assistant 1705; long clock, 11-in. dial, marquetry case with domed hood, about 1700, Wetherfield collection.

"Whereas an old Silver Watch in a black studded case made by one Puller, was taken away from a gentleman on Bagshot Heath, on Monday, April 29. This is to desire them by any hand to send it to Thomas Newman at the Naked Boy in West Smithfield, and no questions shall be asked, but a Reward of 2 guineas shall be given to the Person that brings it" (*Postman*, 11th May, 1706).

"A large House-Clock supposed to be stolen 16 or 18 months since is now in the hands of Jonathan Puller Clockmaker in Red Lion Court in Fleet St." (*Lond. Gaz.*, July 24–28, 1690).

PULLIN, CHARLES. *London*. Apprenticed 1783, C.C. 1745–72.

PUNCHARD, WM. Apprenticed 1676 to R. Seignior, C.C.

PURDEN, CHARLES. *London*. C.C. 1777.

PURDEN, GEORGE. *London*. C.C. 1820.

PURDEN, JOHN. *London*, about 1795.

PURRIER, RICHARD. C.C. 1705.

PURSE, GEORGE. *487 Strand*, 1804–25.

PURSE, THOMAS. *Baltimore, U.S.A.*, 1807. Watches and clocks.

PURSE, WILLIAM. *336 Strand*, 1804.

PURTON, FRANCIS. *2 Carey St.*, 1793.

PURVIS, ALEXANDER. *4 North Audley St.*, 1825–42.

PURVIS, WM. *Edinburgh*. Made a 'Knock' for St. Mary's Church, Dundee, in 1540.

PUTLAND, G. & J. *287 High Holborn*, 1793.

PUTLEY, FRANCIS. *40 Newington Causeway*, 1806–42. Livery C.C. 1812.

PUXTON. See PAXTON.

PUZELAT, ANTOINE. *Blois*. Master 1600–50.

PUZELAT, NICOLAS. *Blois*. Master 1616–39.

PUZY, ISAAC. *London*. Apprenticed in 1651 to Jno. Freeman; C.C. 1658; 12-hour lantern clock, about 1665, inscribed 'Isaac Puzzy'.

PYBUS, F. G. Watch, 1822.

PYBUS, WILLIAM. *66 Threadneedle St.*, 1789–94.

PYE, CHAS. *High St., Birmingham*, 1780.

PYKE, GEORGE, son of Jno. C.C. 1753.

PYKE, JNO. *Newgate St.*; "clock and watch maker to the Prince of Wales", 1755; centre seconds watch, about 1770.

PYKE, JNO. *High St., Eltham*, 1820–42. An excellent maker, formerly Arnold's foreman.

PYKE, JOHN. Watch motion maker, *Bedford Row*. C.C. 1720.

PYKE, STEPHEN. *London*. Long-case clock, about 1750.

PYM, THOMAS. *London*. Apprenticed 1713, C.C. 1721.

PYNE, NATHANIEL. C.C. 1677; a long marquetry case month clock.

PYOTT. See BARCLAY, JAS.

QUAIFE, WILLIAM. *Rye*. Mid-eighteenth century. Watch, shagreen case.

QUARE, DANIEL. *St. Martin's-le-Grand*. Afterwards at the *King's Arms, Exchange Alley*. A Quaker, born 1648; brother C.C. 1671; master 1708; died 1724; a celebrated maker, inventor of the repeating watch.

QUARE & HORSEMAN, at the *King's Arms, Exchange Alley*, 1718–33. Partnership with Daniel Quare, the style continuing after Quare's death until bankrupt in 1733, when the business was probably taken over by Peckover; pair-case gold repeating watch and repeating movement, G.M.; gold repeating *repoussé* watch, set topazes and diamonds, Winter Palace, Petrograd; the Nos. of watches signed Quare & Horseman are known from 4677 to 5503, and of repeaters from 843 to 1129.

QUARI (or QUARIE). *London*. Table clock in engraved brass case, about 1700, V. & A., inscribed 'De Jean Quari, London'.

QUARMAN, JOSEPH. *Temple Cloud*, about 1760–80.

QUARMAN, SAML. *Temple Cloud*. Long-case clocks, also watch with day of the month hand, silver cases, the outer one *repoussé*, h.m., 1768; he died 1772; long-case clock showing 'High water at Bristol Key', about 1775, signed 'Geo. Quarman, Temple Cloud'.

QUARREL, RICHD. Apprenticed 1691 to Phil. Corderoy, C.C.

QUARTERMAINE, JOSEPH. *Aylesbury*, 1755–1802. Watch, tortoise-shell case, about 1757.

QUASH, JOSEPH. Apprenticed 1637 to Geo. Smith, C.C. 1646; watch, about 1650, signed 'Josephus Quash Londini', silver engraved case, V. & A.

QUELCH, JEREM. *London.* Long-case clock, 1735; watch, 1754.

QUELCH, JOHN. C.C. 1646; maker of lantern clocks.

QUELCH, RICHARD. *Oxford.* Octagonal watch, Whitcombe Green collection, about 1650.

QUESNOY (QUESNAY), CLAUDE. *Rouen,* 1575–92. In charge of town clock, and repaired several others.

QUESNOY (QUESNAY), VINCENT. *Rouen,* 1524; *Hampton Court* or *London,* 1532; *Rouen,* 1532–63. There was paid to him from the Privy Purse 11 li. 8s. 8d.; keeper of Rouen town clock; re-made Rouen Cathedral clock 1540.

QUENONAULT, CHAS. *London.* Watch, 1760.

QUENTIN, GILLES. *Paris.* Clockmaker to Louis XIV, 1657.

QUESTED, THOS. *Wye.* Long-case clock, about 1800.

QUICK, THOS. *London.* Watch, 1780.

QUILLAN, —. *Airvalt.* French lantern clock, about 1650.

QUILLET, PARIS. Made the Bastille clock, for which, including three bells with flat tops, he received £3,767 in 1762; he had charge of the clock till his death; his widow in 1776 attended to some repairs.

QUILLIAM. *Liverpool.* See Townley.

QUIMBY, WILLIAM. *Belfast, Me.,* 1821–50.

QUIN, EDWARD. *London (Blackfriars Rd.).* Livery C.C. 1805, died 1825.

QUINTON, STEPHEN. *London.* Maker of long-case clocks, about 1750.

QUINTON, WILLIAM BRETT. *London.* Apprenticed 1761, C.C. 1769–1806.

QUONIAM, JOSEPH. *Paris.* Master 1740, died 1779.

QUY, —. *Bath,* 1798.

R. Cruciform watch, stackfreed movement, signed 'A. R.', Pierpont Morgan collection. Watch marked 'N. R.', about 1620, Pierpont Morgan collection.

RABERT, JOHANN CONRAD. *Berlin,* 1785–1816. Clock.

RACINE, CHAS. FREDK. *Chaux de Fonds.* Celebrated enameller and dial painter, died 1832; watch, Pierpont Morgan collection, modern movement, signed 'Racine Berlin'; watch, about 1750, marked 'Racine, London'.

RADCLIFFE, CHARLES. *Liverpool,* 1680.

RADFORD, HENRY. C.C. 1721.

RADFORD, JAS. *75 Gray's Inn Lane,* 1793.

RADFORD, THOMAS. *London (Gray's Inn Lane).* Apprenticed 1732, C.C. 1749, died 1774.

RADFORD, THOS. *Leeds,* 1770.

RADFORD, WILLIAM, brother of Thos. *Leeds,* 1793–1826. In partnership with his brother in 1792 and continued the business; watch movement.

RADSMA, MARTIN TJEERDS, son. *Harlingen.* Born 1761, died 1836.

RADSMA, TJEERD JACOBS. *Harlingen,* 1731. Died about 1790; long-case astronomical and several bracket clocks.

RAE, CHARLES. *London.* C.C. 1816.

RAE, THE REV. PETER. *Kirkconnel,* 1703–48. Astronomical clock.

RAFE, THOS. Lantern clock, 1661.

RAFFORD, F. *London.* Watch, 1780.

RAFQUIST, ANDERS. *Landskrona,* 1820–40. Wall clocks.

RAGER, JAMES. *London.* Apprenticed 1755, C.C. 1769.

RAGUET-LÉPINE, CLAUDE PIERRE. *Dôle* and later *Paris.* Born 1753, died 1810; son-in-law of and succeeded Jean Antoine Lépine in 1783; watch signed 'Raguet', New York University.

RAGSDALE, GEORGE. *25 New Bond St.,* 1769–83.

RAIGUEL, JEAN HENRI, brother. *St. Imier* and *Paris,* about 1790–1808.

RAILLARD (RAILLART), CLAUDE. *Paris,* 1646. Juré 1675; signatory to Status of Paris corporation. *v.* RALLART.

RAILLARD (RAILLART), CLAUDE, son. *Paris.* Master 1676, juré 1692; fins Boulle bracket clock, Pal. de Pau, Paris.

RAILLARD (RAILLART), CLAUDE. *Paris.* Master 1691, died 1762.

RAILLARD (RAILLART), CLAUDE. *Paris,* 1739–89. Juré 1745; published *Extraits des principaux Statuts des Horlogers de Paris.*

RAIMENT, THOMAS. C.C. 1719.

RAINALDI, CARL, son of Giovannia. Assisted his father.

RAINALDI, GIOVANNIA P. Maker of the first clock in the square of St. Mark, Venice, 1495.

RAINBOW, WM. *London.* Long-case clock, about 1770.

RAINE, JOSEPH. *Silver Street, Durham,* 1804–20.

RAINES (RAYNES), WILLIAM. *Butcher Row, East Smithfield.* C.C. 1660; maker of lantern clocks.

RAINGO, M. *Paris.* Orrery clock, Windsor Castle, 1823; a similar one in the Soane Museum.

RAINIER, DANIEL, son. *London.* Apprenticed 1800, livery C.C. 1806.

RAINIER, JOHN. Livery C.C. 1787.

RAINSFORD, BENJAMIN. *London.* C.C. 1708–15.

RAINSFORD, BERNARD. Apprenticed 1657 to Ed. Clough; C.C. 1677.

RAINSFORD, FRANCIS. *Charing Cross.* Apprenticed to Robt. Gregory, 1680; C.C. 1689.

RAINSFORD, FRANCIS. Apprenticed to Brounker Watts; C.C. 1708.

RAINSFORD, JNO. *New St. Sq.* C.C.; Clock, brass and silvered dial, engraved laurel border, chimes quarters on six bells, shows days of the month, about 1725; in the Wetherfield collection is a regulator by him.

RAITT, ALEXANDER. *London.* Maker of long-case clocks, with striking racks between the plates; 1685–1710.

RAKE, JOHN. *London.* C.C. 1780–96.

RAKER, P. *95 Bishopsgate St.,* 1775.

RALLART, —. *Paris.* Watch, 1630.

RAM, HEWETT. Apprenticed 1691 to Thos. Hickmann, C.C.

RAMAGE, JAMES. *Edinburgh.* Apprenticed 1780–1820.

RAMBLEY, WM. *407 Oxford St.,* 1775–94.

RAMBRANT, JAS. *London.* Watch, 1805.

RAMSAY. Of *Dundee:* PATRICK, 1604, then JOHN, then SILVESTER.

RAMSAY, DAVID. Near *Temple Bar.* Watchmaker to James I; first master of the C.C.; 1600–50.

RAMSAY, JOHN. Oval watch, Pierpont Morgan collection, signed 'John Ramsay, Londres', about 1620; tangent wheel and screw adjustment, balance-cock pinned on.

RAMSAY, JOHN, son of Patrick. *Dundee,* 1610–46.

RAMSAY, SILVESTER, brother. *Dundee,* 1610–46.

RAMSBOTTOM, JNO. *Hall Green.* Clock, about 1770.

RAMSDEN, J. *Hall Green.* Clock, about 1785.

RAMSDEN, JNO. Apprenticed 1654 to Thos. Loomes, C.C.

RAMSDEN, THOMAS. C.C. 1648.

RAMSEY, —. *Islington,* 1800–08.

RAMSEY, JNO. C.C. 1637.

RAMSTEDT, PETTER. *Stockholm,* 1770–1816. Watch movement, Nord. Museum.

RAMUSAT, JEAN LOUIS. *Geneva,* about 1755–70.

RAND, DANIEL. *Boston, U.S.A.,* 1825. Watch.

RAND, WM. *London.* Repeating watch, 1760.

RANDALL, HY. Apprenticed 1660 to Wm. Dobb.

RANDALL, JOHN. *Wine Office Court, Fleet St.,* 1790–94.

RANDALL, MORRIS. Apprenticed 1680 to Jno. Dearmar, C.C.

RANDALL, RICHD. Apprenticed 1665 to Francis Bicknell, C.C.

RANDALL, TIMOTHY. Apprenticed 1683 to Francis Hill, C.C.

RANDALL, WILLIAM. *Newbury*, 1795–1812. Clocks and watches; church clock with Cumming's escapement.

RANEAGE, ISAAC. C.C. 1635.

RANNA, —. *Vienna*. Small watch in lyre-shaped enamelled case, about 1790.

RANSOM, GEORGE. *18 King St.*, *Soho*, 1825.

RANSOM, M. *London*. Watch, 1802.

RANSOM, T. *London*. Watch, about 1790.

RANSON, ROBERT HILL. *London*. Apprenticed 1769, C.C. 1777.

RANT, GEO. C.C. 1687.

RANT, JOHN. *London*. Apprenticed 1676, C.C. 1687–1708.

RANT, JONATHAN. C.C. 1687; bracket quarter repeating time-piece, arched dial, with calendar, ebony case, Wetherfield collection, about 1710.

RAPHARD, —. *London*. Watch, gold case, Schloss collection, 1760.

RAPIER, JNO., 'in Wisbech, fecit', clock, about 1700.

RAPSON, THOS. *4 Montague St.*, *Portman Sq.*, 1814–18.

RAPTON, JOHN STEWART. *London*. C.C. 1773.

RASHER, JOHN. *London*. Apprenticed 1695, C.C. 1703–21.

RATCLIFFE, BENJAMIN. *Welshpool*, 1743–59. Sundial and clock.

RATCLIFFE, JOHN. *Chester*, 1763–97 C.C.

RATCLIFFE, JOHN. *Wrexham*, about 1735–63. Long-case clock.

RATHERAIN, C. *25 Cursitor St.*, 1825.

RATZENHOFER (RAZENHOFER), MATHIAS. *Vienna*. Master 1799; long-case clock of 1827, Uhren Museum, Vienna.

RAUENECKER, MARTIN. *Augsburg*. Comp. 1727; master 1736; juré 1740–70.

RAULET, SAMUEL. *Monmouth, U.S.A.*, 1800.

RAVEN, CRISPIN. *London*. Long solid walnut-case clock, about 1780.

RAVEN, SAMUEL. *London*, about 1795.

RAVENAT, —. *Paris*, 1807–25. Succeeded Gravereau.

RAWFORD, JAMES. *75 Gray's Inn Lane*, 1770–90. Livery C.C. 1787.

RAWLINGS, CHARLES. *Brook St.*, *Holborn*. C.C. 1818, livery 1826; died 1864.

RAWLINGS, GEORGE. *88 Whitechapel*, 1790.

RAWLINS, HENRY. C.C. 1706.

RAWLINS, JAMES. Livery C.C. 1787.

RAWORTH, JOHN. *Penrith*, 1770–1810.

RAWSON, JNO. *Penrith*, 1770.

RAWSON, THOMAS. *Penrith*. Born 1718, died 1811; clocks and watches.

RAXHALL, CHRIS. Apprenticed 1657 to Jas. Seabourne, C.C.

RAY, DANIEL. *Sudbury*. Long-case clock, about 1730.

RAY, SAMUEL. *35 Great Castle St.*, *Oxford St.*, 1820–30.

RAY, WILLIAM. *Sudbury*, 1762–90 C.C.; watch.

RAY & MONTAGUE. *22 Denmark St.*, *Soho*, 1804–19.

RAYLEY, JNO. *London*. Watch, 1830.

RAYMENT, JOHN. *Huntingdon*, 1751–95. Watch. Also RAYMOND. Circular wall clock.

RAYMENT, RICHD. *St. Edmunds Bury*. A good maker of lantern clocks, about 1700. A later specimen, with arched dial, signed 'Richd. Rayment, Bury'; long-case clock, about 1705.

RAYMENT, THOS. Apprenticed to Thos. Taylor; C.C. 1719; watch, *repoussé* gold case, Schloss collection, about 1768; another, painted tortoiseshell case, about 1765.

RAYMENT, THOS. *Stamford*, 1760. Clock, long-case with Oriental lacquer.

RAYMENT, WM. *Stowmarket*, 1750.

RAYMOND, JNO. *Leadenhall St.*, 1774.

RAYMOND, LAZARE TOUSSAINT. *Geneva*, about 1775–91.

RAYMOND, WILLIAM. *Dublin*, 1774–95. Watch.

RAYMONDE. Water clock, dated 1581, and marked 'Raymonde, Chester'.

RAYNER, DOVE. *London* (*Little Old Bailey*). Apprenticed 1693, C.C. 1701–65; bankrupt.

RAYNER, JOHN. *London*. C.C. 1697; watch, h.m., 1727.

RAYNER, STEP. Jno. Baldwin was apprenticed to him in 1691; watch, V. & A., about 1730.

RAYNESFORD. See RAINSFORD.

READ, GEO. *10 Rotherhithe St.*, 1815–25.

READ, GEORGE. *Old Sq.*, *Lincoln's Inn*, 1820.

READ, ISAAC. *Philadelphia*, 1819–25.

READ, THOMAS. *Dublin*, 1765.

READ, THOS. *Manchester*, 1770.

READ, W. *Grantham*, about 1790 C.C.

READ, WILLIAM. *84 Jermyn St.*, *Piccadilly*, 1825.

READ, WM. *Newcastle Pl.*, *Clerkenwell*, 1820.

READER, J. *London*, 1825.

READER, WM. *Hull*. Long-case clock, about 1760.

READING, DANIEL. *London*. Apprenticed 1735, C.C. 1743, died 1777.

READING, ROBERT. *London* (*Shoe Lane* and *New St.*). Apprenticed 1754, C.C. 1761–70; watch.

REBOUL, DANIEL ANTOINE. *Geneva*, about 1775–91.

RECORDON, LOUIS. *Greek St.*, *Soho*, 1780. Afterwards succeeded Emery at *33 Cockspur St.*, *Charing Cross*. In 1780 he patented (No. 1,249) a pedometer winding for watches; 1778–1810. See DESGRANGES.

RED, CR. *London*. Watch, 1783.

REDKNAP, ENOS. *London*. Apprenticed 1785, C.C. 1792–1817.

REDPATH, HENRY. *Stirling*, 1787–1820.

REDRUPP, ELI. *Chesham*, 1780.

REDSTALL, FRANCIS. *Overtons*. Long-case clock, about 1700.

REEAD, THOS. C.C. 1632.

REED, ALEXANDER. Admitted C.C. 1706; clock-watch, Schloss collection, about 1710.

REED, BENJAMIN. *Bristol*, 1775–97. Clocks and watches.

REED, GEORGE JEREMIAH. *London*. Apprenticed 1794, C.C. 1816; livery C.C. 1819–23.

REED, RICHARD, brother. *Chelmsford*, 1772–87. Clocks and watches.

REED, STEPHEN. *New York*, 1805.

REED, WILLIAM, JUN. *London*. C.C. 1824.

REED, WM. *Chelmsford*, 1770.

REEVE, GERVAIS. *London*. Apprenticed 1716, C.C. 1730–61; watch movement.

REEVE, GOWAR. *The Fleet*. C.C. 1730.

REEVE, HENRY. C.C. 1682.

REEVE, JARVIS. C.C. 1731.

REEVE, JOHN. C.C. 1712.

REEVE, JOSEPH. *Yarmouth*, 1700.

REEVE, ROBERT. *York*, f., 1660.

REEVE, SAM. *Stonham*, 1770.

REEVE, THOMAS, in *Pope's Head Alley*, C.C. 1632; assistant 1655.

REEVE, THOS. *Harlestone*, 1660.

REEVE, WM. *24 Ludgate St.*, 1830; *13 Vigo St.*, *Regent St.*, 1835.

REEVES, BENJAMIN. *Lamberhurst.* a. 1774, died 1790; watch; long-case clock.

REEVES, RICHARD. *208 High St., Shoreditch,* 1820–42.

REEVES, WM. *37 Newington Causeway,* 1825–42.

REGARD, REYMOND. Clockmaker at the upper end of *Russell St.,* near *Drury Lane.* Admitted C.C. 1677; mentioned in *Lond. Gaz.,* Jan. 25–28, 1691.

REGNAULD (or REGNAULT), —. *Chalons, France.* Devised a compensated pendulum 1733; Thiout mentions a repeating clock by him.

REGNAULD (or REGNAULT), PIERRE, père, *Rue Vielle-du-Temple, Paris.* Garde visiteur in 1769; clocks and bells of the Bastille placed in his custody, 1789.

REGNAULT, JEROSME FRANÇOIS. *Paris.* Master 1747–89.

REGNAULT, PIERRE ANTOINE. *Paris.* Master 1754, juré 1768–89; took down the clock of the Bastille in 1789.

REGNELL, CARL AXEL. *Vrigstad.* Born 1776, died 1841.

REGNIER, 'MAÎTRE'. *Paris,* 1605. Octagonal watch, late sixteenth century, case of crystal, movement signed 'J. Regnier, Paris'.

REGYNOLDS, GEO. *York,* f., 1641. Died 1680.

REHLE, J. *Freiburg.* Table clock, 1690.

'REICARDLEDERT in *Strassburg'.* Oval alarum watch, about 1595.

REICHENEDER, LEOPOLD. *Burckhausen.* Brass box-shaped circular watch, two dials, numerals up to twenty-four, engraved with views of a town; on back is engraved the Wisdom of Solomon, about 1550; Pierpont Morgan collection.

REID, ADAM. *Clerkenwell* and *Woolwich.* Inventor of an adjustment for Graham's pendulum, 1779–1835. Henderson, in his *Life of Ferguson,* speaks of Andrew Reid, a clever watchmaker, who died at Brixton, in 1835, aged 85.

REID, ALEXANDER. *London.* Apprenticed 1698, C.C. 1707.

REID, ANDREW. *Biggar.* Born 1767, died 1860.

REID, F., & SONS. *Glasgow,* 1786; Reid & Todd, 1825–42.

REID, FRANCIS. *Glasgow,* 1789–1806. Also FRANCIS, & SONS.

REID, J. *Ball Alley, Lombard St.,* 1800–16.

REID, JNO. *Edinburgh.* Long-case clock, about 1820.

REID, THOMAS. Born 1746, died 1831; a celebrated Edinburgh clockmaker, apprenticed to Jas. Cowan, whom he succeeded in 1781; watch, 'Thos. Reid & Co., Edinburgh, 1800'; from 1806 he was in partnership with Wm. Auld till 1823, when he retired from business; Thos. Reid was author of *Treatise on Clock and Watchmaking,* published in 1826, the major part of which was taken from an article by him in Brewster's *Edinburgh Cyclopaedia,* published in 1819; hon f., C.C. 1825.

REID, WILLIAM. *Edinburgh.* Apprenticed 1781–1819.

REID, WILLIAM, JUNR. *London.* C.C. 1824; watch.

REID, WM. *32 Rosoman St., Clerkenwell,* 1790–1820. Fine pocket chronometer, Arnold escapement, h.m.; 1795.

REID & AULD. *Edinburgh,* 1806–23. E. J. Thompson gave to the Horological Institute a fine regulator, inscribed 'Reid & Auld, 1818'.

REIDL, JOSEPH. *Vienna.* Watch, 1770.

REILY, FREDRICK. *Kilkenny,* 1820.

REILLY, J. C. *12 Middle Row, Holborn,* 1815–25.

REILLY, JOHN. *Dublin,* 1778.

REILLY, JOHN. *Philadelphia,* 1785–97.

REINHARDT, CARL GOTTHELF. *Dresden.* Master 1764, died 1800.

REINHOLD, HANS. *Augsburg.* Born 1587, died about 1640; calendar watch, Fränkel collection.

REINHOLD, JOHAN GEORG. *Augsburg,* 1584. Died a. 1600; striking clock in V. & A. by him and Georgius Roll,

dated 1584; celestial globe clock by him and G. Roll, dated 1586, M.P.S., Dresden; large octagonal crystal watch, M.M.A.; clockwork globe C.A. & M.

REISNER, MICHAEL. *Cologne,* 1797–1813.

REITH, JAMES. Repeating watch, about 1700, in pierced and engraved gold case, signed 'James Reith Versailles', V. & A.; admitted C.C. 1705; long-case clock, about 1715.

REMMERDELL, THOS. *Wigan.* Watch, 1776.

RENARD, ARMAND (AMAND). *Paris.* Master 1751–89.

RENCHING, EDMD. Apprenticed 1659 to Robt. Robinson, C.C.

RENIER, MICHAEL E. *Kronstadt.* Table clock, about 1590.

RENSHAW, THOMAS. *Ship Alley, Wellclose Sq.,* 1825.

RENSTRÖM, JOHAN GUSTAF. *Stockholm,* 1824–59.

RENTNOW. WONTNER reversed.

RENTZSCH, SIGISMUND. *2 St. George St., St. James's Sq.* A clever mechanician and excellent workman; he devised and made a peculiar chronometer escapement; his regulator had original features, among them a pendulum, with the mercury divided in several small tubes; he patented in 1813 an automatic timekeeper somewhat similar to Horstmann's; 1813–42.

RETTFORD, JNO. *London.* Watch, 1798.

REVEL, J. *Palais-Royal, Paris,* 1770.

REVELL, JNO. *Eye,* 1775.

REVELL, SAM. Apprenticed 1664 to Thos. Loomes, C.C.

REWALLING, THOMAS. C.C. 1715; watch, about 1720, signed 'Thos. Rewalling, London'.

REY, CHARLES. *Paris.* Master 1770, juré 1786–89.

REY, HUGUES. *Lyons.* 1659 master–1703.

REY, J. Enamelled watch, about 1785, signed 'Jn. Ant. Rey & Fils'.

REY, JEAN ANTOINE. *Geneva.* Born 1682, died 1787.

REY, JEAN FRANÇOIS. *Geneva.* Master 1712, died 1748.

REYMOND, —. *Charleston, U.S.A.,* 1785. From Paris; clocks and watches.

REYNER, STEPHEN, at ye *Dial, Bishopsgate Within.* Admitted C.C. 1691.

REYNER, THOS. *Oxon.* Bracket clock, about 1740.

REYNOLDS, ALBAN. Apprenticed 1670 to Jno. Wise, C.C.

REYNOLDS, FRANCIS. *Kensington,* 1776.

REYNOLDS, G. *10 Gough Sq.,* 1830.

REYNOLDS, JACOB. *Shaston.* Long-case clock, about 1750.

REYNOLDS, JAS. *Holborn Hill.* Livery C.C. 1760.

REYNOLDS, JNO. Blacksmith, *Hagbourn, Berks.* Made a clock and chimes for Brampton Church, for which he was paid £34, 1732.

REYNOLDS, JOSEPH. C.C. 1691.

REYNOLDS, THOMAS. Apprenticed to H. Bradshaw; C.C. 1706; small bracket chiming clock, two trains only, arch dial, with strike-silent hand, inscribed 'Thomas Reynolds, St. Martin's-le-Grand', about 1740.

REYNOLDS, THOS., son and late apprentice of the preceding T. R., *2 St. Martin's-le-Grand.* Admitted C.C. 1736; watch, G.M., about 1770.

REYNOLDS, THOS. *Warwick.* Watch, silver cock, silver name-plate, steel index disc, about 1730.

REYNOLDS, THOS. *Holywell, Oxon.,* 1770–85.

REYNOLDS, THOS., & SON. *1 Sparrow Corner, Minories,* 1783–94.

REYNOLDS, WM. *Launceston,* 1750.

RHETORICK, WALTER. Apprenticed 1651 to David Moody, C.C.

RHODENHURST, WILLIAM. *London.* Apprenticed 1768, C.C. 1776–1820.

RHODES, WILLIAM. *London.* Apprenticed 1755, C.C. 1762.

RIACH, H. *London,* about 1790.

RIBART, ANTOINE, son of Thomas. *Blois.* Born 1608–37.

RIBART, T. *Blois.* Watch, about 1590, Garnier collection.

RIBART, T. *Paris.* Oval watch, about 1630.

RIBOULEAU, LASON. *London.* Apprenticed 1736, C.C. 1746–62.

RICE, BENJAMIN. *Neath.* Born 1757, died 1813; watch.

RICE, JOSEPH. *Baltimore,* 1784. Clocks and watches; entered into partnership with Standish Barry in 1785.

RICE, JOSEPH T. *Albany, U.S.A.,* 1813–23.

RICE, STEPHEN. *20 Pall Mall,* 1793.

RICE, THOMAS. *London.* Apprenticed 1792, C.C. 1800.

RICH, JNO. *London.* Watch on chatelaine, Pierpont Morgan collection, about 1750; repeating watch; 1775.

RICH, JOHN. *Bristol, Conn.,* 1820.

RICH, T. *Cheltenham,* 1788–1810. Bracket clock.

RICHARD, AUGUSTE. Silver watch, signed 'Auguste Richard sur la Port à Rouen', has 'John Mattin' round the dial instead of figures, about 1820; Pierpont Morgan collection.

RICHARD, CHRISTOPHE. *Paris.* 1750 master–1789; repaired clock on La Samaritaine.

RICHARD, DANIEL JOHN. Born at *La Sagne* 1672, died at *Locle,* 1741; is said to have introduced watchmaking into Neuchâtel in 1692; his five sons devoted themselves to the new industry.

RICHARD, FRANÇOIS. *Hambourg.* Watch, V. & A., about 1780.

RICHARD, FRANÇOIS. *Vevey,* 1761–1798.

RICHARD, JEAN JACQUES. *Le Locle,* 1740–66. Watchmaker of repute.

RICHARD, JEAN LOUIS. *Geneva,* about 1775–91.

RICHARD, PETER. C.C. 1679.

RICHARDS, B. *London.* Watch, 1790.

RICHARDS, E. *Guernsey,* about 1790 C.C.

RICHARDS, HENRY. *London.* C.C. 1699; watch, 1725.

RICHARDS, HUGH. *Broad St.* Apprenticed 1691 to Hy. Bradley, master C.C. 1735.

RICHARDS, JAMES. *London.* Apprenticed 1763, C.C. 1770.

RICHARDS, JNO. Apprenticed in 1654 to Wm. Pettitt, C.C.

RICHARDS, JNO. *London.* C.C. 1770; several watches, 1780–96.

RICHARDS, LUKE. C.C. 1648.

RICHARDS, RICHD. Free of C.C. by redemption, 1652.

RICHARDS, S. & J., 1817.

RICHARDS, THEOPHILUS & Co. Centre seconds watch, about 1820.

RICHARDS, THOMAS. *114 Strand,* 1770–72.

RICHARDS, THOMAS. *17 Bridgewater Sq., Barbican,* 1804; *96 Shoreditch,* 1830.

RICHARDS, W. *49 Oxford St.,* 1830.

RICHARDS, WILLIAM. *Albemarle St., Clerkenwell.* Liveryman C.C. 1776.

RICHARDS, WILLIAM. *43 Brick Lane, Old St.,* 1794.

RICHARDS & MORRELL. *240 Pearl St., New York,* 1809.

RICHARDSON, CHARLES. *London.* C.C. 1739.

RICHARDSON, CHARLES. *London.* Apprenticed 1749, C.C. 1760.

RICHARDSON, FRANCIS. *Philadelphia,* 1736.

RICHARDSON, HENRY. *London,* about 1770.

RICHARDSON, HENRY. *London.* C.C. 1813.

RICHARDSON, JAMES. *Bradford.* Clock; 'Jas. Richardson. — Bradforth', about 1760.

RICHARDSON, JAMES. *Lutton,* 1780; *Pentonville,* 1800; master C.C. 1788.

RICHARDSON, JOHN. *Racquet, Court,* 1798–1811; liveryman C.C. 1810.

RICHARDSON, JOHN. *London (Bell Yd.).* Apprenticed 1731, C.C. 1738, died 1774.

RICHARDSON, JOHN. *London,* 1798. C.C. 1807.

RICHARDSON, RICHARD. C.C. 1675; "a good wheel cutter" (Hatton).

RICHARDSON, RICHARD. *Hexham,* 1780.

RICHARDSON, RICHARD. *Liverpool,* about 1780–1803. Long-case clock; watch.

RICHARDSON, THOMAS KELLY. *London (Fore St.).* Apprenticed 1767, C.C. 1775–82.

RICHARDSON, THOS. *Weaverham.* Long-case clock, about 1780.

RICHARDSON, WILLIAM. *Alloa,* 1769–90.

RICHARDSON, WM. Apprenticed 1647 to Jas. Starnell, C.C.

RICHMOND, JAMES. *Bradford,* about 1770–95.

RICHMOND, JOSEPH. *York,* f., 1810.

RICHMOND, ROBT. *Lancaster,* 1817, f.

RICHTER, F. J. *Nürnberg,* late seventeenth century. Watch.

RICKARD, JOHN. *London.* Apprenticed 1649, C.C. 1657.

RICKARD, JOHN. *Exeter,* about 1760–95. Watch, Exeter Museum.

RICKETT, THOS. *High Wycombe,* 1780.

RICKMAN, W. *35 Great Pulteney St.,* 1820.

RICORD, JNO. C.C. 1657.

RICORD, RICHARD. C.C. 1649.

RIDDEL, CHARLES. *Old Meldrum,* 1800–37.

RIDDLESDON, JNO. Watch-spring maker, *Red Cross Sq.,* 1790–94.

RIDDLESDON, SAMUEL. C.C. 1766.

RIDER, JOB. *Belfast.* Advertisement 1791: "Job Rider, from London and Dublin, and last from Hillsborough has commenced business at 'The Reflecting Telescope' *Shambles Street,* where he makes clocks and watches of all kinds to the common manner, with Harrison's and other modern improvements. His turret and steeple clocks are in an entirely new construction"; made a self-winding barometric clock somewhat on the plan of Cox; he removed to *High St., Belfast,* and retired from the clock and watch business in 1807.

RIDER, THOS. Apprenticed 1691 to John Johnson, C.C.

RIDEREAU, S. Established at *Place Maubert, Paris,* in 1769; presented the Academy of Science with a clock striking hours, quarters, and repeating all with the same striking train.

RIDGDALE, N. Oval watch, V. & A., about 1610.

RIDLEY, JOSEPH. Received a reward of 20 guineas from the Society of Arts, for a sector and depthing tool, 1788. In 1793 Joseph, son of Joseph Ridley, watchmaker of St. Margarets, Westminster, was apprentice to Francis Fether, citizen and cutler.

RIDLEY, JOSIAH. C.C. 1685; fine long marquetry case chiming clock, about 1700.

RIEPPOLT (RIEBOLD), JOHANN S. *Regensburg.* Master in *Augsburg* 1727, juré 1735–59, died a. 1770; gold engraved watch; fine watch Rijks Museum, Amsterdam.

RIEUSSEC, —. *Paris,* 1807–25. Well-known maker; invented chronograph making ink mark on dial; chronometer, C.A. & M.

RIGAUD, —. *London.* Watch, about 1740.

RIGAULT, PAUL. *Blois.* Comp. 1619, died about 1638; clockmaker to the duc d'Orléans.

RIGAULT, PAUL, son. *Blois,* 1661–92. Clockmaker to the duc d'Orléans.

RIGBY, E., & SON. *6 Berkeley St., Clerkenwell,* 1795–1800.

RIGBY, JAMES. *35 Rosoman St., Clerkenwell,* 1804.

RIGBY, JAMES. *8 Charing Cross,* 1806–30 (succeeded Leroux, see MORSE, RICHD).

RIGBY, JAS. *Liverpool*, 1830.

RIGBY, JOSHUA. *5 Berkeley St., Clerkenwell*. Hon. freeman C.C. 1781; spoken of by Hatton and by Earnshaw; maker of a repeater watch for the Duke of Sussex; 1765–1800.

RIGBY, JOSHUA. *8 King St., Goswell Rd.*, 1820.

RIGBY, THOS. *29 Alfred Pl., Goswell Rd.*, 1816–18.

RIGGS, WILLIAM H. C. *Philadelphia*, 1819–25.

RIGMAIDEN, —. *Dublin*, about 1760.

RILEY, G. *Halifax*, 1809. See RYLEY.

RILEY, JAMES. *London*. C.C. 1752.

RILEY, JOHN. *Gillingham, Halifax*, 1804.

RILEY, JOHN. *Philadelphia*, 1783–1808. Clocks and watches.

RILEY, PATRICK. Probably *London*, a. 1769. Watch.

RILEY, RILEY. *New York*, 1805. Watch.

RILEY, ROBERT. *Philadelphia*, 1806–08. Watch.

RIMBAULT. This family of clockmakers flourished from about 1700 till nearly the end of the century.

RIMBAULT, PAUL. *9 Denmark St., St. Giles's*, 1779–85.

RIMBAULT, STEPHEN. *7 Great St. Andrew St.*, 1760–81.

RIMER, WM. *Liverpool*. Watch, 1769.

RIMOND, CHARLES. *Geneva*, about 1755–72.

RING, JOHN. *London*. Apprenticed 1686, C.C. 1693.

RING, JOSEPH. C.C. 1693.

RINSES, SIPKE. *Grouw*, 1792. Died 1830; automatic clock.

RIPLEY, JNO. *York*, f., 1471.

RIPPIN, WILLIAM. *Holbeath, Lincolnshire*. Worked at his trade as watch and clock repairer for thirty years after he lost his sight; vouched for by his daughter and many other persons; he died in 1857.

RIPPON, RICHARD. *46 King St., Seven Dials*, 1816; afterwards of *Cooks' Court, Long Acre*. A well-known maker of English repeating work for watches. E. J. Dent married his widow; fine watch movement by him, G.M.

RISBRIDGER (or RIBRIDGER), JOHN. *Brentford*. Long-case clock, square dial, one hand, with date '1740' scratched on back of dial and also '1777 cleaned'.

RISBRIDGER (or RIBRIDGER), JOHN. *New Brentford*, 1800–20.

RISBRIDGER (or RIBRIDGER), WILLIAM. *Dorking*. Lantern and 30-hour long-case clocks, about 1700.

RISDON, FRANCIS. *London*. Watch, about 1780.

RISHTON, JAMES. *Rochdale*, 1821.

RISING, NILS. *Stockholm*. Born 1722; *Göteborg*, 1756. Died 1784; long-case lacquer clock.

RISING, OLOF. *Stockholm*. Apprenticed 1732; *Göteborg*, 1747. Died 1783; watch and long-case clock.

RISOLIERE, ISAAC. *London*. Apprenticed 1749, C.C. 1756–64; died a. 1795.

RITCHIE, DAVID. *Clerkenwell*. Devised a compensation pendulum in 1812.

RITCHIE, GEORGE. *Philadelphia*, 1785–93.

RITCHIE, JAS. *Leith St., Edinburgh*, 1809–42.

RITCHIE, SAMUEL. *Cupar-Fife*, 1800–37.

RITHE, JNO. Apprenticed in 1654 to R. Scrivener, C.C.

RITHERDON, GEO. *Aldgate*, 1753–83.

RITHERDON, ROBERT. *3 Aldgate Within*, 1758–1800.

RITTENHOUSE, DAVID. *Philadelphia*, 1751–77. Astronomical clock, 1767. An important maker.

RITTER, J. LOUIS. *Geneva*, 1754–about 1790. 4-colour gold watch.

RIVAL, DAVID. *Geneva*. Born 1696, died a. 1770.

RIVAL, JEAN JAQUES ANTOINE LOUIS. *Geneva*, about 1775–91.

RIVAL, JEAN PIERRE, son. *Geneva*, about 1750. Went to *Versoix*, 1770.

RIVAZ, PIERRE DE. *Paris*. A celebrated horologist of the mid-eighteenth century. He experimented with marine timekeepers. He converted clocks going a fortnight only into twelve months without winding, and claimed that by adding another wheel his clocks could be made to show the true time, exactly following the sun, even in his equalities.

RIVERS, DAVID. *3 Bridgewater Sq.*, 1753–75.

RIVERS, DAVID. *3 Sweeting's Alley*. Livery C.C. 1766; master 1773; 1760–83; watch, David Rivers & Son, h.m., 1782.

RIVERS, DAVID. *London*. C.C. 1789–95.

RIVERS, JNO. *1 Holborn Bars*, 1783.

RIVERS, SAMUEL. *London*. C.C. 1785.

RIVERS, THOMAS, son of J. J. *London*. Apprenticed 1775, C.C. 1784.

RIVERS, WILLIAM. *33 Cornhill*, 1818–20.

RIVERS, WILLIAM. *London*. C.C. 1776, master C.C. 1801–20.

RIVERS & SON (successors to D. St. Leu). *38 Cornhill*, 1790–1812. Wm. Rivers, master C.C. 1794.

RIVIERE, CHARLES. *London*. C.C. 1815.

RIVIERE, JACOB. *London (Marylebone)*. Apprenticed 1746, C.C. 1756, died 1815.

RIVIERE, LUBIN. *Blois*. Master 1670, died 1694.

RIVIERE, SAMUEL NEWTON. *63 New Bond St.*, 1790–1804.

RIVOIRE, HENRI. *Geneva*, about 1775–90.

RIVONNEAU, JOSEPH. *Paris*. Juré 1784.

RIX, —. *London*. Watch, 1750; clock, about 1760, inscribed 'I. Rix, London'.

ROACH, WILLIAM. *New York*, 1783. Watch.

ROBARTS, B. *London*. Watch, 1783.

ROBB, WM. *Montrose*, 1780.

ROBBIN, FABIAN. *London*. Walnut marquetry long-case month clock, square dial, bull's-eye in front of pendulum bob, 1690–1700. See ROBINS, FABIAN.

ROBERSON, JAS. *London*, 1760.

ROBERT, ABRAM. *Chaux-de-Fonds*, 1750–54. *Basle*, 1759.

ROBERT, ABRAM LOUIS. *Chaux-de-Fonds*, 1756–87. Clock; said to have invented the depth tool.

ROBERT, AIMÉ, son of LOUIS B. *Chaux-de-Fonds*. Born 1758, died 1834; member of firm J. Robert et Fils, *Chaux-de-Fonds*.

ROBERT, CLAUDE ALEXANDRE. *Paris*. Master 1767–89.

ROBERT, DAVID, son of Josué. *Chaux-de-Fonds*. Born 1717, died 1769. 'Très expert horloger'; made 'Toutes sortes de pendules curieuses'; many clocks signed 'Robert l'aîné'.

ROBERT, FRANÇOIS. *Switzerland* and *Besançon*, 1798–1815. A maker of repute.

ROBERT, FRÉDÉRIC. *Chaux-de-Fonds*. Apprenticed 1757–86. Clock.

ROBERT, J. *Chaux-de-Fonds*. Quarter repeating work described by Thiout in 1741.

ROBERT, JACQUES. *Cortaillod*, 1716–22.

ROBERT, LOUIS BENJAMIN, brother. *Chaux-de-Fonds*. Born 1732, died 1781; clockmaker of repute.

ROBERT, NICOLAS. *Paris*. Master 1769–89.

ROBERT, THÉODORE. *Chaux-de-Fonds*, 1745. Died 1775; able clockmaker.

ROBERT & COURVOISIER. *Geneva*, 1790–1800.

ROBERTS, C. *London*. Watch, 1820.

ROBERTS, GEORGE. *27 Marchmont St., Brunswick Sq.*, 1820.

ROBERTS, GIDEON. *Bristol, Conn.*, 1780–1804; then JNO.; then JACOB.

ROBERTS, HUGH. Apprenticed 1657 to David Bouquett; C.C. 1664; in the British Museum is a large astronomical watch by him.

ROBERTS, J. *Dudley.* Watch, about 1800, around bezel, 'Keep me clean and use me well, then I to you the time will tell.'

ROBERTS, J. B. *London.* Watch, 1795.

ROBERTS, JNO. *Trawfynndd,* 1774–1845.

ROBERTS, JNO. *St. James's Market,* 1790.

ROBERTS, JOHN. *London (Mays Bdgs.).* Apprenticed 1764, C.C. 1771.

ROBERTS, JOHN, son of Sam. (2). *London.* C.C. 1776.

ROBERTS, JOHN. *London (Clerkenwell).* C.C. 1805–20.

ROBERTS, JOSIAH. *88 Bishopsgate St.,* 1793.

ROBERTS, PIERCY. *London (Blackfriars).* C.C. 1816.

ROBERTS, RICHARD. Apprenticed 1653 to Eliza Fletcher, C.C.

ROBERTS, SAMUEL. C.C. 1776; watch, G.M., h.m., 1778.

ROBERTS, SAMUEL. *Llanfair Caereinion,* 1755. Died 1800; many long-case clocks.

ROBERTS, TIMOTHY. *Otley,* 1770.

ROBERTS, WM. Apprenticed 1692 to Mordecai Fox, C.C.

ROBERTS, WM. *St. James's Market,* 1806; *5 St. Alban's Place, Pall Mall,* 1820–30.

ROBERTS, WM. *Bath,* 1825.

ROBERTSON, BENJ. *14 Jewin St.,* 1783.

ROBERTSON, CHARLES. *Coupar-Angus,* 1814–37.

ROBERTSON, JAMES. *Dundee,* 1811–28.

ROBERTSON, JAMES. *Leith,* 1818–36.

ROBERTSON, JOHN. *Edinburgh,* 1783–1821.

ROBERTSON, WILLIAM. *Edinburgh,* 1764–80.

ROBERT-THEURER, ÉDOUARD. *Chaux-de-Fonds.* Born 1793, died 1877; great grandson of Josué Robert.

ROBERT-TISSOT, ABRAM. *Le Locle* and *Chaux-de-Fonds,* 1630. Died 1668.

ROBIN, —. *Paris (Rue de Richelieu),* about 1790–1825. Clockmaker to Louis XVIII; mantel clock, Mobilier National, Paris.

ROBIN, ROBERT. *Paris.* Born 1742; died 1809; clockmaker to Louis XVI; two excellent examples of his work are in the Jones collection at V. & A., and one in the Wallace collection; a very fine maker.

ROBINET, PIERRE. *Paris.* 1776 master, juré 1778–1812.

ROBINS, FABIAN. *London.* Walnut marquetry long-case month clock, square dial, glass in front of pendulum bob, about 1695.

ROBINS, JOHN. *67 Aldersgate St.,* 1783–94.

ROBINS, JOHN. *13 Clerkenwell Green,* 1800–04; *65 Charing Cross,* 1817.

ROBINS, JOHN. *13 Frith St.,* 1823–30.

ROBINS, JOSHUA. *London (Bow).* Apprenticed 1791, C.C. 1808–20; watch.

ROBINS, THOMAS. *London (Aldermanbury).* Apprenticed 1763, C.C. 1774; watch.

ROBINS, WM. *13 Fleet St.,* 1783. Master C.C. 1813.

ROBINSON, ANDRES. *Galway,* 1820.

ROBINSON, ANTHONY. *232 Strand,* 1783.

ROBINSON, DAN. Apprenticed 1681 to Wm. Arthur, C.C.

ROBINSON, FRANCIS, 'in the Temple'; apprenticed to Henry Jones, C.C. 1707; master 1725; repeating watch with silver case in the G.M. inscribed 'Servant to His Royal Highness'; another example, a small square-case clock, square dial with cherub corners, 1707–26.

ROBINSON, GEO. Apprenticed 1631 to Simon Hackett, C.C.

ROBINSON, GEO. *London,* 1806. Clock so inscribed in the lighthouse at St. Agnes, Scilly Islands.

ROBINSON, HENRY. *London.* Apprenticed 1724, C.C. 1733–39.

ROBINSON, JAMES, at the Dial in *Grace's Alley, Well Close Sq.* Maker of long-case clocks and watches, 1730–70, afterwards Samuel Robinson.

ROBINSON, JNO. Apprenticed 1681 to Wm. Robinson.

ROBINSON, JNO. *Lancaster,* 1783, f.

ROBINSON, JOSEPH. *London (Holborn* and *Old St.).* Apprenticed 1750, C.C. 1769–96.

ROBINSON, M. Repeating watch, gold *repoussé* case, Schloss collection, 1780.

ROBINSON, MARTIN. *London.* C.C. 1812.

ROBINSON, OLIVER. *London.* Apprenticed 1720, C.C. 1727.

ROBINSON, OWEN. An escapement maker who worked for Arnold, mentioned by Reid as the maker of a double chronometer escapement, 1710–1810.

ROBINSON, PHILIP. *Fleet St.,* 1737–40.

ROBINSON, ROBERT. C.C. 1652; lantern clock, inscribed 'Robert Robinson in Red Cross St of London', about 1655, dial 3 in. in diameter of silver, days of the month engraved outside the hour band with indicator on rotating ring; another lantern clock, marked 'Robert Robinson at the Style in Lothbury, London', about 1670.

ROBINSON, RUHAMER. *Gracechurch St.,* 1713.

ROBINSON, SAMUEL. *London.* C.C. 1785.

ROBINSON, THOMAS. C.C. 1703.

ROBINSON, THOMAS. *Liverpool,* 1790–1829. Watch.

ROBINSON, THOS. *London.* Watch, 1780.

ROBINSON, THOS. *London.* Apprenticed to Paul Barraud; C.C. 1812; watch, 1825.

ROBINSON, WILLIAM. C.C. 1667.

ROBINSON, WILLIAM. Apprenticed to Daniel Delander; C.C. 1720.

ROBINSON, WILLIAM. *Liverpool,* 1795–1824. Lever watch, Chamb. collection; watch, New York University.

ROBINSON, WM. *Leyburn,* 1822–40.

ROBINSON & CAVE. '232 Strand, near Temple Barr', card, Ponsonby collection, about 1770.

ROBOTHAM, F. *Leicester,* about 1740.

ROBOTHAM, FRANCIS JONATHAN. *Hampstead.* About 1790 C.C.–1824.

ROBSON, WILLIAM. Musical-clock maker, *48 Red Cross St.,* 1797–1810. Master C.C. 1809.

ROBSON, WM. *Curtain Rd.,* 1780–94.

ROBSON, WM. *North Shields,* 1807–24.

ROBY, JAMES. *2 Prince's St., Leicester Sq.,* 1793–1800.

ROCHAT, FRÈRES. *Geneva.* Watch, about 1810.

ROCHAT, JEAN MARC DAVID. *Geneva,* about 1775–91.

ROCHFORD, F. *49 Jermyn St.,* 1830.

ROCHFORD, M. F. *212 Piccadilly,* 1804–25.

ROCKWELL, E. & S. S. *New York,* 1822. Watch.

ROCQUET, JACQUES MARTIN. *Paris.* Master 1759–89.

RODET, I. *London.* Quarter repeating watch in gold case beautifully pierced with birds and scrolls; outer case pierced and ornamented in *repoussé* with medallions, escallop shells, and flowers, about 1740, Pierpont Morgan collection; another watch of Dutch character similarly inscribed about 1750; watch, 'Isa Rodet, London', about 1770.

RODGERS, BENJ. *London,* 1720.

RODGERS, J. *39 St. Paul's Churchyard.* Rack-lever watch, 1818.

ROE, JOSHUA. Apprenticed 1687 to Edmd. Appley, C.C.

ROEMER, OLOW (OLAF). *Aarhus.* Born 1644, died 1710; astronomical clocks; recommended the epicycloid for clock.

ROGER, —. Repaired the clock at Exeter Cathedral, 1424.

ROGER, JACQUES. *Lyons.* Master 1643–83 juré. Also Rogier and Rougier.

ROGER, PIERRE. *Angers,* about 1600–26. Re-made cathedral clock in 1626; oval watch Bourges Museum.

ROGERS, —. *Leominster,* about 1730.

ROGERS, B. *London*. Watch, 1735.

ROGERS, C. *59 Charlton St., Somers Town*, 1820.

ROGERS, CHAS. Apprenticed 1649 to Wm. Almond; C.C. 1657.

ROGERS, ISAAC. *White Hart Court, Gracechurch St.* C.C. 1776; master 1824; succeeded to his father's business 1776; removed to *24 Little Bell Alley, Coleman St.*, in 1802; died 1839. A maker of good watches; a specimen in gold *repoussé* outer case is in the British Museum; did a good trade in Turkish markets; 1750–94; large travelling watch, dated 1759, Pierpont Morgan collection.

ROGERS, JAMES. *Leominster*, 1778–95.

ROGERS, JNO. *Hackney*. Watch, 1780.

ROGERS, JOHN. C.C. 1731.

ROGERS, ROBERT. *Bristol*, 1767–90.

ROGERS, S. *Fenchurch St.*, 1774–82.

ROGERS, SAMUEL. *Plymouth, U.S.A.*, 1790–1804.

ROGERS, THOMAS. *63 Charing Cross*. Liveryman C.C. 1810.

ROGERS, THOMAS. *Bath*, 1742. Died 1781; clocks and watches.

ROGERS, THOMAS. *London*. Apprenticed 1754, C.C. 1763.

ROGERS, THOMAS. *London*. Apprenticed 1802, C.C. 1820.

ROGERS, WILLIAM. C.C. 1641; Nicasius Russell was apprenticed to him in 1653.

ROGERS, WILLIAM. *Broad St. Buildings*. Liveryman C.C. 1776.

ROGERS, WM. Apprenticed 1682 to Thos. Taylor, Holborn.

ROGERSON, HENRY. *London*, about 1780.

ROGERSON, JOSHUA. *London*. Apprenticed 1766, C.C. 1773, livery C.C. 1779, died 1782.

ROGERSON, WILLIAM. *London (R. Exchange)*. Apprenticed 1747, C.C. 1754, m.C.C. 1774–78.

ROGET, —. *London*. Watch, about 1740; another, 1755.

ROHR, JOHN A. *Philadelphia*, 1811.

ROIZIN, —. *Rue de Charonne, Paris*, 1770.

ROJARD, JEAN DANIEL. —, about 1750–70.

ROLF, JOSEPH, & SON. *17 Foster Lane*, 1769–88.

ROLL, GEORGE. *Augsburg*. In 1588 he made a clockwork globe, which Rudolph II bought for 1,000 florins; at the V. & A. is a striking clock in a celestial sphere of gilt brass on four feet; the sphere is inscribed 'Elaborabat Georgivs Roll et Johannes Reinhold in Avgvsta Anno Domini 1584'.

ROLLAND, JEAN JOSEPH. *Geneva*, about 1775–91.

ROLLISON, DOLLY. *Halton*. Died 1752; long-case clock, inscribed 'Dollif Rolisson, Halton', long case clock, signed 'Dolf Rollinson, Halton, Essex'.

ROMAN, BORDIER & Co. Watch, about 1825.

ROMEAU, ISAAC. *London*. C.C. 1635–41.

ROMER, FLACK. C.C. 1661.

ROMER, ISAAC. *London*. C.C. 1661.

ROMER, THOS. *20 George St., Adelphi*, 1817.

ROMEUX, LEWIS DE. C.C. 1706.

ROMIEU, — à *Rouen*. Enamelled watch, about 1660.

ROMIEU, L. *Rouen*. Watch in silver case, outer case of leather *piqué* with silver, centre of dial enamelled green, hours on white ring of enamel, about 1630, Pierpont Morgan collection.

ROMIEU, PAUL. *Edinburgh*. Long-case clock, about 1700.

ROMILLY, JOHN. Born in *Geneva*, 1714. A clever watchmaker who migrated to Paris and set up business in the Place Dauphin, where he was very successful; also advocated 8-day watches and made several, also watches with cylinder escapements and very large

balances to vibrate seconds, as well as equation watches; is said to have produced a self-winding watch, possibly on the plan patented in England by Recordon in 1780, and of which Breguet made several; a fine watch by him with enamelled case forms part of the Pierpont Morgan collection; at V. & A. is a watch signed 'I. Romilly à Paris', dating from about 1760; the case is inlaid with tinted gold; died 1796, aged 82.

ROMILLY, PETER. *17 Frith St., Soho*, 1769–94. Long-case chiming clock, inscribed 'Romilly, London', about 1770.

ROMLEY, CHRIS. Apprenticed to Wm. Addis; C.C. 1755. Ludlam quotes both Chris. and Rob. Romley.

ROMLEY, ROBERT, in *Horse Shoe Alley, Middle Moor Fields*, 1765–75.

ROMNEY, JOSEPH. Admitted C.C. 1664.

RONDIN, GUY, à *Nantes*, about 1680.

RONT, WM. *Enfield*. Watch, 1765.

ROOF, DANIEL. C.C. 1676.

ROOKE, JOHN. *26 Berkeley Sq.*, 1765–94. Hon. f. C.C. 1781.

ROOKER, RICHARD. *Chelsea*. C.C. 1728; large silver watch, silver chased dial, having an aperture behind which an imitation pendulum swings, about 1740.

ROOKER, RICHD. Apprenticed 1685 to Jno. Clowes; C.C. 1694.

ROOKES, BARLOW. Admitted C.C. 1667.

ROOKESBY, ROBERT. *London*. 1684 C.C.

ROOKSBY, —. A small timepiece with repeating work, dial brass gilt, beautifully engraved, inscribed 'J. Rooksby in Yorke', about 1690.

"Stolen on the 23rd instant, out of Mr. Jeffreys. House in Yorke, a gold pendulum watch with minutes and seconds, made by Mr. Rooksby, of Hull, with a gold studdied case. Notice to be given to Mr. Hill, Goldsmith, in the Strand" (*Lond. Gaz.*, Nov. 26–30, 1691).

ROOKSBY, JOHN. *York*, f., 1647.

ROPER, MARTIN. *Penrith*, 1820–29.

ROQUE, J. *Passage du Saumon, Paris*, 1770.

ROSANY, L. *Paris*, about 1775.

ROSCOW, ROBERT. *Liverpool*, 1813–29. Watch, New York University.

ROSE, —, JUNR. *St. Ann's Lane*, 1774.

ROSE, DANIEL. *Reading, U.S.A.*, 1820–40.

ROSE, DANIEL. *London*. 1685–89 C.C.

ROSE, JOHN. *Bishopsgate*. C.C. 1730.

ROSE, JOHN. *96 Fleet Market*, 1830.

ROSE, JOHN. *London*. Apprenticed 1736, C.C. 1748, gold watch.

ROSE, JOSEPH. *London*, about 1750. Musical clock in a long case, the base of which is kettle-shape.

ROSE, JOSEPH, & SON. *19 Foster Lane*, 1765–68.

ROSE, JOSEPH, SON & PAYNE. *17 Foster Lane*, 1771–94.

ROSE, MICHAEL. C.C. 1676; 8-day chiming clock in long case with scroll marquetry decoration, signed 'Rose & Son', about 1720.

ROSE, T. *St. Clements, Oxon.*, 1780.

ROSE, WILLIAM. *London*. Watch in painted tortoise-shell case, about 1750.

ROSE, WILLIAM. *London (Bloomsbury)*. Apprenticed 1752, C.C. 1767–1806.

ROSELET, —. *Geneva*. Watch, 1809.

ROSENTRETER, PAULUS. *Nürnberg*. Master 1566; Kleinuhrmacher; clock, K.H.M., about 1600 signed 'P. R.', possibly by him.

ROSIER, JOHN. *Geneva*. Watch, 1815.

ROSKELL, JOHN. *Liverpool*, 1805–21. Watch.

ROSKELL, ROBERT, the elder. *Liverpool*. Many rack lever

and cylinder watches by him; he was also a collector of curious horological specimens, 1800–30.

ROSS, JNO. *Tain*, 1775.

ROSS, THOS. *Hull*, 1770.

ROSS, WM. *Cork*. Watch, handsome *repoussé* case, h.m., 1793.

ROSS & PECKHAM. *41 Bedford St., Covent Garden*, 1810.

ROSSE, DANIEL. *London*. 1688 C.C.

ROSSE, SAMUEL. C.C. 1672.

ROSSE, WILLIAM. *London*. Apprenticed 1683, C.C. 1691.

ROSSI, W. *5 Blackman St.*, 1830.

ROTH, FRANZ ANTON. *Augsburg*. Master 1759–90.

ROTHERHAM, RICHARD KEVITT. *Coventry*, about 1760–1832. *v.* VALE.

ROTHERHAM, THOMAS. Apprenticed to Simon Hacket 1654; C.C. 1662.

ROTHERODD, BENJAMIN. Silver rose-shaped watch in the Bernal collection, seventeenth-century work.

ROTHWOOD, ROBERT. C.C. 1632.

ROTHWOOD, ROBERT. C.C. 1648.

ROTTI, GEORG LEOPOLD. *Augsburg*. Comp. about 1746, master 1755, died 1791.

ROTZENHOFER, MATTHEUS. *Vienna*. Complicated clocks and automata; died 1839.

ROU (LEROUX), GILLES, son of Pierre (1). *Blois*. 1630–81.

ROU (LEROUX), JEAN. *Blois*, 1654–84.

ROU (LEROUX), MARTIN. *Blois*, 1653–72.

ROU (LEROUX), PIERRE. *Blois*, 1623. Died 1662; large striking watch, New York University.

ROU (LEROUX), PIERRE. *Blois*, 1652–89.

ROUBELL, JNO. *4 Orange Grove, Bath*, 1798. See WADHAM.

ROUCKLEIFFE, JNO. *Bridgwater*. Maker of brass clocks, 1770. See BRIMBLE.

ROULEAU, BENJAMIN. *London*. Apprenticed 1765, C.C. 1777.

ROULLET, GABRIEL. *London*. Apprenticed 1742, C.C. 1753.

ROULSTONE, JOHN. *Boston, U.S.A.*, 1789–1803. Watch.

ROUMIEU, ADAM. C.C. 1695.

ROUMIEU, ADAM. C.C. 1726.

ROUMIEU, ADAM. *London*. Apprenticed 1657, C.C. 1687; watch case maker; case marked A.R.

ROUMIEU. JAMES. *London*, 1689. C.C. 1692–1707. Also ROUMYEU.

ROUMIEU, JOHN. C.C. 1720.

ROUMIEU, JOHN. *London*. Apprenticed 1711, C.C. 1720–38; died a. 1742.

ROUMIEU, LEWIS DE. *London*. Apprenticed 1700, C.C. 1707. Also ROMIEU.

ROUMIEU, P. *Rouen*. Watch, about 1740.

ROUMIEU, PAUL. *Edinburgh*. Probably from Rouen; submitted his essay, made in his own chamber and vouched for by George Mill and Andrew Brown, and was admitted to the incorporation of Hammermen 1677; died 1693; watch, about 1680.

ROUMIEU, PAUL. *Edinburgh*, son of the foregoing. Admitted 1682, his essay masters being Richard Mill and Jno. Sympson; died 1710. "Stolen this day in the Parliament House, out of a gentleman's pocket, a silver pendulum watch with a minute hand and a green shagreen case, some of the studs broken off. Whoever can give notice of the said watch to Mr. Romieu, watchmaker, shall be thankfully rewarded" (*Edinburgh Gaz.*, 1699).

ROUMYEU, JAMES. C.C. 1692.

ROUNDELL, THOMAS. *London*. Apprenticed 1729, C.C. 1749.

ROUNTREE, ROBT. *York*, f., 1828.

ROUSBY, JNO. *York*, f., 1683.

ROUSE, ROBERT. Apprenticed 1682 to Chas. Baxter, C.C.

ROUSSATIER, ABRAHAM LOUIS. *Nyon*. 1761 master; then *Vevey* and *Geneva*; 1792; established a factory with PERDONNET.

ROUSSEAU, ANTOINE. *Lyon*, 1664–86.

ROUSSEAU, DAVID. Sixteenth-century cruciform watch.

ROUSSEAU, ISAAC, grandson of Jean. *Geneva*. Born 1672, died 1747; in *Constantinople* a. 1711; went to *Nyon* 1722; father of Jean Jacques Rousseau; made watches for Turkey.

ROUSSEAU, JEAN. A clever watchmaker; a crystal cased watch in the form of a cross by him in the Fellows collection, about 1590.

ROUSSEAU, JEAN, son of the above. Born 1609; died 1684; silver watch, V. & A., engraved with figures of the seasons and with flowers.

ROUSSEAU, JEAN FRANÇOIS, son of Noé. *Geneva*. Born 1685, died 1763.

ROUSSEL, —. Master Horologer of *Paris*, mentioned by Thiout in 1741.

ROUSSEL, ADRIEN. *The Hague*, mid-seventeenth century.

ROUSSEL, GILLES EDME. *Paris*. Master 1749–79.

ROUSSEL, JOHANNES. *The Hague*, mid-seventeenth century.

ROUTH, SAML. C.C.; to him Jno. Marshall was apprenticed in 1682; clock by him about 1720.

ROUTLEDGE, GEO. *Lydford, Devon*. Died 1801; curious epitaph in Lydford churchyard.

ROUX, ALEXANDER. *London*. Apprenticed 1700–10 C.C.

ROUX, BORDIER & ROMAN. *Geneva*, about 1810.

ROUZIER & MELLY. *Geneva* and *Paris*, late eighteenth century. Gold watch, showing on back the time in different places, M.M.A.; small engraved watch, British Museum; 4-colour gold watch set stones, Feill collection.

ROWDEN, JOHN. *London*. Apprenticed to Dinnis 1683; C.C. 1691; watch, silver dial, with raised figures, square pillars, about 1700.

ROWE, BENJAMIN. C.C. 1708.

ROWE, GEORGE, son of Benj. *London*. C.C. 1739.

ROWE, JOHN. *St. Paul's Churchyard*. Liveryman C.C. 1770–82.

ROWE, THOMAS. C.C. 1699.

ROWELL, GEORGE. *Oxford*. About 1790–1813 C.C.; watch movement, Ashmolean Museum.

ROWLAND, JNO. *Manchester*, 1765.

ROWLAND & CO. *8 Coventry St.*, 1825.

ROWLANDS, CHRISTOPHER. *132 Long Acre*, 1815; *9 Coventry St.*, 1835; *33 Leadenhall St.*, 1840.

ROWLANDS, DAVID. *Llanuwchllyn*, about 1780–1850.

ROWLANDS, JAMES. *Bristol*, 1801–18. Watch.

ROWLANDS, JOHN. *Berwick-on-Tweed*. a. 1772–1830; long-case clock.

ROWLANDS, WALTER. *Berwick*, 1775.

ROWLEY, ELIZA. Apprenticed 1694 to Andrew Yeatman and Mary his wife, C.C.

ROWLEY, FRANCIS. Removed from *Birmingham* 1792 to *Turnmill St., Clerkenwell*; died 1824, aged 70. His son FRANCIS, *Faulkner's Alley*, died 1837, aged 49, the business being carried on by his widow Elizabeth; she died in 1870, aged 88.

ROWLEY, JAMES. *London*. Apprenticed 1714, C.C. 1721, died 1788.

ROWLEY, JOHN. *London*, 1716. Made an orrery with Graham; four orreries Old Ashmolean Museum.

ROWLEY, JOHN. *London*. Apprenticed 1780, C.C. 1793.

ROWNING, J. "Once a bad clockmaker in Cambridge" (Ludlam, 1758); John Rowning, M.A., in 1732 patented a clock, and reference is made in the *Dictionary of National Biography* to a brother a watchmaker. In *East Anglian Notes and Queries* are mentioned, as early clockmakers, J. Rowning, Newmarket; Stephen Rowning, Thetford; and Rowning of Brandon; these all probably lived about the middle of the eighteenth century.

ROY, DAVID. C.C. 1682.

ROY, HENRI LOUIS, son of Samuel. *Chaux-de-Fonds.* Born 1770, died 1843; succeeded his father as head of S. Roy et Fils in 1804.

ROY, SAMUEL & FILS. *Chaux-de-Fonds.* One-wheel regulator, about 1780.

ROY, WILLIAM. *30 Bell Yard, Lincoln's Inn,* 1804.

ROY, WILLIAM. *Dunfermline,* 1786–1811.

ROYCROFT, THOMAS. Admitted C.C. 1699.

ROYD, STEPHEN JOSEPH. C.C.; to him was apprenticed Dymoke Evans in 1800.

ROYER, WILLIAM. *40 Gee St., Goswell Rd.,* 1820.

ROYLANDS, WILLIAM. Watch movement maker, *29 Chiswell St.,* 1790–94.

ROYLE, JOS. *Chorley,* 1780.

RUBINS, RICHARD. *Grantham,* 1780.

RUBOTTOM, WM. *Liverpool,* 1770.

RÜCKEN, HINDRICK. *Stockholm,* 1694. Master 1696–1723.

RÜCKERT, THOMAS. *Augsburg,* 1574–1606. Went to the Dresden Court about 1580, and later to the Court of Prague; maker of pedometers.

RUDD, J. *Bradford,* early eighteenth century.

RUDKIN, THOMAS. C.C. 1683.

RUDRUPP, HENRY PHILLIPS. *London.* Apprenticed 1783, C.C. 1791.

RUDRUPP, JNO. *Amersham.* Maker of lantern clocks, about 1710.

RUEGGER, E. M. *Geneva,* 1800–10.

RUEL, SAMUEL. *Rotterdam,* 1765–1705. Watch movement G.M.; watch Denham collection.

RUEL, SAMUEL. *Rotterdam.* Calendar watch, Schloss collection; nicely pierced work on movement, 'The Triumph of Venus', h.m., 1788.

RUETSCHMANN, JOSEPH. *Vienna.* Partner of Cajetano q.v. fine complicated bracket clocks with perpetual calendar, died 1801.

RUGEND, —. *Auch.* Tulip watch, Soltykoff collection, about 1570.

RUGENDAS, NICHOLAS. *Augsburg,* 1605 30.

RUGENDAS, NICOLAUS, son. *Augsburg.* Master 1662, died 1694; fine table clock Neue Hofburg, Vienna.

RUGENDAS, NICOLAUS, son. *Augsburg.* Master 1699, died 1645; sundial, Stuttgart Museum.

RUGG & THAINE. *15 Cheapside.* Enamelled watch; 1769–94.

RULAND (RUHLAND), JOHANN GEORG. *Dresden.* Master 1800, died 1840.

RULE, JAS. *Portsmouth.* Watch, 1779.

RULE, JAS. *York,* f., 1797.

RULMAULT, —. *Abbeville.* Oval striking watch, about 1570.

RUMFORD, JNO. *Bishop Auckland,* 1776.

RUMMEL, JOHANN GRAZ. about 1714. Fine long-case clocks with very fine *repoussé* dials.

RUMPELSBERGER, GEORGE JOSEPH. *Würzburg.* Apprenticed 1747, master 1760–94; court watchmaker.

RUNDELL, EDWD. *Norton St. Phillip's.* Fine musical clock, about 1710.

RUNDELL, PHILIP. *Ludgate Hill.* Livery Drapers' Company, 1770.

RUNDELL & BRIDGE. *32 Ludgate Hill,* 1788–1824. Watch, marked 'Rundell, Bridge, & Rundell, 1830'; Rundell & Bridge succeeded Picket & Rundell; they were silversmiths to the Crown, and their shop one of the attractions of London; the business was purchased by Francis Lambert, and transferred to Coventry St.

RUSH, SAMUEL. *16 Ludgate Hill,* and *Porter St., Leicester Fields,* 1759–90.

RUSH & SHIPMAN. *Hull,* 1822.

RUSSELL, A. C. *London.* Watch, Schloss collection, about 1800.

RUSSELL, BENJ. *Thirsk,* 1822.

RUSSELL, CHARLES. *18 Barbican,* 1790.

RUSSELL, CHARLES, & THOMAS. *18 Barbican,* 1787–1815.

RUSSELL, CORNELIUS. Apprenticed 1686 to Ab. Clyatt, C.C.

RUSSELL, JNO. C.C. about 1660.

RUSSELL, JOHN. *Falkirk,* 1783. Died 1817; watchmaker to the Prince Regent; a well-known maker of musical clocks.

RUSSELL, NICHOLAS. Apprenticed to William Rogers in 1653; C.C. 1663; master 1692; died 1700. "A plain hour-watch goes but 24 hours, the name on it is Nicolus Russell, Londini, fecit" (*Lond. Gaz.*, Dec. 22–27, 1697).

RUSSELL, THOMAS. Watch-case maker, *18 Barbican,* 1775.

RUSSELL, THOMAS. *Lancaster.* 1797 master–1832; watch.

RUSSELL, THOMAS, at the *Clock Case* in *Barbican.* Liveryman C.C. 1776.

RUSSELL, THOS. *Lancaster,* 1797, f., 1832.

RUST, DANIEL. *London.* C.C. 1782–88.

RUST, WILHELM JOACHIM. *Hamburg,* 1804–21.

RUST, WM. *Lincoln,* 1775. *Hull,* 1780.

RUST & SHIPMAN, 1822.

RUTH, CARL AD. *Nörrkoping.* Born 1770, died 1819; watches and clocks.

RUTHERFORD, MICHAEL. *Hawick,* 1803.

RUTLAND, JAMES. *83 Oxford St.,* 1822–30.

RUTLAND, JONATHAN. *110 Oxford St.,* 1793–1804.

RUTTER, JNO. *St. James's Walk,* 1793.

RUTTER, MOSES. *Baltimore, U.S.A.,* 1802–07.

RYCROFT, THOS. A watch by him is mentioned in the *Lond. Gaz.,* Sept. 21–25, 1693.

RYDER, JOSH. *London.* Watch, h.m., 1761.

RYDER, THOMAS. C.C. 1698.

RYDER, THOMAS. C.C. 1712.

RYLAND, JNO. *London.* Watch, 1780.

RYLANDER, N. GUSTAF. *Jönköping.* Born 1777, master 1805, died 1832; watch.

RYLER, WILLIAM. C.C. 1712.

RYLEY, ERASMUS. *Wood's Close.* C.C. 1730.

RYLEY, GEO. Apprenticed C.C. 1683.

RYLEY, JNO. *Coventry,* 1812–18.

RYLEY, LAURENCE. Apprenticed C.C. 1662.

RYLEY, THOMAS. C.C. 1704.

RYLY, WILLIAM. *London.* Apprenticed 1700, C.C. 1712.

RYMER, HY. *6 George St., Adelphi,* 1817.

RYPPLAY, JNO. *York,* f., 1471.

S. Sixteenth-century tambourine case watch marked 'V. S.'

S., H. See SCHNIER.

SABER, EDWD. *Cannon St.,* 1783.

SABEROWSKY, JOHANN GOTTLIEB. *Hamburg,* 1801–21.

SABERTY, J. *London.* Watch, 1765.

SACHEVERELL, BENASSIR. Apprenticed 1680 to W. Thoroughgood; turned over to Tompion; admitted C.C. 1687.

SACK, SOLOMON. *Augsburg.* Master about 1735, juré 1740, died 1751.
SACRÉ, LE JEUNE. *Paris (Rue de Martrois),* 1792–1825. Made watches and clocks 'à l'ivrogne', winding whichever way the key was turned.
SADD, THOMAS. *East Windsor, U.S.A.,* 1750.
SADLEIR, SAMUEL. *Hackney.* Warden C.C. 1723.
SADLEIR, SAMUEL. *London.* C.C. 1735–47.
SADLER, EDWARD. *London.* Apprenticed 1802, C.C. 1817.
SADLER, ROBERT. *London.* Long-case clock, about 1740.
SADLER, SAM. Apprenticed 1687 to Sam. Vernon, C.C.; long marquetry-case clock, about 1700.
SADLER, STEPHEN. *134 Bishopsgate Without,* 1830.
SADLER, THOS. *Norwich.* Long-case clock, about 1770.
SADTLER, PHILIP B. *Baltimore, U.S.A.,* 1802–07. Watch.
SAER, JOSEPH. Admitted C.C. 1687; maker of a square-dial brass 8-day clock, two hands, inscription, 'Joseph Saer, in Penpool Lane, London', 1686–1700.
SAFELY (SAFLEY), JOHN. *Edinburgh,* 1764. Died 1803; long-case clock.
SAFFELL, CHARLES WILSON. *London.* C.C. 1773, livery C.C. 1803, died 1816.
SAFFELL, CHARLES WILSON. *London.* C.C. 1816.
SAFFORD, THOMAS JEFFREY. *Bristol,* 1767–87. Watch.
SAFFORY, JOHN. *13 Tokenhouse Yard,* 1760–75.
SAGAR, EDMUND. *Middleham,* 1750.
SAGAR, ROBT. *Blackburn,* 1818.
SAGE, MATTHEW. *Oxon.* Watch about, 1760.
SAGNIER, FRANÇOIS. *Geneva,* about 1775–91.
SAINSBURY, ROBERT. *Chippenham,* 1775. *Bridgwater.* Long-case clock, about 1780.
ST. ANDREW, G. *London.* Watch, 1790.
ST. GEORGE, JNO. Apprenticed 1674 to Barlow Rookes, C.C.
ST. LEU. See DE ST. LEU.
SALÉN, JOHAN FREDRIC. *Stockholm,* 1821. Died 1859.
SALISBURY, WM. *London.* Watch, 1730.
SALMON, C. E. *151 Bishopsgate Without,* 1823.
SALMON, CHARLES. *London.* C.C. 1821.
SALMON, EDWARD. *London.* C.C. 1798.
SALMON, HENRY. *Coventry St., Piccadilly,* 1769–82.
SALMON, JNO. *Bristol.* Bracket clock, repeating on eight bells, ebony case, about 1700.
SALMON, JOHN. *London.* Apprenticed 1648, C.C. 1654. Also SAMON.
SALMON, JOHN. *London.* Apprenticed 1776, C.C. 1784.
SALMON, PETER. *Stockholm,* 1785. Died 1800.
SALMON, ROBERT. *49 Strand,* 1790–94.
SALMOON, GIDEON ABRAHAM, son. *Kalmar.* Born 1724, died 1791.
SALMOON, JACOB. *Stockholm,* 1720–54.
SALTBY, THOS. *Grantham,* 1770.
SALTER, EDWARD. *20 Cannon St.,* 1788–94.
SALTER, JOHN. *35 Strand,* 1804; *73 Strand,* 1825–30.
SAMBROOK, JOHN. C.C. 1680.
SAMLEY, —. *Gutter Lane,* 1775.
SAMMER, JOSEPH ANTON. *Augsburg.* Apprenticed 1752, master 1770–98.
SAMON, JOHN. C.C. 1654.
SAMPSON, ROBERT. *Westminster.* Invented a two-part chime clock, described in *Transactions of the Society of Arts,* vol. iv., 1786; card, B.M., 'Robert Sampson, 2 Petty France, Westminster, 1788'.
SAMPSON, UMFREVIL. Apprenticed to Chas. Cabrier, C.C. 1735.
SAMPSON, WM. *London,* about 1800.
SAMSON. *London.* On many watches, Dutch style, 1760–96.

SAMSON, J. *11 Denmark St., Soho.* Watch with engraving of the Crucifixion in white metal fastened above the balance on a semicircular metal ground, decorated with rubies, emeralds, and topazes, 1800–05.
SAMSON, SAMUEL. *Westminster.* Watch, British Museum, about 1780; also a silver *repoussé* pair-case watch, apparently for the Dutch market, h.m., 1800; other examples are a long-case musical clock, inscribed 'Samson, maker to His Majesty'; and a musical and mechanical bracket clock; 1778–1805.
SAMSON & GRANDIN. *Denmark St., Soho,* 1810.
SAMUEL, ABRAHAM. *11 Little Alie St., Goodman's Fields,* 1820–25.
SAMUEL, DAVID. *York, f.,* 1820.
SAMUEL, HUMPHREY. *Panton St., Haymarket,* 1790.
SAMUEL, MOSES, LOUIS, & CO., SOLOMON, all of *Liverpool,* about 1818.
SAMUEL, SAMUEL. *London.* a. 1772–1810; watch movement; Buckley collection.
SAMUEL & HILL. *3 Charing Cross,* 1793.
SAMWELL, JNO. Lantern clock, 1665.
SAN CAJETANO, DAVID. *Vienna.* Born 1726, died 1796; lay brother in Marienbrunn monastery; lay name David Rutschmann; able maker of complex astronomical clocks; one at Zwettl, one in Uhren Museum, Vienna, and another Hofburg, Vienna; published 1793 and 1794 *Neues Rädergebäude.*
SANDBLOM, LARS. *Uddevalla,* 1794–1840.
SANDE, THOS. Watch, British Museum, 1620.
SANDERS, ALEX. Apprenticed 1665 to Hugh Roberts, C.C.
SANDERS, CHAS. Apprenticed 1672 to Isaac Carver, C.C.
SANDERS, DANIEL. C.C. 1632.
SANDERS, GEORGE. *57 Sion Gardens, Aldermanbury,* 1790–94.
SANDERS, GEORGE. *8 Gee St., Goswell Rd.,* 1820.
SANDERS, JAS. *46 St. John St.,* 1790–94.
SANDERS, JOHN. *3 Holborn Hill,* 1810–15.
SANDERS, JOHN. *London.* Apprenticed 1714, C.C. 1721. Also SAUNDERS.
SANDERS, JOSEPH. *London (Long Acre).* Apprenticed 1746, C.C. 1753–68.
SANDERS, NATH. *Manchester,* 1770.
SANDERS, RICHARD. *London.* a. 1774, C.C. 1780. See SAUNDERS.
SANDERSON, GEORGE. *Exeter.* Patentee of tools for duplicating parts of watches (1761, No. 763); also a lunar and calendar watch-key (1762, No. 777).
SANDERSON, HY, at the *Dial and Sun, Strand,* 1770–81.
SANDERSON, JNO. *Wigton.* Long-case clock, about 1690; another about 1715; he removed to Carlisle about 1730.
SANDERSON, JNO. *Newcastle,* eldest son of the foregoing, 1750.
SANDERSON, ROBERT. *Strand.* C.C. 1703; afterwards Sanderson & Son; Hatton in 1773 speaks of the late Mr. Sanderson as an improver of calendar work, and the son as clever; 1703–50; silver alarum watch, 'Robert Sanderson, London', h.m., 1769, Pierpont Morgan collection.
SANDERSON, THOS. *105 Bishopsgate Within,* 1815.
SANDERSON, W. *Doncaster.* 1795 C.C.; clocks and watches.
SANDFORD, WILLIAM. *15 Conduit St.,* 1800–25.
SANDIFORD, JAS. *Manchester,* 1780.
SANDLER, JNO. *Feckenham,* about 1790.
SANDOZ, AÎNÉ, ET CIE. *Paris,* 1808–25.
SANDOZ, JACQUES. *Geneva.* Fine travelling repeating watch, about 1750.
SANDOZ, JACQUES. *Les Planchettes* and *Chaux-de-Fonds.* Born 1664, died 1738; sundials and clocks.

SANDOZ ET TROT. *Besançon*, 1792; *Geneva*, 1804–16. Then called Sandoz et Rossel and, in 1821, Rossel et Cie.

SANDS, JNO. Apprenticed 1668 to Isaac Puzzy, C.C.

SANDS, JNO. *St. Dunstan's Alley*, 1790.

SANDS, STEPHEN. *New York*, 1786.

SANDYS, JAS. *137 St. John's St.*, 1800.

SANDYS, WM. Apprenticed 1662 to Robert Grinkin, C.C.

SANFORD, EATON. *Plymouth, U.S.A.*, 1760–76.

SANGSTER, JAMES. *Youghal*, 1820.

SANGSTER, JOHN TROWER. *Bradwell*. C.C. 1803, livery C.C. 1812–40.

SARBITT, JOHN. *11 St. Martin's Court*, 1804.

SARGEANT, JACOB. *Hartford, U.S.A.*, 1828.

SARGENT, BENJAMIN. *133 Fleet St.*, 1769–88.

SARGENT, JOSH. *106 Jermyn St.*, 1794–1818.

SARGENT, NATHANIEL. *London.* C.C. 1769, m.C.C. 1783; long-case clock.

SARGENT, ROBERT. C.C. 1720.

SARGENT, WILLIAM, son. *London.* C.C. 1756.

SARRABEL, T. *Tours*, 1670.

SARRASIN, VINCENT. *Avignon*, 1726–48. Town clock.

SARTON, HEBERT. *Liège*. Watch, about 1775 to 1800.

SATCHABELL, THOMAS. *9 Bridgewater Sq.*, 1804.

SATCHELL, EDWARD. *London*, 1728–48. 'Eminent' watch-maker.

SATCHER, THOMAS. *London.* Apprenticed 1759, C.C. 1775–86.

SATCHER, THOMAS, son. *London.* Apprenticed 1786, C.C. 1798.

SATHER, THOS. *London.* Bracket clock, 1730.

SATTELL, C. Watch-case maker, *36 Clerkenwell Green*, 1795–1800.

SAUDE, PIERRE. *Paris.* Clockmaker to the King, 1658.

SAUNDERS, D. *Parkside, Knightsbridge*, 1800–40.

SAUNDERS, DANIEL. *London*, 1622. C.C. 1632. Also SANDERS.

SAUNDERS, JOHN. C.C. 1721.

SAUNDERS, JOHN. C.C. 1730.

SAUNDERS, JOSEPH. *London (Chick Lane)*. C.C. 1792–1810.

SAUNDERS, JOSHUA. *Cripplegate Buildings*, 1765–70. In 1787, Isaac, son of Isaac Saunders, watch-motion maker of *Golden Lane, Cripplegate*, deceased, was apprenticed to Thos. Allen, citizen and cutler.

SAUNDERS, ROBT. Apprenticed 1675 to Robt. Halstead, C.C.

SAUNDERS, SAMUEL. *London.* Apprenticed 1723, C.C. 1730.

SAUNDERS, THOS. *258 Whitechapel*, 1817.

SAURIN. *Paris*, 1720.

SAUVAGE. *Paris*, on French clock, about 1790.

SAUZER, ABRAM. *Chaux-de-Fonds*, 1786–1806. Clock.

SAVAGE, ABRAHAM. Apprenticed 1648 to Hy. Child, C.C.

SAVAGE, G. *Huddersfield*, 1775.

SAVAGE, GEORGE. A watchmaker who, in the early part of last century, did much to perfect the lever escapement, besides inventing the two-pin variety; he lived at *Huddersfield*, where in 1808 he patented a remontoire; afterwards at *5 St. James's St., Clerkenwell*; in 1822 he received the large Silver Medal from the Society of Arts for a detached escapement for watches, which was a combination of the lever and the chronometer; he in his old age emigrated to Canada, and founded a flourishing retail business in *Montreal*, where he died.

SAVAGE, SAMUEL. *8 Red Lion St., Clerkenwell*, 1825.

SAVAGE, T. *Clifton, Cumberland.* Long-case clock, about 1740.

SAVAGE, THOMAS. *London*, 1677. "Stolen out of the house of John Shorren, Esq., Norfolk Street, a gold watch made by Thomas Savage, of London" (*Lond. Gaz.*, Sept. 10–14, 1691).

SAVAGE, THOS. Apprenticed 1659 to Joseph Quash, C.C.

SAVAGE, THOS. Livery C.C. 1804.

SAVAGE, THOS. *3 Red Lion St.*, 1816–40.

SAVAGE, W. *8 Chapel St., Bedford Row*, 1820–25.

SAVAGE DE SALOP, fecit '98, signature on 30-hour square dial long-case clock.

SAVAGE & VINCENT. *60 Red Lion St.*, 1802–15.

SAVILLE, JOHN. C.C. 1656; assistant 1675; died 1679; maker of a watch reputed to have belonged to William of Orange, dated 1656, silver box, outer case of tortoise-shell decorated with silver, 1656–79.

SAVILLE, JOHN. C.C. 1678; there was a brass lantern clock of his production at Blackburn in 1887.

SAVILLE, WM. Apprenticed 1686 to Jas. Wolverstone, C.C.; eighteenth century long-case clock marked 'Wm. Saville, Dublin'.

SAVORY, A. *54 Cheapside*, 1825.

SAVORY, ANDREW. Apprenticed 1668 to Thos. Parker; C.C. 1676; maker of lantern and bracket clocks.

SAVORY, FARRAND, & CO. *48 Cheapside*, 1793–1800.

SAVORY, JOSEPH. *48 Cheapside*, 1788.

SAVORY, JOSEPH, & CO., 1820.

SAVORY, WILLIAM. *London.* Apprenticed 1770, C.C. 1777–94.

SAWEN & DYER. *Boston, Mass.*, 1800–20.

SAWTELL, E.

SAWYER, JNO. *Leeds*, 1770.

SAWYER, JOHN. *1 Poultry*, 1804.

SAWYER, PAUL. C.C. 1718.

SAXEBY, CHRISTOPHER. Apprenticed to Charles Cabrier, C.C. 1749.

SAXON, JAS. *Liverpool.* Long-case clock, about 1795.

SAXTON & LUKENS. *Philadelphia*, 1828–40.

SAY, NEHEMIAH. C.C. 1654.

SAY, RICHARD. Apprenticed 1688 to Jno. Johnson.

SAYER, MATT. *Oxon.* Watch, 1757.

SAYER, MATHEW. *Exeter*, 1763.

SAYES, NEHEMIAH. *London.* Apprenticed 1648, C.C. 1656.

SAYLLER, JNO. Oval watch by him, Vienna Treasury, about 1650.

SAYRE, JOHN. *New York*, 1800.

SAYRE & RICHARDS. *New York*, 1805.

SCAFE, JOSEPH. *London.* 1729 C.C.

SCAFE, WILLIAM, "at ye sign of the clock in King Street, near Guild Hall"; C.C. by redemption, 1721; master in 1749. The Hon. B. Fairfax, writing to his nephew in 1727, said, "One William Scaife, a watchmaker, born at Bushy, near Denton (co. York) served his time to his father, a blacksmith, but now the most celebrated workman, perhaps, in London and Europe".

SCALE, HENRY. Of him was bought Huggerford's watch with false jewelling used as evidence against Facio; 1705.

SCALES, EDWD. *33 Strand*, 1775–80.

SCANDER, PIERRE. *Blois.* Master 1633–54; clockmaker to the duc d'Orléans from 1641. Also SCANDE and SCANDRE.

SCANDRETT, JOHN. *Worcester.* Master 1782–1816; watch.

SCANDRETT, THOS. *Kingston*, 1740.

SCANTLEBURY, W. *17 Golden Lane*, 1780–92.

SCARDEVILE, JNO. Apprenticed 1663 to Gregory Dossett, C.C.

SCHAGER, ROBERT R. *Uddevalla*, 1819–35.

SCHALCK, JOHANN. *Engel, Prague.* Cruciform watch, Soltykoff collection, about 1580.

SCHALIN, MICHAEL. *Lilla Malma.* Born 1738, died 1782; long-case clock.

SCHARDEES, THO. *London.* Watch, about 1715.

SCHARP (SCHARFF), JOH. ERIK. *Kristinehamn.* Born 1765, died 1825.

SCHAUDT, PHILIPP MATTHÄUS. *Onstmettingen.* Born 1766, died 1855; bracket clock, Furt. Museum.

SCHEGS, ABRAHAM. *Nürnberg.* Enamelled watch, about 1730, Cluny Museum.

SCHEILIN, JACOB. *Dresden,* 1614–28. Court clockmaker.

SCHEIRER, JOHAN. Hexagonal clock, about 1675, Schloss collection.

SCHELHORN, ANDREAS. *Schneeberg, Saxony.* Clock, Green Vaulted Chambers, Dresden, 1570.

SCHENK, ALOIS. *Vienna,* about 1800–about 1840. Gold engraved harp watch; skeleton clock, Uhren Museum, Vienna.

SCHEURLIN, ABRAHAM. *Augsburg.* Born 1616, died 1694; apprenticed to Martin Zoller; table clock, about 1650.

SCHEURLIN, JACOB. *Dresden,* 1614. 'Electoral Saxonian Court Clockmaker'.

SCHIBANI, MARTIN. *Würzburg.* Master 1727, died 1759; a good maker; stand and wall clock, Würzburg Museum.

SCHIETZEL, FRIEDRICH AUGUST. *Dresden.* 1779, master 1806, died 1847.

SCHLOTHEIM, HANS. *Augsburg.* Celebrated 'Tower o' Babel' clock by him in the Green Vaulted Chamber, Dresden, 1602.

SCHLOTT, HANNS. In the British Museum is a clock in the form of a ship by him, said to have been made for the Emperor Rudolph II; 1578–81.

SCHMID. Pendulum watch, about 1700, handsome bridge with bust of William and Mary, by 'Iohan-Jacob Schmid in Basel'.

SCHMIDT, CARL. Oval clock-watch, strikes 1 to 6, brass case, Pierpont Morgan collection, about 1600.

SCHMIDT, J. *Hamburg.* Table clock, about 1710.

SCHMIDT, JOHAN ANDREAS. *Copenhagen.* Master 1783; London, 1801; in 1808 patented a mysterious clock with watch movement in a pivoted hand; agate watch, M.M.A.

SCHMIDT, JOHANNES. *Amsterdam.* Clock, about 1700.

SCHMIDT, JOHN. *St. Mary Axe.* Patentee of mysterious clock (1808, No. 3,185).

SCHMIDT, NICOLAUS. Clock with automata, signed 'Nicolaus Schmidt der junger'; ebony case with the Augsburg work mark, about 1620.

SCHMIDT, ULRICH. Watch, about 1610; finely enamelled case, Pierpont Morgan collection; another watch, signed 'Jo. Ul. Sch.', about the same date.

SCHNACK (SNACK), JOHAN ERLAND, brother. *Stockholm,* 1710–62.

SCHNACK (SNACK), PETTER. *Stockholm.* Born about 1705, died 1742; a famous maker; made turret clock for Abo and large musical clock for the King; started 'Stockholms Manufabrique', by which his clocks were signed; six long-case clocks, one Nord. Museum; eight bracket clocks, two illuminated Sidenbladh.

SCHNEIDER. Octagonal pedestal gilt-metal clock, signed 'Johannes Schneider Augustæ', about 1620.

SCHNEIDER, JOHANN HEINRICH, son. *Basle,* 1763–98. Turret and other clocks.

SCHNIER, HANS. Sixteenth-century book-shaped watch, Pierpont Morgan collection, signed 'H. S.'

SCHOFIELD, EDMUND, son of Major. Born 1730, died 1792.

SCHOFIELD, JNO. *29 Bell Yard, London,* 1793.

SCHOFIELD, JOHN. *Barnish.* In 1789 a new clock, with chimes for the parish church, ordered of him, to cost £193; he was living in 1821.

SCHOFIELD, MAJOR. *Rochdale.* Born 1707, died 1783.

SCHOFIELD, WILLIAM. *Barnish,* 1776.

SCHOFIELD, WILLIAM. *2 Clerkenwell Close,* 1830–32.

SCHOFIELD, WM. *35 Cheyne Walk, Chelsea.* Long-case clocks, 1815–25.

SCHOLER, JOHANN. *Bavaria.* Table clock, about 1570.

SCHOLFIELD, JAMES. *London.* Long-case clock, about 1770.

SCHOLFIELD, JOHN. Long-case clock, lantern movement, about 1690; case 'Halifax' clock, signed 'Johannes Scholfield', about 1720.

SCHOLFIELD, MAJOR. *Manchester,* 1775.

SCHOLLET, JOHN BAPTIST. *Boston, U.S.A.,* 1796–1803. Watch.

SCHÖNER (SCHONNER, SCHONER), CHRISTOPH. *Augsburg.* Master 1681–1710; magnificent table clock and astronomical clock, National Museum, Munich.

SCHORRER, JOSEPH XAVER. *Augsburg.* Master 1765–70, died a. 1790.

SCHRETGER, JOHANN. *Augsburg,* 1660–90.

SCHRINER, CHARLES W. *Philadelphia,* 1813–25.

SCHRINER, CHRISTEN JENSEN. *Copenhagen.* Comp. 1772, master 1781; Master of Corporation 1800–08.

SCHRINER, MARTIN. *Lancaster, U.S.A.,* 1790–1830.

SCHRINER, MARTIN, son of Martin. *Lancaster,* 1830–36. Continued his father's business.

SCHRINER, PHILIP, brother. *Lancaster,* 1830–36. Worked with his brother.

SCHROETER, —. *Lilienthal,* 1789. Used varnished wood pendulum rod.

SCHROETER, CHARLES. *Baltimore, U.S.A.,* 1807–17. Clockmaker.

SCHROETER, DAVIDT. *Elbing,* about 1680. Falling ball clock, National Museum, Cracow.

SCHRÖTER, DAVIDT, 1680–90.

SCHUBARDT, CARL. *Nürnberg.* Born 1631, died 1693; town clock.

SCHUETZE (SCHIOTZ, SCHOTTE), JOSIAS. *Copenhagen,* 1636. Died 1676; travelling clock, National Museum, Copenhagen, illuminated Liisberg.

SCHUHMANN, JOHANN FRIEDRICH. *Dresden.* Master 1784, died 1817; court clock, 1808; chronometer, M.P.S., Dresden.

SCHROEDER, CHRISTEN JENSEN. *Copenhagen.* Comp. 1772, master 1781; Master of Corporation, 1800–08.

SCHULTZ, —. *Augsburg.* Latin cross watch, Schloss collection, about 1570.

SCHULTZ, VINCENT. *Stockholm.* 1728 master–1737; died about 1762; bracket and two long-case clocks and watch.

SCHURICHT, AUGUST CHRISTIAN. *Dresden.* Born 1726, master 1756, died 1793.

SCHURICHT, CHRISTIAN TRAUGOTT. *Dresden.* Master 1784, died 1808; court clock.

SCHURICHT, FRIEDRICHT CHRISTIAN. *Dresden.* Born 1728, master 1756, died 1792.

SCHÜLZ, MICHAEL. *Riga,* seventeenth century. Table clock.

SCHUSTER, PAUL.

SCHUSTER, PAULUS. *Nürnberg,* 1591. Died 1634; complex clock, with 11 dials and automatic and enamel plaques; automatic clock with astrolabe, M.P.S., Dresden; watch, Gélis collection; made clocks for the Dresden Court.

SCHUTE, JASPER. C.C. 1648.

SCHUYLER, PETER C. *New York,* 1802–06. Clocks and watches.

SCHWERER, LAURENCE. *Sheffield,* 1818–36. Clocks and watches.

SCHWERER, MATTHEW. *Hull,* 1814–34.

SCHWILGUE, JEAN B. Born 1776, died 1856; restored Strassburg clock, 1838.

SCIENCE, JOHN. C.C. 1724.

SCOLDING, JOHN. *7 Great Prescot St.*, 1794–1810.

SCOTSON, ELLEN. *9 Pemberton's Alley, Liverpool*, 1790.

SCOTSON, ISAAC. *Merlin's Cave, Old Shambles, Liverpool*, 1767–77.

SCOTSON, JOSEPH. *9 Old Shambles*, 1781.

SCOTT, —. *Gracechurch St.*, 1770–82.

SCOTT, A., & Co. *64 West Smithfield*, 1828–32.

SCOTT, DANIEL. C.C. 1697.

SCOTT, EDWD. Apprenticed 1650 to Wm. Rogers, C.C.

SCOTT, GEO. 'Cannon Gate'; long-case clock, about 1740.

SCOTT, GEORGE. *Edinburgh*, 1716–55.

SCOTT, JAMES. *Leith*, 1774–91.

SCOTT, JAMES. Apprenticed to John Jackson, 1752; C.C. 1766; in 1809 James Scott, watchmaker, of *Grafton St., Dublin*, communicated to *Nicholson's Journal* a paper on platinum balance-springs; in 1820 he took out patents for obtaining motive power.

SCOTT, JAMES AMOS. *London (Clerkenwell)*. C.C. 1809–16. Watch.

SCOTT, JOHN. *London*. C.C. 1772.

SCOTT, JOHN. *40 Gloucester St., Red Lion Sq.* Bracket clock, Wetherfield collection, about 1775; honorary freeman, C.C. 1781; 1770–94.

SCOTT, JOHN. *London*. C.C. 1777.

SCOTT, JOHN. *Newcastle-on-Tyne*, 1782–1811. Long-case clocks.

SCOTT, JOHN. *Edinburgh*. Apprenticed 1779, died 1798. Maker to the Prince of Wales.

SCOTT, JOSEPH. Apprenticed 1674 to Cornelius Herbert, C.C.

SCOTT, JOSHUA. The Minutes of the Cutlers' Company for 1705 record that "Joshua Scott of the parish of St. Botolph without Aldgate, watchmaker, his son Caleb bound to Ephraim How, cutler", &c.

SCOTT, ROBERT. *20 Bell Yard, Temple Bar*, 1815–40.

SCOTT, ROBERT. *Virginia, U.S.A.*, 1779.

SCOTT, SIMON. Apprenticed 1647 to Wm. Comfort, C.C.

SCOTT, STEPHEN. *Elham*. Born 1725, died 1798.

SCOTT, THOS. *Gainsboro'*, 1790.

SCOTT, THOS. *65 Charing Cross*, 1810–20.

SCOTT, WM. *Beith*, 1780.

SCOTT, WM. *39 Dartmouth St.*, 1790–94.

SCOTT, WM. *40 Skinner St., Clerkenwell*, 1830–42.

SCOTT & THORPE, *Strand*. Watch, 1796.

SCRIMGEOUR, JAMES. *Glasgow*. Invented a remontoire about 1810.

SCRIVENER, RICHD. C.C. 1639; Henry Adeane was apprenticed to him in 1668; long-case clock, about 1710, signed 'Richard Scrivener, London'.

SCURR, RICHD. *Thirsk*, 1822; died 1887; long-case clock.

SEA, FREDERICK. *18 Bartholomew Close*, 1820–30.

SEABOURNE, JAMES. Apprenticed to Richd. Seabourne, 1642; C.C. 1649.

SEABOURNE, THOMAS. *London*. 1649 C.C.

SEABOURNE, WM. Apprenticed 1651 to Sam. Horne; C.C. 1659.

SEAGER, JNO. *Liverpool*, 1817–36.

SEAGRAVE, MATTHEW. C.C. 1730.

SEAGRAVE, ROBERT. *35 Gutter Lane*, 1790.

SEALE, RICHARD. *London*. Apprenticed 1766, C.C. 1780–98.

SEALL, FREDERICK. *London*. Apprenticed 1776, C.C. 1789–1810.

SEAMAN, —. *London*. Watch, Dutch style, about 1765.

SEAMAN, WILLIAM. *London*. C.C. 1659; watch.

SEAMER (or SEYMOUR). *York*.

SEAMER (or SEYMOUR). ABEL. f., 1649; also JOSEPH, same date.

SEAMER (or SEYMOUR), PETER. f., 1636.

SEAMER (or SEYMOUR), WM. f., 1627.

SEAMORE, W. *Minories*. Watch, about 1750.

SEATOUN, G. *29 Gutter Lane, Cheapside*. Card, Ponsonby collection, about 1795.

SECHAYE, JEAN. *Geneva*, about 1755–70.

SECHTING, JOHANN GOTTFRIED. ——, 1749–1814. Pupil of P. M. Hahn.

SEDDON, D. *Frodsham*, 1785.

SEDDON, HUMPHREY. *Southwark*, about 1730.

SEDDON, JAMES, in *St. James's*. C.C. 1662.

SEDDON, JOHN. A quaker, died 1740.

SEDDON, JOHN. *Frodsham*, 1780.

SEDDON, NATHANIEL, in *St. James's*. C.C. 1691; watch.

SEDGWICK, SAM. Apprenticed 1692 to Thos. Beasley, C.C.

SEDLEY, JOHN. *London*. Apprenticed 1686, C.C. 1701–32; watch movement.

SEDLEY, THOS. *London*. Watch, 1710.

SEDWELL, EDWARD. Apprenticed to Thomas Loomes; C.C. 1664.

SEFFIN, THOMAS. *London*. C.C. 1720.

SEFTON, EDWARD. *Tadcaster*. Long-case clock, 1775.

SEGNER, GEO. C.C. 1689.

SEGOND, PIERRE. *Geneva*, about 1770–87.

SEHEULT, J., à *Paris*. Watch, about 1650.

SEIGNEURET, P. *Paris*. Clock, V. & A., about 1750 in hanging case of gilt and blued bronze; signed on face 'Seigneuret H'ger de M'gneur le Com^t D'Artois'.

SEIGNIOR, ROBERT. C.C. 1667; an eminent maker; received, in 1682, £20 for a clock set up in the Treasury Chambers; month long clock, 10-in. dial, locking-plate striking; laburnum and olive wood case, domed hood with metal fret and spiral pillars, Wetherfield collection, about 1685; bracket clock in case of red tortoise-shell and ebony, same collection.

"Lost at Somer Hill a gold chain watch in a new fashioned case round hours, the chrystal and Pendant Ring broken off, made by Robert Signior, on the outside of the shagreen shell a cipher of 2 L.L.'s. There was tyed to the watch 2 seals, one a small gold seal with a Coat of Arms, the other enameled set with Cornelian, and thereon engraved the Figure of Plenty. Whoever can give notice thereof so that it be recovered by the owner, or to Mr. Hoare, Goldsmith at the Golden Bottle in Cheapside, or to Mr. Robert Signior in Exchange Alley, shall have five pounds reward, and if bought the money that shall be paid with content" (*Lond. Gaz.*, 9 Dec., 1678).

"A silver Pendulum watch, with a Tortoise-shell case inlaid with silver, made by Mr. Seignior, Exchange Alley" (*Lond. Gaz.*, Dec. 16–19, 1695). See also Senior.

SELBY, JOHN & SON. *Cirencetser*. Two generations to 1793, when son died.

SELBY, PETER. *Wareham*. Long-case clock, about 1760.

SELBY, THOMAS. *London* and *Leeds*. Went *Knaresborough* 1765–95.

SELBY, THOS. C.C.; he worked for Chater in 1730.

SELBY, THOS. *Knaresboro'*, 1765.

SELLAR, JOHN. *Elgin*, 1820–37.

SELLARS, BEZER. *London*. Apprenticed 1758, C.C. 1765–73; died a. 1788.

SELLARS, BEZER, son. *London*. C.C. 1801.

SELLARS, DITON, brother. *London*. C.C. 1814.

SELLARS, JOHN. C.C. 1667; warden, 1692; excused from serving as master in 1696, on account of ill-health.

SELLARS, WILLIAM. Apprenticed 1681 to Jno. Clowes; C.C. 1691; Long Acre, 1700–40.

SELSON, CHARLES. *London.* Apprenticed 1795, C.C. 1802.

SELWOOD, JOHN. C.C. 1641.

SELWOOD, WILLIAM, *ye Mermaid,* in *Lothbury.* C.C. 1633; maker of lantern clocks, 1620–36.

SENÉ, —. Watch, 'Jean Sené à Myes', about 1825.

SENEBIER, A. Cruciform watch, V. & A., about 1595; watch, G.M., signed 'A. Senebier à Geneve', about 1630.

SENEY, G., 'orloger du Roy, à Rouen', crystal case watch in the form of a fleur-de-lis, V. & A., about 1640.

SENIOR (SEIGNIOR?). A watch by him mentioned *Lond. Gaz.*, Aug. 1690.

SENS, WILLIAM. Admitted C.C. 1711.

SERGEANT, BENJAMIN. *133 Fleet St.*, 1754–68.

SERGEANT, NATHANIEL. *London.* Watch, h.m., 1762; Nathaniel Sergeant, who was admitted to the C.C. in 1763 and who served as master in 1783, was possibly his son, but he does not appear to have practised the craft.

SERGEANT, NATHANIEL. *London (Cannon St.).* C.C. 1768–90; watch G.M.

SERGEANT, NATHANIEL. *London.* C.C. 1823.

SERGEANT, PRETTYMAN. Apprenticed 1664 to Hy. Child; C.C. 1671.

SERGEANT, ROBT. *Foster Lane.* C.C. 1730.

SERMAND, JACQUES. *Geneva.* Tulip watch, about 1680, signed 'F. Sermand'; a similar specimen of about the same date, signed 'J. Sermand', Pierpont Morgan collection; watch, Marfels collection, outer case *piqué* with gold pins, about 1675, signed 'J. Sermand, Geneva'; hexagonal crystal watch.

SERMON, JOSEPH. Apprenticed C.C. 1675.

SERRÉ, —. *London.* Repeating watch in finely enamelled case, about 1750, Czar of Russia's collection.

SERVANT, H. *68 Salisbury Court,* 1775.

SERVIER. See GROLLIER.

SEUGNET, E. *London.* Long-case clock, about 1750.

SEUR, CHAS. *London,* 1700.

SEVERBERG, CHRISTIAN. *New York,* 1755–75.

SEWELL, G. *Bury, Lancs.,* 1814.

SEWELL, GEO. *47 Blackman St.,* 1790–94.

SEWELL, WILLIAM, JUN. *London.* C.C. 1825.

SEXTY, R. *71 Carlisle St., Lambeth,* 1830–40.

SEYDELL, FERD. *London.* Repeating watch, 1775.

SEYFFERT, FREDERICK W. *St. John St., Clerkenwell,* patented in 1818 (No. 8,317) a repeating motion.

SEYFFERT, HEINRICH. *Dresden.* Born 1751, died 1818; chronometer and precision clock; chronometer and cylinder watches, M.P.S., Dresden.

SEYLER, JOHANN TOMAS. A clockmaker, 1620.

SEYMORE, JAMES, brother. *London.* C.C. 1789.

SEYMORE, JNO. *Wantage.* Long-case clock, 1712.

SEYMORE, JOHN. *Cherry Tree Court.* C.C. 1711.

SEYMORE, JOHN, son of John Seymore. C.C. 1744; watch, G.M., about 1760.

SEYMORE, ROBERT. *Waterbury, U.S.A.,* 1814.

SEYMORE, WILLIAM. *Minories.* Mahogany case bracket clock, handle on top, brass dial, style 1750; watch, h.m., 1780.

SEYMORE, WILLIAM, son of John (2). *London (Hoxton and Chelsea).* C.C. 1766–1825; watch and bracket clock.

SEYMORE, WILLIAM, brother. *London.* Apprenticed, 1770, C.C. 1789.

SHAKESHAFT, JOSEPH. *Preston.* Also LAURENCE and WILLIAM, all 1800–24.

SHALCROSS, JOSIAH. Maker of cylinder escapements with ruby cylinders, and of duplex escapements; for many years in the employ of McCabes; born 1800, died 1866.

SHALLER, NICHOLAS. Apprenticed 1672 to Jas. Grimes, C.C.

SHALLOW, PHILLIP. *Waterford,* 1820.

SHARP, GEORGE. 1822–25.

SHARP, J. *20 Little Tower St.,* 1794–1808.

SHARP, JNO. Apprenticed 1647 to Hy. Child, C.C.

SHARP, JOHN. *30 Fish St. Hill,* 1806–25.

SHARP, T. *9 Postern Row, Tower Hill,* 1816.

SHARP, THOS. Apprenticed 1667 to Robt. Whitwell, C.C.

SHARP, THOS. *Stratford-on-Avon.* The sexton's clock by him spoken of by Washington Irving in his *Sketch Book* is at the Red Horse, Stratford-on-Avon; died 1799.

SHARP, THOS. *Leighton,* 1780.

SHARP & WILLIAMS. *6 Strand,* 1790.

SHARPE, CHRISTOPHER. *Dublin,* 1820.

SHARPE, WILLIAM. C.C. 1681.

SHARPE, WM. *75 Holborn Bridge,* 1793.

SHARPLES, JAS. *Liverpool,* 1817.

SHARPNELL. See SHRAPNELL.

SHAW, ANNA MARIA. Apprenticed to Isaac Loddington and his wife, 1733.

SHAW, EDWARD. Apprenticed 1689 to Clem. Forster, C.C. Lancaster.

SHAW, JAMES F. *Halifax,* 1790–1830.

SHAW, JAS. *Kember.* Watch, h.m., 1777.

SHAW, JNO. *Liverpool.* Watch, h.m., 1786.

SHAW, JOHN, 'near the Bars in Holborn'; apprenticed to Thos. Taylor of Holborn in 1672; C.C. 1682; master in 1712; splendid marquetry case clock as above; another fine specimen bore the signature 'John Shaw at the Dyall in Holborne'; 1682–1714.

SHAW, JOHN. *London.* Apprenticed 1675, C.C. 1682.

SHAW, ROBT. 1789, f.

SHAW, THOMAS. *Lancaster,* 1766–95. Clock.

SHAW, THOS. 1726, f.

SHAW, WILLIAM. *22 Wood St., Cheapside,* 1760–72.

SHAW, WILLIAM. *Botesdale,* 1760–90. Clocks and watches; long-case clock.

SHAYLER, RICHARD. *Ball Alley, Lombard St.,* 1753–56.

SHAYLER, WILLIAM. *44 Lombard St.,* 1755–75.

SHEAFE, THOMAS. *London (College Hill).* Apprenticed 1737, C.C. 1749–81. Also SHEAF.

SHEARER, MICHAEL. *Edinburgh,* 1786–1825.

SHEAVE, THOS. To him was apprenticed Wm. Howells, 1773.

SHEAVE, WILLIAM. *16 Bell Alley, Coleman St.,* 1770–94. Watch with 'E. Mason, Greenwich', on dial.

SHEARER, JAMES. *23 Devonshire St., Queen Sq.* 1825–42.

SHEARMAN, ROBERT. *Wilmington, Del.,* 1760–70; *Philadelphia, Pa.,* 1799.

SHEARWOOD, JAS. *London.* Watch, 1767.

SHEDDEN, CHARLES. *Perth,* 1813–71.

SHEDEL, JAS. *London.* Small bracket clock, about 1750.

SHEILY, SAMUEL. *61 St. Paul's Churchyard,* 1775.

SHELDRICK, EDWARD. *48 Cheapside,* 1798–1803.

SHELLEY, CHARLES. *London.* Apprenticed 1716–34 C.C.

SHELLEY, JNO. *London.* Lantern clock, 1636.

SHELLY, JOSEPH. C.C. 1717.

SHELLY & KING. *149 Shoreditch,* 1772–75.

SHELTON, JNO. Apprenticed 1662 to Thos. Mills, C.C. "Whereas there was a Silver Minute Pendulum Watch dropt on my Lord Mayor's day between the hours of 9 and 10 at night, the name John Shelton, London. If the person who took it up will bring it or send it to John Collins, Watchmaker, 'The White Horse and Black Boy', in the Great Old Bailey he shall receive full satisfaction even to the whole value if desired (*The Post Man,* Nov. 1, 1705).

SHELTON, JOHN. *London.* Apprenticed 1695, C.C. 1702.

SHELTON, JOHN. *Shoe Lane.* C.C. 1720; livery 1766; in a letter to the Royal Society from Jas. Short in 1752, Jno. Shelton is referred to as "the principal person employed by Mr. Graham in making astronomical clocks"; he published a description of the dead-beat escapement in the *Gentleman's Magazine* for September, 1754. Nevil Maskelyne in 1761 tested a clock of his make.

SHELTON, JOHN. *London (Shoe Lane).* Apprenticed 1737, C.C. 1745.

SHELTON, SAMSON. Member of the Blacksmiths' Company; active in obtaining the charter of the C.C., of which he was one of the first wardens in 1631; died 1649, leaving £50 to the C.C.; fine clock-watch by him, British Museum; 1623–49.

SHEPARD, JNO. *Sheffield,* 1723.

SHEPHARD, JNO. *Whitehaven,* 1770.

SHEPHEARD, THOS. *London.* C.C. 1632; maker of an oval watch, about 1620.

SHEPHERD, HENRY. *4 Pope's Head Alley, Cornhill,* 1760–75.

SHEPHERD, JNO. Apprenticed 1674 to Robt. Storr, C.C.

SHEPHERD, MATTHEW. *Charleston, U.S.A.* From 1774; *New York* from 1760; from *London.* Watch.

SHEPHERD, THOS. Apprenticed 1689 to Jno. Barnard, C.C.

SHEPHERD, THOS. *Liverpool,* 1770.

SHEPHERD, THOS. *Wootton-under-Edge,* 1792.

SHEPHERD, WILLIAM. *Liverpool,* 1763–84.

SHEPHERD, WILLIAM ROBERT. *Pontefract,* 1822–40. SHEPPARD.

SHEPHERD, WM. *199 Strand,* 1815–25.

SHEPLEY, EDWD. *Manchester,* 1780.

SHEPLEY, JOHN. *Stockport.* Died 1749; long oak case clocks.

SHEPLEY, WILLIAM, 1780.

SHEPPARD, SAMUEL. *1 Hanover St., Hanover Sq.,* 1830.

SHEPPERD, SARAH. *199 Strand,* 1830.

SHEPPERD, THOS. See SHEPHEARD.

SHERBIRD, J. *Turk's St., Bethnal Green,* 1820.

SHERBORNE, THOS. *6 Strand,* 1793–1800.

SHERE, HENRY & ARNOLD. *46 Lombard St.,* 1753–68.

SHERWIN, —. *London.* Watch, about 1705.

SHERWOOD, JAMES. *Yarm,* 1816.

SHERWOOD, JNO. Apprenticed 1690 to Hy. Jones, C.C.

SHERWOOD, JOHN. Apprenticed to John Jeffs, and turned over to George Graham, C.C. 1721.

SHERWOOD, THOMAS. *Leeds.* 1801–34; watch.

SHERWOOD, THOS. *Yarm,* 1823.

SHERWOOD, THOS. *Leeds,* 1830.

SHERWOOD, WILLIAM. Apprenticed to James Delander, 1686, C.C. 1695.

SHERWOOD, WILLIAM. C.C. 1720; master in 1740.

SHICK, WILLIAM. *43 Brick Lane, Old St.,* 1820.

SHIEL, ALEX. *London.* Bracket clock, about 1710.

SHIELD, THOS. Apprenticed 1691 to Jno. Harris, C.C.

SHINDLER, THOMAS. *Canterbury.* Maker of long-case clocks, about 1720.

SHIPLEY, JOHN. *Hyde, Cheshire.* Very fine marquetry long-case clock, about 1705.

SHIPPEN, WILLIAM. *Philadelphia,* 1819–24. Watch.

SHIPWAY, JOHN. *London.* C.C. 1813.

SHIRLEY, JAS. Apprenticed 1679 to Jas. Delander, C.C.

SHIRLEY, JOHN. C.C. 1720; in 1724 paid £20 to be transferred to the Vintners' Company.

SHIRT, WM. *25 Coleman St., Bunhill Row,* and *10 City Rd.,* 1815–35. A capable man; he published a 'train card' for watchmakers.

SHOLE, SIM. *Deptford,* 1825.

SHORROCK, THURSTON. *Preston,* 1770.

SHORT, JAMES. *Surrey St., Strand,* 1740–70. A maker of repute who sent to the Royal Society in 1752 an interesting letter on compensated pendulums; Harrison's son, before starting on his voyage to Barbados, in 1764, set his chronometer by Short's regulator.

SHORT, JOSHUA. C.C. 1665.

SHORTALL, THOMAS. *London.* C.C. 1718.

SHORTER. In 1798 Edward Shorter, clockmaker, *Giltspur St.,* was associated with Wm. Anthony, of Clerkenwell, in a patent for carriages, etc.

SHORTER, E. *4 Bridge Rd., Southwark,* 1830.

SHORTGRAVE, ROBERT. *Northampton,* 1734. Died 1751; watch.

SHORTLAND, THOMAS. *London.* Apprenticed 1745, C.C. 1764.

SHOWELL, HY. Apprenticed 1660 to Lionel Wythe, C.C.

SHOWELL, JAS. Apprenticed 1691 to David Minuel, C.C.

SHRAPNELL, JAMES. *36 Ludgate St.,* 1761–70; *60 Charing Cross,* 1775; afterwards Jas. Shrapnell & Son.

SHRUBB, THOS. Apprenticed 1689 to Phil. Browne.

SHUCKBURG, CHARLES. C.C. 1719.

SHURWOOD, THOS. *Yarm,* 1775.

SHUTE, GEO. *London.* Bird and flower marquetry long-case clock, about 1705.

SHUTTLEWORTH, FRANCIS. *23 Duke St., Piccadilly,* 1806–10.

SHUTTLEWORTH, FRAS. *Sarum,* 1760.

SHUTTLEWORTH, HENRY. C.C. 1669.

SHUTZ, GUSTAVUS. *Philadelphia,* 1825.

SHWERER, JOSEPH. *Hull,* 1822.

SHWERER, MATTHEW. Also at *Hull,* 1822.

SIBBALD, WILLIAM. *4 Cannon St. Rd.,* 1815–35.

SIBELIN, JEAN. *Neuchâtel* district. Apprenticed 1706, died 1742; some signed sundials; watches and clocks.

SIBELIN, JOSUÉ. *Neuchâtel.* Apprenticed 1684, died 1738; watch.

SIBELIN L'AÎNÉ. *Neuchâtel,* about 1700.

SIBBERN, JØRGEN. *Nyborg.* Born 1615, died 1700.

SIDEY, —, JUNR. *London.* Watch, 1798.

SIDEY, BENJAMIN. *Cow Lane, Moorfields.* C.C. 1730; master 1761 and 1789; known as a good watchmaker, and active in matters affecting the interests of the trade.

SIDLEY, BENJAMIN. *Watling St.* C.C. 1710.

SIDLEY, JOHN. C.C. 1701.

SIDWELL. See SEDWELL.

SIGG, HANNS JAKOB, son. *Basle.* Born 1644, apprenticed 1663–99.

SILK (or SILKE), JNO. *Elmstead.* Lantern clock, about 1670; long-case clock, about 1710.

SILLITO, CHAS. *Uttoxeter,* 1760.

SILLS, J. *Manchester.* Watch, 1809, another 1811.

SILLS, SILVANI. *Paris,* 1750.

SILVER, FREDK. Livery C.C. 1810.

SILVER, J. & J. *28 Hatton Garden,* 1825–30.

SILVER, JON. *London.* Watch, 1645.

SILVER, JOSEPH. *28 Hatton Garden,* 1793.

SILVESTER, JOHN. Apprenticed to Thomas Bates, and turned over to Henry Jones; C.C. 1693.

SIMCOCK, THOS. *Warrington,* 1818.

SIMCOCK, JOSIAH. Apprenticed 1675 to Hy. Adeane, C.C.

SIMCOX, SAMUEL. C.C. 1708.

SIMCOX, WILLIAM. C.C. 1682.

SIMERY, JAQUES. *Geneva,* about 1775–91.

SIMISTERE, RICHARD. *Birmingham.* Long-case clock, about 1765.

SIMKIN, BEN. *16 High St., Boro',* 1788–93.

SIMKINS, JNO. Apprenticed 1694 to Thos. Taylor.

SIMKINS, ROBERT. *London.* Apprenticed 1695, C.C. 1709–21.

SIMKINS, THOMAS. *London (Trinity Lane)*. Apprenticed 1694, C.C. 1711–29; insolvent.

SIMKINS, THOMAS. *London*. Apprenticed 1723, C.C. 1733.

SIMMONDS, THOS. *London*. Clock, about 1730.

SIMMONS, EBENEZER. *1 Pavement, Moorfields*, 1816; *26 Coleman St.*, 1825–76.

SIMMONS, JOHN. *Fleet St.*, 1753–56.

SIMMS, ISAAC. Watch, British Museum, about 1600.

SIMNER, JAMES. *Liverpool*, 1796–1816.

SIMNER, RICHARD. *London (Roebuck Ct., Old St.)*. Apprenticed 1751, C.C. 1760–95; watch.

SIMNET, JOHN. *New York*, 1770–75. Watch and 'Periodical Titivator'; from *London*; cleaned watches for two shillings. *v.* NIXON.

SIMONDS, J. L. *19 Holborn Hill*, 1820–30.

SIMONDS, THOMAS. *Fleet St.* C.C. 1661; lantern clock, balance escapement; 1661–70.

SIMONS, JOHN. Watch-case coverer, *Sutton St.*, 1790–93.

SIMPKIN, BENJ. *6 Tooley St.*, 1800.

SIMPKIN, JOHN. *Rillington*. Born 1767, died 1834.

SIMPKINS, BENJAMIN. *35 Frith St.*, 1800.

SIMPKINS, GEORGE. *London (Gt. Turnstile, Holborn)*. Apprenticed 1731, C.C. 1766. Also SIMPSON.

SIMPKINS, JOHN. *London*. Apprenticed 1701, C.C. 1710.

SIMPKINS, JOHN. *London*. Apprenticed 1759.

SIMPKINS, THOMAS. C.C. 1710.

SIMPKINS, THOMAS. *London*. Apprenticed 1764, C.C. 1772.

SIMPKINS, WILLIAM. *London*. Apprenticed 1741, C.C. 1749.

SIMPKINSON, ROGER. *41 Fleet St.*, 1758–75.

SIMPSON, ANTHONY. *Cockermouth*, 1810.

SIMPSON, ARCHIBALD. *10 Prince's St., Leicester Sq.*, 1790–94.

SIMPSON, BENJ. *Halifax*, 1776.

SIMPSON, DANIEL. *Workington*, 1810.

SIMPSON, GEORGE. *London (Gt. Turnstile, Holborn)*. Apprenticed 1731, C.C. 1766. Also SIMPKINS.

SIMPSON, HECTOR. Card, B.M., 'H. Simpson, 9 Old Bond St., foreman to the late Mr. Fladgate', 1785; *127 Pall Mall*, 1788–94.

SIMPSON, JOHN. C.C. 1723.

SIMPSON, JOHN. *London*. Apprenticed 1701, C.C. 1710.

SIMPSON, JOHN. *Wigton*, 1770–1820.

SIMPSON, JOHN. *6 Middle Row, Holborn*, 1815–40.

SIMPSON, JOHN. *Wigton*, 1820.

SIMPSON, MARY. *Cockermouth*, 1820.

SIMPSON, R. *Yarmouth*, 1790.

SIMPSON, R. *481 Strand*, 1805–15.

SIMPSON, ROBT. *Halifax*, 1785.

SIMPSON, STEPHEN. *Greta Bridge*. Long-case clock, with 'Peter & Mary Winder' in the centre of the dial, about 1770.

SIMPSON, STEPHEN. *Gibraltar*, about 1790 C.C.

SIMPSON, THOMAS. *London*. Apprenticed 1766, C.C. 1772. *Hertford*, 1775–95; watch. Also SIMSON.

SIMPSON, WILLIAM. C.C. 1700.

SIMPSON, WILLIAM. *London*. Apprenticed 1741, C.C. 1749; watch.

SIMPSON, WILLIAM ELLISON. Hon. f. C.C. 1781; fine long-case repeating clock signed 'Simpson Wigton', about 1775.

SIMPSON & WARD. *Fleet St.*, 1737–40.

SIMS, GEO. 1738. See ADDIS, W.

SIMS, GEO. *Canterbury*, 1745–91.

SIMS, GEO. *Rochester*, 1760.

SIMS, GEO. *Prescot*, 1770.

SIMS, GEORGE, son. *London*. C.C. 1761.

SIMS, HENRY. *London (Harp Lane)*. a. 1760, C.C. 1771–92; watch.

SIMS, HENRY. *Canterbury*. Maker of long-case clocks, 1758–80.

SIMS, JOHN. *64 Lombard St.*, 1773–78.

SIMS, WM. Apprenticed 1693 to Thos. Bradford.

SIMS & SON. *London*. Watch, 1830.

SIMSON, —. *Hartford*, 1780.

SIMSON, GUSTAF. *Göteborg*. Born 1776, died 1833; watch.

SIMSON, LARS (LAURENT). *Göteborg*. Born 1733, master 1763, died 1794; turret clocks.

SINCLARE, G. D. *Dublin*. Watch, 1782.

SINDERBY, FRANCIS H. *14 Devereux Court, Strand*, 1790. Livery C.C. 1810; *18 Bull and Mouth St.*, 1816–42.

SINDREY, LAWRENCE. C.C. 1661.

SING, JOHANN MICHAEL. *Augsburg*. Born 1684, master 1723, juré, died 1767.

SING, MORITZ. *Augsburg*. Master 1732, died 1772.

SINGLETON, JOHN. *Lancaster*, 1806, f.

SKARRAT (SKARRETT), JOHN. *Worcester*. 1794 C.C.; watch.

SKARRAT (SKARRETT), THOMAS. *London*. Apprenticed 1772, C.C. 1782.

SKEGGS, L. *355 Rotherhithe St.*, 1788–1810.

SKEGGS, WM. *London*. Long-case clock, about 1780.

SKEGGS, WM. *355 Rotherhithe St.*, 1816–40.

SKELTON, C. *Malton*, 1823. See SHELTON.

SKELTON, GEORGE. *Edinburgh*. Apprenticed 1773, died 1834; partner in, and successor in 1787 to, Brown & Skelton.

SKEPPER, THOS. Apprenticed 1675 to Thos. Taylor, Strand.

SKILKELTHORPE, WM. Clock at St. Cross Hospital, Winchester, 1737.

SKINNER, ALVAH. *Boston, U.S.A.*, early nineteenth century.

SKINNER, BENJ. *Islington*. Bracket clock, about 1770.

SKINNER, JOHN. *Exeter*. a. 1780, died 1818; watch.

SKINNER, MATTHEW. Apprenticed to Francis Hill; C.C. 1713; master 1746; watch, G.M., about 1750.

SKINNER, ROBERT. *London (Moorfields)*. Apprenticed 1783, C.C. 1792, died 1821.

SKINNER, WILLIAM. *London*. C.C. 1821.

SKIPWORTH, FRANCIS. Apprenticed 1670 to Robt. Lynch, C.C.

SKIRROW, —. 1818.

SKIRROW, JAS. *Wigan*, 1780.

SKIRROW, JAS. *Lancaster*, 1783, f.

SKITTLETHORPE, RICHARD. *Southwark Rd.* Lantern clock, about 1690.

SLACK, —. *Ipstones*. Long-case clock, about 1790.

SLACK, JOSEPH. C.C. 1723.

SLADE, J. L. *London*. Watch, 1790.

SLATER, ROBERT. *London*. C.C. 1775–85.

SLATFORD, JOHN. *London*. Apprenticed 1802, C.C. 1810.

SLEATH, JOHN. *London*. Apprenticed 1747, C.C. 1758.

SLIPPER, JERE. *Maiden Lane*. C.C. 1726.

SLOCOMB, SAMUEL. *Cork*, 1735–50.

SLOUGH, WILLIAM. C.C. 1687.

SLY, ROBERT. C.C. 1720.

SMALL, WM. Apprenticed 1684 to Richd. Farmer, C.C.; pendulum watch, about 1705.

SMALLE, LEWIS. Received payments for 'keeping the clocke' of Lambeth parish church, 1585–1605.

SMALLEY, JOHN. *Lancaster*, 1721, f.

SMALLEY, THOMAS. C.C. 1687; maker of a clock at Battle Abbey, Sussex; 1687–1700.

SMALLPAGE, JAS. *Sandback*, 1790.

SMALLPAGE, JOSH. *Leeds*, 1829.

SMALLWOOD, ED. *Dublin*, 1780.

SMALLWOOD, JNO. *Litchfield.* Long-case clock, about 1730.

SMART, BENJAMIN. *35 Frith St.*, 1800–18.

SMART, JOHN. C.C. 1682.

SMART, ORPHEUS. 1750.

SMART, THOMAS. *4 Little Ryder St., St. James's*, 1816–30.

SMEATON, JNO. At Trinity House is a clock bearing the name of Jno. Smeaton, the celebrated engineer, the initials 'J. S.' being on the hour socket. There is also preserved at Trinity House a long-case clock, on a brass plate affixed to the door of which is inscribed, 'This timepiece was placed in the old Eddystone Lighthouse by John Smeaton, C.E., F.R.S., on the 8th October, 1759'; in Smeaton's book on the building of the Eddystone Lighthouse the following reference is made to it: "This timepiece by a simple contrivance being made to strike a blow every half-hour, would thereby warn the keepers to snuff the candles." Mr. T. P. Cooper says Smeaton and Hindley of York were lifelong friends; he corresponded with John Holmes in 1779, and with Thos. Reid in 1786.

SMEATON, JOHN. *York*, f., 1646; in the British Museum is a rather large silver watch by him, silver dial, outer case of leather *piqué*, about 1650.

SMEATON, TOBIAS. Apprenticed 1664 to Hy. Harland, C.C.

SMELLIE, THOMAS. *London.* Apprenticed 1809, C.C. 1816.

SMELT, ROBERT. *London.* C.C. 1785–94.

SMINT. Calendar watch, inscribed 'Smint London', silver dial with gilt rosettes between the figures; outer case embossed by 'Mavris', about 1775, Pierpont Morgan collection.

SMISON, THOS. *Hartford.* Watch, 1796.

SMIT (SMITT), J. L. *Groningen*, about 1800. Died 1825; published posthumously *Horologie en Uurwerkmakers Handboek.*

SMITH, ABRAHAM. Wooden clock-maker, *Manchester*, 1770.

SMITH, ALEXANDER. *Dundee*, 1718–42.

SMITH, B. *12 Duke St., Lincoln's Inn Fields*, 1830.

SMITH, BENJAMIN. *London.* Apprenticed 1734, C.C. 1742–78; watch.

SMITH, CHARLES. *London (Lombard St.).* Apprenticed 1766, C.C. 1783.

SMITH, CHARLES. *Liskeard.* About 1790 C.C.

SMITH, CHAS. *118 Bunhill Row*, 1790–1823.

SMITH, DAN. *Dorking.* Sheep's-head clock, dial 11½ in. square, long pendulum, about 1730.

SMITH, DANL. *Aldermanbury*, 1775.

SMITH, DAVID. C.C. 1662.

SMITH, EDWARD. *Bury.* Lantern clock, about 1730.

SMITH, EDWARD, at the Parrot and Pearl in *Foster Lane*, 1770.

SMITH, EDWARD. *Newark*, 1770–90. Long-case clocks; watch.

SMITH, EDWD. *Richmond*, 1780.

SMITH, EDWD. *Newark*, 1780.

SMITH, FREDERICK. *London.* Apprenticed 1791, C.C. 1807.

SMITH, G. *11 St. Martin's Churchyard*, 1823–30.

SMITH, GABRIEL. *Chester*, 1752–97. Watch.

SMITH, GABRIEL. Long-case clock, signed 'Gabriel Smith, Bartholmey', about 1695.

SMITH, GABRIEL. *Chester*, 1773.

SMITH, GEO. *Artillery Ground.* C.C. 1730.

SMITH, GEO. *110 Wood St.*, 1770–76.

SMITH, GEO. *4 Huggin Lane*, 1783–90.

SMITH, GEORGE. C.C. 1632.

SMITH, GEORGE. *Charlotte Terrace, New Cut*, 1820.

SMITH, H. Watch movement maker, *12 Berkeley St., Clerkenwell*, 1825–35.

SMITH, H. D. *London.* Watch, with hare and snail on plate as a guide to regulation, 1808.

SMITH, HENRY. *London.* Apprenticed 1650, C.C. 1658.

SMITH, HENRY. C.C. 1703; probably successor to Thomas; pull repeating clock in mahogany case, about 1720, inscribed 'Henry Smith, Gray's Inn'.

SMITH, HENRY. *Reading*, 1794–1803 C.C. Watch, Ilbert collection.

SMITH, HENRY C. *Waterbury, U.S.A.*, 1814.

SMITH, HORATIO. *York*, f., 1822–32.

SMITH, J. *40 Duke St., Manchester Sq.*, 1780.

SMITH, J. *256 Borough*, 1825–30.

SMITH, JABEZ. *16 Fenchurch St.*, 1790.

SMITH, JAMES. *Edinburgh*, 1629. Died 1660.

SMITH, JAMES. *Stow-on-the-Wold.* Clock, about 1740.

SMITH, JAMES. *Gosport*, 1746.

SMITH, JAMES. *115 Fleet St.*, 1760–80.

SMITH, JAMES. *London (Jermyn St.)*, 1776. C.C. 1781–94; clockmaker to George III.

SMITH, JAMES. *Edinburgh*, 1790–1806.

SMITH, JAMES (clockmaker to George III). *Jermyn St.* 1776–94. Hon. f. C.C. 1781.

SMITH, JAS. *Chiswell St.*, 1758–60.

SMITH, JAS. & SON. *118 Bunhill Row*, 1769–88.

SMITH, JAS. *White Horse Court, Bishopsgate*, 1776–90. All sorts of clocks and watches made, mended, and sold by James Smith in White Horse Court, Whitecross St., watch paper, Ponsonby collection, about 1770; *Bishopsgate*, 1776–90.

SMITH, JAS. *98 Oxford St.*, 1790–1815.

SMITH, JNO. *York*, f., 1750. In 1754 he made a new clock for St. Martin's Church, projecting into Coney St., being paid £30 for this work.

SMITH, JNO. *Thirsk*, 1775.

SMITH, JNO. *Chester*, 1785.

SMITH, JNO. *Wrexham.* Watch, 1807.

SMITH, JOHN. Petitioner for incorporation of C.C., and one of the first assistants, 1631–49.

SMITH, JOHN. *London.* Apprenticed 1647, C.C. 1654.

SMITH, JOHN. C.C. 1656; in 1657 Jno. Smith was fined 10s. by C.C. for putting the name Estine Hubert on a watch.

SMITH, JOHN. C.C. 1674, clockmaker and author of "Horological Dialogues, by J. S., clockmaker, in three parts, showing the nature, use and right managing of clocks and watches; with an appendix containing Mr. Oughtred's method for calculating of numbers"; 120 pp. 12 mo, London; published at 'The Three Roses', in Ludgate St., 1675; this was probably the first book in English on watch and clock making. J. S. quite appreciated the pendulum as a controller; he remarks, "As to their regularity I shall say only thus much, that those clocks who have their motion regulated by a pendulum are more excellent than those regulated by a balance, and those that are regulated by a long pendulum are far more excellent than those that are regulated by a short one." Rules are given for calculating the length of a pendulum, and a three-second pendulum is mentioned which "will be 28 ft. 8 in. from the term of suspension to the centre of the bob". In 1694 he published 'Horological Disquisitions', of which a second edition was issued in 1708; his observations covered a wide field; he discoursed on the Baroscope or quicksilver weather glass, on painting, and on the plentiful use of cold water as a preservative of health. He was a Unitarian and plunged into theological discussion; the Rev. Francis Gregory answered him and advised him to go back to the noise of his hammers and the use of his pincers. St. Augustine, in the city of London, is given as his residence; but Hatton says he was originally a Lancashire tool maker, and his 'engines' the best in use; he died prior to 1730, at which date it was advertised that his books could be obtained of Mary Smith, at the Fan and Flower de Luce, over against Somerset House in the Strand, and nowhere else.

SMITH, JOHN. *London*. Apprenticed 1727, C.C. 1738.

SMITH, JOHN. *Charleston, U.S.A.*, 1754.

SMITH, JOHN. *London*. Apprenticed 1749, C.C. 1764.

SMITH, JOHN. C.C. 1703; maker of the turret clock at Westminster Abbey, 1730; the movement of this clock was replaced in 1860.

SMITH, JOHN, son of Benjamin Smith, C.C. 1768.

SMITH, JOHN. *Pittenweem*. Musical clocks, 1770–1814.

SMITH, JOHN, son of John, York. *Thirsk*. Apprenticed 1758–1807.

SMITH, JOHN. *Glasgow*, 1783–1806.

SMITH, JOHN. *143 Houndsditch*. Livery C.C. 1776–90.

SMITH, JOHN. *27 Cornhill*, 1825.

SMITH, JOHN JAMES. *London*, 1781–90.

SMITH, JOSEPH. *London*. Apprenticed 1718, C.C. 1742.

SMITH, JOSEPH. C.C. 1700.

SMITH, JOSEPH. *Bristol*. Long-case clock, about 1730.

SMITH, JOSEPH. *Chester*. Bracket clock, about 1740.

SMITH, JOSEPH. Apprenticed to Daniel Delander; C.C. 1742.

SMITH, JOSEPH. *London*. C.C. 1788.

SMITH, JOSEPH. *49 Lombard St.*, 1783–90.

SMITH, MAURICE. *Royal Exchange*, 1705–32.

SMITH, MORRIS (or MAURICE). C.C. 1702.

SMITH, NAT. Apprenticed 1647 to Wm. Bunting, C.C.

SMITH, NATHANIEL. *London*. Apprenticed 1680, C.C. 1689–1719.

SMITH, OBADIAH. C.C. 1725.

SMITH, PHILIP. C.C. 1776.

SMITH, RICHARD. *Newport*. I. of W., 1730.

SMITH, RICHD. *Cloak Lane*, 1780–85.

SMITH, ROBERT. Watch, Pierpont Morgan collection, about 1630, inscribed 'Robert Smith at Popeshead Alley'; C.C. 1648; warden in 1650, and died during his year of office.

SMITH, ROBERT. *London*. C.C. 1659.

SMITH, ROBERT. *London*. C.C. 1697.

SMITH, ROBERT. C.C. 1695; on the disc of a long walnut case clock appeared the inscription, 'Robert Smith, Dunstable'; 1680–1700.

SMITH, ROBERT. *London (Nixon Sq.)*. C.C. 1750.

SMITH, ROBERT. *Philadelphia*, 1819.

SMITH, RUTH. Apprenticed 1674 to Thos. Birch and Jane his wife, C.C.

SMITH, SAM. *Walford*. Watch, 1787.

SMITH, SAMUEL HENRY. *London (Swan Alley)*. Apprenticed 1708, C.C. 1715, died a. 1774.

SMITH, SAMUEL. *Coventry*. Patented (1812, No. 3,620) a vertical escape wheel with five teeth; several watches were made on this plan; *7 Clerkenwell Close*, 1819–22.

SMITH, STEPHEN. *London*. Apprenticed 1651, C.C. 1658.

SMITH, SUSANNA. Apprenticed to Hannah, wife of Jas. Wilson, 1747.

SMITH, T. W. *27 Fenchurch St.*, 1820–30.

SMITH, THOMAS. *Gray's Inn*. Admitted C.C. 1700; long-case clock, about 1710, with very fine scroll marquetry over the whole surface of the case.

SMITH, THOMAS. C.C. 1718.

SMITH, THOMAS. *London (Princes St., Aldgate)*. Apprenticed 1763, C.C. 1770.

SMITH, THOMAS. *17 John St., Oxford St.*, 1820–35.

SMITH, THOMAS WILLIAM. *London*. C.C. 1819; watch.

SMITH, TUDOR. C.C. 1717.

SMITH, WALTER. C.C. 1641.

SMITH, WALTER. *Cuckfield*, 1773–91. Clocks and watches.

SMITH, WALTER. *98 Bishopsgate St.*, 1795.

SMITH, WILLIAM. *Cheapside*. Livery Blacksmiths' Company, 1759; *32 Cornhill*, 1769–80.

SMITH, WILLIAM. *Keighley*, 1780–1810.

SMITH, WILLIAM. *London*. C.C. 1805.

SMITH, WILLIAM. *Philadelphia*, 1819–25. Watch.

SMITH, WILLIAM. *Irvine*, 1821–50.

SMITH, WILLIAM. *35 Poultry*, 1823.

SMITH, WM. C.C. 1651.

SMITH, WM. *Lancaster*, 1767, f.

SMITH, WM. (from *London*), "at the Dial, in upper end of High St.," Bristol," 1775.

SMITH, WM. *170 Wapping*, 1800–04.

SMITH, WM. *3 Bridgewater Sq.*, 1803–10.

SMITH & ASPREY. *4 Bruton St.*, 1817.

SMITH & CO. *Piccadilly*, 1825.

SMITH & SHARP. *14 Bartholomew Close*, 1780–85.

SMITH & WAREHAM. *Davies St., Berkeley Sq.*, 1790.

SMITHFIELD, W. *Romford*, about 1760.

SMITHER, WILLIAM. *London*. Livery C.C. 1823–40.

SMITHYES, JNO. *London*. Bracket clock, about 1750.

SMITHYES, WM. *Holborn*. Long-case clock, about 1740.

SMITTON, PETER. *12 Crown St., Russell Sq.*, 1820–35.

SMOD, —. *Geisheim*. Watch.

SMORTHWAITE, —. *Colchester*. Lantern clock, about 1680.

SMOULT, JAS. 1739, f., died 1768.

SMOULT, THOS. *Lancaster*, 1708, f., Mayor of Lancaster in 1739.

SMYTH, JOSHUA. 'Steyning in Sussex'. Maker of lantern clocks, 1690.

SMYTH, WM. *Woodbridge*. Long-case clock, about 1800.

SMYTHIES, JAS. Apprenticed 1679 to Geo. Hamilton, C.C.

SMYTHIES, JNO. *London*. Bracket clock, about 1750.

SNATT, JNO. *Ashford*. Brass clock, about 1700.

SNEEBERGER, MICHAEL. *Prague*. Pupil of Burgi, 1605. Crystal travelling clock.

SNELL, E. *Barnstaple*, 1790.

SNELL, GEORGE. C.C. 1688–1700; maker of long-case clocks.

SNELLING, HENRY. *Ball Alley, Lombard St.*, 1769–75.

SNELLING, HENRY. *London*, 1770–75; *Philadelphia*, 1776. Watches and clocks.

SNELLING, JAMES. *Poultry*. C.C. 1712; master in 1736; watch, British Museum.

SNELLING, JOHN. *Alton*, 1761–95. Clocks and watches.

SNELLING, THOMAS. C.C. 1680.

SNIDAL, JAS. *Sheffield*, 1770–1814. His second quality watches were signed 'Dalsni'.

SNIDAL, SAMUEL. *Sheffield*, 1814–40. Watch.

SNOW, DANIEL. Lantern clock, 1664.

SNOW, JNO. *London*. Lantern clock inscribed 'Jno. Snow Aº dmi 1630'.

SNOW, JNO. *Frome*, about 1760.

SNOW, JOHN. *Sarum*. "A watch the hours in the form of Diamonds, the Outcase holes with bizels for the sound of the Bell" (*Lond. Gaz.*, April 1, 1680).

SNOW, RICHARD. *London*. Apprenticed 1750, C.C. 1758–63.

SNOW, RICHD. *Pateley Bridge*, 1822.

SNOW, THOMAS. *London (Fetter Lane* and *Coldbath Fields)*. Apprenticed 1763, C.C. 1773–78.

SNOW, THOS. *Otley*, 1780.

SNOW, WM. About 1780.

SNOW, W. *Marlborough.* Mid-seventeenth century. One of the first high-quality provincial watch-makers.

SNOW, Z. *Bury,* 1814.

SNOWE, JO. *Lavington,* about 1680.

SOAR, JAS. *5 Paradise St., Finsbury,* 1823.

SOCTERYK, DANIEL. *Dortrecht.* The Comte de Lambilly has a watch by him with outer case chased by Cochin.

SÖDERBERG, VICTOR. *Visby,* 1825–40.

SÖDERLING, CARL. *Göteborg.* Born 1745, died 1807.

SÖDERMAN, PETTER. *Stockholm,* 1769–1810. Watch, long-case clock, two bracket clocks, two wall clocks illuminated Sidenbladh.

SOFFLEUR, THOS. *London,* 1680.

SOGDEN, T. *Chichester.* Long-case clock, about 1800.

SOIRON, JEAN FRANÇOIS. *Geneva.* Born 1756, died 1812; painter on engraving of repute; one of the few watch enamellers who signed his work.

SOLIANS, —. *Paris.* Clock, Windsor Castle, about 1790.

SOLLINGER, JACOB. *Vienna,* 1760. Afterwards at Paris; complicated clock with dancing figures, etc.

SOLOMON, EDWD. *Margate.* Watch, 1799.

SOLOMON, HY. *Coventry St.,* 1775.

SOLOMON, MOSES. *King St.* 1810; *Bevis Marks,* 1820; *Great Alie St.,* 1830.

SOLOMON, S. C. *13 St. Mary Axe,* 1794–1804.

SOLTIN, ADAM. *Björneborg,* 1769–1807.

SOMERSALL, FREDERICK. *London.* C.C. 1781.

SOMERSALL, GEORGE. *Leadenhall St.,* 1750; *Finsbury, Moorfields,* 1779.

SOMERSALL, GEORGE, brother. *London (Finsbury).* C.C. 1752–73.

SOMERSALL, JOHN. *Cripplegate Church;* C.C. 1708.

SOMERSALL, JOHN, son of George. *London (Barbican).* C.C. 1743–68.

SOMERSALL, MANDEVILLE. *Fore St.* C.C., lantern clock, about 1685.

SOMERSALL, RICHARD. *Finsbury Pl., Moorfields,* 1776–1804. Livery C.C. 1786.

SOMERVILLE, DAVID. *St. Ninians,* 1805–20.

SOMILLIER, JNO. Apprenticed 1649 to Luke Richards, C.C.

SOMMERSON, G. *Minories.* Lantern clock with Turkish numerals, about 1710.

SOMNER, JNO. Apprenticed 1663 to Wm. Raines, C.C.

SONLEY, J. *Dunlop,* 1770.

SONNEREAU à *Rochelle.* French octagonal watch, about 1640, V. & A.

SÖRDET, ÉTIENNE MARC. *Geneva,* about 1775–91.

SORET, ABRAHAM. *Dublin,* about 1750.

SORET, DAVID, son. *Geneva.* Born 1705, died 1780; watch.

SORET, ISAAC. *Geneva.* Born 1673, died 1760; pair-case silver repeating travelling clock, Feill collection; watch, Geneva Museum.

SORET, ISAAC ET FILS. *Geneva.* Watch, 1765.

SORET, JEAN ROBERT. *Geneva.* Watch with representation's of hammermen striking on bells, G.M., about 1780.

SORET, JEAN ROBERT. *Geneva,* 1740–80. Automatic repeating watch, G.M.; 4-colour gold watch, engraved and set stones, Fränkel collection; similar watch, Gemeente Museum, The Hague; gold engraved watch.

SORET, PIERRE. Watch in enamelled case, about 1620.

SÖRLING, CARL MAG. *Nyköping,* 1794–1813. Two watch movements, Nord Museum.

SÖRLING, JOHAN. *Norrköping,* 1774.

SOUBEYRAN à *Geneva.* Watch, 1760.

SOUNDY (SOUNDS), THOMAS. *London.* C.C. 1752; watch.

SOURDEN, —. *Paris.* 1699.

SOUTER, JEREMIAS. Night clocks; maker of Carillon at Salzburg-Dred, 1710.

SOUTH, HENRY. *Rotherham,* 1710.

SOUTH, JOSEPH. C.C. 1709.

SOUTHAN, GEO. *London.* Rack lever watch, about 1810.

SOUTHAN, SAML. *28 Red Lion St.,* 1790–94.

SOUTHCOTE, JOHN. *London.* Apprenticed 1747, C.C. 1767–1808; movement maker.

SOUTHCOTE, JOSIAH. Apprenticed C.C. 1681.

SOUTHERN, JNO. Apprenticed C.C. 1681.

SOUTHEY, —. *Rochester.* About 1790 C.C.

SOUTHWARK, THOS. Apprenticed 1677 to Barlow Brookes, C.C.

SOUTHWOOD, SAM. Apprenticed 1662 to Chas. Fox, C.C.

SOUTHWORTH, JOHN. C.C. 1689.

SOUTHWORTH, PETER. C.C. 1664.

SOUZA, SAMUEL. *Philadelphia,* 1819.

SOWERBY, JAS. *London.* Long-case clock, lacquer decoration, about 1760.

SOWERBY, JNO. *100 Brick Lane,* 1817; *79 Chiswell St.,* 1830.

SOWERBY, THOS. *124 Long Acre,* 1830.

SOWTER, JOHN. Admitted C.C. 1683.

SPACKMAN, GEORGE. *Philadelphia,* 1825. Watch.

SPALDIN, WM. *Liverpool.* Watch, 1784.

SPARCK, PETER. *Philadelphia,* 1797.

SPARKES, NICHOLAS. Presented C.C. with a piece of plate in lieu of serving as steward, 1659.

SPARKS, ANGEL. *Plymouth,* 1770–95.

SPARKS, THOS. *London.* Apprenticed 1689 to Jno. Drew; watch, 1732.

SPARROW, JNO. *15 Leicester St., Leicester Sq.,* 1815–18.

SPARROW, THOS. *113 Leadenhall St.,* 1790–94.

SPAULDING, EDWARD. *Providence, U.S.A.,* 1788.

SPEAKMAN, EDWARD. C.C. 1691.

SPEAKMAN, JNO. Apprenticed 1692 to Wm. Speakman.

SPEAKMAN, JOHN, JUNR. C.C. 1706.

SPEAKMAN, RICHD. Apprenticed 1692 to E. Micklewright.

SPEAKMAN, THOMAS. C.C. 1685; long-case clock, about 1710.

SPEAKMAN, WILLIAM. Apprenticed 1654; C.C. 1661; master 1701.

SPEARING, WILLIAM. *London.* Apprenticed 1701, C.C. 1719.

SPEEDWELL, G. *London.* Bracket clock, red lacquer case, 1760.

SPEIGHT, JAMES. *Tong,* 1785.

SPENCE, —. *Dublin.* Watch, 1750.

SPENCE, JOHN. *London.* In the British Museum is a silver watch by him, silver dial, matted ground with Roman hour numerals engraved on polished lozenge-shaped plaques, day of the month shown on outer circle, glass over dial. 1650–70.

SPENCE, JOHN. *Boston, U.S.A.,* 1821–25. Watch.

SPENCER, ARTHUR. C.C. 1732.

SPENCER, ELI. *Bolton-le-Moors,* 1818.

SPENCER, J. *20 Red Lion St., Clerkenwell,* 1820–30.

SPENCER, JNO. *Colne,* 1772.

SPENCER, JOHN. *London.* C.C. 1787.

SPENCER, JONATHAN. *London.* Apprenticed 1696, C.C. 1704–14.

SPENCER, RICHARD. *Dublin.* Watch, 1725.

SPENCER, THOMAS. *Strand.* Threatened with prosecution by C.C. for undue taking of apprentices, 1682; C.C. 1685; long-case clock, with fine Dutch marquetry, 10-in. dial, inscription at bottom, 'Thos. Spencer, Londini, fecit', about 1695.

SPENCER, THOS. *Manchester,* 1820.

SPENCER, W. *London.* Watch, 1785.

SPENCER, WOOSTER & Co. *Salem Bridge, U.S.A.*, 1828–37.

SPENCER & PERKINS. *44 Snow Hill*, 1775–94.

SPENDLOVE, JNO. *Thetford*, 1775–90.

SPILSBURY, JAS. *London*. Watch, 1758.

SPINK, MARSHALL. *1 and 2 Gracechurch St.*, 1772. Afterwards Spink & Son, 1772–1842.

SPITTLE, RICHARD. Admitted C.C. 1699–1720; tall walnut long-case clock.

SPITZ, GASPAR, *Schwartz*. Clock, square case, filigree covers over the dials, Vienna Treasury, about 1550.

SPRAKEL, JURRIEN. *Zutphen*. Made a striking and chiming clock with pendulum for St. Martin's, Groningen, in 1661.

SPRATLEY, RICHARD. *London*. Apprenticed 1772, C.C. 1780.

SPRATNELL, SAM. *Cockspur St.*, 1793.

SPRIGG, HY. Apprenticed 1637 to Simon Bartram, C.C.

SPRINGER, SAM. Clock, about 1810.

SPRINGFIELD, T. O. *Norwich*. Long marquetry case clock, about 1770.

SPRINGHALL. See MASTERMAN.

SPROGELL, JOHN. *Philadelphia*, 1791.

SPUR, GEO. *Aylesbury*. Lantern clock, about 1710.

SPURGIN, JERE. *Colchester*, 1770.

SPURRIER, JOHN. Admitted C.C. 1684.

SPYER, J., & SOLOMON. *26 Prescot St.*, 1793–1804; *20 Leman St.*, 1825.

SQUIRE. A well-known Bideford family of watch-makers, 1784–1921.

STACEY, JOHN. C.C. 1683.

STACEY, THOS. *Farnsfield, Notts.*, 1759, afterwards at *Southwell*.

STACEY, WILLIAM. *Fleet St.* Bell-top mahogany case bracket clock, about 1750; livery C.C. 1766.

STACH, HEINRICH. *Hanover*. Watch, 1800.

STADLIN, FRANZ LOUIS. *Pekin*. Born 1658; went to *Pekin* 1707; died 1740; clockmaker to K'ang-hi.

STAFFORD, JOHN. C.C. 1708; master 1741.

STAFFORD, T. *Chelsea*, 1810–20.

STAHL, ANDREAS. *Augsburg*. Early seventeenth century. Watches, Louvre, K. H. M. and M.P.S. Dresden signed 'A. S.' possibly by him; watch, Feill collection.

STAINES, JEFFERY. *London*. 1700–12 C.C.

STAINSBURGH, ROBERT. *Chippenham*. "A silver watch with a black Fish-Skin case, studded with silver, Robert Stainsburg, Chippenham, engraven on the Dial Plate" (*Lond. Gaz.*, Aug. 29, Sept. 1, 1698).

STAINTON, MATTHEW. *1 Aldermanbury*, 1772.

STALLARD, PHILIP. *3 New Sq., Shoe Lane*, 1793.

STALP (STALPP), DANIEL GEORG. *Coburg*. Apprenticed 1705, master 1711–36. Apprenticed in *Ansbach*. Court clock.

STALP (STALPP), JOHANN FRIEDRICH. *Dresden*. Master 1767, died 1789; gold engraved jasper watch; gold *repoussé* repeating watch, M.P.S. Dresden.

STAMFORD, —. *London*. 1640 C.C.

STAMFORD, RICHD. Apprenticed 1652 to Peter Willerme, C.C.

STAMP, JAS. *86 Cheapside*. Livery Goldsmiths' Company, 1775. See SUTTON & SON, also GODBEHERE.

STAMPER, FRANCIS, at 'ye Golden Ball in Lumbarde Streete', a good maker; C.C. 1682; in 1687 ordered by the C.C. to be prosecuted for refusing to admit to his workroom master and wardens when they were upon a search, but he submitted himself to the court, and was fined 20s.; maker of a clock with square dial on a lantern movement; watch by him, V. & A., 1682–1700.

STAMPER, JOHN. *148 Fleet St.*, 1772.

STANBOROUGH, JOSEPH. *London*. Apprenticed 1720, C.C. 1722.

STANBURY, HENRY. C.C. 1709; 30-hour long-case clock, 1709–20.

STANBURY, THOS. *Hereford*, 1780.

STANCLIFFE, JNO. *Askrigg*, 1775–90. He was apprenticed to C. Caygill. Long-case clock.

STANCLIFFE, JOHN. *Halifax*, 1720–60.

STANDISH, WILLIAM. Apprenticed to Jeffery Baily; C.C. 1688.

STANDLEY, MILES. *London*. Apprenticed 1810, C.C. 1818.

STANDRING, JAS. *Rochdale*, 1770–92.

STANDRING, JERE. *Bolton*, 1790.

STANES, JEFFERY. C.C. 1686.

STANFORD, JOHN. *London*. C.C. 1718.

STANFORD, WM. *South Walsham*, 1780.

STANLEY, JOHN. C.C. 1732; long-case clock signed 'J. Stanly, Nth Shields'.

STANLEY, THOMAS FRANÇOIS. *Paris*. Master 1776–99.

STANTON (or STAUNTON), EDWD. *Leadenhall St.* Apprenticed 1655 to Francis Bowen; C.C. 1662; master 1696; bracket clock, three trains, ebony case, Wetherfield collection. "A new Gold Clock-Watch graved with a cypher, on the back Edward Staunton, maker" (*Lond. Gaz.*, Nov. 16–19, 1696).

STANTON (or STAUNTON), JOB. *New York*, 1810.

STANTON (or STAUNTON), JOHN. C.C. 1692.

STANTON (or STAUNTON), JOSEPH. C.C. 1703.

STANTON (or STAUNTON), REGINALD. *London*. Left C.C. 1669.

STANTON (or STAUNTON), SAM. Apprenticed 1692 to Thos. Fletcher, C.C.

STANTON (or STAUNTON), SAMUEL. *London*. 1688 C.C.

STANTON (or STAUNTON), SAMUEL. *London*. Maker of lantern clocks; C.C. 1714.

STANTON (or STAUNTON), WILLIAM, son of Jos. *London*. Apprenticed 1725, C.C. 1732.

STAPLES, JAS. *Odiham*. Watch, 1780.

STAPLES, JAS. *7 Rosoman St., Clerkenwell*, 1788–94.

STAPLES, RICHD. Apprenticed 1684 to Henry Jones, C.C.

STAPLETON, GEORGE. *London*. 1689 C.C.

STAPLETON, STEPHEN. *Sutton*. Watch, 1750; another, rather earlier, 'Stephen Staplets, Sutton'.

STAPLETON, THOMAS. C.C. 1694; watch, about 1700.

STAPLETON, W. *London*. Watch, silver dial, about 1730.

STAPTOE, DAVID HINDRICH, son. *Hälsingfors*, 1713. Master 1716. *Stockholm*, 1734. Died 1748; watch.

STAPTOE, WILLIAM. *Charing Cross*. Admitted C.C. 1703; 1703–1710. See STEPTO.

STARCK, THOMAS. *Germany*. Clock, 1620.

STAREY, JOHN. *4 Sweeting's Alley, Cornhill*, 1770–94. C.C. 1785; livery 1787; long-case clock.

STARKEY, JOSEPH. C.C. 1706.

STARLING, CHARLES. *London* (*Ironmonger Row* and *Chequer Alley*). C.C. 1776–1809.

STARLING, JOSEPH. *London* (*Aldersgate St.*). Apprenticed 1786, C.C. 1795–99.

STARNILL, JAS. C.C. about 1660.

STARR, ROBT. C.C. 1667.

STARTRIDGE, ROGER. *Gravesend*. Clock, about 1750.

STATTER, RICHD. D. Wrote a pamphlet on the advantage of a decimal division of the hour; watch on this plan, G.M., is inscribed 'Richd. Dover Statter and Thos. Statter, Liverpool, No. 1', h.m., 1862.

STAUFFER, SAMUEL C. *Manheim, Lancaster, U.S.A.*, early nineteenth century. A good maker; many long-case clocks.

STAUFFER & EBY. *Manheim, U.S.A.* Partnership of Sam. Stauffer and Christian Eby.

STAUNTON. See STANTON.

STAYNE, THOMAS. C.C. 1654.

STEAD, JNO. *Fetter Lane.* C.C. 1730.

STEAD, JNO. Apprenticed to David Hubert; C.C. 1747.

STEAD, THOS. Apprenticed 1668 to Jno. Webb; C.C. 1678.

STEADMAN & VARDEN. *London.* Balloon clock, about 1780.

STEATH, THOS. Apprenticed 1683 to Jno. Wheeler, C.C.

STEBER, J. N. *Dover.* Watch, 1789.

STEDMAN, J. *Red Lion St.*, 1790.

STEDMAN, JAMES. *London.* 1690 C.C.

STEDMAN, RICHD. *Godalming*, 1780.

STEELE, F. *71 Oxford St.*, 1825–33.

STEELE, JAMES. *London (Clerkenwell).* C.C. 1801, died 1825.

STEELE, JAMES. *London (Clerkenwell Close).* Apprenticed 1793, C.C. 1801–40.

STEELE, WM. *Milecross.* Watch, 1819.

STEERS, BARNARD. *London.* C.C. 1769.

STEERS, JNO. *9 Pall Mall*, 1793.

STEERS, WILLIAM. *London.* C.C. 1769, died 1816.

STEGAR, JOHN. C.C. 1699.

STEIBEL (or STEBBELL), CHRISTOPHER. *Augsburg.* Striking clock with minute hand, also square clock with cupola by him, Vienna Treasury, 1635–60.

STEIL, JNO. *Edinburgh.* Watch, h.m., 1752.

STEIN, ABRAHAM. *Philadelphia*, 1797.

STEINER, JEAN. *Couvet.* Born 1726, died 1807; clocks and watches; maker of repute.

STEINER, JEAN LOUIS. *Convers* and *Chaux-de-Fonds*, 1777–96.

STEINER, JOHANN BAPTIST. *Würzburg.* Master 1772, died 1795.

STEINER, PHILIPP JACOB. *Augsburg.* Comp. about 1721, master 1745–70.

STEINMANN, DANIEL. *29 North Audley St.*, 1840–42.

STEM, RICHARD. *London.* Watch, 1760.

STENBUCH, HANS. *Copenhagen* and *Kronberg*, 1620–47. Court clock.

STENNETT, BENJAMIN FRANTHEM, son. *London.* C.C. 1808.

STENNETT, ROBT. *7 Bartlett St.*, *Bath*, 1790–1800.

STENNETT, WILLIAM, brother. *London.* C.C. 1821–40.

STENNETT, WILLIAM. *London.* Apprenticed 1773, C.C. 1784.

STENNETT, WILLIAM. *London.* 1808 C.C., died 1821.

STEINMÜLLER, JOHANN MELCHIOR. *Gera*, about 1725–75. Astronomical clock, Furt. Museum; travelling repeating clock, M.P.S., Dresden; watch.

STEINMÜLLER, LIENHART DER JÜNGERE. *Basle*, 1556–80.

STEINMÜLLER, LUDWIG. *Basle.* Master 1588–1620.

STEPHENS, EDWD. Apprenticed 1693 to Jonathan Jones.

STEPHENS, FRANCIS. C.C. 1632.

STEPHENS, JOHN. "Nephew and successor to the late Mr. Dudds, 6 Coleman St.', 1780.

STEPHENS, JOSEPH. *Whitechapel*, C.C. 1721; master 1752.

STEPHENS, JOSEPH. *32 Aldgate.* Master C.C. 1776.

STEPHENS, PHILIP. *Minories.* C.C. 1730.

STEPHENS, RICHARD. *London.* Apprenticed 1695, C.C. 1715; watch.

STEPHENS, SAMUEL, son of Jos. *London (Whitechapel).* C.C. 1752–1808.

STEPHENS, SAMUEL. *London.* Apprenticed 1761, C.C. 1774.

STEPHENS, THOMAS. *93 Strand*, 1823.

STEPHENS, THOS. Apprenticed 1693 to Jno. Marshall.

STEPHENS, WM. *Godalming*, 1740.

STEPHENSON, BENJAMIN. *5 Ludgate Hill*, 1774–77.

STEPHENSON, D. W. *27 Lombard St.*, 1820–30.

STEPHENSON, GEO. *London.* Watch, 1797.

STEPHENSON, HENRY. *Dorchester*, about 1790 C.C. Watch.

STEPHENSON, JNO. *Leeds*, 1830.

STEPHENSON, THOS. SAM. *Hoxton.* Livery C.C. 1810.

STEPHENSON, WILLIAM. *27 Lombard St.*, 1793. See STEVENSON & FARROW.

STEPNEY, HENRY. *London.* C.C. 1807.

STEPTO, WM. *St. Giles'.* Arabesque marquetry long-case clock, about 1705.

STERCK, WILLIAM. *Portugal St., Lincoln's Inn*, 1760–68; *16 Poland St.*, 1793.

STERK, WILLIAM. *Cockspur St.*, 1772–90.

STERLAND, JNO. *Nottingham*, 1770.

STERLING, JOSH. *London.* Watch, 1791.

STEUART, JAMES. *8 Green St., Leicester Sq.*, 1790.

STEVENS, DANIEL. C.C. 1661.

STEVENS, GEORGE. C.C. 1673.

STEVENS, GEORGE. *Hindon.* a. 1770–95; watch.

STEVENS, GILES. Apprenticed 1671 to Robt. Wilkins, C.C.

STEVENS, JOHN. *London.* Apprenticed 1648, C.C. 1655. Also STEEVENS.

STEVENS, JOHN. Apprenticed 1684 to Jno. Wynne; C.C. 1691; lantern clock, about 1710, signed 'John Stevens, Colchester'.

STEVENS, JOSEPH. *32 Aldgate Without.* Master C.C. 1752 and 1756; 1745–94.

STEVENS, NATHANIEL. C.C. 1712.

STEVENS, RALPH. Apprenticed 1687 to Richd. Warren.

STEVENS, RICHARD. C.C. 1715.

STEVENS, ROBERT. *Milton.* 1781–95 C.C.; clocks and watches.

STEVENS, SAMUEL. *Grub St.* C.C. 1680; threatened in 1682 with prosecution by C.C. for undue taking of apprentices.

STEVENS, SAMUEL. C.C. 1706; square-dial lantern clock, cherub corners, inscribed 'Sam Stevens, Londini, fecit', on circle; 1706–18.

STEVENS, SAMUEL. '20 Princes St., nere Spittlefields Church', card, about 1780; *26 Whitechapel*, 1790–93.

STEVENS, THOMAS. C.C. 1700.

STEVENS, W. *Cirencester*, 1795.

STEVENSON, —. *Penrith*, 1730.

STEVENSON, —. *Dublin.* Centre seconds clock-watch, about 1760.

STEVENSON, ADAM. Livery C.C. 1786.

STEVENSON, ADAM. *Dunfermline.* 1698–1752.

STEVENSON, CHARLES. *Congleton*, 1768. Died 1796; clocks and watches.

STEVENSON, JOHN. *Stafford*, 1770.

STEVENSON, WILLIAM. *London.* C.C. 1794.

STEVENSON & FARROW. *27 Lombard St.*, 1810–24.

STEVER & BRYANT. *Whigville, U.S.A.*, 1830.

STEWARD, HENRY. *York*, f., 1816. Died 1870.

STEWARD, JNO. *99 Wood St.*, 1793.

STEWART, JAMES. *London.* Eight-day striking bracket clock with mechanical figures in arch of dial, about 1760.

STEWART, JAMES. *Glasgow*, 1778–99.

STIEBEL, B. *5 Chandos St.*, 1823.

STIETZ, J. *Cassel*, 1747–72. Clock, Cassel Landes-Museum.

STIFF, WM. Apprenticed 1676 to Simon Chapman, C.C.

STILEMAN, JNO. C.C. 1640.

STILES, JOHN. C.C. 1704.

STILES, NATHANIEL. *Wood St.* C.C. 1725, master 1751; 1725–70.

STILES, RICHARD. Probably son of the above; master C.C. 1790; 1770–90.

STILL, FRANCIS. C.C. 1699.

STILLARD, GEORGE. *London.* Watch, 1815.

STILLAS, JOHN. *Philadelphia,* 1785–93.

STILLETTO, SAM. Apprenticed to Jno. Spurrier, 1686, C.C.

STILLMAN, WILLIAM. *Burlington, U.S.A.,* 1789–95.

STILWELL, THOMAS. *London.* Apprenticed 1755, C.C. 1762.

STIMNER, RICHD. *Roe Buck Court, Chiswell St.,* 1780.

STIMSON, —. *London.* Bracket clock, engraved plate, knife suspension, about 1710.

STIMSON, H. *Sleaford, Lincolnshire,* 1780.

STIRLING, JOHN. *38 Abchurch Lane,* 1788.

STIRLING, ROBERT. *Stirling,* 1820–60.

STIRRUP, THOMAS. Published *Horometer; or, Complete Dialist,* 1652.

STJÄRNSUNDS URFABRIK, 1711–67. Many long-case clocks, two in Nord. Museum, illuminated Sidenbladh.

STOCK, JABEZ. *Whitechapel.* Long black narrow-case clock, with Japanese decoration, about 1700.

STOCKAR, HENRY. *London.* Marquetry long-case clock, about 1700; another about 1725.

STOCKDON, MATHEW. *London.* C.C. 1717.

STOCKELL, HUGH. *Newcastle.* Watch, 1765, signed 'Hugh Stokell, Newcastle', 1765–1800.

STOCKLER, T. *Bolney.* Bracket clock, about 1730.

STOCKTON, FRANCIS. *Yarm,* 1820–27.

STOCKTON, PETER. *Liverpool,* 1734–61. Watch.

STOCKWELL, HY. *Bell's Buildings,* 1793.

STODDART, JAMES. *13 Red Lion St.,* 1825–42.

STODDART, ROBERT. *61 Red Lion St., Clerkenwell,* 1815–42.

STOGDEN (STOCKTEN), MATTHEW. Worked for Graham; invented improved repeating motion about 1712; admitted C.C. 1717; died in abject poverty, at an advanced age, in 1770.

STOKEL, JOHN. *New York,* 1820–43.

STOKES, HENRY. *Turnmill St., Clerkenwell.* Bequeathed his best clock to Robert Stokes, 1586.

STOKES, JNO. *Bewdley,* 1760.

STOKES, JOHN. *London,* about 1770–87. Watches, Ilbert and Denham collections.

STOKES, SAM. *London.* Long-case clock, about 1695.

STOLLEWERCK à *Paris.* Clock in ormolu case, Jones collection, V. & A., about 1740; two clocks, Wallace collection; a handsome regulator, signed 'Alexandre Fortier invenit, Stollewerck fecit à Paris', finely chased gilt mounts, about 1740; also a cartel clock, signed 'Stollewerck à Paris', about 1770; a clock by Stollewerck in ormolu case chased with masks and festoons and surmounted by a vase, fetched £69 at the Hamilton sale in 1882.

STONE, ANDREW. C.C. 1699.

STONE, CHAS. *Liverpool.* Watch, 1798.

STONE, DAVID. *Hull,* 1822.

STONE, FRANCIS. *Bristol,* 1790.

STONE, GEORGE. *London.* Apprenticed 1765, C.C. 1774.

STONE, J. *Aylesbury,* 1822–30.

STONE, JOHN, 'at the Dial in Aylesbury', 1760–75.

STONE, JOHN. *Reading.* About 1790 C.C.

STONE, RICHD. *Thame.* Watch, h.m., 1771.

STONE, ROGER. C.C. 1710.

STONE, SAMUEL. *8 London Rd.,* 1820.

STONE, THOMAS. *London.* 1689 C.C.–1712.

STONE, WILLIAM. C.C. 1700.

STONEHOUSE, JONATHAN. *Leeds,* 1798–1817. Clock.

STONEHOUSE, RICHARD. *Whitby,* 1715–65. 30-hour long-case clock.

STONEHOUSE, ROBT. & JNO. *Leeds,* 1829.

STONES, SIMON. *Sheffield.* Made a clock for Marston Church in 1654.

STONES, THOMAS. *Lothbury,* C.C. 1692, master 1730; small striking and alarum long-case clock, dial 6 in. square, about 1695; watch, 1735.

STOOKES, J. *London.* Watch, Dutch style, Schloss collection; another, about 1780.

STOOSS, GOTTFRIED. *Elbing,* 1804. Died 1823; town clock.

STOPFORTH, EDWD. Apprenticed 1691 to Hy. Merriman.

STOPPES, AYLMER. *London.* Long-case clock, about 1740; on another clock, oak long case, the inscription, 'Elias Aylʳ Stopes, London'.

STORE, JNO. *Chester.* Clock, about 1790.

STORER, ROBERT. *London (Berkeley Court).* Born 1746, C.C. 1781–1820.

STORER, ROBERT. *London (Berkeley Court).* C.C. 1782.

STORER, ROBERT. Born 1721; started business at 11 *Berkeley Court, Clerkenwell,* about 1743.

STORER, ROBERT and JAMES, his sons, at the same address, 1768; James retired; Robt. Storer & Son, 1788; Robert Storer, the elder partner, who was grandson of the first-named Robert, retired to Olney, Bucks, in 1820, and died in 1832, aged 86; Robert & Walter Storer, 1822. WALTER, who was great-grandson of the first-named Robert, retired about 1840, closing a business carried on at the same address for nearly a century, and died at Olney in 1865, aged 65.

STOREY, CHARLES. *Sidney Alley, Leicester Fields,* 1758–60; 1 *Poultry,* 1743.

STOREY, J. *176 Regent St.,* 1830.

STOREY, JAMES. C.C. 1703. See STORY, JAS.

STORIE, W. *8 Warwick St., Charing Cross.* Card, Hodgkin collection, about 1810.

STORR (& GIBBS, *London.* Watch, 1745).

STORR, BATTY. *York.* Born 1710, died 1793; watch.

STORR, JONATHAN. *York,* 1765–80.

STORR, MARMADUKE. *20 Lombard St.,* 1760–74.

STORR, WILLIAM. *Jermyn St.,* 1765; *44 St. James's St.,* 1779–94; hon. f. C.C. 1781.

STORRS, N. *Utica, New York,* early nineteenth century; long-case maple clock, M.M.A.

STORY, HY. *7 Charterhouse Lane,* 1820.

STORY, JAS. *London.* Long-case clock, scroll, marquetry case, about 1710.

STORY, SAMUEL. Clock, long red lacquer case.

STORY, WILLIAM. *Red Lion St., Clerkenwell,* 1760–72.

STOS, VELANTIN. *Ulm.* Born 1709, died 1785; travelling clock, Ulm Museum.

STOTHARD, BENJ. *South Cave, Yorks.,* 1822.

STOWELL, JOHN. *Medford, Mass.,* 1815–25; *Boston,* 1825–36.

STRACEY, JOHN. *34 Prince's St., Lothbury,* 1790.

STRACHAN, A. & J. *125 Long Acre,* 1830. See MCCABE, and also MURRAY.

STRACHAN, ANDREW, a Scotsman; to avoid prosecution for practising his art in the city of London he bound himself apprentice to Thomas Warden; the Chamberlain ordered the indenture to be cancelled, as Strachan was between thirty and forty years old, 1691; long-case clock, A. Strachan, Newcastle, about 1730.

STRACHAN, ARCHIBALD. *Newcastle.* Watch, about 1775; clock, Arch. Strachan, Tanfield, about 1790.

STRACHAN, CHARLES. *London.* C.C. 1815, livery C.C. 1819.

STRACHAN, JOHN. *Hull.* About 1790 C.C.–1822; bracket clock.

STRACHAN, THOMAS. *London (Threadneedle St.).* C.C. 1771.

STRAHAN, JNO. *London.* Long-case clock, about 1780.

STRAITON, ALEXANDER. A clever watchmaker; apprenticed to Reid & Auld, *St. Martin's Lane,* 1820; *146 Leadenhall St.,* 1825; *15 Little Knightrider St.,* 1842; died 1873, aged 83.

STRAITON, ARCHIBALD (or STRATON). *Edinburgh,* about 1780.

STRAND, PETTER. *Stockholm,* 1791–1815. Musical clock Nord. Museum, illuminated Sidenbladh.

STRANGE, THOS. *Kingston.* Watch, 1799.

STRANGFELLOW, THOMAS. *London.* Apprenticed 1681, C.C. 1691.

STRATFORD, GEORGE. C.C. 1704.

STRATFORD, JAS. *London.* Enamelled watch, about 1790.

STRATTON, JOSEPH. *Church St., Hackney,* 1810–35.

STRATTON, JNO. *133 Bunhill Row,* 1816–25.

STRATTON, RICHARD. C.C. 1720.

STRAUGHAM, JOHN. *London.* 1687 C.C.

STREBELL, CHRISTOPHER. Watch, Vienna Treasury, oval case, of brass gilt, about 1625.

STRECH, PETER. *Philadelphia,* 1750–80.

STREELIN (STREETIN), RICHARD. *London (Cursitor St. and Holborn).* Apprenticed 1738, C.C. 1745–76; watch.

STREET. Long-case month clock by 'John Street Londres', which he presented about 1685 to his friend Abraham Martin, an engraver; Martin was made free of the C.C. in 1682.

STREET, GEO. Apprenticed to Roger Nicholls 1687, C.C.

STREET, RICHARD. *Shoe Lane.* C.C. 1687, warden 1715; maker of a clock costing £50, which was presented by Sir Isaac Newton to Dr. Bentley, Master of Trinity College, Cambridge, in 1708; long clock, 12-in. dial, walnut case, Wetherfield collection, about 1710; clock by him had the hour band shaped like a heart, the tip of the hand being caused to move in a corresponding path; watch, 1784, signed, 'Richard Street, Kepples, Surrey'.

STRELLER, JACOB. *Nuremberg.* Clock, Green Vaulted Chambers, Dresden, about 1700.

STRELLY, FRANCIS. C.C. 1665.

STRENGBERG, PETER. *Stockholm,* 1807–25. Four bracket clocks, two watch movements, Nord. Museum.

STRETCH, BENJ. *Bristol.* Quarter repeating watch, about 1750.

STRETCH, JAS. *Birmingham.* Watch, V. & A., about 1740.

STRETCH, SAM. *Birmingham.* Watch, h.m., 1712.

STRETCH, SAMUEL. *Bristol.* Born 1657, died 1743; 'eminent watchmaker'; watches, Ilbert and Denham collections.

STRETCH, SAMUEL. *Philadelphia,* 1717. Freeman of town; watch.

STRETCH, SAMUEL. *High St., Birmingham,* 1770. A family of Philadelphia clockmakers. Peter emigrated from the Midlands 1702, aged 32. Thomas his son, and William succeeded.

STRETCHE, SAMUEL. *Leke (Leek).* Lantern clock, about 1670.

STRETTON, SARAH. C.C. 1710.

STRIBLING, BENJAMIN. *Stowmarket.* Lantern clocks, about 1700.

STRIGEL, GEORGE PHILIP. *Stafford Row near Buckingham Gate,* 1760–88. Hon. f. C.C. 1781.

STRIGEL, JNO. C. 1790.

STRIGEL, WILLIAM F. *St. James's St.,* 1760–75.

STRIGELL, JOHAN. *Christopher Kreilsheim.* Handless watch, silver pair cases, Schloss collection, about 1700.

STRIGNER, ——. In the British Museum is a watch by him in an outer case of carnelian. It was made for James II, and by him given to his daughter Catherine, Countess of Anglesey and Duchess of Buckingham, about 1687.

STRINGER, JOSIAH. *Stockport,* 1742–50.

STRINGFELLOW, JNO. *London.* C.C. 1691; lantern clock, about 1698.

STRIPLING, THOS. *Barwell,* about 1700.

STRIPLING, THOS. *Litchfield.* Watch, 1816.

STRIPLING & GILBERT. *Lichfield.* From 1775. Firm of Hannah, widow of Thos., and Thos. Gilbert, nephew; clocks signed Thos. Stripling up to 1817 probably by this firm.

STRIXNER, ——. *London.* Watch, about 1745.

STRONG, T. *London.* Watch, 1823.

STRONGFELLOW. See STRINGFELLOW.

STROPP, GOTTLOB WILHELM. *Berlin,* 1785–1804.

STROUD, BENJAMIN. *Ware.* 1784 C.C.; watch.

STROUD, ROBT. *London.* Watch, 1822.

STRUGGLE, CHRISTOPHER. Apprenticed 1671 to Isaac Puzzy, C.C.

STRUTT, J. D. *London.* Watch, 1790.

STUART, BERNARD (Scotsman). Born 1706, died 1755; clock, Imperial collection, Vienna, 1735.

STUART, GEORGE. *Newcastle-on-Tyne,* 1790–1820.

STUBB, THOS. *London.* Long-case clock, about 1690.

STUBBS, GABRIEL. C.C. 1675; 'a small clockmaker' (watchmaker) and a celebrated member of the Company; 1675–77.

STUBBS, J. *Prince's St., Leicester Sq.,* 1830; *28 Panton St., Haymarket,* 1830. Gold chronometer half-quarter repeater; gold dial, raised numerals, 1819.

STUBBS, JOHN. *London (Gt. Arthur St.).* Apprenticed 1747, C.C. 1758, died 1794.

STUBBS, JOSEPH. *241 Holborn,* 1793.

STUBBS, NATHANIEL, son of Jno., 'clock-maker, of St. Andrew, Holborne', bound to Job Worail, citizen and cutler, 1719.

STUBBS, THOS. C.C. 1685.

STUBBS & CO. *London.* On watch movement, about 1760; on dial, Leyden, London.

STUDLEY, DAVID. *Hanover, U.S.A.,* 1806–35.

STUK, WILLIAM. *Cockspur St.,* 1781.

STUMBELS, B. *London.* Watch, about 1760.

STUMBELS (STUMBLES), WILLIAM. *Totnes,* 1754. Watch, Glasgow Art Galleries and Ilbert collection; long-case chiming clock.

STYLE, JOHN, son of Nathaniel. *London.* C.C. 1772–99.

STYLE, NATHANIEL. *Wood St.* C.C. 1725; master 1751; livery 1766; long-case clock, about 1750, signed 'Nathaniel Styles, London'.

STYLE, RICHARD. *3 Carey Lane, Foster Lane.* Livery C.C. 1766; master 1790; 1764–96.

SUDBURY, JOHN. C.C. 1686.

SUDELL, JNO. Apprenticed 1683 to Ben. Bell, C.C.

SUDLOW, BENJ. *Yarmouth.* Watch, about 1780; monogram, 'J.D.C.', on balance-cock.

SUGGATE, GEO. *Halesworth.* Lantern and 30-hour long-case clocks, about 1700; watch, same name and address, 1781.

SULLY, HENRY. Born in 1680, apprenticed to Charles Gretton, C.C. 1704; an eminent man who settled in France; died 1728.

SULMAN. See HOPGOOD.

SUMER, JNO. C.C. 1634.

SUMERALL, THOS. *Dublin,* 1683.

SUMMER, FRANCIS. *26 Greek St., Soho,* 1790–94.

SUMMER, WILLIAM. C.C. 1662.

SUMMERHAYES, ROBERT. *Ilminster*. Afterwards at *Taunton*; died 1857.

SUMMERS, CHAS. *London*. Watch, Schloss collection, case beautifully enamelled, about 1785.

SUMMERS, J. R. *Bedale*. Died 1823.

SUNDBERG, ERIK. *Stockholm*, 1743–65. Court clock; six watches, one Nord Museum; two bracket and wall.

SUNDWALL, PEHR. *Norrköping*, 1810–40.

SUPPLE, JOHN. *Vigo Lane, Piccadilly*, 1783.

SURMOICE, JOHN. *London*. 1640 C.C.

SURRIDGE, JAMES. *London*. C.C. 1786.

SUTHERLAND, D. *Leith*. Clock with moving figures representing Adam and Eve in the Garden of Eden, apparently about 1775.

SUTHERLAND, GEORGE. *Elgin*, 1803–37.

SUTHERLAND, THOS. *2 Vigo Lane*, 1793.

SUTOR, WM. *Edinburgh*, 1712.

SUTTER, EMILE. *Geneva*, 1760–1800. Engraved watch.

SUTTON, ISAAC. C.C. 1662; to him in 1664 was apprenticed Joseph Aberley.

SUTTON, JAMES. *London*. Apprenticed 1795, C.C. 1828.

SUTTON, JNO. Apprenticed 1661 to Ed. Norris, C.C.

SUTTON, JOHN. *London*, 1751. C.C. 1760.

SUTTON, ROBERT. *Whitehaven*, 1840.

SUTTON, ROBERT. *Stafford*, a. 1774–95. Watch.

SUTTON, THOMAS. *London*. Apprenticed 1698, C.C. 1705.

SUTTON, THOMAS. *Liverpool*, 1811–29.

SUTTON, THOS. *Maidstone*, 1760.

SUTTON, WM. *Liverpool*, 1770.

SUTTON, WM., & Co. *85 Cheapside*, 1790–93. Card, Ponsonby collection, 'successors to Mr. Stamp'.

SVANBERG, PETER. *Linköping*, 1792–1821.

SWAIN, ——. *London*. Watch, 1832; *Leeds*, 1820.

SWALE, JAQUES (alien). Threatened with prosecution for working as clockmaker in liberties of C.C. 1668.

SWAN, BENJAMIN. *Haverhill, Mass.*, 1810–40.

SWAN, EDWD. Apprenticed 1650 to Ralph Ash, C.C.

SWAN, ROBT. *Bridlington*, 1770.

SWAN, WM. Apprenticed 1692 to Thos. Tompion; C.C. 1703.

SWANNELL & Co. *Staples Inn, Holborn*, 1790–94.

SWANNICK, G. *38 Banner St.*, 1820.

SWANSON, ROBERT. C.C. 1730.

SWEARER & SONS. Wooden clockmakers, *7 Upper East Smithfield*, 1820.

SWEEBY, JOHN. C.C. 1671; fine long inlaid-case clock, about 1700.

SWEMAN, ——. *London*. Watch, probably Dutch, about 1730.

SWEMAN, WILLIAM. *5 Banner St.*, 1790.

SWETMAN, THOS. *London*, 1735–65; watch marked 'Swettman, London', h.m., 1738; another engraved 'Swetman, London', *repoussé* case with enamelled centre, Schloss collection, about 1760.

SWIFT, M. *68 Red Lion St., Clerkenwell*, 1793.

SWINBURN, JNO. *Bishop Auckland*, 1775; *Sunderland*, 1785.

SWINDELLS, JNO. *Macclesfield*, 1792–1825.

SWINDEN, FRANCIS CHARLES. Born in *Brentford*, settled in *Birmingham*; at *Bath St.*, 1824; *91 New St.*, 1825; afterwards at *Temple St.*

SWINGLER, JAS. *Holbeach*. Watch, 1802.

SWINNEY, HENRY. *London*. Apprenticed 1761, C.C. 1773.

SWINTON, GEORGE. Water clock, 1661.

SYDENHAM, H. & J. *126 New Bond St.*, 1800–04.

SYDENHAM, J. *126 Bond St.*, 1816–23.

SYBERBERG, CHRISTOPHER. *Charleston, U.S.A.*, 1768. Clocks and watches.

SYDERMAN, PHILIP. *Philadelphia*, 1785.

SYKES, GEO. *Malton*, 1823.

SYKES, W. *Holbeck*, 1790.

SYLVANDER, JACOB. *Åbo*, 1778–1805. Wall clocks and watches.

SYLVANDER, MICH. *Uppsala*, 1790. Died 1820.

SYLVESTER, JOHN. C.C. 1693.

SYMES, ROBT. *London*. Long-case clock, about 1800.

SYMMS, ISAAC. *Aldgate*, about 1600. Watch, Pierpont Morgan collection, signed 'Isaac Symmes at Aldgette', about 1620.

SYMONDS, JOSEPH, & Co. *Liverpool*, 1780.

SYMONDS, RICHD. Apprenticed 1668 to Fras. Strelly; C.C. 1691.

SYMONDS, THOMAS. *57 Cheapside*, 1770–75; *20 Fleet St.*, 1755–88.

SYMONS, MOSES. *Hull*, 1822.

SYMONS, THOMAS. *London*. Apprenticed 1655, C.C. 1661; lantern clock.

TABER, THOS. *29 Compton St., Clerkenwell*, 1825.

TACKLEY, C. *London*. Watch, 1826.

TAF, JOHN JAMES. *Philadelphia*, 1794.

TAILOUR, EDWARD. Clockmaker, admitted to Blacksmith's Company, 1629.

TAIT, WILLIAM. *Wigtown*, 1820–37.

TALBOT, THOMAS. Lantern clock, about 1675.

TALBOYS, JACOB. *London*. Apprenticed 1756, C.C. 1763.

TALLANS, GABRIEL. About 1720.

TALLIS, AARON. C.C. 1722.

TALLON, ——. *Paris*. Watch, 1720.

TANNER, ——. Clock engraver and varnisher, *Fleet Market*, 1790–94.

TANNER, JOSEPH. C.C. 1682.

TANQUERAY, JAMES. *London*, 1770–80.

TANSLEY, THOS. *Birmingham*, 1818–36.

TANTUM. Bracket clock, about 1700, inscribed 'Dan. Tantum, in Derby, fecit'.

TAPP, FRANCIS. *85 Strand*, 1775–85.

TAPP, GEO. Apprenticed 1691 to Sam. Bowtell, C.C.

TAPPAN, WILLIAM B. *Philadelphia*, 1819. Clock.

TAPPY, ABRAHAM. Watch, 1778, 'Abe Tappy, Totveeren'; bracket timepiece, small movement in large mahogany case, about 1790.

TAQUET, ——. Watch, 1790.

TARBUCK, JOHN. *St. Mary's Gate, Manchester*. Died 1739.

TARBUCK, ROBT. Apprenticed 1686 to Thos. Stubbs, C.C.

TARLES, JNO. C.C. 1690.

TARLETON, JERE. Apprenticed 1690 to Walter Henshaw, C.C.

TARLETON, RICHD. *Liverpool*, 1760.

TARLETON, WM. *Liverpool*, 1770–95. He made good watches and did much to advance the reputation of Liverpool as a manufacturing centre.

TARMAN, J. B. *34 Regent St., Piccadilly*, 1825.

TARRANT, WILLIAM. *London*. Apprenticed 1813, C.C. 1821.

TARRY, WILLIAM. *Saffron Walden*. Master 1702; died 1729; maker of repute.

TARTS, J. *London*. Watches for the Dutch market, 1755–90.

TASKER, ——. *Folkingham*. Long-case clock, about 1780.

TASMA, DOUWE JELLES. *Grouw* and *Gorredijk*. Born 1753, died 1845; bracket clock.

TASSEL, PIERRE. *Rouen*. Juré 1696.

TATE, RUTH. *East Sheen*. Oak long-case clock, about 1790.

TATE, THOS. *Winterton*. Succeeded Wm. Godfrey; died 1821.

TATE, THOS. *Fenkle Street, Alnwick*, 1820.

TATUM, JNO. *53 Dorset St., Salisbury Sq.*, 1817.

TAVAN, ANTOINE. Born at *Aost, France*, 1742, died at *Geneva*, 1836. An excellent watchmaker who wrote an analysis of various escapements and made models of them; now at *Geneva*.

TAVERNIER, ETIENNE, second son of J.P. An eminent watchmaker, born 1756, died 1839; in 1772 he, from the *Rue de Bussy*, advertised watches in rings, bracelets, tops of canes, and other small articles; his keys were particularly admired; he constructed one to show the days of the week, the days of the month, the age and phases of the moon; adjusting the key to wind the watch actuated the mechanism concealed in the middle part of the key; this was a device for which a patent had been obtained in England by George Sanderson in 1762.

TAVERNIER, JEAN PIERRE. *Paris*. Died 1793.

TAVERNIER, LOUIS. Eldest son of J. P. Born 1754, died 1840.

TAWNY, JAMES. *London*. Apprenticed 1751, C.C. 1759.

TAWNY, PEPE. Watch, about 1700.

TAYLOR. A well-known name among London watchmakers from 1640 till past the middle of the nineteenth century; the two Thomas Taylors, who were active members of the C.C. during the seventeenth century, are distinguished as 'of Holborn' and 'of the Strand'; in 1676 Thomas Taylor, of Essex House Gate, is mentioned.

TAYLOR, ABRAHAM. C.C. 1668.

TAYLOR, BENJ. *Ball Alley, Cornhill*, 1793; *45 Lombard St.*, 1798–1800.

TAYLOR, CHARLES. C.C. 1723.

TAYLOR, EDWARD. Livery C.C. 1810; in the British Museum is a curious watch of his, with symbolical figures and texts of Scripture in the enamel on the dial and case, 1800–30.

TAYLOR, EDWARD. *25 Leadenhall St.*, 1822–25.

TAYLOR, EDWD. Apprenticed 1637 to Wm. Almond, C.C.

TAYLOR, ELLIOTT. *London (Holborn Hill)*. C.C. 1795, livery C.C. 1800–40.

TAYLOR, G. R. *Sunderland*, 1820.

TAYLOR, GEO. Apprenticed 1648 to Ben. Hill, C.C.

TAYLOR, GEO. *Liverpool*, about 1720.

TAYLOR, GEORGE. *London*. C.C. 1699.

TAYLOR, GEORGE. C.C. 1703; to him and his wife Lucy, Rebecca Fisher was apprenticed in 1715.

TAYLOR, HENRY. *London*. Watch, 1760.

TAYLOR, HENRY CLEAVER. *London*. Apprenticed 1737 C.C. 1746.

TAYLOR, J. & S. *Liverpool*, 1818.

TAYLOR, JAMES. *Ashton-under-Lyne*. In 1754 he took out a patent for spinning; in 1769 one for raising weights; died 1813, aged 89.

TAYLOR, JAMES. *London*. C.C. 1802, livery C.C. 1811, died 1821; watch.

TAYLOR, JASPER. In *Gray's Inn*. Apprenticed 1685 to Thos. Taylor; C.C. 1694; pair-case copper verge watch, outside case of leather, with many small rivets, lock-spring projecting through the dial, inscription, 'Jasper Taylor, in Holbourn'.

TAYLOR, JASPER, of *Barnard's Inn*. Admitted C.C. 1729; took an active part in the affairs of the Company; was master in 1754, and clerk from 1760 to 1770 when he died, leaving £10 to C.C. for the poor.

TAYLOR, JNO. *Petworth*. Watch, 1762.

TAYLOR, JNO. *Lancaster*, 1772, f.

TAYLOR, JOHN. C.C. 1687; two clocks by him seen at Moscow; one in large mahogany case, silvered dial, verge escapement, chimed on eight bells and played a tune.

TAYLOR, JOHN. C.C. 1702.

TAYLOR, JOHN. *Manchester*, 1750–81. Clock.

TAYLOR, JOHN. *Bath*, 1770.

TAYLOR, JOHN S. *8 Wilderness Row*, 1809–40.

TAYLOR, JON. *Ormskirk*. Long-case clock, about 1690.

TAYLOR, JOSEPH. *2 Bouverie St.*, 1825.

TAYLOR, KENNARD & CO. *3 Crescent, Jewin St.*, 1822–30.

TAYLOR, LUTHER. *Philadelphia*, 1823–25.

TAYLOR, RICHARD. C.C. 1655.

TAYLOR, RICHARD. C.C. 1724.

TAYLOR, ROB. Apprenticed 1693 to Jas. Hatchman, C.C.

TAYLOR, SAMUEL. *Maiden Lane, Wood St.*, 1774. Livery Goldsmiths' Company; afterwards at *10 Ball Alley, Lombard St.*; master C.C. 1807; 1774–1810.

TAYLOR, SAMUEL. *Philadelphia*, 1799.

TAYLOR, SAMUEL. *London*. Watch, about 1800.

TAYLOR, THOMAS. *Strand*. Apprenticed 1638 to Simon Hackett; C.C. 1646, master 1668; watch, Pierpont Morgan collection, signed 'Thos. Taylor, Londini', balance-cock pinned on, not later than 1650.

TAYLOR, THOMAS. *Holborn*, at the end of *Fetter Lane*. apprenticed 1678 to Thos. Taylor, Holborn; C.C, 1685, master 1710; fine pair-case *repousseé* repeating watch, gold dial. "Lost between Pickadilly and St. James Street, a gold watch made fast in a gold studded case, with high pins at each hour; made by Mr. Taylor, at the Upper End of Fetter Lane, in Holborn. Whoever brings it to Mr. Harrison, Goldsmith, etc., the Three Flower-de-Luces, in the Strand, shall have a guinea reward" (*Lond. Gaz.*, 9–12, 1692).

TAYLOR, THOS. Lantern clock. See TAYLOR.

TAYLOR, THOS. *Holborn*. C.C. about 1660.

TAYLOR, WILLIAM. Apprenticed to John Wright and turned over to Isaac Webb; C.C. 1682.

TAYLOR, WILLIAM. *Bridgnorth*, 1743. Died 1781; clocks and watches.

TAYLOR, WILLIAM. *London*. Apprenticed 1743, C.C. 1753.

TAYLOR, WM. *Whitehaven*, 1775.

TAYLOR, WM. *Dumfries*, 1817.

TAYLOR & SON. *Bristol*. Watch, 1797.

TEAMS, JOHN. *25 Red Cross Sq.*, 1790–94.

TEARE, JOHN. *Dublin*, 1699.

TEARSON, STEPHEN. *Ipswich*. Watch, about 1700.

TEBBATT, BENONI (or BENOMI). *Little Old Bailey*. Apprenticed to Robt. Doore 1676; C.C. 1683. C.C. in 1688 seized at his shop a gold watch-case, both for that it was of coarse and unwarrantable gold, and also so extremely thin that it was insufficient in strength. William Brafield who made the case, admitted his fault, and was fined 5s., the case being broken up.

TELFORD, JOHN. *Wigton*, 1820.

TELFORTH, ISAAC. *London*. Watch, 1765.

TEMPEST, HY. Apprenticed 1638 to Robt. Grinkin, C.C.

TEMPLE, J. *London*. Watch, 1780; another, 1800.

TEMPLE, THOMAS. C.C. 1720.

TEMPLER, CHARLES. C.C. 1673.

TENANT, LEONARD. Paid £37 for a new clock and chimes for St. Margaret's Church, Westminster, 1617.

TENNANT, THOMAS. C.C. 1668.

TEROLD, HENRY. *Ipswich*. Round silver watch-case with interlacing bands, silver dial, Fellows collection, about 1640.

TERREY, JAS. *London.* Long-case clock, about 1770.

TERRIER, D. *Paris.* Clock-watch, Pierpont Morgan collection; numerals on porcelain enamel plaques; single brass case covered with leather *piqué*, 1700.

TERRIER, JAMES. C.C. 1694.

TERRIER, MARY. C.C. 1713.

TERRIER, THOMAS. C.C. 1694.

TERROT, PH., & FAZY. *Geneva.* Watch, 1770; watch, 'Ph. Terrot, Geneva', 1780.

TERROT, PHILIPPE. *Geneva*, 1740–50. Watch in silver case, shaped like a cockle shell, G.M.

TERROT & THUILLIER. *Geneva*, 1760–76.

TERROUS L'AÎNÉ. *Geneva*, 1770–85.

TERRY, —. *Thoralby*, 1730.

TERRY, —. *Richmond, Yorks.*, 1820–50.

TERRY, ELI. *Plymouth, Litchfield County, Connecticut, U.S.A.* Said to be the Sam Slick of Haliburton; patented an equation clock in 1797, and in 1816 patented the well-known type of cheap American shelf or mantel clock which became popular all over the world; he died in 1853.

TERRY, ELI, son of Eli. *Plymouth Hollow* (now *Thomaston*), *U.S.A.* Born 1799, died 1841.

TERRY, ELI & SAMUEL. *U.S.A.*, early nineteenth century. Shelf clock, M.M.A.

TERRY, GARNET. *54 Paternoster Row*, 1785–93; clock-watch, silver embossed case, Schloss collection, probably by him, though apparently of rather an earlier date.

TERRY, HENRY, brother. *Plymouth, U.S.A.* Born about 1802, died 1877; retired from clockmaking about 1830.

TERRY, HY. Apprenticed 1688 to Richd. Farmer, C.C.

TERRY, ISAAC. *Richmond (Yorks)*, 1820–50.

TERRY, JNO. *York*, f., 1759. Watch, 1770.

TERRY, JOHN. *York*, 1705. Died 1757; watch; in 1706 made clock for cupola in Thursday Market. See TIRRY.

TERRY, JOHN. *York*, f., 1713. Died 1783; in 1716 he made a turret clock for York Castle.

TERRY, LEONARD. *York*, f., 1822.

TERRY, SAMUEL, brother of Eli (1). *Bristol, U.S.A.*, 1825–35. Wooden clocks and looking-glass clocks.

TERRY, SILAS BURNHAM, brother of Eli (2). *Thomaston, U.S.A.* Born about 1801, died 1876; made clocks with torsion pendulums.

TERRY, THOMAS & HOADLEY. *Greystone, U.S.A.*, 1809. Firm which started making wooden clocks, but lasted only one year, becoming Thomas & Hoadley.

TERRY, THOMAS. *Boston, U.S.A.*, 1810–25. Watch.

TERRY, WILLIAM. *Masham (Yorks.)*, 1822–40.

TERRY, WM. *Bedale.* Long-case clock, about 1770.

TERRY, WM. *Richmond, Yorks*, 1822.

TERWEER, HY. Watch, Dutch style, about 1750.

TESSEYMAN, GEO. *Northallerton*, 1822–40.

TETLEY, JAMES. *London.* Apprenticed 1784, C.C. 1794.

TEULINGS, C. *15 Charing Cross*, 1793.

TEW, THOS. Apprentice. C.C. 1674.

THACKE, PHILIP. C.C. 1685; marquetry long-case clock, square dial, about 1770.

THACKE, ROBT. Apprenticed 1681 to Jno. Benson, C.C.

THATCHE, ROBERT. *London.* Apprenticed 1684, C.C. 1689–1706.

THATCHER, GEO. *Cranbrook.* Watch, about 1760.

THEAD & PICKETT. *Ludgate Hill*, 1758–65. See PICKETT & RUNDELL.

THEODRICKE, HY. Apprenticed to Jno. Curtis 1679, C.C.

THERASBY (or THORESBY), PETER. *York*, f., 1666.

THÉVENOT, ACHILLE RENÉ. *Paris.* Master 1756–73.

THIBAUT, PIERRE BARTHÉLEMY. *Paris.* Master 1758–89.

THIERRY, —. CAEN. Watch, 1790.

THIERRY, JEAN B. *Paris*, 1774–1812.

THILLIER, I. P. *London.* Watch, 1745.

THIOUIST, NICOLAS. *L.* Calendar clock, about 1730.

THIOUT, ANTOINE L'AÎNÉ. Born 1692, died 1767; *Quai Lepelletier, Paris.* Inventor of many ingenious forms of repeating work, curious clocks, etc., described in his *Traité d'Horlogerie*, Paris, 1741; clockmaker to the Duke of Orleans, 1752; garde-visiteur in 1769.

THIOUT LE JEUNE. *Paris.* Bracket clock, about 1780.

THIRKELD (THRELKELD), DEODATUS. *Newcastle-on-Tyne*, 1657. Master 1699–1732; challenged in 1698 by Wm. Provost, a French clockmaker, that the maker of the best clock should have both, Ed. Burgis and Sam. Watson to decide. Thirkeld won. Watch.

THOMAQUE, ABRAHAM. C.C. 1675.

THOMAQUE, ISAAC. Silver repeating watch, about 1729.

THOMAS, DAN. Apprenticed to Jno. Browne 1675; C.C. 1682.

THOMAS, DANIEL, son. *Blois.* Comp. 1618; *Orléans*, 1628–48.

THOMAS, F. L., & J. W. *153 New Bond St.*, 1821–30.

THOMAS, FRANCIS. *Dublin.* Watch, 1750.

THOMAS, HUGH. Apprenticed 1686 to Richd. Ellis, C.C.

THOMAS, JEAN. *Blois.* Master 1602, died a. 1617.

THOMAS, JNO. *Crewkerne*, 1780.

THOMAS, JNO. *153 New Bond St.*, 1810.

THOMAS, JOHN. *Worcester.* 1790–96 C.C.; watch movement, Worcester Museum.

THOMAS, M., & SONS. *Caernarvon.* Long-case clock, about 1780.

THOMAS, MORRIS. *Caernarvon*, 1769–94. Long-case clocks.

THOMAS, PHILIPPES. *Paris (Rue des Vieux Augustins).* Master 1779–1825; clock.

THOMAS, RICHARD. *98 Strand*, 1793–1804; *17 Bridgewater Sq.*, 1817.

THOMAS, RICHARD. *Helston.* About 1790 C.C.

THOMAS, ROBERT. *Caernarvon*, 1788. Died 1827; long-case clocks.

THOMAS, SAM. *Nantwich*, 1790.

THOMAS, SAMUEL. *Keynsham*, 1785.

THOMAS, SETH. *Plymouth, Conn.* He learnt clockmaking of Eli Terry, whose business he (in conjunction with Silas Hoadley, another of Terry's workmen) acquired in 1810; died 1859.

THOMAS, THOMAS. *314 Borough*, 1825.

THOMAS, THOMAS JOHN. *55 St. James's St.* Verge watch movement, G.M.; another example, watch with cylinder escapement, 1790–1804.

THOMAS, WILLIAM. *London.* Apprenticed 1762, C.C. 1772; bracket clock.

THOMAS & EVANS. *Staining Lane*, 1793.

THOMAS & SON. *3 Strand*, 1825–30.

THOMASEN, TS. *Amsterdam.* Fine long-case clock, about 1760.

THOMEGAY, MARK. *Moorfields*, 1760–68.

THOMEGUEX, JAQUES. *Geneva*, about 1755–70.

THOMLINSON, GEO. Apprenticed 1669 to Thos. Bayley; C.C. 1678; lantern clock, about 1680, inscribed 'Geo. Thomlinson, in George Yard, in Lumbard Street, fecit'.

THOMPSON, ANN, & SON. *Red Lion St., Clerkenwell*, 1790–94.

THOMPSON, C. *London*, about 1760; pair-cased watch, outer case enamelled blue.

THOMPSON, GEO. Apprenticed 1676 to L. Sindrey, C.C.

THOMPSON, HENRY. *London (St. Martin's-le-Grand).* C.C. 1748–59.

THOMPSON, HY. *Bartholomew Close.* C.C. 1730.

THOMPSON, ISAAC. C.C. 1699.

THOMPSON, ISAAC. *London.* 1689 C.C.

THOMPSON, JAMES. *Bride Lane, Fleet St.,* 1790–94.

THOMPSON, JAMES. *Darlington,* 1786. Died 1825. Watch.

THOMPSON, JEREMIAH. *London.* C.C. 1770–83.

THOMPSON, JNO. *York,* f., 1692.

THOMPSON, JOHN. C.C. 1662.

THOMPSON, JOHN. C.C. 1720; large silver watch, 1759, inscribed 'J. Thompson, London', in an outer case of fine English chasing, Pierpont Morgan collection.

THOMPSON, JOHN. *10 Red Lion St., Clerkenwell,* 1765–94.

THOMPSON, JOHN. *Liverpool,* 1734–73. Watch.

THOMPSON, JOS. *London.* Balloon timepiece, Sheraton style, about 1790.

THOMPSON, JOSEPH. *Atherstone.* Clock, about 1800.

THOMPSON, ROBERT. C.C. 1681.

THOMPSON, ROWLAND. Apprenticed 1674 to Kath. Bestwick, widow.

THOMPSON, SAMUEL. *London (Aldgate).* C.C. 1789.

THOMPSON, TROUGHTON. C.C. 1731.

THOMPSON, THOS. *Lancaster,* 1747, f.

THOMPSON, W. *Skinner St., Clerkenwell,* 1790.

THOMPSON, WILLIAM. Apprenticed to Thos. Tompion; C.C. 1703; watch, 1725; watch, 'William Thompson, Chester', date mark, 1703.

THOMPSON, WILLIAM. *London.* Apprenticed 1698, C.C. 1708.

THOMPSON, WILLIAM. *Chester,* 1743–about 1767. Watch, G.M.

THOMPSON, WILLIAM. *Annapolis, U.S.A.,* 1762. Clocks and Watches.

THOMPSON, WILLIAM. *New York,* 1775. Clocks and watches; 'lately arrived from Britain'. See WM., *Baltimore,* below.

THOMPSON, WILLIAM. *Wolverhampton,* 1780–1805. Clocks and watches.

THOMPSON, WILLIAM. *Baltimore, U.S.A.,* 1799–1807. Watches and clocks. See WM., *New York,* above.

THOMSON, ARCHIBALD. *Edinburgh,* 1794–1836. Watch.

THOMSON, GEORGE. *Kilmarnock,* 1820–37.

THOMSON, JAMES. *Pittsburg, U.S.A.,* 1815.

THOMSON, JOHN. *Perth,* 1706–37.

THOMSON, JOHN. *Edinburgh,* 1794–1814.

THOMSON, PHILIP, & SON. *11 Exeter Court, Strand,* 1769.

THOMSON, ROBERT. *Bo'ness,* 1760–88.

THORELET, DAVID. *London,* 1626; *Rouen,* 1630–1661. Called himself "Premier orloger reçu par chef d'oeuvre à Rouen". Published description of the clock of the Hôtel des Consuls made by him in 1657.

THORELET, JONAS. *London.* Watch in plain silver case, dial with gold centre and large figures on white enamel ring, about 1720. Pierpont Morgan collection; long-case clock, about 1746.

THORN, THOMAS. *23 Wood St., Cheapside,* 1758–75.

THORNDIKE, SAM. *Ipswich,* 1760–94.

THORNE, JOHN. *56 Whitechapel,* 1790–1818. John, & Son, *56 Whitechapel,* 1820.

THORNE, ROBERT. *12 Wood St., Cheapside,* 1760–68. Repeating watch in gold *repoussé* case, with outer case of shagreen *piqué,* Pierpont Morgan collection.

THORNE, SIM. *Tiverton,* 1740.

THORNE, SIMON. *London.* Fine bracket clock, pull repeater on eight bells, about 1750.

THORNE, WM. *London.* Clock, about 1800.

THORNHAM, GEO. *Hull,* 1822.

THORNHILL, BRYAN. Apprenticed 1683 to Thos. Bradford.

THORNTON, ANDREW. *Philadelphia,* 1811.

THORNTON, HENRY. C.C. 1699; long-case clock, playing six tunes, seen in Moscow; Mr. E. Alfred Jones mentions two large chiming clocks bearing his name, one in the Winter Palace at St. Petersburg, and the other in the Troitsa Monastery near Moscow. The collection of the Czar of Russia contained two watches by him; one, a repeater, has cases of gold, the inner bears the hall-mark for 1729–30, and the outer *repoussé* decoration representing St. Christophorus carrying the infant Jesus; it is suspended from a chatelaine. The other watch, also in gold cases and furnished with a chatelaine.

THORNTON, JAS. *London.* Watch, British Museum, h.m., 1771.

THORNTON, JOHN. C.C. 1731.

THORNTON, SAMUEL. *London.* Livery C.C. 1812.

THORNTON, THOS. *London.* Watch, 1796.

THORNTON, WILLIAM. *York,* f., 1747.

THORNTON, WILLIAM. *London.* Apprenticed 1783, C.C. 1792.

THOROGOOD, EDWD. C.C. 1668.

THOROGOOD, ETINNE. *9 Burrows Buildings, Blackfriars Bridge.*

THOROGOOD, FREDERICK, son of Luke. *London (Wood St., Cheapside).* C.C. 1810, livery C.C. 1813–23.

THOROGOOD, JAMES. Apprenticed to Jno. 1660.

THOROGOOD, JOHN. C.C. 1660.

THOROGOOD, RICHARD. *175 Fenchurch St.,* 1783–90.

THOROGOOD, STEFANO. Same address; card, British Museum, about 1770; watch, 'Thoroughgood, S., *London',* about 1772.

THOROGOOD, WILLIAM, brother. *London.* C.C. 1820.

THOROGOOD, WM. C.C. 1660.

THOROWGOOD, LUKE. Apprenticed to Thos. Hunter; C.C. 1768, London; long-case clock, about 1770.

THORPE, EDWARD. *London (Cornhill).* C.C. 1780–90.

THORPE, JNO. C.C. 1657.

THORPE, RICHARD. *Market Weighton,* 1822–41.

THORPE, THOMAS. *London (Clerkenwell).* Apprenticed 1811, C.C. 1820.

THOUVEROT (THOUVEREZ), LOUIS. *Paris.* Master 1788–1825; equation and calendar clock. *v.* TOUVEREZ.

THRELKELD, D. *Newcastle-on-Tyne,* 1810.

THRELKELD, RALPH. *London.* Bracket clock, about 1740; seen at the Hague.

THRELKELD, WILLIAM, 'in ye Strand', 1700. "A silver watch with an engraved Case and a Cipher, G. K., in the middle, the Dial Plate having Flower-de-luces at the half-hours, the Maker's name, W. Threlkeld, London" (*Lond. Gaz.,* May 12–15, 1701). In the Soane Museum is a clock by him in a long-case decorated with fine English marquetry in panel, about 1710.

THRELKELL, —. C.C. about 1632.

THRELKELL, R. *London.* Watch, 1730.

THRISTLE, —. *Williton.* Hood clock, about 1730.

THULLIER. See TERROT.

THURET, ISAAC. *Paris.* Lodged at the Louvre, 1686.

THURET, JACQUES, son of Isaac. Obtained the reversion of his father's privileges in 1694; Boulle clock, V. & A., about 1700; another with reclining figure of Time below the dial, Wallace collection.

THWAITES, AINSWORTH. *Rosoman St., Clerkenwell.* Made the Horse Guards clock, 1756; 1740–80.

THWAITES, BENJAMIN, son of Ainsworth. *London.* Apprenticed 1762, C.C. 1770.

THWAITES, JAS. *Ratcliff Highway;* 1768–90.

THWAITES, JOHN. *4 Rosoman St., Clerkenwell.* Master C.C. three times, 1815, 1819, 1820; presented to the C.C. Sully's timekeeper; 1780–1816.

THWAITES & REED. *4 Rosoman St., Clerkenwell*, 1817–42. The firm still exists.

THWING, JAMES. *London*. Apprenticed 1679, C.C. 1707–1712; watch.

THYLET. *London*, 1705. Watch and chatelaine which had belonged to Queen Anne fetched £150 at Christie's in 1904.

TIBBOT, JOHN. *Newtown, Wales*. Born 1757, died 1820; worked from 1777–97; sent a clock to Soc. Arts giving impulse to pendulum once a minute, with cycloidal cheeks; several clocks.

TICHBOURNE, JOHN. *London*. Apprenticed 1750, C.C. 1771.

TICKLE, JNO, JUNR. *Crediton*. 30-hour clock, lantern movement about 1730.

TICKLE, WM. *Newcastle*, 1765–85.

TIDBURY & SON. *206 Oxford St.*, 1822–25.

TIEDE, CHRISTIAN FRIEDRICH. *Berlin*. Born 1794, died 1877; a fine maker of chronometers and observatory clocks; Royal astronomical and Court clock in 1838.

TIESE, J. *London*. Oval watch, 1620.

TIGHT, GEORGE, son of Geo. *London (Islington)*. Apprenticed 1798, C.C. 1791–1811.

TILLBROOKE, JNO. *Bury*. Watch, 1785.

TILLIER, JOHN. *London*. a. 1761–99; watch.

TILLS, RICHD. *London*, 1760.

TILLY, JOSEPH. C.C. 1703; walnut long-case clock, square dial, 1703–20.

TIMNER, RICHD. *London*. Watch, 1805.

TINELLY à *Aix*. Cruciform watch, British Museum, about 1580.

TINGES, CHARLES. *Baltimore, U.S.A.*, 1799–1807. Watch.

TINGLEY, THOS. Apprenticed 1686 to Wm. Glazier, C.C.

TINHAM. Long-case clock, bird and flower marquetry in panels, about 1690, inscribed 'Samuel Tinham, Sarum, fecit'; another, about 1725, with the inscription, 'Saml. Tinham in New Sarum'.

TINSON, THOS. *1 Charing Cross*, 1793.

TINTRELIN, JEAN BAPTISTE. *Paris*. Master 1747–89.

TIPPIN, THOS. *Liverpool*, 1740.

TIPPING, GEORGE. C.C. 1674.

TIRRY, JNO. *York*, about 1680.

TISSOT-DAGUETTE, ABRAM. *Neuchâtel* district, 1727–54.

TITCHENER, BENJAMIN. *London*. Apprenticed 1747, C.C. 1763, died a. 1771.

TITFORD, JOHN. *London*. C.C. 1723.

TITHERTON, JNO. *London*. Long-case clock, about 1700.

TOBIAS, ESAU. *Llandilo*, 1818–35.

TOBIAS, ISAAC. *Liverpool*, 1805–11.

TOBIAS, MICHAEL ISAAC, & CO. *Liverpool*, 1810–29. Watch movement, London Museum; rack lever watch with seconds hand turning four times a minute, Chamb. collection.

TOBIAS, MORRIS. *68 Bell Dock Yard, Wapping*, 1798–1800.

TOBIAS, MORRIS, & CO. *68 Bell Dock Yard, Wapping*, 1804. In 1812 Morris Tobias patented (No. 3,584) a binnacle timepiece, to show the time by 'bells' as watches are kept on board ship; rack lever watches, 'Tobias & Co., Liverpool and London', 1808–25.

TOBIAS & LEVITT. *31 Minories*, 1816–42.

TODD, BEN. *Aldersgate St.*, C.C. 1730.

TODD, JAS. *Bradford*. Clock, about 1760.

TODD, JNO. *York*, f., 1665.

TODD, JOHN. *London*. Apprenticed 1696, C.C. 1707–56; watch.

TODD, JOSEPH. *Hull*, 1806–41.

TODD, ROBT. Apprenticed 1684 to Dan. Quare, C.C.

TODD, SAMUEL. *York*, f., 1686.

TOLBY, CHARLES. C.C. 1720.

TOLEMAN, WILLIAM. *Carnarvon*, 1795–about 1840; watch, National Museum, Cardiff.

TOLESON, RALPH. *London*. Watch, 1695.

TOLKIEN, GEORGE. Same address, 1800–11.

TOLKIEN & DANCER. *145 St. John St.*, 1807.

TOLLER, BOSTOCK. *London*. Apprenticed 1742, C.C. 1766; watch movement.

TOLLER, THOMAS. *London*. Apprenticed 1734, C.C. 1741.

TOLLER BROS. *London*. Watch, 1760.

TOLLEY, CHARLES. C.C. 1683.

TOLLEY, CHARLES, son. *London*. C.C. 1720–26.

TOLLISON, JOHN. C.C. 1714.

TOLLODAY, THOMAS. *London*. Apprenticed 1788.

TOLLOT, PIERRE. *France*. Born 1671, died 1742; watches, Schloss Museum, Berlin and Geneva Museum.

TOLSON, RALPH. Apprenticed 1693 to Cuth. Lee, C.C.; watch, about 1700, signed 'Ralph Tolson, London'.

TOMES, JAS. Apprenticed to Jno. Saville 1678, C.C.

TOMEY, JOSHUA. *Dublin*, 1774–80. Watch.

TOMKINS, WILLIAM. *11 Winchester St.*, 1768–72.

TOMKINS, WILLIAM. *London*. Apprenticed 1789, C.C. 1819.

TOMLIN, EDWD. *69 Threadneedle St.*, 1770–98. Bracket clock, mahogany case, round enamelled dial, marked 'Tomlin, Royal Exchange'.

TOMLINS, NICH. Apprenticed 1639 to Ed. Stevens; C.C. 1646.

TOMLINS, WILLIAM. *London*. 1650 C.C.

TOMLINSON, THOMAS. C.C. 1647.

TOMLINSON, WILLIAM. Brother C.C. 1699; master in 1733; died 1750, a Quaker; chiming bracket clock in ebony case, about 1710, Wetherfield collection; watch by him in V. & A., h.m. 1719; inside a fine 8-day Oriental lacquer clock-case by him were directions to set up and keep a pendulum clock, and underneath, "The said clocks with all other sorts and all sorts of watches are made by William Tomlinson at the Dial and Three Crowns in Birchin Lane, near the Royal Exchange, London, now in White Hart Court, Gracechurch St."; he retired to Stoke Newington.

TOMLYNS, NICHOLAS. C.C. 1647.

TOMPION, CHARLES. Probably *London*. a. 1764; watch.

TOMPION, G. *London*, about 1715. Repeating watch.

TOMPION, RICHARD. *Liverpool*, late eighteenth century. Watch.

TOMPION, THOMAS. *London*. Born 1639, C.C. 1671, master C.C. 1704, died 1713. One of the greatest clock and watchmakers; to his work is due the supremacy of English horology in the eighteenth century; he made some of the first watches with balance-springs. He took Edward Banger into partnership about 1701, then, apparently, worked alone, and took Geo. Graham into partnership about 1711. On his death, in 1713, Graham continued alone.

TOMPION, THOMAS, JUNR, nephew. *London*. Apprenticed 1694, C.C. 1702. Imprisoned for theft in 1720; heir to his uncle and probably retired in 1713.

TOMPION & E. BANGER. *London*, about 1701–08. Banger was nephew, apprentice and assistant of Tompion, senior.

TOMPION & GRAHAM. *London*, about 1711–13. Nephew and, from 1696, pupil of Tompion, senior, and succeeded him in his business.

TOMPKINSON, HUMPHERY. *Maiden Lane, Covent Garden*, 1768–75.

TOMS, T. *7 Swan St., Minories*, 1820.

TOMSON, JOHN. *London*, early nineteenth century. Watch.

TOMSON, SN. *London*. Pair-case watch, about 1770.

TONCKHURE, FRANCIS. *Baltimore, U.S.A.*, early nineteenth century. Watches and clocks.

TOOKE, W. *Lynn.* Watch, 1790.

TOOTELE, WM. *Chorley*, 1770.

TOPHAM, EDWARD. *Castlebar*, 1790–1824.

TOPHAM, J. *9 Basing Lane*, 1788–1800.

TOPPING, JNO. *London.* Apprenticed 1691 to Wm. Grimes, C.C.

TORADO, FRANCIS. *Gray's Inn.* Brother C.C. 1633; oval watch in G.M. His widow became a pensioner of C.C. in 1690.

TORIN, DANIEL. *Hoxton Sq.*, 1766.

TORIN, JAMES LEWIS. *30 Throgmorton St.*, 1738–80.

TORKLER, PETER. *9 Red Lion St., Clerkenwell*, 1782–90.

TORNIQUE, J. *London.* Silver alarm watch, about 1670.

TORRIANO, GIOVANNI. *Cremona, Toledo* and *San Yuste.* 1529. Died 1585; one of the greatest early clockmakers. Brought by Charles V in 1529 to repair Giovanni de Dondi's planetarium clock of 1364; he largely re-made it; Toriano and the clock were taken to Spain by Charles V, who retained him in his service in the Cloister of San Yuste in 1556. Torriano's works are known only from descriptions. Bust in Toledo Museum; account of his life in von Bassermann-Jordan's *Alte Uhren und ihre Meister.* Called by Cardan, Jannellus Turrianus, and by Sacco, Giovanni Janellus or Gianello.

TORTORRE, JAS. *London*, 1770.

TORY, SARAH. Apprenticed 1660 to Richd. Bowen and Mary his wife, C.C.

TOTHAKER, WILLIAM. C.C. 1703.

TOUCH, CHAS. *St. Albans.* Watch, 1744.

TOULMIN, SAMUEL. *London.* Watch, about 1745; Wm. Curteen apprenticed to him in 1759.

TOULMIN, SAMUEL. *27 Strand*, 1765–83. Centre-seconds watch, beating full seconds, cylinder escapement, in the G.M.

TOURLE, WILLIAM. *London.* Apprenticed 1748, C.C. 1776–1805.

TOUTIN, HENRY. *Blois* (brother of Jean). 1614; died 1683.

TOUTIN, JEAN. *Château Surr.* Celebrated enamel painter; 1619; died 1660.

TOVEY, WM. Apprenticed 1655 to Simon Dudson, C.C.

TOVEY, WM. Watch and clock spring maker, *64 Red Lion St., Clerkenwell*, 1798; *53 Upper Moorfields*, 1804.

TOWELL, NICH. Apprenticed 1669 to Sam. Davis, C.C.

TOWER, REUBEN. *Plymouth, U.S.A.*, 1813–20.

TOWERS, WILLIAM. *Wincanton*, 1830.

TOWLE, EDWARD. *London.* Apprenticed 1753, C.C. 1760.

TOWNE, JOSEPH. *Horncastle.* Watch, silver dial, about 1700.

TOWNESON, SAMUEL. *London.* Apprenticed 1695, C.C. 1702–38.

TOWNESON, WILLIAM. *London.* Apprenticed 1708, C.C. 1716–60.

TOWNLEY. Lantern clock, signed 'William Townley Bourton', with heraldic fret engraved 'B.R.F. 1724'.

TOWNLEY, THOS., & SON. *Liverpool*, 1818.

TOWNSEND, CHARLES. *Philadelphia*, 1811.

TOWNSEND, DAVID. *Boston, U.S.A.*, 1789–1806. Watch.

TOWNSEND, ELIZABETH. *119 Fetter Lane*, 1804.

TOWNSEND, ELIZABETH & JOHN. *61 St. Paul's Churchyard*, 1760–69.

TOWNSEND, ISAAC. *Boston, U.S.A.*, 1789–1806. Watch.

TOWNSEND, JAMES. *Helmsdon*, 1720.

TOWNSEND, JNO. Forbidden to work by C.C. 1632.

TOWNSEND, JOHN. *Newport, R.I., U.S.A.*, 1769. On case of long-case clock, M.M.A.

TOWNSEND, JOSEPH. *Helmdon*, 1710.

TOWNSEND, R. *London.* Watch, 1815.

TOWNSEND, RT. *Greenock*, 1770–90. He was paid £2 for keeping the town clock in 1785; long-case clock.

TOWNSEND, SAMUEL. C.C. 1702 (Townson (?)).

TOWNSEND, WILLIAM. *74 Fleet St.*, 1773; *99 Guildford Place, Spafield*, 1842.

TOWSON, JNO. THOS. *Devonport.* Received Vulcan medal and £10 from Society of Arts for chronometer banking, 1826.

TRABET, —. *London.* Watch, apparently Dutch, about 1750.

TRACY, RICHD. Apprenticed 1660 to Nich. Coxeter, C.C.

TRACY, STEP. *London.* Striking watch, Marfels collection, about 1700.

TRACY, STEVEN. *Rotterdam*, 1683.

TRAFFORD, THOS. *London*, about 1665.

TRAIL, WILLIAM. *London*, 1802–24.

TRAMIERI, J., à *Turin.* Watch in case of rock crystal formed as an escalop shell, about 1600, Pierpont Morgan collection.

TRAP, EDWARD. *Bristol*, 1765. Died 1784; watch.

TRAP, RICHARD. *London.* Watch, 1762.

TRATTLE, JOSEPH. *Newport.* Clock, about 1780.

TRAUNER, JOHANN. *Würzburg.* Master 1749, died 1772; a good maker; partner with his father-in-law, Johann Henner, 1753–56; pair-case *repoussé* watch Würzburg Museum.

TRAVER, JNO. Watch, h.m., 1748.

TRAVERS, ADAM. *Liverpool*, 1775; *9 Red Lion St., Clerkenwell*, 1783–94.

TRAVERS, MATHEW. Watch-case maker, *12 Great Sutton St.*, 1810.

TRAVERS, WM. *Red Lion St., Clerkenwell*, 1788–1810.

TRAVIS, GEO. *Rotherham*, 1770.

TRAVIS, GEORGE. *Thorne*, about 1770–1882. Watch.

TRAVIS, J. *Thorne*, 1780.

TRAVIS, JAMES. *Rotherham*, about 1770–95.

TRAVIS, T. *Newcastle-on-Tyne*, 1710.

TRAVIS, WM. *Leek.* Born 1781, apprenticed to Joseph Wild, Macclesfield; died 1875.

TRECHSLER, CHRISTOPH. *Dresden.* Master 1571, died about 1624; mathematical instrument maker.

TREGENT, JAMES. *35 Strand*, 1775; *29 Cranbourne St., Leicester Sq.*, 1780. Hon. f. C.C. 1781; watchmaker to the Prince of Wales; was intimate with Garrick, Sheridan, and other notabilities of the theatre. Kelly refers to him as "Mr. Tregent the celebrated French watchmaker", and relates how Sheridan, by attributing his proverbial unpunctuality to the lack of a timekeeper, obtained from Harris, proprietor of Covent Garden Theatre, a watch of Tregent's make. The Duke of Sussex paid him £400 for a repeater and alarum travelling watch. Long-case clock by him, about 1770, silvered dial with festoons, etc., day of the month, strike-silent; bracket clock with Battersea enamel face, V. & A., signed on face 'James Tregent, Leicester Square, London', 1770–1804.

TRELEGEN, JAMES. *Strand*, 1775.

TRELEGON & OCKLEY. *54 New Bond St.*, 1793.

TREMBLAY, PIERRE. *Blois.* Master 1676–94.

TREMBLEY, DAVID. *Geneva*, about 1750.

TREMBLEY, J. L. *Geneva*, about 1710.

TRENHOLME, WM. C.C. 1728; in 1735 he worked for Bayley.

TRENT, WM. *London.* Watch, 1770.

TREU, ISAAC. *Basle*, 1620–50.

TREU, JAKOB. *Basle*, 1650. Died 1690.

'TREVAN, *Marseille*'. Watch, 1780.

TREVEEN, JARRETT. *London.* C.C. 1688 : watch. Also TERVEEN and TURVEEN.

TREVOR, THOS. Apprenticed 1654 to Peter Delandre, C.C.

TREWIN, —. *Hereford*, about 1770.

TREWINNARD, EDWARD. *Grand Rd., Bermondsey*, 1825.

TREWINNARD, JOSHUA & JAMES. *16 Rotherhithe Wall*, 1790–1842.

TREWINNARD, JOSHUA. *40 Strand*, 1807–10.

TRIBE, JOHN. *Petworth*. Died 1728; hanging clock by him repeats hours and quarters.

TRIGG, THOMAS. C.C. 1701.

TRIGGS, THOMAS. C.C. 1708.

TRIM, JOHN. *London*. Maker of house clocks, 1790–1800.

TRIMOLET, FRANÇOIS LOUIS. *Geneva*, about 1775–91.

TRINGHAM, GEO. *15 Golden Lane*, 1828–42.

TRINGHAM, J. *London*. Watch, 1790.

TRIPP, JOB. *Bridge St.*, 1772.

TRIPPETT, JNO. *Kingston*. C.C. 1668.

TRIPPETT, ROBERT. C.C. 1700; long-case clock, about 1705.

TRIPPETT, THOS. Apprenticed 1654 to Geo. Poole, C.C.

TRIPPETT, WILLIAM. C.C. 1706.

TRIQUET, JAS. *35 Strand*, 1768–72.

TROTH, JAMES. *Pittsburg, U.S.A.*, 1815.

TROTT, ANDREW C. *Boston, U.S.A.*, 1806–09. Watch.

TROTT, PETER. *Boston, U.S.A.*, 1800–05. Watch.

TROTTER, ALEXANDER. *Jedburgh*, 1788–1815. Long-case clocks. Watch.

TROTTER, JOSEPH. *Newcastle-on-Tyne*, 1820–36.

TROUGHTON, BRYAN. *35 Fenchurch St.* Livery Clothworkers' Company, 1760–75.

TROUGHTON, EDWARD. *Fleet St.* Invented a wheel-cutting engine in 1780, and a compensated pendulum in 1790; died 1835, aged 81.

TROUGHTON, JOSEPH. *London*, f. of Lancaster, 1779.

TROUGHTON, NATHANIEL. *25 Rood Lane*, 1768.

TROUGHTON, THOMAS. *London*. Apprenticed 1782, C.C. 1796–1809.

TROUP, JAS. *233 Tooley St.*, 1822.

TROUP, W. *London*. Bracket clock, about 1760.

TROUT, THOMAS. *Bond St.* Long-case clock, about 1710; watch in silver-gilt case, inscribed 'Trout, Westminster', about 1790, Hilton Price collection.

TROVEY, CHARLES. *London*. Apprenticed 1754, C.C. 1776–99; watch.

TROWE, GILBERT. C.C. 1722.

TROWE, JNO. Apprenticed 1685 to Wm. Speakman, C.C.

TRUBSHAW, JOHN. Apprenticed to Robt. Halsted 1679; Admitted C.C. 1686; bracket clock chiming on six bells, about 1700; a gilt metal-cased repeating watch by him, V. & A., about 1710.

TRUSCOTT, LEWIS. *Mevagessey*, late eighteenth century. Long-case clock.

TRUSCOTT, LEWIS. *Haverfordwest*, 1822–44.

TRUSTY, STEPHEN. *London*. C.C. 1770–78.

TRYGG, PETTER. *Falun*, 1750–94. Long-case clock.

TUCK, J. & L. *8 Haymarket*, 1800–30.

TUCKER, JOHN. *Portsmouth*. Clock, about 1715.

TUCKEY, EDWD. Apprenticed 1681 to Robt. Ayres, C.C.

TUCKEY, GILES. *London*. Repeating watch, 1776.

TUCKEY, THOS. C.C. 1646.

TUCKEY, TUDMAN, JAMES. *The Crown, Lombard St.*, 1697–1710. Long marquetry case clock, about 1700.

TUITE, WILLIAM. *41 Great Queen St.*, 1761–75.

TUNNELL, JNO. Successor to Geo. Flashman, *18 Fleet St.*, 1816–30. Livery C.C. 1826; watch duplex escapement compensation balance, h.m., 1821.

TUNSTAL, STEPHEN. *Skipton*. Long-case clock, about 1725.

TUPLING, B. *191 Strand*, 1820.

TUPMAN, GEO. *Vigo St.*, 1790; *6 Charles St., Grosvenor Sq.*, 1806–30; *6A Old Bond St.*, 1842.

TURGES, JAS. Apprenticed 1660 to Ahasuerus Fromanteel.

TURGES, JOSIAH. *London (St. Sepulchre)*. Apprenticed 1752, C.C. 1764–70; pair-case watch, London Museum.

TURKS. *London*, 1731; *Windsor*, 1791.

TURMEAU & KETTLEWELL. *23 Villiers St.*, 1793.

TURNBULL, FRANCIS. Apprenticed 1692 to Sam Marchant, C.C.; 1740.

TURNBULL, ROBERT. *Greenock*, 1790–1832.

TURNBULL, THOS. *Whitby*, 1818.

TURNBULL, WILLIAM. *Edinburgh*, 1758–82.

TURNBULL, WILLIAM. *Darlington* and *Newcastle-on-Tyne*, 1761–80. Watch.

TURNBULL, WM. *Whitby*, 1823.

TURNELL, WILLIAM. *London*. Apprenticed 1821, C.C. 1828.

TURNER, CHARLES. *London*. Apprenticed 1777, C.C. 1786.

TURNER, CHARLES THOMAS. *London (Old St.* and *Goswell St. Rd.)*. Apprenticed 1793, C.C. 1811–22.

TURNER, EDWARD. *London*. C.C. 1769.

TURNER, FRANCIS. *Rochford (Essex)*. About 1800 C.C.

TURNER, HY. Apprenticed 1694 to Richd. Westwood, C.C.

TURNER, J. & CHARLES. *58 and 59 New Bond St.*, 1830.

TURNER, JAMES. *London*. Apprenticed 1792, C.C. 1801.

TURNER, JOHN. *10 London Wall*, 1788–94.

TURNER, JOSEPH. C.C. 1717.

TURNER, THOS. *London*. Fine long-case clocks, about 1745.

TURNER, WILLIAM. *Church St., Spitalfields*, 1760–72.

TURNER, WILLIAM. *London*. C.C. 1821.

TURNER, WM. *18 Cornhill*, 1775; *Fenchurch St.*, 1825–40. See BIRCH.

TURNHAM, RD. *London*. Watch, 1785.

TURRELL, SAMUEL, *Boston, U.S.A.* 1789–1800. Watch.

TURTON, NATH. *Manchester*, 1818.

TURTON & WALBANCKE. *8 Fore St.*, 1793.

TURVEE, JARRET. C.C. 1688.

TUSSINGHAM, JNO. Apprenticed 1682 to Richd. Prince, C.C.

TUTET, EDWARD. *10 Fenchurch St.* Livery C.C. 1766; master 1786; bracket clock, enamel dial, Wetherfield collection; 1760–94.

TUTET, EDWARD, son. *London*. C.C. 1792–1811; abroad in 1813.

TUTTELL, THOMAS. C.C. 1695; pocket sun-dial and 'Perpetuall Almanacke', about 1700.

TUTTON, C. *Bath*, 1826.

TWELL, GEO. Apprenticed 1685 to Wm. Hawkins, C.C.

TWELLS, WM. *High St., Birmingham*, 1770.

TWING, JAMES. C.C. 1688.

TWYCROSS, STEPHEN. *Gough Sq.*, 1793.

TWYCROSS, STEPHEN, & SON. *8 Haymarket*, 1800–04; *13 Newcastle St.*, 1817.

TWYFORD, JOHN. *Bank Top, Manchester*. Died 1789.

TWYFORD, JOSIAH. *Manchester*, 1765. *35 Deansgate, Manchester*, 1794.

TWYFORD, JOSIAH. *Manchester*, 1818.

TWYFORD, R. *20 Salisbury St., Strand*, 1815–19.

TWYFORD, ROBERT. *40 Strand*. Hon. f. C.C. 1781; 1770–82.

TWYFORD, ROBERT, & CO. *9 Finch Lane, Cornhill*, 1790; *10 Salisbury St., Strand*, 1800–10.

TWYFORD, WILLIAM. *88 Bank Top, Manchester*, 1794.

TWYFORD, WM. *Manchester*, 1775.

TYAS, W. T. *Thavis Inn, Holborn*, 1820–35.

TYLER, GEORGE. *Pope's Head Alley*. Apprenticed to Robt. Dingley, 1691, C.C.; bracket clock in Japanese tortoise-shell case, about 1715; bracket clock in walnut case, pull repeating quarters on six bells, about 1720, Wetherfield collection; clock watch, 1735.

TYLER, JNO. Apprenticed 1667 to Jno. Matchett, C.C.

TYLER, RICHD. *Wallingford*, about 1740.

TYMMS, A. *6 Kennington Lane*, 1820.

TYMMS, JNO. Apprenticed 1656 to Nich. Tomlins, C.C.

TYMMS, M. *5 Kennington Lane*, 1820.

TYRELL, WALTER. *London (Shoe Lane)*. Apprenticed 1732, C.C. 1740, died 1789.

TYRER, JAS. HY. *32 Northampton St., Clerkenwell*, 1806–30.

TYRER, THOMAS. *Red Lion St., Clerkenwell*. Patented in 1782 (No. 1,311) the duplex escapement. His specification says, "Horizontal scapement for a watch to act with two wheels".

TYSON, LEECH. *Philadelphia*, 1823–25.

UDALL, J. *5 Great New St., Shoe Lane*, 1819–22.

UDALL, THOS. *8 Flower-du-luce Court*, 1793.

UFFINGTON, JNO. *53 Bunhill Row*, 1793.

UFFINGTON, JOHN. *London*. Apprenticed 1695, C.C. 1702–67.

UFFINGTON, JOHN, son of John. *London*. Apprenticed 1727, C.C. 1739; clock.

UFFINGTON, SAMUEL. *London*. 1740.

ULLMEYER, CHRISTOPH. *Augsburg*. Clock, Green Vaulted Chambers, Dresden.

UNDERHILL, BENJAMIN. *London*. Apprenticed 1762, C.C. 1785.

UNDERHILL, CAVE. Admitted C.C. 1655.

UNDERWOOD, CÆSAR. *3 Panton St.*, 1798–1800; *Ranelagh St., Pimlico*, 1820.

UNDERWOOD, JOHN. *36 Noble St., Cheapside*, 1754–75.

UNDERWOOD, JOHN, & SONS. *Foster Lane*, 1758–63.

UNDERWOOD, ROBT. *3 Falcon St.*, 1769–1810.

UNDERWOOD, WM. *London*. Clock, about 1720.

UNEMAN, JOHN & WILLIAM. Dutch clockmakers in England, 1368.

UNWIN, EDWARD. *30 Upper Lisson St., Paddington*, 1820.

UNWIN, WM. *Newark*, 1776–1804. Afterwards Unwin & Holt.

UPJOHN, —. *Brentford*. Watch, 1810.

UPJOHN, FRANCIS. *1 Bridgewater Sq.* Livery C.C. 1786; suggested distinctive marks on foreign watches 1780–87.

UPJOHN, JAMES. *Threadneedle St.*, 1760–63; *Lombard St.*, 1779. Watch in gold and enamelled cases, V. & A., h.m., 1778.

UPJOHN, JAMES. *London*. Apprenticed 1766, C.C. 1781, livery C.C. 1790; went to *U.S.A.* 1802.

UPJOHN, JAMES & WIRGMAN. *18 Red Lion St., Clerkenwell*, 1769–81. Jas. & Co., 1794.

UPJOHN, PETER. *Bideford*. Watch, 1780.

UPJOHN, PETER. *11 Red Lion St.*, 1783–1835.

UPJOHN, RICHD. *Exon*. Long-case clock, about 1730.

UPJOHN, T. J. *London*, about 1805–10.

UPJOHN, THOS. *Exeter*, about 1760.

UPJOHN, W. J. *11 St. John's Sq.*, 1815–20.

UPJOHN, WM. *Exon*. Watch, silver dial, raised figures, h.m., 1741.

UPTON, NAT. Apprenticed 1674 to Jno. Nash, C.C.

UPTON, RICH. *London*. Watch, about 1755.

URICK, VALENTINE. *Reading, U.S.A.*, 1760.

URNIKA, JARONIMUS. *Stockholm*, 1644–59.

URQUHART, JOHN. *Perth*, 1805–37.

URSEAU, NICHOLAS. Entry of a payment to him as a clockmaker in 1553, and on New Year's Day, 1556, he presented a clock to Queen Elizabeth.

URSEAU, NICHOLAS. Probably a son of the preceding, clockmaker to Queen Elizabeth, 1572–90.

USHERWOOD, WILLIAM. *19 Strand*, 1830.

UTTING, THOS. *Yarmouth*, 1730.

UYTEMVEER, C. *Rotterdam*. Watch, about 1705.

VAART, H. G. *Strassburg*. Spherical watch, about 1560.

VACHERON, ABRAHAM. *Geneva*. Born 1760, died 1843; started in 1785; master a Girod in 1786 and took the name of Vacheron-Girod.

VACHERON, JACQUES BARTHÉLEMY, son. *Geneva*. Born 1787, retired 1844, died 1864. Associated with his uncle Barthélemy Girod in representing the firm of Vacheron in Paris till 1816, and in 1819 with François Constantin. Virgule musical watches; gold engraved watches signed Vacheron & Girod, M.M.A. and Carnegie Museum.

VACHERON & CONSTANTIN. *Geneva*. Title of the firm 1819–67; signature 'Abraham Vacheron' used in 1822 for second quality watches; other signatures were: 'Vacheron & Constantin à Genève', 'Chossat & Comp. à Genève'. In 1839, the firm engaged Georges Leschot to make machine tools for watches; he remained in the firm till 1882. Two engraved watches, M.M.A.

VAILLANT, JACQUES FRANÇOIS. *Paris*. Master 1750, juré 1770, died 1786; clock.

VAILLANT, LOUIS JACQUES. *Paris*. Master 1787–1821.

VALE, HOWLETT, & CARR. *Coventry*, 1754–90. Watch, 'Vale & Howlett, London', 1782.

VALE, SAMUEL. *Coventry*, 1747.

VALE, WILLIAM. Musical clockmaker, *32 Paul St. Finsbury*, 1816–40.

VALE, WM. *6 Colmore Row, Birmingham*, 1770. See also Gimblet.

VALE, WM. *12 Bunhill Row*. A good maker, mentioned by Earnshaw, 1776–94.

VALE & KENYON, about 1780.

VALE & ROTHERHAM. *Coventry* (R. K. Rotherham apprenticed to Vale, Howlett, & Carr), 1790–1840.

VALENTINE, BART. *London*. Watch, 1800.

VALENTINE, CHAS. D. F. Livery C.C. 1810.

VALENTINE, JOHN. *London*. Apprenticed 1762, C.C. 1771–1811.

VALENTINE, WILLIAM. 'At the Dial and Sun, Royston', 1770.

VALERAN, —. Hexagonal table clock, Wallace collection, stamped on the bottom 'E. Valeran, Paris', with the Royal Crown of France and fleur-de-lis, about 1600.

'VALÉRE, *Paris*'. Watch, 1789.

VALLANCE, THOS. *5 Wilderness Row*, 1820.

VALLERAN, FLEURENT. *Paris*, 1544.

VALLETTE, LÉONARD. *Geneva*, about 1755–71.

VALLETTE, SD. & FILS. *Geneva*. Watch, about 1785.

VALLERY, NICOLAS. *Paris*. 1767 master–1789.

VALLIER, JEAN. *Lyons*. In the Pierpont Morgan collection is a triangular watch, on one side portrait of Charles V and on another the arms of Besançon, with the date 1564; cruciform watch, about 1590, Garnier collection; small ornamental watch, British Museum; fine astronomical watch, uncased, by him, British Museum, about 1610; watch, Vienna Treasury, case in the form of a star, mounted in brass and silver, covered on both sides with rock crystal, about 1605.

VALLIN, N. In the Pierpont Morgan collection is a very small oval watch, signed 'N. Vallin', late sixteenth-century. On the back is a representation of St. George and the Dragon in raised enamel work, and around the band of the case, the inscription 'Honi soit qui mal y pense'. Brass clock, British Museum, signed 'N. Vallin, 1600'; with arms of Viscount Montagu, who died 1629; probably from Courdray House, Sussex; modern enamel dial, named 'John Monkhouse, London'. Clock with carillon of thirteen bells, 1598, Ilbert collection.

VAN ALEURS, H. *Amsterdam.* Watch, about 1775.

VAN BLADE, LAURENS. *Hague.* Watch, about 1780.

VANBROFF, JAS. Watch, about 1695.

VAN CEULE, J. LE JEUNE. *Hague.* Repeating watch, Pierpont Morgan collection, about 1750.

VAN CEULEN, JOHN. *Hague.* Clock on Huygens' plan, about 1660; clock-watch, Schloss collection, about 1700; a watch with large balance and primitive arrangement of spring, in the Pierpont Morgan collection, dating from about 1680; bears the signature, 'Jo. Gannes Van Ceulen fecit Hagæ'.

VAN CEULEN, PHILLIPUS. *Hague.* Watch, British Museum, the case enamelled by J. L. Durant, about 1690.

VAN DER CLOESEN, BERNARD. *The Hague,* 1688–1719. A maker of repute, who worked for Huygens; oval watch with hand varying in length to follow the oval, Ilbert collection.

VANDEN BERGH, A. Large late-seventeenth-century Dutch clock, in silver filigree case, V. & A.; movement signed 'Adriaen Vanden Bergh fecit, Hague'; case signed 'J. H. C. Breghtel'.

VANDENBURG, J. *8 Owen's Row,* 1830.

VANDERWOOD, —. Long-case clock, about 1780, inscribed 'Wm. Vanderwood, London'.

VANENHOVE, —. *Amsterdam.* Enamel watch, about 1730.

VANGALAND (VANGALE, VANGANDE), (GILES, GYLES). *London,* 1565–85. "Clockmaker borne under the obedyence of the King of Spain, payeth tribute to no companye & is of the Dutche Church."

VANHAM, LEONARD. *Addle St.,* 1737–40.

VANLONE, MATT. Brother C.C. 1692.

VANLOVE (VANLOUE, VAULOVE), MATTHEW (MATHIEU). *London* (*St. Martin's Lane*), 1689–1708. C.C. 1692; French; watch.

VAN MEIORS, OTTO. *Amsterdam,* 1780.

VANS, CHAS. Apprenticed 1682 to Edwd. Norris, C.C.

VANS, PAT. Apprenticed 1672 to Joseph Knibb, C.C.

VAN SCHILFGAARDEN (SCHLIFGAARDE), ANDRIES. *Gouda,* 1734. Died 1802; from *Rotterdam;* watch.

VANSCOLINA, JERE. Apprenticed to Wm. Ericke; turned over to Francis Atkins; C.C. 1776.

VANTROLLIER, JAMES. One of the first assistants C.C. 1630; watch of an earlier date, Nelthropp collection.

VAN VOOST. Watch, about 1730, inscribed 'Hendrick Van Voost in de Rye'.

VARDON, SAMUEL & THOMAS. *29 Firth St., Soho,* 1783–94.

VARIER, SAMUEL. *Pont Nedd Fechan,* 1731–54. Clocks.

VARIN (VOIRIN, VUARIN), JACQUES. *Lyons.* Master 1642. 1681. From *Varenne.*

VARLEY, WM. 1763.

VARNEAUX, FRANÇOIS. *Paris.* Juré 1760. See VERNEAUX.

VARNISH, JNO. *Rochdale,* 1770.

VASEY, JOHN. *London.* C.C. 1766.

VASLET, ANDREW. C.C. 1717.

VASSALIEU (VASSELY), HUMBERT. *Lyons,* 1523–57.

VASSE, DAVID. *Paris.* Master 1782–1824.

VASSIERE, THOMAS. *London.* C.C. 1698.

VAUCANSON, J. Born at Grenoble, 1709; constructor of automatic movements.

VAUCHER, CLAUDE. *Fleurier,* 1800–20. Introduced train of 18,000.

VAUCHER, DANIEL. *Paris.* Master 1767–86; an eminent maker; watches in most museums illuminated Baillie; fine 4-colour gold engraved repeating watch, F.W.M., signed 'Vaughé à la Cité'; watch movement, Ilbert collection signed 'Vauchez en la Cité'; gold engraved repeating watch set diamonds, Lincoln Museum. A Vaucher, probably Daniel, was granted in 1778 by the Government a premium for a file-cutting machine. Also VAUCHEZ and VAUCHÉ.

VAUCHER, DAVID JEAN JACQUES HENRI. *Fleurier,* 1734–49. Introduced watchmaking into Fleurier.

VAUCHER, FRÈRES. Swiss watch, 1780; another watch, inscribed 'Presented by Napoleon I to Thalma', now at the museum of the 'Sons of the Revolution', New York.

VAUCHER, FRÈRES. *Fleurier* and *Canton,* 1800–66. A different firm from that of Geneva, composed of Claude and César; gold engraved centre-seconds watch.

VAUCHER, JEAN HENRI DAVID, son. *Paris.* Master 1779, juré 1780–89.

VAUCHEZ, —. *Paris,* 1790.

VAUGHAN, CHARLES. *Pontypool,* about 1730–about 1780. Long-case clock, National Museum, Cardiff.

VAUGHAN, EDWARD. *London.* Apprenticed 1706, C.C. 1715–23. Also VAUGHTON.

VAUGHAN, GEO. *Pontypool.* Clock about 1760.

VAUGHAN, GEO. *Greville St., Hatton Garden,* 1816–28.

VAUGHAN, ROBT. Apprenticed 1655 to Jno. Broome, C.C.

VAUGUION, DANIEL, "to their Royal Highnesses the Duke of Gloucester and Prince Henry, at the Duke of Gloucester's Arms at the New Opening, Spring Gardens, Charing Cross", 1760–93.

VAUQUER, ROBT. *Blois.* A celebrated painter in enamel of watch cases; died 1670.

VAUTIER, —. Calendar watch, about 1600, signed 'Loys Vautier, Blois'; died 1623.

VAUTIER (VAUQUER), ABRAHAM. *Blois,* 1578. Died a. 1600.

VAUTIER (VAUQUER), GILLES. *Blois.* Master 1558, died about 1576. Also VAUTHIER and VAULTHYER.

VAUTIER (VAUQUER), LOYS, son. *Blois.* Born 1591, died 1638. A very fine maker; fine engraved watch, British Museum, illuminated Baillie; watch Louvre.

VAUTROLLIER. See VANTROLLIER.

VAUTROLLIER (VAULTROLLIER), JAMES. *London,* 1622. C.C. 1632; one of the first assistants C.C.; watches G.M., M.M.A., Mallett and Blot-Garnier collections.

VAUTYER, —. *Blois.* Handsome octagonal watch, British Museum, case decorated with filigree work and jewels, 1620.

VECUE, THOMAS. C.C. 1632.

VEIGNEUR, —. *Geneva.* Watch, 1775.

VEIGNEUR, FRÈRES. Watch, about 1810.

VÉDIE, LOUIS. *Rouen.* Juré 1691.

VEIRAS, JEAN JAQUES. *Geneva,* about 1755–70.

VEITCH, WILLIAM. *Haddington,* 1754–81.

VENABLES, GEORGE. *London.* Apprenticed 1762, C.C. 1769.

VENABLES, GEORGE. *London.* Apprenticed 1768, C.C. 1795–1805.

VENAULT, —. *Paris.* Watch, 1790.

VENN, THOMAS. *London.* Apprenticed 1752, C.C. 1772–75, watch.

VERBACK, WM. Apprenticed C.C. 1681.

VERDIER, —. *Paris.* 1730 master.

VERDIER, JEAN JACQUES. *Paris.* Master 1737, juré 1773–89; gold engraved watch.

VERE, JOHN HENRY. *48 Lombard St.*, 1769.

VERGO, —. Thiout credits him with the invention of a fusee to wind both ways (see MOORE, THOS.), about 1730.

VERITÉ, —. *Paris*, 1820–30.

VERMEULE, NICHOLAS. *Rotterdam.* Pendulum watch, about 1714; another watch, about 1732, signed 'Nicholas Vermeule Amsterdam'.

VERMEULEN, A. *Amsterdam*, about 1750.

VERNEAUX, HENRY FRANÇOIS. *Paris.* Master 1757; juré 1767–89; engraved watch, F.W.M. See VARNEAUX.

VERNEUIL, —. *Dijon*, about 1800.

VERNEUIL, JNO. *Paris.* Clock, about 1780.

VERNEY, MOSES. *Dublin*, 1743.

VERNEZOBRE DE LAURIEUX, —. *Paris*, 1812.

VERNEZOBRE DE LAURIEUX, JEAN BAPTISTE LOUIS. *Paris.* Master 1769–89.

VERNON, —. C.C. 1685.

VERNON, CHRISTOPHER, in 'ye Great Turnstyle, Holborne'; C.C. 1638; lantern clocks, about 1650.

VERNON, SAMUEL. C.C. 1649, master 1679.

VERNON, SAMUEL, son. *London.* Apprenticed 1677, C.C. 1685–1705.

VERNON, THOMAS. *Liverpool*, 1734–66. Watch.

VERNON, THOS. Watch, *repoussé* case, about 1710; bracket clock, about 1740; bracket clock, inscribed 'Vernon, London', about 1725, plays four tunes on twelve bells, curious motive force consisting of heavy straight springs outside of back plate.

VERNON, THOS. *Ludlow*, 1780.

VERNON & EDEN. *Liverpool.* Watch, 1789.

VEROW, JNO. *Hinckley.* Watch, with curiously shaped fluted pillars, about 1795.

VESEY, CHRIS. Apprenticed 1692 to Jno. Sowter, C.C.

VESPER, J. *Fore St., Limehouse*, 1820.

VEVERS, RICHARD. *2 Cateaton St.*, 1825–30.

VEYRASSAT, PAUL LOUIS. *Vevey* from 1774–98. Master in *Gex*.

VEYRIN, —. *Paris*, 1775–92.

VIAL, CHARLES. 1685. "Silver pendulum watch made by Charles Vial, with a tortoise-shell case inlaid" (*Lond. Gaz.*, Jan. 17–20, 1697).

VIBRANDI, W. *Leuwarden.* Watch, about 1610.

VICARY, GEO. Apprenticed 1682 to Thos. Brafield, C.C.

VICK, RICHARD, in the *Strand.* C.C. 1702; master 1729; repeating watch, inscribed 'Richard Vick, watchmaker to his late Majesty'; another, about 1740 or 1750.

VICK, THOS. *London*, about 1780.

VICKER, ISAAC. *Lancaster*, 1850.

VICKER, JOSEPH. *Lancaster*, 1850.

VICKERMAN, THOS. 'Maiden Lane, opposite Goldsmiths' Hall, Cheapside', card, about 1760.

VIDAL, A. *St. Giroud.* Fine repeating watch, about 1800.

VIDION, JOHN. *Faversham*, 1774–1801. Watch.

VIEL, CHAS. Apprenticed 1678 to Richd. Jarrett; C.C. 1686.

VIEL, RICHD. Apprenticed 1651 to Dan. Fletcher, C.C.

VIET. Early seventeenth-century striking and alarum watch, inscribed 'Jean Viet, Aorlcan'.

VIET, CHARLEMAGNE, son of Paul. *Blois.* Master 1673, died 1695.

VIET, CLAUDE. C.C. 1698; his daughter Marianne was bound apprentice to him in 1715; gold watch, inscribed 'C. Viet, London, watchmaker to Her Majesty', h.m., 1729, outer case engraved. See also MITCHELL & VIET.

VIET, MARIANE, daughter of Claude. *London.* Apprenticed 1714–38 C.C; in partnership with Thomas Mitchell.

VIET, PAUL. *Blois.* Fine watch by him, British Museum, about 1635, case beautifully painted in enamel by Henry Toutin.

VIEUSSEUX, JEAN ET MT. *Geneva*, mid-eighteenth century. Watch.

VIEUSSEUX & RAMERU. ——, about 1735–about 1775. Watches, Ilbert and Feill collections.

VIEVAR, GEO. Apprenticed 1693 to Dan Lecount, C.C.

VIGER, F. Musical clock, Wallace collection, signed 'Viger à Paris', about 1740.

VIGNE, JAMES. *2 Strand*, 1770–94. Hon. f. C.C. 1781.

VIGNE, PETER. *15 Green St., Bath*, 1798–1800.

VIGNE & LAUTIER. *19 Union St.*, 1809.

VIGNEAU, PETER. *London.* C.C. 1709.

VIGNIAUX, P. *Toulouse*, 1788 wrote book.

VILBAR, —. *Paris.* Horloger de la Reine, 1787.

VILLEREUX (VILLECEUX), FRANÇOIS. *Paris.* Master 1758–89.

VILLETTE, JOACHIM. *Lyons*, 1658–60.

VILLETTE, PHILIPPE EMMANUEL. *Lyons.* Born about 1614, died 1694.

VILLISCUN, STEPHEN. *Church Alley, Basinghall St,.* 1780–85.

VINCENT, CHAS. *London.* Watch, 1820.

VINCENT, WM. *Portsmouth*, 1730.

VINCENT, WM. *York*, 1770.

VINCO, DAN. Apprenticed 1691 to Richd. Baker, C.C.

VINE, JAS. *2 Charing Cross*, 1790–94.

VINER, CHARLES EDWARD. *151 New Bond St.* and *Royal Exchange*, 1776–1820; card, British Museum; *19 Sackville St.*, 1840–2; livery C.C. 1819.

VINER, CHARLES EDWARD, & HOPKINS. *8 Sweeting's Alley*, 1829; also *235 Regent St.*, 1829–42. Alarum watches with pendant setter.

VIOLLIER, JACQUES. Crystal cased oval watch, about 1600.

VIPONT, JNO. Apprenticed 1682 to Hy. Morgan, C.C.

VIRGOE, THOMAS. C.C. 1682.

VIRIDET, MARC FRANÇOIS EMANUEL. *Geneva*, about 1775–91.

VIRIDET & CIE. *Paris.* Watch, about 1780; Geneva repeating watch, about 1810.

VISBACH, —. Spring clock, G.M., inscribed 'Pieter Visbach, fecit Hague met privilege', about 1700.

VISBACH, PIETER. *The Hague*, 1690–about 1700. A famous maker, who worked for Huygens; engraved watch, V. & A., illuminated Baillie; spring clock, G.M.; long-case clock.

VISCONTI, G. Clock at Pavia, about 1410.

VISE. See VYSE.

VITROLLE, —. Fine bracket clock, signed 'Vitrolle à Paris', about 1650.

VIZIER, BARNABY. *Dublin*, 1790–1820.

VOAK, JAMES. *35A South Audley Street, London.* Watch, about 1795.

VOGEL, ESIAS. *Nürnberg*, 1553–65. Petitioned in 1565 with Hanns Praun and Marx Steppinger for a separate Guild for Kleinuhrmacher.

VOGEL, NICLAS, son. *Göteborg*, 1705–54. Watch, Nord. Museum.

VOGEL, NICOLAUS. *Stockholm.* Master 1695, died 1723; travelling clock.

VOGHT (& CO. *35 Wigmore St.*, 1830).

VOGLER, JOHANN GEORG. *Augsburg.* Master 1754, died 1765; instrument maker; sundial, British Museum and M.P.S., Dresden.

VOIGHT, HENRY. *Philadelphia*, 1775–93; then SEBASTIAN; then THOS. 1813–25.

VOISIN, A., L'AÎNÉ. *Rue Hyacinthe, Paris*.Garde-visiteur in 1769.

VOISIN, ANTOINE HENRY. *Paris (Rue Dauphine)*. Master 1755, juré 1765–89; fine mantel clock.

VOISIN, ANTOINE L'AÎNÉ. *Paris (Rue Hyacinthe St. Michel)*, 1740. Master 1743, juré 1754–89.

VOISIN, CHARLES. *Paris*, about 1695–about 1730. Porcelain clock, Munich Residenz; lantern clock; watch. Ilbert collection.

VOISIN, HENRY. *Paris (Rue de Thionville)*. a. 1773–1807, Watch.

VOISIN, HENRY. Clock, about 1770.

VOISIN, LE JEUNE. *Rue Dauphine, Paris*, 1769.

VOKINS, JNO. *Newton*. Long-case clock, centre seconds, dead beat, about 1800.

VOLANT, ELIAS (ELIÈ). *London*, 1622. B.C. 1628, C.C. 1632–34; Frenchman. Also VOLUNT and VOLLANT. Oval silver watch about 1640, Ilbert collection.

VOLK, P. *38 Goodge St.*, 1835–40.

VOLLENHAUSS (VALINGHAUSS, WOLLINHAUSS), CARL ANDREAS FRIEDRICH. *Berlin*, 1785–1800. Clock.

VON GUERICKE, OTTO. *Magdeburg*. 1692–80. Inventor of the vacuum pump; long-case clock made by him Magdeburg Stadtbibliothek.

VON SCHNEIDAU, CARL ANTON. *Stockholm*. Born 1751, died 1817. Watch.

VOSSIÈRE, THOMAS. C.C. 1698.

VOTTER, PETER. *Vienna*. Watch, 1764.

VÕTTER, PHILIPP. *Vienna*. Master 1731–63; maker of repute; fine silver travelling clock, Carnegie Museum; fine miniature watch with three cases of gold, tortoise-shell and outer of jasper. Also VOTER.

VOUGHAN, DANIEL. *Charing Cross*, 1775.

VOUGHAN, EDWARD. C.C. 1715.

VOUGHAN, GEORGE. *11 Granville St., Hatton Garden*, 1820 (see Vauguion).

VOYCE, GAMALIEL. Apprenticed 1687 to Sarah Payne; C.C. 1694; arch-top ebony bracket clock, pull quarters, original rise and fall, about 1710.

VOYCE, RICHD. Apprenticed 1693 to Geo. Ethrington, C.C.

VRYTHOFF, JAS. *Berns, Hague*. Enamel watch, about 1740.

VRYTROFT, L. *Hague*. Clock, about 1790.

VUICAR, J. B. *Zug*. Small round watch, silver dial, about 1610.

VUILLE, ALEXANDER. *Baltimore*, 1766.

VUILLEUMIER, MOÏSE. *Tramelan*, about 1730–60.

VULLIAMY, BENJAMIN. *Pall Mall*, son of Justin, and father of Benjamin Lewis. Hon. f. C.C. 1781; 1775–1820.

VULLIAMY, BENJAMIN LEWIS. *68 Pall Mall*. An eminent maker, 1810–54.

VULLIAMY, JUSTIN. Carried on business at Pall Mall, in partnership with Benjamin Gray, whose daughter he married; 1730–75.

VULLIAMY, JUSTIN THEODORE. *London*. Livery C.C. 1813, w.C.C. 1820–23; duplex watches G.M. and S.M.S.K.

VULLIAMY & SON. *76 Pall Mall*, 1793–1820.

VUOLF, J. C. Skull watch in the British Museum, 1600.

VYSE. *Wisbech*.

VYSE, JNO. 1760.

VYSE, WM. 1730.

WADE, BURTT. *London*. Apprenticed 1757, C.C. 1764–about 1800; long-case clock.

WADE, HENRY. Apprenticed to William Webster, and turned over to John Rainsford; C.C. 1728.

WADE, HENRY. *London*. C.C. 1768.

WADE, JOHN. *London*. 1680 C.C., died 1693.

WADE, JOS. *Clerkenwell Close*, 1793.

WADSWORTH, ELI. *Halifax*. Born 1780, died 1861.

WADY, JAMES. *Newport, U.S.A.*, 1750–55.

WADY, JNO. *London*. Bracket clock in japanned case, about 1740.

WADY, WILLIAM. *Bristol*, 1763–1801. Partner with T. CHILETT till 1772; watch.

WADDY, JNO. *London*, 1730.

WAGDON, STEPHEN. C.C. 1724.

WAGGITT, CHARLES. *York*, f., 1818.

WAGGITT, MICHAEL. *Richmond, Yorks.*, 1753.

WAGGITT, MICHAEL. *York*, 1822.

WAGNER, BERNARD HENRI. *Paris*, end eighteenth century–1836. Able maker of Turret clocks; invented gear shaping machine.

WAGNER, E. M. *Berne*. Watch, pendulum vibrating under dial, very fine painting on enamel over balance-cock, about 1760.

WAGNER, J. Born 1800, settled in Paris 1821; died 1875.

WAGNER, JOHAN HEINRICH, à *Pirna*. Square table clock, about 1650.

WAGNER, MICHAEL. *Breslau*. Master 1681, died after 1704; made watches with moving hour figures; stand clock; watch movement, Arts Museum, Prague.

WAGNON, JEAN PIERRE. *Geneva*, about 1775–92.

WAGSTAFF, EDWD. Apprenticed 1650 to Edward East, C.C.

WAGSTAFF, THOMAS. *33 Gracechurch St.*, 1766–94. Long plain mahogany case clock in the Kasan Cathedral, St. Petersburg; bracket clock playing four tunes at the hour, black wood case; in the Pierpont Morgan collection is a repeating watch in silver pierced cases, the thumb piece or opener of the outer case being a diamond; there are a number of long-case clocks by him in America, generally in the possession of Quakers and their descendants; Wagstaff was a Quaker, and members of the Society of Friends, when visiting London, were accustomed to lodge at Wagstaff's house, and on their return frequently took one of his clocks with them; watch, h.m., 1770, with cap and two train wheels of silver.

WAHLSTROM, JAKOB. *Stockholm*. Born 1745, died 1815; watch; court clock.

WAIGHT, WM. *Birmingham*. Watch, 1792.

WAIN, J. *Queen St.*, 1774.

WAIN, WM. *Burslem*, 1803.

WAINWRIGHT, HUMPHRY. *Bunny, Nottingham*. Musical clock, about 1790.

WAINWRIGHT, JNO. *Manchester*, 1765.

WAINWRIGHT, JOHN. C.C. 1679.

WAINWRIGHT, JOHN. *Nottingham*, 1780–99. Long-case clock; watch.

WAINWRIGHT, SAMUEL. *Northampton*. a. 1763–95; watch.

WAIT, JNO., & SON. *Gun Dock, Wapping*, 1765–72.

WAITHMAN, ANTHONY. *Leeds*, 1830.

WAKEFIELD, ROBT. *Tanfield, Durham*, 1820.

WAKEFIELD, TIMOTHY, 1811, f.

WAKEFIELD, WM. *Lancaster*, 1782, f.

WAKELIN & GARRARD. *Panton St.*, 1800–05.

WAKELIN & TAYLOR. *Panton St.*, 1788–94.

WAKELING, SAMUEL. *London*. C.C. 1767–86.

WAKER, PETER. *London*. Apprenticed 1656, C.C. 1663.

WAKLIN, —. Lantern clock, about 1700.

WALBANK, WILLIAM. *London*. Apprenticed 1759, C.C. 1767, died 1806.

WALDEGRAVE, THOS. Apprenticed 1654 to Thos. Belson, C.C.

WALDEN, THOMAS. *Dorchester*, 1620–39. Keeper of town clock.

WALDOE, JOHN. C.C. 1677.

WALDRON, JOHN. *38 Cornhill*, 1790–82. Watch, gold case, *repoussé*, about 1770.

WALDRON, JOHN. *London*. Apprenticed 1756, C.C. 1763–88; watch.

WALE, ANDREW. Apprenticed 1664 to Rich. Ricord, C.C.

WALFORD, J. G. *Banbury*, 1790–1832.

WALFORD, JOHN. C.C. 1717.

WALFORD, THOS. C.C. 1690.

WALKDEN, THOMAS. Apprenticed 1682 to Dorcas Bouquet, C.C. 1694.

WALKER, ALLEN. *London*. Watch, Schloss collection, handsome *repoussé à jour* outer case, 1738; gold watch, three-case, 1782.

WALKER, CHAS. *Coventry*, 1815.

WALKER, D., & SON. *49 Red Lion St., Clerkenwell*, 1806–16; *46 Clerkenwell Close*, 1820.

WALKER, EZEKIEL. *Lynn*, 1770–1804. Wrote an article in *Nicholson's Journal* on longitude and the use of chronometers.

WALKER, GEO. *Hull*, 1822.

WALKER, GEORGE. *London*. Apprenticed 1684.

WALKER, GEORGE. *Dublin*, 1774–95. Watch.

WALKER, GEORGE. C.C. 1683.

WALKER, J. Musical watchmaker, *7 Nassau St., Soho*, 1820.

WALKER, JAMES. *Montrose*, 1820–37.

WALKER, JAS. C.C. 1632; lantern clock, inscribed 'James Walker in Lowthbery, fecit'.

WALKER, JNO. *Newcastle-on-Tyne*, 1770.

WALKER, JNO. Watch-case maker, *York*, f., 1772.

WALKER, JOHN. *London*. C.C. 1632; lantern clock.

WALKER, JOHN. *London*. Apprenticed 1764, C.C. 1771.

WALKER, JOHN, son of Wm. *London*. C.C. 1788–93.

WALKER, JOHN. *Fleet St.*, and afterwards at the *White Horse and Bell*, near *Cheapside Conduit*. C.C. 1717; inventor of a lamp clock, 1710–30.

WALKER, JOHN. *Newcastle-on-Tyne*, 1795.

WALKER, JOHN. *29 Gloucester St., Queen's Sq.*, 1816.

WALKER, JONADAB. C.C. 1687.

WALKER, JONAH. Apprenticed to Langley Bradley; C.C. 1734.

WALKER, JOS. *Nantwich*, 1800.

WALKER, JOSEPH. *Workington*, about 1790–1847. Watch movement, Buckley collection.

WALKER, JOSEPH. *1 Warwick Court, Holborn*, 1790–94.

WALKER, PETER. Apprenticed 1681 to Andrew Savory, C.C.; lacquered long-case clock, about 1730.

WALKER, R. *London*. Watch, 1800.

WALKER, ROBERT. *York*, 1820.

WALKER, SAMUEL. *London*. 1699 C.C.

WALKER, T. *Louth*, 1790.

WALKER, THOMAS. *London*. 1689 C.C.

WALKER, THOMAS. *London*. Apprenticed 1796, C.C. 1803.

WALKER, THOMAS. *17 Castle St., Oxford St.*, 1815.

WALKER, THOS. & SON. Same address, 1820–30.

WALKER, WILLIAM. *London*. Apprenticed 1752, C.C. 1759.

WALKER, WM. *38 Fetter Lane*, 1790–94.

WALKER, WM. *Loughborough*. Watch, 1804.

WALL, B. *Richmond*, 1800.

WALL, JNO. Apprenticed 1676 to Thos. Davis, C.C.

WALL, JNO., & CO. *Coventry*, 1810.

WALL, JOHN. *London*. Apprenticed 1798, C.C. 1809; livery C.C. 1812.

WALL, PETER. *Västerås*, 1758–88.

WALL, WM. *Wandsworth*. Patented an escapement in 1817 (No. 4,097).

WALL & ALNEY. *New Bedford, Mass.*, 1820–23.

WALL & WESTLAKE. *Chatham*. Watch, 1805.

WALLACE, BLACKETT. *Brampton*, 1760.

WALLACE, HY. *Royal Exchange*, 1775.

WALLACE, JOHN. *Leven*. Born 1766, died 1835.

WALLACE, MICHAEL. *Chester-le-Street*, 1770.

WALLACE, THOS. *Brampton*, 1780–1810.

WALLBANK, WILLIAM, son. *London*. Apprenticed 1786, C.C. 1796.

WALLEN, J. *Henley-on-Thames*, 1790. Watch.

WALLEN, WILLIAM. *Henley-on-Thames*, 1725. Also *Reading*, 1756. Watch, Ashmolean Museum.

WALLEN, WILLIAM. *London*. Apprenticed 1728, C.C. 1738.

WALLÉN, JOHAN. *Stockholm*. Born 1752, died 1816. Watch.

WALLER, J. *17 Shoreditch*, 1790.

WALLER, RICHARD. Sun and moon watch, said to have belonged to William of Orange; another, showing regulator on dial, about 1740.

WALLEY, SAM. *Manchester*, 1770.

WALLINGTON, SAM. Apprenticed 1689 to Jno. Shaw, C.C.

WALLIS, HENRY. *Red Lion St.*, 1765–68.

WALLIS, JACOB. *London*. Clock, about 1780.

WALLIS, JNO. *14 Skinner St., Bishopsgate*, 1825–40.

WALLIS, PETER. *Fleet St.*, 1737–40.

WALLIS, WILLIAM. C.C. 1715.

WALLITT, RICHARD. C.C. 1693.

WALLOON, H. *London*. Watch, 1812.

WALMSLEY, ALEX. *London*, f. of Lancaster, 1779.

WALTER, NICHOLAS. Oval watch in the British Museum, about 1620; subscribed to incorporation of C.C. 1630.

WALTERS, HENRY. *Charleston, U.S.A.*, 1757. From *London*. Clocks and watches.

WALTERS, JNO. Apprenticed 1638 to Thos. Howse; C.C. 1645.

WALTERS, JOHN. *London*. Bracket clock, about 1750, strikes one at the hour, plays a tune every three hours.

WALTHALL, JNO. Apprenticed 1684 to Wm. Coward, C.C.

WALTON, CHRISTOPHER. *24 Ludgate St.*, 1823–35.

WALTON, J. *London*. Watch, 1807.

WALTRIN, CHARLES HENRY, son. *Paris*. Master 1767–89.

WALTRIN, JOSEPH. *Paris*. Juré 1773.

WALTRIN, LOUIS RENÉ. *Paris*. Master 1771–89.

WANFIELD, EDMD. Apprenticed 1655 to Nich. Coxeter, C.C.

WANFORD, JNO. Apprenticed 1686 to Ed. Whitfield, C.C.

WANGERIN, CARL FRIEDRICH. *Berlin*, 1785–1801. Clock.

WANGERIN, JOHAN GOTTLIEB. *Stockholm*, 1759; *Linköping* and *Falun*, 1773–94.

WANNER, JOHANN GEORG. *Augsburg*. Comp. 1733, master 1746–70.

WANOSTROCHT (WONOSTROCHT), VINCENT. *London*. Apprenticed 1796, livery C.C. 1812.

WANSEY, HY. Apprenticed 1662 to Jno. Hiccock, C.C.

WAPLES, —. *London*, a. 1765. Watch.

WAPLES, NATHANIEL. *Philadelphia*, 1817–19.

WARBURTON, JNO. *Liverpool*, 1818.

WARBURTON, WILLIAM. C.C. 1693.

WARD, ALEXANDER, son. *London*. Apprenticed 1683, C.C. 1692–1719; watch, Denham collection.

WARD, ANTHONY. *Truro*. Long-case clock, about 1700.

WARD, ANTHONY. *New York*, f., 1724–50; then JOHN.

WARD, BENJAMIN. *London Rd., Southwark*. Fine bracket clock, about 1770.

WARD, BENJAMIN. *London Rd., Southwark*, 1780; *45 Upper Moorfields*, 1790–1808.

WARD, EDWARD. *London*. Apprenticed 1723, C.C. 1732.

WARD, EDWD. C.C. 1638.

WARD, HENRY. *Blandford*. A well-known clockmaker, from about 1775 to 1820; in 1814 the Society of Arts awarded him a silver medal and five guineas for equation work for clocks.

WARD, HENRY. *York*, f. 1830.

WARD, ISAAC. *Philadelphia*, 1811; then JEHU.

WARD, JAS. *Birmingham*. Watch, 1790.

WARD, JOHN. *New St.*, C.C. 1731.

WARD, JOHN. *London*. Apprenticed 1721, C.C. 1730.

WARD, JOHN. *London*. Apprenticed 1722, C.C. 1731.

WARD, JOHN. *London (Cripplegate)*. C.C. 1772, livery C.C. 1774, master C.C. 1797, died 1813.

WARD, JOHN. *39 Greek St.*, 1790–94.

WARD, JOHN. *9 Fore St.* Master C.C. 1797.

WARD, JOSEPH, f. of New York, 1735.

WARD, NATHAN. *Freybury (Maine?)*, 1801.

WARD, RICH. *27 Banner St.*, 1826–42.

WARD, RICHARD. *London*, 1729. Insolvent.

WARD, RICHARD. *Winchester*. Long-case clock, about 1770.

WARD, RICHARD. *Liverpool*, 1780.

WARD, RICHARD. *New Broad St.*, 1780; *18 Tower St.*, 1790–94.

WARD, RICHARD. *Bath* to 1776; *Dublin*, 1776–95.

WARD, RICHARD. *Liverpool*, 1790–1818. Watch.

WARD, ROBERT. *19 Abchurch Lane, Cannon St.*, 1762–85.

WARD, ROBERT. Musical clockmaker, *20 Plumtree St., Bloomsbury*, 1790.

WARD, THOMAS. *Baltimore, U.S.A.*, 1777. Clocks and watches.

WARD, THOS. C.C. 1632.

WARD, W. JOHN. *Barbican*. Livery C.C. 1766; a tiny pair-case gold watch, diameter of a sixpence, nearly a ball, inscribed 'W. J. Ward, London', about 1780.

WARD, WILLIAM, son of Edw. *London (Holborn Hill)*. C.C. 1767–94; watch, S.M.S.K.

WARD, WILLIAM H. *Liverpool*, 1796–1829. Watch.

WARD, WILLIAM. *London*. Apprenticed 1793, C.C. 1800.

WARD & GOVETT. *Philadelphia*, 1813.

WARDEN, ROBT. *London*. Watch, 1790.

WARDEN, SAMUEL. *London* and *Lewes*. Apprenticed 1763, C.C. 1785.

WARDEN, THOMAS. 1691.

WARDEN, WM. Apprenticed 1666 to Thos. Loomes, C.C.

WARE, ROBERT. C.C. 1701.

WAREHAM, JOHN. *18 Davies St., Berkeley Sq.*, 1816–23.

WAREING, JAS. *Liverpool*, 1818.

WARFIELD, JOHN. *London*. Apprenticed 1629 under B.C.–1662.

WARHAM, WILLIAM. *London*. Apprenticed 1765, C.C. 1773.

WARMINGHAM, ANDREW. *Manchester*, 1775.

WARNE, JAMES. *7 Queen St., Cheapside*, 1760–85. Repeating watch, Pierpont Morgan collection.

WARNE, NICH. Apprenticed 1680 to Hy. Adeane, C.C.

WARNE, ROBT. Apprenticed 1693 to Sam Stevens, C.C.

WARNER, CUTHBERT. *Baltimore, U.S.A.*, 1799–1807. Watch.

WARNER, GEORGE T. *New York*, 1795–1806. Watch.

WARNER, JNO. *Draycott*. Made the church clock at Chipping Campden, Gloucestershire, for £8, 1695.

WARNER, JOHN. *Golden Anchor*, near *Temple Bar*. C.C. 1682–92.

WARNER, JOHN. *Temple Bar*. Apprenticed to Wm. Warner 1689; C.C. 1696.

WARNER, THOS. *Chipping Campden*. Descendant of Jno. of Draycott.

WARNER, WM. C.C. about 1675.

WARNER & HINDS. *Dublin*, late eighteenth century–1824.

WARNES, ROBERT. *2 Leicester Sq.*, 1822–25.

WARNITZER, CARL FRIEDRICH. *Berlin*, 1816–47.

WARR, ROBERT. *London*. 1713 C.C.

WARREN, JNO. Apprenticed 1693 to Richd. Medhurst, C.C.

WARREN, RICHARD. C.C. 1668.

WARREN, THOMAS. *London*. Apprenticed 1788, C.C. 1803.

WARREN, THOS. Apprenticed 1667 to Ben Bell, C.C.

WARREN & SON. *Canterbury*, 1820–40.

WARRINGTON, J. & S. R. *Philadelphia*, 1823–25.

WARRINGTON, JOHN. *Philadelphia*, 1811.

WARWICK, JAS. Apprenticed 1656 to Ed. Gilpin, C.C.

WARWICK, JAS. *Newcastle Place*. Watch, h.m., 1829.

WARWICK, WM. *88 London Wall*, 1793.

WASBERG, ERIC, son. *Eskilstuna*. Born 1727, died about 1790; long-case clock.

WASBERG, JOHANNES. *Lilla Malma*. Born 1696, died 1774. Two long-case clocks.

WASHBORN, JOHN. 30-hour clock, about 1710. Several generations of Washborns were clockmakers of Gloucester; long-case clock by Nat. Washbourne, Gloucester, about 1750.

WASHBOURN, GEO. *Gloucester*. Watch, 1770.

WASHBOURN, THOMAS. *Queen Sq., Bartholomew Close*, 1750–60.

WASHINGTON, MARK. Apprenticed 1687 to Rich. Brown, C.C.

WASSE, THOS. Apprenticed C.C. 1682.

WASSELL, J. *9 Picket St., Strand*, 1830.

WASTNESSE, FRANCIS. Apprenticed 1671 to Jno. Trippett, C.C.

WATCH, JOHN. *London*. 1726 C.C.

WATERFALL, W. & J. *Coventry*, 1814.

WATERMAN, WM. Apprenticed 1682 to Amos Winch, C.C.

WATERS, JOHN. C.C. 1646; to him in 1687 was apprenticed the elder Jno. Ellicott.

WATERS, JOHN. C.C. 1682.

WATERS, JOHN. *4 Cornhill*, 1775.

WATERS, JONATHAN. Apprenticed 1686 to Ed. Hine, C.C.

WATERS, ROBERT. *London*. Apprenticed 1729, C.C. 1767. *Cheshunt* in 1793.

WATERS, THOMAS. C.C. 1731.

WATFORD, JNO. C.C. in 1729 Jas. Freeman was apprenticed to him.

WATKIN, OWEN. *Llanrwst*. Watch, 1791.

WATKINS, —. *126 Drury Lane*, 1820.

WATKINS, GEORGE. *London*. Apprenticed 1703, C.C. 1716.

WATKINS, JOHN. *9 Giltspur St., Smithfield*. Received £33 from Society of Arts for improvement in the spring detent escapement, 1804; livery C.C. 1820; *Great Sutton St.*, 1838.

WATKINS, JOHN. *London*. Apprenticed 1801, C.C. 1810.

WATKINS, JOSEPH. *21 Great Warner St., Coldbath Fields*, 1800–19; he attested the value of Earnshaw's Improvements in 1804.

WATMORE, WILLIAM. *London*. 1672 C.C.

WATRIN, JOSEPH. *Paris*. 1768 juré. See VATRIN.

WATSON, *67 Red Lion St., Clerkenwell*, 1820.

WATSON, ALEXANDER. *London*. Apprenticed 1735, C.C. 1742–45.

WATSON, CHRISTOPHER. *York*, of., 1822.

WATSON, EDWARD. *London.* Apprenticed 1696, C.C. 1704.

WATSON, EDWARD. *6 King St., Cheapside*, 1820–42. Livery C.C. 1820.

WATSON, FRANCIS. *Beverley*, 1822.

WATSON, G. *Nassau, New Providence, U.S.A.*, early nineteenth century.

WATSON, GEORGE. *London* (*Southwark*). Livery C.C. 1822.

WATSON, HENRY. *Blackburn*, 1760.

WATSON, JAMES. *24 Arundel St., Strand*, 1788–1805.

WATSON, JNO. *Kirby Moorside*, 1770.

WATSON, JNO. *Pocklington*, 1770.

WATSON, JOHN. *Michael's Alley, Cornhill.* Apprenticed to John Hacker; C.C. 1744–85.

WATSON, JOHN. *London.* C.C. 1781–85; watch movement, V. & A.

WATSON, ROBT. Apprenticed 1689 to Jno. Warner, C.C.

WATSON, SAMUEL. *Coventry.* Admitted C.C. 1692; inventor and maker of a curious piece of clockwork; in 1682 is mentioned a payment of £215 for a clock he sold to his late Majesty, Charles I; the clock "showes the rising and setting of the sun and many other motions" (*Lond. Gaz.*, Sept. 4–8, 1690). Very small bracket clock in black case, about 1710, inscribed 'Samuel Watson, London'. "Lost the 15th Instant on Cheshunt Common, a gold watch in a black Shagreen case with Gold Studs, tyed with a black Taffaty Ribon to a Steel Hooke, Engraven on the Inside Samuel Watson. Whoever gives notice of the same to Mr. Howell at the Penny Post Office in St. Martin's Lane, Westminster, shall have a Guinea Reward" (*Lond. Gaz.*, Oct. 18, 1687). Under the head of Celestial Motions, Derham speaks of an elaborate and curious piece by Mr. Watson; in the Wetherfield collection is an 8-day bracket quarter clock, chiming on three bells, by Samuel Watson, London, dating from about 1700.

WATSON, THOMAS. *23 Aldersgate St.*, 1785–94.

WATSON, THOS. Apprenticed 1662 to Jno. Hillersden.

WATSON, THOS. *Blackburn*, 1770.

WATSON, WALTER. C.C. 1720; Hatton, in 1773, mentions the astronomical or complicated work of Mr. Watson as being rare.

WATSON, WILLIAM. C.C. 1691; long-case clock, chiming quarter and half hours, about 1720; name-plate inscribed 'William Watson, Angel Alley in Leadenhall Street'.

WATSON, WILLIAM. *Elland* (*Yorks.*), 1822–40.

WATSON, WM. *Blackburn*, 1780.

WATSON, WM. *Glasgow*, 1785.

WATSON, WM. *190 Strand*, 1793–1805.

WATSON, WM. *York*, f., 1815.

WATTES, JOHN. C.C. 1664.

WATTS, BROUNKER. Apprenticed to Joseph Knibb, 1684; C.C. 1693; a repeating watch by him in the Guildhall Museum, engraved cap, gold dial, well engraved and pierced inner case; 8-day long-case clock; watch, h.m., 1720; long-case clock, signed 'Brounker Watts & Co.', about 1720. "Lost on the 21st instant, in Gutter Lane, Cheapside, a Silver Watch with Tortoiseshell Outcase, with a Lion Rampant and 3 oaken leaves for the coat, engraven on the Backside, made by Bro. Watts; the movements are the hours, minutes, and seconds. Whoever brings it to the sign of the Goldsmiths' Hall in Gutter Lane, or to Bro. Watts in Fleet Street, shall have a Guinea reward" (*Lond. Gaz.*, April 27–30, 1696).

WATTS, CHAS. *Frome*, 1770.

WATTS, JAMES. C.C. 1720.

WATTS, JNO. *Stamford*, 1690.

WATTS, JOHN. *Canterbury.* a. 1751, died 1775; watch.

WATTS, JOHN. C.C. 1712.

WATTS, RICHARD. C.C. 1680. "Lost the 22nd Inst. out of a Gentleman's Pocket, a Silver Pendulum Watch, with the name Rich. Watts. Whoever brings it to Charles Ferrers at the Chirurgeons Arms in Queen Street, London, shall have 20s. Reward" (*Lond. Gaz.*, Aug. 30, 1688).

WATTS, ROBERT. *London.* Apprenticed 1764, C.C. 1785.

WATTS, ROBERT. *Stamford*, 1760.

WATTS, THOS. Apprenticed 1681 to Ed. Stanton, C.C.

WATTS, THOS. *Lavenham.* Long-case clock, about 1730.

WATTS, THOS. *St. Edmunds Bury*, 1760.

WATTS, WALTER. Apprenticed 1688 to Chas. Halstead, C.C.

WATTS, WILLIAM. *8 Cripplegate Buildings*, 1770; *8 Fore St.*, 1775.

WATTS, WM. *Wotton-under-Edge.* Watch, 1779.

WAUGH, JOHN. *London.* Apprenticed 1795, C.C. 1804.

WAUGH, JOHN. *Wigton*, 1820–41.

WAUGH, WILLIAM. *Liverpool*, about 1820.

WAVRE, JEAN JACQUES ANDRÉ, son. *Neuchâtel*, 1755–1828.

WAWEN, GERVAS. Apprenticed 1689 to Richd. Conyers, C.C.

WAY, JAS. Apprenticed 1681 to Dan Lecount, C.C.

WAY, JNO. Apprenticed 1659 to Thos. Taylor, C.C.

WAYCOTT, PETER. *Ashburton*, 1799. Also at *Holne, Staverton* and *Totnes.* Many long-case clocks.

WAYCOTT, ROBERT, son. *Paignton* and *Torquay*, about 1820–45. Long-case clocks.

WAYLAND, HENRY. *Stratford, Essex.* Apprenticed to Wm. Bushman, 1820.

WAYLETT, JAS. *7 Mark Lane*, 1793.

WAYLETT, JOHN. *9 Ball Alley, Lombard St.*, 1795–1810.

WAYND, RICHARD. *York*, f., 1667.

WEADON, WILLIAM. C.C. 1695.

WEAKMAN, WILLIAM. C.C. 1661.

WEARE, JOSEPH. *Wincanton*, 1813. Died 1886.

WEARNE, RICHARD. *Camborne*, about 1750.

WEATHERALL, THOS. *Hexham*, 1796.

WEATHERBY, DAVID. *Philadelphia*, 1806–25.

WEATHERBY, THOMAS. *Berwick-on-Tweed*, about 1770–95. Watch. Also WEATHERLY.

WEATHERHEAD, LEONARD. *Kirby Lonsdale.* Died 1774.

WEATHERHILT, JOHN. *Liverpool*, about 1780–1829. Long-case clock.

WEATHERHILT, S. *Liverpool.* Watch, about 1760.

WEATHERLEY, DAVID. *Philadelphia*, 1811.

WEATHERLEY, THOS. *Berwick*, 1775.

WEATHERLEY & ROBERTS. *9 Poultry*, 1800–05.

WEATHERLEY & SON. *9 Poultry*, 1810–23.

WEAVER, CUTHBERT. C.C. 1682.

WEAVER, FRANCIS. *London.* Apprenticed 1733, C.C. 1748.

WEAVER, GEO. *Fetter Lane.* C.C. 1730.

WEAVER, SIMON. Apprenticed 1684 to Jas. Wightman, C.C.

WEBB, AMBROSE. *London.* Apprenticed 1712, C.C. 1721.

WEBB, ARTHUR. *86 Portland St.*, 1780–94.

WEBB, BENJAMIN, 'maker to His Majesty', *21 St. John's Sq.*, 1778–90. Hon. f., C.C. 1787; *3 Red Lion St.*, 1806–10. Watch, with compass in dial, inscribed 'By the King's Patent'; this appears to have been patented by Hy. Peckham in 1798.

WEBB, CHARLES. *Cheapside*, 1737–40.

WEBB, DAN. Apprenticed 1692 to Peter Southworth, C.C.

WEBB, EDWARD. *Chewstoke.* Lantern clock; dated 1681, long-case clock, 'Edward Webb Chewstoke 1688', lantern movement, plays three tunes on eight bells; surmounting them is one larger bell.

WEBB, EDWARD. *Bristol*, 1734. Died 1761; watch.

WEBB, EDWARD. *245 Tottenham Court Rd.*, 1816–20.

WEBB, FRANCIS. *Watlington, Oxon.* Hood clock, about 1710; long-case clock, about 1730.

WEBB, ISAAC. Apprenticed 1650 to Richard Masterton; C.C. 1660.

WEBB, J. *Seward St.*, 1820.

WEBB, MATT. *Chewstoke.* Lantern clock, 1688.

WEBB, PETER. *28 Throgmorton St.*, 1753–68.

WEBB, ROBERT. *14 Berkeley St., St. John Sq.*, 1815–19.

WEBB, THOMAS. *London.* Apprenticed 1776, C.C. 1789, livery C.C. 1802.

WEBB, THOMAS. *London.* 1794 C.C.

WEBB, THOS. In 1672 Joana Deacle was apprenticed to Eliza, widow of Thos. Webb, C.C.

WEBB, WM. *London.* Watch, about 1780.

WEBB, WM., & CO. *19 Wilderness Row*, 1816–20.

WEBBER, W. *Woolwich*, 1817.

WEBER, DAVID. *Augsburg*, 1685. Juré 1702, died about 1726.

WEBSTER. Many generations of this family have carried on business in the city of London from 1675.

WEBSTER, GEORGE. C.C. 1703.

WEBSTER, HENRY. C.C. 1709.

WEBSTER, HENRY, brother. *London.* C.C. 1742.

WEBSTER, JNO. *Whitby*, 1822.

WEBSTER, JOHN. *London.* Apprenticed 1686, C.C. 1695–1700.

WEBSTER, JOHN. Apprenticed 1676 to Thos. Tompion; C.C. 1695 (see PENNY, R.).

WEBSTER, JOHN. *Liverpool*, 1800–16. Watch.

WEBSTER, MARGARET. *London.* C.C. 1711.

WEBSTER, RICHARD, son of William Webster. C.C. 1779; livery 1787.

WEBSTER, RICHARD. *26 Change Alley*, 1784–1840. Livery C.C. 1810.

WEBSTER, ROBERT. Brother C.C. 1675; watch, G.M.; in 1688 Sarah Webster was apprenticed to Robt. Webster her father, C.C.

WEBSTER, ROBT. C.C. 1721.

WEBSTER, ROBT. *Whitby, Yorks.* In 1772 he patented (No. 1,021) a repeater.

WEBSTER, SAMUEL. Livery C.C. 1766.

WEBSTER, THOMAS. C.C. 1709.

WEBSTER, THOS. *Dundee.* 'cnocksmith', 1689.

WEBSTER, WILLIAM. From the books of the C.C. he appears to have been apprenticed to Jno. Barnett and to have been free in 1710, though the following extract from the *Lond. Gaz.*, from Nov. 24–28, 1713, seems to refer to him; "On the 20th instant, Mr. Tompion, noted for making of all Sorts of the best Clock and Watches, departed this Life: This is to certify all Persons of whatever Quality or Distinction that William Webster, at the Dial and Three Crowns in Exchange Alley, London, served his apprenticeship, and served as a Journeyman a considerable Time with the said Mr. Tompion, and by his Industry and Care is fully acquainted with his secrets in the said Art." William Webster was warden C.C. 1734, and died in office 1734.

WEBSTER, WILLIAM. *26 Change Alley.* C.C. 1734; master 1755; livery 1766.

WEBSTER, WILLIAM, son of and apprenticed to William Webster, C.C. 1763; in the Pierpont Morgan collection are two watches by William Webster, one a clock-watch and the other, of later date, a repeater; they are both in finely pierced gold cases.

WEBSTER & SON. *11 Change Alley*, 1781–1800.

WECKHERLIN, ELIAS. *Augsburg*, 1646–88. Alarum watch, British Museum; oval watch, Fränkel collection; octagonal crystal watch; watch movement, Ilbert collection; clock movement, Damiano collection; silver gilt *repoussé* watch formerly in Shandon collection.

WEEDON, WM. Apprenticed 1686 to Nat. Barrow; C.C. 1695.

WEEKES, THOMAS. C.C. 1654; fined by C.C. in 1657 for abuse to Warden Coxeter.

WEEKES, THOMAS, son. *London.* C.C. 1688–1710.

WEEKS, —. *Coventry St., London.* English clock movement, dead beat escapement, in French Empire case, about 1810.

WEEKS, CHARLES. C.C. 1713.

WEEKS, JOHN. Clock-case maker, *Great Sutton St.*, 1810–23.

WEEKS, JOHNSON. C.C. 1683.

WEGELIN, G. JOSUA. *Augsburg*, about 1670–1700. Fine square table clock; repeating clock; clock, Cassel Landes-Museum; gilt metal case bracket clock, Prestige collection.

WEIGHT, HENRY. *Gloucester*, 1810–42.

WEINHARD, MARTIN. *Graz.* Fine long-case clocks with *repoussé* dials, about 1714.

WEISSE (WEISE), CARL AUGUST, brother. *Dresden.* Master 1814, died 1860; balanced hand with watchwork for mysterious clock, M.P.S., Dresden.

WEISSE (WEISE), CARL HEINRICH. *Dresden.* Born 1722, master 1756, died 1784; gilt engraved watch.

WEISSE (WEISE), CHRISTIAN EHREGOTT. *Dresden.* Master 1788, died 1818.

WEISSE (WEISE), CHRISTIAN HEINRICH. *Dresden.* Master 1775, died 1793.

WEISSE (WEISE), CHRISTIAN HEINRICH, son of Chr. H. *Dresden.* Born 1768, master 1803, died 1842; court clock 1820.

WEISSE (WEISE), JOH. CONRAD SALOMO, brother. *Dresden.* Master 1814, died 1855; court clock 1845.

WEITZE, JOHANN GOTTLIEB. *Berlin*, 1785–1801. Clock.

WELBORNE, WILLIAM. *Leather Lane, Holborn.* In 1813 fined £15 by C.C. for refusing to take up the livery, 1800–13.

WELCH, WILLIAM. *London (Skinner St.).* Apprenticed 1802, C.C. 1811, livery C.C. 1824.

WELCHER, FREDRIC. *Eskilstuna*, 1788–1824. Long-case clock.

WELCOME, JOHN. C.C. 1705.

WELDER, RICHARD. *St. Anne's, Westminster.* Livery Turners' Company 1774.

WELDER, THOS. *40 Foster Lane*, 1780–85.

WELDON, SAML. *London.* Watch, Nelthropp collection, date letter, 1774.

WELKE. See DE WELKE.

WELLDON, W. Silver *repoussé* and tortoise-shell watch, 1744.

WELLDON, W. Pierpont Morgan collection, bridge over balance, Dutch style, about 1790.

WELLE, ROBT. *30 Red Lion Sq.*, 1825.

WELLENIUS, ERIC. *Norrköping.* Born 1731, died 1802; watch with crown and monogram of Gustavus III on cock Chamb. collection; watches Nord. Museum and National Museum, Stockholm.

WELLER (& MAGSON, long narrow marquetry case clock, about 1705).

WELLER, FRANCIS. *Philadelphia*, 1777. From *London.* Watch.

WELLER, GEORGE. *Exeter*, eighteenth century. Long-case clock.

WELLER, JOHN. C.C. 1713; the Prince of Wales exhibited at the Guelph Exhibition a clock-watch by him; on the back three plumes, 'Ich Dien' and also 'Pro Principe Semper'.

WELLER, THOMAS. *Croydon*, 1802–24.

WELLINGTON, JAS. *London*. Watch, 1778.

WELLINGTON, JOHN. C.C. 1726.

WELLS, ALFRED. *Boston, U.S.A.*, 1803–05 C.C. Watch.

WELLS, A. & G. *Boston, U.S.A.*, 1806. Watch.

WELLS, ISAAC. C.C. 1668.

WELLS, JOHN. C.C. 1682; long-case clock; arabesque marquetry, about 1700.

WELLS, JOHN. *4 Cheapside*, 1758–68.

WELLS, JONATHAN, 1700.

WELLS, JOSEPH. C.C. 1667.

WELLS, MATTHEW. *Russell Court, Covent Garden*, 1755–60.

WELLS, NEDDY. *Shipley*. Fine long-case clock, about 1700.

WELLS, WM. C.C. 1689.

WELSH, ROBT. *Dalkeith*, about 1790.

WELSH, WILLIAM. *New York*, 1805. Watch.

WELTZIEN, DANIEL. *Hamburg*, 1754. Died 1771; watches and clocks and instrument maker.

WENDAY, ANNE. Apprenticed in 1685 to Hy. Jevon and Christian his wife, C.C.

WENHAM, DAVID. *Dereham*. Long-case clock, about 1780; watch, Rochdale Museum, h.m., 1819.

WENHAM, JOHN. *Dereham*. Watch, 1763.

WENTLE, JAS. *147 Aldersgate St.*, 1793.

WENTWON, J. *London*. Watch, Blackburn Museum, 1780.

WENTWORTH, GEORGE. *London (Fleet Market)*. Apprenticed 1729, C.C. 1738–56.

WENTWORTH, WOMBWELL. Apprenticed 1656 to Hy. Harland.

WENTWORTH, WM. *Sarum*. Long-case clock, about 1740.

WENTZ, HILARY. *Philadelphia*, 1823.

WERNER, CASPAR. *Nürnberg*, 1528–57. Dopplmayr says he died in 1545. If this be not an error, there was a second maker of the same name in 1557. A locksmith who gained great repute by his small watches (kleine Uhren).

WESENCRAFT, JOSEPH. *Dublin*, 1692.

WESSMAN, HANS. *Stockholm*. Born 1736, died 1805; four bracket clocks.

WEST, JACOB. *London (Ludgate St.)*. Apprenticed 1749, C.C. 1757–71.

WEST, JAMES. *London*. Apprenticed 1732, C.C. 1741–65; watch movement, Ilbert collection.

WEST, SAMUEL. *Royal Exchange*. Livery C.C. 1766; 8-day bracket clock, verge escapement, in black wood case, with brass mounts and brass dial silvered, has a landscape painted at the top, with two men in the foreground playing tennis, the ball being represented by a small brass button, attached by a wire to the staff of the verge, and working backwards and forwards in a slot cut in the dial; 1750–67.

WEST, THOMAS. *London*. Completed his apprenticeship in 1694; long-case clock, Wetherfield collection, about 1700; large metal pair-case watch, elaborate dial and movement, inscribed 'Thomas West, London', about 1710; long-case clock, about the same date, with the signature, 'Thos. Westt, London'; long marquetry case clock, about 1700.

WEST, THOMAS. *London*. Apprenticed 1687, C.C. 1695, died 1723.

WEST, THOMAS. *Reading*, a. 1762–about 1780. Watch and long-case clock.

WEST, THOMAS G. *Philadelphia*, 1819.

WEST, THOS. *Reading*. Watch, 1780.

WEST, WILLIAM. C.C. 1697.

WEST, WILLIAM. *London*. Apprenticed 1774, C.C. 1782.

WESTBERG, CLAES. *Västerås*, 1816–46.

WESTBROOK, WILLIAM. *London*. Long-case clocks, about 1700 and 1730.

WESCOTT, JNO. *London*. Long-case clock, about 1750.

WESTCOTT, JOHN. C.C. 1703.

WESTEN, ROBERT. *London*. C.C. 1721.

WESTER, LORENTS ADAMSON. *Stockholm*, 1780–95. Four bracket clocks, one in Nord. Museum.

WESTERMAN, ANDREAS. *Laholm*, 1750–70.

WESTERMAN, RICHD. *Leeds*, 1828. He retired in 1850.

WESTFIELD, ROBT. *St. James's St., Clerkenwell*. Patented in 1813 (No. 3,732) a cylinder wheel with teeth of unequal height.

WESTLAKE, JOHN. *33 High St., Boro.*, 1820; *41 Castle St., Boro.*, 1835–42.

WESTMORE, ROBT. *Lancaster*, 1761.

WESTMORE, ROBT. 1785, f.

WESTMORE, THOS. 1779, f.

WESTOBY, JOHN. C.C. 1677. "Lost out of a Gentleman's Pocket on the 12th Inst., between the Rose Tavern without Temple Bar and West Smithfield, a silver Minute Pendulum Watch in tortoise-shell case, inlaid with this figure in the bottom, viz.: A man driving a Hog into a House, the name of the watch, Westobe, London. It had a narrow Ribband flowered with silver and gold to hand the key by when lost. Whoever brings it to Edw. Crouch, Watchmaker, under St. Dunstan's Church, in Fleet Street, shall have a guinea Reward" (*Post Boy*, 13th April, 1697).

WESTON, ABRA. *Lewes*, 1783. Watch.

WESTON, ABRAM. *Lewes*. Long-case clock, about 1690.

WESTON, JAMES, son. *Newark*, 1825–40. Long-case clocks.

WESTON, SAM. *Stratford*. Clock, in lacquer case, about 1730.

WESTON, WILLIAM. *Sowerby (Yorks)*. Born 1789, died 1859.

WESTON, WM. *Newark*, 1810. Afterwards JAMES; then JAMES and JOHN.

WESTON & WILLIS. Enamellers, *23 Greenhill's Rents*, Smithfield, 1810.

WESTPHALL, FERDINAND. *Philadelphia*, 1819. Watch.

WESTWOOD, RICHARD. C.C. 1691; maker of lantern clocks.

WESTWOOD, ROBERT. *Prince's St., Leicester Sq.* In 1829 he patented (No. 5,850) an 8-day watch with large barrel extending over the train.

WETHERED, GEO. Apprenticed 1677 to Hy. Wynne, C.C.

WETHERELL, NATHAN. *Philadelphia*, 1830–40.

WETHERELL, THOS. Apprenticed 1664 to Jno. Clarkson, C.C.

WETHERELL & JANAWAY. *114 Cheapside*, 1785–94.

WETHERSTON, JNO. *Newcastle-on-Tyne*, 1770.

WEYLETT, JOS. *7 Mark Lane*, 1790–94.

WHALEY, BARNABY. Apprenticed 1675 to Jno. Fitter C.C.

WHALLEY, SAM. *Manchester*, 1770–86.

WHAM, W. *13 Knightsbridge*, 1820.

WHAPLETT, THOS. Prior to 1686 he presented a tankard to C.C.; *Wharton Rd., London*. Watch, 1785.

WHARTON, JNO. Apprenticed 1687 to Thos. Speakman, C.C .

WHATLEY, ROBERT, son. *London*. Apprenticed 1814, C.C. 1821.

WHEATLEY, CHARLES. *London*. C.C. 1819.

WHEATLEY, JOHN. Apprenticed to Jeffery Bailey, C.C. 1668.

WHEATLEY, JOHN. *18 Bull and Mouth St.*, 1820–25.

WHEATLEY, WILLIAM. C.C. 1698; long-case clock, about 1700, signed 'Georgius Wheatley'.

WHEATON, CALEB. *Providence, U.S.A.*, 1785–1822.

WHEELER, JOHN. C.C. 1680.

WHEELER, THOMAS. Apprenticed to Nich. Coxeter, 1647; C.C. 1655; master 1684; lantern clock, dolphin frets, altered balance escapement, inscribed 'Thomas Wheeler, near the French Church in Londini'; died 1694.

WHEELER, THOS. *114 Oxford Street*, 1793. Marquetry long-case clock by him with peculiar high dome, surmounted by carved gilt ornaments, about 1700. Wetherfield collection.

WHEELER, VINCENT. Apprenticed 1683 to Ed. Holliday, C.C.

WHEELER, WILLIAM. *London.* Apprenticed 1767, C.C. 1774. Watch.

WHEELS, SAM. *London.* Calendar watch, 1790.

WHEELWRIGHT, OXFORD. *London*, 1701. C.C.; watch.

WHELLAN, THOS, 'in Bishops Gate Street, Londini'. Lantern clock, about 1680.

WHELLER, JOHN. *17 Shoreditch*, 1787–94.

WHELLER, MAURICE. Invented a rolling clock, 1684.

WHELLER, WHEYNARD, EDWD. *London.* watch, 1784.

WHICHCOTE, SAMUEL. *Crane Court, Fleet St.* C.C. 1724; master in 1748.

WHICHCOTE, SAMUEL. *175 Fleet St.* Master C.C. 1764; livery 1766.

WHINFIELD, PHILIP. Apprenticed 1651 to Sam Davis, C.C.

WHIPHAM, THOS. *61 Fleet St.*, 1775.

WHIPHAM & NORTH. 1793.

WHIPP, THOS. *Rochdale.* Long-case clocks, 1820–42.

WHITAKER, EDWARD. *London.* C.C. 1712; watch.

WHITAKER, S. *12 Lang Lane*, 1830.

WHITBY, ROBT. *Chester*, 1814–18.

WHITCHURCH, SAMUEL. *Kingswood, Bristol*, 1760–80. Long-case chiming clock, phases of moon and high water at Bristol in arch, inscribed 'Samuel Whitchurch, Kingswood', presented to King Haakon of Norway by the Corporation of London in 1906.

WHITE, AMOS. *Fetter Lane.* C.C. 1730.

WHITE, CÆSAR. C.C. 1692.

WHITE, EDWARD. Apprenticed 1647 to Jno. White, C.C.

WHITE, J. *New York*, early nineteenth century. Long-case clock, M.M.A.

WHITE, JOHN. Brother C.C. 1647.

WHITE, JOHN. Apprenticed to Thomas Loomes and turned over to Thomas Bagley, C.C. 1670.

WHITE, JOHN. *London.* Apprenticed 1684, C.C. 1692.

WHITE, JOHN. Watch, 1829; *3 Northampton Ter., City Rd.*, 1838–42.

WHITE, JOSEPH. *Philadelphia*, 1811–17.

WHITE, JOSEPH. C.C. 1713.

WHITE, PEREGRINE. *Woodstock.* Long-case chimney clock, at top of dial list of tunes, 'Marquis of Granby' and others, about 1760, at Massachusetts.

WHITE, SEBASTIAN. *Philadelphia*, 1795.

WHITE, THOMAS. C.C. 1683; watch, gold *repoussé* case, outer case of shagreen, Schloss collection, 1743.

WHITE, WM. *306 Oxford St.*, 1830.

WHITEAR & RAVES. *30 Fleet St.*, 1790–94.

WHITEAVES, RICHARD. *30 Fleet St.*, 1804–40. Livery C.C. 1812.

WHITEBREAD, WILLIAM. *High Holborn.* C.C. 1728.

WHITEHEAD, CHAS. Apprenticed 1693 to Whitehead, C.C.

WHITEHEAD, EDWARD. *Wetherby*, about 1770–91. Long-case clock; watch.

WHITEHEAD, JOSEPH. *Liverpool*, 1796–1829. Watch.

WHITEHEAD, RICHARD. C.C. 1671.

WHITEHEAD, ROBT. *3 St. James's St., Clerkenwell*, 1810–15.

WHITEHEAD, SIMON. Apprenticed 1677 to Richard Whitehead, C.C.

WHITEHEAR, RICHARD. C.C. 1648; seems to have settled at Reading; lantern clock, dolphin frets, inscribed 'Richard Whitheare, Reading, fecit'.

WHITEHURST, JOHN. *Derby*, and afterwards of *Bolt Court, Fleet St.*, F.R.S.; a well-known maker of turret and other clocks, inventor of tell-tale clocks; born at *Congleton* 1713, died in *London* 1788; his descendants continued the business at *Derby*; clock in 'The Chauntry', Newark, inscribed 'Made 1807, and fixed here 1808, by Mr. John Whitehurst, senior, of Derby'.

WHITEHURST & SON. *Derby.* Rack-lever watch, about 1805; Whitehurst of Derby was one of three clockmakers invited to tender for the Westminster clock in 1846.

WHITELAW, DAVID. *Edinburgh*, 1815–25. A maker of repute; published in *Edinburgh Phil. Jl.* 1823 'An account of a new escapement'.

WHITELAW, JAMES. *Edinburgh.* Born 1776, died 1846.

WHITEMAN, THOMAS. *London.* 1706–32 C.C. Watch.

WHITESIDE, THOMAS. *Liverpool*, 1777–1805. Watch.

WHITESIDE, JAS. *Ormskirk*, 1800.

WHITEWICK & MOSS. *24 Ludgate Hill*, 1790–94.

WHITFIELD, EDW. C.C. 1663.

WHITFIELD, J. *London*, about 1749.

WHITFORD, GEORGE. *1 Smithfield Bars*, 1830–42.

WHITFORD, SAMUEL. *London (Soho).* C.C. 1819–25.

WHITFORD, THOMAS. *1 Smithfield Bars*, 1790–1800. Whitford & Son, 1810–23.

WHITHAM, JONATHAN. *Sheffield*, 1770.

WHITING, RILEY. *Winchester* and *Winsted, U.S.A.*, 1798–1820.

WHITLACH, JNO. Admitted C.C. 1637; presented a cup to the Company prior to 1652.

WHITLOCK (WHITTLOCK), JAMES. *London.* Apprenticed 1697, C.C. 1704.

WHITLOCK (WHITTLOCK), JAMES, son of James. *London.* C.C. 1744.

WHITLOW, SEARLE. *London.* Apprenticed 1819, C.C. 1826.

WHITMAN, EZRA. *Bridgewater, U.S.A.*, 1790–1840.

WHITMORE, WM. *Northampton.* Watch, 1811.

WHITNEY, ASA. *New York*, 1805. Watch.

WHITNEY, EBENEZER. *New York*, 1822.

WHITNEY, MOSES. *Boston, U.S.A.*, 1822–25. Watch.

WHITTAKER, EDWARD. C.C. 1711.

WHITTAKER, JAMES. Long-case clock, about 1700.

WHITTAKER, WILLIAM, f. of New York, 1731–55.

WHITTINGHAM, EDW., 'at the Dial in Oxford Road near Berwick St.', 1770.

WHITTINGHAM, WILLIAM. Cited by C.C., he not having served ten years, 1688.

WHITTLE, THOMAS. Apprenticed to Henry Harper, C.C. 1683. "Lost in Lincoln's Inn Fields, on the 15th Instant, betwixt 5 and 6 o'clock, a Pendulum Watch in a black seal skin case, studded with silver, a cipher on the back and lined with Red Sattin, made by Angil Whitle. Whoever brings it to Mr. Wilson's, at the Fleece Tavern, in Fleet Street, shall have a guinea Reward" (*Lond. Gaz.*, Oct. 22, 1688).

WHITTON, CHAS. Apprenticed 1690 to Jno. Higgs, C.C. 1698–1709.

WHITTON, RICHARD. *London.* Apprenticed 1731, C.C. 1740–48.

WHITWAY, SAML. *Cheapside*, 1735-40.

WHITWELL, ROBERT. Apprenticed to Robt. Grinkin, 1641; C.C. 1648; in 1651 he presented one cup and three spoons to the Company; early minute-hand watch.

WHITWELL, WM. Apprenticed 1649 to Robt. Whitwell, C.C. In 1678, at *Cutler's Hall*, HUGH WHITWELL, son of Robert, late Citizen and clockmaker, was bound apprentice to Edmond Whitwell, member of the Cutlers' Company.

WHOLLEY, JONATHAN. *London*. C.C. 1825.

WHOOD, ISAAC. Apprenticed 1680 to Thos. Fenn, C.C.

WIBERG, ANDERS PETTER. *Falun*, 1824-46.

WIBERG, JOHAN. *Norrköping*, 1787-91. Watch.

WIBRANDT, JACOB. *Leuwarden*. Small watch, about 1630.

WICH, GABRIEL. *Nantwich*, 1780.

WICHELL, SAMUEL. *St. James's St.* Marquetry long-case clock, about 1710; another long-case clock bears the address, 'Pickadilly'.

WICHENS, JOHN. *London*. Apprenticed 1749, C.C. 1755.

WICHOTE. See WHICHOTE.

WICKES, ALFRED NELSON. *London* (*Clement's Lane*). Apprenticed 1821, C.C. 1833.

WICKES, JOHN. *27 Cannon St.* Livery C.C. 1786; *8 Clement's Lane*, 1804.

WICKES, JOHN HAUGHTON. *8 Clement's Lane*, 1806. Livery C.C. 1810; J. H. Haughton & Son, same address, 1810-35.

WICKES, JOHN. *London* (*Cannon St.*). Apprenticed 1771, livery C.C. 1784, died 1807.

WICKES, JOSEPH. *London* (*Islington Rd.*). Apprenticed 1786, C.C. 1794.

WICKES, W. G. *114 Leadenhall St.*, 1823.

WICKES, WILLIAM GIBSON. *London* (*Bermondsey*). C.C. 1814-25.

WICKES, WM. *Threadneedle St.*, 1680. Geo. Wickes, his son, removed to *Leadenhall St.*, and from thence, in 1720, to the *King's Arms, Panton St.*. For continuation of this business see WICKES & NETHERTON, PARKER & WAKELIN, WAKELIN & TAYLOR, WAKELIN & GARRARD, and GARRARD, ROBT.

WICKMAN, ANDERS. *Stockholm*. Born 1746, died 1796.

WICKS (& NETHERTON, *Panton St.*, 1753-60).

WICKS, WILLIAM. *London*. Long-case clocks, about 1800.

WICKS, WM. Watch-case maker, *34 Percival St.*, 1820.

WICKS & BISHOP. *170 New Bond St.*, 1820-25.

WICKSTEED, EDWARD. *9 Fore St.*, 1768; *114 Bunhill Row*, 1795.

WIDDOWSON, JOSEPH. *100 Fleet St.*, 1830.

WIDEMAN (WIDTENMAN), JOHAN. *Stockholm*, 1675. Died 1717; German; clockmaker to the King; three long-case clocks, one National Museum, Stockholm; wall clock Nord. Museum, illuminated Sidenbladh; six watches. Also WIDMAN. *v.* WIEDEMANN.

WIDENHAM, RICHARD. *6 East St.*, *Clerkenwell*, 1830; *13 Lombard St.*, 1835.

WIDMAN, JACOB. *Augsburg*, 1680. Clock inscribed 'Jacob Widman, Augustanus', an English dial engraved 'William Barbaull, London', had been added.

WIEDEMAN, T. In the Horological Museum, Copenhagen, is a curious watch signed 'Theodor Wiedeman, Wienna'. It has three balances geared together, and dates probably from about 1700.

WIELAND, JOHANN GEORG. *Salem, U.S.A.*, about 1780. Bracket clock, Furt. Museum.

WIELANDY, ABRAHAM. *Paris*. Master 1767-89.

WIGAN, THOMAS. *Bristol*, 1760. Died 1790; watch.

WIGGIN, ROBT. *Colne, Lancs.*, 1818.

WIGGINTON, JNO. Apprenticed 1663 to Bernard Gernon.

WIGGINTON, WM. *11 St. James's Walk*, 1806-20.

WIGHT, JAS. *12 Union St., Southwark*, 1806-20.

WIGHTMAN, GEORGE, son of Thos. *London*. C.C. 1738.

WIGHTMAN, JAS. Apprenticed in 1663 to Ed. Eyston, C.C. 1670.

WIGHTMAN, JNO. Apprenticed 1688, to Jno. Jones, C.C.

WIGHTMAN, THOMAS. *George Yard, London*, about 1800.

WIGHTMAN, THOMAS. *95 St. Martin's Lane*, 1798-1818.

WIGHTMAN, THOS. Apprenticed 1692 to Hy Hester, junr.; watch, about 1700; gold watch, h.m., 1745.

WIGHTMAN, WILLIAM. C.C. 1696; long-case clock, about 1700.

WIGHTWICK & MOSS. *24 Ludgate St.*, 1775-1804 (John Wightwick, hon. freeman C.C. 1781).

WIGNALL (or WIGNELL), JNO. Also F., *Ormskirk*. Long-case clocks, 1760-85.

WIGRAM, THOS. *67 St. James's St.*, 1804.

WIGSON, WILLIAM. *London*. C.C. 1781, livery C.C. 1792.

WIGSON, WILLIAM. *Colchester*, 1792-1825 C.C.

WILBUR, JOB. *Newport, U.S.A.*, 1815-40.

WILCOCKS (WILCOCK, WILCOX), DANIEL, son. *London* (*Aldersgate St.*). Apprenticed 1748, C.C. 1757-72.

WILCOCKS, T. *2 Red Lion St., Clerkenwell*, 1817.

WILCOCKS (WILCOCK, WILCOX), THOMAS. *London*. Apprenticed 1716-48 C.C.

WILD, E. (tools). *2 St. John's Sq.*, 1798-1810.

WILD, JAS. *Frith St., Soho*, 1790.

WILD, JOSEPH. *Macclesfield*. William Travis was apprenticed to him about 1794.

WILD, MRS., 'in the New Market, near the Borough Market, Southwark', 1780.

WILDE, J. *Preston*, 1814.

WILDE, JOSH. *Macclesfield*, 1782.

WILDE, MICHAEL. *Wakefield*, 1775.

WILDE, SAML. *Islington*. Maker of lever escapements, a remarkably good workman and sound horologist, 1800-42.

WILDE, THOMAS. *London* (*Borough Market*). Apprenticed 1755, C.C. 1766. Watch.

WILDE, THOMAS. *Reading*. From 1775-99. Lacquer inn clock.

WILDE, WM. C.C. 1717-24.

WILDER, EZRA. *Hingham, U.S.A.*, 1800.

WILDER, JNO. C.C. 1790.

WILDER, JOSHUA. *Hingham, U.S.A.*, 1780-1800. Long-case clock, Museum of Fine Arts, Boston, illuminated Milham.

WILDER, RICHARD. *Richmond Buildings, Soho*. C.C. 1776; watch, h.m., 1785.

WILDER, WILLIAM. *London*. a. 1760-88. Watch.

WILDERS, J. *London*. Many watches, Dutch style, 1760-80.

WILDMAN, CHAS. *6 Great Newport St.*, 1800.

WILDMAN, SAMUEL. *63 Cheapside*, 1760-88.

WILDMAN, WATKINSON. *Cheapside*, 1753-63.

WILKES, JNO. *London*. Watch, 1740.

WILKIE, ROBERT. *Cupar-Fife*, 1792-1830.

WILKIE, ROBERT. *London*. C.C. 1819.

WILKIESON, JOHN. *Kendal*, 1771.

WILKINS, GEORGE. *36 Frith St., Soho*, 1810-25. Card, British Museum.

WILKINS, JNO. Apprenticed 1693 to Jno. Howse, C.C.

WILKINS, JOHN. *Bath*, 1770.

WILKINS, JOHN. *Marlborough*, 1770.

WILKINS, JONATHAN. *London* (*Plumbtree Ct., Holborn*) Apprenticed 1744, C.C. 1753-65.

WILKINS, RALPH. *Stamford*, 1775.

WILKINS, ROBT. C.C. 1670.

WILKINS, ROBT. *London*. Watch, 1750.

WILKINS, SPEED. *London*. Apprenticed 1694, C.C. 1704.
WILKINS, WILLIAM. *London*. C.C. 1748, livery C.C. 1794–1840.
WILKINS, WM. *Devizes*, about 1730.
WILKINS & SON. *Long Acre*, 1805.
WILKINSON, —. *Wigton*, about 1740.
WILKINSON, EDWARD. Apprenticed C.C. 1655.
WILKINSON, J. *London*. Watch, 1765.
WILKINSON, JAMES. *18 Castle St.*, 1830; *19 Farringdon St.*, 1835.
WILKINSON, JNO. *Leeds*. Long-case clock, about 1695.
WILKINSON, T. *32 Piccadilly; 8 Cornhill*, 1793; 1825–30.
WILKINSON, THOS. *London*. Fine musical long-case clock, about 1760; plays at the hour either Lady Coventry's Minuet, or the 101st Psalm.
WILKINSON, THOS. *York*, f., died 1776.
WILKINSON, WILLIAM. C.C. 1718.
WILKINSON, WILLIAM. *London*. C.C. 1749.
WILKINSON, WILLIAM. *Penrith*, about 1790 C.C.
WILKINSON, WILLM. *Leeds*. Long-case clock; dial, 16½ in.
WILKINSON, WM. *Congleton*, 1780.
WILKS, WM. *Wolverton*, near *Stratford-on-Avon*. In 1779 he was paid £20 for "erecting and setting up a church clock" for the parish of Clarendon.
WILLANS, JOSEPH. *London*. 1785–1807 C.C.
WILLANS, WILLIAM. *London*. 1792 livery C.C., died 1810.
WILLANS, WILLIAM, son of Jos. *London (City Rd.)*. Apprenticed 1800, C.C. 1807, livery C.C. 1810.
WILLARD, —. *Philadelphia*, 1778. Watch. Also WILLAR.
WILLARD, —. *Boston, U.S.A.* Several generations beginning with BENJAMIN about 1770. In the *Boston Gazette* for 22nd Feb. 1773, was announced, "Benjamin Willard, at his shop in Roxbury Street, pursues different branches of clock and watch work, has for sale musical clocks playing different tunes, a new tune every day of the week and on Sunday a Psalm tune. These tunes perform every hour without any obstruction to the motion or going of the clock, and new invention for pricking barrels to perform the music, and his clocks are made much cheaper than any yet known. All the branches of the business likewise carried on at his shop in Grafton." He was followed early in the nineteenth century by Aaron, who had a shop in Boston, and by Simon. 'Willard' or 'Banjo' clocks, well known in the neighbourhood of Boston, are of the hanging variety, and have below the dial a long trunk, narrow for the greater part of its length, and a square panelled enlargement near the bottom, which is in some instances painted with figures or a landscape, in others having inserted a circular glass through which the motion of the pendulum bob could be seen. Many of these bore the name, 'Willard, Jr.'
WILLARD, AARON, brother. *Roxbury* and *Boston, U.S.A.* Born 1757, died 1844. *Boston* in 1800. Simon was the most important maker of the three brothers, who were famous in Massachusetts; they made a few long-case clocks and high mantel or shelf clocks, but mainly 'banjo' clocks, with a circular top, narrow trunk, and wide rectangular base; many illuminated Milham; succeeding members of the family are among the following.
WILLARD, AARON, son of Aaron. *Roxbury* and *Boston*, 1816–63. Clock. Continued his father's business.
WILLARD, BENJAMIN. *Grafton, Lexington* and *Roxbury, U.S.A.* Born 1743, died 1803; long-case clocks and musical clocks. Also WILLIARD.
WILLARD, BENJAMIN, son of Simon (1). ——, about 1825.
WILLARD, EPHRAIM. *Medford, Roxbury* and *New York*. 1755–1805; long-case clocks.

WILLARD, JOHN. *Boston, U.S.A.*, 1803. Watch.
WILLARD, SIMON, brother. *Grafton* and *Roxbury*. Born 1753, died 1848; made long-case clocks and in 1801 invented the 8-day banjo clock and discontinued long-case clocks; made turret clock for the University of Virginia at Charlottsville.
WILLARD, SIMON, son of Simon. *Boston*. Born 1795. Watch. In Boston from 1828.
WILLARD & NOLAN. *Boston*, 1806. Clock.
WILLCOCKS, RICHARD. *46 Red Lion St., Clerkenwell*, 1785–1800.
WILLCOCKS, THOMAS. *London (Goswell St.)*. C.C. 1819–24.
WILLEBRAND, JOHANN MARTIN. *Augsburg*, 1682. Died 1726; dials British Museum, M.M.A., Old Ashmolean Museum and Stuttgart Museum; pedometer, Old Ashmolean Museum.
WILLEN, JOHAN. *London*. Watch, 1720.
WILLERTON, SKULL & GREEN. *21 New Bond St.*, 1783–94.
WILLETT, JAS. *London*. Watch, silver cock, 1727; long Oriental lacquer case clock, about 1730.
WILLIAMS, ALEXANDER. *Chichester*. C.C. 1790, livery C.C. 1798, died 1811.
WILLIAMS, CHARLES. *London (Aldersgate St., Silver St. and Monkwell St.)*. Apprenticed 1763, C.C. 1771–78, died a. 1787. Watch.
WILLIAMS, DAVID. 'Endfield', 1774.
WILLIAMS, DAVID. *Newport, U.S.A.*, 1810.
WILLIAMS, E. *London*, mid-eighteenth century. Watch.
WILLIAMS, E. *1 Albany, Saville Row*, 1825.
WILLIAMS, EVAN. *Newport, Wales*, about 1780–1830. Long case-clocks.
WILLIAMS, GEO. *7 Bridgwater Sq.*, 1817.
WILLIAMS, GEORGE. *Bristol*, 1782–1830.
WILLIAMS, GEORGE. *Bristol*, 1801–30.
WILLIAMS, GEORGE *London (Monkwell St.)*. Apprenticed 1793, C.C. 1801, livery C.C. 1813.
WILLIAMS, JAS. *35 Goodge St.*, 1794.
WILLIAMS, JAS. *14 Market Place, Bath*, 1798.
WILLIAMS, JNO. *Leeds*. Long-case clock, about 1700.
WILLIAMS, JNO. *11 Old Bond St.*, 1769.
WILLIAMS, JNO. ('from Mr. Graham's'). *Clements, Lancs.*, 1770.
WILLIAMS, JOHN. *168 Shoreditch*, 1800–04.
WILLIAMS, JOHN. Watch-case maker, *56 Great Sutton St.*, 1820.
WILLIAMS, JOHN. *4 Amen Corner*, 1821; *70 St. Paul's Churchyard*, 1831.
WILLIAMS, JOHN. *London*. Apprenticed 1782, C.C. 1792.
WILLIAMS, JOHN. *London*. Apprenticed 1784, C.C. 1796.
WILLIAMS, JOHN. *London*. Apprenticed 1746, C.C. 1753–63.
WILLIAMS, JOHN. *London*. C.C. 1768–1802.
WILLIAMS, JOHN. *London*. Apprenticed 1808, C.C. 1815.
WILLIAMS, JOSEPH (*Ireland*). C.C. 1685.
WILLIAMS, P. *Lombard St.*, 1770.
WILLIAMS, R. *Liverpool*. Watch, 1810.
WILLIAMS, REES. *Cwmwysg, Brecknock*, 1737–1827. Long-case clock.
WILLIAMS, THOMAS. *Chepstow*, 1750–85. From *Bristol*.
WILLIAMS, THOS. Apprenticed 1689 to Isaac Day, C.C.
WILLIAMS, THOS. *Haverfordwest*. 1780–90.
WILLIAMS, WILLIAM. *Cwmwysg, Brecknock*, 1774–1825.
WILLIAMSON, CHRISTOPHER. *London*. C.C. 1821; watch.
WILLIAMSON, EDWARD. Apprenticed to Jonathan Puller for seven years ending 1694; long marquetry case clock, about 1710; long-case clock, about 1700, by Dave Williamson.

WILLIAMSON, J. *London*. Watch, 1790.

WILLIAMSON, JOHN. C.C. 1682; late-seventeenth-century alarm watch, signed 'John Williamson in Leeds', V. & A., silver case pierced and engraved.

WILLIAMSON, JOHN. *Edinburgh*. Apprenticed 1778–1825.

WILLIAMSON, JOSEPH. A first-rate horologist, inventor and maker of equation clocks; outside of the craft his reputation here was not commensurate with his merits; he held the appointment of watchmaker of the cabinet of Charles II of Spain, for whom he made a 400–day long-case equation clock; master of C.C. 1724, and died in office, 1725.

WILLIAMSON, MICHAEL, son of Robert. *London*. C.C. 1714.

WILLIAMSON, ROBERT. *St. Bartholomew Lane*. Apprenticed 1658 to Jas. Letts; C.C. 1666, master 1698; watch with a shagreen case in the British Museum; another in case of white agate, about 1740, Pierpont Morgan collection.

WILLIAMSON, SHAW. *Dublin*, a. 1777–95. Watch, Ilbert collection.

WILLIAMSON, THOMAS. C.C. 1668. "Lost on the 19th day of August, from Mr. Will. Clinch's house at Epsom, a silver Minute Pendulum Watch with a scollop-shell case studded with silver, made by Thomas Williamson, London, with a silk string and a silver seal with a Coat of Arms. Whoever brings it to Mr. Robert Dingly, watchmaker in George Yard, Lombard Street, shall have 2 guineas Reward" (*Lond. Gaz.*, Sept. 5–8, 1692).

WILLIAMSON, TIMOTHY. *196 Fleet St.*, 1769–75; *90 Great Russell St.*, 1788. Large watch, silver-gilt case, taken from Peking.

WILLIAMSON, WILLIAM. C.C. 1664.

WILLIAMSON, WILLIAM. *London*. C.C. 1689–about 1710; watch, Glasgow Art Galleries.

WILLIAMSTON, RALPH. C.C. 1706; watch, 'R. Williamston, London', V. & A., h.m., 1749.

WILLIARME, PIERRE. Admitted C.C. 1648. A correspondent of *Notes and Queries* has a MS. return of strangers dwelling within Aldersgate Ward, October 1635, which states that Peter Williarme, watchmaker, resided in the parish of St. Botolph, and had then been in England twelve years, being a native of Geneva.

WILLIN, WM. *Percival St.*, 1800–11. Livery C.C. 1810.

WILLING, —. *London*. Calendar watch, one hand, nicely engraved dial, Schloss collection, about 1720.

WILLIS, AMBROSE. Apprenticed 1687 to Thos. Baldwin, C.C.

WILLIS, GEORGE. *London*. Apprenticed 1716.

WILLIS, JNO. Enameller, *23 Greenhill's Rents*, 1823; afterwards *Percival St.*

WILLIS, MARY. *81 Bishopsgate St., Without*, 1822–25.

WILLIS, RICHARD. *Truro*, about 1770–85.

WILLIS, RICHARD OCKSHUT. *London*. Apprenticed 1752, C.C. 1760.

WILLIS, WILLIAM. *London*. 1716 C.C.

WILLMOT, JOHN. *86 St. Margaret's Hill*, 1762–75.

WILLMOT, THOMAS. C.C. 1715.

WILLOUGHBY, BENJ. *Bristol*. Watch, about 1730; another, about 1765.

WILLOUGHBY, BENJAMIN. *High Cross*. Apprenticed 1676 to Robt. Dingley, C.C.

WILLOUGHBY, JOHN. C.C. 1686.

WILLOUGHBY, JOHN. *London*. Apprenticed 1704, C.C. 1711–28.

WILLOWE, JOHN. *Fleet St.* One of the first wardens C.C., master 1635; watch, British Museum, in a fancy case of escallop shape, 1620–40.

WILLS, JNO. Apprenticed 1682 to Wm. Hillier, C.C.

WILLS, JOHN. *London (St. John's Lane)*. Apprenticed 1758, C.C. 1770, died 1824.

WILLS, R. *Truro*, 1775–95.

WILLSHIRE, JAMES. *Glasshouse Yard, Goswell St.*, 1769–80; long-case clock.

WILLSHIRE, JAMES. *19 High Holborn*, 1781.

WILLSON, GEORGE. C.C. 1692.

WILLSON, JAS. *London*. Watch, 1768.

WILLSON, JOHN. *King's Head Court, Holborn*. C.C. 1714.

WILLSON, THOMAS. C.C. 1659, assistant 1685.

WILLSON, WILLIAM. C.C. 1693.

WILMER, THOS. *London*, about 1760.

WILMOT, GEORGE. Apprenticed to Jeffery Baily and turned over to John White; C.C. 1670.

WILMOT, ISAAC. Apprenticed 1662 to Jno. Bayes, C.C.

WILMOT, JNO. Apprenticed 1676 to G. Stubbs, C.C., *Upper Rosoman Street*, about 1810.

WILMOT, STEPHEN. *London*. Apprenticed 1667 to Ed. Staunton; C.C. 1674; 30-hour long-case clock, square dial, about 1720.

WILMOT, THOS. Apprenticed 1653 to Thos. Loomes, C.C.

WILMSHURST, STEPHEN. *Basingstoke*, 1770.

WILMSHURST, T. *Deal*. Watch, Schloss collection, 1746.

WILMSHURST & SON. *Brighthelmstone* (now *Brighton*); watch, 1765.

WILSON, ALEXANDER. *132 Drury Lane*. Hon. f., C.C. 1781; maker of a verge watch, pair of brass cases, with outside case of tortoise-shell, on which are representations of ferns, 1770–94.

WILSON, CHARLES. *London*. Apprenticed 1811, C.C. 1824.

WILSON, EDWD. Apprenticed 1663 to Richard Nau; C.C. 1670.

WILSON, G. *17 Craven Buildings, Drury Lane*, 1820.

WILSON, GEORGE. C.C. 1730.

WILSON, JAMES, against St. Lawrence Church; C.C. 1723; Susannah Smith was apprenticed to his wife Hannah Wilson in 1747.

WILSON, JAMES. *Hawick*. Born 1748, died 1821.

WILSON, JAMES. *4 King St., Westminster*, 1770–94; hon. f., 1781.

WILSON, JAMES. *Ettrick*. Born 1748, died 1821.

WILSON, JAMES. *London (Threadneedle St.).* C.C. 1802–09; watch.

WILSON, JAMES. *27 Threadneedle St.*, 1804; *Sweeting's Alley, Royal Exchange*, and afterwards at *53 Lombard St.*; died 1810.

WILSON, JAS. *Nuneaton*, 1742.

WILSON, JAS. *Askrigg*. Died 1786.

WILSON, JN. *Ulverstone*, 1775.

WILSON, JNO. *Edinburgh*. Apprenticed to Andrew Brown in 1711.

WILSON, JNO. Clock in America, dating from about 1740, marked 'John Wilson from London'.

WILSON, JNO. *London*. Watch, 1772.

WILSON, JNO. *Dublin*. Watch, 1804.

WILSON, JOHN. *Corn Market, Belfast*, 1750, afterwards at *Linen Hall St., Belfast*.

WILSON (or WILLSON), JOSHUA. *London*. Apprenticed 1688 to Wm. Fuller, C.C.; lantern clock, finely engraved dial, about 1700; long clock, 11-in. dial, fine marquetry case, about 1705, Wetherfield collection; watch, h.m., 1707.

WILSON, NAT. Apprenticed 1658 to Edward East, C.C.

WILSON, NICH. *Kendal*, 1765.

WILSON, RICHARD. *York*, f., 1586.

WILSON, ROBERT, son of Josh. *London*. C.C. 1733; watch.

WILSON, THOMAS. *Guisborough*, 1790–1825. Long-case clock. Later T. & J.

WILSON, THOS. Apprenticed 1651 to Simon Hackett, C.C.

WILSON, THOS. *London.* Watch, 1791.

WILSON, THOS. *Spalding.* Clock, about 1800.

WILSON, TITUS. *Lancaster,* 1779, f.

WILSON, W. *38 Southampton St., Strand,* 1829–42. Afterwards Wilson & Gander. See JESSOP.

WILSON, WILL. *Kendal,* 1790.

WILSON, WILLIAM, his son, f., 1607.

WILSON, WILLIAM. *London.* C.C. 1809; watch.

WILTER, JOHN. Watch, G.M., silver dial, silver *repoussé* case, signed Cochin; another example, a silver *repoussé* pair-case watch, Dutch style; another, a calendar watch in the Schloss collection, has a painting of the Queen of the Poppies on the back of the case; watch, 1769; 1760–84.

WILTON, CLAY. C.C. 1697; watch, with embossed case by Cochin.

WILTON, JOHN. *London.* Watch, silver inner case, outer one green shagreen with *piqué* ornament, about 1767, Hilton Price collection.

WILTSHIRE & SONS. *136 Cornhill,* 1822–30.

WIMBLE, NEMIH. *Maidstone,* about 1760.

WIMEN, GEORGE. *Philadelphia,* 1820. Watch.

WIMER, ANDREW. *Philadelphia,* 1819. Watch.

WIMPER, DAVID. *Hammersmith.* Long-case clock, about 1740.

WINCH, AMOS. C.C. 1677.

WINCKLES, JNO. *London.* Watch, 1782.

WINDER, of *Lancaster:* THOS, 1795, f.; STEPHEN, 1823, f.; THOS, 1825, f.; WM. 1830, f.

WINDESS, *Lancaster:* THOS. 1795; STEPHEN, 1823; THOS, 1825; WM. 1830.

WINDOW, DAVID. *London.* C.C. 1718; watch.

WINDMILLS, J. & T. *Great Tower St.* (Thomas Windmills, master C.C. 1718); many excellent long-case clocks by them are to be met with; 1710–40.

WINDMILLS, JOSEPH. *St. Martin's-le-Grand,* afterwards in *Mark Lane.* Well known as a good maker of clocks and watches; C.C. 1671, master 1702; fine lantern clock; clock, engraved brass dial, on the upper part of which is inscribed 'Thomas Pardey, 1697'; another production is a bracket clock, inscribed 'Joseph Windmills, at Mark Lane End, next Tower Streete, Londini, Fecit'; long-case clock, 10-in. dial, bolt and shutter maintaining power, inlaid laburnum and olive wood case, sliding hood, with spiral pillars, about 1690; another with an 11-in. dial marquetry case, about 1700; in the British Museum is a handsome watch by him, silver dial, in which is a semicircular opening above the centre; through it appears a representation of blue sky, with the sun pointing to the hour by day, and the moon by night; tortoise-shell case; there is a similar watch by Joshua Hutchin. "Gold watch lost, made by Mr. Windmills, in Mark Lane. Give notice as above, or to Mr. Rudge, over against the Swan Tavern, in King's Street, Westminster" (*Lond. Gaz.,* April 25th, 1687).

WINDMILLS, THOMAS. Apprenticed to Joseph Windmills, 1686; C.C. 1695, master 1719; a repeating watch by him in the G.M.

WINDMILLS & BENNETT. Long-case clock, about 1725.

WINDMILLS & ELKINS. *London.* Bracket clock, about 1725.

WINDMILLS & WIGHTMAN. *London.* Long-case clock, about 1720.

WINDON, DANIEL. C.C. 1718.

WINDSOR, JAMES. *London.* Apprenticed 1778, C.C. 1787–96; watch.

WINEROW, WILLIAM. C.C. 1718.

WING, MARK. *27 Goswell St.,* 1816–42.

WINGATE, FREDERICK. *Augusta, U.S.A.,* 1800.

WINGATE, PAINE. *Boston, U.S.A.,* 1789; *Newburyport,* 1803.

WINGHAM, JOHN. *London.* C.C. 1785–1800.

WINGROVE, JNO. *St. John's Sq.,* C.C. 1730; watch, about 1745, inscribed 'Sarah Wingrove, London'.

WINKLEY, JNO. *Canterbury,* about 1760.

WINNE, HY. See WYNNE.

WINNOCK, DANIEL. C.C. 1707.

WINNOCK, JOSHUA. Apprenticed to Ahasuerus Fromanteel the Elder; C.C. 1672.

WINROWE, WM. *London.* Watch, 1760.

WINSMORE, JOHN. C.C. 1712.

WINSMORE, WILLIAM. *London.* Apprenticed 1699, C.C. 1712.

WINSON, THOS. *London.* Watch, 1782.

WINSTANLEY, ALEX. *Wigan,* about 1780.

WINSTANLEY, E. *London.* Watch, with minute circle inside hour circle, about 1780.

WINSTANLEY, EDWARD. *Liverpool,* 1770.

WINSTANLEY, EDWD. *Wigan,* 1820.

WINSTANLEY, JERE. Apprenticed 1687 to Jno. Wheeler, C.C.; long-case clock, about 1750, inscribed 'Winstanley, Holy Well, North Wales'.

WINSTANLEY, PETER. *Huyton.* Watch, silver balance-cock, about 1775.

WINSTANLEY, ROBT. *Ormskirk,* 1818.

WINSTENDLEY, THOS. *Modely.* Watch, h.m., 1774.

WINSTON, WM. 'Opposite the Cross', *Hereford,* 1770. Died 1785.

WINT, DAN. Apprenticed 1693 to J. Clowes, C.C.

WINT, DANL. 'At the Dial and Crown', *West Smithfield,* 1774.

WINTER, GEORG ERNST GOTTHELF. *Dresden.* Master 1808, died. 1856; town clock.

WINTER, ROBT. *59 Cannon St. Ratcliffe,* 1817.

WINTER, SAM. Apprenticed 1683 to Ed. Stanton, C.C.

WINTER, WM. Apprenticed to Robert Dingley, C.C.

WINTERHALDER, —. *London.* Watch, 1810.

WINTLE, DAVID. *London.* Clock, about 1680.

WINTLE, THOS. *9 Poultry,* 1760–68.

WINTWORTH, THOS. *Sarum.* Lantern clocks, 1700–40.

WIRGMAN, C. *5 George St.,* 1830.

WIRGMAN, C. & G. *31 Castle St., Holborn,* 1804.

WIRGMAN, G. *Hewitt's Court, Strand,* 1825.

WIRGMAN, PETER. *79 St. James's St.,* 1775–94.

WIRGMAN, THOMAS. *68 St. James's St.,* 1823.

WIRRALL, COPLEY. C.C. 1648.

WISE (or WYSE). Several generations among the early makers.

WISE (or WYSE), FEATHERSTONE. *Hull,* 1822.

WISE (or WYSE), JNO. Apprenticed 1638 to Peter Closon; C.C. 1646.

WISE (or WYSE), JOHN. C.C. 1669; clock, inscribed 'John Wise Londini, fecit', given to Zion College in 1672.

WISE (or WYSE), JOHN. C.C. 1683; on 1st Nov. 1693, "John Wise dwelling neere the popes head in Moore-fields citizen and clockmaker of London", became a joint surety for Richard Wise, Renter to the Cutlers' Company for 1693–94.

WISE (or WYSE), JOHN. C.C. 1710.

WISE (or WYSE), JOSEPH. C.C. 1687; in the same year was apprenticed to him the celebrated Langley Bradley.

WISE (or WYSE), LUKE. *Reading,* 1686; watch, about 1720, stolen from Newington Free Library.

WISE (or WYSE), LUKE. C.C. 1694.

WISE (or WYSE), MARK. C.C. 1719; *Wantage*, 1730.

WISE (or WYSE), MATTHEW. *London*. Watch, 1740; *Daventry*, 1780.

WISE (or WYSE), PETER, son of John. Admitted C.C. 1693, master 1725; bracket clock; 1693–1726.

WISE (or WYSE), RICHARD. C.C. 1679.

WISE (or WYSE), ROBERT. C.C. 1694.

WISE (or WYSE), THOMAS. *Fenchurch St.*; C.C. 1686; long-case clock in the Vestry of Westminster Abbey, square dial, rings round winding holes; another, signed 'Thos. Wise, Fenchurch St.', from the Dunn collection, fetched fifty-eight guineas at Christie's in 1912.

WISE (or WYSE), WILLIAM. *Wantage*, 1660–1703. Lantern clock.

WISEMAN, JOHN. C.C. 1647.

WISS, FRÈRES. *Geneva*, about 1775.

WISS & MENU. *Geneva*, 1790.

WISWALL, THOS. *20 Ely Pl.*, 1800.

WISWALL & CO. *52 Red Lion St.*, 1810.

WITCHELL, ROBERT. *London (Hatton Garden)*. Apprenticed 1735, C.C. 1744, livery C.C. 1766–72.

WITH, THOS. *London*. Fine bracket clock, date of the month hand, Sheraton case, about 1790.

WITHER, JAS. Apprenticed 1637 to R. Child, C.C.

WITHER, JOHN. C.C. 1699; maker of long-case clocks.

WITHER, RICHD. Apprenticed 1681 to Andrew Prime, C.C.

WITHERS, JOHN. *London (Blackfriars)*. C.C. 1790–1816.

WITHERS, WM. *London*. Long-case clock at the Church of the Cappucins, Cadiz, about 1760.

WITHERS, WM. *Bristol*, 1820–43. Lever watch in French case, about 1825.

WITNESS, FRANCIS. Apprenticed 1650 to Job Betts, C.C.

WITSON, H. *London*. Watch, 1825.

WITTAM, JAS. *Dublin*, 1695.

WITTE, JACOB NICOLAI. *Copenhagen*. Master 1699, died a. 1741; silver watch, National Museum, Copenhagen, illuminated Liisberg. Also VIET, VEIT and HUEIT.

WITTE, SAMUEL. C.C. 1660.

WITTINGHAM, CHAS. *London*. Watch, 1820.

WITTINGHAM, WM. *London*. Watch, about 1700.

WITTIT, JAMES. *London*. Watch, G.M., about 1750.

WIWEL, CHRISTIAN HENRY. *London*. C.C. 1823.

WOGDEN, STEPHEN. *Greenwich*. Small arch-dial, about 1730.

WOLF, J. *Wienne*. Maker of a book-shaped watch, 1627.

WOLF, JEREMIAS. *Vienna*. Born 1663, died 1724; automata maker; book watch; clock on pillar, Bernal sale; table clock, Webster collection.

WOLFE, JNO. *Noble St.* C.C. 1730.

WOLFE, JOSEPH. *Mitre Court, near Aldgate*, 1762–72.

WOLFF, AUGUST. *Kriegshaber*, 1756–70.

WOLFF, ÉTIENNE AUGUSTE. *Geneva*, about 1775–91.

WOLFF, PETER HEINRICH. *Berlin*, 1785–1801. Clock.

WOLFGANG, JOHANN. *Pollinger, Fridtberg*. Repeating watch, V. & A., about 1730.

WOLKSTEIN, DAVID. *Augsburg*. Associated with Dasypodius in the superintendence of the second Strassburg clock in 1570. He is said to have invented the Carillon.

WOLLER, MATT. *Coventry*, 1816.

WOLVERSTONE, BENJAMIN. Apprenticed to Richd. Richardson in 1647; C.C. 1656; alarum watch, silver dial, one hand, in the G.M.

WOLVERSTONE, JAMES. *London*. C.C. 1690.

WOLVERSTONE, JAS. C.C. 1670.

WOLVERSTONE, THOMAS. C.C. 1650.

WOLVERSTONE, THOMAS. *London*. Apprenticed 1667, C.C. 1670.

WOMERSLEY. Long-case clock, square dial, rings round winding holes, signed 'Geo. Womersley', about 1720.

WONTNER, JOHN. *Minories*. A well-known maker, 1770–1812; livery C.C. 1810.

WONTNER, JOHN, & SON. *125 Minories*, 1804–12. See also RENTNOW.

WONTNER, JOHN, son of John. *London*. Apprenticed 1798, C.C. 1807, livery C.C. 1810.

WOOBORN, GEO. *London*. Watch, 1798.

WOOD, BARTHOLOMEW. *London (Barbican)*. Apprenticed 1773, C.C. 1780–92.

WOOD, BENJ. *London*. Watch, 1800.

WOOD, DAN. *London*. Watch, 1745.

WOOD, DAVID. *Newburyport, U.S.A.*, 1765–90.

WOOD, F. *Scarboro'*, 1770–90.

WOOD, G. *Exon*. Lantern clock, about 1660.

WOOD, GEO. *19 Orange Grove, Bath*, 1798.

WOOD, HENRY. C.C. 1720.

WOOD, JAMES. Apprenticed to Joseph Miller, C.C. 1745; Samuel Alvey apprenticed to him in 1750; watch, G.M., about 1780.

WOOD, JAMES. *Brighton*. 1799 C.C.

WOOD, JAS. Apprenticed 1668 to Ed. Gilpin, C.C.

WOOD, JNO. *Grantham*, 1780.

WOOD, JOHN. C.C. 1701.

WOOD, JOHN. *Stroud*, 1769–92. Watch.

WOOD, JOHN. *Liverpool*. 1796–1824 C.C.; watch.

WOOD, JOHN. *Philadelphia*, 1770–93. "Clocks, watches, gold & silver work made, mended, and sold at the sign of the Dial, the corner of Front & Chestnut Streets".

WOOD, JOHN. *32 Minories*, 1775.

WOOD, JOSEPH. *Scarboro'*. Long-case clock, about 1760, Mr. Logan.

WOOD, JOSEPH. *Bristol*, 1775. died 1791; watch.

WOOD, JOSIAH. *New Bedford*, 1797–1810.

WOOD, PETER. Long-case clock, about 1750.

WOOD, RICHD. Apprenticed 1651 to Jno. Cooke, C.C.

WOOD, ROBERT. C.C. 1670.

WOOD, ROBERT. *Horse Shoe Alley, Moorfields*, 1785–1810; fine bracket clock, about 1790.

WOOD, ROBERT. *4 Harley Pl., Kent Rd.*, 1820–35.

WOOD, THOMAS. C.C. 1691.

WOOD, THOMAS. *Barbican*. C.C. 1727.

WOOD, THOMAS JAS. *86 Charlotte St., Rathbone Pl.*, 1822–30.

WOOD, WILLIAM. *London*. C.C. 1755.

WOODALL, F. 1817.

WOODALL, T. J. *3 Birchin Lane*, 1804–10.

WOODALL, THOS. Apprenticed to G. C. Addis; C.C. 1796.

WOODDEN, CHARLES. *London*. Apprenticed 1743, C.C. 1755–78.

WOODFINE, RT. *Liverpool*. Watch, 1809.

WOODFORD, JONATHAN. Apprenticed 1684 to Jno. Ebsworth, C.C.; watch, 1736.

WOODHILL, JABEZ. *63 St. Paul's Churchyard*, 1830.

WOODINGTON, WM. Apprenticed 1638 to Ed. Gilpin, C.C.

WOODMAN, JNO. *London*, about 1780.

WOODRUFF & SON. *43 Kirby St., Hatton Garden*, 1822–30.

WOODS, JNO. *Liverpool*, 1770.

WOODS, THOMAS. C.C. 1713.

WOODWARD, JNO. Apprenticed 1656 to Ben. Hill, C.C.

WOODWARD, JOSEPH. *London*. Apprenticed 1803, C.C. 1820.

WOODWARD, THOS. Apprenticed 1671 to Jno. Frowde, C.C.

WOOLARD, JOHN. *14 Bridge Rd., Lambeth*, 1810–18.

WOOLEY, THOS. *41 Hutton St.*, 1793.

WOOLFE, JAMES. *London.* 1747 C.C.

WOOLHEAD, MAJ. *London.* Watch, 1780.

WOOLLETT, JOHN. *Maidstone.* About 1790 C.C.

WOOLLEY, —. *Tenterden.* Act of Parliament clock, about 1797.

WOOLRIDGE, STEPHEN. Apprenticed 1652 to Jere. Gregory, C.C.

WOOLVERTON, JAMES. C.C. 1690.

WOOLVERTON, JAS. C.C. 1677.

WOPSHOT, THOS. *London.* Watch, 1773.

WORBOYS, ARTHUR. *4 Wine Office Court, Fleet St.*, 1769–85.

WORBOYS, JNO. *30 Ludgate Hill*, 1780–94.

WORGAN, MATTHEW. *Bristol.* 1754–94 C.C.; clocks and watches.

WORKE, JNO. *London.* Many watches, Dutch style, 1760–85.

WORLIDGE, NAT. Apprenticed 1661 to Ed. Norris, C.C.

WORMESLEY, —. *Macclesfield*, 1814.

WORRALL, JOHN. *71 Goswell Rd.*, 1836–42.

WORRELL, JNO. *London.* Long-case clock, about 1760.

WORSFOLD, JNO. *Dorking.* Long-case clock, about 1720.

WORSFOLD, JNO. *Hampton Wick.* Watch, 1733.

WORSFOLD, THOMAS. *Hampton Wick.* 1775–90 C.C.; watch.

WORSLEY, JOHN. *London.* Watch, 1802.

WORSLEY, THOS. *22 Cheapside*, 1783–1805.

WORSLEY, THOS. *Liverpool.* Watch by him said to have been presented to Robert Burns by his brother ploughmen of Ayr in 1785.

WORSWICK, THOS. *Lancaster*, 1753, f.

WORTHINGTON, BASIL, brother. *London.* C.C. 1752–55.

WORTHINGTON, EDWD. Apprenticed 1655 to Jas. Cowpe, C.C.

WORTHINGTON, JOHN. C.C. 1721; watch, 1740.

WORTHINGTON, JOHN, son. *London.* C.C. 1746.

WORTLEY, HUMPHREY. Apprenticed 1653 to Ab. Gyott, C.C.

WOTTON, THOMAS. *Fleet St.* Maker of lantern clocks, 1690–94.

WRAGG, HOUBLON. C.C. 1724, known as a maker of long-case clocks.

WRANCH (? Wrench), JNO. *Chester.* Lantern clock, about 1700.

WRANGLES, JNO. *Scarborough*, 1800.

WRAPSON, I. *Chichester.* Long-case clock, about 1800.

WRAY, HILTON. *London.* Apprenticed 1752, C.C. 1769, master C.C. 1785, died 1812.

WREGHIT, JOHN. *Patrington (Yorks.)*, 1822–41.

WREN, JOHN. *96 Bishopsgate Without*, 1780–85.

WRENCH, CHARLES, 'near the Turnpike, Shoreditch', card, Ponsonby collection, about 1780; *57 Bishopsgate St. Within*, 1790; *25 Camomile St.*, 1798; *29 Paternoster Row*, 1810–15.

WRENCH, CHARLES JAMES, son. *London.* C.C. 1814, livery C.C. 1815.

WRENCH, EDWD. Watch, about 1690.

WRENCH, JOHN. *Chester.* Died 1716; lantern clock engraved 'John Wrench in Chester', dating from about 1680.

WRENCH, JOHN. *Chester.* Died 1751; long inlaid case clock by him, about 1730.

WRENCH, W. *Chester.* Long-case clock, about 1760.

WRENCH, WILLIAM. *Chester*, 1746–61. Watch.

WRESSELL, ROBERT. *London.* C.C. 1795.

WRIGHT, BENJAMIN. *Bell Alley, Coleman St.* Apprenticed to Abraham Prime, 1678; C.C. 1685.

WRIGHT, CHARLES CUSHING. *New York.* Arter 1812 settled in Utica.

WRIGHT, CHAS. *9 Avemary Lane*, 1780; *76 Strand*, 1788; *94 Watling St.*, 1790.

WRIGHT, EDMD. Apprenticed 1682 to Joseph Knibb, C.C.

WRIGHT, EDWD. *London.* Watch, 1775.

WRIGHT, ELIZABETH. *141 Ratcliff Highway*, 1825..

WRIGHT, JAMES. *London.* C.C. 1733.

WRIGHT, JAS. *181 Union St., Borough*, 1820–35.

WRIGHT, JNO. *New York*, 1712–35; f. 1713.

WRIGHT, JNO. Hon. f., C.C. 1781.

WRIGHT, JNO. *Chesterfield*, 1785.

WRIGHT, JOHN. Oval watch, British Museum, inscribed 'Wm. Heade, the owner', representation of the Crucifixion engraved inside, about 1620; part of a circular watch movement, dating from about 1640, and engraved 'Johannes Wright in Covent Garden', is in the Guildhall Museum.

WRIGHT, JOHN. *London.* C.C. 1671.

WRIGHT, JOHN. C.C. 1661.

WRIGHT, JOHN *London.* C.C. 1715.

WRIGHT, JOHN. C.C. 1700.

WRIGHT, JOSH. *Warwick*, about 1790.

WRIGHT, RICHARD. *Chelmsford*, 1776. Died 1816; watch.

WRIGHT, RICHARD. C.C. 1696.

WRIGHT, ROBT. C.C. 1634.

WRIGHT, S. *141 Ratcliff Highway*, 1820.

WRIGHT, THOMAS. *London (Poultry).* C.C. 1770, died 1792; watchmaker to the King; patented a bimetallic strip for varying the length of a pendulum in 1783; watch G.M.; bracket clock.

WRIGHT, THOMAS. *Duke St., St. Martin's Lane*, 1765–75.

WRIGHT, THOMAS. *6 Poultry.* Admitted C.C. 1770; 'maker to the King' on a bracket clock; he was a Quaker and a leading watchmaker; in 1783 he patented (No. 1,354) a form of detent escapement and compensation balance; died 1792; 1770–92, afterwards Wright & Thorp.

WRIGHT, THOMAS. *Dorking*, about 1800.

WRIGHT, WILLIAM. *Baltimore, U.S.A.*, 1802. Watch.

WRIGHT, WILLIAM. *London (Brixton).* C.C. 1817.

WRIGHT, WM. *London.* Apprenticed 1684 to Hy. Brigden, C.C.; long clock, 11-in. dial, panelled marquetry case, with spiral pillars to hood, about 1695, Wetherfield collection; at Goldsmiths' Hall is à long-case clock by him.

WRIGHT & SELLON. Watch, 1769.

WRIGHT & MOSS. *Ludgate Street, London.* Watch, h.m., 1791.

WRIGHTMAN, THOMAS. Admitted C.C. 1701.

WRIGHTSON, THOMAS. Master C.C. 1737; 1724–38.

WRIGHTWICK, JNO. Long-case clock, about 1770 (? Wightwick).

WRITS, W. *Amsterdam.* Watch, 1767.

WROLEY, GEO. *Bristol*, 1843.

WROTH, EDWARD. *London.* Apprenticed 1778, C.C. 1797.

WURTH, FERDINAND. *Donaueschingen.* Born 1775, died 1872. Wall clock, Furt. Museum, by him or his son.

WUTKY, —. Clock-watch, signed 'Johann Wutky in Breslau', about 1660, Pierpont Morgan collection.

WYATT, ANTHONY. *367 Oxford St.*, 1800–18.

WYATT, RICHARD. *Dublin*, 1731. Died 1755.

WYBERD, WM. *Hertford*, 1750.

WYCH, DAVID. Next door to the *Cross Keys Tavern, Strand.* C.C. 1694.

WYCH, JNO. Apprenticed 1677 to Jno. Fitter, C.C.

WYER, JOSEPH. *London.* Apprenticed 1760, C.C. 1770–91.

WYETH, JOHN. Brother C.C. 1655.

WYETH, LIONEL. See WYTHE.

WYKE, ARTHUR. Apprenticed 1691 to Thos. Wood, C.C.

WYKE, JNO. *Liverpool.* Long-case clock, about 1760.

WYKE, JNO. *Prescot*, 1780. Good maker of tools for watch and clock makers; afterwards at Liverpool, with Green.

WYKE & GREEN. *Wyke's Court, Dale St., Liverpool.* Makers of watches and clocks and parts thereof and watchmakers' tools; published a quarto illustrated catalogue of tools, about 1810.

WYKES, R. *2 Evelyn's Buildings, Oxford St.*, 1825.

WYKES, NEHEMIAH. *Liverpool*, 1758. Died 1787; famous for watch and clockmaking tools.

WYLD, JOHN. *Nottingham.* Clock, about 1720.

WYLDE, JNO. *London.* Watch, 1810.

WYLDER & HALL. *16 Sun St., Bishopsgate St.*, 1794.

WYLIE, JAMES. *Thirsk*, 1822–40.

WYMARK, MARK. *5 Percival St.*, 1816–42.

WYMARK, PHILIP. *Brighton*, about 1800–22.

WYNN, RICHARD, son of Geo. (1). *London.* Apprenticed 1764, C.C. 1773–1800. Also WYNNE.

WYNN, W. M. *135 Fleet St.*, 1804.

WYNN, WILLIAM, at *Farnham* in 1817, when he was awarded the Isis gold medal and twenty guineas by the Society of Arts for a timekeeper and compensation pendulum; in 1822 he was at *19 Dean St., Soho*, and received a prize of twenty guineas from the Society for an improved method of lifting the hammers in striking clocks; maker of an exceedingly fine clock for Boston (Lincolnshire) Church, no dials, hours and quarters on bells; is said to have died in Clerkenwell workhouse; 1810–35.

WYNNE, HENRY. Apprenticed to Ralph Greatorex, 1654; C.C. 1662, master in 1690.

WYNNE, JNO. Apprenticed 1670 to Wm. Watmore, C.C.

WYNNE, ROBT. Apprenticed 1641 to Jas. Vantrollier, C.C.

WYSE. See WISE.

WYTHE, LIONEL. C.C. 1646; a good maker; to him was apprenticed Charles Gretton, in 1662.

WYTHE, RICHD. Apprenticed 1682 to Jno. Johnson, C.C.

YARDE, THOMAS. Watch, British Museum, about 1580.

YARDLEY, JAMES. *Bishop's Stortford.* Long-case clock, arch dial, date on back of day of month circle, 1763.

YATE, WM. Oval watch, about 1605.

YATES, GEORGE. *Malden.* Watch, G.M., h.m., 1746.

YATES, HENRY. *Liverpool*, 1770.

YATES, JNO. Opposite the church, *Wandsworth*, 1800.

YATES, MICHAEL. Apprenticed 1664 to Isaac Plovier, C.C.

YATES, RICHD. *London.* Clock, 1760.

YATES, SAMUEL. C.C. 1648.

YATES, SAMUEL. C.C. 1685.

YATES, SAMUEL. *Kingston, Jamaica*, about 1800 C.C.

YATES, WM. C.C. about 1660.

YEADEN, RICHARD. *Charleston, U.S.A.*, 1771. Clocks and watches.

YEADON, WM. *Stourbridge*, 1830.

YEAMAN, JOHN. *Edinburgh*, 1734–49.

YEATMAN, ANDREW. Apprenticed in 1684 to Jas. Woolverton; C.C. 1692; silver watch, in the G.M., about 1700.

YELAH, JNO. *Wrexham*, 1780.

YELVERTON, WM. *115 Portland St.*, 1780–94.

YEOMANS, JAMES. *Birmingham*, 1767. Watch. In *New York* and partner with John Collins, 1769. Alone in 1771. Died 1773; long-case clock.

YEOMANS, RALPH. C.C. 1722.

YERIAF, FAIREY reversed, *q.v.*

YERIAF. See FAIREY.

YEWDALL, JNO. *Bradford.* Watch, 1803.

YOAKLEY, THOS. *London.* Watch, 1760; long-case clock, signed 'Thomas Yoakley, Ratcliff Cross'.

YONGE, GEORGE. *131 Strand*, 1798. Yonge succeeded the celebrated Holmes (the shop was pulled down to make the entrance to Waterloo Bridge in 1824).

YONGE, GEORGE, & SON. *156 Strand*, 1823.

YONGE, ROBERT. *Bennet St., Westminster.* C.C. 1730.

YORKE, JOSEPH W. *Turnagain Lane.* Apprenticed 1735.

YORKE, THOMAS. *Turnagain Lane.* C.C. 1716.

YORKE, THOMAS. *London (Shoe Lane).* C.C. 1799–1804.

YOUELL, ROBT. Apprenticed 1691 to Michael Knight, C.C.

YOUNG, CHAS. *London.* Centre seconds, duplex watch, free balance-spring, stud screwed to plate, about 1805; marine chronometer, G.M., about 1815; pocket chronometer, about 1817.

YOUNG, FRANCIS. Apprenticed 1680 to Hy. Young, C.C.

YOUNG, HENRICUS. *London.* C.C. 1672; long-case clock about 1685.

YOUNG, HENRY. Near the *Wine House in the Strand.* C.C. 1672. "A Gold Watch made by Mr. H. Young, that went with a chain, the Hour of the day and day of the Month. Having a studded Shagrine case, and the square in the inner case where the ring is riveted" (*Lond. Gaz.*, April 26–29, 1680).

YOUNG, HENRY. *89 Fleet St.*, 1679–1700.

YOUNG, HENRY. *Swaffham*, 1790–1800.

YOUNG, HY. *18 Ludgate St.*, 1783–88.

YOUNG, J. *40 Old Gravel Lane*, 1820.

YOUNG, JAMES. *Perth*, 1764–92.

YOUNG, JAMES. *Portsmouth.* About 1790 C.C.

YOUNG, JAMES. *32 Aldersgate St.*, 1783. Livery C.C. 1786.

YOUNG, JOHN. *44 Great Russell St., Bloomsbury*, 1778–1807. Livery C.C. 1781; very small bracket clock by him, round enamelled dial fitted in square brass plate.

YOUNG, RICHARD. *Newcastle-on-Tyne.* Born 1773, died 1815; clocks and watches.

YOUNG, RICHD. Apprenticed 1669 to Ed. Fage, C.C.

YOUNG, RICHD. *London.* Watch, 1775.

YOUNG, ROBERT. *London.* Apprenticed 1740, C.C. 1747.

YOUNG, SAML. *Perth.* Watch, 1781.

YOUNG, STEPHEN. *New York*, 1805.

YOUNG, THOMAS. C.C. 1699.

YOUNG, THOMAS. *Perth.* Apprenticed 1789–1848.

YOUNG, THOMAS. *Edinburgh*, 1823–50.

YOUNG, W. *London*, about 1800.

YOUNG, WILLIAM. *Charing Cross.* C.C. 1661, assistant 1695; maker of a long oak case clock, square dial, day of month circle.

YOUNG, WILLIAM. *Charing Cross.* C.C. 1682; small walnut and ebony long-case clock, solid hood, spiral pillars, square dial, cherub corners, about 1700.

YOUNG, WILLIAM, son of John. *London (Abchurch Lane).* Apprenticed 1793, C.C. 1801–25.

YOUNG, WILLIAM. *Harrogate*, 1827. Long-case clock with the old sulphur well painted on the dial; died 1876.

YOUNG, WM. *Bath.* Watch, 1790.

YOUNG, WM. *15 Butcherhall Lane*, 1825.

YVER, ÉLIE. *Angouleme.* Born 1661, died 1744.

YVER, F., à *Saintes.* Watch, about 1675.

ZACHARIE, ANTOINE. *Lyons*, 1672. Master 1674, dead in 1702.

ZACHARIE LE JEUNE. Clever horologer in *Lyons*, 1769.

ZACHARY, JOHN. Apprenticed to William Simcox, and turned over to Daniel Quare; admitted C.C. 1694.

ZECH, JACOB. *Prague* in 1525. died 1540; maker of earliest known fusee clock, 1525, Society of Antiquaries, London.

ZEITZ, JOHANN GEORG. *Munich*, 1765. Court clockmaker 1797–1803; son-in-law of ARZT.

ZELLER, JOHANN JAKOB. *Basle*. Born 1701, died 1778; a maker of repute; veilleuse clock in Basle Historical Museum.

ZIEGENHIRT (ZIEGELHART), ERNST NICOLAI. *Copenhagen*. Master 1724; first master of Copenhagen Corporation 1755; died 1756; made long-case clock with carillon for Hørsholm castle illuminated Liisberg.

ZINZANTH, HY. Apprenticed 1657 to Jno. Coulson, C.C.

ZOLLER (or ZOLLNER), MARTIN. *Augsburg*. Clock by him, Vienna Treasury, about 1590; Abraham Scheurlin apprenticed to him, 1633.

ZUCKER, JNO. *Tiverton*, 1710.

INDEX

Index

523

Going Train — Nos. 1, [1a],
4, 5, 6,
Striking Train — A, B,
Rack Train — α, β,

C [REVERSE]

C₁

1 & A

CRESSWELL

BACK PLATE